JAWAHARLAL NEHRU

Glimpses of World History

JAWAHARLAL NEHRU

Glimpses of World History

BEING FURTHER LETTERS TO HIS DAUGHTER,
WRITTEN IN PRISON, AND CONTAINING
A RAMBLING ACCOUNT OF HISTORY
FOR YOUNG PEOPLE

WITH 50 MAPS BY
J. F. HORRABIN

JAWAHARLAL NEHRU MEMORIAL FUND
OXFORD UNIVERSITY PRESS

First published in two volumes 1934–35 by
Kitabistan, Allahabad

This edition
Published by Jawaharlal Nehru Memorial Fund
First Impression 1982
Second Impression 1983
Third Impression 1984
Fourth Impression 1987
Fifth Impression 1988
Sixth Impression 1989
Seventh Impression 1989
Eighth Impression 1992

SBN 19 561323 6

Distributed by Oxford University Press

Printed by Indraprastha Press (CBT), Nehru House,
4, Bahadur Shah Zafar Marg, New Delhi 110002
Published by Jawaharlal Nehru Memorial Fund
Teen Murti House, New Delhi 110011

FOREWORD

My father's three books — *Glimpses of World History, An Autobiograpy* and *The Discovery of India* — have been my companions through life. It is difficult to be detached about them.

Indeed *Glimpses* was written for me. It remains the best introduction to the story of man for young and growing people in India and all over the world. The *Autobiography* has been acclaimed as not merely the quest of one individual for freedom, but as an insight into the making of the mind of new India. I had to correct the proofs of *Discovery* while my father was away, I think in Calcutta, and I was in Allahabad ill with mumps! The *Discovery* delves deep into the sources of India's national personality. Together, these books have moulded a whole generation of Indians and inspired persons from many other countries.

Books fascinated Jawaharlal Nehru. He sought out ideas. He was extraordinarily sensitive to literary beauty. In his writings he aimed at describing his motives and appraisals as meticulously as possible. The purpose was not self-justification or rationalization, but to show the rightness and inevitability of the actions and events in which he was a prime participant. He was a luminous man and his writings reflected the radiance of his spirit.

The decision of the Jawaharlal Nehru Memorial Fund to bring out a uniform edition of these three classics will be widely welcomed.

Indira Gandhi

New Delhi
4 November 1980

PREFACE

TO ORIGINAL EDITION

I DO not know when or where these letters will be published, or whether they will be published at all, for India is a strange land to-day and it is difficult to prophesy. But I am writing these lines while I have the chance to do so, before events forestall me.

An apology and an explanation are needed for this historical series of letters. Those readers who take the trouble to go through them will perhaps find the apology and the explanation. In particular, I would refer the reader to the last letter, and perhaps it would be as well, in this topsy-turvy world, to begin at the end.

The letters have grown. There was little of planning about them, and I never thought that they would grow to these dimensions. Nearly six years ago, when my daughter was ten years old, I wrote a number of letters to her containing a brief and simple account of the early days of the world. These early letters were subsequently published in book form and they had a generous reception. The idea of continuing them hovered in my mind, but a busy life full of political activity prevented it from taking shape. Prison gave me the chance I needed, and I seized it.

Prison-life has its advantages; it brings both leisure and a measure of detachment. But the disadvantages are obvious. There are no libraries or reference books at the command of the prisoner, and, under these conditions, to write on any subject, and especially history, is a foolhardy undertaking. A number of books came to me, but they could not be kept. They came and went. Twelve years ago, however, when, in common with large numbers of my countrymen and countrywomen, I started my pilgrimages to prison, I developed the habit of making notes of the books I read. My note-books grew in number and they came to my rescue when I started writing. Other books of course helped me greatly, among them inevitably, H. G. Wells's *Outline of History*. But the lack of good reference books was very real, and because of this the narrative had often to be slurred over, or particular periods skipped.

The letters are personal and there are many intimate touches in them which were meant for my daughter alone. I do not know what to do about them, for it is not easy to take them out without considerable effort. I am therefore leaving them untouched.

Physical inactivity leads to introspection and varying moods. I am afraid these changing moods are very apparent in the course of these letters, and the method of treatment is not the objective

vii

one of a historian. I do not claim to be a historian. There is an
unfortunate mixture of elementary writing for the young and a
discussion at times of the ideas of grown-ups. There are numerous
repetitions. Indeed, of the faults that these letters contain there
is no end. They are superficial sketches joined together by a thin
thread. I have borrowed my facts and ideas from odd books, and
many errors may have crept in. It was my intention to have these
letters revised by a competent historian, but during my brief period
out of prison I have not had the time to make any such arrangement.

In the course of these letters I have often expressed my opinions
rather aggressively. I hold to those opinions, but even as I was
writing the letters my outlook on history changed gradually. To-day
if I had to re-write them, I would write differently or with a
different emphasis. But I cannot tear up what I have written
and start afresh.

JAWAHARLAL NEHRU.

January 1, 1934.

CONTENTS

FROM CENTRAL PRISON, NAINI

FROM ON BOARD SS. CRACOVIA IN THE ARABIAN SEA

FROM DISTRICT GAOL, BAREILLY

CONTENTS

x

CONTENTS

CONTENTS

CONTENTS

CONTENTS

LIST OF MAPS

LIST OF MAPS

A CHRONOLOGY OF
WORLD HISTORY

TO INDIRA

Indu

Dates are not very attractive things. And yet they help in putting things in their right place, so that we may have an ordered sequence in our minds.-A long list of dates is a most depressing affair. I have arranged some important dates in a different form, as you will see. Various parts of the world are represented by different columns so that you can have a very rough idea at a glance of what the world was like at a particular stage or date. Of course the idea will be very very rough. This chronology is meant to be used for reference purposes. Having finished with it I now feel that I could have made a better one! But this will have to do for the present. It represents a few days' hard work.

Papu

Dehra Dun Jail
August 22, 1933

A CHRONOLOGY OF WORLD HISTORY

For the very early periods of human history dates are sometimes pure guesswork. Sometimes they are so uncertain that experts differ about them by a thousand years. The earliest remains of human culture so far discovered take us back to beyond 5000 B.C., that is to about 7000 years ago. Egyptian history is supposed to begin then. It was the end of the age of stone. Egypt was then split up into many small states. Archaeologists have also discovered the early remains of a civilization, dating from about 5000 B.C., in Chaldea or Elam (Mesopotamia). The capital city of this was Susa. Most of the archaeological discoveries have been made in Egypt and in Mesopotamia because most of the digging has taken place there. Probably similar discoveries, of a like date, will be made in other countries also. This idea is strengthened by the next batch of archaeological finds which dates from about 3500 B.C. These discoveries take us right across Asia: from Egypt–Chaldea–Eastern Persia–Indus Valley in India–Western Turkestan–to the Yellow River or Hoang-Ho in China. In all these places a common stage of development is found. It is the end of the age of polished stone and copper is beginning to be used. There is agriculture, and domestic animals; and trade, and tools of the same type, and beautiful jewellery of gold and silver, and painted pottery with many similar designs. Writing had already appeared. It appears that a common civilization existed at this period, about 5500 years ago, from Egypt to North India and China. Because of the common pottery this has been called the 'Painted Pottery Civilization.' This civilization is already so advanced, its culture and fine arts are so developed, that it has thousands of years of cultural growth behind it. This is the period of Mohenjo Daro in India with its fine houses and streets and artistic development. In Egypt the separate states now join together to form one state under the Pharoahs–the god-kings. In Chaldea two powerful states appear about this time–Sumer and Akkad–with a high degree of culture; and on the banks of the Euphrates stands the famous city of Ur––'Ur of the Chaldees' it is called in the Bible. From this common 'Painted Pottery Civilization' the four great eastern civilizations–Egyptian, Mesopotamian (including Persian or

Iranian), Indian, and Chinese—diverge and develop separately. Thus we have:—

B.C	Egypt	Chaldea or Elam (Mesopotamia)	India	China
c. 3500		Common Painted Pottery Civilization		
3300	Becomes one state under Pharoahs.	Two powerful states—Sumer and Akkad city of Ur.	Mohenjo Daro and Harappa in the Indus Valley (Three cities one on top of the other from B.C. 3300 to B.C. 2700).	Settlements on the Yellow River or Hoang-Ho.

It is probable that contemporaneous with the Painted Pottery Civilization in the East, there existed a similar civilization in the eastern Mediterranean, in the Greek Islands and the western coasts of Asia Minor. This early Mediterranean civilization led to the high Minoan civilization of Knossos of about 2000–1500 B.C., which gradually decayed and became the Mycenaean or Aegean civilization (of the Greek Islands) of about 1600–1100 B.C. About this time (from c. 1300 onwards) the Semitic Phoenicians, the great traders of the ancient western world, come into prominence and their settlements grow up all along the Mediterranean Coast. The city of Tyre in Asia Minor was the most important of these settlements. It was about this time also that the Aryans spread out in Europe. It was these Aryan Greeks, the Hellenes, that laid siege to Troy in the 12th century B.C. Hellenic civilization gradually developed and Hellenic colonies sprung up in Asia Minor, South Italy, Sicily, and the South of France. Homer wrote his epics in the eleventh century B.C.

Meanwhile much had happened in the older centres of civilization in the East. In Egypt and Chaldea empires had already flourished and decayed. In India the Aryans had established themselves in the north and were pushing down to the south. They seem to have come to India long before they appear in Greece. They found the civilized and cultured Dravidians already established in the country and they drove them towards South India. The Vedas were written in the early days of the Aryan invasion, and they were followed, long afterwards, by the epics. In China consolidation was taking place and a great State was growing up. Silk culture was already known.

And now for our chart. But remember that the various names of civilizations and historic periods (such as Minoan, Mycenaean, Aegean, etc.), must not be taken as mutually exclusive or as indicating clearly defined periods. They are vague terms used by present day archaeologists and historians to distinguish various civilizations and periods which often overlap and run into each other. Remember also that it is impossible to give the dates in the chart according to scale, that is, giving the same space to the same length of time. It would be far better and more accurate to have such a scale, for this would give a more correct idea of history. But such a chart would become enormously long for we have to deal with thousands of years in the early stages of history, and of course the pre-historic periods are vastly bigger. So that we have to give up the idea of the scale, and sometimes an inch will do duty for a thousand years or more, and in another place, it may represent a bare ten years or less.

NOTE:—*c.* before a date means that the date is not exact but is approximate only. It is from the Latin *circa*—about.

Mediterranean Coasts Greece—Carthage—Rome	Egypt	Date	Western Asia Chaldea—Palestine—Persia	India	China Korea and Japan
	Memphite Empire 2800—2300 great pyramids built by Cheops, etc. Great Sphinx at Gizeh.	B.C. 2800		Indus Valley civilization in North-west.	
Early Mediterranean civilization		2300			2356 Yao Emperor.
	Hyksos invasion of Egypt. First Theban Empire from 2160 to 1660.			Dravidians in greater part of India.	2205 Hsia dynasty begins (to 1765) Silk culture.
	Temples of Karnak and Luxor built by Rameses II.	2100	2100 Hammurabi establishes Babylonian Empire. City of Babylon.		
Minoan Civilization of Knossus (c. 2000-1500).		2000		Successive waves of Aryans enter from North west and establish themselves in North.	
			1925 Hittites destroy Babylonian Empire.		
				Vedic periods.	
		1700			1765 Shang or Yin dynasty (to 1122).
Mycenaean civilization (a. 1600—1100).	1580 Second Theban Empire (to 1100).			Epic period—Ramayana and Mahabharat (but books were written down much later).	
		1500		Aryanization of South India.	
			Rise of Assyrians—King Tiglath—Pilesar.		
Phoenician settlements in the Mediterranean city of Tyre in Asia Minor.		1300			
Aryans spread out in Europe.					1122 Chou dynasty (to 255).
Siege of Troy by Hellenic Greeks 1184				Village republics of ancient India.	1122 Korea: Kitse establishes Kingdom of Chosen (which lasts till 193 B.C.).
		1100	Palestine Saul King of Israel. David c. 1000. Solomon 977—937		
c. 1000 Homer writes Epics: Iliad and Odyssey.					
Hellenic colonies in Asia Minor, South Italy, Sicily and South France.		800			
800 Phoenicians found Carthage in North Africa. Greek City States: Athens, Sparta, Thebes, Corinth, etc.					
776 Olympic games established in Greece					
753 Rome built					
			728 Assyrians conquer Babylon and found Assyrian Empire. Capital City Nineveh.		
		700	c.700 (or earlier) Zarathushtra or Zoroaster.	Panini the great grammarian.	
					660 Japan: Small Yamato State. Legendary first emperor Jimmu Tenno.
			612 Aryan Medes capture Nineveh and destroy Assyrian Empire.		
c. 600 Sappho the great poetess in Lesbos.		600			

[Probably beginnings of ancient American civilizations in Mexico, Central America and Peru, about this time— Sixth Century B.C.]

Greece and Rome and Carthage	Egypt	Western Asia Persia
Carthage great trade centre—dominant power in Mediterranean.		
Pythagoras in Samos c.570–504.		586 Babylonian captivity of Jews by Nebuchadnezzar.
		550 Cyrus (Persian Aryan) conquers Medes. Defeats Croesus of Lydia. Great Achaemenid dynasty begins. Empire from Hellespont to India.
	525 Persian King Cambyses conquers Egypt.	
Roman Republic begins c.500. 490 Battle of Marathon—Greeks repulse Persians. 480 Thermopylae and Salamis.		Darius and Xerxes attempt to conquer Greece and fail. Great City of Persepolis.
Golden age of Greece: Socrates, Euripides, Pericles, Aeschylus, Sophocles, Plato, Pindar, Aristophanes, Pheidias. 404 Destruction of Athens by Sparta. 359 Philip King of Macedonia.		
336 Alexander the Great.	332 Alexander in Egypt. The Greek Ptolemys rule Egypt.	Alexander defeats Darius III and ends Persian Empire of Achaemenids. He dies at Babylon 323. His Empire splits up.
	Alexandria—a great centre of Greek culture.	Seleucus rules in West Asia. Hellenic dynasty of the Seleucids.
264 (to 241) First Punic War—Rome against Carthage.		
		250 Iranian Parthians free themselves, from Seleucids and establish Arsacid dynasty (lasts to A.D. 224).
219 (to 202) Second Punic War. Hannibal. Roman Empire spreads to Spain, Greece, Asia Minor.		
149 Third Punic War. Carthage destroyed.		
91 Civil Wars in Italy.		
73 Revolt of slaves under Spartacus in Rome. Conquest of Gaul, Britain by Julius Caesar and of eastern territories by Pompey.		Roman conquests in Asia Minor, etc. 53 Parthians defeat Romans at Carrhae.
48 Caesar defeats Pompey at Pharsalos. 44 Caesar killed in Rome.	Cleopatra last Ptolemy ruler.	
	30 Egypt becomes a Roman province	

Date	India (and Central Asia)	Farther India—Malaysia, etc.	China (and Korea and Japan)
B.C.	Buddha c.620–540.		Lao-Tse 605—531.
600			
			Confucius 551–429.
500	Mahavira (died c.467 or earlier).		
400	Pallavas dominant in extreme South of India.	Pallava traders and seamen visit Malaysian ports.	c.400 Silk exported to Europe.
300	Alexander's raid in North India 326. 321 Chandragupta—Chanakya—Maurya Empire begins—'Arthashastra'. 303 Seleucus defeated Pataliputra great Capital City Taxila—Ujjain—Mathura. 268 Ashoka (to 226) Great Empire almost whole India and part of Central Asia. Buddhist missionaries sent to foreign lands.	Chinese settle in Indo-China. Early Pallava settlements—Farther India, Eastern Islands, etc.	255 Ch'in dynasty. 249–209 Shih Huang Ti. Burning of Books. Great Wall completed 204.
200	220 Growth of Andhra power in South. Great Southern Empire lasting to 3rd century A.C. Pallavas in extreme South. Indo-Scythians come from north-west and settle in Punjab—Rajputana—Kathiawar. c.150 Patanjali.		202 Han dynasty (to 221 A.C.) [KOREA: 193 Ki-Tse dynasty ends]
100	Kushan Empire in North India and Central Asia—from Benares to Yarkand. Buddhist Turki dynasty. Capital Peshawar (Purushapura)—Lasts till 3rd cent. A.C. contemporaneous with Andhra Empire in South. Close intercourse between India and Graeco-Roman world and Central Asia.	Chinese conquer and annex Annam.	140–86 Wu Ti Emperor. Contacts with Japan and Rome. 108 North Korea conquered by Chinese. [JAPAN: Yamato still a small state.] Literary Civil Service Examination system begins in China. Lasts 2000 years. Printing from wooden blocks invented.

Roman Empire	Western Asia	Date
		B.C. 100
27 B.C. Octavian Caesar becomes Princeps. The Chief and Imperator. Roman Empire begins.		
	Jesus born at Nazareth in Palestine.	B.C. A.C.
14—180 Emperors: Tiberius, Caligula, Claudius, Nero, Vespasian, Titus, Domitian, Nerva, Trojan, Hadrian, Antonius, Marcus Aurelius.		A.C. 100
[Maya and Aztec Civilizations in America develop in second century A.C. Strongly organized States, many cities—art—architecture, etc.]		200
	224 Sasanid Empire in Persia begins. Strongly nationalist Iranian and Zoroastrian (lasts till 652).	
	272 Arab desert state of Palmyra ends. Zenobia Queen.	300
306 Constantine the Great. Emperor. Capital taken to Byzantium which becomes Constantinople. Christianity becomes official religion of Empire. Division of Empire into Western and Eastern.		
c.400 Barbarian attacks on Rome		400
410 Goths under Alaric capture and sack Rome.		
450 Huns under Attila overrun Gaul and Italy and are finally defeated in 451 at the Battle of Chalous in France.		
455 Vandals under Genseric sack Rome. 476 Western Empire ceases to exist. The Goth Odoaca King in Italy. Other Goth Kings. 481 Clovis of France.		
Eastern Roman Empire with Capital at Constantinople continues though much weakened by Barbarian and Hun attacks. Revives under Justinian who reigns from 527 to 565.		500

India	Farther India—Malaysia, etc.	China	Japan and Korea
Great schism in Buddhism—Mahayana and Hinayana.			
Organized expeditions of Pallavas to found colonies in Malaysia and Eastern Islands. Development of maritime trade.	Important Indian (Pallava) colonies established especially at Cambodia, Sri Vijaya in Sumatra. South Malay, Central Java, Eastern Borneo.	Buddhism introduced into China. Later Han Emperors drive Tartars west. (These go later to Europe and India as Huns, etc.).	
		221 Han dynasty falls.	
		Three kingdoms.	
320 Gupta Empire in North India begins Nationalist revival—Renaissance. Capital Ayudhya. Golden age of Sanskrit. 320 Chandragupta.			Yamato (Japan) expands about 350.
335 Samudragupta. Extensive conquests.			
380 Vikramaditya Kalidas, the poet.			
Fa-Hien, Chinese pilgrim, visits India.			
c.450 Hun invasion of India.			
Toroman the Hun establishes himself in North India. 495.			
Mihiragula, the Hun. 510–28.	Hindu States in Indo-China.	Bodhi dharma reaches Canton.	
525 Bodhidharma the patriarch of Indian Buddhism leaves India to settle in China.			

Western Europe	Eastern Europe	Western Asia	Central Asia
	Frequent wars between Byzantine (Constantinople) Empire and Sasanid (Persian) Empire weakening both.		
		570 Mohamad born (dies 632) at Mecca, Sasanid Empire extends to Egypt, Syria, Asia Minor, Persia under Khusrau II. 619.	Mixed Indo-Chinese—Persian culture in Central Asia. Buddhism widespread among Turks and other races.
		622 Hegira. The flight to Medina.	
		632. Abu Bakr Caliph.	
		634 Omar Caliph.	
	Byzantine Empire defeated by Arabs but preserves itself.	632–70 Arabs defeat Byzantine Empire and conquer Persia, Egypt, North Africa and parts of Central Asia. Capital Damascus. Ommayad Caliphs (Sasanid Empire ended by Arab Conquest).	Chinese Tangs extend in the North towards the Caspian Sea. Arab conquests in Central Asia.
711 Arab conquest of Spain from North Africa.			
Invasion of France.			
732 Battle of Tours in France. Charles Martel defeats Arabs and stops Arab invasion.			
750 Arab kingdom of Cordoba in Spain. Famous city and University.		750 Ommayad Caliphs overthrown. Abbaside Caliphate begins. Spain becomes independent. Arab kingdom under Ommayades. Arab Empire shrinks but consolidation. Capital goes to Baghdad.	Arab Empire
		786 (to 809) Haroun-al-Rashid Caliph. Brilliant reign. Embassies to China and Charlemagne.	
800 Charlemagne crowned Emperor of the West. Holy Roman Empire begins.	Eastern Roman (Byzantine) Empire manages to continue in a shrunken state although hard pressed on all sides.		
		850 Decline of Abbasides and Arab Empire. Independent Moslem kingdoms rise up.	Transoxiana and other independent Moslem Kingdoms rise up in Central Asia. Persian and Turkish dynasties.
		Seljuk Turks in Western Asia.	
962 Otto the Great of Germany becomes Emperor of Holy Roman Empire.		969 Egypt becomes independent. Separate Fatirnide Caliphate.	
		Seljuk Turks dominate over West Asia.	
987 Hugh Capet King of France.			
			Mahmud of Ghazni.

Date	India	Farther India, Malaysia etc.	China	Japan and Korea
A.C. 550	c.550 Chalukyan Empire dominant in South India, Pulakesin.			Buddhism introduced into Japan via Korea. Becomes court religion 552.
600	Harshavardhan's Empire in North India Capital Kanauj. (Harsha dies 648) Hiuen Tsang, Chinese pilgrim visits India c.630. Brahmagupta, great mathematician, first evolves decimal system.	Buddhist state of Sri Vijaya in Sumatra.	618 Tang dynasty begins (lasts till 907) famous capital Si-an-fu. 635 Nestorian Christianity comes to China.	Chinese conquer Korea.
	Arabs reach Baluchistan	Annam and Cambodia tributary to Chinese Tangs.		650 Direct intercourse of Japan with China.
700			Tangs drive Turks west; extend empire to Caspian Sea; come up against advancing Arabs. Maritime commerce and foreign trade develops.	
	710 Arabs conquer Sindh			
800	Rashtrakutas end Chalukyan hegemony in south and dominate west coast and centre (Maratha country) till end 10th century when (973) Rashtrakutas come back. Ellora: Kailas Temple begun. Shankaracharya (died c.828)		Chinese teach paper making to Arabs (from whom Europe learns it later)	Name of Yamato changed to Nippon. 794 Kyoto made capital of Nippon.
	c.850 Chola Empire in Tamil Land (South India). Pallavas overshadowed.	Jayavarman establishes Cambodian Empire (in indo-China) which lasts 400 years till 13th century. Angkor famous city. Angkor Vat Temple. Great buildings—sculpture.		c.850 Fujiwara family dominant in Japan
900	Shukracharya's Nitisara. Semi-independent village panchayats throughout India. Chola Empire expands. Rajaraja 985.		907 Yang dynasty ends. 960 Sung dynasty begins.	

Western Europe (and America)	Eastern Europe	Western Asia Asia Minor—Palestine—Iraq—Persia	Central Asia	Date
				A.C. 1000
[*Central America*: Great City of Uxmal grows up: c 1000 A League of three Central American States formed—the League of Mayapan.]			Mahmud of Ghazni (died 1030). Firdusi—Alberuni.	
		Omar Khayyam the Persian poet (born c. 1040 dies c. 1123).	1037 Ibn Sina or Avicenna the great physician of Bokhara dies.	
1066 William of Normandy conquers England.				
1073 Hildebrande becomes Pope as Gregory VII.		1071 Seljuk Turks under Alp Arslan win great victory of Melasgird over Byzantine Empire and conquer all Asia Minor (Anatolia) right upto Constantinople.		
1096 First Crusade. Large numbers of people massacred. Gothic architecture in Western Europe during 11th and 12th centuries.	Crusaders loot and misbehave in Eastern Europe.	Europe alarmed at this revival of Moslem energy.		
		1099 Crusaders under Godfrey de Bouillon capture Jerusalem. Terrible slaughter.		1100
1147 Second Crusade.		1147 Second Crusade.		
1147 Portugal won from the Moslem kingdom of Cordoba and a Christian kingdom established there.				
1152 Frederick Barbarossa of Hohenstaufen dynasty. Emperor of Holy Roman Empire.				
		1169 Saladin ruler of Egypt. He recaptures Jerusalem in 1187.		
1189 Third Crusade. Richard I of England Coeur de Lion. [Central America: c. 1190 Mayapan destroyed].		1189 Third Crusade ends in failure.		
1202 Fourth Crusade attacks Eastern (Byzantine) Empire.	1204 Crusaders capture Constantinople and a Latin Emperor set up (till 1261)	Empire of Khwarism (Khiva) over Persia and Central Asia.	Khwarism Empire.	1200
		Shaikh Sadi of Shiraj—great Persian poet (c. 1184—1282). Jalal-al-Din Rumi—great Persian mystic (1207—73).		
1212 Children's Crusade. 1215 Magna Carta signed by King John of England. 1221 Fifth Crusade. 1228 Frederic II of Hohenstaufen Emperor of Holy Roman Empire (1212—50) leads 6th Crusade although Pope excommunicates him. 1233 Spanish Inquisition established.	Mongols under Chengiz invade South Russia.	1221 Fifth Crusade. Frederick II acquires Jerusalem by negotiation with Sultan 1228.	1218 Chengiz Khan invades Central Asia, destroys Khwarism. Great cities Bokhara, Samarqand, Balkh, etc., utterly destroyed. Central Asia made almost a desert.	
	1240 Mongol invasion of Russia, Poland, etc. Russia tributary to Mongols. 1241 Mongol victory at Liegnitz in Silesia.			
1250 Frederick II died. Hohenstaufen dynasty ends. 1250 Kingdom of Cordoba in Spain ends—Small Arab kingdom of Granada in South Spain begins.		1244 Egyptian Sultan re-takes Jerusalem.		1250
		1258 Mongols under Hulagu invade Western Asia, destroy Baghdad and break power of Seljuk Turks. At last stopped and repulsed by Sultan Baibers of Egypt the 'bandukdar.' 1259 Ilkhan dynasty of Mongols rules over Persia, Iraq, etc.		
1265 Dante Alighieri born. 1273 Rudolph of Hapsburg elected Emperor of Holy Roman Empire. During 13th and 14th centuries growth of European cities: Republic of Venice—Genoa, Florence, Bologna, Pisa, Milan, Naples. Paris—Antwerp—Hamburg—Frankfurt, Cologne, Munich, etc.	1261 Greeks re-capture Constantinople from Latins.			
	Mongols of the Golden Horde established in greater part of Russia.			1300

India	Farther India, Malaysia, etc.	China and Mongolia	Japan and Korea
Numerous raids by Mahmud in North India. Mathura, Somnath, etc. Vast treasure taken away. Punjab annexed by him.	Highest development of Buddhist Empire of Sri Vijaya of Sumatra. All eastern islands (except East Java) under it. Sea-power, trade and ship building.		
Chola Empire in South grows under Rajendra (1013–44) conquests of Ceylon, Gaur (Bengal) and Burma. Sea-trade.			
			1072 The Cloistered Emperors (in Japan).
Ramanuja lived in South India.			
	Beginnings of Siam	1127 Kin Tartars establish themselves in North China. 1127 (to 1260) Sungs rule in South China only. Called Southern Sungs.	
	Hindu State in East Java continues as an independent trade rival of Sri Vijaya. Great Borubudar temple built in Java.		
		c.1155 Chengiz Khan born in Mongolia.	
1192 Shahabuddin defeats Prithwi Raj Muslim rule begins in India (to 1333).			1192 Yoritomo establishes Kamakura Shogunate.
1206 Qutbuddin—Slave King—Delhi Empire Qutb Minar built.		1206 Chengiz Khan chosen Kagan or great Khan at Karakorum in Mongolia. Mongol conquest of China, Central Asia, South Russia.	
		1227 Chengiz Khan dies. Oghatai becomes Great Khan. Second Mongol invasion of Europe.	
		1251 Oghatai dies—Mangu Khan becomes Great Khan.	
		1260 Kublai Khan becomes Great Khan. Capital removed from Karakoram to Peking.	
Decline of the Cholas in the South. Marco Polo visits South India—Pandyas leading Tamil power. 1296 Alauddin Sultan of Delhi. Mongol raids in North repulsed.	Burma, Annam, etc, added to Chinese Empire of Mongols. Angkor city destroyed by silting up of river. Cambodian Empire ends.	Yuan dynasty begins (to 1368)—conquests of Burma, Annam, etc. Marco Polo visits China. Chinese intercourse with Europe.	

Western Europe (and America)	Eastern Europe	Western Asia Asia Minor—Syria—Iraq—Persia (and Egypt)	Central Asia
[*Central America* and *Mexico* c. 1325 Aztecs conquer Maya country. Found great city of Tenochtitlan.]		Ibn Battuta's travels from Africa (Morocco) to Asia Minor, South Russia, Central Asia, India and China.	
		1336 Mongol Ilkhan dynasty ends. Hafiz—great Persian poet (1320–89).	1336 Timur born.
c. 1348 The Great Plague—Black Death—in Europe, North Africa and parts of Asia. Populations wiped out in all countries affected.	Great Plague in South Russia.	Great Plague in Asia Minor—Egypt, etc. Ottoman Turks grow in power in Asia Minor.	Great Plague.
	1353 Ottoman Turks cross over to Europe and conquer Balkans, make Adrianople Capital. Byzantine Empire still continues in Constantinople.		
1378 The Great Schism in Western Christianity. Two Popes—one at Rome, the other at Avignon in France. Schism ends by compromise in 1417.			
			Timur's conquest in Central Asia.
		c. 1396 Timur conquers Persia and ends Ilkhan dynasty—defeats Ottoman Sultan Bayarid at Angora.	
		Prince of Moscow, having driven out Mongols of the Golden Horde, becomes independent, and develops into 'Tsar' of Russia.	
1430 Jeanne d'Arc burnt by the English at Rouen.			1405 Death of Timur Timurid dynasty in Central Asia—Shah Rukh.
	1453 Ottoman Turks capture Constantinople. End of Eastern Roman (Byzantine) Empire.		Timurid Renaissance in art, etc.
1473 Copernicus born.			
1486 Diaz goes round the Cape of Good Hope.			Bihzad—famous painter of Herat (and later Tabriz).
1492 Arab kingdom of Granada ends. Moors driven out of Spain.	Ottoman Empire spreads in South-east Europe.		
1492 Columbus crosses Atlantic and reaches America.			
1498 Vasco da Gama reaches India via Cape.			
Renaissance begins in Italy: Leonardo da Vinci, Michelangelo, Raphael.		1502 Persian Safavi dynasty begins (to 1736) Shah Abbas I.	
1513 Balboa reaches Pacific Ocean.			
1519 Magellan sails round the world. 1519 Cortes conquers the Aztecs of Mexico.	1520 Sulaiman the Magnificent Sultan of Ottoman Empire which spreads and includes Hungary and all Balkans	Ottoman Empire includes West Asia to Baghdad and also Egypt. (To east of Ottoman Empire the Persian Safavi dominions).	
1530 Pizarro's conquest of the Incas of Peru. Spanish American Empire develops. 1530 Hapsburg Charles V Emperor Holy Roman Empire, King of Spain, Netherlands, American Dominions, etc.			

Date	India	Farther india, Malaysia, etc.	China	Japan and Korea
A.C. 1300	Ibn Battuta visits India.			1333 Ashikaga Shogunate begins in Japan.
1350	1350 Firuz Shah Sultan (to 1388).		Great Plague.	
		1377 Hindu State of Madjapahit in East Java develops sea power and destroys its trade rival Sri Vijaya of Sumatra Empire of Madjapahit at its greatest extent. 1380 Malacca founded.	1368 Ming dynasty begins. Break up of Mongol Empire. Great period of prosperity and culture in China. (Mings end in 1644).	Suzerainty of Chinese Ming Emperors acknowledged by Shoguns of Japan.
	1388 On death of Firuz Shah break up of Delhi Empire: kingdoms of Gaur (Bengal) Jaunpur, Kulbarga, Ahmednagar, Gujarat.			1392 *Korea:* On decline ofMongol influence Yi-Tai-Jo becomes ruler. His dynasty lasts over 600 years (to Japanese annexation in 1910)— Seoul made capital.
1400	1399 Timur's raid—Massacre and destruction of Delhi.	Cheng Ho's expeditions 1405–33. Empire of Madjapahit declines.	1405 Chinese admiral Cheng Ho's naval expeditions all over eastern seas-islands, etc.	
1450.				1467–1567 Civil wars in Japan.
	Kingdoms of Bijapur and Vijayanagar in South India.	1478 Moslem Arabs from Malacca capture Madjapahit. Empire of Malacca.		
1500	1498 Vasco da Gama reaches Calicut. Guru Nanak in North India (died *c.* 1528) Chaitanya in Bengal (d. 1533)	1511 Portuguese capture Malacca and establish wide-spread Eastern Empire—control eastern trade.	1516 Portuguese reach Canton. They misbehave and try forcible methods. Are driven out by the Chinese.	
	1526 Babar wins battle of Panipat—Mughal Empire in India begins.			

North and South America	Western Europe	Eastern Europe	Date
	Martin Luther (died 1546). The Reformation Protestantism begins in North-west Europe.		A.C. 1500
			1550
	1558 (to 1603) Elizabeth's reign in England.		
	1564 Shakespeare born.		
	1567 Revolt of the Netherlands against Spain.		
1577 Francis Drake sails round the world.			
		c.1581 Russian bandit Yermak crosses Urals with Cossacks and goes East.	
		Ottoman Empire over Balkans, Hungary, etc.	
	1600 British East India Company formed.		1600
	1602 Dutch East India Company formed.		
1620 'Mayflower' brings Puritan settlers from England to North America.			
		1636 Russians push on in East and reach Pacific Ocean.	
	1642 Louis XIV 'Grande Monarque' of France begins 72-year reign.		
	1648 Treaty of Westphalia. Holland and Switzerland recognized as independent.		
	1649 Civil War in England—Victory of Parliament over King. Execution of Charles I. English Republic till 1660. Oliver Cromwell.		1650
		1683 Ottoman Turks checked at the gates of Vienna.	
	1688 British Revolution.	1689 Peter the Great in Russia. Reigns 1689 to 1725.	
European Settlements on eastern coasts of North America growing up. Spanish Empire in South America except in Brazil where Portuguese rule.		Treaty with China. Embassies sent to China. Peter ends the seclusion of women in Russia (purdah).	1700
		1730 Russo-Turkish War (the first of many throughout 18th and 19th centuries).	

Western Asia	India	Farther India, Malaysia, etc.	China (and Siberia)	Japan
	1540 Sher Shah defeats Humayun.			1542 Portuguese arrive. Christianity introduced.
	1556 Mughal Restoration. Akbar's reign begins. Conquest of the Deccan.			
	1564 Bijapur defeats and sacks Vijayanagar.			
Ottoman Empire over Arabia, Syria, Asia Minor, Iraq and Egypt. In Persia Safavi dynasty, renaissance of art, etc.		1571 Spanish rule over Philippine Islands begins. 'Missionary Empire'. Islands isolated. 'Manila Galleon. Dutch and English attack Portuguese all over Eastern waters.	1581 Yermak with his Cossacks conquers little state of Sibir in North Asia (from which Siberia).	1596 Anti-Christian Policy. Iyeyasu (dies 1616). 1603 Tokugava Shoguns begin
	1605 Akbar dies—Jehangir Mughal Emperor.			
	1627 Shivaji born. 1628 Shah Jehan Mughal Emperor. Taj Mahal built at Agra.	1623'Massacre of Amboyna.' Dutch Governor executes entire staff of British East India Company at Amboyna on charge of conspiracy. Thereupon English withdraw from East Indian islands. 1641 Dutch capture Malacca from Portuguese whose Eastern Empire practically ends.	1636 Russians reach Pacific Ocean, north of Chinese Empire. 1644 Manchu conquest. End of Ming dynasty. Manchu dynasty till 1912.	1641 Japan closed to all foreigners for over 200 years (till 1853)
	1658 Aurungzeb Mughal Emperor. 1680 Shivaji dies.	Dutch supreme in East Indian islands (Java, Sumatra, etc.) Control trade. No rivals.	1661Emperor Kang Hi (Manchu) rules 61 years over largest and most populous empire in the world (till 1722). Powerful State. 1689 Treaty of Nerchinsk between China and Russia.	
c. 1732 Nadir Shah dominates Persia.	1707 Aurungzeb dies—Mughal Empire goes to pieces. Sikh Guru Govind Singh dies (10th and last guru).		1728 Behring reaches Alaska from across Siberia. Russian advance east in North Asia continues.	

North and South America	Western Europe	Eastern Europe	Western Asia
Right through eighteenth century African slave trade carried on by European countries. At its height at end of eighteenth century. Liverpool and New York centres of this trade.	1740 Frederick the Great of Prussia begins reign. Voltaire (1694–1778).	Ottoman Empire weakening, Russia advancing lured by Constantinople. Repeated wars.	Civil War in Persia.
1763 Canada ceded by France to England.	1756–63 Seven Years' War—Worldwide struggle between England and France for dominion ends in English victory.		
1775 North American colonies at war with England. 1776 American Revolution. Declaration of Independence. George Washington.	Goethe (1749–1832). Beethoven, the great musician (1770–1827).	1774 Russia takes Crimea from Turkey and reaches Black Sea. 1782 Catherine II the Great Tsarina.	
	1789 Storming of the Bastille in Paris. French Revolution begins.		
	1792 France becomes a Republic.	Russian boundary advancing towards Constantinople, Turkey retreating.	
	1799 Napoleon Bonaparte. First consul.		1798 Napoleon in Egypt.
Revolutions in South America. Independent republics established	1804 Napoleon Emperor. 1806 'Holy Roman Empire' ends formally.		
	1815 Battle of Waterloo. Treaty of Vienna.		
Simon Bolivar. End of Spanish and Portuguese American Empires.	Industrial Revolution in England (from end of 18th century onwards).		
African slave trade prohibited by most countries but extensive illegal trade still carried on and Negroes taken to Southern States of United States of America.	1825 First railway (in England). 1830 Revolutions in Europe. Louis Philippe becomes King of France. Belgium becomes independent. 1832 British Reform Bill.	1829 Greece frees herself from Ottoman rule and becomes independent.	Ottoman Empire continues over Asia Minor—Palestine—Syria—Arabia and Iraq. But Egypt is semi-independent under Mehemet Ali (dies 1849).
United States of America spread westward. Acquire California.	1848 Year of Revolution in Europe. Republic established in France.		
	1852 Second French Republic ends. Napoleon III Emperor of the French. Charles Darwin (1809–82). Karl Marx (1818–83).	1854–6 Crimean War. England and France help Turkey against Russia.	1856 British War with Persia.
		1860 Russian Empire reaches Pacific Ocean.	

Date	India	Farther India, Malaysia, etc.	China	Japan
A.C. 1700			1736 Chien Lung Emperor—reigns 60 years (to 1796).	
	c. 1737 Marathas dominant in Central and South India. At the gates of Delhi. 1739 Nadir Shah's raid in Northern India. Struggle between French and English for mastery in India ends in destruction of French power. (1737–57)—Dupleix—Clive.			
1750	1757 Battle of Plassey. English dominant power.			
	Sikh power growing in the Punjab. 1790–99 Mysore Wars of the British against Haider Ali and Tippu Sultan.	1782 New Siamese dynasty begins—Rama I (This dynasty still reigning).	Chien Lung's Empire reaches widest limits in Chinese history—includes Manchuria, Mongolia, Tibet and Central Asia; and Vassal States: Korea, Annam, Siam, Burma. Nepal also invaded and made Tributary.	
1800	1814 British War against Nepal.	1798 Dutch East India Co. ends. Netherlands government takes over direct charge of Dutch East Indies.	British embassies to China (in 1792 and 1816). 1800 Chinese government prohibit opium. Illegal opium trade carried on by foreigners especially British East India Company.	
	1819 Ranjit Singh ruler of Sikh State in the Punjab and Kashmir. (He dies in 1839).	1819 British acquire Singapore from where British authority extends over Malay Peninsula. Singapore attracts all the trade and ruins. Dutch port of Malacca.		
	1824 English make war on Burma. Assam annexed.	1824 First Burma War.		
	1839 First Anglo-Afghan War. Fear of Russian advance through Central Asia towards India. 1845 and 1848 Anglo-Sikh Wars. Punjab annexed by the British.		1840 The Opium War—Anglo-Chinese. 1842 First Treaty settlements. Hong Kong ceded to British. Five ports opened to foreign trade. Extra territoriality, etc. (Treaty of Nanking).	
1850	1856 Second Burma War of British. More annexations. 1857 Sepoy Mutiny and great Revolt against British in Northern and Central India. 1858 End of British East India Company. Direct rule of British Parliament.	1856 Second Anglo-Burmese War.	1850 Great Taiping Rebellion begins—lasts till 1864. 1858 Second China War —Britain and France against China. 1858–1860 Chinese treaties with Russia ceding large territories in eastern Siberia to Russia. Thus Russian Empire reaches Pacific Ocean. 1860 British and French destroy imperial (Chinese) Summer Palace.	1853 American Squadron under Perry, visits Japan. Japan opened up again to foreign trade, etc. after over 200 years.

North and South America	Western Europe	Eastern Europe	Western Asia and Egypt	Date
				A.C. 1850
1861–65 American Civil War. Emancipation of Negroes. President Abraham Lincoln.	1861 Italy becomes united and independent. Mazzini—Garibaldi—Cavour.		1869 Suez Canal opened	
Right through 19th century in North America and North-West Europe especially, and partly elsewhere, great progress of science and growth of industry and mechanical transport. Development of democracy—capitalism—nationalism—imperialism.		Nationalism in Balkans—Turkey's subject nationalities gradually freeing themselves.		
	1870–71 Franco-Prussian War—France defeated. German Empire proclaimed at Versailles. Bismarck. France becomes a Republic. Shortlived commune in Paris.		1883 England occupies Egypt.	
		1876 Sultan grants constitution to Turkey and then suspends it. 1877 Russo-Turkish War.		
	1878 Treaty of Berlin after Russo-Turkish War. Development of the Labour Movement especially in North-west Europe. Trade Unions—Internationals Socialism. Karl Marx.	1878 Bulgaria, Serbia, Rumania and Montenegro gain independence from Turkish rule.		
1898 Spanish-American War—U.S. take Philippines. Cuba becomes free.	Western Powers scramble for Africa in second half of 19th century. 1899–1902 Anglo-Boer War in South Africa.		1906 Constitution granted by Shah of Persia—Majlis. Anglo-Russian aggression in Persia.	1900
		1905 Russian defeat by Japan leads to unsuccessful revolution in Russia. Duma established.		
		1908 Turkish Revolution. Constitution of 1876 restored. Committee of Union and Progress.		
		1911 Italian War with Turkey over Tripoli. 1912 Balkan Wars. Turkey almost driven out of Europe.		
	1914–18 Great War	Great War	Great War	
1917 United States join War.		1917 Two Russian Revolutions. Bolsheviks seize power. Civil War and wars of intervention in Russia and Siberia.	Turkish Ottoman Empire breaks up. Nationalist movements develop all over Western Asia and Egypt. 1919 Rising in Egypt. Saad Zaghlul Pasha	
1919–29 Ten year period of great prosperity in United States.	1918 Revolutions in Germany, Austria, etc. End of imperial dynasties. Republics established. 1919 Peace of Versailles. Many new States in Europe. Reparations—Mandates—League of Nations. Labour troubles—financial difficulties—Fall of currencies—numerous international conferences. 1920–22 Anglo-Irish War—Sinn Fein—Irish Free State established. 1922 Fascism triumphs in Italy: Benito Mussolini. Dictatorships in many countries of Europe.			
		1923 Union of Socialist and Soviet Republics established.		
	1926 General strike in Great Britain.		1922 Turkish victory over Greece. Mustafa Kemal Pasha. 1922 Sultanate abolished. Republic established in Turkey. 1924 Khilafat abolished. 1925 Riza Khan becomes Shah of Persia.	
1929 Slump and crisis	1929 Great trade depression and slump begins all over world—fall in prices—defaults of Governments bank failures. International trade dries up. (Depression still on in 1933). 1931 Revolution in Spain. Republic established.	1929 Soviet Union's Five Year Plan for rapid industrialization.	1925 Syrian rising against French Mandate. Damascus partly destroyed by French. 1926 Ibn Saud King of Hejaz.	
1930 Revolutions in South America—Argentine, Brazil, Chile, etc. Defaults of governments.				
1933 President Roosevelt given dictatorial powers by Congress to meet crisis. Starts great drive for higher wages, etc. State control of industry.	1933 Nazi triumph in Germany. Adolf Hitler. Republic suppressed. Persecution of labour and Jews, etc. Rise of Fascism in many countries of Europe.	1933 Soviet's Second Five Year Plan begins.	Palestine—Trans Jordan under British Mandate. Iraq nominally free but under British influence.	1933

India	Farther India, Malaysia, etc.	China	Japan
		1861 Dowager Empress Tzu Hsi (to 1908).	1867 Shogunate ended. Emperor Mutsuhito assumes charge (to 1912). Reforms. Tokyo made capital.
1879 Second Anglo-Afghan War.			
1885 Third Anglo-Burman War—Whole country annexed. 1885 Indian National Congress started. Rise of national movement.	1884 French rule in Annam (Indo-China). 1885 All Burma annexed by England.	1884 War between China and France.	
	1896 Fresh annexations by England and France in Malay and Siam. Federated Malay States formed under British rule. A small part of Siam remains free. 1898 Philippine Islands under United States of America.	1894 Japan defeats China. Treaty of Shimonosehi. Three Power intervention.	1889 New Constitution but Emperor remains supreme. Rapid industrialization and Westernization. 1894 War with China.
		1897 Scramble of Western Powers for concessions in China—Germany, Russia, France, and England all coerce China by displays of naval force.	
		1900 Boxer outbreak. International siege of Peking. Russians in Manchuria.	1902 Anglo-Japanese alliance.
			1904–5 Russo-Japanese War—Japan becomes a World Power. Great industrial and economic progress.
			1905 Japanese suzerainty over *Korea*.
			1910 *Korea*: Japanese turn out Korean king and annex Korea. Korean independence movement crushed.
		1912 Proclamation of Chinese Republic. Abdication of Manchu dynasty. Sun Yat-Sen. Yuan Shih-Kai.	
		1915 Japan's 21 demands—Great resentment in China.	1914 Japan joins Anglo-French allies in Great War.
		1917 China joins Anglo-French allies in War.	
1919 Third Anglo-Afghan War—Afghanistan becomes independent. 1919 Jallianwala Bagh Massacre in Amritsar. Martial Law in the Punjab.	Nationalist movements in Dutch East Indies, Philippines, French Indo-China, etc.	Rise of Tuchuns—Civil War.	
1920 Noncooperation movement under Gandhi. National struggle continues on mass lines.		1922 Washington Conference proclaims independence and integrity of China.	
	1927 Nationalist rising in Java suppressed.	1926 Victory of Kuo-Ming Tang followed by break-up of Party. Disintegration of China.	
		1929 Communist State established in interior.	
1930 National Congress declares for independence. Civil Disobedience movement. Suspension and truce in 1931. Again renewed 1932–33.	1932 Peaceful revolution in Siam. A constitution agreed to.	1932–33 Japanese invasion of Manchuria and North China.	Japanese aggression in China. On being censured by League of Nations, Japan retires from League.

A BIRTHDAY LETTER

FOR INDIRA PRIYADARSHINI
ON HER THIRTEENTH BIRTHDAY

Central Prison, Naini
October 26,[1] *1930*

ON your birthday you have been in the habit of receiving presents
and good wishes. Good wishes you will still have in full measure,
but what present can I send you from Naini Prison ? My presents
cannot be very material or solid. They can only be of the air and
of the mind and spirit, such as a good fairy might have bestowed
on you—things that even the high walls of prison cannot stop.

You know, sweetheart, how I dislike sermonizing and doling out
good advice. When I am tempted to dó this I always think of the
story of a " very wise man " I once read. Perhaps one day you will
yourself read the book which contains this story. Thirteen hundred
years ago there came a great traveller from China to India in search
of wisdom and knowledge. His name was Hiuen Tsang, and over
the deserts and mountains of the north he came, braving many
dangers, facing and overcoming many obstacles, so great was his
thirst for knowledge. And he spent many years in India learning
himself and teaching others, especially at the great university of
Nalanda, which existed then near the city that used to be called
Pātaliputra and is now known as Patna. Hiuen Tsang became
very learned himself and he was given the title of " Master of the
Law "—the Law of the Buddha—and he journeyed all over India
and saw and studied the people that lived in this great country in
those far-off days. Later he wrote a book of his travels, and it is
this book which contains the story that comes to my mind. It is
about a man from South India who came to Karnasuvarna, which
was a city somewhere near modern Bhagalpur in Bihar ; and this
man, it is written, wore round his waist copper-plates, and on his
head he carried a lighted torch. Staff in hand, with proud bearing
and lofty steps, he wandered about in this strange attire. And
when any one asked him the reason for his curious get-up, he told
him that his wisdom was so great that he was afraid his belly would
burst if he did not wear copper-plates round it ; and because he
was moved with pity for the ignorant people round about him, who
lived in darkness, he carried the light on his head.

Well, I am quite sure that there is no danger of my ever bursting
with too much wisdom and so there is no need for me to wear
copper-plates or armour. And in any event, I hope that my

[1] Indira's birthday takes place, according to the Gregorian Calendar, on
November 19. It was observed, however, on October 26, according to the
Samvat era.

1

wisdom, such of it as I possess, does not live in my belly. Wherever it may reside, there is plenty of room still for more of it and there is no chance of there being no room left. If I am so limited in wisdom, how can I pose as a wise man and distribute good advice to others? And so I have always thought that the best way to find out what is right and what is not right, what should be done and what should not be done, is not by giving a sermon, but by talking and discussing, and out of discussion sometimes a little bit of the truth comes out. I have liked my talks with you and we have discussed many things, but the world is wide and beyond our world lie other wonderful and mysterious worlds, so none of us need ever be bored or imagine, like the very foolish and conceited person whose story Hiuen Tsang has told us, that we have learned everything worth learning and become very wise. And perhaps it is as well that we do not become very wise; for the very wise, if any such there are, must sometimes feel rather sad that there is nothing more to learn. They must miss the joy of discovery and of learning new things—the great adventure that all of us who care to may have.

I must not therefore sermonize. But what am I to do, then? A letter can hardly take the place of a talk; at best it is a one-sided affair. So, if I say anything that sounds like good advice do not take it as if it were a bad pill to swallow. Imagine that I have made a suggestion to you for you to think over, as if we really were having a talk.

In history we read of great periods in the life of nations, of great men and women and great deeds performed, and sometimes in our dreams and reveries we imagine ourselves back in those times and doing brave deeds like the heroes and heroines of old. Do you remember how fascinated you were when you first read the story of Jeanne d'Arc, and how your ambition was to be something like her? Ordinary men and women are not usually heroic. They think of their daily bread and butter, of their children, of their household worries and the like. But a time comes when a whole people become full of faith for a great cause, and then even simple, ordinary men and women become heroes, and history becomes stirring and epoch-making. Great leaders have something in them which inspires a whole people and makes them do great deeds.

The year you were born in—1917—was one of the memorable years of history when a great leader, with a heart full of love and sympathy for the poor and suffering, made his people write a noble and never-to-be-forgotten chapter of history. In the very month in which you were born, Lenin started the great Revolution which has changed the face of Russia and Siberia. And to-day in India another great leader, also full of love for all who suffer and passionately eager to help them, has inspired our people to great endeavour and noble sacrifice, so that they may again be free and the starving and the poor and the oppressed may have their burdens removed from them. Bapuji [1] lies in prison, but the magic of his message

[1] Mahatma Gandhi.

steals into the hearts of India's millions, and men and women, and even little children, come out of their little shells and become India's soldiers of freedom. In India to-day we are making history, and you and I are fortunate to see this happening before our eyes and to take some part ourselves in this great drama.

How shall we bear ourselves in this great movement? What part shall we play in it? I cannot say what part will fall to our lot; but, whatever it may be, let us remember that we can do nothing which may bring discredit to our cause or dishonour to our people. If we are to be India's soldiers we have India's honour in our keeping, and that honour is a sacred trust. Often we may be in doubt as to what to do. It is no easy matter to decide what is right and what is not. One little test I shall ask you to apply whenever you are in doubt. It may help you. Never do anything in secret or anything that you would wish to hide. For the desire to hide anything means that you are afraid, and fear is a bad thing and unworthy of you. Be brave, and all the rest follows. If you are brave, you will not fear and will not do anything of which you are ashamed. You know that in our great Freedom Movement, under Bapuji's leadership, there is no room for secrecy or hiding. We have nothing to hide. We are not afraid of what we do and what we say. We work in the sun and in the light. Even so in our private lives let us make friends with the sun and work in the light and do nothing secretly or furtively. Privacy, of course, we may have and should have, but that is a very different thing from secrecy. And if you do so, my dear, you will grow up a child of the light, unafraid and serene and unruffled, whatever may happen.

I have written a very long letter to you. And yet there is so much I would like to tell you. How can a letter contain it?

You are fortunate, I have said, in being a witness to this great struggle for freedom that is going on in our country. You are also very fortunate in having a very brave and wonderful little woman for your Mummie, and if you are ever in doubt or in trouble you cannot have a better friend.

Good-bye, little one, and may you grow up into a brave soldier in India's service.

With all my love and good wishes.

1

A NEW YEAR'S GIFT

New Year's Day, 1931

Do you remember the letters I wrote to you, more than two years ago, when you were at Mussoorie and I was at Allahabad? You liked them, you told me then, and I have often wondered if I should not continue that series and try to tell you something more about this world of ours. But I have hesitated to do so. It is very interesting to think of the past story of the world and of the great men and women and of the great deeds that it contains. To read history is good, but even more interesting and fascinating is to help in making history. And you know that history is being made in our country to-day. The past of India is a long, long one, lost in the mists of antiquity; it has its sad and unhappy periods which make us feel ashamed and miserable, but on the whole it is a splendid past of which we may well be proud and think with pleasure. And yet to-day we have little leisure to think of the past. It is the future that fills our minds, the future that we are fashioning, and the present that absorbs all our time and energy.

I have had time enough here in Naini Prison to read or write what I wanted to. But my mind wanders and I think of the great struggle that is going on outside; of what others are doing and what I would do if I were with them. I am too full of the present and the future to think of the past. And yet I have felt that this was wrong of me. When I cannot take part in the work outside, why should I worry?

But the real reason—shall I whisper it to you?—why I put off writing was another one. I am beginning to doubt if I know enough to teach you! You are growing up so fast, and becoming such a wise little person, that all that I learnt at school and college and afterwards may not be enough for you, and at any rate may be rather stale. After some time, it may be that you will take up the rôle of teacher and teach me many new things! As I told you, in the letter I wrote to you on your last birthday, I am not at all like the Very Wise Man who went about with copper-plates round about him, so that he might not burst with excess of learning.

When you were at Mussoorie it was easy enough for me to write about the early days of the world. For the knowledge that we have of those days is vague and indefinite. But as we come out of those very ancient times, history gradually begins, and man begins his curious career in various parts of the world. And to follow man in this career, sometimes wise, more often mad and foolish, is no easy matter. With the help of books one might make an attempt. But Naini Prison does not provide a library. So I am afraid it is not possible for me to give you any connected account of world history, much as I should have liked to have done so. I dislike very much boys and girls learning the history of just one country, and that, too, very often through learning by heart some dates and a few facts. But history is one connected whole and you cannot understand even the history of any one country if you do not know what has happened in other parts of the world. I hope that you will not learn history in this narrow way, confining it to one or two countries, but will survey the whole world. Remember always that there is not so very much difference between various people as we seem to imagine. Maps and atlases show us countries in different colours. Undoubtedly people do differ from one another, but they resemble each other also a great deal, and it is well to keep this in mind and not be misled by the colours on the map or by national boundaries.

I cannot write for you the history of my choice. You will have to go to other books for it. But I shall write to you from time to time something about the past and about the people who lived in the days gone by, and who played a big part on the world's stage.

I do not know if my letters will interest you or awaken your curiosity. Indeed, I do not know when you will see them, or if you will see them at all. Strange that we should be so near and yet so far away ! In Mussoorie you were several hundred miles away from me. Yet I could write to you as often as I wished, and run up to you when the desire to see you became strong. But here we are on either side of the Jumna river—not far from each other, yet the high walls of Naini Prison keep us effectively apart. One letter a fortnight I may write, and one letter a fortnight I may receive, and once a fortnight I may have a twenty-minute interview. And yet these restrictions are good. We seldom value anything which we can get cheaply, and I am beginning to believe that a period in prison is a very desirable part of one's education. Fortunately there are scores of thousands in our country who are having this course to-day !

I cannot say if you will like these letters when you see them. But I have decided to write them for my own pleasure. They bring you very near to me, and I feel almost that I have had a talk with you. Often enough I think of you, but to-day you have hardly been absent from my mind. To-day is New Year's Day. As I lay in bed, very early in the morning, watching the stars, I thought of the great year that was past, with all its hope and anguish and joy, and all the great and gallant deeds performed. And I thought of Bapuji, who has made our old country young and vigorous again by his magic touch, sitting in his prison cell in Yeravada. And I thought of Dadu [1] and many others. And especially I thought of Mummie and you. Later in the morning came the news that Mummie had been arrested and taken to gaol. It was a pleasant New Year's gift for me. It had long been expected and I have no doubt that Mummie is thoroughly happy and contented.

But you must be rather lonely. Once a fortnight you may see Mummie and once a fortnight you may see me, and you will carry our messages to each other. But I shall sit down with pen and paper and I shall think of you. And then you will silently come near me and we shall talk of many things. And we shall dream of the past, and find our way to make the future greater than the past. So on this New Year's Day let us resolve that, by the time this year also grows old and dies, we shall have brought this bright future dream of ours nearer to the present, and given to India's past a shining page of history.

[1] Indira's grandfather, Pandit Motilal Nehru.

2

THE LESSON OF HISTORY

January 5, 1931

WHAT shall I write to you, my dear? Where shall I begin? When I think of the past, vast numbers of pictures rush through my mind. Some of the pictures stay longer than others. They are my favourites and I begin to muse about them, and, unconsciously almost, I compare past happenings with what is taking place to-day, and try to find a lesson in them for my guidance. But what a strange jumble is one's mind, full of disconnected thoughts and ill-arranged images, like a gallery with no order in the arrangement of pictures. And yet perhaps the fault is not entirely ours. Most of us could certainly arrange the order of events in our minds better. But sometimes the events themselves are strange and difficult to fit into any scheme of things.

I think I wrote to you once that a study of history should teach us how the world has slowly but surely progressed, how the first simple animals gave place to more complicated and advanced animals, how last of all came the master animal—Man, and how by force of his intellect he triumphed over the others. Man's growth from barbarism to civilization is supposed to be the theme of history. In some of my letters I have tried to show you how the idea of co-operation or working together has grown, and how our ideal should be to work together for the common good. But sometimes, looking at great stretches of history, it is difficult to believe that this ideal has made much progress or that we are very much civilized or advanced. There is enough of want of co-operation to-day, of one country or people selfishly attacking or oppressing another, of one man exploiting another. If after millions of years of progress we are still so backward and imperfect, how much longer will it take us to learn to behave as sensible and reasonable persons? Sometimes we read about past periods of history which seem to be better than ours, more cultured and civilized even, and this makes us doubt if our world is going forward or backward. Our own country has surely had brilliant periods in the past, far better in every way than our present.

It is true that there have been brilliant periods in the past in many countries—in India, Egypt, China, Greece, and elsewhere— and that many of these countries have relapsed and gone back. But even this should not make us lose heart. The world is a big place and the rise and fall of any country for a while may not make much difference to the world at large.

Many people nowadays are apt to boast of our great civilization and of the wonders of science. Science has indeed done wonders, and the great men of science are worthy of all respect. But those who boast are seldom the great. And it is well to remember that in many ways man has not made very great progress from the other

animals. It may be that in certain ways some animals are superior
to him still. This may sound a foolish statement, and people who
do not know better may laugh at it. But you have just read Maeter-
linck's Life of the Bee, of the White Ant, and the Ant, and you must
have wondered at the social organization of these insects. We
look down upon the insects as almost the lowest of living things, and
yet these tiny things have learnt the art of co-operation and of
sacrifice for the common good far better than man. Ever since I
read of the White Ant and of its sacrifices for its comrades, I have
developed a soft corner in my heart for it. If mutual co-operation
and sacrifice for the good of society are the tests of civilization, we
may say that the White Ant and the Ant are in this respect superior
to man.

In one of our old Sanskrit books there is a verse which can be
translated as follows : " For the family sacrifice the individual, for
the community the family, for the country the community, and for
the Soul the whole world ". What the Soul is few of us can know or
tell, and each one of us can interpret it in a different way. But the
lesson this Sanskrit verse teaches us is the same lesson of co-operation and sacrifice for the larger good. We in India had forgotten
this sovereign path to real greatness for many a day, and so we had
fallen. But again we seem to have glimpses of it, and all the
country is astir. How wonderful it is to see men and women, and
boys and girls, smilingly going ahead in India's cause and not
caring about any pain or suffering ! Well may they smile and be
glad, for the joy of serving in a great cause is theirs; and to those
who are fortunate comes the joy of sacrifice also. To-day we are
trying to free India. That is a great thing. But an even greater
is the cause of humanity itself. And because we feel that our
struggle is a part of the great human struggle to end suffering and
misery, we can rejoice that we are doing our little bit to help the
progress of the world.

Meanwhile, you sit in Anand Bhawan, and Mummie sits in
Malacca Gaol, and I here in Naini Prison—and we miss each other
sometimes, rather badly, do we not ? But think of the day when we
shall all three meet again ! I shall look forward to it, and the
thought of it will lighten and cheer up my heart.

3

INQILĀB ZINDABĀD[1]

January 7, 1931

PRIYADARSHINI[2]—dear to the sight, but dearer still when sight
is denied ! As I sat here to-day to write to you, faint cries, like
distant thunder, reached me. I could not make out at first what

---

[1] *Inqilāb zindabād* means " long live revolution ".
[2] *Priyadarshini* is Indira's second name and means " dear to the sight ".

they were, but they had a familiar ring and they seemed to find an answering echo in my heart. Gradually they seemed to approach and grow in volume, and soon there was no doubt as to what they were. " *Inqilāb zindabād !* " " *Inqilāb zindabād !* " the prison resounded with the spirited challenge, and our hearts were glad to hear it. I do not know who they were who shouted our war-cry so near us outside the gaol—whether they were men and women from the city or peasants from the villages. Nor do I know the occasion for it to-day. But whoever they were, they cheered us up, and we sent a silent answer to their greeting and all our good wishes went with it.

Why should we shout " *Inqilāb zindabād* " ? Why should we want revolution and change ? India of course wants a big change to-day. But even after the big change that we all want has come and India is independent, we cannot rest quiescent. Nothing in the world that is alive remains unchanging. All Nature changes from day to day and minute to minute, only the dead stop growing and are quiescent. Fresh water runs on, and if you stop it, it becomes stagnant. So also is it with the life of man and the life of a nation. Whether we want to or not, we grow old. Babies become little girls, and little girls big girls and grown-up women and old women. We have to put up with these changes. But there are many who refuse to admit that the world changes. They keep their minds closed and locked up and will not permit any new ideas to come into them. Nothing frightens them so much as the idea of thinking. What is the result ? The world moves on in spite of them, and because they and people like them do not adapt themselves to the changing conditions, there are big burst-ups from time to time. Big revolutions take place, like the great French Revolution of a hundred and forty years ago, or the Russian Revolution thirteen years ago. Even so in our own country, we are to-day in the middle of a revolution. We want independence, of course. But we want something more. We want to clear out all the stagnant pools and let in clean fresh water everywhere. We must sweep away the dirt and the poverty and misery from our country. We must also clean up, as far as we can, the cobwebs from the minds of so many people which prevent them from thinking and co-operating in the great work before us. It is a great work, and it may be that it will require time. Let us, at least, give it a good push on— *Inqilāb zindabād !*

We are on the threshold of our Revolution. What the future will bring we cannot say. But even the present has brought us rich returns for our labours. See the women of India, how proudly they march ahead of all in the struggle ! Gentle and yet brave and indomitable, see how they set the pace for others. And the *purdah*, which hid our brave and beautiful women, and was a curse to them and to their country, where is it now ? Is it not rapidly slinking away to take its rightful place in the shelves of museums, where we keep the relics of a bygone age ?

See also the children—the boys and girls—the Vānar Sēnās and the Bāl and Bālikā Sabhās. The parents of many of these children may have behaved as cowards or slaves in the past. But who dare doubt that the children of our generation will tolerate no slavery or cowardice ?

And so the wheel of change moves on, and those who were down go up and those who were up go down. It was time it moved in our country. But we have given it such a push this time that no one can stop it.

Inqilāb zindabād !

4

ASIA AND EUROPE

January 8, 1931

EVERYTHING changes continually, I said in my last letter. What is history, indeed, but a record of change ? And if there had been very few changes in the past, there would have been little of history to write.

The history we learn in school or college is usually not up to much. I do not know very much about others, but about myself I know that I learnt very little in school. I learnt a little—very little—of the history of India, and a little of the history of England. And even the history of India that I learnt was largely wrong or distorted and written by people who looked down upon our country. Of the history of other countries I had the vaguest knowledge. It was only after I left college that I read some real history. Fortunately, my visits to prison have given me a chance of improving my knowledge.

I have written to you in some of my earlier letters about the ancient civilization of India, about the Dravidians and the coming of the Aryans. I have not written much about the days before the Aryans, because I do not know much about them. But it will interest you to know that within the last few years the remains of a very ancient civilization have been discovered in India. These are in the north-west of India round about a place called Mohen-jo Daro. People have dug out these remains of perhaps 5000 years ago and have even discovered mummies, similar to those of old Egypt. Imagine ! all this was thousands of years ago, long before the Aryans came. Europe must then have been a wilderness.

To-day Europe is strong and powerful, and its people consider themselves the most civilized and cultured in the world. They look down upon Asia and her peoples, and come and grab everything they can get from the countries of Asia. How times have changed ! Let us have a good look at Europe and Asia. Open an atlas and see little Europe sticking on to the great Asiatic Continent. It seems to be just a little extension of it. When you read history you will find that for long periods and stretches of time

Asia had been dominant. Her people went in wave after wave and conquered Europe. They ravaged Europe and they civilized Europe. Aryans, Scythians, Huns, Arabs, Mongols, Turks—they all came from somewhere in Asia and spread out over Asia and Europe. Asia seemed to produce them in great numbers like locusts. Indeed, Europe was for long like a colony of Asia, and many people of modern Europe are descended from these invaders from Asia.

Asia sprawls right across the map like a big, lumbering giant. Europe is small. But, of course, this does not mean that Asia is great because of her size or that Europe is not worthy of much attention. Size is the poorest test of a man's or a country's greatness. We know well that Europe, though the smallest of continents, is to-day great. We know also that many of her countries have had brilliant periods of history. They have produced great men of science who have, by their discoveries and inventions, advanced human civilization tremendously and made life easier for millions of men and women. They have had great writers and thinkers, and artists and musicians and men of action. It would be foolish not to recognize the greatness of Europe.

But it would be equally foolish to forget the greatness of Asia. We are apt to be taken in a little by the glitter of Europe and forget the past. Let us remember that it is Asia that has produced great leaders of thought who have influenced the world perhaps more than any one or anything elsewhere—the great founders of the principal religions. Hinduism, the oldest of the great religions existing to-day, is of course the product of India. So also is its great sister-religion Buddhism, which now spreads all over China and Japan and Burma and Tibet and Ceylon. The religion of the Jews and Christianity are also Asiatic religions, as their origin was in Palestine on the west coast of Asia. Zoroastrianism, the religion of the Parsis, began in Persia, and you know that Mohammed, the prophet of Islam, was born in Mecca in Arabia. Krishna, Buddha, Zoroaster, Christ, Mohammed, and Confucius and Lao-Tse, the great philosophers of China—you could fill pages with the names of the great thinkers of Asia. You could also fill pages with the names of the great men of action of Asia. And in many other ways I could show you how great and vital was this old continent of ours in the days gone by.

How times have changed ! But they are changing again even before our eyes. History usually works slowly through the centuries, though sometimes there are periods of rush and burst-ups. To-day, however, it is moving fast in Asia, and the old continent is waking up after her long slumber. The eyes of the world are upon her, for everyone knows that Asia is going to play a great part in the future.

5

THE OLD CIVILIZATIONS AND OUR INHERITANCE

January 9, 1931

I READ yesterday in the *Bharat*, the Hindi newspaper which brings us some news of the outside world twice a week, that Mummie was not being properly treated in the Malacca Gaol. Also that she is going to be sent to Lucknow Gaol. I was put out a little and I worried. Perhaps there was no truth in the rumour given in the *Bharat*. But even a doubt about it is not good to have. It is easy enough to put up with discomfort and suffering oneself. It does every one good, as otherwise we might grow too soft. But it is not very easy or comforting to think of the suffering of others who are dear to us, especially if we can do nothing for them. And so the doubt that the *Bharat* raised in my mind made me worry about Mummie. She is brave and has the heart of a lioness, but she is weak in body, and I would not like her body to become weaker. What can we do, however stout-hearted we may be, if our bodies fail us ? If we want to do any work well, we must have health and strength and perfect bodies.

Perhaps it is as well that Mummie is going to be sent to Lucknow. She may be more comfortable and happier there, and there will be some companions in Lucknow Gaol. Probably she is alone in Malacca. Still, it was pleasant to think that she was not far, just four or five miles away from our prison. But this is a foolish fancy. Five miles or a 150 miles are much the same when the high walls of two prisons intervene.

I was so glad to learn to-day that Dadu had come back to Allahabad and that he was better. I was also very pleased to learn that he had gone to see Mummie in Malacca Gaol. Perhaps, with luck, I may see all of you to-morrow. For to-morrow is my interview day, and in gaol the *mulāqāt kā din* is a great day. I have not seen Dadu for nearly two months. I shall see him, I hope, and satisfy myself that he is really better. And I shall see you after a long, long fortnight, and you will bring me news of yourself and of Mummie.

Heigh-ho ! I write on of foolish things although I sat down to write to you about past history. Let us try to forget the present for a while and go back 2000 or 3000 years.

Of Egypt and of ancient Knossos in Crete, I wrote to you a little in some of my previous letters. And I told you that the ancient civilizations took root in these two countries as well as in what is now called Iraq or Mesopotamia, and in China and India and Greece. Greece, perhaps, came a little later than the others. So that the civilization of India takes rank in age with its sister-civilizations of Egypt and China and Iraq. And even ancient Greece is a younger sister of these. What happened to these ancient civilizations ? Knossos is no more. Indeed, for nearly 3000 years it has been no more. The people of the younger civilization of Greece came and destroyed it. The old civilization of Egypt, after a splendid history lasting for thousands of years, vanished and left no trace behind it, except the great Pyramids and the Sphinx, and the ruins of great temples and mummies and the like. Of course Egypt, the country, is still there and the river Nile flows through it as of old, and men and women live in it as in other countries. But there is no connecting link between these modern people and the old civilization of their country.

Iraq and Persia—how many empires have flourished there and followed each other into oblivion! Babylonia and Assyria and Chaldæa, to mention the oldest only. And the great cities of Babylon and Nineveh. The Old Testament in the Bible is full of the record of these people. Later, in this land of ancient history, other empires flourished, and then ceased to flourish. Here was Baghdad, the magic city of the *Arabian Nights*. But empires come and empires go, and the biggest and proudest of kings and emperors strut on the world's stage for a brief while only. But civilizations endure. In Iraq and Persia, however, the old civilization went utterly, even as the old civilization of Egypt.

Greece in her ancient days was great indeed, and people read even now of her glory with wonder. We stand awed and wonder-struck before the beauty of her marble statuary, and read the frag-ments of her old literature that have come down to us with reverence and amazement. It is said, and rightly, that modern Europe is in some ways the child of ancient Greece, so much has Europe been influenced by Greek thought and Greek ways. But the glory that was Greece, where is it now? For ages past, the old civilization has been no more, and other ways have taken its place, and Greece to-day is but a petty country in the south-east of Europe.

Egypt, Knossos, Iraq, and Greece—they have all gone. Their old civilizations, even as Babylon and Nineveh, have ceased to exist. What, then, of the two other ancients in this company of old civilizations? What of China and India? As in other countries, they too have had empire after empire. There have been invasions and destructions and loot on a vast scale. Dynasties of kings have ruled for hundreds of years and then been replaced by others. All this has happened in India and China, as elsewhere. But nowhere else, apart from India and China, has there been a real continuity of civilization. In spite of all the changes and battles and invasions, the thread of the ancient civilizations has continued to run on in both these countries. It is true that both of them have fallen greatly from their old estate, and that the ancient cultures are covered up with a heap of dust, and sometimes filth, which the long ages have accumulated. But still they endure and the old Indian civilization is the basis of Indian life even to-day. New conditions have arisen in the world now; and the coming of the steamship and the railway and the great factory has changed the face of the world. It may be, it is indeed probable, that they will change as they are already changing, the face of India also. But it is interesting and rather wonderful to think of this long range and continuity of Indian culture and civilization, right from the dawn of history, through long ages, down to us. In a sense, we in India are the heirs of these thousands of years. We are in the direct line, it may be, with the ancients, who came down through the north-western mountain passes into the smiling plains of what was to be known as Brahmāvarta and Aryavarta and Bhāratavarsha and Hindustān. Can you not see them trekking down the mountain passes into the unknown land below ? Brave and full of the spirit of adventure, they dared to go ahead without fear of the consequences. If death came, they did not mind, they met it laughing. But they loved life and knew that the only way to enjoy life was to be fearless, and not to worry about defeat and disaster. For defeat and disaster have a way of keeping away from those who are not afraid. Think of them, those distant ancestors of ours, marching on and on, and suddenly reaching the banks of the noble Ganga flowing majestically down to the sea. How the sight must have filled them with joy ! And is it any wonder that they bowed down to her and praised her in their rich and melodious language ?

It is indeed wonderful to think that we are the heirs of all these ages. But let us not become conceited, for if we are the heirs of the ages, we are the heirs of both the good and the bad. And there is a great deal of evil in our present inheritance in India, a great deal that has kept us down in the world, and reduced our noble country to great poverty, and made her a plaything in the hands of others. But have we not decided that this must no longer continue ?

6

THE HELLENES

January 10, 1931

NONE of you came to-day to interview us, and the *mulāqāt kā din* has been rather a blank day. It was a disappointment. And what was worse was the reason given for the postponement of the interview. We were told that Dadu was not well. More we could not find out. Well, when I found that the interview was not taking place to-day, I went to my *charkha* and did some spinning. I find that spinning on the *charkha* and weaving *niwār* are delightfully soothing. So, when in doubt, spin !

We compared and contrasted Europe and Asia in my last letter. Let us have a brief look at old Europe, as it is supposed to have been. For a long time, Europe meant the countries round about the Mediterranean Sea. We have no records of the northern countries of Europe in those days. Germany and England and France were supposed by the people of the Mediterranean to be inhabited by wild and barbarous tribes. Indeed, to begin with, civilization is supposed to have been confined to the eastern Mediterranean. As you know, Egypt (which, of course, is in Africa and not in Europe) and Knossos were the first countries to go ahead. Gradually the Aryans poured westwards from Asia, and invaded Greece and the neighbouring countries. These were the Aryan Greeks whom we now know and admire as the ancient Greeks. To begin with, I suppose, they were not very different from the Aryans who, perhaps earlier, had descended into India. But changes must have crept in, and gradually the two branches of the Aryan race became more and more different. The Indian Aryans were influenced greatly by the still older civilization of India—that of the Dravidians, and perhaps the remains of the civilization whose ruins we see at Mohen-jo Daro. The Aryans and the Dravidians gave much to each other and took much from each other also, and thus built up a common culture for India.

In the same way the Aryan Greeks must have been greatly influenced by the older civilization of Knossos which they found flourishing in the Grecian homelands. But though influenced by it, they destroyed Knossos and much of its outer civilization also, and on its ruins they built their own civilization. We must remember that the Aryan Greeks as well as the Aryan Indians were, in those early days, rough and hard fighters. They were vigorous, and they destroyed or absorbed the softer and more civilized people they came across.

So Knossos was destroyed nearly 1000 years before Christ was born. And the new Greeks established themselves in Greece and the islands round about. They went by sea to the west coast of Asia Minor, to southern Italy and Sicily, and even to the south of France. Marseilles in France was founded by them; but perhaps even before they went, there was a Phœnician settlement there. You will remember that the Phœnicians were a great seafaring people of Asia Minor who went far and wide in search of trade. They even managed to reach England in those early days when England was a barbarous country, and the long sea voyage through the straits of Gibraltar must have been a perilous one.

In the mainland of Greece famous cities grew up : Athens and Sparta and Thebes and Corinth. The early days of the Greeks, or the Hellenes as they were called, were celebrated in two famous epics, the *Iliad* and the *Odyssey*. You know something about these two epics, which in a way correspond to our own epics, the *Rāmāyana* and *Mahābhārata*. They are said to have been written by Homer, who was blind. The *Iliad* tells us how Paris carried away the beautiful Helen to his town of Troy, and how the Greek kings and chiefs then laid siege to Troy to recover her. The *Odyssey* is the story of the wanderings of Odysseus or Ulysses on his way back from the siege of Troy. In Asia Minor, not far from the coast, stood this little town of Troy. It exists no more, and for ages past it has ceased to be; but the genius of a poet has made it immortal.

As the Hellenes or Greeks were growing rapidly to their brief but splendid manhood, it is interesting to notice the quiet birth of

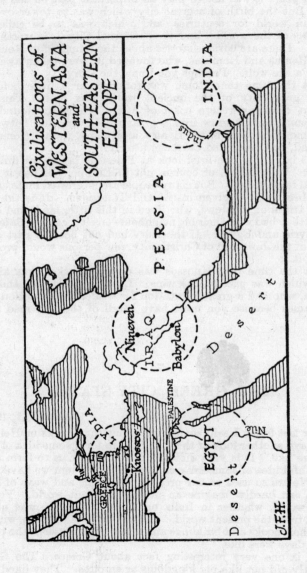

Civilisations of
WESTERN ASIA
and
SOUTH-EASTERN
EUROPE

another Power, which was later to conquer and supplant Greece. Rome is said to have been founded about this time. For several hundred years it was not to play an important part on the world's stage. But the birth of a great city which was to tower over the European world for centuries, and which was to be called the " mistress of the world " and the " Eternal City ", is worth mentioning. There are curious stories about the founding of Rome and of how Remus and Romulus, who founded it, were taken away and kept by a she-wolf. Perhaps you know the story.

About the time that Rome was founded, or a little before it, another great city of the ancient world was built. This was Carthage, on the northern coast of Africa, which was founded by the Phœnicians. It grew into a great sea-Power, and between it and Rome there was bitter rivalry and many wars. Rome won in the end, and destroyed Carthage utterly.

Let us have just one brief look at Palestine before we finish for the day. Palestine is, of course, not in Europe, nor has it much historical importance. But many people are interested in its ancient history because it is given in the Old Testament. It is the story of some tribes of the Jews, who lived in this little land, and of the troubles they had with their big neighbours on either side—Babylonia and Assyria and Egypt. If the story had not become part of the religion of the Jews and of Christianity, few persons would probably know of it.

About the time that Knossos was destroyed, Saul was king of Israel, which was part of Palestine. Later came David, and then Solomon, who had a great reputation for wisdom. I mention these three names because you must have heard of them or read about them.

7

THE GREEK CITY-STATES

January 11, 1931

IN my last letter I said something about the Greeks or Hellenes. Let us have another look at them and try to form some idea of what they were like. It is very difficult, of course, for us to form a real and truthful idea of something or some people whom we have never seen. We are so used to our present conditions and ways of living that we can hardly imagine an utterly different world. Yet the ancient world, whether in India or China or Greece, was utterly different from the present world. All we can do is to guess, with the help of their books and buildings and other remains, what the people in those days were like.

There is one very interesting fact about Greece. The Greeks apparently did not like big kingdoms or empires. They liked little City-States—that is to say, each city was an independent State.

They were little republics, with the city in the centre and some fields round about from which the food of the city came. A republic, as you know, has no king. These Greek City-States had no kings, but were governed by the rich citizens. The average man there had little or no say in the government. There were many slaves who had no rights in the government, and women also had no rights. So that only a part of the population of the City-States were citizens, and as such could vote on public questions. It was not difficult for these citizens to vote, as all of them could be gathered together in one place. This could only be done because it was a small City-State and not a great big country under one government. Imagine all the voters of India, or even of a province like Bengal or Agra, meeting together ! It simply can't be done. This difficulty had to be faced later in other countries, and a solution was found in what is called " representative government ". This means that instead of all the voters of a country meeting together to decide on a question, they elect their " representatives ", who meet together and consider public questions relating to the country and make laws for it. In this way the ordinary voter is supposed to help indirectly in the government of his country.

But this has nothing to do with Greece. Greece avoided this difficult question by not having anything bigger than a City-State. Although the Greeks spread out, as I have told you, all over Greece and southern Italy and Sicily and other coasts of the Mediterranean, they did not try to have an empire or one government for all these places under their control. Everywhere they went they formed their separate City-State.

In India also you will find that in the early days there were small republics or kingdoms rather like the Greek City-State. But apparently they did not last long, and they were absorbed into larger kingdoms. Even so, however, for a very long time our village *panchāyats* had a great deal of power. Perhaps the first impulse of the old Aryans was to have small City-States wherever they went. But geographical conditions and contact with older civilizations gradually made them give up this idea in many of the countries they inhabited. In Persia especially, we find large States and empires grew up; in India also there was a tendency for larger kingdoms to grow up. But in Greece the City-State continued for long, till a Greek, famous in history, made the first attempt we know of to conquer the world. This was Alexander the Great. We shall have something to say of him later.

So the Greeks refused to join their little City-States together to form a large State, kingdom or republic. Not only did they keep separate and independent, but they were almost always fighting each other. There was great rivalry between them, often resulting in war.

And yet there were many common links joining these City-States together. They had a common language, a common culture and the same religion. Their religion was one of many gods and goddesses, and they had a rich and beautiful mythology like the old Hindu mythology. They worshipped the beautiful. Even now we have a few of their old statues in marble and stone, and they are wondrously beautiful. They believed in having healthy and beautiful bodies, and for this purpose organized games and races. These games used to take place from time to time on a big scale at Olympia, in Greece, and people from all over Greece gathered together there. You must have heard of the Olympic games that take place even now. The name has been taken from the old Greek games at Olympia and applied to games and championships between different countries.

So the Greek City-States lived separately, meeting each other at their games and fighting each other frequently. When a great danger came from outside, however, they united to resist it. This was the Persian invasion, about which we shall have something to say at a later stage.

8

EMPIRES IN WESTERN ASIA

January 13, 1931

It was good to see you all yesterday. But I had a shock when I saw Dadu. He was looking so weak and ill. Look after him well and make him fit and strong again. I could hardly speak to you yesterday. What can one do in a short interview? I try to make up for all the interviews and talks we have not had by writing these letters. But they are poor substitutes, and the make-believe does not last long! Still it is good sometimes to play at make-believe.

Let us go back to the ancients. We have been with the old Greeks lately. What were the other countries like about this time? We need not trouble ourselves much about the other countries of Europe. We do not, or at any rate I do not, know anything very interesting about them. The climate of northern Europe had probably been changing, and this must have resulted in new conditions. Long, long ago, you may perhaps remember, it was very cold all over northern Europe and northern Asia. This was called the Ice Age, and huge glaciers came right down to Central Europe. Man did not exist then probably, or even if he did he was more animal than human. You may wonder how we can say now that there were glaciers in those days. There can, of course, be no record of them in any books, for there were no books or writers of books in those days. But you have not forgotten the book of Nature, I hope. Nature has a way of writing her own history in her rocks and stones, and all who wish to may read it there. It is a kind of auto biography—that is, one's own history. Now, glaciers have a way of leaving very peculiar marks of their existence. You can hardly mistake them once you get to recognize them. And if you want to study these marks, all you have to do is to go to any of our present glaciers in the Himalayas or the Alps or elsewhere. You have yourself seen the glaciers round about Mont Blanc in the Alps, but perhaps no one pointed out to you then these special marks. There are plenty of fine glaciers in Kashmir and in other parts of the Himalayas. The nearest glacier for us is the Pindari glacier, which is about a week's march from Almora. I went there once when I was a small boy—much younger than you are now—and I still remember it vividly.

Instead of history and the past, I have drifted into glaciers and the Pindari ! That comes of the game of make-believe. I want, if possible, to talk to you as if you were here, and if I do so we must surely have little excursions occasionally to glaciers and the like.

We started discussing glaciers because of my reference to the Ice Age. We can say that glaciers came down to Central Europe and to England, because we can still find the peculiar marks of glaciers in these countries. They are to be found on the old rocks, and this makes us think that it must have been very cold all over central and northern Europe then. Later it became warmer and the glaciers gradually shrank. Geologists—the people who study the history of the earth—tell us that this cold spell was succeeded by a warm spell when it was even warmer than it is to-day in Europe. Owing to this warmth, dense forests grew up in Europe.

The Aryans in their wanderings reached central Europe also. They do not appear to have done anything very remarkable there at this period, so we can for the moment ignore them. The civilized peoples of Greece and the Mediterranean probably looked upon these people of central and northern Europe as barbarians. But these " barbarians " were living a healthy and warlike life in their forests and villages, and unconsciously preparing themselves for the day when they were to swoop down and topple over the governments of the more civilized peoples of the south. But this happened long afterwards and we need not anticipate.

If we know little about northern Europe, we know nothing at all about great continents and tracts of country. America is supposed to have been discovered by Columbus, but that does not mean, as we are finding out now, that civilized people did not exist there before Columbus went there. But anyhow, we know nothing of America in those early days of which we are speaking. Nor do we know anything about the continent of Africa, Egypt of course being excepted, and also the coast of the Mediterranean. Egypt was at this period probably at the decline of her great and ancient civilization. But, even so, it was a very advanced country in those days.

We have now to consider what was happening in Asia. Here, as you know, there were three centres of ancient civilization : the Mesopotamian, the Indian, and the Chinese.

In Mesopotamia and Persia and Asia Minor, empire after empire came and went even in those early days. There was the Assyrian Empire, the Median, the Babylonian, and later the Persian. We need not go into the details of how these empires fought each other, or remained at peace for a while side by side, or destroyed each other. You will notice the difference between the Greek City-States and the empires of western Asia. From very early days there appears to have been a passion for a great State or empire in these countries. Perhaps it was due to their older civilization, or there may have been other causes.

One name might interest you. It is that of Crœsus of whom you must have heard. To be as rich as Crœsus has become a well-known saying in English. You may also have read stories of this Crœsus, of how rich and proud he was and how he was humbled. Crœsus was the king of a country called Lydia, which was on the west coast of Asia, where Asia Minor is to-day. Being a country touching the sea, probably there was a great deal of trade there. In his time the Persian Empire under Cyrus was growing and becoming powerful. Cyrus and Crœsus came into conflict and Cyrus defeated Crœsus. The story of this defeat, and how in his misery wisdom and sense came to the proud Crœsus, is told us by a Greek writer of history, Herodotus.

Cyrus had a great empire probably extending right up to India in the east. But one of his successors, Darius, had an even greater empire. It included Egypt and a bit of Central Asia, and even a small part of India near the Indus river. It is said that a huge quantity of gold dust used to be sent to him from this Indian province of his as tribute. In those days there must have been gold dust near the Indus river. There is none to be found there now, and indeed the country is largely waste land. This shows how the climate must have changed.

As you will read history and think of past conditions and compare them with present conditions, one of the things that will interest you most is the change that has taken place in Central Asia. This was the place from where issued innumerable tribes, hordes of men and women, who spread out over distant continents. This was the place which had great and mighty cities in the past, rich and populous, comparable to the great European capitals of to-day, cities far bigger than Calcutta or Bombay to-day. There were gardens and greenery everywhere, and the climate was delightfully temperate, neither too cold nor too hot. All this it was. And now, for many hundreds of years, it has been a bare, inhospitable country, almost a desert. Some of the great cities of the past still linger on—Samarqand and Bokhara, their very names bring up hosts of memories—but they are ghosts of their former selves.

But I am again anticipating. It the ancient days which we were considering there was no Samarqand or Bokhara. All this was to come. The veil of the future hid it, and the greatness and the fall of central Asia were still to be.

9

THE BURDEN OF OLD TRADITION

January 14, 1931

I HAVE developed strange habits in prison. One of these is the habit of getting up very early—earlier even than the dawn. I began this last summer, for I liked to watch the coming of the dawn and the way it gradually put out the stars. Have you ever seen the moonlight before the dawn and the slow change to day? Often I have watched this contest between the moonlight and the dawn, in which the dawn always wins. In the strange half-light it is difficult to say for some time whether it is the moonlight or the light of the coming day. And then almost suddenly there is no doubt of it and it is day, and the pale moon retires, beaten, from the contest.

According to my habit, I got up to-day when the stars were still out, and one could only guess that the morning was coming by that strange something which is in the air just before the dawn. And as I sat reading, the calm of the early morning was broken by distant voices and rumblings, ever growing stronger. I remembered that it was the *Sankrānti* day, the first big day of the *Māgh Melā*, and the pilgrims were marching in their thousands for their morning dip at the Sangam, where the Ganga meets the Jumna and the invisible Sarasvatī is also supposed to join them. And as they marched they sang and sometimes cheered mother Ganga—*Gangā Māi ki Jai*— and their voices reached me over the walls of Naini Prison. As I listened to them I thought of the power of faith which drew these vast numbers to the river and made them forget for a while their poverty and misery. And I thought how year after year, for how many hundreds or thousands of years, the pilgrims had marched to the *Trivenī*. Men may come and men may go, and governments and empires may lord it awhile and then disappear into the past; but the old tradition continues, and generation after generation bows down to it. Tradition has much of good in it, but sometimes it becomes a terrible burden, which makes it difficult for us to move forward. It is fascinating to think of the unbroken chain which connects us with the dim and distant past, to read accounts of these *melās* written 1300 years ago—and the *melā* was an old tradition even then. But this chain has a way of clinging on to us when we want to move on, and of making us almost prisoners in the grip of this tradition. We shall have to keep many of the links with our past, but we shall also have to break through the prison of tradition wherever it prevents us from our onward march.

In our last three letters we have been trying to form a picture of what the world was like between 3000 and 2500 years ago. I have not mentioned any dates. I do not like them, and I do not want you to trouble yourself much with them. It is also difficult to know the correct dates of happenings in these olden times. Later, it may be necessary occasionally to give and to remember a few dates to help

us to keep the facts in proper order in our minds.   For the present
we are trying to form an idea of the ancient world.

We have had a glimpse of Greece and the Mediterranean, of Egypt,
of Asia Minor and Persia.   Let us now come back to our own country.
We have one great difficulty in studying the early history of India.
The early Aryans here—or the Indo-Aryans as they are called—cared
to write no histories.   We have seen already in our earlier letters
how great they were in many ways.   The books they have produced—the *Vedas*, the *Upanishads*, the *Rāmāyana*, the *Mahābhārata*,
and other books—could only have been written by great men.
These books and other material help us in studying past history.
They tell us about the manners and customs, the ways of thinking
and living of our ancestors.   But they are not accurate history.
The only real history in Sanskrit, but of a much later period, is a
history of Kashmir.   This is called the *Rājatarangini*, the chronicle
of the kings of Kashmir, and was written by Kalhana.   You will be
interested to learn that as I am writing these letters to you, Ranjit
Puphā [1] is translating this great history of Kashmir from the
Sanskrit.   He has nearly finished half of it.   It is a very big book.
When the full translation appears we shall all, of course, read it
eagerly, for unfortunately most of us do not know enough Sanskrit
to read the original.   We shall read it not only because it is a fine
book, but also because it will tell us a great deal about the past, and
especially about Kashmir, which, as you know, is our old homeland.

When the Aryans entered India, India was already civilized.
Indeed, it now appears certain from the remains at Mohen-jo Daro
in the north-west that a great civilization existed here for a long time
before the Aryans came.   But about this we do not know much yet.
Probably within a few years we shall know more, when our archæologists—the men who make a special study of old ruins—have dug
out all that there is to be found there.

Even apart from this, however, it is clear that the Dravidians had
a rich civilization then in southern India, and perhaps also in
northern India.   Their languages, which are not the daughters of
the Aryan Sanskrit, are very old and have fine literatures.   These
languages are Tamil, Telugu, Kanarese and Malayālam.   All these
languages still flourish in South India.   Perhaps you know that the
National Congress, unlike the British Government, has divided India
on the basis of language.   This is far better, as it brings one kind of
people, speaking one language and generally having similar customs,
into one provincial area.   The Congress provinces in the south are
the Andhra-desha or the Andhra province in northern Madras,
where Telugu is spoken; the Tāmil Nād, or the Tamil province
where Tamil is spoken; the Karnataka, which is south of Bombay,
and where Kannada or Kanarese is spoken; and Kerala, which
corresponds roughly with Malabar, where Malayālam is spoken.
There can be no doubt that in future provincial divisions of India
a great deal of attention will be paid to the language of the area.

[1] Ranjit S. Pandit, the author's brother-in-law, who was in prison with him
at the time.

Here I might as well say a little more about the languages of India. Some people in Europe and elsewhere imagine that there are hundreds of languages in India. This is perfectly absurd, and any one who says so only shows his own ignorance. In a big country like India there are, of course, numerous dialects—that is, local variations of a language. There are also many hill tribes and other small groups in various parts of the country with special languages. But all these are unimportant when you take India as a whole. Only from the point of view of the census are they important. The real languages of India, as I think I mentioned in one of my earlier letters, belong to two families, the Dravidian, to which we have referred above, and the Indo-Aryan. The principal Indo-Aryan language was Sanskrit, and all the Indo-Aryan languages of India are daughters of Sanskrit. These are Hindi, Bengali, Gujrati, and Marathi. There are also some other variations. In Assam there is Assamese, and in Orissa or Utkal the Uriya language is used. Urdū is a variation of Hindi. The word Hindustani is used to mean both Hindi and Urdū. Thus the principal languages of India are just ten. Hindustani, Bengali, Gujrati, Marathi, Tamil, Telugu, Kanarese, Malayālam, Uriya and Assamese. Of these, Hindustani, which is our mother-tongue, is spoken all over northern India—in the Punjab, United Provinces, Bihar, Central Provinces, Rajputana, Delhi and central India. This is a huge area inhabited by about 150,000,000 people. So you see that already 150,000,000 speak Hindustani, with minor variations, and, as you know well, Hindustani is understood in most parts of India. It is likely to become the common language of India. But this of course does not mean that the other principal languages, which I have mentioned above, should disappear. They should certainly remain as provincial languages, for they have fine literatures, and one should never try to take away a well-developed language from a people. The only way for a people to grow, for their children to learn, is through their own language. In India to-day everything is topsy-turvy, and we use English a great deal even amongst ourselves. It is perfectly ridiculous for me to write to you in English—and yet I am doing so! We shall get out of the habit soon, I hope.

10

THE VILLAGE REPUBLICS OF ANCIENT INDIA

January 15, 1931

How are we to make any progress with our review of past history? I am always leaving the main line and going along side-tracks. In my last letter, just when I was getting on to the subject, I started off on the languages of India.

Let us go back to old India. You know that what is Afghanistan to-day was then, and for a long time afterwards, a part of India. The north-west of India was called Gāndhāra. All over the north, in the plains of the Indus and the Ganges, there were big settlements of the Aryans. These Aryan immigrants probably knew the art of building well, for many of them must have come from the Aryan settlements in Persia and Mesopotamia, where there were great cities even then. In between the Aryan settlements there were many forests and especially between North India and the south there was a great forest. It is unlikely that any large numbers of Aryans crossed this forest to settle down in the south. But many individuals must have gone to explore and to trade and to carry the Aryan culture and traditions to the south. The old tradition tells us that the first Aryan to go to the south was the Rishi Agastya who carried the message of Aryan religion and culture to the Deccan.

A considerable trade already flourished between India and foreign countries. The pepper and gold and pearls of the south attracted foreign traders across the sea. Rice also was probably exported. Teakwood from Malabar has been found in ancient palaces in Babylonia.

Gradually the Aryans evolved their village system in India. This was a mixture of the old Dravidian village and the new Aryan ideas. These villages were almost independent and were governed by their elected *panchāyats*. A number of villages or small towns were joined together under a raja or chief, who was sometimes elected and sometimes hereditary. Often different village groups co-operated with each other in order to build roads, rest-houses, canals for irrigation, and such-like communal things, which were for the common good. It appears that the raja, although he was the chief man in his State, could not do just what he liked. He was himself subject to Aryan laws and customs, and he could be deposed or fined by his people. There was no such thing as *L'état c'est moi*, to which I referred in my earlier letters. Thus there was a kind of democracy in the Aryan settlements—that is to say, the Aryan inhabitants could to some extent control the government.

Compare these Indo-Aryans to the Aryan Greeks. There were many differences, and yet there were many points in common. There was some kind of democracy in both places. But let us always remember that this democracy was more or less confined to the Aryans themselves. Their slaves, or those whom they placed in low castes, had no democracy or freedom. The caste system, with its innumerable divisions, as we know it, did not exist then. In those days there were, among the Indian Aryans, four divisions of society, or four castes. These were the *Brahmans* or learned men, priests, sages; the *Kshattriyas* or rulers; *Vaishyas* or merchants and the men engaged in commerce; and *Shūdras* or the labourers and workers. These divisions were thus based on occupation. It is possible that the caste system was partly based on the desire of the Aryans to keep themselves aloof from the conquered race. The

Aryans were sufficiently proud and conceited to look down upon all other races, and they did not want their people to get mixed up with them. The very word for caste in Sanskrit is *varna* or colour. This also shows that the Aryans who came were fairer in complexion than the original inhabitants of India.

Thus we have to bear in mind that, on the one side, the Aryans kept down the working class and did not allow it any share in their democracy; on the other, they had a great deal of freedom among themselves. They would not allow their kings or rulers to misbehave; and if any ruler misbehaved, he was removed. The kings were usually *Kshattriyas*, but sometimes, during wars and times of difficulty, even a *Shūdra*, or a member of the lowest class, could win a throne, if he were able enough. In later days the Aryans degenerated and their caste system became rigid. Too many divisions made the country weak, and it fell. They also forgot their old idea of freedom. For, in the old days it was said that never shall an Aryan be made a slave, and that for him death was preferable to dishonour of the Aryan name.

The settlements of the Aryans, the towns and villages, did not grow up in a haphazard way. They were made according to plan; and geometry, you will be interested to know, had a good deal to do with these plans. Indeed, geometrical figures were also used then in Vedic *pūjās*. Even now in many Hindu households some of these figures are used during various *pūjās*. Now geometry is very closely connected with the building of houses and towns. The old Aryan village was at first probably a kind of fortified camp, for there was always fear of attack in those days. Even when there was no danger of hostile attacks, the same plan continued. The plan would be a rectangle, with walls all round, and four big gates and four small ones. Inside these walls were the streets in a special order and the houses. In the centre of the village there was the *Panchāyat ghar*, where the village elders met. In small villages instead of this *Panchāyat ghar* there would be just a big tree. Every year all the freemen of the village would meet to elect their *panchāyat*.

Many learned men used to retire into the forests, near the towns and villages, in order to lead simple lives, or to study and work in quiet. Pupils gathered round them, and gradually fresh settlements grew up of these teachers and their students. We can consider these settlements as universities. There were not many fine buildings there, but those who sought knowledge came from long distances to these places of learning.

Opposite Anand Bhawan [1] is Bharadwāj Ashram. You know it well. Perhaps you also know that Bharadwāj is supposed to have been a very learned man in the old days of the *Rāmāyana*, and Rāmachandra is said to have visited him during his exile. It is stated that thousands of pupils and students lived with him. There must have been quite a university, with Bharadwāj as its head. In those days the Ashram was on the banks of the Ganga. This is very likely, although now the river is nearly a mile away. The soil

[1] The author's house in Allahabad.

of our garden is, in some places, very sandy, and may have been part of the bed of the Ganga in those days.

Those early days were the great period of the Aryans in India. Unfortunately we have no history of this period, and can only rely on non-historical books for such facts as we know. Among the kingdoms and republics of those days were Magadha, in South Bihar; Videha, in North Bihar; Kāshī, or Benares; Koshala, of which the capital was Ayodhyā (the modern Fyzabad); and the Panchālas, between the Ganga and the Jumna. In the country of these Panchālas the two chief cities were Mathurā and Kānyakubja. Both these cities were famous in later history also. Both exist still, Kānyakubja under the name Kanauj, near Cawnpore. Ujjain also existed in those early days; it is now a small town in Gwalior State.

Near Pātaliputra or Patna, there was the city of Vaisāli. This was the capital city of a clan famous in early Indian history—the Lichchhavi clan. This State was a republic, and was governed by an assembly of notables with an elected president, who was called the *Nāyaka*.

As time passed, large towns and cities grew up. Trade increased and the arts and crafts of the artisan prospered. The cities became big trading centres. The *ashrams* in the forests, where the learned Brahmans lived with their pupils, also grew up into large university towns. And in these centres of learning every kind of subject that was then known was taught. The Brahmans even taught the science of war. You will remember that the great teacher of the Pāndavas in the *Mahābhārata* was Dronāchārya, a Brahman, who taught them. among other things, the way to fight.

11

A THOUSAND YEARS OF CHINA

January 16, 1931

NEWS has come from the outside world—news that disturbs and grieves, and yet that fills one with pride and joy. We have heard of the fate of the Sholapur people. We have also had some brief accounts of what happened all over the country when this sad news was known. It is difficult to sit here quietly when our young men are giving their lives and thousands of men and women are facing the brutal *lāthi*. But it is good training for us. I suppose each one of us will have opportunities to test himself or herself to the utmost. Meanwhile it does one's heart good to know how our people dare to go ahead to meet suffering, how each additional weapon and blow of the enemy makes them stronger and more determined to resist.

It is difficult to think of other matters when the news of the day fills one's mind. But empty musing does not help much, and if we have to do any solid work we must control our minds. Let us

The Beginning of
CHINESE
CIVILISATION

JAPAN

CHOSEN

Hoang-ho

Yang-tse

Desert

Mountain country

J.F.H.

therefore go back to old times and live for a while far away from our present troubles.

Let us go to India's sister in ancient history—China.   In China and in the other countries of eastern Asia, like Japan, Korea, Indo-China, Siam and Burma, we have not to deal with the Aryan people. We have here the Mongolian races.

About 5000 years ago or more there was an invasion of China from the west.   These invading tribes also came from Central Asia, and were fairly advanced in their civilization.   They knew agriculture and kept large flocks and herds of cattle.   They built good houses and had a well-developed society.   They settled down near the Hoang Ho, which is also called the Yellow River, and organized their State.   For many hundreds of years they continued spreading over China and improving their arts and crafts.   The Chinese people were largely farmers, and their chiefs were really patriarchs of the kind I have described to you in my earlier letters.   Six or seven hundred years later—that is, more than 4000 years ago from now— we find a man named Yao calling himself emperor.   But in spite of this title he was more of a patriarch than an emperor of the kind Egypt or Mesopotamia had.   The Chinese people continued to live as farmers, and there was not much of a central government.

I have told you how the patriarchs used to be elected by their people, and later how they became hereditary.   We see that happening in China.   Yao was not succeeded by his son, but he nominated another person who was considered the most capable man in the country.   Soon, however, the title became hereditary, and it is said that for more than 400 years the Hsia dynasty ruled China. The last Hsia ruler was very cruel and there was a revolution which overthrew him.   Another dynasty, called the Shang or Yin dynasty, then came into power and this lasted for nearly 650 years.

In a little paragraph, in two or three short sentences, I have disposed of China's history for more than 1000 years.   Wonderful, is it not, what one can do with these expanses of history?   But you must realize that my little paragraph does not lessen the length of these 1000 or 1100 years.   We are used to thinking in terms of days and months and years.   It is difficult for you to have a clear idea of even 100 years.   Your thirteen years seem a lot, do they not ? And each additional year makes you so much bigger.   How then can you get hold, in your mind, of 1000 years of history ?   It is a long time.   Generation after generation comes and goes, and towns grow into great cities and then crumble away, and fresh cities take their place.   Think of the last 1000 years of history, and then perhaps you will have some idea of this long period.   What amazing changes have taken place in these 1000 years in the world !

It is a wonderful thing, the history of China, with its long tradition of culture, and its dynasties, each lasting for 500 years or even 800 years or more.

Think of the slow progress and development of China during these 1100 years I have disposed of in a paragraph.   Gradually the patriarchal system gives way and the central government develops. A well-organized State appears.   Even in these ancient times China knew the art of writing. But Chinese writing, as you know, is very different from our writing or from the writing of English and French. It has not got an alphabet. It is written in symbols or pictures.

The Shang dynasty after 640 years of rule was upset by a revolution, and a new dynasty, the Chou dynasty, came into power. This had an even longer period of power than the Shang. It lasted for 867 years. It was under the Chou dynasty that a well-organized Chinese State appeared. It was also during this period that the two great philosophers of China, Confucius and Lao-Tse, lived. We shall have something to say about them later.

When the Shang dynasty was driven out, one of its high officials named Ki-Tse preferred exile to serving the Chous. So he marched with 5000 followers out of China into Korea. He called the country *Chosen* or the " Land of the Morning Calm ". Korea, or Chosen, is east of China, so Ki-Tse went east towards the rising sun. Perhaps he then thought that he had reached the easternmost country, and therefore gave it this name. With Ki-Tse began the history of Korea from 1100 years before Christ. Ki-Tse brought to his new country Chinese arts and crafts, and house-building, and agriculture, and silk-making. More Chinese immigrants followed Ki-Tse. Ki-Tse's descendants ruled Chosen for over 900 years.

Chosen was not, of course, the most easterly country. East of it, as we know, is Japan. But we have no knowledge of what was happening in Japan when Ki-Tse went to Chosen. Japanese history is not nearly so old as that of China, or even Korea or Chosen. The Japanese say that their first emperor was named Jimmu Tenno and that he ruled 600 or 700 years before Christ. He is supposed by them to have been a descendant of the Sun goddess, for the Sun was considered a goddess in Japan. The present Emperor of Japan is said to be a direct descendant of this Jimmu Tenno, and is thus also believed by many Japanese to be a descendant of the sun.

You know that in our country the Rajputs also in the same way claim that they go back to the sun and the moon. Their two principal houses are the *Sūryavañshi*, or the Race of the Sun, and the *Chandravañshi*, or the Race of the Moon. The Maharana of Udaipur is the head of the Sūryavañshis, and he traces his pedigree far back into the past. Wonderful people are our Rajputs, and of the stories of their valour and chivalry there is no end.

12

THE CALL OF THE PAST

January 17, 1931

WE have now had a brief look at the ancient world as it probably was up to about 2500 years ago. Our survey has been very brief and very limited. We have only dealt with the countries which were fairly advanced or which have some kind of definite history. In Egypt we have just mentioned the great civilization which produced the Pyramids and the Sphinx and many other things which we cannot go into now. This great civilization had had its day, and was on the decline even at this early period which we are considering. Knossos was also nearing its end. In China we have traced vast periods of time during which it grew into a great central empire and developed writing and silk-making and many beautiful things. We have had a glimpse of Korea and Japan. In India we have just hinted at the old civilization represented now by the ruins at Mohenjo Daro in the Indus valley; and the Dravidian civilization with its trade with foreign countries; and lastly the Aryans. We have referred to some of the famous books which the Aryans produced in those days, the *Vedas* and *Upanishads*, and the epics, the *Rāmāyana* and the *Mahābhārata*. And we have followed them spreading out over northern India, and even penetrating to the south and, in contact with the old Dravidians, building up a new civilization and culture, which had something of the Dravidian in it and a great deal of the Aryan. Especially have we seen how their village communities grew up on a democratic basis and developed into towns and cities, and forest *ashrams* became universities. In Mesopotamia and Persia we have only briefly referred to the growth of empire after empire; one of these later empires, that of Darius, extending to the river Indus in India. In Palestine we have had a glimpse of the Hebrews, who, though few in number and living in a tiny corner of the world, have attracted a great deal of attention. Their kings, David and Solomon, are remembered when greater kings have been forgotten, because they find mention in the Bible. In Greece we have seen the new Aryan civilization grow up on the ruins of the older civilization of Knossos. The City-States have grown up and Greek colonies have sprung up on the borders of the Mediterranean. Rome, which was to be great, and Carthage, its bitter rival, are just appearing on the horizon of history.

All this we have barely glimpsed. I could have told you something of the countries which we have not mentioned—the countries of northern Europe and south-eastern Asia. Even in these early days Indian seamen from South India ventured across the Bay of Bengal to the Malay peninsula and to the islands south of it. But we must draw the line somewhere, or else we shall never get on.

The countries we have dealt with are supposed to belong to the ancient world. But remember that in those days there was not much communication between distant countries. Adventurous sailors went across the seas, and some people undertook long land journeys for trade or other purposes. But this must have been rare, for the peril was great. Geography was little known. The earth was supposed to be flat, and not round. So that no one knew much about any countries except those which were near. Thus people in Greece knew practically nothing of China or India, and the Chinese or Indians knew very little about the countries of the Mediterranean.

Have a look at a map of the ancient world, if you can find one. Some of the descriptions of the world and maps given by the old writers are amusing. In those maps the several countries assume extraordinary shapes. Maps of ancient times prepared now are much more helpful, and I hope you will often consult them when reading about these times. A map helps greatly. Without it, we can have no real idea of history. Indeed, to learn history one should have as many maps and as many pictures as possible; pictures of old buildings, ruins, and such other remains of those times as have come down. These pictures fill up the dry skeleton of history and make it live for us. History, if we are to learn anything from it, must be a succession of vivid images in our mind, so that when we read it, we can almost see events happening. It should be a fascinating play which grips us, a comedy sometimes, more often a tragedy, of which the stage is the world, and the players are the great men and women of the past.

Pictures and maps help a little to open our eyes to this pageant of history. They should be within reach of every boy and girl. But better even than pictures is a personal visit to the ruins and remains of old history. It is not possible to see all of these, for they are spread out all over the world. But we can always find some remains of the past within easy reach of us, if we keep our eyes wide open. The big museums collect the smaller remains and relics. In India there are plenty of remains of past history, but of the very ancient days there are very few. Mohen-jo Daro and Harappa are perhaps the only instances so far. It may be that many of the very old buildings crumbled to dust in the hot climate. It is much more likely, however, that many of them still lie under the surface of the soil, waiting to be dug up. And as we dig them up and find old relics and inscriptions, the past history of our country will gradually open its pages to us, and we shall read in these pages of stone and brick and mortar what our ancestors did in the old, old times.

You have been to Delhi, and you have seen some of the ruins and old buildings round about the present city. When you see them again, think of the past, and they will carry you back and tell you more history than any book. Right from the days of the *Mahābhārata* have people lived in Delhi city or near it, and they have called it by many names: Indraprastha, Hastināpur, Tughlaqābād, Shāhjahānābād—I do not even know all these names. Tradition tells us that there have been seven cities of Delhi on seven different sites, always moving because of the vagaries of the river Jumna. And now we see an eighth city—Raisina or New Delhi—rising up at the command of the present rulers of this country. Empire after empire has flourished in Delhi and has gone.

Go to Benares or Kāshī, that most ancient of cities, and give ear to her murmuring. Does she not tell you of her immemorial past—of how she has gone on while empires have decayed, of Buddha who came to her with his new gospel, of the millions who have gone to her through the ages to find peace and solace? Old and hoary, decrepit, dirty, smelly, and yet much alive and full of the strength of ages, is Benares. Full of charm and wonder is Kāshī, for in her eyes you can see the past of India, and in the murmur of her waters you can hear the voices of ages long gone by.

Or, go nearer still, to the old Ashoka pillar in our city of Allahabad or Prayag. See the inscription carved on it at the bidding of Ashoka, and you can almost hear his voice across 2000 years.

13

WHERE DO RICHES GO TO?

January 18, 1931

IN my letters to you which I sent to Mussoorie, I tried to show you how different classes of people developed as man advanced. The early men had a hard life even to find food. They hunted and gathered nuts and fruits from day to day, and wandered from place to place in search of food. Gradually tribes grew up. These were really large families living together and hunting together, because it was safer to be together than alone. Then came a great change— the discovery of agriculture, which made a tremendous difference. People found it much easier to grow food on the land by the methods of agriculture than to hunt all the time. And ploughing and sowing and harvesting meant living on the land. They could not just wander about as they used to, but had to remain near their fields. So grew up villages and towns.

Agriculture also brought about other changes. The food that was produced by the land was much more than could be used up at once. This excess or surplus was stored up. Life became a little more complicated than it used to be in the old days of hunting, and different classes of people did the actual work in the fields and elsewhere, and some did the managing and organizing. The managers and organizers gradually became more powerful, and became patriarchs and rulers and kings and nobles. And, having the power to do so, they kept for themselves a great deal of the excess or surplus food that was produced. Thus they became richer, while those who worked in the fields got just enough food to live on. A time came later when these managers and organizers became too lazy or incompetent to do even the work of organizing. They did nothing, but they took good care to take a fat share of the food produced by the workers. And they began to think that they had every right to live in this way on the labour of others without doing anything themselves.

So you will see that the coming of agriculture made a vast difference to life. By improving the method of getting food, by making it easier to get it, agriculture changed the whole basis of society. It gave people leisure. Different classes grew up. Everybody was not busy in getting food, and so some people could take to other work. Various kinds of crafts grew up and new professions were formed. Power, however, chiefly rested with the organizing class.

You will find in later history also how great changes have been brought about by new ways of producing food and other necessaries.

Man began to require many other things almost as much as food.   So that any great change in the methods of production resulted in great changes in society.   To give you one big instance of it : when steam was applied to working factories and moving railways and ships, a great change was made in the methods of production and distribution.   The steam factories could make things far more quickly than the artisans and craftsmen could with their hands or simple tools.   The big machine was really an enormous tool.   And the railway and the steamship helped in taking food and the products of factories quickly to distant countries.   You can well imagine what a difference this must have made all over the world.

New and quicker ways of producing food and other things have been discovered in history from time to time.   And you would, of course, think that if better methods were used for production, much more would be produced, and the world would be richer and every one would have more.   You would be partly right and partly wrong.   Better methods of production have certainly made the world richer.   But which part of the world ?   It is obvious enough that there is great poverty and misery still in our country, of course, but even in a rich country like England this is so.   Why ?   Where do the riches go to ?   It is a strange thing that in spite of more and more wealth being produced, the poor have remained poor.   They have made some little progress in certain countries, but it is very little compared to the new wealth produced.   We can easily see, however, to whom this wealth largely goes.   It goes to those who, usually being the managers or organizers, see to it that they get the lion's share of everything good.   And, stranger still, classes have grown up in society of people who do not even pretend to do any work, and yet who take this lion's share of the work of others !   And—would you believe it ?—these classes are honoured ; and some foolish people imagine that it is degrading to have to work for one's living !   Such is the topsy-turvy condition of our world.   Is it surprising that the peasant in his field and the worker in his factory are poor, although they produce the food and wealth of the world ?   We talk of freedom for our country, but what will any freedom be worth unless it puts an end to this topsy-turvydom, and gives to the man who does the work the fruits of his toil ?   Big, fat books have been written on politics and the art of government, on economics and how the nation's wealth should be distributed.   Learned professors lecture on these subjects.   But, while people talk and discuss, those who work suffer.   Two hundred years ago a famous Frenchman, Voltaire, said of politicians and the like that " they have discovered in their fine politics the art of causing those to die of hunger who, cultivating the earth, give the means of life to others ".

Still, ancient man advanced and gradually encroached upon wild Nature.   He cut the forests and built the houses and tilled the land.   Man is supposed to have conquered Nature to some extent.   People talk of the conquest of Nature.   This is loose talk and is not quite correct.   It is far better to say that man has begun to understand Nature, and the more he has understood, the more he has been able to co-operate with Nature and to utilize it for his own purposes.   In the old days men were afraid of Nature and of natural phenomena. Instead of trying to understand them, they tried to worship and offer peace offerings, as if Nature were a wild beast which had to be appeased and cajoled.   Thus thunder and lightning and epidemic diseases frightened them, and they thought that these could be prevented only by offerings.   Many simple people think that an eclipse of the sun or moon is a terrible calamity.   Instead of trying to understand that it is a very simple natural occurrence, people needlessly excite themselves about it, and fast and bathe to protect the sun or the moon !   The sun and the moon are quite capable of looking after themselves.   We need not worry about them.

We have talked of the growth of civilization and culture, and we have seen the beginnings of this when people settled down to live in villages and towns.   The greater quantity of food that they got gave them more leisure and they could thus think of other matters than hunting and eating.   With the growth of thought developed the arts and crafts and culture generally.   As the population increased, people had to live closer to each other.   They were continually meeting each other and having business with each other.   If people have to live together they must be considerate to each other.   They must avoid doing anything which might hurt their companions or neighbours, otherwise no social life is possible.   Take a family, for instance.   A family is a tiny bit of society which will live happily if its members have consideration for each other.   This is not very difficult as a rule in a family, as there is a bond of affection between its members.   Even so it sometimes happens that we forget to be considerate and show that we are not very cultured and civilized after all.   In the case of a larger group than the family, it is exactly the same—whether we take our neighbours, or the people of our city, or our countrymen, or the people of other countries even.   So the growth of population resulted in more social life and more restraint and consideration for others.   Culture and civilization are difficult to define, and I shall not try to define them.   But among the many things that culture includes are certainly restraint over oneself and consideration for others.   If a person has not got this self-restraint and has no consideration for others, one can certainly say that he is uncultured.

14

THE SIXTH CENTURY BEFORE CHRIST, AND RELIGION

January 20, 1931

LET us march on the long road of history.   We have reached a big milestone, 2500 years ago, or, to put it a little differently, about 600 years before Christ.   Do not think this is an accurate date.   I am merely giving you a rough period of time.   About this time we find a number of great men, great thinkers, founders of religions, in different countries, from China and India to Persia and Greece. They did not live at exactly the same time.   But they were near enough to each other in point of time to make this period of the sixth century before Christ a period of great interest.   There must have been a wave of thought going through the world, a wave of discontent with existing conditions and of hope and aspiration for something better.   For remember that the great founders of religions were always seeking something better and trying to change their people and improve them and lessen their misery.   They were always revolutionaries who were not afraid of attacking existing evils. Where old tradition had gone wrong or where it prevented future growth, they attacked it and removed it without fear.   And, above all, they set an example of noble living which for vast numbers of people, generation after generation, became an ideal and an inspiration.

In India, in that sixth century before Christ, we had the Buddha and Mahāvīra; in China, Confucius and Lao-Tse; in Persia, Zarathushtra or Zoroaster [1]; in the Greek island of Samos, Pythagoras.   You may have heard these names before, though perhaps in different connections.   The average school boy or girl thinks of Pythagoras as a busybody who proved a theorem in geometry, which he or she, unhappy person, has to learn now !   This theorem deals with the squares on the sides of a right-angled triangle and is to be found in Euclid or any other geometry.   But, apart from his discoveries in geometry, Pythagoras is supposed to have been a great thinker.   We do not know much about him and indeed some people doubt if he ever existed !

Zoroaster of Persia is said to have been the founder of Zoroastrianism; but I am not sure if it is quite correct to call him the founder. It is better perhaps to say that he gave a new direction and a new form to the old thought and religion of Persia.   For a long time past this religion has hardly existed in Persia.   The Parsis, who long ago came to India from Persia, brought it with them, and they have practised it ever since.

In China, there were two great men, Confucius and Lao-Tse, during this period.   A more correct way of writing Confucius is Kong Fu-Tse.   Neither of these men was a founder of a religion in the ordinary sense of the word.   They laid down systems of morals and social behaviour, what one should do and what one should not do.   But after their deaths numerous temples were built to their memory in China, and their books were as much respected by the Chinese as the *Vedas* by the Hindus or the Bible by the Christians. And one of the results of the Confucian teaching has been to make the Chinese people the most courteous and perfect-mannered and cultured in the world.

In India there were Mahāvīra and the Buddha.   Mahāvīra started the Jain religion as it exists to-day.   His real name was Vardhamana,

---

[1] Zarathushtra probably lived in the eighth century B.C.

Mahāvīra being the title of greatness given to him.   Jains live largely
in western India and in Kathiawad, and to-day they are often included among the Hindus.   They have beautiful temples in Kathiawad and in Mount Abu in Rajputana.   They are very great believers
in *ahimsa* or non-violence, and are wholly against doing anything
which might cause injury to any living being.   In this connection, it
might interest you to know that Pythagoras was a strict vegetarian
and insisted on all his pupils and *chelās* being vegetarians.

We come now to Gautama, the Buddha.   He was, as you no
doubt know, a *Kshattriya*, a prince of a royal house, and Siddhārtha
was his name.   His mother was Queen Māyā—" joyously reverenced
by all, even as the young moon strong and calm of purpose as the
earth, pure of heart as the lotus was Maya, the great Lady," says
the old chronicle.   His parents brought him up in comfort and
luxury, and tried to keep him away from all sight of suffering or
misery.   But this was not possible, and tradition says that he did
see poverty and suffering and death, and that he was greatly
affected by them.   There was no peace for him then in his palace,
and all the luxury with which he was surrounded, and even his
beautiful young wife whom he loved, could not keep his mind away
from suffering humanity.   And the thought grew in him and the
desire to find a remedy for these evils, till he could bear it no longer;
and, in the silence of the night, he left his palace and his dear ones,
and marched out alone into the wide world to find answers to the
questions which troubled him.   Long and weary was his search for
these answers.   At last, many years later, it is said that, sitting
under a *peepal* tree in Gaya, enlightenment came to him, and he
became the Buddha, the " Enlightened ".   And the tree under which
he had sat came to be known as the Bodhi tree, the Tree of Enlightenment.   In the Deer Park at Sarnath, called Isipatana then,
under the shadow of ancient Kāshī, Buddha began his teaching.
He pointed out the " path of good living ".   He condemned the
sacrifices of all manner of things to the gods, and said we must
sacrifice, instead, our anger and hatred and envy and wrong-thinking.

When Buddha was born the old Vedic religion prevailed in India.
But already it had changed and fallen from its high estate.   The
Brahman priests had introduced all manner of rites and *pūjās* and
superstition, for the more there is of *pūjā* the more do the priests
flourish.   Caste was becoming stricter, and the common people
were frightened by omens and spells and witchcraft and quackery.
The priests got the people under their control by these methods and
challenged the power of the *Kshattriya* rulers.   There was thus
rivalry between the *Kshattriyas* and the Brahmans.   Buddha came
as a great popular reformer, and he attacked this priestly tyranny
and all the evils which had crept into the old Vedic religion.   He laid
stress on people living a good life and performing good deeds, and
not performing *pūjās* and the like.   He organized the Buddhist
Saṅgha, an association of monks and nuns, who followed his teaching.

Buddhism, as a religion, did not spread much in India for some
time.   Later, we shall see how it spread and how again, in India, it
almost ceased to exist as a separate religion.   While it triumphed in

distant countries from Ceylon to China, in India, the land of its birth, Buddhism was absorbed back into Brahminism or Hinduism. But it exercised a great influence on Brahminism, and rid it of some at least of its superstition and ritual.

Buddhism to-day is the religion of the greatest number of people in the world. Other religions which have the largest number of followers are Christianity, Islam and Hinduism. There are, besides, the religions of the Hebrews, of the Sikhs, of the Parsis, and others. Religions and their founders have played a great part in the history of the world, and we cannot ignore them in any survey of history. But I find some difficulty in writing about them. There can be no doubt that the founders of the great religions have been among the greatest and noblest men that the world has produced. But their disciples and the people who have come after them have often been far from great or good. Often in history we see that religion, which was meant to raise us and make us better and nobler, has made people behave like beasts. Instead of bringing enlightenment of them, it has often tried to keep them in the dark; instead to broadening their minds, it has frequently made them narrow-minded and intolerant of others. In the name of religion many great and fine deeds have been performed. In the name of religion also thousands and millions have been killed, and every possible crime has been committed.

What, then, is one to do with religion? For some people religion means the other world : heaven, paradise or whatever it may be called. In the hope of going to heaven they are religious or do certain things. This reminds me of the child who behaves in the hope of being rewarded with a jam puff or *jalebi*! If the child is always thinking of the jam puff or the *jalebi*, you would not say that it had been properly trained, would you? Much less would you approve of boys and girls who did everything for the sake of jam puffs and the like. What, then, shall we say of grown-up persons who think and act in this way? For, after all, there is no essential difference between the jam puff and the idea of paradise. We are all more or less selfish. But we try to train up our children so that they may become as unselfish as possible. At any rate, our ideals should be wholly unselfish, so that we may try to live up to them.

We all desire to achieve, to see the result of our actions. That is natural. But what do we aim at? Are we concerned with ourselves only or with the larger good—the good of society, of our country, or of humanity? After all, this larger good will include us also. Some days ago I think I gave you a Sanskrit verse in one of my letters. This stated that the individual should be sacrificed for the family, the family for the community, and the community for the country. I shall give you the translation of another verse from Sanskrit. This is from the *Bhāgavata*. It runs thus : " I desire not the supreme state of bliss with its eight perfections, nor the cessation of re-birth. May I take up the sorrow of all creatures who suffer and enter into them so that they may be made free from grief."

One religious man says this, and another says that. And, often enough, each one of them considers the other a fool or a knave.

Who is right ?   As they talk of things which cannot be seen or proved, it is difficult to settle the argument.   But it seems rather presumptuous of both of them to talk with certainty of such matters and to break each other's heads over them.   Most of us are narrow-minded and not very wise.   Can we presume to imagine that we know the whole truth and to force this down the throat of our neighbour ?   It may be we are right.   It may be that our neighbour is also right.   If you see a flower on a tree, you do not call it the tree. If another person sees the leaf only, and yet another the trunk, each has seen part of the tree only.   How foolish it would be for each one of them to say that the tree was the flower only or the leaf or the trunk, and to fight over this !

I am afraid the next world does not interest me.   My mind is full of what I should do in this world, and if I see my way clearly here, I am content.   If my duty here is clear to me, I do not trouble myself about any other world.

As you grow up, you will meet all kinds of people : religious people, anti-religious people, and people who do not care either way.   There are big churches and religious organizations possessing great wealth and power, sometimes using them for good purposes, sometimes for bad.   You will meet very fine and noble people who are religious, and knaves and scoundrels who, under the cloak of religion, rob and defraud others.   And you will have to think about these matters and decide for yourself.   One can learn much from others, but everything worth while one has to find out or experience oneself. There are some questions which each person has to answer for himself or herself.

Do not be in a hurry to decide.   Before you can decide anything big or vital you will have to train yourself and educate yourself to do so.   It is right that people should think for themselves and decide for themselves, but they must have the ability to decide.   You would not ask a new-born babe to decide anything !   And there are many people who, though grown in years, are almost like new-born babes so far as their minds are concerned.

I have written a longer letter than usual to-day, and you may find it dull.   But I wanted to have my little say on this subject.   If you do not understand anything now it does not matter.   You will understand soon enough.

15

PERSIA AND GREECE

January 21, 1931

YOUR letter came to-day, and it was good to know that Mummie and you were getting on well.   But I wish Dadu would get rid of his fever and his troubles.   He has worked so hard all his life, and even now he can have no peace and no rest.

So you have read many books from the library and want me to suggest more. But you do not tell me what you have read. It is a good habit to read books, but I rather suspect those who read too many books quickly. I suspect them of not reading them properly at all, of just skimming through them, and forgetting them the day after. If a book is worth reading it is worth reading with some care and thoroughness. But, then, there are such vast numbers of books which are not worth reading at all, and it is no easy matter to pick and choose good books. You may tell me that if you choose books from our library, they should be good books, or else why should we have got them? Well, well, read on, and I shall give you such help as I can from Naini Prison. Often I think of the speed with which you are growing in mind and body. How I should like to be with you! Perhaps you may outgrow these very letters that I am writing to you by the time they reach you. I suppose that Chand [1] will be old enough to read them then, so that anyhow there will be some one to appreciate them.

Let us go back to old Greece and Persia and consider for a while their wars with each other. In one of our letters we discussed the Greek City-States and the great empire of Persia under a ruler called by the Greeks Darius. This empire of Darius was a great one not only in extent but also in organization. It extended from Asia Minor to the Indus, and Egypt was part of it, and so also were some Greek cities of Asia Minor. Right across this vast empire ran good roads along which went regularly the imperial post. Darius, for some reason or other, decided to conquer the Greek City-States, and during these wars some very famous battles of history took place.

The accounts that we have of these wars were written by a Greek historian named Herodotus, who lived very soon after the events he recorded. He was, of course, partial to the Greeks, but his account is very interesting, and I shall, in the course of these letters, give you some quotations from his history.

The first Persian attack on Greece failed because the Persian army suffered greatly during its march from disease and lack of food. It did not even reach Greece, but had to go back. Then came the second attack in 490 B.C. The Persian army avoided the land route this time and came by sea, and landed at a place called Marathon, near Athens. The Athenians were greatly alarmed, for the fame of the Persian Empire was great. In their fear, the Athenians tried to make up with their old enemies the Spartans and appealed to them for help against the common enemy. But even before the Spartans could arrive, the Athenians succeeded in defeating the Persian army. This was at the famous battle of Marathon, which took place in 490 B.C.

It seems curious that a small Greek City-State could have defeated the army of a great empire. But this is not so strange as it might appear. The Greeks were fighting near their home and for their home whilst the Persian army was far from its homelands. It

[1] Indira's little cousin, Chandralekha Pandit.

was a mixed army of soldiers from all parts of the Persian Empire. They fought because they were paid for it; they were not interested very much in the conquest of Greece.   The Athenians, on the other hand, fought for their freedom.   They preferred to die rather than lose their freedom, and those who are prepared to die for any cause are seldom defeated.

So Darius was defeated at Marathon.   He died in Persia later, and was succeeded by Xerxes.   Xerxes also had the ambition to conquer Greece, and he fitted out an expedition for this purpose. And here I shall take you to the fascinating story as told by Herodotus.   Artabanus was the uncle of Xerxes.   He thought there was danger to the Persian army in going to Greece, and he tried to induce his nephew Xerxes not to war against Greece.   Herodotus tells us that Xerxes answered him as follows :

> " There is reason in what you say, but you ought not to see danger everywhere or to reckon every risk.   If whatever comes up you are going to weigh everything alike, you will never do anything.   It is better to be always an optimist and to suffer half the amount of evil, than always to be full of gloomy anticipations and never suffer anything at all.   If you attack every proposal made without showing us the right course to follow, you will come to grief as much as those whom you oppose.   The scales are evenly balanced.   How can a human being know certainly which way they will incline ?   He cannot.   But success generally attends those who wish to act; and it does not attend those who are timid and balance everything.   You see the great power which Persia has attained.   If my predecessors on the throne had held your views, or without holding them had had counsellors like you, you would never have seen our kingdom become so great.   It is by taking risks that they made us what we are.   Great things are achieved through great dangers."

I have given this long quotation because these words of his make us understand the Persian King better than any other account. As it happened, the advice of Artabanus turned out to be correct and the Persian army was defeated in Greece.   Xerxes lost, but his words still ring true and contain a lesson for all of us.   And to-day, when we are trying to achieve great things, let us remember that we must pass through great dangers before we can reach our goal.

Xerxes, the King of kings, took his great army across Asia Minor and crossed to Europe across the Dardanelles, or the Hellespont as it was called in those days.   On his way, it is said, Xerxes paid a visit to the ruins of Troy town, where the Greek heroes of old had battled for Helen.   A great bridge was put across the Hellespont for the army to cross; and as the Persian army went across, Xerxes surveyed it, seated on a marble throne on top of a hill near by.

> " And," Herodotus tells us, " seeing all the Hellespont covered over with the ships and all the shores and the plains of Abydos full of men, then Xerxes pronounced himself a happy man, and then he fell to weeping.   Artabanus, his uncle, therefore perceiving him— the same who at first boldly declared his opinion advising Xerxes

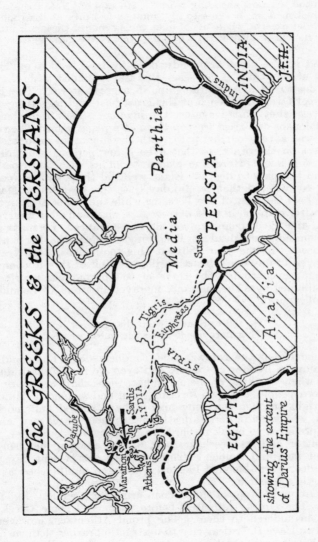

The GREEKS & the PERSIANS

showing the extent of Darius' Empire

not to march against Hellas—this man, I say, having observed that Xerxes wept, asked as follows : ' O King, how far different from one another are the things which thou hast done now and a short while before now ! For having pronounced thyself a happy man, thou art now shedding tears.' He said : ' Yea, for after I had reckoned up, it came to my mind to feel pity at the thought how brief was the whole life of man, seeing that of these multitudes not one will be alive when a hundred years have gone by '."

And so the great army advanced by land, and a multitude of ships accompanied it by sea. But the sea sided with the Greeks and destroyed most of the ships in a great storm. The Hellenes or Greeks were frightened at this great host, and forgetting all their quarrels, they united against the invader. They retreated before the Persians and tried to stop them at a place named Thermopylæ. This was a very narrow path, with the mountain on one side and the sea on the other, so that even a few persons could defend it against a host. Here was placed Leonidas with 300 Spartans to defend the pass to death. Right well did these gallant men serve their country on that fateful day, just ten years after Marathon. They held the host of the Persians while the Greek army retreated. Man after man fell in that narrow pass, and man after man replaced them, and the Persian army could not advance. Leonidas and his 300 comrades lay dead at Thermopylæ before the Persians could go ahead. In the year 480 B.C. this took place, 2410 years ago, and even to-day one's heart thrills to think of this unconquerable courage ; even to-day the traveller to Thermopylæ may see with tear-dimmed eyes the message, engraved in stone, of Leonidas and his colleagues :

" Go tell to Sparta, thou that passest by,
    That here obedient to her words we lie."

Wonderful is the courage that conquers death ! Leonidas and Thermopylæ live for evermore, and even we in distant India feel a thrill when we think of them. What, then, shall we say or feel of our own people, our own forbears, men and women of Hindustan, who right through our long history have smiled and mocked at death, who have preferred death to dishonour or slavery, and who have preferred to break rather than bow down to tyranny ? Think of Chittor and its peerless story, of the amazing heroism of its Rajput men and women ! Think also of our present day, of our comrades, warm-blooded like us, who have not flinched at death for India's freedom.

Thermopylæ stopped the Persian army for a while. But not for long. The Greeks retreated before them and some Greek cities even surrendered to them. The proud Athenians, however, preferred to leave their dear city to destruction rather than surrender ; and the whole population went away, mostly on the ships. The Persians entered the deserted city and burnt it. The Athenian fleet had, however, not yet been defeated, and a great battle took place near Salamis. The Persian ships were destroyed, and Xerxes, thoroughly disheartened by this disaster, went back to Persia.

Persia remained a great empire for some time longer, but Marathon and Salamis pointed the way to its decline. Later we shall see how it fell. For those who lived in those days it must have been amazing to see this vast empire totter. Herodotus thought over it and drew a moral from it. He says that a nation's history has three stages : success ; then as a consequence of success, arrogance and injustice ; and then, as a consequence of these, downfall.

16

THE GLORY THAT WAS HELLAS

January 23, 1931

THE victories of the Hellenes or Greeks over the Persians had two results. The Persian Empire gradually declined and grew weaker, and the Greeks entered into a brilliant period of their history. This brilliance was short-lived in the life of a nation. It lasted less than 200 years altogether. It was not a greatness of wide empire, like Persia or the other empires that had gone before. Later the great Alexander arose and for a brief while astonished the world by his conquests. But we are not now dealing with him. We are discussing the period between the Persian wars and the coming of Alexander—a period of about 150 years from Thermopylæ and Salamis. The Persian danger had united the Greeks. When this danger was removed, they again fell apart and soon started quarrelling with each other. In particular the City-States of Athens and Sparta were bitter rivals. But we shall not trouble ourselves about their quarrels. They have no importance, and we only remember them because of the greatness of Greece in those days in other ways.

We have only a few books, a few statues, a few ruins of those days of Greece. Yet these few are such as to fill us with admiration and to make us wonder at the many-sided greatness of the men of Hellas. How rich their minds must have been and how deft their hands, to produce their beautiful statuary and their buildings ! Phidias was a famous sculptor of those days, but there were many others of renown also. Their plays—tragedies and comedies—are still among the greatest of their kind. Sophocles and Æschylus and Euripides and Aristophanes and Pindar and Menander and Sappho and others can only be names for you now. But you will read their works when you grow up, I hope, and realize something of the glory that was Greece.

This period of Greek history is a warning to us as to how we should read the history of any country. If we paid attention merely to the petty wars and all the other pettiness that prevailed in the

Greek States, what would we know of them? If we are to understand them we must enter into their thought and try to appreciate
what they felt and did. It is the inner history that really counts,
and it is this that has made modern Europe a child in many ways of
the ancient Greek culture.

It is strange and fascinating how in the lives of nations such
periods of brilliant life come and go. For a while they brighten up
everything and enable the men and women of that period and
country to create things of beauty. People seem to become inspired
Our country, too, has had such periods. The earliest of these that
we know of was the period which gave birth to the *Vedas* and the
Upanishads and other books. Unfortunately, we have no record
of those ancient days, and many beautiful and great works may
have perished or may still await discovery. But we have enough to
show what giants of mind and thought were those Indians of old.
In later Indian history we have also had such brilliant periods, and
perhaps in our wanderings through the ages we may come across
them too.

Athens especially became famous during this period. It had a
great statesman for its leader. Pericles was his name, and for
thirty years he held power in Athens. During this period Athens
became a noble city, full of beautiful buildings and great artists
and great thinkers. Even now it is spoken of as the Athens of
Pericles and we talk of the Age of Pericles.

Our friend Herodotus, the historian, who lived about this time
in Athens, thought about this growth of Athens and, as he was fond
of moralizing, he drew a moral from it. He says in his history
that :

> " The power of Athens grew; and here is evidence—and there
> is proof of it everywhere—that libertyis a good thing. While the
> Athenians were despotically governed, they were not superior in
> war to any of their neighbours, but when they got rid of their
> despot, they far surpassed them. This shows that in subjection
> they did not exert themselves, but they were working for a master,
> but when they became free each individual keenly did his best on
> his own account."

I have mentioned the names of some of the great ones of those
times. One of the greatest of that, or any time, I have not yet
mentioned. His name was Socrates. He was a philosopher, always
searching for truth. To him the only thing worth having was
true knowledge, and he often discussed difficult questions with his
friends and acquaintances, so that out of the discussions truth
might emerge. He had many disciples or *chelās*, and the greatest
of these was Plato. Plato wrote many books which have come
down to us, and it is from these books that we know a great deal
of his master, Socrates. Evidently governments do not like people
who are always trying to find out things; they do not like the
search for truth. The Athenian Government—this was just after
the time of Pericles—did not like the methods of Socrates, and they
held a trial and condemned him to death. They told him that if

he promised to give up his discussions with people and changed his ways they would let him off. But he refused to do so and preferred the cup of poison, which brought him death, to giving up what he considered his duty. On the point of death almost he addressed his accusers and judges, the Athenians, and said :

> "If you propose to acquit me on condition that I abandon my search for truth, I will say : I thank you, O Athenians, but I will obey God, who as I believe set me this task, rather than you, and so long as I have breath and strength I will never cease from my occupation with philosophy. I will continue the practice of accosting whomever I meet and saying to him, 'Are you not ashamed of setting your heart on wealth and honours while you have no care for wisdom and truth and making your soul better?' I know not what death is—it may be a good thing, and I am not afraid of it. But I do know that it is a bad thing to desert one's post and I prefer what may be good to what I know to be bad."

In life Socrates served the cause of truth and knowledge well, but better still he served it in his death.

In these days you will often read or hear discussions and arguments on many problems—on Socialism and Capitalism and many other things. There is a great deal of suffering and injustice in the world, and many people are thoroughly dissatisfied with it, and they seek to change it. Plato also thought of problems of government, and he has written about them. Thus even in those days people were thinking of how to shape the government of a country and society so that there may be greater happiness all round.

When Plato was getting old, another Greek, who has become famous, was coming to the front. His name was Aristotle. He had been the private tutor of Alexander the Great, and Alexander helped him greatly with his work. Aristotle did not trouble himself with problems of philosophy, like Socrates and Plato. He was more interested in observing things in Nature and in understanding the ways of Nature. This is called Natural Philosophy or, more often now, Science. Thus Aristotle was one of the early scientists.

We must now go on to Aristotle's pupil, the great Alexander, and follow his swift career. But that must be to-morrow. I have written enough for to-day.

To-day is *Vasanta Pañchamī*, the coming of spring. The all-too-short winter is past and the air has lost its keenness. More and more birds come to us and fill the day with their songs. And to-day, just fifteen years ago, in Delhi city, your Mummie and I got married to each other !

17

A FAMOUS CONQUEROR, BUT A CONCEITED YOUNG MAN

January 24, 1931

IN my last letter, and even before that, I have referred to Alexander the Great. I think I have called him a Greek. It is not quite correct to say so, for he was really a Macedonian—that is, he came from a country just north of Greece. The Macedonians were in many ways like the Greeks; you might call them their cousins. Philip, the father of Alexander, was King of Macedonia. He was an able king and he made his little kingdom strong, and built up a very efficient army. Alexander is called " the Great ", and he is very famous in history. But a great deal of what he did was made possible by the careful work of his father Philip before him. Whether Alexander was a really great man or not is a doubtful matter. He is certainly no hero of mine. But he succeeded in a short life in impressing his name on two continents, and in history he is supposed to be the first of the world-conquerors. Far away in the heart of Central Asia, he is still remembered as Sikandar, and whatever he may have been in reality, history has succeeded in attaching a glamour to his name. Scores of cities have been named after him and many of these still exist. The greatest of these was Alexandria, in Egypt.

Alexander was only twenty when he became king. Full of ambition to achieve greatness, he was eager to march towards the old enemy, Persia, with the fine army which his father had made for him. The Greeks did not like either Philip or Alexander, but they were cowed down a little by their strength. And so they acknowledged each of them, one after the other, as the captain-general of all the Greek forces which were to invade Persia. Thus they bowed down to the new power that was rising. One Greek city, Thebes, rebelled against him, and he struck at it with great cruelty and violence. He destroyed this famous city and knocked down its buildings and massacred many of its people and sold many thousands into slavery. By this barbarous behaviour he terrified Greece. But this and other instances of barbarism in his life do not make him admirable for us and only repel and disgust us.

Egypt, which was then under the Persian King, was easily conquered by Alexander, who had already defeated the Persian King, Darius III, a successor of Xerxes. Later he went again towards Persia and defeated Darius a second time. The great palace of Darius, the " King of kings ", was destroyed by Alexander, in revenge, he said, for the burning of Athens by Xerxes.

There is an old book in the Persian language, written nearly 1000 years ago, by a poet named Firdausi. The book is called the

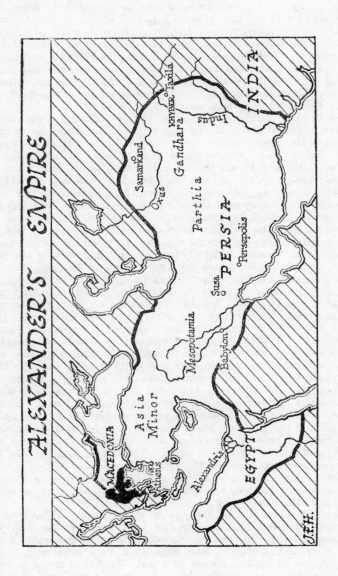

ALEXANDER'S EMPIRE

INDIA

KHYBER Taxila

Gandhara

Indus

Samarkand

Oxus

Parthia

PERSIA

Persepolis

Susa

Mesopotamia

Babylon

Asia Minor

MACEDONIA

Athens

Alexandria

EGYPT

J.F.H.

Shāhnāmah; it is a chronicle of the Kings of Persia. This book describes, very fancifully, the battles of Alexander and Darius. It tells us that on being defeated Darius sought help from India. " A camel with the pace of wind he sent " to Fūr or Porus, who was a king in the north-west of India. But Porus could not help him at all. He himself had to face the onslaught of Alexander soon afterwards. In this book, the *Shāhnāmah* of Firdausi, it is interesting to find numerous references to Indian swords and daggers being used by the Persian King and nobles. This indicates that even in Alexander's day India was making swords of fine steel, which were welcomed in foreign countries.

Alexander wandered on from Persia. Through the country where Herat and Kabul and Samarqand now stand he went and reached the upper valleys of the river Indus. Here he met the first Indian ruler who opposed him. Greek historians call him Porus, after the Greek fashion. His real name must have been similar to this, but we do not know it. It is said that Porus fought bravely and it was not easy for Alexander to overcome him. Very chivalrous and very tall, Porus is said to have been, and Alexander was so impressed by his courage and chivalry that, even after defeating him, he left him in charge of his kingdom. But from being King Porus he became a *satrap*, or governor, of the Greeks.

Alexander entered India through the Khyber Pass in the north-west, and *via* Taxila, which lies a little north of Rawalpindi. Even now you can see the ruins of this ancient city. After defeating Porus, Alexander appears to have considered marching south towards the Ganges. But he did not do so, and, following the Indus valley, he returned. It is interesting to think what might have happened if Alexander had marched towards the heart of Hindustan. Would he have continued to win? Or would the Indian armies have overcome him? A frontier king like Porus gave him sufficient trouble, and it is quite possible that the bigger kingdoms of Middle India might have been strong enough to check Alexander. But whatever Alexander may or may not have wished, his soldiers decided for him. They were tired and weary of many years' wanderings. Perhaps they were impressed by the fighting qualities of the Indian soldiers and did not wish to take the risk of a defeat. Whatever the reason was, the army insisted on going back, and Alexander had to agree. The return journey was, however, a disastrous one, and the army suffered from lack of food and water. Soon afterwards, in 323 B.C., Alexander died at Babylon. He never saw his home country Macedonia again after he set out for his Persian campaign.

So died Alexander at the age of thirty-three. What had this " great " person done during his brief career? He won some brilliant battles. He was undoubtedly a great general. But he was vain and conceited, and sometimes very cruel and violent. He thought of himself almost as a god. In fits of anger or whims of the moment he killed some of his best friends, and destroyed great cities together with their inhabitants. He left nothing solid behind him in his empire—not even proper roads—that he had built. Like a meteor in the sky he came and went, and left little of himself behind him except a memory. His family people killed each other off after his death, and his great empire fell to pieces. A world-conqueror he is called, and it is said that once he sat down and wept because there was nothing more left for him to conquer ! But India, except for a little bit in the north-west, was still unconquered by him; and China even then was a great State, and Alexander went nowhere near China.

On his death his empire was divided up between his generals. Egypt fell to Ptolemy, who established a strong government there and founded a dynasty. Under this government, with Alexandria as its capital, Egypt was a powerful country, and Alexandria was a great city famous for its science and philosophy and learning.

Persia and Mesopotamia and part of Asia Minor fell to the lot of another general, Seleucus. To his share fell also the part of north-western India which Alexander had conquered. But he was unable to keep any part of India, and the Greek garrison was driven out from there after Alexander's death.

Alexander came to India in 326 B.C. His coming was just a raid and it made very little difference to India. Some people think that this raid helped to begin intercourse between the Indians and the Greeks. But, as a matter of fact, even before Alexander's day there was a highway between the East and the West, and India was in continual touch with Persia, and even Greece. This contact must, of course, have been increased by Alexander's visit, and the two cultures—the Indian and the Greek—must have mixed to a greater extent.

Alexander's raid and his death led, in India, to the founding of a great empire, the Mauryan Empire. This was one of the great periods in Indian history, and we must spend some little time over it.

18

CHANDRAGUPTA MAURYA AND THE ARTHASHĀSTRA

January 25, 1931

IN one of our letters I mentioned Magadha. This was an old kingdom, situated where the province of Bihar now lies. The capital of this kingdom was Pātaliputra, the modern Patna. About the time we are now considering, a line of kings belonging to the Nanda dynasty or family ruled over Magadha. When Alexander came on his raid to the north-west of India, a Nanda king ruled at Pātaliputra. Probably related to this king, there was a young man there named Chandragupta. Chandragupta appears to have been a very clever, energetic and ambitious person, and the Nanda king, thinking him too clever, or not liking something that he had done, exiled him from his country. Chandragupta went north to Taxila, attracted perhaps by stories of Alexander and the Greeks. With him was a very able Brahman named Vishnugupta, also called Chānakya. The two of them, Chandragupta and Chānakya, were not meek and mild persons bowing down to fate or whatever might happen to them. They had great and ambitious schemes in their heads and they wanted to go ahead and succeed. Perhaps Chandragupta was dazzled and attracted by the glory of Alexander and wanted to follow his example. In Chānakya he had an ideal friend and counsellor for this purpose. Both kept their eyes open and watched carefully what was happening in Taxila. They bided their time.

Soon their opportunity came. As soon as news of Alexander's death reached Taxila, Chandragupta knew that the time had come for action. He roused up the people round about and, with their help, he attacked and drove away the Greek garrison that Alexander had left. Having taken possession of Taxila, Chandragupta and his allies marched south to Pātaliputra and defeated the Nanda king. This was in 321 B.C., just five years after Alexander's death; and from this date begins the reign of the Mauryan dynasty. It is not quite clear why Chandragupta was called Maurya. Some people think that this was due to his mother's name being Mura; others say that his mother's father was the keeper of the king's peacocks, and a peacock is called *mayūra* in Sanskrit. Whatever the origin of the word may have been, Chandragupta Maurya is the name he is known by, to distinguish him from another famous Chandragupta, who was a great ruler in India many hundreds of years later.

The *Mahābhārata* and other old books and old stories tell us of great kings—chakravartī rājās—who ruled over the whole of Bhārata. But we have no clear knowledge of those days and cannot even say what was the extent of Bhārata or Bhāratavarsha then. It may be that the stories coming down to us exaggerate the might of the old rulers. However that may be, the first instance that we find in history of a strong and widespread empire in India is that of Chandragupta Maurya. As we shall see, this was a very advanced and powerful government. It is clear that such a government and State could not have come into existence suddenly. For a long time past there must have been various processes going on—processes of amalgamation of the smaller kingdoms and of advancement in the art of government.

During Chandragupta's reign Seleucus, the general of Alexander who had inherited the countries from Asia Minor to India, crossed the Indus with an army and invaded India. He repented very soon of his rashness. Chandragupta defeated him badly and Seleucus went back the way he had come. Instead of gaining anything, he had to give up a good part of Gāndhāra, or Afghanistan, up to Kabul and Herat, to Chandragupta. Chandragupta also married the daughter of Seleucus. His empire now covered the whole of North India and part of Afghanistan, from Kabul to Bengal, and from the Arabian Sea to the Bay of Bengal. Only South India was not under him. Pātaliputra was the capital of this great empire.

Seleucus sent an ambassador named Megasthenes to represent him at the Court of Chandragupta. Megasthenes has left us an interesting account of those days. But we have another and a more interesting account which gives us full details of the government of Chandragupta. This is Kautilya's *Arthashāstra*. Kautilya is none other than our old friend Chānakya or Vishnugupta, and *Arthashāstra* means " the science of wealth ".

This book, the *Arthashāstra*, deals with so many subjects and discusses such a variety of matters that it is not possible for me to tell you much about it. It deals with the duties of the king, of his ministers and counsellors, of council meetings, of departments of government, of trade and commerce, of the government of towns and villages, of law and law courts, of social customs, of the rights of women, of the maintenance of the old and helpless, of marriage and divorce, of taxation, of the army and navy, of war and peace, of diplomacy, of agriculture, of spinning and weaving, of artisans, of passports, and even of gaols ! I could go on adding to this list, but I do not want to fill this letter with the chapter-heads of Kautilya.

The king, on receiving the royal authority from the people's hands at the time of the coronation, had to take an oath of service of the people. " May I ", he had to affirm, " may I be deprived of heaven, of life, and of offspring if I oppress you." The king's daily work and routine are given. He had to be ready always for urgent work, for public work could not suffer or await a king's pleasure. " If a king is energetic, his subjects will be equally energetic." " In the happiness of his subjects lies his happiness, in their welfare, whatever pleases himself he shall consider as not good, but whatever pleases his subjects, he shall consider as good." Kings are disappearing from this world of ours. There are very few left, and they too will go soon enough. It is interesting, however, to see that the idea of kingship in ancient India meant service of the people. There was no divine right of kings, no autocratic power. And if the king misbehaved, his people had the right to remove him and put another in his place. This was the idea and the theory. Of course, there were many kings who fell short of this ideal and who brought misfortune to their country and people by their folly.

The *Arthashāstra* also lays stress on the old doctrine that " never shall an *Ārya* be subjected to slavery ". Apparently there were some kind of slaves, brought from outside the country or belonging to the country, but so far as the *Āryas* were concerned, care was taken that they should never become slaves.

The capital city of the Mauryan Empire was Pātaliputra. This was a magnificent city with a nine-mile frontage along the Ganges river. There were sixty-four main gates and hundreds of smaller ones. The houses were chiefly made of wood, and as there was danger of fire, elaborate precautions were taken to prevent it. The principal streets had thousands of vessels always kept filled with water. Each householder was also made to keep vessels of water ready for use in case of fire, as well as ladders, hooks and other articles that might be necessary.

One rule for the cities, recorded by Kautilya, will interest you. Whoever threw dirt in the street was punished with a fine. If any one allowed mud or water to collect in the street, he was also fined. If these rules were enforced, Pātaliputra and the other cities must have been fine and clean and sanitary. I wish some such rules could be introduced by our municipalities !

Pātaliputra had a municipal council to manage its affairs. This was elected by the people. It had thirty members, there being six committees of five members each. These committees dealt with the industries and handicrafts of the city, arrangements for travellers and pilgrims, deaths and births for taxation purposes, manufactures and other matters. The whole council looked after sanitation, finance, water-supply, gardens and public buildings.

There were *panchāyats* for administering justice and courts of appeal. Special measures were taken for famine relief, and half the stores in all the State warehouses were always kept in reserve for times of famine.

Such was the Mauryan Empire as organized by Chandragupta and Chānakya 2200 years ago. I have just mentioned some of the matters mentioned by Kautilya and Megasthenes. Even these will give you a rough idea of North India in those days. The country must have hummed with life from the capital city of Pātaliputra to the many other great cities and the thousands of towns and villages of the Empire. Great roads led from one part of the Empire to the other. The principal *Rājapattra*, the King's Way, passed through Pātaliputra to the north-west frontier. There were many canals and a special irrigation department to look after them; and a navigation department for the harbours, ferries, bridges, and the numerous boats and ships that plied from one place to another. Ships went across the seas to Burma and China.

Over this empire Chandragupta ruled for twenty-four years. He died in 296 B.C. We shall carry on the story of the Mauryan Empire in our next letter.

19

THREE MONTHS!

S.S. " Cracovia,"
April 21, 1931

It is long since I wrote to you. Nearly three months have gone by—three months of sorrow and difficulty and strain; three months of change in India, and change above all in our family circle. India has stopped for a while the campaign of *Satyagraha*, or Civil Disobedience, but the problems that face us are not easier of solution; and our family has lost its dearly loved head, who gave us strength and inspiration, and under whose sheltering care we grew up and learnt to do our bit for India, our common mother.

How well I remember that day in Naini Prison! It was the 26th of January, and I sat down, as was my usual practice, to write to you about the days that have gone by. Only the day before I had written about Chandragupta and of the Mauryan Empire which he founded. And I had promised to carry on the story and to tell you of those who followed Chandragupta Maurya, of Ashoka the Great, beloved of the gods, who shone like a bright star in the Indian sky and passed away, leaving a deathless memory. As I thought of Ashoka, my mind wandered and came back to the present, to the 26th of January, the day I sat with pen and paper to write to you. That day was a great day for us, for a year ago we had celebrated that very day all over India, in city and in village, as Independence Day, *Pūrna Swarāj* day, and all of us in our millions had taken the pledge of Independence. Since then a year had passed by, a year of struggle and suffering and triumph, and again India was going to celebrate that great day. And as I sat in barrack No. 6 of Naini Prison, I thought of the meetings and processions and the *lāthi* charges and arrests that would take place that day all over the country. I thought of this with pride and joy and anguish, when suddenly my musing was cut short. A message was brought to me from the outside world that Dadu was very ill and I was to be released immediately to go to him. Full of anxiety, I forgot my musings, and put away the letter to you I had just begun, and left Naini Prison for Anand Bhawan.

Ten days I was with Dadu before he left us. Ten days and nights we watched his suffering and agony and his brave fight with the Angel of Death. Many a fight had he fought during his life, and many a victory won. He did not know how to surrender, and even face to face with Death, he would not give in. As I watched this last struggle of his, full of anguish at my inability to help him whom I loved so much, I thought of some lines which I had read long ago in a tale of Edgar Allan Poe : " Man doth not yield himself to the angels, nor even unto death utterly, save by the weakness of his feeble will."

It was on the 6th of February, in the early morning, that he left us. We brought his body, wrapped in the Flag he loved so well, from Lucknow to Anand Bhawan. Within a few hours it was reduced to a handful of ashes and the Ganga carried away this precious burden to the sea.

Millions have sorrowed for him; but what of us, children of his, flesh of his flesh and bone of his bone! And what of the new Anand Bhawan, child of his also, even as we are, fashioned by him so lovingly and carefully. It is lonely and deserted and its spirit seems to have gone; and we walk along its verandahs with light steps, lest we disturb, thinking ever of him who made it.

We sorrow for him and miss him at every step. And as the days go by the sorrow does not seem to grow less or his absence more tolerable. But, then, I think that he would not have us so. He would not like us to give in to grief, but to face it, as he faced his troubles, and conquer it. He would like us to go on with the work he left unfinished. How can we rest or give in to futile grief when work beckons and the cause of India's freedom demands our service? For that cause he died. For that cause we will live and strive and, if necessary, die. After all, we are his children and have something of his fire and strength and determination in us.

The deep blue Arabian Sea stretches out before me as I write; and on the other side, in the far distance, is the coast of India, passing by. I think of this vast and almost immeasurable expanse and compare it to the little barrack, with its high walls, in Naini Prison, from where I wrote my previous letters to you. The sharp outline of the horizon stands out before me, where the sea seems to meet the sky; but in gaol, a prisoner's horizon is the top of the wall surrounding him. Many of us who were in prison are out of it to-day and can breathe the freer air outside. But many of our colleagues remain still in their narrow cells deprived of the sight of the sea and the land and the horizon. And India herself is still in prison and her freedom is yet to come. What is our freedom worth if India is not free?

20

THE ARABIAN SEA

S.S. " Cracovia,"
April 22, 1931

STRANGE that we should be travelling by this boat—the *Cracovia* —from Bombay to Colombo! I remember well waiting for the *Cracovia* to arrive in Venice nearly four years ago. Dadu was on board, and I had gone to Venice to meet him, leaving you at your school at Bex in Switzerland. Again, some months later, it was by the *Cracovia* that Dadu returned home from Europe and I met

him in Bombay.   Some of his fellow-passengers of that voyage are
with us now, and they are full of stories of him.

I wrote to you yesterday of the past three months of change.
One thing that took place during these last few weeks I would have
you remember, as India will remember it for long years to come.
Less than a month ago in Cawnpore city died a gallant soldier of
India, Ganesh Shankar Vidyarthi, done to death even as he sought
to save others.   Ganeshji was a dear friend of mine, a noble and
selfless comrade with whom it was a privilege to work.   When madness broke out in Cawnpore last month and Indian killed Indian,
Ganeshji rushed out into the fray, not to fight any one of his countrymen, but to save them.   He saved hundreds, himself he could not
save, and did not care to save, and by the hands of the very people
he sought to save, he met his death.   Cawnpore and our province
have lost a bright star and many of us a dear and wise friend.   But
what a glorious death was his, as he faced calm-eyed and without
flinching the madness of the mob, and even in the midst of danger
and death thought only of others and how to save them !

Three months of change !   A drop in the ocean of time, a bare
second in the life of a nation !   Only three weeks ago I went to see
the ruins of Mohen-jo Daro in the Indus valley in Sind.   You were
not with me there.   I saw a great city coming out of the earth, a
city of solid brick houses and wide thoroughfares, built, they say,
5000 years ago.   And I saw beautiful jewellery and jars found in
this ancient city.   I could almost imagine men and women, decked
out in gay attire, walking up and down its streets and lanes, and
children playing, as children will, and the bazaars, bright with
merchandise, and people buying and selling, and the temple bells
ringing.

For these 5000 years India has lived her life and seen many a
change.   And I sometimes wonder if this old mother of ours, so
ancient and yet so young and beautiful, does not smile at the
impatience of her children and their petty worries and their joys
and sorrows, which last for a day and then are no more !

21

A HOLIDAY AND A DREAM JOURNEY

March 26, 1932

FOURTEEN months have passed by since I wrote to you from
Naini Prison about past history.   Three months later I added two
short letters to that series from the Arabian Sea.   We were on
board the *Cracovia* then, hurrying to Lankā.[1]   As I wrote, the great

----

[1] Lankā is the old name for Ceylon.

big sea stretched out before me and my hungry eyes gazed at it and could not take their fill. Then came Lankā, and for a month we made glorious holiday and tried to forget our troubles and worries. Up and down that most beautiful of islands we went, wondering at its exceeding loveliness and at the abundance of Nature. Kandy and Nuwara Eliya and Anurdahapura, with its ruins and relics of old greatness; how pleasant it is to think of the many places we visited ! But, above all, I love to think of the cool tropical jungle with its abundant life, looking at you with a thousand eyes; and of the graceful areca tree, slender and straight and true; and the innumerable coconuts; and the palm-fringed sea-shore where the emerald green of the island meets the blue of the sea and the sky; and the sea-water glistens and plays on the surf, and the wind rustles through the palm leaves.

It was your first visit to the tropics, and for me also, but for a brief stay long ago, the memory of which had almost faded, it was a new experience. I had not been attracted to them, as I feared the heat. It was the sea and the mountain, and above all the high snows and glaciers, that fascinated me. But even during our short stay in Ceylon I felt something of the charm and the witchery of the tropics, and I came back, somewhat wistfully, hoping to make friends with them again.

Our month of holiday in Ceylon ended too soon, and we crossed the narrow seas to the southern tip of India. Do you remember our visit to Kanyā-Kumāri, where the Virgin Goddess is said to dwell and keep guard, and which Westerners, with their genius for twisting and corrupting our names, have called Cape Comorin ? We sat, literally, at the feet of mother India then, and we saw the Arabian Sea meet the waters of the Bay of Bengal, and we liked to imagine that they were both paying homage to India ! Wonderfully peaceful it was there, and my mind travelled several thousand miles to the other extremity of India where the eternal snows crown the Himalayas and peace also dwells. But between the two there is strife enough and misery and poverty !

We left the Cape and journeyed northwards.

Through Travancore and Cochin we went, and over the backwaters of Malabar—how beautiful they were, and how our boat glided along in the moonlight between the wooded banks, almost as if in a dream ! Then we passed on to Mysore and Hyderabad and Bombay and, at last, to Allahabad. That was nine months ago, in the month of June.

But all roads in India in these days sooner or later lead to one destination; all journeys, dream ones or real, end in prison ! And so here I am back again behind my old familiar walls, with plenty of time to think of or write to you, though my letters may not reach you. Again the fight is on and our people, men and women, boys and girls, go forth to battle for freedom and to rid this country of the curse of poverty. But freedom is a goddess hard to win; she demands, as of old, human sacrifice from her votaries.

I complete three months in prison to-day. It was on this very day three months ago—December 26—that I was arrested for the sixth time. I have taken long in resuming these letters to you, but you know how difficult it is sometimes to think of the distant past when the present fills the mind. It takes some little time for me to settle down in gaol and to avoid worrying about happenings outside. I shall try to write to you regularly. But I am in a different prison now, and the change is not to my liking and interferes a little with my work. My horizon is higher than ever here. The wall which faces me must bear some relation, in height at least, to the Great Wall of China! It seems to be about 25 feet high, and the sun takes an extra hour and a half to climb over it every morning before it can visit us.

Our horizon may be limited for a while. But it is good to think of the great blue sea and the mountains and the deserts, and of the dream journey we took—it hardly seems real now—you and Mummie and I, ten months ago.

22

MAN'S STRUGGLE FOR A LIVING

March 28, 1932

LET us pick up again the threads of world-history and try to have some glimpses into the past. It is a tangled web, difficult to unravel and difficult even to see as a whole. We are so apt to lose ourselves in a particular bit of it and give it more importance than it deserves. Nearly all of us think that the history of our own country, whichever that might be, is more glorious and more worthy of study than the histories of other countries. I have warned you against this once before, and I shall warn you again. It is so easy to fall into the trap. It was, indeed, to prevent this happening that I began writing these letters to you, and yet, sometimes, I have felt that I am making this very mistake. What am I to do if my own education was defective and the history I was taught was topsy-turvy? I have tried to make amends for it by further study in the seclusion of prison, and perhaps I have succeeded to some extent. But I cannot remove from the gallery of my mind the pictures of persons and events which I hung there in my boyhood and youth. And these pictures colour my outlook on history, which is sufficiently limited as it is by incomplete knowledge. I shall make mistakes, therefore, in what I write; and many an unimportant fact I shall mention, and many an important one rorget to write about. But these letters are not meant to take the place of books of history. They are—or at least I please myself by imagining them to be—little talks *entre nous*, which we might have had if 1000 miles and many solid walls did not separate us.

I cannot help writing to you about many famous men who fill the pages of history books. They are often interesting in their own way, and they help us to understand the times in which they lived. But history is not just a record of the doings of big men, of kings and emperors and the like. If it were so, history might as well shut up shop now; for kings and emperors have almost ceased to strut about the world's stage. But the really great men and women do not, of course, require thrones or crowns or jewels or titles to show them off. It is only the kings and the princelets, who have nothing in them but their kingships and princedoms, who have to put on their liveries and uniforms to hide the nakedness underneath. And unhappily many of us are taken in and deluded by this outward show and make the mistake of

> "Calling a crowned man royal
> That was no more than a king."

Real history should deal, not with a few individuals here and there, but with the people who make up a nation, who work and by their labour produce the necessaries and luxuries of life, and who in a thousand different ways act and react on each other. Such a history of man would really be a fascinating story. It would be the story of man's struggle through the ages against Nature and the elements, against wild beasts and the jungle and, last and most difficult of all, against some of his own kind who have tried to keep him down and to exploit him for their own benefit. It is the story of man's struggle for a living. And because, in order to live, certain things, like food and shelter and clothing in cold climates, are necessary, those who have controlled these necessities have lorded it over man. The rulers and the bosses have had authority because they owned or controlled some essential of livelihood, and this control gave them the power to starve people into submission. And so we see the strange sight of large masses being exploited by the comparatively few; of some who earn without working at all, and of vast numbers who work but earn very little.

The savage, hunting alone, gradually forms a family; and the whole household work together and for each other. Many households co-operate together to form the village, and workers and merchants and artisans of different villages later join together to form guilds of craftsmen. Gradually you see the social unit growing. To begin with, it was the individual, the savage. There was no society of any kind. The family was the next bigger unit, and then the village and the group of villages. Why did this social unit grow? It was the struggle for a living that forced growth and co-operation, for co-operation in defence against the common enemy and in attack was obviously far more effective than single-handed defence or attack. Even more so was co-operation in work helpful. By working together they could produce far more food and other necessaries than by working singly. This co-operation in work meant that the economic unit was also evolving, from the individual savage, who hunted for himself, into large groups. Indeed, it was probably this growth of the economic unit, ever pushed on by man's struggle for a living, that resulted in the growth of society and of the social unit.   Right through the long stretches of history we see this growth in the midst of almost interminable conflict and misery, and sometimes even a relapse. But do not imagine that this growth means necessarily that the world has progressed greatly or is a far happier place than it was. Perhaps it is better than it was; but it is very far from perfection, and there is misery enough everywhere.

Life becomes more and more complicated as these economic and social units grow.   Commerce and trade increase.   Barter takes the place of gift, and then money comes and makes a tremendous difference to all transactions.   Immediately trade goes ahead, for payment by gold or silver coin makes an exchange easy. Later, even coin is not always used and people use symbols. A piece of paper with a promise to pay is considered good enough. Thus come into use bank-notes and cheques. This means doing business on credit. The use of credit again helps trade and commerce greatly. As you know, cheques and bank-notes are frequently used nowadays and sensible people do not carry about bags of gold and silver with them.

Thus we see, as history progresses out of the dim past, people producing more and more and people specializing in different trades, exchanging their goods with each other, and in this way increasing trade.   We see also new and better means of communication developing, especially during the last hundred years or so, after the steam engine came.   As production grows, the wealth of the world increases, and some people at least have more leisure.   And so what is called civilization develops.

All this happens, and people boast of our enlightened and progressive age, and of the wonders of our modern civilization and of our great culture and science; and yet the poor remain poor and miserable, and great nations fight each other and slaughter millions; and great countries like our own are ruled by an alien people. What is the good of civilization to us if we cannot even have freedom in our own households?   But now we are up and doing.

How fortunate we are to live in these stirring times, when each one of us can take part in the great adventure and see not only India but the whole world in process of change !   You are a lucky girl.   Born in the month and year of the great revolution which ushered in a new era in Russia, you are now witne ss to a revolution in your own country, and soon you may be an act or in it.   All over the world there is trouble and change.   In the Far East, Japan is at the throat of China; in the West, and indeed all over the world, the old system totters and threatens to collapse.   Countries talk of disarmament, but look suspiciously at each other and keep armed to the teeth.   It is the twilight of Capitalism, which has lorded it for so long over the world.   And when it goes, as go it must, it will take many an evil thing with it.

23

A SURVEY

March 29, 1932

How far have we reached in our journey through the ages? We have talked a little already of the old days in Egypt and India and China and Knossos. We have seen the ancient and wonderful civilization of Egypt, which produced the Pyramids, gradually decay and lose its strength and become an empty shadow, a thing of forms and symbols, with little of real life in it. We have seen Knossos destroyed by the sister race from the Grecian mainland. In India and China we have glanced at the dim and distant beginnings, unable for want of material to know much, but conscious of their rich civilization even in those days; and wondering at the unbroken links which join the two countries culturally to their respective pasts, many thousands of years ago. In Mesopotamia we have had just a glimpse of empire after empire flourishing for a while, and then going the way of all empires.

We have also said something of a number of great thinkers who appeared in different countries about 500 or 600 years before Christ. Buddha and Mahāvīra in India, Confucius and Lao-Tse in China, Zoroaster in Persia, and Pythagoras in Greece. We noticed that Buddha attacked priestcraft and the existing forms of the old Vedic religion in India; for he found that the masses were being imposed upon and deluded by all manner of superstition and *pūjās*. He attacked the caste system and preached equality.

We went back then to the West, where Asia and Europe join each other, and followed the fortunes of Persia and Greece—how a great empire rose in Persia and Darius, the " King of kings ", extended it right up to Sindh in India; how this empire tried to swallow up little Greece, but found, to its great amazement, that the little thing could fight back and hold its own. Then followed the short but brilliant period of Greek history of which I have told you something, when a host of geniuses and great men lived there and produced literature and art of the highest beauty.

The golden age of Greece did not last long. Alexander of Macedon spread the fame of Greece far and wide by his conquests, but with his coming the high culture of Greece gradually faded. Alexander destroyed the Persian Empire and even crossed the borders of India as a conqueror. He was undoubtedly a great general, but tradition has woven innumerable legends round his name and he has acquired a fame which he hardly deserves. Only the well-read know anything of Socrates or Plato or Phidias or Sophocles or the other great men of Greece. But who has not heard of Alexander?

Alexander did comparatively little. The Persian Empire was

old and tottering and was hardly likely to survive for long.   In India Alexander's visit was just a raid and had little significance. Perhaps if Alexander had lived longer he might have done something more substantial.   But he died young, and his empire fell to pieces immediately.   But though his empire did not last, his name endures.

One great effect of Alexander's march to the East was the fresh contacts established between East and West.   Large numbers of Greeks went east and settled down in the old cities or in new colonies which they established.   Even before Alexander there was contact and trade between East and West.   But after him this increased greatly.

Another possible effect of Alexander's invasions was, if true, very unfortunate for the Greeks.   A theory has been advanced that his soldiers took back with them the malaria mosquito from the swamps of Mesopotamia to the Greek lowlands; and thus malaria spread and weakened and enfeebled the Greek race.   This is one of the explanations given of the decline of the Greeks.   But it is just a theory, and no one knows how much truth it contains.

Alexander's brief-lived empire came to an end.   But in its place arose several smaller empires.   Among these was that of Egypt under Ptolemy and that of western Asia under Seleucus.   Both Ptolemy and Seleucus were Alexander's generals.   Seleucus tried to encroach on India, but he found to his dismay that India could hit back with vigour.   Chandragupta Maurya had established a powerful State all over northern and central India.   Of Chandragupta and his famous Brahman minister Chānakya and the book he wrote—the *Arthashāstra*—I have already, in my earlier letters, told you something.   Fortunately for us, this book gives us a good picture of those times in India over 2200 years ago.

We have completed our look back, and we shall go ahead with the story of the Mauryan Empire and of Ashoka in the next letter. I promised, indeed, to do so over fourteen months ago, on January 25, 1931, in Naini Prison.   I have still to keep this promise.

24

ASHOKA, THE BELOVED OF THE GODS

March 30, 1932

I AM afraid I am a little too fond of running down kings and princes.   I see little in their kind to admire or do reverence to. But we are now coming to a man who, in spite of being a king and emperor, was great and worthy of admiration.   He was Ashoka, the grandson of Chandragupta Maurya.   Speaking of him in his *Outline of History*, H. G. Wells (some of whose romances you must have read) says : " Amidst the tens of thousands of names of monarchs that crowd the columns of history, their majesties and graciousnesses and serenities and royal highnesses and the like, the name of Ashoka shines, and shines almost alone, a star.   From the Volga to Japan his name is still honoured.   China, Tibet, and even India, though it has left his doctrine, preserve the tradition of his greatness. More living men cherish his memory to-day than have ever heard the names of Constantine or Charlemagne."

This is high praise indeed.   But it is deserved, and for an Indian it is an especial pleasure to think of this period of India's history.

Chandragupta died nearly 300 years before the Christian era began.   He was succeeded by his son Bindusāra, who seems to have had a quiet reign of twenty-five years.   He kept up contacts with the Greek world, and ambassadors came to his Court from Ptolemy of Egypt, and Antiochus, who was the son of Seleucus of western Asia.   There was trade with the outside world and, it is said, the Egyptians used to dye their cloth with indigo from India.   It is also stated that they wrapped their mummies in Indian muslins. Some old remains have been discovered in Bihar which seem to show that some kind of glass was made there even before the Mauryan period.

It will interest you to know that Megasthenes, the Greek ambassador who came to the Court of Chandragupta, writes about the Indian love of finery and beauty, and specially notes the use of the shoe to add to one's height.   So high heels are not entirely a modern invention.

Ashoka succeeded Bindusāra in 268 B.C. to a great empire, which included the whole of north and central India and extended right up to Central Asia.   With the desire, perhaps, of bringing into his empire the remaining parts in the south-east and south, he started the conquest of Kalinga in the ninth year of his reign.   Kalinga lay on the east coast of India, between the Mahanadi, Godāvari and Kistna rivers.   The people of Kalinga fought bravely, but they were ultimately subdued after terrible slaughter.   This war and slaughter affected Ashoka so deeply that he was disgusted with war and all its works.   Henceforth there was to be no war for him.   Nearly the whole of India, except a tiny tip in the south, was under him ; and it was easy enough for him to complete the conquest of this little tip.   But he refrained.   According to H. G. Wells, he is the only military monarch on record who abandoned warfare after victory.

Fortunately for us, we have Ashoka's own words, telling us of what he thought and what he did.   In numerous edicts which were carved out in the rock or on metal, we still have his messages to his people and to posterity.   You know that there is such an Ashoka Pillar in the fort at Allahabad.   There are many others in our province.

In these edicts Ashoka tells us of his horror and remorse at the slaughter which war and conquest involve.   The only true conquest, he says, is the conquest of self and the conquest of men's hearts by the *Dharma*. But I shall quote for you some of these edicts. They make fascinating reading and they will bring Ashoka nearer to you.

" Kalinga was conquered by His Sacred and Gracious Majesty", so runs an edict, " when he had been consecrated eight years. One hundred and fifty thousand persons were thence carried away captive, one hundred thousand were there slain, and many times that number died.

" Directly after the annexation of the Kalingas began His Sacred Majesty's zealous protection of the Law of Piety, his love of that Law, and his inculcation of that Law (*Dharma*).   Thus arose his sacred Majesty's remorse for having conquered the Kalingas, because the conquest of a country previously unconquered involves the slaughter, death and carrying away captive of the people.   That is a matter of profound sorrow and regret to His Sacred Majesty."

The edict goes on to say that Ashoka would not tolerate any longer the slaughter or captivity of even a hundredth or thousandth part of the number killed and made captive in Kalinga.

" Moreover, should any one do him wrong, that too must be borne with by His Sacred Majesty, so far as it can possibly be borne with.   Even upon the forest folk in his dominions His Sacred Majesty looks kindly and he seeks to make them think aright, for, if he did not, repentance would come upon His Sacred Majesty. For His Sacred Majesty desires that all animate beings should have security, self-control, peace of mind, and joyousness."

Ashoka further explains that true conquest consists of the conquest of men's hearts by the Law of Duty or Piety, and to relate that he had already won such real victories, not only in his own dominions, but in distant kingdoms.

The Law, to which reference is made repeatedly in these edicts, was the Law of the Buddha.   Ashoka became an ardent Buddhist and tried his utmost to spread the *Dharma*.   But there was no force or compulsion.   It was only by winning men's hearts that he sought to make converts.   Men of religion have seldom, very seldom, been as tolerant as Ashoka.   In order to convert people to their own faith they have seldom scrupled to use force and terrorism and fraud.   The whole of history is full of religious persecution and religious wars, and in the name of religion and of God perhaps more blood has been shed than in any other name.   It is good therefore to remember how a great son of India, intensely religious, and the head of a powerful empire, behaved in order to convert people to his ways of thought.   It is strange that any one should be so foolish as to think that religion and faith can be thrust down a person's throat at the point of the sword or a bayonet.

So Ashoka, the beloved of the gods—*devānāmpriya*, as he is called in the edicts—sent his messengers and ambassadors to the kingdoms of the West in Asia, Europe and Africa.   To Ceylon, you will remember, he sent his own brother Mahendra and sister Sanghamitra, and they are said to have carried a branch of the sacred peepal tree from Gaya. Do you remember the peepal tree we saw in the temple at Anuradhapura? We are told that this was the very tree which grew out of that ancient branch.

In India Buddhism spread rapidly. And as the *Dharma* was for Ashoka not just the repetition of empty prayers and the performance of *pūjās* and ceremonies, but the performance of good deeds and social uplift, all over the country public gardens and hospitals and wells and roads grew up. Special provision was made for the education of women. Four great university towns—Takshashila or Taxila in the far north, near Peshawar; Mathurā, vulgarly spelt Muttra now by the English; Ujjain in Central India; and Nalanda near Patna in Bihar—attracted students not only from India, but from distant countries—from China to western Asia—and these students carried back home with them the message of Buddha's teaching. Great monasteries grew up all over the country—*Vihāra* they were called. There were apparently so many round about Pātaliputra or Patna that the whole province came to be known as Vihara, or, as it is called now, Bihar. But, as often happens, these monasteries soon lost the inspiration of teaching and of thought, and became just places where people followed a certain routine and worship.

Ashoka's passion for protecting life extended to animals also. Hospitals especially meant for them were erected, and animal-sacrifice was forbidden. In both these matters he was somewhat in advance of our own time. Unhappily, animal-sacrifice still prevails to some extent, and is supposed to be an essential part of religion; and there is little provision for the treatment of animals.

Ashoka's example and the spread of Buddhism resulted in vegetarianism becoming popular. Till then *Kshattriyas* and Brahmans in India generally ate meat and used to take wines and alcoholic drinks. Both meat-eating and wine-drinking grew much less.

So ruled Ashoka for thirty-eight years, trying his utmost to promote peacefully the public good. He was always ready for public business " at all times and at all places, whether I am dining or in the ladies' apartments, in my bedroom or in my closet, in my carriage or in my palace gardens, the official reporters should keep me constantly informed of the people's business ". If any difficulty arose, a report was to be made to him immediately " at any hour and at any place ", for, as he says, " work I must for the commonweal ".

Ashoka died in 226 B.C. Some time before his death he became a Buddhist monk.

We have few remains of Mauryan times. But what we have are practically the earliest so far discovered of Aryan civilization in India—for the moment we are not considering the ruins of Mohen-jo-Daro. In Sarnāth, near Benares, you can see the beautiful Ashoka pillar with the lions on the top.

Of the great city of Pātaliputra, which was Ashoka's capital, nothing is left. Indeed over 1500 years ago, 600 years after Ashoka, a Chinese traveller, Fa-Hien, visited the place. The city flourished

then and was rich and prosperous, but even then Ashoka's palace
of stone was in ruins.   Even these ruins impressed Fa-Hien, who
says in his travel record that they did not appear to be human work.

The palace of massive stone is gone, leaving no trace behind, but
the memory of Ashoka lives over the whole continent of Asia, and
his edicts still speak to us in a language we can understand and
appreciate.   And we can still learn much from them.   This letter
has grown long and may weary you.   I shall finish it with a small
quotation from one of Ashoka's edicts :

> " All sects deserve reverence for one reason or another.   By thus
> acting a man exalts his own sect and at the same time does service
> to the sects of other people."

25

THE WORLD OF ASHOKA'S TIME

March 31, 1932

WE have seen that Ashoka sent missions and ambassadors to
distant countries and that there was continuous contact and trade
between India and these countries.   Of course you must remember,
when I talk of these contacts and of trade in those days, that it was
nothing like what we have now.   It is easy enough now for people
and for merchandise to go by train and steamer and aeroplane.
But in those days of the distant past every journey was a perilous
and a lengthy one, and only the adventurous and the hardy undertook it.   There can, therefore, be no comparison between trade
then and now.

What were these " distant countries " referred to by Ashoka ?
What was the world like during his time ?   We know nothing of
Africa, except of Egypt and of the Mediterranean coast.   We know
very little of northern and central and eastern Europe, or of northern
and central Asia.   Of America also we know nothing ; but there
are many people who think that highly developed civilizations existed
in the American continents from early times.   Columbus is said to
have " discovered " America long after—in the fifteenth century
after Christ.   We know that a high civilization existed then in
Peru in South America and in the surrounding countries.   It is
therefore quite possible that cultured people dwelt in America and
formed well-organized societies in the days when India had Ashoka,
in the third century before Christ.   But we have no facts about
them, and it is not of much use to guess.   I mention them
because we are all so apt to think that civilized people lived only in
those parts of the world of which we have heard and read.   For a
long time Europeans imagined that ancient history meant only the

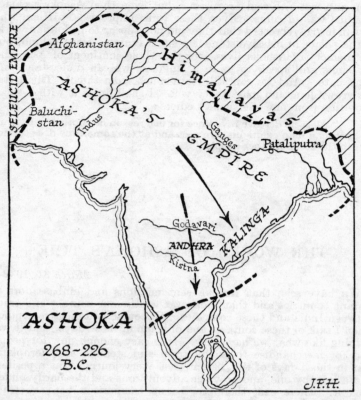

ASHOKA
268~226
B.C.

J.F.H.

history of Greece and of Rome and of the Jews. All the rest of the
world apparently was a wilderness in those days, according to their
old way of thinking. Later they discovered how limited was their
knowledge, when their own scholars and archæologists told them
of China and India and other countries. So we must be on our
guard, and must not think that our limited knowledge compasses
all that has taken place in this world of ours.

For the present, however, we may say that the civilized ancient
world of Ashoka's day—that is, the third century before Christ—
consisted principally of the Mediterranean countries of Europe and
Africa; western Asia, China and India. China was probably more
or less cut off then from direct contact with the western countries
or even western Asia, and fantastic notions prevailed in the West
about China or Cathay. India seems to have been the connecting
link between the West and China.

We have already seen that after the death of Alexander his empire
was divided up by his generals. There were three principal divisions:
(1) Western Asia, Persia, and Mesopotamia, under Seleucus; (2)

Egypt under Ptolemy; and (3) Macedonia, under Antigonus. The
first two lasted for a long time. You will remember that Seleucus
was the neighbour of India and was greedy enough to want to add
a bit of India to his empire. But he met more than his match in
Chandragupta, who drove him back and made him give up a part
of what is now Afghanistan.

Macedonia was less fortunate. It was harried by Gauls and
others from the north, and only one part of this kingdom managed
to hold out against these Gauls and to remain independent. This
was Pergamum in Asia Minor, where Turkey is situated to-day. It
was a little Greek State, but for more than 100 years it became a
home of Greek culture and art, and beautiful buildings grew up,
and a library and museum. In a small way it was a rival to
Alexandria across the sea.

Alexandria was the capital of the Ptolemys in Egypt. It became
a great city, famous in the ancient world. The glory of Athens
had diminished greatly, and gradually Alexandria took its place
as the cultural centre of the Greeks. Its great library and museum
attracted large numbers of students from far countries, who discussed philosophy and mathematics and religion and other problems
that filled the minds of the ancient world. Euclid, of whom you
and every boy and girl who has been to school has heard, was a
resident of Alexandria, and a contemporary of Ashoka's.

The Ptolemys were, as you know, Greeks, but they adopted many
Egyptian ways and customs. They even took to some of the old
gods of Egypt. Jupiter and Apollo and the other gods and goddesses
of the old Greeks, who, like the Vedic gods in the *Mahābhārata*,
appeared so often in Homer's epics, had to retire or change their
names and appear in a different guise. Between the gods and
goddesses of old Egypt—Isis and Osiris and Horus—and those of
old Greece there was a mingling and an amalgamation, and new
gods were put before the multitude for its worship. What did it
matter to whom they bowed down and paid worship, and by what
name it was known, so long as they had something to which to do
pūjā! Of the new gods the most famous was called Serapis.

Alexandria also was a great trading centre, and merchants from
other parts of the civilized world came to it. We are told that
there was a colony of Indian merchants in Alexandria. We also
know that Alexandrian merchants had a settlement in South India
on the Malabar coast.

Not far from Egypt, across the Mediterranean, was Rome, already
grown great, and destined to grow far greater and more powerful.
And facing it, on the African coast, was Carthage, its rival and
enemy. We shall have to consider their story at some length,
before we can have any idea of the ancient world.

In the East, China was growing as great as Rome in the West,
and we shall have to consider this also before we can form a proper
picture of the world in Ashoka's time.

26

THE CH'INS AND THE HANS

April 3rd, 1932

In my letters to you last year from Naini I wrote to you something about the early days of China, of the settlements on the Hoang-Ho river, and of the early dynasties, the Hsia, the Shang or Yin, and the Chou, how the Chinese State gradually grew up and a centralized government was developed during these vast periods of time.   There followed a long period then, still nominally under the Chou dynasty, when this process of centralization stopped and there was disorganization.   Petty rulers of local areas became practically independent and quarrelled with each other.   This unfortunate state of affairs lasted for several hundred years—everything in China seems to run into several hundred or 1000 years !— till one of these local rulers, the Duke of Ch'in, managed to drive out the ancient and effete Chou dynasty.   His descendants are called the Ch'in dynasty, and it is interesting to note that the name China is derived from this Ch'in.

The Ch'ins began their career thus in China in 255 B.C.   Thirteen years previously Ashoka had begun his reign in India.   We are thus now dealing with the contemporaries of Ashoka in China.   The first three Ch'in emperors had very short reigns.   Then, in 246 B.C. came the fourth, who was in his own way a remarkable man.   His name was Wang Cheng, but later he adopted another name—Shih Huang Ti—and he is usually known by his second name, which means "The First Emperor".   He had evidently a very high opinion of himself and his times, and was no respecter of the past.   Indeed, he wanted people to forget the past and to imagine that history began with him—the great First Emperor !   It mattered little that there had already been successive emperors in China for more than 2000 years.   Even their memory was to be wiped out from the land.   And not only the old emperors but all other famous men of the past were also to be forgotten.   So the order went forth that all books giving an account of the past, especially books of history and the Confucian classics, were to be burnt and destroyed utterly.   The only books excepted were books on medicine and some sciences.   In his edict he said :

" Those who shall make use of antiquity to belittle modern times shall be put to death with their relations."

And he kept his word.   Hundreds of scholars who tried to hide books which they loved were buried alive.   A nice, kind-hearted and amiable person he must have been, the First Emperor !   I remember him always, and not without some sympathy, when I hear too much praise of the past in India.   Some of our people are always looking back to the past, always glorifying it and always seeking inspiration from it. If the past inspires to great deeds, by all means let us be inspired by it. But it does not seem to me to be healthy for any person or for any nation to be always looking back. As some one has said, if man was meant to go back or always to look back he would have had eyes at the back of his head. Let us study our past by all means, and admire in it whatever is worthy of admiration, but our eyes must always look in front and our steps must go ahead.

Undoubtedly Shih Huang Ti acted in a barbarous way by having the old books and the readers of those books burnt or buried. And the result was that almost all his work ended with him. He was the First Emperor, to be followed by a second and a third, and so on till the end of time. Such was his intention. And yet of all China's dynasties, the Ch'in was the shortest. Many of these dynasties, as I have told you, lasted hundreds and hundreds of years; one of them, the predecessor of the Ch'ins, lasted as much as 867 years. But the great Ch'ins rose and triumphed and ruled a powerful empire, and decayed and ended—all in a brief fifty years. Shih Huang Ti was to have been the first of a great line of powerful emperors, and yet three years after his death in 209 B.C., his dynasty came to an end. And soon, after all, the books and the classics of Confucius were dug out of hiding, and took the same pride of place as before.

As a ruler Shih Huang Ti was one of the most powerful that China has had. He put an end to the pretensions of the numerous local rulers, destroyed feudalism and built up a strong central government. He conquered the whole of China and even Annam. It was he who started building the Great Wall. This was an expensive job. But the Chinese apparently preferred spending money over this wall, which was to protect them from foreign enemies, to keeping a large standing army for defence. The Wall could hardly prevent a big invasion. All it did was to stop petty raids. It shows, however, that the Chinese wanted peace and, in spite of their strength, were not lovers of military glory.

Shih Huang Ti, the First Emperor, died, and there was hardly a second of that dynasty to follow. But from his day China has always had a tradition of unity.

Another dynasty then comes upon the scene—the Han dynasty. This flourished for over 400 years, and among the early rulers was a woman-empress. Sixth of the line was Wu-Ti, who was also one of China's most powerful and famous rulers. He was emperor for over fifty years. He defeated the Tartars who were continually raiding the north. From Korea in the east right up to the Caspian Sea in the west, the Chinese Emperor was supreme, and all the tribes of Central Asia acknowledged him as their over-lord. Look at the map of Asia and you will have some idea of the tremendous extent of his influence and of the power of China in the first and second centuries before Christ. We read a great deal of the greatness of Rome during this period, and one is apt to think that Rome overshadowed the world. " Mistress of the world " Rome has been called. But though Rome was great then and growing greater, China was a vaster and a more powerful empire.

It was probably in the days of Wu-Ti that China and Rome established their contacts. Trade between the two countries took place through the Parthians, who inhabited the regions called Persia and Mesopotamia to-day. Later, when there was war between Rome and Parthia, this trade was interrupted, and Rome then tried direct trade by sea, and a Roman ship actually came to China. But this was in the second century after Christ. We are still in the period before the Christian era.

Buddhism came to China during the reign of the Han dynasty. It had been heard of in China even before the Christian era, but it began to spread later when the emperor of the day is said to have seen a wonderful dream of a man 16 feet tall, with a bright halo round his head. As he saw this vision in the west, he sent messengers in this direction, and these messengers returned with an image of Buddha and Buddhist writings. With Buddhism came the influence of Indian art to China, and from China this spread to Korea, and from there to Japan.

During the Han period two other important events are worthy of note. The art of printing from wooden blocks was invented, but it was not much used for nearly 1000 years. Even so China was 500 years ahead of Europe.

The second noteworthy fact was the introduction of the examination system for public officials. Boys and girls do not love examinations, and I sympathize with them. But this Chinese system of appointing public officials was a remarkable thing in those days. In other countries, till recently, officials were appointed by favouritism chiefly, or out of a special class or caste. In China any one passing the examination could be appointed. This was not an ideal system, as a person may pass an examination in the Confucian classics and yet may not be a very good public official. But the system was a vast improvement over favouritism and the like, and for 2000 years it lasted in China. It was only recently that it was ended.

27

ROME AGAINST CARTHAGE

April 5, 1932

FROM the Far East we shall now go to the West, and trace the growth of Rome. It is said that Rome was founded in the eighth century before Christ. The early Romans, who were probably descendants of the Aryans, had some settlements on the seven hills near the Tiber, and these settlements slowly grew into a city.

And this City-State went on growing and expanding in Italy till it reached the southern tip at Messina, facing Sicily.

You will perhaps remember the City-States of Greece. Wherever the Greeks went, they carried this idea of their City-State with them, and dotted all over the Mediterranean coast were Greek colonies and City-States. But now in Rome we are dealing with something very different. To begin with, perhaps Rome was not unlike the Greek City-State, but soon it spread by defeating the neighbouring tribes. The territory of the Roman State thus grew and comprised the great part of Italy. Such a big area could not be a City-State. It was governed from Rome, and Rome itself had a very peculiar type of government. There was no big emperor or king; nor was there the modern type of republic. Still, the government was a kind of republic, dominated over by the rich families owning land. The Senate was supposed to govern, and this Senate was nominated by two elected persons called " Consuls ". For a long time only the aristocrats could become senators. The Roman people were divided into two classes : the patricians or the rich aristocrats, usually landowners; and the plebeians, who were the common citizens. The history of the Roman State or Republic for several hundred years is one of conflict between these two classes. The patricians have all the power, and with the power goes money ; the plebeians, or plebs, are the under-dogs with neither power nor money. The plebeians go on struggling and fighting to gain power and slowly some crumbs fall to their lot. It is interesting to note that in this long struggle the plebs successfully tried non-co-operation of a kind. They marched out of Rome in a body and setted down in a new city. This frightened the patricians, as they could not get on without the plebs, and so they compromised with them and gave them some slight privileges. Gradually it became possible for a plebeian to attain high office, and even to become a member of the Senate.

We talk of the struggles of the patricians and the plebeians, and we are apt to think that no one else counted. But besides these two groups there was in the Roman State an enormous number of slaves who had no rights of any kind. They were not citizens; they had no vote ; they were the private and personal property of their master, like dogs or cows. They could be sold or punished at the sweet will of the master. They could be freed also under certain conditions, and when they became free they formed a special class called freedmen. In the ancient world in the West slaves were always in great demand, and in order to fulfil this demand huge slave-markets arose, and expeditions went out to capture men and women, and even children, in distant lands and sell them into slavery. The glory and the majesty of ancient Greece and Rome, as of ancient Egypt, had for their foundation a system of widespread slavery.

Was this system of slavery equally prevalent then in India ? Very probably it was not. Nor did China have it. This does not mean that there was no slavery in ancient India or China. But such slavery as existed was more or less of the domestic kind. A few domestic servants were considered slaves. India and China do not seem to have had labour slaves—huge gangs working on the land or elsewhere. Thus these two countries escaped the most degrading aspects of slavery.

So Rome grew, and the patricians profited thereby and grew richer and more prosperous. The plebeians, meanwhile, remained poor and were sat upon by the patricians; and both patrician and plebeian combined to sit upon the poor slave.

As Rome grew, how was it governed? By the Senate, I have said; and the Senate was nominated by two elected Consuls. Who elected the Consuls? The citizens who were voters. To begin with, when Rome was small like a City-State, all the citizens lived in or near Rome. It was not very difficult for them to meet together and vote. But as Rome grew, there were many citizens living far from Rome and it was not easy for them to vote. " Representative government ", as it is called now, was not evolved or practised then. Now you know that each area or constituency elects its representative for the national Assembly or Parliament or Congress, and so, in a way, the whole nation is represented in a small gathering. This had not apparently struck the old Romans. So they carried on with their voting in Rome when it was almost impossible for the distant voters to come. Indeed, the distant voters seldom knew what was happening. There were no newspapers or pamphlets or printed books and very few people could read. Thus the power of the vote given to people living far from Rome was of no practical use to them. They had the franchise, but distance disfranchised them.

So that you will notice that it was really only the voters in Rome itself that had any real share in elections and in important decisions. They voted in the open air by going into enclosures. Of these voters many were the poor plebeians. The rich patricians who wanted high office and power bribed these poor people to vote for them. So that Roman elections had quite as much bribery and trickery as sometimes even modern elections have.

As Rome was growing in Italy, Carthage was growing in power in North Africa. The Carthaginians were the descendants of the Phœnicians and had the tradition of seamanship and of trade. Theirs was also a republic, but it was, even more than that of Rome, a republic of rich men. It was a city republic with a huge slave population.

Between Rome and Carthage there were, in the early days, Greek colonies in southern Italy and Messina. But Rome and Carthage united to drive out the Greeks and, having succeeded in doing so, Carthage took Sicily, and Rome came right up to the tip of the Italian boot. The friendship and alliance of Rome and Carthage did not last long. Very soon there were clashes between the two, and bitter rivalry developed. The Mediterranean was not big enough for two strong Powers facing each other across the narrow seas. Both were ambitious. Rome was growing and had the ambition and confidence of youth. Carthage, to begin with, perhaps looked down a little on upstart Rome and felt confident of its command of the seas. For over 100 years they fought each other, with intervals of peace in between; and they fought like wild animals, bringing misery to vast populations. There were three wars between them—the Punic Wars they are called. The first Punic War lasted twenty-three years from 264 to 241 B.C. and ended in a victory for Rome. Twenty-two years later came the second Punic War, and Carthage sent a general, famous in history, named Hannibal. For fifteen years Hannibal harassed Rome and terrorized the Roman people. He defeated their armies with great slaughter—notably at Cannæ in 216 B.C. And he did all this with little help from Carthage, from which he was cut off, as the Romans held command of the sea. But in spite of defeat and disaster and in spite of the perpetual menace of Hannibal, the Roman people did not give in, and fought on against their hated enemy. Afraid of meeting Hannibal in open battle, they avoided such battles and merely tried to harass him and cut off his communications. The Roman general who was specially fond of avoiding battle in this way was a man called Fabius. For ten years he thus avoided battle. I mention his name not because he was a great man and therefore worthy of remembrance, but because his name has given birth to a word in the English language—Fabian. There are " Fabian " tactics which do not force the issue; they avoid battle or a crisis and hope to gain their end by slow attrition. There is a Fabian Society in England which believes in socialism but does not believe in hurry or sudden changes.

Hannibal made a great part of Italy a desert, but Rome's persistence and doggedness won in the end. In 202 B.C., at the battle of Zama, Hannibal was defeated. He fled from place to place, pursued by the unquenchable hatred of Rome. At last he poisoned himself.

There was peace for half a century between Rome and Carthage, which had been humbled sufficiently and hardly dared challenge Rome now. Even so Rome was not content, and it forced a third Punic War on the Carthaginians. This ended in great slaughter and in the complete destruction of Carthage. Indeed, the plough was made to till the earth where the proud city of Carthage had once stood, the Queen of the Mediterranean.

28

THE ROMAN REPUBLIC BECOMES AN EMPIRE

April 9, 1932

WITH the final defeat and destruction of Carthage, Rome was supreme and without a rival in the western world. It had already conquered the Greek States; it now took possession of the territories belonging to Carthage. Thus Spain came to Rome after the second Punic War. But still the Roman dominions comprised the Mediter-

ranean countries only.   The whole of northern and central Europe
was independent of Rome.

In Rome, the result of victory and conquest was wealth and
luxury, and gold and slaves poured in from the conquered lands.
But where did they go to ?   The Senate, as I have told you, was the
governing body in Rome, and it consisted of people from rich aristocratic families.   This group of rich people controlled the Roman
Republic and its life, and as the power and extent of Rome grew,
the wealth of these people grew with it.   So that the rich became
richer, while the poor remained poor or actually became poorer.
The slave populations grew, and luxury and misery advanced side
by side.   When this happens there is usually trouble.   It is an
amazing thing how much human beings will put up with, but there
is a limit to human endurance, and when this is reached there are
burst-ups.

The rich people tried to lull the poor by games and contests in
circuses, where gladiators were forced to fight and kill each other
just to amuse the spectators.   Large numbers of slaves and prisoners
of war were thus killed for what was called, I suppose, sport.

But disorders increased in the Roman State.   There were insurrections and massacres, and bribery and corruption during the
elections.   Even the poor, down-trodden slaves rose in revolt under
a gladiator named Spartacus.   But they were crushed ruthlessly,
and it is said that 6000 of them were crucified on the Appian Way in
Rome.

Adventurers and generals gradually become more important and
overshadow the Senate.   There is civil war and desolation, and rival
generals fighting each other.   In the East, in Parthia (Mesopotamia),
the Roman legions suffered a great defeat at the battle of Carrhae in
53 B.C., where the Parthians destroyed the Roman army sent against
them.

Among these crowds of Roman generals two names stand out—
Pompey and Julius Cæsar.   Cæsar, as you know, conquered France,
or Gaul as it was called, and Britain.   Pompey went east and had
some success there.   But between the two there was bitter rivalry ;
both were ambitious and could not tolerate a rival.   The poor
Senate receded into the background, although each paid lip-homage
to it.   Cæsar defeated Pompey, and thus became the chief man in
the Roman world.   But Rome was a republic, and so he could not
officially be the boss of everything.   Attempts were made, therefore,
to crown him king or emperor.   He was willing enough, but the long
republican tradition made him hesitate.   Indeed, this tradition
was too strong for him, and he was stabbed to death by Brutus
and others on the very steps of the Forum.   You must have
read Shakespeare's play *Julius Cæsar*, in which this scene is
given.

Julius Cæsar was killed in the year 44 B.C., but his death did not
save the Republic.   Cæsar's adopted son and great-nephew,
Octavian, and his friend Marc Antony avenged Cæsar's death.   And
then kingship came back, and Octavian became the chief of the

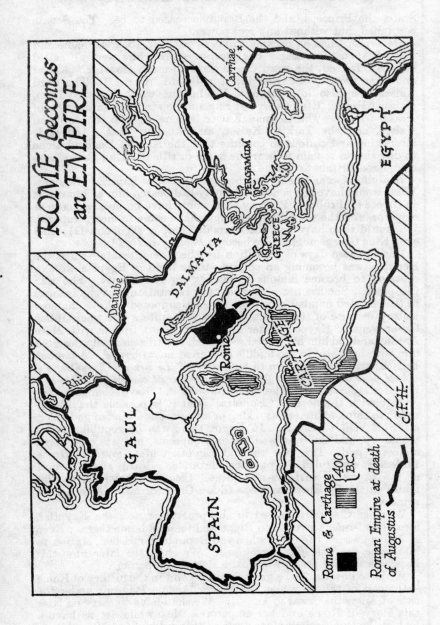

State, the Princeps, and the Republic ceased to be. The Senate continued, but without any real power.

Octavian, when he became Princeps or Chief, took the name and title of Augustus Cæsar. His successors after him were all called Cæsars. Indeed, the word Cæsar came to mean emperor. Kaiser and Tsar are derived from this same word "Cæsar". The word Kaiser has also long been a Hindustani word—Kaisar-i-Rūm, Kaisar-i-Hind. King George of England now rejoices in the title of *Kaisar-i-Hind*. The German Kaiser is gone, so also the Austrian Kaiser, and the Turkish Kaiser, and Russian Tsar. And it is interesting and curious to consider that the King of England alone to-day should remain to bear the name or title of Julius Cæsar, who conquered Britain for Rome.

So Julius Cæsar's name has become a word of imperial grandeur. What would have happened if Pompey had beaten him at Pharsalus in Greece? Probably Pompey then would have become princeps or emperor, and the word Pompey might have come to mean emperor. We would then have had the German Pompey (Wilhelm II); and even King George might have become *Pompey-i-Hind* !

During these days of transition for the Roman State—when the Republic was becoming an empire—there lived in Egypt a woman destined to become famous in history for her beauty. She was Cleopatra. She has not a very savoury reputation, but she belongs to that limited number of women who are supposed to have changed history because of their beauty. She was quite a girl when Julius Cæsar went to Egypt. Later she became great friends with Marc Antony and did him little good. Indeed, she treacherously deserted him with her ships in the middle of a great naval battle. A famous French writer, Pascal, wrote long ago : " *Le nez de Cléopâtre, s'il eût été plus court, toute la face de la terre aurait changé* ". This is a bit of exaggeration. The world would not have changed very greatly with the nose of Cleopatra. But it is possible that Cæsar began to think of himself as a king or emperor, as a kind of god-ruler, after his visit to Egypt. In Egypt there was no republic, but a monarchy, and the ruler was not only supreme, but was considered almost a god. This was the old Egyptian idea, and the Greek Ptolemys, who ruled Egypt after Alexander's death, adopted most of the Egyptian customs and ideas. Cleopatra belonged to this family of the Ptolemys, and was thus a Greek or rather Macedonian princess.

Whether Cleopatra helped in the process or not, the Egyptian idea of god-ruler travelled to Rome and found a home there. Even in Julius Cæsar's life-time, when the Republic flourished, statues to him were put up and worshipped. We shall see later how this became a regular practice with the Roman Emperors.

We have now reached a great turning-point in the history of Rome —the end of the Republic. Octavian became Princeps under the title of Augustus Cæsar in A.D. 27. We shall have to carry on later this story of Rome and her emperors. Meanwhile, let us have a look at the Roman dominions during the last days of the Republic.

Rome ruled Italy, of course, and Spain and Gaul (France) in the west.   In the east she had Greece and Asia Minor, where, you will remember, there was the Greek State of Pergamum.   In northern Africa, Egypt was supposed to be an allied and protected State; Carthage and some other parts of the Mediterranean countries were also under Rome.   Thus, in the north, the boundary of the Roman dominions ran along the Rhine.   All the peoples of Germany and Russia and northern and central Europe were outside the Roman world.   So also were all the people to the east of Mesopotamia.

Rome was great in those days, but many people in Europe, ignorant of the history of other countries, imagine that it dominated the world.   This was very far from being the case.   At this very period, you will remember, the great Han dynasty of China ruled or was over-lord of an area which stretched right across Asia to the Caspian Sea.   At the battle of Carrhæ, in Mesopotamia, where the Romans were badly defeated, it is probable that the Parthians were helped by the Mongolians.

But Roman history, especially the history of the Roman Republic, is dear to the European, as he considers the old Roman State to be a kind of ancestor of the modern European States, and to some extent this is true.   And so English school-boys, whether they knew modern history or not, were made to learn Greek and Roman history.   I well remember being made to read, in the original Latin, Julius Cæsar's account of his campaign in Gaul.   Cæsar was not only a warrior but a graceful and effective writer also, and his *De Bello Gallico* is still read in thousands of schoolrooms in Europe.

We began, a little while ago, to survey the world at the time of Ashoka.   We have not only finished that survey, but have gone beyond it in China and in Europe.   We are now almost on the threshold of the Christian era, and we shall have to go back to India to bring our knowledge of her people up to date.   For great changes took place there after Ashoka's death, and new empires arose in the south and the north.

I have tried to make you think of world-history as one continuous whole.   But you will remember, I hope, that in these early days the contacts between distant countries were of the most limited kind. Rome, which was advanced in many ways, knew little of geography and maps and took no special steps to learn.   A school-boy or school-girl to-day knows far more of geography than the great generals and the wise men of the Roman Senate knew, although they considered themselves masters of the world.   And just as they considered themselves masters of the world, some thousands of miles away, across the great continent of Asia, the rulers of China also considered themselves the masters of the world.

29

SOUTH INDIA OVERSHADOWS THE NORTH

April 10, 1932

WE return to India after our long journeys to China in the Far East, and Rome in the West.

The Mauryan Empire did not last long after Ashoka's death. Within a few years it withered away. The northern provinces fell away, and in the south a new power arose—the Andhra power. Ashoka's descendants continued to rule the vanishing empire for nearly fifty years, till they were forcibly removed by their commander-in-chief, a Brahman named Pushyamitra. This man made himself king, and there is said to have been a revival of Brahminism in his time. Buddhist monks were also persecuted to some extent. But you will find, as you read Indian history, that the way Brahminism attacked Buddhism was much more subtle. It did not do anything so crude as to persecute it much. Some persecution there was, but this was probably political, and not religious. The great Buddhist *Sañghas* were powerful organizations, and many rulers were afraid of their political powers; hence their attempts to weaken them. Brahminism ultimately succeeded in almost driving out Buddhism from the country of its birth by assimilating it to some extent and absorbing it and trying to find a place for it in its own house.

Thus the new Brahminism was not a mere reversion to the old state of affairs and a negation of all that Buddhism had tried to do. The old leaders of Brahminism were much cleverer and from of old it had been their practice to absorb and assimilate. When the Aryans first came to India they assimilated much of Dravidian culture and custom, and all through their history they have, consciously or unconsciously, acted in this way. They did likewise with Buddhism, and made of Buddha an *avatār* and a god—one of many in the Hindu pantheon. Buddha remained a person to be worshipped and adored by the multitude, but his special message was quietly put aside, and Brahminism or Hinduism, with minor variations, continued the even tenor of its ways. But this process of Brahminising Buddha was a long one, and we are anticipating, for Buddhism was to remain in India for many hundred years after Ashoka's death.

We need not trouble ourselves with the kings and dynasties that followed each other in Magadha. About 200 years after Ashoka's death Magadha ceased to be the premier State of India, but even then it continued to be a great centre of Buddhist culture.

Meanwhile, important events were taking place both in the north and the south. In the north there were repeated invasions by various peoples of Central Asia called Baktrians and Sakas and Scythians and Turkis and Kushans. I think I wrote to you once how Central Asia has been a breeding-ground for hordes of people

and how these people have come out, again and again in history, and
spread out all over Asia and even over Europe.   There were several
such invasions of India during the 200 years before Christ.   But you
must remember that these invasions were not just for conquest and
loot.   They were for land to settle down in.   Most of these Central
Asian tribes were nomads, and as their numbers grew, the land they
lived in was not sufficient to support them.   So they had to migrate
and seek fresh lands.   An even more forceful reason for these great
migrations was the pressure from behind.   One great tribe or clan
would drive away others, and these, in their turn, would be compelled to invade other countries.   Thus the people who came as
invaders to India were often themselves refugees from their own
pastures.   The Chinese Empire also, whenever it was strong enough
to do so, as in the days of the Hans, drove these nomads away and
thus compelled them to seek new homes.

You must also remember that these nomadic tribes of Central
Asia did not look upon India wholly as an enemy country.   They
are referred to as " barbarians ", and undoubtedly, compared to the
India of those days, they were not as civilized.   But most of them
were ardent Buddhists, and they looked up to India, which had given
birth to the *Dharma*.

Even in Pushyamitra's time there was an invasion in the north-
west by Menander of Baktria who was a pious Buddhist.   Baktria
was the country just across the Indian border.   It used to be part
of Seleucus's empire, but later it became independent.   Menander's
invasion was repulsed, but he managed to keep Kabul and Sindh.

Later came the invasion of the Sakas, who came in great numbers
and spread out all over northern and western India.   The Sakas
were a great tribe of Turki nomads.   They were pushed out of their
pastures by another great tribe, the Kushans.   They overran
Baktria and Parthia and gradually established themselves in
northern India, more particularly in the Punjab, Rajputana and
Kathiawad.   India civilized them, and they gave up their nomadic
habits.

It is interesting to observe that these Baktrian and Turki rulers
in parts of India did not make much difference to Indo-Aryan
society.   These rulers, being Buddhist, followed the Buddhist
church organization, which was itself based on the old Indo-Aryan
plan of democratic village communities.   Thus India continued to
be, even under these rulers, largely a collection of self-governing
village communities or republics, under the central power.   During
this period also Takshashila and Mathurā continued to be great
centres of Buddhist learning, attracting students from China and
western Asia.

But repeated invasions from the north-west and the gradual
break-up of the Mauryan State organization had one effect.   The
southern Indian States became truer representatives of the old Indo-
Aryan system.   Thus the centre of Indo-Aryan power moved south.
Probably many able persons from the north migrated to the south
on account of the invasions.   You will see later on that this process

was repeated 1000 years later when the Muslims invaded India. Even now southern India has been far less affected by foreign invasions and contacts than the north. Most of us living in the north have grown up in a composite culture—a mixture of Hindu and Muslim with a dash of the West. Even our language—Hindi or Urdū, or Hindustani, call it what you like—is a composite language. But the south is still, as you have seen yourself, pre-dominantly Hindu and orthodox. For many hundreds of years it tried to protect and preserve the old Aryan tradition, and in this attempt it built up a rigid society which is amazing in its intolerance even to-day. Walls are dangerous companions. They may occasionally protect from outside evil and keep out an unwelcome intruder. But they also make you a prisoner and a slave, and you purchase your so-called purity and immunity at the cost of freedom. And the most terrible of walls are the walls that grow up in the mind which prevent you from discarding an evil tradition simply because it is old, and from accepting a new thought because it is novel.

But South India did a real service by preserving through 1000 years and more the Indo-Aryan traditions not only in religion, but in art and in politics. If you want to see specimens of old Indian art now, you have to go to South India. In politics, we have it from Megasthenes, the Greek, that the popular assemblies of the south restrained the power of kings.

Not only the learned men but the artists and builders and artisans and craftsmen went south when Magadha declined. A considerable trade flourished between South India and Europe. Pearls, ivory, gold, rice, pepper, peacocks, and even monkeys, were sent to Babylon and Egypt and Greece, and later to Rome. Teakwood from the Malabar Coast went even earlier to Chaldæa and Babylonia. And all this trade, or most of it, was carried in Indian ships, manned by Dravidians. This will enable you to realize what an advanced position South India occupied in the ancient world. Large numbers of Roman coins have been discovered in the south, and, as I have already told you, there were Alexandrian colonies on the Malabar Coast and Indian colonies in Alexandria.

Soon after Ashoka's death the Andhra State in the south became independent. Andhra, as you perhaps know, is a Congress province now, along the east coast of India, north of Madras. Telugu is the language of Andhra-desha. The Andhra power extended rapidly after Ashoka till it spread right across the Deccan from sea to sea.

From the south great colonizing enterprises were undertaken, but of these we shall speak later.

I have referred above to the Sakas and Scythians and others who invaded India and settled down in the north. They became part of India, and we in North India are as much descended from them as from the Aryans. In particular, the brave and fine-looking Rajputs and the hardy people of Kathiawad are their descendants.

30

THE BORDERLAND EMPIRE OF THE KUSHANS

April 11, 1932

I HAVE told you in my last letter of the repeated Saka and Turki invasions of India. I have also told you of the growth of a powerful Andhra State in the south stretching from the Bay of Bengal to the Arabian Sea. The Sakas were driven forward by the Kushans, and some time later these Kushans themselves appeared on the scene. In the first century before Christ they established a State on the Indian borderland, and this State grew into a great empire. This Kushan Empire extended down to Benares and the Vindhya mountains in the south, and to Kashgar and Yarkand and Khotan in the north, and the borders of Persia and Parthia in the west. Thus the whole of northern India, including the United Provinces, Punjab and Kashmir, and a good bit of Central Asia were under the Kushan rulers. This empire lasted for nearly 300 years, just about the time when the Andhra State flourished in South India. The Kushan capital at first seems to have been Kabul; later it was shifted to Peshawar, or Purushapura as it was called, and there it remained.

This Kushan Empire is interesting in many ways. It was a Buddhist empire, and one of its famous rulers—the Emperor Kanishka—was ardently devoted to the *Dharma*. Near Peshawar, the capital, was Takshashila, which had for a long time been a centre of Buddhist culture. The Kushans, as I think I have told you, were Mongolians, or allied to them. From the Kushan capital there must have been a continuous coming and going to the Mongolian homelands, and Buddhist learning and Buddhist culture must have gone to China and Mongolia. In the same way, western Asia must have come into intimate touch with Buddhist thought. Western Asia had been under Greek rule since Alexander's day, and large numbers of Greeks had brought their culture to it. This Greek Asiatic culture mingled now with Indian Buddhist culture.

Thus China and western Asia were influenced by India. But in the same manner India was also influenced by them. The Kushan Empire sat, like a colossus astride the back of Asia, in between the Græco-Roman world on the west, the Chinese world in the east and the Indian world in the south. It was a halfway house both between India and Rome, and India and China.

As you might expect, this central position helped to bring about close intercourse between India and Rome. The Kushan period corresponded with the last days of the Roman Republic, when Julius Cæsar was alive, and the first 200 years of the Roman Empire. It is said that the Kushan Emperor sent a great embassy to Augustus Cæsar. Trade flourished both by land and sea. Among the articles which were sent by India to Rome were perfumes, spices, silks, brocades, muslins, cloth of gold and precious stones. A

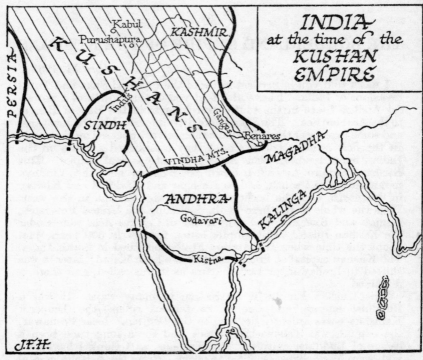

Roman author, named Pliny, actually complained bitterly of the drain of gold from Rome to India. He said that these luxuries cost the Roman Empire one hundred million sesterces annually. This would be about a crore and a half of rupees or a million pounds sterling.

During this period there was great debate and argument in the Buddhist monasteries and at the meetings of the *Sañgha*. New ideas, or old ideas in novel attire, were coming from the south and the west, and the simplicity of Buddhist thought was being gradually affected. This process of change went on till it resulted in Buddhism splitting up into two sections—called the Mahāyāna (the Great Vehicle) and the Hinayāna (Little Vehicle). And as the outlook on life and religion changed with the new interpretations and ideas, the manifestations of these ideas in art and architecture also changed. It is not easy to say how these changes were brought about. Perhaps there were two main influences which both tended to deflect Buddhist thought in the same direction : Brahminic and Hellenic.

Buddhism was, I have told you several times, a revolt against caste and priestcraft and ritualism. Gautama did not approve of image-worship. He did not claim to be a god to be worshipped. He was the Enlightened One, the Buddha. In accordance with this ideology, Buddha was not represented in images, and the archi-tecture of those days avoided all images. But the Brahmans wanted to bridge the gap between Hinduism and Buddhism and were always trying to introduce Hindu ideas and symbolism into Buddhist thought ; and the craftsmen from the Græco-Roman world were also used to making images of the gods. Thus gradually images crept into the Buddhist shrines. To begin with they were not of the Buddha but of the Bodhi-Sattvas, who, in Buddhist tradition, are said to be previous incarnations of Buddha. The process continued till Buddha himself was depicted in images and worshipped.

The Mahāyāna school of Buddhism approved of these changes. It was nearer to the Brahman way of thinking. The Kushan emperors accepted the Mahāyāna school and helped it to spread. But they were by no means intolerant of the Hinayāna school, or even of other religions. Kanishka is said to have encouraged Zoroastrianism also.

It is interesting to read of the great debates that used to take place between the learned about the relative merits of Mahāyāna and Hinayāna. Huge gatherings of the *Sangha* used to be held for this purpose. Kanishka held a general assembly of the *Sangha* in Kashmir. The debates and the controversy on this question lasted many hundreds of years. Mahāyāna triumphed in northern India, Hinayāna in the south, till both of them, in India, were absorbed by Hinduism. To-day the Mahāyāna form of Buddhism exists in China, Japan and Tibet ; the Hinayāna exists in Ceylon and Burma.

The art of a people is a true mirror of their minds, and so, as the simplicity of early Buddhist thought gave place to elaborate symbolism, even so Indian art became more and more elaborate and ornate. In particular, the Mahāyāna sculpture of the north-west, in Gandhara, was full of elaboration of statuary and ornament. Even the Hinayāna architecture could not keep itself wholly untouched by this new phase, and it lost gradually the restraint and simplicity of its earlier style and took to rich carving and symbolism.

There are a few monuments of this period with us still. The most interesting are some of the beautiful frescoes at Ajanta.

We shall now bid good-bye to the Kushans. But remember this. Like the Sakas and other Turki peoples, the Kushans hardly came to India or ruled over India as aliens governing a conquered country. The bond of religion tied them to India and her people, but besides this they adopted the principles of government of the Aryan people in India. And because they fitted in with the Aryan system to a large extent, they succeeded in ruling northern India for nearly 300 years.

31

JESUS AND CHRISTIANITY

April 12, 1932

THE Kushan Empire in the north-west of India and the Han dynasty in China have carried us beyond an important landmark in history, and we must go back to it. So far we have been dealing with dates B.C.—before Christ. Now we are in the Christian Era— A.D., or A.C. The era, as its name implies, dates from Christ, from the supposed date of birth of Christ. As a matter of fact, it is probable that Christ was born four years before this date, but that makes little difference. It is customary to refer to dates after Christ as A.D.—Anno Domini—in the year of the Lord. There is no harm in following this widespread practice, but it seems to me more scientific to use the letters A.C.—after Christ—for these dates just as we have been using B.C. I propose to do so.

The story of Christ or Jesus, as his name was, is given in the New Testament of the Bible, and you know something about it. In these accounts given in the Gospels little is said about his youth. He was born at Nazareth, he preached in Galilee, and he came to Jerusalem when he was over thirty. Soon after he was tried and sentenced by the Roman governor, Pontius Pilate. It is not clear what Jesus did or where he went before he started his preaching. All over Central Asia, in Kashmir and Ladakh and Tibet and even farther north, there is still a strong belief that Jesus or Isā travelled about there. Some people believe that he visited India also. It is not possible to say anything with certainty, and indeed most authorities who have studied the life of Jesus do not believe that Jesus came to India or Central Asia. But there is nothing inherently improbable in his having done so. In those days the great universities of India, specially Takshashila in the north-west, attracted earnest students from distant countries, and Jesus might well have come there in quest of knowledge. In many respects the teaching of Jesus is so similar to Gautama's teaching that it seems highly probable that he was fully acquainted with it. But Buddhism was sufficiently known in other countries, and Jesus could well have known of it without coming to India.

Religions, as every school-girl knows, have led to conflict and bitter struggles. But it is interesting to watch the beginnings of the world-religions and to compare them. There is so much that is similar in their outlook and their teaching that one wonders why people should be foolish enough to quarrel about details and un-essentials. But the early teachings are added to and distorted till it is difficult to recognize them; and the place of the teacher is taken by narrow-minded and intolerant bigots. Often enough religion has served as a handmaiden to politics and imperialism. It was the old Roman policy to cultivate superstition for the benefit, or rather for the exploitation, of the masses, for it was easier to keep down the people if they were superstitious. The Roman aristocrats would consent to dabble in high philosophy, but what was good for them was not good or safe for the masses. Machiavelli, a famous Italian of a later day, who has written a book on politics, states that religion is necessary for government, and that it may be the duty of a ruler to support a religion which he believes to be false. Even in recent times we have had innumerable instances of imperialism advancing under the cloak of religion. It is not surprising that Karl Marx wrote that " Religion is the opium of the masses ".

Jesus was a Jew, and the Jews were and are a peculiar and strangely persevering people. After a brief period of glory in the days of David and Solomon they fell on evil days. Even this glory was on a small scale, but it was magnified in their imaginations till it became a kind of Golden Age of the past, which would come again at the appointed time when the Jews would become great and powerful. They spread out all over the Roman Empire and elsewhere, but held together, firm in the belief that their day of glory was coming and that a messiah would usher this in. It is one of the wonders of history how the Jews, without a home or a refuge, harassed and persecuted beyond measure, and often done to death, have preserved their identity and held together for over 2000 years.

The Jews expected a messiah, and perhaps they had hopes of Jesus. But they were soon disappointed. Jesus talked a strange language of revolt against existing conditions and the social order. In particular he was against the rich and the hypocrites who made of religion a matter of certain observances and ceremonial. Instead of promising wealth and glory, he asked people to give up even what they had for a vague and mythical Kingdom of Heaven. He talked in stories and parables, but it is clear that he was a born rebel who could not tolerate existing conditions and was out to change them. This was not what the Jews wanted, and so most of them turned against him and handed him over to the Roman authorities.

The Roman people were not intolerant so far as religions went, for the Empire tolerated all religions, and even if someone chose to blaspheme or curse any of the gods, he was not punished. As one of the emperors, Tiberius, said : " If the gods are insulted, let them see to it themselves." The Roman governor, Pontius Pilate, before whom Jesus was produced, could not therefore have worried about the religious aspect of the matter. Jesus was looked upon as a political, and by the Jews as a social, rebel; and as such he was tried and sentenced and crucified at Golgotha. In the hour of his agony even his chosen disciples deserted him and denied him, and by their betrayal made his suffering almost unbearable, so that, before he died, he uttered those strangely moving words : "My God ! My God ! why hast thou forsaken me ? "

Jesus was quite young, being only a little over thirty when he died. We read in the beautiful language of the Gospels the tragic story of his death, and are moved. The growth of Christianity in after ages has made millions revere the name of Jesus, although they have seldom followed his teachings. But we must remember that when he was crucified, he was not widely known outside Palestine. The people in Rome knew nothing about him, and even Pontius Pilate must have attached little importance to the incident.

The immediate followers and disciples of Jesus were frightened into denying him, but soon after his death a newcomer, Paul, who had not seen Jesus himself, started spreading what he considered to be the Christian doctrine. Many people think that the Christianity that Paul preached was very different from the teachings of Jesus. Paul was an able and learned person, but he was not a social rebel such as Jesus was. Paul succeeded, however, and Christianity gradually spread. The Romans attached little importance to it to begin with. They thought Christians were a sect of the Jews. But the Christians became aggressive. They were hostile to all other religions and they refused absolutely to worship the Emperor's image. The Romans could not understand this mentality and, as it appeared to them, narrow-mindedness. They considered the Christians therefore as cranks who were pugnacious and uncultured and opposed to human progress. As a religion, they might have tolerated Christianity, but the Christian refusal to pay homage to the Emperor's image was looked upon as political treason and was made punishable with death. The Christians also strongly criticized the gladiatorial shows. Then followed the persecution of the Christians, and their property was confiscated and they were thrown to the lions. You must have read stories of these Christian martyrs and perhaps you have also seen cinema films of them. But when a person is prepared to die for a cause, and indeed to glory in such a death, it is impossible to suppress him or the cause he represents. And the Roman Empire wholly failed to suppress the Christians. Indeed, it was Christianity that came out triumphant in the conflict, and early in the fourth century after Christ one of the Roman emperors himself became a Christian, and Christianity became the official religion of the Empire. This was Constantine, who founded Constantinople. We shall come to him later.

As Christianity grew, violent disputes arose about the divinity of Jesus. You will remember my telling you how Gautama the Buddha, who claimed no divinity, came to be worshipped as a god and as an *avatār*. Similarly, Jesus claimed no divinity. His repeated statements that he was the son of God and the son of man do not necessarily mean any divine or superhuman claim. But human beings like to make gods of their great men, whom, having deified, they refrain from following ! Six hundred years later the Prophet Mohammad started another great religion, but, profiting perhaps by these instances, he stated clearly and repeatedly that he was human, and not divine.

So, instead of understanding and following the teachings of Jesus, the Christians argued and quarrelled about the nature of Jesus' divinity and about the Trinity. They called each other heretics and persecuted each other and cut each other's heads off. There was a great and violent controversy at one time among different Christian sects over a certain diphthong. One party said that the word *Homo-ousion* should be used in a prayer; the other wanted *Homoi-ousion*—this difference had reference to the divinity of Jesus. Over this diphthong fierce war was raged and large numbers of people were slaughtered.

These internal disputes took place as the Church grew in power. They have continued between various Christian sects till quite recent times in the West.

You may be surprised to learn that Christianity came to India long before it went to England or western Europe, and when even in Rome it was a despised and proscribed sect. Within 100 years or so of the death of Jesus, Christian missionaries came to South India by sea. They were received courteously and permitted to preach their new faith. They converted a large number of people, and their descendants have lived there, with varying fortunes, to this day. Most of them belong to old Christian sects which have ceased to exist in Europe. Some of these have their headquarters now in Asia Minor.

Christianity is politically the dominant religion to-day, because it is the religion of the dominant peoples of Europe. But it is strange to think of the rebel Jesus preaching non-violence and *ahimsā* and a revolt against the social order, and then to compare him with his loud-voiced followers of to-day, with their imperialism and armaments and wars and worship of wealth. The Sermon on the Mount and modern European and American Christianity— how amazingly dissimilar they are ! It is not surprising that many people should think that Bapu is far nearer to Christ's teaching than most of his so-called followers in the West to-day.

32

THE ROMAN EMPIRE

April 23, 1932

I HAVE not written to you for many days, my dear. I have been disturbed and thrilled by news from Allahabad, and, above all, by news of Dol Amma, your old grandmother. And I have chafed a little at my comparative comfort in gaol when my mother, frail and weak, has had to face and receive the *lāthi* blows of the police. But I must not allow my thoughts to run away with me and to interfere with my story.

We shall go back to Rome, or Romaka as the old Sanskrit books

have it. You will remember that we have talked of the end of the
Roman Republic and of the coming of the Roman Empire.
Octavian, the adopted son of Julius Cæsar, became the first monarch,
under the name of Augustus Cæsar. He did not call himself king,
partly because the title was not considered big enough for him, and
partly because he wanted to keep up the outward forms of the
Republic. He therefore called himself " Imperator " or commander. This word imperator thus came to be the highest title,
and, as you perhaps know, the English word " emperor " comes
from it. So the early empire in Rome gave two words, which were
long coveted and used by monarchs all over the world almost—
emperor and Cæsar or Kaiser or Tsar. Originally, it was supposed
that there could only be one emperor at one time, a kind of boss
of the whole world. Rome was called Mistress of the World, and
people in the West thought that the whole world was overshadowed
by Rome. This was of course incorrect and only displayed ignorance
of geography and history. The Roman Empire was largely a
Mediterranean empire and never went beyond Mesopotamia in the
east. There were bigger and more powerful and more cultured
States in China and India from time to time. None the less, so far
as the western world was concerned, Rome was the sole empire,
and as such represented a kind of world-empire to the ancients.
It had tremendous prestige.

The most wonderful thing about Rome is this idea behind it—
the idea of world-dominion, of the headship of the world. Even
when Rome fell, this idea protected it and gave it strength. And
the idea persisted even when it was cut off completely from Rome
itself. So much so that the Empire itself vanished and became a
phantom, but the idea remained.

I find it a little difficult to write of Rome and of its successors.
It is not easy to pick and choose what to tell you, and my mind is,
I am afraid, a bit of a jumble of ill-assorted pictures gathered from
old books that I have read, largely in prison. Indeed, one of the
famous books on Roman history I would probably not have read if
I had not come to prison. The book is so big that it is difficult to
find time, in the midst of other activities, to read it right through.
It is called *The Decline and Fall of the Roman Empire*, and is by an
Englishman named Gibbon. It was written quite a long time ago—
about 150 years—on the shores of Lac Leman in Switzerland, but
it makes fascinating reading even now, and I found its story, given
in somewhat pompous but melodious language, more engrossing
than any novel. Nearly ten years ago I read it in Lucknow District
Gaol, and for over a month I lived with Gibbon for a close companion,
wrapped up in the images of the past that his language evoked. I
was suddenly discharged before I had quite finished the book.
The charm was broken, and I found some difficulty in finding the
time and the mood to go back to ancient Rome and Constantinople
and read the hundred or so pages that remained.

But this was nearly ten years ago and, of course, I have forgotten
a very great deal of what I read then. Still, enough remains in

my mind to fill it and confuse it, and I do not want the confusion to pass on to you.

Let us, first of all, cast a look at the Roman Empire or Empires through the ages. Later perhaps one may try to fill in the picture a little.

The Empire begins with Augustus Cæsar on the eve of the Christian era. For a little while the Emperors pay deference to the Senate, but almost the last traces of the Republic disappear soon enough, and the Emperor becomes all-powerful, a wholly autocratic monarch—indeed, almost a god. During his lifetime he is worshipped as semidivine. After his death he becomes a full god. All the writers of the day endow most of the early Emperors with every virtue—specially Augustus. They call it the Golden Age, the Age of Augustus, when every virtue flourished and the good were rewarded and the wicked punished. That is the way writers have in despotic countries, where it is obvious that the praise of the ruler pays. Some of the most famous of Latin authors—Virgil, Ovid, Horace—whose books we had to read at school, lived about this time. It is possible that after the civil wars and troubles which took place continually during the latter days of the Republic, it was a great relief to have a period of peace and respite when trade and some measure of civilization could flourish.

But what was this civilization? It was a rich man's civilization, and these rich were not even like the artistic and keen-witted rich of ancient Greece, but a rather commonplace and dull crowd, whose chief job was to enjoy themselves. From all over the world foods and articles of luxury came for them, and there was great magnificence and show. The tribe of such people is not extinct even yet. There was pomp and show and a succession of gorgeous processions and games in the circus and gladiators done to death. But behind this pomp was the misery of the masses. There was heavy taxation which fell on the common people chiefly, and the burden of work fell on the innumerable slaves. Even their doctoring and philosophizing and thinking the great ones of Rome left largely to Greek slaves ! There was exceedingly little attempt to educate or to find out facts about the world of which they called themselves the masters.

Emperor followed emperor, and some were bad and some were very bad. And gradually the army became all-powerful and could make and unmake emperors. So it came about that there was bidding to gain the favour of the army and money was squeezed from the masses or from conquered territories to bribe the army. One of the great sources of revenue was the slave-trade, and there were regular organized slave-hunts by Roman armies in the East. Slave merchants accompanied the armies to buy up the slaves on the spot. The island of Delos, sacred to the old Greeks, became a great slave-market, where sometimes as many as 10,000 slaves were sold in a day ! In the great Colosseum of Rome, a popular emperor used to display as many as 1200 gladiators at a time—slaves who were to die to provide sport for the emperor and his people.

Such was Roman civilization in the days of the Empire. And yet our friend Gibbon writes that : " If a man were called upon to fix the period in the history of the world when the human race was most happy and prosperous, he would, without hesitation, name that which elapsed from the death of Domitian to the accession of Commodus "—this means the eighty-four years from 96 A.C. to 180 A.C. I am afraid Gibbon, with all his learning, has said something with which most people will certainly hesitate to agree. He talks of the human race, meaning thereby the Mediterranean world chiefly, for he could have had little or no knowledge of India or China or ancient Egypt.

But perhaps I am a little hard on Rome. It must have been a pleasant change to have some measure of peace within the Roman dominions. There were frequent wars on the frontiers, but within the Empire there was, during the early days at least, the *Pax Romana*—the Roman Peace. There was some security, and this brought trade. Roman citizenship was extended to the whole Roman world—but remember that the poor slaves had nothing to do with it. And also remember that the Emperor was all-powerful and the citizen had few rights. Any discussion on politics would have been considered treason against the Imperator. For the upper classes there was a measure of uniform government and one law. This must have been a great gain to many people who had previously suffered under worse despotisms.

Gradually the Romans became too lazy or otherwise unfit even to fight in their own armies. The farmers in the countryside became poorer under the burdens they had to carry, and so did the people in the city. But the emperors wanted to keep the city-folk pleased, so that they might not give trouble. For this purpose free bread was given to the people of Rome and free games in the circus to amuse them. Thus they were kept in good humour, but this free distribution could only take place in a few places, and even this was done at the cost of misery and suffering to the slave populations in other countries like Egypt, who provided the free flour.

As the Roman people did not readily join the armies, people from outside the Empire—" barbarians " as they were called—were enlisted, and the Roman armies came largely to consist of people who were allied or related to the " barbarian " enemies of Rome. On the frontiers these " barbarian " tribes continually pressed and hemmed in the Romans. As Rome grew weaker the " barbarians " seemed to grow stronger and more daring. From the east especially there was danger, and as this frontier was far from Rome, it was not easy to defend it. Three hundred years after Augustus Cæsar, an emperor named Constantine took a great step which was to have far-reaching consequences. He actually shifted the seat of his empire from Rome to the East. Near an old city called Byzantium on the shores of the Bosphorus, between the Black Sea and the Mediterranean, he founded a new city, which he called, after himself, Constantinople. Constantinople, or New Rome as it was also called, became then the capital and seat of the Roman Empire.

Even to-day in many parts of Asia Constantinople is known as Rūm or Roum.

33

THE ROMAN EMPIRE SPLITS UP AND FINALLY BECOMES A GHOST

April 24, 1932

WE shall continue to-day our survey of the Empire of Rome. Early in the fourth century of the Christian era—in 326 A.C.— Constantine founded the city of Constantinople, near the site of old Byzantium, and he shifted the capital of his empire all the way from old Rome to this New Rome on the Bosphorus. Have a look at the map. You will see that this new city of Constantinople stands on the edge of Europe looking out towards mighty Asia ; it is a kind of link between the two continents. Many great trade-routes passed through it, both by land and sea. It is a fine position for a city and for a capital. Constantine chose well, but he or his successors had to pay for this change of capital. Just as old Rome was a bit too far from Asia Minor and the East, so the new eastern capital was too far from the western countries, like Gaul and Britain.

To get over this difficulty for a while there were joint emperors, one sitting in Rome, the other in Constantinople. This led to a regular division of the Empire into the Western and the Eastern. But the Western Empire, which had Rome for its capital, did not long survive the shock. It could not defend itself against those whom it called the " barbarians ". The Goths, a Germanic tribe, came and sacked Rome, and then came the Vandals and the Huns, and the Western Empire collapsed. You must have heard the word Hun used. During the last Great War it was commonly applied by the English to the Germans in order to make out that the Germans were very cruel and barbarous. As a matter of fact in war-time everybody, or almost everybody, loses his head and forgets all that he has learnt of civilization and good manners and behaves cruelly and barbarously. The Germans behaved in this way; so did the English and the French. There was little to choose between them in this respect.

The word Hun has become a terrible term of reproach. So also has the word Vandal. Probably these Huns and Vandals were rather coarse and cruel and did a lot of damage, but we must re- member that all the accounts of them that we have got are from their enemies the Romans, and one can hardly expect them to be im- partial. Anyhow, the Goths and the Vandals and the Huns knocked down the Western Roman Empire like a house of cards. One of the reasons why they succeeded so easily was probably because the

Roman peasantry were so utterly miserable under the Empire, and were so heavily taxed and so much in debt, that they welcomed any change.   Just as the poor Indian peasant to-day would welcome any change in his terrible poverty and misery.

The Western Roman Empire thus collapsed.   Some centuries later it was to rise again in a different form.   The Eastern Empire, however, continued, although it was hard put to it to withstand the attacks of the Huns and others.   Not only did it survive these attacks, but it carried on century after century in spite of continuous fighting against the Arabs, and later, against the Turks. For the amazing period of 1100 years it survived, till at last it fell in 1453 A.C. when Constantinople was captured by the Ottoman Turks or the Osmanlis.   Ever since then, for nearly 500 years now, Constantinople, or Istanbul as they call it, has been in the possession of the Turks.   From there they repeatedly marched into Europe and came right up to the walls of Vienna.   They were driven back gradually in later centuries, and a dozen years ago, after their defeat in the Great War, they nearly lost Constantinople.   The English were in possession of this city and the Turkish Sultan was a puppet in their hands.   But a great leader, Mustafa Kemal Pasha, came to rescue his people and, after a heroic struggle, he succeeded.   To-day Turkey is a republic and the Sultan has vanished for ever.   Kemal Pasha [1] is the President of the Republic.   Constantinople, the seat of an empire for 1500 years, first the Eastern Roman and then the Turkish, is still part of the Turkish State, but it is not even its capital.   The Turks have preferred to keep away from its imperial associations and to have their capital at Angora (or Ankara), far away in Asia Minor.

We have hurried through nearly 2000 years and followed rapidly the changes which came, one after another, the founding of Constantinople and the transfer of the capital of the Roman Empire to the new city.   But Constantine did another novel thing.   He turned Christian and, as he was the Emperor, that meant, of course, that Christianity became the official religion of the Empire.   It must have been a strange thing, this sudden change in the position of Christianity—from that of a persecuted faith to an imperial religion. The change did not do it much good for a while.   Different sects of Christians started quarrelling with each other.   Ultimately there was a great break between two sections—the Latin section and the Greek.   The Latin section had its headquarters in Rome and the Bishop of Rome was looked up to as its head—later to become the Pope of Rome; and the Greek section had its headquarters in Constantinople.   The Latin Church spread all over northern and western Europe and came to be known as the Roman Catholic Church.   The Greek Church was known as the Orthodox Church.   After the fall of the Eastern Roman Empire, Russia was the chief country where the Orthodox Church flourished.   Now with Bolshevism in Russia this Church, or any other Church, has no official position there.

I refer to the Eastern Roman Empire, and yet this had little to do with Rome.   Even the language they used was Greek, not Latin.

---

[1] Kemal Pasha died in 1939.

In a sense, it might almost be considered to have been a continuation of Alexander's Greek Empire. It had little contact with western Europe, although for long it would not admit the right of western countries to be independent of it. And yet the Eastern Empire stuck to the word Roman and the people were called Roman, as if there was some magic in the word. And, stranger still, the city of Rome, in spite of its fall from the headship of empire, did not lose its prestige, and even the barbarians who came to conquer it seemed to hesitate, and treated it with deference. Such is the power of a great name and the power of ideas !

Having lost the empire, Rome started carving out a new empire, but of a different kind. It was said that Peter, the disciple of Jesus, had come to Rome and become the first bishop there. This gave sanctity to the place in the eyes of many Christians and added special importance to the bishopric of Rome. The Bishop of Rome was, to begin with, not unlike other bishops, but he grew in importance after the Emperor went to Constantinople. There was no one to overshadow him then, and, as the successor to the chair of Peter, he came to be regarded as the chief of the bishops. Later he came to be called the Pope, and as you know the Popes exist to this day and are the heads of the Roman Catholic Church.

It is curious to note that one of the reasons for the split between the Roman Church and the Greek Orthodox Church was the use of images. The Roman Church encouraged the worship of the images of its saints, and especially of Mary, the mother of Jesus, while the Orthodox Church objected to this strongly.

Rome was occupied and ruled for many generations by chiefs of the northern tribes. But even they often acknowledged the overlordship of the Emperor at Constantinople. Meanwhile the power of the Bishop of Rome, as a religious head, grew, till he felt strong enough to defy Constantinople. When trouble came over the question of image-worship, the Pope decided to cut Rome off completely from the East. Much had happened meanwhile of which we shall have to speak later—a new religion, Islam, had arisen in Arabia, and the Arabs had overrun all northern Africa and Spain, and were attacking the heart of Europe; new States were being formed in northern and western Europe; and the Eastern Roman Empire was being fiercely assailed by the Arabs.

The Pope begged for assistance from a great leader of the Franks, a Germanic tribe of the north, and later, Karl or Charles, the head of the Franks, was crowned Emperor in Rome. This was quite a new empire or State, but they called it the " Roman Empire " and later, the " Holy Roman Empire ". They could not think of an empire without its being Roman, and although Charlemagne, or Charles the Great, as he is called, had little to do with Rome, he became Imperator and Cæsar and Augustus. The new Empire was supposed to be a continuation of the old one, but there was an addition to its name. It had become " Holy ". It was holy because it was specially a Christian empire, with the Pope for its godfather.

Again you see the strange power of ideas. A Frank or a German living in Central Europe becomes Roman Emperor ! And the future history of this " Holy " Empire is stranger still. As an empire, it became a very shadowy affair. While the Eastern Roman Empire at Constantinople carried on as a State, this Western one changed and vanished and appeared again from time to time. It was indeed a phantom and ghostly empire, continuing to exist in theory by the prestige of the Roman name and the Christian Church. It was an empire of the imagination with little of reality. Someone —I think it was Voltaire—defined this " Holy Roman Empire " as something which was neither holy, nor Roman, nor an empire ! Just as someone else once defined the Indian Civil Service, with which we are unfortunately still afflicted in this country, as neither Indian, nor civil, nor a service !

Whatever it was, this phantom Holy Roman Empire carried on in name at least for 1000 years, and it was only a little over 100 years ago, in Napoleon's time, that it finally ended. The end was not very remarkable or dramatic. Indeed, few people must have noticed it, as in reality it had not existed for a long time. But the ghost was laid at last, though not finally, for it rose up again in different guises as Kaisers and Tsars and the like. Most of these were laid to rest during the Great War which ended fourteen years ago.

34

THE IDEA OF THE WORLD STATE

April 25, 1932

I FEAR I must tire you and perplex you often enough with these letters. Especially my last two letters about the Roman Empires must be a trial for you. I have gone backwards and forwards through thousands of years and across thousands of miles, and if I have succeeded in creating some confusion in your mind, the fault is entirely mine. Don't be downhearted. Carry on. If you do not follow what I say at any place, do not trouble about it, but go on. These letters are not meant to teach you history, but just to give you glimpses of it and to awaken your curiosity.

You must be rather tired of the Roman Empires   I confess I am. But we shall bear with them a little more to-day, and then take leave of them for a while.

You know that there is a great deal of talk now-a-days of nationalism and patriotism—the love of one's country. Nearly all of us in India to-day are intense nationalists. This nationalism is quite a new thing in history, and perhaps we may study its beginning and growth in the course of these letters. There was hardly any such feeling at the time of the Roman Empires. The Empire was supposed to be one great State ruling the world. There never has been an empire or State which has ruled the whole world, but, owing to ignorance of geography, and the great difficulty of transportation and travelling across long distances, people often thought in olden times that such a State did exist. Thus, in Europe and round the Mediterranean the Roman State even before it became an empire was looked up to as a kind of super-State to which all the others were subordinate. So great was its prestige that some countries, like Pergamum, the Greek State in Asia Minor, and Egypt were actually presented to the Roman people by their rulers. They felt that Rome was all-powerful and irresistible. And yet, as I have told you, whether as a republic or as an empire, Rome never ruled over much more than the Mediterranean countries. The " barbarians " of the north of Europe would not submit to it, and it did not care much about them. But whatever the extent of Rome's authority might have been, it had the idea of a World-State behind it, and this idea was accepted by most people of the day in the West. It was because of this that the Roman Empires survived for so long, and their name and prestige were great even when there was no substance behind them.

This idea of one great State dominating over the rest of the world was not peculiar to Rome. We find it in China and India in the old days. As you know, the Chinese State was often a vaster one than the Roman Empire, extending right up to the Caspian Sea. The Chinese Emperor, " the son of Heaven " as he was called, was considered by the Chinese as the Universal Sovereign. It is true there were tribes and people who gave trouble and who did not obey the Emperor. But they were the " barbarians ", just as the Romans called the north Europeans " barbarians ".

In the same way in India from the earliest days you find references to these so-called universal sovereigns—*Chakravarti Rājās*. Their idea of the world was very limited, of course. India itself was so enormous that it seemed the world to them, and the overlordship of India appeared to them to be the overlordship of the world. The others outside were the " barbarians ", the *mlechchhas*. The mythical Bharat who has given his name to our country—Bharat-varsha—is supposed by tradition to have been such a *chakravarti* sovereign. Yudhishthira and his brothers fought, according to the *Mahābhārata*, for this world-sovereignty. The *ashwamedha*—the great horse-sacrifice—was a challenge and symbol of world-dominion. Ashoka probably aimed at it before, overcome by remorse, he stopped all fighting. Later on you will see other imperialist sovereigns of India, like the Guptas, who also aimed at this.

You will thus see that in the old days people often thought in terms of universal sovereigns and World-States. Long afterwards came nationalism and a new kind of imperialism, and between the two they have played sufficient havoc in this world Again there is talk to-day of a World-State, not a great empire, or a universal sovereign, but a kind of World-Republic which would prevent the exploitation of one nation or people or class by another. Whether or not anything like this will take place in the near future, it is difficult to say. But the world is in a bad way, and there seems to be no other way to get rid of its illness.

I have referred repeatedly to the " barbarians " of northern Europe. I use the word because they are referred to as such by the Romans. These people, like the nomads and other tribes of Central Asia, were certainly less civilized than their neighbours in Rome or in India. But they were more vigorous, as they lived an open-air life. Later they became Christians, and even when they conquered Rome they did not come, as a rule, as ruthless enemies. The modern nations of northern Europe are descended from these " barbarian " tribes—the Goths and Franks and others.

I have not given you the names of the Roman Emperors. There were crowds of them and, barring a few, they were bad enough Some were monsters of evil. You have no doubt heard of Nero, but there were many far worse than he was. One woman, Irene, actually killed her own son, who was emperor, in order to become empress. This was in Constantinople.

One Emperor of Rome stands out above the others. His name was Marcus Aurelius Antoninus. He is supposed to have been a philosopher, and a book of his, containing his thoughts and meditations, is well worth study. To make up for Marcus Aurelius, his son, who succeeded him, was one of the worst villains that Rome produced.

For the first 300 years of the Roman Empire, Rome was the centre of the western world. It must have been a great city, full of mighty buildings, and people must have come to it from all over the Empire and even beyond it. Numerous ships brought dainties from distant countries—rare foods and costly stuffs. Every year, it is said, a fleet of 120 ships went from an Egyptian port in the Red Sea to India. They went just in time to take advantage of the monsoon winds, and this helped them greatly. Usually they went to South India. They loaded their precious goods and returned, with the help again of the prevailing winds, to Egypt. From Egypt the goods were sent overland and by sea to Rome.

But all this trade was largely for the benefit of the rich. Behind the luxury of the few was the misery of the many. For over 300 years Rome was supreme in the West, and afterwards, when Constantinople was founded, it shared supremacy with it. It is curious that during this long period it did not produce anything great in the realm of thought, as ancient Greece did in a short time. Indeed, Roman civilization seems to have been in many respects a pale shadow of Hellenic civilization. In one thing Romans are supposed to have given a great lead. This is law. Even now lawyers in the West have to learn Roman Law, as it is said to be the foundation of a great deal of law in Europe.

The British Empire is often compared with the Roman Empire— usually by the English, to their own great satisfaction. All empires are more or less similar. They fatten on the exploitation of the many. But there is one other strong resemblance between the Romans and the English people—they are both singularly devoid of imagination ! Smug and self-satisfied, and convinced that the world was made specially for their benefit, they go through life untroubled by doubt or difficulty.

35

PARTHIA AND THE SASSANIDS

April 26, 1932

WE must leave the Roman Empire and Europe now for a visit to other parts of the world. We have to see what has been happening in Asia and to carry on the story of India and of China. Other countries now appear on the horizon of known history, and we shall have to say something about them also. Indeed, as we proceed there will be so much to be said about so many places that I am likely to give up the job in despair.

In one of my letters I referred to a great defeat of the armies of the Roman Republic at the battle of Carrhæ in Parthia. I did not stop to explain about the Parthians and how they had managed to establish a State where Persia and Mesopotamia are now. You will remember that after Alexander his general Seleucus and his descendants ruled an empire extending from India to Asia Minor in the west. For about 300 years they flourished, till they were driven away by another of the Central Asian tribes, called the Parthians. It was these Parthians in Persia or Parthia, as it was called, that defeated the Romans during the last days of the Republic, and the Empire that came later never succeeded in defeating them utterly. For two and a half centuries they ruled Parthia, till an internal revolution drove them out. The Persians themselves rose against their alien rulers and put in their place one of their own race and religion. This was Ardeshir I and his dynasty is called the Sassanid dynasty. Ardeshir was an ardent supporter of Zoroastrianism, which you will remember is the religion of the Parsis, and he was not very tolerant of other religions. Between the Sassanids and the Roman Empire there was almost constant war. They even succeeded in capturing one of the Roman Emperors. On several occasions the Persian armies almost reached Constantinople; once they conquered Egypt. The Sassanid Empire is chiefly notable for its religious zeal in favour of Zoroastrianism. When Islam came in the seventh century it put an end both to the Sassanid Empire and the official religion. Many Zoroastrians preferred to leave their country because of this change and for fear of persecution, and they came to India, which welcomed them as she has welcomed all others who have come to her seeking refuge. The Parsis in India to-day are the descendants of these Zoroastrians.

It is curious and rather wonderful to compare other countries
with India in the matter of treatment of different religions. In
most places, and especially in Europe, you will find, in the past,
intolerance and persecution of all who do not profess the official
faith. There was compulsion almost everywhere. You will read
about the terrible Inquisition in Europe, and of the burning of so-
called witches. But in India, in olden times there was almost full
tolerance. The slight conflict between Hinduism and Buddhism
was nothing compared to the violent conflicts of religious sects in
the West. It is well to remember this, for, unhappily, we have had
religious and communal troubles recently, and some people, ignorant
of history, imagine that this has been India's fate right through the
ages. This is wholly wrong. Such troubles are largely of recent
growth. You will find that after Islam began, for many hundred
years Musalmans lived in all parts of India in perfect peace with
their neighbours. They were welcomed when they came as traders
and encouraged to settle down. But I am anticipating.

So India welcomed the Zoroastrians, just as a few hundred years
before, she had also welcomed many Jews who fled from Rome in
the first century after Christ on account of persecution.

During the period of Sassanid rule in Persia, a little desert State
flourished in Palmyra in Syria, and it had its brief day of glory.
Palmyra was a trading market in the middle of the Syrian desert.
Great ruins, to be seen even to-day, tell us of its mighty buildings.
At one time the ruler of the State was a woman named Zenobia.
But she was defeated by the Romans and they were unchivalrous
enough to take her in chains to Rome.

Syria was a pleasant land at the beginning of the Christian era.
The New Testament tells us something about it. There were great
towns and a dense population, in spite of misgovernment and
tyranny; there were large canals and an extensive trade. But
continuous fighting and misrule reduced it in 600 years almost to a
wilderness—the great towns were deserted and the old buildings were
in ruins.

If you fly by aeroplane from India to Europe, you will pass over
these ruins of Palmyra and Baalbak. You will see where Babylon
was, and many another place famous in history, and now no more.

36

SOUTH INDIA COLONIZES

April 28, 1932

WE have wandered far. Let us now return to India again and
try to find out what our forbears in this country were doing. You
will remember the borderland empire of the Kushans—the great

Buddhist State comprising the whole of northern India and a good bit of Central Asia—with its capital at Purushapura or Peshawar. You will also perhaps remember that about this period in the south of India there was a great State stretching from sea to sea—the Andhra State. For about 300 years the Kushans and the Andhras flourished. About the middle of the third century after Christ these two empires ceased to be, and for a period India had a number of small States. Within 100 years, however, another Chandragupta arose in Pātaliputra and started a period of aggressive Hindu imperialism. But before we go on to the Guptas, as they are called, we might have a look at the beginnings of great enterprises in the south, which were to carry Indian art and culture to distant islands of the East.

You know well the shape of India, as she lies between the Himalayas and the two seas. The north is far removed from the sea. Its main preoccupation in the past has been the land frontier, over which enemies and invaders used to come. But east and west and south we have a tremendous sea-coast, and India narrows down till the east meets the west at Kanya Kumari or Cape Comorin. All these people living near the sea were naturally interested in it, and one would expect many of them to be seafaring folk. I have told you already of the great trade which South India had from the remotest times with the West. It is not surprising therefore to find that from early times shipbuilding existed in India and people crossed the seas in search of trade, or may be adventure. Vijaya is supposed to have gone from India and conquered Ceylon about the time Gautama the Buddha lived here. In the Ajanta caves, I think there is a representation of Vijaya crossing to Ceylon, with horses and elephants being carried across in ships. Vijaya gave the name Sinhala to the Island—" Sinhala Dweep ". Sinhala is derived from *Sinha*, a lion, and there is an old story about a lion, current in Ceylon, which I have forgotten. I suppose the word Ceylon is derived from Sinhala.

The little crossing from South India to Ceylon was, of course, no great feat. But we have plenty of evidence of shipbuilding and people going across the seas from the many Indian ports which dotted the coastline from Bengal to Gujrat. Chānakya, the great Minister of Chandragupta Maurya, tells us something about the navy in his *Arthashāstra*, about which I wrote to you from Naini. Megasthenes, the Greek ambassador at Chandragupta's Court, also mentions it. Thus it appears that even at the beginning of the Mauryan period shipbuilding was a flourishing industry in India. And ships are obviously meant to be used. So quite a considerable number of people must have crossed the seas in them. It is strange and interesting to think of this, and then to think of some of our people even to-day who are afraid of crossing the seas and think it against their religion to do so. We cannot call these people relics of the past, for, as you see, the past was much more sensible. Fortunately, such extraordinary notions have largely disappeared now, and there are few people who are influenced by them.

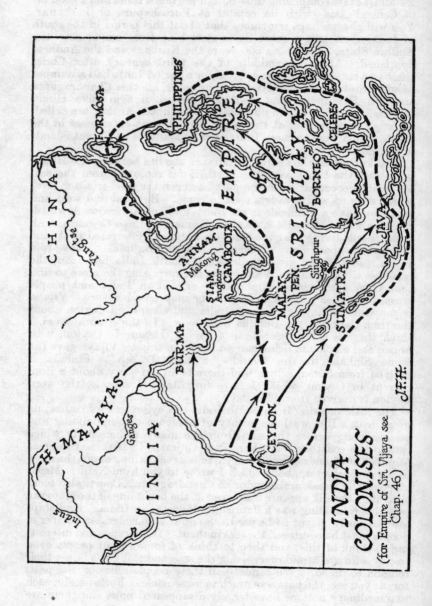

INDIA
COLONISES
(for Empire of Sri Vijaya see
Chap. 46)

The south naturally looked more to the sea than the north.   Most
of the foreign trade was with the south, and Tamil poems are full of
references to " yavana " wines and vases and lamps.   " Yavana "
was chiefly used for Greeks, but perhaps vaguely for all foreigners.
The Andhra coins of the second and third centuries bear the device
of a large two-masted ship, which shows how very much interested
the old Andhras must have been in shipbuilding and sea-trade.

It was the south, therefore, which took the lead in a great enterprise which resulted in establishing Indian colonies all over the
islands in the East.   These colonizing excursions started in the first
century after Christ and they continued for hundreds of years.   All
over Malay and Java and Sumatra and Cambodia and Borneo they
went, and established themselves and took Indian culture and Indian
art with them.   In Burma and Siam and Indo-China there were
large Indian colonies.   Many even of the names they gave to their
new towns and settlements were borrowed from India—Ayodhyā,
Hastinapur, Taxila, Gāndhāra.   Strange how history repeats itself !
The Anglo-Saxon colonists who went to America did likewise, and in
the United States to-day the names of old English cities are repeated.

No doubt these Indian colonists misbehaved wherever they went,
as all such colonists do.   They must have exploited the people of
the islands and lorded it over them.   But after a while the colonists
and the old inhabitants must have intermixed, for it was difficult
to keep up regular contacts with India.   Hindu States and empires
were established in these eastern islands, and then Buddhist rulers
came, and between the Hindu and the Buddhist there was a tussle
for mastery.   It is a long and fascinating story—the history of
Further or Greater India, as it is called.   Mighty ruins still tell us
of the great buildings and temples that adorned these Indian settlements.   There were great cities, built by Indian builders and craftsmen—Kamboja, Sri Vijaya, Angkor the Magnificent, Madjapahit.

For nearly 1400 years these Hindu and Buddhist States lasted in
these islands, contending against each other for mastery, changing
hands, and occasionally destroying each other.   In the fifteenth
century the Muslims finally obtained control, and soon after came the
Portuguese and the Spaniards, the Dutch and the English, and last
of all the Americans.   The Chinese, of course, had always been close
neighbours, sometimes interfering and conquering; oftener living
as friends and exchanging gifts; and all the time influencing them
with their great culture and civilization.

These Hindu colonies of the East have many things to interest us.
The most striking feature is that the colonization was evidently
organized by one of the principal governments of the day in southern
India.   At first many individual explorers must have gone;   then
later as trade developed families and groups of people must have gone
on their own account.   It is said that the early settlers were from
Kalinga (Orissa) and the eastern coast.   Perhaps some people went
from Bengal also.   There is also a tradition that some people from
Gujrat, pushed out from their own homelands, went to these islands.
But these are conjectures.   The principal stream of colonists went

from the Pallava country—the southern portion of the Tamil land, where a great Pallava dynasty was ruling. And it was this Pallava government that seems to have organized this colonization of Malaysia. Perhaps there was pressure of population owing to people pushing down from northern India. Whatever the reason may have been, settlements in widely scattered places, far from India, were deliberately planned and colonies were started in these places almost simultaneously. These settlements were in Indo-China, Malay Peninsula, Borneo, Sumatra, Java and in other places. All these were Pallava colonies bearing Indian names. In Indo-China the settlement was called Kamboja (the present Kambodia), a name which came all the way from a Kamboja in the Kabul Valley in Gāndhāra.

For 400 or 500 years these settlements remained Hindu in religion; then gradually Buddhism spread all over. Much later came Islam and spread in part of Malaysia, part remaining Buddhist.

Empires and kingdoms came and went in Malaysia. But the real result of these colonizing enterprises of southern India was to introduce Indo-Aryan civilization in this part of the world, and to a certain extent the people of Malaysia to-day are the children of the same civilization as we are. They have had other influences also, notably the Chinese, and it is interesting to observe the mixture of these two powerful influences—the Indian and the Chinese—on the different countries of Malaysia. Some have been more Indianized; in others the Chinese element is more in evidence. On the mainland, in Burma, Siam and Indo-China, the Chinese influence is predominant—but not in Malay. In the islands, Java, Sumatra and others, Indian influence is more obvious, with a recent covering of Islam.

But there was no conflict between the Indian and the Chinese influences. They were very dissimilar, and yet they could work on parallel lines without difficulty. In religion, of course, India was the fountain-head, whether it was Hinduism or Buddhism. Even China owed her religion to India. In art also Indian influence was supreme in Malaysia. Even in Indo-China, where Chinese influence was great, the architecture was wholly Indian. China influenced these continental countries more in regard to their methods of government and their general philosophy of life. So that to-day the people of Indo-China and Burma and Siam seem to be nearer akin to the Chinese than to the Indian. Of course, racially they have more of Mongolian blood in them, and this makes them resemble, to some extent, the Chinese.

In Borobodur in Java are to be seen now the remains of great Buddhist temples built by Indian artisans. The whole story of the Buddha's life is carved on the walls of these buildings, and they are a unique monument not only to the Buddha, but to the Indian art of that day.

Indian influence went farther still. It reached the Philippines and even Formosa, which were both part, for a time, of the Hindu Sri Vijaya kingdom of Sumatra. Long afterwards the Philippines were ruled by the Spaniards, and now they are under American control. Manila is the capital city of the Philippines. A new legislative building was put up there some time ago and on its façade four figures have been carved representing the sources of Philippine culture. These figures are Manu, the great law-giver of ancient India; Lao-Tse, the philosopher of China; and two figures representing Anglo-Saxon law and justice, and Spain.

37

HINDU IMPERIALISM UNDER THE GUPTAS

April 29, 1932

WHILE men from South India were crossing the high seas and founding settlements and towns in distant places, in the north of India there was a strange ferment. The Kushan Empire had lost its strength and greatness and was becoming smaller and shrinking away. All over the north there were small States, often ruled by the descendants of the Sakas or Scythians or Turkis, who had come to India over the north-western frontier. I have told you that these people were Buddhists and that they came to India not as enemies to raid but to settle down here. They were pushed inexorably from behind by other tribes in Central Asia, who in their turn were often pushed away by the Chinese kingdom. On coming to India these people largely adopted Indo-Aryan customs and traditions. They looked upon India as the parent country for religion and culture and civilization. The Kushans themselves had followed Indo-Aryan traditions to a large extent. This was indeed the reason why they managed to stay in India and rule over large parts of it for such a long time. They tried to behave as Indo-Aryans, and wanted the people of the country to forget that they were aliens. They succeeded in some measure, but not quite, for among the *Kshattriyas* especially the feeling rankled that aliens were ruling over them. They chafed under this foreign rule, and so the ferment grew and people's minds were troubled. Ultimately these disaffected people found a capable leader, and under his banner they started a " holy war ", as it is called, to free Aryavarta.

This leader was named Chandragupta. Do not mix him up with the other Chandragupta, the grandfather of Ashoka. This man had nothing to do with the Mauryan dynasty. It so happened that he was a petty Raja of Pātaliputra, but the descendants of Ashoka had retired into obscurity by then. You must remember that we are now in the beginning of the fourth century after Christ—that is, about 308 A.C. This was 534 years after Ashoka's death.

Chandragupta was ambitious and capable. He set out to win over the other Aryan chiefs in the north and to form a kind of federation with them. He married Kumara Devi of the famous and powerful Lichchhavi clan, and thus secured the support of this clan. Having prepared his ground carefully, Chandragupta proclaimed his " holy war " against all foreign rulers in India. The *Kshattriyas* and the Aryan aristocracy, deprived of their power and positions by the aliens, were at the back of this war. After a dozen years of fighting, Chandragupta managed to gain control of a part of northern India, including what are now known as the United Provinces. He then crowned himself King of kings.

Thus began what is known as the Gupta dynasty. It lasted for about 200 years, till the Huns came to trouble it. It was a period of somewhat aggressive Hinduism and nationalism. The foreign rulers —the Turkis and Parthians and other non-Aryans—were rooted out and forcibly removed. We thus find racial antagonism at work. The Indo-Aryan aristocrat was proud of his race and looked down upon these barbarians and *mlechchhas*. Indo-Aryan States and rulers who were conquered by the Guptas were dealt with leniently. But there was no leniency for the non-Aryans.

Chandragupta's son, Samudragupta, was an even more aggressive fighter than his father. He was a great general, and when he became Emperor he carried on victorious campaigns all over the country, and even in the south. He extended the Gupta Empire till it spread over a great part of India. But in the south his suzerainty was nominal. In the north the Kushans were pushed back across the Indus river.

Samudragupta's son, Chandragupta II, was also a warrior king, and he conquered Kathiawad and Gujrat, which had been under the rule of a Saka or Turki dynasty for a long time. He took the name of Vikramaditya, and by this he is usually known. But this name, like that of Cæsar, became the title of many rulers, and is therefore rather confusing.

Do you remember seeing an enormous iron pillar near the Qutub Minar in Delhi ? This pillar is said to have been built by Vikramaditya as a kind of Victory Pillar. It is a fine piece of work, and on the top is a lotus flower, a symbol of empire.

The Gupta period was the period of Hindu imperialism in India. There was a great revival of old Aryan culture and Sanskrit learning. The Hellenistic, or Greek, and Mongolian elements in Indian life and culture, which had been brought by the Greeks, Kushans and others, were not encouraged, and were in fact deliberately superseded by laying stress on the Indo-Aryan traditions. Sanskrit was the official Court language. But even in those days Sanskrit was not the common language of the people. The spoken language was a form of Prakrit, which was nearly allied to Sanskrit. But even though Sanskrit was not the vernacular of the time, it was living enough. There was a great flowering of Sanskrit poetry and drama and of Indo-Aryan art. In the history of Sanskrit literature this period is perhaps the richest after the great days which gave the

Vedas and the Epics. Kalidasa, that wonderful writer, belonged to this period. Vikramaditya is said to have had a brilliant Court, where he assembled the greatest writers and artists of the day. Have you not heard of the Nine Jewels of his Court—the *Navaratna* ? Kalidasa is said to have been one of these nine.

Samudragupta changed the capital of his empire from Pātaliputra to Ayodhyā. Perhaps he felt that Ayodhyā offered a more suitable background for his aggressive Indo-Aryan outlook—with its story of Ramachandra immortalized in Valmiki's epic.

The Gupta revival of Aryanism and Hinduism was naturally not very favourably inclined towards Buddhism. This was partly because this movement was aristocratic, with the *Kshattriya* chiefs backing it, and Buddhism had more of democracy in it; partly because the Mahāyāna form of Buddhism was closely associated with the Kushans and other alien rulers of northern India. But there seems to have been no persecution of Buddhism. Buddhist monasteries continued and were still great educational institutions. The Guptas had friendly relations with the rulers of Ceylon, where Buddhism flourished. Meghavarna, the King of Ceylon, sent costly gifts to Samudragupta and founded a monastery at Gaya for Sinhalese students.

But Buddhism declined in India. This decline was due, as I have told you previously, not so much to outside pressure on the part of the Brahmans or the Government of the day, as to the power of Hinduism to absorb it gradually.

It was about this time that one of the famous travellers from China visited India—not Hiuen Tsang, about whom I have told you, but Fa-Hien. He came as a Buddhist in search of Buddhist sacred books. He tells us that the people of Magadha were happy and prosperous; that justice was mildly administered; and that there was no death penalty. Gaya was waste and desolate; Kapilavastu had become a jungle; but at Pātaliputra people were " rich, prosperous and virtuous ". There were many rich and magnificent Buddhist monasteries. Along the main roads there were *dharmashālās*, where travellers could stay and were supplied with food at public expense. In the great cities there were free hospitals.

After wandering about India, Fa-Hien went to Ceylon, and spent two years there. But a companion of his, Tao-Ching, liked India greatly, and was so much impressed by the piety of the Buddhist monks that he decided to remain here. Fa-Hien returned by sea from Ceylon to China, and after many adventures and many years' absence, he reached home.

Chandragupta the Second, or Vikramaditya, ruled for about twenty-three years. After him came his son, Kumaragupta, who had a long reign of forty years. The next was Skandagupta, who succeeded in 453. A.C. He had to face a new terror, which ultimately broke the back of the great Gupta Empire. But of this I shall tell you in my next letter.

Some of the finest frescoes of Ajanta, as well as the halls and chapel, are examples of Gupta art. When you see them you will realize how wonderful they are. Unfortunately the frescoes are slowly disappearing, as they cannot stand exposure for long.

What was happening in other parts of the world when the Guptas held sway in India ? Chandragupta the First was the contemporary of Constantine the Great, the Roman Emperor who founded Constantinople. During the times of the later Guptas, the Roman Empire split up into the Eastern and Western, and the Western was ultimately overthrown by the northern " barbarian " tribes. Thus, just about the time when the Roman Empire was weakening, India had a very powerful State with great generals and mighty armies. Samudragupta is sometimes spoken of as the " Indian Napoleon ", but, ambitious as he was, he did not look beyond the frontiers of India for his conquests.

The Gupta period was one of aggressive imperialism and conquest and victory. But there are many such imperialistic periods in the history of every country, and they have little importance in the long run. What makes the Gupta times stand out, however, and worthy of being remembered with some pride in India, is the wonderful renaissance of art and literature which they witnessed.

38

THE HUNS COME TO INDIA

May 4, 1932

THE new terror which descended on India across the north-western mountains was the Hun terror. I said something about the Huns in a previous letter when we were discussing the Roman Empire. In Europe their greatest leader was Attila, who for many years terrorized over both Rome and Constantinople. Allied to these tribes were the Huns—called the White Huns—who came to India about the same time. They were also nomads from central Asia. For a long time past they had been hovering along the Indian frontier and giving a lot of trouble to all concerned there. As their numbers grew, and perhaps because they were pushed from behind by other tribes, they undertook a regular invasion.

Skandagupta, fifth of the Gupta line, had to face this Hun invasion. He defeated them and hurled them back; but a dozen years later they came again. Gradually they spread over Gāndhāra and the greater part of northern India. They tortured the Buddhists and committed all manner of frightfulness.

There must have been continuous warfare against them, but the Guptas could not drive them away. Fresh waves of Huns came and spread over Central India, and their chief, Toroman, installed himself as king. He was bad enough, but after him came his son, Mihiragula, who was an unmitigated savage and fiendishly cruel. Kalhana in his history of Kashmir—the *Rājatarangini*—tells us that one of Mihiragula's amusements was to have elephants thrown over great precipices into the valley below. His atrocities roused up Aryavarta at length, and the Aryas under Baladitya of the Gupta line and Yashodharman, a ruler of Central India, defeated the Huns and made Mihiragula a prisoner. But, unlike the Huns, Baladitya was chivalrous, and he spared Mihiragula and told him to go away outside the country. Mihiragula took refuge in Kashmir and later treacherously attacked Baladitya, who had treated him so generously.

Soon, however, the Hun power weakened in India. But many of the descendants of the Huns remained and gradually got mixed up with the Aryan population. It is possible that some of our Rajput clans of Central India and Rajputana have a trace of this White Hun blood.

The Huns ruled northern India for a very short time—less than fifty years. Afterwards they settled down peacefully. But the Hun wars and their frightfulness made a great impression on the Indian Aryans. Hun methods of life and government were very different from those of the Aryans. The Aryans were still in a large measure a freedom-loving race. Even their kings had to bow down to the popular will, and their village assemblies had great power. But the coming of the Huns and their settling down and mixing with the Indian people made some difference to these Aryan standards and lowered them.

Baladitya, who was the last of the great Guptas, died in 530 A.C. It is interesting to note that this ruler of a typical Hindu line was himself attracted towards Buddhism and that his *guru* was a Buddhist monk. The Gupta period is specially known for its revival of Krishna-worship, but even so there appears to have been no marked conflict with Buddhism.

Again we find, after the 200 years of Gupta rule, many States rising up in the north, independent of any central authority. In the south of India, however, a great State now develops. A ruler of the name of Pulakesin, who claimed descent from Ramachandra, established an empire in the south, known as the Chalukyan Empire. These southern people must have been closely connected with the Indian colonies in the eastern islands, and there must have been constant traffic between these islands and India. We also learn that Indian ships frequently carried merchandise to Persia. The Chalukyan kingdom exchanged ambassadors with the Sassanids in Persia, especially with one of their great rulers, Khusrau II.

39

INDIA'S CONTROL OF FOREIGN MARKETS

May 5, 1932

RIGHT through this old period of history which we are considering, for more than 1000 years, we find Indian trade flourishing both in the west in Europe and western Asia, and in the east right up to China. Why was this so? Not merely because the Indians in those days were good sailors and good merchants, which they certainly were; and not merely because of their skill in handicrafts, great as was this skill. All this helped. But one of the chief reasons for the control of distant markets by India seems to have been her progress in chemistry, especially in dyeing. The Indians of those days seem to have discovered special methods for the preparation of fast dyes for cloth. They also knew a special method of preparing the indigo dye from the plant. You will notice that the very name " indigo " comes from India. It is also probable that the old Indians knew how to temper steel well, and thus to make fine steel weapons. You may remember my telling you that in the old Persian stories of Alexander's invasion, whenever a good sword or dagger is mentioned it is stated that it was from India.

Because India could make these dyes and other articles better than the other countries, it was natural that she should command the markets. The person or the country having a better tool, or a better or cheaper method of making any article, is bound, in the long run, to drive out another person or country which has not got as good a tool or as good a method. And this is the reason why Europe has gone ahead of Asia during the last 200 years. New discoveries and inventions gave Europe new and powerful tools and new methods of manufacture. With the help of these she captured the markets of the world and became rich and powerful. There were other causes, too, which helped her. But for the moment I would like you to consider how important a thing a tool is. Man, a great man once said, is a tool-making animal. And man's history, from the earliest days to the present, is a history of more and more efficient tools—from the early stone arrows and hammers of the Stone Age to the railway and steam-engine and the enormous machines of to-day. Indeed, almost everything we do requires a tool. Where would we be without tools?

A tool is a good thing; it helps to lighten work. But of course a tool may be misused. A saw is a useful tool, but a child may hurt itself with it. A knife is one of the most useful things you can have. Every scout must have it. And yet a foolish person may kill another with the knife. It is not the fault of the poor knife. The fault lies with the person misusing the tool.

In the same way modern machinery, good in itself, has been and is being misused in many ways. Instead of lightening the burden of work on the masses, it has often made their lot even worse than before. Instead of bringing happiness and comfort to millions of people, as it should, it has brought misery to many; and it has placed so much power in the hands of governments that they can slaughter millions in their wars.

But the fault lies not in machinery, but in the misuse of it. If the big machinery were controlled not by irresponsible persons who want to make money for themselves out of it, but on behalf of and for the good of the people generally, there would be a tremendous difference.

So in those days, unlike to-day, India was ahead of the world in her methods of manufacture. And so Indian cloth and Indian dyes and other articles went to far countries and were eagerly sought after. To India this trade brought wealth. Besides this trade, South India supplied pepper and other spices. These spices also came from the eastern islands and passed *via* India to the West. Pepper was greatly valued in Rome and the West, and it is said that Alaric, a chief of the Goths who captured Rome in 410 A.C. took 3000 lb. of pepper from there. All this pepper must have come from or *via* India.

40

THE UPS AND DOWNS OF COUNTRIES AND CIVILIZATIONS

May 6, 1932

WE have kept away from China for a long time now. Let us go to it again and carry on our tale, and see what was happening to it when Rome was falling in the West, and India was having a national revival under the Guptas. The rise or fall of Rome affected China very little. They were too far removed from each other. But I have already told you that the driving back of the Central Asian tribes by the Chinese State sometimes had disastrous consequences for Europe and India. These tribes, or others whom they pushed, went west and south. They upset kingdoms and States and created confusion. Many settled down in eastern Europe and in India.

There were, of course, direct contacts between Rome and China, and embassies were exchanged. The earliest of such embassies mentioned in the Chinese books is said to have come from the Emperor An-Tun of Rome in 166. A.C. This An-Tun is no other than Marcus Aurelius Antoninus, whom I mentioned in one of my letters to you.

The fall of Rome in Europe was a mighty thing. It was not merely the fall of a city or the fall of an empire. In a way the Roman Empire continued at Constantinople for long afterwards, and the ghost of the Empire hovered all over Europe for 1400 years or so. But the fall of Rome was the end of a great period. It was the end of the ancient world of Greece and Rome. A new world, a new culture and civilization were rising in the West on the ruins of Rome. We are misled by words and phrases, and because we find the same words used, we are apt to think that they mean the same thing. After Rome fell, western Europe continued to talk in the language of Rome, but behind that language were different ideas and different meanings. People say that the countries of Europe to-day are the children of Greece and Rome. And this is true to some extent, but still it is a misleading statement. For the countries of Europe represent something quite different from what Greece and Rome stood for. The old world of Rome and Greece collapsed almost completely. The civilization that had been built up in 1000 years or more ran to seed and decayed. It was then that the semi-civilized, half-barbarous countries of western Europe appear on the page of history and build up slowly a new culture and civilization. They learned much from Rome; they borrowed from the old world. But the process of learning was difficult and laborious. For hundreds of years culture and civilization seemed to have gone to sleep in Europe. There was the darkness of ignorance and bigotry. These centuries have therefore been called the Dark Ages.

Why was this so? Why should the world go back; and why should the knowledge accumulated through hundreds of years of labour disappear, or be forgotten? These are big questions, which trouble the wisest of us. I shall not attempt to answer them. Is it not strange that India, which was great in thought and action, should fall so miserably and for long periods should remain a slave country? Or China, with her splendid past, be a prey to interminable fighting? Perhaps the knowledge and the wisdom of the ages, which man has gathered together bit by bit, do not disappear. But somehow our eyes close and we cannot see at times. The window is shut and there is darkness. But outside and all around is the light, and if we keep our eyes or our windows shut, it does not mean that the light has disappeared.

Some people say that the Dark Ages in Europe were due to Christianity—not the religion of Jesus, but the official Christianity which flourished in the West after Constantine, the Roman Emperor, adopted it. Indeed, these people say that the adoption of Christianity by Constantine in the fourth century " inaugurated a millennium " (that is, 1000 years) " in which reason was enchained, thought was enslaved, and knowledge made no progress ". Not only did it bring persecution and bigotry and intolerance, but it made it difficult for people to make progress in science and in most other ways. Sacred books often become obstacles to progress. They tell us what the world was like at the time that they were written; they tell us the ideas of that period, and its customs. No one dare challenge those ideas or those customs because they are written in a " sacred " book. So, although the world may change tremendously, we are not allowed to change our ideas and customs to fit in with the changed conditions. The result is that we become misfits, and of course there is trouble.

Some people therefore accuse Christianity of having brought this period of darkness over Europe. Others tell us that it was Christianity and Christian monks and priests who kept the lamp of learning alight during the Dark Ages. They kept up art and painting, and valuable books were carefully preserved and copied by them.

Thus do people argue. Perhaps both are right. But it would be ridiculous to say that Christianity is responsible for all the evils that followed the fall of Rome. Indeed, Rome fell because of these evils.

I have wandered far. What I wanted to point out to you was that while in Europe there was a sudden social collapse and a sudden change there was no such sudden change in China or even in India. In Europe we see the end of a civilization and the early beginnings of another which was to develop slowly into what it is to-day. In China we see the same high degree of culture and civilization continuing without any such break. There are ups and downs. Good periods and bad kings and emperors come and go, and dynasties change. But the cultural inheritance does not break. Even when China splits up into several States and there is mutual conflict, art and literature flourish, lovely paintings are made, and beautiful vases and fine buildings. Printing comes into use, and tea-drinking comes into fashion and is celebrated in poetry. There is a continuing grace and artistry in China which can come alone from a high civilization.

So also in India. There is no sudden break, as in Rome. Certainly there are bad times and good. Periods of fine literary and artistic production, and periods of destruction and decay. But civilization continues, after a fashion. It spreads from India to the other countries of the East. It absorbs and teaches even the barbarians who come to plunder.

Do not think that I am trying to praise India or China at the expense of the West. There is nothing to shout about in the condition of India or China to-day, and even the blind can see that, with all their past greatness, they have sunk low in the scale of nations. If there was no sudden break with their past culture, this does not mean that there has been no change for the worse. If we were up and we are down, obviously we have come down in the world. We may feel pleased at the continuity of our civilization, but that is small comfort when that civilization itself has run to seed. Perhaps it might have been better for us if we had had sudden breaks with the past. This might have shaken us up and given new life and vitality. It may be that the events that are happening in India and the world to-day are giving this impetus to our old country and filling her with youth and new life again.

The strength and perseverance of India in the past seem to have lain in her widespread system of village republics or self-governing *panchāyats*. There were no big landlords and no big *zamindars*, such as we have to-day. Land belonged to the village community or *panchāyat* or to the peasants who worked on it. And these *panchāyats* had a great deal of power and authority. They were elected by the village folk, and thus there was a basis of democracy in this system. Kings came and went, or quarrelled with each other, but they did not touch or interfere with this village system or venture to take away from the liberties of the *panchāyats*. And so while empires changed, the social fabric which was based on the village system continued without great change. We are apt to be misled by the accounts of invasions and fighting and change of rulers into thinking that the whole population was affected by them. Of course, populations were sometimes affected, especially in the north of India, but on the whole it may be said that they worried little and carried on in spite of changes at the top.

Another factor that strengthened the social system in India for a long time was the caste system as it originally existed. Caste then was not so rigid as it became later; nor did it depend on birth alone. It held Indian life together for thousands of years, and it could only do so, not by preventing change or growth, but by allowing this to take place. The old Indian outlook in religion and life was always one of tolerance and experiment and change. That gave it strength. Gradually, however, repeated invasions and other troubles made caste rigid, and with it the whole Indian outlook became more rigid and unyielding. This process went on till the Indian people were reduced to their present miserable condition, and caste became the enemy of every kind of progress. Instead of holding together the social structure, it splits it up into hundreds of divisions and makes us weak and turns brother against brother.

Thus caste helped in the past in strengthening India's social system. But even so it had the seeds of decay in it. It was based on perpetuating inequality and injustice, and any such attempt was bound to fail in the end. No sound and stable society can be built up on the basis of inequality and injustice, or on the exploitation of one class or group by another. Because to-day there is still this unfair exploitation, we see so much trouble and unhappiness all over the world. But everywhere people have come to realize this and are working hard to get rid of it.

As in India, so also in China, the strength of the social system lay in the villages, and the hundreds of thousands of peasants who owned and tilled the land. There also there were no big *zamindars*. Religion was never permitted to dogmatize or to become intolerant. Of all the people in the world, perhaps the Chinese have been and still are the least bigoted in the matter of religion.

Again, you will remember that both in India and China there was no such labour slavery as in Greece or Rome, or earlier still in Egypt. There were some domestic servants who were slaves, but they made little difference to the social system. This system would have gone on in the same way without them. Not so in ancient Greece or Rome, where the large numbers of slaves were an essential part of the system, and the real burden of all work lay on them. And in Egypt, where would the great Pyramids have been but for this slave labour ?

I began this letter with China and I intended to carry on her story.   But I have drifted to other subjects, not an unusual thing for me !   Perhaps next time we may stick to China.

41

CHINA FLOURISHES UNDER THE TANGS

May 7, 1932

I HAVE told you of the Han dynasty in China ; and of the coming of Buddhism ; and of the invention of printing ; and the introduction of the examination system for choosing public officers.   In the third century after Christ the Han dynasty ends and the empire is divided up into three States.   This period of division into " The Three Kingdoms ", as they are called, lasts for several hundred years, till China is reunited again and made into a powerful single State by a new dynasty, called the Tang Dynasty.   This was early in the seventh century.

But even during this period of division Chinese culture and art continued in spite of Tartar attacks from the north.   We are told of large libraries and of fine paintings.   India continued to export not only her fine cloth and other goods, but her thought and religion and art.   Many Buddhist missionaries went to China from India, and they carried with them the traditions of Indian art, and it is possible that Indian artists and master-craftsmen also went.   The coming of Buddhism and of new ideas from India had a great effect on China.   China of course was and had been a highly civilized country.   It was not as if the religion or thought or art of India went to a backward country and took possession of it.   In China this had to come up against China's own ancient art and ways of thought.   The result of the impact of these two was to produce something different from either—something with much of India in it but still essentially Chinese and moulded according to the Chinese pattern.   Thus the coming of these thought-currents from India gave an impetus and a kick to the artistic and mental life of China.

In the same way the message of Buddhism and of Indian art went farther east to Korea and Japan, and it is interesting to see how these countries were affected by it.   Each country adapted it to suit its own particular genius.   Thus although Buddhism flourishes in China and Japan, it bears a different aspect in each country ; and both these perhaps differ in many ways from the Buddhism that went out from India.   Art also varies and changes with the skies and with the people.   In India we have now, as a

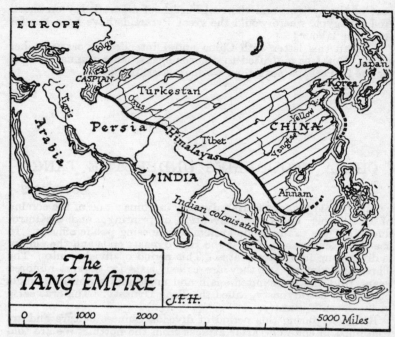

EUROPE

Volga

CASPIAN

Turkestan

Oxus

Tigris

Arabia

Persia

Himalayas

Tibet

CHINA

Yellow

Yangtze

INDIA

Annam

Japan

Korea

Indian colonisation

The
TANG EMPIRE

J.F.H.

0   1000   2000   5000 Miles

people, forgotten art and beauty. Not only have we not produced
anything of great beauty for long, but most of us have even forgotten how to appreciate the beautiful. How can beauty and art
flourish in a country which is not free? They wither away in the
darkness of subjection and restraint. But already, with the vision
of freedom before us, our sense of beauty is slowly waking up.
When freedom comes you will see a great revival of art and beauty
in this country, and I hope this will sweep away the ugliness of our
homes and our cities and our lives. China and Japan have been
more fortunate than India and they have preserved still a great
deal of their sense of beauty and artistry.

As Buddhism spread in China more and more Indian Buddhists
and monks went there, and Chinese monks travelled to India and
to other countries. I have told you of Fa-Hien. You know also
of Huien Tsang. Both of these came to India. There is a very
interesting report of the journey of a Chinese monk named Hui
Sheng across the eastern seas. He came to the capital of China in
499 A.C. and said that he had visited a land, which he called Fu
Sang, several thousand miles east of China. East of China and
Japan there is the Pacific Ocean, and it is possible that Hui Sheng
had crossed this ocean. Perhaps he visited Mexico, for in Mexico
there was even then an old civilization.

Attracted by the spread of Buddhism in China, the head and

patriarch of Indian Buddhism, whose name or title was Bodhidharma, sailed from South India for Canton in China. Perhaps the gradual weakening of Buddhism in India induced him to go. He was an old man when he went in 526 A.C. With him and after him went many other monks to China. It is said that in one province of China alone—Lo-Yang—there were at this time more than 3000 Indian monks and 10,000 Indian families.

Buddhism had another period of revival in India soon after, and as the birthplace of the Buddha and the place where the sacred writings were, India continued to attract pious Buddhists. But the glory seems to have departed from Buddhism in India, and China now becomes the leading Buddhist country.

The Tang dynasty was started by the Emperor Kao Tsu in 618 A.C. Not only did he unite the whole of China, but he spread his authority over an immense area—over Annam and Cambodia in the south and right up to Persia and the Caspian Sea in the west. Part of Korea was also included in this mighty empire. The capital of the Empire was Si-an-Fu, a city which was famous in eastern Asia for its splendour and culture. Embassies and commissions came to it from Japan and southern Korea, which was still free, to study its arts, philosophy, and civilization.

The Tang Emperors encouraged foreign trade and foreign visitors. Special laws were made for the foreigners who settled or came to China, so that they might be judged according to their own customs wherever possible. We find especially the Arabs settling down in South China, near Canton, about 300 A.C. This was before Islam came—that is, before the birth of the Prophet Mohammad. With the help of these Arabs an overseas trade developed and was carried in Arab as well as Chinese ships.

You will be surprised to learn that the census—that is, the counting of people in a country so that its population may be known—is a very old institution in China. As long ago as 156 A.C. it is said that a census took place. This must have been during the time of the Hans. The counting used to be by families and not by individuals. Each family was roughly supposed to have five persons in it. According to this reckoning China had a population of about 50,000,000 in 156 A.C. This is not a very accurate method, of course, but just remember that this census is quite a new thing in the West. I believe the first census was held in the United States of America about 150 years ago.

In the early days of the Tangs, two other religions appeared in China—Christianity and Islam. Christianity was brought by a sect which had been declared heretic and driven away from the West. They were called Nestorians. I wrote to you some time ago of the disputes and fights between Christian sects. It was as a result of one of these disputes that the Nestorians were driven away by Rome. But they spread in China and Persia and in many other parts of Asia. They came to India also and had some success. But later other branches of Christianity and Islam swallowed up the Nestorians and there is little trace of them left. I was greatly surprised to find a small colony of them at a place in South India which we visited last year. Do you remember ? Their bishop entertained us to tea. He was a delightful old man.

It took some time for Christianity to reach China. But Islam came more swiftly. It came, indeed, a few years before the Nestorians and during the lifetime of its Prophet. The Chinese Emperor received both the embassies—Islamic and Nestorian—with courtesy and listened to what they had to say. He appreciated their views and showed favour impartially. The Arabs were permitted to build a mosque in Canton. This mosque still exists, although it is 1300 years old, and is one of the oldest mosques in the world.

So also the Tang Emperor permitted the building of a Christian church and monastery. The contrast between this tolerant attitude and the intolerance of Europe in those days is very marked.

It is said that the Arabs learnt the art of making paper from the Chinese and then taught it to Europe. In 751 A.C. there was a battle in Turkestan in Central Asia between the Chinese and the Muslim Arabs. The Arabs made several Chinese prisoners, and these prisoners taught them how to make paper.

The Tangs lasted for 300 years, till 907. A.C. These 300 years are said by some to be China's greatest period, when there was not only a high level of culture, but a high level of general happiness for the people. Many things that the West got to know much later, the Chinese knew then. Paper I have already mentioned. Gunpowder was another. They were good engineers, and generally, in almost every particular, they were far in advance of Europe. If they were so far ahead, then why could they not keep ahead and lead Europe in science and discovery ? But Europe gradually crept up to them, like a youth overtaking an elderly person, and was soon ahead, in some respects at any rate. Why this kind of thing happens in the history of nations is a most difficult question for philosophers to ponder over. As you are not yet a philosopher who will worry about this question, I need not worry either.

The greatness of China during this period had naturally great influence over the rest of Asia, which looked up to China for guidance in art and civilization. India's star was not shining very brightly after the Gupta Empire ended. As usual, however, progress and civilization in China led to too much luxury and easy living. Then there was corruption in the State, and this made heavy taxation necessary. And so the people got fed up with the Tangs and put an end to their dynasty.

42

CHOSEN AND DAI NIPPON

May 8, 1932

As we proceed with our story of the world, more and more countries will come into our ken. So we must now have a look at Korea and Japan, close neighbours of China and, in many ways, children of Chinese civilization. They are at the extreme end of Asia—the Far East—and beyond is the great Pacific Ocean. Till recent years there was, of course, no contact with the American continent. So their sole contacts were with the great nation on the mainland—China. From China and through China they got their religion and art and civilization. The debt of both Korea and Japan to China is tremendous; and something they owe also to India. But whatever of India they got was through China and coloured by the Chinese spirit.

Situated as they are, both Korea and Japan had little to do with big events in Asia or elsewhere. They were far from the centre of things, and to some extent they were fortunate, especially Japan. We might therefore almost ignore their history, till recent times, without any great difficulty. This would not make much difference to our understanding events in the rest of Asia. But we need not ignore it, just as we are not ignoring the past story of Malaysia and the eastern islands. Korea, poor little country, is almost forgotten to-day. Japan has swallowed her up and made her part of her empire. But Korea dreams still of freedom and struggles for independence. Japan is very much in evidence now and the newspapers are full of her attacks on China. As I write there is something like a war going on in Manchuria. So it would be well if we were to know something of the past of Korea and Japan, as this would help us to understand the present.

The first thing to remember is their isolation for long periods. Japan, indeed, has a remarkable record of isolation and freedom from invasion. In the whole course of her history there have been few attempts at invading her and no success has attended them. All her troubles, till recently, have been her own internal troubles. For a period, Japan even cut herself off from the rest of the world completely. It was hardly possible for a Japanese to go out of the country or for foreigners, even the Chinese, to enter it. This was done to protect themselves from foreigners from Europe and Christian missionaries. It was a dangerous and foolish thing to do, for it meant putting the whole nation in prison and cutting it off from all outside influences, good or bad. And then suddenly Japan threw open her doors and her windows and rushed out to learn everything that Europe had to teach. And she learnt this with such right good will that within a generation or two she had become outwardly like any European country, and had even copied all their bad habits ! All this took place within the last seventy years or so.

Korean history begins long after Chinese, and Japanese history begins long after Korean. I told you in one of my letters last year how a Chinese exile named Ki-Tse, not approving of a change of dynasty in China, marched eastwards with 5000 followers. He settled down in Korea, calling it " Chosen "—the Land of the Morning Calm. This was in 1122 b.c. Ki-Tse brought with him Chinese arts and crafts, agriculture and silk-making. For over 900 years Ki-Tse's descendants ruled Chosen. Chinese immigrants used to come from time to time and settle down in Chosen, and thus there was fairly close contact with China.

A big batch of Chinese came when Shih Huang Ti was emperor in China. You will perhaps remember this Chinese emperor who was a contemporary of Ashoka. He is the man who called himself " First Emperor " and had all the old books burnt. Driven away by Shih Huang Ti's ruthless methods, many Chinese took refuge in Korea, driving away the feeble descendants of Ki-Tse. After this, Chosen was divided up into several States for over 800 years. These States often quarrelled with each other. Once one of these States asked China for help—a dangerous request to make. The help came, but it refused to go back ! That is the way of powerful countries. China stayed on and added part of Chosen to her empire. Even the rest of Chosen, for some hundreds of years, acknowledged the suzerainty of the Tang Emperors in China.

It was in 935 a.c. that Chosen became a united independent kingdom. Wang Kien was the man who succeeded in establishing this and for 450 years his successors managed to rule this kingdom.

In two or three paragraphs I have given you more than 2000 years of Korean history ! What is worth remembering is Korea's great debt to China. The art of writing came to Korea from China. For 1000 years they used the Chinese characters, which, you will remember, represent ideas and words and phrases and not letters. Then they evolved out of this a special alphabet more suitable to their own language.

Buddhism came *via* China, and the Confucian philosophy also came from China. Artistic influences from India travelled through China to Korea and Japan. Korea produced beautiful works of art, especially of sculpture. Their architecture resembled the Chinese. Great progress was also made in shipbuilding. Indeed, at one time the people of Korea had a powerful navy, with which they invaded Japan.

Probably the ancestors of the present Japanese came from Korea or Chosen. Some of them may have come from the south, from Malaysia. As you know, the Japanese are a Mongolian race. There are still some people in Japan, called the Ainus, who are supposed to be the original inhabitants of the country. These people are fair and rather hairy, quite different from the average Japanese. The Ainus have been driven to the northern part of the islands.

We find that a certain Empress Jingo was head of Yamato State about 200 a.c. Yamato was the original name of Japan, or that part of it where these immigrants had settled. Note the name of

this lady—Jingo. It is a curious coincidence that this should be
the name of one of the earliest Japanese rulers. The word " Jingo "
has come to have a definite meaning in English. It means a
blustering and bumptious imperialist, or we might say just simply
an imperialist, for every such person is bound to be, to some extent,
blustering and bumptious. Japan is supposed to suffer also from
this disease of imperialism or Jingoism, and in recent years she has
misbehaved greatly towards Korea and China. So it is curious
that Jingo should have been the name of her first historical ruler.

Yamato kept up close relations with Korea and it was through
Korea that Chinese civilization reached Yamato. The Chinese
written language also came about 400 A.C. through Korea. So also
came Buddhism. In 552 A.C. the ruler of Pakche (which was then
one of the three kingdoms into which Korea was divided) sent to
the ruler of Yamato a golden image of Buddha and Buddhist
missionaries with their scriptures.

The old religion of Japan was Shinto. This is a Chinese word
meaning " the way of the Gods ". It was a mixture of Nature-
worship and ancestor-worship. It did not trouble itself much
with the future life or with mysteries and problems. It was the
religion of a race of warriors. The Japanese, so near to the Chinese
and so much in their debt for their civilization, are yet utterly
different from the Chinese. The Chinese have been and are an
essentially peaceful people. The whole of their civilization and
philosophy of life is peaceful. The Japanese, on the other hand,
have been and still are a fighting people. The chief virtue of a
soldier is loyalty to his leader and to his comrade. This has been
a virtue of the Japanese, and much of their strength is due to this.
Shinto taught this virtue—" Honour the Gods and be loyal to their
descendants "—and so Shinto has survived to this day in Japan and
exists alongside with Buddhism.

But is this a virtue ? To be loyal to a comrade or to a cause is
certainly a virtue. But Shinto and other religions have often tried
to exploit our loyalties so as to benefit a group of people who rule
over us. The worship of authority, that is what they have taught
in Japan and in Rome and elsewhere, and you will see later how
much harm this has done us.

There was some conflict between the new Buddhism, when it
came, and the old Shinto. But soon they settled down side by
side, and so they have continued till now. Shinto is still the more
popular of the two, and it is encouraged by the ruling classes
because it teaches obedience and loyalty to them. Buddhism is a
slightly more dangerous religion, for the founder himself was a
rebel.

The artistic history of Japan begins with Buddhism. Japan or
Yamato began then to develop direct contacts with China. There
were constant embassies to China, especially during the Tang period,
when the new capital Si-an-fu was famous all over eastern Asia.
Indeed, the Japanese, or the people of Yamato, themselves established a new capital, called Nara, and tried to make this an exact

copy of Si-an-fu. The Japanese always seem to have had an amazing capacity for copying and imitating others.

Throughout Japanese history one finds great families opposing each other and struggling for power. Elsewhere, too, you will find this in the old days. In these families the old clan-idea persists. So Japanese history is the story chiefly of the rivalries of families. Their Emperor, the Mikado, is supposed to be all-powerful, an autocrat and semi-divine, descended from the Sun. Shinto and ancestor-worship have helped to make the people accept the autocracy of the Emperor and made them obedient to the powerful men of the land. But the Emperor himself has very often in Japan been a puppet without any real power. The power and authority were with some great family or clan who were the kingmakers and made kings and emperors of their choice.

The first great Japanese family that appears in history controlling the State was the Soga family. It was their adoption of Buddhism that made of this a Court and official religion. One of their leaders, Shotuku Taishi, is one of the greatest men in Japanese history. He was a sincere Buddhist and an artist of great ability. He got his ideas from the Chinese Confucian classics, and tried to build up the government on a moral foundation and not just force. Japan was then full of clans whose chiefs were almost independent, and who fought each other and obeyed no authority. The Emperor, in spite of his high-sounding title, was just a big clan chief. Shotuku Taishi set about changing this and making the Central Government strong. He made the various clan chiefs and nobles " vassals " or subordinates to the Emperor. This was about 600. A.C.

But after Shotuku Taishi's death the Soga family was driven away. A little later another man very famous in Japanese history comes on the scene. His name was Kakatomi no Kamatori. He made all manner of changes in the government and copied many Chinese methods. But he did not imitate the examination system of appointing public officials, which was peculiar to China. The Emperor now becomes something much more than a clan chief and the Central Government becomes strong.

It was during this period that Nara became the capital, but this was only for a short time. Kyoto was made capital in 794 A.C., and for nearly 1100 years it remained so, till it was displaced, only a short while ago, by Tokio. Tokio is a great big modern city. But it is Kyoto which tells us something of the soul of Japan, and which carries about her the memories of 1000 years.

Kakatomi no Kamatori became the founder of the Fujiwara family which was to play a great rôle in Japanese history. For 200 years they ruled, making the emperors mere puppets and forcing them often to marry their womenfolk. Afraid of able men in other families, they forced them to enter monasteries.

When the capital was at Nara, the Chinese Emperor sent a message to the Japanese ruler addressing him as the Emperor of Tai-Nyih-Pung-Kok, which means " Great-Sun-Rise-Kingdom ". The Japanese rather liked this name. It sounded much more

imposing than Yamato. So they began calling their country
"Dai Nippon "—" the Land of the Rising Sun "—and this is still
their own name for Japan. The name Japan itself came in a curious
way from Nippon. Six hundred years later a great Italian traveller,
named Marco Polo, visited China. He never went to Japan, but
he wrote about it in his book of travels. He had heard the name
Nyih-Pung-Kok. He wrote this as " Chipango " in his book, and
from this came the word Japan.

Have I told you, or do you know, how our country came to be
called India and Hindustan? Both names come from the river
Indus or Sindhu, which thus becomes *the* river of India. From
Sindhu the Greeks called our country Indos, and from this came
India. Also from Sindhu, the Persians got Hindu, and from that
came Hindustan.

43

HARSHA-VARDHANA AND HIUEN TSANG

May 11, 1932

WE shall go back to India again. The Huns have been defeated
and driven back, but many remain in odd corners. The great
Gupta dynasty fades away after Baladitya, and there are many
kingdoms and States in northern India. In the south Pulakesin
has established the Chalukyan Empire.

Not far from Cawnpore is the little town of Kanauj. Cawnpore
is now a big city, but an ugly one with its factories and chimneys,
and Kanauj is a modest place, hardly bigger than a village. But
in the days of which I speak, Kanauj was a great capital, famous
for its poets and artists and philosophers, and Cawnpore was still
unborn, and was to remain unborn for many hundreds of years.

Kanauj is the modern name. The real name is Kānya-Kubja—
the " hunch-backed girl ". The story is that some ancient sage
or *rishi*, made angry at a fancied slight, cursed the hundred daughters
of a king and made them hunch-backed! And since then the
city where they lived was called the " City of Hunch-backed Girls "
—Kānya-Kubja.

But we shall call it Kanauj for short. The Huns killed the Raja
of Kanauj and made his wife Rājashrī a prisoner. Thereupon
Rājashrī's brother, Raja-Vardhana, came to fight the Huns and
rescue his sister. He defeated them, but was treacherously killed.
The younger brother, Harsha-Vardhana, now went out to search
for his sister Rājashrī. The poor girl had managed to escape to
the mountains and, overcome by her sufferings, had decided to
end her life. It is said that she was on the point of becoming a
sati when Harsha found her and saved her from this.

Having found and rescued his sister, the next thing Harsha
did was to punish the petty raja who had killed his brother

treacherously. Not only did he punish him, but he succeeded in conquering the whole of northern India, from sea to sea, and up to the Vindhya Mountains in the south. Beyond the Vindhyas was the Chalukyan Empire, and Harsha was stopped by this.

Harsha-Vardhana made Kanauj his capital. Being himself a poet and dramatist, he gathered round himself a host of poets and artists, and Kanauj became a famous city. Harsha was a keen Buddhist. Buddhism, as a separate faith, had weakened greatly in India; it was being swallowed up by the Brahmans. Harsha appears to have been the last great Buddhist sovereign in India.

It was during Harsha's reign that our old friend, Hiuen Tsang,[1] came to India, and the book of his travels that he wrote on his return tells us a lot about India and the countries of Central Asia which he crossed on his way to India. He was a pious Buddhist, and he came to visit the sacred places of Buddhism and to take with him the scriptures of the faith. Right across the desert of Gobi he came, visiting many a famous city on the way—Tashkand and Samarqand and Balkh and Khotan and Yarkand. All over India he travelled, perhaps even visiting Ceylon. His book is a strange and fascinating jumble of accurate observations of the countries he visited, wonderful character-sketches of peoples in different parts of India, which seem true even to-day, fantastic stories which he heard, and numerous miracle-stories of the Buddha and the Bodhisattvas. One of his delightful stories, about the Very Wise Man who went about with copper-plates round his belly, I have already told you.

Many years he spent in India, especially in the great university of Nalanda, which was not far from Pātaliputra. Nalanda, which was a monastery and university combined, is said to have had as many as 10,000 students and monks in residence. It was the great centre of Buddhist learning, a rival to Benares, which was the stronghold of Brahman learning.

I told you once that India was known of old as the Land of the Moon—Indu-land ! Hiuen Tsang also tells us about this, and describes how suitable the name is. Apparently even in Chinese In-Tu is the name for the moon. So it is quite easy for you to adopt a Chinese name ![2]

Hiuen Tsang came to India in 629 A.C. He was twenty-six years old when he started on his journey from China. An old Chinese record tells us that he was handsome and tall. " His colouring was delicate, his eyes brilliant. His bearing was grave and majestic, and his features seemed to radiate charm and brightness. . . . He had the majesty of the great waters that surround the earth, the serenity and brilliance of the lotus that rises from the midst of the waters."

Alone, in the saffron garb of the Buddhist *bhikshu*, he started on his mighty journey, even though the Chinese Emperor had

---

[1] Hiuen Tsang's name is also spelt Yuen Chang or Yuan Chwang or Hsuan tsang.

[2] Indira's pet name is Indu.

refused his permission. He crossed the Gobi desert, barely surviving the ordeal, and reached the kingdom of Turfan, that stood
on the very edge of this desert. A strange little oasis of culture
was this desert kingdom. It is a dead place now where archæologists
and antiquarians dig for old remains. But in the seventh century,
when Hiuen Tsang passed through it, it was full of life and a high
culture.. And this culture was a remarkable combination of India,
China, Persia, and even bits of Europe. Buddhism flourished and
Indian influence through Sanskrit was marked; and yet the ways
of life were borrowed largely from China and Persia. Their language
was not Mongolian, as one might expect, but Indo-European,
resembling in many ways the Celtic languages of Europe. And,
stranger still, on their frescoes in stone appear figures that are
similar to European types. Very beautiful are these frescoes with
their Buddhas and Bodhisattvas and gods and goddesses. The
goddesses often have Indian draperies or Grecian head-dresses and
draperies, presenting, so says the French critic M. Grousset, " the
happiest combination of Hindu suppleness, Hellenic eloquence, and
Chinese charm ".

Turfan still exists, and you can find it in the map. But it is a
place of little importance. How wonderful it is that in the far-off
seventh century, rich streams of culture should have flown from
distant regions to meet here and unite to form a harmonious
synthesis !

From Turfan the pilgrim Hiuen Tsang went on to Kucha, yet
another famous centre of Central Asia then, with a rich and brilliant
civilization, known especially for the fame of its musicians and the
charm of its women. Its religion and art came from India ; Iran
contributed to its culture and to its merchandise ; and its language
was related to Sanskrit, old Persian, Latin and Celtic. Another
fascinating mixture !

And so Hiuen Tsang travelled on through the lands of the Turks
from where the Great Khan, who was a Buddhist, exercised dominion
over the greater part of Central Asia ; to Samarqand, which was
already then an ancient city with memories of Alexander, who had
passed by it nearly 1000 years earlier ; to Balkh ; and then the
valley of the Kabul river, and Kashmir and India.

These were the early days of the Tang dynasty in China, when
Si-an-fu, their capital, was a centre of art and learning, and China
led the world in civilization. You must remember, therefore, that
Hiuen Tsang came from this highly civilized country, and his
standards of comparison must have been high. His testimony
about Indian conditions is thus important and valuable. He
praises the Indian people and the administration. " With respect
to the ordinary people," he says, " although they are naturally
light-minded, yet they are upright and honourable. In money
matters they are without craft, and in administering justice they
are considerate. . . . They are not deceitful or treacherous in their
conduct, and are faithful in their oaths and promises. In their
rules of government there is remarkable rectitude, whilst in their

behaviour there is much gentleness and sweetness. With respect
to criminals or rebels, these are few in number, and only occasionally
troublesome."

He further says : " As the administration of the government is
founded on benign principles, the executive is simple. . . . People
are not subject to forced labour."   " In this way taxes on people
are light and the personal service required of them is moderate.
Each one keeps his own worldly goods in peace, and all till the
ground for their subsistence. Those who cultivate the royal estates
pay a sixth part of the produce as tribute. The merchants who
engage in commerce come and go in carrying out their transactions,
and so on."

Hiuen Tsang found that the education of the people was organized
and began early. After the primer had been learnt, the boy or
girl was supposed to begin the study of the five *Shastras* at the age
of seven.   " *Shastras* " are now supposed to mean purely religious
books, but in those days they meant knowledge of all kinds. Thus
the five *Shastras* were : (1) Grammar; (2) Science of arts and
crafts; (3) Medicine; (4) Logic; (5) Philosophy. The study of
these subjects went on in the universities and was usually completed at the age of thirty. I suppose not very many people could
go on up to that age. But it appears that primary education was
comparatively widespread, as all the monks and priests were the
teachers, and there was no lack of them. Hiuen Tsang was much
struck by the love of learning of the Indian people, and right
through his book he refers to this.

Hiuen gives us a description of the great Kumbh Mela at Prayag.[1]
When you see this *mela* again, think of Hiuen Tsang's visit to it
1300 years ago, and remember that even then it was an old *mela*
coming right down from the Vedic times. Compared to this
ancient one, of hoary lineage, our city of Allahabad is but of yesterday. It was founded by Akbar less than 400 years ago. Far older
was Prayag, but older still is that attraction which, for thousands
of years, has drawn millions, year after year, to the meeting-place
of the Ganga and the Jumna.

Hiuen Tsang tells us how Harsha, though a Buddhist, went to
this typical Hindu festival. On his behalf an imperial decree
invited all the poor and needy of the " Five Indies " to come and
be his guests at the *mela*. It was a brave invitation, even for an
emperor. Needless to say, many came; and 100,000 are said to
have fed daily as Harsha's guests ! At this *mela*, every five years,
Harsha used to distribute all the surplus of his treasury : gold,
jewellery, silk—indeed everything he had. He even gave away his
crown and rich clothing and took from his sister Rájashrí a common
garment which had already been worn.

As a pious Buddhist, Harsha stopped the killing of animals for
food. This was probably not objected to much by the Brahmans,
as they had taken more and more to vegetarianism since Buddha's
coming.

[1] Prayag is the old name for Allahabad. *Mela* is a fair.

There is a little tit-bit of information in Hiuen's book which might interest you. He tells us that when a person fell ill in India he immediately fasted for seven days. Most people recovered during this fast. But if the illness continued, then they took medicine. Illness could not have been popular in those days, nor would doctors be much in demand !

A striking feature of India in those days was the great deference and respect shown by rulers and military men to learned and cultured people. In India and in China a deliberate attempt was made, and with great success, to give the place of honour to learning and culture, and not to brute force or riches.

After spending many years in India, Hiuen Tsang journeyed back home, crossing again the northern mountains. He was nearly drowned in the Indus and many of his valuable books were washed away. But still he managed to take a large number of manuscripts, and the translation of these into Chinese kept him busy for many years. He was welcomed back with great warmth by the Tang Emperor at Si-an-fu, and it was this Emperor who made him write the account of his travels.

Hiuen tells us of the Turks he met in Central Asia—this new tribe which in later years was to go west and upset many a kingdom. He tells us of Buddhist monasteries all over Central Asia. Indeed, Buddhist monasteries were to be found in Persia, Iraq or Mesopotamia, Khorasan, Mosul—right up to the frontiers of Syria. Of the Persian people, Hiuen tells us that they " care not for learning, but give themselves entirely to works of art. All they make the neighbouring countries value very much."

Wonderful travellers there were in those days ! Even the journeys to the heart of Africa or the North or South Pole now seem feeble compared with the giant journeys of old. For years they moved on and on, across mountains and deserts, and cut off completely from all friends. Sometimes, perhaps, they felt a little home-sick, but they are much too dignified to say so. One of these travellers, however, lets us have a glimpse into his mind as, standing in a distant land, he thought of home and hungered for it. His name was Sung-Yun, and he came to India 100 years before Hiuen Tsang. He was in the mountain country in Gāndhāra, north-west of India. He tells us that " the gentle breeze which fanned the air, the songs of the birds, the trees in their springtide beauty, the butterflies that fluttered over the numerous flowers— all this caused Sung-Yun, as he gazed on this lovely scenery in a distant land, to revert to home thoughts; and so melancholy were his reflections, that he brought on a severe attack of illness ! "

44

SOUTH INDIA PRODUCES MANY KINGS AND WARRIORS AND A GREAT MAN

May 13, 1932

KING HARSHA died in 648 A.C. But even before his death a little cloud appeared on the north-west frontier of India, in Baluchistan—a cloud which was the forerunner of a mighty storm that was breaking in western Asia, northern Africa and southern Europe. A new prophet had arisen in Arabia, and Mohammad was his name; and he had preached a new religion called Islam. Fired with zeal for their new faith, and full of confidence in themselves, the Arabs dashed across continents, conquering as they went. It was an amazing feat, and we must examine this new force which came into the world and made so much difference to it. But before we consider it, we must pay a visit to South India and try to make out what it was like in those days. The Muslim Arabs reached Baluchistan in Harsha's time, and soon after they took possession of Sindh. But there they stayed, and for another 300 years there was no further Muslim invasion of India. And when this invasion came it was not the doing of the Arabs, but of some of the Central Asian tribes who became converted to Islam.

So we go to the south. In the west and centre there is the Chalukyan kingdom, largely consisting of the Maharashtra country, with Badami as their capital. Hiuen Tsang praises the Maharashtrians and speaks highly of their courage. They are " warlike and proud-spirited, grateful for favours and revengeful for wrongs ". The Chalukyans had to hold Harsha in the north, the Pallavas in the south, and Kalinga (Orissa) in the east. They grew in power and spread from sea to sea, and then they were pushed away by the Rashtrakutas.

And so big empires and kingdoms flourished in the south— sometimes balancing each other, sometimes one of them growing and overshadowing the others. Under the Pandyan kings Madura was a great centre of culture, and poets and writers of the Tamil language gathered there. Most of the classics of Tamil date from the beginning of the Christian era. The Pallavas, whose capital was Kanchipura—the modern Conjeevaram, also had their day of glory. They were largely responsible for the colonization of Malaysia.

Later, the Chola Empire grew to power, and about the middle of the ninth century it dominated the south. It was a sea-power and had a big navy, with which it swept the Bay of Bengal and the Arabian sea. Its chief port was Kaviripaddinam at the mouth of the Kaveri river. Vijayalaya was their first great ruler. They went on spreading north till the Rashtrakutas suddenly defeated them, but they recovered soon under Rajaraja, who restored the

Chola fortunes. This was near the end of the tenth century, just about the time when Muslim invasions were taking place in northern India. Rajaraja was, of course, little affected by what was happening in the far north, and he carried on his imperialist ventures. He conquered Ceylon, and the Cholas ruled there for seventy years. His son Rajendra was equally aggressive and warlike. He conquered southern Burma, taking his war-elephants with him in his ships. He came to northern India also and defeated the King of Bengal. The Chola Empire thus became very extensive, the biggest since the days of the Guptas. But it did not last. Rajendra was a great warrior, but he appears to have been cruel, and he did nothing to win over the States he had conquered. He reigned from 1013 to 1044, and after his death the Chola Empire broke up, many of the tributary States revolting.

Apart from their success in war, the Cholas were long famous for their sea-trade. Their fine cotton goods were much sought after, and their port, Kaviripaddinam, was a busy place, with ships carrying merchandise coming from and going to distant places. There was a settlement of Yavanas or Greeks there. There is mention of the Cholas even in the *Mahābhārata*.

I have tried to tell you, as briefly as possible, about several hundred years of South Indian history. Probably this attempt at brevity will only confuse you. But we cannot afford to lose ourselves in the maze of different kingdoms and dynasties. We have the whole world to consider, and if a small part of it, even though it may be the part where we live, took up much of our time, we would never get on with the rest.

But more important than the kings and their conquests is the cultural and artistic record of those times. Artistically, there are far more remains in the south than the north has to offer. Most of the northern monuments and buildings and sculptures were destroyed during the wars and Muslim invasions. In the south they escaped even when the Muslims reached there. It is unfortunate that numerous beautiful monuments were destroyed in the north. The Muslims who came there—and remember they were the Central Asians and not the Arabs—were full of zeal for their religion and wanted to destroy idols. But another reason for their destruction was perhaps the use of old temples as citadels and fighting places. Many of the temples in the south even now seem to resemble citadels where people can defend themselves if attacked. These temples thus served many purposes, apart from that of worship. They were the village school, the village meeting-place, *panchāyat ghar* or parliament, and finally, if this became necessary, the village fort for defence against the enemy. Thus all the life of the village revolved round the temple, and naturally the people who must have bossed over everything were the temple priests and Brahmans. But the fact that temples were used sometimes as citadels may explain why the Muslim invaders destroyed them.

Of this period there is a beautiful temple at Tanjore built by Rajaraja, the Chola ruler. At Badami there are also fine temples—

so also at Conjeevaram. But the most wonderful of the temples we have of those days is the Kailasa temple of Ellora—a marvel carved out of the solid rock. This was begun in the second half of the eighth century. There are also beautiful pieces of sculpture in bronze, notably the famous Nataraja—Shiva's dance of life.

Rajendra I, the Chola King, had remarkable irrigation works constructed at Cholapuram—an embankment of solid masonry, sixteen miles long. A hundred years after these were made an Arab traveller, Alberuni, visited them and he was amazed. He says of them : " Our people, when they see them, wonder at them and are unable to describe them, much less construct anything like them."

I have mentioned in this letter the names of some kings and dynasties, who lived their brief life of glory and then disappeared and were forgotten. But a more remarkable man arose in the south, destined to play a more vital part in India's life than all the kings and emperors. This young man is known as Shankara-charya. Probably he was born about the end of the eighth century. He seems to have been a person of amazing genius. He set about reviving Hinduism, or rather a special intellectual kind of Hinduism called Saivism—the worship of Shiva. He fought against Buddhism—fought with his intellect and arguments. He established an order of *sanyāsins* open to all castes, like the Buddhist Sangha. He established four centres for this order of *sanyāsins*, situated at the four corners of India, north, west, south, east. He travelled all over India, and wherever he went he triumphed. He came to Benares as a conqueror, but a conqueror of the mind and in argument. Ultimately he went to Kedarnath in the Hima-layas, where the eternal snows begin, and he died there. And he was only thirty-two, or maybe a little more, when he died.

Shankaracharya's record is a remarkable one. Buddhism, which had been driven south from the north, now almost disappears from India. Hinduism, and the variety of it known as Saivism, becomes dominant all over the country. The whole country is stirred up intellectually by Shankara's books and commentaries and arguments. Not only does he become the great leader of the Brahman class, but he seems to catch the imagination of the masses. It is an unusual thing for a man to become a great leader chiefly because of his powerful intellect, and for such a person to impress himself on millions of people and on history. Great soldiers and conquerors seem to stand out in history. They become popular or are hated, and sometimes they mould history. Great religious leaders have moved millions and fired them with enthusiasm, but always this has been on the basis of faith. The emotions have been appealed to and have been touched.

It is difficult for an appeal to the mind and to the intellect to go far. Most people unfortunately do not think : they feel and act according to their feelings. Yet Shankara's appeal was to the mind and intellect and to reason. It was not just the repetition of a dogma contained in an old book. Whether his argument was right or wrong is immaterial for the moment.   What is interesting is his intellectual approach to religious problems, and even more so the success he gained in spite of this method of approach.   This gives us a glimpse into the mind of the ruling classes in those days.

It may interest you to know that among Hindu philosophers there was a man, named Charvaka, who preached atheism—that is, who said that there was no God.   There are many people to-day, especially in Russia, who do not believe in God.   We need not enter into that question here.   But what is very interesting is the freedom of thought and writing in India in the olden days.   There was what is known as freedom of conscience.   This was not so in Europe till very recent times, and even now there are some disabilities.

Another fact which Shankara's brief but strenuous life brings out is the cultural unity of India.   Right through ancient history this seems to have been acknowledged.   Geographically, as you know, India is more or less of a unit.   Politically she has often been split up, though occasionally, as we have seen, she has almost been under one central authority.   But right from the beginning, culturally she has been one, because she had the same background, the same traditions, the same religions, the same heroes and heroines, the same old mythology, the same learned language (Sanskrit), the same places of worship spread out all over the country, the same village *panchāyats* and the same ideology and polity.   To the average Indian the whole of India was a kind of *punya-bhūmi*—a holy land—while the rest of the world was largely peopled by *mlechchhas* and barbarians !   Thus there rose a common Indian consciousness which triumphed over, and partly ignored, the political divisions of the country.   Especially was this so as the village system of *panchāyat* government continued, whatever the changes at the top might be.

Shankara's choice of the four corners of India for his *maths*, or the headquarters of his order of *sanyāsins*, shows how he regarded India as a cultural unit.   And the great success which met his campaign all over the country in a very short time also shows how intellectual and cultural currents travelled rapidly from one end of the country to another.

Shankara preached Saivism, and this spread especially in the south, where many of the old temples are Saiva temples.   In the north, during Gupta times, there was a great revival of Vaishnavism and Krishna-worship.   The temples of these two branches of Hinduism are different from each other.

This letter has become long enough.   But I have still to say much about the condition of India during these Middle Ages.   That must wait till the next letter.

45

INDIA IN THE MIDDLE AGES

May 14, 1932

You will remember my telling you of the *Arthashāstra*, the book written by Chānakya or Kautilya, who was the chief Minister of Chandragupta Maurya, the grandfather of Ashoka. In this book we were told all manner of things about the people and methods of government of those days. It was almost as if a window were opened which enables us to have a peep at India in the fourth century before Christ. Such books giving intimate details of administration are far more helpful than exaggerated accounts of kings and their conquests.

We have another book which helps us a little to form an idea of India in the Middle Ages. This is the *Nītisāra* of Shukrācharya. This is not so good or helpful as the *Arthashāstra*, but with its help and that of some inscriptions and other accounts we shall try to open a window into the ninth or tenth century after Christ.

The *Nītisāra* tells us that " neither through colour, nor through ancestors can the spirit worthy of a Brahman be generated ". Thus, according to it, caste division should not be by birth, but by capacity. Again, it says : " In making official appointments work, character, and merit were to be regarded—neither caste nor family ". The king was not to act upon his own opinions, but upon the opinion of the majority of the people. " Public opinion is more powerful than the king as the rope made of many fibres is strong enough to drag a lion."

These are all excellent maxims, good even to-day in theory. But as a matter of fact, they do not take us very far in practice. A man can rise by capacity and merit. But how is he to acquire the capacity and merit ? A boy or a girl may be quite smart and may become a clever and efficient person if suitable education and training are given. But if no arrangements are made for the education or training what is the poor boy or girl to do ?

In the same way, what is public opinion ? Whose opinion is to count as the opinion of the public ? Probably the writer of the *Nītisāra* did not consider the large number of shūdra workers as entitled to give any opinion. They hardly counted. Public opinion was perhaps just the opinion of the upper and ruling classes.

Still, it is interesting to notice that in Indian polity in the Middle Ages, as before, autocracy or the divine right of kings had no place.

Then we are told of the king's Council of State and of the high officers in charge of public works and parks and forests; of the organization of town and village life; of bridges, ferries, rest-houses, roads and—most important for a town or village—drains.

The village *panchāyat* had full control over the affairs of the village, and the *panches* were treated with great respect by the king's officers. It was the *panchāyat* that distributed lands and collected taxes and then paid the government tax on behalf of the village. There appears to have been a big *panchāyat* or *mahasabha*, which supervised the work of these *panchāyats* and could interfere if there was need for it. These *panchāyats* also had judicial powers and could act as judges and try people.

Some old inscriptions from South India tell us how the members of the *panchāyats* were elected, their qualifications and disqualifications. If any member did not render accounts of public funds he was disqualified. Another very interesting rule seems to have been that near relatives of members were disqualified from office. How excellent if this could be enforced now in all our councils and assemblies and municipálities !

There is mention of a woman's name as a member of a committee. So it appears that women could serve on these *panchāyats* and their committees.

Committees were formed out of the elected members of the *panchāyats*, each committee lasting for a year. If a member misbehaved he could be removed at once.

This system of village self-government was the foundation of the Aryan polity. It was this that gave it strength. So jealous were the village assemblies of their liberties that it was laid down that no soldier was to enter a village except with a royal permit. The *Nitisāra* says that when the subjects complain of an officer, the king " should take the side not of his officers but of his subjects "; and if a large number of people complain, the officer was to be dismissed, " for," says the *Nitisāra*, " who does not get intoxicated by drinking of the vanity of office ? " Wise words which seem to apply especially to the crowds of officials who misbehave and misgovern us in this country to-day !

In the larger towns, where there were many artisans and merchants, guilds were formed. Thus there were craft guilds, banking corporations and mercantile associations. There were, of course, religious organizations also. All these organizations had a great measure of control over their domestic affairs.

The king was enjoined to tax people lightly so as not to injure them or bear heavily on them. He was to levy taxes as a garland-maker gathers flowers and leaves from the trees in the forest, not like a charcoal-burner.

Such is the fragmentary information that we can pick up about the Middle Ages in India. It is a little difficult to find out how far practice fitted in with the theory laid down in the books. It is easy enough to write of fine theories and ideals in books, but it is more difficult to live up to them. The books, however, help us to realize what the ideology or the ideas of the people were at the time, even though they may not have practised them wholly. We find that the kings and rulers were far from being autocratic rulers. Their power was kept in check by elected *panchāyats*. We find also that there was a fairly advanced system of self-government

in the villages and towns, and that there was little interference
with this by the Central Government.

But when I talk of the ideology of the people, or self-government,
what do I mean? The whole social structure in India was based
on the caste system. In theory, this may not have been rigid,
and may have been open to merit or capacity, as the *Nitisāra* says.
But in reality this means very little. The ruling classes or castes
were the Brahmans and *Kshattriyas*. Sometimes there was conflict between them for mastery, more often they ruled jointly and
accommodated each other. The others they kept down. Gradually,
as trade and commerce increased, the merchant-class became rich
and important, and as it grew in importance, it was given certain
privileges and freedom to arrange the domestic affairs of its guilds.
But even then it had no real share in the power of the State. As
for the poor Shūdras, they remained the bottom dogs right through.
And even below them were others still.

Occasionally men from the lower castes made good. Shūdras
were even known to become kings. But this was a rare thing. A
more frequent method of rising in the social scale was for a whole
sub-caste to go up a step. New tribes were often absorbed into
Hinduism at the bottom; slowly they worked themselves up.

You will see, therefore, that although there was no labour slavery
in India as in the West, our whole social structure was one of
gradations—one class over another. The millions at the bottom
were exploited by and had to bear the weight of all those at the
top. And the people at the top took care to perpetuate this system
and to keep the power for themselves by not giving opportunities
of education or training to these poor people at the bottom of the
ladder. In the village *panchāyats* perhaps the peasantry had some
say and could not be ignored, but it is highly likely that a few
clever Brahmans dominated these *panchāyats* also.

The old Aryan polity seems to continue from the days when the
Aryans came to India and came into touch with the Dravidians to
the Middle Ages of which we are speaking. But there appears to
be a progressive deterioration and weakening. Perhaps it was
growing old; and perhaps the repeated incursions from outside
gradually wore it down.

It might interest you to know that India was great in mathematics in the old days, and among the great names is that of a
woman—Lilāvati. It is said that it was Lilāvati and her father,
Bhāskarāchārya, and perhaps another man, Brahmagupta, who
first evolved the decimal system. Algebra is also said to be of
Indian origin. From India it went to Arabia, and from there to
Europe. The word Algebra is from the Arabic.

46

ANGKOR THE MAGNIFICENT AND SRI VIJAYA

May 17, 1932

WE shall now pay a brief visit to Farther India—the colonies and settlements of people from South India in Malaysia and Indo-China. I have already told you how these settlements were deliberately organized and arranged. They did not just grow up anyhow. There must have been frequent journeys across the seas and a sufficient mastery over the seas, to permit of this deliberate colonization simultaneously at several places. I have also told you that these colonies began in the first and second centuries of the Christian era. They were Hindu colonies bearing South Indian names. After some centuries Buddhism gradually spread, till nearly the whole of Hindu Malaysia had become Buddhist.

Let us go to Indo-China first. The earliest colony was named Champa, and was in Annam. There we find in the third century the city of Pandurangam growing up. Two hundred years later the great city of Kamboja flourished. It was full of great buildings and temples of stone. All over these Indian colonies you will find mighty buildings growing up. Architects and master builders must have been taken across from India, and they carried on the Indian traditions in building there. Between the different States and islands there was a great deal of competition in building, and this competition resulted in a high type of artistic development.

The people living in these settlements were naturally seafaring folk. They or their ancestors had already crossed the seas to reach these places, and all round them was the sea. Seafaring folk take to trade easily. So these people were traders and merchants, carrying their wares across the seas to the different islands, to India in the west and to China in the east. The different States in Malaysia were thus controlled largely by the merchant classes. Often there was conflict between these States and great wars and massacres. Sometimes a Hindu State waged war against a Buddhist State. But the real motive for many of these wars in those days seems to have been trade rivalry. Just as in these days wars take place between great Powers for markets for the goods they manufacture.

For 300 years or so, up to the eighth century, there were three different Hindu States in Indo-China. In the ninth century a great ruler arose—Jaya-varman, who united all these and built up a great empire. He was probably a Buddhist. He began building his capital at Angkor, and his successor, Yaso-varman, completed it. This Cambodian Empire lasted for nearly 400 years. As empires go, it was supposed to be splendid and powerful. The royal city of Angkor Thom was known all over the East as " Angkor the Magnificent." It was a city of over a million people, larger than the Rome of the Cæsars had been. Near it was the wonderful temple of Angkor Vat. In the thirteenth century Cambodia was attacked on several sides. The Annamese attacked in the east, the local tribes in the west. And in the north the Shan people were driven south by Mongols, and finding no other way of escape, they attacked Cambodia. The kingdom was tired out by this constant fighting and defending itself. Still the city of Angkor continued to be one of the most splendid cities in the East. In 1297 a Chinese envoy, who had been sent to the Cambodian king, wrote a glowing description of its wonderful buildings.

But suddenly Angkor suffered a terrible catastrophe. About 1300 A.C. the mouth of the river Mekong became blocked by deposits of mud. The waters of the river could not flow through, and they backed up and flooded the entire region round the great city, turning fertile fields into a great area of useless marshlands. The large population of the city began to starve. It could not stay on, and was forced to leave the city and migrate. So " Angkor the Magnificent " was abandoned, and the jungle came and took possession of it, and its wonderful buildings housed wild animals for a while, till the jungle reduced the palaces to dust and reigned unchallenged.

The Cambodian State could not survive this catastrophe for long. It collapsed gradually and became a province sometimes ruled by Siam, sometimes by Annam. But even now the ruins of the great temple of Angkor Vat tell us something of the days when a proud and splendid city stood near by, drawing merchants with their wares from distant lands, and sending out to other countries the fine goods that its citizens and artisans made.

Across the sea, not very far from Indo-China, lay the island of Sumatra. Here also the Pallavas from South India had established their earliest colonies in the first or second century after Christ. These grew gradually. The Malay Peninsula early became part of the Sumatran State, and for long afterwards the histories of Sumatra and the Malay Peninsula were closely allied. The capital of the State was the large city of Sri Vijaya, situated inland in the mountains of Sumatra, and having a port at the mouth of the Palembang river. About the fifth or sixth century Buddhism became the predominant religion of Sumatra. Indeed, Sumatra took the lead in carrying on active missionary work for Buddhism and ultimately succeeded in converting most of Hindu Malaysia to Buddhism. This Sumatran empire is therefore known as the Buddhist Empire of Sri Vijaya.

Sri Vajaya went on growing bigger and bigger till it included not only Sumatra and Malay, but Borneo, Philippines, Celebes, half of Java, half of the island of Formosa (which belongs to Japan now), Ceylon, and even a port in the south of China near Canton. Probably it also included a port in the southern tip of India, facing Ceylon. You will thus see that it was a widespread empire, covering the whole of Malaysia. Commerce and trade and shipbuilding were the chief occupations of these Indian colonies. The Chinese and Arabian writers of the time give us long lists of ports and new colonies subject to the Sumatran State. These lists go on growing.

The British Empire to-day is spread out all over the world and everywhere it has got seaports and good coaling-stations : Gibraltar, the Suez Canal (which is largely under British control), Aden, Colombo, Singapore, Hongkong and so on. The British have been a nation of traders during the last 300 years and their trade and strength have depended on sea power. They have thus required ports and coaling-stations at convenient distances all over the world. The Sri Vijaya Empire was also a sea Power based on trade. Hence you find that it had ports wherever it could get the smallest footing. Indeed, a remarkable feature of the settlements of the Sumatran State was their strategic value—that is to say, they were carefully located at places where they could command the surrounding seas. Often they were in pairs to help each other in maintaining this command.

Thus Singapore, which is a great city now, was originally a settlement of the Sumatran colonists. The name, as you will notice, is a typical Indian name : Singhpur. The Sumatran people had another settlement just opposite the Straits, facing Singapore. Sometimes they would stretch an iron chain right across the Strait and so stop all ships from passing till they paid heavy tolls.

So the Empire of Sri Vijaya was not unlike the British Empire, though of course it was much smaller. But it lasted longer than the British Empire is likely to last. Its period of highest development was in the eleventh century, just about the time when the Chola Empire flourished in South India. But it long outlived this Chola Empire. There were friendly relations between the two for a long time, but both were aggressive seafaring folk with strong navies and widespread trade connections. Early in the eleventh century they came into conflict and there was war. The Chola king, Rajendra I, sent an overseas expedition which humbled Sri Vijaya. But Sri Vijaya soon recovered from this shock.

At the beginning of the eleventh century the Chinese Emperor sent a gift of a number of bronze bells to the Sumatran King. In return the latter sent pearls and ivory and Sanskrit books. There was also a letter inscribed on a golden plate in " Indian characters ", it is said.

Sri Vijaya flourished for quite a long time, from its early beginnings about the second century to the fifth or sixth century, when it turned Buddhist, and then, gradual and continuous growth till the eleventh century. For another 300 years it remained a great empire controlling the trade and commerce of Malaysia. It was overthrown ultimately in 1377 A.C. by another of the old Pallava colonies.

I have told you that the Sri Vijaya Empire spread from Ceylon to Canton in China. It included most of the islands in between. But one little bit it could not subdue. This was the eastern part of Java, which continued to remain an independent State and which also remained Hindu and refused to turn Buddhist. Thus while western Java was under Sri Vijaya, eastern Java was independent. This Hindu State of East Java was also a commercial State, and it depended for its prosperity on trade. It must have looked with envious eyes on Singapore, which, because of its fine position, had become a great trade centre. Thus there was rivalry between Sri Vijaya and East Java, and this developed into bitter enmity. From the twelfth century onwards the Javan State grew slowly at the expense of Sri Vijaya and, as I have said, in the fourteenth century—in 1377 A.C.—it defeated Sri Vijaya completely. It was a cruel war and there was great destruction. Both the cities of Sri Vijaya and Singapore were destroyed. Thus ended the second of the great empires of Malaysia—the Empire of Sri Vijaya— and over its ruins rose the third of these empires, that of Madjapahit.

In spite of the cruelty and barbarity shown by the East Javans in their war with Sri Vijaya, it appears from the many books we still have of that period in Java that this Hindu State had attained a high degree of civilization. What it excelled in was building, and especially the building of temples. There were over 500 temples, and among these are said to be some of the world's finest and most artistic specimens of stone architecture. Most of these great temples were built between the middle of the seventh and the middle of the tenth century—that is, between 650 and 950 A.C. The Javanese must have brought large numbers of builders and master-craftsmen from India and other neighbouring countries to help them to build these mighty temples. We shall follow the fortunes of Java and Madjapahit in a subsequent letter.

I might mention here that both Borneo and the Philippines learnt the art of writing from India, through these early Pallavan colonies. Unfortunately many of the old manuscripts in the Philippines were destroyed by the Spaniards.

Remember also that the Arabs had their colonies all over these islands from the early days, long before Islam. They were great traders, and wherever trade was to be found, the Arabs went.

47

ROME RELAPSES INTO DARKNESS

May 19, 1932

I FEEL often enough that I am not at all a good guide for you through the maze of past history. I get lost myself. How, then, can I guide you aright? But again I think that perhaps I might be of a little help to you, and so I continue these letters. To me certainly they are of great help. As I write them and think of you, my dear, I forget that the temperature in the shade and where I sit is 112 degrees and the hot *loo* is blowing. And I forget even sometimes that I am in the District Gaol of Bareilly.

My last letter carried you right up to the end of the fourteenth century in Malaysia. And yet in northern India we have not gone beyond King Harsha's time—the seventh century; and in Europe we have still more time to make up. It is very difficult to keep to the same time-scale everywhere. I try to do so, but sometimes, as in the case of Angkor and Sri Vijaya, I shoot ahead a few hundred years, so that I might complete their story. But remember that while the Cambodian Empire and the Sri Vijaya Empire flourished in the East, all manner of changes were taking place in India and in China and in Europe. Remember also that my last letter contains, in a few pages, the history of 1000 years of Indo-China and Malaysia. These countries are cut off from the main currents of Asiatic and European history, and therefore little attention is paid to them. But theirs is a rich and long history— rich in achievement, in trade, in art, in architecture especially— and it is well worthy of study. To Indians their story must be of particular interest, for they were almost a part of India; men and women from India crossing the eastern seas and carrying with them Indian culture and civilization and art and religion.

So, although we have gone on ahead in Malaysia, we are really still in the seventh century. We have still to go to Arabia and consider the coming of Islam and the great changes that this brought in Europe and Asia. And we have to follow the course of events in Europe.

Let us have another look at Europe and let us go back a little. You will remember that Constantine, the Roman Emperor, founded the city of Constantinople, where Byzantium was, on the shores of the Bosphorus. To this city, the New Rome, he shifted the capital of the Empire from the old Rome. Soon afterwards the Roman Empire split up into two : the Western with Rome for its capital and the Eastern Empire with its seat at Constantinople. The Eastern Empire had to face great difficulties and many enemies. And yet, strange to say, it managed to carry on century after century, for 1100 years, till the Turks put an end to it.

The Western Empire had no such existence. In spite of the great prestige of the Roman name and the imperial city of Rome, which had for so long dominated the western world, it collapsed with remarkable rapidity. It could not withstand the attacks of any of the northern tribes. Alaric, the Goth, marched down into Italy and captured Rome in 410 A.C. Later came the Vandals, who also sacked Rome. The Vandals were a Germanic people who had crossed France and Spain, and, entering Africa, had established a kingdom on the ruins of Carthage. From old Carthage they crossed the seas and captured Rome. It seems almost as though it were a belated revenge for the Roman victory in the Punic Wars.

About this time the Huns, who had originally come from central Asia or Mongolia, became powerful. These people were nomads. They had settled down east of the Danube river and north and west of the Eastern Roman Empire. Under Attila, their leader, they became very aggressive, and the Constantinople Emperor and government lived in constant terror of them. Attila bullied them and made them pay large sums of money to him. Having humiliated the Eastern Empire sufficiently, Attila decided to attack the Western Empire. He invaded Gaul and destroyed many towns in southern France. The imperial forces would have been no match for him, but the Germanic tribes, the " barbarians " of the Romans, were frightened at this Hun invasion, and so the Franks and Goths joined the imperial army and together they fought the Huns under Attila at a great battle at Troyes. Over 150,000 people are said to have been killed at this battle, at which Attila was defeated and the Mongolian Huns repulsed. This was in 451 A.O. But Attila, though defeated, was full of fight. He went down to Italy and burnt and looted many towns in the north. He died soon afterwards, leaving an enduring reputation for cruelty and ruthlessness. Attila the Hun is even to-day almost the embodiment of ruthless destruction. The Huns quietened down after his death and settled on the land and got mixed up with many other populations. You may remember that it was roughly about this time that the White Huns came to India.

Forty years later a Goth, Theodoric, became King of Rome, and that was almost the end of the Western Empire. A successful attempt was made a little later by an Eastern Emperor, Justinian, to include Italy in his empire. He conquered both Italy and Sicily, but they broke away soon after, and the Eastern Empire had enough to do to protect itself.

Is it not strange that Imperial Rome and her empire should have collapsed so quickly and so easily before almost every tribe that chose to attack it ? One would think that Rome had gone to pieces, or that it was just a hollow shell. Probably this would be correct. The strength of Rome for a lengthy period lay in her prestige. Her past history had led other peoples to think of her as the leader of the world, and they treated her with respect and almost with superstitious fear. So Rome continued, outwardly as the powerful mistress of an empire, but in reality with no strength behind her. There was outward calm, and there were crowds in her theatres and stadiums and market-places. But inevitably she was heading for collapse, not merely because she was weak, but because she had built up a rich man's civilization on the misery and slavery of the masses. I told you, in one of my letters, of the revolts and insurrections of the poor; also of a great slaves' revolt which was ruthlessly put down. These revolts show us how rotten was the social structure of Rome. It was going to pieces of itself, and the coming of the northern tribes—the Goths and the others— helped this process, and therefore they met with little opposition. The Roman peasant was fed up with his miserable lot and welcomed any change. As for the poor labourer and the slave, they were far worse off.

With the end of the Western Roman Empire we see the new peoples of the West coming to the front—the Goths and Franks and others with whose names I shall not trouble you. These peoples are the ancestors of the western Europeans of to-day—the Germans, French, etc. Slowly we see these countries taking shape in Europe. At the same time we find a very low type of civilization. The end of Imperial Rome had also been the end of the pomp and luxury of Rome, and the superficial civilization which had dragged on in Rome vanished almost in a day, its roots having long been sapped. Thus we see actually one of the strange instances of humanity visibly moving backwards. We have this in India, in Egypt, in China, in Greece and Rome and elsewhere. After knowledge and experience have been laboriously gathered and a culture and civilization built up, there is a stop. And not only a stop, but a going back. A veil seems to be cast over the past, and though we have occasional glimpses of it, the mountain of knowledge and experience has to be climbed afresh. Perhaps each time one goes a little higher and makes the next ascent easier. Just as expedition after expedition goes up Mount Everest, each subsequent expedition goes nearer to the summit, and it may be that the highest peak will be conquered before long.

So we find darkness in Europe. The Dark Ages begin and life becomes rude and crude, and there is almost no education, and fighting seems to be the only occupation or amusement. The days of Socrates and Plato seem very far off indeed.

So much for the West. Let us look at the Eastern Empire also. Constantine, you will remember, made Christianity the official religion. One of his successors, the Emperor Julian, refused to accept Christianity. He wanted to go back to the worship of the old gods and goddesses. But he could not succeed, for the old gods had had their day, and Christianity was too powerful for them. Julian was called Julian the Apostate by the Christians, and that is the title by which he is known in history.

Soon after Julian came another Emperor who was very unlike him. His name was Theodosius, and he is called the Great, I suppose because he was great in destroying the old temples and the old statues of the gods and goddesses. He was not only strongly opposed to those who were not Christians : he was equally aggressive against Christians who were not orthodox according to his way of thinking. He would tolerate no opinion or religion of which he did not approve. Theodosius for a short while joined the Eastern and Western Empires and was Emperor of both. This was in 392 A.C., before the barbarian invasions of Rome.

Christianity continued to spread. Its struggles now were not against non-Christians. All the fighting was done by Christian sects against each other, and the amount of intolerance shown by them is amazing. All over northern Africa and western Asia, as well as in Europe, there were many battle-grounds where Christians sought to convince their brother-Christians of the true faith by means of blows and cudgels and such-like gentle measures of persuasion.

From 527 to 565 A.C. Justinian was Emperor at Constantinople. As I have already told you, he turned out the Goths from Italy and for some time Italy and Sicily were parts of the Eastern Empire. Later the Goths recovered Italy.

Justinian built the beautiful cathedral of Sancta Sophia in Constantinople, which is still one of the finest of Byzantine churches. He also had all the existing laws brought together and arranged by able lawyers. Long before I knew anything of the Eastern Roman Empire and its emperors, I knew of Justinian's name from this law-book, which is called the *Institutes of Justinian*, and which I had to read. But although Justinian founded a university at Constantinople, he closed the academy or the old schools of philosophy of Athens which had been founded by Plato and had lasted 1000 years. Philosophy is a dangerous thing for any dogmatic religion; it makes people think.

And so we have arrived at the sixth century. We see Rome and Constantinople gradually drifting farther apart; Rome taken possession of by the Germanic tribes of the north; Constantinople becoming the centre of a Greek empire, although it was called Roman; Rome going to pieces and sinking to the low level of civilization of its conquerors, whom it used to call the " barbarians " in the days of its glory; Constantinople carrying on the old tradition in a way, but also going down in the scale of civilization; Christian sects fighting each other for mastery; and Eastern Christianity, which had spread right up to Turkestan and China and Abyssinia, becoming cut off from both Constantinople and Rome. The Dark Ages commence. Learning, so far, was classical learning—that is, Greek or old Latin, which derived its inspiration from Greek. But these old Greek books dealing with gods and goddesses and with philosophies were not considered to be fit literature for the pious and devout and intolerant Christians of those early days. So they were not encouraged, and learning suffered, as did also many forms of art.

But Christianity did something also to preserve learning and art. Monasteries like the Buddhist *saṅgha* were founded and spread rapidly. In these monasteries sometimes the old learning found a home. And here also the beginnings of a new art were laid down which was to blossom forth in all its beauty many centuries later. These monks just managed to keep the lamp of learning and art burning dimly. It was a service they rendered by preventing it from going out. But the light was confined to a narrow place; outside there was general darkness.

In these early days of Christianity there was another strange tendency. Many people, fired by religious zeal, retired into the deserts and solitary places, far from the haunts of man, and lived in a wild state there. They tortured themselves and did not wash at all, and generally tried to bear as much pain as possible. This was especially so in Egypt, where many such hermits lived in the desert. Their idea seems to have been that the more they suffered and the less they washed the holier they became. One of these hermits sat on the top of a column for many years ! These hermits gradually ceased to exist, but for a long time many devout Christians believed that to enjoy anything was almost a sin. This idea of suffering coloured the Christian mentality. There is not much of this in Europe to-day ! Indeed, everybody there seems bent on rushing about madly and having what is called a good time. And the rushing about often ends in weariness and *ennui* and not in the good time.

But in India we see sometimes even to-day people behaving to some extent as the Christian hermits did in Egypt. They hold up one arm till it dries up and atrophies, or sit on spikes, or do many other absurd and foolish things. Some do it, I suppose, just to impose on ignorant people and get money out of them, others perhaps because they feel that they become more holy thereby ! As if it can ever be desirable to make your body unfit for any decent activity.

I am reminded of a story of Buddha, for which again I go to our old friend Hiuen Tsang. A young disciple of his was doing penance. Buddha asked him : " You, dear youth, when living as a layman, did you know how to play the lute ? " He said : " I knew." " Well, then," said Buddha, " I will draw a comparison derived from this. The cords being too tight, then the sounds were not in cadence ; when they were too loose, then the sounds had neither harmony nor charm ; but when not tight and not slack, then the sounds were harmonious. So also," Buddha continued, " in regard to the body. If it is harshly treated, it becomes wearied and the mind is listless ; if it is too softly treated, then the feelings are pampered and the will is weakened."

48

THE COMING OF ISLAM

May 21, 1932

WE have considered the history of many countries and the ups and downs of many kingdoms and empires. But Arabia has not yet come into our story, except as a country which sent out mariners and traders to distant parts of the world. Look at the map. To the west is Egypt ; to the north Syria and Iraq, and a little to the east of this Persia or Iran ; a little farther to the north-west are Asia Minor and Constantinople. Greece is not far ; and India also is just across the sea on the other side. Except for China and the Far East, Arabia was very centrally situated so far as the old civilizations were concerned. Great cities rose on the Tigris and Euphrates in Iraq, Alexandria in Egypt, Damascus in Syria, Antioch in Asia Minor. The Arab was a traveller and a trader, and he must have gone to these cities frequently enough. But still Arabia plays no notable part in history. There does not seem to be as high a degree of civilization there as in neighbouring countries. It neither attempted to conquer other countries, nor was it easy to subdue it.

Arabia is a desert country, and deserts and mountains breed hard people who love their freedom and are not easily subdued. It was not a rich country and there was little in it to attract foreign conquerors and imperialists. There were just two little towns—Mecca and Yethrib by the sea. For the rest there were dwellings in the desert, and the people of the country were largely Bedouins or Baddus—the "dwellers of the desert". Their constant companions were their swift camels and their beautiful horses, and even the ass was a faithful friend valued for its remarkable powers of endurance. To be compared to the donkey or the ass was a compliment, and not a term of reproach, as in other countries. For life is hard in a desert country, and strength and endurance are even more precious qualities there than elsewhere.

They were proud and sensitive, these men of the desert, and quarrelsome. They lived in their clans and their families and quarrelled with other clans and families. Once a year they made peace with each other and journeyed to Mecca on pilgrimage to their many gods whose images were kept there. Above all, they worshipped a huge black stone—the Kaaba.

It was a nomadic and patriarchal life—the kind of life led by the primitive tribes in Central Asia or elsewhere, before they settled down to city life and civilization. The great empires which rose up round Arabia often included Arabia in their dominions, but this was more nominal than real. It was no easy matter to subdue or govern nomadic desert tribes.

Once, as you may perhaps remember, a little Arab State rose in Palmyra in Syria, and it had its brief period of glory in the third century after Christ. But even this was outside Arabia proper. So the Bedouins lived their desert lives, generation after generation, and Arab ships went out to trade, and Arabia went on with little change. Some people became Christians and some became Jews but mostly they remained worshippers of the 360 idols and the Black Stone in Mecca.

It is strange that this Arab race, which for long ages had lived a sleepy existence, apparently cut off from what was happening elsewhere, should suddenly wake up and show such tremendous energy as to startle and upset the world. The story of the Arabs, and of how they spread rapidly over Asia, Europe and Africa, and of the high culture and civilization which they developed, is one of the wonders of history.

Islam was the new force or idea which woke up the Arabs and filled them with self-confidence and energy. This was a religion started by a new prophet, Mohammad, who was born in Mecca in 570 A.C. He was in no hurry to start this religion. He lived a quiet life, liked and trusted by his fellow-citizens. Indeed, he was known as " Al-Amīn "—the Trusty. But when he started preaching his new religion, and especially when he preached against the idols at Mecca, there was a loud outcry against him, and ultimately he was driven out of Mecca, barely escaping with his life. Above all he laid stress on the claim that there was only one God, and that he, Mohammad, was the Prophet of God.

Driven away by his own people from Mecca, he sought refuge with some friends and helpers in Yethrib. This flight from Mecca is called the *Hijrat* in Arabic, and the Muslim calendar begins from this date—622 A.C. This Hegira calendar is a lunar calendar—that is, it is calculated according to the moon. It is therefore five or six days shorter than the solar year which we usually observe, and the Hegira months do not stick to the same seasons of the year. Thus the same month may be in winter this year and in the middle of summer after some years.

Islam may be said to begin with the flight—the *Hijrat*—in 622 A.C., although in a sense it had begun a little earlier. The city of Yethrib welcomed Mohammad and, in honour of his coming the name of the city itself was changed to " Madīnat-un-Nabī "—the city of the Prophet—or, just shortly, Madina, or Medina, as it is known now. The people of Medina who helped Mohammad were called *Ansār*—the helpers. Descendants of these " helpers " were proud of this title, and even to this day they use it.

Before we start on Islam's and the Arabs' career of conquest, let us have one brief look around. We have just seen that Rome had collapsed. The old Græco-Roman civilization had ended, and the whole social structure which it had built up had been upset. The northern European tribes and clans were now coming into some prominence. Trying to learn something from Rome, they were really building up an entirely new type of civilization. But this was just the beginning of it, and there was little of it visible. Thus the old had gone and the new had not taken its place; so there was darkness in Europe. At the eastern end of it, it is true, there was the Eastern Roman Empire, which still flourished. The city of Constantinople was even then a great and splendid city—the greatest in Europe. Games and circuses took place in its amphitheatres, and there was a great deal of pomp and show. But still the Empire was weakening. There were continuous wars with the Sassanids of Persia. Khusrau the Second of Persia had indeed taken away from Constantinople part of its dominions and even claimed a nominal overlordship over Arabia. Khusrau also conquered Egypt and went right up to Constantinople, but was then defeated by Heraclius the Greek Emperor there. Later, Khusrau was murdered by his own son, Kavadh.

So you will notice that both Europe in the West and Persia in the East were in a bad way. Add to this the quarrels of the Christian sects, which had no end. A very corrupt and quarrelsome Christianity flourished in the West as well as in Africa. In Persia, the Zoroastrian religion was part of the State and was forced on the people. So the average person in Europe or Africa or Persia was disillusioned with the existing religion. Just about this time, early in the seventh century, great plagues swept all over Europe, killing millions of people.

In India, Harsha-Vardhana ruled, and Hiuen Tsang paid his visit about this time. During Harsha's reign India was a strong Power, but soon after, northern India grew divided and weak. Farther east, in China, the great Tang dynasty had just begun its career.

In 627 A.C. Tai Tsung, one of their greatest emperors, came to the throne, and during his time the Chinese Empire extended right up to the Caspian Sea in the west. Most of the countries of Central Asia acknowledged his suzerainty and paid tribute to him. Probably there was no centralized government of the whole of this vast empire.

This was the state of the Asiatic and European world when Islam was born. China was strong and powerful, but it was far; India was strong enough for a period at least, but we shall see that there was no conflict with India for a long time to come; Europe and Africa were weak and exhausted.

Within seven years of the flight, Mohammad returned to Mecca as its master. Even before this he sent out from Medina a summons to the kings and rulers of the world to acknowledge the one God and his Prophet. Heraclius, the Constantinople Emperor, got it while he was still engaged in his campaign against the Persians in Syria; the Persian King got it; and it is said that even Tai-Tsung got it in China. They must have wondered, these kings and rulers, who this unknown person was who dared to command them! From the sending of these messages we can form some idea of the supreme confidence in himself and his mission which Mohammad must have had. And this confidence and faith he managed to give to his people, and with this to inspire and console them, this desert people of no great consequence managed to conquer half the known world.

Confidence and faith in themselves were a great thing. Islam also gave them a message of brotherhood—of the equality of all those who were Muslims. A measure of democracy was thus placed before the people. Compared to the corrupt Christianity of the day, this message of brotherhood must have had a great appeal, not only for the Arabs, but also for the inhabitants of many countries where they went.

Mohammad died in 632 A.C., ten years after the *Hijrat*. He had succeeded in making a nation out of the many warring tribes of Arabia and in firing them with enthusiasm for a cause. He was succeeded by Abu Bakr, a member of his family, as Khalifa or Caliph or chief. This succession used to be by a kind of informal election at a public meeting. Two years later Abu Bakr died, and was succeeded by Omar, who was Khalifa for ten years.

Abu Bakr and Omar were great men who laid the foundation of Arabian and Islamic greatness. As Khalifas they were both religious heads and political chiefs—King and Pope in one. In spite of their high position and the growing power of their State, they stuck to the simplicity of their ways and refused to countenance luxury and pomp. The democracy of Islam was a living thing for them. But their own officers and emirs took to silks and luxury soon enough, and many stories are told of Abu Bakr and Omar rebuking and punishing these officers, and even weeping at this extravagance. They felt that their strength lay in their simple and hard living, and that if they took to the luxury of the Persian or Constantinople Courts, the Arabs would be corrupted and would fall.

Even in these short dozen years, during which Abu Bakr and Omar ruled, the Arabs defeated both the Eastern Roman Empire and the Sassanid King of Persia. Jerusalem, the holy city of the Jews and Christians, was occupied by the Arabs, and the whole of Syria and Iraq and Persia became part of the new Arabian Empire.

49

THE ARABS CONQUER FROM SPAIN TO MONGOLIA

May 23, 1932

LIKE the founders of some other religions, Mohammad was a rebel against many of the existing social customs. The religion he preached, by its simplicity and directness and its flavour of democracy and equality, appealed to the masses in the neighbouring countries who had been ground down long enough by autocratic kings and equally autocratic and domineering priests. They were tired of the old order and were ripe for a change. Islam offered them this change, and it was a welcome change, for it bettered them in many ways and put an end to many old abuses. Islam did not bring any great social revolution in its train which might have put an end to a large extent to the exploitation of the masses. But it did lessen this exploitation so far as the Muslims were concerned, and made them feel that they belonged to one great brotherhood.

So the Arabs marched from conquest to conquest. Often enough they won without fighting. Within twenty-five years of the death of their Prophet, the Arabs conquered the whole of Persia and Syria and Armenia and a bit of Central Asia on the one side; and Egypt and a bit of northern Africa on the west. Egypt had fallen to them with the greatest ease, as Egypt had suffered most from the exploitation of the Roman Empire and from the rivalry of Christian sects. There is a story that the Arabs burnt the famous library of Alexandria, but this is now believed to be false. The Arabs were too fond of books to behave in this barbarous manner. It is probable, however, that the Emperor Theodosius of Constantinople, about whom I have told you something already, was guilty of this destruction, or part of it. A part of the library had been destroyed long before, during a siege at the time of Julius Cæsar. Theodosius did not approve of old pagan Greek books dealing with the old Greek mythologies and philosophies. He was much too devout a Christian. It is said that he used these books as fuel with which to heat his baths.

The Arabs went on advancing both in the east and the west. In the east, Herat and Kabul and Balkh fell, and they reached the Indus river and Sindh. But beyond this they did not go into

India, and for several hundred years their relations with the Indian
rulers were of the friendliest. In the west they marched on and on.
It is said that their general Okba went right across northern Africa
till he reached the Atlantic Ocean, on the western coast of what is
now known as Morocco. He was rather disappointed at this obstacle,
and he rode as far as he could into the sea and then expressed his
sorrow to the Almighty that there was no more land in that direction
for him to conquer in His name !

From Morocco and Africa, the Arabs crossed the narrow sea into
Spain and Europe—the Pillars of Hercules, as these narrow straits
were called by the old Greeks. The Arab general who crossed into
Europe landed at Gibraltar, and this name itself is a reminder of
him. His name was Tariq, and Gibraltar is really Jabal-ut-Tariq,
the rock of Tariq.

Spain was conquered rapidly, and the Arabs then poured into
southern France. So, in about 100 years from the death of Mohammad, the Arab Empire spread from the south of France and Spain
right across northern Africa to Suez, and across Arabia and Persia
and Central Asia to the borders of Mongolia. India was out of it
except for Sindh. Europe was being attacked by the Arabs from
two sides—directly at Constantinople, and in France, *via* Africa.
The Arabs in the south of France were small in numbers and they
were very far from their homeland. Thus they could not get much
help from Arabia, which was busy then conquering Central Asia. But
still these Arabs in France frightened the people of western Europe,
and a great coalition was formed to fight them. Charles Martel
was the leader of this coalition and in 732 A.C. he defeated them at
the battle of Tours in France. This defeat saved Europe from the
Arabs. " On the plains of Tours," a historian has said, " the
Arabs lost the empire of the world when almost in their grasp."
There can be no doubt that if the Arabs had won at Tours, European
history would have been tremendously changed. There was no
one else to stop them in Europe and they could have marched right
across to Constantinople and put an end to the Eastern Roman
Empire and the other States on the way. Instead of Christianity,
Islam would then have become the religion of Europe, and all manner
of other changes might have taken place. But this is just a flight
of imagination. As it happened, the Arabs were stopped in France.
For many hundreds of years afterwards, however, they remained
and ruled in Spain.

From Spain to Mongolia the Arabs triumphed, and these nomads
from the deserts became the proud rulers of a mighty empire.
Saracens they were called, perhaps from *Sahrā* and *nashīn*—the
dwellers of the desert. But the dwellers of the desert took soon
enough to luxury and city life, and palaces grew up in their cities.
In spite of their triumphs in distant countries, they could not get
rid of their old habit of quarrelling amongst themselves. Of course,
there was something worth quarrelling about now, for the headship
of Arabia meant the control of a great empire. So there were
frequent quarrels for the place of the Khalifa. There were petty

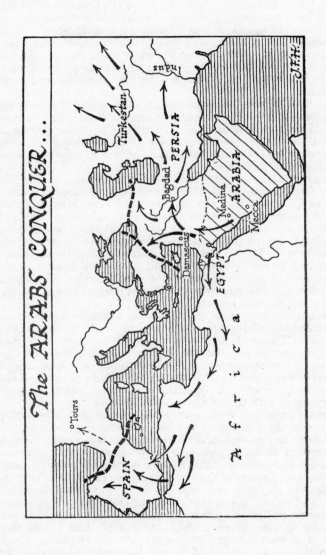

quarrels, family quarrels, leading to civil war. These quarrels resulted in a big division in Islam and two sects were formed—the Sunnis and Shiahs—which still exist.

Trouble came soon after the régimes of the first two great Khalifas —Abu Bakr and Omar. Ali, the husband of Fatima, who was the daughter of Mohammad, was Khalifa for a short while. But there was continuous conflict. Ali was murdered, and some time later his son Hussain, with his family, were massacred on the plain of Karbala. It is this tragedy of Karbala that is mourned year after year in the month of Moharram by the Muslims, and especially the Shiahs.

The Khalifa now becomes an absolute king. There is nothing of democracy or election left about him. He was just like any other absolute monarch of his day. In theory he continued to be the religious head also, the Commander of the Faithful. But some of these rulers actually insulted Islam, of which they were supposed to be the chief protectors.

For about 100 years the Khalifas belonged to a branch of Mohammad's family, known as the Ommeyades. Damascus was made their capital, and this old city became very beautiful, with its palaces, mosques, fountains and kiosks. The water-supply of Damascus was famous. During this period the Arabs developed a special style of architecture which has come to be known as Saracenic architecture. There is not much of ornamentation in this. It is simple and imposing and beautiful. The idea behind this architecture was the graceful palm of Arabia and Syria. The arches and the pillars and the minarets and domes remind one of the arching and doming of palm groves.

This architecture came to India also, but here it was influenced by Indian ideas and a mixed style was evolved. Some of the finest examples of Saracenic architecture are still in Spain.

Wealth and empire brought luxury and the games and arts of luxury. Horse-racing was a favourite amusement of the Arabs, so also were polo and hunting and chess. There was quite a fashionable craze for music and especially for singing, and the capital was full of singers with their trains and hangers-on.

Another great but very unfortunate change gradually took place. This was in the position of women. Among the Arabs women did not observe any *purdah*. They were not secluded and hidden away. They moved about in public, went to mosques and lectures, and even delivered lectures. But success made the Arabs imitate more and more the customs of the two old empires on either side of them— the Eastern Roman and the Persian. They had defeated the former and put an end to the latter, but they themselves succumbed to many an evil habit of these empires. It is said that it was due especially to the influence of Constantinople and Persia that the seclusion of women began among the Arabs. Gradually the *harem* system begins, and men and women meet each other less and less socially. Unhappily this seclusion of women became a feature of Islamic society, and India also learnt it from them when the Muslims came here. It amazes me to think that some people put up with this barbarity still. Whenever I think of the women in *purdah*, cut off from the outside world, I invariably think of a prison or a zoo ! How can a nation go ahead if half of its population is kept hidden away in a kind of prison ?

Fortunately, India is rapidly tearing the *purdah* away. Even Muslim society has largely rid itself of this terrible burden. In Turkey, Kamal Pasha has put an end to it completely, and in Egypt it is going fast.

One thing more and I shall finish this letter. The Arabs, especially at the beginning of their awakening, were full of enthusiasm for their faith. Yet they were a tolerant people and there are numerous instances of this toleration in religion. In Jerusalem the Khalifa Omar made a point of it. In Spain there was a large Christian population which had the fullest liberty of conscience. In India the Arabs never ruled except in Sindh, but there were frequent contacts, and the relations were friendly. Indeed, the most noticeable thing about this period of history is the contrast between the toleration of the Muslim Arab and the intolerance of the Christian in Europe.

50

BAGHDAD AND HARUNAL-RASHID

May 27, 1932

LET us continue the story of the Arabs before reverting to other countries.

For nearly 100 years, as I told you in my last letter, the Caliphs belonged to the Ommeyade branch of the Prophet Mohammad's family. They ruled from Damascus, and during their rule the Muslim Arabs carried the standard of Islam far and wide. While the Arabs conquered in distant lands, they quarrelled at home and there was frequent civil war. Ultimately the Ommeyades were overthrown by another branch of Mohammad's family, descended from his uncle Abbas, and hence called the Abbasides. The Abbasides came as avengers of the cruelties of the Ommeyades, but they excelled them in cruelty and massacre after their victory was won. They hunted out all the Ommeyades they could find and killed them in a barbarous way.

This was the beginning in 750 A.C. of the long reign of the Abbaside Caliphs. It was not a very happy or auspicious beginning, and yet the Abbaside period is a bright enough period in Arab history. But there were great changes now from the days of the Ommeyades. The civil war in Arabia shook up the whole of the Arab Empire. The Abbasides won at home, but in far Spain the Arab Governor was an Ommeyade, and he refused to recognize the Abbaside Caliph. North Africa, or the viceroyalty of Ifrikia as it was called, also became more or less independent soon afterwards. And Egypt did likewise, and indeed went so far to proclaim another Caliph. Egypt was near enough to be threatened and forced to submit, and this was done from time to time. But Ifrikia was not interfered with, and as for Spain, it was much too far away for any action. So we see that the Arab Empire split up on the accession of the Abbasides. The Caliph was no longer the head of the whole Muslim world, he was not now the Commander of all the Faithful. Islam was no longer united, and the Arabs in Spain and the Abbasides disliked each other so much that each often welcomed the misfortunes of the other.

In spite of all this, the Abbaside Caliphs were great sovereigns and their empire was a great empire, as empires go. The old faith and energy which conquered mountains and spread like a prairie fire were no more in evidence. There was no simplicity and little of democracy left, and the Commander of the Faithful was little different from the Persian King of kings, who had been defeated by the earlier Arabs, or the Emperor at Constantinople. In the Arabs of the time of Mohammad the Prophet, there was a strange life and strength which were very different from the strength of kings' armies. They stood out in the world of their time, and armies and princes crumpled up before their irresistible march. The masses were weary of these princes, and the Arabs seemed to bring to them the promise of change for the better and of social revolution.

All this was changed now. The men of the desert lived in palaces now, and instead of dates had the most gorgeous foods. They were comfortable enough, so why should they bother about change and social revolution? They tried to rival the old empires in splendour and they adopted many an evil custom of theirs. One of these, as I told you, was the seclusion of women.

The capital now went from Damascus to Baghdad in Iraq. This change of capital itself was significant, for Baghdad used to be the summer retreat of the Persian kings. And as Baghdad was farther away from Europe than Damascus, henceforth the Abbasides looked more towards Asia than to Europe. There were to be still many attempts to capture Constantinople, and there were many wars with European nations, but most of these wars were defensive. The days of conquest seem to have ended, and the Abbaside Caliphs tried to consolidate such of the empire as was left to them. This was great enough even without Spain and Africa.

Baghdad! Do you not remember it? And Harunal-Rashid and Shaherazade and the wonderful stories contained in the *Arabian Nights*? The city that now grew up under the Abbaside Caliphs was the city of the *Arabian Nights*. It was a vast city of palaces and public offices and schools and colleges, and great shops, and parks and gardens. The merchants carried on a vast trade with the East and West. Crowds of Government officials kept in continuous touch with the distant parts of the Empire, and the government, becoming more and more complicated, was divided up into many departments. An efficient postal system connected all the corners of the Empire to the capital. Hospitals abounded. Visitors came to Baghdad from all over the world, especially learned men and students and artists, for it was known that the Caliph welcomed all who were learned or who were skilful in the arts.

The Caliph himself lived in great luxury surrounded by slaves, and his women-folk had taken to the *harem*. The Abbaside Empire was at the height of its outward glory during the reign of Harunal-Rashid from 786 to 809 A.C. Embassies came to Harun from the Emperor of China and Emperor Charlemagne in the West. Baghdad and the Abbaside dominions were far in advance of the Europe of those days, except for Arab Spain, in all the arts of government, in trade, and in the development of learning.

The Abbaside period is especially interesting for us because of the new interest in science which it started. Science, as you know, is a very big thing in the modern world, and we owe a great deal to it. Science does not simply sit down and pray for things to happen, but seeks to find out why things happen. It experiments and tries again and again, and sometimes fails and sometimes succeeds—and so bit by bit it adds to human knowledge. This modern world of ours is very different from the ancient world or the Middle Ages. This great difference is largely due to science, for the modern world has been made by science.

Among the ancients we do not find the scientific method in Egypt or China or India. We find just a bit of it in old Greece. In Rome again it was absent. But the Arabs had this scientific spirit of inquiry, and so they may be considered the fathers of modern science. In some subjects, like medicine and mathematics, they learnt much from India. Indian scholars and mathematicians came in large numbers to Baghdad. Many Arab students went to Takshashila in North India, which was still a great university, specializing in medicine. Sanskrit books on medical and other subjects were especially translated into Arabic. Many things—for example, paper-making—the Arabs learnt from China. But on the basis of the knowledge gained from others they made their own researches and made several important discoveries. They made the first telescope and the mariner's compass. In medicine, Arab physicians and surgeons were famous all over Europe.

Baghdad was, of course, the great centre of all these intellectual activities. In the West, Cordoba, the capital of Arab Spain, was another centre. There were many other university centres in the Arab world, where the life of the intellect flourished—there was Cairo or al-Qahira, " the Victorious ", Basra and Kufa. But over all these famous cities towered Baghdad, " the capital of Islam, the eye of Iraq, the seat of empire, the centre of beauty, culture and arts ", as an Arab historian describes it. It had a population of over 2,000,000 and thus was far bigger than modern Calcutta or Bombay.

It may interest you to know that the habit of wearing socks and stockings is said to have begun in Baghdad among the rich. They

were called " mozas ", and the Hindustani word for them must be
derived from this. So also the French " chemise ", which comes
from " kamis ", a shirt. Both the *kamis* and the *moza* went from
the Arabs to the Byzantines in Constantinople and from there to
Europe.

The Arabs had always been great travellers. They continued
their long journeys across the seas and established colonies in Africa,
on the coasts of India, in Malaysia and even in China. One of their
famous travellers was Alberūnī, who came to India and left, like
Hiuen Tsang, a record of his travels.

The Arabs were also historians, and we know a great deal about
them from their own books and histories. And all of us know what
fine stories and romances they could write. Thousands and thousands of people have never heard of the Abbaside Khalifas and of
their empire, but they know of Baghdad of the *Alf Laila wa Laila*,
the " Thousand and one Nights ", the city of mystery and romance.
The empire of the imagination is often more real and more lasting
than the empire of fact.

Soon after the death of Harunal-Rashid trouble came to the
Arab Empire. There were disorders, and different parts of the
empire fell away, the provincial governors becoming hereditary
rulers. The caliphs became more and more powerless, till a time
came when a caliph ruled over the city of Baghdad only and a few
villages around it. A caliph was even dragged out of his palace
by his own soldiery and killed. Then for a while some strong men
rose who ruled from Baghdad and made the caliph a dependant of
theirs.

Meanwhile the unity of Islam was a thing of the distant past.
Separate kingdoms arose everywhere from Egypt to Khorasan in
Central Asia. And from farther east still the nomad tribes moved
west. The old Turks of Central Asia became Muslims and came and
took possession of Baghdad. They are known as the Seljuq Turks.
They defeated the Byzantine army of Constantinople utterly, much
to the surprise of Europe. For Europe had thought that the Arabs
and Muslims had spent their strength and were getting weaker and
weaker. It was true that the Arabs had declined greatly, but the
Seljuq Turks now came on the scene to uphold the banner of Islam
and to challenge Europe with it.

This challenge was soon taken up, as we shall see, and the Christian
nations of Europe organized crusades to fight the Muslims and
reconquer Jerusalem, their holy city. For over 100 years Christianity
and Islam fought for mastery in Syria and Palestine and Asia Minor
and exhausted each other, and soaked every inch of the soil almost
of these countries with human blood. And the flourishing cities
of these parts lost their trade and greatness, and the smiling fields
were often converted into a wilderness.

So they fought each other. But even before their fighting was
over, across Asia in Mongolia there arose Chengiz Khan, the Mongol
Shaker of the Earth, as he was called, who was indeed going to shake
Asia and Europe. He and his descendants finally put an end to

Baghdad and its empire. By the time the Mongols had finished with the great and famous city of Baghdad, it was almost a heap of dust and ashes and most of its 2,000,000 inhabitants were dead. This was in 1258 A.C.

Baghdad is now again a flourishing city and is the capital of the State of Iraq. But it is only a shadow of its former self, for it never recovered from the death and desolation which the Mongols brought.

51

FROM HARSHA TO MAHMUD IN NORTH INDIA

June 1, 1932

WE must interrupt our story of the Arabs or Saracens and have a look at other countries. What was happening in India, in China, and in the countries of Europe, while the Arabs grew in power and conquered and spread and then declined? Some little glimpses we have already had—the defeat of the Arabs at Tours in France in 732 by a joint army under Charles Martel, their conquest of Central Asia, and their coming up to Sindh in India. Let us first turn to India.

Harsha-Vardhana of Kanauj died in 648 A.C., and with his death the political degeneration of North India became more obvious. For some time past this had been going on, and the conflict between Hinduism and Buddhism had helped the process. During Harsha's time there was outwardly a brave show, but for a while only. After him a number of small States grew up in the north, sometimes enjoying a brief glory, sometimes quarrelling with each other. It it curious that even in these 300 years or more after Harsha, art and literature flourished and there were many fine public works constructed. Several famous Sanskrit writers, like Bhavabhuti and Rajasekhara, lived in these times, and several kings, not important politically, were famous for the art and learning which grew under them. One of these rulers—Raja Bhoja—has become almost a mythical type of the model king, and even to-day people refer to him as such.

But in spite of these bright spots the north was declining. South India was again taking the lead and overshadowing the north. I have told you a little of the south in these days in a previous letter (44); of the Chalukyas, and the Chola Empire, and the Pallavas, and the Rashtrakutas. I have also told you of Shankaracharya, who in a short life managed to impress both the learned and the unlearned all over the country, and almost succeeded in putting an end to Buddhism in India. Strange that even as he did so a new religion should knock at the gates of India, and later come in a flood of conquest, to challenge the existing order !

The Arabs reached the borders of India soon enough, even while Harsha was alive. They stopped there for a while and then took possession of Sindh. In 710 A.C. a young boy of seventeen, Mohammad ibn Kasim, commanding an Arab army, conquered the Indus valley up to Multan in western Punjab. This was the full extent of the Arab conquest of India. Perhaps if they had tried hard enough they might have gone farther. It should not have been difficult, as North India was weak. But, although there was plenty of fighting going on between these Arabs and the neighbouring rulers, there was no organized attempt at conquest. Politically, therefore, this Arab conquest of Sindh was not an important affair. The Muslim conquest of India was to come several hundred years later. But culturally the contact of the Arabs with the people of India had great results.

The Arabs had friendly relations with the Indian rulers of the south, especially the Rashtrakutas. Many Arabs settled along the west coast of India and built mosques in their settlements. Arab travellers and traders visited various parts of India. Arab students came in large numbers to the northern University of Takshashila or Taxila, which was especially famous for medicine. It is said that in the days of Harunal-Rashid Indian scholarship had a high place in Baghdad and physicians from India went there to organize hospitals and medical schools. Many Sanskrit books on mathematics and astronomy were translated into Arabic.

Thus the Arabs took much from the old Indo-Aryan culture. They took also much from the Aryan culture of Persia, and also something from Hellenic culture. They were almost like a new race, in the prime of their vigour, and they took advantage of all the old cultures they saw around them, and learnt from them; and on this foundation they built something of their very own—the Saracenic culture. This had a comparatively brief life, as cultures go, but it was a brilliant life, which shines against the dark background of the Middle Ages in Europe.

It is strange to find that while the Arabs profited by their contacts with Indo-Aryan, Persian and Hellenic cultures, the Indians and Persians and Greeks did not profit much by their contacts with the Arabs. Perhaps this was due to the fact that the Arabs were new and full of vigour and enthusiasm, while the others were old races, going along the old ruts, and not caring over-much for change. It is curious how age seems to have the same effect on a people or a race as it has on an individual—it makes them slow of movement, inelastic in mind and body, conservative and afraid of change.

So India was not greatly affected or much changed by this contact with the Arabs, which lasted for some hundreds of years. But during this long period India must have got to know something of the new religion, Islam. Muslim Arabs came and went and built mosques, and sometimes preached their religion, and sometimes even converted people. There seems to have been no objection to this in those days, no trouble or friction between Hinduism and Islam. It is interesting to note this because in later days friction and trouble did arise between the two religions. It was only when in the eleventh century Islam came to India in the guise of a conqueror, sword in hand, that it produced a violent reaction, and the old toleration gave way to hatred and conflict.

This wielder of the sword who came to India with fire and slaughter was Mahmud of Ghazni. Ghazni is now a little town in Afghanistan. Round about Ghazni grew up a State in the tenth century. Nominally the Central Asian States were under the Caliph of Baghdad, but, as I have told you already, after Harunal-Rashid's death the Caliph weakened and a time came when his empire split up into a number of independent States. This is the period of which we are now speaking. A Turkish slave named Subuktagin carved a State for himself around Ghazni and Kandahar about 975 A.C. He raided India also. In those days a man named Jaipal was Raja of Lahore. Very venturesome, Jaipal marched to the Kabul valley against Subuktagin and got defeated.

Mahmud succeeded his father Subuktagin. He was a brilliant general and a fine cavalry leader. Year after year he raided India and sacked and killed and took away with him vast treasure and large numbers of captives. Altogether he made seventeen raids and only one of these—into Kashmir—was a failure. The others were successful, and he became a terror all over the north. He went as far south as Pātaliputra, Mathura and Somnath. From Thaneshwara he took away, it is said, 200,000 captives and vast wealth. But it was in Somnath that he got the most treasure. For this was one of the great temples, and the offerings of centuries had accumulated there. It is said that thousands of people took refuge in the temple when Mahmud approached, in the hope that a miracle would happen and the god they worshipped would protect them. But miracles seldom occur, except in the imaginations of the faithful, and the temple was broken and looted by Mahmud and 50,000 people perished, waiting for the miracle which did not happen.

Mahmud died in 1030 A.C. The whole of the Punjab and Sindh was under his sway at the time. He is looked upon as a great leader of Islam who came to spread Islam in India. Most Muslims adore him; most Hindus hate him. As a matter of fact, he was hardly a religious man. He was a Mohammedan, of course, but that was by the way. Above everything he was soldier, and a brilliant soldier. He came to India to conquer and loot, as soldiers unfortunately do, and he would have done so to whatever religion he might have belonged. It is interesting to find that he threatened the Muslim rulers of Sindh, and only on their submission and payment of tribute did he spare them. He even threatened the Caliph at Baghdad with death and demanded Samarqand from him. We must therefore not fall into the common error of considering Mahmud as anything more than a successful soldier.

Mahmud took large numbers of Indian architects and builders with him to Ghazni and built a fine mosque there which he called the "Celestial Bride". He was very fond of gardens.

Of Mathura, Mahmud has given us a glimpse, which shows us

what a great city it was. Writing to his Governor at Ghazni, Mahmud says : " There are here (at Mathura) a thousand edifices as firm as the faith of the faithful; nor is it likely that this city has attained its present condition but at the expense of many millions of *dinars*, nor could such another be constructed under a period of 200 years."

This description of Mathura by Mahmud we read in an account given by Firdausi. Firdausi was a great Persian poet who lived in Mahmud's time. I remember mentioning his name and the name of his chief work, the *Shāhnāmah*, in one of my letters to you last year. There is a story that the *Shāhnāmah* was written at the request of Mahmud, who promised to pay him a gold *dinar* (a coin) for every couplet of verses. But Firdausi apparently did not believe in conciseness or brevity. He wrote at tremendous length, and when he produced his many thousands of couplets before Mahmud, he was praised for his work, but Mahmud regretted the rash promise of payment he had made. He tried to pay him something much less, and Firdausi was very angry and refused to accept anything.

We have taken a long step from Harsha to Mahmud, and surveyed 350 years and more of Indian history in a few paragraphs. I suppose much could be said of this long period which would be interesting. But I am ignorant of it, and so it is safer for me to preserve a discreet silence. I could tell you something of various kings and rulers who fought each other and sometimes even established large kingdoms in northern India, like the Panchala Kingdom; of the trials of the great city of Kanauj; how it was assailed and captured for a while by the rulers of Kashmir, and then by the King of Bengal, and later still by the Rashtrakutas from the south. But this record would serve little purpose and would only confuse you.

We have now arrived at the end of a long chapter of Indian history, and a new one begins. It is difficult, and often enough wrong, to divide up history into compartments. It is like a flowing river : it goes on and on. Still it changes, and sometimes we can see the end of one phase and the beginning of another. Such changes are not sudden : they shade off into each other. So we reach the end of an act in the unending drama of history, as far as India is concerned. What is called the Hindu period is gradually drawing to a close; the Indo-Aryan culture which had flourished for some thousands of years has to struggle now against a new-comer. But remember that this change was not sudden; it was a slow process. Islam came to the north with Mahmud. The south was not touched by Islamic conquest for a long time to come, and even Bengal was free from it for nearly 200 years more. In the north we find Chittor, which was to be so famous in after-history for its reckless gallantry, becoming a rallying-point for Rajput clans. But surely and inexorably the tide of Muslim conquest spread, and no amount of individual courage could stop it. There can be no doubt that the old Indo-Aryan India was on the decline.

Being unable to check the foreigner and the conqueror, Indo-

Aryan culture adopted a defensive attitude. It retired into a shell in its endeavours to protect itself. It made its caste system, which till then had an element of flexibility in it, more rigid and fixed. It reduced the freedom of its womenfolk. Even the village *panchā-yats* underwent a slow change for the worse. And yet even as it declined before a more vigorous people, it sought to influence them and mould them to its own ways. And such was its power of absorption and assimilation that it succeeded in a measure in bringing about the cultural conquest of its conquerors.

You must remember that the contest was not between the Indo-Aryan civilization and the highly civilized Arab. The contest was between civilized but decadent India and the semi-civilized and occasionally nomadic people from Central Asia who had themselves recently been converted to Islam. Unhappily, India connected Islam with this lack of civilization and with the horrors of Mahmud's raids, and bitterness grew.

52

THE COUNTRIES OF EUROPE TAKE SHAPE

June 3, 1932

SHALL we pay a visit to Europe now, my dear? When we were there last it was in a bad way. The collapse of Rome had meant the collapse of civilization in western Europe. In eastern Europe, except for that part of it which was under the Constantinople Government, conditions were even worse. Attila the Hun had spread fire and destruction over a good part of the continent. But the Eastern Roman Empire, though declining, had endured, and had even shown occasional bursts of energy.

In the West things began to settle down in a new way after the shake-up which the fall of Rome gave. It took a long time to settle down. But one can just make out the new pattern as it develops. Christianity spreads, helped sometimes by its saints and men of peace, sometimes by the sword of its warrior kings. New kingdoms rise up. In France and Belgium and part of Germany the Franks (whom you must not confuse with the French yet) formed a kingdom under a ruler named Clovis, who ruled from 481 to 511 A.O. This is called the Merovingian line, from the name of Clovis's grandfather. But these kings were soon put into the shade by an official of their own Court—the Mayor of the Palace. These mayors became all-powerful and became hereditary mayors. They were the real rulers, the so-called kings were just puppets.

It was one of these Mayors of the Palace, Charles Martel, who defeated the Saracens at the great battle of Tours in France in 732. A.O. By this victory he stopped the Saracen wave of conquest and, in Christian eyes, he saved Europe. His prestige and reputation gained greatly by this. He was looked up to as the champion

of Christendom against the enemy. The Popes of Rome were not
then on good terms with the Constantinople Emperor. So they
began to look up to Charles Martel for help. His son Pepin decided
to call himself king and remove the puppet who was there, and the
Pope of course gladly agreed.

Pepin's son was Charlemagne. The Pope was in trouble again,
and he invited Charlemagne to come to his rescue. Charles did so
and drove away his enemies, and on Christmas day 800 A.C. there was
a great ceremony in the Cathedral when the Pope crowned Charlemagne Roman Emperor. From that day began the Holy Roman
Empire of which I wrote to you once before.

It was a strange empire and its later history is stranger still, as it
vanishes gradually, like the Cheshire cat in *Alice*, leaving just the
smile behind with no trace of body. But this was yet to come, and
we need not pry into the future.

This Holy Roman Empire was not a continuation of the old
Western Roman Empire. It was something different. It considered itself *the* Empire, the Emperor being boss over everybody else
in the world—except perhaps the Pope. Between the Emperor and
Pope there was for many centuries a contest as to who was the
greater. But this also was to come later. What is interesting to
note is that this new empire was supposed to be a revival of the old
Roman Empire, when this was supreme, and Rome was said to be
the mistress of the world. But to this was added a new idea—that
of Christianity and Christendom. Hence the Empire was " holy ".
The Emperor was supposed to be a kind of Viceroy of God on earth,
and so was the Pope. One dealt with political matters, the other
with spiritual. This was the idea, at any rate, and it was from this, I
suppose, that the idea of the Divine right of kings arose in Europe.
The Emperor was the Defender of the Faith. You will be interested
to know that the English King is still styled the Defender of the
Faith.

Compare this emperor with the Khalifa or Caliph, who was
styled the Commander of the Faithful. The Khalifa was really an
emperor and Pope combined, to begin with. Later, as we shall see,
he became just a figurehead.

The Constantinople emperors, of course, did not at all approve
of this newly-arisen " Holy Roman Empire " in the west. At the
time that Charlemagne was crowned, a woman, Irene, had made
herself Empress at Constantinople. She was the creature who killed
her own son to become Empress, and things were in a bad way in
her time. This was one of the reasons which emboldened the Pope
to break away from Constantinople by crowning Charlemagne.

Charlemagne was now the head of Western Christendom, the
Viceroy of God on earth, the Emperor of a holy empire. How
pompous these phrases sound ! But they serve their purpose by
deluding and hypnotizing the people. By calling God and religion
to its help, authority has often enough sought to fool others and
increase its own power. The king and the emperor and the high
priest become, for the average person, vague and shadowy beings,

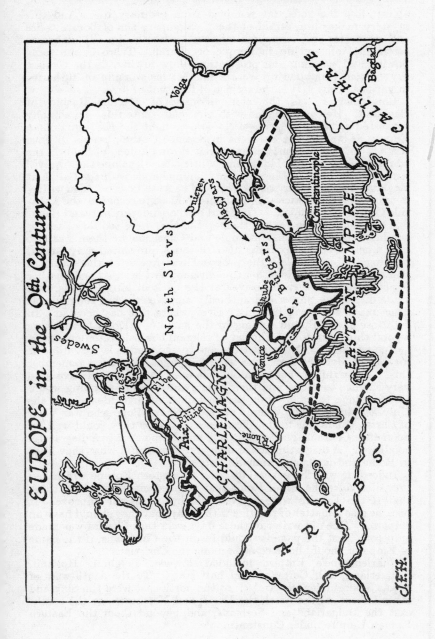

almost like the gods, far removed from ordinary life. And this mystery makes him afraid of them. Compare the elaborate codes and etiquettes and ceremonial of courts with the equally elaborate ceremonial of worship in temple or church. There is the same bowing and scraping and prostration—kow-towing, as the Chinese say. From childhood up we are taught this worship of authority in various forms. It is the service of fear, not of love.

Charlemagne was the contemporary of Harunal-Rashid of Baghdad. He corresponded with him, and—note this—he actually suggested an alliance between the two to fight the Eastern Roman Empire as well as the Saracens in Spain. Nothing seems to have come of this suggestion, but even so it throws a flood of light on the working of the minds of kings and politicians. Imagine the " holy " Emperor, the head of Christendom, joining hands with the Caliph at Baghdad against a Christian Power and an Arab Power. You will remember that the Saracens of Spain had refused to recognize the Abbaside Caliphs of Baghdad. They had become independent, and Baghdad had a grievance against them. But they were too far apart for conflict. Between Constantinople and Charlemagne there was also not much love lost. Here also distance prevented any actual fighting. None the less the proposal was made for the Christian and the Arab to join together to fight another Christian and another Arab Power. The real motives at the back of kings' minds were those of gaining power and authority and wealth, but religion was often made the cloak for this. Everywhere this has been so. In India we saw Mahmud coming in the name of religion but making a good thing out of it. The cry of religion has paid often enough.

But people's ideas change from age to age, and it is very difficult for us to judge of others who lived long ago. We must remember this. Many things that seem obvious to us to-day would have been very strange to them, and their habits and ways of thinking would seem strange to us. While people talked of high ideals, and the Holy Empire, and the Viceroy of God, and the Pope who was Vicar of Christ, conditions in the West were as bad as they could well be. Soon after Charlemagne's reign Italy and Rome were in a disgraceful condition. A disgusting lot of men and women did what they liked in Rome and made and unmade Popes.

Indeed, it was the general disorder in western Europe which had prevailed since the fall of Rome that induced many people to think that if the Empire were revived, conditions would improve. It became also a matter of prestige with many that they should have an emperor. One old writer of those days says that Charles was made emperor " lest the pagans should insult the Christians, if the name of Emperor should have ceased among the Christians ".

Charlemagne's Empire included France, Belgium, Holland, Switzerland, half Germany and half Italy. To the south-west of it was Spain under the Arabs; to the north-east were the Slav and other tribes; to the north the Danes and Northmen, to the south-east the Bulgarians and Serbians, and beyond them the Eastern Roman Empire under Constantinople.

Charlemagne died in 814, and soon afterwards troubles arose for a division of the spoils of empire. His descendants, who are called the Carlovingians (Carolus, the Latin for Charles), were not up to much, as can be gathered from the titles of some of them : the Fat, the Bald, the Pious. From the division of Charlemagne's Empire we now see Germany and France shaping themselves. Germany is supposed to date as a nation from 843 A.C., and it is said that it was the Emperor Otto the Great, who reigned from 962 to 973, who made the Germans more or less a single people. France was already no part of Otto's Empire. In 987 Hugh Capet drove away the feeble Carlovingian kings and obtained control of France. This was not much in the way of control, as France was divided up into big areas under independent nobles, and they often fought each other. But they feared the Emperor and Pope more than each other and united to resist them. With Hugh Capet France begins as a nation, and even in these early beginnings we can see the rivalry between France and Germany, which has endured for 1000 years, right up to our day. Strange that two neighbouring countries and peoples so cultured and highly endowed as the French and the Germans should go on nursing this ancient feud from generation to generation. But perhaps the fault is not so much theirs as that of the systems under which they have lived.

About this time Russia also comes upon the stage in history. Rurik, a man from the north, is said to have laid the foundations of the Russian State about 850 A.C. In the south-east of Europe we find the Bulgarians settling down, and indeed becoming rather aggressive; also the Serbians. The Magyars or Hungarians and the Poles also begin to form States between the Holy Roman Empire and the new Russia.

Meanwhile, from northern Europe men came down in ships to the western and southern countries and burned and killed and looted. You have read of the Danes and other Northmen who went to England to harry and sack. These Northmen or Norsemen or Normans, as they came to be called, went to the Mediterranean, sailed up the big rivers in their ships, and wherever they went they robbed and killed and looted. There was anarchy in Italy, and Rome was in a deplorable condition. They sacked Rome, and threatened even Constantinople. These robbers and plunderers seized the north-west of France, where Normandy is, and South Italy and Sicily, and gradually settled down there and became lords and landowners, as robbers often do when they are prosperous. It was these Normans from Normandy in France that went and conquered England in 1066 A.C. under William, known as the Conqueror. So we see England also taking shape.

We have now arrived roughly at the end of the first millennium or 1000 years of the Christian era in Europe. About this time Mahmud of Ghazni was raiding India, and about this time the Abbaside Caliphs of Baghdad were breaking up and the Seljuq Turks were reviving Islam in western Asia. Spain continued to be under the Arabs, but they were cut off completely from their home-lands in Arabia, and indeed were not on good terms with the Baghdad rulers. North Africa was practically independent of Baghdad. In Egypt there was not only an independent govern- ment, but a separate caliphate, and for some time the Egyptian Caliph ruled over North Africa also.

53

THE FEUDAL SYSTEM

June 4, 1932

IN our last letter we had a glimpse of the beginnings of France and Germany and Russia and England, as we know them to-day. But do not imagine that people in those days thought of these countries in the same way as we do now. We think of different nations, of Englishmen and Frenchmen and Germans, and each one of these thinks of his country as his motherland or fatherland or *patrie*. This is the feeling of nationality which is so obvious in the world to-day. Our struggle for freedom in India is our " national " struggle. But this idea of nationality did not exist in those days. There was some idea of Christendom, of belonging to a group or society of Christians as against the heathen or Muslims. In the same way the Muslims had the idea of belonging to the world of Islam as against all others who were unbelievers.

But these ideas of Christendom and Islam were vague notions which did not touch the daily life of the people. Only on special occasions were they worked up to fill the people with religious zeal to fight for Christianity or Islam, as the case might be. Instead of nationality there was a peculiar relation between man and man. This was the feudal relation arising out of what is known as the Feudal System. After the downfall of Rome the old order in the West had collapsed. There was disorder and anarchy and violence and force everywhere. The strong seized what they could and held on to it as long as a stronger person did not come to throw them out. Strong castles were built and the lords of these castles went out with raiding-parties and harried the countryside, and sometimes fought others like themselves. The poor peasants and workers on the land of course suffered the most. Out of this disorder grew up the feudal system.

The peasants were not organized, and could not defend themselves against these robber-barons. There was no central government strong enough to protect them. So they made the best of a bad job and came to terms with the lord of the castle who plundered them. They agreed to give him part of what they produced in their fields and also to serve him in some ways, provided that he would not plunder and harass them and would protect them from others of his kind. The lord of the small castle in the same way came to terms with the lord of the bigger castle. But the little lord could not give the big lord the produce of the field, as he was not a peasant or a producer. So he promised to give him military service—that is, to fight for him whenever need arose. In return the big one was to protect the little one, and the latter was the vassal of the lord. And so, step by step, they went up to yet bigger lords and nobles, till at last they arrived at the king at the top of this feudal structure. But they did not stop even there. To them even heaven had its own bit of the feudal system with its Trinity, presided over by God !

This was the system that grew up gradually out of the disorder that prevailed in Europe. You must remember that there was practically no central government at the time; there were no policemen or the like. The owner of a piece of land was the governor and lord of it as well as of all the people who lived upon it. He was a kind of little king and was supposed to protect them in return for their service and part of the produce of their fields. He was the liege-lord of these people, who were called villeins or serfs. In theory, he held his land from his superior lord, whose vassal he was and to whom he gave military service.

Even the officials of the Church were parts of the feudal system. They were both priests and feudal lords. Thus, in Germany nearly half the land and wealth was in the hands of the bishops and abbots. The Pope was himself a feudal lord.

This whole system, you will notice, was one of gradations and classes. There was no question of equality. At the bottom were the villeins or serfs, and they had to carry the whole weight of the social structure—the little lords and the big lords, and the bigger lords and the king. And the whole cost of the Church—of the bishops and abbots and cardinals and ordinary priests—fell on them also. The lords, little or big, did not do any work which might produce food or any other kind of wealth. This was considered beneath them. Fighting was their chief occupation, and when not engaged in this, they hunted or indulged in mock-fights and tournaments. They were a rough and illiterate lot who did not know many ways of amusing themselves besides fighting and eating and drinking. Thus the whole burden of producing the food and the other necessaries of life fell on the peasants and the artisans. At the top of the whole system was the king, who was supposed to be a kind of vassal of God.

This was the idea behind this feudal system. In theory the lords were bound to protect their vassals and serfs, but in practice they were a law unto themselves. Their superiors or the king seldom checked them, and the peasantry were too weak to resist their demands. Being far the stronger, they took from their serfs the utmost they could and left them barely enough to carry on a miserable existence. That has been the way of owners of land always and in every country. The ownership of land has given nobility. The robber knight who seized land and built a castle became a noble lord respected by everybody. This ownership has also given power, and the owner has used this power to take away as much from the

peasant and the producer or the worker as he could.   Even the laws
have helped the owners of land, for the laws have been made by them
and their friends.   And this is the reason why many people think
that land should not belong to individuals, but to the community.
If it belongs to the State or community, that means that it belongs
to all who live there, and no one can then exploit others on it, or get
an unfair advantage.

   But these ideas were yet to come.   During the time of which we
are speaking people did not think along these lines.   The masses
of the people were miserable, but they saw no way out of their
difficulties.   They put up with them, therefore, and carried on their
life of hopeless labour.   The habit of obedience had been dinned
into them, and once this is done, people will put up with almost
anything.   So we find a society growing up consisting of the feudal
lords and their retainers on the one side and the very poor on the
other.   Round the stone castle of the lord would cluster the mud or
wooden huts of the serfs.   There were two worlds, far removed from
each other—the world of the lord, and the world of the serf; and
the lord probably considered the serf as only some degrees removed
from the cattle he tended.

   Sometimes the smaller priests tried to protect the serfs from their
lords.   But as a rule the priests and clergy sided with the lords, and
as a matter of fact the bishops and abbots were themselves feudal
lords.

   In India we have not had this kind of feudal system, but we have
had something similar to it.   Indeed, our Indian States, with their
rulers and nobles and lordlings, still preserve many feudal customs.
The Indian caste system, though wholly different from the feudal
system, yet divided society into classes.   In China, as I think I
have told you, there has never been any autocracy or privileged
class of this kind.   By their ancient system of examinations they
opened the gate to the highest office to each individual.   But of
course in practice there may have been many restrictions.

   In the feudal system there was thus no idea of equality or of
freedom.   There was an idea of rights and obligations—that is, a
feudal lord received as his right service and part of the produce of
the land; and considered it as his obligation to give protection.
But rights are always remembered and obligations are often ignored.
We have even now great landowners in some European countries
and in India who take enormous sums as rent from their tenants,
without doing a scrap of work, but all idea of any obligation has
long been forgotten.

   It is strange to notice how the old barbarian tribes of Europe who
were so fond of their freedom gradually resigned themselves to this
feudal system which denied it completely.   These tribes used to
elect their chiefs and to hold them in check.   Now we find despotism
and autocracy everywhere and no question of election.   I cannot
say why this change occurred.   It may be that the doctrines spread
by the Church helped the spread of undemocratic ideas.   The king
became the shadow of God on earth, and how can you disobey or

argue with even the shadow of the Almighty? The feudal system seemed to include heaven and earth in its fold.

In India also we find the old Aryan ideas of freedom gradually changing. They become weaker and weaker till they are almost forgotten. But in the early Middle Ages, as I showed you, they were still remembered to some extent, as the *Nitisāra* of Shukrācharya and the South Indian inscriptions tell us.

Some freedom slowly came to Europe again through the new forms that were rising up. Besides the owners of land and those who worked on it, the lords and their serfs, there were other classes of people—artisans and traders. These people, as such, were not part of the feudal system. In the period of disorder there was little enough trade, and handicrafts did not flourish. But gradually trade increased and the importance of mastercraftsmen and merchants grew. They became wealthy, and the lords and barons went to them to borrow money. They lent the money, but they insisted on the lords allowing them certain privileges. These privileges added to their strength. So we find now, instead of the serfs' huts clustering round the lord's castle, little towns growing up with houses all round a cathedral or church or guild-hall. The merchants and artisans formed guilds or associations, and the headquarters of these associations became the guild-halls which later became the town-halls.

These cities that were growing up—Cologne and Frankfurt and Hamburg and many others—became rivals of the power of the feudal lords. A new class was growing up in them, the merchant and trading class, which was wealthy enough to defy even the nobles. It was a long struggle, and often the king, afraid of the power of his own nobles and barons, sided with the cities. But I am going too far ahead.

I began this letter by telling you that there was no feeling of nationality in those days. People thought of their duty and allegiance to their superior lord. They had taken the oath to serve him, not the country. Even the king was a vague person, too far away. If the lord rebelled against the king, that was his look-out. His vassals had to follow him. This was very different from the idea of nationality which was to come much later.

54

CHINA PUSHES THE NOMADS TO THE WEST

June 5, 1932

I HAVE not written to you about China and the Far Eastern countries for a long time—nearly a month, I think. We have discussed many changes in Europe and India and western Asia; we have watched the Arabs spread out and conquer many lands, and Europe fall back into darkness and struggle to come out of it. All this time China was, of course, carrying on and, as a rule, carrying on rather well.   In the seventh and eighth centuries, China under the Tang emperors was probably the most civilized and prosperous and the best governed country in the world.   Europe, of course, could not be compared with it, as it was very backward after the collapse of Rome.   North India was at a low ebb for most of the time.   She had her bright periods, as when Harsha ruled, but on the whole she was going downhill.   South India was certainly more vigorous than the north; and across the seas her colonies, Angkor and Sri Vijaya, were on the eve of a great period.   The only States that could rival China during this period in some respects were the two Arab States of Baghdad and Spain.   But even these were at the height of their glory for a comparatively short period.   It is interesting to note, however, that a Tang Emperor, who had been driven away from his throne, appealed to the Arabs for help, and it is was through their help that he regained power.

So China was well in the van of civilization in those days, and could with some justification regard the Europeans of the time as a set of semi-barbarians.   In the known world she was supreme.   I say the known world because I do not know what was happening then in America.   This we know, that both in Mexico and in Peru and the neighbouring countries civilizations had been existing for several hundred years.   In some respects they were remarkably advanced;   in other respects they appear to have been just as remarkably backward.   But I know so little about them that I dare not say much.   I should like you, however, to keep them in mind— the Maya civilization of Mexico and Central America, and the Peruvian State of the Incas.   Others, wiser than I am, may tell you something worth while about them.   I must confess that they fascinate me, but my fascination is only equalled by my ignorance of them.

Another matter I should like you to remember.   We have seen in the course of our letters that many nomadic tribes have appeared in Central Asia and gone west to Europe or descended on India. The Huns, the Scythians, the Turks, and many others have gone, one after another, in wave after wave.   You will remember the White Huns who came to India and Attila's Huns in Europe.   The Seljuq Turks who took possession of the Baghdad Empire also came from Central Asia.   Later another branch of the Turks—the Otto- man Turks—were to come and finally conquer Constantinople and go right up to the walls of Vienna.   Out of Central Asia or Mongolia also were to come the terrible Mongols who conquered right up to the heart of Europe, and even brought China under their rule; and one of whose descendants was to found a dynasty and an empire in India which was to produce some famous rulers.

With these nomadic tribes of Central Asia and Mongolia, China waged ceaseless war.   Or perhaps it would be more correct to say that these nomads were almost always giving trouble to China, and China was obliged to defend itself.   It was to protect itself against these that the Great Wall was built.   It did some good, no doubt, but it was poor enough protection against raids. Emperor after emperor had to drive back the nomads, and it was in this process of driving back that the Empire of China spread far into the west, right up to the Caspian Sea, as I have told you. The Chinese people were not given over-much to imperialism. Some of their emperors were certainly imperialists and ambitious of conquest. But compared to many other peoples, they were peace-loving and not fond of war and conquest. The learned man in China has always had more honour and glory than the warrior. If in spite of this the Chinese Empire became very extensive at times, it was largely due to irritation against the continuous pin-pricks and raids of the nomads to the north and west. The strong emperors drove them far to the west to get rid of them once for all. They did not solve the question for ever, but they got some relief at least.

But the relief the people of China got was at the expense of other peoples and countries. For the nomads who were driven out by the Chinese went and attacked other countries. They came to India. They went to Europe again and again. The drives of the Han Emperors of China gave other countries the Huns and the Tartars and other nomads; the Tangs presented the Turks to Europe.

So far the Chinese had succeeded to a large extent in defending themselves from these nomadic tribes. We shall now come to a period when they were not so successful.

The Tang dynasty, as always happens with these dynasties everywhere, gradually tapered off into a number of incompetent rulers, who had none of the strong points of their predecessors, but only their love of luxury. Corruption spread in the State, and this was accompanied by heavy taxation, which of course fell mostly on the poorer classes. Discontent increased, and at the beginning of the tenth century, in 907 A.C., the dynasty fell.

For half a century there was a succession of petty and unimportant rulers. In 960 A.C., however, another of China's big dynasties begins. This was the Sung dynasty, founded by Kao-Tsu. But trouble, both at the frontiers and in the interior of China, continued. The heavy land taxes were a great burden on the peasantry and were much resented. As in India, the whole land system was too much of a burden for the people, and there could be no peace or progress till this was completely changed. But it is always difficult to make these root-and-branch changes. The people at the top profit by the existing system and shout a lot when change is proposed. But if the change is not made in time, it has a habit of coming without invitation and of upsetting the whole apple-cart !

The Tang dynasty fell because it did not make the necessary changes. The Sungs had continuous troubles also because of this. One man arose who might have succeeded. He was Wang An-Shih, a prime minister of the Sungs in the eleventh century. China was, as I have told you, a land governed by the ideas of Confucius. All officials had to pass examinations in the Confucian classics, and nobody dared to go against anything that Confucius had said. Wang An-Shih did not go against them, but he interpreted them in a remarkable way. That is a way clever people have of getting round a difficulty. Some of Wang's ideas were remarkably modern. His whole object was to lessen the burden of taxation on the poor and increase it on the rich who could afford to pay. He lowered the land taxes and permitted the peasants to pay them in kind—that is, in grain or other produce—if they found payment in money difficult. On the rich he levied an income-tax. This is supposed to be quite a modern tax, and yet we find it proposed in China 900 years ago. To help the farmers, Wang proposed that the government should lend them money which could be repaid at harvest time. Another difficulty which had to be got over was the rise and fall of the price of grain. When the market price falls, the poor peasants can get very little for the produce of their fields. They cannot sell it, and thus have no money with which to pay taxes or to buy anything. Wang An-Shih tried to face this problem and suggested that the government should buy and sell grain to keep the price from rising and falling.

Wang also proposed that there should be no forced labour for public works, and that every man who worked must be paid his full wage. He also instituted a local militia called the Pao Chia. But Wang was unfortunately too far ahead of his times, and after a while his reforms lapsed. Only the militia continued for more than 800 years.

Not being bold enough to solve the problems that faced them, the Sungs gradually succumbed to them. The northern barbarians, the Khitans, were too much for them. Unable to drive them back, they asked another tribe from the north-west—the Kins or the Golden Tartars—to come to their help. The Kins came and drove out the Khitans, but they stayed themselves and refused to budge ! That is often the fate of a weak person or country seeking aid from a strong one. The Kins made themselves masters of northern China and made Peking their capital. The Sungs retired to the south and went on shrinking before the advancing Kins. Thus there was a Kin Empire in northern China and a Sung Empire in. southern China. These Sungs were called the Southern Sungs. The Sung Dynasty in the north lasted from 960 to 1127 A.C. The Southern Sungs ruled in southern China for 150 years, till the Mongols came and put an end to them in 1260 A.C. But China, as India of old, retaliated by absorbing and assimilating even the Mongols and making them almost typical Chinamen.

So China succumbed at last to the nomad tribes. But even in the process of doing so it civilized them, and so did not suffer from them as other parts of Asia and Europe did.

The Sungs in the north and in the south were not politically as powerful as their predecessors, the Tangs. But they carried on the artistic tradition of the great days of the Tangs, and indeed improved upon it. South China under the Southern Sungs excelled in art and poetry, and beautiful paintings were made, especially of scenes from Nature, for the Sung artists loved Nature. Porcelain also appears, made beautiful by the touch of the artist's fingers. This was to become more and more beautiful and wonderful until 200 years later, under the Ming monarchs, marvellously fine porcelain was produced. A vase of the Ming period in China is even to-day a thing of rare delight.

55

THE SHOGUN RULES IN JAPAN

June 6, 1932

FROM China it is easy to cross the Yellow Sea and visit Japan, and now that we are so near to it we might as well do so. Do you remember our last visit ? We saw the rise of great families fighting for mastery, and a central government coming more and more into evidence. The emperor from being the chief of a big and powerful clan became the head of the central government. Nara, the capital, was established as a symbol of central authority. And then the capital was changed to Kyoto. Chinese methods of government were copied and much was taken from or *via* China—art, religion, politics. Even the name of the country—Dai Nippon—came from China.

We saw also a powerful family—the Fujiwara family—seizing all the power and treating the emperors as puppets. For 200 years they ruled until the emperors got desperate and abdicated and entered monasteries. But in spite of becoming a monk the ex-emperor interfered a great deal in the affairs of government by advising the reigning emperor who was his son. By this method the emperors managed to get round the Fujiwara family to some extent. It was rather a complicated way of doing things, but anyhow it succeeded in reducing the power of the Fujiwaras. The real power lay with the emperors, who abdicated one after the other and became monks. They are called, therefore, the Cloistered Emperors.

Meanwhile, however, other changes took place and a new class of large landholders who were also military men arose. The Fujiwaras had created these landholders and asked them to collect taxes for the government. They were called " Daimyos ", which means " great names ". It is curious to compare this with the rise of a similar class in our province just before the British came. In Oudh, especially, the king who was a weakling appointed tax-collectors. These people kept little armies of their own to help them to collect forcibly, and of course they kept most of the collections for themselves. These tax-collectors in some cases developed into the big *taluqdars*.

The Daimyos became very powerful with their retainers and little armies, and fought each other and ignored the Central Government at Kyoto. The two chief Daimyo families were the Taira and the Minamoto. They helped the Emperor in suppressing the

Fujiwaras in 1156 A.C. But then they attacked each other. The Tairas won, and, perhaps to make sure that the rival family would not trouble them in future, they killed them. They killed all the leading Minamotos except four children, one of these being a twelve-year old boy, Yoritomo. The Taira family, in spite of their attempts, had not been thorough enough. This boy Yoritomo, who was spared as of no great consequence, grew up a bitter enemy of the Taira family, full of the desire for vengeance. He succeeded. He drove them out of the capital, and then smashed them up at a naval battle.

Yoritomo now became all powerful, and the Emperor gave him the high-sounding title of Sei-i-tai-Shogun, which means the Barbarian-subduing-great-general. This was in 1192 A.C. The title was hereditary, and with it went full power to govern. The Shogun was the real ruler. In this way began the Shogunate in Japan. It was to last a very long time, nearly 700 years, almost to recent times, when modern Japan was to rise out of her feudal shell.

But this does not mean that Yoritomo's descendants ruled as Shoguns for 700 years. There were several changes in the families out of which Shoguns came. There was civil war repeatedly, but the system of the Shogun being the real ruler, and governing in the name of an emperor, who had little or no power, continued for this long period. Often it so happened that even the Shogun became a mere figurehead and a number of officials held the power.

Yoritomo was afraid of living in the luxury of the capital, Kyoto, as he felt that soft living would weaken him and his colleagues. So he established his military capital at Kamakura, and this first Shogunate is called therefore the Kamakura Shogunate. It lasted till 1333 A.C., that is, for nearly 150 years. Japan had peace during most of this period. After the many years of civil war the peace was very welcome and there was an era of prosperity. The condition of Japan during this period was certainly much better, and the government was more efficient, than that of any country of contemporary Europe. Japan was an apt pupil of China, although there was a vast difference in the two outlooks. China, as I have said, was an essentially peaceful and quiet country. Japan, on the other hand, was an aggressive military country. In China a soldier was looked down upon and the trade of fighting was not considered very honourable; in Japan the topmost men were soldiers, and the ideal was that of a Daimyo or fighting knight.

So Japan took much from China, but took it in its own way and adapted and moulded everything to suit its racial genius. Intimate contacts with China continued, and so did trade, chiefly on Chinese ships. There was a sudden stop to this towards the end of the thirteenth century, for the Mongols had come to China and Korea. The Mongols even attempted to conquer Japan, but they were repulsed. Thus the Mongols, who changed the face of Asia and shook Europe, had no marked effect on Japan. Japan carried on in her old way, cut off even more than before from external influences.

There is a story in the old official annals of Japan of how the cotton-plant first came to the country. It is said that some Indians who were shipwrecked near the coast of Japan brought the cotton seeds in 799 A.C.

The tea-plant came later. It was first introduced early in the ninth century, but it had no success then. In 1191 a Buddhist monk brought seeds of the tea-plant from China, and very soon tea became popular. This drinking of tea created a demand for fine pottery. Late in the thirteenth century a Japanese potter went to China to study the art of making porcelain. He spent six years there. On his return he started making fine Japanese porcelain. Tea-drinking is now a fine art in Japan and there is an elaborate ceremonial about it. When you go to Japan you must drink it the right way, or you will be considered a bit of a barbarian.

56

THE QUEST OF MAN

June 10, 1932

FOUR days ago I wrote to you from Bareilly Gaol. That very evening I was told to gather up my belongings and to march out of the prison—not to be discharged, but to be transferred to another prison. So I bade good-bye to my companions of the barrack, where I had lived for just four months, and I had a last look at the great twenty-four-foot wall under whose sheltering care I had sat for so long, and I marched out to see the outside world again for a while. There were two of us being transferred. They would not take us to Bareilly station lest people might see us, for we have become *purdahnashins*,[1] and may not be seen! Fifty miles out they drove us by car to a little station in the wilderness. I felt thankful for this drive. It was delightful to feel the cool night air and to see the phantom trees and men and animals rush by in the semi-darkness, after many months of seclusion.

We were brought to Dehra Dun. Early in the morning we were again taken out of our train, before we had reached the end of our journey, and taken by car, lest prying eyes should see us.

And so here I sit in the little gaol of Dehra Dun, and it is better here than at Bareilly. It is not quite so hot, and the temperature does not rise to 112 degrees, as it did in Bareilly. And the walls surrounding us are lower and the trees that overlook them are greener. In the distance I can even see, over our wall, the top of a palm tree, and the sight delights me and makes me think of Ceylon and Malabar. Beyond the trees there lie the mountains, not many miles away, and, perched up on top of them, sits Mussoorie. I cannot see the mountains, for the trees hide them, but it is good to be near them and to imagine at night the lights of Mussoorie twinkling in the far distance.

Four years ago—or is it three?—I began writing these series of letters to you when you were at Mussoorie. What a lot has happened

[1] People who live behind the veil.

during these three or four years, and how you have grown! With
fits and starts and after long gaps I have continued these letters,
mostly from prison. But the more I write the less I like what I
write; and a fear comes upon me that these letters may not interest
you much, and may even become a burden for you. Why, then,
should I continue to write them?

I should have liked to place vivid images of the past before you,
one after another, to make you sense how this world of ours has
changed, step by step, and developed and progressed, and sometimes apparently gone back; to make you see something of the old
civilizations and how they have risen like the tide and then subsided; to make you realize how the river of history has run on from
age to age, continuously, interminably, with its eddies and whirl-
pools and backwaters, and still rushes on to an unknown sea. I
should have liked to take you on man's trail and follow it up from
the early beginnings, when he was hardly a man, to to-day, when
he prides himself so much, rather vainly and foolishly, on his great
civilization. We did begin that way, you will remember, in the
Mussoorie days, when we talked of the discovery of fire and of
agriculture, and the settling down in towns, and the division of
labour. But the farther we have advanced, the more we have got
mixed up with empires and the like, and often we have lost sight of
that trail. We have just skimmed over the surface of history. I
have placed the skeleton of old happenings before you and I have
wished that I had the power to cover it with flesh and blood, to
make it living and vital for you.

But I am afraid I have not got that power, and you must rely
upon your imagination to work the miracle. Why, then, should I
write, when you can read about past history in many good books?
Yet, through my doubts I have continued writing, and I suppose I
shall still continue. I remember the promise I made to you, and
I shall try to fulfil it. But more even than this is the joy that the
thought of you gives me when I sit down to write and imagine that
you are by me and we are talking to each other.

Of man's trail I have written above, since he emerged stumbling
and slouching from the jungle. It has been a long trail of many
thousands of years. And yet how short a time it is if you compare
it to the earth's story and the ages and æons of time before man
came! But for us man is naturally more interesting than all the
great animals that existed before him; he is interesting because he
brought a new thing with him which the others do not seem to have
had. This was mind—curiosity—the desire to find out and learn.
So from the earliest days began man's quest. Observe a little
baby, how it looks at the new and wonderful world about it; how
it begins to recognize things and people; how it learns. Look at a
little girl; if she is a healthy and wide-awake person she will ask so
many questions about so many things. Even so, in the morning of
history when man was young and the world was new and wonderful,
and rather fearsome to him, he must have looked and stared all
around him, and asked questions. Who was he to ask except

himself? There was no one else to answer. But he had a wonderful little thing—a mind—and with the help of this, slowly and painfully, he went on storing his experiences and learning from them. So from the earliest times until to-day man's quest has gone on, and he has found out many things, but many still remain, and as he advances on his trail, he discovers vast new tracts stretching out before him, which show to him how far he is still from the end of his quest—if there is such an end.

What has been this quest of man, and whither does he journey? For thousands of years men have tried to answer these questions. Religion and philosophy and science have all considered them, and given many answers. I shall not trouble you with these answers, for the sufficient reason that I do not know most of them. But, in the main, religion has attempted to give a complete and dogmatic answer, and has often cared little for the mind, but has sought to enforce obedience to its decisions in various ways. Science gives a doubting and hesitating reply, for it is of the nature of science not to dogmatize, but to experiment and reason and rely on the mind of man. I need hardly tell you that my preferences are all for science and the methods of science.

We may not be able to answer these questions about man's quest with any assurance, but we can see that the quest itself has taken two lines. Man has looked outside himself as well as inside; he has tried to understand Nature, and he has also tried to understand himself. The quest is really one and the same, for man is part of Nature. "Know thyself", said the old philosophers of India and Greece; and the *Upanishads* contain the record of the ceaseless and rather wonderful strivings after this knowledge by the old Aryan Indians. The other knowledge of Nature has been the special province of science, and our modern world is witness to the great progress made therein. Science, indeed, is spreading out its wings even farther now, and taking charge of both lines of this quest and co-ordinating them. It is looking up with confidence to the most distant stars, and it tells us also of the wonderful little things in continuous motion—the electrons and protons—of which all matter consists.

The mind of man has carried man a long way in his voyage of discovery. As he has learnt to understand Nature more he has utilized it and harnessed it to his own advantage, and thus he has won more power. But unhappily he has not always known how to use this new power, and he has often misused it. Science itself has been used by him chiefly to supply him with terrible weapons to kill his brother and destroy the very civilization that he has built up with so much labour.

57

THE END OF THE FIRST MILLENNIUM AFTER CHRIST

June 11, 1932

IT may be worth while for us to stop a little at the stage we have reached in our journey and have a look around. How far have we got? Where are we now? And what does the world look like? Let us then take seats on Aladdin's Magic Carpet and pay brief visits to various parts of the world of that day.

We have travelled through the first millennium or 1000 years of the Christian era. In some countries we have gone on a little ahead, and in some we are a little behind this stage.

In Asia, we see China under the Sung dynasty. The great Tang dynasty is over, and the Sungs have to face both domestic trouble and foreign attack from the northern barbarians, the Khitans. For 150 years they hold on, but then they are weak enough to ask for the help of another barbarian tribe, the Golden Tartars or Kins. The Kins come and stay, and the poor Sungs have to shrink away to the south, where, as the Southern Sungs, they carry on for another 150 years. Meanwhile beautiful arts, painting and porcelain-making, flourish.

In Korea, after a period of division and conflict, a united independent kingdom was established in 935 A.C. and this lasted for a long time—about 450 years. Korea takes much of her civilization and art and methods of government from China. Religion and also something of art go to her, as well as to Japan, from India, through China. Japan, situated far to the east, almost like a sentinel of Asia, carries on her existence, more or less cut off from the rest of the world. The Fujiwara family is supreme, and the emperor, who has recently become something more than a clan chief, is kept in the shade. Later comes the Shogun.

In Malaysia the Indian colonies flourish. Angkor the Magnificent is the capital of Cambodia, and this State is at the height of its power and development. In Sumatra, Sri Vijaya is the capital of a great Buddhist Empire which controls all the eastern islands and carries on an extensive trade between them. In Eastern Java there is an independent Hindu State which is soon to grow and, competing with Sri Vijaya for trade and the wealth that trade brings, is to wage bitter war with it, as the modern European nations do for trade, and is ultimately to conquer and destroy it.

In India, north and south are cut off from each other more than they have been for some time. In the north, Mahmud of Ghazni sweeps down again and again and destroys and plunders. He carries away vast wealth and attaches the Punjab to his kingdom. In the south, we find the Chola Empire expanding and gaining in

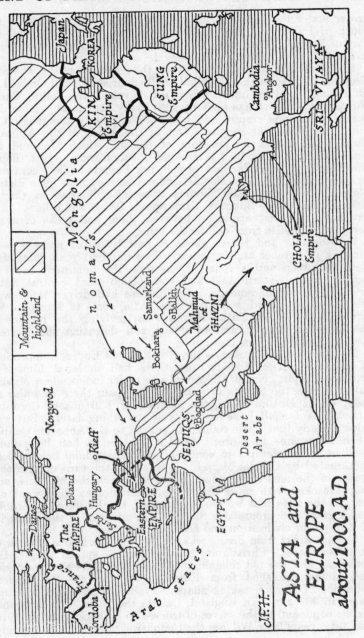

Japan

KOREA

KIN Empire

SUNG Empire

Cambodia
Angkor

SRI VIJAYA

Mongolia

n o m a d s

Samarkand
Bokhara   oBalkh

Mahmud
of
GHAZNI

CHOLA Empire

Mountain &
highland

Novgorod

SELJUCS
Bagdad

Desert
Arabs

Danes

France

The EMPIRE

Poland

Hungary oKief

Serbs

Eastern
EMPIRE

EGYPT

Cordoba

Arab states

ASIA and
EUROPE
about 1000 A.D.

J.F.H.

power under Rajaraja and his son Rajendra. They dominate the
south of India, and their navies sweep the Arabian Sea and the
Bay of Bengal. They carry out aggressive expeditions of conquest
to Ceylon, South Burma and Bengal.

In central and western Asia we see the remnants of the Abbaside
Empire of Baghdad. Baghdad still flourishes, and indeed is
increasing in power under a new set of rulers, the Seljuq Turks.
But the old Empire has split up into many kingdoms. Islam has
ceased to be one empire and has become merely the religion of
many countries and peoples. Out of the wreck of the Abbaside
Empire has arisen the kingdom of Ghazni, which Mahmud has
ruled and from which he has swooped down on India. But though
the Empire of Baghdad has broken up, Baghdad itself continues
to be a great city, attracting artists and learned men from distant
places. Many great and famous cities also flourish in Central
Asia at this time—Bokhara, Samarqand, Balkh and others. And
extensive trade is carried on between them and great caravans
carry merchandise from one to the other.

In Mongolia and round about it new tribes of nomads were
growing in number and in power. Two hundred years later they
were to sweep across Asia. Even now the dominant races in
central and western Asia had come from that central Asian
breeding-ground of nomads. The Chinese had driven them west
and they had spread, some down to India, some to Europe. We
now find the Seljuq Turks, driven west, reviving the fortune of
the Baghdad Empire, and attacking and defeating the Eastern
Roman Empire of Constantinople.

So much for Asia. Across the Red Sea was Egypt, independent
of Baghdad. The Muslim ruler there had declared himself a
separate Caliph. North Africa was also under independent Muslim
rule. Across the Straits of Gibraltar in Spain there was also an
independent Muslim State, the Emirate of Kurtuba or Cordoba.
About this I shall have to tell you something later. But you
know already that Spain refused to submit to the Abbaside Caliphs
when they came to power. Ever since then it had been independent. Its attempts to conquer France had, long before, been
checkmated by Charles Martel. It was now the turn of Christian
States in the northern part of Spain to attack the Muslims, and
they attacked with more and more confidence as time went on.
But, at the time that we are speaking of, the Emirate of Cordoba
was a great and progressive State, far in advance of the countries
of Europe, in civilization and science.

Europe, apart from Spain, was divided up now into a number of
Christian States. Christianity had by this time spread all over the
continent and the old religions of heroes and gods and goddesses
had almost vanished from Europe. We can see the modern
countries of Europe taking shape. France appears under Hugh
Capet in 987 A.C. In England, Canute the Dane, who is famous
for his command to the waves of the sea to go back, ruled in 1016.
and fifty years later William the Conqueror came from Normandy.

Germany was part of the Holy Roman Empire, but it was definitely becoming one country, although it was still divided up into many smaller States. Russia was spreading in the east and often threatening Constantinople with her ships. This was the beginning of the strange fascination for Constantinople which Russia has always felt. She has coveted this great city for 1000 years and hoped at last to get it as the result of the Great War which ended fourteen years ago. But the Revolution came suddenly and upset all the plans of old Russia.

You will also see on the map of Europe of 900 years ago Poland and Hungary, where the Magyars lived, and the kingdoms of the Bulgarians and Serbs. And, of course, you will see the Eastern Roman Empire surrounded by a host of enemies, but still carrying on. The Russians attacked it, the Bulgarians annoyed it, the Normans harassed it continually by sea, and now, most dangerous of all, the Seljuq Turks threatened its very life. But it was not going to collapse for another 400 years, in spite of all these enemies and difficulties. This amazing persistence is partly explained by the strength of the position of Constantinople. It was so well situated that it was difficult for an enemy to take it. Partly also it is explained by the discovery by the Greeks of a new method of defence. This was what was called "Greek Fire"; it was some stuff which caught fire when it touched water. By means of this Greek fire the people of Constantinople played havoc with the invading armies which tried to cross the Bosphorus by setting fire to their ships.

Such was the map of Europe after the first 1000 years of the Christian era. You would have found also the Northmen or Normans coming down in their ships and harassing and plundering towns on the sea coasts in the Mediterranean and ships on the high seas. They were, indeed, becoming respectable by success. In France they had established themselves in Normandy in the west; England they had conquered from their base in France; the island of Sicily they conquered from the Muslims and added to it South Italy, making a kingdom called the Kingdom of Sicilia.

In the centre of Europe, from the North Sea to Rome, sprawled the Holy Roman Empire, consisting of many States with one head, the Emperor. Between this German Emperor and the Pope of Rome there was a continuous tussle for mastery. Sometimes the Emperor prevailed, sometimes the Pope, but gradually the Popes increased in power. In their threat of excommunication—that is, to cast a man out of society and make an outlaw of him—they had a terrible weapon. One proud emperor, indeed, was brought so low by the Pope of the day that to beg forgiveness he had to go barefoot in the snow and to wait thus outside the Pope's residence at Canossa in Italy till the Pope was kind enough to admit him!

We see these countries of Europe fashioning out, but they would be very different from what they are to-day, and especially their people would be different. They would hardly speak of themselves as Frenchmen, or Englishmen, or Germans. The poor cultivators were a miserable lot and knew nothing of country or geography. All they knew was that they were the serfs of their lord and must do the lord's bidding. The nobles, if you asked them who they were, would tell you that they were the lords of this or that place and the vassals of some superior lord or of the king. This was the feudal system which spread all over Europe.

Gradually we find large cities growing in Germany and northern Italy especially. Paris also was a prominent city then. These cities are the centres of trade and commerce, and wealth accumulates there. The cities do not like the feudal lords, and there is always a tussle between the two, but money tells in the end. With the help of their money, which they lend to the lords, they buy privileges and power. And so slowly a new class grows in the city which does not fit in with the feudal system.

Thus we find that society in Europe is divided up in layers according to the feudal pattern, and even the Church gives its sanction and blessing to this order. There is no feeling of nationality. But there is a certain feeling all over Europe, especially amongst the upper classes, an idea of Christendom, something which unites the Christian nations of Europe. The Church helps to spread this idea, for it strengthens the Church and increases the power of the Pope of Rome, who is now the unquestioned head of the Church in western Europe. You will remember that Rome had cut itself away from Constantinople and the Eastern Roman Empire. Constantinople still continued its old Orthodox Church and Russia also took its religion from it. The Pope was not recognized by the Greeks of Constantinople.

But in the hour of peril, when Constantinople was surrounded by enemies, and more especially threatened by the Seljuq Turks, it forgot its pride and its hatred of Rome, and appealed to the Pope for help against the Muslim infidel. Rome had a great Pope then —Hildebrande, who became Pope Gregory the Seventh. It was Hildebrande before whom the proud German Emperor had appeared barefoot in the snow at Canossa.

Another event had excited the imagination of Christian Europe then. Many devout Christians believed that the world would come to a sudden end just 1000 years after Christ. The word millennium means a thousand years. It comes from two Latin words : *mille* meaning thousand, and *annus*, year. As the end of the world was expected then, the millennium came to mean a sudden change to a better world. As I have told you, there was great misery then in Europe, and this prospect of the " millennium " brought relief to many a weary person. Many sold up their lands and journeyed to Palestine to be present in their Holy Land when the end of the world came.

But the end of the world did not come, and the thousands of pilgrims who had journeyed to Jerusalem were ill-treated and harassed by the Turks. They returned to Europe full of anger and humiliation, and spread the story of their sufferings in the Holy Land. One famous pilgrim, Peter the Hermit, especially, went

about, staff in hand, preaching to the people to rescue their holy
city Jerusalem from the Muslims. Indignation and enthusiasm
grew in Christendom, and, seeing this, the Pope decided to lead the
movement.

About this time had come the appeal from Constantinople for
help against the infidel. All Christendom, both Roman and Greek,
now seemed to be ranged against the oncoming Turks. In 1095
a great Church Council decided to proclaim a holy war against the
Muslims for the recovery of the Holy City of Jerusalem. Thus
began the Crusades—the fight of Christendom against Islam, of
the Cross against the Crescent.

58

ANOTHER LOOK AT ASIA AND EUROPE

June 12, 1932

WE have finished our brief survey of the world—of Asia and
Europe and a bit of Africa—at the end of 1000 years after Christ.
But look again.

Asia. The old civilizations of India and China still continue
and flourish. Indian culture spreads to Malaysia and Cambodia
and brings rich fruit there. Chinese culture spreads to Korea and
Japan and, to some extent, Malaysia. In western Asia, Arabian
culture prevails in Arabia, Palestine, Syria and Mesopotamia; in
Persia or Iran, there is a mixture of the old Iranian and the newer
Arabian civilization. Some of the countries of Central Asia have
also imbibed this mixed Iranian-Arabian civilization, and have also
been influenced by India and China. In all these countries there
is a high level of civilization; trade and learning and the arts
flourish; great cities abound; and famous universities attract
students from afar. Only in Mongolia and in some parts of Central
Asia, as well as in Siberia in the north, is the level of civilization
low.

Europe now. It is backward and semi-barbarous compared to
the progressive countries of Asia. The old Græco-Roman civilization is just a memory of the distant past. Learning is at a discount; the arts are not much in evidence; and trade is far less
than in Asia. There are two bright spots. Spain, under the
Arabs, carries on the traditions of the great days of the Arabs,
and Constantinople, even in her slow decay, is a great and
populous city, sitting on the border, between Asia and Europe.
Over the greater part of Europe there is frequent disorder and,
under the feudal system which prevails, each knight and lord is a
little king in his domain. Rome, the imperial capital of old, at
one time had been hardly bigger than a village, and wild animals
had lived in its old Colosseum. But it is growing again.

So if you compared the two, Asia and Europe, 1000 years after

Christ, the comparison would have been greatly to the advantage of Asia.

Let us have another look and try to see below the surface of things. We find that all is not so well with Asia as a superficial observer might imagine. India and China, the two cradles of ancient civilization, are in trouble. Their troubles are not merely those of invasion from outside, but the more real troubles which sap away the inner life and strength. The Arabs in the west have come to the end of their great days. It is true that the Seljuqs rise to power, but their rise is simply due to their fighting qualities. They do not, like the Indians or Chinese or Persians or Arabs, represent the culture of Asia, but the fighting quality of Asia. Everywhere in Asia the old cultured races seem to be shrinking. They have lost confidence in themselves and are on the defensive. New peoples arise, strong and full of energy, who conquer these old races in Asia, and even threaten Europe. But they do not bring a new wave of civilization with them or a new impetus for culture. The old races slowly civilize them and assimilate their conquerors.

So we see a great change coming over Asia. While the old civilizations continue and the fine arts flourish and there are refinements in luxury, the pulse of civilization weakens, and the breath of life seems to grow less and less. For long they are to continue. There is no definite break or end to them, except in Arabia and Central Asia when the Mongols come. In China and India there is a slow fading off, till the old civilization becomes like a painted picture, beautiful to look at from a distance, but lifeless; and if you come near it, you see that the white ants have been at it.

Civilizations, like empires, fall, not so much because of the strength of the enemy outside, as through the weakness and decay within. Rome fell not because of the barbarians; they merely knocked down something that was already dead. The heart of Rome had ceased beating when the arms and legs were cut off. We see something of this process in India and China and in the case of the Arabs. The collapse of Arabian civilization was sudden, even as their rise had been. In India and China the process is long-drawn-out and it is not easy to spot it.

Long before Mahmud of Ghazni came to India this process had started. We can see the change in the minds of the people. Instead of creating new ideas and things, the people of India busied themselves with repetition and imitation of what had been done. Their minds were keen enough still, but they busied themselves in interpreting and explaining what had been said and written long ago. They still produced wonderful sculpture and carvings, but they were heavy with too much detail and ornament, and often almost a touch of the grotesque crept in. Originality was absent and so was bold and noble design. The polished graces and arts and luxury continued among the rich and the well-to-do, but little was done to relieve the toil and misery of the people as a whole or to increase production.

All these are the signs of the evening of a civilization. When this takes place you may be sure that the life of that civilization is vanishing; for creation is the sign of life, not repetition and imitation.

Some such processes are in evidence in China and India then. But do not mistake me. I do not mean that China or India cease to be because of this or relapse into barbarism. I mean that the old urge of the creative spirit that China and India had received in the past was exhausting its energy and not renewing itself. It was not adapting itself to changed surroundings; it was merely carrying on. This happens with every country and civilization. There are periods of great creative effort and growth and periods of exhaustion. It is amazing that in India and China the exhaustion came so late, and, even so, it has never been complete.

Islam brought a new impulse for human progress to India. To some extent it served as a tonic. It shook up India. But it did less good than it might have done because of two reasons. It came in the wrong way, and it came rather late. For hundreds of years before Mahmud of Ghazni raided India, Muslim missionaries had wandered about India and had been welcomed. They came in peace and had some success. There was little, if any, ill-feeling against Islam. Then came Mahmud with fire and sword, and the manner of his coming as a conqueror and a plunderer and killer injured the reputation of Islam in India more than anything else. He was, of course, just like any other great conqueror, killing and plundering, and caring little for religion. But for a very long time his raids overshadowed Islam in India and made it difficult for people to consider it dispassionately, as they might otherwise have done.

This was one reason. The other was that it came late. It came about 400 years after it began, and during this long period it had exhausted itself somewhat, and lost a great deal of its creative energy. If the Arabs had come to India with Islam in the early days, the rising Arabian culture would have mixed with the old Indian culture and the two would have acted and reacted on each other, with great consequences. It would have been the mixing of two cultured races; and the Arabs were well known for their toleration and rationalism in religion. At one period, indeed, there was a club in Baghdad, under the patronage of the Caliph, where men of all religions and no religion met together to discuss and debate about all matters from the point of view of rationalism alone.

But the Arabs did not come to India proper. They stopped in Sindh, and India was little influenced by them. Islam came to India through the Turks and others who did not have the tolerance or the culture of the Arab, and who were primarily soldiers.

Still, a new impulse came to India for progress and creative effort. How this put some new life in India and then worked itself out, we shall consider later.

Another result of the weakening of Indian civilization is now in evidence. Attacked from outside, it sought to defend itself against the incoming tide by building a shell round itself and almost

imprisoning itself.   This again was a sign of weakness and fear; and
the remedy only increased the disease.   The real disease was not
foreign invasion, but stagnation.   By this exclusiveness the stagnation grew and all avenues of growth were stopped.   Later we shall
see that China did this also in its own way, and so did Japan.   It
is a little dangerous to live in a society which is closed up like a
shell.   We petrify there and grow unaccustomed to fresh air and
fresh ideas.   Fresh air is as necessary for societies as for individuals.

So much for Asia.   Europe, we saw, was backward and quarrelsome at that time.   But behind all this disorder and uncouthness
you can detect energy at least and life.   Asia, after her long dominance, was on the down-grade; Europe was struggling up.   But she
had still far to go before she could come up anywhere near Asia's
level.

To-day Europe is dominant and Asia struggles painfully for freedom.   Yet look below the surface again.   You will find a new
energy in Asia, a new creative spirit, and a new life.   Asia is up
again, there can be no doubt.   And Europe, or rather western
Europe, in spite of her greatness, shows some signs of decay.   There
are no barbarians who are strong enough to destroy European
civilization.   But sometimes civilized people themselves act barbarously, and if this happens, civilization may destroy itself.

I talk of Asia and Europe.   But they are just geographical
expressions, and the problems that face us are not Asiatic or
European problems, but world problems or problems of humanity.
And unless we solve them for the whole world, there will continue
to be trouble.   Such a solution can only mean the ending of poverty
and misery everywhere.   This may take a long time, but we must
aim at this, and at nothing less than this.   Only then can we have
real culture and civilization based on equality, where there is no
exploitation of any country or class.   Such a society will be a
creative and progressive society, adapting itself to changing circumstances, and basing itself on the co-operation of its members.   And
ultimately it must spread all over the world.   There will be no
danger of such a civilization collapsing or decaying, as the old
civilizations did.

So while we struggle for the freedom of India, we must remember
that the great aim is human freedom, which includes the freedom
of our people as well as other peoples.

59

THE MAYA CIVILIZATION OF AMERICA

June 13, 1932

IN these letters I am trying to trace world history, so I tell you.
But in effect this has been the history of Asia and Europe and the
north of Africa.   Of America and Australia I have said nothing,

or next to nothing. I have warned you, however, that there was a civilization in America in these early days. Not much is known of this, and I certainly know very little indeed. Still, I cannot resist the temptation to tell you something about it here, so that you may not make the common mistake of thinking that America was just a savage country till Columbus and other Europeans reached there.

Probably as long ago as the Stone Age, before man had settled down anywhere and was a wanderer and hunter, there was land communication between Asia and North America. Groups and tribes of men must have passed from one continent to another *via* Alaska. Later these communications were cut off and people in America slowly developed their own civilization. Remember that, so far as we know, there was nothing to connect them with Asia or Europe. There are no accounts of any effective contacts till the so-called discovery of the New World late in the sixteenth century. This world of America was a distant and different world, uninfluenced by the happenings in Europe or Asia.

It appears that there were three centres of civilization: in Mexico, in Central America, and in Peru. It is not clear when they started, but the Mexican calendar began with a date corresponding with 613 B.C. We find in the early years of the Christian era, the second century onwards, already many cities growing. There is stonework and pottery and weaving and very fine dyeing. Copper and gold are abundant, but there is no iron. Architecture develops and the cities vie with each other in building. There is a special kind of rather intricate writing. Art, and especially sculpture, is much in evidence and is of considerable beauty.

There were several States in each of these areas of civilization. There were several languages and a considerable literature in them. Well-organized and strong governments existed, and the cities contained a cultured and intellectual society. Both the legislation and the financial system of these States were highly developed. About 960 A.C. the city of Uxmal was founded, and it is said that this soon developed into a great city comparable to the great cities of Asia in those days. There were also other large cities: Labua, Mayapan, Chaomultun.

The three leading States of Central America formed an alliance, which is now called the League of Mayapan. This was just about 1000 years after Christ, the period we have reached in Asia and Europe. So a millennium after Christ there was a powerful combination of civilized States in Central America. But all these States and the Maya civilization itself were priest-ridden. Astronomy was the science most honoured, and the priests by their knowledge of this science played on the ignorance of the people: Just as millions in India have been induced to bathe and fast during eclipses of the sun and moon.

For over 100 years the League of Mayapan lasted. There appears to have been a social revolution then, and a foreign Power from the border intervened. About 1190 A.C. Mayapan was

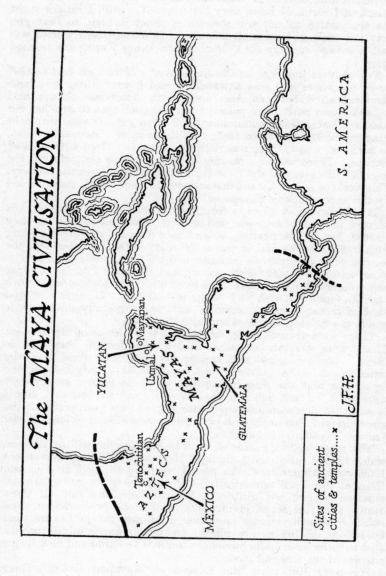

The MAYA CIVILISATION

YUCATAN

oMayapan
Uxmal x

MAYAS

GUATEMALA

A Z T E C S
Tenochtitlan
o x

MEXICO

S. AMERICA

Sites of ancient
cities & temples....x

J.F.H.

destroyed. The other great cities, however, continued. In another 100 years another people came on the scene. These were the Aztecs from Mexico. Early in the fourteenth century they conquered the Maya country and about 1325 A.D. they founded the city of Tenochtitlan. Soon this became the capital city of the whole Mexican world, the centre of the Empire of the Aztecs, with a vast population.

The Aztecs were a military nation. They had military colonies and garrisons, and a network of military roads. It is even said that they were clever enough to make their dependent States quarrel with each other. It was easier to rule them if they were divided. That has been the old policy of all empires. Rome called it : *Divide et impera !*—divide and rule.

The Aztecs, in spite of their cleverness in other matters, were also priest-ridden, and, worse still, their religion was full of human sacrifice. Thousands of human beings were sacrificed in this way in a most horrible manner every year.

For nearly 200 years the Aztecs ruled their empire with a rod of iron. There was outward security and peace in the empire, but the people were ruthlessly exploited and impoverished. A State so built and so carried on could not endure. And so it happened. Early in the sixteenth century (in 1519), when the Aztecs were apparently at the height of their power, the whole empire came down with a crash before a handful of foreign bandits and adventurers ! This is one of the most amazing examples of the collapse of an empire. And this was brought about by a Spaniard, Hernan Cortés, and a small troop with him. Cortés was a brave man, and daring enough. He had two things which were of great help to him—firearms and horses. Apparently there were no horses in the Mexican Empire, and there were certainly no firearms. But neither Cortés's courage nor his guns and horses would have availed him if the Aztec Empire had not been rotten at heart. It had decayed inside, just keeping the outer form, and even a little kick was enough to bring it down.   The empire was based on exploitation and was much resented by the people. So when it was attacked, the people at large welcomed the discomfiture of the imperialists. As usual when this happens, there was a social revolution also.

Cortés was once driven away, and he barely escaped with his life. But he returned, and then, helped by some of the inhabitants, he conquered. Not only did this end the Aztec rule, but it is curious to find that the whole of Mexican civilization collapsed with it, and soon of the imperial and giant city of Tenochtitlan little was left. Not a stone remains of it now, and on the site of it the Spaniards erected a cathedral. The other great Mayan cities also went to pieces, and the forests of Yucatan engulfed them, till even their names were forgotten, and many of them are now remembered by the names of villages near by. All their literature also perished and only three books survive, and even these no one has so far been able to read.

It is extraordinarily difficult to explain this sudden disappearance

of an ancient people and an ancient civilization, which had lasted
for nearly 1500 years, as soon as they come in contact with the new
people from Europe.   Almost it seems as if this contact was of the
nature of a disease, a new plague that wiped them off.   With all
their high civilization in some respects, they were very backward
in other respects.   They were a curious mixture of the various periods
of history.

In South America there was another seat of civilization in Peru,
and the Inca ruled it.   He was a kind of divine monarch.   It is
strange that this Peruvian civilization was, in its later days at least,
completely cut off from the Mexican civilization.   They were not
far from each other, and yet they knew nothing of each other,
and this itself shows their remarkable backwardness in some
respects.   A Spaniard also put an end to this Peruvian State soon
after Cortés had succeeded in Mexico.   This was Pizarro.   He came
in 1530 and he seized the Inca by treachery.   The seizure of the
" divine " monarch itself terrified the people.   Pizarro tried to rule
in the name of the Inca for some time and extorted vast wealth.
Later this pretence was ended and the Spaniards made Peru a part
of their dominions.

When Cortés first saw the city of Tenochtitlan he was astounded
at its greatness.   He had seen nothing like it in Europe.

Many relics of Mayan and Peruvian art have been recovered and
can be seen in American museums, especially, I think, in Mexico.
They show a fine artistic tradition.   The Peruvian goldsmith's
work is said to be superb.   Some of the pieces of sculpture found,
especially some serpents in stone, are very fine.   Others were
apparently meant to be works of horror, and they do horrify !

60

A JUMP BACK TO MOHENJO-DARO

June 14, 1932

I HAVE just been reading about Mohenjo-daro and the old Indus
Valley civilization of India.   A great new book has come out
describing this and telling us all that is so far known about it.   It
has been prepared and written by the men who have been in charge
of the excavations and diggings, and who have themselves seen the
city come out, as it were, of mother Earth, as they dug deeper and
deeper.   I have not seen this book yet.   I wish I could get it here.
But I have read a review of it, and I want to share with you some
of the quotations given in it.   It is a wonderful thing, this civilization of the Indus Valley, and the more one learns of it, the more
it amazes.   So you will not mind, I hope, if we break our account
of past history and jump back in this letter to 5000 years ago.

Mohenjo-daro is said to be as old as that at least.   But Mohenjo-
daro, as we find it, is a fine city, the home of a cultured and civilized
people.   Behind it there must have been a long period of growth

already. So we are told by this book. Sir John Marshall, who is in charge of the excavations tells us :

> " One thing that .stands out clear and unmistakable both at Mohenjo-daro and Harappa is that the civilization hitherto revealed at these two places is not an incipient civilization, but one already age-old and stereotyped on Indian soil, with many millennia of human endeavour behind it. Thus India must henceforth be recognized, along with Persia, Mesopotamia, and Egypt as one of the most important areas where the civilizing processes were initiated and developed."

I do not think I have told you of Harappa yet. This is another place where old ruins, similar to those at Mohenjo-daro, have been excavated. It is in western Punjab.

So we find that in the Indus Valley we go back not only 5000 years but many more thousands, till we are lost in the dim mists of antiquity when man first settled down. The Aryans had not come to India when Mohenjo-daro flourished, and yet there is no doubt that—

> " the Punjab and Sind, if not other parts of India as well, were enjoying an advanced and singularly uniform civilization of their own, closely akin but in some respects even superior, to that of contemporary Mesopotamia and Egypt."

Excavations in Mohenjo-daro and Harappa have revealed this ancient and fascinating civilization to us. How much more lies buried elsewhere under the soil of India ! It seems probable that this civilization was fairly widespread in India and was not merely confined to Mohenjo-daro and Harappa. Even these two places are far apart.

This was an age " in which arms and utensils of stone continue to be used side by side with those of copper and bronze ". Sir John Marshall tells us of the points of difference and superiority of the Indus Valley people to their contemporaries of Egypt and Mesopotamia.

> " Thus," he says, " to mention only a few salient points, the use of cotton for textiles was exclusively restricted at this period to India and was not extended to the western world until 2000 or 3000 years later. Again, there is nothing that we know of in prehistoric Egypt or Mesopotamia or anywhere else in western Asia to compare with the well-built baths and commodious houses of the citizens of Mohenjo-daro. In those countries, much money and thought were lavished on the building of magnificent temples for the gods and on the palaces and tombs of kings, but the rest of the people seemingly had to content themselves with insignificant dwellings of mud. In the Indus Valley the picture is reversed, and the finest structures are those erected for the convenience of the citizens."

Again we are told that—

> " equally peculiar to the Indus Valley and stamped with an individual character of their own are its art and its religion. Nothing that we know of in other countries at this period bears any resemblance, in point of style, to the faience models of rams, dogs,

and other animals or to the intaglio engravings on the seals, the best of which—notably the humped and short-horn bulls—are distinguished by a breadth of treatment and a feeling for line and plastic form that have rarely been surpassed in glyptic art; nor would it be possible, until the classic age of Greece, to match the exquisitely supple modelling of the two human statuettes from Harappa figured in Plates X and XI. In the religion of the Indus people there is much, of course, that might be paralleled in other countries. This is true of every prehistoric and most historic religions as well. But, taken as a whole, their religion is so characteristically Indian as hardly to be distinguished from still living Hinduism. . . . "

You may not understand a few words in this quotation. *Faience* means earthenware or porcelain work; *intaglio* and *glyptic* works are carvings and engravings on something hard, often some precious stone or gem.

I wish I could see the statuettes found at Harappa, or even their pictures. Perhaps, some day, you and I may journey to Harappa and Mohenjo-daro and take our fill of these sights. Meanwhile we shall carry on—you at your school at Poona, and I at my school, which is called the District Gaol of Dehra Dun.

61

CORDOBA AND GRANADA

June 16, 1932

WE have journeyed on in Asia and Europe through the years and we have halted at the end of 1000 years after Christ, and had a look back. But Spain has somehow been left out of our account—Spain under the Arabs—and we must go back and fit her into the picture.

Something you know already, if you still remember it. It was in 711 A.C. that the Arab general crossed to Spain from Africa. He was Tariq, and he landed at Gibraltar (the *Jabal-ut-Tariq*, the rock of Tariq). Within two years the Arabs had conquered the whole of Spain, and a little later Portugal was added. They went on and on; marched into France and spread all over the south. Thoroughly frightened at this, the Franks and other tribes joined together under Charles Martel, and made a great effort to stop the Arabs. They succeeded, and at the great battle of Tours near Poitiers in France the Franks defeated the Arabs. It was a great defeat and put an end to Arab dreams of the conquest of Europe. Many times after that the Arabs and the Franks and other Christian people in France fought each other; and sometimes the Arabs won and entered France, and sometimes they were pushed back in Spain. Even Charlemagne attacked them in Spain, but he was defeated. On the whole, however, for a long period the balance was kept up, and the Arabs ruled in Spain but went no further.

Spain was thus made part of the great Arab Empire, which spread right across Africa to the borders of Mongolia. But not for long. You will remember that there was civil war in Arabia and the Abbasides pushed out the Ommeyade Caliphs. The Arab Governor in Spain was an Ommeyade, and he refused to recognize the new Abbaside Caliph. So Spain cut itself off from the Arab Empire, and the Caliph at Baghdad was too far away and too full of his own troubles to do anything in the matter. But bad blood continued between Spain and Baghdad, and the two Arab States, instead of helping each other in the hour of trial, rather welcomed the difficulties of each other.

It was somewhat rash of the Spanish Arabs to break loose from their homeland. They were in a far country amid an alien population, and were surrounded by enemies. They were small in numbers. In the event of danger and difficulty there was no one to help them. But in those days they were full of self-confidence and cared little for these dangers. As a matter of fact they did remarkably well in spite of the continuous pressure of the Christian nations in the north, and, single-handed, they maintained their dominion over the greater part of Spain for 500 years. Even after this they managed to hold on to a smaller kingdom in the south of Spain for another 200 years. And so they actually outlasted the great Empire of Baghdad; and the city of Baghdad itself had long been reduced to dust when the Arabs said their last farewell to Spain.

These 700 years of Arab rule in parts of Spain are surprising enough. But what is more interesting is the high civilization and culture of the Spanish Arabs, or Moors as they were called. A historian, carried away by his enthusiasm a little, has said that:

> "The Moors organized that wonderful kingdom of Cordova, which was the marvel of the Middle Ages, and which, when all Europe was plunged in barbaric ignorance and strife, alone held the torch of learning and civilization bright and shining before the Western world."

Kurtuba was the capital of this kingdom for just 500 years. This is usually called Cordoba in English, sometimes Cordova. I am afraid I have a way of spelling the same name differently at times. But I shall try to stick to Cordoba. This was a great city of a million inhabitants, a garden city ten miles in length, with twenty-four miles of suburbs. There are said to have been 60,000 palaces and mansions, 200,000 smaller houses, 80,000 shops, 3800 mosques and 700 public baths. These figures may be exaggerations, but they give some idea of the city. There were many libraries, the chief of these, the Imperial Library of the Emir, containing 400,000 books. The University of Cordoba was famous all over Europe and even in western Asia. Free elementary schools for the poor abounded. A historian says that:

> "In Spain almost everybody knew how to read and write, whilst in Christian Europe, save and except the clergy, even persons belonging to the highest ranks were wholly ignorant."

Such was the city of Cordoba, competing with the other great Arab city of Baghdad. Its fame spread all over Europe and a German writer of the tenth century called it " the ornament of the world ". To its university came students from distant places. The influence of Arab philosophy spread to the other great universities of Europe, Paris, Oxford and the universities of northern Italy. Averroes or Ibn Rushd was a famous philosopher of Cordoba in the twelfth century. In his later years he fell out with the Spanish Emir and was banished. He went and settled in Paris.

As in other parts of Europe, there was a kind of feudal system in Spain also. Great and powerful nobles grew up, and between them and the Emir, who was the ruler, there was frequent fighting. It was this civil war which weakened the Arab State more than the attacks from outside. At the same time the power of some small Christian States in northern Spain was growing and they were pushing away at the Arabs.

About 1000 A.C.—that is, just at the end of the millennium—the kingdom of the Emir extended almost all over Spain. It even included a bit of southern France. But collapse came soon, and, as usual, it was due to internal weakness. The fine fabric of Arab civilization, with its arts and luxury and chivalry, was, after all, a rich man's civilization. The starving poor revolted and there were labour riots. Gradually civil war spread, and the provinces fell away, and the Spanish Empire of the Arabs went to pieces. Still the Arabs continued, split up as they were, and it was not till 1236 A.C. that Cordoba finally fell to the Christian King of Castile.

The Arabs were driven south, but still they resisted. In the south of Spain they carved out a little kingdom, the kingdom of Granada, and held on there. It was a little affair, this kingdom, so far as size went, but it reproduced Arab civilization in miniature. The famous Alhambra still stands in Granada, with its beautiful arches and columns and arabesques, a reminder of those days. It was originally called in Arabic " Al-Hamra ", the red palace. Arabesques are the beautiful designs you often see on Arab and other buildings influenced by Islam. The painting of figures was not encouraged by Islam. So the builders took to making fancy and intricate designs. Often they wrote Arabic verses from the Quran over the arches and elsewhere and made of them a beautiful decoration. The Arabic script is a flowing script which lends itself easily to such decoration.

The kingdom of Granada lasted for 200 years. It was pressed and harassed by the Christian States of Spain, especially Castile, and sometimes it agreed to pay tribute to Castile. It would probably not have lasted so long if the Christian States had themselves not been divided. But in 1469 A.C. a marriage took place between the rulers of two of these principal States, Ferdinand and Isabella, and this united Castile, Aragon and Leon. Ferdinand and Isabella put an end to the Arab kingdom of Granada. The Arabs fought bravely for several years till they were surrounded and hemmed in in Granada. Starved out, they surrendered in 1492 A.C.

Many of the Saracens or Arabs left Spain and went to Africa. Near Granada, overlooking the city, there is a spot which still bears the name of " El ultimo sospiro del moro ", the last sigh of the Moor.

But a large number of Arabs remained in Spain. The treatment of these Arabs is a very dark chapter in the history of Spain. There was cruelty and massacre, and the promises made to them about toleration were forgotten. About this time the Inquisition, that terrible weapon which the Roman Church forged to crush all who did not bow down to it, was established in Spain. Jews, who had prospered under the Saracens, were now forced to change their religion and many were burnt to death. Women and children were not spared. " The infidels " (that is the Saracens), so says a historian, " were ordered to abandon their picturesque costume, and to assume the hat and breeches of their conquerors, to renounce their language, their customs and ceremonies, even their very names, and to speak Spanish, behave Spanishly, and re-name themselves Spaniards ". Of course there were risings and revolts against these barbarities. But they were mercilessly crushed.

The Spanish Christians seem to have been very much against washing and bathing. Perhaps they objected to these simply because the Spanish Arabs were very fond of them and had erected great public baths all over the place. The Christians even went so far as to issue orders " for the reformation of the Moriscos " or Moors or Arabs, that " neither themselves, their women, nor any other persons, should be permitted to wash or bathe themselves either at home or elsewhere; and that all their bathing-houses should be pulled down and destroyed ".

Apart from the sin of washing, another great charge brought against the " Moriscos " was that they were tolerant in religion. It is extraordinary to read of this, and yet this was one of the main charges in an account of the " Apostacies and Treasons of the Moriscos " drawn up by the Archbishop of Valencia in 1602, when he was recommending the expulsion of Saracens from Spain. Referring to this he says, " that they [the Moriscos] commended nothing so much as that liberty of conscience in all matters of religion, which the Turks, and all other Mohammedans, suffer their subjects to enjoy ". What a great compliment was thus paid unwittingly to the Saracens in Spain, and how different and intolerant was the outlook of the Spanish Christians !

Millions of Saracens were driven out forcibly from Spain, mostly into Africa, some to France. But you must remember that the Arabs had been in Spain for seven hundred years; and during this long period they had become to a large extent merged in the people of Spain. Originally Arabs, they had gradually become more and more Spanish. Probably the Spanish Arabs of later years were quite different from the Arabs of Baghdad. Even to-day the Spanish race has much of Arab blood in its veins

The Saracens had also spread to the south of France and even to Switzerland, not as rulers, but as settlers. Sometimes even now one comes across an Arab type of face among the Frenchmen from the *midi*.

Thus ended, not only Saracen rule in Spain, but also Arab civilization. For, even earlier, this civilization had collapsed in Asia, as we shall presently see. It influenced many countries and many cultures, and left many a bright souvenir. But it did not rise again by itself in after-history.

After the Saracens left, Spain, under Ferdinand and Isabella, grew in power. Soon afterwards, the discovery of America brought vast wealth to it, and for a while it was the most powerful country in Europe, dominating others. But its fall was rapid and it sank into insignificance, and while the other countries of Europe advanced, Spain remained stagnant, dreaming still of the Middle Ages and not realizing that the world had changed since then.

An English historian, Lane Poole, writing of the Saracens in Spain says :

> " For centuries Spain had been the centre of civilization, the seat of arts and sciences, of learning and every form of refined enlightenment. No other country in Europe had so far approached the cultivated dominion of the Moors. The brief brilliancy of Ferdinand and Isabella, and of the Empire of Charles, could found no such enduring pre-eminence. The Moors were banished; for a while Christian Spain shone, like the moon, with a borrowed light; then came the eclipse, and in that darkness Spain has grovelled ever since. The true memorial of the Moors is seen in desolate tracts of utter barrenness, where once the Moors grew luxuriant vines and olives and yellow ears of corn; in a stupid, ignorant population where once wit and learning flourished; in the general stagnation and degradation of a people which has hopelessly fallen in the scale of nations, and has deserved its humiliation."

This is a hard judgment. About a year ago there was a revolution in Spain and the King was removed. There is a republic there now. Perhaps this young republic will do better, and bring Spain again into line with other countries.

62

THE CRUSADES

June 19, 1932

I TOLD you in a recent letter (No. 57) of the declaration by the Pope and his Church Council of a holy war against the Muslims for the recovery of the city of Jerusalem. The rising power of the Seljuq Turks frightened Europe, and especially the Constantinople government, which was directly threatened. Stories of the ill-treatment of Christian pilgrims to Jerusalem and Palestine by the Turks excited the people of Europe and filled them with anger. So a " holy war " was declared, and the Pope and the Church called upon all the Christian peoples of Europe to march to the rescue of the " holy " city.

Thus began the Crusades in 1095 A.C., and for more than 150 years the struggle continued between Christianity and Islam, between the Cross and the Crescent. There were long periods of rest in between, but there was almost a continuous state of war, and wave after wave of Christian Crusaders came to fight and mostly to die in the " holy " land. This long warfare yielded no substantial results to the Crusaders. For a short while Jerusalem was in their hands, but later it went back to the Turks, and there it remained. The chief result of the Crusades was to bring death and misery to millions of Christians and Muslims and again to soak Asia Minor and Palestine with human blood.

What was the state of the Empire of Baghdad at this time ? The Abbasides continued at the head of it. They were still the Caliphs, the Commanders of the Faithful. But they were nominal heads, having little power. We have already seen how their empire split up and the provincial governors became independent. Mahmud of Ghazni, who raided India so often, was a powerful sovereign who threatened the Caliph, if the latter did not behave according to his wishes. Even in Baghdad itself the Turks were really masters. Then came another branch of the Turks—the Seljuqs—and they rapidly established their power and spread, victorious, to the gates of Constantinople itself. But the Caliph still remained the Caliph, though with no political power. He gave the title of Sultan to the Seljuq chiefs, and the Sultan ruled. The Crusaders had thus to fight against these Seljuq Sultans and their followers.

In Europe the Crusades increased the idea of " Christendom "— the world of Christianity, as opposed to all non-Christians. Europe had a common idea and purpose—the recovery of the " holy land " from the so-called infidel. This common purpose filled people with enthusiasm, and many a man left home and property for the sake of the great cause. Many went with noble motives. Many were attracted by the promise of the Pope that those who went would have their sins forgiven. There were other reasons also for the Crusades. Rome wanted once for all to become the boss of Constantinople. You will remember that the Constantinople Church was different from that of Rome. It called itself the Orthodox Church and it disliked the Roman Church intensely and considered the Pope an upstart. The Pope wanted to put an end to this conceit of Constantinople and to bring it within his fold. Under the cloak of a holy war against the infidel Turk, he wanted to obtain what he had long desired. That is the way of politicians and those who consider themselves statesmen ! It is well to remember this conflict between Rome and Constantinople, as it continually crops up during the Crusades.

Another reason for the Crusades was a commercial one. The business people, especially of the growing ports of Venice and Genoa, wanted them because their trade was suffering. The Seljuq Turks had closed many of their trade routes to the East.

The common people, of course, knew nothing about these reasons. No one told them. Politicians usually hide their real reasons and talk pompously of religion and justice and truth and the like. It was so at the time of the Crusades. It is so still. People were taken in then; and still the great majority of people are taken in by the soft talk of politicians.

So large numbers gathered for the Crusades. Among them were good and earnest people; but there were also many who were far from good who were attracted by the hope of plunder. It was a strange collection of pious and religious men and the riffraff of the population, who were capable of every kind of crime. Indeed, these Crusaders, or many of them, going out to serve in what was to them a noble cause, committed the vilest and most disgusting of crimes. Many were so busy with plundering and misbehaving on the way that they never reached anywhere near Palestine. Some took to massacring Jews on the way; some even massacred their brother-Christians. Fed up with their misbehaviour, sometimes the peasantry of the Christian countries they passed through rose and attacked them, killing many and driving the others away.

The Crusaders at last managed to reach Palestine under a Norman, Godfrey of Bouillon. Jerusalem fell to them and then the " carnage lasted for a week ". There was a terrible massacre. A French eyewitness of this says that " under the portico of the mosque the blood was knee deep and reached the horses' bridles ". Godfrey became King of Jerusalem.

Seventy years later Jerusalem was re-taken from the Christians by Saladin, the Sultan of Egypt. This excited the people of Europe again and several Crusades followed. This time the kings and emperors of Europe came in person, but they had little success. They quarrelled among themselves for precedence and were jealous of each other. It is a dismal story of ghastly and cruel war and petty intrigue and sordid crime. But sometimes the better side of human nature prevailed over this horror, and incidents took place when enemies behaved with courtesy and chivalry to each other. Among the foreign kings in Palestine was Richard of England, Cœur de Lion, the Lion-Hearted, noted for his physical strength and courage. Saladin was also a great fighter, and famous for his chivalry. Even the Crusaders who fought Saladin came to appreciate this chivalry of his. There is a story that once Richard was very ill and was suffering from the heat. Saladin, hearing of this, arranged to send him fresh snow and ice from the mountains. Ice could not be made artificially then by freezing water, as we do now. So natural snow and ice from the mountains had to be taken by swift messengers.

There are many stories of the time of the Crusades. Perhaps you have read Walter Scott's *Talisman*.

One batch of Crusaders went to Constantinople and took possession of it. They drove out the Greek Emperor of the Eastern Empire and established a Latin kingdom and the Roman Church. Terrible massacres also took place in Constantinople and the city itself was partly burnt by the Crusaders. But this Latin kingdom did not last long. The Greeks of the Eastern Empire, weak as they were, came back and drove away the Latins after a little over fifty years. The Eastern Empire of Constantinople continued for another 200 years, till 1453, when the Turks finally put an end to it.

This capture of Constantinople by the Crusaders brings out the desire of the Roman Church and the Pope to extend their influence there. Although the Greeks of this city had, in a moment of panic, appealed to Rome for help against the Turks, they helped the Crusaders little, and disliked them greatly.

But the most terrible of all these Crusades was what is called the Children's Crusade. Large numbers of young boys, chiefly French and some from Germany, in their excitement, left their homes and decided to go to Palestine. Many of them died on the way, many were lost. Most of them reached Marseilles, and there these poor children were tricked and their enthusiasm was taken advantage of by scoundrels. Under the pretext of taking them to the " holy land ", slave-traders took them on their ships, carried them to Egypt, and sold them into slavery.

Richard of England on his way back from Palestine was captured by his enemies in eastern Europe and a very heavy ransom had to be paid for his release. A King of France was captured in Palestine itself, and had to be ransomed. An Emperor of the Holy Roman Empire, Frederick Barbarossa, was drowned in a river in Palestine. Meanwhile, as time went on, all the glamour went out of these Crusades. People got fed up with them. Jerusalem remained in Muslim hands, but the kings and people of Europe were no longer interested in wasting more lives and treasure for its recovery. Since then for nearly 700 years Jerusalem continued to be under the Muslims. It was only recently, during the Great War, in 1918, that it was taken from the Turks by an English general.

One of the later Crusades was interesting and unusual. Indeed, it was hardly a crusade at all in the old sense of the word. The Emperor Frederick II, of the Holy Roman Empire, came and, instead of fighting, had an interview with the then Sultan of Egypt and they came to a friendly understanding ! Frederick was an extraordinary person. At a time when most kings were hardly literate, he knew many languages, including Arabic. He was known as the " Wonder of the World ". He cared little for the Pope, and the Pope thereupon excommunicated him, but this had little effect on him.

The Crusades thus failed to achieve anything. But this continuous fighting weakened the Seljuq Turks. Even more than this, however, feudalism sapped the foundations of the Seljuq Empire. The big feudal lords considered themselves practically independent. They fought each other. Sometimes they even went so far as to ask for Christian help against each other. It was this internal weakness of the Turks that played into the hands of the Crusaders sometimes. When, however, there was a strong ruler like Saladin, they made little progress.

There is another view of the Crusades, a recent view put forward by the English historian, G. M. Trevelyan (the author of the Garibaldi books which you know). This is interesting. " The Crusades," says Trevelyan, " were the military and religious aspect of a general urge towards the East on the part of the reviving energies of Europe. The prize that Europe brought back from the Crusades was not the permanent liberation of the Holy Sepulchre or the potential unity of Christendom, of which the story of the Crusades was one long negation. She brought back instead the finer arts and crafts, luxury, science, and intellectual curiosity—everything that Peter the Hermit would most have despised."

Saladin died in 1193, and gradually what remained of the old Arab Empire went to pieces. In many parts of western Asia there was disorder under the petty feudal lords. The last Crusade took place in 1249. It was headed by Louis IX, King of France, who was defeated and taken prisoner.

Meanwhile big things had been happening in Eastern and Central Asia. The Mongols, under a mighty chieftain, Chengiz or Jenghiz Khan, were advancing and covering the eastern horizon like a huge dark cloud. Crusader and defender, Christian and Muslim alike, saw this coming invasion with fear. We shall deal with Chengiz and the Mongols in a later letter.

One thing I should like to mention before I end this letter. In Bokhara, in Central Asia, there lived a very great Arab physician, who was famous in Asia as well as Europe. His name was Ibn Sina, but he is better known in Europe as Avicenna. The Prince of Physicians he was called. He died in 1037, before the Crusades began.

I mention Ibn Sina's name because of his fame. But remember that right through this period, even when the Arab Empire was on the decline, Arab civilization continued in western and part of Central Asia. Saladin, busy as he was fighting the Crusaders, built many colleges and hospitals. But this civilization was on the eve of a sudden and complete collapse. The Mongols were coming from the East.

63

EUROPE AT THE TIME OF THE CRUSADES

June 20, 1932

In my last letter we saw something of the clash between Christianity and Islam in the eleventh, twelfth and thirteenth centuries. The idea of Christendom develops in Europe. Christianity has by this time spread all over Europe, the last comers being the Slav races of Eastern Europe—Russians and others. There is an interesting story—I do not know how far it is true—that the old Russian people, before they became Christian, discussed the question of changing their old religion and adopting a new one. The two new religions they had heard of were Christianity and Islam. So, quite in the modern style, they sent a deputation to visit the countries where these religions were practised, to examine them and report on them. It is said that this deputation visited some places in western Asia, where Islam prevailed, and then they went to Constantinople. They were amazed at what they saw at Constantinople. The ceremonial of the Orthodox Church was rich and gorgeous, with music and beautiful singing. The priests came in splendid garments and there was burning of incense. This ceremonial impressed the simple and semi-civilized people from the north tremendously. Islam had nothing so gorgeous. So they decided in favour of Christianity, and on their return they reported accordingly to their king. The king and his people thereupon became Christians, and because they took their Christianity from Constantinople, they were followers of the Orthodox Greek Church and not of Rome. At no subsequent time did Russia acknowledge the Pope of Rome.

This conversion of Russia took place long before the Crusades. The Bulgarians also, it is said, at one time were half inclined to become Mohammedans, but then the attraction of Constantinople was greater. Their king married a Byzantine princess (you will remember that Byzantium was the old name for Constantinople) and became a Christian. In the same way other neighbouring people had adopted Christianity.

What was happening in Europe during these Crusades? You have seen that some of the kings and emperors journeyed to Palestine and several of them got into trouble there. The Pope meanwhile sat in Rome and issued commands and appeals for the " holy war " against the " infidel " Turk. This was the time, perhaps, when the power of the Popes was at its highest. I have told you how a proud emperor stood barefooted in the snow at Canossa waiting to be admitted to the Pope's presence to beg forgiveness. It was this Pope Gregory VII, whose previous name was Hildebrand, who had fixed up a new method for the election of Popes. The cardinals were the highest priests in the Roman Catholic world. A college of cardinals was created—the Holy College it was called—and this college elected a new Pope. This was the system introduced in 1059 A.C. and it has continued, perhaps with some modifications, to this day. Even now when a Pope dies, the College of Cardinals meets immediately, and they sit in a locked chamber. No one can come in or go out from that room till the election is over. Often they have sat there for many long hours unable to agree about their choice. But they cannot come out ! So they are forced to agree at last, and as soon as a choice is made white smoke is sent up so that the waiting crowds outside can know.

Just as the Pope was chosen by election, the Emperor of the Holy Roman Empire also came to be elected. But he was elected by the great feudal lords. There were seven of these—the elector-princes as they were called. In this way they tried to prevent the

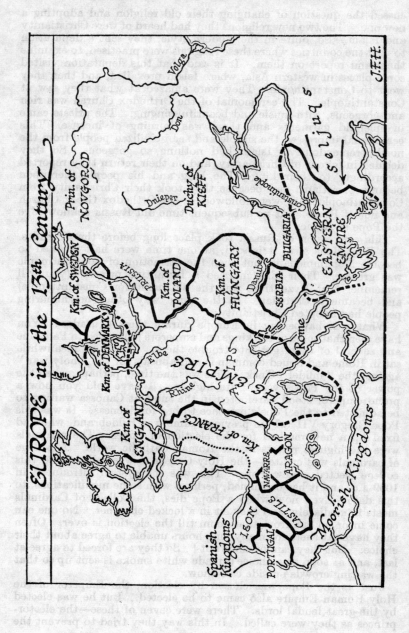

EUROPE in the 13th Century

J.F.H.

Emperor always coming from one family. In practice, however, one family often dominated these elections for long periods.

Thus we find in the twelfth and thirteenth centuries the Hohenstaufen dynasty dominating the Empire. Hohenstaufen is, I believe, some small town or village in Germany. The family originally coming from there took their name from it. Frederick I of Hohenstaufen became Emperor in 1152. He is usually called Frederick Barbarossa. He it was who got drowned on his way to the Crusades. It is said that his reign was the most brilliant in the history of the Empire. To the German people he has long been a hero, a half-mythical figure round whom many legends have gathered. It is said that he sleeps in a deep cavern in a mountain and that when the right time comes he will wake up and come out to save his people.

Against the Pope, Frederick Barbarossa carried on a great struggle, but this ended in victory for the Pope, and Frederick had to bow down to him. He was an autocratic monarch, but his great feudal vassals gave him a lot of trouble. In Italy, where large cities were growing up, Frederick tried to crush their freedom. But he did not succeed. In Germany also great cities were growing, especially on the banks of rivers : Cologne, Hamburg, Frankfurt, and many others. Here Frederick's policy was different. He supported the free German cities in order to lessen the power of the nobles and feudal lords.

I have told you on several occasions what the old Indian idea of kingship was. From the old Aryan days to Ashoka's time, and from the *Arthashāstra* to the *Nītisāra* of Sukrācharya, it is repeatedly stated that the King must bow down to public opinion. It is the public that is the ultimate master. This was the Indian theory, although in practice kings in India, as elsewhere, were autocratic enough. Compare this to the old European view. According to the lawyers of those days the Emperor had absolute authority. His will was law. " The Emperor is the living law upon Earth," they said. Frederick Barbarossa himself said : " It is not for the people to give laws to the prince, but to obey his command."

Compare this also with the Chinese view. The emperor or king there was called by high-sounding titles, like the Son of Heaven, but this must not mislead us. In theory his position was very different from that of the all-powerful European Emperor. An old Chinese writer, Meng-tse, has written : " The people is the most important element in the country ; next come the useful gods of the soil and the crops, and last in importance comes the ruler."

The Emperor in Europe was thus supposed to be supreme on earth, and it was from this that the notion of the divine right of kings arose. In practice, of course, he was very far from supreme. Even his feudal vassals were turbulent enough, and gradually, as we shall see, new classes arose in the cities, which claimed some share of power. On the other hand the Pope also claimed to be supreme on earth. Where two " supremes " meet there is bound to be trouble.

The grandson of Frederick Barbarossa was also called Frederick. He became Emperor at an early age and was called Frederick II. He was the man who was called *stupor mundi*, the Wonder of the World, and who went to Palestine and had a friendly talk with the Egyptian Sultan. He also, like his grandfather, defied the Pope and refused to obey him. The Pope retaliated by excommunicating him. This was the old and mighty weapon of the Popes, but it was growing a little rusty. Frederick II cared little for the anger of the Pope, and the world also was changing. Frederick wrote long letters to all the princes and rulers of Europe, pointing out that the Pope had no business to interfere with the kings; it was the business of the Popes to look after religious and spiritual matters and not to meddle with politics. He also described the corruption of the clergy. Frederick had by far the best of the argument with the Popes. His letters are very interesting, as they are the first indication of the modern spirit being introduced into the old struggle between Emperor and Pope.

Frederick II was very tolerant in religion, and Arab and Jewish philosophers came to his Court. It is said that it was through him that the Arabic numerals and algebra (which you will remember came originally from India) came to Europe. He also founded the university of Naples and a great medical school at the ancient university of Salerno.

Frederick II ruled from 1212 to 1250. With his death ended the Hohenstaufen control of the Empire. Indeed the Empire itself practically ended. Italy fell away, Germany went to pieces and for many years there was frightful disorder. Robber knights and bandits plundered and looted, and there was no one to check them. The weight of the Holy Roman Empire had been too great for the German kingdom to bear. In France and England the kings were gradually consolidating their positions, and putting down the big feudal vassals who were troublesome. In Germany the King was also Emperor, and he was far too busy fighting the Pope or the Italian cities to curb his nobles. Germany had the doubtful honour of having the Emperor, but it paid for this by weakness and dissension at home. France and England grew to be strong nations long before Germany was even united. For hundreds of years there were numerous petty princes in Germany. It was only about sixty years ago that Germany was united, and even then the little kings and princes continued. The Great War of 1914–18 put an end to this crowd.

There was so much disorder in Germany after Frederick II that for twenty-three years no emperor was elected. In 1273 Rudolph, Count of Hapsburg, was elected emperor. A new family—that of Hapsburg—now comes upon the scene. This was going to stick to the Empire to the end. This family also came to an end, as a ruling one, during the Great War. The Emperor of Austria-Hungary at the time of the War was a Hapsburg named Francis Joseph. He was a very old man, having been on the throne for over sixty years. His nephew and the heir to the throne was Franz Ferdinand, who was murdered with his wife in Serajevo in Bosnia (in the Balkans) in 1914. It was this murder which brought on the Great War, and the War put an end to many things, among them the old dynasty of the Håpsburgs.

So much for the Holy Roman Empire. To the west of it, France and England were frequently at war with each other, and, more frequently, the king of each was at war with his big nobles. The kings triumphed over their nobles, far more than the emperor or king in Germany, and so England and France grew to be much more compact countries, and their unity gave them strength.

In England an event happened about this time of which you might have read. This was the signing of the Magna Charta by King John in 1215. A.C. John had succeeded his brother, Richard *Cœur de Lion*. He was very grasping, but he was also weak and he succeeded in irritating everybody. The nobles cornered him at the island of Runnymede in the Thames and, almost at the sword's point, forced him to sign this Magna Charta, or Great Charter, which contained a promise that he would respect certain liberties of the nobles and people of England. This was the first big step in the long fight for political liberty in England. It was especially laid down that the king could not interfere with the property and liberty of any citizen without the consent of the man's equals. Out of this arose the jury system, where equals are supposed to judge. Thus in England we find that the king's power was checked early. The theory of the supremacy of the ruler, which prevailed in the Holy Roman Empire, was not accepted in England even then.

It is interesting to note that this rule laid down in England over 700 years ago does not apply to India even in 1932 under British rule. To-day one individual, the Viceroy, has power to issue Ordinances, framing laws and depriving people of their liberty and their property.

Soon after Magna Charta another notable event took place in England. A national council gradually grew up to which knights and citizens were sent from the different country areas and the cities. This was the beginning of the English Parliament. The knights and citizens came to form the Commons' House; the nobles and the bishops formed the Lords' House. This Parliament had little power to begin with, but this grew gradually. Ultimately there came the final test between the King and Parliament, as to who was supreme. The King lost his head, and Parliament became undisputed master. But this was to take place after nearly 400 years, in the seventeenth century.

In France also there was a Council of the Three Estates, as they were called. These Three Estates were the Lords, the Church and the Commons. This Council sometimes met, when the king willed it. But its meetings were very infrequent, and it did not succeed in gaining the power which the English Parliament did. In France also a king had to lose his head before the power of the kings was broken.

In the east, the Eastern Roman Empire of the Greeks still

continued. From its earliest days it had been at war with someone or other, and often it seemed at the point of succumbing. Yet it survived, first the attack of northern barbarians and then that of the Muslims. Of all the attacks that fell on the Empire, from the Russians or Bulgarians or Arabs or the Seljuq Turks, the most deadly and harmful was the attack of the Crusaders. These Christian knights did more injury to Christian Constantinople than any " infidel " had done. From this great catastrophe the Empire and the city of Constantinople never recovered.

The world of western Europe was quite ignorant of the Eastern Empire. It cared little for it. It was hardly part of " Christendom ". Its language was Greek, while the learned language of western Europe was Latin. As a matter of fact, even in the days of its decline there was far more learning and literary activity in Constantinople than in the West. But it was the learning of the aged, without any strength or creative power behind it. The West had little learning, but it was young and had creative power, and soon this power was to break out in the creation of works of beauty.

In the Eastern Empire there was no conflict between the Church and the Emperor, as in Rome. The Emperor there was supreme, and he was quite despotic. There was no question of any freedom. The throne was the prize of the strongest or the most unscrupulous. By murder and trickery, through blood and crime, men gained the crown, and the people sheepishly obeyed them. It seemed to be immaterial to them who ruled.

The Eastern Empire stood as a kind of sentinel at the gates of Europe, guarding them from Asiatic invasion. For many hundreds of years it succeeded. The Arabs could not take Constantinople; the Seljuq Turks, although they came near it, could not take it; the Mongols passed it by and went north into Russia. Last came the Ottoman Turks and to them fell the great prize of the imperial city of Constantinople in 1453 A.C. And with the fall of the city, fell also the Eastern Empire.

64

THE RISE OF EUROPEAN CITIES

June 21, 1932

THE period of the Crusades was the great period of faith in Europe, of common aspiration and belief, and the people sought relief from their daily misery in this faith and hope. There was no science; there was very little learning; for faith and science and learning do not easily go together. Learning and knowledge make people think, and doubt and questioning are difficult companions for faith to have. And the way of science is the way of inquiry and experiment, which is not the way of faith. We shall see later how this faith weakened and doubt arose.

But for the moment we see faith flourishing and the Roman Church putting itself at the head of the "faithful" and often exploiting them. Many, many thousands of the "faithful" were sent to the Crusades in Palestine, never to return. The Pope also began to declare crusades against Christian people or groups in Europe who did not obey him in everything. The Pope and the Church even took advantage of this faith by issuing, and often selling, "dispensations" and "indulgences". "Dispensations" were permissions to break some law or convention of the Church. Thus the very laws which the Church made, it allowed to be set aside in special cases. Respect for such laws could hardly continue for long. "Indulgences" were even worse. According to the Roman Church, after death a soul goes to purgatory, which is a place somewhere between heaven and hell, and there it suffers for the sins committed in this world. Afterwards the soul is supposed to go to heaven. The Pope issued promises to people, for payment, that they would escape purgatory and go straight to heaven. Thus the faith of the simple was exploited by the Church, and even out of crimes and what it considered sins, it made money. This practice of selling "indulgences" grew up some time after the Crusades. It became a great scandal, and was one of the reasons why many people turned against the Church of Rome.

It is strange how much people with simple faith will put up with. It is because of this that religion has become one of the biggest and most paying businesses in many countries. See the priests in the temples, how they try to fleece the poor worshipper. Go to the banks of the Ganga, and you will see the *pandās* refusing to perform some ceremony till the unhappy villager pays up. Whatever happens in the family—a birth, a marriage, a death—the priest steps in and payment is required.

In every religion this is so—Hinduism, Christianity, Islam, Zoroastrianism. Each has its own methods of making money out of the faith of the faithful. In Hinduism the methods are obvious enough. In Islam there is supposed to be no priesthood, and in the past this helped a little in protecting its followers from religious exploitation. But individuals and classes arose, calling themselves specialists in religion, learned men, *maulavis* and *mullas* and the like, and they imposed upon the simple Muslims of faith and exploited them. Where a long beard, or a tuft of hair on the crown of the head, or a long mark on the forehead, or a fakir's dress, or a *sanyasin's* yellow or ochre garb is a passport to holiness, it is not difficult to impose on the public.

If you go to America, most advanced of countries, you will find there also that religion is a big industry living on the exploitation of the people.

I have wandered far from the Middle Ages and the age of faith. We must go back to them. We find this faith taking visible and creative shape. In the eleventh and twelfth centuries there is a great building period and cathedrals spring up all over western

Europe. A new architecture appears such as had not been seen in Europe before. By a clever device the weight and stress of the heavy roofs are distributed to great buttresses outside the building Inside one is surprised to see delicate columns apparently supporting the massive weight on top. There is a pointed arch, taken from the Arab style of architecture. Above the whole building there is a spire climbing up to the sky. This was the Gothic style of architecture, which was evolved in Europe. It was wondrously beautiful, and it seemed to represent soaring faith and aspiration. Truly it represents that age of faith. Such buildings can only be built by architects and craftsmen in love with their work and co-operating together in a great undertaking.

This rise of the Gothic in western Europe is a surprising thing. Out of the welter of disorder and anarchy and ignorance and intolerance, grew up this thing of beauty, almost like a prayer going up to the heavens. In France, northern Italy, Germany and England, Gothic cathedrals grew up almost simultaneously. No one knows exactly how they began. No one knows the names of their architects. They seem to represent more the joint will and labour of the people as a whole than that of a single architect. Another new thing was the stained glass of the windows of the cathedrals. There were fine paintings in beautiful colours on these windows, and the light that came through them added to the solemn and awe-inspiring effect created by the building.

Some little time ago, in one of my recent letters to you, I compared Europe with Asia. We saw that Asia was far more cultured and civilized than Europe at the time. And yet in India there was not much of creative work being done, and creation, I said, is the sign of life. This Gothic architecture coming out of semi-civilized Europe shows us that there was life enough there. In spite of the difficulties which disorder and a backward state of civilization present, this life breaks out and seeks methods of manifesting itself. The Gothic buildings were one of these manifestations. Later we shall see it coming out in painting and sculpture and the love of adventure.

You have seen some of these Gothic cathedrals. I wonder if you remember them. You visited the beautiful cathedral at Cologne in Germany. At Milan in Italy there is a very fine Gothic cathedral; so also at Chartres in France. But I cannot name all these places. These cathedrals are spread out over Germany, France, England and northern Italy. It is strange that in Rome itself there is no Gothic building of note.

During this great building period of the eleventh and twelfth centuries non-Gothic churches were also put up, like the great cathedral of Notre Dame in Paris, and probably St. Mark's in Venice. St. Mark's, which you have seen, is an example of Byzantine work and has beautiful mosaics.

The age of faith declined, and with it the building of churches and cathedrals. Men's thoughts turned in other directions, to their business and trade, to their civic life. Instead of cathedrals, city halls began to be built. So we find from the beginning of the fifteenth century beautiful Gothic town-halls or guild-halls scattered over northern and western Europe. In London the Houses of Parliament are Gothic, but I do not know when they were built. I have an idea that the original Gothic building was burnt down and another one, also Gothic in style, was then built.

These great Gothic cathedrals that rose up in the eleventh and twelfth centuries were situated in the towns and cities. The old cities were waking up, and new towns were growing. There was a change all over Europe, and everywhere town life was increasing. In the old days of the Roman Empire there were, of course, great towns all round the Mediterranean coast. But with the fall of Rome and Graeco-Roman civilization, these towns also decayed. Except for Constantinople there was hardly a big city in Europe, apart from Spain, where the Arabs were. In Asia—in India, China and the Arabian world—great cities flourished at this time. But Europe did not have them. Cities and culture and civilization seem to go together, and Europe had none of these for a long time after the collapse of the Roman order.

But now again there was a revival of city life. In Italy especially these cities grew. They were a thorn in the side of the Emperor of the Holy Roman Empire, for they would not agree to the suppression of certain liberties they had. These cities in Italy and elsewhere represent the growth of the merchant classes and the *bourgeoisie* or middle classes.

Venice, lording it over the Adriatic Sea, had become a free republic. Beautiful as it is to-day, as the sea goes in and out through its winding canals, it is said that it was marshy land before the city was built. When Attila the Hun came down with fire and sword into Aquileia, some fugitives managed to escape to the marshes of Venice. They built themselves the city of Venice there and, situated as they were between the Eastern Roman Empire and the Western, they managed to remain free. Trade came to Venice from India and the East and brought her riches, and she built up a navy and became a power on the sea. It was a republic of rich men with a president who was called a Doge. This republic lasted till Napoleon entered Venice as a conqueror in 1797. It is said that the Doge, who was a very old man, dropped down dead on that day. He was the last Doge of Venice.

On the other side of Italy was Genoa, also a great trading city of seafaring folk, a rival of Venice. In between was the university town of Bologna, and Pisa, and Verona and Florence, which was to produce soon so many great artists and which was going to shine brilliantly under the rule of the famous Medici family. Milan, also in northern Italy, was already an important manufacturing centre; and, in the south, Naples was growing.

In France, Paris, which Hugh Capet had made his capital, was growing with the growth of France. Always Paris has been the nerve-centre and heart of France. There have been other capitals of other countries, but none of them, during the last 1000 years, has dominated the country so much as Paris has dominated France. Other towns in France which become important are Lyons and Marseilles (which was a very old port), Orléans, Bordeaux and Boulogne.

In Germany, as in Italy, the growth of the free cities is most notable, especially in the thirteenth and fourteenth centuries. Their population grows, and as their power and wealth increase, they grow bolder, and fight the nobles. The Emperor sometimes encouraged them, as he wanted to subdue the big nobles. These cities formed big commercial leagues and associations for defending themselves. Sometimes these associations or confederacies, as they were called, actually made war on counter associations of nobles. Hamburg, Bremen, Cologne, Frankfurt, Munich, Danzig, Nuremberg and Breslau were some of these growing cities.

In the Netherlands (known as Holland and Belgium now) there were the cities of Antwerp, Bruges and Ghent, commercial cities with an ever-growing business. In England, of course, there was London, but it could not then compete with the important cities of the Continent in size or wealth or trade. The two universities of Oxford and Cambridge were growing in importance as centres of learning. In the east of Europe there was the city of Vienna, one of the oldest in Europe; and in Russia there were Moscow and Kiev and Novgorod.

These new cities, or most of them, must be distinguished from the old-style imperial cities. The importance of the rising cities of Europe was not due to any emperor or king, but to the trade that they controlled. Their strength lay therefore not in the nobles, but in the merchant classes. They were merchant cities. The rise of the cities therefore means the rise of the *bourgeoisie*. This *bourgeoisie*, we shall see later, went on increasing in power, till it successfully challenged king and noble and seized power from them. But this was to happen long after the period we are considering.

Cities and civilization often go together, I have just said. With the growth of cities learning also grows and the spirit of freedom. Men living in rural areas are scattered and are often very superstitious. They seem to be at the mercy of the elements. They have to work hard and have little leisure, and they dare not disobey their lords. In cities large numbers live together; they have the opportunity of living a more civilized life, of learning, of discussing and criticizing, and of thinking.

So the spirit of freedom grows both against political authority as represented by the feudal nobles, and against the spiritual authority as represented by the Church. The age of faith declines and doubt begins. The authority of the Pope and of the Church is not always blindly obeyed. We saw how the Emperor Frederick II treated the Pope. We shall see this spirit of defiance growing.

There was also a revival of learning from the twelfth century onwards. Latin was the common language of the learned in Europe, and men in quest of knowledge travelled from one university to another. Dante Alighieri, the great Italian poet, was born in 1265. Petrarch, another great poet of Italy, was born in 1304. A little later, Chaucer, the earliest of the great English poets, flourished in England.

But even more interesting than the revival of learning were the faint beginnings of the scientific spirit, which was to grow so much in after-years in Europe. You will remember my telling you that the Arabs had this spirit and worked according to it to some extent. It was difficult for such a spirit of inquiry with an open mind and of experiment to exist in Europe during the Middle Ages. The Church would not tolerate it. But in spite of the Church it begins to be visible. One of the first persons who had this scientific spirit at this time in Europe was an Englishman, Roger Bacon. He lived at Oxford in the thirteenth century.

65

THE AFGHANS INVADE INDIA

June 23, 1932

MY letter to you was interrupted yesterday. As I sat down to write, I forgot the gaol and my surroundings here and travelled, with the speed of thought, back to the world of the Middle Ages. But I was brought back, with even greater speed, to the present, and was made rather painfully conscious of the gaol. I was told that orders had come from above forbidding interviews with Mummie and Diddaji [1] for a month. Why? I was not told. Why should a prisoner be told? They have been here in Dehra Dun for ten days now waiting for the next interview day, and now their waiting has been to no purpose, and they must go back. Such is the courtesy extended to us. Well, well, we must not mind. It is all in the day's work, and prison is prison, and we had better not forget it.

It was not possible for me to leave the present for the past after this rude awakening. But I feel a little better to-day, after a night's rest. So I begin afresh.

We shall come back to India now. We have been away long enough. What was happening here while Europe was trying to struggle out of the darkness of the Middle Ages; when the people there were crushed under the weight of the feudal system and the general disorder and misgovernment that prevailed; when Pope and Emperor struggled against each other, and the countries of Europe took shape; when Christianity and Islam struggled for mastery during the Crusades?

Already we have had a glimpse of India during the early Middle Ages. We have also seen Sultan Mahmud swoop down from Ghazni in the north-west to the rich plains of northern India and

[1] Indira's grandmother.

plunder and destroy. Mahmud's raids, terrible as they were, produced no great or lasting change in India. They gave a great shock to the country, especially the north, and numerous fine monuments and buildings were destroyed by him. But only Sindh and a part of the Punjab remained in the Empire of Ghazni. The rest of the north recovered soon enough; the south was not even touched, nor was Bengal. For another 150 years or more after Mahmud, neither Muslim conquest nor Islam made much progress in India.

It was towards the end of the twelfth century (about 1186 A.C.) that a fresh wave of invasion came from the north-west. An Afghan chief had arisen in Afghanistan, who captured Ghazni and put an end to the Ghaznavite Empire. He is called Shahab-ud-din Ghuri (Ghur being some little town in Afghanistan). He came down to Lahore, took possession of it, and then marched to Delhi. The King of Delhi was Prithwi Raj Chauhan, and under his leadership many other chiefs of northern India fought against the invader and defeated him utterly. But only for a while. Shahab-ud-din returned next year with a great force, and this time he defeated and killed Prithwi Raj.

Prithwi Raj is still a popular hero, and there are many legends and songs about him. The most famous of these is about his eloping with the daughter of Raja Jaichandra of Kanauj. But the elopement cost him dear. It cost him the lives of his bravest followers and the enmity of a powerful king. It sowed the seeds of dissension and mutual conflict, and thus made it easy for the invader to win.

Thus in 1192 A.C. was won the first great victory by Shahab-ud-din, which resulted in the establishment of Muslim rule in India. Slowly the invaders spread, east and south. In another 150 years (by 1340) Muslim rule extended over a great part of the south. Then it began to shrink in the south. New States arose, some Muslim, some Hindu, notably the Hindu empire of Vijayanagar. For 200 years Islam lost ground to some extent, and it was only when the great Akbar came, in the middle of the sixteenth century, that it spread again across nearly the whole of India.

The coming of the Muslim invaders into India produced many reactions. Remember that these invaders were Afghans, and not Arabs or Persians or the cultured and highly civilized Muslims of western Asia. From the point of view of civilization these Afghans were backward as compared to Indians; but they were full of energy and far more alive than India was at the time. India was too much in a rut. It was becoming unchanging and unprogressive. It stuck to the old ways and made no attempt to better them. Even with regard to methods of warfare India was backward, and the Afghans were far better organized. So, in spite of courage and sacrifice, the old India went down before the Muslim invader.

These Muslims were fierce and cruel enough to begin with. They came from a hard country where "softness" was not much appreciated. Added to this was the fact that they were in a newly conquered country, surrounded by enemies, who might revolt at any moment. Fear of rebellion must have been ever present, and fear often produces cruelty and frightfulness. So there were massacres to cow down the people. It was not a question of a Muslim killing a Hindu because of his religion; but a question of an alien conqueror trying to break the spirit of the conquered. Religion is almost always brought in to explain these acts of cruelty, but this is not correct. Sometimes religion was used as a pretext. But the real causes were political or social. The people from Central Asia, who invaded India, were fierce and merciless even in their homelands and long before they were converted to Islam. Having conquered a new country, they knew only one way of keeping it under control—the way of terror.

Gradually, however, we find India toning down these fierce warriors and civilizing them. They begin to feel as if they were Indians, and not foreign invaders. They marry women of the country, and the distinction between invader and the invaded slowly lessens.

It will interest you to know that Mahmud of Ghazni, who was the greatest destroyer that northern India had known, and who is said to have been a champion of Islam against the " idolaters ", had a Hindu army corps under a Hindu general, named Tilak. He took Tilak and his army to Ghazni and used him to put down rebellious Muslims. So you will see that for Mahmud the object was conquest. In India he was prepared to kill " idolaters " with the help of his Muslim soldiers; in central Asia he was equally prepared to kill Muslims with the help of his Hindu soldiers.

Islam shook up India. It introduced vitality and an impulse for progress in a society which was becoming wholly unprogressive. Hindu art, which had become decadent and morbid, and heavy with repetition and detail, undergoes a change in the north. A new art grows up, which might be called Indo-Muslim, full of energy and vitality. The old Indian master-builders draw inspiration from the new ideas brought by the Muslims. The very simplicity of the Muslim creed and outlook on life influenced the architecture of the day, and brought back to it simple and noble design.

The first effect of the Muslim invasion was an exodus of people to the south. After Mahmud's raids and massacres, Islam was associated in northern India with barbarous cruelty and destruction. So when the new invasion came and could not be checked, crowds of skilled craftsmen and learned men went to southern India. This gave a great impetus to Aryan culture in the south.

I have told you already something of the south. How the Chalukyas were the dominant power in the west and centre (the Maharashtra country) from the middle of the sixth century onwards for 200 years. Hiuen Tsang visited Pulakesin II, who was the ruler then. Then came the Rashtrakutas, who defeated the Chalukyas and dominated the south for another 200 years, from the eighth to nearly the end of the tenth century. These Rashtrakutas were on

the best of terms with the Arab rulers of Sindh, and many Arab
traders and travellers visited them.   One such traveller has left an
account of his visit.   He tells us that the ruler of the Rashtrakutas
of the time (ninth century) was one of the four great monarchs of the
world.   The other three great monarchs were, in his opinion, the Caliph
of Baghdad, the Emperor of China, and the Emperor of Rum (that is,
Constantinople).   This is interesting as showing what the prevalent
opinion in Asia must have been at the time.   For an Arab traveller
to compare the kingdom of the Rashtrakutas with the Caliph's
Empire, when Baghdad was at the height of its glory and power,
means that this kingdom of Maharashtra must have been very
strong and powerful.

These Rashtrakutas gave place again to the Chalukyas in the
tenth century (973 A.C.), and these remained in power again for
over 200 years (up to 1190 A.C.).   There is a long poem about one
of these Chalukyan kings, and in this it is stated that he was chosen
by his wife at a public *swayamvar*.[1]   It is interesting to find this
old Aryan custom surviving for so long.

Farther south and east in India lay the Tamil country.   Here
from the third century to the ninth, for about 600 years, the
Pallavas ruled; and for 200 years, beginning from the middle of
the sixth century, they dominated the south.   You will remember
that it was these Pallavas who sent out colonizing expeditions to
Malaysia and the eastern islands.   The capital of the Pallava state
was Kanchi or Conjeevaram, a beautiful city then, and even now
remarkable for its wise town-planning.

The Pallavas give place to the aggressive Cholas early in the
tenth century.   I have told you something of the Chola Empire of
Rajaraja and Rajendra, who built great fleets and went conquering
to Ceylon, Burma and Bengal.   More interesting is the information
we have of the elective village *panchāyat* system they had.   This
system was built up from below, village unions electing many committees to look after various kinds of work, and also electing district
unions.   Several districts formed a province.   I have often, in
these letters, laid stress on this village *panchāyat* system, as this was
the backbone of the old Aryan polity.

About the time of the Afghan invasions in northern India, the
Cholas were dominant in southern India.   Soon, however, they
began to decline, and a little kingdom, which was subordinate to
them, became independent and grew in power.   This was the
Pandya kingdom, with Madura for its capital and Kayal as its port.
A famous traveller from Venice, Marco Polo, about whom I shall
have something more to say later, visited Kayal, the port, twice,
in 1288 and in 1293.   He describes the town as " a great and noble
city ", full of ships from Arabia and China, and humming with
business.   Marco himself came by ship from China.

Marco Polo also tells us that the finest muslins, which " look like
tissue of spider's web ", were made on the east coast of India.

[1] In ancient India it was a custom for a daughter of a king to choose her
husband at a gathering to which all the eligible kings and princes were invited.

Marco mentions that a lady—Rudramani Devi—was the queen in the Telugu country—that is, the east coast north of Madras. This lady ruled for forty years, and she is highly praised by Marco.

Another interesting piece of information we get from Marco is that large numbers of horses were imported into southern India by sea from Arabia and Persia. The climate of the south was not suitable for horse-breeding. It is said that one of the reasons why the Muslim invaders of India were better fighters was their possession of the better horses. The best horse-breeding grounds in Asia were under their control.

The Pandya Kingdom was thus the leading Tamil Power in the thirteenth century, when the Cholas declined. Early in the fourteenth century (in 1310) the Muslim wedge of invasion reached south. It drove into the Pandya kingdom, which rapidly collapsed.

I have surveyed south Indian history in this letter, and perhaps repeated what I had previously said. But the subject is a little confusing, and people get mixed up between the Pallavas and the Chalukyas and Cholas and the rest of them. And yet if you look at it as a whole you may be able to fit the broad framework into your mind. Ashoka, you will remember, ruled over the whole of India (except for a tiny tip at the bottom) and Afghanistan and part of Central Asia. After him rose, in the south, the Andhra power, which extended right across the Deccan, and lasted for 400 years, about the time that the Kushans had their borderland empire in the north. As the Telugu Andhras decline, the Tamil Pallavas rise on the east coast and the south and for a very long period they hold sway. They colonize in Malaysia. After 600 years of rule, they give place to the Cholas, who conquer distant lands and sweep the seas with their navies. Three hundred years later they retire from the scene, and the Pandyan kingdom emerges into prominence, and the city of Madura becomes a centre of culture and Kayal a great and busy port in touch with distant countries.

So much for the south and east. On the west, in the Maharashtra country, there were the Chalukyas and then the Rashtrakutas, and then again, for a second time, the Chalukyas.

All these are just names. But consider the long periods for which these kingdoms lasted and the high degree of civilization attained. There was an inner strength which seems to have given more stability and peace to them than the kingdoms of Europe had. But the social structure had outlived its day and the stability had gone. It was soon to topple over when the Muslim armies moved southward early in the fourteenth century.

66

THE SLAVE KINGS OF DELHI

June 24, 1932

I HAVE told you of Sultan Mahmud of Ghazni, and I have also said something of the poet Firdausi, who wrote the *Shāhnāma* in Persian at Mahmud's request. But I have not told you yet of another distinguished man of Mahmud's time, who came with him to the Punjab. This was Alberuni, a learned man and a scholar, very different from the fierce and bigoted warriors of the day. He travelled all over India, trying to understand the new country and its people. So keen was he to appreciate the Indian viewpoint that he learnt Sanskrit and read for himself the principal books of the Hindus. He studied the philosophy of India and the sciences and arts as taught here. The *Bhagawad Gita* became quite a favourite of his. He went south to the Chola kingdom and was amazed at the great irrigation works he saw there. The record of his wanderings in India is one of the great travel books of old days that we still have. In a welter of destruction and massacre and intolerance, he stands out, the patient scholar, observing and learning, and trying to find out where truth lay.

After Shahab-ud-din, the Afghan, who defeated Prithwi Raj, there came a succession of Sultans of Delhi called the Slave Kings. The first of them was Qutub-ud-din. He had been a slave of Shahab-ud-din, but even slaves could rise to high positions, and he managed to become the first Sultan of Delhi. Some others after him were also originally slaves, and hence this is called the slave dynasty. They were all pretty fierce, and conquest and destruction of buildings and libraries and terrorization went together. They were fond of building also, and they liked size in building. Qutub-ud-din started building the Qutub Minar, the great tower near Delhi which you know so well. His successor, Iltutmish, finished the tower and also built near it some beautiful arches, which still exist. The materials for these buildings were almost all taken from old Indian buildings, chiefly temples. The master-builders were all of course Indian, but, as I have told you, they were greatly influenced by the new ideas brought by the Muslims.

Every invader of India from Mahmud of Ghazni onwards took back with him crowds of Indian artisans and master-builders. The influence of Indian architecture thus spread in Central Asia.

Bihar and Bengal were conquered by the Afghans with the greatest ease. They were audacious, and took the defenders completely by surprise, and audacity often pays. This conquest of Bengal is almost as surprising as the conquests of Cortés and Pizarro in America.

It was during the reign of Iltutmish (from 1211 to 1236) that a great and terrifying cloud hovered over the frontiers of India. This was composed of the Mongols under Chengiz Khan. Right up to the Indus he came, pursuing an enemy, but there he stopped. India escaped him. It was nearly 200 years later that another of his breed, Timur, came down to India to massacre and destroy. But although Chengiz did not come, many Mongols made a practice of raiding India, and even coming right up to Lahore. They spread terror and frightened even the Sultans, who sometimes bribed them off. Many thousands of them settled down in the Punjab.

Among the Sultans there is a woman named Razia. She was the daughter of Iltutmish. She seems to have been an able person and a brave fighter, but she had a hard time with her fierce Afghan nobles and the fiercer Mongols raiding the Punjab.

The Slave kings ended in 1290. Soon after came Ala-ud-din Khilji, who came to the throne by the gentle method of murdering his uncle, who was also his father-in-law. He followed this up by having all the Muslim nobles whom he suspected of disloyalty killed. Fearing a Mongol plot, he ordered that every Mongol in his territories should be killed, so that " not one of the stock should be left alive upon the face of the earth ". And so 20,000 or 30,000 of them, most of them of course quite innocent, were massacred.

I am afraid these references to massacres repeatedly are not very pleasing. Nor are they very important from the larger viewpoint of history. Still, they help one to realize that conditions in northern India at this time were far from secure or civilized. There was a reversion to some extent to barbarism. While Islam brought an element of progress to India, the Muslim Afghans brought an element of barbarism. Many people mix up the two, but they should be distinguished.

Ala-ud-din was intolerant, like the others. But it seems as if the outlook of these Central Asian rulers of India was now changing. They were beginning to think of India as their home. They were no longer strangers here. Ala-ud-din married a Hindu lady, and so did his son.

Under Ala-ud-din there seems to have been an attempt made to have a more or less efficient system of government. The lines of communication were especially kept in order for the movements of the army, and the army was the special care of Ala-ud-din. He made it very powerful, and with it he conquered Gujrat and a great part of the south. His general returned from the south with enormous wealth. It is said that he brought 50,000 maunds of gold, a vast quantity of jewels and pearls, and 20,000 horses and 312 elephants.

Chittor, the home of romance and chivalry, full of courage, but even then old-fashioned and sticking to outworn methods of warfare, was overwhelmed by Ala-ud-din's efficient army. There was a sack of Chittor in 1303. But before this could take place, the men and women of the fortress, obedient to old custom, performed the terrible rite of *jauhar*. According to this, when defeat threatens and there is no other way, in the last extremity, it was better for the men to go out and die in the field of battle and for the women to burn themselves on a pyre. A terrible thing this was, especially for the women. It would have been better if the women, too, had gone out sword in hand and died on the battlefield. But, in any event, death was preferable to slavery and degradation, as conquest in war meant in those days.

Meanwhile the people of the country, the Hindus, were being slowly converted to Islam. The process was not rapid. Some changed their religion because Islam appealed to them, some did so because of fear, some because it is natural to want to be on the winning side. But the principal reason for the change was economic. People who were not Muslims had to pay a special tax, a poll tax—*jezia*, as it was called. This was a great burden on the poor. Many would change their religion just to escape it. Among the higher classes desire to gain Court favour and high office was a powerful motive. Ala-ud-din's great general, Malik Kafur, who conquered the south, was a convert from Hinduism.

I must tell you about another Sultan of Delhi, a most extra-ordinary individual. He was Mohammad bin Tughlaq. He was a most learned and accomplished man both in Persian, and Arabic. He had studied philosophy and logic, even Greek philosophy. He knew something of mathematics and science and medicine. He was a brave man, and was for his times quite a paragon of learning and a wonder. And yet, and yet, this paragon was a monster of cruelty and seems to have been quite mad! He came to the throne by killing his own father. He had fantastic notions of conquering Persia and China. Naturally they came to grief. But his most famous exploit was his decision to ruin Delhi, his own capital, because some of the people of the city had dared to criticize his policy in anonymous notices. He ordered that the capital should be transferred from Delhi to Deoghiri in the south (in Hyderabad State now). This place he called Daulatabad. Some compensation was paid to the owners of houses, and then every one, without exception, was ordered to leave the city within three days.

Most people left. Some hid themselves. When they were found they were punished cruelly, even though one was a blind man and another a paralytic. It was forty days' march to Daulatabad from Delhi. One can imagine what the terrible condition of the people must have been during this march and how many must have dropped on the way.

And the city of Delhi, what became of it? Two years later Mohammad bin Tughlaq tried to re-people Delhi. But he did not succeed. He had previously made it into a " perfect desert ", as an eye-witness tells us. It is possible to make a garden into a wilderness quickly; but it is not easy to re-convert the wilderness into a garden. Ibn Battuta, an African Moorish traveller, who was with the Sultan, returned to Delhi, and he says that " it is one of the greatest cities in the universe. When we entered this capital we found it in the state which has been described. It was empty, abandoned, and had but a small population." Another person describing the city as spreading over eight or ten miles : " All was destroyed. So complete was the ruin, that not a cat or a dog was left among the buildings of the city, in its palaces or in its suburbs."

This madman ruled as Sultan for twenty-five years, right up to 1351. It is amazing how much knavery and cruelty and incompetence in their rulers people will put up with. But in spite of the servility of the people Mohammad bin Tughlaq was successful in breaking up his empire. The country was ruined by his mad schemes and by heavy taxation. There were famines, and at last there were revolts. Even in his lifetime, from 1340 onwards, large areas of the empire became independent. Bengal became independent. In the south several States arose. Chief of these was the Hindu State of Vijayanagar, which arose in 1336 and within ten years was a great Power in the south.

Near Delhi you can still see the ruins of Tughlaqabad, which was built by Mohammad's father.

67

CHENGIZ KHAN SHAKES UP ASIA AND EUROPE

June 25, 1932

IN many of my recent letters I have referred to the Mongols and hinted at the terror and destruction that they caused. In China our account of the Sung dynasty stopped with the coming of the Mongols. In western Asia again we come up against them, and there is an end of the old order. In India the Slave Kings escaped them, but none the less they created enough commotion. All Asia seems to have been brought low by these nomads from Mongolia. And not Asia only, but half Europe too. Who were these amazing people who suddenly burst forth and astounded the world? The Scythians and the Huns and Turks and the Tartars —all from Central Asia—had already played a notable part in history. Some of these peoples were still prominent; the Seljuq Turks in western Asia, the Tartars in northern China and elsewhere. But the Mongols had so far done nothing much. Probably no one in western Asia knew much about them. They belonged to many unimportant tribes in Mongolia and were subject to the Kin Tartars, who had conquered the north of China.

Suddenly they seemed to gain power. Their scattered tribes joined together and elected a single leader, the Great Khan, and swore allegiance and obedience to him. Under him they marched to Peking and put an end to the Kin Empire. They marched west and swept away the great kingdoms they found on their way. They went to Russia and subdued it. Later they wiped off completely Baghdad and its empire and went right up to Poland and central Europe. There was none to stop them. India escaped by

a sheer chance. One can well imagine what the amazement of the
Eurasian world must have been at this volcanic eruption. It almost
seemed like a great natural calamity, like an earthquake, before
which man can do little.

Strong men and women they were, these nomads from Mongolia,
used to hardship, and living in tents on the wide steppes of northern
Asia. But their strength and hard training might not have availed
them much if they had not produced a chief who was a most remarkable man. This was the person who is known as Chengiz Khan
(or Genghiz or Jenghiz or Jengiz Khan—there are many ways of
spelling it). He was born in 1155 A.C. and his original name was
Timuchin. His father,Yesugei-Bagatur,died when he was a little boy.
" Bagatur ", by the way, was a favourite name for Mongol nobles.
It means " hero " and I suppose the Urdu *bahadur* comes from it.

Although just a little boy of ten, with no one to help him, he
struggled on and on, and ultimately made good. Step by step he
advanced till at last the great Mongol Assembly, called the *Kurul-
tai*, met and elected him the Great Khan or Kagan or Emperor.
A few years before he had been given the name of Chengiz.

A *Secret History of the Mongol People* written in the thirteenth
century, and published in China in the fourteenth century, describes
this election :

> " And so, when all the generations living in felt tents became
> united under a single authority, in the year of the Leopard, they
> assembled near the sources of the Onon, and raising the White
> Banner on Nine Legs, they conferred on Chengiz the title of
> Kagan."

Chengiz was already fifty-one years of age when he became the
Great Khan or Kagan. He was not very young, and most people
at this age want peace and quiet. But this was only the beginning
of his career of conquest. This is worthy of notice, as most great
conquerors do their conquering when fairly young. This also
reminds us that Chengiz did not simply dash across Asia in a fit of
youthful enthusiasm. He was a cautious and careful middle-aged
man, and every big thing he did was preceded by thought and
preparation.

The Mongols were nomads, hating cities and the ways of cities.
Many people think that because they were nomads they must have
been barbarians. But this is a mistaken idea. They did not
know, of course, many of the city arts, but they had developed a
way of life of their own and had an intricate organization. If they
won great victories on the field of battle, it was not because of their
numbers, but because of their discipline and organization. And
above all it was due to the brilliant captainship of Chengiz. For
Chengiz is, without doubt, the greatest military genius and leader
in history. Alexander and Cæsar seem petty before him. Chengiz
was not only himself a very great commander, but he trained many
of his generals and made them brilliant leaders. Thousands of
miles away from their homelands, surrounded by enemies and a

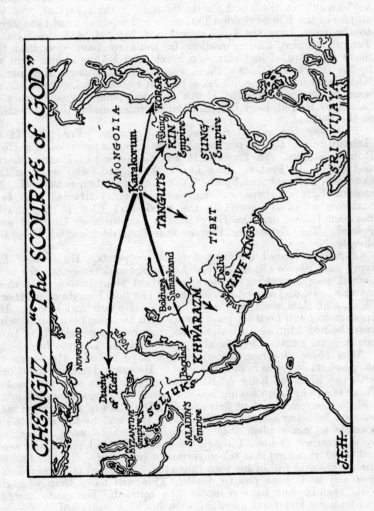

hostile population, they carried on victorious warfare against superior numbers.

What was the map of Asia and Europe like when Chengiz appeared striding over it ?   China to the east and south of Mongolia was split up.   To the south was the Sung Empire, where the Southern Sungs held sway; to the north, with Peking for their capital, was the empire of the Kin or Golden Tartars, who had driven out the Sungs; to the west, over the Gobi desert and beyond, was the Hsia or Tangut Empire, also nomadic.   In India we have seen that the Slave Kings ruled in Delhi.   In Persia and Mesopotamia, right up to the frontiers of India, there was the great Muslim kingdom of Khwarazm or Khiva, with its capital at Samarqand.   West of this were the Seljuqs, and in Egypt and Palestine the successors of Saladin.   Round Baghdad, the Caliph ruled under the protection of the Seljuqs.

This was the period of the later Crusades.   Frederick II of Hohenstaufen, the *stupor mundi*, was the Emperor of the Holy Roman Empire.   In England it was the period of Magna Charta and after.   In France, King Louis IX reigned, who went to the Crusades, got captured by the Turks and was then ransomed.   In eastern Europe, there was Russia, apparently divided into two States, that of Novgorod in the north and Kiev in the south. Between Russia and the Holy Roman Empire were Hungary and Poland.   The Byzantine Empire still flourished round Constantinople.

Chengiz prepared carefully for his conquests.   He trained his army and, above all, he trained his horses and remounts, for to a nomad people nothing is more important than horses.   He then marched east and almost put an end to the Kin Empire of northern China and Manchuria, and took Peking.   He subdued Korea.   He appears to have been on good terms with the Southern Sungs who even helped him against the Kins, not realizing that their turn might come next.   Chengiz also conquered the Tanguts later.

After these victories Chengiz might have rested.   He seems to have had no desire to invade the west.   He wanted friendly relations with the Shah or King of Khwarazm.   But this was not to be. There is an old Latin saying which means that those whom the gods wish to destroy they first drive mad.   The Shah of Khwarazm was bent on bringing about his own destruction and he did everything possible to accomplish this.   Mongol merchants were massacred by a governor of his.   Chengiz even then wanted peace and sent ambassadors asking that the governor be punished.   But the foolish Shah, vain and full of his own importance, insulted these ambassadors and had them put to death.   This was more than Chengiz could stand; but he was not to be hurried.   He made careful preparations and then marched with his host westward.

This march, begun in 1219, opened the eyes of Asia, and partly of Europe too, to this new terror, this great roller which came on inexorably, crushing down cities and men by the million.   The Empire of Khwarazm ceased to exist.   The great city of Bokhara, full of palaces, and with over a million population, was reduced to ashes. Samarqand, the capital, was destroyed, and out of a million people that lived there, only 50,000 remained alive. Herat, Balkh and many other flourishing cities were all destroyed. Millions were killed. All the arts and crafts that had flourished in Central Asia for hundreds of years disappeared, civilized life seemed to cease in Persia and in central Asia. There was desert where Chengiz had passed.

The son of the Shah of Khwarazm, Jalaluddin, fought bravely against this flood. He retreated right up to the Indus river and, pressed hard there, he is said to have jumped on horseback 30 feet down into the great river and swum across. He found shelter at the Delhi Court. Chengiz did not think it worth while to pursue him there.

Fortunately for the Seljuq Turks and Baghdad, Chengiz left them in peace and marched north into Russia. He defeated and took prisoner the Grand Duke of Kiev. He returned east to crush a rebellion of Hsias or Tanguts.

Chengiz died in 1227 at the age of seventy-two. His empire extended from the Black Sea in the west to the Pacific Ocean, and it was still vigorous and growing. His capital was still the little town of Karakorum in Mongolia. Nomad as he was, he was an extremely able organizer, and he was wise enough to employ able ministers to help him. His empire, so rapidly conquered, did not break up at his death.

To Persian and Arab historians Chengiz is a monster—the " Scourge of God " as he is called. He is painted as a very cruel person. He was very cruel, no doubt, but he was not very different from many of the rulers of his day. In India the Afghan kings were much the same, on a smaller scale. When Ghazni was captured by the Afghans in 1150 they revenged themselves for an old blood-feud by sacking and burning the city. For seven days " plunder, devastation and slaughter were continuous. Every man that was found was slain, and all the women and children were made prisoners. All the palaces and edifices of the Mahmudi Kings (that is, descendants of Sultan Mahmud), which had no equals in the world, were destroyed." This was the behaviour of Muslims towards brother-Muslims. There was nothing to choose in quality between this and what took place in India under the Afghan kings and Chengiz's career of destruction in Central Asia and Persia. Chengiz was particularly angry with Khwarazm because his ambassador had been killed by the Shah. For him it was a kind of blood-feud. Elsewhere there was great destruction done by Chengis. But perhaps it was not so great as in Central Asia.

There was another motive behind Chengiz's destruction of towns. He had the spirit of a nomad, and he hated towns and cities. He liked living in the steppes or great plains. At one time Chengiz considered the desirability of destroying all the cities in China, but fortunately he desisted ! His idea was to combine civilization with a nomadic life. But this was not, and is not, possible.

You might perhaps think from Chengiz Khan's name that he was a Mohammedan. But this was not so. The name is a Mongol name. Chengiz was a very tolerant person in religion. His religion, such as it was, was Shamaism, a worship of the " Everlasting Blue Sky ". He used to have long talks with Chinese Tao-ist sages, but he stuck to Shamaism, and when in difficulty, consulted the sky.

You must have noticed, earlier in this letter, that Chengiz was " elected " Great Khan by an assembly of the Mongols. This assembly was really a feudal assembly, not a popular one, and Chengiz was thus the feudal head of the clan.

He was illiterate, and so also were all his followers. Probably he did not even know that there was such a thing as writing for a long time. Messages were sent by word of mouth, and were usually in verse in the form of allegories and proverbs. It is amazing how business could be carried on in a vast empire by means of oral messages. When Chengiz learnt that there was such a thing as writing, he felt immediately that this was very useful and valuable, and he ordered his sons and chief officers to learn it. He also ordered that the old customary law of the Mongols must be put down in writing, also his own sayings. The idea was that this customary law was the " unchangeable law " for ever and ever, and no one could disobey it. Even the Emperor was subject to it. But this " unchangeable law " is lost now, and even the present-day Mongols have no recollection or tradition of it.

Every country and every religion has its old customary law and written law, and often it imagines that this is the " unchangeable law " which will endure for ever. Sometimes it is considered as " revelation "—that is, something " revealed " by God—and what God is supposed to reveal cannot be considered as changing or transitory. But laws are meant to fit existing conditions, and they are meant to help us to better ourselves. If conditions change, how can the old laws fit in ? They must change with changing conditions, or else they become iron chains keeping us back while the world marches on. No law can be an " unchangeable law " It must be based on knowledge, and as knowledge grows, it must grow with it.

I have given you more details and information about Chengiz Khan than was perhaps necessary. But the man fascinates me. Strange, is it not, that this fierce and cruel and violent feudal chief of a nomadic tribe should fascinate a peaceful and non-violent and mild person like me, who am a dweller of cities and a hater of everything feudal !

68

THE MONGOLS DOMINATE THE WORLD

June 26, 1932

WHEN Chengiz Khan died, his son, Oghotai, became the Great Khan. Compared to Chengiz and to the Mongols of his time, he was humane and peacefully inclined. He was fond of saying that : " Our Kagan Chengiz built up our imperial house with great labour. Now it is time to give the peoples peace and prosperity, and to alleviate their burdens." Notice how he thinks as a feudal chief, in terms of his clan.

But the era of conquest was not over, and the Mongols were still overflowing with energy. There was a second invasion of Europe under the great general, Sabutai. The armies and generals of Europe were no match for Sabutai. Carefully preparing his ground by sending spies and advance agents to the enemy countries to bring information, he knew well what the political and military situation of these countries was before he advanced. On the field of battle he was the master of the art of war, and the European generals seemed to be just beginners at it in comparison with him. Sabutai marched straight to Russia, leaving Baghdad and the Seljuqs in peace on the south-west. For six years he marched on and on, plundering and destroying Moscow, Kiev, Poland, Hungary, Cracow. In 1241 a Polish and German army was annihilated at Liebnitz in Lower Silesia in Central Europe. The whole of Europe seemed to be doomed. There was nobody to stop the Mongols. Frederick II, wonder of the world though he was called, must have paled before this real wonder which had come out of Mongolia. The kings and rulers of Europe gasped, when suddenly unexpected relief came.

Oghotai had died, and there was some trouble about the succession. So the Mongol armies in Europe, undefeated though they were, turned back and marched east to their homelands in 1242. Europe breathed again.

Meanwhile the Mongols had spread in China, and finished off completely the Kins in the north and even the Sungs in South China. Mangu Khan became the Great Khan in 1252, and he appointed Kublai the Governor of China. To Mangu's Court at Karakorum came a great concourse of people from Asia and Europe. Still the Great Khan lived in tents, after the way of the nomads. But the tents were rich and full of the plunder and wealth of continents. Merchants came, especially Muslim merchants, and found the Mongols generous buyers. Artisans and astrologers and mathematicians and men who dabbled in the science of the day, all gathered together in this city of tents which seemed to lord it over the world There was a measure of peace and order over the vast Mongol Empire, and the great caravan routes across the continents were full of people going to and fro.   Europe and Asia were brought into closer contact with each other.

And then there was a race between the men of religion to Kara-korum.   They all wanted to convert these conquerors of the world to their own particular brand of religion.   The religion that suc-ceeded in getting these all-powerful people on its side would surely itself become all-powerful and would triumph over all others.   The Pope sent envoys from Rome; the Nestorian Christians came; the Muslims were there; and so also were the Buddhists.   The Mongols were in no great hurry to adopt any new religion.   They were not an over-religious people.   It appears that at one time the Great Khan flirted with the idea of adopting Christianity, but he could not tolerate the claims of the Pope.   Ultimately the Mongols drifted into the religions of the areas where they settled down.   In China and Mongolia most of them became Buddhists; in Central Asia they became Muslims; perhaps some in Russia and in Hungary became Christians.

There is still in existence in the Pope's library at the Vatican in Rome an original letter of the Great Khan (Mangu) to the Pope. It is in Arabic.   It appears that the Pope had sent an envoy warning the new Khan, after Oghotai's death, not to invade Europe again. The Khan replied that he had invaded Europe because the Europeans did not behave properly towards him.

Yet another wave of conquest and destruction took place in Mangu's time.   His brother Hulagu was Governor in Persia. Annoyed with the Caliph at Baghdad about something, Hulagu sent a message to him chiding him for not keeping his promises, and telling him to behave better in future or else he would lose his empire.   The Caliph was not a very wise man, nor could he profit by experience.   He sent an offensive reply, and the Mongol envoys were insulted by a mob in Baghdad.   Hulagu's Mongol blood was up at this.   In a rage he marched on Baghdad, and after forty days' siege he took it.   That was the end of the city of the *Arabian Nights*, and all the treasures that had accumulated there during 500 years of empire.   The Caliph and his sons and near relatives were put to death.   There was a general massacre for weeks, till the river Tigris was dyed red with blood for miles.   It is said that a million and a half people perished.   All the artistic and literary treasures and libraries were destroyed.   Baghdad was utterly ruined.   Even the ancient irrigation system of western Asia, thousands of years old, was destroyed by Hulagu.

Aleppo and Edessa and many another city shared the same fate, and the shadow of night fell over western Asia.   A historian of the time says that this was a " period of famine for science and virtue ".   A Mongol army sent to Palestine was defeated by Sultan Baibers of Egypt.   This Sultan had an interesting surname —" Bandūkdār "—because of a regiment of men armed with *bandūks* or firearms.   We now come to the era of the firearms. The Chinese had long known gunpowder.   The Mongols probably learnt it from them and it may be that firearms helped them in their victories. It was through the Mongols that firearms were introduced into Europe.

The destruction of Baghdad in 1258 put an end finally to what remained of the Abbaside Empire. This was the end of the distinctive Arab civilization in western Asia. Far away in southern Spain, Granada still carried on the Arab tradition. It was to last for over 200 years more before it too collapsed. Arabia itself sank rapidly in importance, and its people have played no great part in history since. Later they became part of the Ottoman Turkish Empire. During the Great War of 1914–18 there was an Arab rebellion against the Turks, engineered by the English, and since then Arabia has been more or less independent.

There was no Caliph for two years. Then Sultan Baibers of Egypt nominated a relative of the last Abbaside Caliph as Caliph. But he had no political power and was just a spiritual head. Three hundred years later the Turkish Sultan of Constantinople obtained this title of Caliph from the last holder. The Turkish Sultans continued to be Caliph till both Sultan and Caliph were ended a few years ago by Mustafa Kamal Pasha.

I have digressed from my story. Mangu, the Great Khan, died in 1239. He had conquered Tibet before his death. Kublai Khan, the Governor of China, now became the Great Khan. Kublai had long been in China, and this country interested him. He therefore moved his capital from Karakorum to Peking, changing the name of the city to Khanbalik, the " City of the Khan ". Kublai's interest in Chinese affairs made him neglect his great empire, and gradually the great Mongol governors became independent.

Kublai completed the conquest of China, but his campaigns were very different from the old Mongol campaigns. There was much less cruelty and destruction. China had already toned down and civilized Kublai. The Chinese also took to him kindly and treated him almost as one of themselves. He actually founded an orthodox Chinese dynasty—the Yuan dynasty. Kublai added Tongking, Annam and Burma to his empire. He tried to conquer Japan and Malaysia, but failed because the Mongols were not used to the sea and did not know ship-building.

During the reign of Mangu Khan, an interesting embassy came to him from the King of France—Louis IX. Louis suggested an alliance between the Mongols and the Christian Powers of Europe against the Muslims. Poor Louis had had a bad time when he was taken prisoner during the Crusades. But the Mongols were not interested in such alliances; nor were they interested in attacking any religious people as such.

Why should they ally themselves with the petty kings and princes of Europe ? And against whom ? They had little to fear from the fighting qualities of the western European States or of the Islamic States. It was by sheer chance that western Europe escaped them. The Seljuq Turks bowed down to them and paid tribute. Only the Sultan of Egypt had defeated a Mongol army, but there is little doubt that they could have subdued him if they seriously attempted it. Right across Asia and Europe the mighty Mongol Empire sprawled. There had never been in history anything to compare with the Mongol conquests; there had never been such a vast empire. The Mongols must indeed have seemed at the time the lords of the world. India was free from them at the time simply because they had not gone that way. Western Europe, just about the size of India, was also outside the Empire. But all these places existed almost on sufferance, and only so long as the Mongols did not take it into their heads to swallow them up. So it must have seemed in the thirteenth century.

But the tremendous energy of the Mongol seemed to be lessening; the impulse to go on conquering waned. You must remember that in those days people moved slowly on foot or on horseback. There were no quicker methods of locomotion. For an army to go from its home in Mongolia to the western frontier of the Empire in Europe would itself take a year of journeying. They were not keen enough on conquest to take these mighty journeys through their own empire, when there was no chance of plunder. Besides, repeated success in war and plunder had made the Mongol troopers rich in booty. Many of them may have even had slaves. So they quietened down and began to take to sober and peaceful ways. The man who has got everything he wants is all in favour of peace and order.

The administration of the vast Mongol Empire must have been a very difficult task. It is not surprising therefore that it began to split up. Kublai Khan died in 1292. After him there was no Great Khan. The Empire divided up into five big areas:

(1) The Empire of China, including Mongolia and Manchuria and Tibet. This was the principal one, under Kublai's descendants of the Yuan dynasty;

(2) To the far west in Russia, Poland and Hungary was the Empire of the Golden Horde (as the Mongols there were called);

(3) In Persia and Mesopotamia and part of Central Asia, there was the Ilkhan Empire—which had been founded by Hulagu, and to which the Seljuq Turks paid tribute;

(4) North of Tibet in Central Asia there was Great Turkey, as it was called, the Empire of Zagatai; and

(5) Between Mongolia and the Golden Horde, there was a Siberian Empire of the Mongols.

Although the great Mongol Empire was split up, each one of these five divisions of it was a mighty empire.

69

MARCO POLO, THE GREAT TRAVELLER

June 27, 1932

I HAVE told you of the Court of the Great Khan at Karakorum; how crowds of merchants and artisans and learned men and missionaries came there, attracted by the fame of the Mongols and the glamour of their victories. They came also because the Mongols encouraged them to do so. They were a strange people, these Mongols; highly efficient in some ways, and almost childish in other matters. Even their ferocity and cruelty, shocking as it was, has a childish element in it. It is this childishness in them, I think, that makes these fierce warriors rather attractive. Some hundreds of years later a Mongol, or Moghal, as they were called in India, conquered this country. He was Babar, and his mother was a descendant of Chengiz Khan. Having conquered India, he sighed for the cool breezes and the flowers and gardens and water-melons of Kabul and the north. He was a delightful person, and the memoirs that he wrote make him still a very human and attractive figure.

So the Mongols encouraged visitors from abroad to their Courts. They had a desire for knowledge and wanted to learn from them. You will remember my telling you that as soon as Chengiz Khan learned that there was such a thing as writing, he immediately grasped the significance of it and ordered his officers to learn it. They had open and receptive minds and could learn from others. Kublai Khan, after settling down in Peking and becoming a respectable Chinese monarch, especially encouraged visitors from foreign countries. To him journeyed two merchants from Venice, the brothers Nicolo Polo and Maffeo Polo. They had gone right up to Bokhara in quest of business, and there they met some envoys sent by Kublai Khan to Hulagu in Persia. They were induced to join this caravan, and thus they journeyed to the Court of the Great Khan in Peking.

Nicolo and Maffeo were well received by Kublai Khan, and they told him about Europe and Christianity and the Pope. Kublai was greatly interested, and seems to have been attracted towards Christianity. He sent the Polos back to Europe in 1269 with a message for the Pope. He asked that 100 learned men, " intelligent men acquainted with the seven arts " and able to justify Christianity, should be sent to him. But the two Polos on their return found Europe and the Pope in a bad way. There were no such 100 learned men to be had. After two years' delay they journeyed back with two Christian friars or monks. What was far more important, they took with them Nicolo's son, a young man named Marco.

The three Polos started on their tremendous journey and crossed the whole length of Asia by the land routes. What mighty journeys they were! Even now, to follow the route of the Polos would take the best part of a year. Partly the Polos followed the old route of Hiuen Tsang. They went *via* Palestine to Armenia and then to Mesopotamia and the Persian Gulf, where they met merchants from India. Across Persia to Balkh, and over the mountains to Kashgar, and then to Khotan and the Lop-Nor, the Wandering Lake. Again the desert, and so on to the fields of China and Peking. They had a sovereign passport with them—a gold tablet given by the Great Khan himself.

This was the old caravan route between China and Syria in the days of ancient Rome. A short while ago I read of a journey across the Gobi Desert by Sven Hedin, the Swedish explorer and traveller. He went from Peking west, crossing the desert, touching the Lake —Lop-Nor—on to Khotan and beyond. He had every modern convenience with him, and yet his expedition had to face trouble and suffering. What must the journey have been like 700 and 1300 years ago, when the Polos and Hiuen Tsang went that way! Sven Hedin made an interesting discovery. He found that Lop-Nor, the lake, had changed its position. Long ago, in the fourth century, the river Tarin, which flows into the Lop-Nor, changed its course, and the desert sands quickly came and covered its old deserted course. The old city of Loulan that stood there was cut off from the outside world and its inhabitants left it to its ruin. The lake also changed its position because of this river, and the old caravan and trade route did likewise. Sven Hedin found that very recently, only a few years ago, the Tarin river had again changed its course and gone back to its old position. The lake has followed it. Again the Tarin goes by the ruins of the old city of Loulan, and it may be that the old route, unused for 1600 years, may again come into fashion, but the place of the camel may be taken by the motor-car. It is because of this that Lop-Nor is called the Wandering Lake. I have told you of the wanderings of the Tarin river and the Lop-Nor, as it will give some idea of how water-courses change large areas, and thus affect history. Central Asia, in the old days, as we have seen, had a teeming population; and wave after wave of its people went conquering to the west and to the south. To-day it is almost a deserted area, with few towns and a sparse population. Probably there was much more water there at that time, and so it could support a big population. As the climate became drier and water less abundant, the population lessened and dwindled away.

There was one advantage in these long journeys. One had time to learn the new language or languages. The three Polos took three and a half years to reach Peking from Venice, and during this long period Marco mastered the Mongol language, and perhaps Chinese also. Marco became a favourite with the Great Khan, and for nearly seventeen years he served him. He was made governor, and went on official missions to different parts of China. Although Marco and his father were homesick and wanted to return to Venice, it was not easy to get the Khan's permission. At last they had a chance of returning. The Mongol ruler of the

Ilkhan Empire in Persia, who was a cousin of Kublai's, lost his wife. He wanted to marry again, but his old wife had made him promise not to marry any woman outside their clan. So Argon (that was his name) sent envoys to Kublai Khan to Peking and begged him to send a suitable woman of the clan to him.

Kublai Khan selected a young Mongol princess, and the three Polos were added to her escort as they were experienced travellers. They went by sea from the south of China to Sumatra and stayed there for some time. The Buddhist Empire of Sri Vijaya flourished in Sumatra then, but it was shrinking. From Sumatra the party came to South India. I have already told you of Marco's visit to the flourishing port of Kayal in the Pandya kingdom of South India. The Princess and Marco and the party made a fairly long stay in India. They seem to have been in no hurry, and it took them two years to reach Persia. But meanwhile the expectant bridegroom had died ! He had waited long enough. Perhaps it was not such a great misfortune that he died. The young Princess married Argon's son, who was much more her age.

The Polos left the Princess and went on towards home *via* Constantinople. They reached Venice in 1295, twenty-four years after they had left it. No one recognized them, and it is said that to impress their old friends and others, they gave a feast, and in the middle of it they ripped open their shabby and padded clothes. Immediately valuable jewels—diamonds, rubies, emeralds and other kinds—came out in heaps and astonished the guests. But still, few people believed the stories of the Polos about their adventures in China and India. They thought that Marco and his father and uncle were exaggerating. Used to their little republic of Venice, they could not imagine the size and wealth of China and other Asiatic countries.

Three years later, in 1295, Venice went to war with the city of Genoa. They were both sea Powers and rivals of each other, and there was a great naval battle between them. The Venetians got beaten, and many thousands of them were made prisoners by the Genoese. Among these prisoners was our friend Marco Polo. Sitting in his prison in Genoa, he wrote, or rather dictated, an account of his travels. In this way the *Travels of Marco Polo* came into existence. What a useful place prison is in which to do good work !

In these travels Marco describes China especially, and the many journeys he made through it; he also describes to some extent Siam, Java, Sumatra, Ceylon and South India. He tells us of the great Chinese seaports crowded with ships from all parts of the Orient, some so large as to carry crews of 300 or 400 men. He describes China as a smiling and prosperous country with many cities and boroughs; and manufactures of " cloth of silk and gold and many fine taffetas "; and " fine vineyards and fields and gardens "; and " excellent hostelries for travellers " all along the routes. He tells of a special messenger service for imperial messages. These messages travelled at the rate of 400 miles in twenty-four hours by relays of horses—which is very good going indeed. We

are informed that the people of China used black stones, which they
dug out of the ground, in place of firewood. This obviously means
that they worked coal-mines and used coal as fuel. Kublai
Khan issued paper money—that is, he issued paper notes with the
promise to pay in gold, as is done to-day. This is most interesting
as showing that a modern method of creating credit was used by
him. Marco mentioned, much to the excitement and amazement of
people in Europe, that a Christian colony, under a ruler, Prester
John, lived in China. Probably these were some old Nestorians in
Mongolia.

About Japan and Burma and India, he also wrote : sometimes
what he had seen, and sometimes what he had heard. Marco's
story was, and still is, a wonderful story of travel. To the people
of Europe in their tight little countries with their petty jealousies
it was an eye-opener. It brought home to them the greatness and
wealth and marvels of the larger world. It excited their imaginations, and called to their sense of adventure, and tickled their
cupidity. It induced them to take to the sea more. Europe was
growing. Its young civilization was finding its feet and struggling
against the restrictions of the Middle Ages. It was full of energy,
like a youth on the verge of manhood. This urge to the sea and
the quest of wealth and adventure carried the Europeans later to
America, round the Cape of Good Hope, to the Pacific, to India, to
China and Japan. The sea became the highway of the world, and
the great caravan routes across continents lessened in importance.

The Great Khan, Kublai, died soon after Marco Polo left him.
The Yuan dynasty, which he had founded in China, did not long
survive him. The Mongol power declined rapidly, and there was a
Chinese nationalist wave against the foreigner. Within sixty years
the Mongols had been driven out from South China, and a Chinaman
had established himself as Emperor at Nanking. In another dozen
years—in 1368—the Yuan dynasty fell finally and the Mongols
were driven beyond the Great Wall. Another great Chinese
dynasty—the " Tai Ming " dynasty—comes upon the scene now.
For a long period, nearly 300 years, this dynasty ruled in China,
and this period is looked upon as one of good government, prosperity
and culture. No attempt was made at foreign conquests or
imperialistic ventures.

The break-up of the Mongol Empire in China resulted in ending
the intercourse between China and Europe. The land routes were
not safe now. The sea routes were not much in use yet.

70

THE ROMAN CHURCH BECOMES MILITANT

June 28, 1932

I HAVE told you that Kublai Khan sent a message to the Pope
asking him to send 100 learned men to China. But the Pope did

no such thing. He was in a bad way at the time. If you remember it, this was the period, after the death of Emperor Frederick II, when there was no Emperor, from 1250 to 1273. Central Europe was in a frightful condition then, and there was disorder, and robber knights plundering everywhere. Rudolph of Hapsburg became Emperor in 1273, but this did not improve matters much. Italy was lost to the Empire.

Not only was there political disorder, but there were the beginnings of what might be called religious disorder, from the point of view of the Roman Church. People were no longer so docile and obedient to the orders of the Church. They had begun to doubt, and doubt is a dangerous thing in matters religious. Already we have seen the Emperor Frederick II treating the Pope casually and not caring much about being excommunicated. He even started an argument with him in writing, and the Pope did not come off well in this argument. There must have been many doubters like Frederick in Europe in his time. There were many also who, though not doubting or objecting to the claims of the Church or the Pope, resented the corruption and luxury of the big men of the Church.

The Crusades were tapering off rather ignominiously. They had started off with great hopes and enthusiasm, but they failed to achieve anything, and such failures always bring about a reaction. Not wholly satisfied with the Church as it was, people began, rather vaguely and gradually, to look elsewhere for light. The Church retaliated by violence, and tried to retain control over men's minds by methods of terrorism. It forgot that the mind of man is a very tricky thing and that brute force is a poor weapon against it. So it tried to strangle the stirrings of conscience in individuals and groups; it tried to meet doubt not by argument and reason, but by the club and the stake.

As early as 1155, the wrath of the Church fell on a popular and earnest preacher, Arnold of Brescia in Italy. Arnold preached against the corruption and luxury of the clergy. He was seized and hanged, and then his dead body was burnt and the ashes were thrown into the river Tiber, so that people might not keep them as relics ! To the last Arnold was constant and calm.

The Popes even went so far as to declare whole groups and Christian sects, who differed in some small matter of belief or who criticized the clergy too much, as outcasts. Regular crusades were proclaimed against these people and every kind of disgusting cruelty and frightfulness was practised against them. In this way were treated the Albigeois (or the Albigenses) of Toulouse in the south of France, and the Waldenses, the followers of a man named Waldo.

About this time, or rather a little earlier, there lived a man in Italy who is one of the most attractive figures in Christianity. He was Francis of Assisi. He was a rich man who gave up his riches and, taking a vow of poverty, went out into the world to serve the sick and the poor. And because lepers were the most unhappy and uncared for, he devoted himself especially to them. He founded an order—the Order of St. Francis, it is called—something like the *Sangha* of the Buddha. He went about preaching and serving from place to place, trying to live as Christ had lived. Great numbers of people came to him, and many became his disciples. He even went to Egypt and Palestine, while the Crusades were going on. But, Christian as he was, the Muslims respected this gentle and lovable person, and did not interfere with him in any way. He lived from 1181 to 1226. His Order came into conflict with the high officials of the Church after his death. Perhaps the Church did not fancy this stress on a life of poverty. They had outgrown this primitive Christian doctrine. Four Franciscan friars were burnt alive as heretics in Marseilles in 1318.

A few years ago there was a great celebration at the little town of Assisi in honour of St. Francis. I forget why it was held then. Probably it was the seven hundredth anniversary of his death.

Like the Franciscan Order, but very unlike it in spirit, another Order rose inside the Church. This was founded by St. Dominic, a Spaniard, and it is called the Dominican Order. This was aggressive and orthodox. To them everything was to be subordinated to the grand duty of maintaining the faith. If this could not be done by persuasion, then it would be done by violence.

The Church started the reign of violence in religion, formally and officially, in 1233, by starting what is called the Inquisition. This was a kind of court which inquired into the orthodoxy of people's beliefs, and if they did not come up to the standard, their usual punishment was death by burning. There was a regular hunt for " heretics ", and hundreds of them were burnt at the stake. Even worse than this burning was the torture inflicted on them to make them recant. Many poor unfortunate women were accused of being witches and were burnt. But this was often done, and especially in England and Scotland, by the mob, and not by order of the Inquisition.

The Pope issued an " Edict of Faith " calling upon every man to be an informer ! He condemned chemistry and called it a diabolical art. And all this violence and terror was done in all honesty. They believed that by burning the man at the stake, they were saving his soul or the souls of other people. Men of religion have often thrust themselves on others, forced down their own views on them and believed that they were doing a public service. In the name of God they have killed and murdered; and talking about saving the " immortal soul ", they have not hesitated to reduce the mortal body to ashes. The record of religion is very bad. But I do not think there is anything to beat the Inquisition for cold-blooded cruelty. And yet it is an amazing thing that many of the men who were responsible for this did it, not for any personal gain, but in the firm belief that they were doing the right thing.

While the Popes were letting loose this reign of terror on Europe, they were losing the commanding position they had come to occupy, as the lords of kings and emperors. The days of their excommunicating an emperor and frightening him into submission were gone.

When the Holy Roman Empire was in a bad way, and there was no emperor, or the Emperor kept far from Rome, the King of France began to interfere with the Popes. In 1303, the King was displeased at something the Pope had done. He sent a man to him, who forced his way to the Pope's bedroom in his own palace, and insulted him to his face. There was no disapproval of this insulting treatment in any country. Compare this with the bare-footed emperor in the snow at Canossa !

A few years later, in 1309, a new Pope, who was a Frenchman, took up his residence at Avignon, in France. Here the Popes lived till 1377 very much under the influence of the French kings. Next year, in 1378, there was a split in the College of Cardinals, called the Great Schism. Two Popes were elected, one by each group of cardinals. One Pope lived at Rome and the Emperor and most countries of northern Europe acknowledged him ; the other, who came to be called the anti-Pope, lived at Avignon, and the King of France and some of his allies supported him. For forty years this continued, and Pope and anti-Pope cursed each other and excommunicated each other. In 1417 there was a compromise and a new Pope, living in Rome, was elected by both parties. But this unseemly quarrel between two Popes must have had a very great effect on the people of Europe. If the vicars and representatives of God on earth, as they called themselves, behave in this way, people begin to doubt their holiness and bona fides. So this quarrel helped greatly in shaking people out of a blind obedience to religious authority. But they required much more shaking yet.

One of the men who started criticizing the Church rather freely was Wycliffe, an Englishman. He was a clergyman and a professor at Oxford. He is famous as the first translator of the Bible into English. He managed to escape the anger of Rome during his lifetime, but in 1415, thirty-one years after his death, a Church Council ordered that his bones should be dug up and burnt ! And this was done.

Although Wycliffe's bones were desecrated and burnt, his views could not easily be stifled, and they spread. They even reached far Bohemia, or Czechoslovakia as it is called now, and influenced John Huss, who became the head of the Prague University. He was excommunicated by the Pope for his views, but they could do little to him in his native town, as he was very popular. So they played a trick on him. He was given a safe conduct by the Emperor and invited to Constance in Switzerland, where a Church Council was sitting. He went. He was told to confess his error. He refused to do so unless he was convinced of it. And then in spite of their promise and safe conduct, they burnt him alive. This was in 1415 A.C. Huss was a very brave man and he preferred a painful death to saying what he knew to be false. He died a martyr to freedom of conscience and freedom of speech. He is one of the heroes of the Czech people, and his memory is honoured to this day in Czechoslovakia.

John Huss's martyrdom was not in vain. It was a spark which

lighted a fire of insurrection among his followers in Bohemia. The Pope proclaimed a crusade against them. Crusades were cheap and cost nothing and there were plenty of scoundrels and adventurers who took advantage of them. These Crusaders committed " the most horrible atrocities " (as H. G. Wells tells us) on innocent people. But when the army of the Hussites came singing their battle-hymn, the Crusaders vanished. They went back rapidly the way they had come. So long as innocent villagers could be killed and plundered, the Crusaders were full of martial enthusiasm, but on the approach of organized fighters, they fled.

So began the series of revolts and insurrections against autocratic and dogmatic religion which were to spread all over Europe and divide it into rival camps, and which were to split Christianity into Catholic and Protestant.

71

THE FIGHT AGAINST AUTHORITARIANISM

June 30, 1932

I AM afraid you will find my accounts of religious conflict in Europe rather dull. But they are important, as they show us how modern Europe developed. They help us to understand Europe. The fight for religious freedom, which we see developing in Europe in the fourteenth century and after, and the fight for political freedom, which will come next, are really two aspects of the same struggle. This is the struggle against authority and authoritarianism. Both the Holy Roman Empire and the Papacy represented absolute authority, and they tried to crush the spirit of man. The Emperor was there by " divine right ", even more so the Pope, and no one had the right to question this, or disobey the orders issued to him from above. Obedience was the great virtue. Even the exercise of private judgment was considered sinful. Thus the issue between blind obedience and freedom was quite clear. A great fight was waged in Europe for many centuries for freedom of conscience and, later, political freedom. After many ups and downs and great suffering, a measure of success was obtained. But just when people were congratulating themselves that the goal of freedom had been reached, they found that they were mistaken. There could be no real freedom without economic freedom, and so long as poverty remained. To call a starving man free is but to mock him. So the next step was the fight for economic freedom, and that fight is being waged to-day all over the world. Only in one country can it be said that economic freedom has been won by the people generally, and that is Russia, or rather the Soviet Union.

In India there was no such fight for freedom of conscience because from the earliest days this right never seems to have been denied. People could believe in almost anything they liked and there was no compulsion. The method of influencing the minds of people was by argument and debate, and not by the club and the stake. There may, of course, have been compulsion or violence used occasionally, but the right of freedom of conscience was admitted in the old Aryan theory. The result of this was not wholly good, strange as this may seem. Being assured of a theoretical freedom, people were not vigilant enough about it, and gradually they got more and more entangled in the rites and ceremonials and superstitions of a degraded religion. They developed a religious ideology which took them back a long way and made them slaves to religious authority. That authority was not that of a Pope or other individual. It was the authority of the " sacred books " and customs and conventions. So while we talked of freedom of conscience and were proud to have it, we were really far from it, and were chained up by the ideas which had been impressed upon us by the old books and our customs. Authority and authoritarianism reigned over us and controlled our minds. The chains which sometimes tie up our bodies are bad enough; but the invisible chains consisting of ideas and prejudices which tie up our minds are far worse. They are of our own making, and though often we are not conscious of them, they hold us in their terrible grip.

The coming of the Muslims to India as invaders introduced an element of compulsion in religion. The fight was really a political one between conqueror and conquered, but it was coloured by the religious element, and there was, at times, religious persecution. But it would be wrong to imagine that Islam stood for such persecution. There is an interesting report of a speech delivered by a Spanish Muslim when he was driven out of Spain, together with the remaining Arabs, in 1610. He protested against the Inquisition and said: " Did our victorious ancestors ever once attempt to extirpate Christianity out of Spain, when it was in their power? Did they not suffer your forefathers to enjoy the free use of their rites at the same time as they wore their chains? . . . If there may have been some examples of forced conversions, they are so rare as scarce to deserve mentioning, and only attempted by men who had not the fear of God and the Prophet before their eyes, and who in doing so, have acted directly and diametrically contrary to the holy precepts and ordinances of Islam, which cannot, without sacrilege, be violated by any who would be held worthy of the honourable epithet of Musalman. You can never produce, among us, any bloodthirsty formal tribunal, on account of different persuasions in points of faith, that any wise approaches your execrable Inquisition Our arms, it is true, are ever open to receive all who are disposed to embrace our religion; but we are not allowed by our sacred Qurar to tyrannize over consciences."

So religious toleration and freedom of conscience, which were such marked features of old Indian life, slipped away from us to some extent, while Europe caught up to us and then went ahead in establishing, after many a struggle, these very principles. To-day, sometimes, there is communal conflict in India, and Hindus and

Muslims fight each other and kill each other. It is true that this happens only occasionally in some places, and that mostly we live in peace rnd friendship, for our real interests are one. It is a shameful thing for any Hindu or Muslim to fight his brother in the name of religion. We must put an end to it, and we will of course do so. But what is important is to get out of that complex ideology of custom, convention and superstition which, under the guise of religion, enchains us.

As in the case of religious toleration, India started off fairly well in regard to political freedom. You will remember our village republics, and how originally the king's powers were supposed to be limited. There was no such thing as the divine right of the kings of Europe. Because our whole polity was based on village freedom, people were careless as to who was the king. If their local freedom was preserved to them what did it matter to them who was the boss above? But this was a dangerous and foolish idea. Gradually the boss on top increased his powers and encroached on the freedom of the village. And a time arrived when we had absolutely autocratic monarchs and there was no village self-government and no shadow of freedom anywhere from the top to the bottom.

72

THE PASSING OF THE MIDDLE AGES

July 1, 1932

LET us look at Europe again from the thirteenth to the fifteenth centuries. There seems to be a tremendous amount of disorder and violence and conflict. The conditions in India were pretty bad also, but almost one would think that India was peaceful compared to Europe.

The Mongols had brought gunpowder to Europe and firearms were being used now. The kings took advantage of this to crush their rebellious feudal nobles. In this work they got the help of the new merchant classes in the cities. The nobles were in the habit of carrying on little private wars of their own amongst themselves. This weakened them, but it harassed the countryside also. As the king grew in power, he put down this private warfare. In some places there were civil wars between two rival claimants for the crown. Thus in England there was a conflict between two families, the House of York and the House of Lancaster. Each party adopted a rose for its emblem, one a white rose, the other a red one. These wars are therefore called the Wars of the Roses. Large numbers of feudal nobles were killed in these civil wars. The Crusades also killed off many of them. Thus gradually the feudal lords were brought under control. But this did not mean that power was transferred from the nobles to the people. It was the king who grew more powerful. The people remained much the same, except that they were slightly better off by the lessening of private warfare. The king, however, developed more and more into an all-powerful and auto-cratic monarch. The conflict between the king and the new mer-chant classes was still to come.

More terrible than war and massacre even, there came the Great Plague to Europe about 1348. It spread all over Europe from Russia and Asia Minor to England; it went to Egypt, northern Africa, Central Asia and then spread westward. It was called the Black Death, and it killed off people by the million. About a third of the population of England died, and in China and elsewhere the death-roll was stupendous. It is surprising that it did not come to India.

This awful calamity reduced the population greatly and often there were not enough people to till the land. Owing to the lack of men, the wages of workers tended to rise from their miserable level. But the landlords and property-owners controlled the parliaments, and they passed laws to force people to work at the old miserable wage and not to ask for more. Crushed and exploited beyond endurance, the peasants and the poor revolted. All over western Europe these peasant revolts took place one after the other. In France there was what is called a *jacquerie* in 1358. In England there was Wat Tyler's rebellion, in which Tyler was killed in front of the English King in 1381. These revolts were put down, often with much cruelty. But new ideas of equality were slowly spreading. People were asking themselves why they should be poor and starve when others were rich and had an abundance of everything. Why should some be lords and others serfs ? Why should some have fine clothes and others not even rags enough to cover themselves ? The old idea of submission to authority, on which the whole feudal system was based, was breaking down. So the peasants rose again and again, but they were weak and disorganized, and were put down, only to rise again some time later.

England and France were almost continually at war with each other. From early in the fourteenth century to the middle of the fifteenth century there was what is called the Hundred Years' War between them. To the east of France there was Burgundy. This was a powerful State, nominally vassal to the King of France. But Burgundy was a turbulent and troublesome vassal, and the English intrigued with it, as well as with other Powers, against France. France was for a while hemmed in on all sides. A good part of western France was for long in English possession, and the King of England began to call himself King of France also. When France was at the lowest ebb of her fortunes and there seemed no hope for her, hope and victory came in the form of a young peasant girl. You know something of Jeanne d'Arc (or Joan of Arc), the Maid of Orleans. She is a heroine of yours. She gave confidence to her dispirited people and inspired them to great endeavour, and under her lead they drove out the English from their country. But for all this the reward she got was a trial and sentence of the Inquisition and the stake. The English got hold of her, and they made the

Church condemn her, and then in the market-place of Rouen they burnt her in 1430. Many years later the Roman Church sought to undo what had been done by reversing the decision condemning her; and long afterwards they made her a saint !

Jeanne spoke of France and of saving her *patrie* from the foreigner. This was a new way of speaking. At that time people were too full of feudal ideas to think of nationalism. So the way Jeanne spoke surprised them and they hardly understood her. We can see the faint beginnings of nationalism in France from the time of Jeanne d'Arc.

Having got the English out of his country, the French King turned to Burgundy, which had given so much trouble. This powerful vassal was finally brought under control, and Burgundy became part of France about 1483. The French King now becomes a powerful monarch. He had crushed or brought under control all his feudal nobles. With the absorption of Burgundy into France France and Germany came face to face. Their frontiers touched each other. But while France was a strong centralized monarchy, Germany was weak and split up into many States.

England was also trying to conquer Scotland. This too was a long struggle, and Scotland was often on the side of France against England. In 1314 the Scots under Robert Bruce defeated the English at Bannockburn.

Even earlier than this, in the twelfth century, the English began their attempts to conquer Ireland. Seven hundred years ago that was, and since then there has been frequent war and revolt and terror and frightfulness in Ireland. This little country refused to submit to an alien domination and, generation after generation, has risen in revolt to proclaim that it will not submit.

In the thirteenth century another small nation of Europe— Switzerland—asserted its right to freedom. It formed part of the Holy Roman Empire, and Austria ruled it. You must have read the story of William Tell and his son, but probably this is not true. But even more wonderful is the revolt of the Swiss peasants against the great empire and their refusal to submit to it. Three of the cantons revolted first and formed an " Everlasting League ", as they called it, in 1291. Other cantons joined them and in 1499 Switzerland became a free republic. It was a federation of the different cantons, and it was called the Swiss Confederation. Do you remember the bonfires we saw on many a mountain-top in Switzerland on the first of August ? That was the national day of the Swiss, the anniversary of the beginning of their revolution, when the bonfire was the signal to rise against the Austrian ruler.

In the east of Europe, what was happening to Constantinople ? You will remember that the Latin crusaders captured this city from the Greeks in 1204 A.C. In 1261 these people were driven out by the Greeks, who re-established the Eastern Empire again. But another and a greater danger was coming.

When the Mongols had advanced across Asia, 50,000 Ottoman Turks had fled before them. These were different from the Seljuq

Turks. They looked up to an ancestor, or founder of a dynasty, named Othman or Osman. Hence they were called Ottoman or Osmanli Turks. These Ottomans took refuge under the Seljuqs in western Asia. As the Seljuq Turks weakened, the Ottomans seem to have grown in power. They went on spreading. Instead of attacking Constantinople, as many others had done before them, they passed it by and crossed over to Europe in 1353. They spread rapidly and occupied Bulgaria and Serbia and made Adrianople their capital. Thus the Ottoman Empire spread on either side of Constantinople in Asia and Europe. It surrounded Constantinople, but this city remained outside it. But the proud Eastern Roman Empire of 1000 years was reduced to just this city and practically nothing more. Although the Turk was rapidly swallowing up the Eastern Empire, there appear to have been friendly relations between the Sultans and the Emperors, and they married into each other's families. Ultimately in 1453 Constantinople fell to the Turks. We shall now refer to the Ottoman Turks only. The Seljuqs have dropped out of the picture.

The fall of Constantinople, though long expected, was a great event which shook Europe. It meant the final end of the 1000-year-old Greek Eastern Empire. It meant another Muslim invasion of Europe. The Turks went on spreading, and sometimes it almost seemed that they would conquer Europe, but they were checked at the gates of Vienna.

The great cathedral of Saint Sophia, which had been built by the Emperor Justinian in the sixth century, was turned into a mosque—Aya Sufiya it was called—and there was some plundering of its treasures. Europe was excited about this, but it could do nothing. As a matter of fact, however, the Turkish Sultans were very tolerant of the Orthodox Greek Church, and after the capture of Constantinople, Sultan Mohammad II actually proclaimed himself the protector of the Greek Church. A later Sultan, who is known as Suleiman the Magnificent, considered himself the representative of the Eastern Emperors and took the title of Cæsar. Such is the power of ancient tradition.

The Ottoman Turks do not seem to have been very unwelcome to the Greeks of Constantinople. They saw that the old empire was collapsing. They preferred the Turks to the Pope and the western Christians. Their experience of the Latin Crusaders had been bad. It is said that during the last siege of Constantinople in 1453 a Byzantine nobleman said : " Better the turban of the Prophet than the tiara of the Pope."

The Turks built up a peculiar corps, called the Janissaries. They took little Christian children, as a kind of tribute from the Christians, and gave them special training. It was cruel to separate young boys from their parents, but these boys had some advantages also, as they were well trained and became a kind of military aristocracy. This corps of Janissaries became a pillar of the Ottoman Sultans. The word Janissary comes from *Jan* (life) *nisar* (sacrifice)—one who sacrifices his life.

In a similar way in Egypt a corps of " Mamelukes," corresponding to the Janissaries, was formed.   This became all-powerful, and even supplied the Sultans to Egypt.

The Ottoman Sultans, by taking Constantinople, seem to have inherited many of the evil habits of luxury and corruption from their predecessors, the Byzantine emperors.   The whole degraded imperial system of the Byzantines enveloped them and gradually sapped their strength.   But for some time they were strong and Christian Europe was in fear of them.   They conquered Egypt and took the title of Caliph from the weak and powerless representative of the Abbasides who then possessed it.   From that time onwards the Ottoman Sultans called themselves the Caliphs till some years ago, when Mustafa Kamal Pasha put an end to it by abolishing both the Sultanate and the Khalifate.

The date of the fall of Constantinople is a great date in history. It is supposed to be the end of one era and the beginning of another. The Middle Ages are over.   The 1000 years of the Dark Ages end, and there is a quickening in Europe, and fresh life and energy are visible.   This is called the beginning of the Renaissance—the re- birth of learning and art.   People seem to wake up, as from a long sleep, and they look back across the centuries to ancient Greece, in the days of her glory, and draw inspiration from her.   There is almost a revolt of the mind against the sombre and dismal view of life encouraged by the Church, and the chains that encompassed the human spirit.   The old Grecian love of beauty appears, and Europe blossoms out with fine works of painting and sculpture and architecture.

All this, of course, was not caused suddenly by the fall of Con- stantinople.   It would be absurd to think so.   The capture of the city by the Turks did just a little to speed up the change, as it resulted in large numbers of learned men and scholars leaving it and going west.   They brought with them to Italy the treasures of Greek literature just when the West was in a mood to appreciate them.   In this sense the fall of the city helped slightly in launching the Renaissance.

But this was only a petty reason for the great change.   The old Greek literature and thought was not a new thing in Italy or the West of the Middle Ages.   In the universities people studied it still and learned men knew of it.   But it was confined to a few, and because it did not fit in with the prevailing view of life, it did not spread. Slowly the ground was prepared for a new view of life by the be- ginnings of doubt in the minds of the people.   They were dissatisfied with things as they were and searched for something which might satisfy them more.   While they were in this state of doubt and expectancy their minds discovered the old pagan philosophy of Greece, and they drank deep of her literature.   This seemed to them just the thing they sought, and the discovery filled them with enthusiasm.

The Renaissance first began in Italy.   Later it appeared in France, England and elsewhere.   It was not just a re-discovery of Greek thought and literature. It was something far bigger and greater. It was the outward manifestation of the process that had been going on under the surface in Europe for a long time. This ferment was to break out in many ways. The Renaissance was one of them.

73

THE DISCOVERY OF THE SEA ROUTES

July 3, 1932

WE have now reached the stage in Europe when the medieval world begins to break up and give place to a new order. There is discontent and dissatisfaction against existing conditions, and this feeling is the parent of change and progress. All the classes that were exploited by the feudal system and the religious system were discontented. We have seen that peasant revolts, or *jacqueries*, as they are called in French (from Jacques, a peasant name), were taking place. But the peasants were still very backward and weak and, in spite of their revolts, could gain little. Their day was yet to come. The real conflict was between the old feudal class and the new wide-awake middle class, which was growing in power. The feudal system meant that wealth was based on land—was, in fact, land. But now a new kind of wealth was being accumulated, which was not from land. This was from manufactures and trade, and the new middle class or *bourgeoisie* profited by this, and this gave them power. This conflict was already an old one. What we now see is a change in the relative positions of the two parties. The feudal system, though still continuing, is on the defensive. The *bourgeoisie*, confident of its new strength, takes up the offensive. The struggle goes on through hundreds of years, ever more and more in favour of the *bourgeoisie*. It varies in different countries of Europe. In eastern Europe there is little of the struggle. It is in the west that the *bourgeoisie* first comes into prominence.

The breaking down of the old barriers meant an advance in many directions—in science, in art, in literature, in architecture, in new discoveries. That is always so when the human spirit breaks its bonds; it expands and spreads out. Even so, when freedom comes to our country, will our people and our genius expand and spread out in all directions.

As the hold of the Church relaxes and grows weaker, people spend less money on cathedrals and churches. Beautiful buildings grow up in many places, but they are town-halls and the like. The Gothic style also retires, and a new one develops.

Just about this time, when western Europe was full of a new energy, came the lure of gold from the East. Stories of Marco Polo and other travellers who had been to India and China excited the imagination of Europe, and this stimulus of untold wealth in the East drew many to the sea. Just then came the fall of Constantinople. The Turks controlled the land and the sea routes to the East, and they did not encourage trade much. The big merchants and traders chafed at this; the new class of adventurers, who wanted to get at the gold of the East, were also annoyed. So they tried to find out new ways of reaching the golden East.

Every schoolgirl knows now that our earth is round and that it goes round the sun. This is such an obvious thing to all of us. But it was not very obvious in the old days, and those people who ventured to think so and say so got into trouble with the Church. But in spite of the fear of the Church, more and more persons began to think that the earth was round. If it was round, then it should be possible to reach China and India by going west. So some thought. Others thought of reaching India by going round Africa. You must remember that there was no Suez Canal then and ships could not go from the Mediterranean to the Red Sea. Goods and merchandise used to be sent overland, probably on the backs of camels, between the Mediterranean Sea and the Red Sea, and were transferred to fresh ships on the other side. This was not convenient at any time. With Egypt and Syria under the Turks, this route became even more difficult.

But the lure of India's wealth continued to excite and draw people. Spain and Portugal took the lead in the voyages of exploration. Spain was just then driving out the last of the Moors or Saracens from Granada. The marriage of Ferdinand of Aragon and Isabella of Castile had united Christian Spain, and in 1492, nearly fifty years after the Turks took Constantinople on the other side of Europe, Granada, of the Arabs, fell. Spain immediately became a great Christian Power in Europe.

The Portuguese tried to go east, the Spaniards west. The first great advance was the discovery by the Portuguese in 1445 of Cape Verde. This cape is the westernmost point of Africa. Look at the map of Africa. You will see that as one sails down from Europe towards this cape, one has to go south-west. At Cape Verde one goes round the corner and begins going south-east. The discovery of this cape was a very hopeful sign, for it made people believe that they would be able to go round Africa towards India.

It took another forty years, however, before Africa was rounded. In 1486 Bartholomew Diaz, also a Portuguese, went round the southern tip of Africa—that is, what is called the Cape of Good Hope. Within a few years yet another Portuguese, Vasco da Gama, took advantage of this discovery and came to India, *via* the Cape of Good Hope. Vasco da Gama reached Calicut on the Malabar Coast in 1498.

So the Portuguese won in the race to reach India. But meanwhile great things were happening on the other side of the world and Spain was to profit by them. Christopher Columbus had reached the American world in 1492. Columbus was a poor Genoese and, believing that the world was round, he wanted to go to Japan and India by sailing west. He did not think that the journey would be nearly as long as it turned out to be. He went about from Court to

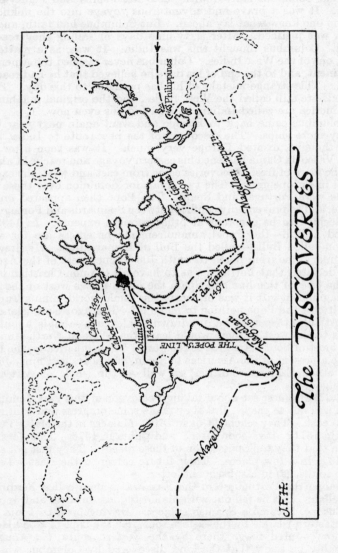

The DISCOVERIES

Philippines

Magellan Exped. (return)

da Gama 1498

V. da Gama 1497

Cabot 1497

Cabot 1498

Columbus 1492

THE POPE'S LINE

Magellan 1519

Magellan

J.F.H.

Court trying to induce some prince to help him in his voyage of exploration. At last Ferdinand and Isabella of Spain agreed to do so, and Columbus started with three little ships and eighty-eight men. It was a brave and adventurous voyage into the unknown, for no one knew what lay ahead. But Columbus had faith, and his faith was justified. After sixty-nine days of sailing they reached land. Columbus thought this was India. It was, as a matter of fact, one of the West Indies. Columbus never reached the American continent, and to the end of his days he believed that he had reached Asia. This strange mistake of his has persisted to this day. These islands are still called the West Indies, and the original inhabitants of America are called Indians or Red Indians even now.

Columbus came back to Europe and went again next year with many more ships. The discovery of the new route to India, as it was thought, excited Europe very much. It was soon after this that Vasco da Gama hastened his eastern voyage and reached Calicut. As the news of fresh discoveries came from east and west, the excitement in Europe grew. The two rivals for dominion over these new lands were Portugal and Spain. The Pope then appeared on the scene, and to prevent any conflict between Spaniards and Portuguese, he decided to be generous at other people's expense. In 1493 he issued a Bull—the Papal announcements or edicts are for some reason called Bulls—called the Bull of Demarcation. He drew an imaginary line from north to south 100 leagues west of the Azores, and declared that Portugal was to have all the non-Christian lands to the east of this line and Spain the lands to the west of the line. A magnificent gift it was of nearly the whole world, minus Europe, and it cost the Pope nothing to make it ! The Azores are islands in the Atlantic Ocean, and a line drawn 100 leagues—that is, about 300 miles to the west of them would leave the whole of North America and most of South America to the west. Thus, practically, the Pope made a present of the Americas to Spain, and of India, China, Japan and other Eastern countries, as well as the whole of Africa, to Portugal !

The Portuguese set about taking possession of this vast dominion. This was not so easy. But they made some progress and continued to go east. They reached Goa in 1510; Malacca in the Malay Peninsula in 1511; Java soon after; and China in 1576. This does not mean that they took possession of these places. They just got some footings in a few places. Their future career in the East we shall have to discuss in a subsequent letter.

Among the Portuguese in the East was a man called Ferdinand Magellan. But he fell out with his Portuguese masters and, returnto Europe, became a Spanish subject. Having been to India and the Eastern islands by the eastern route, *via* the Cape of Good Hope, he now wanted to go there by the western route, *via* America. Probably he knew that the land discovered by Columbus was far from being Asia. Indeed, in 1513 a Spaniard named Balboa had crossed the mountains of Panama in Central America and had reached the Pacific Ocean. For some reason or other he called this the South

Sea, and standing on the shore of it, he claimed the new sea and all lands washed by it as possessions of his master, the King of Spain.

In 1519 Magellan started on his western voyage, which was going to be the greatest voyage of them all. He had five ships and 270 men. He crossed the Atlantic to South America and continued going south till he reached the end of the continent. He had lost one ship by shipwreck and another had deserted; three ships remained. With these he crossed the narrow strait between the South American continent and an island, and came out into the open sea on the other side. This was the Pacific Ocean, so called by Magellan because it was very peaceful compared to the Atlantic. It had taken him just fourteen months to reach the Pacific. The strait he passed through is still known after him—the Strait of Magellan.

Magellan then bravely continued north and then north-west across the unknown sea. This was the most terrible part of the voyage. No one knew that it would take so long. For nearly four months, 108 days to be exact, they were in mid-ocean with little to eat or drink. At last, after great privation, they reached the Philippine Islands. The people they met there were friendly to them and gave them food and exchanged gifts. But the Spaniards were offensive and overbearing. Magellan took part in some petty war between two chieftains and was killed. Many other Spaniards were killed by the people of the island because of their overbearing attitude.

The Spaniards were looking for the Spice Islands, where the precious spices came from. They went on in search for them. Another ship had to be given up and burnt; only two remained. It was decided that one of these should go back to Spain *via* the Pacific, and the other *via* the Cape of Good Hope. The former ship did not go far, as it was captured by the Portuguese. But the other one, named the *Vittoria*, crept round Africa and reached Seville in Spain with eighteen men in 1522, just three years after it had sailed. It had gone round the world, and it was the first ship to do so.

I have written at some length about the voyage of the *Vittoria* because it was a wonderful voyage. We cross the seas now in every comfort and take long journeys in big ships. But think of these early voyagers, who faced all manner of danger and peril, and plunging into the unknown, discovered the sea routes for those who came after them. The Spaniards and Portuguese of those days were proud and overbearing and cruel people; but they were wonderfully brave and full of the spirit of adventure.

While Magellan was going round the world, Cortés was entering the city of Mexico and conquering the Aztec Empire for the Spanish King. I have already told you something of this and of the Maya civilization of America. Cortés reached Mexico in 1519. Pizarro reached the Inca Empire (where Peru is now) in South America in 1530. By courage and audacity, and treachery and cruelty, and taking advantage of internal dissensions of the people, Cortés and Pizarro succeeded in putting an end to two old empires. But both of these empires were out of date and, in some ways, very primitive. So they fell down, like a house of cards, at the first push.

Where the great explorers and discoverers had gone, hordes of adventurers followed, eager for loot and plunder. Spanish America especially suffered from this crowd, and even Columbus was treated very badly by them. At the same time gold and silver flowed unceasingly to Spain from Peru and Mexico. Enormous quantities of these precious metals came, dazzling Europe, and making Spain the dominating Power of Europe. This gold and silver spread to other countries of Europe, and thus there was an abundant supply of money with which to buy the products of the East.

The success of Portugal and Spain naturally fired the imaginations of the people of other countries, especially of France and England and Holland and the north German towns. They tried hard at first to find a passage to Asia and America by a northern route, north of Norway to the east, and *via* Greenland to the west. But they failed in this, and then took to the well-known routes.

What a wonderful time this must have been, when the world seemed to be opening out and showing her treasures and marvels ! New discoveries came one after another, oceans and new continents, and wealth beyond measure, just waiting for the magic call—" open sesame ". The very air must have breathed of the magic of these adventures.

The world is a narrower place now, and there is little to discover in it. So it seems. But that is not so, for science has opened up tremendous new vistas which wait to be explored, and of adventure there is no lack. Especially in India to-day !

74

THE BREAK-UP OF THE MONGOL EMPIRES

July 9, 1932

I HAVE written to you of the passing of the Middle Ages and of the awakening of the new spirit in Europe, and a new energy which found outlets in many ways. Europe seems to be bustling with activity and creative effort. Her people, after being cooped up in their little countries for centuries, burst out and cross the wide oceans and go to the uttermost corners of the world. They go forth as conquerors, confident in their own strength ; and this very confidence gives them courage and makes them perform wonderful deeds.

But you must have wondered how this sudden change took place. In the middle of the thirteenth century the Mongols dominated Asia and Europe. Eastern Europe was in their possession, western Europe trembled before these great and seemingly invincible warriors. What were the kings and emperors of Europe compared to even a general of the Great Khan ?

Two hundred years later, the Ottoman Turks were in possession of the imperial city of Constantinople and a good bit of south-eastern Europe. After 800 years of fighting between Muslim and Christian, the great prize, which had lured the Arabs and the Seljuqs, had fallen into the hands of the Ottomans. Not content with this, the Ottoman Sultans looked with hungry eyes to the west, even at Rome itself. They threatened the German (Holy Roman) Empire and Italy. They conquered Hungary and reached the walls of Vienna and the frontiers of Italy. In the east they added Baghdad to their dominions; in the south, Egypt. In the middle of the sixteenth century Sultan Suleiman, called the Magnificent, ruled over this great Turkish Empire. Even on the seas his fleets were supreme.

How, then, did this change occur? How did Europe get rid of the Mongol menace? How did it survive the Turkish danger? and not only survive it, but become aggressive itself and a menace to others?

The Mongols did not threaten Europe for long. They went away of their own accord to elect a new Khan and they did not come back. Western Europe was too far away from their homelands in Mongolia. Perhaps also it did not attract them because it was woody country and they were used to the wide open plains and steppes. In any event western Europe saved itself from the Mongols not by any valour of its own, but by the indifference and the preoccupations of the Mongols. In eastern Europe they remained for some time longer, till the Mongol power gradually broke up.

I have already told you that the capture of Constantinople by the Turks in 1452 is supposed to be a turning-point in European history. It marks, for the sake of convenience, the passing of the Middle Ages and the coming of the new spirit, the Renaissance, which flowered out in a variety of ways. Thus, curiously, just when Europe was threatened by the Turks, and the Turks seemed to have a good chance of success, Europe found her feet and developed strength. The Turks went on advancing in western Europe for a while; and while they advanced, European explorers were discovering new countries and seas and rounding the globe. Under Suleiman the Magnificent, who reigned from 1520 to 1566, the Turkish Empire spread from Vienna to Baghdad and Cairo. But there was no advance after that. The Turks were succumbing to the old weakening and corrupting traditions of the Constantinople of the Greeks. As Europe increased in power, the Turks lost their old energy and became weaker.

In the course of our wanderings through past ages we have seen many invasions of Europe by Asia. There were some invasions of Asia by Europe, but they were of little moment. Alexander went across Asia to India without any great result. The Romans never went beyond Mesopotamia. Europe, on the other hand, was repeatedly overrun by Asiatic tribes from the earliest times. Of these Asiatic invasions the Ottoman invasion of Europe was the last. Gradually we find the rôles are reversed, and Europe takes up the aggressive. This change might be said to occur about the middle of the sixteenth century. America, newly discovered, goes down quickly before Europe. Asia is a more difficult problem. For 200 years Europeans try to find footholds in various parts of the Asiatic continent, and by the middle of the eighteenth century they begin to dominate parts of Asia. It is well to remember this, as some people, ignorant of history, imagine that Europe has always bossed it over Asia. This new rôle of Europe is quite a recent one, as we shall see, and already the scene is changing and the rôle appears out of date. New ideas are astir in all the countries of the East, and powerful movements aiming at freedom are challenging and shaking the domination of Europe. Wider and deeper even than these nationalistic ideas are the new social ideas of equality which want to put an end to all imperialism and exploitation. There should be no question in future of Europe dominating Asia or Asia dominating Europe, or any country exploiting another.

This has been a long preface. We come back to the Mongols. Let us follow their fortunes for a while and see what happened to them. You will remember that Kublai Khan was the last Great Khan. After his death in 1292 the vast empire, which stretched right across Asia from Korea to Poland and Hungary in Europe, split up into five empires. Each of these five empires was in reality a very big empire. In a previous letter (No. 68) I have given you the names of these five.

The principal one was the Empire of China, including Manchuria, Mongolia, Tibet, Korea, Annam, Tongking and part of Burma. The Yuan dynasty, descendants of Kublai, succeeded to this; but not for long. Very soon bits of it dropped off in the south, and as I have told you, in 1368, just seventy-six years after Kublai's death, his dynasty fell and the Mongols were driven away.

In the far west was the Empire of the Golden Horde—what a fascinating name these people had ! The Russian nobles paid tribute to it for nearly 200 years after Kublai's death. At the end of this period (1480) the Empire was weakening a little and the Grand Duke of Moscow, who had managed to become the chief Russian noble, refused to pay tribute. This Grand Duke is called Ivan the Great. In the north of Russia there was the old republic of Novgorod, which was controlled by merchants and traders. Ivan defeated this republic and added it to his dukedom. Constantinople meanwhile had fallen to the Turks and the family of the old emperors had been driven out. Ivan married a girl of this old imperial family, and thus claimed to be in the imperial line and an heir to old Byzantium. The Russian Empire, which was finally ended by the revolutions of 1917, began in this way, under Ivan the Great. His grandson, who was very cruel, and was therefore called Ivan the Terrible, gave himself the title of Tsar, which was the equivalent of Cæsar or Emperor.

Thus the Mongols finally retired from Europe. We need not trouble ourselves much about the remains of the Golden Horde or the other Mongol empires of Central Asia. Besides, I do not know much about them. But one man claims our attention.

This man was Timur, who wanted to be a second Chengiz Khan. He claimed to be descended from Chengiz, but he was really a Turk. He was lame and is therefore called Timur-i-lang or Timur the Lame or Tamurlane. He succeeded his father and became ruler of Samarqand in 1369. Soon afterwards, he started on his career of conquest and cruelty. He was a great general, but he was a complete savage. The Mongols of central Asia had meanwhile become Muslims and Timur himself was a Muslim. But the fact that he was dealing with Muslims did not soften him in the least. Wherever he went he spread desolation and pestilence and utter misery. His chief pleasure was the erection of enormous pyramids of skulls. From Delhi in the east to Asia Minor in the west he caused to be massacred hundreds of thousands of persons and had their skulls arranged in the form of pyramids !

Chengiz Khan and his Mongols were cruel and destructive, but they were like others of their time. But Timur was much worse. He stands apart for wanton and fiendish cruelty. In one place, it is said, he erected a tower of 2000 live men and covered them up with brick and mortar !

The wealth of India attracted this savage. He had some difficulty in inducing his generals and nobles to agree to his proposal to invade India. There was a great council in Samarqand, and the nobles objected to going to India because of the great heat there. Ultimately Timur promised that he would not stay in India. He would just plunder and destroy and return. He kept his word.

Northern India was then, you will remember, under Muslim rule. There was a Sultan at Delhi. But this Muslim State was weak, and constant warfare with the Mongols on the frontiers had broken its backbone. So when Timur came with an army of Mongols there was no great resistance and he went on gaily with his massacres and pyramids. Both Hindus and Muslims were slain. No distinction seems to have been made. The prisoners becoming a burden, he ordered all of them to be killed and 100,000 were massacred. At one place, it is said, both the Hindus and Muslims jointly performed the Rajput ceremony of *jauhar*—marching out to die in battle. But why should I go on repeating this story of horror ? It was the same all along his route. Famine and disease followed Timur's army. For fifteen days he remained in Delhi, and converted that great city into a shambles. He returned to Samarqand, after plundering Kashmir on the way.

Savage as he was, Timur wanted to put up fine buildings in Samarqand and elsewhere in central Asia. So he collected, as Sultan Mahmud had done long before him, artisans and skilled mechanics and master-builders in India and took them with him. The best of these master-builders and craftsmen he kept in his own imperial service. The others were spread in the chief cities of western Asia. Thus developed a new style of architecture.

After Timur's departure, Delhi was a city of the dead. Famine and pestilence reigned unchecked. There was no ruler or organization or order for two months. There were few inhabitants. Even the man Timur had appointed as his Viceroy in Delhi retired to Multan.

Timur then went west spreading desolation across Persia and Mesopotamia. At Angora he met a great army of the Ottoman Turks in 1402. By brilliant generalship he defeated these Turks. But the sea was too much for him, and he could not cross the Bosphorus. So Europe escaped him.

Three years later, in 1405, Timur died, as he was marching towards China. With him collapsed his great empire, which covered nearly the whole of Western Asia. The Ottomans paid tribute to him, so did Egypt, so did the Golden Horde. But his ability was confined to his generalship, which was remarkable. Some of his campaigns in the snows of Siberia were extraordinary. But at heart he was a barbarous nomad, and he built up no organization and left behind him no competent men, as Chengiz had done, to carry on the empire. So the Empire of Timur ended with him and left a memory only of massacre and desolation. In Central Asia, of the hordes of adventurers and conquerors who have passed through it, four men are remembered still—Sikandar or Alexander, Sultan Mahmud, Chengiz Khan, and Timur.

Timur shook up the Ottoman Turks by his defeat of them. But they recovered soon and, as we know, in another fifty years (1453) they took Constantinople.

We must take leave of Central Asia now. It goes back in the scale of civilization and sinks into obscurity. Nothing of note happens which will demand our attention. Only the memory of old civilizations remains, destroyed by the hand of man. Nature also laid a heavy hand on it, and gradually made the climate drier and less habitable.

We must also bid good-bye to the Mongols, except for a branch of them which subsequently came to India and built a great and famous empire here. But the Empire of Chengiz Khan and his descendants breaks up, and the Mongols revert to their petty chieftains and their tribal habits.

75

INDIA BEGINS TO TACKLE A DIFFICULT PROBLEM

July 12, 1932

I HAVE written to you of Timur and his massacres and pyramids of heads. How horrible and barbarous all this seems ! Such a thing could not happen in our civilized age. And yet, do not be so sure. We have only recently seen and heard of what can and does happen even in our own times. The destruction of life and property caused by Chengiz Khan or Timur, great as it was, pales almost into insignificance before the destruction during the Great War of 1914–18. And every Mongol cruelty can be rivalled by modern instances of frightfulness.

Yet it is undoubted that we have progressed in a hundred ways since the days of Chengiz or Timur. Life is not only vastly more complicated, but it is richer; and many of the forces of Nature have been explored and understood and brought to the use of man. Certainly the world is more civilized and cultured now. Why, then, do we relapse back into barbarism during periods of war? Because war itself is a negation and denial of civilization and culture, except in so far as it takes advantage of the civilized brain to invent and use more and more powerful and horrible weapons. With the coming of war most people who are involved in it work themselves up into a terrible state of excitement, forget much that civilization has taught them, forget truth and the graces of life, and begin to resemble their savage ancestors of a few thousand years ago. Is it, then, surprising that war, whenever waged, is a horrible thing?

What would a stranger to this world of ours say if he were to visit us during war-time? Suppose he only saw us then, and not during peace-time. He would only judge by the war, and come to the conclusion that we were cruel and relentless, savages occasionally showing courage and sacrifice, but, on the whole, with few redeeming features, and with one master-passion—to kill and destroy each other. He would misjudge us and form a distorted view of our world, because he would see only one side of us at a particular, and not very favourable, time.

So also, if we think of the past in terms of wars and massacres only, we shall misjudge it. Unfortunately wars and massacres have a way of attracting a great deal of attention. The day-to-day life of a people is rather dull. What is the historian to say about it? So the historian swoops down on a war or battle and makes the most of it. Of course we cannot forget or ignore such wars, but we must not attach more importance to them than they deserve. Let us think of the past in terms of the present, and of the people in those days in terms of ourselves. We shall then get a more human view of them, and we shall realize that what really counted were the day-to-day life and the thoughts of those people, and not the occasional wars. It is well to remember this, as you will find your history books over-full of such wars. Even these letters of mine are apt to stray in that direction. The real reason for this is the difficulty in writing about the day-to-day life of past times. I do not know enough about it.

Timur, as we have seen, was one of the worst afflictions that befell India. One shudders to think of the trail of horror which he left behind him wherever he went. And yet southern India was wholly unaffected by him, so also the east and west and central India. Even the present United Provinces practically escaped him, except for a bit in the north, near Delhi and Meerut. The Punjab, besides Delhi city, was the province that suffered most by Timur's raid. Even in the Punjab the main sufferers lay along the route taken by

Timur. The vast majority of the people of the Punjab carried on their ordinary work without any interruption. So we must be on our guard not to exaggerate the importance of these wars and raids.

Let us look at the India of the fourteenth and fifteenth centuries. The Delhi Sultanate shrinks till it vanishes away on Timur's coming. There are a number of large independent States all over India, mostly Muslim; but there is one powerful Hindu State—Vijayanagar— in the south. Islam is no longer a stranger or a newcomer in India. It is well established. The fierceness and cruelty of the early Afghan invaders and the Slave kings have been toned down, and the Muslim kings are as much Indians as the Hindus. They have no outside connections. Wars take place between different States, but they are political and not religious. Sometimes a Muslim State employs Hindu troops, and a Hindu State Muslim troops. Muslim kings often marry Hindu women and Hindus are often employed as ministers and high officials by the Muslim kings. There is little of the feeling of conqueror and conquered or ruler and ruled. Indeed, most of the Muslims, including some of the rulers, are Indians converted to Islam. Many of these become converted in the hope of gaining Court favour or economic advantage, and in spite of their change of religion they stick to most of their old customs. Some Muslim rulers adopt forcible methods to bring about conversion, but even this is largely with a political object, as it is thought that the converts would be more loyal subjects. But force does not go far in bringing about conversions. A more effective method is the economic. Non-Muslims are made to pay a poll-tax called the *jizya*, and many of them, wishing to escape this, become Muslims.

But all this takes place in the cities. The villages are little affected, and the millions of villagers carry on in the old way. It is true that the king's officers interfere more in village life. The powers of the village *panchāyats* are less now than they used to be, but still the *panchāyats* continue and are the centre and backbone of village life. Socially, and in the matter of religion and custom, the village is almost unchanged. India, as you know, is still a country of hundreds of thousands of villages. The towns and cities sit on the surface, as it were, but the real India has been, and still is, village India. This village India was not much changed by Islam.

Hinduism was shaken up in two ways by the coming of Islam; and, strange to say, these ways were contrary to each other. On the one side it became conservative; it hardened and retired into a shell in an attempt at protecting itself against the attack on it. Caste became stiffer and more exclusive; the *purdah* and seclusion of women became commoner. On the other hand, there was a kind of internal revolt against caste and too much *pūjā* and ceremonial. Many efforts were made to reform it.

Of course right through history, from the earliest times, reformers have risen in Hinduism, who have tried to rid it of its abuses. Buddha was the greatest of these. I have also told you of Shankara-charya, who lived in the eighth century. Three hundred years later, in the eleventh century, there lived in the south, in the Chola Empire, another great reformer who was the leader of a rival school of thought to that of Shankara. His name was Ramanuja. Shankara was a Shaivite and a man of intellect. Ramanuja was a Vaishnavite and a man of faith. Ramanuja's influence spread all over India. I have told you how, right through history, India has been culturally united, even though politically it may have been split up into many warring States. Whenever a great man or a great movement arose, it spread all over India regardless of political boundaries.

After Islam had settled down in India, a new type of reformer rose among the Hindus, as well as among the Muslims. He tried to bring the two religions nearer to each other by laying stress on the common features of both and attacking their rites and ceremonials. An effort was thus made to bring about a synthesis of the two—that is to say, a kind of mixture of the two. It was a difficult task, as there was much ill feeling and prejudice on both sides. But we shall see that century after century this effort was made. Even some of the Muslim rulers, and notably the great Akbar, tried to bring about this synthesis.

Ramanand, who lived in the south in the fourteenth century, was the first well-known teacher who preached this synthesis. He preached against caste and ignored it. Among his disciples was a Muslim weaver named Kabir, who became even more famous later on. Kabir became very popular. His songs in Hindi, as you perhaps know, are very well known now even in remote villages in the north. He was neither Hindu nor Muslim; he was both, or something between the two, and his followers came from both religions and all castes. There is a story that when he died his body was covered with a sheet. His Hindu disciples wanted to take it for cremation; his Muslim disciples wanted to bury it. So they argued and quarrelled. But when they lifted up the sheet they found that the body for the possession of which they were quarrelling had disappeared and in its place there were some fresh flowers. The story may be quite imaginary, but it is a pretty one.

A little after Kabir there rose another great reformer and religious leader in the north. This was Guru Nanak, who was the founder of Sikhism. He was followed, one after the other, by the ten *gurus* of the Sikhs, the last of whom was Guru Govind Singh.

One other name, famous in Indian religious and cultural history, I should like to mention here. This was Chaitanya, a famous scholar of Bengal early in the sixteenth century, who suddenly decided that his scholarship was not worth while and left it, and took to the ways of faith. He became a great *bhakta*, who went about singing *bhajans* with his disciples all over Bengal. He founded also a Vaishnavite order, and his influence is still great in Bengal.

So much for religious reform and synthesis. In all other departments of life also there was this synthesis going on, sometimes consciously, more often unconsciously. A new culture, a new architecture, a new language was growing up. But remember that all this took place far more in the cities than in the villages, and especially in Delhi, the imperial capital, and the other great capitals of States and provinces. At the top the king was more autocratic than ever before. The old Indian rulers had custom and convention to check their autocracy. The new Muslim rulers did not have even this. Although in theory there is far more equality in Islam, and, as we have seen, even a slave could become sultan, still the autocratic and unchecked power of the king increased. What more amazing instance of this can one have than that of the mad Tughlaq who moved the capital from Delhi to Daulatabad ?

The practice of keeping slaves, especially by the sultans, also increased. A special effort was made to capture these in war. Artisans were specially valued amongst them. The others were enrolled in the sultan's guard.

What of the great universities of Nalanda and Takshashila or Taxila ? They had long ceased to exist, but many new university centres of a new type had arisen. *Tols* they were called, where the old Sanskrit learning was imparted. They were not up to date. They lived in the past and probably kept up a spirit of reaction. Benares has all along been one of the biggest of such centres.

I have spoken above of Kabir's songs in Hindi. Hindi was thus in the fifteenth century already not only a popular but a literary language. Sanskrit had long ceased to be a living language. Even in the days of Kalidas and the Gupta kings, Sanskrit was confined to the learned. The ordinary people talked a Prakrit, a variation of Sanskrit. Slowly the other daughters of Sanskrit developed— Hindi, Bengali, Marathi and Gujrati. Many Muslim writers and poets wrote in Hindi. A Muslim king of Jaunpur in the fifteenth century had the *Mahābhārata* and the *Bhagawad* translated from the Sanskrit into Bengali. The accounts of the Muslim rulers of Bijapur in the south were kept in Marathi. So we find that already in the fifteenth century these daughter languages of Sanskrit had grown up considerably. In the south, of course, the Dravidian languages—Tamil and Telugu and Malayālam and Kanarese—were much older.

The Muslim Court language was Persian. Most educated people learnt Persian if they had anything to do with the Courts or government offices. Thus large numbers of Hindus learnt Persian. Gradually a new language developed in the camps and bazaars, called " Urdū ", which means ' camp ". In reality this was not a new language. It was Hindi with a slightly different dress on; there were more of Persian words in it, but otherwise it was Hindi. This Hindi-Urdū language, or as it is sometimes called Hindustani, spread all over northern and Central India. It is to-day spoken, with minor variations, by about 150,000,000 people and understood by a far greater number. Thus it is, from the point of numbers, one of the major languages of the world.

In architecture, new styles were developed and many noble buildings arose—in Bijapur and Vijayanagar in the south ; in Golkonda ; in Ahmedabad, which was then a great and beautiful city, and in Jaunpur, not far from Allahabad. Do you remember our visit to the old ruins of Golkonda near Hyderabad ? We went up the great fortress and saw, spread out beneath us, the old city, with its palaces and markets—all in ruins now.

So, while kings quarrelled and destroyed each other, silent forces in India worked ceaselessly for a synthesis, in order that the people of India might live harmoniously together and devote their energies jointly to progress and betterment. In the course of centuries they achieved considerable success. But before their work was completed there was another upset, and we went back part of the way we had come. Again we have to-day to march the same way and work for a synthesis of all that is good. But this time it must be on surer foundations. It must be based on freedom and social equality, and it must fit in with a better world-order. Only then will it endure.

The problem of this synthesis of religion and culture engrossed the better mind of India for many hundreds of years. It was so full of it that political and social freedom were forgotten, and just when Europe shot ahead in a dozen different directions, India remained behind, unprogressing and vegetating.

There was a time, as I have already told you, when India controlled foreign markets because of her progress in chemistry—in the making of dyes—in tempering steel, and for many other reasons. Her ships carried her merchandise to distant places. India had long lost this control at the time of which we are speaking. In the sixteenth century the river began to flow back to the East. It was a small trickle to begin with. But it was to grow till it became a mighty stream.

76

THE KINGDOMS OF SOUTH INDIA

July 14, 1932

LET us have another look at India and see the shifting panorama of States and empires. Almost it is like a great and unending movie film with silent pictures coming one after the other.

You will remember, perhaps, the mad Sultan Mohammad Tughlaq and how he succeeded in breaking up the Delhi Empire. The great provinces in the south fell away and new States arose there, chief among these being the Hindu State of Vijayanagar and the Muslim State of Gulbarga. To the east, the province of Gaur, which included Bengal and Bihar, became independent under a Muslim ruler.

Mohammad's successor was his nephew Firoz Shah. He was saner than his uncle and more humane. But there was still intolerance. Firoz was an efficient ruler, and he introduced many reforms in his administration. He could not recover the lost provinces in the south or east, but he managed to check the process of the breaking up of the empire. He was particularly fond of building new cities and palaces and mosques and planning gardens. Firozabad, near Delhi, and Jaunpur, not far from Allahabad, were founded by him. He also built a great canal on the Jumna, and repaired many of the old buildings which were falling to pieces. He was quite proud of this work of his, and left a long list of the new buildings he had put up and the old ones he had repaired.

Firoz Shah's mother was a Rajput woman, Bibi Naila, the daughter of a big chief. There is a story that she was at first refused in marriage to Firoz's father. Thereupon there was war and Naila's country was attacked and desolated. Bibi Naila, on learning of the suffering of her people on her account, was much upset and decided to put an end to it and save her people by surrendering herself to the father of Firoz Shah. Thus Firoz Shah had Rajput blood. You will find that such intermarriages between Muslim rulers and Rajput women became frequent, and this must have helped in developing a sentiment of a common nationality.

Firoz Shah died in 1388 after a long reign of thirty-seven years. Immediately the fabric of the Delhi Empire which he had held together fell to pieces. There was no central government and petty rulers bossed it everywhere. It was during this period of disorder and weakness that Timur came down from the north, just ten years after Firoz Shah's death. He nearly killed Delhi. Slowly the city recovered, and fifty years later it again became the seat of a central government with a Sultan at the head. But it was a little State and could not compare with the great kingdoms of the south and west and east. The Sultans were Afghans. They were a poor lot, and even their own Afghan nobles got fed up with them ultimately, and, in sheer disgust, invited a foreigner to come and rule over them. This foreigner was Babar, a Mongol, or Moghal, as we shall call them now, after they settle down in India. He was directly descended from Timur and his mother was a descendant of Chengiz Khan. He was at the time ruler of Kabul. He gladly accepted the invitation to come to India; indeed, he would probably have come even without the invitation. On the plains of Panipat, near Delhi, in 1526, Babar won the Empire of Hindustan. A great empire rose again, known as the Moghal Empire of India, and Delhi again attained prominence and became the seat of this empire. But before we consider this we must look at the rest of India and see what was happening there during these 150 years of the decline of Delhi.

Quite a number of States, little and great, existed in India during this period. In Jaunpur, newly founded, there was a small Muslim State ruled by the Sharqi kings. It was not big and powerful, and politically it was not important. But for nearly 100 years in the fifteenth century it was a great seat of culture and toleration in religion. The Muslim colleges of Jaunpur spread these ideas of toleration, and one of the rulers even tried to bring about that synthesis between Hindus and Muslims of which I wrote to you in my last letter. Art and fine building were encouraged, and so were the growing languages of the country, like Hindi and Bengali. In the midst of a great deal of intolerance, the little and short-lived State of Jaunpur stands out, a haven of scholarship and culture and toleration.

To the east, coming almost right up to Allahabad, was the great

State of Gaur, which included Bihar and Bengal. The city of Gaur
was a seaport communicating by sea with the coastal towns of
India. In central India, west of Allahabad and almost up to Gujrat,
was Malwa, with its capital at Mandu, which was a city and fortress
combined. Here in Mandu many beautiful and splendid buildings
arose, and their ruins attract visitors still.

North-west of Malwa was Rajputana, with many Rajput States,
and especially Chittor. There was frequent fighting between
Chittor and Malwa and Gujrat. Chittor was small compared to these
two powerful States, but the Rajputs have always been brave
fighters. Sometimes, in spite of their small numbers, they won.
Such a victory by the Rana of Chittor over Malwa was celebrated
by his building a fine tower of victory—the *Jaya Stambha*—in Chittor. The Sultan of Mandu, not to be outdone, built a high tower at
Mandu. The Chittor tower still remains; the Mandu one has
vanished.

To the west of Malwa lay Gujrat. Here was established a powerful kingdom, and its capital, Ahmedabad, founded by Sultan Ahmad
Shah, became a great city of nearly 1,000,000 inhabitants. Beautiful buildings arose in this city and, it is said that for 300 years, from
the fifteenth to the eighteenth centuries, Ahmedabad was one of the
finest cities in the world. It is curious to find that the great Jami
Masjid of the city resembles the Jaina temple built at Ranpur by
the Rana of Chittor, which was built about the same time. This
shows how the old Indian architects were being affected by the new
ideas, and were producing a new architecture. Here again you see
the synthesis in the field of art of which I have already written.
Even now there are many of these fine old buildings in Ahmedabad
with wonderful carvings in stone, but the new industrial city that
has grown up around them is not a thing of beauty.

It was about this time that the Portuguese reached India. You
will remember that Vasco da Gama was the first to come round the
Cape of Good Hope. He reached Calicut in the south in 1498.
Of course many Europeans had previously visited India, but they
came as traders or just simply as visitors. The Portuguese now
came with different ideas. They were full of pride and self-confidence; they had the Pope's gift of the Eastern world. They came
with the intention of conquest. They were small in numbers to
begin with, but more and more ships came, and some coast towns were
seized, notably Goa. The Portuguese never did much in India.
They never got inland. But they were the first of the Europeans to
come by sea to attack India. They were followed much later by the
French and English. Thus the opening of the sea-routes showed the
weakness of India by sea. The old Powers of South India had
dwindled and their attention was diverted to dangers from
inland.

The Gujrat Sultans fought the Portuguese even by sea. They
allied themselves with the Ottoman Turks and defeated a Portuguese
fleet, but the Portuguese won later and controlled the sea. Just then
the fear of the Moghals at Delhi made the Gujrat Sultans seek peace
with the Portuguese, but the latter played them false.

In South India there had arisen early in the fourteenth century two great kingdoms : Gulbarga, also called the Bahmani kingdom, and, to the south of this, Vijayanagar. The Bahmani kingdom spread all over the Maharashtra area and partly over the Karnataka. It lasted for over 150 years, but its record is an ignoble one. There is intolerance and violence and murder, and the luxury of the Sultan and nobles side by side with extreme misery of the people. Early in the sixteenth century the Bahmani kingdom collapsed through sheer ineptitude and was split up into five sultanates—Bijapur, Ahmednagar, Golkonda, Bidar and Berar. The State of Vijayanagar had meantime carried on for nearly 200 years, and was still flourishing. Between these six States there were frequent wars, each attempting to gain the mastery of the south. There were all manner of combinations between them, and these were always changing. Sometimes a Muslim State fought a Hindu State ; sometimes a Muslim and a Hindu State jointly fought another Muslim one. The struggles were purely political, and whenever any one State seemed to become too powerful, the others allied themselves against it. Ultimately Vijayanagar's strength and wealth induced the Muslim States to combine against it, and in 1565, at the battle of Talikota, they succeeded in crushing it completely. The Empire of Vijayanagar ended after two and a half centuries, and the great and splendid city was utterly destroyed.

The victorious allies fell out amongst themselves soon after and fought each other, and before long the shadow of the Moghal Empire of Delhi fell on them all. Another of their troubles were the Portuguese, who captured Goa in 1510. This was in Bijapur State. In spite of every effort to dislodge them, the Portuguese stuck to Goa, and their leader, Albuquerque, who had the fine title of Viceroy of the East, indulged in disgusting cruelties. The Portuguese carried out a massacre of the people and did not spare even women and children. Ever since then, to this day, the Portuguese have remained in Goa.

Beautiful buildings were made in these southern States, specially in Vijayanagar and Golkonda and Bijapur. Golkonda is in ruins now ; Bijapur still has many of these fine buildings ; Vijayanagar was reduced to dust and is no more. The city of Hyderabad was founded near Golkonda about this time. The builders and craftsmen of the south are said to have gone later to the north and helped in the building of the Taj Mahal at Agra.

In spite of general toleration of each other's religions, there were occasional bursts of bigotry and intolerance. The wars were often accompanied by frightful slaughters and destruction. Yet it is interesting to remember that the Muslim State of Bijapur had Hindu cavalry, and that the Hindu State of Vijayanagar had some Muslim troops. There appears to have been a fairly high degree of civilization, but it was a rich man's show, and the man in the field was out of it. He was poor, and yet, as always happens, he bore the burden of the great luxury of the rich.

77

VIJAYANAGAR

July 15, 1932

Of all the kingdoms of the south that we discussed in our last letter, Vijayanagar has the longest history. It so happened that many foreign visitors came to it and left accounts of the State and the city. There was an Italian, Nicolo Conti, who came in 1420; and Abdur-Razzaq of Herat, who came from the Court of the Great Khan in Central Asia in 1443; and Paes, a Portuguese, who visited the city in 1522; and many others. There is also a history of India which deals with the South Indian States, and especially Bijapur. This was written in Persian by Ferishta in Akbar's time, not long after the period we are considering. Contemporary histories are often very partial and exaggerated, but they are of great help. There are hardly any of these known to us for the pre-Muslim periods, with the exception of the *Rājatarangini* of Kashmir. Ferishta's history was thus a great innovation. Others followed him.

The descriptions of foreign visitors to Vijayanagar give us a good and impartial picture of the city. They tell us more than the accounts of the wretched wars which were frequently taking place. I shall therefore tell you something of what these people say.

Vijayanagar was founded about 1336. It was situated in what is known as the Karnataka area of South India. Being a Hindu State, it naturally attracted large numbers of refugees from the Muslim States in the south. It grew rapidly. Within a few years the State dominated the south, and the capital city attracted attention by its wealth and beauty. Vijayanagar became the dominant Power in the Dekhan.

Ferishta tells us of its great wealth and describes the capital in 1406, when a Muslim Bahmani king from Gulbarga went there to marry a princess of Vijayanagar. He says that for six miles the road was spread with cloth of gold and velvet and similar rich stuffs. What a terrible and scandalous waste of money !

In 1420 came the Italian, Nicolo Conti, and he tells us that the circumference of the city was sixty miles. This area was so vast because there were numerous gardens. Conti was of opinion that the ruler of Vijayanagar, or Raya as he was called, was the most powerful ruler in India at the time.

Then comes Abdur-Razzaq from central Asia. On his way to Vijayanagar, near Mangalore, he saw a wonderful temple made of pure molten brass. It was 15 feet high, and 30 feet by 30 at its base. Further up, at Belur, he was still more amazed at another temple. Indeed, he does not attempt to describe it, as he fears that if he did so, he would be " charged with exaggeration " ! Then he reached the city of Vijayanagar, and he goes into ecstasies over this. He says : " The city is such that eye has not seen nor ear heard of any place resembling it upon the whole earth." He describes the many bazaars : " At the head of each bazaar there is a lofty arcade and magnificent gallery, but the palace of the King is loftier than all of them." "The bazaars are very long and broad. . . . Sweet-scented flowers are always procurable fresh in that city and they are considered as even necessary sustenance, seeing that without them they could not exist. The tradesmen of each separate guild or craft have their shops close to one another. The jewellers sell their rubies and pearls and diamonds and emeralds openly in the bazaar." Abdur-Razzaq goes on to describe that " in this charming area, in which the palace of the King is contained, there are many rivulets and streams flowing through channels of cut stone, polished and even. . . . The country is so well populated that it is impossible in a reasonable space to convey an idea of it." And so he goes on, this visitor from Central Asia in the middle of the fifteenth century, waxing eloquent over the glories of Vijayanagar.

It may be thought that Abdur-Razzaq was not acquainted with many big cities, and so he was almost overcome when he saw Vijayanagar. Our next visitor, however, was a well-travelled man. He was Paes, the Portuguese, and he came in 1522, just about the time when the Renaissance was influencing Italy and beautiful buildings were rising up in the Italian cities. Paes apparently knew these Italian cities, and his testimony is thus very valuable. The city of Vijayanagar, he says, is as " large as Rome and very beautiful to the sight ". He describes at length the wonders of the city, and the charms of its innumerable lakes and waterways and fruit gardens. It is, he says, " the best-provided city in the world . . . for the state of the city is not like that of other cities, which often fail of supplies and provisions, for in this everything abounds." One of the rooms he saw in the palace was " all of ivory, as well the chamber as the walls from top to bottom, and the pillars of the cross-timbers at the top had roses and flowers of lotuses all of ivory, and all well executed, so that there could not be better—it is so rich and beautiful that you would hardly find anywhere another such."

Paes also describes the ruler of Vijayanagar at the time of his visit. He was one of the great rulers of South Indian history, and his reputation as a great warrior, and as one who was chivalrous to his enemies, as a patron of literature, and a popular and generous king, still survives in the south. His name was Krishna Deva Raya. He reigned for twenty years, from 1509 to 1529. Paes tells of his height and figure and even complexion, which he says was fair. " He is the most feared and perfect king that could possibly be, cheerful of disposition and very merry; he is one that seeks to honour foreigners, and receives them kindly, asking about all their affairs whatever their condition may be." Giving the King's many titles, Paes adds : " But it seems that he has in fact nothing compared to what a man like him ought to have, so gallant and perfect is he in all things."

High praise indeed ! The Empire of Vijayanagar at this time spread all over the south and the east coast. It included Mysore, Travancore and the whole of the present Madras presidency.

One thing else I might mention. Great irrigation works were erected about 1400 A.O. to bring good water to the city. A whole river was dammed up and a big reservoir was made. From this the water went to the city in an aqueduct, 15 miles in length, often cut out of the solid rock.

Such was Vijayanagar. It was proud of its wealth and beauty and over-confident of its strength. No one thought that the end of the city and empire was near. Only forty-three years after the visit of Paes, danger suddenly loomed up. The other States of the Dekhan, jealous of Vijayanagar, formed a league against it and determined to destroy it. Even then Vijayanagar felt foolishly confident. The end came soon, and it was terrible in its completeness.

As I have told you, Vijayanagar was defeated by this league of States in 1565. There was terrible slaughter, and the sack of the great city followed soon after. All the beautiful buildings and temples and palaces were destroyed. The exquisite carvings and sculptures were smashed, and huge bonfires were lit to burn up everything that could be burnt. Destruction went on till only a heap of ruins was left. " Never," says an English historian, " never perhaps in the history of the world has such havoc been wrought, and wrought so suddenly, on so splendid a city; teeming with a wealthy and industrious population in the full plenitude of prosperity one day, and on the next seized, pillaged, and reduced to ruins, amid scenes of savage massacre and horrors beggaring description."

78

THE MALAYSIAN EMPIRES OF MADJAPAHIT AND MALACCA

July 17, 1932

WE have been rather neglectful of Malaysia and the Eastern Islands, and it is long since I wrote about them. I have looked back, and I find that my last account of them was in letter 46 ; since then we have had thirty-one letters, and have now reached number 78. It is difficult to keep all the countries in line.

Do you remember something of what I wrote to you just two months ago to-day ? Of Cambodia and Angkor and Sumatra' and Sri Vijaya ? How in Indo-China the old Indian colonies developed in the course of many hundred years into one big State—the Empire of Cambodia ? And then Nature intervened and, harshly and suddenly, put an end to the city and the empire. This took place about 1300 A.C.

Almost contemporaneous with—that is, existing at the same time as—the Cambodian State was another great State across the sea in

the island of Sumatra. But Sri Vijaya started a little later in its
career of empire, and outlasted Cambodia. Its end was also rather
sudden, but it was man, and not Nature, that brought it about.
For 300 years the Buddhist Empire of Sri Vijaya flourished and
controlled almost all the islands of the East, and for a while even
had a footing in India and Ceylon and China. It was a merchant
empire, and trade was its chief function. But then arose another
merchant State near by in the eastern part of the island of Java—
a Hindu State which had refused to be subdued by Sri Vijaya.

For 400 years, from the beginning of the ninth century, this Eastern
Javan State was menaced by the growing power of Sri Vijaya. But
it succeeded in retaining its independence, and at the same time in
building an amazing number of fine stone temples. The greatest
of these, known as the Borobodur temples, are still to be seen, and
attract numerous visitors. Having escaped the dominion of Sri
Vijaya, East Java itself became aggressive, and in its turn became a
menace to its old rival Sri Vijaya. Both were merchant States,
crossing the seas for trade, and so they were often coming into
conflict with each other.

I feel tempted to compare this rivalry of Java and Sumatra with
the rivalries of modern Powers, say, of Germany and England.
Java, feeling that the only way to check Sri Vijaya and increase its
own trade was to add to its naval strength, developed its sea power
greatly. Great naval expeditions were sent out, but often they did
not come to grips with the enemy for years. So Java went on
growing and became more and more aggressive. Towards the end
of the thirteenth century a city was founded, named Madjapahit,
and this became the capital of the growing Javan State.

So presumptuous and arrogant did this Javan State become that
it actually insulted some envoys of Kublai, the Great Khan, who
had sent them for tribute. Not only was no tribute paid, but one of
the envoys had an insulting message tattooed on the forehead !
It was a very foolish and dangerous game to play with a Mongol
Khan. A similar insult had resulted in the destruction of Central
Asia by Chengiz, and later of Baghdad by Hulagu. And yet the
little island State of Java dared to offer it. But, fortunately for it,
the Mongols had toned down a great deal and had no desire for conquest. Naval fighting was also not much to their liking; they felt
stronger on solid land. Still Kublai sent an expedition to Java to
punish the guilty ruler. The Chinese defeated the Javanese and
killed the king. But they do not seem to have done much damage.
How the Mongols had changed under Chinese influence !

Indeed, the Chinese expedition, seems ultimately to have resulted
in making Java, or the Madjapahit Empire as we shall now call it,
stronger. This is because the Chinese introduced firearms into
Java, and it was probably the use of these firearms that brought
victory to Madjapahit in subsequent wars.

The Empire of Madjapahit went on expanding. This was not
by chance or in a haphazard way. It was imperialist expansion
organized by the State and carried on by an efficient army and

navy. A woman, Queen Suhita, was the ruler during part of this period of expansion. The government appears to have been highly centralized and efficient. It is stated by Western historians that the system of taxation, customs, tolls and internal revenues was excellent. Among the separate departments of government were : a Colonial Department, a Commerce Department, a Department of Public Welfare and Public Health, a Department of the Interior, and a War Department. There was a Supreme Court consisting of two presiding officers and seven judges. The Brahman priests seem to have had a good deal of power, but the King was supposed to control them.

These departments, and even some of the names for them, remind us to some extent of the *Arthashāstra*. But the Colonial Department was new. The Minister in charge of the Department for the Interior, which dealt with the affairs of the home State, was called *mantri*. This shows that Indian traditions and culture continued in these islands 1200 years after the first settlements were made by the Pallava colonists from South India. This could only be so if the contacts were kept up. There is no doubt that such contacts were kept up by means of trade.

As Madjapahit was a trading empire, it is natural that the export and import trades—that is to say, the trades relating to the goods that were sent out and those that were received from other countries —were carefully organized. These trades were chiefly with India, China and its own colonies. So long as there was a state of war with Sri Vijaya it was not possible to have peaceful trade with it or its colonies.

The Javan State lasted for many hundreds of years, but the great period of the Empire of Madjapahit was from 1335 to 1380, just forty-five years. It was during this period, in 1377, that Sri Vijaya was finally captured and destroyed. With Annam, Siam and Cambodia there were alliances.

The capital city of Madjapahit was a fine and prosperous city, with a mighty Shiva temple in the centre. There were many splendid buildings. Indeed, all the Indian colonies in Malaysia specialized in fine buildings. There were several other great cities and many ports in Java.

This imperialist State did not long survive its old enemy, Sri Vijaya. There was civil war and trouble with China, which resulted in a great Chinese fleet coming to Java. The colonies gradually dropped off. In 1426 there was a great famine, and two years later Madjapahit ceased to be an empire. It carried on, however, as an independent State for another fifty years, when the Muslim State of Malacca captured it.

Thus ended the third of the empires which had grown out of the old Indian settlements in Malaysia. In our short letters we have dealt with long periods. The first colonists came from India almost at the beginning of the Christian era, and we are now in the fifteenth century. So we have surveyed 1400 years of the history of these settlements. Each of the three empire States we have especially considered—Cambodia, Sri Vijaya and Madjapahit—lasted for hundreds of years. It is well to remember these long periods, as they give some idea of the stability and efficiency of these States. Fine architecture was their special love, and trade their main business. They carried on the tradition of Indian culture and mixed with it harmoniously many elements from Chinese culture.

You will remember that there were many other Indian settlements besides the three I have especially mentioned. But we cannot consider each one separately. Nor can I say much about two neighbouring countries—Burma and Siam. In both these countries powerful States arose and there was a great deal of artistic activity. Buddhism spread in both of them. Burma was invaded by the Mongols once, but Siam was never invaded by China. Both Burma and Siam, however, often paid tribute to China. It was a kind of offering which a respectful younger brother might make to an elder. In return for this tribute rich gifts came from China to the younger brother.

Before the Mongol invasion of Burma, the capital of the country was the city of Pagan in North Burma. For over 200 years this city was the capital, and it is said that it was a very beautiful city, its only rival being Angkor. Its finest building was the Anand temple, one of the most beautiful examples of Buddhist architecture. in the world. There were many other magnificent buildings. Indeed, even the ruins of Pagan city now are beautiful. Pagan's days of greatness were from the eleventh to the thirteenth century. There was some trouble and confusion in Burma for some time afterwards, and North and South Burma were separate. In the sixteenth century a great ruler arose in the south, and he united Burma again. His capital was Pegu in the south.

I hope this short and sudden reference to Burma and Siam will not confuse you. We have arrived at the end of a chapter in the history of Malaysia and Indonesia, and I wanted to complete our survey. So far, the principal influences, political and cultural, which affected these parts had their origin in India and China. As I have told you already, the continental countries in the south-east of Asia, like Burma, Siam, Indo-China, were more influenced by China; the islands and the Malay Peninsula were more influenced by India.

Now a new influence comes on the scene. This is brought by the Arabs. Burma and Siam were not affected by this, but Malay and the islands succumb to it, and soon a Muslim empire grows up.

Arab traders had visited these islands and settled there for 1000 years or more. But they were intent on business, and did not otherwise interfere with the governments. In the fourteenth century Arab missionaries came out from Arabia, and they met with success, especially in converting some of the local rulers.

Meanwhile political changes were taking place. Madjapahit was expanding and crushing Sri Vijaya. When Sri Vijaya fell, large numbers of refugees went to the south of the Malay Peninsula and founded the city of Malacca there. This city, as well as the States, grew rapidly, and by 1400 it was already a large city. The Javanese people of Madjapahit were not liked by their subject peoples. As is usual with imperialists, they were tyrannous, and many people preferred going to the new State of Malacca to remaining under Madjapahit. Siam was also at the time rather aggressive. So Malacca became a place of refuge for many people. There were both Buddhists and Muslims. The rulers were at first Buddhists, but later they adopted Islam.

The young State of Malacca was menaced by Java on the one side and Siam on the other. It tried to find friends and allies among the other small Muslim States in the islands. It even appealed to China for protection. At that time the Mings, who had displaced the Mongols, ruled in China. It is remarkable how all the little Islamic States in Malaysia turned to China for protection at the same time. This shows that there must have been some immediate threat from powerful enemies.

China had always followed a policy towards the Malaysian countries of friendly but dignified isolation. She was not keen on conquest. She felt that it had little to gain from them, but she was prepared to teach them her civilization. The Ming Emperor apparently decided to vary this old policy and to take greater interest in these countries. He does not seem to have approved of the aggression of Java and of Siam. So, to check these and to make the power of China felt by others, he sent out a vast fleet under Admiral Cheng Ho. Some of the ships in this fleet were 400 feet in length.

Cheng Ho made many trips and visited almost all the islands—Philippines, Java, Sumatra, Malay Peninsula, etc. He even came to Ceylon and conquered it and carried off the king to China. In his last expedition he went as far as the Persian Gulf. Cheng Ho's voyages in the early years of the fifteenth century had great influence over all the countries he visited. Wishing to check Hindu Madjapahit and Buddhist Siam, he deliberately encouraged Islam, and the State of Malacca became firmly established under the protection of his great fleet. Cheng Ho's motives were, of course, purely political, and had nothing to do with religion. He himself was a Buddhist.

So the State of Malacca became the head of the opposition to Madjapahit. Its strength grew and gradually it seized the colonies of Java. In 1478 the city of Madjapahit itself was captured. Islam then became the religion of the Court and of the cities. But in the countryside, as in India, the old faith and myths and customs continued.

The Malaccan Empire might have become as great and as long-lived as Sri Vijaya and Madjapahit, but it did not have the chance. The Portuguese intervened, and within a few years—in 1511—Malacca fell to them. So the fourth of these empires gave place to a fifth, which itself was not to have a long life. And for the first time in history Europe became aggressive and dominant in these eastern waters.

79

EUROPE BEGINS TO GRAB IN EASTERN ASIA

July 19, 1932

WE ended our last letter with the appearance of the Portuguese in Malaysia. You will remember my telling you a short while ago of the discovery of the sea routes, and how the Portuguese and the Spanish had a kind of race to reach the East first. Portugal went east; Spain went west. Portugal managed to come round Africa to India; Spain stumbled by mistake on America, and later came round South America to Malaysia. We can now join up some of our threads, and carry on our story of Malaysia.

Spices (pepper, etc.), as you perhaps know, are produced in hot climates, in countries near the equator. Europe does not produce them at all. South India and Ceylon produce some. But most of these spices came from the Malaysian islands, called the Moluccas. These islands are, in fact, called the Spice Islands. From the earliest times there was a great demand in Europe for these spices, and they were regularly sent. By the time they reached Europe they were very valuable. In Roman times pepper was worth its weight in gold. Although spices were so valuable and were in such demand in the West, Europe took no steps to get them itself. For a long time the spice trade was in the hands of Indians; later the Arabs controlled it. It was the lure of the spices that drew the Portuguese and Spaniards on and on from different sides of the world, till they met in Malaysia. The Portuguese had a lead in this quest, as the Spanish got busy, and very profitably busy, in America on the way to the East.

Soon after Vasco da Gama reached India *via* the Cape of Good Hope, many Portuguese ships came the same way, and they went farther east. Just then the new Empire of Malacca controlled the spice and other trade. So immediately the Portuguese came into conflict with it and with the Arab traders generally. Their Viceroy, Albuquerque, seized Malacca in 1511 and put an end to Muslim trade. The Portuguese now controlled the trade to Europe, and their capital in Europe, Lisbon, became the great commercial centre for distributing spices and many other Eastern goods in Europe.

It is worth noting that although Albuquerque was a harsh and cruel enemy to the Arabs, he tried to be friendly with the other commercial people in the East. In particular, he treated all the Chinese he came across with especial courtesy, with the result that favourable reports of the Portuguese were carried to China. Probably hostility to the Arabs was due to the Arab predominance in Eastern trade.

Meanwhile the search for the Spice Islands continued and Magellan, who later crossed the Pacific and went round the world, was a member of the expedition which found the Moluccas. For over sixty years the Portuguese had no rival in the spice trade to Europe.

Then in 1565 Spain occupied the Philippine Islands, and thus a second European Power appeared in Eastern waters. But Spain made little difference to Portuguese trade, as the Spanish were not primarily a commercial people. They sent soldiers and missionaries to the East. Meanwhile Portugal had a monopoly of the spice trade, so much so that even Persia and Egypt had to get their spices through the Portuguese. They would not even allow anyone else to trade directly with the Spice Islands. So Portugal grew rich, but it made no attempt to develop colonies. As you know, it is a small country, and it did not have enough men to send out. It is surprising enough what this little country was able to do for a 100 years—the whole of the sixteenth century—in the East.

Meanwhile the Spanish stuck to the Philippines and tried to make as much money from them as possible. They did little except extort tribute. With the Portuguese they had come to terms to avoid conflict in Eastern waters. The Spanish Government would not allow the Philippines to trade with Spanish America, as they were afraid that the gold and silver of Mexico and Peru might flow out to the East. Only one ship a year came and went. This was called the "Manilla Galleon," and you can imagine how eagerly this annual visit must have been awaited by the Spanish in the Philippines. For 240 years this "Manilla Galleon" crossed the Pacific between the Islands and America.

In Europe these successes of Spain and Portugal were making other nations turn green with envy. As we shall see later, Spain dominated over Europe at that time. England was hardly a first-rate Power. In the Netherlands—that is, Holland and part of Belgium—there had been a revolt against Spanish rule. The English people, sympathizing with the Dutch and envious of Spain, helped the Dutch privately. Some of their seamen went about committing what amounted to piracy on the high seas by capturing the Spanish treasure-ships from America. The leader at this rather risky but profitable game was Sir Francis Drake, and he called it singeing the King of Spain's beard.

In 1577 Drake went out with five ships to plunder the Spanish colonies. He was successful in the raid, but he lost four of his ships. Only one of the ships—the *Golden Hind*—reached the Pacific, and Drake came back to England in this *via* the Cape of Good Hope. Thus he went right round the world, and the *Golden Hind* was the second ship to do so, the first being Magellan's *Vittoria*. It took three years to go round.

The singeing of the Spanish King's beard could not go on for long without leading to trouble, and soon war came between England and Spain. The Dutch were already fighting Spain. Portugal was also involved in this war, as for some years past the same king had been ruling over Spain and Portugal. With a great deal of good luck and determination, England, to the surprise of Europe, came well out of this war. The "Invincible Armada" sent by Spain to conquer Britain was, you will remember, wrecked. But we are for the present concerned with the East.

Both the English and the Dutch invaded the Far East and attacked the Spanish and Portuguese. The Spanish were all concentrated in the Philippines, and they could easily defend it. But the Portuguese were hard hit. Their Eastern Empire spread for 6000 miles from the Red Sea to the Moluccas, the Spice Islands. They were established near Aden, in the Persian Gulf, in Ceylon, in many places on the Indian coast, and of course all over the Eastern islands and in Malay. Gradually they lost their Eastern Empire; town after town, settlement after settlement, went to the Dutch or the English. Even Malacca fell in 1641. All that remained were a few small outposts in India and elsewhere. Goa in western India was the chief of these, and the Portuguese are still there, and it forms part of the Portuguese Republic which was established some years ago. The great Akbar tried to take Goa from the Portuguese, but even he did not succeed.

So Portugal passes out of Eastern history. The little country had taken an enormous mouthful. It could not swallow it, and it exhausted itself in the attempt. Spain sticks on to the Philippines, but plays little part in Eastern affairs. The mastery of the valuable Eastern trade now passes to Holland and England. Both these countries had already laid themselves out for this by the formation of trading companies. In England Queen Elizabeth gave a charter in 1600 to the East India Company. Two years later the Dutch East India Company was formed. Both these companies were meant for trade only. They were private companies, but they were often helped by the State. They were mostly interested in the Malaysian spice trade. India was at the time a powerful country under the Moghal Emperors and could not be safely angered

The Dutch and the English often fell out amongst themselves, and the English ultimately withdrew from the Eastern islands and paid more attention to India. The great Moghal Empire was then weakening, and this afforded an opportunity to foreign adventurers. We shall see later how such adventurers came from England and France and tried, by intrigue and fighting, to get parts of this dissolving empire.

80

AN AGE OF PEACE AND PROSPERITY IN CHINA

July 22, 1932

So you have been ill, my dear, and, for aught I know, may still be laid up. It takes time for news to reach the inside of a gaol. I can do very little to help you, and you will have to look after yourself. But I shall think of you a great deal. Strange, how we are all spread out—you, far away in Poona; Mummie, unwell in Allahabad; and the rest of us in various prisons !

For some days I have found it a little difficult to write these letters

to you. It was not easy to keep up the pretence of having a talk
with you. I thought of you lying ill in Poona, and I wondered
when I would see you again; how many more months or years
would pass before we met; and how you would have grown during
the interval.

But too much of musing is not good, especially in gaol, and I must
pull myself up, and forget to-day for a while, and think of yesterday.

We were in Malaysia, were we not? And we saw a strange happening. Europe was becoming aggressive in Asia; the Portuguese
came, and then the Spanish; and later came the English and the
Dutch. But the activities of these Europeans were for a long time
largely confined to Malaysia and the islands. To the west there was
a strong India under the Moghals; to the north was China, also well
able to look after herself. So India and China had little interference
from the Europeans.

It is but a step from Malaysia to China. Let us go there now.
The Yuan dynasty founded by Kublai Khan, the Mongol, is gone.
A popular rebellion drove the last of the Mongol forces beyond the
Great Wall in 1368. The leader of rebellion was Hung Wu, who
began life as the son of a poor labourer and had little school education. But he was a good pupil in the larger school of life, and he
became a successful leader, and later a wise ruler. He did not get
puffed up with conceit and pride because he had become an emperor,
but throughout his life he remembered that he was a son of the
people. He reigned for thirty years, and his reign is remembered
still for his continuous efforts to better the ordinary people from
whom he had come. To the end he retained his early simplicity of
tastes.

Hung Wu was the first Emperor of the new Ming dynasty. His
son, Yung Lo, was also a great ruler. He was Emperor from 1402
to 1424. But I must not inflict these Chinese names upon you.
There were several good rulers and then, as usually happens, there
was deterioration. But let us forget the emperors and consider this
period in China's history. It is a bright period, and there is a
singular charm about it. The word " Ming " itself means bright.
The Ming dynasty lasted for 276 years—from 1368 to 1644. It is
the most typically Chinese of all dynasties, and during their rule the
genius of the Chinese people had full scope. It is a period of peace,
both domestic and foreign. There is no aggressive foreign policy;
no imperialist adventure. There is friendship with the neighbouring countries. Only in the north there is some danger from the
nomadic Tartar tribes. For the rest of the eastern world China is
very much the elder brother, the clever, favoured and cultured one,
very conscious of his superiority, but wishing well to the younger
brothers and willing to teach them and share with them his own
culture and civilization. And they in their turn all looked up to
him. For some time Japan even acknowledged the suzerainty of
China, and the Shogun, who ruled Japan, called himself the vassal
of the Ming Emperor. From Korea and from the Indonesian
islands—Java, Sumatra, etc.—and Indo-China came tribute.

It was in Yung Lo's reign that the great naval expedition under Admiral Cheng Ho went out to Malaysia. For nearly thirty years Cheng Ho wandered all over the eastern seas right up to the Persian Gulf. This looks like an imperialist attempt to overawe the island States. Apparently, however, there was no intention of conquest or other gain. The growing power of Siam and Madjapahit probably induced Yung Lo to send out this expedition. But, whatever the reason may have been, the expedition had very great results. It checked Madjapahit and Siam, and encouraged the new Muslim State of Malacca; and it spread Chinese culture all over Indonesia and the East.

Because there was peace and friendship between China and her neighbours, more attention could be given to domestic affairs. There was good government, and the burden on the peasantry was lessened by a lowering of the taxes. The roads and waterways and canals and reservoirs were improved. Public granaries were established to make provision for bad harvests and hard times. The government issued paper money, and thus increased credit and facilitated trade and the exchange of commodities. This paper money was widely used, and 70 per cent. of the taxes could be paid in it.

Even more notable was the cultural history of this period. The Chinese have for ages been a cultured and artistic people. The good government of the Ming period and the encouragement given to art brought out the genius of the people. Splendid buildings arose, and great paintings, and the Ming porcelains are famous for their graceful shapes and beautiful workmanship. The paintings rivalled those great ones which Italy was then producing under the urge of the Renaissance.

China at the end of the fifteenth century was far ahead of Europe in wealth, industry, and culture. During the whole of the Ming period, no country in Europe or elsewhere could compare with China in the happiness and artistic activity of its people. And remember that this covered the great Renaissance period in Europe.

One of the reasons why the Ming period is very well known artistically is because it has left for us numerous examples of its fine work. There are big monuments, and fine carving in wood and ivory and jade, and bronze vases and porcelains. Towards the end of the Ming period the designs have a tendency to become too elaborate, and this rather spoils the carving or painting.

It was during this period that the Portuguese ships first came to China. They reached Canton in 1516. Albuquerque had taken good care to treat all the Chinese he came across well, and favourable reports had reached China. So they were well received. But soon afterwards the Portuguese started misbehaving in many ways and erected forts at several places. The Chinese Government was surprised at this barbarity. It took no hasty action, but ultimately it drove the whole lot of them out. The Portuguese then realized that their usual methods did not pay in China. They became more peaceful and humble, and in 1557 they obtained permission to settle down near Canton. Macao was then founded by them.

With the Portuguese came Christian missionaries. One of the most famous of these was St. Francis Xavier. He spent a good deal of his time in India, and you will find many missionary colleges named after him. He also went to Japan. He died in a Chinese port before he was allowed to land. Christian missionaries were not encouraged by the Chinese. Two Jesuit priests, however, disguised themselves as Buddhist students and studied Chinese for several years. They became great Confucian scholars and also won reputations as scientists. One of these was named Matteo Ricci. He was a very able and brilliant scholar, and was also tactful enough to get round the Emperor. He threw off his disguise later, and through his influence Christianity attained a much better position in China.

The Dutch came to Macao early in the seventeenth century. They asked for permission to trade. But there was little love between them and the Portuguese and the latter tried their best to prejudice the Chinese against them. They told the Chinese that the Dutch were a nation of ferocious pirates. So the Chinese refused to give permission. A few years later the Dutch sent a big fleet from their city of Batavia in Java to Macao. Very foolishly they tried to take Macao by force, but the Chinese and Portuguese were much too strong for them.

The English followed the Dutch, but they also had little success. It was after the Ming period was over that they got a share in the China trade.

The Ming period, like all things, good and bad, came to an end about the middle of the seventeenth century. The little Tartar cloud in the north grew and grew till it cast its shadow on China itself. You will remember the old Kin or Golden Tartars. They had driven away the Sungs to the south of China, and they in their turn were driven out by the Mongols. A new tribe, cousin to these Kins, now became prominent north of China, where Manchuria is now. They called themselves Manchus. It was these Manchus who finally replaced the Mings.

But the Manchus would have had great difficulty in conquering China if China had not been split up in rival factions. Foreign invasions in almost every country—China, India, etc.—have always succeeded because of the weakness of that country and the internal conflicts of its people. So in China there were disturbances all over the country. Perhaps the later Ming emperors were corrupt and incompetent, or economic conditions were such as to bring about a social revolution. The struggle against the Manchus was also costly, and became a great strain. Brigand leaders cropped up everywhere, and the biggest of these was actually emperor for a short time. The general of the Mings who was leading the armies against the Manchus was Wu San-Kwei. He was hard put to it to know what to do between the brigand emperor and the Manchus. Very foolishly, or perhaps traitorously, he asked the Manchus to help him against the brigand. The Manchus gladly did so—and of course remained in Peking ! Wu San-Kwei then, convinced of the helplessness of the Ming cause, deserted it and joined the foreign invaders, the Manchus.

It is not surprising that this man, Wu San-Kwei, is loathed in China to this day and regarded as one of the great traitors of their history.   Entrusted with the defence of the country, he went over to the enemy and actually helped him to bring about the submission of the southern provinces.   His reward came by his appointment by the Manchus as the viceroy of these very provinces he had won for them.

By 1650 the city of Canton was captured by the Manchus and the conquest of China was complete.   They won perhaps because they were better fighters than the Chinese.   Perhaps too long a period of peace and prosperity had weakened the Chinese in a military sense. But the rapidity of the Manchu conquest was due to other reasons also, notably the great care they took to conciliate the Chinese   In former times the Tartar invasions were often accompanied by cruelty and massacre.   On this occasion every effort was made to win over the Chinese officials and these very persons were appointed again to offices.   Thus Chinese officials occupied the highest posts.   The old Ming methods of government were also not changed.   The system appeared to be the same, but the guiding hands at the top were altered.

But two important facts denoted that the Chinese were under foreign rule.   Manchu troops were stationed at important centres; and the Manchu custom of wearing the queue or pigtail was imposed on the Chinese as a sign of submission.   Most of us have always associated the Chinese with these pigtails.   But it was not a Chinese custom at all.   It was a sign of slavery, like the many signs which some Indians adopt to-day without feeling the shame and the degradation of it.   The Chinese have now given up the pigtail.

So ended this bright Ming period in China.   One wonders why it fell so rapidly after nearly three centuries of good government.   If the government was as good as it is supposed to be, why were there revolts and internal troubles ?   Why could not the foreign invaders from Manchuria be stopped ?   Probably the government became oppressive towards the end.   And it may be that too much parental government weakened the people.   Spoon-feeding is not good for children or nations.

One wonders also why China during these days, highly cultured as she was, did not advance in other directions—science, discovery, etc.   The peoples of Europe were far behind her ; yet you can see them, during the days of the Renaissance, full of energy and adventure and the spirit of inquiry.   You can compare the two to a cultured person of middle age, rather fond of a quiet life, not keen on new adventure and a disturbance of his routine, busy with his classics and his art ; and a young boy, rather uncouth, but full of energy and inquiry and seeking adventure everywhere.   There is a great beauty in China, but it is the calm beauty of the afternoon or evening.

81

JAPAN SHUTS HERSELF UP

July 23, 1932

FROM China we might as well go on to Japan, making a very brief stay in Korea on the way. The Mongols had of course dominated Korea. They had tried to attack Japan also, but without success. Kublai Khan sent several expeditions to Japan, but they were repelled. The Mongols never seem to have felt at ease on the sea. They were essentially continental people. Japan, being an island, escaped them.

Soon after the Mongols were driven out of China, there was a revolution in Korea, and the rulers who had submitted to the Mongols were driven out. The leader of this revolt was a patriot Korean, Yi Tai-jo. He became the new ruler and the founder of a dynasty which lasted over 500 years—from 1392 till quite recent times when Japan annexed Korea. Seoul was then made the capital, and it has remained so ever since. We cannot go into these 500 years of Korean history. Korea, or Chosen, as it was again called, carried on, an almost independent country, but under the shadow of China and often paying tribute to it. With Japan there were several wars, and on some occasions Korea was successful. But now there is no comparison between the two. Japan is a great and powerful empire, with all the vices of imperialist Powers ; poor Korea is a bit of this empire, ruled and exploited by the Japanese, and struggling rather helplessly, but bravely, for her freedom. But this is recent history, and we are still in the distant past.

In Japan, you will remember that the Shogun had become the real ruler towards the end of the twelfth century. The Emperor was almost a figurehead. The first Shogunate, known as the Kamakura Shogunate, lasted for nearly 150 years and gave the country efficient government and peace. The usual decline of the ruling dynasty followed, and inefficiency and luxury and civil war. There were conflicts between the Emperor who wanted to assert himself, and the Shogun. The Emperor failed, and so did the old Shogunate, and a new line of Shoguns rose to power in 1338. This was the Ashikaga Shogunate, which lasted for 235 years. But this was a period of conflict and war. It was almost contemporaneous with the Mings in China. One of these Shoguns was very anxious to win the goodwill of the Mings, and he went so far as to acknowledge himself the vassal of the Ming Emperor. Japanese historians are very annoyed at this slight to Japan and bitterly denounce this man.

Relations with China were naturally very friendly, and a new interest arose in Chinese culture which was then flowering under the Mings. Everything Chinese was studied and admired—painting, poetry, architecture, philosophy, and even the science of war. Two famous buildings, the Kinkakuji (the Golden Pavilion) and the Ginkakuji (the Silver Pavilion), were built at this time.

Side by side with this artistic development and luxury, there was much suffering of the peasantry. Taxation of the peasants was exceedingly heavy, and the burden of the civil wars fell largely on them. Conditions became worse and worse till the Central Government hardly functioned outside the capital.

The Portuguese arrived in 1542 during these wars. It is interesting to note that firearms were first brought to Japan by them. This seems very strange, as China had long known them, and indeed Europe had got to know of them from China, through the Mongols.

Three men ultimately rescued Japan from the hundred-years-old civil war. They were Norbunaga, a Daimyo or noble, Hideyoshi, a peasant, and Tokugawa Iyeyasu, one of the great nobles. By the end of the sixteenth century the whole of Japan was again united. Hideyoshi, the peasant, was one of the ablest statesmen of Japan. But it is said that he was very ugly—short and stumpy with a face like that of an ape.

Having united Japan, these people did not know what to do with their large army. So for want of any other occupation they invaded Korea. But they repented soon enough. The Koreans defeated the Japanese navy and controlled the Sea of Japan between the two countries. They did this largely with the help of a new kind of ship with a roof like the back of a tortoise and with iron plates. These ships were called "Tortoise Boats". They could be rowed backwards or forwards at will, and the Japanese warships were destroyed by these boats.

Tokugawa Iyeyasu, the third of the men named above, managed to profit greatly by the civil wars. So much so that he became vastly rich and owned nearly one-seventh of Japan. It was he who built the city of Yedo in the middle of his possessions. This later became Tokyo. Iyeyasu became Shogun in 1603, and thus began the third and last Shogunate, the Tokugawa Shogunate, which lasted for over 250 years.

Meanwhile the Portuguese had been carrying on trade in a small way. They had no European rivals for quite fifty years, the Spanish coming in 1592, and the Dutch and English even later. Christianity seems to have been introduced by St. Francis Xavier in 1549. Jesuits were allowed to preach, and were even encouraged. This was for political reasons, as the Buddhist monasteries were supposed to be hotbeds of intrigue. For this reason these monks were suppressed and favour was shown to the Christian missionaries. But soon enough the Japanese came to feel that these missionaries were dangerous, and immediately they changed their policy and tried to drive them out. As early as 1587 an Anti-Christian decree was issued ordering all missionaries to leave Japan within twenty days on pain of death. This was not aimed at merchants. It was stated that merchants could remain and trade, but if they brought a missionary on their ships, both the ship and the goods in it would be confiscated. This decree was passed for purely political reasons.

Hideyoshi scented danger. He felt that the missionaries and their converts might become politically dangerous. And he was not much mistaken.

Soon after this an incident occurred which convinced Hideyoshi that his fears were justified, and enraged him. The Manilla Galleon, which, you may remember, used to go once a year between the Philippines and Spanish America, was driven by a typhoon on to the Japanese coast. The Spanish captain tried to frighten the local Japanese by showing them a map of the world, and especially pointing out the vast possessions of the Spanish King. The captain was asked how Spain had managed to get this huge empire. Nothing so simple, he replied. The missionaries went first, and when there were many converts, soldiers were sent to combine with the converts and overthrow the government. When a report of this reached Hideyoshi he was not over-pleased and became still more bitter against the missionaries. He allowed the Manilla Galleon to go, but he had some of the missionaries and their converts put to death.

When Iyeyasu became Shogun he was more friendly to foreigners. He was especially interested in developing foreign trade, particularly with his own port, Yedo. But after Iyeyasu's death the persecution of Christians began again. Missionaries were forcibly driven out and Japanese converts were made to give up Christianity. Even the commercial policy changed, so afraid were the Japanese of the political designs of the foreigners. At any cost they wanted to keep the foreigner out.

One can understand this reaction of the Japanese. What surprises one is that they should have been penetrating enough to spot the wolf of imperialism in the sheep's clothing of religion, even though they had had little intercourse with Europeans. In later years and in other countries, we know well how religion has been exploited by the European Powers for their own aggrandizement.

And now began a unique thing in history. This was the closing up of Japan. Deliberately, the policy of isolation and exclusion was adopted, and, once adopted, it was pursued with amazing thoroughness. The English, not finding themselves welcome, gave up going to Japan in 1623. Next year the Spaniards, who were feared most of all, were deported. It was laid down that only non-Christians could go abroad for trade; and even they could not go to the Philippines. Finally, a dozen years later, in 1636, Japan was sealed up. The Portuguese were expelled; all Japanese, Christians or non-Christians, were forbidden to go abroad for any reason whatsoever; and no Japanese living abroad could return to Japan, on pain of death! Only some Dutch people remained, but they were absolutely forbidden to leave the ports and to go into the interior of the country. In 1641 even these Dutch people were removed to a little island in Nagasaki harbour and were kept almost like prisoners there. Thus, just ninety-nine years after the first Portuguese came, Japan cut off all foreign intercourse and shut herself up.

A Portuguese ship came in 1640 with an embassy asking for the restoration of trade. But there was nothing doing. The Japanese killed the envoys and most of the crew, and left some of the crew alive to go back and report.

For over 200 years Japan was almost completely cut off from the world, even from its neighbours, China and Korea.   The few Dutch-men on the island, and an occasional Chinaman, under strict super-vision, were the only links with the outer world.   This cutting off is a most extraordinary thing.   At no period in recorded history, and in no country, is there another example of this.   Even mysterious Tibet or central Africa communicated often enough with their neighbours.   It is a dangerous thing to isolate oneself; dangerous both for an individual and for a nation.   But Japan survived it, and had internal peace, and recovered from the long wars.   And when at last, in 1853, she opened her door and windows again, she per-formed another extraordinary thing.   She went ahead with a rush, made up for lost time, caught up to the European nations, and beat them at their own game.

How dull is the bald outline of history, and how thin and lifeless are the figures that pass through it !   Yet sometimes, when one reads a book written in the olden time, life seems to pour into the dead past, and the stage seems to come quite near to us, and living and loving and hating human beings move on it.   I have been reading about a charming lady of old Japan, the Lady Murasaki, who lived many hundreds of years ago—long before the civil wars of which I have written in this letter.   She has written a long account of her life at the Emperor's Court in Japan, and as I read extracts from this, with its delightful touches, and intimacies, and courtly futilities, the Lady Murasaki became very real to me, and a vivid picture arose of the limited but artistic world of the Court of old Japan.

82

EUROPE IN TURMOIL

August 4, 1932

I HAVE not written these letters to you for many days; it must be nearly two weeks since I wrote.   One has moods in prison—as indeed one has in the world outside too—and lately I have felt little inclined to write these letters, which no one sees but myself.   They are pinned together and put away to await the time, months or years hence, when perhaps you may see them.   Months or years hence ! when we meet again, and have a good look at each other, and I am surprised to find how you have grown and changed.   We shall have plenty to talk of and to do then, and you will pay little attention to these letters.   There will be quite a mountain of them by that time, and how many hundreds of hours of my prison life will be locked up in them !

But still I shall carry on with these letters and add to the pile of those already written. Perhaps they may interest you; and certainly they interest me.

We have been in Asia for some little time now, and we have followed her story in India, in Malaysia, and in China and Japan. We left Europe, rather suddenly, just when it was waking up and beginning to get interesting. There was a "renaissance", a re-birth. Or perhaps it would be more correct to say that there was a new birth, because the Europe which we find developing in the sixteenth century was no copy of any older period. It was a new thing, or at least an old thing with an entirely new covering on it.

Everywhere in Europe there is turmoil and restlessness, and a bursting out of an enclosed place. For many hundreds of years a social and economic structure modelled on feudal lines had covered Europe and held it in its grip. For a while this shell prevented growth. But the shell was cracking now in many places. Columbus and Vasco da Gama and the early discoverers of the sea-routes broke through the shell, and the sudden and astounding wealth of Spain and Portugal from the Americas and the East dazzled Europe and hastened the change. Europe began to look beyond its narrow waters and to think in terms of the world. Great possibilities of world trade and dominion opened out. The *bourgeoisie* grew more powerful, and feudalism became more and more of a hindrance in western Europe.

Feudalism was already out of date. The essence of this system had been the shameless exploitation of the peasantry. There had been forced labour, unpaid work, all manner of special dues and payments to the lord, and this lord himself was the judge. The suffering of the peasantry had been so great that, as we have seen, peasant riots and wars had broken out frequently. These peasant wars spread and became more and more frequent, and the economic revolution which took place in many parts of Europe, replacing the feudal system with the middle class or *bourgeois* State, followed, and was largely brought about by these agrarian revolts and *jacqueries*.

But do not think that these changes were brought about quickly. They took long, and for scores of years civil war raged in Europe. A great part of Europe was, indeed, ruined by these wars. They were not only peasant wars, but, as we shall see, religious wars between Protestant and Catholic, national wars of freedom, as in the Netherlands, and the revolt of the *bourgeoisie* against the absolute power of the king. All this sounds very confusing, does it not? Well, it is confusing and complicated. But if we look at the big events and movements, we shall be able to make something out of it.

The first thing to remember is that there was great distress and suffering among the peasantry, which resulted in the peasant wars. The second thing which we must note is the rise of the *bourgeoisie* and the growth of the productive forces. More labour was applied in producing things and there was more trade. The third thing to note is the fact that the Church was the greatest of the landowners. It was a tremendous vested interest, and was thus, of course, very much interested in the feudal system continuing. It wanted no economic change which might deprive it of a great deal of its wealth and property. Thus when the religious revolt from Rome took place, it fitted in with the economic revolution.

This great economic revolution was accompanied by, or followed by, changes in all directions—social, religious, political. If you take a distant and large enough view of Europe in the sixteenth and seventeenth centuries, you will be able to make out how all these activities and movements and changes were inter-related and connected together. Usually three great movements of this period are emphasized—Renaissance, Reformation, and Revolution. But behind all these, remember, was the economic distress and turmoil leading to the economic revolution, which was far the most important of all the changes.

The Renaissance was the re-birth of learning—the growth of art and science and literature, and the languages of European countries. The Reformation was a revolt against the Roman Church. It was a popular revolt against the corruption of the Church; it was also a revolt of the princes of Europe against the claims of the Pope to lord it over them; and thirdly it was an attempt to reform the Church from within. Revolution was the political struggle of the *bourgeoisie* to control the kings and limit their power.

Behind all these movements lay another factor—printing. You will remember that the Arabs learned paper-making from the Chinese and Europe learnt it from the Arabs. Still, it took a long time before paper was cheap and abundant. Towards the end of the fifteenth century books began to be printed in various parts of Europe—in Holland, Italy, England, Hungary, etc. Try to think of what the world was like before paper and printing became common. We are so used to books and paper and printing now that a world without them is most difficult to imagine. Without printed books it is almost impossible to teach many people even reading and writing. Books have to be copied out laboriously by hand and can reach only a small number of people. Teaching has to be largely oral, and students have to learn everything by heart. You see that even now in some primitive *maktabs* and *pāthshālās*.

With the coming of paper and printing an enormous change takes place. Printed books appear—school books and others. Very soon there are many people who can read and write. The more people read, the more they think (but this applies to the reading of thoughtful books, not to much of the trash that appears to-day). And the more one thinks, the more one begins to examine existing conditions and to criticize them. And this often leads to a challenge of the existing order. Ignorance is always afraid of change. It fears the unknown and sticks to its rut, however miserable it may be there. In its blindness it stumbles on anyhow. But with right reading comes a measure of knowledge, and the eyes are partly opened.

It was this opening of the eyes by means of paper and printing that helped tremendously all these great movements of which we have been speaking. Among the earliest books to be printed were

Bibles, and many persons who had only heard the Latin text of the Bible till then and had not understood it, were now able to read the book in their own language. This reading often made them very critical and somewhat independent of the priests. School books also appeared in large numbers. From this time onwards we find that the languages of Europe develop rapidly. Till now Latin had overshadowed them.

The history of Europe is full of the names of great men during this period. We shall come across some of them later. Always, when a country or continent breaks through the shell which has prevented growth, it shoots ahead in many directions. We find this in Europe, and the story of Europe at this period is most interesting and instructive because of the economic and other great changes that take place. Compare it to the history of India, or even of China during the same period. As I have told you, both these countries were ahead of Europe in many ways at the time. And yet there is a passivity about their history as compared with the dynamic nature of European history of this period. There are great rulers and great men in India and China and a high degree of culture, but, and especially so in India, the masses seem to be spiritless and passive. They put up with changes of rulers without any great objection. They seem to have been broken in, and have become too much used to obedience to challenge authority. Thus their history, though interesting occasionally, is more a record of events and rulers than of popular movements. I am not sure how far this is true of China; but of India it certainly has been true for many hundred years. And all the ills that have come to India during this period have been due to this unhappy condition of our people.

Another tendency to be noticed in India is the desire to look back and not forward; to the heights we once occupied and not to the heights we hope to occupy. And so our people sighed for the past, and, instead of getting a move on, obeyed anyone who chose to order them about. Ultimately empires rest not so much on their strength as on the servility of the people over whom they dominate.

83

THE RENAISSANCE

August 5, 1932

OUT of the turmoil and travail that were spreading all over Europe rose the fine flower of the Renaissance. It grew in the soil of Italy first, but it looked across the centuries to old Greece for inspiration and nourishment. From Greece it took its love of beauty, and added to the beauty of bodily form something that was deeper, that came from the mind and was of the spirit. It was an urban growth, and the cities of northern Italy gave shelter to it. In particular, Florence was the home of the early Renaissance.

Florence had already produced, in the thirteenth and fourteenth centuries, Dante and Petrarch, the two great poets of the Italian language. During the Middle Ages it was for a long time the financial capital of Europe, where the big money-lenders congregated. It was a little republic of rich and not very admirable people, who often ill-treated their own great men. "Fickle Florence", it has been called. But, in spite of the money-lenders and the despots and tyrants, this city produced, in the second half of the fifteenth century, three remarkable men : Leonardo da Vinci, Michelangelo, and Raphael. All three of them were very great artists and painters; Leonardo and Michelangelo were great in other directions also. Michelangelo was a wonderful sculptor, hewing mighty figures out of the solid marble; and he was a great architect, and the mighty Cathedral of St. Peter's in Rome was largely fashioned by him. He lived to a tremendous age—nearly ninety—and almost to his dying day he laboured at St. Peter's. He was an unhappy man, always seeking for something behind the surface of things, always thinking, always attempting amazing tasks. "One paints with his head, not with his hands," he once said.

Leonardo was the oldest of the three, and in many ways the most wonderful. Indeed, he was the most remarkable man of his age, and, remember, it was an age which produced many great men. A very great painter and sculptor, he was also a great thinker and scientist. Always experimenting, always probing, and trying to find out the reason for things, he was the first of the great scientists that have laid the foundations of modern science. "Kindly nature," he said, "sees to it that you may find something to learn everywhere in the world." He was a self-taught man, and began teaching himself Latin and mathematics at the age of thirty. He became a great engineer also, and he was the first to discover that blood circulated through the body. He was fascinated by the structure of the body. "Coarse people," he said, " of bad habits and shallow judgments do not deserve so beautiful an instrument, such a complex anatomical equipment, as the human body. They should merely have a sack for taking in food and letting it out again, for they are nothing but an alimentary canal ! " He was himself a vegetarian, and was very fond of animals. A habit of his was to buy caged birds in the market and set them free immediately.

Most amazing of all were Leonardo's attempts at aviation or flying in the air. He did not succeed, but he went a good way towards success. There was no one to follow up his theories and experiments. Perhaps if there had been a couple of Leonardos to follow him, the modern aeroplane might have been invented 200 or 300 years ago. This strange and wonderful man lived from 1452 to 1519. His life, it is said, " was a dialogue with Nature ". He was always asking questions, and trying to find answers to them by experiment; he seemed to be ever reaching forward, trying to grasp the future.

I have written about these three men of Florence, and especially about Leonardo, because he is a favourite of mine. The history of the republic of Florence is not very pleasant or edifying, with its intrigues and despots and knavish rulers. But much may be forgiven Florence—we may excuse even her money-lenders !—because of the great men she has produced. The shadow of these great sons of hers lies on her still, and as you pass the streets of this beautiful city, or look at the lovely Arno as it flows by under the medieval bridges, an enchantment seems to come over you, and the past becomes vivid and alive. Dante goes by, and Beatrice, the lady he loved, passes, leaving faint perfume trailing behind her. And Leonardo seems to march along the narrow streets, lost in thought, pondering over the mysteries of life and Nature.

So the Renaissance flowered in Italy from the fifteenth century, and gradually travelled to other western countries. Great artists tried to put life in stone and canvas, and the galleries and museums of Europe are full of their paintings and sculptures. In Italy there was a decline in the artistic renaissance by the end of the sixteenth century. In the seventeenth century Holland produced great painters, one of the most famous being Rembrandt, and in Spain about this time there was Velasquez. But I shall not mention more names. There are so many of them. If you are interested in the great master-painters, go to the galleries and look at their works. Their names are of little account ; it is their art and the beauty they created that have a message for us.

During this period—the fifteenth to the seventeenth centuries—science also gradually forges ahead and comes into its own. It had a stiff fight with the Church, for the Church did not believe in making people think and experiment. For it the earth was the centre of the universe and the sun went round it and the stars were fixed points in the heavens. Any one who said otherwise was a heretic and might be dealt with by the Inquisition. In spite of this a Pole, named Copernicus, did challenge this belief and proved that the earth went round the sun. Thus he laid the foundations of the modern idea of the universe. He lived from 1473 to 1543. Somehow he managed to escape the wrath of the Church for his revolutionary and heretical opinions. Others who came after him were not so fortunate. Giordano Bruno, an Italian, was burned in Rome by the Church in 1600 for insisting that the earth went round the sun, and the stars were themselves suns. A contemporary of his, Galileo, who made the telescope, was also threatened by the Church, but he was weaker than Bruno, and thought it more expedient to recant. So he admitted to the Church that he was mistaken in his folly and that the earth was of course the centre of the universe, and the sun went round it. Even so, he had to spend some time in prison doing penance.

Among the prominent men of science in the sixteenth century was Harvey, who finally proved the circulation of the blood. In the seventeenth century comes one of the greatest names in science—Isaac Newton, who was a great mathematician. He discovered what is called the law of gravitation—of how things fall—and thus wrested another of Nature's secrets.

So much, or rather so little, for science. Literature also forged ahead during this period. The new spirit that was abroad affected the young European languages powerfully. These languages had existed for some time, and we have seen that Italy had already produced great poets. In England there had been Chaucer. But Latin, the speech and language of the learned and of the Church all over Europe, overshadowed them all. They were the vulgar tongues —the vernaculars, as many people very curiously call the Indian languages still. It was almost undignified to write in them. But the new spirit, and paper and printing, pushed these languages ahead. Italian was the first in the field; then followed French and English and Spanish and, last of all, German. In France a band of young writers in the sixteenth century resolved to write in their own language and not in Latin, and to improve their " vulgar tongue " till it became a suitable medium for the best of literature.

So the languages of Europe progressed and gained in richness and power till they became the fine languages they are to-day. I shall not mention the names of many famous writers; I shall give just a few. In England there was the famous Shakespeare from 1564 to 1616; and immediately following him in the seventeenth century was Milton, the blind poet of *Paradise Lost*. In France there were the philosopher Descartes and the dramatist, Molière, both in the seventeenth century. Molière was the founder of the Comédie Française, the great State theatre in Paris. A contemporary of Shakespeare in Spain was Cervantes, who wrote *Don Quixote*.

One other name I shall mention, not because of its greatness, but because it is well known. This is Machiavelli, another Florentine. He was just an ordinary politician in the fifteenth–sixteenth centuries, but he wrote a book, called *The Prince*, which became famous. This book gives us a glimpse into the minds of the princes and politicians of the day. Machiavelli tells us that religion is necessary for a government—not, mind you, to make people virtuous, but to help to govern them and keep them down. It may even be the duty of the ruler to support a religion which he believes to be false! " A prince," says Machiavelli, " must know how to play at once man and beast, lion and fox. He neither should nor can keep his word when to do so will turn against him. . . . I venture to maintain that it is very disadvantageous always to be honest; useful on the other hand, to appear pious and faithful, humane and devout. Nothing is more useful than the appearance of virtue."

Pretty bad, is it not ? The greater the scoundrel, the better the prince ! If this was the state of an average prince's mind in those days in Europe, it is not surprising that there was continuous trouble there. But why go so far back ? Even to-day the imperialist Powers behave much like the prince of Machiavelli. Beneath the appearance of virtue, there is greed and cruelty and unscrupulousness; beneath the kid glove of civilization there is the red claw of the beast.

84

THE PROTESTANT REVOLT AND THE PEASANTS' WAR

August 8, 1932

I HAVE written several letters to you already about Europe during the fifteenth to the seventeenth centuries. I have told you something about the passing of the Middle Ages, and the great distress of the peasantry, and the rise of the *bourgeoisie*, and the discovery of America and the seaways to the East, and the progress of art, and science, and the languages of Europe. But much still remains to be told about this period to complete the outlines of the picture. Remember that my last two letters, as well as the one about the sea-routes, and this one that I am writing, and perhaps one or two others to follow, deal with the same period in Europe. I write separately about different movements and activities, but they took place more or less at the same time, and each influenced the other.

Even before the times of the Renaissance there had been rumblings in the body of the Roman Church. Both the princes and peoples of Europe were beginning to feel the heavy hand of the Church, and to grumble a little, and to doubt. Frederick II, the Emperor, you will remember, had quite an argument with the Pope, and cared little even for excommunication. These signs of doubt and disobedience angered Rome, and it resolved to crush the new heresy. For this purpose the Inquisition was created, and there was the burning of unhappy men who were styled heretics, and women who were accused of being witches, all over Europe. John Huss of Prague was tricked and burnt, and thereupon his followers in Bohemia, the Hussites, raised the banner of revolt. Not all the terrors of the Inquisition could put down this new spirit of revolt against the Roman Church. It spread, and to it was added, no doubt, the feeling of the peasantry against the Church as a big landowner. And the princes in many places encouraged this spirit for selfish reasons. They were casting envious and covetous eyes on the vast properties of the Church. The printing of books and Bibles added to the smouldering fire.

Early in the sixteenth century there rose in Germany Martin Luther, who was to become the great leader of the revolt against Rome. He was a Christian priest who after a visit to Rome became disgusted with the corruption and luxury of the Church. This controversy grew and grew till it split up the Roman Church into two, and divided western Europe into two camps, religious as well as political. The old orthodox Greek Church of Russia and eastern Europe kept apart from this controversy. So far as it was concerned Rome was itself far removed from the true faith.

In this way began the Protestant revolt. It was called Protestant

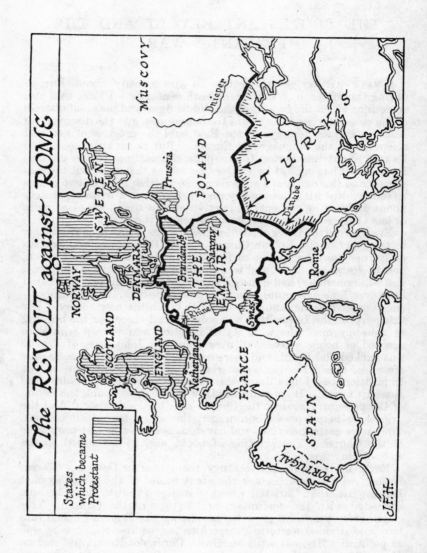

because it *protested* against various dogmas of the Roman Church. Ever since then there have been two main divisions of Christianity in western Europe—Roman Catholic and Protestant. But the Protestants are divided up into many sects.

This movement against the Church is called the Reformation. It was in the main a popular revolt against corruption as well as the authoritarianism of the Church. Side by side with this, many princes wanted to put an end to all attempts by the Pope to dominate over them. They resented very much the interference of the Pope in their political affairs. There was also a third phase of the Reformation, an attempt by loyal Churchmen to reform the Church of its abuses from within.

You will perhaps remember the two orders of the Church—the Franciscan and the Dominican. In the sixteenth century, just about the time Martin Luther was gaining in strength, a new Church order was started by a Spaniard, Ignatius of Loyola. He called it the "Society of Jesus", and its members were called Jesuits. I have already referred to the Jesuits visiting China and the East. This "Order of Jesus" was a very remarkable society. It aimed at training people for efficient and whole-time service of the Roman Church and the Pope. It gave a hard training, and so successful was this, that it produced remarkably efficient and faithful servants of the Church. So faithful were they to the Church, that they obeyed it blindly and without questioning, and they gave their all to it. Where the Church stood to gain by it, they would sacrifice themselves willingly to it; indeed, they have had a reputation of being wholly without scruple in the service of the Church. The good of the Church justified and excused everything.

This remarkable body of men was of the greatest help to the Roman Church. Not only did they carry its name and message to distant lands, but they raised the standard of the Church in Europe. Partly on account of the internal movement for reform, and largely because of the menace of the Protestant revolt, there was much less corruption in Rome. Thus the Reformation split the Church into two and at the same time reformed it internally to some extent.

As the Protestant revolt developed some of the kings and princes of Europe sided with one party, some with the other. Religious motives had little to do with this. It was mostly a question of politics and the desire for gain. The Emperor of the Holy Roman Empire at that time was Charles V, a Hapsburg. Owing to the marriages of his father and grandfather, he happened to inherit a large empire which included Austria, Germany (nominally), Spain, Naples and Sicily, the Netherlands and Spanish America. It was a favourite method in Europe in those days, this way of adding to one's dominions by marriage. Thus Charles, for no merit of his own, happened to rule over half Europe, and for a while he seemed to be a great man. He decided to side with the Pope against the Protestants. The idea of the Reformation was not in keeping with the idea of empire. But many of the smaller German princes sided with the Protestants, and there were two factions throughout Germany—

the Roman and the Lutheran. This naturally resulted in civil war in Germany.

In England the much-married Henry VIII went against the Pope and favoured the Protestants, or rather himself. He coveted the property of the Church and, after breaking with Rome, he confiscated all the rich lands of the abbeys and monasteries and the churches. A personal reason for his break with the Pope was because he wanted to divorce his wife, and marry another woman.

In France the position was peculiar. The Chief Minister of the King was the famous Cardinal Richelieu, who practically ruled the kingdom. Richelieu kept France on the side of Rome and Pope and crushed Protestantism there. But, such are the intrigues of politics, he encouraged Protestantism in Germany so that there might be civil war there and Germany might become weak and disunited ! The antagonism of France and Germany to each other runs like a thread through the history of Europe.

Luther was the great Protestant, and he opposed the authority of Rome. But do not imagine that he was tolerant in religion. He was as intolerant as the Pope he was fighting. So the Reformation did not bring religious liberty to Europe. It bred a new type of fanatic— the puritan and the Calvinist. Calvin was one of the later leaders of the Protestant movement. He was a good organizer, and for a while he controlled the city of Geneva. Do you remember the great monument to the Reformation in the park at Geneva ? The huge expanse of wall with statues of Calvin and others ? Calvin was so intolerant that he burnt many persons because they simply did not agree with him and were free thinkers.

Luther and the Protestants were helped greatly by the mass of the people because there was a strong feeling against the Roman Church. As I have told you, the peasantry were very miserable and there were frequent riots. These riots developed into a regular Peasants' War in Germany. The poor peasants rose against the evil system which crushed them and demanded the most ordinary and reasonable rights—that serfdom should cease, and the right to fish and hunt. But even these were denied them, and the princes of Germany tried to crush them with every species of barbarity. And Luther, the great reformer, what was his attitude ? Did he side with the poor peasants and support their just demands ? Not he ! On the peasants' demand that serfdom should end, Luther, said : " This article would make all men equal and so change the spiritual kingdom of Christ into an external worldly one. Impossible ! An earthly kingdom cannot exist without inequality of persons. Some must be free, others serfs, some rulers, others subjects." He curses the peasants and calls for their destruction. " Therefore let all who are able hew them down, slaughter and stab them, openly or in secret, and remember that there is nothing more poisonous, noxious and utterly diabolical than a rebel. You must kill him as you would a mad dog; if you do not fall upon him, he will fall upon you and the whole land." Pretty language this, especially coming from a religious leader and a reformer.

So one sees that all the talk of freedom and liberty was meant for the upper classes only, not for the masses. The masses had lived, almost in every age, a life not far removed from that of the animals. They must continue to do so, according to Luther, because that was laid down by Heaven. The Protestant revolt against Rome had been largely caused by the great economic distress of the people. It had fitted in with it and had utilized it. But when it was feared that the serfs might go too far and gain their freedom from serfdom—this was a little enough thing—the Protestant leaders joined the princes in crushing them. The day of the masses was still far distant. The new age that was dawning was the age of the middle classes, the *bourgeoisie*. From all the conflicts and wars of the sixteenth and seventeenth centuries, one can see this class, almost inevitably, rising step by step.

Wherever this rising *bourgeoisie* was fairly strong, there Protestantism spread. There were many kinds and sects of Protestants. In England the King made himself the head of the Church—the " Defender of the Faith "—and the Church practically ceased to be a Church and became just a department of the government. The Church of England has continued to be so ever since.

In other countries, especially in Germany, Switzerland and the Netherlands, other sects grew in prominence. Calvinism spread because it was in keeping with the growth of the *bourgeoisie*. In religious matters Calvin was terribly intolerant. There was torture and burning for the heretics, and the strictest discipline of the faithful. But in business matters his teaching was more in keeping with growing trade and industry, which the Roman teaching was not. Profits in business were blessed, and credit was encouraged. So the new *bourgeoisie* adopted this new version of the old faith and, with a perfectly easy conscience, went on making money. They had utilized the masses in their fights against the feudal nobles. Now, having triumphed over the nobles, they ignored or sat upon the masses.

But the *bourgeoisie* had to face many obstacles yet. There was the king still in the way. The king had joined with the men of the town in fighting the nobles. Now that the nobles had been reduced to powerlessness, the king was much stronger, and he seemed to be master of the field. The contest between him and the middle classes was yet to come.

85

AUTOCRACY IN SIXTEENTH- AND
SEVENTEENTH-CENTURY EUROPE

August 26, 1932

I HAVE again been very negligent. It is long since I wrote these letters. There is none to question me or keep me up to the mark, and so I slacken occasionally and busy myself with other things. If we were together it would be different, would it not? But why should I write then, if you and I could talk to each other?

My last letters to you were about Europe at a time of great turmoil and change. They dealt with the great changes in the sixteenth and seventeenth centuries, the changes that came with or followed the economic revolution which put an end to the Middle Ages and raised up the *bourgeoisie*. In our last letter we saw Christendom in western Europe breaking up into two factions— Catholic and Protestant. Germany was the special battle-ground of the religious struggles between these two factions because the two parties were more or less evenly balanced. The other countries of western Europe were also involved to some extent in these struggles. England kept apart from the continental religious struggle. Under her king, Henry VIII, she cut herself off from Rome without much internal disturbance, and established a Church of her own which was something between the Catholic and the Protestant. Henry cared little for religion. He wanted the Church lands, and he got them; and he wanted to marry again, and he did so. Thus the main result of the Reformation was to free the kings and princes from the leading-strings of the Pope.

While these movements of the Renaissance and Reformation and the economic turmoil were changing the face of Europe, what was the political background like? What was the map of Europe like in the sixteenth and seventeenth centuries? It was, of course, a changing map during these 200 years. Let us then look at the map as it was early in the sixteenth century.

In the south-east the Turks hold Constantinople and their empire advances into Hungary. In the south-west corner the Muslim Saracens, descendants of the Arab conquerors, have been driven away from Granada, and Spain has emerged as a Christian Power under the joint rule of Ferdinand and Isabella. The long centuries of conflict between Christian and Muslim in Spain have made the Spaniard cling to his Catholic religion passionately and with bigotry. It is in Spain that the terrible Inquisition is established. Under the glamour of the discovery of America and the wealth that this is bringing her, Spain is beginning to play a leading part in European politics.

Look at the map again. We recognize England and France, much as they are now. In the centre of the map is the Empire, divided up into many German States, each of which was more or less independent. It is a curious collection of little States under princes, dukes, bishops, electors and such-like persons. There are also many towns with special privileges, and the northern commercial towns have joined up and formed a confederation. Then there is the republic of Switzerland, in fact free, but not yet formally recognized to be so; the republic of Venice, and also other city-republics in northern Italy; the territory belonging to the Popes, round about Rome, called the Papal States; and the kingdom of Naples and Sicily to the south of them. To the east there is Poland between the Empire and Russia, and the kingdom of Hungary, with the Ottoman Turks casting their shadow on it. Farther to the east is Russia, newly developing into a strong State, after it had got rid of the Mongols of the Golden Horde. And to the north and west there are some other countries.

Such was Europe early in the sixteenth century. In 1520 Charles V became Emperor. He was a Hapsburg and, as we have seen, he managed to inherit the kingdoms of Spain, and of Naples and Sicily, and the Netherlands. It is strange how whole countries and peoples changed masters in Europe because of certain royal marriages. Millions of people and great countries were just inherited. Sometimes they were given as dowries. The island of Bombay thus came to an English king, Charles II, as the dowry of his wife Catharine of Braganza (in Portugal). By careful marriage, therefore, the Hapsburgs gathered together an empire, and Charles V became head of this. He was a very ordinary man, chiefly noted for eating enormously, but for the moment his great dominions made him seem a colossus in Europe.

In the same year that Charles became Emperor, Suleiman became head of the Ottoman Empire. During his reign this empire spread in all directions, and especially in eastern Europe. The Turks came right up to the gates of Vienna, but just missed capturing this beautiful old city. But they terrified the Hapsburg Emperor, and he thought it expedient to buy off Suleiman by paying him tribute. Imagine the great Emperor of the Holy Roman Empire paying tribute to the Sultan of Turkey. Suleiman is known as Suleiman the Magnificent. He took the title of emperor himself, as he considered himself the representative of the Eastern Byzantine Cæsars.

There was a great deal of building activity in Constantinople at the time of Suleiman and many beautiful mosques were made. The artistic Renaissance in Italy seems to have had its counterpart in the East also. Not only in Constantinople was there artistic activity, but in Persia and in Khorasan in Central Asia beautiful paintings were being made.

In India we have seen Babar, the Moghal, come down from the north-west and establish a new dynasty. This was in 1526, when Charles V was Emperor in Europe and Suleiman was ruling in Constantinople. We shall have a great deal to say of Babar and his brilliant descendants. It is interesting to note here, however, that Babar was himself a Renaissance type of prince, though a better one than the European type of the period. He was an adventurer, but a gallant knight, with a passion for literature and art. In the Italy of that period there were also princes who were adventurers and lovers of literature and art, and their petty Courts had a superficial brilliance. The Medici family of Florence and the Borgias were famous then. But these Italian princes, and most others in Europe at the time, were true followers of Machiavelli, unscrupulous, intriguing, and despotic, using the poison cup and the dagger of the assassin for their opponents. It is hardly fair to compare the knightly Babar with this crowd, just as it would be out of place to compare their petty Courts with the Court of the Moghal emperors at Delhi or Agra—Akbar and Shah Jahan and others. It is said that these Moghal Courts were magnificent, and were perhaps the richest and most splendid that have ever existed.

We have drifted, almost unawares, to India from Europe. But I wanted you to realize what was happening in India and elsewhere during the days of the European Renaissance. There was artistic activity then in Turkey and Persia and Central Asia and India. In China these were the peaceful and prosperous days of the Mings, when a high level of artistic production was reached. But all this art of the Renaissance period, except perhaps in China, was more or less courtly art. It was not an art of the people. In Italy, after the great artists, some of whose names I have mentioned, passed away, the later Renaissance art became trivial and unimportant.

So Europe in the sixteenth century was divided up between Catholic and Protestant princes. Princes counted then, not their people. Italy, Austria, France, and Spain were Catholic; Germany half Catholic and half Protestant; England Protestant simply because her King chose to be so. And because England was Protestant, this was enough reason for Ireland, whom England tried to conquer and oppress, to remain Catholic. But it is not quite correct to say that the religion of the people did not matter. It did matter in the end, and many a war and revolution took place because of it. It is difficult to separate the religious aspect from the political and the economic. I think I have told you already that the Protestant revolt against Rome took place especially where the new trading class was becoming strong. We can thus see that there was a connection between religion and trade. Again, many of the princes were afraid of the religious reformation because they thought that under cover of it there might be civil revolution and their authority might be overthrown. If a man was prepared to challenge the religious authority of the Pope, why, then he might also challenge the political authority of the king or prince. This was dangerous doctrine for the kings. They still clung to the divine right of their kind to rule. Even the Protestant princes were not prepared to give this up.

And yet, in spite of the Reformation, kings were all-powerful in Europe. At no previous period were they so autocratic. Previously the great feudal nobles checked them, and often challenged their authority. The merchants and *bourgeoisie* did not like these nobles; neither did the king. So with the help of the merchant class, as well as the peasantry, the king crushed the nobles, and became all-powerful. The *bourgeoisie*, although they had grown in power and importance, were not strong enough yet to check the king. But soon the middle classes began to object to many things that the king did. In particular, they objected to repeated and heavy taxation, and to interference in religion. The king did not like this at all. He was annoyed at their presumption in objecting to anything that he did. So he put them in gaol and punished them otherwise. There was arbitrary imprisonment, just as there is to-day in India because we refuse to submit to the British Government. The king also interfered with trade. All this made matters worse and resistance to the king grew. This fight of the *bourgeoisie* for power against the autocracy of the kings lasted many hundred years, till recent times, and many a king's head had to fall before the idea of the divine right of kings was finally buried, and kings were put in their proper places. In some countries the victory was won early, in others later. We shall follow the fortunes of the fight in subsequent letters.

But in the sixteenth century the king was boss almost everywhere in Europe—almost, but not quite. You will remember that in Switzerland the poor peasants of the mountains had dared to defy the great Hapsburg monarch and had won their freedom. So, in the European sea of absolutism and autocracy, the little peasant republic of Switzerland stood out as an island where kings had no place.

Soon matters came to a head in another place—the Netherlands—and the fight for popular and religious liberty was fought out and won. It is a little country, but it was a great fight against the greatest Power in Europe then—Spain. Thus the Netherlands gave a lead to Europe. Then came a struggle for popular freedom in England which cost a king his head and gave the victory to the Parliament of the day. The Netherlands and England thus took the lead in these struggles of the *bourgeoisie* against autocracy. And because the *bourgeoisie* won in these countries, it was able to take advantage of the new conditions and forge ahead of other countries. Both built powerful navies later; both developed trade with distant countries; and both laid the foundations of empire in Asia.

We have not said much about England so far in these letters. There was little to say, as England was not a very important country in Europe. But a change takes place now and, as we shall see, England rapidly forges ahead. We have referred to Magna Charta and the early beginnings of Parliament, and to the peasant troubles and civil wars between different dynasties. During these wars murder and assassination by the kings were common enough. Large numbers of the feudal nobles died in the battles, and thus their class lost its strength. A new dynasty—the Tudors—came to the throne, and they played the autocrat well enough. Henry VIII was a Tudor. So was his daughter, Elizabeth.

After the Emperor Charles V, the Empire split up. Spain and the Netherlands went to his son Philip II. Spain at the time towered over Europe as the most powerful monarchy. You will remember that it possessed Peru and Mexico, and gold poured from the Americas. But, in spite of Columbus and Cortés and Pizarro, Spain could not take advantage of the new conditions. It was not interested in trade. All that it cared for was religion of the most bigoted and cruel kind. All over the country the Inquisition flourished and the most horrible tortures were inflicted on so-called heretics. From time to time great public festivals were arranged when batches of these " heretics ", men and women, were burned alive on huge pyres in the presence of the king and royal family and ambassadors and thousands of people. *Autos-da-fé*, acts of faith, these public burnings were called. Terrible and monstrous all this seems. The whole history of Europe of this period is so full of violence and horrible and barbarous cruelty and religious bigotry as to be almost unbelievable.

The Empire of Spain did not last long. The gallant fight of little Holland shook it up thoroughly. A little later, in 1588, an attempt to conquer England failed miserably, and the " Invincible Armada " which carried the Spanish troops never even reached England. It was wrecked on the high seas. This is not surprising, as the man in command of the Armada knew nothing about ships or the sea. Indeed, he went to King Philip II and " humbly requested His Majesty to relieve him from the post, for, he said, he knew nothing of sea strategy and, moreover, was a bad sailor. But the King answered that the fleet would be led by the Lord Himself ! "

So gradually the Empire of Spain faded away. In the days of Charles V it was said that the sun never set on his empire, a saying which is often repeated about another proud and overbearing empire to-day.

86

THE NETHERLANDS FIGHT FOR FREEDOM

August 27, 1932

I TOLD you in my last letter how kings became supreme, almost all over Europe, in the sixteenth century. In England there were the Tudors, in Spain and Austria the Hapsburgs. In Russia and in great parts of Germany and Italy there were autocratic monarchs. France was perhaps typical of this kind of king ruling through a personal monarchy, the whole kingdom being considered almost the personal property of the king. A very able minister, the Cardinal Richelieu, helped in strengthening France and her monarchy. France has always thought that her strength and security lay in the weakness of Germany. So Richelieu, who was a great Catholic priest, and who crushed Protestants mercilessly in France, actually encouraged Protestants in Germany. This was intended to encourage mutual conflict and disorder in Germany, and thus to weaken her. This policy met with great success. There was, as we shall see, civil war of the worst kind in Germany, which ruined her.

In France also there was civil war in the middle of the seventeenth century—the war of the Fronde it is called. But the King crushed both the nobles and the merchants. The nobles had no real power left, but to keep them on his side the King allowed them innumerable privileges. They paid practically no tax. Both the nobility and clergy were exempt from taxation. The whole burden of taxation fell on the common people, and particularly the peasantry. With the money extorted from these poor miserable wretches, great and magnificent palaces arose and a splendid Court surrounded the King. Do you remember visiting Versailles, near Paris? Those great palaces there, that we go to see now, grew up in the seventeenth century out of the blood of the French peasantry. Versailles was the symbol of absolute and irresponsible monarchy; and it is not surprising that Versailles became the forerunner of the French Revolution, which put an end to all monarchy. But the revolution was still far off in those days. The King was Louis XIV—the Grand Monarque he was called, the Roi-Soleil, the sun round whom revolved the planets of his Court. For the enormous period of seventy-two years he reigned, from 1643 to 1715, and for his chief minister he had another great Cardinal, Mazarin. There was a great deal of luxury on the top, and royal patronage of literature and science and art, but under a thin covering of splendour there was misery and suffering. It was a world of beautiful wigs and lace cuffs and fine clothing covering a body that was seldom washed and was full of dirt and filth.

We are all of us influenced a great deal by pomp and pageantry, and it is not surprising that Louis XIV influenced Europe greatly during his long reign. He was the model king and others tried to copy him. But this Grand Monarque, what was he? " Strip your Louis Quatorze of his king-gear," says a well-known English writer, Carlyle, " and there is left nothing but a poor forked radish with a head fantastically carved." It is a hard description, probably applicable to most people, kings and commoners.

Louis Quatorze carries us to 1715, the beginning of the eighteenth century. Meanwhile, much had happened in the other countries of Europe, and some of these events deserve notice from us.

I have told you already of the revolt of the Netherlands against Spain. The story of their gallant fight is worthy of closer study. An American named J. L. Motley has written a famous account of this struggle for freedom, and he has made it an absorbing and fascinating tale. I hardly know of a novel that is more gripping than this moving account of what took place 350 years ago in this little corner of Europe. The book is called *The Rise of the Dutch Republic*, and I read it in prison.

The Netherlands include both Holland and Belgium. Their very name tells us that they are low lands. Holland comes from hollow-land. Great parts of them are actually below sea-level, and enormous dykes and walls have to protect them from the North Sea. Such a country, where one has to fight the sea continually, breeds hardy seafaring folk, and people who cross the seas frequently take to trade. So the people of the Netherlands became traders. They produced woollen and other goods, and the spices of the East also went to them. Rich and busy cities arose—Bruges and Ghent and, especially, Antwerp. As the trade with the East developed, these cities grew in wealth, and Antwerp became in the sixteenth century the commercial capital of Europe. In its house of exchange it is said that 5000 merchants gathered daily to do business with each other; in its harbour there were as many as 2500 vessels at one time. Nearly 500 vessels came to it and went from it every day. These merchant classes controlled the city governments.

This was just the kind of trading community that would be attracted by the new religious ideas of the Reformation. Protestantism spread there, especially in the north. The chances of inheritance made the Hapsburg Charles V, and after him his son Philip II, rulers of the Netherlands. Neither of them could tolerate any kind of freedom—political or religious. Philip tried to crush the privileges of the cities as well as the new religion. He sent as governor-general the Duke of Alva, who has become famous for his oppression and tyranny. The Inquisition was established, and a "Blood-Council" which sent thousands to the stake or the scaffold.

It is a long story, and I cannot tell it here. As the tyranny of Spain increased, the strength of the people to combat it increased also. A great and wise leader rose amongst them—Prince William of Orange, known as William the Silent—who was more than a match for the Duke of Alva. The Inquisition actually condemned in one sentence in 1568 all the inhabitants of the Netherlands to death as heretics, with a few named exceptions. This was an amazing sentence unique in history—three or four lines condemning 3,000,000 of people!

At first the fight seemed to be between the Netherland nobles and the King of Spain. It was almost like the struggles between king and nobles in other countries. Alva tried to crush them, and many a great noble had to mount the scaffold at Brussels. One of the popular and famous nobles who was executed was Count Egmont. Later, Alva, hard up for money, tried new and heavy taxation. This touched the pockets of the merchant classes, and they rebelled. Added to this was the struggle between Catholic and Protestant.

Spain was a mighty Power, in the full pride of her greatness; the Netherlands were just a few provinces of merchant folk and effete and extravagant nobles. There was no comparison between the two. Yet Spain found it difficult enough to crush them. There were massacres repeatedly, whole populations being wiped out. Alva and his generals rivalled Chengiz Khan and Timur in their destruction of human life. Often they improved on the Mongols. City after city was besieged by Alva, and the untrained men, and often the women of the city, fought the trained soldiers of Alva on land and water till starvation made it impossible for them to carry on. Preferring even absolute destruction of all they valued to the Spanish yoke, the Hollanders broke open the dykes and let in the North Sea to drown and drive away the Spanish troops. As the struggle proceeded it became more and more ruthless, and both sides became exceedingly cruel. The siege of beautiful Haarlem stands out, bravely defended to the last, but ending in the usual massacre and plunder by the Spanish soldiery; the siege of Alkmaar, which escaped by the piercing of the dykes; and Leyden, surrounded by the enemy, with starvation and disease killing thousands. There were no green leaves left on the trees in Leyden; they had all been eaten. Men and women fought with famishing dogs on dunghills for scraps. Still they held out, and from the ramparts haggard and starving people hurled defiance at the enemy, and told the Spaniards that they would live on rats and dogs and anything rather than surrender. "And when all has perished but ourselves, be sure that we will each devour our left arms, retaining our right to defend our women, our liberty and our religion, against the foreign tyrant. Should God, in His wrath, doom us to destruction, and deny us all relief, even then we will maintain ourselves for ever against your entrance. When the last hour has come, with our hands we shall set fire to the city, and perish men, women, and children together, in the flames, rather than suffer our homes to be polluted, and our liberties to be crushed."

Such was the spirit of the people of Leyden. But despair reigned there as day after day went by without relief; and they sent a message to their friends of the Estates of Holland outside. The Estates took the great decision to drown their dear land rather than allow Leyden to fall to the enemy. "Better a drowned land than a lost land." And to Leyden, their sorely stricken sister-city, they sent this answer: "Rather will we see our whole land and all our possessions perish in the waves, than forsake thee, Leyden!"

At last dyke after dyke was broken and, helped by a favourable wind, the sea-waters rushed in, carrying the Dutch ships, bringing food and relief. And the Spanish troops, fearful of this new enemy, the sea, departed in haste. So Leyden survived, and, in memory of the heroism of her inhabitants, the University of Leyden, famous since then, was established in 1575.

There are many such tales of heroism, and many of horrible butchery. In beautiful Antwerp there was terrible massacre and looting, 8000 being killed. The "Spanish Fury" it was called.

But the great struggle was largely carried on by Holland, and not by the southern part of the Netherlands. By bribery and coercion the Spanish rulers succeeded in winning over many of the nobles of the Netherlands and made them crush their own countrymen. They were helped by the fact that there were far more Catholics than Protestants in the south. They tried to win over the Catholics, and partly succeeded. And the nobles! It was shameful to what treason and trickery many of them stooped to win favour and wealth for themselves from the Spanish King, even though their country might perish.

Addressing the General Assembly of the Netherlands, William of Orange said: " 'Tis only by the Netherlands that the Netherlands are crushed. Whence has the Duke of Alva the power of which he boasts, but from yourselves—from Netherland cities? Whence his ships, supplies, money, weapons, soldiers? From the Netherland people."

So, ultimately, the Spaniards succeeded in winning over that part of the Netherlands which is roughly Belgium to-day. But Holland they could not subdue, try as they did. It is curious to notice that right through the struggle, almost to the end, Holland did not disclaim allegiance to Philip II of Spain. They were prepared to keep him as king if he would recognize their liberties. At last they were forced to cut themselves away from him. They offered the crown to their great leader William, but he would not have it. Circumstances thus forced them, almost against their will, to become a republic. So great was the kingly tradition of those days.

The struggle in Holland went on for many years. It was not till 1609 that Holland became independent. But the real fight in the Netherlands took place from 1567 to 1584. Philip II of Spain, unable to defeat William of Orange, had him killed by an assassin's hand. He offered a public reward for his assassination, such was the morality of Europe at that time. Many attempts to kill William failed. The sixth attempt succeeded in 1584, and the great man—" Father William " he was called all over Holland— died; but he had done his work. The Dutch Republic had been forged through sacrifice and suffering. Resistance to tyrants and despots does good to a country and to a people. It trains and strengthens. And Holland, strong and self-reliant, immediately became a great naval Power and spread out to the Far East. Belgium, separated from Holland, continued under Spanish rule.

Let us look at Germany to complete our picture of Europe. There was a terrible civil war here from 1618 to 1648, called the Thirty Years' War. It was between Catholic and Protestant, and the little princes and electors of Germany fought each other and the Emperor; and the Catholic King of France had a look in on the side of the Protestants just to add to the confusion; and ultimately the King of Sweden, Gustavus Adolphus—the " Lion of the North " he was called—came down and defeated the Emperor, and thus saved the Protestants. But Germany was a ruined country. The mercenary soldiers were like brigands. They went about looting and plundering. Even generals of armies, having no money to pay their soldiers or even to feed them, took to looting. And—think of it !—this lasted for thirty years : massacre and destruction and looting going on year after year. There could be little or no trade; there could be hardly any cultivation. And so there was less and less food, and more and more starvation. And this of course resulted in more brigands and more looting. Germany became a kind of nursery for professional and mercenary soldiers.

At last this war came to an end, when, perhaps, there was nothing left to plunder. But it took a long, long time for Germany to recover and pull herself together again. In 1648 the Peace of Westphalia put an end to the German civil war. By this the Emperor of the Holy Roman Empire became a shadow and a ghost with no power. France took a big slice, Alsace; to keep it for over 200 years, and then to be forced to give it back to a new Germany; and again to take it back after the Great War of 1914–1918. France thus profited by this peace. But another Power now arose in Germany which was going to be a thorn in the side of France. This was Prussia, ruled by the House of Hohenzollern.

The Peace of Westphalia finally recognized the republics of Switzerland and Holland.

What a tale of war and massacre and plundering and bigotry, I tell you! And yet this was Europe just after the Renaissance, when there had been such an outburst of energy and artistic and literary activity. I have compared Europe to the countries of Asia, and pointed out the new life that was stirring in Europe. One can see this new life trying to struggle through. The birth of a new child and of a new order is accompanied with much suffering. When there is economic instability at the base, society and politics shake at the top. That a new life was stirring in Europe is obvious enough. But all round it what barbarous behaviour! It was a maxim of the time that " the science of reigning was the science of lying ". The whole atmosphere reeks with lies and intrigue, violence and cruelty, and one wonders how people put up with it.

87

ENGLAND CUTS OFF THE HEAD OF HER KING

August 29, 1932

WE shall spend some little time on England's history now. We have largely ignored this so far, as there was little of interest there during the Middle Ages. The country was more backward than France or Italy. The University of Oxford, however, early became a famous seat of learning, and, a little later, Cambridge followed. It was Oxford that produced Wycliffe, about whom I have already written to you.

The chief interest in early English history centres round the development of Parliament. From early days efforts were made by the nobles to limit the power of the king. There was the Magna Charta in 1215. A little later the beginnings of Parliament are visible. They are crude beginnings. There are the great nobles and bishops who develop into a House of Lords. But more important ultimately was an elected council consisting of knights and the smaller landowners and some representatives of the towns. This elected council developed into the House of Commons. Both these Councils or Houses consisted of landowners and wealthy men. Even the men in the House of Commons represented a small number of rich landowners and merchants only.

The House of Commons had little power. They petitioned and

pointed out grievances to the king and gradually began to interfere with taxation. Without their approval it was difficult for new taxes to be imposed or collected and so the king began the practice of asking for their approval for such taxation. The power of the purse is always a great power, and Parliament, and especially the Commons' House, increased in strength and prestige as it gained this power. Often there was friction between the king and the Commons. But still Parliament was a feeble thing, and the Tudor rulers, as I have told you, were more or less absolute monarchs. But the Tudors were clever, and they avoided forcing a struggle with Parliament.

England escaped the bitter religious struggles of the Continent. There was a great deal of religious conflict and rioting and bigotry, and a scandalous number of women were burnt alive because they were considered to be witches. But compared to the Continent, England was peaceful. With Henry VIII the country was supposed to turn Protestant. Of course there were many Catholics in the land, and there were also many extreme Protestants. The new Church of England, however, was something between the two; calling itself Protestant, but perhaps more Catholic than Protestant, and in reality a department of State with the king for its head. The break with Rome and the Pope, however, was complete, and there was many an " anti-Popery " riot. In Queen Elizabeth's time (she was the daughter of Henry VIII), the opening of the new sea-routes to the East and to America, and the new opportunities for trade, lured many people. Fascinated by the success of Spanish and Portuguese seamen, and covetous of the wealth to be gained, England took to the sea. Sir Francis Drake and others like him at first became the pirates of the seas, plundering Spanish vessels from America. Drake then went for a mighty voyage round the world. Sir Walter Raleigh crossed the Atlantic and tried to found a settlement on the east coast of what is now the United States. This was called Virginia, as a compliment to Elizabeth, the Virgin Queen. It was Raleigh who first brought the habit of smoking tobacco to Europe from America. Then came the Spanish Armada, and the complete failure of this proud enterprise encouraged England a great deal. All this has little to do with the struggle between king and Parliament, except that it kept people's minds occupied and turned to foreign affairs. But even in Tudor times trouble brewed under the surface.

The Elizabethan period is one of the brightest in England. Elizabeth was a great queen, and England produced many a great man of action in her time. But greater than the Queen and her adventurer knights were the poets and dramatists of this generation, and above them all towers the immortal William Shakespeare. His plays are, of course, known the world over to-day, although we know little enough about him personally. He was one of a brilliant band which has enriched the English language with numerous precious gems which fill us with delight. Even the small lyrical poems of the Elizabethan period have a peculiar charm which none others have. In the simplest and sweetest of language they trip along merrily, telling us of everyday happenings in a way all their own. Writing of this period, an English critic, Lytton Strachey, has told us of the "noble band of Elizabethans whose strong and splendid spirit gave to England, in one miraculous generation, the most glorious heritage of drama that the world has ever known".

Elizabeth died in 1603, just two years before the great Akbar died in India. She was succeeded by the then King of Scotland because he was supposed to be next in the line of succession. He became James I, and England and Scotland thus became one kingdom. What England had failed to do by violence was done peacefully. James I was a believer in the divine right of kings, and disliked Parliament. He was not as clever as Elizabeth, and very soon trouble arose between him and Parliament. It was during his reign that many stiff-necked Protestants in England left their native country for good and sailed in the *Mayflower* in 1620 to settle in America. They objected to the autocratic method of James I and they disliked the new Church of England, and did not consider it Protestant enough. So they left home and country and set sail for the wild new land across the Atlantic. They landed on the northern coasts in a place which they called New Plymouth. More colonists followed them, and gradually the settlements increased till there were thirteen colonies all along the eastern coast. These colonies ultimately developed into the United States of America. But that was a long way off yet.

The son of James I was Charles I, and matters very soon came to a head after he became King in 1625. Parliament therefore presented to him in 1628 the "Petition of Right", which is a famous document in English history. In this petition the King was told that he was not an absolute monarch and could not do many things. He could not tax or imprison people illegally. He could not even do in the seventeenth century what the English Viceroy of India does in the twentieth—issue ordinances and imprison people under them.

Annoyed at being told what he could do and what he could not, Charles dissolved Parliament and ruled without it. After some years, however, he was so hard up for money that he had to call another Parliament. There had been great anger at all that Charles had been doing without Parliament, and the new Parliament was spoiling for a fight with him. Within two years, in 1642, civil war began, the King on one side, supported by many nobles and a great part of the army, the Parliament on the other, supported by the rich merchants and the city of London. For several years this war dragged on, till there arose on the side of Parliament a great leader, Oliver Cromwell. He was a great organizer, a stern disciplinarian and a man full of religious enthusiasm for the cause. "In the dark perils of war," says Carlyle about Cromwell, "in the high places of the field, hope shone in him like a pillar of fire, when it had gone out in all the others." Cromwell built up a new army, the "Ironsides" they were called, and filled them with his own disciplined enthusiasm. The "Puritans" of the army of Parliament faced the "Cavaliers" of Charles. Cromwell won in the end, and Charles, the King, became a prisoner of Parliament.

Many members of Parliament still wanted to compromise with the King, but Cromwell's new army would not listen to this, and an officer of this army, Colonel Pride, boldly marched into the Parliament House and turned out all such members. Pride's Purge this has been called. It was a drastic remedy, and not very complimentary to Parliament. If Parliament objected to the King's autocracy, here was another power, their own army, which paid little attention to their legal quibbles. Such is the way of revolutions.

The remaining members of the House of Commons, called the Rump Parliament, decided to try Charles, in spite of the objection of the House of Lords, and they condemned him to death " as a tyrant, traitor, murderer, and enemy of his country " And in 1649 this man, who had been their King, and who had talked of his divine right to rule, was beheaded in Whitehall in London.

Kings die like other people. Indeed, many of them in history have died violent deaths. Autocracy and kingship breed assassination and murder, and English royalties had had enough of assassination in the past. But that an elected assembly should presume to constitute itself into a court, and try the King, and condemn him to death, and then have him beheaded, was a novel and an amazing thing. It was curious that the English people, who have always been very conservative and averse to rapid changes, should thus set an example of how a tyrant and traitorous king should be treated. But the deed was done not so much by the English people as a whole as by the new " Ironsides " under Cromwell.

All the kings and Cæsars and princes and petty royalties of Europe were greatly shocked. What would happen to them if the common people became so presumptuous and followed the example of England ? Many of them would have attacked England and crushed her, but the destinies of England were not in charge of an incompetent king then. England was for the first time a republic, and Cromwell and his army were there to defend her. Cromwell was practically dictator. He was called the " Lord Protector " Under his stern and efficient rule England's strength grew and her fleets drove away the Dutch and French and Spanish fleets. For the first time England became the chief naval Power in Europe.

But the English Republic had a very short life—hardly eleven years after the death of Charles I. Cromwell died in 1658, and two years later the Republic fell. The son of Charles I, who had taken refuge in foreign countries, came back to England, and he was welcomed and crowned as Charles II. This second Charles was a low and disreputable person, and his idea of kingship was just to have a good time. But he was clever enough not to go against Parliament too much. He was actually in the secret pay of the French King. England lost the position she had gained in Europe during Cromwell's time, and the Dutch actually came up and burnt the English fleet in the Thames.

Charles' brother, James II, succeeded him, and immediately there was trouble with Parliament. James was a devout Catholic, and he wanted to establish the Pope's ascendancy again in England. But whatever ideas the English people had on religion—and they were vague enough—most of them were bitter against the Pope and all "Popery". James II could do nothing against this widespread feeling and, having angered Parliament, he had to fly to France for refuge.

Again Parliament had triumphed over the king, and this time quite peacefully and without civil war. There was no king in the country. But England was not going to be a republic again. The Englishman loves a lord, it is said, and, even more, he loves the pomp and pageantry of royalty. So Parliament searched for a new king, and found one in the House of Orange, which, 100 years before, had given William the Silent to lead the great struggle of the Netherlands against Spain. There was another William, Prince of Orange, now, and he had married Mary of the English royal family. So William and Mary were made joint sovereigns in 1688 Parliament was supreme now, and the English revolution, giving power to the people represented in Parliament, was complete. No British king or queen has dared to challenge the authority of Parliament since that date. But, of course, there are many ways of intriguing and influencing, without definitely opposing or challenging, and several British kings have adopted these methods.

Parliament became supreme. But what was this Parliament? Do not imagine that it represented the people of England. It represented only a very small part of them. The House of Lords represented, as its name signifies, the lords or great landowners and the bishops. Even the House of Commons was an assembly of rich men, either owners of landed property or big merchants. Very few people had the vote. Till 100 years ago there were any number of what are called "pocket boroughs" in England—that is to say constituencies which were practically in somebody's pocket. The whole constituency might consist of just one or two voters electing a member ! In 1793 it is said that 306 members of the House of Commons were elected by 160 persons in all. One hamlet, named Old Sarum, returned two members to Parliament. Thus you will see that the vast majority of the people had no votes and were not represented in Parliament. The House of Commons was very far from being a popular assembly. It did not even represent the new middle classes that were rising up in the towns. It just represented the landowning class and some rich merchants. Seats in Parliament were bought and sold, and there was a great deal of bribery. And this took place right down to 1832, just 100 years ago, when a Reform Bill was passed after much agitation, and more people got the vote.

So we see that the victory of Parliament over the king meant the victory of a handful of rich people. England was governed really by this handful of landowners with a sprinkling of merchants.

All other classes, comprising practically the whole nation, had no say in the matter.

In the same way, you will remember that the Dutch Republic, which came into existence after the great struggle with Spain, was also a rich man's republic.

After William and Mary, Anne, Mary's sister, was Queen of England. At her death in 1714, there was again some difficulty about the next king. Parliament ultimately went to Germany for their choice. They chose a German, who was then the Elector of Hanover, and made him George I of England. Probably Parliament chose him because he was dull and not at all clever, and it was safer to have a foolish king than a clever one who might interfere with Parliament. George I could not even speak English; the English King was ignorant of English. Even his son, who became George II, knew hardly any English. In this way was established in England the House of Hanover, or the Hanoverian dynasty, which still flourishes there. It can hardly be said to reign, as the reigning and ruling is done by Parliament.

In the sixteenth and seventeenth centuries there was a great deal of trouble and friction between Ireland and England. There were attempts at the conquest of Ireland and rebellions and massacres right through the reigns of Elizabeth and James I. James confiscated a great deal of landed property in Ulster, in the north of Ireland, and brought over Protestants from Scotland to settle in these areas. Ever since then these Protestant colonists have remained there and Ireland has been divided into two parts : the native Irish and the Scotch colonists; Roman Catholic and Protestant. There has been bitter hatred between the two, and of course the English have profited by this division. As ever, the rulers believe in a policy of " divide and rule ". Even now the biggest question in Ireland is the Ulster question.

During the English civil war there was a massacre of the English in Ireland. Cromwell avenged this cruelly by a massacre of the Irish, and to this day this is remembered bitterly by the Irish. There was more fighting, and there were settlements and treaties, and these were broken by the English—it is a long and painful history, the history of the agony of Ireland.

It may interest you to know that Jonathan Swift, the author of *Gulliver's Travels*, lived about this time, from 1667 to 1745. The book is a famous children's classic, but it is really a bitter satire on the England of his day. Daniel Defoe, who wrote *Robinson Crusoe*, was a contemporary of Swift.

88

BABAR

September 3, 1932

LET us come back to India. We have spent some time over Europe, and in many a letter tried to look under the turmoil and struggle and warfare, and to understand what was happening there during the sixteenth and seventeenth centuries. I wonder what impressions you have gathered of this period in Europe. Whatever your impressions may be, they must be very mixed, and that is not surprising, for Europe was a very mixed and curious place just then. Continuous and barbarous warfare, religious bigotry and cruelty unmatched in history, autocracy and the " divine right " of kings, a degenerate aristocracy, and shameless exploitation of the people. China seemed to be ages ahead of all this— she was a cultured, artistic, tolerant and more or less peaceful country. India, in spite of disruption and degeneration, compared favourably in many ways.

But Europe also showed a different and a pleasanter face. There were the beginnings of modern science visible, and the idea of popular freedom begins to grow and shake the thrones of kings. Underneath these, and the cause of these and of most other activities, is the commercial and industrial development of the western and north-western European countries. Large cities grow up, full of merchants trading with distant countries, and humming with the industrial activity of the artisans. All over western Europe craft guilds—that is, associations of artisans and craftsmen—grow up. These merchant and industrial classes form the *bourgeoisie*—the new middle class. This class grows, but it finds many obstacles— political, social, and religious. In politics and social organization there are the remains of the feudal system. This system belonged to an age that was past and did not fit in with the new conditions and hindered trade and industry. Feudal lords used to charge all manner of tolls and taxes which irritated the trading classes. So the *bourgeoisie* set itself out to remove this class from power. The king did not like the feudal nobles either, as they wanted to encroach on his power. So the king and the *bourgeoisie* became allies against the feudal lords and deprived them of real influence. As a result the king becomes more powerful and autocratic.

In the same way it was felt that the religious organization of the day in western Europe, and the prevailing religious ideas and notions of doing business, came in the way of the growth of trade and industry. Religion itself was connected with the feudal system in many ways, and the Church, as I have told you, was the biggest feudal landlord. For many years previously individuals and groups had risen to criticize and challenge the Roman Church. But they did not make any great difference. Now, however, the whole rising *bourgeoisie* wanted a change, and so the movement for reform became a mighty one.

All these changes, and many others which we have already considered together, were the different aspects and phases of the revolution which brought the *bourgeoisie* to the front. The process seems to have been more or less the same in the western European countries, but it took place at different times in the different countries. Eastern Europe, meanwhile, and for long afterwards, was very backward industrially, and so no such change took place there.

In China and India there were also craft guilds and hosts of artisans and craftsmen. Industry was as advanced, and often more so, than in western Europe. But we do not find there the growth of science at this stage as in Europe, nor is there the same kind of urge for popular freedom. In both countries there were long traditions of religious freedom and local freedom in towns and villages and in guilds. People cared little for the king's power and autocracy so long as they were not interfered with in their local matters. Both countries had built up a social organization which had lasted for a very long time and was far more stable than anything in Europe. It was perhaps the very stability and rigidity of this organization which prevented growth. In India we have seen disruption and degeneration finally ending in the conquest of the north by the Moghal Babar. The people seem to have completely forgotten their old Aryan ideas of freedom and have become servile and resigned to any ruler. Even the Muslims who had brought a new life to the country seem to have become as degenerate and servile as the others.

Thus Europe, endowed with a freshness and energy which the old civilizations of the East seemed to lack, slowly steals ahead of them. Her sons go to the far corners of the world. The lure of trade and wealth draws her seamen to the Americas and Asia. In south-eastern Asia we saw the Portuguese put an end to the Arab Empire of Malacca. They establish outposts on the Indian coast-line and all over the eastern seas. But soon their mastery of the spice trade is challenged by two new sea Powers, Holland and England. Portugal is driven away from the East and her eastern empire and trade perish. The Dutch take Portugal's place to some extent and many of the eastern islands are occupied by them. In 1600 Queen Elizabeth grants a charter to the East India Company, a company of London merchants, to trade in India, and two years later the Dutch East India Company is formed. Thus begins the period of grabbing by Europe in Asia. For a long time this is almost confined to Malay and the eastern islands. China is too strong for Europe, under the Mings and the early Manchus who came in the middle of the seventeenth century. Japan actually goes so far as to turn out every foreigner and shut herself up completely in 1641. And India? Our story has lagged behind in India, and we must fill up the gap. As we shall see, India rose to be a powerful monarchy under the new Moghal dynasty, and there was little danger or chance of European invasion. But Europe was already dominant on the seas.

So we come back to India. In Europe and China and Japan and

Malaysia we have reached the end of the seventeenth century and we are on the verge of the eighteenth. But in India we are still in the early sixteenth, when Babar came.

Babar's victory over the feeble and contemptible Afghan Sultan of Delhi in 1526 begins a new epoch and a new empire in India—the Moghal Empire. With a brief interval, it lasted from 1526 to 1707, a period of 181 years. These were the years of its power and glory, when the fame of the Great Moghal of India spread all over Asia and Europe. There were six big rulers of this dynasty, and then the empire went to pieces, and the Marathas and Sikhs and others carved out States from it. And after them came the British, who, profiting by the breakdown of the central power and the confusion in the country, gradually established their dominion.

I have told you something of Babar already. Descended from Chengiz and Timur, he had something of their greatness and military ability. But the Mongols had become more civilized since the days of Chengiz, and Babar was one of the most cultured and delightful persons one could meet. There was no sectarianism in him, no religious bigotry, and he did not destroy as his ancestors used to do. He was devoted to art and literature, and was himself a poet in Persian. Flowers and gardens he loved, and in the heat of India he thought often of his home in Central Asia. " The violets are lovely in Ferghana," he says in his memoirs; " it is a mass of tulips and roses."

Babar was only a boy of eleven when his father died and he became ruler of Samarqand. It was not a soft job. There were enemies all around him. So, at an age when little boys and girls are at school, he had to take to the field with his sword. He lost his throne and won it back, and had many a great adventure in his stormy career. And yet he managed to cultivate literature and poetry and art. Ambition drove him on. Having conquered Kabul, he crossed the Indus to India. He had a very small army, but he had the new artillery which was then being used in Europe and western Asia. The huge Afghan host that went to fight him went to pieces before this little well-trained army and its artillery, and victory came to Babar. But his troubles were not over, and his fate hung in the balance many a time. Once when grave danger threatened him, his generals advised him to retreat to the north. But he was made of sterner stuff and said that he preferred facing death to retreating. He loved the wine-cup. He decided, however, at this crisis in his life, to give up drinking, and he broke all his drinking-cups. He happened to win, and he kept his pledge about wine.

Babar was barely four years in India when he died. They were four years of fighting and little rest, and he remained a stranger to India and knew little about her. In Agra he laid out a splendid capital and sent to Constantinople for a famous architect. Those were the days when Suleiman the Magnificent was building in Constantinople. Sinan was a famous Ottoman architect and he sent his favourite pupil Yusuf to India.

Babar wrote his memoirs, and this delightful book gives intimate glimpses of the man. He tells us of Hindustan and of its animals and flowers and trees and fruits—not forgetting the frogs! He sighs for the melons and grapes and flowers of his native country. And he expresses his extreme disappointment at the people. According to him they have not a single good point in their favour. Perhaps he did not get to know them in his four years of war, and the more cultured classes kept away from the new conqueror. Perhaps also a new-comer does not easily enter into the life and culture of another people. Anyway he found nothing that was admirable, either in the Afghans who had been the ruling classes for some time, or in the majority of the people. He is a good observer and, even allowing for the partiality of a new-comer, his account shows that North India was in a poor way at the time. He did not visit South India at all.

"The Empire of Hindustan," Babar tells us, "is extensive, populous, and rich. On the east, the south, and even the west, it is bounded by the great ocean. On the north it has Kabul, Ghazni, and Kandahar. The capital of all Hindustan is Delhi." It is interesting to note that the whole of India was looked upon as a unit by Babar, although when he came it was split up into many kingdoms. This idea of the unity of India has persisted throughout history.

Babar goes on with his description of India :

" It is a remarkably fine country. It is quite a different world compared with our countries. Its hills and rivers, its forests and plains, its animals and plants, its inhabitants and their language, its winds and rains, are all of a different nature. . . . You have no sooner passed Sindh than the country, the trees, the stones, the wandering tribes, the manners and customs of the people, are all entirely those of Hindustan. Even the reptiles are different. . . . The frogs of Hindustan are worthy of notice. Though of the same species as our own, yet they will run six or seven *gaz* on the face of the water."

He then gives lists of the animals, flowers, trees, and fruits of Hindustan.

And then we come to the people.

" The country of Hindustan has few pleasures to recommend it. The people are not handsome. They have no idea of the charms of friendly society, or of frankly mixing together or of familiar intercourse. They have no genius, no comprehension of mind, no politeness of manner, no kindness or fellow feeling, no ingenuity or mechanical invention in planning or executing their handicraft works, no skill or knowledge in design or architecture ; they have no good horses, no good flesh, no grapes or musk-melons, no good fruits, no ice or cold water, no good food, or bread in their bazaars, no baths or colleges, no candles, no torches, not a candlestick."

What *have* they got ? one is tempted to ask ! Babar must have been thoroughly fed up when he wrote this.

" The chief excellence of Hindustan [says Babar] is that it is a large country and has abundance of gold and silver. . . . Another convenience of Hindustan is that the workmen of every profession and trade are innumerable and without end. For any work and any employment, there is always a set ready, to whom the same employment and trade have descended from father to son for ages."

I have quoted at some length from these memoirs of Babar. Such books often give us a better idea of a man than any description of him.

Babar died in 1530, when he was forty-nine years of age. There is a well-known story concerning his death. Humayun, his son, was ill, and Babar, in his love for him, is said to have offered his own life if his son got well. It is said that Humayun recovered and Babar died within a few days of this incident.

They carried Babar's body to Kabul, and there they buried it in a garden he loved. He had gone back at last to the flowers he longed for.

89

AKBAR

September 4, 1932

BABAR had conquered a great part of northern India by his generalship and military efficiency. He had defeated the Afghan Sultan of Delhi, and later, and this was the more difficult task, the Rajput clans under the leadership of the gallant Rana Sanga of Chittor, a famous hero in Rajput history. But he left a difficult task for his son Humayun. Humayun was a cultured and learned person, but no soldier like his father. He had trouble all over his new empire, and ultimately in 1540, ten years after Babar's death, an Afghan chief in Bihar, named Sher Khan, defeated and drove him out of India. So the second of the Great Moghals became a wanderer, hiding himself and suffering all manner of privations. It was during these wanderings in the Rajputana desert that his wife gave birth to a son in November 1542. This son, born in the desert, was to become Akbar.

Humayun escaped to Persia, and Shah Tamasp, the ruler of the place, gave him shelter. Meanwhile Sher Khan was supreme in northern India, and for five years he ruled as Sher Shah. Even during this brief period he showed that he was a very capable person. He was a brilliant organizer, and his government was active and efficient. In the midst of his wars he found time to start a new and a better land-revenue system for assessing taxes on the cultivators. He was a stern and hard man, but of all the Afghan rulers of India, and of many others also, he was certainly the ablest and best.   But, as often happens with efficient autocrats, he was all in all in his government, and with his death the whole structure went to pieces.

Humayun took advantage of this disorganization and returned from Persia in 1556 with an army.   He won, and after an interval of sixteen years he was again on the throne of Delhi. But not for long.   Six months later he fell down a staircase and died.

It is interesting to contrast the tombs or mausoleums of Sher Shah and Humayun.   The Afghan's tomb is at Sahasram in Bihar, a stern, strong, imperious-looking building, like the man.   Humayun's tomb is at Delhi.   It is a polished and elegant building. And from these structures of stone one can form a good idea of these two rivals for empire in the sixteenth century.

Akbar was only thirteen years old then.   Like his grandfather, he came to the throne early.   He had a guardian and protector, Bairam Khan—the Khan Baba, he was called.   But within four years Akbar wearied of guardianship and other people's direction and took the government into his own hands.

For nearly fifty years Akbar ruled India, from early in 1556 to the end of 1605.   This was the period of the revolt of the Netherlands in Europe, and of Shakespeare in England.   Akbar's name stands out in Indian history, and sometimes, and in some ways, he reminds one of Ashoka.   It is a strange thing that a Buddhist Emperor of India of the third century before Christ, and a Muslim Emperor of India of the sixteenth century after Christ, should speak in the same manner and almost in the same voice.   One wonders if this is not perhaps the voice of India herself speaking through two of her great sons.   Of Ashoka we know little enough, except what he has himself left carved in stone.   Of Akbar we know a great deal.   Two contemporary historians of his Court have left long accounts, and the foreigners who visited him, and especially the Jesuits who tried hard to convert him to Christianity, have written at length.

He was the third in the line from Babar.   But the Moghals were still new to the country.   They were regarded as foreigners and their hold was military.   It was Akbar's reign that established the Moghal dynasty and made it of the soil and wholly Indian in outlook.   It was in his reign that the title of Great Moghal came to be used in Europe.   He was very autocratic and had uncontrolled power.   There seems to have been no whisper in India then of checking a ruler's powers.   As it happened, Akbar was a wise despot, and he worked hard for the welfare of the Indian people. In a sense he might be considered to be the father of Indian nationalism.   At a time when there was little of nationality in the country and religion was a dividing factor, Akbar deliberately placed the ideal of a common Indian nationhood above the claims of separatist religion.   He did not wholly succeed in his attempt. But it is amazing how far he did go and what great success attended his efforts.

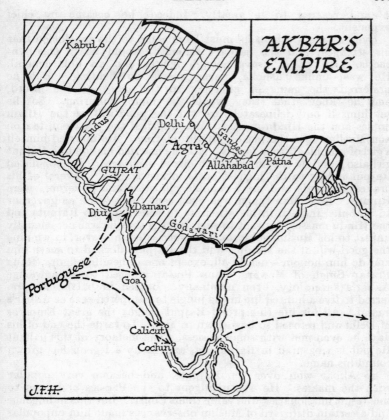

And yet Akbar's success, such as it was, was not due entirely to his unaided self. No man can succeed in great tasks unless the time is ripe and the atmosphere is favourable. A great man often forces the pace and creates his own atmosphere. But the great man himself is a product of the times and of the prevailing atmosphere. So Akbar also was the product of the times in India.

In a previous letter I told you how silent forces in India worked for the synthesis of the two cultures and religions that had been thrown together in this country. I told you of new styles of architecture and of the growth of the Indian languages, and especially of Urdū or Hindustani. And I also told you of reformers and religious leaders, like Ramananda and Kabir and Gurū Nanak, who sought to bring Islam and Hinduism nearer to each other by laying stress on the common features and attacking their rites and ceremonials. This spirit of synthesis was abroad, and Akbar, with his finely sensitive and receptive mind, must have absorbed it and reacted to it greatly. Indeed, he became its chief exponent.

Even as a statesman he must have come to the conclusion that his strength, and the nation's strength, would lie in this synthesis. He was a brave enough fighter and an able general. He was, unlike Ashoka, never averse to fighting. But he preferred the gains of affection to the gains of the sword, and he knew that they would be more enduring. So he set himself out deliberately to win the good-will of the Hindu nobles and the Hindu masses. He abolished the *jizya* poll tax on non-Muslims and the tax on Hindu pilgrims. He married himself a girl of a noble Rajput family; later he married his son to a Rajput girl also; and he encouraged such mixed marriages. He appointed Rajput nobles to the highest posts in his Empire. Several of his bravest generals and most capable ministers and governors were Hindus. Raja Man Singh was even sent for a while as governor to Kabul. Indeed, in his attempts to conciliate the Rajputs and the Hindu masses, he went to such lengths that he was occasionally unjust to his Muslim subjects. He succeeded, however, in winning the good-will of the Hindus, and the Rajputs flocked to serve him and do him honour—nearly all, except one unbending figure, Rana Pratap Singh of Mewar. Rana Pratap refused to acknowledge Akbar's suzerainty, even nominally. Beaten in battle, he preferred to live a hunted life in the jungle to pampered ease as Akbar's vassal. All his life this proud Rajput fought the great Emperor of Delhi and refused to bow down to him. Towards the end of his days he even met with some success. The memory of this gallant Rajput is treasured in Rajputana, and many a legend has grown round his name.

So Akbar won over the Rajputs, and became very popular with the masses. He was indulgent to the Parsees and even to the Jesuit missionaries who came to his Court. But this indulgence and a certain disregard of Muslim observances made him unpopular with the Muslim nobles, and there were several revolts against him.

I have compared him to Ashoka, but do not be misled by this comparison. In many ways he was unlike him. He was very ambitious, and to the end of his days he was a conqueror, intent on extending his empire. The Jesuits tell us that he

" possessed an alert and discerning mind; he was a man of sound judgment, prudent in affairs, and above all, kind, affable, and generous. With these qualities he combined the courage of those who undertake and carry out great enterprises. . . . He was interested in, and curious to learn about many things, and possessed an intimate knowledge not only of military and political matters, but of many of the mechanical arts . . . the light of clemency and mildness shone forth from this prince, even upon those who offended against his own person. He seldom lost his temper. If he did so, he fell into a violent passion; but his wrath was never of long duration.''

Remember that this description is not by a courtier, but by a stranger from another land who had plenty of opportunities to observe Akbar.

Physically, Akbar was extraordinarily strong and active, and he loved nothing better than hunting wild and dangerous animals. As a soldier he was brave to the point of recklessness. His amazing energy can be judged from a famous march of his from Agra to Ahmedabad in nine days. A revolt had broken out in Gujrat, and Akbar rushed with a little army across the desert of Rajputana, a distance of 450 miles. It was an extraordinary feat. There were no railways or motor cars then, I need hardly remind you.

But great men have something besides all these qualities : they have, it is said, a magnetism which draws people to them. Akbar had this personal magnetism and charm in abundant measure; his compelling eyes were, in the wonderful description of the Jesuits, " vibrant like the sea in sunshine ". Is it any wonder that this man should fascinate us still, and that his most royal and manly figure should tower high above the crowds of men who have been but kings ?

As a conqueror, Akbar triumphed all over North India and even the South. He added Gujrat, Bengal, Orissa, Kashmir and Sindh to his Empire. He was victorious in Central India and South India also and took tribute. His defeat of Rani Durgavati, a ruler in the Central Province, does him little credit. The Rani was a brave and good ruler and she did him no harm. But ambition and the desire for empire care little for such obstacles. In South India his armies fought another woman ruler, the famous Chand Bibi, regent of Ahmednagar. This lady had courage and ability, and the fight she put up impressed the Moghal army so much that they granted her a favourable peace. Unfortunately she was killed later by some discontented soldiers of her own.

Akbar's armies also laid siege to Chittor—this was before Rana Pratap's time. Chittor was defended very gallantly by Jaimal. On his death there was the terrible *jauhar* ceremony again, and Chittor fell.

Akbar managed to gather round himself many efficient lieutenants who were devoted to him. Chief among these were the two brothers, Faizi and Abul Fazl, and Birbal, about whom innumerable stories are still told. Todar Mal was his finance minister. It was he who revised the whole revenue system. In those days, you may be interested to know, there was no *zamindari* system and no *zamindars* or *taluqdars*. The State settled with the individual cultivators or *ryots*. It is what is called now the *ryot-wari* system. Present-day *zamindars* are the creation of the British.

Raja Man Singh of Jaipur was one of Akbar's best generals. Another famous person in Akbar's Court was Tansen, the great singer, who has become the patron saint of all singers in India.

Akbar's capital was at Agra to begin with and he built the fort there. Then he built a new city at Fatehpur-Sikri, which is about fifteen miles from Agra. He chose this site as a saintly person,

Shaikh Salim Chishti, lived there. Here he built a splendid city, "much greater than London", according to an English traveller of the day, and for over fifteen years this was the capital of his Empire. Later he made Lahore his capital. "His Majesty", says Abul-Fazl, the friend and minister of Akbar, "plans splendid edifices, and dresses the work of his mind and heart in the garment of stone and clay." Fatehpur-Sikri still stands with its beautiful mosque and great *Buland Darwāza* and many other fine buildings. It is a deserted city and there is no life in it; but through its streets and across its wide courts the ghosts of a dead empire still seem to pass.

Our present city of Allahabad was also founded by Akbar, but of course the site is a most ancient one and Prayaga has flourished there since the days of the *Rāmāyana*. The fort at Allahabad was built by Akbar.

It must have been a busy life of conquest and consolidation of a vast empire. But right through it one can see another of Akbar's remarkable traits. This was his boundless curiosity and his search for truth. Whoever could throw light on any subject was sent for and questioned. The men of different religions gathered round him in the *Ibādat Khāna*, each hoping to convert this mighty monarch. They often quarrelled with each other, and Akbar sat by, listening to their arguments and putting many questions to them. He seems to have been convinced that truth was no monopoly of any religion or sect, and he proclaimed that his avowed principle was one of universal toleration in religion.

A historian of his reign, Badauni, who must have participated in many of these gatherings himself, gives an interesting account of Akbar, which I shall quote. Badauni himself was an orthodox Muslim, and he thoroughly disapproved of these activities of Akbar.

"His Majesty [he says] collected the opinions of everyone, especially of such as were not Muslims, retaining whatever he approved of, and rejecting everything which was against his disposition and ran counter to his wishes. From his earliest childhood to his manhood, and from his manhood to old age, his Majesty has passed through the most various phases, and through all sorts of religious practices and sectarian beliefs, and has collected everything which people can find in books, with a talent of selection peculiar to him, and a spirit of enquiry opposed to every (Islamic) principle. Thus a faith based on some elementary principles traced itself on the mirror of his heart, and as a result of all the influences brought to bear on his Majesty, there grew, gradually as the outline on a stone, the conviction in his heart that there were sensible men in all religions, and abstemious thinkers, and men endowed with miraculous powers, among all nations. If some true knowledge was thus everywhere to be found, why should truth be confined to one religion ? . . .

At this time, you will remember, there was the most extraordinary intolerance in Europe in matters of religion. The Inquisition flourished in Spain and the Netherlands and elsewhere, and both

Catholic and Calvinist thought tolerance of the other a deadly sin.

Year after year Akbar continued his religious talks and arguments with the professors of all faiths, till these professors got rather tired of it and gave up hope of converting him to their particular faith. When each faith had something of the truth, how could he fix upon one? " For the Gentiles ", he is reported by the Jesuits to have remarked, " regard their law as good; and so likewise do the Saracens and the Christians. To which, then, shall we give our adherence? " (By the Gentiles, the Jesuits meant the Hindus, and the Saracens referred, of course, to the Muslims. The Jesuit fathers, being Portuguese, knew the Saracens of Spain, and called the Indian Muslims by the same name.) Akbar's question was a very pertinent one, but it annoyed the Jesuits, who say, in their book, that " thus we see in this Prince the common fault of the atheist, who refuses to make reason subservient to faith, and, accepting nothing as true which his feeble mind is unable to fathom, is content to submit to his own imperfect judgment matters transcending the highest limits of human understanding ". If this is the definition of an atheist, the more we have of them the better.

What Akbar was aiming at is not clear. Did he look upon the question purely as a political one? In his desire to evolve a common nationality did he want to force the different religions into one channel? Or was he religious in his motives and his quest? I do not know. But I am inclined to think that he was more of a statesman than a religious reformer. Whatever his object may have been, he actually proclaimed a new religion—the *Din Ilahi*—of which he himself was the head. In religion, as in other matters, his autocracy was to be unchallenged, and there was a lot of disgusting prostration and kissing the feet and the like. The new religion did not catch. All it did was to irritate the Muslims.

Akbar was the very essence of authoritarianism. And yet it is interesting to speculate what his reaction to politically liberal ideas might have been. If there was to be liberty of conscience, why not greater political freedom for the people? To science he would certainly have been greatly attracted. Unhappily, these ideas, which were beginning to trouble some people in Europe then, were not current in India at the time. Nor does there seem to have been any use of the printing-press, and education was thus very limited. Indeed, you will be amazed to learn that Akbar was illiterate—that is, he could not read or write! But none the less he was highly educated and was very fond of having books read to him. Under his orders many Sanskrit books were translated into Persian.

It is interesting to note that he issued orders forbidding the practice of *sati* by Hindu widows, and also the practice of making prisoners of war slaves.

Akbar died in October 1605 in his sixty-fourth year, after a reign of nearly fifty years.　He lies buried in a beautiful mausoleum at Sikandra, near Agra.

In Akbar's reign there flourished in northern India—mostly in Benares—a man whose name is known to every villager in the United Provinces.　He is far better known there, and is more popular, than Akbar or any king can be.　I refer to Tulsi Das, who wrote the *Rāmacharitmanas* or the *Rāmāyana* in Hindi.

90

THE DECLINE AND FALL OF THE MOGHAL EMPIRE IN INDIA

September 9, 1932

I FEEL tempted to tell you something more of Akbar, but I must restrain myself.　I cannot, however, resist giving you some more quotations from the accounts of the Portuguese missionaries. Their opinions are of far greater value than those of courtiers, and it is well to remember that they were greatly disappointed in Akbar because he did not become a Christian.　Still they say that "indeed he was a great king; for he knew that the good ruler is he who can command, simultaneously, the obedience, the respect, the love and the fear of his subjects.　He was a prince beloved of all, firm with the great, kind to those of low estate, and just to all men, high and low, neighbour or stranger, Christian, Saracen or Gentile; so that every man believed that the king was on his side."　"At one time," the Jesuits further tell us, " he would be deeply immersed in state affairs, or giving audience to his subjects, and the next moment he would be seen shearing camels, hewing stones, cutting wood, or hammering iron, and doing all with as much diligence as though engaged in his own particular vocation." Powerful and autocratic monarch though he was, he did not think manual labour beneath his dignity, as some people seem to think to-day.

We are further told that " he ate sparingly, taking flesh only three or four months in the year. . . . With great difficulty he spared three hours of the night for sleep. . . . He had a wonderful memory.　He knew the names of all his elephants, though he had many thousands of them, also the names of his horses, deer and even pigeons ! "　This amazing memory seems hardly credible, and there may be some exaggeration in the account.　But that he had a wonderful mind there can be no doubt.　" Though he could neither read nor write, he knew everything that took place in his kingdom."　And " his eagerness for knowledge " was such that he

" tried to learn everything at once, like a hungry man trying to swallow his food at a single gulp ".

Such was Akbar. But he was the complete autocrat, and although he gave a large measure of security to the people, and reduced the burden of taxation on the peasantry, his mind was not directed to raising the general level by education and training. It was the age of autocracy everywhere, and compared to other autocratic monarchs he shines brilliantly as a king and a man.

Although third in the line from Babar, Akbar was the real founder of the Moghal dynasty in India. Like Kublai Khan's Yuan dynasty in China, the Moghal rulers become, from Akbar onwards, an Indian dynasty. And because of the great work that Akbar had done in consolidating his empire, his dynasty endured for over a 100 years after his death.

There were three able rulers after Akbar, but there was nothing extraordinary about them. Whenever an emperor died, there was an unseemly scramble among his sons for the throne. There were palace intrigues and wars of succession, and revolts of sons against fathers, and brothers against brothers, and murders and blinding of relatives—all the revolting accompaniments of autocracy and absolute rule. There was pomp and splendour, unequalled anywhere. This was the time, you will remember, when Louis XIV, the Roi-Soleil, flourished in France and built Versailles and held a magnificent Court. But the Roi-Soleil's magnificence paled before the magnificence of the Grand Moghal. Probably these Moghal rulers were the richest sovereigns of the age. And yet famine came sometimes, and pestilence and disease, and wiped off vast numbers, while the imperial Court lived in luxury.

The toleration of religions of Akbar's time continued in his son Jahangir's reign, but then it faded away and there was some persecution of Christians and Hindus. Later on, in the reign of Aurangzeb, there was a determined attempt to persecute Hindus by destruction of temples and a re-imposition of the hated *jizya* poll-tax. So the foundations of the empire, which Akbar had laboriously laid, were removed one by one, and suddenly the empire tottered and fell.

Akbar was succeeded by Jahangir, his son by a Rajput wife. He carried on to some extent his father's traditions, but he was probably more interested in art and painting, and gardens and flowers, than in government. He had a fine art-gallery. Every year he went to Kashmir, and I think it was he who laid out the famous gardens near Srinagar—the Shalamar and Nishat Baghs. Jahangir's wife, or rather one of his many wives, was the beautiful Nur Jahan, who was the real power behind the throne. It was in Jahangir's reign that the beautiful building containing the tomb of Itmad-ud-Daula was built. Always, when I go to Agra, I try to visit this gem of architecture to feast my eyes on its beauty.

After Jahangir came his son Shah Jahan, who ruled for thirty years (1628–1658). In his reign—he was the contemporary of

Louis XIV of France—came the climax of Moghal splendour, and in his reign also are clearly visible the seeds of decay. The famous Peacock Throne, covered with expensive jewels, was made for the King to sit on. Then also was made the Taj Mahal, that dream of beauty by the side of the Jumna at Agra. This is, as perhaps you know, the tomb of the wife he loved, Mumtaz Mahal. Shah Jahan did much that does him no credit or honour. He was intolerant in religion, and he did next to nothing to give relief to the Dekhan and Gujrat when a terrible famine raged there. His wealth and magnificence appear most odious when contrasted with the misery and poverty of his people. And yet much, per-haps, may be forgiven him for the marvels of loveliness in stone and marble that he has left behind. It was in his time that Moghal architecture reached its height. Besides the Taj, he built the Moti Masjid—the Pearl Mosque in Agra; and the great Jami Masjid of Delhi, and the *Dīwān-i-ām* and *Dīwān-i-khās* in the palace in Delhi. These are buildings of a noble simplicity; some of them enormous and yet graceful and elegant, and fairy-like in their beauty.

But behind this fairy-like beauty were the poverty-stricken people, who paid for the palaces, though many did not even have mud huts to live in. There was unrestrained despotism, and fierce punishments were given to those who happened to displease the Emperor or his great viceroys and governors. The principles of Machiavelli governed the intrigues of the Court. Akbar's clemency and toleration and good government were things of the past. Affairs were heading for trouble.

Then came Aurangzeb, the last of the Great Moghals. He started off his reign by imprisoning his old father. For forty-eight years he reigned, from 1659 to 1707. He was no lover of art or literature, like his grandfather Jahangir, or of architecture like his father, Shah Jahan. He was an austere puritan, a bigot, tolerating no religion but his own. The pomp of the Court continued, but in his personal life Aurangzeb was simple and almost an ascetic. De-liberately he laid down a policy of persecuting the followers of the Hindu religion. Deliberately he reversed Akbar's policy of con-ciliation and synthesis, and thus removed the whole foundation on which the Empire had so far rested. He reimposed the *jizya* tax on Hindus; he excluded Hindus from office as far as possible; he gave offence to the Rajput nobles, who had supported the dynasty since Akbar's time, and brought on a Rajput war; he destroyed Hindu temples by the thousand, and many a beautiful old building of the past was thus reduced to dust. And while his empire spread in the south, and Bijapur and Golkonda fell to him, and tribute came to him from the far south, its foundations were sapped and it grew weaker and weaker, and enemies sprang up on every side. A Hindu petition to him against the *jizya* tax stated that the tribute " is repugnant to justice; it is equally foreign from good policy, as it must impoverish the country; moreover, it is an innovation and an infringement of the laws of Hindustan." Referring to the conditions prevailing in the empire, it said : " During your Majesty's reign many have been alienated from the Empire and further loss of territory must necessarily follow, since devastation and rapine now universally prevail without restraint. Your subjects are trampled under foot, and every province of your Empire is impoverished, depopulation spreads, and difficulties accumulate."

It was this general misery that was the prelude to the great changes that were to come over India during the next fifty years or so. Among these changes was the sudden and complete collapse of the great Moghal Empire after the death of Aurangzeb. Great changes and great movements almost always have economic causes at their backs, and we have seen the fall of great empires in Europe and China heralded and accompanied by economic collapse and subsequent revolution. So also in India.

The Moghal Empire fell, as almost all empires fall, because of its own inherent weakness. It literally went to pieces. But this process was greatly helped by a new consciousness of revolt among the Hindus, which was brought to a head by Aurangzeb's policy. But this religious Hindu nationalism of a kind had its roots even earlier than Aurangzeb's reign and it may be that it was partly because of this that Aurangzeb became so bitter and intolerant. The Marathas and Sikhs and others were the spearheads of this Hindu revival, and the Moghal Empire was finally overthrown by them, as we shall see in the next letter. But they were not to profit by this rich inheritance. The British, quietly and cleverly, were to step in and take possession of the booty while others fought each other for it.

It may interest you to know what the royal camp of the Moghal Emperors was like when they set out with an army. It was a tremendous affair, with a circumference of thirty miles and a population of half a million ! This population included the army accompanying the Emperor, but there were vast numbers of other people, and hundreds of bazaars in this huge city on the march. It was in these moving camps that Urdū—the " camp " language—developed.

There are many portraits of Moghal times still existing, fine and delicate paintings. There is a regular gallery of the portraits of the Emperors. They bring out wonderfully the personality of these men from Babar to Aurangzeb.

The Moghal Emperors used to display themselves at least twice a day from a balcony to the people and receive petitions. When the English King George V came to India for the coronation durbar at Delhi in 1911 he was made to display himself in a like manner. The British consider themselves the successors of the Moghals to the dominion of India and try to copy them in pomp and vulgar display. As I have told you, the English King has even been given the title of the Moghal rulers—the Kaiser-i-Hind. Even now, probably there is nowhere in the world so much pomp and pageantry as there is round the person of the English Viceroy in India.

I have not told you yet of the relations of the later Moghals with foreigners. In Akbar's Court the Portuguese missionaries were great favourites, and Akbar's contacts with the European world were mainly through the Portuguese. To him they appeared to be the most powerful of European nations, and they controlled the seas. The English were not in evidence. Akbar coveted Goa and even attacked it, but without success. The Moghals did not take to the sea kindly and were powerless before a naval Power. This is curious, as there was much ship-building in eastern Bengal at the time. But these ships were mostly meant for carrying merchandise. One of the reasons for the fall of the Moghal Empire is said to have been this powerlessness at sea. The day of the naval powers had come.

When the English tried to come to the Moghal Court, the Portuguese were jealous of them and tried their best to prejudice Jahangir against them. But Sir Thomas Roe, an ambassador of James I of England, managed to reach Jahangir's Court in 1615, and he gained concessions from the Emperor and laid the foundations of the East India Company's trade. Meanwhile the English fleet had defeated Portuguese ships in Indian seas. The star of England was slowly rising over the horizon; Portugal was fading away in the west. The Dutch and the English gradually drove the Portuguese from eastern waters, and, you will remember, even the great port of Malacca fell to the Dutch in 1641. In 1629 there was war between Shah Jahan and the Portuguese in Hugli. The Portuguese were carrying on a regular slave trade and were making forcible conversions to Christianity. Hugli was captured by the Moghals after a gallant defence. The little country of Portugal was exhausted by these repeated wars. She retired from the contest for empire, but she clung on to Goa and a few other places, and there she is still.

The English meanwhile started factories in the Indian coast towns near Madras and Surat. Madras itself was founded by them in 1639. In 1662 Charles II of England married Catherine of Braganza of Portugal and he got the island of Bombay as dowry. A little later he sold this for a trifle to the East India Company. This took place during Aurangzeb's reign. The East India Company, proud of having driven away the Portuguese, and thinking that the Moghal Empire was weakening, tried to increase its possessions in India by force in 1685. But it came to grief. Warships came all the way from England and attacks were made on Aurangzeb's dominions both in the east in Bengal and in the west in Surat. But the Moghals were still strong enough to defeat them severely. The English learnt a lesson from this, and were much more careful in future. Even on Aurangzeb's death, when the Moghal power was obviously going to pieces, they hesitated for many years before venturing on big enterprises. In 1690 one of them, Job Charnock, founded the city of Calcutta. Thus the three cities of Madras, Bombay and Calcutta were founded by Englishmen, and they grew up in the beginning largely with British enterprise.

Now France also appears in India. A French trading company is formed, and in 1668 they start a factory at Surat, and some at other places. A few years later they buy the town of Pondicherry, which becomes the most important commercial port on the east coast.

In 1707 Aurangzeb dies at the great age of nearly ninety. The stage is set for the struggle to possess the magnificent prize left by him—India.   There are his own incompetent descendants and some of his great governors; there are the Marathas and Sikhs; and men looking covetously from across the north-west frontier; and the two foreign nations from across the seas—the English and the French. And what of the poor people of India ?

91

THE SIKHS AND THE MARATHAS

September 12, 1932

A STRANGE patchwork was India during the hundred years following Aurangzeb's death, a kaleidoscope, ever changing, but not very beautiful to look at. Such a period is an ideal one for adventurers and those who are bold and unscrupulous enough to seize opportunities without caring for the means or methods adopted. So adventurers rose all over India, adventurers who were native to the soil, and those who came across the north-west frontier, and those, like the English and French, who came across the seas. Each man or group played his or its own hand and was prepared to send all the others to the devil; sometimes two or more combined to crush a third, only, later, to fall out among themselves. There were frantic attempts to carve out kingdoms and to get rich quickly, and to plunder, often undisguised and unashamed, sometimes under a thin disguise of trade. And behind all this was the vanishing Moghal Empire, disappearing like the Cheshire cat, till not even the smile remained, and the so-called Emperor was an unhappy pensioner or prisoner of others.

But all this upheaval and turmoil, and turning and twisting, were the outward indications of a revolution going on below the surface. The old economic order was breaking up; feudalism had had its day and was collapsing. It was not in keeping with the new conditions in the country. We have seen this process in Europe, and we have seen the merchant classes rise, only to be checked by absolute monarchs. Only in England, and to some extent in Holland, were the monarchs subdued. When Aurangzeb came to the throne, England was under the short-lived republic which followed the execution of Charles I. And it was during

Aurangzeb's reign also that the British revolution was completed by the running away of James II and the victory of Parliament in 1688. The fact that England had a semi-popular council like Parliament helped greatly in the struggle. There was something which could be set up against the feudal nobles and later, the king.

In most other countries of Europe conditions were different. In France there was still the Grand Monarque, Louis XIV, who was a contemporary of Aurangzeb right through his long reign, and who survived him by eight years. Absolute rule continued there till almost the end of the eighteenth century, when there was a famous and a tremendous outburst—the great French Revolution. In Germany, as we saw, the seventeenth century was a terrible period. It was during this century that the Thirty Years' War took place, which broke up the country and ruined it.

Conditions in India in the eighteenth century were, to some extent, comparable to the Thirty Years' War period of Germany. But do not drive the comparison too far. In both the countries there was an economic breakdown and the old feudal class was out of place. Although feudalism was collapsing in India, it did not disappear for a long time. And even when it had practically disappeared its outward form continued. Indeed, even to-day there are many relics of feudalism in India and in some parts of Europe.

The Moghal Empire broke up because of these economic changes, but there was no middle class ready to take advantage of this break-up and seize power. There was also no organization or council representing these classes, as there had been in England. Too much despotic rule had made the people generally rather servile, and the old ideas of freedom, such as they were, were almost forgotten. Yet, as we shall see later, in this very letter, there were attempts, partly feudal, partly *bourgeois* and partly peasant, to seize power, and some of these attempts came near success. The main thing to note, however, is that there seems to have been a gap between the fall of feudalism and the rise of the middle class, sufficiently prepared to assume power. When there is such a gap there is trouble and turmoil, as there was in Germany. So it happened in India. Petty kings and princes fight for mastery in the country, but they are representatives of a decaying order, and have no secure foundations. They come up against a new class of persons : the representatives of the British *bourgeoisie*, which had triumphed recently in its own country. This British middle class represents a higher social order than the feudal; it is in keeping with the new conditions developing in the world; it is better organized and is more efficient; it has better tools and weapons and can thus wage war more effectively; and it has the command of the sea. The feudal princes of India cannot possibly compete with this new Power, and, one by one, they go down before it.

This is a long enough prelude to this letter. We must now go back a little. I have referred in my last letter and in this to popular risings and to a religious Hindu nationalistic revival during the later days of Aurangzeb's reign. We must now say something more about this. We find quite a number of semi-religious popular movements growing up in various parts of the Moghal Empire. They are peaceful movements for a time, having little to do with politics. Songs and religious hymns are written in the languages of the country—in Hindi, Marathi, Punjabi—and become popular. These songs and hymns raise mass consciousness. Religious sects are formed round popular preachers. Pressure of economic circumstances gradually turns these sects to political questions; there is friction with the ruling authority—the Moghal Empire—then there is repression of the sect. This repression converts the peaceful religious sect into a military brotherhood. This was the development of the Sikhs, and of many other sects. The Marathas have a more complicated history, but there also we find a mixture of religion and nationalism taking up arms against the Moghals. The Moghal Empire was not overthrown by the British, but by these religious-nationalist movements, and especially by the Marathas. These movements naturally gained strength by Aurangzeb's policy of intolerance. It is also quite possible that Aurangzeb became more bitter and intolerant because of this rising religious consciousness against his rule.

As early as 1669 the Jat peasants of Mathurā rose in rebellion. They were suppressed repeatedly, but they rose again and again for over thirty years, till Aurangzeb's death. Remember that Mathurā is quite near Agra, and these rebellions were thus taking place near the capital. Another rebellion was that of the Satnamis, a Hindu sect consisting mainly of common folk. Thus this was also a poor people's rising, and was quite different from the revolts of nobles and governors and the like. A Moghal noble of the time describes them in disgust as " a gang of bloody miserable rebels, goldsmiths, carpenters, sweepers, tanners, and other ignoble beings ". In his opinion it must have been a scandalous thing for such " ignoble persons " to rise against their superiors.

We now come to the Sikhs, and we must trace their history from an earlier period. You will remember my telling you of Gurū Nanak. He died soon after Babar came to India. He was one of those who tried to find a common platform between Hinduism and Islam. He was succeeded by three other *gurūs*, who, like him, were perfectly peaceful and were only interested in religious matters. Akbar gave the site of the tank and the golden temple at Amritsar to the fourth *gurū*. Since then Amritsar has been the headquarters of Sikhism.

Then came the fifth *gurū*, Arjun Singh, who compiled the *Granth*, which is a collection of sayings and hymns, and is the sacred book of the Sikhs. For a political offence Jahangir had Arjun Singh tortured to death. This was the turning-point in the career of the Sikhs. The unjust and cruel treatment of their *gurū* filled them with resentment and turned their minds to arms. Under their sixth *guru*, Hargovind, they became a military brotherhood, and from that time onwards they were often in conflict with the ruling power. Guru Hargovind was himself imprisoned for ten years by Jahangir. The ninth *guru* was Tegh Bahadur, who lived in Aurangzeb's reign. He was ordered by Aurangzeb to embrace Islam, and on his refusal, he was executed. The tenth and the last *guru* was Govind Singh. He made the Sikhs into a powerful military community, mainly to oppose the Delhi Emperor. He died a year after Aurangzeb. There has been no *guru* since then. It is said that the powers of the *guru* now rest in the whole Sikh community, the *Khalsa*, or the " chosen ", as it is called.

Soon after Aurangzeb's death there was a Sikh rebellion. This was put down, but the Sikhs continued to grow in strength and to consolidate themselves in the Punjab. Later, at the end of the century, a Sikh State was to emerge in the Punjab under Ranjit Singh.

Troublesome as were all these rebellions, the real danger to the Moghal Empire came from the rising power of the Marathas in the south-west. Even in Shah Jahan's reign, a Maratha chieftain, Shahji Bhonsla, gave trouble. He was an officer of the Ahmednagar State, and later of Bijapur. But it was his son, Shivaji, born in 1627, who became the glory of the Marathas and the terror of the Empire. When only a boy of nineteen he started on his predatory career and captured his first fort near Poona. He was a gallant captain, an ideal guerilla leader and adventurer, and he built up a band of brave and hardened mountaineers, who were devoted to him. With their help he captured many forts and gave Aurangzeb's commanders a bad time. In 1665 he suddenly appeared at Surat, where there was the English factory, and sacked the city. He was induced to visit Aurangzeb's Court at Agra, but he felt humiliated and insulted by not being treated as an independent prince. He was kept a prisoner, but escaped. Even then Aurangzeb tried to win him over by giving him the title of raja.

But soon Shivaji was on the war-path again, and the Moghal officers in the south were so terrified of him that they paid him money for protection. This was the famous *chauth* or fourth part of the revenue which the Marathas claimed wherever they went. So the Maratha power went on increasing and the Delhi Empire weakening. In 1674 Shivaji had himself crowned with great ceremony at Raigarh. His victories continued to his death in 1680.

You have been living at Poona, in the heart of the Maratha country, for some time now, and you must know how Shivaji is loved and adored by the people there. He represented a religious-nationalist revival of the kind I have already mentioned. The economic breakdown and general misery of the people prepared the soil; and two great Marathi poets, Ramdas and Tukaram, nurtured this soil by their poetry and hymns. The Maratha people thus gained in consciousness and unity, and just then came a brilliant captain to lead them to victory.

Shivaji's son, Sambhaji, was tortured and killed by the Moghals, but the Marathas, after some setbacks, continued to grow in strength. With the death of Aurangzeb his great empire began to vanish into air. Various governors became independent of headquarters. Bengal fell away. So did Oudh and Rohilkhand. In the south the Vazir Asaf Jah founded a kingdom, the modern Hyderabad State. The present Nizam is a descendant of Asaf Jah. Within seventeen years of Aurangzeb's death the Empire had almost disappeared. But in Delhi or Agra there was a succession of nominal emperors without an empire.

As the Empire weakens, the Marathas grow stronger. Their prime minister, called the Peshwa, becomes the real power, overshadowing the Raja. The office of Peshwas becomes hereditary, like that of the Shogun in Japan, and the Raja sinks into the background. The Delhi Emperor, in his weakness, recognizes the right of the Marathas to collect their *chauth* tax all over the Dekhan. Not content with this, the Peshwa conquers Gujrat, Malwa and central India. His troops appear at the very gates of Delhi in 1737. The Marathas seemed to be destined for the overlordship of India. They dominated the land. But suddenly, in 1739, there was an intrusion from the north-west, which upset the balance of power and changed the face of northern India.

92

THE ENGLISH TRIUMPH OVER THEIR RIVALS IN INDIA

September 13, 1932

WE have seen that the Delhi Empire was in a pretty bad way. Indeed, one could almost say that, as an empire, it was in no way at all. Yet Delhi and northern India were to sink much lower still. As I have told you, it was the day of adventurers in India. A prince of adventurers suddenly swooped down from the northwest, and after much killing and plundering, walked off with enormous treasure. This was Nadir Shah, who had made himself the ruler of Persia. He took away with him the famous peacock throne which Shah Jahan had had made. This terrible visitation took place in 1739, and northern India was prostrate. Nadir Shah brought his dominions right up to the Indus. Thus Afghanistan was cut off from India. From the days of the *Mahābhārata* and Gāndhāra, right through Indian history, Afghanistan was intimately connected with India. It is now cut adrift.

Delhi saw yet another invader and plunderer within seventeen years. This was Ahmad Shah Durrani, who had succeeded Nadir

Shah in Afghanistan. Yet, in spite of these invasions, the Maratha power continued to spread, and in 1758 the Punjab was under them. They did not attempt to organize a government over all this territory. They realized their famous *chauth* tax and left the ruling to the local people. Thus they had practically inherited the Delhi Empire. But then came a great check. Durrani came down again from the north-west and, in alliance with others utterly defeated a great host of the Marathas at the old battlefield of Panipat in 1761. Durrani was then the master of the north of India, and there was no power to check him. But in the moment of his triumph he had to face trouble and revolt among his own people and he returned home.

For a while the Marathas seemed to have ended their days of domination and ceased to count for much. They had lost the great prize they sought after. But they recovered gradually and again became the most formidable internal power in India. Meanwhile, however, as we shall see, other and even more powerful forces had come into play, and the fate of India was being decided for a few generations. About this time there arose several Maratha chieftains who were supposed to be dependants of the Peshwa. Most prominent of these was Scindia of Gwalior; there were also the Gaekwar of Baroda and Holkar of Indore.

Now we must consider the other events I have referred to above. The dominating fact of this period in South India is the struggle between the English and the French. Often during the eighteenth century England and France were at war in Europe and their representatives fought each other in India. But sometimes the two fought in India even when their countries were officially at peace. On both sides there were bold and unscrupulous adventurers, over-eager to gain wealth and power, and there was naturally intense rivalry between them. On the French side the most prominent man in these days was Dupleix; on the English, Clive. Dupleix started the profitable game of taking part in local disputes between two States, hiring out his trained troops, and grabbing afterwards. French influence increased; but the English followed his methods soon enough and improved upon them. Both sides, like hungry vultures, looked for trouble, and there was enough of this to be found. Whenever there was a disputed succession in the south, you would probably find the English supporting one claimant, and the French another. England won against France after fifteen years of struggle (1746–1761). The English adventurers in India received full support from their home country; Dupleix and his colleagues had no such help from France. This is not surprising. Behind the English in India were the British merchants and others holding shares in the East India Company and they could influence Parliament and the government; behind the French was King Louis XV (grandson and successor of the Grand Monarque, Louis XIV), heading merrily for disaster. The British mastery of the sea also helped greatly. Both the French and the British trained Indian troops—sepoys they were called,

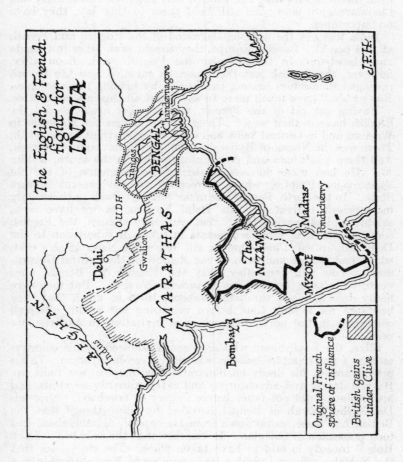

from *sipāhī*—and as they were better armed and disciplined than the local armies, their services were in great demand.

So the English defeated the French in India and completely destroyed the French cities of Chandarnagore and Pondicherry. Such was the destruction that not a roof is said to have been left in either place. The French faded out from the Indian scene from this time onwards, and though they got back Pondicherry and Chandarnagore later, and still hold them to this day, they have no importance.

India was not the only battleground of the English and French at this period. Besides Europe, they fought each other in Canada and elsewhere. In Canada also the English won. Soon after, however, the English lost the American colonies, and the French revenged themselves against the British by helping these colonies. But we shall have much more to say about all this in a later letter.

Having got rid of the French, what further obstacles did the English have in their way? There were of course the Marathas in Western and in Central India and even to some extent in the north. There was the Nizam of Hyderabad, but he did not count for much. And there was a new and powerful opponent in the south, Haider Ali. He had made himself master of the remnants of the old Vijayanagar Empire, which correspond to the present Mysore State. In the north, Bengal was under Siraj-ud-Daula, a thoroughly incompetent individual. The Delhi Empire, as we have seen, existed in imagination only. Yet, curiously enough, the English continued to send humble presents in token of submission to the Delhi Empire till 1756—that is, till long after Nadir Shah's raid, which had put an end even to the shadow of the Central Government. You will remember that the English in Bengal once ventured to take the offensive in Aurangzeb's time. But they were badly defeated, and the defeat sobered them so much that they hesitated for a long time before venturing out again, although conditions in the north were an open invitation to any resolute person.

Clive, the Englishman who is so much admired by his countrymen as a great empire-builder, was such a resolute person. In his person and in his deeds he illustrates how empires are built up. He was daring and adventurous and extraordinarily covetous, and his resolution did not falter before forgery or falsehood. Siraj-ud-Daula, the Nawab of Bengal, irritated by many things that the British had done, came down from his capital, Murshidabad, and took possession of Calcutta. It was then that the so-called "Black Hole" tragedy is said to have taken place. The story goes that the Nawab's officers locked a large number of English people in a small and stifling room for the night, and that most of them were suffocated and died. Undoubtedly such a deed is barbarous and horrible, but the whole story is based on the narrative of one person who is not considered very reliable. It is thus thought by many people that the story is largely untrue and, in any event, is greatly exaggerated.

Clive took revenge for the Nawab's success in capturing Calcutta. But the empire-builder set about it in his own way by bribing the Nawab's minister, Mir Jafar, to play the traitor, and by forging a document, the story of which is too long to relate. Having prepared the ground by forgery and treason, Clive defeated the Nawab at Plassey in 1757. This was a small battle, as battles go, and indeed it had been practically won by Clive by his intrigues even before the fighting began. But the little battle of Plassey had big results. It decided the fate of Bengal, and British dominion in India is often said to begin from Plassey. On this unsavoury foundation of treason and forgery was built up the British Empire in India. But such, more or less, is the way of all empires and empire-builders.

This sudden turn in fortune's wheel went to the heads of the adventurous and covetous Englishmen in Bengal. They were masters of Bengal and there was no one to hold their hands. So, headed by Clive, they dipped into the public treasury of the province and completely drained it. Clive made a present to himself of about two and a half million rupees in cash and, not content with this, took also a very valuable *jāgīr* or estate yielding several lakhs a year! All the other English people " compensated " themselves in a like way. There was a shameless scramble for riches, and the greed and unscrupulousness of the officials of the East India Company passed all bounds. The English became the nawab-makers of Bengal and changed nawabs at will. With each change there was bribery and enormous presents. They had no responsibility for government—that was the poor, changing nawab's job; their job was to get rich quick.

A few years later, in 1764, the British won another battle, at Buxar, which resulted in the nominal Emperor at Delhi submitting to them. He became their pensioner. The mastery of the British in Bengal and Bihar was now unchallenged. They were not content with the vast plunder they were taking from the country, and they set about finding new ways of making money. They had nothing to do with internal trade. Now they insisted on carrying on this trade without paying the transit duties which all other merchants dealing with home-made goods had to pay. This was one of the first blows struck by the British at India's manufacturers and trade.

The position of the British in northern India was now one of power and wealth without any responsibility. The merchant adventurers of the East India Company did not trouble to distinguish between bona-fide trade and unfair trade and plunder pure and simple. These were the days when Englishmen returned to England from India overflowing with Indian money, and were called " Nabobs ". If you have read Thackeray's *Vanity Fair* you will remember such a bloated person in it.

Political insecurity and troubles, want of rain, and the British policy of grab, all combined to bring about a most terrible famine in Bengal and Bihar in 1770. It is said that more than a third of

the population of these areas perished.   Think of this awful figure !
How many millions died of slow starvation !   Whole areas were
depopulated, and jungles grew up and swallowed cultivated fields
and villages.   Nobody did anything to help the starving people.
The Nawab had no power or authority or inclination.   The East
India Company had the power and authority, but they felt no
responsibility or inclination.   Their job was to gather money and
to collect revenue, and they did this so efficiently and satisfactorily
for their own pockets that, wonderful to relate, in spite of the
great famine, and although over a third of the population disappeared, they collected the full amount of revenue from the survivors !   Indeed, they collected even more, and they did this, as
the official report puts it, " violently ".   It is difficult to grasp fully
the inhumanity of this forcible and violent collection from the
starved and miserable survivors of a mighty calamity.

In spite of the victory of the English in Bengal and over the
French, they had to face great difficulties in the south.   There
were defeats and humiliations for them before final victory came.
Haider Ali of Mysore was their bitter opponent.   He was an able
and fierce leader, and he repeatedly defeated the English forces.
In 1769 he dictated terms of peace favourable to himself under the
very walls of Madras.   Ten years later he was again successful in
a large measure, and after his death his son, Tippu Sultan, became
a thorn in the side of the British.   It took two more Mysore wars
and many years to defeat finally Tippu.   An ancestor of the present
Maharaja of Mysore was then installed as a ruler under the protection of the British.

The Marathas also defeated the British in the south in 1782.
In the north, Scindia of Gwalior was dominant and controlled the
poor hapless Emperor of Delhi.

Meanwhile Warren Hastings was sent from England, and he
became the first Governor-General.   The British Parliament now
began to take interest in India.   Hastings is supposed to be the
greatest of English rulers in India, but even in his time the government was well known to be corrupt and full of abuses.   Some
instances of extortion of large sums of money by Hastings have
become famous.   On his return to England Hastings was impeached
before Parliament for his Indian administration and, after a long
trial, was acquitted.   Previously, Clive had also been censured by
Parliament, and he actually committed suicide.   So England satisfied her conscience by censuring or trying these men, but in her
heart she admired them, and was willing enough to profit by their
policy.   Clive and Hastings may be censured, but they are the
typical empire-builders, and so long as empires have to be forcibly
imposed on subject people, and these people exploited, such men will
come to the front and will gain admiration.   Methods of exploitation
may differ from age to age, but the spirit is the same.   Clive may have
been censured by the British Parliament, but they have put up a
statue to him in front of the India Office in Whitehall in London, and
inside, his spirit dwells and fashions British policy in India.

Hastings started the policy of having puppet Indian princes under British control. So we have to thank him partly for the crowds of gilded and empty-headed maharajas and nawabs who strut about the Indian scene, and make a nuisance of themselves.

As the British Empire grew in India there were many more wars with the Marathas, Afghans, Sikhs, Burmans, etc. But the unique thing about these wars was that although they were carried on for England's benefit, India paid for them. No burden fell on England or the English people. They only reaped the profit.

Remember that the East India Company—a trading company— was governing India. There was growing control by the British Parliament, but, in the main, India's destinies were in the hands of a set of merchant adventurers. Government was largely trade, trade was largely plunder. The lines of distinction were thin. Enormous dividends of 100 per cent. and 150 per cent. and over 200 per cent. per year were paid by the Company to its share-holders. And, apart from this, its agents in India picked up tidy little sums, as we have seen in the case of Clive. The officials of the Company also took trade monopolies and built up huge fortunes in this way with great rapidity. Such was the Company's régime in India.

93

A GREAT MANCHU RULER IN CHINA

September 15, 1932

I AM shaken up completely and I know not what to do. News has come, terrible news, that Bapu has determined to starve him-self to death. My little world, in which he has occupied such a big place, shakes and totters, and there seems to be darkness and emptiness everywhere. His picture comes before my eyes again and again—it was the last time I saw him, just over a year ago, standing on the deck of the ship that was taking him away from India to the West. Shall I not see him again ? And whom shall I go to when I am in doubt and require wise counsel, or am afflicted and in sorrow and need loving comfort ? What shall we all do when our beloved chief who inspired us and led us has gone ? Oh, India is a horrid country to allow her great men to die so ; and the people of India are slaves and have the minds of slaves to bicker and quarrel about trivial nothings and forget freedom itself.

I have been in no mood to write and I have thought even of ending this series of letters. But that would be a foolish thing. What can I do in this cell of mine but read and write and think ? And what can comfort me more when I am weary and distraught than thought of you and writing to you ? Sorrow and tears are poor companions in this world. " More tears have been shed than the waters that are in the great ocean," said the Buddha, and

many more tears will be shed before this unhappy world is put
right. Our task still lies ahead of us, the great work still beckons,
and there can be no rest for us and for those who follow us till
that work is completed. So I have decided to carry on with my
usual routine, and I shall write to you as before.

My last few letters have been about India, and the latter part
of the tale I have told has not been an edifying one. India was
lying prostrate, a prey to every brigand and adventurer. China,
her great sister in the East, was in a much better way, and to China
we must go now.

You will remember my telling you (Letter 80) of the prosperous
days of the Ming period, and how corruption and disruption came,
and China's northern neighbours, the Manchus, came down and
conquered. From 1650 onwards the Manchus were firmly established all over China. Under this semi-foreign dynasty China grew
strong, and even aggressive. The Manchus brought a new energy,
and, while they interfered as little as possible with China internally,
they spent their superfluous energy in extending their empire to
the north and west and south.

A new dynasty usually produces some capable rulers to begin
with and then tails off into incompetents. So also the Manchus
produced some unusually able and competent rulers and statesmen.
The second Emperor was Kang Hi. He was only eight years old
when he came to the throne. For sixty-one years he was the
monarch of an empire which was larger and more populous than
any other in the world. But his place in history is not secured
because of this or because of his military prowess. He is remembered because of his statesmanship and his remarkable literary
activities. He was the Emperor from 1661 to 1722—that is, for
fifty-four years he was the contemporary of Louis XIV, the " Grand
Monarque " of France. Both of them reigned for tremendously
long periods, Louis winning in this race for setting up a record
by reigning for seventy-two years. It is interesting to compare
the two, but the comparison is all to the disadvantage of Louis.
He ruined his country and exhausted and burdened her with vast
debts. He was intolerant in religion. Kang Hi was an earnest
Confucian, but he was tolerant of other faiths. Under him, indeed
under the first four Manchu emperors, the Ming culture was left
undisturbed. It retained its high standard and in some respects
improved upon it. Industry, art, literature and education flourished
as in the days of the Mings. Wonderful porcelain continued to be
produced. Colour-printing was invented, and copper-engraving
learnt from the Jesuits.

The secret of the statesmanship and success of the Manchu rulers
lay in their identifying themselves completely with Chinese culture.
Absorbing Chinese thought and culture, they did not lose the
energy and activity of the less civilized Manchus. And so Kang
Hi was an unusual and curious mixture—a diligent student of
philosophy and literature, absorbed in cultural activities, and an
efficient military head, rather fond of conquest. He was no mere

dilettante or superficial lover of literature and the arts. Among his literary activities the three following works, prepared at his suggestion, and often under his personal supervision, will give you some idea of the depth of his interest and learning.

The Chinese language, you will remember, consists of characters, not words. Kang Hi had a lexicon or dictionary of the language prepared. This was a mighty work containing over 40,000 characters, with numerous phrases illustrating them. It is said to be unrivalled even to-day.

Another of the productions which we owe to Kang Hi's enthusiasm was a huge illustrated encyclopædia, a wonderful work running into several hundred volumes. This was a complete library in itself; everything was dealt with, every subject considered. The book was printed from movable copper plates after Kang Hi's death.

The third important work I shall mention here was a concordance of the whole of Chinese literature—that is, a kind of dictionary in which words and passages are collected and compared. This also was an extraordinary piece of work, as it involved a close study of the whole of literature. Full quotations from poets, historians and essayists were given.

There were many literary activities of Kang Hi, but these three are enough to impress any one. I can think of no similar modern work to compare with any of these except the great *Oxford English Dictionary*, which took over fifty years' labour of a large number of scholars, and was only completed a few years ago.

Kang Hi was quite favourable to Christianity and Christian missionaries. He encouraged foreign trade and threw open all the ports of China to it. But soon he discovered that the Europeans misbehaved and had to be kept in check. He suspected the missionaries, not without good reason, of intriguing with the imperialists of their home governments to facilitate conquest. This made him give up his tolerant attitude to Christianity. His suspicions were confirmed later by a report received from a Chinese military officer at Canton. In this report it was pointed out how close the connection was in the Philippines and in Japan between European governments and their merchants and missionaries. The officer therefore recommended that in order to safeguard the Empire from invasion and foreign intrigue, foreign trade should be restricted and the spread of Christianity stopped.

This report was presented in 1717. It throws a flood of light on foreign intrigues in eastern countries and on the motives which led some of these countries to restrict foreign trade and the spread of Christianity. Some such development also took place, you may remember, in Japan, which led to the shutting up of the country. It is often stated that the Chinese and others are backward and ignorant and hate foreigners and put difficulties in the way of trade. As a matter of fact our review of history has shown to us clearly enough that there was abundant intercourse between India and China and other countries from the earliest times. There was no question of hating foreigners or foreign trade. For a long time, indeed, India controlled many foreign markets. It was only when foreign trade missions became the recognized methods of imperialist expansion of the western European Powers, that they became suspect in the East.

The report of the Canton officer was considered by the Chinese Grand Council of State and approved. Thereupon the Emperor Kang Hi took action accordingly, and issued decrees strictly limiting foreign trade and missionary activity.

I am now going to leave China proper for a while and take you to the north of Asia—Siberia—and tell you what was happening there. The vast expanse of Siberia connects China in the far east with Russia in the west. I have told you that the Manchu Empire in China was an aggressive one. It included Manchuria, of course; it spread to Mongolia and beyond. Russia also, having driven out the Mongols of the Golden Horde, had become a strong centralized State, and was spreading out to the east, across the Siberian plains. The two empires now meet in Siberia.

The rapid weakening and decay of the Mongols in Asia is one of the strange facts of history. These people, who thundered across Asia and Europe, and conquered the greater part of the known world under Chengiz and his descendants, sink into oblivion. Under Timur they rose again for a while, but his empire died with him. After him, some of his descendants, called the Timurids, reigned in Central Asia, and we know that a well-known school of painting flourished in their Courts. Babar, who came to India, was a Timurid. In spite of these Timurid rulers, however, the Mongol race, right across Asia, from Russia to its homeland in Mongolia, decayed and lost all importance. Why it did so, no one seems to know. Some suggest that changes in climate had something to do with it; others are of a different opinion. Anyway, the old conquerors and invaders are now themselves invaded from right and left.

After the break-up of the Mongol Empire the overland routes across Asia were closed up for nearly 200 years. In the second half of the sixteenth century, however, the Russians sent an embassy overland to China. They tried to establish diplomatic relations with the Ming emperors, without success. Soon after, a Russian bandit of the name of Yermak crossed the Ural Mountains at the head of a band of Cossacks and conquered the little State of Sibir. It was from the name of this State that the name of Siberia is derived.

This was in 1581, and from that date the Russians went farther and farther to the east, till they reached the Pacific Ocean in about fifty years. Soon they came in conflict with the Chinese in the Amur Valley, and there was fighting between the two, resulting in the defeat of the Russians. In 1689 there was a treaty between the two countries—the Treaty of Nerchinsk. Boundaries were fixed and trade arrangements made. This was the first Chinese treaty with a European country. The treaty checked Russian advance, but a considerable caravan trade developed. At that time the Russian Tsar was Peter the Great, and he was anxious to develop close relations with China. He sent two embassies to Kang Hi and then kept a permanent envoy at the Chinese Court.

From the earliest days China was in the habit of receiving foreign embassies. I think I mentioned in one of my letters that the Roman Emperor, Marcus Aurelius Antonius, sent an embassy in the second century after Christ. It is interesting to find that in 1656 Dutch and Russian embassies went to the Chinese Court and they found envoys from the Great Moghal there. These must have been sent by Shah Jahan.

94

A CHINESE EMPEROR WRITES TO AN ENGLISH KING

September 16, 1932

THE Manchu emperors seem to have been extraordinarily long-lived. The grandson of Kang Hi was the fourth Emperor, Chien Lung. He also reigned for the tremendous period of sixty years, from 1736 to 1796. He was like his grandfather in other respects also; his two main interests were literary activities and extension of empire. He had a great search made for all literary works worthy of preservation. These were collected and were catalogued in great detail. Catalogue is hardly the word for it, as all the facts known about each work were put down and critical remarks were added. This mighty descriptive catalogue of the Imperial Library was under four heads : classics, that is, Confucianism ; history, philosophy; and general literature. It is said that there is no parallel to such a work anywhere.

About this time also Chinese novels, short stories and plays developed, and attained a high standard. It is interesting to note that in England also the novel was then developing. Chinese porcelain and other fine works of art were in demand in Europe, and there was a continuous trade in them. More interesting was the beginning of the tea trade. This began in the days of the first Manchu emperor. Tea reached England probably in the reign of Charles II. Samuel Pepys, a famous diarist in English, has an entry in his diary in 1660 about drinking for the first time " Tee (a China drink) ". The tea trade developed tremendously, and 200 years later, in 1860, the export of tea from one Chinese port alone, Foochow, in one season, was one hundred million pounds. Later tea was cultivated in other places also, and, as you know, it is now extensively grown in India and Ceylon.

Chien Lung extended his empire by conquering Turkestan in Central Asia and occupying Tibet. Some years later, in 1790, the Gurkhas of Nepal invaded Tibet. Chien Lung thereupon not only drove out the Gurkhas from Tibet, but pursued them over the Himalayas into Nepal, and compelled Nepal to become a vassal State of the Chinese Empire. This conquest of Nepal was a remarkable achievement. For a Chinese army to cross Tibet and then the Himalayas and beat a warlike people like the Gurkhas in their very homeland, is amazing. As it happened, the British in India had trouble with Nepal only twenty-two years later, in 1814. They sent an army to Nepal, but this met with great difficulties, although it had no Himalayas to cross.

At the end of Chien Lung's reign in 1796 the Empire directly governed by him included Manchuria, Mongolia, Tibet and Turkestan. Vassal states admitting his suzerainty were : Korea, Annam, Siam and Burma. But conquest and the quest of military glory are expensive games to play. They result in heavy expenditure, and the burden of taxation grows. This burden always falls most on the poorest. Economic conditions were also changing, and this added to the discontent. Secret societies were formed all over the country. China, like Italy, has had quite a reputation for secret societies. Some of these had interesting names : White Lily Society, Society of Divine Justice, White Feather Society, Heaven and Earth Society.

Meanwhile, in spite of all restrictions, foreign trade was growing. There was great dissatisfaction among the foreign merchants at these restrictions. The East India Company, which had spread out to Canton, had the biggest share of the trade, and felt the restrictions most. These were the days, as we shall see in subsequent letters, when the so-called Industrial Revolution was beginning, and England was taking a lead in this. The steam engine had been made, and new methods and the use of machinery were making work easier and increasing production, especially of cotton goods. These extra goods that were made had to be sold, and new markets were therefore sought. England was very fortunate in controlling India just at this period, as she could take steps, as she in fact did, to force the sale of her goods there. But she wanted the China trade also.

So in 1792 the British Government sent an embassy, under Lord Macartney, to Peking. George III was then King of England. Chien Lung received them in audience and there was an exchange of presents. But the Emperor refused to make any change in the old restrictions on foreign trade. The answer which Chien Lung sent to George III is a very interesting document, and I shall give you a long extract from it. It runs thus :

" . . . You, O King, live beyond the confines of many seas, nevertheless, impelled by your humble desire to partake of the benefits of our civilization, you have despatched a mission respectfully bearing your memorial. . . . To show your devotion, you have also sent offerings of your country's produce. I have read your memorial : the earnest terms in which it is cast reveal a respectful humility on your part which is highly praiseworthy. . . .

" Swaying the wide world, I have but one aim in view, namely, to maintain a perfect governance and to fulfil the duties of the

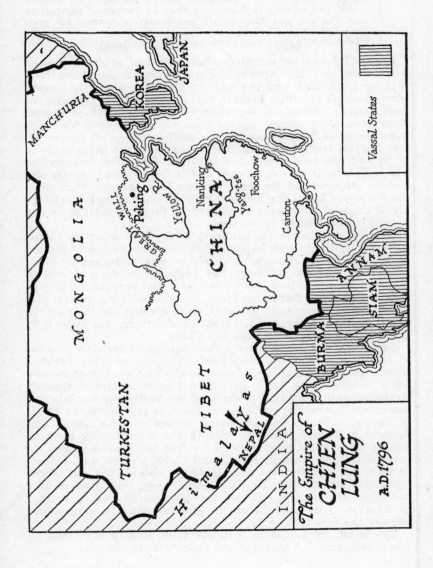

The Empire of CHIEN LUNG

A.D. 1796

State; strange and costly objects do not interest me. I . . . have no use for your country's manufactures. It behoves you, O King, to respect my sentiments and to display even greater devotion and loyalty in future, so that by perpetual submission to our Throne, you may secure peace and prosperity for your country hereafter. . .

" Tremblingly obey and show no negligence ! "

George III and his ministers must have had a bit of a shock when they read this answer ! But the serene confidence in a superior civilization and the majesty of power which the answer shows had no enduring basis in fact. The Manchu Government looked strong, and was strong, under Chien Lung. But its foundations were being sapped by the changing economic order. The secret societies I have mentioned were indications of discontent. But the real trouble was that the country was not being made to fit in with the new economic conditions. The West, meanwhile, was the leader in this new order, and it forged ahead rapidly and became stronger and stronger. In less than seventy years after the Emperor Chien Lung had sent his very superior reply to George III of England, China was humiliated by England and France and her pride was dragged in the dust.

I must keep that story, however, for my next letter on China. With the death of Chien Lung in 1796 we reach practically the end of the eighteenth century. But before this century had ended much that was extraordinary had happened in America and in Europe. It was indeed due to the wars and troubles in Europe that the Western pressure on China was lessened for a quarter of a century. So in our next letter we go to Europe and take up the tale from the beginning of the eighteenth century, and make it fit in with developments in India and China.

But before I end this letter I shall tell you of Russia's progress in the East. After the Treaty of Nerchinsk in 1689 between Russia and China, Russian influence in the East went on increasing for a century and a half. In 1728 a Danish captain in Russia's service, named Vitus Bering, explored the strait between Asia and America. This strait, perhaps you know, is still called the Strait of Bering, after his name. Bering crossed over to Alaska and declared it Russian territory. Alaska was a great place for furs, and as there was a large demand for furs in China, a special fur trade developed between Russia and China. There was, indeed, so much demand for furs, etc., in China towards the end of the eighteenth century that Russia imported them from Hudson Bay in Canada, via England, and then sent them to the great fur market in Kiakhta near Lake Baikal in Siberia. What a tremendous journey the furs took !

This letter, for a change, is shorter than most of my letters to you in this series. I hope you will appreciate the change.

95

THE WAR OF IDEAS IN EIGHTEENTH-CENTURY EUROPE

September 19, 1932

WE shall go back to Europe now and follow its changing destiny. It is on the eve of mighty changes which impressed themselves on the world's history. To understand these changes we shall have to pry underneath the surface of things, and try to find out what was passing in the minds of men. For action, as we see it, is the result of a complex of thoughts and passions, prejudices and superstitions, hopes and fears; and the action by itself is difficult to understand unless we consider with it the causes that led up to it. But this is no easy matter; and even if I were capable of writing pertinently about these causes and motives which fashion the outstanding events of history, I would not think of making these letters duller and heavier than they already are. Sometimes I fear that in my enthusiasm for a subject, or for a certain point of view, I rush into deeper water than I should. You will have to put up with that, I am afraid. We cannot therefore go deeply into these causes. But it would be exceedingly foolish to ignore them; and indeed if we did so we would miss the fascination and significance of history.

We have considered the upheavals and disorders of Europe during the sixteenth and the first half of the seventeenth centuries. In the middle of the seventeenth century there was the Treaty of Westphalia (1648) which ended the terrible Thirty Years' War; and, the year after, the civil war in England ended and Charles I lost his head. There followed a period of comparative peace. The continent of Europe was thoroughly exhausted. Trade with the colonies in America and elsewhere brought money to Europe, and this gave relief and lessened the tension between different classes.

In England there came the peaceful revolution which drove away James II and gave the victory to Parliament (1688). The real fight had been won by Parliament in the civil war against Charles I. The peaceful revolution merely confirmed the decision arrived at forty years previously by force of arms.

The king had thus to take a back seat in England, but on the continent it was otherwise, except in a few small areas, like Switzerland and Holland. Absolute and irresponsible monarchs were still the fashion there, and Louis XIV of France, the Grand Monarque, was the model and the paragon to be followed by others. The seventeenth century is practically the century of Louis XIV on the continent of Europe. Heedless of the doom that awaited their kind, and not even taking a lesson from the fate of Charles I of England, the kings of Europe went on playing the autocrat with all pomp and circumstance and folly. They claimed all the power and all the wealth of the land, and their country was to them almost like a private estate. Over 400 years ago a famous Dutch scholar, Erasmus, wrote :

"Of all the birds the eagle alone has seemed to wise men the type of royalty—not beautiful, not musical, not fit for food, but carnivorous, greedy, hateful to all, the curse of all, and, with its great powers of doing harm, surpassing them in its desire of doing it."

Kings have almost disappeared to-day, and such as remain are relics of a past age, with little or no power. We can now ignore them. But other and more dangerous people have taken their place, and the eagle is still a fitting emblem for these latter-day imperialists and kings of iron and oil and silver and gold.

The monarchies of Europe developed strong centralized States. The old feudal ideas of lord and vassal were dead or dying. The new idea of country as a unit and an entity took its place. France, under two very able ministers, Richelieu and Mazarin, was the leader in this. So nationalism grew, and a measure of patriotism. Religion, which had so far been the most important element in men's lives, retired into the background and new ideas took its place, as I hope to tell you later in this letter.

The seventeenth century is even more notable, in that the foundations of modern science were laid in it, and a world market was created. This vast new market naturally upset the old economy of Europe, and much that subsequently happened in Europe and Asia and America can only be understood if this new market is kept in view. Science developed later, and provided means to supply the needs of this world market.

In the eighteenth century the race for colonies and empire, especially between England and France, resulted in war not only in Europe but in Canada and, as we have seen, in India. After these wars in the middle of the century there was again a period of comparative peace. The surface of Europe appeared to be calm and almost unruffled. The numerous Courts of Europe were full of very polite and cultured and fine ladies and gentlemen. But the calm was on the surface only. Underneath there was turmoil, and the minds of men were troubled and agitated by new thoughts and ideas; and the bodies of men, apart from the charmed circle of the Courts and some of the upper classes, were subjected to greater and greater suffering owing to increasing poverty. The calm in the second half of the eighteenth century in Europe was thus a very deceptive one; it was the prelude to a storm. On the 14th of July, 1789, the storm broke in the capital of the greatest of European monarchies—Paris. It swept away this monarchy and a hundred other out-of-date and moss-grown customs and privileges.

This storm and subsequent change were long prepared in France, and partly in other European countries also, by new ideas. Right through the Middle Ages religion was the dominant factor in Europe. Even afterwards, during the days of the Reformation, this continued to be so. Every question, whether it was political or economic, was considered from the point of view of religion. Religion was organized and meant the views of the Pope or the high officials of the Church. The organization of society was rather like caste in India. The idea of caste originally was a division according to professions or functions. It was this very idea of social classes according to functions that lay at the basis of the ideas of the Middle Ages on society. Within a class, as within a caste in India, there was equality. As between two or more classes, however, there was inequality. This inequality was at the very basis of the whole social structure, and no one challenged it. Those who suffered under this system were told to " expect their reward in heaven ". In this way religion tried to uphold the unjust social order and tried to distract people's minds from it by talking of the next world. It also preached what is called the doctrine of trustee-ship—that is to say, that the rich man was a kind of trustee for the poor; the landlord held his land " in trust " for his tenant. This was the Church's way of explaining a very awkward situation. It made little difference to the rich man, and it brought no comfort to the poor. Clever explanations cannot take the place of food in a hungry stomach.

The bitter religious wars between Catholic and Protestant, the intolerance of both the Catholic and the Calvinist, and the Inqui-sition, all resulted from this intense religious and communal outlook. Think of it ! Many hundreds of thousands of women are said to have been burnt in Europe as witches, mostly by Puritans. New ideas in science were suppressed because these were supposed to be in conflict with the Church's view of things. It was a static, an unmoving view of life; there was no question of progress.

We find that these ideas begin to change gradually from the sixteenth century onwards; science appears and the all-embracing hold of religion lessens; politics and economics are considered apart from religion. There is, it is said, a growth of rationalism—that is, of reason as opposed to blind faith—in the seventeenth and eigh-teenth centuries. The eighteenth century, indeed, is supposed to have established the victory of toleration. This is partly true. But the victory really meant that people had given up attaching as much importance to their religion as they used to. Toleration was very near to indifference. When people are terribly keen about anything they are seldom tolerant about it; it is only when they care little for it that they graciously proclaim that they are tolerant. With the coming of industrialism and the big machine, the indiffer-ence to religion grew even more. Science sapped the foundations of the old belief in Europe; the new industry and economics pre-sented new problems which filled people's minds. So people in Europe gave up (but not entirely) the habit of breaking each other's heads on questions of religious belief or dogma; instead, they took to breaking heads on economic and social issues.

It is interesting and instructive to compare this religious period of Europe with India to-day. India is often called, both in praise and in derision, a religious and spiritual country. It is contrasted with Europe, which is called irreligious and too fond of the good things of life. As a matter of fact this " religious " India is extraordinarily like Europe in the sixteenth century in so far as religion colours the Indian outlook. Of course we cannot carry the comparison too far. But it is very clear that we have the same phenomena here in our over-emphasis on questions of religious faith and dogma, in our mixing up political and economic questions with the interests of religious groups, in our communal quarrels, and similar questions, as existed in medieval Europe. There is no question of a practical and materialistic West and a spiritual and other-worldly East. The difference is between an industrial and highly mechanized West, with all its accompanying good and bad points, and an East which is still largely pre-industrial and agricultural.

This growth of toleration and rationalism in Europe was a slow process. It was not helped much at first by books, as people were afraid to criticize Christianity publicly. To do so meant imprisonment or some other punishment. A German philosopher was banished from Prussia because he had praised Confucius too much. This was interpreted as a slight on Christianity. In the eighteenth century, however, as these new ideas became clearer and more general, books came out dealing with these subjects. The most famous writer of the time on rationalistic and other subjects was Voltaire, a Frenchman, who was imprisoned and banished, and who ultimately lived at Ferney near Geneva. When in prison he was not allowed paper or ink. So he wrote verses with pieces of lead between the lines of a book. He became a celebrity when quite young. Indeed, he was only ten when he attracted attention by his unusual ability. Voltaire hated injustice and bigotry and he waged war against them. His famous cry was *Ecrasez l'infâme*. He lived to a great old age (1694–1778) and wrote an enormous number of books. Because he criticized Christianity he was fiercely hated by orthodox Christians. In one of his books he says that " a man who accepts his religion without examining it is like an ox which allows itself to be harnessed ". Voltaire's writings had great influence in making people incline towards rationalism and the new ideas. His old house at Ferney is still a place of pilgrimage for many.

Another great writer, a contemporary of Voltaire but younger than him, was Jean Jacques Rousseau. He was born in Geneva, and Geneva is very proud of him. Do you remember his statue there ? Rousseau's writings on religion and politics raised quite an outcry. None the less, his novel and rather daring social and political theories set the minds of many afire with new ideas and new resolves. His political theories are out of date now, but they played an important part in preparing the people of France for the great revolution. Rousseau did not preach revolution, probably he did not even expect one. But his books and ideas certainly sowed the seed in men's minds which blossomed out in the revolution.

His best known book is the "Social Contract"—*Du Contrat Social*—and this begins with a famous sentence (I quote from memory) : "Man is born free, but is everywhere in chains."

Rousseau was also a great educationist, and many of the new methods of teaching he suggested are now used in schools.

Besides Voltaire and Rousseau there were many other notable thinkers and writers in France in the eighteenth century. I shall only mention one other name—Montesquieu, who wrote, besides other books, the *Esprit des Lois*. An Encyclopædia also came out in Paris about this time, and this was full of articles by Diderot and other able writers on political and social subjects. Indeed, France seemed to be full of philosophers and thinkers, and, what is more, they were widely read and they succeeded in making large numbers of ordinary people think their thoughts and discuss their theories. Thus there grew up in France a strong body of opinion opposed to religious intolerance and political and social privilege. A vague desire for liberty possessed the people. And yet, curiously, neither the philosophers nor the people wanted to get rid of the king. The idea of a republic was not a common one then, and people still hoped that they might have an ideal prince, something like Plato's philosopher king, who would remove their burdens and give them justice and a measure of liberty. At any rate this is what the philosophers write. One is inclined to doubt how far the suffering masses loved the king.

In England there was no such development of political thought as in France. It is said that the Englishman is not a political animal, whilst the Frenchman is. Apart from this the English revolution of 1688 had relieved the tension somewhat. There was, however, plenty of privilege still enjoyed by certain classes. New economic developments, about which I shall tell you something in another letter soon, and trade and entanglements in America and India, kept the English mind busy. And when social tension became great, a temporary compromise averted the danger of a break. In France there was no room for such compromise, and hence the upset.

It is interesting to note, however, that the modern novel developed in England about the middle of the eighteenth century. *Gulliver's Travels* and *Robinson Crusoe* both appeared, as I have already told you, early in the eighteenth century. They were followed by real novels. A new reading public comes into evidence in England at this time.

It was in the eighteenth century also that the Englishman Gibbon wrote his famous *Decline and Fall of the Roman Empire*. I have, already referred to him and his book in a previous letter of mine when I dealt with the Roman Empire.

96

EUROPE ON THE EVE OF GREAT CHANGES

September 24, 1932

WE have tried to have a little peep into the minds of the men and women of the eighteenth century in Europe, especially in France. It has been just a glimpse revealing to us some new ideas growing and battling with the old. Having been behind the scenes, we shall now have a look at the actors on the public stage of Europe.

In France old Louis XIV finally succeeded in dying in 1715. He had outlived several generations, and he was succeeded by his great-grandson, who became Louis XV. There was another long reign of fifty-nine years. Thus two successive kings of France, Louis XIV and XV, reigned for a total period of 131 years! Surely this must be a world record. The two Manchu emperors in China, Kang Hi and Chien Lung, each reigned for over sixty years, but they did not follow each other, and there was a third reign in between.

Apart from its extraordinary length, the reign of Louis XV was chiefly remarkable for its disgusting corruption and intrigue. The resources of the kingdom were used for the pleasures of the king. There was extravagance at Court based on graft. The men and women at Court who happened to please the king got free gifts of land and sinecure offices, which meant income without work. And the burden of all this fell more and more on the masses. Autocracy and incompetence and corruption went hand in hand, merrily forward. Is it surprising that before the century was over, they came to the end of their path and stepped into the abyss? What does surprise us is that the path was such a long one and the fall came so late. Louis XV escaped the people's judgment and vengeance; it was his successor in 1774, Louis XVI, who had to face this.

In spite of his incompetence and depravity, Louis XV had no doubts about his absolute authority in the State. He was everything, and no one could challenge his right to do anything he chose. Listen to what he said, addressing an assembly in Paris in 1766 :

> "*C'est en ma personne seul que reside l'autorité souveraine.* . . . *C'est à moi seul qu'appartient le pouvoir législatif sans dépendance et sans partage. L'ordre public tout entier émane de moi ; j'en suis le gardien suprême. Mon peuple n'est qu'un avec moi ; les droits et les intérêts de la nation, dont on ose faire un corps séparé du monarque, sont nécessairement unis avec les miens et ne reposent qu'entre mes mains.*"

Such was the ruler of France for the greater part of the eighteenth century. He seemed to dominate Europe for a while, but then he came into conflict with the ambitions of other kings and peoples, and had to acknowledge defeat. Some of the old rivals of France no longer played a dominant part on the European stage, but others arose to take their place and challenge the French power. Proud Spain had fallen back both in Europe and elsewhere after her brief day of imperial glory. But she still held large colonies in America and the Philippine Islands. The Hapsburgs of Austria, who had so long monopolized the headship of the Empire and, through this, the leadership of Europe, were also no longer so prominent as they used to be. Austria was not the leading State of the Empire now; another, Prussia, had risen and become equally important. There were wars about the Austrian succession to the crown, and for a long period a woman, Maria Theresa, occupied it.

The Treaty of Westphalia of 1648, you will remember, had made Prussia one of the important Powers of Europe. The House of Hohenzollern ruled there and challenged the supremacy of the other German dynasty—the House of Hapsburg in Austria. For forty-six years (1740-1786) Prussia was ruled by Frederick, who has been called, because of his military success, the Great. He was an absolute monarch, like the others in Europe, but he put on the pose of a philosopher and tried to be friends with Voltaire. He built up a strong army and was a successful general. He called himself a rationalist and is reported to have said that " everyone should be allowed to get to heaven in his own way ".

From the seventeenth century onwards French culture was dominant in Europe. In the middle years of the eighteenth century this became even more marked, and Voltaire had a tremendous European reputation. Indeed, some people even call this century " the century of Voltaire ". French literature was read in all the Courts of Europe, even in backward St. Petersburg, and cultured and educated people preferred writing and speaking in French. Thus Frederick the Great of Prussia almost always wrote and spoke in French. He even tried writing French poetry, which he wanted Voltaire to correct and polish up for him.

East of Prussia lay Russia, already growing into the giant of later years. We have seen, when we were considering Chinese history, how Russia spread across Siberia to the Pacific, and even crossed to Alaska. Towards the end of the seventeenth century Russia had a strong ruler, Peter the Great. Peter wanted to put an end to many of the old Mongolian associations and outlook that Russia had inherited. He wanted to " westernize " her, as they say. So he left his old capital, Moscow, which was full of the old traditions, and built himself a new city and a new capital. This was St. Petersburg, in the north, on the banks of the Neva, at the head of the Gulf of Finland. This city was quite unlike Moscow with its golden cupolas and domes; it was more like the great cities of western Europe. Petersburg became the symbol of " westernization ", and Russia began to play a greater part in European politics. Perhaps you know that Petersburg, the name, is no more. Twice in the course of the last twenty years it has changed its name. The first change was to Petrograd, and the second one, which now holds, to Leningrad.

Peter the Great made many changes in Russia. I shall mention

one which will interest you. He put an end to the practice of the
seclusion of women, called *terem*, which prevailed in Russia at the
time. Peter had his eyes on India and knew the value of India in
international politics. In his will he wrote : " Bear in mind that
the commerce of India is the commerce of the world; and that he
who can exclusively command it is dictator of Europe ". His last
words were justified by the rapid growth in England's power after
she gained dominion over India. The exploitation of India gave
England prestige and wealth, and made her for several generations
the leading Power of the world.

Between Prussia and Austria, on the one side, and Russia, on
the other, lay Poland. It was a backward country with a poor
peasantry. There was little trade or industry and no great towns.
It had a curious constitution with an elected king, and with the
power in the hands of the feudal aristocrats. As the countries
surrounding it became stronger, Poland became weaker. Prussia
and Russia and Austria eyed it hungrily.

And yet it was the King of Poland that had beaten back the last
Turkish attack on Vienna in 1683. The Ottoman Turks were not
aggressive again. They had exhausted their energy and the tide
turned gradually. Henceforward they were on the defensive, and
slowly the Turkish Empire in Europe began to shrink. But in the
first half of the eighteenth century, the period we are considering,
Turkey was a powerful country in the south-east of Europe, and
her empire extended over the Balkans and across Hungary to
Poland.

Italy in the south was split up under different rulers and did not
count for much in European politics. The Pope no longer played
a commanding rôle, and the kings and princes, while treating him
with deference, ignored him in political matters. Gradually a new
system was arising in Europe, the system of great Powers. Strong
centralized monarchies, as I told you, helped to develop the idea of
a nation. People began to think of their countries in a peculiar
way, which is common enough to-day, but was uncommon before
this period. France, England or Britannia, Italia and other similar
figures, begin to emerge. They seem to symbolize the nation.
Later on, in the nineteenth century, these figures take definite shape
in the minds of men and women and move their hearts strangely.
They become the new goddesses at whose altar every patriot is
supposed to worship, and in their name and on their behalf patriots
fight and kill each other. You know how the idea of *Bhārat Mātā*
—mother India—moves all of us, and how for this mythical and
imaginary figure people gladly suffer and give their lives. So
people in other countries felt also for their idea of their motherland.
But all this was a later development. For the present I want to
tell you that the eighteenth century saw this idea of nationality
and patriotism take root. The French philosophers helped in this
process, and the great French Revolution put the seal on this idea.

These nations were the " Powers ". Kings came and went, but
the nation continued. Of these Powers gradually some stood out

as more important than the others. Thus in the early eighteenth-century France, England, Austria, Prussia and Russia were definitely " Great Powers ". Some others, like Spain, were in theory great, but they were declining.

England was rapidly gaining in wealth and importance. Up to the time of Elizabeth she had not been an important country in the European sense, and much less so in the world sense. Her population was small; probably it did not exceed 6,000,000 at the time, which is far less than the population of London now. But with the Puritan revolution and the victory of Parliament over the king, England adapted herself to the new conditions and went ahead. So also did Holland, after the yoke of Spain had been shaken off.

In the eighteenth century there was a scramble for colonies in America and Asia. Many European Powers took part in this, but the chief contest ultimately lay between two—England and France. England had got a great lead in the race, both in America and India. France, apart from being incompetently governed by Louis XV, was too much involved in European politics. From 1756 to 1763 war was waged between these two Powers, as well as several others, in Europe and Canada and India to decide as to who was to be master. This war is called the Seven Years' War. We saw a bit of it in India when France was defeated. In Canada also England won. In Europe, England followed a policy, for which she has become well known, of paying others to fight for her. Frederick the Great was her ally.

The result of this Seven Years' War was very favourable to England. Both in India and Canada she had no European rival left. On the seas her naval supremacy was established. Thus England was in a position to establish and extend her empire and to become a world Power. Prussia also increased in importance.

Europe was again exhausted by this fighting, and again there appeared to be comparative calm over the continent. But this calm did not prevent Prussia, Austria and Russia from swallowing up the kingdom of Poland. Poland was in no position to fight these Powers, and so these three wolves fell on her, and by partitioning her repeatedly, put an end to Poland as an independent country. There were three partitions—in 1772, 1793 and 1795. After the first of these, the Poles made a great effort to reform and strengthen their country. They established a parliament, and there was a revival of art and literature. But the autocratic monarchs surrounding Poland had tasted blood, and they were not to be baulked; besides, they had no love for parliaments. So, in spite of the patriotism of the Poles and the brave fight they put up under their great hero Kosciusko, Poland disappeared from the map of Europe in 1795. It disappeared then, but the Poles kept alive their patriotism and continued to dream of freedom, and 123 years later their dream was realized, when Poland reappeared as an independent country after the Great War.

I have said that there was a measure of calm in Europe in the

second half of the eighteenth century. But this did not last long,
and it was mostly on the surface. I have also told you of various
happenings in this century. But the eighteenth century is really
famous for three events—three revolutions—and everything else
that happened in Europe during these 100 years fades into insignificance when put beside these three. All these three revolutions
took place in the last quarter of the century. They were of three
distinct types—political, industrial, and social. The political
revolution took place in America. This was the revolt of the
British colonies there, resulting in the formation of an independent
republic, the United States of America, which was to become so
powerful in our own time. The Industrial Revolution began in
England and spread to other western European countries and then
elsewhere. It was a peaceful revolution, but a far-reaching one,
and it has influenced life all over the world more than anything in
recorded history before. It meant the coming of steam and the
big machine, and ultimately the innumerable offshoots of industrialism that we see around us. The social revolution was the
great French Revolution, which not only put an end to monarchy
in France, but also to innumerable privileges, and brought new
classes to the front. We shall have to study all these three
revolutions separately in some slight detail.

We have seen that on the eve of these great changes monarchies
were supreme in Europe. In England and Holland there were
parliaments, but they were controlled by aristocrats and the rich.
The laws were made for the rich, to protect their property and
rights and privileges. Education also was only for the rich and
privileged classes. Indeed, government itself was for these classes.
One of the great problems of the time was the problem of the poor.
Although conditions improved a little at the top, the misery of the
poor remained, and indeed became more marked.

Right through the eighteenth century the nations of Europe
carried on a cruel and heartless slave trade. Slaves, as such, had
ceased to exist in Europe, although the serfs or villeins, as the cultivators on the land were called, were little better than slaves. With
the discovery of America, however, the old slave trade was revived
in its most cruel form. The Spanish and Portuguese began it by
capturing Negroes on the African coast and taking them to America
to work on the land. The English took their full share in this
abominable trade. It is difficult for you or for any of us to have
any idea of the terrible sufferings of the Africans as they were hunted
and caught like wild beasts and then chained together, and so
transported to America. Vast numbers died before they could
even reach their journey's end. Of all those who have suffered in
this world, the Negroes have perhaps borne the heaviest burden.
Slavery was formally abolished in the nineteenth century, England
taking the lead. In the United States a civil war had to be fought
to decide this question. The millions of Negroes in the United
States of America to-day are the descendants of these slaves.

I shall finish this letter on a pleasant note by telling you of the great development of music in this century in Germany and Austria. As you know, Germans are the leaders in European music. Some of their great names appear even in the seventeenth century. As elsewhere, music in Europe was almost a part of religious ceremonial. Gradually this is separated, and music becomes an art by itself, apart from religion. Two great names stand out in the eighteenth century—Mozart and Beethoven. They were both infant prodigies, both composers of genius. Beethoven, perhaps the greatest musical composer of the West, became, strange to say, quite deaf, and so the wonderful music he created for others he could not hear himself. But his heart must have sung to him before he captured that music.

97

THE COMING OF THE BIG MACHINE

September 26, 1932

WE shall now consider what is called the Industrial Revolution. It began in England, and in England therefore we shall study it briefly. I can give no exact date for it, for the change did not take place on a particular date as if by magic. Yet it was rapid enough, and from the middle of the eighteenth century onwards, in less than 100 years, it changed the face of life. We have followed the course of history, you and I in these letters, from the earliest days for several thousand years, and we have noted many changes. But all these changes, great as they sometimes were, did not vitally alter the way life was lived by the people. If Socrates or Ashoka or Julius Cæsar had suddenly appeared in Akbar's Court in India, or in England or France in the early eighteenth century, they would have noticed many changes. They might have approved of some of these changes and disapproved of others. But on the whole they would have recognized the world, outwardly at any rate, for ideas would not have differed greatly. And, again so far as outward appearances went, they would not have felt wholly out of place in it. If they wanted to travel, they would have done so by horse or carriage drawn by horses, much as they used to do in their own time, and the time occupied in the journey would have been about the same.

But if any of the three came to our present-day world, he would be mightily surprised, and it may be that his surprise would often be a painful one. He would find that people travel now far faster than the fastest horse, swifter almost than the arrow from the bow. By railway and steamship and automobile and aeroplane they rush about at a terrific pace all over the world. Then he would be interested in the telegraph and the telephone and the wireless, and the vast number of books that modern printing-presses throw out, and newspapers and a host of other things—all children of the new forms of industry which the Industrial Revolution of the eighteenth century and after introduced. Whether Socrates or Ashoka or

Julius Cæsar would approve of these new methods or disapprove
of them, I cannot say, but there is no doubt that they would find
them radically different from the methods prevailing in their own
times.

The Industrial Revolution brought the big machine to the world.
It ushered in the Machine Age or the Mechanical Age. Of course
there had been machines before, but none had been so big as the
new machine. What is a machine? It is a big tool to help man
to do his work. Man has been called a tool-making animal, and
from his earliest days he has made tools and tried to better them.
His supremacy over the other animals, many of them more powerful
than he was, was established because of his tools. The tool was an
extension of his hand; or you may call it a third hand. The
machine was the extension of the tool. The tool and the machine
raised man above the brute creation. They freed human society
from the bondage of Nature. With the help of the tool and the
machine, man found it easier to produce things. He produced
more, and yet had more leisure. And this resulted in the progress
of the arts of civilization, and of thought and science.

But the big machine and all its allies have not been unmixed
blessings. If it has encouraged the growth of civilization, it has
also encouraged the growth of barbarism by producing terrible
weapons of warfare and destruction. If it has produced abundance,
this abundance has not been mainly for the masses, but chiefly for
the limited few. It has made the difference between the luxury of
the very rich and the poverty of the poor even greater than it was
in the past. Instead of being the tool and servant of man, it has
presumed to become his master. On the one side, it has taught
certain virtues—co-operation, organization, punctuality; on the
other, it has made life itself a dull routine for millions, a mechanical
burden with little of joy or freedom in it.

But why should we blame the poor machine for the ills that have
followed from it? The fault lies with man, who has misused it,
and with society, which has not profited by it fully. It seems to
be unthinkable that the world, or any country, can go back to the
old days before the Industrial Revolution, and it hardly seems
desirable or wise that, in order to get rid of some evils, we should
throw away the numerous good things that industrialism has brought
us. And, in any event, the machine has come and is going to stay.
Therefore the problem for us is to retain the good things of industrialism and to get rid of the evil that attaches to it. We must
profit by the wealth it produces, but see to it that the wealth is
evenly distributed among those who produce it.

This letter was meant to tell you something about the Industrial
Revolution in England. But, as is my habit, I have gone off at a
tangent and started discussing the effects of industrialism. I have
put before you a problem that is troubling people to-day. But
before we reach to-day we have to deal with yesterday; before we
consider the results of industrialism we must study when and how
it came. I have made this preamble so long in order to impress

you with the importance of this revolution. It was not a mere political revolution changing kings and rulers at the top. It was a revolution affecting all the various classes, and indeed everybody. The triumph of the machine and of industrialism meant the triumph of the classes that controlled the machine. As I told you long ago, the class that controls the means of production is the class that rules. In older times the only important means of production was the land, and therefore those who owned the land—that is, the landlords—were the bosses. In feudal times this was so. Other wealth than land then appears, and the landowning classes begin to share their power with the owners of the new means of production. And now comes the big machine, and naturally the classes that control this come to the front and become the bosses.

In the course of these letters I have told you on several occasions of how the *bourgeoisie* of the towns rose in importance and struggled with the feudal nobles and gained a measure of victory in some places. I have told you of the collapse of feudalism, and I have probably led you to imagine that the *bourgeoisie*—the new middle class—took its place. If so, I want to correct myself, for the rise to power of the middle class was much slower, and it had not taken place at the period we are discussing. It took a great revolution in France and the fear of a similar revolution in England for the *bourgeoisie* to gain power. The English Revolution of 1688 resulted in the victory of Parliament, but Parliament itself, you will remember, was a body representing a small number of people, chiefly landowners. Some big merchants from the towns might get into it, but on the whole the merchant class—the middle class —had no place in it.

Political power was thus in the hands of those who owned landed property. This was so in England, and even more so elsewhere. Landed property was inherited from father to son. Thus political power itself became an inherited privilege. I have already told you of " pocket boroughs " in England—that is, constituencies, returning members to Parliament, consisting of just a few electors. These few electors were usually under someone's control, and thus the borough was said to be in his pocket. Such elections were, of course, farcical, and there was a great deal of corruption and selling of votes and seats in Parliament. Some rich members of the rising middle class could afford to buy a seat in Parliament in this way. But the masses had no look-in either way. They inherited no privileges or power, and obviously they could not buy power. So what could they do when they were sat upon and exploited by the rich and the privileged ? They had no voice inside Parliament, or even in the election of members to Parliament. Even outside demonstrations by them were frowned upon by those in authority and put down by force. They were disorganized and weak and helpless. But when the cup of suffering and misery was over-full they forgot law and order and had a riot. There was thus a great deal of lawlessness in England in the eighteenth century. The general economic condition of the people was bad. It was made worse by the efforts of the big landlords to increase their estates at the expense of the small farmers who were squeezed out. Common land belonging to villages was also grabbed. All this increased the sufferings of the masses. The people also resented having no voice at all in the government, and there was a vague demand for more liberty.

In France the position was even worse, and led to the Revolution. In England the king was unimportant and more people shared the power. Besides, there was no such development of political ideas in England as in France. So England escaped a big outburst and the changes came to it more gradually. Meanwhile the rapid changes made by industrialism and the new economic structure forced the pace.

Such was the political background in England in the eighteenth century. In home industries England had forged ahead chiefly by the immigration of foreign artisans. The religious wars on the Continent forced many Protestants to leave their countries and homes and take refuge in England. At the time when the Spaniards were trying to crush the revolt in the Netherlands, large numbers of artisans fled from the Netherlands to England. It is said that 30,000 of them settled in the east of England, and Queen Elizabeth made it a condition of allowing them to settle that each house should employ one English apprentice. This helped England to build up her own cloth-making industry. When this was established, the English people prohibited the fabrics of the Netherlands from coming to England. Meanwhile the Netherlands were still in the midst of their fierce war for freedom, and their industries suffered. So it happened that while previously numerous vessels laden with the fabrics of the Netherlands went to England, soon after, not only was this stopped, but an opposite flow of English fabrics to the Netherlands began and increased in volume.

Thus the Walloons from Belgium taught the English cloth-making. Later came the Huguenots—Protestant refugees from France—and they taught the English silk-weaving. In the latter half of the seventeenth century large numbers of skilled workers came over from the Continent, and the English learned many trades from them, such as the making of paper, glass, mechanical toys, clocks and watches.

So England, which had so far been a backward country in Europe, grew in importance and wealth. London also grew, and became a fairly important port with a thriving population of merchants and traders. There is an interesting story which shows us that London was a considerable port and trading centre early in the seventeenth century. James I, the King of England who was father of Charles I, who lost his head, was a great believer in the autocracy and the divine right of kings. He did not like Parliament or the upstart merchants of London and, in his anger, threatened the citizens of London with the removal of his Court to Oxford. The Lord Mayor of London was unmoved by this threat, and he said that he hoped " His Majesty would be graciously pleased to leave them the Thames "!

It was this rich merchant class of London that backed Parliament and gave it a great deal of money during the struggle with Charles I.

All these industries that had grown up in England were what is called cottage or home industries. That is to say, the artisans or craftsmen usually worked in their own houses, or in small groups. There were guilds or associations of craftsmen in each trade, not unlike many castes in India, but without the religious element in caste. The master craftsmen took apprentices and taught them their craft. Weavers had their own looms, spinners their own spinning-wheels. Spinning was quite widespread, and was the spare-time industry of girls and women. Sometimes there were small factories where a number of looms were collected and the weavers worked together. But each weaver worked separately at his loom, and there was really no difference between his working at this loom at home or at some other place in company with other weavers and their looms. The small factory was wholly unlike the modern factory, with its big machinery.

This cottage stage of industry flourished not only in England then, but all over the world, in every country where there was industry. Thus in India these cottage industries were very advanced. In England cottage industries have almost completely disappeared, but in India there are still many of them. Both the big machine and the cottage loom still flourish side by side in India, and you can compare and contrast the two. As you know, the cloth we wear is *khadi*. It is hand spun and hand woven, and is thus entirely a product of the cottages and mud-huts of India.

New mechanical inventions, however, made a great deal of difference to cottage industries in England. Machines did more and more the work of man, and made it easier to produce more with less effort. These inventions began in the middle of the eighteenth century, and we shall consider them in our next letter.

I have referred briefly to our *khadi* movement. I do not wish to say much about it here. But I should like to point out to you that this movement and the *charkha* [1] are not meant to compete with the big machine. Many people fall into this mistake, and imagine that the *charkha* means a going back to the Middle Ages, and the discarding of machines and all that industrialism has brought us. This is all wrong. Our movement is decidedly not against industrialism as such or machines and factories. We want India to have the best of everything, and as rapidly as possible. But having regard to existing conditions in India, and especially the terrible poverty of our peasantry, we have urged them to spin in their spare time. Thus not only do they better their own conditions a little, but they help in lessening our dependence on foreign cloth, which has taken so much wealth out of our country.

[1] Spinning wheel.

98

THE INDUSTRIAL REVOLUTION BEGINS IN ENGLAND

September 27, 1932

I MUST now tell you of some of the mechanical inventions which made such a tremendous difference in methods of production. They seem simple enough when we see them now in a mill or factory. But to think of them for the first time and to invent them was a very difficult matter. The first of these inventions came in 1738, when a man named Kay made the flying shuttle for cloth-weaving. Before this invention the thread in the shuttle in the weaver's hand had to be carried slowly across and through the other threads placed lengthwise, called the warp. The flying shuttle quickened this process, and thus doubled the weaver's output. This meant that the weaver could consume much more yarn. Spinners were hard put to it to supply this additional yarn, and they tried to find some way of increasing their output. This problem was partly solved by the invention by Hargreaves in 1764 of the spinning-jenny. Other inventions by Richard Arkwright and others followed; water-power was used and later steam-power. All these inventions were first applied to the cotton industry, and factories or cotton-mills grew up. The next industry to take to the new methods was the woollen industry.

Meanwhile, in 1765, James Watt made his steam engine. This was a great event, and the use of steam in factory production followed from it. Coal was now wanted for the new factories, and the coal industry therefore developed. The use of coal led to new methods of iron-smelting—that is, the melting of the iron ore to separate the pure metal. The iron industry thereupon grew fast. New factories were built near the coal-fields, as coal was cheaper there.

Thus three great industries grew up in England—the textile, iron and coal—and factories sprung up in the coal areas and other suitable places. The face of England changed. Instead of the green and pleasant countryside, there grew up in many places these new factories with their long chimneys belching forth smoke and darkening the neighbourhood. They were not beautiful to look at these factories, surrounded by mountains of coal and heaps of refuse. Nor were the new manufacturing towns, growing around the factories, things of beauty. They were put up anyhow, the only object of the owners being to get on with the making of money. They were ugly and large and dirty, and the starving workers had to put up with these as well as with the terribly unwholesome conditions in the factories.

You may remember my telling you of the squeezing out of the small farmers by the big landowners and the growth of unemployment, resulting in riots and lawlessness in England. The new industries made matters worse to begin with. Agriculture suffered and unemployment increased. Indeed, as each new invention came it resulted in replacing manual labour by mechanical devices. This often led to workers being discharged, and caused great resentment among them. Many of them came to hate the new machines, and they even tried to break them. The machine-wreckers these people were called.

Machine-wrecking has quite a long history in Europe, going back to the sixteenth century, when a simple machine loom was invented in Germany. In an old book written by an Italian priest in 1579 it is stated about this loom that the Town Council of Danzig " being afraid that the invention might throw a large number of the workmen on the streets, had the machine destroyed, and the inventor secretly strangled or drowned " ! In spite of this summary way of dealing with the inventor, this machine appeared again in the seventeenth century, and there were riots all over Europe because of it. Laws were passed in many places against its use, and it was even publicly burned in the market-place. It is possible that if this machine had come into use when it was first invented, other inventions would have followed, and the machine age would have come sooner than it did. But the mere fact that it was not used shows that conditions were not then ripe for it. When these conditions were ripe, then machinery established itself in spite of numerous riots in England. It was natural for the workers to feel resentment at the machine. Gradually they came to learn that the fault did not lie with the machine, but with the way it was used for the profit of a few persons. Let us go back, however, to the development of the machine and of factories in England.

The new factories swallowed up many of the cottage industries and the private workers. It was not possible for these home-workers to compete with the machine. So they had to give up their old crafts and trades and seek employment as wage-earners in the very factories they hated, or to join the unemployed. The collapse of the cottage industries was not sudden, but it was rapid enough. By the end of the century—that is, by about 1800—the big factories were much in evidence. About thirty years later steam railways began in England with Stephenson's famous engine named the *Rocket*. And so the machine went on advancing all over the country and in almost all departments of industry and life.

It is interesting to note that all the inventors, many of whom I have not mentioned, came from the class of manual workers. It is from this class also that many of the early industrial leaders came. But the result of their inventions and the factory system that followed was to make the gulf between the employer and the worker wider still. The worker in the factory became just a cog in a machine, helpless in the hands of vast economic forces he could not even understand, much less control. The craftsman and the artisan first sensed that something was wrong when they found that the new factory was competing with them and making and selling articles far cheaper than they could possibly make them with their

simple and primitive tools at home. For no fault of theirs they had
to shut up their little shops. If they could not carry on with their
own crafts, much less could they succeed with a new one. So
they joined the army of the unemployed and starved. " Hunger ",
it has been said, " is the drill-sergeant of the factory owner," and
hunger ultimately drove them to the new factories to seek employment. The employers showed them little pity. They gave them
work indeed, but at a bare pittance, for which the miserable workers
had to pour out their life-blood in the factories. Women, and little
children even, worked long hours in stifling, unhealthy places till
many of them almost fainted and dropped down with fatigue.
Men worked right down below in the coal-mines the whole day long
and did not see the daylight for months at a time.

But do not think that all this was just due to the cruelty of the
employers. They were seldom consciously cruel; the fault lay with
the system. They were out to increase their business and to conquer
distant world-markets from other countries, and in order to do this
they were prepared to put up with anything. The building of new
factories and the purchase of machinery cost a lot of money. It is
only after the factory begins to produce and these goods are sold in
the market that the money comes back. So these factory-owners
had to economize in order to build and, even when money came
by sale of goods, they went on building more factories. They
had got a lead over the other countries of the world because of their
early industrialization, and they wanted to profit by this—and,
indeed, they did profit. So, in their mad desire to increase their
business and make more money, they crushed the poor workers
whose labour produced the sources of their wealth.

Thus the new system of industry was particularly adapted to the
exploitation of the weak by the strong. Right through history
we have seen the powerful exploiting the weak. The factory
system made this easier. In law there was no slavery, but in fact
the starving worker, the wage-slave of the factory, was little better
than the old slave. The law was all in favour of the employer.
Even religion favoured him and told the poor to put up with their
miserable lot here in this world and expect a heavenly compensation in the next. Indeed, the governing classes developed quite
a convenient philosophy that the poor were necessary for society,
and that therefore it was quite virtuous to pay low wages. If
higher wages were paid the poor would try to have a good time, and
not work hard enough. It was a comforting and useful way of
thinking, because it just fitted in with the material interests of the
factory-owners and the other rich people.

It is very interesting and instructive to read about these times.
One learns so much. We can see what tremendous effect the
mechanical processes of production have on economics and society.
The whole social fabric is upset; new classes come to the front and
gain power; the artisan class becomes the wage-earning class
in the factory. In addition to this, the new economics moulds
people's ideas even in religion and morals. The convictions of the

mass of mankind run hand in hand with their interests or class-feelings, and they take good care, when they have the power to do so, to make laws to protect their own interests. Of course all this is done with every appearance of virtue and with every assurance that the good of mankind is the only motive at the back of the law. We, in India, have enough of pious sentiments from English viceroys and other officials in India. We are always being told how they labour for the good of India. Meanwhile they govern us with ordinances and bayonets and crush the life-blood out of our people. Our *zamindars* tell us how they love their tenants, but they do not scruple to squeeze and rack-rent them till they have nothing left but their starved bodies. Our capitalists and big factory-owners also assure us of their good-will for their workers, but the good-will does not translate itself into better wages or better conditions for the workers. All the profits go to make new palaces, not to improve the mud hut of the worker.

It is amazing how people deceive themselves and others when it is to their interest to do so. So we find the English employers of the eighteenth century and after resisting all attempts to better the lot of their workers. They objected to factory legislation and housing reform, and refused to admit that society had any obligation to remove the causes of distress. They comforted themselves with the thought that it was the idle only who suffered, and in any event they hardly looked upon the workers as human beings like themselves. They developed a new philosophy which is called *laissez-faire*—that is, they wanted to do just what they liked in their business without any interference from government. By having started factories to make things before other countries had done so, they had got a lead, and all they wanted was a free field to make money. *Laissez-faire* became almost a semi-divine theory which was supposed to give an opportunity to everybody if he could but take advantage of it. Each man and woman was to fight the rest of the world to go ahead, and if many fell in the struggle, what did it matter?

In the course of these letters I have told you of the progress of co-operation between man and man, which had been the basis of civilization. But *laissez-faire* and the new capitalism brought the law of the jungle. "Pig philosophy", Carlyle called it. Who laid down this new law of life and business? Not the workers. The poor fellows had little to say in the matter. It was the successful manufacturers at the top who wanted no interference with their success in the name of foolish sentiment. So in the name of liberty and the rights of property they objected even to the compulsory sanitation of private houses and interference with the adulteration of goods.

I have just used the word capitalism. Capitalism of a kind had existed in all countries for a long time—that is to say industry was carried on with accumulated money. But with the coming of the big machine and industrialism far larger sums of money were required for factory production. "Industrial capital" this was called, and the word capitalism is now used to refer to the economic system which grew up after the Industrial Revolution. Under this system capitalists—that is, owners of capital—controlled the factories and took the profits. With industrialization capitalism spread all over the world, except now in the Soviet Union and perhaps one or two other places From its earliest days capitalism emphasized the difference between the rich and the poor. The mechanization of industry resulted in much greater production, and therefore it produced greater wealth. But this new wealth went to a small group only—the owners of the new industries. The workers remained poor. Very slowly the workers' standards improved in England, largely because of the exploitation of India and other places. But the workers' share in the profits of industry was very small. The Industrial Revolution and capitalism solved the problem of production. They did not solve the problem of the distribution of the new wealth created. So the old tussle between the haves and the have-nots not only remained, but it became acuter.

The Industrial Revolution took place in the second half of the eighteenth century. This was the very period when the British were fighting in India and Canada. It was then that the Seven Years' War took place. These events acted and reacted on each other greatly. The enormous sums of money that the East India Company and its servants (you will remember Clive) extorted out of India, after the Battle of Plassey and later, were of great help in starting the new industries. I have told you earlier in this letter that industrialization is an expensive job to begin with. It swallows up money without any return for some time. Unless plenty of money is available, either by loan or otherwise, it results in poverty and distress till such time as the industry begins to work and make money. England was extraordinarily fortunate in getting these vast sums of money from India just when she wanted them most for her developing industries and factories.

Having built up these factories, new wants arose. The factories wanted raw material to convert it into manufactured articles. Thus cotton was required to make cloth. Even more necessary were new markets where the new goods produced by the factories could be sold. England had got a tremendous lead over other countries by starting factories first. But in spite of this lead she would have had difficulties in finding easy markets. Again India came, very unwillingly, to the rescue. The English in India adopted all manner of devices to ruin Indian industries and force English cloth on India. I shall say more of this later. Meanwhile it is important to note how the Industrial Revolution in England was helped by the British holding India and forcing it to fit in with their schemes.

Industrialism spread to all parts of the world during the nineteenth century, and capitalist industry developed elsewhere on the general lines laid down in England. Capitalism led inevitably to a new imperialism, for everywhere there was a demand for raw materials for manufacture and markets to sell the manufactured goods. The easiest way to have the markets and the raw materials was to take possession of the country. So there was a wild scramble among the more powerful countries for new territories. England, again, with her possession of India and her sea power, had a great advantage. But of imperialism and its fruits I shall have to say something later.

With the coming of the Industrial Revolution the English world was more and more dominated by the great cloth manufacturers of Lancashire, and the iron-masters and the mine-owners.

99

AMERICA BREAKS AWAY FROM ENGLAND

October 2, 1932

WE shall now consider the second great revolution of the eighteenth century—the revolt of the American colonies against England. This was a political revolution only, and not so vital as the Industrial Revolution, which we have been studying, or the French Revolution, which was to follow it soon and shake the social foundations of Europe. And yet this political change in America was important and destined to bear great results. The American colonies which became free then have grown to-day into the most powerful, the richest, and industrially the most advanced country in the world.

Do you remember the *Mayflower*, the ship that took a batch of Protestants from England to America in 1620? They did not like the autocracy of James I; nor did they like his religion. So these people, since then called the " Pilgrim Fathers," shook the dust of England from off their feet and went to the strange new land across the Atlantic Ocean, to found a colony where they would have greater freedom. They landed in the north, and called the place New Plymouth. Colonists had gone before them to other parts of the North American coast-line. Many others followed them, till there were little colonies dotted all over the east coast from north to south. There were Catholic colonies, and colonies founded by Cavalier nobles from England, and Quaker colonies—Pennsylvania is named after the Quaker Penn. There were also Dutchmen, and Germans and Danes and some Frenchmen. They were a mixed lot, but by far the greatest number of them were the English colonists. The Dutch founded a town and called it New Amsterdam. When the English took this later they changed the name to New York —so well known now.

The English colonists continued to acknowledge the British King and Parliament. Many of them had left their homes because they were discontented with their lot there and did not approve of much that the King or Parliament did. But they had no desire to break away. The southern colonies, consisting of cavaliers and supporters of the King, were even more attached to England. The colonies lived their separate lives, and had little in common with each other. By the eighteenth century there were thirteen colonies on the east coast, all under British control. To the north was Canada, to the south Spanish territory. The Dutch and Danish and other settlements in these thirteen colonies had all been swallowed up by them and were under British control. But remember that the colonies were along the coast only, and some distance inland. Beyond them, to the west, lay vast territories stretching right up to the Pacific Ocean, nearly ten times the size of the thirteen colonies. These territories were not occupied by any European colonists. They were inhabited by, and were under the control of, various tribes or nations of Red Indians. The chief of these were the Iroquois.

In the middle of the century there was, as you will remember, a world-wide struggle between England and France. This was known as the Seven Years' War (1756–1763), and it was waged not only in Europe, but in India and Canada. England won, and France had to give up Canada to her. France was thus eliminated from America, and England controlled all the settlements in North America. Only in the province of Quebec in Canada was there any French population; otherwise the settlements were predominantly English. Quebec, strange to say, is still an island of French language and culture surrounded by an Anglo-Saxon population. Montreal (from Mont Royal), the biggest city of Quebec Province, has, I believe, more French-speaking people in it than any city other than Paris.

I have told you, in an earlier letter, of the slave trade that was carried on by European countries to bring Negro workers from Africa to America. This terrible and ghastly trade was largely in the hands of the Spanish, Portuguese and English. Labour was needed in America, especially in the southern States, where large tobacco plantations had grown up. The people of the country, the so-called Red Indians, were nomads and did not like to settle down; besides, they refused to work under conditions of slavery. They would not bend; they preferred to be broken, and broken they were in subsequent years. They were practically exterminated, and most of them died off under the new conditions. There are not many left to-day of these people who once inhabited a whole continent.

As the Red Indians would not work in the plantations, and labour was badly needed, the unhappy people of Africa were captured in horrible man-hunts and sent across the seas in a manner the cruelty of which is almost beyond belief. These African Negroes were taken to the southern States—Virginia, Carolina and Georgia—and made to work in gangs on the large plantations, chiefly of tobacco.

In the northern States conditions were different. The old Puritan traditions brought over by the Pilgrim Fathers in the

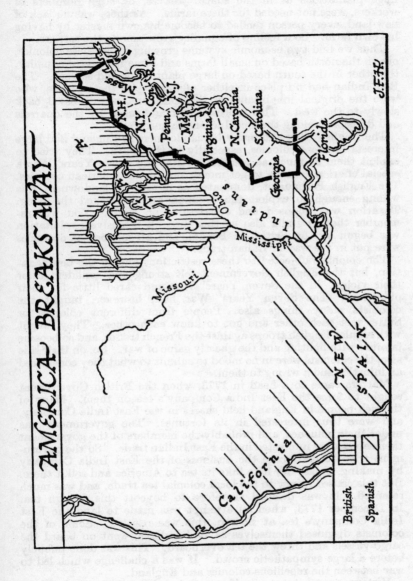

Mayflower still flourished. There were compact farms, and no such huge plantations as in the south. Slaves, or large numbers of workers, were not needed for these farms. As there was no lack of new land, every person tended to become his own master by having his own farm. So a feeling of equality grew among the settlers.

Thus we find two economic systems growing up in these colonies, one in the north based on small farms and some notions of equality, the other in the south based on large plantations and slavery. The Red Indian had no place in either of these. So these people, who were the original inhabitants of the continent, were pressed back slowly to the west. This process was made easier by the quarrels and divisions among the Red Indians themselves.

The English King and many big landowners in England had large interests in these colonies, especially in the south. They tried to exploit them as much as possible. After the Seven Years' War a special effort was made to get money out of the American colonies. The English Parliament, dominated as it was by landowners, was willing enough to exploit the colonies, and it backed the King. Taxation was imposed and restrictions on trade. You will remember that in India also at this time an intensive exploitation was begun by the British in Bengal, and all manner of obstacles were put in the way of Indian trade.

The colonists objected to these restrictions and to the new taxation, but the English Government felt strong and confident after their victory in the Seven Years' War and cared little for their objections. The Seven Years' War had, however, taught the colonists many things also. People from different colonies or States met each other and got to know each other. They fought with regular English troops against the French troops, and so became familiar with fighting and the ghastly game of war. So, on their side also, the colonists were in no mood to submit to what they considered an injustice and a wrong to them.

Matters came to a head in 1773, when the British Government sought to force the East India Company's tea on them. Many of the rich people in England held shares in the East India Company, and were thus interested in its fortunes. The government was under their influence, and probably the members of the government themselves were interested in the East Indian trade. So the government tried to encourage the business of the East India Company by making it easy for it to take its tea to America and sell it there. But this caused injury to the local colonial tea trade, and was much resented. It was decided therefore to boycott this foreign tea. In December 1773, when an attempt was made to land the East India Company's tea at Boston, this was resisted. Some of the colonists disguised themselves as Red Indians, went on board the cargo-vessels and threw the tea overboard. This was done publicly before a large sympathetic crowd. It was a challenge which led to war between the rebellious colonies and England.

History never repeats itself exactly, and yet it is strange how near it comes to it sometimes. This incident of throwing overboard of the tea at Boston in 1773 has become very famous. It is called the " Boston tea-party ". When Bapu, two and a half years ago, started his salt campaign and the great march to Dandi, and the salt raids, many people in America thought of their " Boston tea-party " and compared the new " salt-party " to it. But of course there was a great deal of difference between the two.

A year and a half later, in 1775, war began between England and her American colonies. What were the colonies fighting for ? Not independence, not to cut away from England. Even when fighting had begun and blood had been shed on both sides, the leaders of the colonists continued to address George III of England as their " Most Gracious Sovereign " and to consider themselves as his faithful subjects. It is most interesting to notice this, as you will find the same thing happening often enough. In Holland, Philip II of Spain was called sovereign, although bitter warfare was being carried on against his armies. It was only after many years of fighting that Holland was forced to declare her independence. In India, after many years of doubt and hesitation, and dallying with the idea of Dominion Status and the like, our National Congress declared, on the 1st January, 1930, in favour of independence. Even now there are some people who seem to be afraid of the idea of independence and talk of Dominion rule in India. But history teaches us, and the examples of Holland and America made it clear enough, that the end of such a struggle can only be independence.

In 1774, a little before war began between the colonies and England, Washington stated that no thinking man in all North America desired independence. And yet Washington was to be the first president of the American Republic ! In 1774, after the war had begun, forty-six leading members of the Colonial Congress addressed King George III as his faithful subjects and pleaded for peace and the cessation of the " effusion of blood ". They were ardently desirous of restoring harmony and good-will between England and her American children. All they ask for is some kind of Dominion government, and they declare, in Washington's words, that no thinking man wanted independence. This was called the " Olive Branch Petition ".

But in less than two years twenty-five of the signatories of this petition had signed another document—the Declaration of Independence.

So the colonies did not begin fighting for the sake of independence. Their grievances were taxation and restrictions on trade. They denied the right of the British Parliament to tax them against their will. " No taxation without representation " was their famous cry, and they were not represented in the British Parliament.

The colonists had no army, but they had a vast country to retire and fall back upon whenever necessary. They built up an army, and Washington ultimately became their Commander-in-Chief. They had a few successes and, thinking perhaps that the time was a favourable one for a fling at the old enemy, England, France joined the colonies. Spain also declared war against England. The odds were against England now, but the war dragged on for many years. In 1776 came the famous " Declaration of Independence " of the colonies. In 1782 the war ended, and the Peace of Paris between the warring countries was signed in 1783.

So the thirteen American colonies became an independent republic—the United States of America as they were called. But for a long time each State was jealous of the others and considered itself more or less independent. Only gradually came the feeling of a common nationality. It was a vast country, continually spreading westwards. It was the first great republic of the modern world— tiny Switzerland being the only other real republic at the time. Holland, although republican, was controlled by the aristocracy. England was not only a monarchy, but its Parliament was in the hands of the small rich landowning class. So the United States Republic was a new kind of country. It had no past, as the countries of Europe and Asia had. It had no relics of feudalism, except in the plantation system and slavery in the south. It had no hereditary nobility. The *bourgeoisie* or middle class had thus few obstacles to its growth, and it grew rapidly. Its population at the time of the War of Independence was less than 4,000,000. Two years ago, in 1930, it was nearly 123,000,000.

George Washington became the first president of the United States. He was a great landowner from the State of Virginia. Other great men of this period who are considered the founders of the republic are Thomas Paine, Benjamin Franklin, Patrick Henry, Thomas Jefferson, Adams and James Madison. Benjamin Franklin was an especially distinguished man, and was a great scientist. By flying boys' kites he showed that the lightning in the clouds was the same thing as electricity.

The Declaration of Independence of 1776 stated that " all men are born equal ". This is hardly a correct statement, if analysed, for some are weak and some are strong, some are more intelligent and capable than others. But the idea behind the statement is clear enough and praiseworthy. The colonists wanted to get rid of the feudal inequalities of Europe. That in itself was a very great advance. Probably many of the framers of the Declaration of Independence were influenced by the philosophers and thinkers of eighteenth-century France, from Voltaire and Rousseau onwards.

" All men are born equal "—and yet there was the poor Negro, a slave with few rights ! What of him ? How did he fit in with the constitution ? He did not fit in, and he has not yet fitted in. Many years later there was a bitter civil war between the northern and southern States, and as a result slavery was abolished. But the Negro problem still continues in America.

100

THE FALL OF THE BASTILLE

October 7, 1932

WE have now considered very briefly two of the revolutions of the eighteenth century. In this letter I shall tell you something of the third revolution—the French Revolution. Of the three this one in France created the most stir. The Industrial Revolution, which began in England, was a vastly important one, but it crept on gradually and was almost unnoticed by most people. Few realized at the time its real significance. The French Revolution, on the other hand, burst suddenly on an astonished Europe, like a thunderbolt. Europe was still under a host of monarchs and emperors. The ancient Holy Roman Empire had long ceased to function, but it still existed on paper and its ghost cast a long shadow over Europe. In this world of kings and emperors and courts and palaces, there came, out of the depths of the common people, this strange and terrifying creature, which paid no attention to moss-grown custom or privilege, and which hurled a king from his throne and threatened others with a like fate. Is it surprising that the kings and all the privileged people of Europe trembled before this revolt of the masses, whom they had so long ignored and crushed ?

The French Revolution burst like a volcano. And yet revolutions and volcanoes do not break out suddenly without reason or long evolution. We see the sudden burst and are surprised; but underneath the surface of the earth many forces play against each other for long ages, and the fires gather together, till the crust on the surface can hold them down no longer, and they burst forth in mighty flames shooting up to the sky, and molten lava rolls down the mountain side. Even so the forces that ultimately break out in revolution play for long under the surface of society. Water boils when you heat it; but you know that it has reached boiling point only after getting hotter and hotter.

Ideas and economic conditions make revolutions. Foolish people in authority, blind to everything that does not fit in with their ideas, imagine that revolutions are caused by agitators. Agitators are people who are discontented with existing conditions and desire a change and work for it. Every revolutionary period has its full supply of them; they are themselves the outcome of the ferment and dissatisfaction that exist. But tens and hundreds of thousands of people do not move to action merely at the bidding of an agitator. Most people desire security above everything; they do not want to risk losing what they have got. But when economic conditions are such that their day-to-day suffering grows and life becomes almost an intolerable burden, then even the weak are prepared to take risks. It is then that they listen to the voice of the agitator who seems to show them a way out of their misery.

In many of my letters I have told you of the distress of the people and of peasant risings. In every country of Asia and Europe there have been these revolts of the peasantry, often resulting in much bloodshed and in cruel repression. Their distress drove the peasants to revolutionary action, but usually they had no clear ideas of their goal. Because of this vagueness in thought, this want of an ideology, their efforts often ended in failure. In the French Revolution we find a new thing, at any rate on such a big scale—the union of ideas with the economic urge for revolutionary action. Where there is such a union, there is the real revolution, and a real revolution affects the whole fabric of life and society—political, social, economic and religious. We find this happening in France in the last years of the eighteenth century.

I have told you already of the luxury and incompetence and corruption of the French kings and the grinding poverty of the common people. I have also told you something of the ferment in the minds of the French people; of the new ideas set going by Voltaire and Rousseau and Montesquieu and many others. So there were the two processes—economic distress and the formation of an ideology —going on together and acting and reacting on each other. It takes a long time to build up the ideology of a people, for new ideas have to filter down gradually to them, and few persons are eager to give up their old prejudices and notions. It so happens, often enough, that by the time a new ideology is established and the people have at last succeeded in accepting a new set of ideas, these ideas themselves are somewhat out of date. It is interesting to notice that the ideas of the French philosophers of the eighteenth century were based on the pre-industrial age in Europe; and yet almost at that very time the Industrial Revolution was beginning in England, and this was changing industry and life so much that in reality it was knocking out the bottom from many of the new French theories. The Industrial Revolution really developed later on, and the French philosophers could not of course guess what was going to happen. Yet their ideas, on which to a large extent the French Revolution based its ideology, were partly out of date, with the coming of big industry.

However that might be, it is clear that these ideas and theories of the French philosophers had a very powerful effect on the Revolution. There had previously been many instances of masses in action in risings and revolts; now there was a remarkable instance of conscious masses in action, or rather consciously guided masses in action. Hence the importance of this great revolution in France.

I have told you that Louis XV succeeded his great-grandfather Louis XIV in 1715 and reigned for fifty-nine years. He is reported to have said: *Après moi le déluge*,[1] and he acted accordingly. Merrily he sent his country to the abyss. He took no lesson from the British Revolution and the beheading of the English King. In 1774 he was succeeded by his grandson, Louis XVI, a very foolish and brainless man. His wife was Marie Antoinette, a sister

[1] After me the deluge.

of the Hapsburg Austrian Emperor. She was also very foolish, but she had a kind of obstinate strength, and Louis XVI was entirely under her thumb. She was even more full of the idea of the "divine right of kings" than Louis, and she hated the common people. Between the two of them, wife and husband, they did everything to make the idea of monarchy hateful to the people. The French people, even after the beginning of the Revolution, were not clear on the question of the monarchy, but Louis and Marie Antoinette by their actions and follies made the republic inevitable. And yet wiser people than they were could have done little. Even so the Tsar and Tsarina of Russia behaved with amazing folly on the eve of the Russian Revolution of 1917. It is curious how these people become even more foolish as the crisis deepens, and thus help in their own destruction. There is a famous Latin saying which just fits them—*quem deus perdere vult, prius dementat*, whom God wishes to destroy he first makes mad. There is an almost exact equivalent in Sanskrit—*vināsh kāle viparit buddhi*.

One of the props of monarchy and dictatorship has often been military glory. Whenever there is trouble at home, a king or a government clique is attracted towards military adventure abroad to distract people's minds. But in France the result of the military adventures had been bad. The Seven Years' War had meant defeat for France, and was thus a blow to the monarchy. Bankruptcy came nearer and nearer. The French participation in the American War of Independence meant more expenditure. Where was all this money to come from? The nobles and priests were privileged and exempt from most taxes, and they had no intention of giving up their privileges. Yet money had to be raised not only to pay debts, but also for the extravagances of the Court. What of the masses, the common people? I shall give you a description of them from Carlyle, an English writer on the French Revolution. He has a peculiar style, as you will notice, but he is often very effective in his pen pictures :

> "With the working people again, it is not well. Unlucky! For there are from twenty to twenty-five millions of them. Whom, however, we lump together into a kind of dim compendious unity, monstrous but dim, far off, as the canaille; or, more humanely, as 'the masses.' Masses indeed; and yet singular to say, if, with an effort of imagination, thou follow them, over broad France, into their clay hovels, into their garrets and hutches, the masses consist all of units. Every unit of whom has his own heart and sorrows; stands covered there with his own skin, and if you pinch him he will bleed."

How well the description fits, not only the France of 1789, but the India of 1932! Do not many of us lump together the "masses" of India, the scores of millions of peasants and workers, and think of them as some unhappy, ungainly beast? Beasts of burden they have been for many a long day and still are. We "sympathize" with them and talk patronizingly of doing them good. And yet we hardly think of them as individuals and human beings, not very much unlike us. It is well to remember that in their mud huts they have their separate lives and feel hunger and cold and pain like all of us. Many of our politicians, learned in the law, think and talk of constitutions and the like, forgetting the human beings for whom constitutions and laws are made. Politics for the dwellers of our millions of mud huts and town slums means food for the hungry and clothing and shelter.

So stood France under Louis XVI. Right at the beginning of his reign there were hunger riots. For several years these continued, and then there was a gap, followed later by fresh peasant risings. During one of these food riots at Dijon, the Governor told the starving people : " The grass has sprouted, go to the fields and browse on it ! " Vast numbers of people became professional beggars. It was officially declared that in 1777 there were eleven lakhs of beggars in France. How India comes inevitably to our minds when we think of this poverty and misery !

The peasants were not only hungry for food, but were also hungry for land. Under the feudal system the nobles were lords of the land, and to them went a great part of the income from it. The peasants had no clear ideas, no clear goal, but they wanted to own their land and they hated this feudal system which crushed them, they hated the nobles, and the clergy, and (think of India again !) the *gabelle* or salt tax, which was especially felt by the poor.

Such was the condition of the peasantry, and yet the King and Queen clamoured for money. The government had no money to spend and debts grew. Marie Antoinette was nick-named " Madame Déficit ". There was no way of raising more money. At last, Louis XVI, at his wits' end, summoned the States-General in May 1789. This body consisted of the representatives of the three classes, or Estates of the realm as they were called : nobles, clergy, commons. In composition it was thus not unlike the British Parliament, with its House of Lords, consisting of nobles and clergy, and the House of Commons. But there were many differences between the two. The British Parliament had been meeting more or less regularly for some hundreds of years and had got well established with traditions and rules and methods of doing work. The States-General seldom met and had no traditions. Both bodies represented the upper classes, the British House of Commons even more so than the Commons in the States-General. The peasantry were nowhere represented.

On May 4, 1789, the States-General was opened by the King at Versailles. But soon the King was sorry that he ever called these representatives of the three Estates together. The third Estate— that is, the Commons or the middle classes—began to take the bit between their teeth and insist that no taxation could be levied without their consent. They had the example of England before them, where the Commons' House had established this right. The recent American example was also before them. They thought very mistakenly, that England was a free country. As a matter of fact this was a delusion, as England was controlled and governed by the aristocratic and landowning classes. Parliament itself was a monopoly of theirs, owing to the very limited franchise— that is, the right to vote.

However, whatever little the Third Estate or the Commons did was too much for King Louis. He had them turned out of the hall. The deputies had no intention of going away. They met immediately on a tennis-court near by, and took an oath not to disperse till they had established a constitution. This is known as the Oath of the Tennis-Court. Then came the critical moment when the King tried force and his own soldiers refused to obey his orders. Always in a revolution the crisis comes when the army, which is the main prop of government, refuses to fire on their brethren in the crowd. Louis was frightened and he gave in, and then, in his usual foolish way, intrigued to get foreign regiments to shoot down his own people. This was too much for the people and, on the memorable 14th of July, 1789, they rose in Paris and captured the old prison of the Bastille and set free the prisoners.

The fall of the Bastille is a great event in history. It began the revolution; it was a signal for popular risings all over the country; it meant the end of the old order in France, of feudalism and grand monarchy and privilege; it was a terrible and terrifying portent for all the kings and emperors of Europe. France, which had set the fashion in grand monarchs, was now setting a new fashion, and Europe was amazed. Some looked at the deed with fear and trembling, but many saw hope in it and the promise of a better day. The 14th of July is still the day of the Fête Nationale of France, and every year it is celebrated all over the country.

The 14th of July saw the Bastille fall to the mob of Paris. Yet, so blind often are those in authority, that on the evening before, on the 13th, there was a royal fête at Versailles. There was dancing and singing, and toasts were drunk, before the King and Queen, to the coming victory over rebellious Paris. It is strange how extraordinary was the hold of the idea of the monarchy in Europe. We, in the present age, have got used to republics and hardly take kings seriously. The few kings that remain in the world behave very circumspectly lest worse befall them. Even so, most people are opposed to the idea of monarchy, as it keeps up class divisions and encourages the spirit of exclusion and snobbery. But this was not so in eighteenth-century Europe. For the people of those days a country without a king was a little difficult to imagine. So it happened that in spite of Louis's folly and attempted defiance, there was yet no talk of deposing him. For nearly two years more they put up with him and his intrigues, and it was only when he tried to run away and was caught that France decided to do without a king.

But that was to be later. Meanwhile the States-General became the National Assembly, and the King was supposed to have become a constitutional or limited monarch—that is, a king who did what he was told to do by the Assembly. But he hated this and Marie Antoinette hated it still more, and the people of Paris did not love them over-much and suspected them of all manner of intrigues. Versailles, where the King and Queen held Court at the time, was too far from Paris for the people of the capital to keep an eye on them. Tales and rumours of feasting and luxury at Versailles also excited the hungry people of Paris. So the King and Queen were taken to the Tuileries in Paris in one of the strangest of processions. I shall continue the story of the Revolution in my next letter.

101

THE FRENCH REVOLUTION

October 10, 1932

I FIND it a little difficult to write to you about the French Revolution. This is not for any lack of material, but because of the very abundance of it. The Revolution was an amazing and an ever-changing drama, full of extraordinary incidents that still fascinate us and horrify and thrill. The politics of princes and statesmen have their home in the closet and the private room, and an air of mystery covers them. A discreet veil hides many sins, and decorous language conceals the conflict of rival ambitions and greed. Even when this conflict leads to war and vast numbers of young people are sent to their death for the sake of this greed and ambition, our ears are not offended by mention of any such lowly motives. We are told, instead, of noble ideals and great causes which demand the last sacrifice.

But a revolution is very different. It has its home in the field and the street and the market-place, and its methods are rough and coarse. The people who make it have not had the advantage of the education of the princes and the statesmen. Their language is not courtly and decorous, hiding a multitude of intrigues and evil designs. There is no mystery about them, no veils to hide the working of their minds; even their bodies have little enough covering. Politics in a revolution cease to be the sport of kings or professional politicians. They deal with realities, and behind them are raw human nature and the empty stomachs of the hungry.

So we see in France, during these fateful five years from 1789 to 1794, the hungry masses in action. It is they who force the hands of timid politicians and make them abolish monarchy and feudalism and the privileges of the Church. It is they who pay homage to the terrible Madame Guillotine and take cruel vengeance against those who had crushed them in the past and those whom they suspect of intriguing against their new-found freedom. It is these ragged, barefooted people who, with improvised arms, rush to defend their Revolution on the battlefield, and drive back the trained armies of a Europe united against them. They achieve wonders, these people of France, but after several years of terrible strain and conflict, the Revolution exhausts its energy and turns on itself and begins to eat up its own children. And then comes the counter-revolution, swallowing up the Revolution, and sending the common people who had dared and suffered so much back to be ruled by the " superior " classes. Out of the counter-revolution emerges Napoleon, dictator and emperor. But neither the counter-revolution nor Napoleon could send back the people to their old places. No one could wipe away the principal conquests of the Revolution; and no one could take away from the French people, and indeed the other peoples of Europe, the passionate memory of the days when the under-dog cast off his yoke, even though for a while only.

There were many parties and groups fighting for mastery in the early days of the Revolution. There were the royalists, indulging in the vain hope of keeping Louis XVI as an absolute king; the moderate liberals wanting a constitution and prepared to keep the King as a limited monarch; the moderate republicans, called the party of the Gironde; and the more extreme republicans, named the Jacobins, because they used to meet in the hall of the Jacobin Convent. These were the main groups, and among them all, and outside them, were many adventurers. Behind all these groups and individuals were the masses of France, and especially of Paris, acting under many an unknown leader from their own ranks. In foreign countries, especially in England, there were the *émigrés*, the French nobles who had run away from the Revolution and were continually intriguing against it. All the Powers of Europe were ranged against revolutionary France. Parliamentary but aristocratic England, as well as the kings and emperors of the Continent, were equally afraid of this strange eruption of the common man, and tried to crush it.

The royalists and the King intrigued, and only brought their own ruin nearer. The party which was most important at first in the National Assembly was that of the moderate liberals, who wanted a constitution somewhat after the fashion of England and America. Their leader was Mirabeau. For nearly two years they were in power in the Assembly and, flushed with the success of the first days of the Revolution, they made many brave declarations and brought about some important changes. Twenty days after the fall of the Bastille, on August 4, 1789, there was a dramatic scene in the Assembly. The subject before the Assembly was the abolition of feudal rights and privileges. There was something in the air of France then which went to the heads of the people, and even the feudal lords seem to have been intoxicated for a while by the new wine of freedom. Great nobles and leaders of the Church got up in the Assembly Chamber and vied with each other in giving up their feudal rights and special privileges. It was an honest and generous gesture, though it did not have much effect for some years. Sometimes, but rarely, such generous impulses move a privileged class; or perhaps it may be that a realization comes to it that the end of privilege is near and a virtuous generosity is the best course. Only a few days ago we saw a wonderful gesture of this kind made by the caste Hindus in India when Bapu fasted to remove untouchability and, as if by a magician's wand, a wave of feeling passed through the land. The chains that Hindus had placed over many of their brethren fell from them in some measure, and a thousand doors, that had been closed to these untouchables for ages, opened out to them.

So in a flush of enthusiasm the National Assembly of revolutionary France abolished, by resolution at least, serfdom and privileges and feudal courts and the exemption of nobles and clergy from taxation, and even titles. It was strange that although the King still remained, the nobility lost their titles.

The Assembly then went on to pass a Declaration of the Rights of Man. The idea for this famous declaration was probably taken from the American Declaration of Independence. But the American declaration is short and simple, the French one long and rather complicated. The Rights of Man were the rights which were supposed to ensure him equality and liberty and happiness. Very brave and daring seemed this Declaration of the Rights of Man at the time, and for nearly 100 years afterwards it was the charter of the liberals and democrats of Europe. And yet to-day it is out of date and does not solve any of the problems of our time. It took a long time for people to discover that mere equality before the law and the possession of a vote do not ensure real equality or liberty or happiness, and that those in power have other ways of exploiting them still. Political thought has advanced or changed much since the days of the French Revolution, and probably even most of the conservatives to-day would accept the high-sounding principles of the Declaration of the Rights of Man. But that does not mean, as all of us can find out without much trouble, that they are prepared to grant real equality and freedom. This Declaration, indeed, protected private property. The estates of the big nobles and the Church were confiscated for other reasons relating to feudal rights and special privileges. But the right to own property itself was considered a sacred and inviolable one. As you perhaps know, advanced political thought now considers that private property is an evil and should, as far as possible, be abolished.

The Declaration of the Rights of Man may seem to us to-day a commonplace document. The brave ideals of yesterday often enough become the commonplaces of to-day. But at the time it was proclaimed it sent a thrill through Europe, and it seemed to carry the fair promise of better times to all who suffered and were downtrodden. But the King did not like it; he was amazed at this blasphemy, and he refused to sanction it. He was still at Versailles. It was then that the Paris mob, led by the women, came to the Versailles palace and not only made the King sanction the Declaration, but forced him to go to Paris. It was this strange procession to which I referred at the end of my last letter.

The Assembly brought about many other useful reforms. The vast property of the Church was confiscated by the State. A new division of France was made into eighty departments and this division, I believe, still exists. Better law-courts, to take the place of the old feudal courts, were set up. All, this was to the good, but it did not go far enough. It did not benefit much the peasantry who hungered for land or the common people in the towns who hungered for bread. The Revolution seemed to have been arrested. As I have told you, the masses, the peasantry and the common people of the towns were not represented in the Assembly at all. The Assembly was controlled by the middle classes, under the leadership of Mirabeau; and as soon as they felt that they had gained their objects, they tried their best to stop the Revolution. They even began to ally themselves to King Louis and to shoot down the peasantry in the provinces. Their leader, Mirabeau, actually became the secret adviser of the King. And the common people, who had stormed and captured the Bastille and thought that they had thereby cast aside their chains, wondered what had happened. Their freedom seemed to be as far off as ever, and the new National Assembly was keeping them down almost in the manner of the old lords.

Foiled in the Assembly, the people of Paris, which was the heart of the Revolution, found another outlet for their revolutionary energy. This was the Commune or municipality of Paris. Not only the Commune, but each section of the city, which returned several members to the Commune, had a living organization, in direct touch with the masses. The Commune, and the sections especially, became the standard-bearers of the Revolution and the rivals of the moderate and middle-class Assembly.

Meanwhile the anniversary of the fall of the Bastille came round, and the people of Paris held a great fête on July 14. The Fête of the Federation it was called; and the common people of Paris gave their labour freely to decorate the city, for they felt that the fête was theirs.

So the Revolution stood in 1790 and 1791. The Assembly had lost all its revolutionary ardour and had had enough of changes; but the people of Paris were still simmering with revolutionary energy, the peasantry still looking hungrily at the land. Matters could not continue for long in this way; either the Revolution had to go ahead or to die down. Mirabeau, the moderate leader, died early in 1791. In spite of his secret intrigues with the King he was popular with the people and kept them in check. On June 21, 1791, an event took place which decided the fate of the Revolution. This was the flight of King Louis and Marie Antoinette in disguise. They almost managed to reach the frontier. But some peasants recognized them at Varennes, near Verdun, and they were stopped and brought back to Paris.

This act of the King and Queen sealed their fate so far as the people of Paris were concerned. The idea of the republic now grew rapidly, and yet so moderate and so far removed from public sentiment were the Assembly and the government of the day, that they continued to shoot down people who demanded that Louis be dethroned. Marat, one of the great figures of the Revolution, was hunted by the authorities because he denounced the King, after

his flight, as a traitor.   He had to hide in the sewers of Paris and
contracted a terrible skin disease there.

Still, strange to say, Louis continued in theory as king for over
a year more.   In September 1791 the National Assembly finished
its career and gave place to the Legislative Assembly.   This was
as moderate as the other, and was representative only of the upper
classes.   It did not represent the rising fever of France.   This fever
of revolution spread among the people, and the extreme republicans,
the Jacobins, who came from the people, grew in strength.

Meanwhile the Powers of Europe were watching these strange
happenings with alarm.   For a while Prussia and Austria and Russia
were busy with booty elsewhere.   They were putting an end to the
old kingdom of Poland, but events in France were marching too
far ahead, and claimed their attention.   In 1792 France was at war
with Austria and Prussia.   Austria, I might inform you, was now
in possession of the Belgian part of the Netherlands, and this had a
common frontier with France.   Foreign armies advanced into
French territory and defeated the French troops.   The King was
supposed, not without reason, to be in league with them, and all
royalists were suspected of treachery.   As the dangers grew round
them, the people of France became more and more inflamed and
panicky.   They saw spies and traitors everywhere.   The revolutionary Commune of Paris took the lead at this crisis, hoisted the
Red Flag to signify that the people had proclaimed martial law
against the rebellion of the Court, and on August 10, 1792, ordered
an attack on the King's palace.   The King had them shot down by
his Swiss guards.   But the victory lay with the people, and the
Commune forced the Assembly to depose the King and imprison
him.

The Red Flag, as everybody knows, is now the flag of the workers
everywhere, of socialism and communism.   Formerly it used to be
the official flag to proclaim martial law against the people.   I
imagine, but I am not sure, that the use of this flag by the Paris
Commune was the first use of it on behalf of the people, and it was
from this that it gradually developed into the workers' flag.

The deposition and imprisonment of the King were not enough.
The people of Paris, inflamed at the action of the Swiss guards in
shooting and killing many of them, and full of fear and anger at
traitors and spies, went about arresting the people whom they
suspected and filling the prisons with them.   Many of those arrested
were no doubt guilty, but many innocent persons were also arrested
and imprisoned.   Some days later another fierce wave of passion
came over the people, and they brought out their prisoners from the
prisons and, after a mock trial, killed most of them.   Over 1000 persons were killed in these " September massacres ", as they are called.
This was the first taste of blood on a large scale which the Paris
mob got.   Much more blood was to flow before the thirst for it was
satiated.

In September also occurred the first victory of the French troops
over the invading Austrians and Prussians.   This was at the little

battle of Valmy, small in itself but with big results, for it saved the Revolution.

On September 21, 1792, the National Convention met. This was a new body taking the place of the Assembly. It was more advanced than the two Assemblies that had gone before it, but it still lagged behind the Commune. The first thing that the Convention did was to proclaim a republic. The trial of Louis XVI came soon after; he was condemned to death, and on January 21, 1793, he had to pay with his head for the sins of the monarchy. He was guillotined—that is, beheaded by the guillotine. The people of France had now burned their boats behind them. They had taken the final step and defied the kings and emperors of Europe. There was no going back for them, and from the very steps of the guillotine, which was still covered with a king's blood, Danton, a great leader of the Revolution, addressed the assembled crowds and hurled his challenge at these other kings. "The kings of Europe would challenge us," he cried; "we throw them the head of a king!"

102

REVOLUTION AND COUNTER-REVOLUTION

October 13, 1932

KING LOUIS was gone. But even before his death France had undergone an amazing change. The blood of her people was afire with the fever of revolution; their veins tingled and a flaming enthusiasm took possession of them. Republican France was at bay; the rest of Europe, kingly Europe, was against her. Republican France would show these effete kings and princes how patriots warmed by the sun of liberty could fight. They would fight not only for their own newly won freedom, but for the freedom of all others who were oppressed by kings and nobles. To the nations of Europe the French people sent their message, calling upon them to rise against their rulers, and declaring themselves the friends of all peoples and the enemies of all kingly governments. France, *la patrie*, became the mother of freedom, at whose altar it was a joy to sacrifice. And in this hour of fierce enthusiasm there came to them a wonderful song, in tune with their flaming mood, making them rush forward singing to the battle-front and leap over all obstacles, reckless of the odds. This was Rouget de Lisle's war-song for the army of the Rhine, known since then as the *Marseillaise*, and even now the national song of the French.

> *Allons, enfants de la patrie,*
> *Le jour de gloire est arrivé !*
> *Contre nous de la tyrannie*
> *L'étendard sanglant est levé.*
> *Entendez-vous dans les campagnes,*
> *Mugir ces féroces soldats !*

Ils viennent jusque dans nos bras,
Égorger nos fils, nos compagnes !
Aux armes, citoyens ! formez vos bataillons !
Marchons, marchons, qu'un sang impur abreuve nos sillons !

They did not sing futile songs about long life to kings. Instead they sang of the sacred love of the motherland, and of liberty, beloved liberty.

Amour sacré de la patrie,
Conduis, soutiens nos bras vengeurs !
Liberté, liberté chérie,
Combats avec tes défenseurs !

There were terrible privations. There was not food enough or clothing, or boots or shoes, or even arms. In many places the citizens were asked to give up their boots and shoes for the army; patriots gave up many kinds of food which were scarce and were needed by the army; some even fasted frequently. Leather and kitchen utensils and frying-pans and buckets and many other household articles were requisitioned. And in the streets of Paris there was a hammering at many a forge for the common people, all the *citoyens* and *citoyennes* were helping even in the manufacture of arms. There were great privations; but what did it matter when France, *la patrie*, beautiful France in her rags but with the crown of freedom on her head, was in danger, and the enemy was at her gate? So the youth of France rushed to her rescue and, careless of hunger or thirst, marched to victory. "Seldom," says Carlyle, "do we find that a whole people can be said to have any Faith at all; except in things that it can eat and handle. Whensoever it gets any Faith, its history becomes spirit-stirring, noteworthy." This faith in a great cause came to the men and women of the Revolution, and the history they made in those memorable days, and the sacrifices they endured, have still the power of stirring us and quickening our pulse.

These revolutionary armies of new recruits, half-trained as they were, drove out all foreign troops from French soil and then freed the lower Netherlands (Belgium, etc.) from the Austrians. For the last time the Hapsburgs left the Netherlands, to return no more. The trained professional armies of Europe could not face these revolutionary recruits. The trained soldier fought for pay and fought cautiously; the revolutionary recruit fought for an ideal and was prepared to take great risks to win. The former moved slowly with a mountain of baggage, the latter had little to carry and moved rapidly. The revolutionary armies were thus a new type in war, and they fought with a new technique. They changed the old methods of warfare and became, to some extent, the models for the armies of the next 100 years in Europe. But the real strength of these armies lay in their enthusiasm and their audacity. For their motto, and indeed for the motto of the Revolution itself at this stage, we can give Danton's famous phrase : "*Pour vaincre les ennemis de la patrie il nous faut de l'audace, encore de l'audace et toujours de l'audace.*"

The war spread. England became a powerful enemy because of her navy. Republican France had built up a great land army, but on the sea she was weak. England started a blockade of all French ports. From England also the French *émigrés* poured into France millions of false *assignats* or currency notes of the French Republic. In this way they tried to ruin French currency and finances.

The foreign war dominated everything, and all the energy of the nation went into it. Such wars are dangerous for revolutions, for they turn attention from social problems to fighting the foreign enemy, and thus the real object of the revolution is defeated. War fever takes the place of the fever of revolution. So it happened in France and, as we shall see, the last stage of France was the dictatorship of a great military commander.

There was trouble also at home. In the Vendée, in the west of France, a great peasant revolt broke out, partly because of the refusal of the peasantry there to join the new armies, and partly because of the efforts of the royalist leaders and *émigrés*. The Revolution was really being controlled and directed by the city people of Paris; the peasantry could not understand or appreciate the swift changes in the capital, and they lagged behind. The Vendée revolt was suppressed with great cruelty. During war, and especially civil war, the worst passions are aroused and pity becomes a homeless wanderer. In Lyons there was a counter-revolutionary rising. It was put down and a proposal was made that the great city of Lyons be destroyed as a punishment ! " Lyons made war against liberty—Lyons exists no more ! " Fortunately this proposal was not accepted, but Lyons was made to suffer a great deal.

Meanwhile what was happening in Paris ? Who was in control there ? A newly elected Commune and its sections still dominated the life of the city. In the National Convention there was a struggle for power between the various groups, chief amongst which were the Girondins or the moderate republicans and the Jacobins or the extreme republicans. The Jacobins won, and at the beginning of June 1793 most of the Girondin deputies were excluded from the Convention. The Convention now took the final step to abolish feudal rights, and lands which had belonged to the feudal lords were restored to the local communes or municipalities—that is, these lands became common property.

The Convention, dominated by the Jacobins now, appointed two committees—the Committees of Public Welfare and Public Safety—and gave them wide powers. These committees, and especially the one on Public Safety, soon became very powerful and dreaded. They drove the Convention on from step to step till the Revolution tumbled into the abyss of the Terror. Fear still cast its shadow over everybody : fear of the foreign enemies who surrounded them, of spies and traitors, and there were many of these. Fear blinds and makes desperate, and the Convention, urged on by this ever-haunting fear, passed a terrible law in September 1793—the Law of Suspects. No one who was suspected was safe, and who could be free from being suspected? A month later twenty-two Girondin deputies of the Convention were tried by the Revolutionary Tribunal and rapidly sentenced to death.

Thus began the Terror. Daily there were journeys to the guillotine of those who were condemned; daily the carts—tumbrils they were called—carrying these victims, creaked and rumbled over the cobble-stones of the Paris streets, and the people jeered at the unhappy persons. To speak even in the Convention against the ruling clique was dangerous, for that led to suspicion, and suspicion led to trial and the guillotine. The Convention was controlled by the Committees of Public Welfare and Public Safety. These Committees, with all the power of life and death in their hands, did not like to share it with others. They objected to the Commune of Paris; indeed, they objected to everyone who did not agree with them. Power has an extraordinary way of corrupting people. So these Committees set about to crush the Commune, which, with its sections, had been the backbone of the Revolution. They crushed the sections first, and, having lopped off its supports, they crushed the Commune. Thus does revolution often eat itself up. The sections in each part of Paris were the links which joined the populace with the people on top; they were the veins through which ran the red blood of the Revolution, which gave it strength and life. The crushing of the sections and the Commune early in 1794 meant the cutting off of this life-blood. Henceforth the Convention and the Committees were organs of government on top, not in living touch with the people, trying, like all those in authority, to impose their will on others by means of the Terror. This was the beginning of the end of the real revolutionary period. For another six months the Terror was to continue and the Revolution drag on. But the end was in sight.

Who were the leaders of Paris and France during these days of storm and stress? Many names stand out. Camille Desmoulins, the man who led the attack on the Bastille in 1789, and played a notable part on many another occasion. Pleading for a policy of clemency during the Terror, he himself fell a victim to the guillotine, to be followed only a few days later by his young wife, Lucille, who preferred death to living without him. Fabre d'Eglantine, the poet, Fouquier-Tinville, the dreaded public prosecutor. Marat, perhaps the greatest and ablest of the men of the Revolution, stabbed to death by a young girl, Charlotte Corday. Danton, whom I have twice quoted already, brave and leonine, a great and popular orator, but none the less to end on the guillotine. And Robespierre, the best known of all, the leader of the Jacobins and practically the dictator of the Convention during the days of the Terror. He has become almost the embodiment of the Terror, and many people think of him with a shudder. Yet of this man's honesty and patriotism there is no question; he was known as the " incorruptible ". But simple as he was in his life, he was inordinately self-centred, and he seemed to think that everyone who differed from him was a traitor to the Republic and the Revolution.

Many of the great men of the Revolution, who had been his colleagues, were sent to the guillotine at his instance; till at last the Convention which had been following him so meekly turned upon him. They called him a tyrant and a despot, and put an end to him and his despotism.

All these leaders of the Revolution were young men; revolutions are seldom made by the old. Important as many of these leaders were, none of them, not even Robespierre, plays a dominating part in the great drama. Before the fact of the Revolution itself they seem to shrink; for the Revolution was not brought about, or even controlled, by them. It was one of those elemental human earthquakes which occur from time to time in history, and which social conditions and long-continued misery and despotism prepare, slowly but irrevocably.

Do not imagine that the Convention did nothing except quarrel and guillotine. The energy released by a real revolution is always very great. Much of this was absorbed by the foreign wars, but still much remained, and a great deal of constructive work was done. In particular, the whole system of national education was overhauled. The Metric System, which every child in school learns now, was introduced then, and it simplified all weights and measures of length and volume. This system has spread now to most parts of the civilized world, but conservative England still sticks to an ancient out-of-date system of yards and furlongs and pounds and hundredweights and the like. We in India have to put up with these complicated lengths and weights as well as seers and maunds, etc.

As a logical corollary to the metric system, there was a new republican calendar. It began from the day the Republic was proclaimed, September 22, 1792. The week of seven days was changed to a week of ten days, the tenth day being a holiday. There were twelve months still, but their names were changed. Fabre d'Eglantine, the poet, gave delightful new names to the months, in accordance with the season. The three spring months were Germinal, Floréal, Prairial; the summer months were Messidor, Thermidor, Fructidor; autumn came in Vendémiaire, Brumaire, Frimaire; and winter in Nivôse, Pluviôse, Ventôse. This calendar did not long survive the Republic.

At one time there was a strong movement against Christianity and the worship of Reason was proposed. Temples of Truth were put up. The movement spread rapidly to the provinces. In November 1793 there was a great Fête of Liberty and Reason in Notre Dame Cathedral in Paris, and a beautiful woman personified Reason. But Robespierre was conservative in such matters. He did not approve of this movement. Neither did Danton. The Jacobin Committee of Public Welfare was against it, and the leaders of the movement were therefore guillotined. There was no half-way house between power and the guillotine. As a counterblast to the Fête of Liberty and Reason, Robespierre arranged another celebration---the Fête of the Supreme Being. By a vote of the Convention it was decided that France believed in a Supreme Being ! The Roman Catholic religion crept back again into favour.

After the crushing of the Paris sections and Commune, matters were rapidly coming to a head. The Jacobins were supreme; they controlled the government, but they were falling out among themselves. The guillotining of Hébert and his supporters, who had taken the lead in the Fête of Liberty and Reason, was the first big break in the Jacobin party. Fabre d'Eglantine followed; and when, early in 1794, Danton and Camille Desmoulins and others protested against Robespierre sending too many people to the guillotine, they themselves were struck down. The execution of Danton, in April 1794, carried out in a hurry lest the people should intervene, meant to the people of Paris and the provinces that the Revolution had ended. A lion of the Revolution had fallen, and a narrow clique was now in power. Surrounded by enemies, cut off from the people, this clique spotted treason everywhere and saw no other way of saving itself than to intensify the Terror.

So the Terror grew worse and the tumbrils rolling to the guillotine were more crowded with victims than ever. In June a new law was passed, called the Law of the 22nd Prairial, which made it a crime, punishable by death, to spread false news to divide or stir up the people, to undermine morality and corrupt the public conscience. Everyone who differed from Robespierre and his henchmen could be caught in the wide net of this law. Large groups of persons were tried together and sentenced—as many as 150, a mixture of convicts, royalists and others, being tried together on one occasion.

For forty-six days this new Terror lasted. At last, on the 9th Thermidor (July 27, 1794), the worm turned. The Convention suddenly turned against Robespierre and his supporters, and with cries of " Down with the tyrant ", they arrested them, and would not allow Robespierre even to speak. The next day the tumbril carried him to the guillotine where he had sent so many. Thus ended the French Revolution.

After the fall of Robespierre came the counter-revolution. The Moderates came to the front, and these people now fell on the Jacobins and terrorized over them. After the Red Terror there came what is called the White Terror. Fifteen months later, in October 1795, the Convention broke up and a Directory of five members became the Government. This was definitely a *bourgeois* government, and it tried to keep down the common people. For over four years the Directory ruled France and, such was the prestige and strength of the Republic even after all the internal troubles, it carried on victorious war abroad. There were some insurrections against it, but they were put down. One of these was suppressed by a young general of the Republican Army, Napoleon Bonaparte, who dared to fire at the Paris crowd—this is famous as the " whiff of grapeshot "—and kill many of them. When the old Revolutionary Army could itself be used to kill the common people of France, then obviously there was no shadow of revolution left.

So the Revolution ended, and many of the bright dreams of the

idealists and the hopes of the poor ended with it. And yet it had
gained much that it set out to gain. No counter-revolution could
bring back serfdom again, and not even the Bourbon kings—the
French dynasty was Bourbon—when they came back, could take
back the land which had been distributed among the peasantry.
The common man in the field or in the town was far better off than
he had ever been before. Indeed, even during the Terror he was
better off than before the Revolution. The Terror was not against
him, but against the upper classes; though towards the end some
of the poorer people also suffered under it.

The Revolution fell, but the republican idea spread throughout
Europe, and with it went the principles which had been proclaimed
in the Declaration of the Rights of Man.

103

THE WAYS OF GOVERNMENTS

October 27, 1932

I HAVE not written for two weeks. I am afraid I grow slack.
The thought that I am approaching the end of my story keeps me
back a little. Already we are at the end of the eighteenth century;
the 100 years of the nineteenth century await our inspection, and
then we shall have just two and thirty years of the twentieth to
bring us right up to to-day. But these 132 years that remain will
take a lot of telling. Being quite near us, they loom large and fill
our minds, and seem to us more important than earlier events.
Much that we see around us to-day has its roots in these years, and
indeed I shall have no easy task in leading you through the dense
forest of events and happenings of the last century and more.
Perhaps this is the reason why I shirk it! But I wonder also what
I shall do when, at last, I bring this story of man to the year 1932,
and the past merges into the present and stops before the shadow
of the future. What shall I write to you then, my dear? What
pretext shall I find to sit pen in hand and think of you, or imagine
you sitting by me asking me many a question which I try to answer?

Three letters I have written about the French Revolution—three
long letters about five brief years in the history of France. During
our journey through the ages we have taken centuries at a stride,
and we have seen continents at a glance. But here in France,
between the years 1789 and 1794, we have made a fairly lengthy
stay; and yet you will be surprised to learn that I have tried very
hard to be brief, for my mind was full of the subject and my pen
wanted to run on. The French Revolution is important historically.
It marks the end of an epoch and the beginning of another. But
it fascinates even more by its dramatic character, and it teaches
many a lesson to all of us. The world is to-day again in a ferment,
and we are on the eve of great changes. In our own country we

live in a period of revolution, however peaceful it may be. So we may learn much from the French Revolution and from the other great revolution, which has taken place in Russia in our own day and almost before our eyes. Real revolutions of the people, like these two, cast a fierce light on the grim realities of life; like a flash of lightning they reveal the whole landscape, and especially the dark places. For a while at least the goal seems clearly visible and strangely near. Faith and energy fill one. Doubt and hesitation vanish. There is no question of compromise with the second best. Straight, like an arrow, the men who make the revolution go toward the goal, seeing neither to the right nor to the left; and the straighter and keener their vision the farther goes the revolution. But this occurs only during the high period of the revolution, when its leaders are on the mountain peaks and the masses are marching up the mountain side. But, alas ! there comes a time when they have to come down from the mountains into the dark valleys below, and faith grows dim and energy grows less.

In 1778 old Voltaire, who had been an exile almost all his life, came back to Paris to die. He was eighty-four years old then. Addressing the youth of Paris he said : " The young are fortunate; they will see great things." Indeed they saw and took part in great things, for the Revolution broke out eleven years later. It had been kept waiting long enough. " *L'état c'est moi* ", had said Louis XIV, the Grand Monarque, in the seventeenth century; " *Après moi le déluge* ", said his successor, Louis XV, in the eighteenth ; and after this invitation the deluge came and swept away Louis XVI and his company. Instead of the nobles with their powdered wigs and silken breeches, the " sansculottes "—the men without breeches —came to the front; and everybody in France was a " citoyen " or a " citoyenne." " *Liberté, Égalité, Fraternité* " was the motto of the new Republic shouted out to the world.

The Terror looms large in the days of the Revolution. In less than sixteen months, from the appointment of the special Revolutionary Tribunal to the fall of Robespierre, nearly 4000 persons were guillotined. That is a large number, and when one thinks that many an innocent person must have been sent to the guillotine, one is shocked and grieved. And yet it is well to remember certain facts, so that we may see the French Terror in its true perspective. The Republic was surrounded by enemies and traitors and spies, and many of those condemned to the guillotine were avowed opponents working for the destruction of the Republic. Toward the end of the Terror the innocent suffered with the guilty. When fear comes our vision is clouded, and it becomes difficult to distinguish between the guilty and the innocent. The French Republic had to face at a critical moment the opposition and treachery of some even of their own great generals, like Lafayette. It is no wonder that the nerve of the leaders failed them and they started hitting right and left indiscriminately.

It is also well to remember, as H. G. Wells points out in his History, what was happening in those days in England and America and other countries. The criminal law, especially in defence of property, was savage, and people were hanged for trivial offences. In some places torture was still officially used. Wells says that far more people were hanged in this way in England and America than were sent to the guillotine under the Terror in France during the same period.

Think again of the slave raids of those days with their horrible cruelty and inhumanity. Think also of war, modern war especially, which wipes off hundreds of thousands of young men in their prime. Come nearer, to our own country, and consider recent events. Thirteen years ago, on an April evening in Amritsar, the day of the spring festival, hundreds were done to death and thousands grievously wounded in the Jallianwala Bagh. And all the conspiracy cases and special tribunals and ordinances—what are they but attempts to terrorize and coerce a people ? The intensity of repression and terrorism is a measure of the fear of a government. Every government, reactionary or revolutionary, alien or *swadeshi*, when it fears for its own existence, indulges in terrorism. The reactionary government does so on behalf of some privileged people and against the masses; the revolutionary government acts on behalf of the masses and against the privileged few. The revolutionary government is franker and more straightforward; it is often cruel and harsh, but there is little of subterfuge or deceit in it. The reactionary government lives in an atmosphere of deception, for it knows that it could not last if it were found out. It talks about liberty, and means thereby liberty for itself to do what it pleases. It talks of justice, and means by it the perpetuation of the existing order under which it flourishes, though others perish. Above all, it talks of law and order and, under cover of this phrase, shoots and kills and imprisons and gags and does every illegal and disorderly thing. In the name of " law and order " hundreds of our brethren have been tried by special tribunals and condemned to death. In this name, on an April day two and a half years ago in Peshawar, machine-guns shot down large numbers of our brave Pathan fellow-countrymen, unarmed as they were. And for this " law and order " the British Air Force drops bombs on our frontier villages and in Iraq, and kills or maims for life men and women and little children indiscriminately. Lest people should escape on the approach of an aeroplane, a fiendish ingenuity has devised what are called " time-delayed bombs ", which fall down apparently harmlessly and do not burst for a while. The men and women of the village, thinking that the danger is past, return to their homes, and soon afterwards the bombs burst and kill and destroy.

Think also of the day-to-day terror of starvation which overshadows millions. We get used to the misery around us. We imagine that the workers and the peasants are a coarser lot than we are and not very sensitive to suffering. Vain arguments to still the pricking of our own consciences ! I remember visiting a coalmine in Jharia in Bihar, and I shall never forget the shock I had when I saw men and women working away far underneath the surface of the earth in long, black, dark corridors of coal. People talk of an eight-hour work-day for the mine-workers, and some even oppose this and think that more work should be got out of them. And when I hear or read these arguments, my mind goes back to that visit of mine to the black dungeons below where even eight minutes became a trial for me.

The French Terror was a terrible thing. And yet it was a flea-bite compared to the chronic evils of poverty and unemployment. The costs of social revolution, however great they might be, are less than these evils and the cost of war which comes to us from time to time under our present political and social system. The Terror of the French Revolution looms large because many titled and aristocratic persons were its victims, and we are so used to honouring the privileged classes that our sympathies go out to them when they are in trouble. It is well to sympathize with them as with others. But it is also well to remember that they are just a few. We may wish them well. But those who really matter are the masses, and we cannot sacrifice the many to a few. " 'Tis the people that compose the human race," writes Rousseau; " what is not people is so small a concern that it is not worth the trouble of counting."

I intended telling you of Napoleon in this letter. But my mind has wandered and my pen run on to other subjects, and Napoleon still awaits inspection. He must await our pleasure till the next letter.

104

NAPOLEON

November 4, 1932

OUT of the French Revolution emerged Napoleon. France, Republican France, that had challenged and dared the kings of Europe, succumbed to this little Corsican. A strange, wild beauty had France then. A French poet, Barbier, has compared her to a wild animal, a proud and free mare, with head high and shining skin; a beautiful vagabond, fiercely intolerant of saddle and harness and rein, stamping on the ground, and frightening the world with the noise of her neighing. This proud mare consented to be ridden by the young man from Corsica, and he did many wonderful deeds with her. But he tamed her also and made the wild free thing lose all her wildness and freedom. And he exploited her and exhausted her till she threw him down and fell down herself.

> *O Corse à cheveux plats ! que la France était belle*
> *Au grand soleil de messidor !*
> *C'était une cavale indomptable et rebelle,*
> *Sans frein d'acier, ni rênes d'or ;*
> *Une jument sauvage à la coupe rustique,*
> *Fumante encore du sang des rois,*
> *Mais fière, et d'un pied fort heurtant le sol antique,*
> *Libre pour la première fois !*

Jamais aucune main n'avait passé sur elle
  Pour la flétrir et l'outrager ;
Jamais ses larges flancs n'avaient porté la selle
  Et le harnais de l'étranger ;
Tout son poil reluisait, et, belle vagabonde,
  L'œil haut, la croupe en mouvement,
Sur ses jarrets dressée, elle effrayait le monde
  Du bruit de son hennissement.

What manner of man was Napoleon, then? Was he one of the great ones of the earth, the Man of Destiny, as he was called, a mighty hero and one who helped in freeing humanity from its many burdens? Or was he, as H. G. Wells and some others say, a mere adventurer and a wrecker, who did great injury to Europe and civilization? Probably both these views are exaggerated; probably both contain some measure of the truth. All of us are curious mixtures of the good and the bad, the great and the little. He was such a mixture, but, unlike most of us, extraordinary qualities went to make up this mixture. Courage he had and self-confidence and imagination and amazing energy and vast ambition. He was a very great general, a master of the art of war, comparable to the great captains of old—Alexander and Chengiz. But he was petty also, and selfish and self-centred, and the dominating impulse of his life was not the pursuit of an ideal, but the quest of personal power. "My mistress!" he once said, "Power is my mistress! The conquest of that mistress has cost me so much that I will allow no one to rob me of her, or to share her with me!" Child of the Revolution he was, and yet he dreamt of vast empire, and the conquests of Alexander filled his mind. Even Europe seemed small. The East lured him, and especially Egypt and India. "Only in the East," he said, early in his career when he was twenty-seven, "have there been great empires and mighty changes; in the East where six hundred million people dwell. Europe is a mole-hill!"

Napoleon Bonaparte was born in 1769 in the island of Corsica, which was under France. He had mixed French-Corsican and Italian blood. He was trained in a military school in France, and during the Revolution was a member of the Jacobin Club. But probably he joined the Jacobins merely to advance his own interests, and not because he believed in their ideals. In 1793 he won his first victory at Toulon. The rich people of this place, afraid of losing their property under the revolutionary régime, had actually invited the English and handed over the remains of the French navy to them. This disaster, coupled with others at the time, had been a great blow to the young Republic, and every available man, and even women, were called upon to enlist. Napoleon crushed the rebels and defeated the English force at Toulon by a masterly attack. His star began to shine brightly now, and at the age of twenty-four he was a general. Within a few months, however, he got into trouble when Robespierre was guillotined, and he was suspected of belonging to his party. But the only party he really belonged to had a membership of one only—namely, Napoleon! Then came the Directory, and Napoleon proved that, far from being

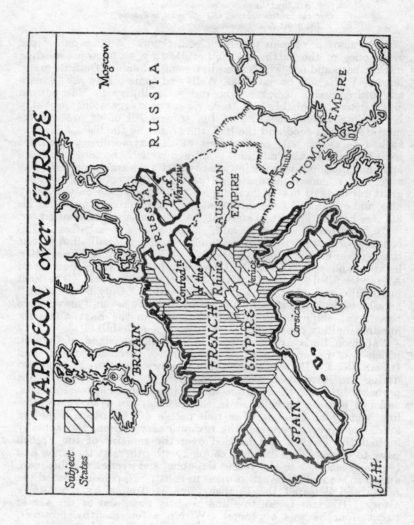

a Jacobin, he was a leader of counter-revolution and could shoot down the common people without turning a hair. This was the famous "whiff of grapeshot", in 1795, of which I have told you in a previous letter. On that day Napoleon wounded the Republic. Within ten years he had put an end to the Republic and become Emperor of the French.

In 1796 he became the commander of the Army of Italy and he astonished Europe by a brilliant campaign in northern Italy. The French army had still something of the fire of revolution. But they were in rags and had neither proper clothes nor shoes nor food nor money. He led this tattered and footsore band across the Alps, promising them food and all good things when they reached the rich Italian plain. To the people of Italy, on the other hand, he promised freedom; he was coming to liberate them from oppressors. A strange mixture of revolutionary jargon with the prospect of loot and plunder! So he played cleverly on the feelings of both the French and the Italians, and, being partly Italian himself, he produced a great impression. As victories came to him, his prestige grew and his fame spread. In his own army he shared in many ways the lot of the common soldier, and he shared also his danger, for an attack usually found him wherever danger threatened most. He was ever on the look out for real merit, and rewarded it immediately, even on the battlefield. To his soldiers he was like a father—a very young father!—known affectionately as the " Petit Caporal ", and often addressed by them as " tu ". Is it any wonder that this young general in his twenties became the darling of the French soldiers?

Having triumphed all over northern Italy and defeated Austria there, and put an end to the old republic of Venice, and made a very undesirable imperialistic peace, he returned to Paris as the great conquering hero. He was beginning to dominate France already. But he felt perhaps that the time was not ripe for him to seize power, and so he arranged to go with an army to Egypt. From his youth onwards he had felt this call of the East, and now he could gratify it, and dreams of vast empire must have floated in his mind. He just managed to escape the English fleet in the Mediterranean and reached Alexandria.

Egypt was then part of the Ottoman Turkish Empire, but this empire had declined, and in effect the Mamelukes ruled Egypt nominally under the Sultan of Turkey. Revolutions and inventions might shake Europe, but the Mamelukes still lived after the fashion of the Middle Ages. It is said that when Napoleon approached Cairo, a Mameluke knight, in brilliant attire of silk and damascened armour, rode up to the French army and challenged the leader to single combat! The poor man was met most unchivalrously by a volley. Soon afterwards, Napoleon won the Battle of the Pyramids. He was fond of dramatic poses. Riding in front of his troops before the Pyramids he addressed them : " Soldiers, forty centuries are looking down upon you ! "

Napoleon was master of war on land and he continued to win.

But on sea he was helpless. He did not understand it, and he does not seem to have had competent admirals. England just then had a genius in command of her navy in the Mediterranean. This was Horatio Nelson. Nelson came, rather audaciously, right into harbour one day and destroyed the French fleet at what is called the Battle of the Nile. Napoleon was thus cut off from France in a foreign country. He managed to escape secretly and reached France, but in doing so he sacrificed his Army of the East.

In spite of victories and some military glory, the great eastern expedition had been a failure. It is interesting to note, however, that Napoleon took with him to Egypt a whole crowd of savants and learned men and professors with books and all manner of apparatus. There were daily discussions of this " Institute ", in which Napoleon joined as an equal, and the savants did a great deal of good work of scientific exploration. The old riddle of the hieroglyphics was solved by the discovery of a granite slab containing an inscription in three scripts—Greek and two variants of Egyptian picture writing. With the help of the Greek the other two scripts were deciphered. It is also interesting to find that a proposal to cut a canal at Suez interested Napoleon greatly.

When in Egypt, Napoleon opened negotiations with the Shah of Persia and Tippu Sultan in South India. But nothing came of them because of his powerlessness at sea. It was sea-power that ultimately broke Napoleon; and it was sea-power that made England great in the nineteenth century.

France was in a bad way when Napoleon returned from Egypt. The Directory was discredited and unpopular, and so everybody turned to him. He was willing enough to assume power. A month after his return, in November 1799, with the help of his brother Lucien, he forcibly dispersed the Assembly, and thus put an end to the constitution as it then existed, under which the Directory had governed. This *coup d'état*, as such forcible State actions are called, made Napoleon the master of the situation. He could only do it because he was popular and the people had faith in him. The Revolution had long been liquidated ; democracy even was now disappearing and a popular general held the field. A new constitution was drafted under which there were to be three consuls (this name was taken from ancient Rome), but the chief of these with full power was Napoleon, who was called First Consul and was appointed for ten years. During the discussions on the constitution someone suggested that there should be a president with no real power, whose chief business would be to sign documents and formally represent the Republic, something like the constitutional kings, or the French President, of to-day. But Napoleon wanted power, not merely the livery of royalty. He would have none of this stately but powerless President. " Away with this fat hog ", he cried.

This constitution, with Napoleon as First Consul for ten years, was put to the vote of the people, and it was almost unanimously adopted by over 3,000,000 votes. Thus the people of France themselves presented all power to Napoleon, in the vain hope that he would bring them freedom and happiness.

But we cannot follow Napoleon's life-story in detail. It is full of intense activity and a hunger for more and more power. On the very first night after the *coup d'état*, before the new constitution was framed or passed, he appointed two committees to draft a legal code. This was the first act of his dictatorship. After long discussions, in which Napoleon joined, this code was finally adopted in 1804. It was called the *Code Napoléon*. Judged by the ideas of the Revolution or by modern standards, this code was not advanced. But it was an advance on existing conditions, and for 100 years it was, in some respects, almost a model for Europe. In many other ways he introduced simplicity and efficiency in the administration. He interfered in everything and had a wonderful memory for details. With his amazing energy and vitality he exhausted all his co-workers and secretaries. One of these co-workers writes about him during this period : " Ruling, administering, negotiating—with that orderly intelligence of his, he gets through eighteen hours' work a day. In three years he has ruled more than the kings ruled in a century." This, no doubt, is exaggerated, but it is clear that Napoleon had, like Akbar, an extraordinary memory and perfectly ordered mind. He said himself : " When I wish to put away any matter out of my mind, I close its drawer and open the drawer belonging to another. The contents of the drawers never get mixed up, and they never worry me or weary me. Do I want sleep ? I close all the drawers and then I am asleep." Indeed, he was known to lie down on the ground in the middle of a battle and sleep for half an hour or so and then get up for another long spell of intensive work.

He had been made First Consul for ten years. The next step in the ladder of power came after three years, in 1802, when he had himself made Consul for life, and his powers were increased. The Republic was at an end, and he was a monarch in all but name, and inevitably, in 1804, he declared himself Emperor, after taking a vote of the people. He was all-powerful in France, and yet there was a great difference between him and the autocratic kings of old. He could not base his authority on tradition and divine right. He had to base it on his efficiency and on his popularity with the people, especially the peasants, who were all along his most faithful supporters because they felt that he had saved their lands for them. " What do I care," said Napoleon once, " for the opinion of drawing-rooms and the babblers ! I recognize only one opinion, that of the peasants." But the peasants also grew weary at last of supplying their sons for the warfare that was almost continuously going on. When this support was withdrawn, the mighty edifice that Napoleon had created began to totter.

For ten years he was Emperor, and during these years he rushed about all over the Continent of Europe and carried on striking military campaigns and won memorable battles. All Europe trembled at his name and was dominated by him as it has never been dominated by anyone else before or since.   Marengo (this was in 1800, when he crossed with his army the Great St. Bernard pass in Switzerland, all covered with the winter snow), Ulm, Austerlitz, Jena, Eylau, Friedland, Wagram, are the names of some of his famous victories on land.   Austria, Prussia and Russia all collapsed before him.   Spain, Italy, the Netherlands, a great part of Germany called the Confederation of the Rhine, Poland called now the Duchy of Warsaw, were all subject States.   The old Holy Roman Empire, which had long existed in name only, was finally ended.

Of the major European Powers, England alone escaped disaster. The sea, which was ever a mystery to Napoleon, saved England. And because of the security given by the sea, England became the greatest and most relentless of his enemies.   I have told you how, right at the beginning of his career, Nelson destroyed Napoleon's fleet in the Battle of the Nile.   On October 21, 1805, Nelson won a greater victory still against the combined French and Spanish fleets off Cape Trafalgar on the south coast of Spain.   It was just before this sea battle that Nelson gave his famous signal to his fleet : " England expects that every man will do his duty."   Nelson died in the hour of triumph, but his victory, proudly cherished by the English people and commemorated in the Nelson column and Trafalgar Square in London, destroyed Napoleon's dream of invading England.

Napoleon retaliated by an order closing all the harbours on the continent of Europe to England.   There were to be no communications with her of any kind, and England, " the nation of shop-keepers ", was to be subdued in this way.   England, on her part, blockaded these ports and prevented trade between Napoleon's Empire and America and other continents.   England also fought Napoleon by ceaseless intrigue on the Continent and lavish distri-bution of gold to his enemies and to neutrals.   She was helped in this by some of the great money houses of Europe, notably the Rothschilds.

Yet another method adopted by England against Napoleon was propaganda.   This was a novel kind of campaign then, but it has since become common enough.   A Press campaign against France, and especially Napoleon, was started.   All manner of articles, pamphlets, news-sheets, cartoons making fun of the new Emperor, and spurious memories, full of falsehoods, were issued from London and smuggled into France.   Nowadays a Press campaign of false-hood has become a regular part of modern war.   During the Great War of 1914–1918 the most extraordinary lies were told unblushingly by all governments of the countries involved, and in this art of manufacturing and circulating falsehood the English Government seems to have been easily first.   It had a long century-old training since the days of Napoleon.   We in India know well enough how truth about our country is suppressed and the most amazing falsehood circulated here and in England.

105

MORE ABOUT NAPOLEON

November 6, 1932

WE must carry on the story of Napoleon from where we left off in our last letter.

Wherever Napoleon went, he carried something of the French Revolution with him, and the peoples of the countries he conquered were not wholly averse to his coming. They were weary of their own effete and half-feudal rulers, who sat heavily upon them. This helped Napoleon greatly, and feudalism fell before him as he marched. In Germany especially was feudalism swept away. In Spain he put an end to the Inquisition. But the very spirit of nationalism that he unconsciously evoked turned against him and ultimately defeated him. He could overpower the old kings and emperors, but not a whole people roused against him. The Spanish people thus rose against him and for years sapped his energy and resources. The German people also organized themselves under a great patriot, Baron von Stein, who became the implacable enemy of Napoleon. There was a German war of liberation. Thus Nationalism, which Napoleon himself had aroused, allied to sea-power, brought about his fall. But in any event it would have been difficult for the whole of Europe to tolerate a dictator. Or perhaps Napoleon himself was correct when he said afterwards : " No one but myself can be blamed for my fall. I have been my own greatest enemy, the cause of my disastrous fate."

This man of genius had the most extraordinary failings. He always had a touch of the *parvenu*, the upstart, about him, and he nourished a strange desire to be treated as an equal by the old and effete kings and emperors. He advanced his own brothers and sisters in the most absurd way, although they were thoroughly incompetent. The only decent brother was Lucien, who had helped Napoleon at a critical moment during the *coup d'état* of 1799, but who subsequently fell out with him and retired to Italy. The other brothers, vain and foolish, were made kings and rulers by Napoleon. He had a curious and vulgar passion for pushing on his family. Almost every one of them played him false and deserted him when he was in trouble. Napoleon was also very keen on founding a dynasty. Early in his career, even before he had gone on the Italian campaign and become famous, he had married Josephine de Beauharnais, a beautiful but rather flighty lady. He was terribly disappointed at having no children by her, for he had set his heart on a dynasty. So he decided to divorce Josephine and marry another woman, although he liked her. He wanted to marry a Russian Grand Duchess, but the Tsar would not agree to this. Napoleon might be almost the master of Europe, but the Tsar considered it somewhat presumptuous of him to aspire to marry into the Russian imperial family ! Napoleon then more or less forced the Hapsburg

Emperor of Austria to give him his daughter Marie Louise in marriage. He had a son by her, but she was dull and unintelligent and did not like him at all and made him a bad wife. When he was in trouble, she deserted him and forgot all about him.

It is very strange how this man, who towered above his generation in some ways, fell a victim to the empty glamour which the old idea of kingship exercised. And yet, often enough, he spoke in terms of revolution and made fun of these effete kings. He had deliberately turned his back on the Revolution and the new order; the old order neither suited him nor was it prepared to have him. So between the two he fell.

Gradually this career of military glory goes to its inevitable tragic end. Some of his own ministers are treacherous and intrigue against him; Talleyrand intrigues with the Tsar of Russia, Fouché intrigues with England. Napoleon catches them in their treachery and yet, strange to say, merely upbraids them and allows them to continue as his ministers. One of his generals, Bernadotte, turns against him and becomes a bitter enemy. His family, except for his mother and his brother Lucien, continue to misbehave, and often work against him. Even in France discontent increases and his dictatorship becomes hard and ruthless, many people being imprisoned without trial. His star is definitely on the decline, and many a rat, foreseeing the end, deserts the ship. Physically and mentally he is also declining, although still young in years. He gets violent colic pains right in the middle of a battle. Power also corrupts him. His old skill is still there, but he moves more heavily now; often he hesitates and is in doubt, and his armies are more cumbrous.

In 1812, with a mighty army—the Grande Armée it was called —he moves to the invasion of Russia. He defeats the Russians and then advances without much opposition. The Russian armies retreat and retreat and refuse to fight. The Grande Armée seeks them in vain, and at last reaches Moscow. The Tsar is inclined to give in, but two men, a Frenchman, Bernadotte, Napoleon's old colleague and general, and the German nationalist leader, Baron von Stein, whom Napoleon had declared an outlaw, prevail upon him not to do so. The Russians set fire to their own beloved city of Moscow to smoke the enemy out. And when news of the burning of Moscow reaches St. Petersburg, Stein, sitting at table, raises his glass to it and cries : " Three or four times, ere this, I have lost my baggage. We must get used to throwing away such things. Since we must die, let us be valiant ! "

It is the beginning of winter. Napoleon decides to leave burning Moscow and to return to France. And so the Grande Armée trudges back wearily through the snow with the Russian Cossacks ever by their sides and at their heels, attacking them, harassing them continuously, cutting down stragglers. The bitter cold and the Cossacks between them take toll of thousands of lives, and the Grande Armée becomes a ghostly procession—all on foot and in rags, footsore and frost-bitten, wearily dragging themselves along.

Napoleon also marches on foot with his grenadiers. It is a terrible and heart-breaking march, and the mighty army becomes smaller and smaller and almost vanishes away. Just a handful of people return.

This Russian campaign was a terrible blow. It exhausted France of her man-power. Even more so it aged Napoleon, and made him careworn and weary of strife. But he was not to be allowed to rest in peace. His enemies surrounded him and, although he was still the brilliant commander winning victories, the net drew closer and closer. Talleyrand's intrigues increased, and some even of Napoleon's trusted marshals turned against him. Weary and disgusted, Napoleon abdicated from the throne in April 1814.

A great congress of the European Powers was held in Vienna to make a new map of Europe, now that Napoleon was out of the way. Napoleon was sent to the little island of Elba in the Mediterranean. Another Bourbon, another Louis, brother of the one who was guillotined, was brought out from wherever he had been living in seclusion and was placed on the throne of France as Louis XVIII. The Bourbons were thus back again, and with them came back much of the old tyranny. So this was the end of all the brave doings of five and twenty years since the Bastille fell ! In Vienna the kings and their ministers argued and quarrelled among themselves, and during the intervals had a good time. They felt enormously relieved. A great terror had been removed, and they could breathe again. Talleyrand, the traitor who had betrayed Napoleon, was popular with this crowd of kings and ministers, and played an important part in the Congress. Another famous diplomatist at the Congress was Metternich, the Foreign Minister of Austria.

In less than a year Napoleon had had enough of Elba, and France had had enough of the Bourbons. He managed to escape in a little boat, and landed at Cannes on the Riviera on February 26, 1815, almost alone. He was received enthusiastically by the peasants. The armies that were sent against him, when they saw their old commander, the " Petit Caporal ", shouted " *Vive l'Empereur* " and joined him. And so, triumphantly, he reached Paris and the Bourbon King fled away. But in all the other capitals of Europe there was terror and consternation. And in Vienna, where the Congress was still dragging on, the dancing and the feasting came to a sudden end, and a common fear made the kings and ministers forget all their squabbling and concentrate on the one task of crushing Napoleon anew. So all Europe marched against him, but France was weary of warfare. And Napoleon, although only forty-six, was a tired old man, forsaken even by his wife, Marie Louise. He won some battles, but finally he was defeated at Waterloo, near the city of Brussels, by the English and Prussian armies, under Wellington and Blücher, just 100 days after he landed. This period of his return is therefore called " The Hundred Days ". Waterloo was a hardly contested battle and victory hung in the balance. Napoleon had very bad luck. It was quite possible for him to have won it, but even so he would have had to go down some time later before a combined Europe. Defeated as he was now, many of his supporters tried to save themselves by turning against him. A struggle was hopeless, and he abdicated for the second time, and going to an English ship in a French port, handed himself over to the captain, saying that he wanted to live quietly in England.

But he was mistaken if he expected liberal and courteous treatment from England or Europe. They were too frightened of him, and his escape from Elba had convinced them that he must be kept far away and securely guarded. So, in spite of his protests, he was declared a prisoner and sent, with a few companions, to the far-away island of St. Helena in the South Atlantic Ocean. He was considered " the prisoner of Europe ", and several Powers sent commissioners to keep watch on him in St. Helena, but in reality the English had the full responsibility for guarding him. Even on that far-away island, cut off from the world, they brought quite an army to keep watch on him. This lonely rock of St. Helena was described at the time by Count Balmain, the Russian Commissioner there, as " that spot in the world which is the saddest, the most isolated, the most unapproachable, the easiest to defend, the hardest to attack, the most unsociable . . ." The English Governor of the island was an extraordinarily uncouth and barbarous person, and he treated Napoleon very shabbily. He was kept in the most unhealthy part of the island in a wretched house, and all manner of irritating restrictions were placed on him and his companions. Sometimes he did not even have enough wholesome food to eat. He was not allowed to communicate with friends in Europe, not even with his little son, whom, in the days of his power, he had given the title of King of Rome. Indeed, even news of his son was not allowed to reach him.

It is surprising how meanly Napoleon was treated. But the Governor of St. Helena was but the tool of his government, and it seems to have been the deliberate policy of the English Government to ill-treat and humiliate their prisoner. The other Powers of Europe were consenting parties to this. Napoleon's mother, in spite of her old age, wanted to join him in St. Helena, but the Great Powers said no ! This shabby treatment given to him is a measure of the terror which he still inspired in Europe, although his wings had been clipped and he lay powerless in a far-away island.

For five and a half years he endured this living death in St. Helena. It is not difficult to imagine how this man of vast energy and ambition must have suffered, cooped up in that little rock of an island and subjected daily to petty humiliations. He died in May 1821, and even after death he was pursued by the hatred of the Governor, and a wretched grave was provided for him. Slowly, as the news of the ill-treatment and persecution of Napoleon reached Europe (news travelled slowly in those days), there was an outcry against it in many countries, including England. Castlereagh, the English Foreign Minister, who was chiefly responsible for this ill-treatment, became very unpopular because of this and also because of his harsh domestic policy. He felt this so much that he committed suicide.

It is difficult to judge great and extraordinary men; and that Napoleon was great in his own way and extraordinary there can be no doubt. He was elemental, almost like a force of Nature. Full of ideas and imagination, he was yet blind to the value of ideals and unselfish motives. He tried to win and impress people by offering them glory and wealth. When therefore his stock of glory and power lessened, there were few ideal motives to keep by him those very people whom he had advanced, and many basely deserted him. Religion was to him just a method of keeping the poor and the miserable satisfied with their lot. Of Christianity he once said : " How could I accept a religion which would damn Socrates and Plato ? " When in Egypt he showed some favour to Islam, no doubt because he thought this might win him popularity with the people there. He was thoroughly irreligious, and yet he encouraged religion, for he looked upon it as a prop to the existing social order. "Religion," he said, "associates with heaven an idea of equality, which prevents the poor from massacring the rich. Religion has the same sort of value as vaccination. It gratifies our taste for the miraculous, and protects us from quacks. . . . Society cannot exist without inequality of property; but this latter cannot exist without religion. One who is dying of hunger when the man next to him is feasting on dainties can only be sustained by a belief in a higher power, and by the conviction that in another world there will be a different distribution of goods." In the pride of his strength, he is reported to have said : " Should the heavens fall down on us we shall hold them off with the points of our lances."

He had the magnetism of the great, and he won devoted friendship from many. His glance, like Akbar's, was magnetic. " I have seldom drawn my sword," he said once; " I won my battles with my eyes, not with my weapons." A strange statement for a man who plunged Europe into war ! In later years, during his exile, he said that force was no remedy, and that the spirit of man was greater than the sword. " Do you know," he said, " what amazes me more than all else ? The impotence of force to organize anything. There are only two powers in the world : the spirit and the sword. In the long run the sword will always be conquered by the spirit." But there was no long run for him. He was in a hurry, and right at the beginning of his career he had chosen the way of the sword; by the sword he triumphed, and by the sword he fell. Again, he said : " War is an anachronism; some day victories will be won without cannon and without bayonets." Circumstances were too much for him—his vaulting ambition, the ease with which he triumphed in war, and the hatred of the rulers of Europe for this upstart and their fear of him, which allowed him no peace to settle down. He was reckless in sacrificing human lives in battle, and yet it is said that the sight of suffering greatly moved him.

In his personal life he was simple, and never indulged in any excesses, except excess of work. According to him, " However little a man may eat he always eats too much. One can get ill from over-eating, but never from under-eating." It was this simple life which gave him splendid health and vast energy. He could sleep when he liked and as little as he liked. To ride 100 miles in the course of the morning and afternoon was not an extraordinary thing for him.

As his ambition carried him across the European Continent, he began to think of Europe as one State, one unit, with one law, one government. "I shall fuse all the nations into one." Later, chastened by his exile in St. Helena, this idea came back to him, and in a more impersonal form : " Sooner or later, this union [of European nations] will be brought about by the force of events. The first impetus has been given; and after the fall of my system, it seems to me that the only way in which an equilibrium can be achieved in Europe is through a league of nations." More than 100 years later, Europe is still groping and experimenting with a League of Nations !

He wrote a last testament in which he left a message for his little son, whom he had called the King of Rome, and news even of whom had been so cruelly kept away from him. He hoped that his son would reign one day, and he told him to reign in peace, and not to have recourse to violence. " I was obliged to daunt Europe by arms; in the present day, the way is to convince by reason." But the son was not destined to reign. He died in Vienna in his youth, eleven years after his father.

But all these thoughts came to him during his exile, when he was much chastened, and perhaps also he wrote to influence posterity in his favour. In the days of his greatness he was too much of a man of action to be a philosopher. He worshipped only at the altar of power; his real and only love was power, and he loved it not crudely but as an artist. " I love power," he said—" yes, I love it, but after the manner of an artist : as a fiddler loves his fiddle in order to conjure from it tone and chords and harmonies." But the quest for over-much power is a dangerous one, and sooner or later downfall and ruin come to the individuals or nations who seek it. So Napoleon fell, and it was as well that he fell.

Meanwhile the Bourbons reigned in France. But it has been said that the Bourbons never learned anything and never forgot anything. Within nine years after Napoleon's death, France had had enough of them and overthrew them. Another monarchy was established and, as a gesture of good-will to the memory of Napoleon, his statue, which had been removed from the top of the Vendôme column, was placed on it again. And the unhappy mother of Napoleon, blind through age, said : " Once again the Emperor is in Paris."

106

A SURVEY OF THE WORLD

November 19, 1932

So Napoleon passed away from the world's stage which he had dominated for so long. More than a 100 years have passed since then, and the dust of many an old controversy has settled down. But, as I have told you, people still differ greatly about him. Probably if Napoleon had been born during some other, and more peaceful, period he would have been just a distinguished general and nothing more, and might have passed almost unnoticed. But revolution and change gave him the chance to forge ahead, and he seized it. His fall and passing out of European politics must have come as a great relief to the people of Europe, for they were weary of war. A whole generation had not seen real peace, and they longed for it. None felt the relief more than the kings and princes of Europe, who had trembled at Napoleon's name for many years.

We have spent a long time in France and Europe, and now we are well advanced into the nineteenth century. Let us have a look round the world and see what it was like when Napoleon fell.

In Europe, you will remember, the old kings and their ministers had gathered together at the Congress of Vienna. The bogeyman was gone, and they could now play at their old game and settle the fate of millions of human beings at their sweet will and pleasure. It did not matter what the people wanted, nor did it matter what the natural and linguistic boundaries of a country were. The Tsar of Russia, England (represented by Castlereagh), Austria (represented by Metternich), and Prussia were the principal Powers; and of course there was Talleyrand, clever and witty and popular, once the minister of Napoleon, now the minister of the Bourbon King of France. These people, in the intervals of feasting and dancing, re-cast the map of Europe, which had been changed so much by Napoleon.

Louis XVIII, the Bourbon, was thrust back on France. In Spain even the Inquisition was restored. The monarchs at the Congress of Vienna did not like republics. So they did not re-establish the old Dutch Republic in Holland. Instead, they lumped up Holland and Belgium in one kingdom of the Netherlands. Poland disappeared again as a separate country and was swallowed up by Prussia, Austria and chiefly Russia. Venice and North Italy went to Austria. A bit of Italy and a bit of France, between Switzerland and the Riviera, became the kingdom of Sardinia. In central Europe there was a curious and vague German Confederation, but the two chief Powers in it continued to be Prussia and Austria. And there were other changes also. So the wise men of the Congress of Vienna ordained, forcing people hither and thither against their will, making them speak a language which was not their own, and generally sowing the seeds of future trouble and war.

What the Congress of Vienna of 1814–1815 was especially concerned with was to make the kings quite secure. The French Revolution had given them the fright of their lives, and they thought, foolishly, that they could prevent the new revolutionary ideas from spreading. The Tsar of Russia, the Emperor of Austria and the King of Prussia even formed what was called " The Holy Alliance " to preserve themselves and other monarchs. Almost it seems as if we are back to the days of Louis XIV and Louis XV. There was suppression all over Europe, including England, of all liberal ideas. How progressive people in Europe must have despaired that the agony of the French Revolution had been in vain !

In the east of Europe, Turkey had weakened greatly. It was undergoing a process of slow decay. Egypt was supposed to be within the Turkish Empire, but was semi-independent. Greece revolted against Turkish dominion in 1821, and after eight years of war won its freedom with the help of England, France and Russia. It was in this war that the English poet Byron died as a volunteer fighting for Greece. He has written some very beautiful poems about Greece which perhaps you know.

I might as well mention here two other political changes that took place in Europe in 1830. France, fed up with the repression and tyranny of the Bourbons, drove them out again. But instead of a republic, another king was chosen. This was Louis Philippe, who behaved a little better, and more or less as a constitutional king. He managed to reign till 1848, when there was another and a bigger outburst. In Belgium also there was a revolt in 1830. This resulted in the separation of Belgium and Holland. The big European Powers of course strongly disapproved of a republic. So they presented a German prince to Belgium and made him king there. Another German prince was made King of Greece. The many states of Germany always seem to have had an abundance of such princes, to be had whenever a throne was vacant. The English royal house that is still reigning, you will remember, came from the little State of Hanover in Germany.

The year 1830 was a year of revolts in many other places in Europe also—in Germany and Italy and especially in Poland. But the revolts were crushed by the kings. There was a great deal of cruel repression in Poland by the Russians, and even the use of the Polish language was forbidden. This year—1830—was a kind of prelude to 1848, which, as we shall see, was a year of revolution in Europe.

So much for Europe. Across the Atlantic, the United States were gradually spreading out towards the west. Far away from European rivalries and wars, and with unlimited land at their disposal, they were making rapid progress and were catching up Europe. In South America, however, great changes took place. These were indirectly caused by Napoleon. When Napoleon conquered Spain and put a brother of his on the throne there, the

Spanish colonies in South America revolted. Thus, strangely enough, it was the loyalty of the Spanish American colonies to the old Spanish dynasty that led them to independence. But this was the immediate excuse. The break would have come anyhow some time later, for the spirit of independence was growing all over South America. The great hero of South American independence was Simon Bolivar, called *El Libertador*, the Liberator. The Republic of Bolivia in South America is named after him. Thus, when Napoleon fell, Spanish America was cut off from Spain and was fighting for independence. The removal of Napoleon made no difference to the struggle, and it continued against the new Spain for many years. Some of the European kings wanted to help their brother-King of Spain to crush the revolutionaries in the American colonies. But the United States put a final stop to this interference. Monroe was President of the United States then, and he told the European Powers that if they interfered anywhere in America, North or South, they would have to fight the United States. This threat frightened the European Powers, and since then they have more or less kept away from South America. President Monroe's threat to Europe has become famous as the " Monroe Doctrine ". It protected the new South American republics from the greed of Europe for a long time, and allowed them to grow. They were protected from Europe well enough, but there was no one to protect them from the protector—the United States. To-day the United States dominate them, and many of the smaller republics are completely under their thumb.

The vast country of Brazil was a colony of Portugal. This also became independent about the same time as the Spanish colonies of America. So we find that by 1830 the whole of South America was free from European domination. In North America there was of course the British colony of Canada.

We now come to Asia. In India the English were now undoubtedly the predominant Power. During the Napoleonic wars in Europe the English had consolidated their position and even taken possession of Java. Tippu Sultan in Mysore had been vanquished, and in 1819 the Maratha power was finally overthrown. In the Punjab, however, there was a Sikh State under Ranjit Singh. All over India the British were creeping on and spreading. In the east, Assam was annexed, and Arakan—Burma—remained for the next mouthful.

While Britain spread in India, another great European Power, Russia, was spreading in Central Asia. Already it touched the Pacific in the east and China. Now it was rolling down through the petty States of Central Asia right to the frontier of Afghanistan. The British in India grew afraid of this giant approaching them, and in their nervousness provoked a war with Afghanistan without the shadow of an excuse. But they burnt their fingers badly.

China was under the Manchus, suspecting, with good reason, the foreigners who came in the name of trade or religion, and trying to keep them out. But the foreigners continued to shout and misbehave at her gates, and especially encouraged the traffic in opium. The East India Company had the monopoly of the British China trade. The Chinese Emperor prohibited the entry of opium, but smuggling continued, and the foreigners carried on an illegal trade in opium. This resulted in a war with England, rightly called the Opium War, and the British forced the Chinese to take opium.

I told you long ago of the shutting up of Japan in 1634. At the beginning of the nineteenth century it was still closed to all outsiders. But within its closed borders the old Shogunate was getting weaker, and new conditions were rising which were going to put a sudden end to the old system. Farther south, in southeastern Asia, European Powers were absorbing territory. The Spanish still held the Philippine Islands. The Portuguese had been driven away by the English and Dutch. The Dutch got back Java and the other islands after the Congress of Vienna. The English were spreading out to Singapore and the Malay Peninsula. Annam, Siam and Burma were still independent, though they paid an occasional tribute to China.

Very roughly this was the political state of the world during the fifteen years from Waterloo to 1830. Europe was definitely coming out as the boss of the world; and in Europe itself reaction was triumphant. The emperors and kings, and even the reactionary Parliament of England, thought that they had finally crushed liberal ideas. They tried to bottle up these ideas. They failed, of course, and there were repeated revolts.

The political changes seem to dominate the scene. Yet far more important was the great revolution in methods of production and distribution and travel that began with the Industrial Revolution of England. Silently but irresistibly this was spreading in Europe and North America, and was changing the outlook and habits of millions, and the relations between different classes. New ideas were emerging out of the clanging of the machinery, and a new world was being built up. Europe was growing more and more efficient and deadly, more and more greedy and imperialistic and callous. The spirit of Napoleon seemed to pervade it. But in Europe also were growing up ideas which were destined to fight and overthrow imperialism.

Also there is the literature and poetry and music of this period that fascinates. But I must not allow my pen to run on. It has done enough duty for to-day.

107

THE HUNDRED YEARS BEFORE THE WORLD WAR

November 22, 1932

NAPOLEON fell in 1814; he returned from Elba next year and was again defeated, but his system had collapsed in 1814. Exactly 100 years later, in 1914, began the Great War, which spread almost all over the world and, during the four years that it lasted, caused terrible loss and suffering. We shall have to consider this period of 100 years in some detail. Already, in my last letter, I have tried to give you a rough idea of the world as it was when this period began. It is worth while, I think, for us to have a look at the century as a whole before we examine bits of it in different countries. In this way, perhaps, we shall have a better idea of the main currents during these 100 years, and thus see the wood as well as the trees.

These 100 years from 1814 to 1914 fell, as you will of course notice, very largely in the nineteenth century. We might as well refer to them, therefore, as the nineteenth century, although this would not be quite accurate.

The nineteenth century is a fascinating period. But the study of it is no easy matter for us. It is a vast panorama, a great picture, and because we are so near to it, it appears to us bigger and fuller than the centuries that preceded it. This bigness and complexity are rather apt to overwhelm us at times, as we try to unravel the thousand threads that go to make it up.

It was the century of marvellous mechanical progress. The Industrial Revolution brought in its train the Mechanical Revolution, and machines became more and more important in man's life. They did a great deal that man had done before, and eased his drudgery, and lessened his dependence on the elements, and produced wealth for him. Science helped greatly, and travel and transport became swifter and ever swifter. The railway came and displaced the stagecoach; the steamship took the place of the sailing-ship, and then came the great ocean liner, powerful and stately, going from continent to continent with speed and regularity. Towards the end of the century came the automobile, and motor-cars spread out all over the world. And lastly came the aeroplane. At the same time man began to control and utilize a new wonder—electricity—and the telegraph and telephone appeared. All this made a vast difference to the world. As the means of communication developed and people travelled faster and faster, the world seemed to shrink and become much smaller. We are used to all this to-day, and we seldom think about it. But all these improvements and changes are newcomers to this world of ours; they have all come within the last 100 years.

It was also the century of Europe, or rather of Western Europe, and especially of England. The Industrial and Mechanical Revolutions had begun and progressed there, and they gave a great lead to western Europe. England was predominant in sea-power and industry, but gradually the other countries of western Europe caught up with it. The United States of America also forged ahead with this new mechanical civilization, and railroads carried them westwards to the Pacific, and made the huge country one nation. They were too busy with their own problems and their expansion to trouble themselves much about Europe and the rest of the world. But they were strong enough to resent and prevent any interference from Europe. The Monroe Doctrine, about which I told you in my last letter, preserved the republics of South America from the greed of Europe. These republics are called the Latin republics, as they were founded by people from Spain and Portugal. These two countries, as well as Italy and France, are called Latin nations. The northern countries of Europe are, on the other hand, Teutonic, England being the Anglo-Saxon branch of the Teutons. The people of the United States of America originally came from this Anglo-Saxon stock, but of course all kinds of immigrants have gone there since.

The rest of the world was backward industrially and mechanically, and could not compete with the new mechanical civilization of the West. The new machine industries of Europe produced goods far more rapidly and abundantly than the old cottage-industries. But to produce these goods raw material was required, and much of this was not to be had in western Europe; and when the goods were produced, they had to be sold, and so markets for them were necessary. So western Europe searched for countries which would provide this raw material and buy the manufactured goods. Asia and Africa were weak, and Europe fell on them like a beast of prey. In the race for empire, England, by virtue of her lead in industry and her sea-power, was easily first.

You will remember that Europeans first came to India and the East to buy spices and other articles in demand in Europe. Thus Eastern goods went to Europe, and many a product of an Eastern handloom went west. But now, with the development of the machine, this process was reversed. The cheaper goods of western Europe came to the East, and the cottage-industries of India were deliberately killed by the East India Company in order to encourage the sale of English goods.

Europe sat on giant Asia. In the north the Russian Empire sprawled across the whole continent. In the south England had firm hold over the biggest prize of all—India. In the west the Turkish Empire was going to pieces, and Turkey was referred to as the " Sick man of Europe ". Persia, nominally independent, was dominated by England and Russia. The whole of south-eastern Asia—Burma, Indo-China, Malay, Java, Sumatra, Borneo, the Philippines, etc.—was absorbed by Europe, with the exception of a bit of Siam. In the Far East China was being nibbled at by all the European powers and concession after concession was forced

out of her.   Only Japan stood upright and faced Europe as an equal.
She had come out of her seclusion and adjusted herself to the
new conditions with remarkable rapidity.

Africa was very backward, except for Egypt.   It could offer no
effective resistance to Europe, and so the European Powers fell
on it in a mad race for empire and divided up this huge continent.
England occupied Egypt, for it was on the way to India, and British
policy henceforth was dominated by the desire to hold on to India.
The Suez Canal was opened in 1869, and this made the journey from
Europe to India much shorter; it also made Egypt more valuable
to England, for Egypt could interfere with the canal, and thus controlled the sea-route to India.

So, as a result of the Mechanical Revolution, capitalist civilization
spread all over the world and Europe was dominant everywhere.
And capitalism led to imperialism.   So that the century might also
be called the century of imperialism.   But this new Imperial Age
was very different from the old imperialisms of Rome and China
and India and the Arabs and Mongols.   There was a new type of
empire, hungry for raw materials and markets.   The new imperialism
was the child of the new industrialism.   " Trade follows the flag ",
it was said, and often enough the flag followed the Bible. Religion,
science, the love of one's own country, all were prostituted to one
end—the exploitation of the weaker and industrially more backward
peoples of the earth, so that the lords of the big machine, the princes
of industrialism, might grow richer and richer.   The Christian
missionary, going in the name of truth and love, was often the out-
post of empire, and if any harm befell him, his country made this
an excuse to seize territory and extort concessions.

The capitalist organization of industry and civilization led inevitably to this imperialism.   Capitalism also led to an intensification of the feeling of nationalism, so that you can also call this century
the century of nationalism.   This nationalism was not merely a
love of one's own country, but a hatred of all others.   From this
glorification of one's own patch of land and contemptuous running
down of others, trouble and friction between different countries
were bound to result.   Industrial rivalry and imperial rivalry between
different European countries made matters worse.   The map of
Europe as settled by the Congress of Vienna in 1814 15 was
another irritating factor.   According to this, some nationalities
had been suppressed and put forcibly under other people's rule.
Poland had disappeared as a nation.   Austria-Hungary became an
ill-assorted empire containing all manner of people cordially disliking
each other.   The Turkish Empire in the south-east of Europe
contained many non-Turkish peoples in the Balkans.   Italy was
split up into many States, and part of it was under Austria.   Repeated attempts were made through war and revolution to change
this map of Europe.   In my last letter I mentioned some which
followed soon after the Vienna settlement.   In the second half of the
century Italy managed to shake off the Austrians in the north
and the Pope's domination in the centre, and became a united

nation. This was followed soon afterwards by the unification of Germany under the leadership of Prussia. France was defeated and humiliated by Germany and deprived of two of her frontier provinces, Alsace and Lorraine, and from that day she dreamt of *revanche* (revenge). In less than fifty years there was a bloody and terrible revenge.

England, with her great lead, was the most fortunate of the European countries. She held all the prizes, and was well content with things as they were. India was the model of the new type of empire, a rich territory from the exploitation of which a river of gold flowed ceaselessly to England. All the other would-be empire-builders envied this possession of India by England. They sought to build empires elsewhere after this Indian model. The French succeeded in some measure; the Germans came rather late into the field, and there was little left for them. So there was political tension all over the world between these " Great Powers " of Europe, each trying to swallow more and more territory and coming up against another engaged in the same process. Between England and Russia especially there was continuous friction, for Russia seemed to threaten England's possession of India from central Asia. So England was always trying to checkmate Russia. When Russia, in the middle of the century, defeated Turkey and coveted Constantinople, England came down on the side of Turkey and drove Russia back. England did this not out of love for Turkey, but from fear of Russia and of losing India.

England's industrial lead gradually grew less and less as Germany and France and the United States crept up to her. By the end of the century matters were coming to a head. The world was too small for the vast ambitions of these European Powers. Each feared and hated and envied the other, and this fear and hatred made them increase their armies and their ships of war. There was a feverish competition in these engines of destruction. There were also alliances between different countries to fight others, and ultimately two systems of alliances faced each other in Europe—one was headed by France, to which England also privately adhered, and the other was headed by Germany. Europe became an armed camp. And there was ever fiercer competition in industry and trade and armaments. And a narrow spirit of nationalism was whipped up in each western country, so that the masses might be misled and made to hate their neighbours in other countries, and thus be kept ready for war.

A blind nationalism thus began to dominate Europe. This was strange, for the speeding up of communications had brought different countries closer to each other and many more people travelled. One would have thought that as people grew to know their neighbours better, their prejudices would lessen and their narrow-mindedness give place to a broader outlook. To some extent this undoubtedly took place, but the whole structure of society under the new industrial capitalism was such that it bred friction between nation and nation, class and class, and man and man.

Nationalism also grew in the East. It took the shape of resistance to the foreigner, who was dominating and exploiting the country. At first the feudal relics in eastern countries resisted foreign domination, because they felt that their position was threatened. They failed, as they were bound to do. A new nationalism then arose tinged with a religious outlook. Gradually this religious colouring faded off and a nationalism of the western type emerged. In Japan, foreign domination was avoided, and an intense half-feudal nationalism was encouraged.

Asia began to resist European aggression from the earliest days, but the resistance became half-hearted when the power and efficiency of the new weapons which the European armies possessed were realized. The growth of science and the mechanical progress made in Europe had made these European armies far more powerful than anything the East had then. Eastern countries therefore felt powerless before them and bowed their heads in despair. Some people say that the East is spiritual and the West material. This kind of remark is very deceptive. The real difference between the East and the West at the time when Europe came as aggressor, in the eighteenth and nineteenth centuries, was the medievalism of the East and the industrial and mechanical progress of the West. India and other eastern countries were dazzled at first, not only by the military efficiency of the West, but also by their scientific and technical progress. All this combined to give them a feeling of inferiority in regard to military and technical matters. In spite of this, however, nationalism grew, and the desire to resist foreign aggression and turn out the foreigner. Early in the twentieth century an event occurred which had a great effect on the mind of Asia. This was the defeat of Tsarist Russia by Japan. For little Japan to defeat one of the greatest and most powerful of European Powers surprised most people; in Asia the surprise was a most pleasant one. Japan was looked upon as the representative of Asia battling against western aggression and, for the moment, became very popular all over the East. Of course Japan was no such representative of Asia, and she fought for her own hand just like any Great Power of Europe. I remember well how excited I used to get when news came of the Japanese victories. I was about your age then.

So, as the imperialism of the West became more and more aggressive, nationalism grew in the East to counter it and fight it. All over Asia, from the Arab nations in the West to the Mongolian nations of the Far East, national movements took shape, advanced cautiously at first and moderately, and then became more and more extreme in their demands. India saw the beginnings and early years of the National Congress. The revolt of Asia had begun.

Our survey of the nineteenth century is far from over yet. But this letter is long enough and must end.

108

THE NINETEENTH CENTURY CONTINUED

November 24, 1932

I TOLD you in my last letter of some of the distinguishing features of the nineteenth century and of the many things that resulted from the industrial capitalism which took possession of western Europe after the coming of the big machine. One of the reasons why western Europe took the lead in this was the possession by it of coal seams and iron ore. Coal and iron were essential for the making and working of the big machines.

This capitalism led, as we saw, to imperialism and nationalism. Nationalism was no new thing; it had existed before. But it became intenser and narrower. At the same time it bound together and separated; those living in one national unit came closer to each other, but they were cut off more and more from others living in a different national unit. While patriotism grew in each country, it was accompanied by dislike and distrust of the foreigner. In Europe, the industrially advanced countries glared at each other like beasts of prey. England, having got most of the booty, wanted naturally to stick to it. But for other countries, notably Germany, there was too much of England all over the place. So friction increased, and ended in open fighting. The whole structure of industrial capitalism, and its offshoot imperialism, leads to this friction and conflict. Inherent in them there seem to be contradictions which cannot be reconciled, based as they are on conflict and competition and exploitation. Thus in the East, nationalism, child of imperialism, became its bitter enemy.

In spite of these contradictions, however, the capitalist form of civilization taught many a useful lesson. It taught organization, for the big machine and large-scale industry require a great deal of organization before they can function. It taught co-operation in large undertakings. It taught efficiency and punctuality. It is not possible to run big factories or a railway system unless these qualities are present. Sometimes it is said that these qualities are typical western qualities and the East does not possess them. In this, as in most other matters, there is no question of the East and the West. The qualities were developed because of industrialism, and the West, being industrialized, possesses them, while the East, being still largely agricultural and not industrialized, is lacking in them.

Industrial capitalism performed one other great service. It showed how wealth could be produced by power production—that is, with the help of the big machine and coal and steam. The old fear that there was not enough in the world to go round, and so there must always be vast numbers of poor people, had the bottom knocked out of it. With the help of science and machinery, enough food and clothing, and every other thing that was necessary, could be produced for the world's population. The problem of production was thus solved, at least in theory. And yet there it stopped. Wealth was undoubtedly produced abundantly, but the poor remained poor and, indeed, became poorer. In the eastern and African countries, under European domination, there was of course naked and unashamed exploitation. There was no one to care for the unhappy people who lived there. But even in western Europe poverty remained and became more and more obvious. For a while the exploitation of the rest of the world brought wealth to western Europe. Most of this wealth remained with the few rich people at the top, but a little percolated through to the poorer classes, and their standard of living went up a little. Population also increased very greatly.

But much of this wealth and the raising of the standard of living was at the expense of exploited people in Asia, Africa, and other non-industrialized areas. This exploitation and flow of wealth hid for a while the contradictions of the capitalist system. Even so, the difference between the rich and the poor grew; the distance became greater. They were two different peoples, two separate nations. Benjamin Disraeli, a great English statesman of the nineteenth century, has described them :

> " Two nations; between whom there is no intercourse and no sympathy; who are as ignorant of each other's habits, thoughts and feelings, as if they were dwellers in different zones, or inhabitants of different planets; who are formed by a different breeding, are fed by a different food, are ordered by different manners, are not governed by the same laws . . . the Rich and the Poor."

The new conditions of industry brought large numbers of workers to the big factories, and so a new class arose—that of the factory-worker. These people were different from the peasants and field-workers in many ways. The peasant has to rely a great deal on the seasons and the rainfall. These are not under his control, and so he begins to think that his misery and poverty are due to supernatural causes. He becomes superstitious and ignores economic causes, and lives a dull, hopeless life, resigned to an unkind fate which he cannot alter. But the factory-worker works with machines, things made by man; he produces goods regardless of the seasons and the rainfall; he produces wealth, but he finds that this very largely goes to others and that he himself remains poor; to some extent he can see economic laws in action. And so he does not think of supernatural causes and is not so superstitious as the peasant. For his poverty he does not blame the gods; he blames society or the social system, and especially the capitalist owner of the factory who takes such a big part of the profits of his labour. He becomes class-conscious, and sees that there are different classes and the upper classes prey on his class. And this leads to discontent and revolt. The first murmurs of discontent are vague and dull; the first uprisings are blind and thoughtless and weak, and they are easily crushed by the government. For the government now wholly represents the interests of the new middle class which controls the great factories and their offshoots. But hunger cannot be crushed for long, and soon the poor worker finds a new source of strength in union with his comrades. So trade unions arise to protect the worker and fight for his rights. They are secret bodies at first, for the government will not even permit the workers to organize themselves. It becomes clearer and clearer that the government is definitely a class government, out to protect by all means the class it represents. Laws also are class laws. Slowly the workers gain strength, and their trade unions become powerful organizations. Different kinds of workers see that their interests are really one as against the exploiting class in power. So different trade unions co-operate together and the factory-workers of a country become one organized group. The next step is for the workers of different countries to unite, for they too feel that their interests are common and the enemy is a common one. Thus arises the cry : " Workers of the World Unite", and international organizations of workers are formed. Capitalist industry also grows meanwhile, and becomes international. And so labour confronts capitalism, wherever this industrial capitalism flourishes.

I have gone ahead too fast and must go back. But this nineteenth-century world is such a jumble of many tendencies, often contradicting each other, that it is difficult to keep them all in view. What will you make, I wonder, of this strange mixture of capitalism and imperialism and nationalism and internationalism and wealth and poverty ? But life itself is a strange mixture. We have to take it as it is, try to understand it, and then to better it.

This jumble of misfits made many people in Europe and America think. Early in the century, after Napoleon fell, there was little liberty in any European country. In some of these countries there was the king's despotism, in some, like England, a small aristocratic and rich class was in power. Everywhere, as I have told you, there was repression of the liberal elements. But in spite of this, the American and the French Revolutions had made the ideas of democracy and political liberty known and appreciated by liberal thinkers. Democracy, indeed, began to be looked upon as the cure for all the ills and troubles of the State and the people. The democratic ideal was that there should be no privilege; every person should be treated by the State as of equal social and political value. Of course people differ greatly from each other in many ways : some are stronger than others, some wiser, some more unselfish. But the believers in democracy said that whatever their differences might be, men should have the same political status. And this was to be brought about by giving everyone the vote. Advanced thinkers and liberals believed in the virtues of democracy fervently, and they tried hard to bring it about. The conservatives and reactionaries opposed them, and everywhere there was a great tussle. In some countries there were revolutions. England was on the verge of civil war before the franchise was extended—that is, votes for electing members to Parliament were given to some more people.

Gradually, however, democracy triumphed in most places, till by the end of the century most men at least had the vote in western Europe and America. Democracy had been the great ideal of the nineteenth century, so much so that the century might also be called the century of democracy. Democracy had triumphed in the end, and yet, when this end came, people had begun to lose faith in it. They found that it had failed to put an end to poverty and misery and many contradictions of the capitalist system. What was the good of a vote to a man who was hungry? And what was the measure of the liberty he had if his vote or his services could be purchased for the price of a meal? So democracy fell into disrepute, or, to be correct, political democracy went out of favour. But this is outside the scope of the nineteenth century.

Democracy dealt with the political aspect of liberty. It was a reaction against autocracy and other despotisms. It offered no special solution of the industrial problems that were arising, or of poverty, or class conflict. It laid stress on a theoretical freedom of each individual to work according to his bent, in the hope that he would try, from self-interest, to better himself in every way, and thus society would progress. This was the doctrine of *laissez-faire*, about which I think I wrote to you in a previous letter. But the theory of individual freedom failed because the man who was compelled to work for a wage was far from free.

The great difficulty that arose under the system of industrial capitalism was this : those who worked and thus served the community were poorly paid, the rewards went to others who did not work. Thus the rewards were divorced from the services. This resulted, on the one hand, in the degradation and impoverishment of those who laboured; and, on the other hand, in the creation of a class who lived, or rather sponged, on industry without themselves working in it or adding in any way to its wealth. It was like the peasantry, who worked on the land, and the *zamindar*, who profited by their labour, without working on the land himself. This distribution of the fruits of labour was manifestly unjust; what is more. the worker, unlike the long-suffering peasant, felt that it was unjust, and resented it; it tended to get worse as time went on. In all the industrialized countries of the West these discrepancies became glaring, and thoughtful and earnest people tried to find a way out of the tangle. Thus arose the set of ideas known as socialism, child of capitalism, and enemy of it, and perhaps destined to supplant it. In England it took a moderate form, in France and Germany it was more revolutionary. In the United States of America the comparatively small population in a vast country had plenty of opportunity for growth, and so the injustices and misery which capitalism brought to western Europe were not apparent to the same extent for a long time.

In the middle of the nineteenth century there arose a man in Germany who was destined to become the prophet of socialism and the father of that form of socialism which is known as communism. His name was Karl Marx. He was not just a vague philosopher or a professor who discussed academic theories. He was a practical philosopher, and his method was to apply the technique of science to the study of political and economic problems, and thus to find a remedy for the world's ills. Philosophy, he said, had hitherto merely set out to explain the world; communist philosophy must aspire to change it. Together with another man, Engels, he issued the "Communist Manifesto" which gave the outline of his philosophy. Later he published a mighty book in German called *Das Kapital* 'or *Capital*, in which he reviewed the world's history scientifically, and showed in what direction society was developing and how this process could be hurried up. I shall not try to explain the Marxian philosophy here. But I should like you to remember that Marx's great book had tremendous influence on the development of socialism, and it is to-day the Bible of Communist Russia.

Another famous book, which came out in England about the middle of the century, and created a great sensation was Darwin's *Origin of Species*. Darwin was a naturalist—that is, he observed and studied Nature, and especially plants and animals. He showed, with the help of many examples, how plants and animals had developed in Nature, how one species had changed into another by a process of natural selection, how simple forms had gradually become more complex. This kind of scientific reasoning was directly opposed to some religious teachings about the creation of the world and the animals and man. There was then a great argument between the scientists and the believers in these teachings. The real conflict was not so much about facts as about the attitude to life generally. The narrow religious attitude was largely one of fear and magic and superstition. Reasoning was not encouraged, and people were asked to believe in what they were told, and were not to question why. Many subjects were wrapped up in a mystic covering of sanctity and holiness, and were not to be uncovered or touched. The spirit and methods of science were very different from this. For science was curious to find out everything. It would not take anything for granted, nor would the supposed holiness of a subject frighten it away. It probed into everything, and discouraged superstition, and believed only in such things as could be established by experiment or reason.

The spirit of science won in this struggle with a fossilized religious outlook. Most people who thought about these matters had already, even as far back as the eighteenth century, become rationalists. You will remember that I told you of the wave of philosophic thought in France before the Revolution. But now the change went deeper into society. The average educated person began to be affected by the progress of science. He did not perhaps think very deeply on the subject, nor did he know much about science. But he could not help being awed by the pageant of discovery and invention that unfolded itself before him. The railway, electricity, the telegraph, telephone, phonograph and ever so many other things came one after the other, and they were all children of the scientific method. They were hailed as the triumph of science. Science was seen, not only to increase human knowledge, but also to increase man's control over Nature. It is not surprising that science triumphed and that people bowed down in worship before this all-powerful new god. And the men of science of the nineteenth century became very complacent and cocksure of themselves, and very definite in their opinions. Science has made vast progress from those days half a century ago, but to-day the attitude is very different from that complacency and cocksureness of the nineteenth century. To-day the real scientist feels that the ocean of knowledge is a vast and boundless one, and though he seeks to sail on it, he is humbler and more hesitating than his predecessors.

Another notable feature of the nineteenth century was the great progress of popular education in the West. This was opposed with great vigour by many members of the ruling classes, who said that it would make the common people discontented, seditious, insolent, and un-Christian! Christianity, according to this argument, consists in ignorance and a willing obedience to the rich and powerful. But in spite of this opposition, elementary schools were introduced and popular education spread. Like many other features of the nineteenth century, this also was a consequence of the new industrialism. For the big factory and big machine required industrial efficiency, and this could only be produced by education. The society of the period was in great need of all kinds of skilled labour; this need was met by popular education.

This widespread elementary education produced a very large class of literate people. They could hardly be called educated, but they could read and write, and the habit of reading newspapers spread. Cheap newspapers came out and had enormous circulations. They began to exercise a powerful influence over people's minds. Often indeed they misled and roused men's passions against a neighbouring country, and thus led to war. But, in any event, the " Press " definitely became a power to be reckoned with.

Much that I have written in this letter applies chiefly to Europe, and particularly to western Europe. To North America, also it applies to some extent. The rest of the world, Asia, with the exception of Japan and Africa, were passive and suffering agents of Europe's policy. The nineteenth century was, as I have said, the century of Europe. Europe seemed to fill the picture; Europe occupied the centre of the world's stage. In the past there had been long periods when Asia dominated Europe. There were periods when the centres of civilization and progress lay in Egypt or Iraq or India or China or Greece or Rome or Arabia. But the old civilizations exhausted themselves and became petrified and fossilized. The vital element of change and progress left them, and life passed on to other regions. It was Europe's turn now, and Europe was all the more dominant because of the progress in communications which made all parts of the world easily and rapidly accessible.

The nineteenth century saw the flowering of European civilization —*bourgeois* civilization it is called, because the *bourgeois* classes, produced by industrial capitalism, dominated it. I have told you of many of the contradictions and bad points of this civilization. We in India and the East saw these bad points especially, and suffered from them. But no country and no people can rise to greatness unless they have something of the stuff of greatness in them, and western Europe had such stuff in her. And the prestige of Europe rested ultimately not so much on her military power as on the qualities which had made her great. There was an abundant life and vitality and creative power evident everywhere. Great poets and writers and philosophers and scientists and musicians and engineers and men of action were produced. And undoubtedly even the lot of the common man in western Europe was far better than it had ever been before. The great capital cities—London, Paris, Berlin, New York—became bigger and bigger, and higher and higher went their buildings, and luxury increased, and science offered a thousand ways of lessening human toil and drudgery and of adding to the comfort and pleasure of life. And life among the well-to-do classes became mellow and cultured, and a certain complacency and self-sufficiency and unctuousness came to them. It seems almost like the pleasant afternoon or evening of a civilization.

So, in the second half of the nineteenth century, Europe bore a pleasant and prosperous aspect, and it seemed, on the surface at least, that this mellow culture and civilization would endure and progress from triumph to triumph. But if you peeped below the surface, you would see a strange commotion and many an unpleasant sight. For this prosperous culture was largely meant for the upper classes of Europe only, and it was based on the exploitation of many countries and many peoples. You would see some of the contradictions that I have pointed out, and the national hatreds and the grim and cruel face of imperialism. You would not then be so sure about the permanence or charm of this nineteenth-century civilization. The outside body was fair enough, but there was a canker in the heart; there was a great deal of talk of health and progress, but decadence was eating at the vitals of this *bourgeois* civilization.

The crash came in 1914. After four and a quarter years of war, Europe emerged indeed, but with terrible wounds which have not yet been healed. But of that I shall have to tell you afterwards.

109

WARS AND REVOLT IN INDIA

November 27, 1932

WE have had a good long survey of the nineteenth century. Let us now look more closely at certain parts of the world. We shall begin with India.

I told you some time back of how the British triumphed over

their rivals in India.   The French were definitely eliminated during
the Napoleonic wars.   The Marathas, Tippu Sultan in Mysore, and
the Sikhs in the Punjab, held the British for a while.   But they
could not resist them for long.   The British were obviously the
strongest and best-equipped Power.   They had better weapons
and better organization, and, above all, they had sea-power to fall
back upon.   Even when defeated, as they often were, they were not
eliminated, as they could draw upon other resources owing to their
command of the sea routes.   For the local Powers, however, defeat
often meant a disaster which could not be remedied.   The British
were not only the better-equipped fighters and the better organizers,
but were also far cleverer than their local rivals, and took every
advantage of their mutual rivalries.   So inevitably the British
power spread and the rivals were knocked down one by one, and often
with the help of others whose turn to go down came next.   It is
surprising how shortsighted these feudal chieftains of India were
at the time.   They never thought of uniting against the foreign
enemy.   Each fought a lone hand and lost, and deserved to lose.

As the British power grew in strength it became more and more
aggressive and truculent.   It made war with or without excuse.
There were many such wars.   I do not propose to weary you with
an account of them.   Wars are not pleasant subjects, and far too
much importance is paid to them in history.   But the picture would
be incomplete if I did not say something about them.

I have already told you of two wars between Haider Ali of Mysore
and the British.   Haider Ali was largely successful in these.   His
son, Tippu Sultan, was a bitter enemy of the British.   It took
two more wars, in 1790–92 and 1799, to put and end to him.   Tippu
died fighting.   Near Mysore city you can still see the ruins of his old
capital, Seringapatam, where he lies buried.

The Marathas remained to challenge British supremacy.   There
was the Peshwa in the west and Scindia of Gwalior and Holkar
of Indore and some other chiefs.   But the Maratha power went to
pieces after the death of two great statesmen, Mahadaji Scindia of
Gwalior who died in 1794, and Nana Farnavis, minister of the
Peshwa, who died in 1800.   Still the Marathas took a lot of beating,
and there were British defeats before the final overthrow of the
Marathas in 1819.   The Maratha chiefs were defeated separately,
each watching the other go down without helping.   Scindia and
Holkar became dependent rulers acknowledging the suzerainty of
the British.   The Gaikwar of Baroda had even previously come to
terms with the foreign Power.

Before taking leave of the Marathas I should like to mention one
name which has become famous in Central India.   This is the name
of Ahalya Bai, a ruler of Indore for thirty years from 1765 to 1795.
She was a young widow of thirty when she came to the *gaddi*, and
she succeeded remarkably well in administering her State.   Of
course she did not observe *purdah*.   The Marathas have never done
so.   She attended to the business of the State herself, sat in open
durbar, and raised Indore from a village to a wealthy city.   She

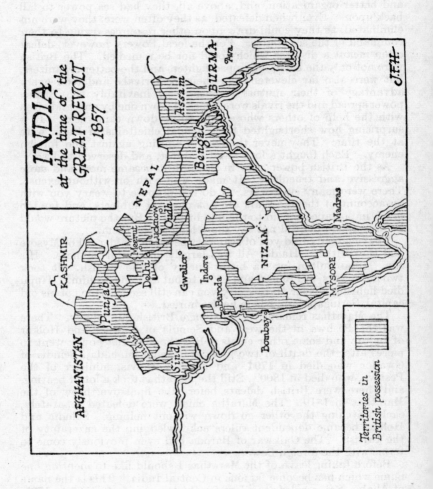

avoided wars and kept peace and made her State prosperous at a time when the greater part of India was in a state of turmoil. It is not surprising that she is still considered a saint and is revered in Central India.

A little before the last Maratha war, the British had a war with Nepal from 1814 to 1816. They had great difficulties in the mountains, but they won in the end, and this district of Dehra Dun, where I sit in prison writing this letter, and Kumaun and Naini Tal came under British rule. You may perhaps remember my telling you, in a letter on China, of the amazing exploit of a Chinese army which crossed Tibet and walked over the Himalayas and beat the Gurkhas in their homeland, Nepal. This was only twenty-two years before the British-Nepal War. Ever since then Nepal formally acknowledged China's suzerainty, but I suppose it does not do so now. It is a peculiar country, very backward, very much cut off from the rest of the world, and yet, from all accounts, a delight-fully situated place, full of natural wealth. It is not a dependent State like Kashmir or Hyderabad. It is called independent, but the British people see to it that this independence is kept within bounds. And the brave and warlike people of Nepal—the Gurkhas —are enrolled in the British army in India and are used to keep down Indians.

In the east, Burma had spread right up to Assam. So there was bound to be conflict with the ever-advancing British. There were three wars with Burma, each time the British annexing some terri-tory. The first war in 1824–26 resulted in Assam coming under the British; in the second war, in 1852, South Burma was annexed. North Burma, with the capital at Ava near Mandalay, was completely cut off from the sea and left high and dry, at the mercy of the British. The end came in 1885, when there was a third Burma War, and the whole of the country was annexed by the British and joined on to the British Empire. But Burma was in theory a vassal of China; and indeed it used to send tribute regularly. It is curious to note that the British, when annexing Burma, agreed to continue this tribute to China. This shows that even in 1885 they were sufficiently impressed by the power of China, although China was so involved in her own troubles that she could not help her vassal when Burma was invaded. The British paid the tribute to China once after 1885, and then discontinued it.

The Burma Wars have taken us to 1885. I wanted to deal with them all together. But now we must go back to North India and to an earlier part of the century. In the Punjab a great Sikh State had risen under Ranjit Singh. Right at the beginning of the century Ranjit Singh became master of Amritsar. By 1820 he was master of nearly the whole of the Punjab and Kashmir. He died in 1839. The Sikh State weakened and began to break up soon after his death. The Sikhs illustrate the old maxim that one rises in adversity and falls after success is attained. It was not possible even for the later Moghals to suppress the Sikhs when they were a hunted minority group. But with political success, the very foundations of success were weakened. There were two wars between the British and the Sikhs, the first in 1845–46 and the second in 1848–49. During the second there was a severe defeat of the British at Chilianwala. In the end, however, the British triumphed completely and the Punjab was annexed. It may interest you to know—because you are a Kashmiri—that Kashmir was sold by the British to a certain Raja Gulab Singh of Jammu for about seventy-five lakhs of rupees. It was a bargain for Gulab Singh ! The poor people of Kashmir of course did not count in the transaction. Kashmir is now one of the States dependent on the British and the present Maharaja there is a descendant of Gulab Singh.

Farther to the north, or rather north-west of the Punjab, lay Afghanistan, and not far from Afghanistan, on the other side, were the Russians. The spread of the Russian Empire in central Asia upset the nerves of the British. They were afraid that Russia might attack India. Almost right through the nineteenth century there was talk of the " Russian menace ". As early as 1839 the British in India made an entirely unprovoked attack on Afghanistan. At that time the Afghan frontier was far from British India, and the independent Sikh State of the Punjab intervened. None the less, the British marched to Kabul, making the Sikhs their allies. But the Afghans took signal revenge. However backward they may be in many respects, they love their freedom and will fight to the last to preserve it. And so Afghanistan has always been a " hornets' nest " for any foreign army that invaded it. Although the British had occupied Kabul and many parts of the country, suddenly there were revolts everywhere, they were driven back, and a whole British army suffered destruction. Later another British invasion took place to avenge this disaster. The British occupied Kabul and blew up the great covered bazaar of the city, and the British soldiery plundered and set fire to many parts of the city. It was clear, however, that Afghanistan could not easily be held by the British without continuous fighting. So they retired.

Nearly forty years later, in 1878, the British in India were again unnerved by the Amir, or ruler, of Afghanistan becoming friendly with Russia. To a large extent history repeated itself. There was another war, and the British invaded the country and seemed to have won, when the British envoy and party were massacred by the Afghans and a British army defeated. The British took some measures of retribution and again withdrew from the " hornets' nest ". For many years afterwards the position of Afghanistan was peculiar. The British would not allow the Amir to have any direct relations with other foreign countries, and at the same time they gave him annually a large sum of money. Thirteen years ago, in 1919, there was a third Afghan War which resulted in Afghanistan becoming fully independent. But this is outside the scope of the period we are discussing now.

There were other little wars also. One of these, a particularly shameless one, was forced on Sindh in 1843. The British Agent there bullied the Sindhis and goaded them to action, and then crushed them and annexed the province. And as a profitable side-line, prize money was distributed to the British officers for this deed; the Agent's (Sir Charles Napier) share being about seven lakhs of rupees ! It is not surprising that the India of that period attracted the unscrupulous and adventurous Britisher.

Oudh also was annexed in 1856. It was in a frightful state of misgovernment at the time. The rulers for some time past had been the Nawab-Viziers, as they were called. Originally, the Nawab-Vizier had been appointed by the Moghal Emperor at Delhi as his Governor of Oudh. But with the decay of the Moghal Empire, Oudh became independent. But not for long. The later Nawab-Viziers were thoroughly incompetent and depraved, and even if they wanted to do any good, they were unable to do it because of the interference of the East India Company. They had no real power left, and the British were not at all interested in the internal government of Oudh. So Oudh went to pieces, and, inevitably, became part of the British dominions.

I have said enough, and perhaps more than enough, of wars and annexations. But all these were just the outward indications of a great process that was going on, and that was bound to go on. In India the old economic order was already breaking up when the British came. Feudalism was cracking up. Even if no foreigners had come to India then, the feudal order could not long have survived. As in Europe, it would have given place slowly to a new order under which the new productive classes had more power. But before this change could take place, when only the break-up had occurred, the British came and, without much difficulty, stepped into the breach. The rulers they fought in India and defeated belonged already to a past and vanishing age. They had no real future before them. The British were thus, under the circumstances, bound to succeed. They hastened the end of the feudal order in India; and yet strangely, as we shall see later, they tried to prop it up outwardly and thus put obstacles in the way of India's progress towards the new order.

Thus the British became the agents of a historical process in India—the process which was to change feudal India into the modern kind of industrialized capitalist State. They did not realize this themselves; and certainly the various Indian rulers who fought them knew nothing about it. An order that is doomed seldom sees the signs of the times, seldom realizes that it has fulfilled its purpose and its function and should retire gracefully before all-powerful events force it into undignified retreat, seldom understands the lesson of history, and seldom appreciates that the world is marching on, leaving it behind in the " dustbin of history ", as somebody has said. Even so, the Indian feudal order did not realize all this and fought unavailingly against the British. Even so, the British in India and elsewhere in the East to-day do not realize that their day is past, the day of empire is past, and that the world marches onward relentlessly pushing the British Empire into the " dustbin of history ".

But the feudal order that prevailed in India, when the British were spreading out, made one more final effort to recover power and drive out the foreigner. This was the great revolt of 1857. All over the country there was a great deal of dissatisfaction and discontent against the British. The East India Company's policy was to make money and to do little else; and this policy, added to the ignorance and rapacity of many of its officers, had resulted in widespread misery. Even the British Indian army was affected, and there were many petty mutinies. Many of the feudal chiefs and their descendants were naturally bitter against their new masters. So a great revolt was organized secretly. This organization spread especially round about the United Provinces and in Central India, and yet, so blind are the British people in India to what Indians do or think, the government had no inkling of it. Apparently a date was fixed for the revolt to begin simultaneously in many places. But some Indian regiments at Meerut went ahead too fast and mutinied on May 10, 1857. This premature outburst upset the programme of the leaders of the revolt, as it put the government on their guard. The revolt, however, spread all over the United Provinces and Delhi and partly in Central India and Bihar. It was not merely a military revolt; it was a general popular rebellion in these areas against the British. Bahadur Shah, the last of the line of the Great Moghals, a feeble old man and a poet, was proclaimed by some as Emperor. The Revolt developed into a war of Indian independence against the hated foreigner, but it was an independence of the old feudal type, with autocratic emperors at the head. There was no freedom for the common people in it, but large numbers of them joined it because they connected their miserable condition and poverty with the coming of the British, and also in some places because of the hold of the big landlords. Religious animosity also urged them on. Both Hindus and Mohammedans took full part in this war.

For many months British rule in North and Central India hung almost by a thread. But the fate of the Revolt was settled by the Indians themselves. The Sikhs and the Gurkhas supported the British. The Nizam in the south, and Scindia in the north, and many other Indian States, also lined up with the British. Even apart from these defections, the Revolt had the seeds of failure in it. It was fighting for a lost cause, the feudal order; it had no good leadership; it was badly organized, and there were mutual squabbles all the time. Some of the rebels also sullied their cause by cruel massacres of the British. This barbarous behaviour naturally set up the backs of the British people in India, and they paid it back in the same coin, but a hundred and a thousand times multiplied. The English were especially incensed by a massacre of English men and women and children in Cawnpore, treacherously ordered, it is stated, after promise of safety had been given, by Nana Sahab, a descendant of the Peshwa. A memorial well in Cawnpore commemorates this horrible tragedy.

In many an outlying station the English were surrounded by crowds. Sometimes they were treated well more often badly.

They fought well and bravely against great odds. The siege of Lucknow stands out, coupled with the names of Outram and Have-lock, as an example of British courage and endurance. The siege and fall of Delhi in September 1857 marked the turning-point of the Revolt. Henceforth and for many months afterwards the British crushed the Revolt. In doing so they spread terror everywhere. Vast numbers were shot down in cold blood; large numbers were shot to pieces from the mouth of cannon; thousands were hanged from the wayside trees. An English general, Neill, who marched from Allahabad to Cawnpore, is said to have hanged people all along the way, till hardly a tree remained by the roadside which had not been converted into a gibbet. Prosperous villages were rooted out and destroyed. It is all a terrible and most painful story, and I hardly dare tell you all the bitter truth. If Nana Sahab had behaved barbarously and treacherously, many an English officer exceeded his barbarity a hundred-fold. If mobs of mutinous Indian soldiers, without officers or leaders, had been guilty of cruel and revolting deeds, the trained British soldiers, led by their officers, exceeded them in cruelty and barbarity. I do not want to compare the two. It is a sorry business on both sides, but our perverted histories tell us a lot about the treachery and cruelty on the Indian side, and hardly mention the other side. It is also well to remember that the cruelty of a mob is nothing compared to the cruelty of an organized government when it begins to behave like a mob. Even to-day, if you go to many of the villages in our province, you will find that the people have still got a vivid and ghastly memory of the horrors that befell them during the crushing of the Revolt.

In the midst of the horrors of the Revolt and its suppression, one name stands out, a bright spot against a dark background. This is the name of Lakshmi Bai, Rani of Jhansi, a girl-widow, twenty years of age, who donned a man's dress and came out to lead her people against the British. Many a story is told of her spirit and ability and undaunted courage. Even the English general who opposed her has called her the " best and bravest " of the rebel leaders. She died while fighting.

The Revolt of 1857–58 was the last flicker of feudal India. It ended many things. It ended the line of the Great Moghal, for Bahadur Shah's two sons and a grandson were shot down in cold blood, without any reason or provocation, by an English officer, Hodson, as he was carrying them away to Delhi. Thus, ignominiously, ended the line of Timur and Babar and Akbar.

The Revolt also put an end to the rule of the East India Company in India. The British Government now took direct charge, and the British Governor-General blossomed out into a " Viceroy ". Nine-teen years later, in 1877, the Queen of England took the title of " Kaiser-i-Hind ", the old title of the Cæsars and of the Byzantine Empire, adapted to India. The Moghal dynasty was no more But the spirit and even symbols of autocracy remained, and another Great Moghal sat in England.

110

THE INDIAN ARTISAN GOES TO THE WALL

December 1, 1932

WE have done with the nineteenth-century wars in India.   I am glad of it.   We can now proceed to consider more important happenings of this period in India.   But remember that these wars for the benefit of England were carried on at the expense of India.   The British people practised with great success the method of making the people of India pay for their own conquest.   The Indian people also paid with blood and treasure for the conquest of neighbouring peoples with whom they had no quarrel—the Burmese and Afghans. The wars impoverished India to some extent, for all war means destruction of wealth.   War also meant prize money for the conquerors, as we have seen in the case of Sindh.   In spite of this impoverishment, due to these and other causes, the flow of gold and silver to the East India Company continued so that fat dividends might be paid to their shareholders.

I think I have told you previously that the early days of the British power in India were the days of merchant adventurers who traded and plundered indiscriminately.   The East India Company and its agents carried off in this way a vast amount of the accumulated wealth of India   This was practically without any return to India.   In the case of ordinary trade there is some give and take, but in the second half of the eighteenth century, after Plassey, the money all went one way—to England.   India was thus deprived of a great deal of its old wealth and this went to help the industrial development of England at a vital period of transition.   This first British period in India, based on trade and naked plunder, ended roughly by the end of the eighteenth century.

The second period of British rule covered the nineteenth century, when India became a great source for raw materials which were sent to the factories of England, and a market for British manufactured goods.   This was done at the expense of India's progress and economic development.   For the first half of the century the East India Company, a trading company, started originally to make money, governed India.   The British Parliament, however, paid more and more attention to Indian affairs.   Then, after the Revolt of 1857–58, as we have seen in the last letter, the British Government took direct charge of India.   But this made no vital difference in the fundamental policy, for the government represented the same class which controlled the East India Company.

Between the economic interests of India and England there was an obvious conflict.   This conflict was always decided in England's favour, as all power lay with England.   Even before the industrialization of England a famous English writer had pointed out the harmful effects of the East India Company's rule in India.   This man was Adam Smith, who is called the father of political economy.

In a famous book of his called *The Wealth of Nations*, which was published as early as 1776, he said, referring to the East India Company :

> " The government of an exclusive company of merchants is perhaps the worst of all governments for any country whatever. . . . It is the interest of the East India Company considered as sovereigns that the European goods which are carried to their Indian dominions should be sold there as cheaply as possible ; and that the Indian goods which are brought from there should be sold there as dear as possible. But the reverse of this is their interest as merchants. As sovereigns their interest is exactly the same with that of the country which they govern. As merchants their interest is directly opposite to that interest."

I have told you that when the British came to India the old feudal order was breaking up. The fall of the Moghal Empire produced political chaos and disorder in many parts of India. But, even so, " India in the eighteenth century was a great manufacturing as well as a great agricultural country, and the Indian hand-loom supplied the markets of Asia and Europe ", as an Indian economist, Romesh Chundra Dutt, has written. In the course of these letters I have told you of India's control over foreign markets in ancient days. Four-thousand-year-old mummies in Egypt were wrapped in fine Indian muslin. The skill of the Indian artisan was famous in the East as well as the West. Even when political downfall came, the artisans did not forget the cunning of their hands. The English and other foreign merchants who came to India in quest of trade came not to sell foreign goods here, but to buy the fine and delicate articles made in India and to sell them at a great profit in Europe. Thus the European traders were attracted first not by raw materials, but by the manufactured wares of India. The East India Company, before it gained dominion in India, carried on a very profitable business by selling Indian-made linens and woollens and silks and embroidered goods. In particular a high degree of efficiency was reached in India in the textile industry—that is, in the making of cotton, silk and woollen goods. " Weaving," says R. C. Dutt, " was the national industry of the people and spinning was the pursuit of millions of women." Indian textiles went to England and other parts of Europe, to China and Japan and Burma and Arabia and Persia and parts of Africa.

Clive has described the city of Murshidabad in Bengal in 1757 as a city " as extensive, populous, and rich as the city of London, with this difference, that there are individuals in the first possessing infinitely greater property than in the last ". This was in the very year of Plassey when the British finally established themselves in Bengal. At the very moment of political downfall, Bengal was rich and full of many industries, and sending out her fine fabrics to different parts of the world. The city of Dacca was especially famous for its fine muslins, and did a huge export trade in them.

Thus India at this period had developed far beyond the purely agricultural and village stage. Of course India was, and still is, and must long remain, predominantly agricultural. But with village life and agriculture a town life had also developed. In these towns the artisans and craftsmen gathered, and collective production took place—that is, there were little factories employing 100 or more artisans. Of course these factories could not be compared to the huge factories of the Machine Age which came later. In western Europe, and especially in the Netherlands, there were many such factories before industrialism began.

India was in a transition stage, It was a manufacturing country, and a *bourgeois* class was being evolved in these towns. The owners of these factories were capitalists who supplied raw material to the craftsmen. In course of time this class would no doubt have grown powerful enough, as in Europe, to replace the feudal class. Just then the British intervened, with fatal results to India's industries.

At first the East India Company encouraged Indian industries because they made money out of them. The sale of Indian goods in foreign countries brought gold and silver to the country. But the manufacturers in England did not like this competition, and so they induced their government, early in the eighteenth century, to tax Indian goods coming to England. Some Indian articles were entirely prohibited from entering England, and I believe it was made a crime for any one to wear in public some Indian material. They could enforce their boycott with the help of the law. Here in India at present a mention of the boycott of British cloth lands one in gaol ! This policy of boycott of Indian goods by England would not, by itself, have done much harm, for many other markets remained. But England happened to control a great part of India at the time, through the East India Company, and England deliberately began a policy of pushing on British industries at the cost of Indian industries. English goods could enter India without the payment of any duty. In India the artisans and craftsmen were harassed and forced to work in the East India Company's factories. Even the internal trade of India was crippled by means of certain transit duties—that is, duties which had to be paid if goods were sent from place to place.

So efficient was the textile industry of India that even the rising English machine-industry could not compete with it, and had to be protected by a duty of about 80 per cent. Early in the nineteenth century some Indian silks and cottons could be sold in the British market at a much lower price than those made in England. But this could not last when England, the ruling Power in India, was bent on crushing Indian industries. In any event the products of the Indian cottage-industries could not long compete with machine-industry as this improved. For machine-industry is a far more efficient way of manufacturing large quantities of goods, which are thus much cheaper than cottage-made goods. But England forcibly hurried the process and prevented India from adapting herself gradually to changed conditions.

So India, which had been for hundreds of years " the Lancashire of the Eastern world ", and had, in the eighteenth century, supplied cotton goods on a vast scale to Europe, lost her position as a manufacturing country, and became just a consumer of British goods. The machine did not come to India, as it might have done in the ordinary course; but machine-made goods came from outside. The current which was flowing from India, bearing Indian goods to foreign countries, and bringing back gold and silver, was reversed. Henceforth foreign goods came to India and gold and silver went out of it.

The textile industry of India was the first to collapse before this onslaught. As machine-industry developed in England, other Indian industries followed the way of the textile industry. Ordinarily it is the duty of a country's government to protect and encourage the country's industries. But far from protecting and encouraging, the East India Company crushed every industry which came into conflict with British industry. Shipbuilding in India collapsed, and the metal workers could not carry on, and the manufacture of glass and paper also dwindled away.

At first foreign goods reached the port towns and the interior near them. As roads and railways were built, foreign goods went farther and farther inland, and drove out the artisan even from the village. The cutting through of the Suez Canal brought England nearer to India, and it became cheaper to bring British goods. So more and more foreign machine-goods came, and they went even to the remote villages. The process went on right through the nineteenth century, and indeed it is going on to some extent still. During the last few years, however, there have been some checks to this which we shall consider later.

This spreading, creeping movement of British goods, chiefly cloth, brought death to the hand-industries of India. But there was another aspect which was more terrible still. What of the millions of artisans who were thrown out of work? What of the vast numbers of weavers and other workers who became unemployed? In England also the artisans were thrown out of work when the big factories came. They suffered greatly, but they found work in the new factories, and so they adapted themselves to the new conditions. In India there was no such alternative. There were no factories to go to; the British did not want India to become a modern industrial country and did not encourage factories. So the poor, homeless, workless, starving artisans fell back on the land. But even the land did not welcome them; there were enough people already on it, and there was no land to be had. Some of the ruined artisans managed to become peasants, but most of them became just landless labourers on the look-out for a job. And large numbers must have simply starved to death. In 1834 the English Governor-General in India is said to have reported that "the misery hardly finds a parallel in the history of commerce. The bones of the cotton-weavers are bleaching the plains of India."

Most of these weavers and artisans had lived in towns and cities. Now that their occupation was gone they drifted back to the land and to the villages. And so the population of the towns went down and the population of the villages went up. That is, to put it in another way, India became less urban and more rural. This ruralization continued right through the nineteenth century, and even now it has not stopped. Now, this is a very curious thing about India during this period. All over the world the effect of machine-industry and industrialization was to draw people from the villages to towns. In India there was the opposite tendency. The cities and towns grew smaller and languished. And more and more people hung on to agriculture to find a very difficult livelihood.

Together with the main industries, many an auxiliary or subsidiary industry also began to disappear. Carding, dying, printing became less and less; and hand-spinning stopped and *charkhas* disappeared from millions of homes. This meant that the peasantry lost an additional source of income, for spinning by the members of the peasant household had helped to add to the income from land. All this had happened, of course, in western Europe when machine-industry had begun. But the change had been natural there, and if there was the death of one order, there was at the same time the birth of a new one. In India the change was violent. The old order of manufacturing cottage-industries was killed, but there was no rebirth; it was not permitted by the British authorities in the interests of British industry.

We have seen that India was a prosperous manufacturing country when the British gained power here. The next stage, in the ordinary course, should have been to make the country industrial and to introduce the big machine. But instead of going forward, India actually went back as a result of British policy. She ceased even to be a manufacturing country, and became, more than ever, an agricultural country.

So poor agriculture had to support all these vast numbers of unemployed artisans and others. The pressure on land became terrible, and yet it still went on increasing. This is the foundation and the basis of the Indian problem of poverty. From this policy most of our ills have resulted. And till this basic problem is solved there can be no ending of the poverty and misery of the Indian peasant and village-dweller.

Too many people having no profession but agriculture, hanging on to the land, cut up their farms and holdings into tiny little bits. There was not more to go round. The little land each peasant household had was too small to support it decently. Poverty and semi-starvation always faced them at the best of times. And often enough the times were far from good. They were at the mercy of the seasons and the elements and the monsoons. And famines came and terrible diseases spread and carried off millions. They went to the *bania*—the village money-lender—and borrowed money, and their debts grew bigger and bigger and all hope and possibility of payment passed, and life became a burden too heavy to be borne. Such became the condition of the vast majority of the population of India under British rule in the nineteenth century.

111
THE VILLAGE, THE PEASANT, AND THE LANDLORD IN INDIA

December 2, 1932

I HAVE told you in my last letter of the British policy in India which resulted in the death of Indian cottage-industries and the driving of the artisan to agriculture and the village. This over-pressure or burden on the land of far too many people who have no other occupation is, as I have said, the great problem in India. It is due to this, largely, that India is poor. If these people could be diverted from the land and given other wealth-producing occupations, they would not only add to the wealth of the country, but the pressure on land would be greatly relieved, and even agriculture would prosper.

It is often said that this over-pressure on land is due to the growth of the population of India, and not so much to British policy. This argument is not a correct one. It is true that the population of India has gone up during the last 100 years, but so have the populations of most other countries. In Europe, indeed, the proportionate increase, especially in England and Belgium and Holland and Germany, has been far greater. The question of the growth of population of a country, or of the world as a whole, and how to provide for it, and how to restrict it, when necessary, is a very important one. I cannot enter into it here, as it might confuse the other issues. But I should like to make it clear that the real cause of the pressure on land in India is the want of occupations other than agriculture, and not the growth of population. The present population of India could probably be easily absorbed and thrive in India if other occupations and industries were forthcoming. It may be that later we shall have to deal with the question of the growth of population.

Let us now examine some other aspects of British policy in India. We shall go to the village first.

I have often written to you about the village *panchāyats* of India, and how they persisted through invasion and change. As late as 1830 a British Governor in India, Sir Charles Metcalfe, described the village communities as follows:

> "The village communities are little republics having nearly everything they want within themselves; and almost independent of foreign relations. They seem to last where nothing else lasts. This union of the village communities, each one forming a separate little State in itself . . . is in a high degree conducive to their happiness, and to the enjoyment of a great portion of freedom and independence."

This description is very complimentary to the old village system. We have a picture of an almost idyllic state of affairs. Undoubtedly

the amount of local freedom and independence that the villages had
was a good thing, and there were other good features also.   But
we must not lose sight of the defects of the system.   To live a self-
sufficient village life cut off from the rest of the world was not
conducive to progress in anything.   Growth and progress consist in
co-operation between larger and larger units.   The more a person
or a group keeps to himself or itself, the more danger there is of him
or it becoming self-centred and selfish and narrow-minded.   Village
folk when compared to town people are often narrow-minded and
superstitious.   So the village communities, with all their good
points, could not be centres of progress.   They were rather primitive
and backward.   Handicrafts and industry flourished mainly in the
towns.   Of course there were large numbers of weavers spread out
in the villages.

The real reason why the village communities lived their separate
lives, without much contact with each other, was the lack of means
of communication.   There were few good roads connecting villages.
It was, indeed, this lack of good roads that made it rather difficult
for the Central Government of the country to intervene too much
in village affairs.   Towns and villages on the banks of, or near,
good-sized rivers could communicate by boats, but there were not
many rivers that could be used in this way.   This want of easy
communications came in the way of internal trade also.

The East India Company, for a great many years, were only
interested in making money and paying dividends to their shareholders.   They spent very little on roads, and nothing at all on
education and sanitation and hospitals and the like.   But later,
when the British began to concentrate on buying raw material and
selling British machine-goods, a different policy regarding communications was adopted.   On the sea coast of India new cities
sprang up to serve the growing foreign trade.   These cities—like
Bombay, Calcutta, Madras, and later Karachi—collected raw
material, such as cotton, etc., for despatch to foreign countries, and
received foreign machine-goods, especially from England, for distribution and sale in India.   These new cities were very different
from the great industrial cities that were growing in the West, like
Liverpool and Manchester and Birmingham and Sheffield.   The
European cities were manufacturing centres, with big factories
making goods, and ports for the despatch of these goods.   The
new Indian cities produced nothing.   They were just depots for
foreign trade, and symbols of foreign rule.

Now, I have told you that owing to British policy India was
becoming more and more rural and people were leaving the towns
and going to the village and the land.   In spite of this, and without
affecting this process, these new cities grew up on the seaboard.
They grew at the expense of smaller cities and towns, and not at the
expense of the villages.   The general process of ruralization
continued.

These new cities on the seaboard had to be connected with the
interior to be able to help in the collection of raw material and the

distribution of foreign goods.   Some other cities also grew up as capitals or administrative centres of provinces.   The need for good communications thus became urgent.   Roads were made and later railways.   The first railway was built in Bombay in 1853.

The old village communities were hard put to it to adapt themselves to the changing conditions produced by the destruction of Indian industries.   But when more good roads and railways came and spread all over the country, the old village system, which had survived for so long, broke up at last and ended.   The little village republic could not keep cut off from the world when the world came knocking at its gate.   The price of articles in one village immediately affected prices in another, for articles could be sent easily from one village to another.   Indeed, as world communications developed, the price of wheat in Canada or the United States of America would affect the price of Indian wheat.   Thus the Indian village system was dragged, by the force of events, into the circle of world prices. The old economic order in the village went to pieces and, much to the astonishment of the peasant, a new order was forced on him. Instead of growing food and other stuffs for his village market, he began to grow for the world market.   He was caught in the whirlpool of world production and prices, and he sank lower and lower. Previously there had been famines in India when a harvest failed, and there was nothing to fall back upon, and no suitable means of obtaining food from other parts of the country.   There were famines of food.   But now a strange thing happened.   People would starve in the midst of plenty, or when food was available.   Even if food were not locally available, it could be brought from elsewhere by train and other swift means.   The food was there, but there was no money to buy it.   Thus there were famines of money, and not food.   And, stranger still, sometimes the very abundance of a harvest brought misery in its train for the peasantry, as we have seen during the last three years of depression.

So the old village system ended, and the *panchāyat* ceased to exist.   We need not express any great regret for this, as the system had outlived its day and did not fit in with modern conditions. But here again it broke up without any rebirth of a new village system in accord with these conditions.   This work of rebuilding and rebirth still remains to be done by us.

We have so far considered the indirect results of British policy on the land and the peasant.   Let us now consider what the actual land policy of the East India Company was—that is, the policy which directly affected the peasant and all connected with the land. This is a complicated affair, and rather dull, I am afraid.   But our country is full of these poor cultivators, and we should make some effort to understand what ails them, and how we can serve them and better their lot.

We hear of *zamindars* and *taluqadars* and their tenants; and there are many kinds of tenants; and there are sub-tenants—that is, tenants of tenants.   I shall not take you into the intricacies of all this.   Broadly speaking, the *zamindars* to-day are middle-men—that is, they stand between the cultivator and the State. The cultivator is their tenant, and he pays them rent, or a kind of tax, for the use of the land, which is supposed to belong to the *zamindar*. Out of this rent the *zamindar* pays a portion as land revenue to the State, as a tax on his land. Thus the produce of the land is divided up into three parts; one part goes to the *zamindar*, another to the State, and the third remains with the tenant-culti-vator. Do not imagine that these parts are equal. The cultivator works on the land, and it is due to his labour, ploughing and sowing and dozens of other activities, that the land produces anything. He is obviously entitled to the fruits of his toil. The State, as representing society as a whole, has important functions to perform in the interests of everybody. Thus it ought to educate all the children, and build good roads and other means of communication, and have hospitals and sanitary services, and parks and museums, and a vast number of other things. For this it requires money, and it is right that it should take a share out of the produce of the land. What that share should be is another question. What the cultivator gives to the State really comes back to him, or ought to come back to him, in the shape of services—roads, education, sanita-tion, etc. At the present moment the State in India is represented by a foreign government, and so we are apt to dislike the State. But in a properly organized and free country the State is the people.

So we have disposed of two parts of the produce of the land—one going to the cultivator and the other to the State. A third part, as we have seen, goes to the *zamindar* or middle-man. What does he do to get it or deserve it? Nothing at all, or practically nothing. He just takes a big share in the produce—his rent—without helping in any way in the work of production. He thus becomes a fifth wheel in the coach—not only unnecessary, but an actual encum-brance, and a burden on the land. And naturally the person who suffers most from this unnecessary burden is the cultivator, who has to give part of his earnings to him. It is for this reason that many people think that the *zamindar* or *taluqadar* is a wholly unnecessary middle-man, and that the *zamindari* system is bad and ought to be changed so that the middle-man disappears. At present we have this *zamindari* system chiefly in three provinces in India—Bengal, Bihar, and the United Provinces.

In the other provinces the peasant cultivators usually pay their land revenue direct to the State and there are no middle-men. These people are sometimes called peasant proprietors; sometimes, as in the Punjab, they are called *zamindars*, but they are different from the big *zamindars* of the United Provinces and Bengal and Bihar.

After this long explanation I want to tell you that this *zamindari* system which flourishes in Bengal, Bihar, and the United Provinces, and about which we hear so much nowadays, is quite a new thing in India. It is a creation of the British. It did not exist before they came.

In the old times there were no such *zamindars* or land-holders or middle-men. The cultivators gave a part of their produce direct to the State. Sometimes the village *panchāyat* acted on behalf of all the cultivators of the village. In Akbar's time, his famous Finance Minister, Raja Todar Mal, had a very careful survey of the land made. The government or State took one-third of the produce from the cultivator, who could, if he so chose, pay in cash. Taxes were on the whole not heavy, and they increased very gradually. Then came the collapse of the Moghal Empire. The Central Government weakened and could not collect their taxes properly. A new way of collection then arose. Tax collectors were appointed, not on salary, but as agents who could keep one-tenth of the collections for themselves. They were called revenue-farmers, or sometimes *zamindars* or *taluqadars*, but remember that these words did not mean what they mean to-day.

As the Central Government decayed, the system became worse and worse. It even came to this, that auctions were held for the revenue-farming of an area, and the highest bidder got it. This meant that the man who got the job had a free hand to extort as much as he could from the unhappy cultivator, and he used this freedom to the full. Gradually these revenue-farmers tended to become hereditary as the government was too weak to remove them.

As a matter of fact, the first so-called legal title of the East India Company in Bengal was that of revenue-farmer on behalf of the Moghal Emperor. This was the grant of the *Diwani* to the Company in 1765. The Company thus became a kind of Diwan of the Moghal Emperor at Delhi. But all this was fiction. After Plassey, in 1757, the British were predominant in Bengal, and the poor Moghal Emperor had little or no power anywhere.

The East India Company and its officers were terribly greedy. As I have told you, they emptied the treasury of Bengal and laid violent hands on money wherever they could find it. They tried to squeeze Bengal and Bihar and extract the maximum of land revenue. They created smaller revenue-farmers and they increased the revenue demand on them most exorbitantly. The land revenue was doubled in a short space and collected pitilessly, any one not paying up punctually being turned out. The revenue-farmers, in their turn, were cruel and rapacious to the cultivators, who were rack-rented and ejected from their holdings. Within twelve years of Plassey, within four years of the grant of the *Diwani*, the policy of the East India Company, added to want of rain, brought about a terrible famine in Bengal and Bihar, when one-third of the whole population perished. I have referred to this famine of 1769-70 in a previous letter to you, and told you that, in spite of it, the East India Company collected the full amount of revenue. The officers of the Company deserve special mention for their remarkable efficiency. Men and women and children died by tens of millions, but they were able to extort money even out of the corpses, so that big dividends might be paid to wealthy men in England.

So matters went on for another twenty years or more, and, despite the famine, the East India Company continued to extort money, and the fair province of Bengal was brought to ruin. Even the big revenue-farmers were reduced to beggary, and from this one can imagine what the state of the miserable cultivator was. Things were so bad that the East India Company woke up and made an attempt to remedy them. The Governor-General of the day, Lord Cornwallis, himself a big landlord in England, wanted to create landlords after the British fashion in India. The revenue-farmers for some time past had been behaving like landlords. Cornwallis came to a settlement with them and treated them as such. The result was that for the first time India got this new type of middle-man, and the cultivators were reduced to the position of mere tenants. The British dealt with these land-holders or *zamindars* directly, and left them to do what they liked with their tenantry. There was no protection of any kind for the poor tenant from the rapacity of the landlord.

This settlement that Cornwallis made with the *zamindars* of Bengal and Bihar in 1793 is called the " Permanent Settlement ". The word " settlement " means the fixing of the amount of land revenue to be paid by each *zamindar* to the Government. For Bengal and Bihar this was fixed permanently. There was to be no change. Later on, as British rule spread in the north-west to Oudh and Agra, the British policy was changed. They had temporary settle-ments with *zamindars*, not permanent as in Bengal. Each tempor-ary settlement was revised periodically, usually every thirty years, and the sum to be paid as land revenue was fixed afresh. Usually it was enhanced at every settlement.

In the south, in Madras and round about, the *zamīndārī* system did not prevail. There was peasant proprietorship there, and so the East India Company settled directly with the peasants. But there, and everywhere, an insatiable greed made the Company's officers fix the land revenue at a very high figure, and this was cruelly extorted. For non-payment there was immediate ejection, but where was the poor man to go to ? Owing to the over-pressure on land there was always a demand for it ; there were always starving people who were willing to accept it on any conditions. Frequently there were troubles and agrarian riots when even the long-suffering peasant could bear no more.

About the middle of the nineteenth century another tyranny arose in Bengal. Certain English people established themselves as landlords in order to carry on trade in indigo. They made very hard terms with their tenants about the cultivation of the indigo plant. The tenants were compelled to grow the indigo plant in a certain part of their holdings, and then had to sell this at a fixed rate to the English landlords or planters, as they were called. This system is called the plantation system. The conditions forced on the tenants were so hard that it was very difficult for them to fulfil them. The British Government then came to the help of the planters, and passed special laws to force the poor tenants to culti-vate indigo according to those conditions. By these laws, with their punishments, the tenants of these plantations became serfs and

slaves of the planters in some respects. They were terrorized over
by the agents of the indigo factories, for these English or Indian
agents felt quite secure with the protection of the government.
Often, when the price of indigo fell, it was far more profitable for the
cultivator to grow something else, such as rice, but he was not permitted to do so. There was a great deal of trouble and misery for
the cultivator, and at last, exasperated beyond measure, the worm
turned. The peasantry rose against the planters and sacked a
factory. They were crushed back into submission.

I have tried in this letter to give you—at some length, I am afraid
—a picture of agrarian conditions in the nineteenth century. I
have tried to explain how the lot of the Indian peasant grew steadily
worse; how he was exploited by everyone who came in contact with
him, by tax-gatherer, and landlord, and *bania*, and the planter and
his agent, and by the biggest *bania* of all, the British Government,
acting either through the East India Company or directly. For at
the basis of all this exploitation lay the policy deliberately pursued
by the British in India. The destruction of cottage-industries with
no effort to replace them by other kinds of industry; the driving of
the unemployed artisan to the village and the consequent over-
pressure on land; landlordism; the plantation system; heavy
taxation on land resulting in exorbitant rent, cruelly collected; the
forcing of the peasant to the *bania* money-lender, from whose iron
grip he never escaped; innumerable ejections from the land for
inability to pay rent or revenue in time; and, above all, the perpetual
terrorism of policeman and tax-gatherer and landlord's agent and
factory agent, which almost destroyed all spirit and soul that he
possessed. What could be the result of all this but inevitable
tragedy and frightful catastrophe?

Terrible famines occurred which wiped off millions of the population. And, strange to say, even when food was lacking and people
were starving for the want of it, wheat and other food-grains were
exported to foreign countries for the profit of the rich traders. But
the real tragedy was not the lack of food, for food could be brought
by railway train from other parts of the country, but the lack of
means to buy it. In 1861 there was a great famine in North India,
especially in our province, and it is stated that over $8\frac{1}{2}$ per cent. of
the population of the affected area died. Fifteen years later, in
1876, and for two years, there was another terrible famine in North
and Central India as well as in South India. The United Provinces
were again the worst sufferers, and also the Central Provinces
and part of the Punjab. About 10,000,000 people died! Again,
twenty years later, in 1896, more or less in this same unhappy area,
there was another famine, more terrible than any other known in
Indian history. This frightful visitation laid North and Central
India low and crushed it utterly. In 1900 there was still another
famine.

In a brief paragraph I have told you of four mighty famines in
the course of forty years. I cannot tell you, and you cannot realize,
the terrible suffering and horror that are contained in this grim

story. Indeed, I am not sure that I want you to realize it, for with this realization would come anger and great bitterness, and I do not want you to be bitter at your age.

You have heard of Florence Nightingale, the brave Englishwoman who first organized efficient nursing of those wounded in war. As long ago as 1878, she wrote : " The saddest sight to be seen in the East—nay, probably in the world—is the peasant of our Eastern Empire." She referred to the " consequences of our laws " producing in " the most fertile country in the world, a grinding, chronic semi-starvation in many places where what is called famine does not exist ".

Yes, there can be few sights that are sadder than the sunken eyes of our *kisāns* with the hunted, hopeless look in them. What a burden our peasantry have carried these many years ! And let us not forget that we, who have prospered a little, have been part of that burden. All of us, foreigner and Indian, have sought to exploit that long-suffering *kisān* and have mounted on his back. Is it surprising that his back breaks ?

But, at long last, there came a glimmering of hope for him, a whisper of better times and lighter burdens. A little man came who looked straight into his eyes, and deep down into his shrunken heart, and sensed his long agony. And there was magic in that look, and a fire in his touch, and in his voice there was understanding and a yearning and abounding love and faithfulness unto death. And when the peasant and the worker and all who were down-trodden saw him and heard him, their dead hearts woke to life and thrilled, and a strange hope rose in them, and they shouted with joy : " *Mahātmā Gāndhī kī jai*," and they prepared to march out of their valley of suffering. But the old machine that had crushed them for so long would not let them go easily. It moved again and produced new weapons, new laws and ordinances, to crush them, new chains to bind them. And then ?—that is no part of my tale or history. That is still part of to-morrow, and when to-morrow becomes to-day, we shall know. But who doubts ?

112

HOW BRITAIN RULED INDIA

December 5, 1932

I HAVE already written you three long letters on India in the nineteenth century. It is a long story and a long agony, and if I compress it too much, I fear that I shall make it still more difficult to understand. I am perhaps paying more attention to this period of India's story than I have paid to other countries or other periods. That is not unnatural. Being an Indian, I am more interested in it, and knowing more about it, I can write more fully. Besides, this period has something much more than a historical interest for us. Modern India, such as we find her to-day, was formed and took shape in this travail of the nineteenth century. If we are to understand India as she is, we must know something of the forces that went to make her or mar her. Only so can we serve her intelligently, and know what we should do and what path we should take.

I have not done with this period of India's history. I have still much to tell you. In these letters I take one or more aspect and tell you something about it. I deal with each aspect separately, so that it may be easier to understand. But you will know, of course, that all these activities and changes that I have told you about, and all those that I shall describe in this letter and afterwards, took place more or less simultaneously, one influencing the other, and between them they produced the India of the nineteenth century.

Reading of these deeds and misdeeds of the British in India, you will sometimes feel angry at the policy they have pursued and the widespread misery that has resulted from it. But whose fault was it that this happened? Was it not due to our own weakness and ignorance? Weakness and folly are always invitations to despotism. If the British can profit by our mutual dissensions, the fault is ours that we quarrel amongst ourselves. If they can divide us and so weaken us, playing on the selfishness of separate groups, our permitting this is itself a sign of the superiority of the British. Therefore if you would be angry, be angry with weakness and ignorance and mutual strife, for it is these things that are responsible for our troubles.

The tyranny of the British, we say. Whose tyranny is it, after all? Who profits by it? Not the whole British race, for millions of them are themselves unhappy and oppressed. And undoubtedly there are small groups and classes of Indians who have profited a little by the British exploitation of India. Where are we to draw the line, then? It is not a question of individuals, but that of a system. We have been living under a huge machine that has exploited and crushed India's millions. This machine is the machine of the new imperialism, the outcome of industrial capitalism. The profits of this exploitation go largely to England, but in England they go almost entirely to certain classes. Some part of the profits of exploitation remain in India also, and certain classes benefit by them. It is therefore foolish for us to get angry with individuals, or even with the British as a whole. If a system is wrong and injures us, it has to be changed. It makes little difference who runs it, and even good people are helpless in a bad system. With the best will in the world, you cannot convert stones and earth into good food, however much you may cook them. So it is, I think, with imperialism and capitalism. They cannot be improved; the only real improvement is to do away with them altogether. But that is my opinion. Some people differ from this. You need not take anything for granted, and, when the time comes, you can draw your own conclusions. But about one thing most people do agree: that what is wrong is the system, and it is useless getting annoyed with individuals. If we want a change, let us attack and change the system. We have seen some of the evil effects of the system in India. When we consider China and Egypt and many other countries we shall see the same system, the same machine of capital-ist-imperialism, at work exploiting other peoples.

We shall go back to our story. I have told you of the advanced stage of Indian cottage-industries when the British came. With natural progress in the methods of production, and without any intervention from outside, it is probable that some time or other machine-industry would have come to India. There was iron and coal in the country and, as we saw in England, these helped the new industrialism greatly, and indeed partly brought it about. Ulti-mately this would have happened in India also. There might have been some delay in this, owing to the chaotic political conditions. The British, however, intervened. They represented a country and a community which had already changed over to the new big machine production. One might think, therefore, that they would favour such a change in India also, and encourage that class in India which was most likely to bring it about. They did no such thing. Indeed, they did the very opposite of this. Treating India as a possible rival, they broke up her industries, and actually dis-couraged the growth of machine-industry.

Thus we find a somewhat remarkable state of affairs in India. We find that the British, the most advanced people in Europe at the time, ally themselves in India with the most backward and conservative classes. They bolster up a dying feudal class; they create landlords; they support the hundreds of dependent Indian rulers in their semi-feudal states. They actually strengthen feudalism in India. Yet these British had been the pioneers in Europe of the middle-class or *bourgeois* revolution which had given their Parliament power; they had also been the pioneers in the Industrial Revolution which had resulted in introducing industrial capitalism to the world. It was because of their lead in these matters that they went far ahead of their rivals and established a vast empire.

It is not difficult to understand why the British acted in this way in India. The whole basis of capitalism is cut-throat competition and exploitation, and imperialism is an advanced stage of this. So the British, having the power, killed their actual rivals and deliber-ately prevented the growth of other rivals. They could not possibly make friends with the masses, for the whole object of their presence in India was to exploit them. The interests of the exploiters and the exploited could never be the same. So they, the British, fell back on the relics of feudalism which India still possessed. These had little real strength left even when the British came; but they were propped up and given a small share in the exploitation of the country. This propping up could only give temporary relief to a class which had outlived its utility; when the props were removed they were sure to fall or adapt themselves to the new conditions. There were as many as 700 Indian States, big and small, depending on the good-will of the British. You know some of these big States :

Hyderabad, Kashmir, Mysore, Baroda, Gwalior, etc. But, curiously, most of the Indian rulers of these States are not descended from the old feudal nobility, just as most of the big *zamindars* have no very ancient traditions. There is one chief, however—the Maharana of Udaipur, the head of the Surya Vanshi, Rajputs of the race of the Sun, who can trace his lineage back to dim prehistoric days. Probably the only living person who can compete with him in this respect is the Mikado of Japan.

British rule also helped religious conservatism. This sounds strange, for the British claimed to profess Christianity, and yet their coming made Hinduism and Islam in India more rigid. To some extent this reaction was natural, as foreign invasion tends to make the religions and culture of the country protect themselves by rigidity. It was in this way that Hinduism had become rigid and caste had developed after the Muslim invasions. Now, both Hinduism and Islam reacted after this fashion. But, apart from this, the British Government in India actually—both deliberately and unconsciously—helped the conservative elements in the two religions. The British were not interested in religion or in conversions; they were out to make money. They were afraid of interfering in any way in religious matters lest the people, in their anger, rose against them. So to avoid even the suspicion of interference, they went so far as actually to protect and help the country's religions, or rather the external forms of religion. The result often was that the outer form remained, but there was little inside it.

This fear of irritating the orthodox people made the government side with them in matters of reform. Thus the cause of reform was held up. An alien government can seldom introduce social reform, because every change it seeks to introduce is resented by the people. Hinduism and Hindu law were in many respects changing and progressive, though the progress had been remarkably slow in recent centuries. Hindu law itself is largely custom, and customs change and grow. This elasticity of the Hindu law disappeared under the British and gave place to rigid legal codes drawn up after consultation with the most orthodox people. Thus the growth of Hindu society, slow as it was, was stopped. The Muslims resented the new conditions even more, and retired into their shells.

A great deal of credit is taken by the British for the abolition of what is (rather incorrectly) called *sati*, the practice of a Hindu widow burning herself on the funeral pyre of her husband. They deserve some credit for this, but as a matter of fact the government only took action after many years of agitation by Indian reformers headed by Raja Ram Mohan Roy. Previous to them other rulers, and especially the Marathas, had forbidden it; the Portuguese Albuquerque had abolished the practice in Goa. It was put down by the British as a result of Indian agitation and Christian missionary endeavours. So far as I can remember, this was the only reform of religious significance which was brought about by the British Government.

So the British allied themselves with all the backward and

conservative elements in the country. And they tried to make India
a purely agricultural country producing raw materials for their
industries. To prevent factories growing up in India they actually
put a duty on machinery entering India. Other countries encouraged their own industries. Japan, as we shall see, simply galloped
ahead with industrialization. But in India the British Government put its foot down. Owing to the duty on machinery, which
was not taken off till 1860, the cost of building a factory in India
was four times that of building it in England, although labour was
far cheaper in India. This policy of obstruction could only delay
matters; it could not stop the inevitable march of events. About
the middle of the century machine-industry began to grow in India.
The jute industry began in Bengal with British capital. The coming
of the railways helped the growth of industry, and after 1880 cotton-
mills, largely with Indian capital, grew up in Bombay and Ahmedabad. Then came mining. Except for the cotton-mills, this slow
industrialization was very largely done with British capital. And all
this was almost in spite of the government. The government talked
of the *laissez-faire* policy, of allowing matters to take their own
course, of not interfering with private initiative. The British
Government had interfered with Indian trade in England and
crushed it with duties and prohibitions when this was a rival in
the eighteenth and early nineteenth centuries. Having got on
top, they could afford to talk of *laissez-faire*. As a matter of fact,
however, they were not merely indifferent. They actually discouraged certain Indian industries, especially the growing cotton
industry of Bombay and Ahmedabad. A tax or duty was put on
the products of these Indian mills; it was called the excise duty on
cotton. The object of this was to help British cotton goods from
Lancashire to compete with Indian textiles. Almost every country
puts duties on some foreign goods, either to protect its own industries
or to raise money. But the British in India did a very unusual
and remarkable thing. They put the duty on Indian goods themselves ! This cotton excise duty was continued, in spite of a great
deal of agitation, till recent years.

In this way modern industry grew slowly in India, despite the
government. The richer classes in India cried out more and more
for industrial development. It was only as late, I think, as 1905
that the government created a department of Commerce and
Industry, but even so, little was done by it till the World War came.
This growth of industrial conditions created a class of industrial
workers who worked in the city factories. The pressure on land, of
which I have told you, and the semi-famine conditions of the rural
areas, drove many villagers to these factories, as well as to the great
plantations that were rising in Bengal and Assam. This pressure
also led many to emigrate to other countries where they were told
they would get high wages. Emigration took place especially to
South Africa, Fiji, Mauritius and Ceylon. But the change did little
good to the workers. The emigrants in some of the countries were
treated almost like slaves. In the tea-plantations of Assam they

were in no better condition. Discouraged and disheartened, many of them sought, later on, to return to their villages from the plantations. But they were not welcome in their own villages, as there was no land to be had.

The workers in the factories soon found that the slightly higher wage did not go very far. Everything cost more in the cities; altogether the cost of living was much higher. The places where they had to live were wretched hovels, filthy, damp and dark and insanitary. Their working conditions were also bad. In the village they had often starved, but they had had their fill of the sun and of fresh air. There was no fresh air and little sun for the factory-worker. His wages were not enough to meet the higher cost of living. Even women and children had to work long hours. Mothers with babes in their arms took to drugging their babies so that they might not interfere with work. Such were the miserable conditions under which these industrial workers worked in the factories. They were unhappy, of course, and discontent grew. Sometimes, in very despair, they had a strike—that is, they stopped work. But they were weak and feeble, and could easily be crushed by their wealthy employers, backed often by the government. Very slowly and after bitter experience they learnt the value of joint action. They formed trade unions.

Do not think that this is a description of past conditions. There has been some improvement in labour conditions in India. Certain laws have been passed giving just a little protection to the poor worker. But even now you have but to go to Cawnpore or Bombay, or a number of other places where factories exist, and you will be horrified to see the houses of the workers.

I have written to you in this and other letters of the British in India and of the British Government in India. What was this like, and how did it function? There was the East India Company at first, but behind it was the British Parliament. In 1858, after the great Revolt, the British Parliament took direct charge, and later the English King, or rather Queen, for there was a queen then, became Kaiser-i-Hind. In India there was the Governor-General, who became a Viceroy also, at the top, and under him were crowds of officials. India was divided up, more or less as it is now, into large provinces and States. The States under Indian rulers were supposed to be half-independent, but as a matter of fact they were wholly dependent on the British. An English official, called the Resident, lived in each of the larger States, and he exercised general control over the administration. He was not interested in internal reform, and it mattered little to him how bad or old-fashioned the government of the State was. What he was interested in was in strengthening British authority in the State.

About a third of India was divided up into these States. The remaining two-thirds were under the direct government of the British. These two-thirds were therefore called British India. All the high officials in British India were British, except towards the end of the century, when a few Indians crept in. Even so all power and authority of course remained, and still remains, with the British. These high officials, apart from the military, were members of what is called the Indian Civil Service. The whole government of India was thus controlled by this service, the I.C.S. Such a government by officials, who appoint each other and are not responsible for what they do to the people, is called a bureaucracy, from the word bureau, an office.

We hear a great deal about this I.C.S. They have been a curious set of persons. They were efficient in some ways. They organized the government, strengthened British rule, and incidentally, profited greatly by it themselves. All the departments of government which helped in consolidating British rule and in collecting taxes were efficiently organized. Other departments were neglected. Not being appointed by, or responsible to, the people, the I.C.S. paid little attention to these other departments which concerned the people most. As was natural under the circumstances, they became arrogant and overbearing and contemptuous of public opinion. Narrow and limited in outlook, they began to look upon themselves as the wisest people on earth. The good of India meant to them primarily the good of their own service. They formed a kind of mutual admiration society and were continually praising each other. Unchecked power and authority inevitably lead to this, and the Indian Civil Service were practically masters of India. The British Parliament was too far away to interfere and, in any event, it had no occasion to interfere, as they served its interests and the interests of British industry. As for the interests of the people of India, there was no way of influencing them to any marked extent. Even feeble criticism of their actions was resented by them, so intolerant were they.

And yet the Indian Civil Service has had many good and honest and capable people in it. But they could not change the drift of policy or divert the current which was dragging India along. The I.C.S. were, after all, the agents of the industrial and financial interests in England, who were chiefly interested in exploiting India.

This bureaucratic government of India grew efficient wherever its own interests and the interests of British industry were concerned. But education and sanitation and hospitals and the many other activities which go to make a healthy and progressive nation were neglected. For many years there was no thought of these. The old village schools died away. Then slowly and grudgingly a little start was made. This start in education was also brought about by their own needs. The British people filled all the high offices, but obviously they could not fill the smaller offices and the clerkships. Clerks were wanted, and it was to produce clerks that schools and colleges were first started by the British. Ever since then this has been the main purpose of education in India; and most of its products are only capable of being clerks. But soon the supply of clerks was greater than the demand in government and other offices. Many were left over, and these formed a new class of educated unemployed.

Bengal took the lead in this new English education, and therefore the early supply of clerks was very largely Bengali. In 1857 three universities were started—in Calcutta, Bombay, and Madras. A fact worth noticing is that the Muslims did not take kindly to the new education. They were thus left behind in the race for clerkships and government service. Later this became one of their grievances.

Another fact worth noticing is that even when the government made a start with education, girls were completely ignored. This is not surprising. The education given was meant to produce clerks, and men-clerks were wanted, and only they were available then, owing to backward social customs. So girls were wholly neglected, and it was long afterwards when some little beginning was made for them.

113

THE REAWAKENING OF INDIA

December 7, 1932

I HAVE told you of the consolidation of British rule in India and of the policy which brought poverty and misery to our people. Peace certainly came, and orderly government also, and both were welcome after the disorders which followed the break-up of the Moghal empire. Organized gangs of thieves and dacoits had been put down. But peace and order were worth little to the man in the field or the factory, who was crushed under the grinding weight of the new domination. But again, I would remind you, it is foolish to get angry with a country or with a people, with Britain or the British. They were as much the victims of circumstances as we were. Our study of history has shown us that life is often very cruel and callous. To get excited over it, or merely to blame people, is foolish and does not help. It is much more sensible to try to understand the causes of poverty and misery and exploitation, and then try to remove them. If we fail to do so, and fall back in the march of events, we are bound to suffer. India fell back in this way. She became a bit of a fossil; her society was crystallized in old tradition; her social system lost its energy and life and began to stagnate. It is not surprising that India suffered. The British happened to be the agents to make her suffer. If they had not been there, perhaps some other people might have acted in the same way.

But one great benefit the English did confer on India. The very impact of their new and vigorous life shook up India and brought about a feeling of political unity and nationality. Perhaps such a shock, painful as it was, was needed to rejuvenate our ancient country and people. English education, intended to produce clerks, also put Indians in touch with current western thought. A new class began to arise, the English-educated class, small in numbers and cut off from the masses, but still destined to take the lead in the new nationalist movements. This class, at first, was full of admiration for England and the English ideas of liberty. Just then people in England were talking a great deal about liberty and democracy. All this was rather vague, and in India England was ruling despotically for her own benefit. But it was hoped, rather optimistically, that England would confer freedom on India at the right time.

The impact of western ideas on India had its effect on Hindu religion also to some extent. The masses were not affected and, as I have told you, the British Government's policy actually helped the orthodox people. But the new middle class that was arising, consisting of government servants and professional people, were affected. Early in the nineteenth century an attempt to reform Hinduism on western lines took place in Bengal. Of course Hinduism had had innumerable reformers in the past, and some of these I have mentioned to you in the course of these letters. But the new attempt was definitely influenced by Christianity and western thought. The maker of this attempt was Raja Ram Mohan Roy, a great man and a great scholar, whose name we have come across already in connection with the abolition of *satī*. He knew Sanskrit and Arabic and many other languages well, and he carefully studied various religions. He was opposed to religious ceremonies and *pūjās* and the like, and he pleaded for social reform and women's education. The society he founded was called the *Brahmo Samāj*. It was, and has remained, a small organization, so far as numbers go, and it has been confined to the English-knowing people of Bengal. But it has had considerable influence on the life of Bengal. The Tagore family took to it, and for long the poet Rabindranath's father, known as Maharshi Debendra Nath Tagore, was the prop and pillar of the *Samāj*. Another leading member was Keshab Chander Sen.

Later in the century another religious reform movement took place. This was in the Punjab, and the founder was Swami Dayananda Saraswati. Another society was started, called the *Arya Samāj*. This also rejected many of the later growths of Hinduism and combated caste. Its cry was " Back to the *Vedas* ". Although it was a reforming movement, influenced no doubt by Muslim and Christian thought, it was in essence an aggressive militant movement. And so it happened, curiously, that the *Arya Samāj* which, of many Hindu sects, probably came nearest to Islam, became a rival and opponent of Islam. It was an attempt to convert the defensive and static Hinduism into an aggressive missionary religion. It was meant to revive Hinduism. What gave the movement some strength was a colouring of nationalism. It was, indeed, Hindu nationalism raising its head. And the very fact that it was Hindu nationalism made it difficult for it to become Indian nationalism.

The *Arya Samāj* was far more widespread than the *Brahmo Samāj*, especially in the Punjab. But it was largely confined to the middle classes. The *Samāj* has done a great deal of educational work, and has started many schools and colleges, both for boys and girls.

Another remarkable religious man of the century, but very different from the others I have mentioned in this letter, was Ramakrishna Paramhansa. He did not start any aggressive society for reform. He laid stress on service, and the *Ramakrishna Sevashrams* in many parts of the country are carrying on this tradition of service of the weak and poor. A famous disciple of Ramakrishna's was Swami Vivekananda, who very eloquently and forcibly preached the gospel of nationalism. This was not in any way anti-Muslim or anti anyone else, nor was it the somewhat narrow nationalism of the *Arya Samāj*. None the less Vivekananda's nationalism was Hindu nationalism, and it had its roots in Hindu religion and culture.

Thus it is interesting to note that the early waves of nationalism in India in the nineteenth century were religious and Hindu. The Muslims naturally could take no part in this Hindu nationalism. They kept apart. Having kept away from English education, the new ideas affected them less, and there was far less intellectual ferment amongst them. Many decades later they began to come out of their shell, and then, as with the Hindus, their nationalism took the shape of a Muslim nationalism, looking back to Islamic traditions and culture, and fearful of losing these because of the Hindu majority. But this Muslim movement became evident much later, towards the end of the century.

Another interesting thing to note is that these reform and progressive movements in Hinduism and Islam tried to fit in, as far as possible, the new scientific and political ideas derived from the West with their old religious notions and habits. They were not prepared to challenge and examine fearlessly these old notions and habits; nor could they ignore the new world of science and political and social ideas which lay around them. So they tried to harmonize the two by trying to show that all modern ideas and progress could be traced back to the old sacred books of their religions. This attempt was bound to end in failure. It merely prevented people from thinking straight. Instead of thinking boldly and trying to understand the new forces and ideas which were changing the world, they were oppressed by the weight of ancient habit and tradition. Instead of looking ahead and marching ahead, they were all the time furtively looking back. It is not easy to go ahead, if the head is always turned and looks back.

The English-educated class grew slowly in the cities, and at the same time a new middle class arose consisting of professional people —that is, lawyers and doctors and the like, and merchants and traders. There had been, of course, a middle class in the past, but this was largely crushed by the early British policy. The new *bourgeoisie*, or middle class, was a direct outcome of British rule; in a sense they were the hangers-on of this rule. They shared to a small extent in the exploitation of the masses; they took the crumbs that fell from the richly laden table of the British ruling classes. They were petty officials helping in the British administration of the country; many were lawyers assisting in the working of

the law courts and growing rich by litigation; and there were
merchants, the go-betweens of British trade and industry, who
sold British goods for a profit or commission.

The great majority of these people of the new *bourgeoisie* were
Hindus. This was due to their somewhat better economic condition,
as compared to the Muslims, and also to their taking to English
education, which was a passport to government service and the
professions. The Muslims were generally poorer. Most of the
weavers, who had gone to the wall on account of the British destruction of Indian industries, were Muslims. In Bengal, which has the
biggest Muslim population of any Indian province, they were poor
tenants or small land-holders. The landlord was usually a Hindu,
and so was the village *bania*, who was the money-lender and the
owner of the village store. The landlord and the *bania* were thus
in a position to oppress the tenant and exploit him, and they took
full advantage of this position. It is well to remember this fact,
for in this lies the root cause of the tension between Hindu and
Muslim.

In the same way the higher-caste Hindus, especially in the south,
exploited the so-called " depressed " classes, who were mostly
workers on the land. The problem of the depressed classes has been
very much before us recently, and especially since Bapu's fast.
Untouchability has been attacked all along the front, and hundreds
of temples and other places have been thrown open to these classes.
But right down at the bottom of the question is this economic
exploitation, and unless this goes, the depressed classes will remain
depressed. The untouchables have been agricultural serfs who
were not allowed to own land. They had other disabilities also.

Although India as a whole and the masses grew poorer, the handful of people comprising the new *bourgeoisie* prospered to some
extent because they shared in the country's exploitation. The
lawyers and other professional people and the merchants accumulated some money. They wanted to invest this, so that they could
have an income from interest. Many of them bought up land from
the impoverished landlords, and thus they became themselves
landowners. Others, seeing the wonderful prosperity of English
industry, wanted to invest their money in factories in India. So
Indian capital went into these big machine factories and an Indian
industrial capitalist class began to arise. This was about fifty
years ago, after 1880.

As this *bourgeoisie* grew, their appetite also grew. They wanted
to get on, to make more money, to have more posts in government
service, more facilities for starting factories. They found the
British obstructing them in every path. All the high posts were
monopolized by the British, and industry was run for the profit
of the British. So they began agitating, and this was the origin
of the new nationalist movement. After the revolt of 1857 and its
cruel suppression, people had been too much broken up for any
agitation or aggressive movement. It took them many years to
revive a little.

Nationalist ideas were soon spreading, and Bengal was taking the lead. New books came out in Bengali, and they had a great influence on the language as well as on the development of nationalism in Bengal. It was in one of these books, *Ananda Matha*, by Bankim Chandra Chatterji, that our famous song *Vande Matram* occurs. A Bengali poem which created a stir was *Nil Darpan*—the mirror of indigo. It gave a very painful account of the miseries of the Bengal peasantry under the plantation system, of which I have told you something.

Meanwhile the power of Indian capital was also increasing, and it demanded more elbow-room to grow. At last in 1885 all these various elements of the new *bourgeoisie* determined to start an organization to plead their cause. Thus was the Indian National Congress founded in 1885. This organization, which you and every boy and girl in India know well, has become in recent years great and powerful. It took up the cause of the masses and became, to some extent, their champion. It challenged the very basis of British rule in India, and led great mass movements against it. It raised the banner of independence and fought for freedom manfully. And to-day it is still carrying on the fight. But all this is subsequent history. The National Congress when it was first founded was a very moderate and cautious body, affirming its loyalty to the British and asking, very politely, for some petty reforms. It represented the richer *bourgeoisie*; even the poorer middle classes were not in it. As for the masses, the peasants and workers, they had nothing to do with it. It was the organ of the English-educated classes chiefly, and it carried on its activities in our step-mother tongue— the English language. Its demands were the demands of the land-lords and Indian capitalists and the educated unemployed seeking for jobs. Little attention was paid to the grinding poverty of the masses or their needs. It demanded the " Indianization " of the services—that is to say, the greater employment of Indians in government service in place of Englishmen. It did not see that what was wrong with India was the machine which exploited the people, and that it made no difference who had charge of the machine, Indian or foreigner. The Congress further complained of the huge expenses of the English officials in the military and civil services, and of the " drain " of gold and silver from India to England.

Do not think that in pointing out how moderate the early Congress was I am criticizing it or trying to belittle it. That is not my purpose, for I believe that the Congress in those days and its leaders did great work. The hard facts of Indian politics drove it step by step, almost unwillingly, to a more and more extreme position. But in the early days it could not have been anything but what it was. And in those days it required great courage for its founders to go ahead. It is easy enough for us to talk bravely of freedom when the crowd is with us and praises us for it. But it is very difficult to be the pioneer in a great undertaking.

The first Congress was held in Bombay in 1885. W. C. Bonnerji of Bengal was the first president. Other prominent names of those early days are Surendra Nath Banerji, Badruddin Tyabji, Pheroze-shah Mehta. But one name towers above all others—that of Dadabhai Naoroji, who became the *Grand Old Man of India* and who first used the word *Swaraj* for India's goal. One other name I shall tell you, for he is the sole survivor to-day of the old guard of the Congress, and you know him well. He is Pandit Madan Mohan Malaviya. For over fifty years he has laboured in India's cause, and, worn down with years and anxiety, he labours still for the realization of the dream he dreamed in the days of his youth.

So the Congress went on from year to year and gained in strength. It was not narrow in its appeal like the Hindu nationalism of an earlier day. But still it was in the main Hindu. Some leading Muslims joined it, and even presided over it, but the Muslims as a whole kept away. A great Muslim leader of the day was Sir Syed Ahmad Khan. He saw that lack of education, and especially modern education, had injured the Muslims greatly and kept them backward. He felt therefore that he must persuade them to take to this education and to concentrate on it, before dabbling in politics. So he advised the Muslims to keep away from the Congress, and he co-operated with the government and founded a fine college in Aligarh, which has since grown into a university. Sir Syed's advice was followed by the great majority of the Muslims, who did not join the Congress. But a small minority was always with it. Remember that when I refer to majorities and minorities I mean the majority or minority of the upper middle class, English-educated, Muslims and Hindus. The masses, both Hindu and Muslim, had nothing to do with the Congress, and very few had even heard of it in those days. Even the lower middle classes were not affected by it then.

The Congress grew, but even faster than the Congress grew the ideas of nationality and the desire for freedom. The Congress appeal was necessarily limited because it was confined to the English-knowing people. To some extent this helped in bringing different provinces nearer to each other and developing a common outlook. But because it did not go down deep to the people, it had little strength. I have told you in another letter of an occur-rence which stirred Asia greatly. This was the victory of little Japan over giant Russia in 1904–5. India, in common with other Asiatic countries, was vastly impressed, that is, the educated middle classes were impressed, and their self-confidence grew. If Japan could make good against one of the most powerful European countries, why not India ? For long the Indian people had suffered from a feeling of inferiority before the British. The long domination by the British, the savage suppression of the Revolt of 1857, had cowed them. By an Arms Act they were prevented from keeping arms. In everything that happened in India they were reminded that they were the subject race, the inferior race. Even the educa-tion that was given to them filled them with this idea of inferiority. Perverted and false history taught them that India was a land where anarchy had always prevailed, and Hindus and Muslims had cut each other's throats, till the British came to rescue the country from this miserable plight and give it peace and prosperity. Indeed, the whole of Asia, the Europeans believed and proclaimed, regardless of fact or history, was a backward continent which must remain under European domination.

The Japanese victory, therefore, was a great pick-me-up for Asia. In India it lessened the feeling of inferiority, from which most of us suffered. Nationalist ideas spread more widely, especially in Bengal and Maharashtra. Just then an event took place which shook Bengal to the depths and stirred the whole of India. The British Government divided up the great province of Bengal (which at that time included Bihar) into two parts, one of these being Eastern Bengal. The growing nationalism of the *bourgeoisie* in Bengal resented it. It suspected that the British wanted to weaken them by thus dividing them. Eastern Bengal had a majority of Muslims, so by this division a Hindu-Muslim question was also raised. A great anti-British movement rose in Bengal. Most of the landholders joined it, and so did Indian capitalists. The cry of *Swadeshi* was first raised then, and with it the boycott of British goods, which of course helped Indian industry and capital. The movement even spread to the masses to some extent, and partly it drew its inspiration from Hinduism. Side by side with it there arose in Bengal a school of revolutionary violence, and the bomb first made its appearance in Indian politics. Aurobindo Ghose was one of the brilliant leaders of the Bengal movement. He still lives, but for many years he has lived a retired life in Pondicherry, which is in French India.

In western India, in the Maharashtra country, there was also a great ferment at this time and a revival of an aggressive nationalism, tinged also with Hinduism. A great leader arose there, Bal Gangadhar Tilak, known throughout India as the Lokamanya, the "Honoured of the People ". Tilak was a great scholar, learned alike in the old ways of the East and the new ways of the West; he was a great politician; but, above all, he was a great mass leader. The leaders of the National Congress had so far appealed only to the English-educated Indians; they were little known by the masses. Tilak was the first political leader of the new India who reached the masses and drew strength from them. His dynamic personality brought a new element of strength and indomitable courage, and, added to the new spirit of nationalism and sacrifice in Bengal, it changed the face of Indian politics.

What was the Congress doing during these stirring days of 1906 and 1907 and 1908 ? The Congress leaders, far from leading the nation at the time of this awakening of the national spirit, hung back. They were used to a quieter brand of politics in which the masses did not intrude. They did not like the flaming enthusiasm of Bengal, nor did they feel at home with the new unbending spirit of Maharashtra, as embodied in Tilak. They praised *Swadeshi* but hesitated at the boycott of British goods. Two parties developed in the Congress—the extremists under Tilak and some Bengal leaders and the moderates under the older Congress leaders. The most prominent of the moderate leaders was, however, a young man,

Gopal Krishna Gokhale, a very able man who had devoted his life to service. Gokhale was also from Maharashtra. Tilak and he faced each other from their rival groups and, inevitably, the split came in 1907 and the Congress was divided. The moderates continued to control the Congress, the extremists were driven out. The moderates won, but it was at the cost of their popularity in the country, for Tilak's party was far the more popular with the people. The Congress became weak and for some years had little influence.

And what of the government during these years? How did it react to the growth of Indian nationalism? Governments have only one method of meeting an argument or a demand which they do not like—the use of the bludgeon. So the government indulged in repression and sent people to prison, and curbed the newspapers with Press laws, and let loose crowds of secret policemen and spies to shadow everybody they did not like. Since those days the members of the C.I.D. in India have been the constant companions of prominent Indian politicians. Many of the Bengal leaders were sentenced to imprisonment. The most noted trial was that of Lokamanya Tilak, who was sentenced to six years, and who during his imprisonment in Mandalay wrote a famous book. Lala Lajpat Rai was also deported to Burma.

But repression did not succeed in crushing Bengal. So a measure of reform in the administration was hurried up to appease some people at least. The policy was then, as it was later and is now, to split up the nationalist ranks. The moderates were to be "rallied" and the extremists crushed. In 1908 these new reforms, called the Morley-Minto reforms, were announced. They succeeded in "rallying the moderates", who were pleased with them. The extremists, with their leaders in gaol, were demoralized and the national movement weakened. In Bengal, however, the agitation against the partition continued and ended with success. In 1911 the British Government reversed the partition of Bengal. This triumph put new heart in the Bengalis. But the movement of 1907 had spent itself, and India relapsed into political apathy.

In 1911 also it was proclaimed that Delhi was to be the new capital—Delhi, the seat of many an empire, and the grave also of many an empire.

So stood India in 1914 when the World War broke out in Europe and ended the 100-year period. That war also affected India tremendously, but of that I shall have something to say later.

I have done, at long last, with India in the nineteenth century. I have brought you to within eighteen years of to-day. And now we must leave India and, in the next letter, go to China and examine another type of imperialist exploitation.

114

BRITAIN FORCES OPIUM ON CHINA

December 14, 1932

I HAVE told you, at considerable length, of the effect of the Industrial and Mechanical Revolutions on India, and of how the new imperialism worked in India.   Being an Indian, I am a partisan, and I am afraid I cannot help taking a partisan view.   But I have tried, and I should like you to try, to consider these questions as a scientist impartially examining facts, and not as a nationalist out to prove one side of the case.   Nationalism is good in its place, but it is an unreliable friend and an unsafe historian.   It blinds us to many happenings, and sometimes distorts the truth, especially when it concerns us or our country.   So we have to be wary, when considering the recent history of India, lest we cast all the blame for our misfortunes on the British.

Having seen how India was exploited in the nineteenth century by the industrialists and capitalists of Britain, let us go to the other great country of Asia, India's old-time friend, that ancient among nations, China.   We shall find here a different type of exploitation by the West.   China did not become a colony or dependency of any European country, as India did.   She escaped this, as she had a strong enough central government to hold the country together till about the middle of the nineteenth century.   India, as we have seen, had gone to pieces more than 100 years before this, when the Moghal Empire fell.   China grew weak in the nineteenth century, but still it held together to the last, and the mutual jealousies of foreign Powers prevented them from taking too much advantage of China's weakness.

In my last letter on China (it was number 94) I told you of the attempts made by the British to increase their trade with China. I gave you a long quotation from the very superior and patronizing letter written by the Manchu Emperor Chien Lung in answer to the English King George III.   This was in 1792.   This date will remind you of the stormy times that Europe was having then—it was the period of the French Revolution.   And this was followed by Napoleon and the Napoleonic wars.   England had her hands full during this whole period and was fighting desperately against Napoleon.   There was no question thus of an extension of the China trade for her till Napoleon fell and England breathed with relief.   Soon after, however, in 1816, another British embassy was sent to China.   But there was some difficulty about the ceremonial to be observed, and the Chinese Emperor refused to see the British envoy, Lord Amhurst, and ordered him to go back.   The ceremony to be performed was called the *kotow*, which is a kind of prostration on the ground.   Perhaps you have heard of the word " kow-towing ".

So nothing happened.   Meanwhile a new trade was rapidly

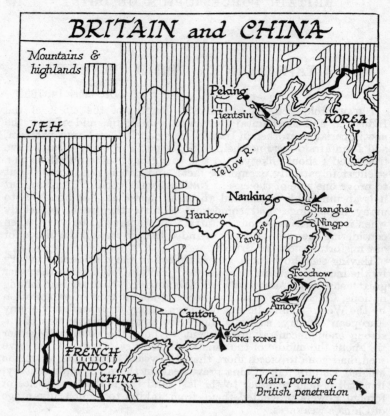

BRITAIN and CHINA

Mountains & highlands

J.F.H.

Peking
Tientsin
KOREA
Yellow R.
Nanking
Hankow
Shanghai
Ningpo
Yangtse
Foochow
Amoy
Canton
HONG KONG
FRENCH INDO-CHINA

Main points of British penetration

growing—the trade in opium. It is not perhaps correct to call this a new trade, as opium was first imported from India as early as the fifteenth century. India had sent in the past many a good thing to China. Opium was one of the really bad things sent by her. But the trade was limited. It grew in the nineteenth century because of the Europeans, and especially the East India Company, which had a monopoly of the British trade. It is said that the Dutch in the East used to mix it with their tobacco and then smoke it as a preventive against malaria. Through them opium-smoking went to China, but in a worse form, for in China pure opium was smoked. The Chinese Government wanted to stop the habit because of its bad effect on the people, and also because the opium trade took away a lot of money from the country.

In 1800 the Chinese Government issued an edict or order prohibiting all importation of opium for any purpose whatsoever. But the trade was a very profitable one for the foreigners. They continued to smuggle opium into the country and bribed Chinese officials to overlook this. The Chinese Government thereupon made a rule that their officials were not to meet foreign merchants. Severe penalties were also laid down for teaching the Chinese or Manchu languages to any foreigner. But all this was to no purpose. The opium trade continued, and there was probably a great deal of bribery and corruption. Indeed, matters became worse after 1834, when the British Government put an end to the monopoly of the East India Company in the China trade, and threw this open to all British merchants.

There was a sudden increase in opium-smuggling, and the Chinese Government at last decided to take strong action to suppress it. They chose a good man for this purpose. Lin Tse-hsi was appointed a special commissioner to suppress the smuggling, and he took swift and vigorous action. He went down to Canton in the south, which was the chief centre for this illegal trade, and ordered all the foreign merchants there to deliver to him all the opium they had. They refused to obey the order at first. Thereupon Lin forced them to obey. He cut them off in their factories, made their Chinese workers and servants leave them, and allowed no food to go to them from outside. This vigour and thoroughness resulted in the foreign merchants coming to terms and handing over to the Chinese 20,000 cases of opium. Lin had this huge quantity of opium, which was obviously meant for smuggling purposes, destroyed. Lin also told the foreign merchants that no ship would be allowed to enter Canton unless the captain gave an undertaking that he would not bring opium. If this promise was broken, the Chinese Government would confiscate the ship and its entire cargo. Commissioner Lin was a thorough person. He did the work entrusted to him well, but he did not realize that the consequences were going to be hard on China.

The consequences were : war with Britain, defeat of China, a humiliating treaty; and opium, the very thing the Chinese Government wanted to prohibit, forced down their throats. Whether opium was good or bad for the Chinese was immaterial. What the Chinese Government wanted to do did not much matter; but what did matter was that smuggling opium into China was a very profitable job for British merchants, and Britain was not prepared to tolerate the loss of this income. Most of the opium destroyed by Commissioner Lin belonged to British merchants. So, in the name of national honour, Britain went to war with China in 1840. This war is rightly called the Opium War, for it was fought and won for the right of forcing opium on China.

China could do little against the British fleet which blockaded Canton and other places. After two years she was forced to submit, and in 1842 the Treaty of Nanking laid down that five ports were to be opened to foreign trade, which meant especially the opium trade then. These five ports were Canton, Shanghai, Amoy, Ningpo, and Foochow. They were called the " treaty ports ". Britain also took possession of the island of Hongkong, near Canton, and extorted a large sum of money as compensation for the opium that had been destroyed, and for the costs of the war which she had forced on China.

Thus the British achieved the victory of opium. The Chinese Emperor made a personal appeal to Queen Victoria, England's Queen at the time, pointing out with all courtesy the terrible effects of the opium trade which was now forced on China. There was no reply from the Queen. Just fifty years earlier his predecessor, Chien Lung, had written very differently to the King of England !

This was the beginning of China's troubles with the imperialist Powers of the West. Her isolation was at an end. She had to accept foreign trade; and she had to accept, in addition, Christian missionaries. These missionaries played an important part in China as the vanguard of imperialism. Many of China's subsequent troubles had something to do with missionaries. Their behaviour was often insolent and exasperating, but they could not be tried by Chinese courts. Under the new treaty, foreigners from the West were not subject to Chinese law or Chinese justice. They were tried by their own courts. This was called " extra-territoriality ", and it still exists, and is much resented. The converts of the missionaries also claimed this special protection of " extra-territoriality ". They were in no way entitled to it; but that made no difference, as the great missionary, the representative of a powerful imperialist nation, was behind them. Thus village was sometimes set against village, and when, exasperated beyond measure, the villagers or others rose and attacked the missionary, and sometimes killed him, then the imperialist Power behind swooped down and took signal reparation. Few occurrences have been so profitable to European Powers as the murders of their missionaries in China ! For they made each such murder the occasion for demanding and extorting further privileges.

It was also a convert to Christianity who started one of the most terrible and cruel rebellions in China. This was the Taiping Rebellion, started about 1850 by a half-mad person, Hung Hsin-Chuan. This religious maniac had extraordinary success and went about with the war-cry " Kill the idolaters ", and vast numbers of people were killed. The rebellion devastated more than half China, and during a dozen years or so it is estimated that at least 20,000,000 people died on account of it. It is not right, of course, to hold the Christian missionaries or the foreign Powers responsible for this outbreak and the massacres which accompanied it. At first the missionaries seemed to bless it, but later they repudiated Hung. The Chinese Government, however, continued to believe that the Christian missionaries were responsible for it. This belief makes us realize how greatly the Chinese resented missionary activities then and later. To them the missionary did not come as a messenger of religion and good-will. He was the agent of imperialism. As an English author has said : " First the missionary, then the gunboat, then the land-grabbing—this is the procession of events in the Chinese mind." It is well to bear this in mind, as the missionary crops up often enough in Chinese troubles.

It is extraordinary that a rebellion led by a mad fanatic should have had such great success before it was finally suppressed. The real reason for this was that the old order in China was breaking up. In my last letter on China, I think I told you of the burden of taxation and the changing economic conditions and the growing discontent of the people. Secret societies were rising everywhere against the Manchu Government, and there was rebellion in the air. Foreign trade, the trade in opium and other articles, made matters worse. Foreign trade China had had, of course, in the past. But now the conditions were different. The big machine-industry of the West was turning out goods fast, and these could not all be sold at home. So they had to find markets elsewhere. This was the urge for markets in India as well as in China. These goods, and especially opium, upset the old trade arrangements, and thus made the economic confusion worse. As in India, the price of articles in the Chinese bazaars began to be affected by the world prices. All this added to the discontent and misery of the people and strengthened the Taiping Rebellion.

This was the background in China during these days of growing arrogance and interference by the western Powers. It is not surprising that China could do little to withstand their demands. These European Powers and much later Japan, as we shall see, took full advantage of China's confusion and difficulties to extort privileges and territory from her. China, indeed, would have gone the way of India, and become the dependency and empire of one or more of the western Powers and Japan, but for the mutual rivalry of these Powers and their jealousy of each other.

I have strayed from my main story in telling you about this general background during the nineteenth century in China, of economic breakdown, Taiping Rebellion, missionaries, and foreign aggression. But one must know something of this to be able to follow intelligently the narrative of events. For events in history do not just happen like miracles. They occur because a variety of causes lead up to them. But these causes are often not obvious; they lie under the surface of events. The Manchu rulers of China, till recently so great and powerful, must have been amazed at the sudden change of fortune's wheel. They did not see, probably, that the roots of their collapse lay in their own past; they did not appreciate the industrial progress of the West and its disastrous consequences on China's economic system. They resented greatly the intrusions of the " barbarian " foreigners. The Emperor at the time, referring to these intrusions, used a delightful old Chinese phrase : he said that he would allow no man to snore alongside of his bed ! But the wisdom and humour of the old classics, though they taught a serene confidence and a magnificent fortitude in misfortune, were not enough to repel the foreigner.

The Treaty of Nanking opened the door to Britain in China. But Britain was not going to have all the fat plums to herself. France and the United States stepped in and also made commercial treaties with China. China was helpless, and this compulsion exercised on her did not make her love or respect the foreigner. She resented the very presence of these " barbarians ". The foreigner, on his side, was still far from content. His appetite for exploiting China grew. The British again took the lead.

It was a very favourable time for the foreigners, as China was busy with the Taiping Rebellion and could offer no resistance. So the British set about to find a pretext for war. In 1856 the Chinese Viceroy of Canton had the Chinese crew of a ship arrested for piracy. The ship belonged to the Chinese, and no foreigner was involved. But it flew the British flag because of a permit from the Hongkong Government. As it happened, even this permit had expired. None the less, as in the fable of the wolf and the lamb at the river, the British Government made this the excuse for war.

Troops were sent to China from England. Just then the Indian Revolt of 1857 broke out, and all these troops were diverted to India. The China War had to wait till the Revolt was crushed. In 1858 this second China War began. The French, meanwhile, had also discovered a pretext for taking part in it, for a French missionary had been killed somewhere in China. So the English and the French swooped down on the Chinese, who had their hands full with the Taiping Rebellion. The British and the French Governments tried to induce Russia and the United States of America to join them, but they did not agree. They were quite prepared, however, to share in the loot. There was practically no fighting, and new treaties, extorting more privileges, were signed by all the four Powers with China. More ports were opened to foreign trade.

But the story of the Second China War is not yet over. There was another act to the play, with a still more tragic sequel to it. When treaties are made it is customary for the governments concerned to ratify or confirm them. It was arranged that this ratification of the new treaties should take place within a year at Peking. When the time came for this, the Russian envoy came direct to Peking, overland from Russia. The other three came by sea and wanted to bring their boats up the river Peiho to Peking. This city was being threatened by the Taiping rebels just then, and the river had been fortified. The Chinese Government therefore asked the British, French and American envoys not to come by the river route, but to travel by a land route farther north. It was not an unreasonable request. The American agreed to it. Not so the British and French envoys. They tried to force their way up the Peiho river in spite of the fortifications. The Chinese fired upon them and forced them back with heavy losses.

Arrogant and over-proud governments, which would not even listen to a request from the Chinese Government to change their travel route, could not tolerate this. More troops were sent for to take vengeance. In 1860 they marched on the old city of Peking, and their vengeance took the form of the destruction and looting and burning of one of the most wonderful buildings in the city. This was the Imperial Summer Palace, the Yuen-Ming-Yuen, completed in the reign of Chien Lung. It was full of rare treasures of art and literature, the finest that China had produced. There were old bronzes of great beauty, and amazingly fine porcelain, and rare manuscripts, and pictures and every kind of curio and work of art for which China had been famous for 1000 years. The Anglo-French soldiery, ignorant vandals that they were, looted these treasures and destroyed them in huge bonfires which kept burning for many days ! Is it any wonder that the Chinese, with a culture of thousands of years behind them, looked upon this vandalism with anguish in their hearts, and considered the wreckers ignorant barbarians who only knew how to kill and destroy ? And memories of the Huns and the Mongols and many other old-time barbarian wreckers must have come to them.

But the foreign " barbarians " cared little what the Chinese thought of them. They felt secure in their gunboats and with their modern weapons of war. What did it matter to them that the rich and rare treasures which had been collected during hundreds of years were no more ? What did they care for Chinese art and culture ?

> " Whatever happens,
> We have got
> The Maxim gun,
> And they have not ! "

115

CHINA IN DIFFICULTIES

December 24, 1932

In my last letter I told you of the destruction by the British and French of the wonderful Summer Palace of Peking in 1860. This was done, it is said, as a punishment for a Chinese violation of a flag of truce. It may have been true that some Chinese troops had been guilty of such an offence, but still the deliberate vandalism of the British and French almost passes one's comprehension. This was not the act of a few ignorant soldiers, but of the men in authority. Why do such things happen ? The English and the French are civilized and cultured peoples, in many ways the leaders of modern civilization. And yet these people, who in private life are decent and considerate, forget all their civilization and decency in their public dealings and conflicts with other people. There seems to be a strange contrast between the behaviour of individuals to each other and the behaviour of nations. Children and boys and girls are taught not to be too selfish, to think of others, to behave properly. All our education is meant to teach us this lesson, and to a small extent we learn it. And then comes war, and we forget our old lesson, and the brute in us shows his face. So decent people behave like brutes.

This is so even when two kindred nations, like the French and Germans, fight each other. But it is far worse when different races are in conflict; when the European faces the races and peoples of Asia and Africa. The different races know little of each other, for each is a closed book to the other; and where there is ignorance there is no fellow-feeling. Racial hatred and bitterness increase, and when there is a conflict between two races, it is not only a political war, but something far worse—a racial war. This explains to some extent the horrors of the Indian Revolt of 1857, and the cruelty and vandalism of the dominant European Powers in Asia and Africa.

It all seems very sad and very silly. But where there is the domination of one nation over another, one people over another, one class over another, there is bound to be discontent and friction and revolt, and an attempt by the exploited nation or people or class to get rid of its exploiter. And this exploitation of one by another is the very basis of our present-day society, which is called capitalism, and out of which imperialism has emerged.

In the nineteenth century the big machines and industrial progress had made the western European nations and the United States of America wealthy and powerful. They began to think that they were the lords of the earth and that the other races were far inferior to them and must make way for them. Having gained some control over the forces of Nature, they became arrogant and overbearing to others. They forgot that civilized man must not only control Nature, but must also control himself. And so we see in this nineteenth century progressive races, ahead of others in many ways, often behaving in a manner which would put a backward savage to shame. This may perhaps help you to understand the behaviour of European races in Asia and Africa, not only in the last century, but even to-day.

Do not imagine that I am comparing the European races to ourselves or to other races to our advantage. Far from it. We all have our dark spots, and some of ours are pretty bad; or else we might not have fallen quite so low as we have done.

We shall go back to China now. The British and French had given a demonstration of their might by destroying the Summer Palace. They followed this up by forcing China to ratify the old treaties and extorted fresh privileges out of her. In Shanghai the Chinese customs service was organized under foreign officials by the Chinese Government in accordance with these treaties. This was called the " Imperial Maritime Customs ".

Meanwhile the Taiping Rebellion, which had enfeebled China and thus given an opportunity to the foreign Powers, was still dragging on. At last, in 1864, it was finally put down by a Chinese Governor, Li Hung Chang, who became a leading statesman of China.

While England and France extorted privileges and concessions out of China by terrorism, Russia in the north achieved a remarkable success by more peaceful methods. Only a few years before, Russia, hungry for the possession of Constantinople, had attacked Turkey in Europe. England and France were afraid of Russia's growing strength, and so they joined the Turks and defeated Russia in what is known as the Crimean War of 1854–56. Defeated in the west, Russia began to look towards the east, and had great success. China was persuaded by peaceful means to cede to Russia a province in the north-east, adjoining the sea, with the city and harbour of Vladivostok. This triumph for Russia was due to a brilliant young Russian officer, Muravieff. In this way, Russia gained far more by friendly methods than England and France had gained after their three years' war and insensate destruction.

So matters stood in 1860. The great Chinese Empire of the Manchus, which by the end of the eighteenth century covered and dominated nearly half Asia, was now humbled and disgraced. Western Powers from distant Europe had defeated and humiliated it; an internal rebellion had almost upset the Empire. All this shook up China completely. It was obvious that all was not well, and some effort was made to reorganize the country to meet the new conditions and the foreign menace. So this year 1860 might almost be considered the beginning of a new era when China prepares to resist foreign aggression. China's neighbour, Japan, was similarly occupied at this time, and this also served as an example. Japan succeeded far more than China, but for a while China did hold back the foreign Powers.

A Chinese mission, under an American named Burlingame, who was a warm friend of China, was sent to the treaty Powers, and he succeeded in getting somewhat better terms from them. A new Sino-American treaty was signed in 1868, and it is interesting to find that in this the Chinese Government agreed, as a favour and a concession to the United States, to permit the emigration of Chinese workers to the States. The United States were busy then developing their western Pacific States, especially California, and labour was scarce there. So they imported Chinese labour. But this became the source of fresh trouble. The Americans began to object to cheap Chinese labour, and there was friction between the two governments. The United States Government later stopped Chinese immigration, and this humiliating treatment was greatly resented by the Chinese people, who boycotted American goods. But all this is a long story which brings us into the twentieth century. We need not go into it.

The Taiping Rebellion had hardly been crushed when another revolt broke out against the Manchus. This was not in China proper, but in the far west, in Turkestan, the centre of Asia. This was largely inhabited by Muslims; and the Muslim tribes, under a leader named Yakub Beg, rose in 1863 and drove out the Chinese authorities. This local revolt has interest for us for two reasons. Russia tried to take advantage of it by seizing Chinese territory. This, of course, was a well-established European manœuvre whenever China was in difficulties. But, to every one's surprise, China refused to agree, and ultimately made Russia disgorge. This was due to an extraordinary campaign by the Chinese General Tso Tsung-tang in Central Asia against Yakub Beg. This general took matters in a most leisurely fashion. He marched slowly, allowing year after year to pass by before he reached the rebels. Twice he actually halted his army long enough to plant and reap a crop of grain to provide for its use ! The problem of providing food supplies for an army is always a difficult one, and this must have been formidable when the Gobi desert had to be crossed. So General Tso solved it in a novel way. He then defeated Yakub Beg and put an end to the rebellion. His campaign in Kashgar and Turfan and Yarkand, etc., is said, from a military point of view, to have been a wonderful one.

Having settled satisfactorily with Russia in central Asia, the Chinese Government soon had trouble in another part of their wide-flung but disintegrating empire. This was in Annam, which was a vassal State of China. The French had designs on it, and there was fighting between China and France. Again, to every one's surprise, China did rather well, and was not cowed down by France. There was a satisfactory treaty in 1885.

The imperialist Powers were sufficiently impressed by these new signs of strength in China. It seemed as if she were recovering from her weakness of 1860 and before. There was talk of reform, and many people thought that she had turned the corner. It was because of this that England, when annexing Burma in 1886, promised to send every ten years the customary tribute to China.

But China was far from having turned the corner yet. There was still a great deal of humiliation and suffering and disruption in store for her. What was wrong with her was not merely the weak-ness of the army or navy, but something which went far deeper. Her whole social and economic structure was going to pieces. As I have told you already, it was in a bad way early in the nineteenth century when many secret societies were formed against the Manchus. Foreign trade and the effects of contact with industrialized countries made matters worse. The appearance of strength which came over China after 1860 had little reality behind it. There were some local reforms by energetic officials here and there, especially by Li Hung Chang. But these could not touch the roots of the problem or cure the disease which enfeebled China.

The chief reason for the outward showing of strength by China during these years was the presence at the head of affairs of a strong ruler. This was a remarkable woman, the Empress Dowager Tzu Hsi. She was only twenty-six when power came into her hands, as the nominal Emperor was her infant son. For forty-seven years she ruled China with vigour. She chose efficient officials and impressed them with some part of her own vigour. It was largely due to this and to her that China made a braver show of strength than she had done for many a year.

But meanwhile, across the narrow seas, Japan was performing wonders and changing out of all recognition. To Japan, therefore, we must now go.

116

JAPAN RUSHES AHEAD

December 27, 1932

It is long since I wrote to you about Japan. Over five months ago I told you (in letter 81) of the strange way in which this country shut herself up in the seventeenth century. From 1641, for over 200 years, the people of Japan lived cut off from the rest of the world. These 200 years saw great changes in Europe and Asia and America, and even in Africa. Of some of the stirring events that took place during this period I have already told you. But no news of them reached this secluded nation; no breath from outside came to disturb the old-world feudal air of Japan. Almost it seemed as if the march of time and change had been stayed, and the mid-seventeenth century held captive. For though time rolled on, the picture seemed to remain the same. It was feudal Japan, with the landowning class in power. The Emperor had little power; the real ruler was the Shogun, the head of a great clan. Like the Kshattriyas in India, there was a warrior class called the Samurai. The feudal lords and the Samurai were the ruling class. Often different lords and clans quarrelled with each other. But all of them joined in oppressing and exploiting the peasantry and all others.

Still, Japan had peace. After the long civil wars which had exhausted the country this peace was very welcome. Some of the great warring nobles—the Daimyos—were suppressed. Slowly Japan began to recover from the ravages of civil war. People's minds turned more to industry and art and literature and religion. Christianity had been suppressed; Buddhism revived, and later Shinto, which is a typical Japanese worship of ancestors. Confucius, the sage of China, became the ideal to be looked up to in matters of social behaviour and morals. Art flourished in the circles of the Court and the nobility. In some ways the picture was similar to that of the Middle Ages of Europe.

But it is not so easy to keep out change, and though outside contacts were stopped, inside Japan itself change worked, though more slowly than it might otherwise have done. As in other countries, the feudal order moved towards economic collapse. Discontent grew, and the Shogun, being at the head of affairs, became the target for this. The growth of Shinto-worship made people look more to the Emperor, who was supposed to be the direct descendant of the Sun. Thus a spirit of nationalism grew out of the prevailing discontents, and this spirit, based as it was on an economic breakdown, would have inevitably led to a change and the opening of Japan to the world.

Many attempts had been made by foreign Powers to open up Japan, but they had all failed. About the middle of the nineteenth century the United States of America became especially interested in this. They had just spread out to the west in California, and San Francisco was becoming an important port. The newly opened trade with China was inviting, but the journey across the Pacific was a long one. So they wanted to call at a Japanese port to break this long journey and take supplies. This was the reason for America's repeated attempts to open up Japan.

In 1853 an American squadron came to Japan with a letter from the American President. These were the first steamships seen in Japan. A year later the Shogun agreed to open two ports. The British, Russians and Dutch, learning of this, came soon after and also made similar treaties with the Shogun. So Japan was open again to the world after 213 years.

But there was trouble ahead. The Shogun had posed as the Emperor before the foreign Powers. He was no longer popular, and a great agitation rose against him and his foreign treaties. Some foreigners were also killed, and this resulted in a naval attack by the foreign Powers. The position became more and more difficult, and ultimately the Shogun was prevailed upon to resign his office in 1867. Thus ended the Tokugawa Shogunate which, you may or may not remember, began with Iyeyasu in 1603. Not only that, but the whole system of the Shogunate, which had lasted for nearly 700 years came to an end.

The new Emperor now came into his own. He was a boy of fourteen who had just succeeded to the throne as the Emperor Mutsihito. For forty-five years he reigned, from 1867 to 1912, and this period is known as the Meiji (or " enlightened rule ") era. It was during his reign that Japan forged ahead, and, copying western nations, became their equal in many respects. This vast change brought about in a generation is remarkable and without parallel in history. Japan became a great industrial nation and, after the manner of the western Powers, an imperialistic and predatory nation. She bore all the outward signs of progress. In industry she even advanced beyond her teachers. Her population increased rapidly. Her ships went round the globe. She became a great Power whose voice was heard with respect in international affairs. And yet all this mighty change did not go very deep down into the heart of the nation. It would be wrong to call the changes superficial, for they were far more than that. But the outlook of the rulers still remained feudal, and they sought to combine radical reform with this feudal shell. They seemed to succeed to a large extent.

The people who were responsible for these great changes in Japan were a band of far-seeing men of the nobility—the " Elder Statesmen " they were called. When the anti-foreign riots in Japan were followed by bombardment by the foreign warships, the Japanese saw their helplessness and felt bitterly humiliated. Instead of cursing their fate and tearing their hair, they decided to learn a lesson from this defeat and degradation. The Elder Statesmen chalked out a programme of reform and they adhered to it.

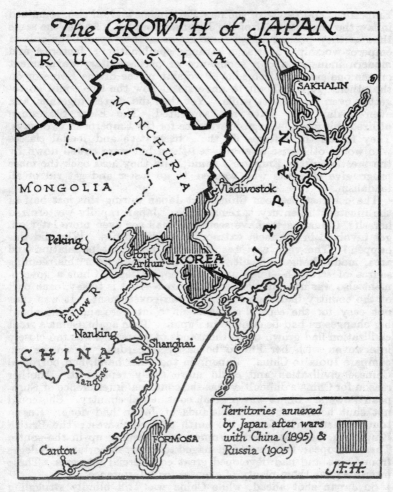

The GROWTH of JAPAN

RUSSIA

MANCHURIA

SAKHALIN

MONGOLIA

Vladivostok

JAPAN

Peking

Port
Arthur KOREA

Yellow R.

Nanking

Shanghai

CHINA

Yangtse

Canton

FORMOSA

Territories annexed
by Japan after wars
with China (1895) &
Russia (1905)

J.F.H.

The old feudal Daimios were abolished. The capital of the Emperor was taken from Kyoto to Yedo, which was now renamed Tokyo. A new constitution was announced with two Houses of Parliament, of which the lower House was elected, the upper nominated. There were changes in education, law, industry, and in almost everything. Factories grew up, and a modern army and navy were formed. Experts were sent for from foreign countries, and Japanese students were sent to Europe and America, not to become barristers and the like, as Indians have done in the past, but to become scientists and technical experts.

All this was done by the Elder Statesmen in the name of the

Emperor, who in spite of the new Parliament and all else, remained in law the absolute ruler of the Japanese Empire. And at the same time as they pushed ahead these reforms, they spread the cult of emperor-worship. It was a strange combination : factories and modern industry and a semblance of parliamentary government on the one side, and a medieval worship of the divine Emperor on the other. It is difficult to understand how the two could go together even for a short while. Yet they did march together, and even to-day they have not separated. The Elder Statesmen utilized this great feeling of reverence for the Emperor in two ways. They forced the reforms on the conservative and feudal classes who would otherwise have resisted them but were cowed down by the prestige of the Emperor's name ; and they held back the more progressive elements who wanted to go faster and get rid of all feudalism.

The contrast between China and Japan during this last half of the nineteenth century is remarkable. Japan rapidly westernized herself ; China, as we have seen and shall see even more later on, got involved in the most extraordinary difficulties. Why did this happen ? The very vastness of China, her great population and area, made change difficult. India also suffers from this seeming source of strength—huge area and population. China's government also was not sufficiently centralized—that is to say, each part of the country had a great deal of self-government. It was thus not easy for the central government to interfere and bring about big changes as had been done in Japan. Then again, China's great civilization had grown up in thousands of years and was too closely interwoven with her life to be easily discarded. Again we can compare India to China. Japan, on the other hand, had borrowed Chinese civilization and could more easily replace it. Another reason for China's difficulties was the continual interference of European Powers. China was a great continental country. She could not shut herself up, as the islands of Japan had done. Russia touched her territories to the north and north-west; the British Empire in the south-west; France was creeping up in the south. These European Powers had managed to extort important privileges from China and had developed great commercial interests. These interests gave them plenty of excuses for interference.

So Japan shot ahead, while China was still blindly struggling on and trying, with little success, to adapt herself to the new conditions. And yet there is another strange fact worth noticing. Japan took to western machinery and industry and, with a modern army and navy, put on the garb of an advanced industrialized Power. But she did not take so readily to the new thought and ideas of Europe; to notions of individual and social freedom; to a scientific outlook on life and society. At heart she remained feudal and authoritarian and tied up to a strange emperor-worship which the rest of the world had long outgrown. The passionate and self-sacrificing patriotism of the Japanese was closely allied to this loyalty to the Emperor. Nationalism and the cult of the divine

Emperor went side by side. China, on the other hand, did not take readily to big machinery and industry; but the Chinese, or at any rate modern China, welcomed western thought and ideas and the scientific outlook. These were not so far removed from their own. Thus we see that although modern China entered more into the spirit of western civilization, Japan outstripped her because she put on the armour of it, ignoring the spirit. And all Europe praised Japan because she was strong in this armour, and they made her one of their fellowship. But China was weak and unprovided with Maxim guns and the like. So they insulted her and preached to her and exploited her, caring little for her thought and ideas.

Japan not only followed Europe in industrial methods, but also in imperialistic aggression. She was more than a faithful pupil of the European Powers : she often improved on them. Her real difficulty was the discordance between the new industrialism and the old feudalism. In her attempts to carry on with both she could not establish economic equilibrium. Taxation was very heavy, and people grumbled. To prevent trouble at home she had recourse to an old device—distracting attention by war and im-perialistic adventures abroad. Her new industries also forced her to look to other countries for raw materials and markets, just as the Industrial Revolution had forced England, and later other western European Powers, to look abroad and conquer. Production increased and there was a rapid growth of population. More and more food and raw materials were required. Where was she to get them ? Her nearest neighbours were China and Korea. China offered opportunities for trade, but she was a thickly populated country. In Manchuria, however, which formed the north-eastern provinces of the Chinese Empire, there was plenty of elbow-room for development and colonization. So to Korea and Manchuria, Japan looked hungrily.

Japan also saw with concern the western Powers getting all manner of privileges from China, and even trying to get territory. She did not like this at all. If these Powers became well established on the mainland opposite to her, her safety might be imperilled and, at any rate, her growth on the continent would be checked.

In less than twenty years after her opening to the outer world, Japan began to be aggressive towards China. A petty dispute about some fishermen, who had been shipwrecked and were murdered, gave Japan an opportunity to demand compensation from China. China refused at first, but then, threatened with war and occupied at the time with the French in Annam, she gave in to Japan. This was in 1874. Japan was elated by this triumph and immediately looked round for further conquests. Korea seemed inviting and, picking a quarrel with her for some petty reason, Japan invaded her and forced her to pay a sum of money and to open some ports for Japanese trade.

Korea had long been a vassal State of China. She looked to China for support, but China was unable to help. The Chinese Government, fearing that Japan might acquire too much influence, advised Korea to give in for the moment and also to make treaties with the western Powers to checkmate Japan. So Korea was thrown open to the world by 1882. But Japan was not going to be satisfied with this. Taking advantage of China's difficulties, she again raised the Korean question and made China agree to a joint protectorate over Korea—that is, poor Korea became a vassal State of both. This was obviously a most unsatisfactory state of affairs for all concerned. There was bound to be trouble. Japan, indeed, wanted trouble, and in 1894 she forced a war on China.

The Sino-Japanese War of 1894–95 was a runaway affair for Japan. Her army and navy were up to date; the Chinese were still old-fashioned and inefficient. Japan won all along the line, and forced a treaty on China which put her on the same level as the western treaty Powers. Korea was declared independent, but this was only a veil for Japanese control. China was also forced to give to Japan the Liaotung peninsula in Manchuria, with Port Arthur, as well as Formosa and some other islands.

This crushing defeat of China by little Japan surprised the world. The western Powers were by no means pleased at this rise of a powerful country in the Far East. Even during the Sino-Japanese War, when Japan was seen to be winning, she was warned by these Powers that they would not consent to Japan annexing any part of China's mainland. In spite of this warning she took the Liaotung peninsula with an important port—Port Arthur. But she was not allowed to keep this. Three great Powers—Russia, Germany and France—insisted on her giving it up, and, much to her annoyance and anger, she had to do so. She was not strong enough to face these three.

But Japan remembered this slight upon her. It rankled and made her prepare for a greater struggle. Nine years later this struggle came with Russia.

Meanwhile Japan, by her victory over China, had established her position as the strongest nation of the Far East. China had appeared in all her weakness, and all fear of her vanished from the western Powers. They swooped down on her like vultures on a dead or dying body, and tried to get as much as possible for themselves. France, Russia, England, and Germany—all scrambled for sea-ports on the China coast and for privileges. There was an unholy and a most unseemly battle for concessions. Every little thing was made an excuse for claiming additional privileges or concessions. Because two missionaries were killed, Germany seized by force Kiauchau in the Shantung peninsula in the east. Because Germany took this, the other Powers insisted on their share of the booty. Russia took Port Arthur, of which she had deprived Japan three years previously. England took Wei-hai-wei to set off Russia's possession of Port Arthur. France took a port and territory in Annam. Russia also got permission to build a railway across North Manchuria, an extension of the Trans-Siberian railway.

It was extraordinary—this shameless scramble. Of course China did not enjoy parting with territory or granting concessions

She was forced to agree on every occasion by displays of naval force and threats of bombardment. What shall we call this scandalous behaviour? Highway robbery? Brigandage? It is the way of imperialism. Sometimes it works in secret; sometimes it covers its evil deeds under a cloak of pious sentiment and hypocritical pretence of doing good to others. But in China in 1898 there was no cloak or covering. The naked thing stood out in all its ugliness.

117

JAPAN DEFEATS RUSSIA

December 29, 1932

I HAVE been writing to you about the Far East, and I shall continue this story to-day. You may wonder why I seek to burden your mind with the wars and disputes of the past. They are not savoury subjects, and they are over and done with. I do not want to lay stress on them. But much that is happening to-day in the Far East has its roots in these very troubles, and some knowledge of them therefore is necessary to the understanding of modern problems. China, like India, is one of the great world problems of to-day. And even as I write, a bitter dispute is going on regarding the Japanese conquest of Manchuria.

I told you in my last letter of the scramble for concessions in China in 1898, backed by the warships of the western Powers. They seized all the good ports, and in the province lying behind the port they secured all manner of rights—to open mines, build railroads, etc. And still the demand continued for further concessions. The foreign governments began to talk of " spheres of influence " in China. This is a gentle way which modern imperialistic governments have of partitioning a country. There are various degrees of possession and control. Annexation is, of course, complete possession; a protectorate is something with slightly less control; " spheres of influence " is less still. But they all point to the same thing; one step leads to another. Indeed, as we shall perhaps have the chance of discussing later, annexation is an old and almost discarded method which brings nationalistic trouble in its train. It is far easier to have economic control of a country and not worry about the rest.

So the partition of China seemed imminent and Japan was thoroughly alarmed. The fruits of her victory over China seemed to have gone to the western Powers, and she gazed in helpless anger at this splitting up of China. Above all, she was wroth with Russia for preventing her from taking possession of Port Arthur and then seizing it herself.

There was one great Power, however, which had so far taken no part in this scramble for concessions in China or the plans for partition. This was the United States of America. They had kept away not because they were more virtuous than the others, but because they were busy developing their vast country. As they spread westwards to the Pacific Ocean fresh areas required development, and all their energies and wealth were poured into this. Indeed, a great deal of European capital was also invested in America for this purpose. But by the end of the century Americans began to look abroad for investments. They looked to China, and saw with disapproval that the European Powers were on the point of dividing it up into " spheres of influence ", with a view perhaps to eventual annexation. America was being left out. So America pressed for what is called the " open-door " policy in China. This meant that equal facilities should be given to all for trade and business in China. The other Powers agreed to this.

This continual aggression thoroughly frightened the Chinese Government, and convinced them that they must reform and reorganize. They tried to do so, but they had little chance to succeed on account of the continuous demands for fresh concessions. The Dowager Empress Tzu Hsi had been living in retirement for some years. The Chinese people began to look to her as a possible saviour. The Emperor at the time, suspecting some intrigue, wanted to put her in prison. But the old lady retaliated by removing him from power and taking control herself. She took no steps for radical reform, as Japan had done, but she concentrated on building up a modern army. She encouraged the formation of local bands of militia for defence. These bodies of local militia called themselves " I Ho Tuan "—Bands of Righteous Harmony. Sometimes they were also called " Fists of Righteous Harmony "—I Ho Chuan. This latter name reached some Europeans in the port towns, and they translated it into " Boxers ", a crude translation of a graceful phrase.

These " Boxers " were a patriotic reaction against foreign aggression and the innumerable insults which had been offered to China and the Chinese by foreigners. It is not surprising that they did not love the foreigner, who seemed to them the embodiment of evil. In particular they disliked missionaries, who had misbehaved greatly, and, as for the Chinese Christians, they considered them traitors to their country. They represented old China making a last effort to protect herself from the new order. The attempt was not likely to succeed in this way.

There was bound to be friction between these patriotic, antiforeign, anti-missionary, conservative people and the Westerners. Conflicts occurred; an English missionary was murdered; many Europeans and a large number of Chinese Christians were killed. Foreign governments demanded the suppression of the patriotic Boxer movement. The Chinese Government punished those who were guilty of killing, but how could it suppress its own child in this way ? Meanwhile the Boxer movement spread rapidly. The foreign ministers, alarmed by it, summoned troops from their warships, and this again made the Chinese think that the foreign invasion had begun. Soon there was conflict. The German Minister was killed, and there was a siege of the foreign legations in Peking.

A great part of China was up in arms in sympathy with the patriotic Boxer movement. But the viceroys of some provinces remained neutral and helped the foreign Powers in this way. The Dowager Empress undoubtedly sympathized with the Boxers, but she was not openly associated with them Foreigners tried to make out that the Boxers were just brigands. But as a matter of fact the rebellion of 1900 was a patriotic effort to free China from foreign interference. A high English officer in China, Sir Robert Hart, who was Inspector-General of the customs there at the time, went through the siege of the legations. He tells us that the foreigners, and especially the missionaries, were to blame for outraging Chinese feelings, and that the rebellion " was patriotic in its origin, and that it was justifiable in much that it aimed at cannot be questioned, and cannot be too much insisted on ".

This sudden turning of the worm irritated the western Powers greatly. They hurried troops, as they were justified in doing, to save and protect their own people who were besieged in Peking. An international force under a German commander marched to relieve the legations. The Kaiser of Germany asked his troops in China to behave like Huns, and probably it is from this order that the English took to calling all Germans Huns during the World War.

The Kaiser's advice was followed not only by his own troops, but by all the foreign armies. As these forces marched to Peking, the treatment they gave to the people was such that large numbers preferred suicide to falling into their hands. Chinese women in those days dwarfed their feet and could not easily run away. So many of them killed themselves. In this way the allied armies marched on, leaving a trail of death and suicide and burning villages. An English war correspondent, who accompanied the allied forces, says :

> There are things that I must not write, and may not be printed in England, which would seem to show that this western civilization of ours is merely a veneer over savagery. The actual truth has never been written about any war, and this will be no exception.

These armies reached Peking and relieved the legations. And then followed the sack of Peking—" the biggest looting excursion since the days of Pizarro ". The art treasures of Peking went into the hands of crude and uncultured people who did not even know their value. And it is sad to note that the missionaries took a prominent part in this looting. Groups of people went from house to house fixing notices on them saying that they belonged to them. The valuables in the house were sold, and then a move was made to another big house.

The rivalry of the Powers, and partly also the attitude of the United States Government, saved China from partition. But she was made to drink the bitterest cup of humiliation. All manner of indignities were heaped on her : a permanent foreign military force was to remain in Peking and also to guard the railway ; many forts were to be destroyed ; membership of an anti-foreign society was made punishable with death ; further commercial privileges were taken and a huge sum of money extorted as an indemnity ; and, most terrible blow of all, the Chinese Government was forced to put to death as "rebels" the patriotic leaders of the Boxer movement. Such was the "Peking Protocol", as it is called, which was signed in 1901.

While all this was taking place in China proper, and especially round Peking, the Russian Government took advantage of the prevailing confusion to send large numbers of troops across Siberia to Manchuria. China was powerless ; all it could do was to protest. But, as it happened, the other Powers disapproved very much of the Russian Government taking possession in this way of a large slice of territory. Even more anxious and alarmed was the Japanese Government at this development. So the Powers pressed Russia to go back, and the Russian Government tried to assume a look of virtuous pain and surprise that its honourable intentions should have been doubted by any one, and assured the Powers that it had absolutely no intention of interfering with China's sovereign rights, and would withdraw its troops as soon as order was restored on the Russian railway in Manchuria. So everybody was satisfied, and, no doubt compliments must have been paid by the Powers to each other for their remarkable unselfishness and virtue. But, none the less, Russian troops remained in Manchuria and spread right up to Korea.

This advance of Russia in Manchuria and to Korea angered the Japanese greatly. Quietly but intensively they prepared for war. They remembered the combination of three Powers against them in 1895, when they had been forced to give up Port Arthur after the China War, and they tried to prevent this happening again. They found in England a Power which feared Russian advance and wanted to check it. So in 1902 an Anglo-Japanese Alliance was made with the object of preventing a combination of Powers from coercing either Power in the Far East. Japan felt safe now, and took up a more aggressive attitude towards Russia. She demanded that Russian troops be withdrawn from Manchuria. But the foolish Tsarist Government of the day looked upon Japan with contempt and never believed that she would fight.

Early in 1904 war began between the two countries. Japan was fully prepared for it, and the Japanese people, egged on by their government's propaganda and their cult of emperor-worship, were aflame with patriotic fervour. Russia, on the other hand, was wholly unprepared, and her autocratic government could only govern by continuous repression of the people. For a year and a half the war raged, and all Asia and Europe and America were witness to Japan's victories on sea and land. Port Arthur fell to the Japanese after amazing deeds of sacrifice and enormous slaughter.

A great fleet of warships was sent by Russia from Europe all the way by sea to the Far East. After having crossed half the world, travel-stained after thousands of miles of voyage, this mighty fleet arrived in the Sea of Japan, and there, in the narrow straits between Japan and Korea, it was sunk by the Japanese, together with its admiral. Nearly the whole fleet went down in this great disaster.

Russia, Tsarist Russia, was hard hit by defeat after defeat. Russia had great reserves of power; was it not she that had humbled Napoleon 100 years before? But just then the real Russia, the common people of Russia, spoke.

In the course of these letters I am continually referring to Russia, England, France, China, Japan, and so on, as if each country were a living entity. This is a bad habit of mine, which I have acquired from books and newspapers. What I mean, of course, is the Russian Government, the English Government of the day, and so on. These governments may represent nobody but a small group, or they may represent a class, and it is not correct to think or say that they represent the whole people. During the nineteenth century the English Government might be said to have represented a small group of well-to-do people, the owners of land and the upper middle classes, who controlled Parliament. The great majority of the people had no say in the matter. In India to-day one hears sometimes of India sending a representative to the League of Nations or a Round-Table Conference or to some other function. This is nonsense. The so-called representatives cannot be the representatives of India unless the people of India choose them. They are thus the nominees of the Government of India, which, in spite of its name, is just a department of the British Government. Russia, at the time of the Russo-Japanese War, was an autocracy. The Tsar was the " autocrat of all the Russias ", and a very foolish autocrat he was. The workers and the peasants were kept down by means of the army, and even the middle classes had no voice of any kind in the government. Many a brave Russian youth raised his head and his hand against this tyranny and sacrificed his life in the fight for freedom. Many a girl went the same way. So, when I talk of " Russia " doing this or doing that, of fighting Japan, all I mean is the Tsarist Government and nothing more.

The Japanese war, with its disaster, brought more suffering to the common people. The workers often went on strike in the factories to bring pressure on the government. On January 22, 1905, several thousands of peaceful peasants and workers, led by a priest, went in procession to the Winter Palace of the Tsar to beg for some relief from their sufferings. The Tsar, instead of hearing what they had to say, had them shot down. There was a terrible slaughter; 200 were killed, and the winter snow of Petersburg was red with blood. It was a Sunday, and, ever since, that day has been called " Bloody Sunday ". The country was deeply stirred. There were strikes of workers, and these led up to an attempted revolution. This revolution of 1905 was put down with great cruelty by the Tsar's Government. It is interesting for us for several reasons.

It was a kind of preparation for the great revolution twelve years later, in 1917, which changed the face of Russia. And it was during this unsuccessful revolution of 1905 that the revolutionary workers created a new organization which was to become so famous later on —the soviets.

From telling you about China and Japan and the Russo-Japanese War I have, as is my way, drifted to the Russian revolution of 1905. But I had to tell you something of this to explain the background in Russia during this Manchurian War. It was largely because of this attempted revolution and the temper of the people that the Tsar came to terms with Japan.

The Russo-Japanese War ended with the Treaty of Portsmouth in September 1905. Portsmouth is in the United States. The American President had invited both parties and the treaty of peace was signed there. By this treaty Japan got back at last Port Arthur and the Liaotung peninsula, which, you will remember, she had been forced to give up after the China War. Japan also took a great part of the railway which the Russians had built in Manchuria, and half of the island of Sakhalien, which lies north of Japan. Further, Russia abandoned all claims on Korea.

So Japan had won, and she entered the charmed circle of the great Powers. The victory of Japan, an Asiatic country, had a far-reaching effect on all the countries of Asia. I have told you how, as a boy, I used to get excited over it. That excitement was shared by many a boy and girl and grown-up in Asia. A great European Power had been defeated; therefore Asia could still defeat Europe as it had done so often in the past. Nationalism spread more rapidly over the eastern countries and the cry of " Asia for Asiatics " was heard. But this nationalism was not a mere return to the past, a clinging on to old customs and beliefs. Japan's victory was seen to be due to her adoption of the new industrial methods of the West, and these ideas and methods became more popular all over the East.

118

CHINA BECOMES A REPUBLIC

December 30, 1932

WE have seen how Japan's victory over Russia pleased and flattered Asiatic nations. The immediate result of it, however, was to add one more to the small group of aggressive, imperialistic Powers. The first effect of this was felt by Korea. Japan's rise meant Korea's fall. Ever since her reopening to the world, Japan had marked out Korea, and partly Manchuria, as her own. Of course she declared repeatedly that she was going to respect the integrity of China and the independence of Korea. The imperialist

Powers have a way of giving fulsome assurances of good-will even while they rob the party concerned, of declaring the sanctity of life even as they kill. So Japan declared solemnly that she would not interfere in Korea, and at the same time carried through her old policy of taking possession of her. Her wars with China and Russia both centred round Korea and Manchuria. Step by step she had advanced, and now with the defeat of China and Russia, her way was clear.

No scruple had ever troubled Japan in the pursuit of her imperial policy. She grabbed openly, not caring even to cover her designs with a veil. As early as 1894, just before the China War, the Japanese had forcibly entered the royal palace at Seoul, the capital of Korea, and removed and imprisoned the Queen, who would not do their bidding. After the Russian War, in 1905; the Japanese Government forced the Korean King to sign away his country's independence and accept Japanese suzerainty. But this was not good enough. In less than five years this unhappy king was removed altogether from the throne, and Korea was annexed to the Japanese Empire. This was in 1910. After a long history of over 3000 years, Korea passed away as a separate State. The king who was thus removed belonged to a dynasty which had driven out the Mongols 500 years before. But Korea, like her elder sister China, became fossilized and stagnant, and had to pay the penalty for this.

Korea was given its old name again—Chosen, the land of the morning calm. The Japanese brought some modern reforms with them, but they ruthlessly crushed the spirit of the Korean people. For many years the struggle for independence continued and there were many outbreaks, the most important one being in 1919. The people of Korea, and especially young men and women, struggled gallantly against tremendous odds. On one occasion, when a Korean organization fighting for freedom formally declared independence, and thus defied the Japanese, the story goes that they immediately telephoned to the police and informed them of what they had done ! Thus deliberately they sacrified themselves for their ideal. The suppression of the Koreans by the Japanese is a very sad and dark chapter in history. You will be interested to know that young Korean girls, many of them fresh from college, played a prominent part in the struggle.

Let us go back to China now. We left her rather suddenly after the crushing of the Boxer movement and the Peking Protocol in 1901. China was thoroughly humiliated, and again there was an attempt at reform. Even the old Dowager Empress seemed to think that something should be done. During the Russo-Japanese War, China remained a passive spectator, although the fighting was taking place on Chinese territory—Manchuria. Japan's victory strengthened the reformers in China. Education was modernized, and many students were sent to Europe and America and Japan to study modern sciences. The old system of literary examinations by which officials used to be appointed was abolished.

This amazing system, typical of China, had lasted for 2000 years— ever since the days of the Han dynasty. It had long outgrown its utility, and was keeping back China; so it was well that it was abolished. And yet, in its way, it was for long ages a wonderful thing. It represented the Chinese outlook on life, which was neither feudal nor priestly, as in most other countries of Asia and Europe, but was based on reason. The Chinese have always been the least religious of people, and yet they have followed their system of an ethical and regulated life more strictly than any religious people. They tried to develop a rational society, but as they limited this within the four corners of the ancient classics, progress and necessary changes were prevented and there was stagnation and fossilization. We in India have much to learn from this Chinese rationalism, for we are still in the grip of caste and dogmatic religion and priest-craft and feudal ideas. The great Chinese sage Confucius gave a warning to his people which is worthy of remembrance : " Never have anything to do with those who pretend to have dealings with the supernatural. If you allow supernaturalism to get a foothold in your country, the result would be a dreadful calamity." In our country unfortunately many a man with a tuft of hair on his head, or matted locks, or long beard, or intricate markings on the forehead, or saffron cloak, poses as an agent of the supernatural and fleeces the common people.

But China, with all her old-time rationalism and culture, had lost grip with the present, and her old institutions gave her little help in her hour of difficulty. The march of events had vitalized many of her children and made them seek diligently for light elsewhere. They had shaken up even the old Dowager Empress, who talked of granting a constitution and self-government, and sent a com-mission to foreign countries to study their constitutions.

The Chinese Government under the old Dowager was moving at last. But the people were moving faster. As early as 1894 Dr. Sun Yat Sen had founded the " China Revival Society ", which many joined as a protest against the unfair and one-sided treaties— the " unequal treaties " they are called by the Chinese—which the foreign Powers had forced on China. This society grew, and attracted to it the youth of the country. In 1911 it changed its name to the Kuo-Min-Tang—the " People's National Party "—and became the centre of the Chinese Revolution. Dr. Sun, the inspirer of the move-ment, looked to the United States for his model. He wanted a re-public, not a constitutional monarchy, as in England, and certainly no emperor-worship, as in Japan. The Chinese had never made a fetish of their emperors, and besides, the reigning dynasty was hardly Chinese. It was Manchu, and there was a good deal of anti-Manchu feeling. It was this ferment in the people that had moved the Dowager Empress. But the old lady died soon after her proclamations about the coming constitution. Strangely enough, both the old Dowager and her nephew the Emperor, whom she had removed from the throne, died within twenty-four hours of each other in November 1908. A babe now became the nominal Emperor.

Again there were loud demands for the calling of a parliament, and anti-Manchu and anti-monarchical feeling rose higher. The revolutionaries gathered strength. The only strong man who might have faced them was the viceroy of a province, Yuan Shih-Kai. This man was a wily old fox, but he happened to control the only modern and efficient army in China, called the " model army ". Very foolishly, the Manchu rulers irritated and dismissed Yuan, and thus lost the only man who might have saved them for a while. In October 1911 revolution broke out in the valley of the Yangtze, and soon a great part of Central and South China was in revolt. On New Year's Day in 1912 these provinces in revolt proclaimed a republic with its capital at Nanking. Dr. Sun Yat Sen was chosen as President.

Meanwhile Yuan Shih-Kai had been watching the drama ready to intervene when it would be to his advantage to do so. The story of Yuan's dismissal by the Regent (who was acting for his son, the infant Emperor) and his subsequent recall is interesting. Everything was done with all courtesy and politeness in the old China. When Yuan had to be dismissed it was announced that he was suffering from a bad leg. Of course everyone knew that his leg was in excellent condition, and that this was just the conventional method of sending him away. But Yuan had his revenge. Two years later, in 1911, when mutiny and revolt had broken out against the Government, the Regent summoned Yuan in alarm. Yuan had no intention of going unless his terms were granted. So he replied to the Regent that he regretted that he could not possibly leave home just then, as his leg was not yet well enough for him to travel ! His leg recovered with remarkable speed when his conditions were accepted a month later.

But it was too late to check the revolution, and Yuan was clever enough not to compromise himself by committing himself to either side. Finally he advised the abdication of the Manchus. With a republic facing them and deserted by their own general, the Manchu rulers had little choice left. On February 12, 1912, an Edict of Abdication was issued, and thus disappeared the Manchu dynasty from the Chinese stage, after over two and a half centuries of memorable rule. According to a Chinese phrase : " They had come in with the roar of a tiger, to disappear like the tail of a snake."

On this same day, February 12, there took place a strange ceremony in Nanking, the new Republican capital, and also the place where stood the mausoleum of the first Ming sovereign—a ceremony which brought together the old and the new in vivid contrast. Sun Yat Sen, President of the Republic, went with his Cabinet to this mausoleum and presented offerings in the old way. And in the course of his address on this occasion, he said : " We are initiating the example to Eastern Asia of a republican form of government; success comes early or late to those who strive, but the good are surely rewarded in the end. Why, then, should we repine to-day that victory has tarried long ? "

For many a long year, at home and in exile, Dr. Sun had laboured for China's freedom, and success seemed to have come at last. But freedom is a slippery friend, and success demands full payment before it comes, and often it mocks us with vain hope, and tests us with many a hardship, before it can be secured. China's and Dr. Sun's journey were far from over. For many a year the young Republic had to fight for its life, and even to-day, twenty-one years after, when it should have come of age, the future of China hangs in the balance.

The Manchus had abdicated, but Yuan still stood in the way of the Republic, and no one seemed to know what he would do. He controlled the North, the Republic the South. For the sake of peace, and to avoid civil war, Dr. Sun effaced himself, retired from the presidentship and had Yuan Shih-Kai elected as president. But Yuan was no republican. He was out to gain power to exalt himself. He borrowed money from foreign Powers to crush the very Republic which had honoured him by electing him President. He dismissed Parliament and dissolved the Kuo-Min-Tang. This led to a split, and a rival government, with Dr. Sun as its head, was set up in the South. The split which Dr. Sun had sought to avoid by all the means in his power had come, and there were two governments in China when the World War broke out. Yuan tried to become emperor, but he failed and died soon after.

119

FARTHER INDIA AND THE EAST INDIES

December 31, 1932

WE have done with the Far East for a while. We have seen something of India also during the nineteenth century, and it is time that we moved westward to Europe and America and Africa. But before we take this long journey, I should like you to have a glimpse of the south-east corner of Asia and bring our knowledge of it up to date. It is long since we considered these countries. I have referred to them in some previous letters rather vaguely and variously and perhaps not very correctly, as Malaysia and Indonesia and the East Indies and Farther India. I doubt if any of these names covers the whole area, but so long as we understand each other, what's in a name ?

Look at a map if you have one handy. To the south-east of Asia you will see a peninsula consisting of Burma and Siam, and what is now called French Indo-China. And from between Burma and Siam a thin tongue of land shoots out—the Malay Peninsula— fattening out towards the end, with the city of Singapore at the tip. From Malay to Australia there lie many islands, big ones and small, curiously shaped, giving the impression of the ruins of a giant bridge connecting Asia and Australia. These islands are the East Indies, and to the north of these lie the Philippines.   A modern map will tell you that Burma and Malay are under the British; Indo-China is French, and, in between, Siam is an independent country.   The East Indies—Sumatra and Java and a great part of Borneo and the Celebes and Moluccas, the famous spice-islands which drew the mariners of Europe across many thousands miles of perilous seas—are Dutch.   The Philippine Islands are under American domination.

That is the present position of these countries of the eastern seas.   But you will remember my telling you of India's children who went and colonized these countries nearly 2000 years ago; of the great empires that flourished there for long ages; of beautiful cities with wonderful buildings; of trade and commerce and a mingling of Indian and Chinese culture and civilization.

In my last letter dealing with these countries (it is number 79) I told you of the fall of the Portuguese Empire of the East and the rise of the British and Dutch East India Companies.   In the Philippines the Spaniards still ruled.

The British and the Dutch had combined to defeat and drive out the Portuguese.   They succeeded, but there was little love between the victors, and they quarrelled with each other frequently. On one occasion, in 1623, the Dutch Governor of Amboyna in the Moluccas had the entire English staff of the East India Company arrested and executed on a charge of conspiring against the Dutch Government.   This wholesale execution is known as the Massacre of Amboyna.

One fact I would have you remember; I have told you of it in earlier letters.   At this period—that is, during the seventeenth century and after—Europe was not an industrial country.   It did not manufacture goods on any large scale for export.   The days of the big machine and the Industrial Revolution were far distant still. Asia was more of a manufacturing and exporting country than Europe.   When the goods of Asia went to Europe, they were paid for partly by European goods and partly out of the treasure that came from Spanish America.   This trade between Asia and Europe was a profitable one.   The Portuguese had controlled it for a long time and had grown rich by it; the British and Dutch East India Companies were formed to share in it.   But the Portuguese looked upon this trade as their peculiar preserve, and would not allow any one to share in it.   They had had no difficulty with the Spaniards in the Philippines, as the Spaniards were more interested in religion than in trade.   There was little of religion about the British and Dutch adventurers who came on behalf of the two new trading companies.   Soon there was conflict.

The Portuguese had been ruling for over a century and a quarter in the East.   They were far from popular with the people they ruled and there was discontent.   The two trading companies of England and Holland took advantage of this discontent and helped these people to get rid of the Portuguese, but, immediately after, they themselves stepped into the place vacated by the Portuguese.   As rulers of India and the East Indies they took tribute from the people

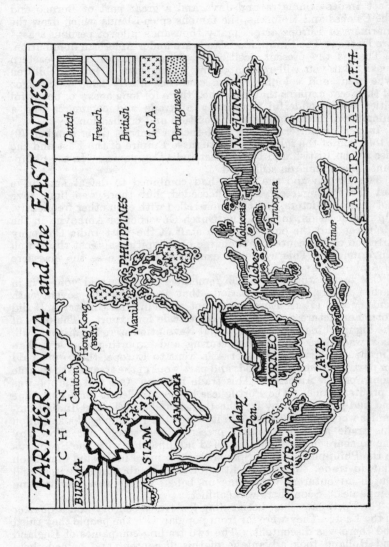

FARTHER INDIA and the EAST INDIES

Dutch.
French.
British.
U.S.A.
Portuguese.

J.F.H.

CHINA
BURMA
ANNAM
SIAM
CAMBODIA
Malay Pen.
Singapore
SUMATRA
JAVA
BORNEO
Canton
Hong Kong (Brit.)
Manila
PHILIPPINES
Celebes
Moluccas
Amboyna
Timor
N. GUINEA
AUSTRALIA

in the shape of heavy taxes and in other ways, and this helped them greatly in carrying on the foreign trade without any great burden on Europe. The great difficulty which Europe had previously experienced in paying for the goods from eastern countries was thus lessened. Even so, as we have seen, England tried to stop the inflow of Indian goods by prohibition and heavy duties. Matters stood thus till the coming of the Industrial Revolution.

The conflict of the Dutch and the British in the East Indies did not last long, because the British withdrew from it. They were beginning to get busy in India, and had their hands full. So these East Indian islands were left entirely to the Dutch East India Company, with the exception of the Philippines, which remained under the Spanish. As the Spanish cared very little for trade and were not trying to conquer any further territory, the Dutch had no rivals now in this area.

The Dutch East India Company, like its namesake the British Company in India, settled down to make as much money as possible. For a 150 years this trading company ruled these islands. They did not pay the slightest attention to the welfare of the people. They oppressed them and extorted as much tribute out of them as was possible. When it was easy to make money by taking tribute, trade became a secondary consideration and languished. The Company was thoroughly inefficient, and the Dutchmen who went out to serve it belonged to the same type of unscrupulous adventurers as the factors or agents of the British Company in India. Money-making, by fair means or foul, was their chief concern. In India the resources of the country were far greater, and even a great deal of mismanagement could be covered up; in India also a number of able British governors made the administration efficient at the top, even though it crushed the people at the bottom, But you will remember that the great Revolt of 1857 put an end to the British East India Company.

The Dutch East India Company went from bad to worse, and ultimately in 1798 the Netherlands Government took direct charge of the Eastern Islands. Soon after, owing to the Napoleonic Wars in Europe and Holland becoming a part of Napoleon's Empire, the English Government took possession of these islands. For five years they were treated as a province of British India, and during this period considerable reforms were introduced. With the fall of Napoleon, the East Indies were returned to Holland. During the five years that Java was connected with the British Indian Government, an able Englishman, Thomas Stamford Raffles, acted as Lieutenant-Governor of Java. Raffles reported that the history of the Dutch colonial administration " is one of the most extraordinary relations of treachery, bribery, massacre, and meanness ". Among other practices, the Dutch officials used to have a regular system of kidnapping people in the Celebes in order to secure slaves for use in Java. This kidnapping was accompanied by devastation and killing.

The direct rule of the Netherlands Government was no better

than that of the Company. In some ways it was even more oppressive for the people. You will remember perhaps what I told you of the Indigo Plantation system in Bengal, which caused so much misery to the cultivators. Something similar to this system, only much worse, was introduced in Java and elsewhere. In the days of the Company the people were made to supply goods. Now, under the "culture system " as it was called, they were forced to work for a certain period every year, which was supposed to be about a third or a quarter of the cultivator's time. In practice, often enough, almost all the cultivator's time was taken up. The Dutch Government worked through contractors, who were given advances of money, free of any interest, by the government. These contractors then exploited the land with the help of forced labour. The produce of the land was supposed to be shared, in certain fixed proportions, between the government, the contractor and the cultivator. Probably the poor cultivator's share was the smallest of all; I do not know exactly what it was. The government also laid it down that certain products that were required in Europe must be grown over part of the land. Among these were tea, coffee, sugar, indigo, etc. As in the case of the indigo plantations in Bengal, these had to be grown even though the profit was less than it otherwise might be.

The Dutch Government made enormous profits; the contractors flourished; the cultivators starved and lived in misery. In the middle of the nineteenth century there was a terrible famine, and vast numbers of people died. Only then was it thought necessary to do something for the unhappy cultivator. Slowly his conditions were bettered, but even as late as 1916 there was still forced labour.

In the latter half of the nineteenth century a number of educational and other reforms were introduced by the Dutch. A new middle class has grown up and a nationalist movement has demanded freedom. As in India, some very halting advance has been made, and feeble assemblies, with little real power, have been established. About five years ago there was a revolution in the Dutch East Indies; it was crushed with great cruelty. But no amount of cruelty or oppression can kill the spirit of freedom which has arisen in Java and the other islands.

The Dutch East Indies are now known as Netherlands India. Every fortnight an air service goes all the way from Holland, across Europe and Asia, to the city of Batavia in Java.

I have finished my outline story of the East Indian islands, and now I want to cross over to the mainland of Asia. Of Burma there is little more to be said. Often the country was divided between North and South, and the two struggled with each other. Sometimes a powerful king united the two and even ventured to conquer neighbouring Siam. And then, in the nineteenth century, came the conflicts with the British. The Burmese King, over-confident of his strength, invaded and annexed Assam. The first Burmese War with the British in India followed in 1824, and Assam went to the British. The British now discovered that the Burmese Government and army were weak, and the desire to annex the whole country came to them. Silly pretexts were found for a second and a third war, and by 1885 the whole kingdom was annexed and made part of the British Indian Empire. Since then Burma's fate has been linked with India's.

South of Burma, the British had also spread in the Malay Peninsula. They took possession of the island of Singapore early in the nineteenth century, and owing to its happy situation it soon became a rising commercial city and a port of call for all ships going to the Far East. The old port of Malacca, farther up in the peninsula, declined. From Singapore the British began to spread north. There were many small States in the Malay Peninsula, most of them vassal to Siam. By the end of the century all these States were British protectorates, and they were joined together in a kind of federation named the " Federated Malay States ". Siam had to give up all the rights she possessed in some of these States to England.

Siam was thus being surrounded by European Powers. To the west and south, in Burma and Malay, England was supreme; to the east France was aggressive and was absorbing Annam. Annam acknowledged China's suzerainty, but that was of little help when China herself was in difficulties. You will remember my telling you in a recent letter on China about fighting between France and China over the French invasion of Annam. France was checked a little, but only for a while. In the second half of the nineteenth century France built up a great colony, called French Indo-China, including Annam and Cambodia. Cambodia, where in the old days the Empire of Angkor the Magnificent had flourished, was a subject-State of Siam. France established its sway over it by threat of war with Siam. It is worth noticing that all the early intrigues of the French in these countries were carried on through French missionaries. One of these missionaries was sentenced to death for some reason or other, and it was to secure reparation for this that the first French expedition was sent in 1857. This expedition seized the port of Saigon in the south, and from there French control spread north.

I am afraid there is a great deal of repetition in these sordid tales of imperialist advance in the countries of Asia. The methods were more or less the same everywhere, and almost everywhere they succeeded. I have dealt with country after country, and finished the story, for the time being at least, by putting it under some European Power. Only one country in south-east Asia escaped this fate, and this was Siam.

Siam was lucky to escape, wedged in as she was between England in Burma and France in Indo-China. Perhaps it was because of the presence of these European rivals to the right and left of her that she escaped. She owed her good fortune also to the fact that she was having a spell of fairly good government and there were no internal troubles, as there had been in many other countries. But good government was, of course, no guarantee against foreign invasion. As it happened, England had her hands full in India and Burma, and France in Indo-China. By the time both of them had reached the frontiers of Siam, late in the nineteenth century, the day for annexations was already passing. The spirit of resistance was rising in the East, and nationalist movements were beginning in the colonies and dependencies. There was danger of war between Siam and France over Cambodia, but Siam gave in and avoided friction with the French. To the west a strong mountain barrier protected Siam from the British in Burma.

I have told you that twice at least in the past the Burmese kings have invaded Siam, and even annexed it. The last invasion was in 1767, when the Siamese capital named Ayuthia or Ayudhia (note how Indian names occur) was destroyed. Soon, however, the Burmese were driven out by a popular rising and a new dynasty began with King Rama I in 1782. Even to-day, just a 150 years later, this dynasty still reigns in Siam, and all the kings seem to be called " Rama ". Under this new dynasty Siam had good but rather paternal government and, very wisely, an effort was made to cultivate good relations with foreign Powers. The ports were opened for foreign trade, commercial treaties were made with certain foreign Powers, and some reforms were introduced in the administration. The new capital was Bangkok. All this was not enough to keep the imperialist wolves away. England spread in Malay and took Siamese territory there; France got Cambodia and other Siamese territory to the east. France and England nearly came to blows over Siam in 1896. But then, in the recognized imperialist fashion, they agreed to guarantee the integrity of the remaining portions of Siamese territory and, at the same time, divided this up into three " spheres of influence ". The eastern part was the French sphere, the western was the British, and in between there was a neutral area where both could have their pickings. Having thus solemnly guaranteed the integrity of Siam, a few years later France took some more territory to the east, and England of course then had to take some compensation in the south.

Still, in spite of all this, a part of Siam has escaped European domination, and that is the only country to do so in this part of Asia. The tide of European aggression has been checked now, and there is little chance of Europe getting more territory in Asia. The time is soon coming when the European Powers in Asia will have to pack up and go home.

Siam was till recently and autocratic monarchy and, in spite of some reforms, there was a good deal of feudalism. A few months ago there was a revolution there—a peaceful one—and the upper middle classes, it seems, came to the front. Some kind of parliament has been established there. The king, of the dynasty of Rama I, wisely agreed to the change, and so the dynasty has remained. Siam has thus now a constitutional monarchy.

One other country of south-east Asia remains for us to consider—the Philippine Islands. I wanted to write about them also in this letter, but it is late and I am tired, and the letter is long enough.

This is the last letter I shall write to you this year—1932—for the old year has run its course and is at its last gasp. In another three hours it will be no more and will become a memory of the past.

120

ANOTHER NEW YEAR'S DAY

New Year's Day, 1933

It is New Year's Day to-day. The earth has completed another cycle round the sun. It recognizes no special days or holidays, as it rushes ceaselessly through space, caring not at all what happens on its surface to the innumerable midgets that crawl on it, and quarrel with each other, and imagine themselves—men and women—in their foolish vanity, the salt of the earth and the hub of the universe. The earth ignores her children, but we can hardly ignore ourselves, and on New Year's Day many of us are apt to rest awhile in our life's journey and look back and grow reminiscent, and then look forward and try to gather hope. So I am reminiscent to-day. It is my third consecutive New Year's Day in prison, though in between I was out in the wider world for many months. Going farther back, I remember that during the last eleven years I have spent five New Years' Days in prison. And I begin to wonder how many more such days and other days I shall see in prison !

But I am an "habitual" now, in the language of the prison, and that many times over, and I am used to gaol life. It is a strange contrast to my life outside, of work and activity and large gatherings and public speaking and a rushing about from place to place. Here all is different; everything is quiet, and there is little movement, and I sit for long intervals, and for long hours I am silent. The days and the weeks and the months pass by, one after the other, merging into each other, and there is little to distinguish one from the other. And the past looks like a blurred picture with nothing standing out. Yesterday takes one back to the day of one's arrest, for in between is almost a blank with little to impress the mind. It is the life of a vegetable rooted to one place, growing there without comment or argument, silent, motionless. And sometimes the activities of the outside world appear strange and a little bewildering to one in prison; they seem distant and unreal—a phantom show. So we develop two natures, the active and the passive, two ways of living, two personalities, like Dr. Jekyll and Mr. Hyde. Have you read this story of Robert Louis Stevenson's ?

One gets used to everything in time, even to the routine and sameness of gaol. And rest is good for the body; and quiet is good for the mind; it makes one think. " *Le repos est une bonne chose, mais l'ennui est son frère !* " And now perhaps you will understand what these letters to you have meant to me. They may be dull reading to you and tedious and prolix. But they have filled up my gaol life and given me an occupation which has brought me a great deal of joy. It was just two years ago to-day, on New Year's Day, that I began them in Naini Prison, and I continued them on my return to gaol. Sometimes I have not written for weeks, sometimes I have written daily. When the mood to write captured me and I sat down with pen and paper, I moved in a different world, and you were my darling companion, and gaol with all its works was forgotten. These letters thus came to represent for me my escapes from gaol.

This letter that I am now writing is numbered 120, and this numbering began only nine months ago in Bareilly Gaol. I am amazed that I have written so much already, and I fear what you will say or feel when this mountain of letters descends upon you in one great mass. But you cannot grudge me my escapes and journeys from prison. It is more than seven months since I saw you, my dear. What a long time it has been !

The story that my letters have contained has not been a very pleasant one. History is not pleasant. Man, in spite of his great and vaunted progress, is still a very unpleasant and selfish animal. And yet perhaps it is possible to see the silver lining of progress right through the long and dismal record of selfishness and quarrelsomeness and inhumanity of man. I am a bit of an optimist and am inclined to take a hopeful view of things, but optimism must not blind us to the dark spots around us and to the danger of an unthinking optimism itself being very much misplaced. For the world as it has been and is still gives little enough ground for optimism. It is a hard place for the idealist and for him who does not take his beliefs on trust. All manner of questions arise for which there is no straight answer; all manner of doubts come which do not easily vanish. Why should there be so much folly and misery in the world ? That is the old question that troubled Prince Siddhartha 2,500 years ago in this country of ours. The story is told that he asked himself this question many a time before enlightenment came to him, and he became the Buddha. He asked himself, it is said :

> " How can it be that Brahm
> Would make a world and keep it miserable,
> Since if all powerful, he leaves it so,
> He is not good, and if not powerful,
> He is not God ? "

In our own country the fight for freedom goes on, and yet many of our countrymen pay little heed to it and argue and quarrel among themselves, and think in terms of a sect or a religious group or narrow class, and forget the larger good. And some, blind to the vision of freedom,

> ". . . took truce with tyrants and grew tame,
> And gathered up cast crowns and creeds to wear,
> And rags and shards regilded."

In the name of law and order, tyranny flourishes and tries to crush those who will not submit to it. Strange that the very thing that should be a refuge of the weak and the oppressed should become a weapon in the hand of the oppressors. This letter has had several quotations already, but I must give you one other which appeals to me and which seems to fit in with our present state. It is from a book of Montesquieu, a French philosopher of the eighteenth century, whom I have mentioned already in one of my earlier letters.

> " Il n'y a point de plus cruelle tyrannie que celle que l'on exerce à l'ombre des lois et avec les couleurs de la justice, lorsqu'on va pour ainsi dire noyer des malheureux sur la planche même sur laquelle ils s'étaient sauvés."

This letter has become much too dismal for a New Year Day letter. That is highly unbecoming. Indeed, I am not dismal, and why should we be dismal ? We have the joy of working and struggling for a great cause; we have a great leader, a beloved friend and a trusty guide, whose sight gives strength and whose touch inspires; and we have the surety that success awaits us, and sooner or later we shall achieve it. Life would be dull and colourless but for the obstacles that we have to overcome and the fights that we have to win.

And you, my darling one, on the threshold of life, must have no dealings with the dismal and the dreary. You will face life and all that it brings with a joyful and serene countenance, and welcome such difficulties as may come your way for the pleasure of surmounting them.

And so, *au revoir*, *bien aimée*, and may this be not too long in coming !

121

THE PHILIPPINES AND THE UNITED STATES OF AMERICA

January 3, 1933

HAVING digressed a little on New Year's Day, we must now get on with our story. We might as well deal with the Philippine Islands so that the picture of the eastern part of Asia might be completed. Why should we pay special attention to these islands ? There are many other islands in Asia and elsewhere which I am not even mentioning in the course of these letters. We are trying to follow the growth of the new imperialism in Asia and its reactions on the older civilizations. India is the model empire for this study; China shows us another and a different, but also a vastly important, aspect of the spread of this industrial imperialism. The East Indies, Indo-China, etc., have also something to teach us. In the same way the Philippines have interest for us. This interest is increased because we find a new Power in action here—the United States of America.

We saw that in China the United States were not as aggressive as the other Powers; on some occasions they even helped China by restraining the other imperialist governments. This was not due to their dislike of imperialism or to a love of China, but to certain internal factors which made them differ from the European countries. These European countries were tightly packed in a small continent, thickly populated, with little elbow-room for each other. There was always friction and trouble. With the coming of industrialism their population grew rapidly, and they began to produce more and more goods which they could not dispose of at home. Food was required for the growing population and raw materials for the factories and markets for the manufactured goods. The urgent economic necessity for fulfilling these wants drove them to distant countries and to wars for empire among themselves.

These considerations did not apply to the United States. Their country was about as big as Europe and the population was small. There was plenty of room for everybody, plenty of opportunities for devoting their energies to the development of their own vast undeveloped territories. As railways were built they went west and spread farther and farther till they reached the Pacific Ocean. All this work in their own country kept the Americans busy, and they had no time or inclination for colonial adventures. Indeed, at one time, as I have told you, a demand for labour on the Californian coast made them ask the Chinese Government for Chinese workers, a request which was complied with and which later created bitterness between the two countries. This preoccupation of the Americans with their own country kept them away from the race for empire in which the European Governments were indulging. They interfered in China only when they felt that they must, and when they feared that the other Powers would divide the country among themselves.

The Philippines, however, came under direct American rule. They tell us of American imperialism, and so have interest for us. Do not imagine that the empire of the United States is confined to the Philippine Islands. Outwardly that is the only empire they have got, but, profiting by the experience and troubles of other imperialist Powers, they have improved on the old methods. They do not take the trouble to annex a country, as Britain annexed India; all they are interested in is profit, and so they take steps to control the wealth of the country. Through the control of the wealth it is easy enough to control the people of the country and, indeed, the land itself. And so without much trouble, or friction with an aggressive nationalism, they control the country and share its wealth. This ingenious method is called economic imperialism. The map does not show it. A country may appear to be free and independent if you consult geography or an atlas. But if you look behind the veil you will find that it is in the grip of another country, or rather of its bankers and big business men. It is this invisible empire that the United States of America possesses. And it is this invisible but none the less effective empire which Britain is trying to preserve for herself, in India and elsewhere, when outwardly she hands over control of the political machine to the people of the country. This is a dangerous thing and we must beware of it.

We need not look into this invisible economic empire at this stage, for the Philippines are part of the visible empire.

There is also another, though a minor and rather sentimental, reason for our interest in the Philippines. To-day they have a Spanish-American appearance, but the whole background of their old culture came from India. Indian culture travelled to them *via* Sumatra and Java and touched almost every aspect of life—social, religious, and political. Old Indian myths and stories and part of our literature reached them. Their languages contain many Sanskrit words. Their art is influenced by India, and so are their laws and handicrafts. Even dress and ornamentation bear this impress. The Spaniards, during their long rule of over 300 years, tried to destroy all evidence of this old Indian culture, and so little remains now.

The Spanish occupation of these islands began as long ago as 1565. They are thus among the earliest footholds of Europe in Asia. They were governed quite differently from the Portuguese or British or Dutch colonies. Trade was not encouraged. Religion was the background of the governments, and the officials were mostly missionaries and churchmen. It has been called a " Missionaries' Empire ". No attempt was made to improve the condition of the people. There was misgovernment and oppression and heavy taxation, and attempts at forced conversions to Christianity. These conditions naturally led to many revolts. Many Chinese came over to the islands to carry on trade. As they refused to become Christians, massacres of them were organized. English and Dutch merchants were not allowed, partly because often they were enemies, and partly because they were Protestant Christians, and thus heretics in the eyes of the Roman Catholic Spaniards.

Conditions worsened. But one good result followed. The different parts and groups of the islands were united, and a national consciousness began to arise in the nineteenth century. The opening out of the islands to foreign merchants about the middle of this century led to some reforms in education and other departments, and trade and business grew. A Filipino middle class developed. There had been inter-marriages between the Spaniards and the Filipinos, and many Filipinos had Spanish blood. Spain came to be looked up to almost as a home country and Spanish ideas spread. None the less, the spirit of nationalism grew, and as it was repressed it became revolutionary. There was no idea at first of separation from Spain : self-government was demanded and some representation in Spain's feeble and ineffective parliament called the " Cortes ". It is curious how national movements everywhere begin moderately and inevitably become more extreme and stand ultimately for separation and independence. A demand for freedom suppressed has to be met later with compound interest. So in the Philippines the demand grew; national organizations were formed to enforce it and secret societies also spread. A " Young Filipino Party ", whose leader was Dr. Jose Rizal, played a prominent part. The Spanish authorities tried to crush the movement by the only method which governments seem to know—terrorism. Rizal and large numbers of other leaders were sentenced to death and executed in 1896.

This was the last straw. Open rebellion then broke out against the Spanish Government, and the Filipinos issued their " declaration of independence ". For a full year the struggle continued, and the Spaniards could not crush the rebellion. Then promise of substantial reforms led to a suspension. Nothing, however, was done by Spain, and in 1898 the rebellion broke out afresh.

Meanwhile the American Government had quarrelled with Spain over some other matter and war was declared between the two countries. An American fleet attacked the Philippines in April 1898. The rebel Filipino leaders, fully expecting that the great American Republic would stand for Filipino freedom, helped the Americans in the war. They again declared their independence and organized a republican government. A Filipino Congress assembled in September 1898, and by the end of November a constitution was adopted. But while this constitution was being discussed by this Congress, Spain was being defeated by the United States. Spain was weak, and before the end of the year confessed herself beaten and the war ended. In the terms of peace Spain handed over the Philippine Islands to the United States. This generous gift cost her nothing at all, as the Filipino rebels had already put an end to Spanish authority.

The United States Government now took steps to take possession of the islands. The Filipinos protested and pointed out that Spain had no business and no power to transfer the islands, as she possessed nothing to transfer at the time. Their protest was in vain, and just when they were congratulating themselves on their newly won freedom, they had to fight afresh and fight a vastly more powerful government than that of Spain. For three and a half years they carried on their gallant struggle, for a few months as an organized government, and later by means of guerrilla warfare.

The revolt was finally suppressed and American rule established. Considerable reforms were introduced, especially in education, but the demand for independence continued. In 1916 the United States Congress passed a bill known as the " Jones Bill ", by which they transferred some powers to an elected legislature. But the American Governor-General has the right to interfere, and he has often done so.

There have been no risings against the United States authorities in the island; but the Filipinos have refused to be content with their present lot and have carried on their agitation and demand for independence. The Americans have often assured them, in the true imperialist manner, that they were there only for the Filipinos' benefit and would leave the islands as soon as the Filipinos were capable of carrying on by themselves. Even in the Jones Bill of 1916 it was stated that " it is, as it always has been, the purpose of the people of the United States to withdraw their sovereignty over the Philippine Islands and to recognize their independence as soon as a stable government can be established therein ". In spite of this there are many people in America who are openly opposed to Philippine independence.

Even as I write news comes in the papers that the United States Congress has passed a resolution, or some such declaration, stating that the Philippines will be granted their independence within ten years.

The United States have certain economic interests in the Philippines which they are anxious to protect. They are particularly interested in rubber plantations there, as rubber is one of the very necessary things that they lack. But their main interest in the occupation of the island is, I believe, fear of Japan. Japan is quite near the Philippines, and Japan is overflowing with an ever-growing population. It is quite likely that the Japanese Government looks greedily on these islands. There is not much love lost between the American and the Japanese Governments, and so the question of the future of the Philippines becomes a part of the larger question of the Pacific Powers and their relations.

122

WHERE THREE CONTINENTS MEET

January 16, 1933

ONE of my New Year wishes has found fulfilment much sooner than I had expected when I wrote a fortnight ago. After my long wait we have had an interview at last, and I have seen you again. And the joy and excitement of seeing you and others have filled me for many a day, and upset my routine and made me neglect my usual work. I have felt in holiday mood. Four days ago it was that we met, and already it seems so long ago! Already I think of the future and wonder when and where our next meeting will be.

Meanwhile no gaol rules can stop me from my game of make-believe, and I shall continue these letters to you.

I have been writing to you for some time past about the nine-teenth century. I tried to give you at first a general survey of this century, which is roughly the 100 years after Napoleon's fall, Then we proceeded to a more detailed survey of some countries. We had a good look at India, and then at China and Japan, and lastly at Farther India and the East Indies. We have so far considered only a part of Asia in this more detailed survey; the rest of the world remains. It is a long story, and it is not easy to keep it straight and clear. I have to take countries and continents one after the other and deal with them separately. Again and again I have to go back and cover the same period of time for a different area. This must necessarily be a little confusing. But you must try to remember that all these nineteenth-century events in different countries took place contemporaneously, more or less at the same time, influencing and reacting on each other. That is why the study of the history of one country by itself is very deceptive; only a world history can give us a right idea of the importance of events and forces that have shaped the past and made it into the present. These letters do not pretend to give you such a world history; that is a task beyond me, and you will find no lack of books on the subject. All that I have tried to do in these letters is to rouse your interest in world history, to show you certain aspects of it, and to make you follow certain threads of human activity from the early times till to-day. I do not know how far I shall succeed; I fear that the result of my labours might be to place before you a hotch-potch which might confuse you more than help you to form a right judgment.

Europe was the driving-force of the nineteenth century. Nationalism reigned there, and industrialism spread and radiated to distant corners of the world and often took the shape of imperialism. We have seen this in our first brief survey of the century, and have followed the effects of imperialism in some detail in India and Eastern India. Before we go to Europe again for a closer look I should like you to pay a brief visit to western Asia. I have neglected this part for a long time, chiefly because I am rather ignorant of its subsequent history.

Western Asia is very different from Eastern Asia and from India. In the distant past, of course, many races and tribes came from Central Asia and the East and overran it. The Turks themselves came in this way. Before the Christian era Buddhism also spread right up to Asia Minor, but it does not appear to have taken root there. Western Asia has, during the ages, looked more towards Europe than towards Asia or the East. In a way it has been Asia's window to Europe. Even the spread of Islam in various parts of Asia did not make much difference to the Western outlook.

India and China and the neighbouring countries never looked at Europe in this way. They were wrapped up in Asia. Between India and China there is a vast difference, in race and outlook and culture. China has never been the slave of religion and has not had any priestly hierarchy. India has always prided herself on her religion, and her society has been priest-ridden in spite of Buddha's attempts to rid her of this incubus. There are many other differences between India and China, and yet there is a strange unity between India and eastern and south-eastern Asia.

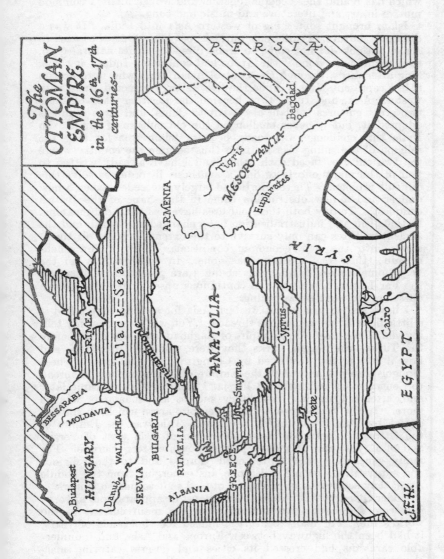

The
OTTOMAN
EMPIRE
in the 16th–17th
centuries—

PERSIA

Bagdad

Tigris

MESOPOTAMIA

Euphrates

ARMENIA

SYRIA

Black Sea

Constantinople

CRIMEA

ANATOLIA

Cyprus

Cairo

Smyrna

EGYPT

Crete

BESSARABIA

MOLDAVIA

HUNGARY

WALLACHIA

Budapest

Danube

SERVIA

BULGARIA

RUMELIA

ALBANIA

GREECE

J.F.H.

This unity has been given by the thread of the Buddha legend which has bound these people together and woven many a common motive in art and literature and music and song.

Islam brought something of western Asia into India. It was a different culture, a different outlook on life. But the western Asian outlook did not come to India direct or in its natural garb, as it might have done if the Arabs had conquered India; it came, long afterwards, through the Central Asian races who were not its fittest representatives. None the less, Islam connected India with western Asia, and India thus became the meeting-place of these two great cultures. Islam also went to China, and large numbers adopted it, but it never challenged the old culture of China. In India this challenge was made because Islam was for long the religion of the ruling class. India thus became the country where the two cultures faced each other, and I have already written to you of the many efforts to find a synthesis in order to solve this difficult problem. These efforts had largely succeeded, when a new danger and a new obstruction came in the shape of the British conquest. To-day both these cultures have lost their old meaning. Nationalism and industrialization have changed the world, and the ancient cultures can only survive to the extent they can fit themselves into the new economic conditions. Their hollow shells remain; their real meaning has gone. In western Asia, in the very homelands of Islam, vast changes are going on. China and the Far East are in a state of continuous upset. In India we can ourselves see what is happening.

I have not written about western Asia for so long that I find it a little difficult to pick up the threads. You will remember my telling you of the great Arab Empire of Baghdad, and how it fell before the Turks—the Seljuq Turks they were, not the Ottomans—and how it was finally destroyed by Chengiz Khan's Mongols. These Mongols also put an end to the Empire of Khwarism which spread to Central Asia and included Persia. Timur the Lame came later and, after a brief day of military success and massacre, was no more. In the west, however, a new empire arose which, in spite of defeat by Timur, continued to spread. This was the Empire of the Ottoman Turks who took possession of Asia west of Persia, and of Egypt, and of a good part of south-eastern Europe. For many generations they threatened Europe, and to the religious and superstitious people of Europe, just emerging from the Middle Ages, they seemed to be a scourge of God sent to punish sinners.

Under Ottoman rule western Asia almost disappears from history; it becomes a back-water cut off from the main current of the world's life. For many centuries, indeed for thousands of years, it had been the highway between Europe and Asia, and innumerable caravans had crossed its cities and deserts carrying merchandise from one continent to another. But the Turks did not encourage trade, and, even if they had done so, they were powerless before a new factor. This was the development of the sea-routes between Asia and Europe. The sea became the new highway, and the ship took the place of the camel of the desert. With this change western Asia lost a great deal of its significance to the world. It lived a life apart. The opening of the Suez Canal, in the second half of the nineteenth century, made the sea-route even more important. This canal became the greatest highway between East and West, bringing the two worlds nearer each other.

And now, in the twentieth century, another change is taking place before our very eyes; and in the old rivalry between land and sea, the land is winning and displacing the sea as the world's chief highway. The coming of the automobile made a difference, and the aeroplane added to this vastly. The ancient trade-routes, deserted for so long, are again busy with traffic, but, instead of the leisurely camel, the automobile rushes across the desert, and overhead flies the aeroplane.

The Ottoman Empire had joined together three continents—Asia, Africa, and Europe. But long before the nineteenth century it had grown weak, and this century saw it going to pieces. From the " Scourge of God " it became the " Sick Man of Europe ". The World War of 1914–18 put an end to it, and out of its ashes arose a new Turkey, self-reliant, strong and progressive, and several other new States.

Western Asia, I have said above, is Asia's window to Europe. It is bounded by the Mediterranean Sea, which has divided and linked together Asia and Europe and Africa. This link has been a powerful one in the past, and the countries bordering on the Mediterranean have had much in common. European civilization begins in the Mediterranean area. Old Greece or Hellas had her colonies dotted about the seaboard of the three continents; the Roman Empire spread around it; Christianity found its early home round the Mediterranean; the Arabs took their culture from the eastern coast to Sicily, and right across the southern African coasts to Spain in the west, and remained there for 700 years.

We see thus how intimate is the connection of the Asiatic Mediterranean countries with South Europe and North Africa. Western Asia thus becomes a definite link in the past between Asia and the other two continents. But it is easy enough to find such links all over the world if we but look for them. The narrow outlook of nationalism has made us think of separate countries far more than of the oneness of the world and the common interests of different countries.

123

A LOOK BACK

January 19, 1933

I HAVE read recently two books which have pleased me greatly, and which I should have liked to share with you. They are both by a Frenchman, René Grousset, who is the conservator or director of the Musée Guimet in Paris. Have you been to this delightful museum of Eastern, and especially Buddhist, art? I do not remember your accompanying me. M. Grousset has written a survey of Eastern—that is, Asiatic—civilizations in four volumes, dealing separately with India, the Middle East (which means Western Asia and Persia), China, and Japan. Being interested in Art, he has dealt with his subject from the point of view of the development of various kinds of artistic activity, and he has given large numbers of beautiful pictures. It is far better and more interesting to learn history in this way than by learning about wars and battles and the intrigues of kings.

I have read only two of M. Grousset's volumes so far, those dealing with India and the Middle East, and they have delighted me. The pictures of fine buildings and noble statuary and wonderful frescoes and paintings have carried me far from Dehra Dun Gaol to distant countries and times long past.

I wrote to you long ago of Mohenjo Daro and Harappa in the Indus Valley in north-west India, the ruins of the ancient civilization which flourished 5000 years ago. In those far-off days when people lived and worked and played in Mohenjo Daro there were many other centres of civilization. Our information is slight; it is limited to certain ruins that have been discovered in various parts of Asia and in Egypt. Perhaps if we dig hard enough and widely enough we may find many more such ruins. But already we know of a high civilization in those days in the Nile Valley in Egypt; in Chaldea (Mesopotamia), where Susa was the capital of the State of Elam; in Persepolis in eastern Persia; in Turkestan in Central Asia; and by the Yellow River or Hoang-Ho in China.

This was the period when copper was beginning to be used, the age of polished stone was passing. All over these wide areas from Egypt to China about the same stage of growth seems to have been reached. Indeed, it is surprising to find some proofs of a common civilization spreading right across Asia, which show that the different centres were not isolated, but were in touch with each other. Agriculture flourished and domestic animals were kept and there was some trade. The art of writing had appeared, but these old picture-writings have not yet been deciphered. Similar tools are found in widely separated areas, and the artistic products are also remarkably similar. Painted pottery, beautiful vases with all manner of designs and decorations, attract special notice. This pottery is so much in evidence that this whole period has been named the " painted pottery civilization ". There was gold and silver jewellery, also alabaster and marble vessels, and even cotton fabrics. Each of these centres of early civilization from Egypt to the Indus Valley and to China had something special to itself and carried on independently, and yet the thread of a common and a connected civilization seems to run through them.

This was, roughly, 5000 years ago. But it is clear that such a civilization was relatively advanced, and must have taken some thousands of years to develop. In the Nile Valley and in Chaldea it can be traced back for at least another 2000 years, and probably the other centres are equally old.

Out of this common and widespread civilization of the early Copper Age, the Mohenjo Daro period of about 3000 B.C., the four great Eastern civilizations diverge and differentiate and develop separately. These four were the Egyptian, the Mesopotamian, the Indian, and the Chinese. It was during this latter period that the Great Pyramids were built in Egypt and the great Sphinx at Gizeh. Later still came the Theban period in Egypt, when the Theban Empire flourished there, about 2000 B.C., and wonderful statues and frescoes were produced. This was a great period of a renaissance of art. The huge temple of Luxor was built about this time. Tutankhamen, whose name everybody seems to know without knowing anything else about him, was one of the Theban Pharaohs.

In Chaldea powerful organized States arose in two regions, Sumer and Akkad. The famous city of Ur of the Chaldees was already producing artistic masterpieces in the days of Mohenjo Daro. After about 700 years of lordship, Ur was overthrown. The Babylonians, who were a Semitic people (that is like the Jews or Arabs) coming from Syria, became the new rulers. The city of Babylon now became the centre of a new empire to which there is frequent reference in the Bible. There was a revival of literature during this period, and epic poems were written and sung. These epic poems describing the beginning of the world and a mighty deluge are supposed to be the stories round which the earlier chapters of the Bible are written.

Then Babylon fell, and many centuries afterwards (about 1000 B.C. and onwards) the Assyrians come on the scene and establish an empire with Nineveh as capital. These people were most extraordinary. They were brutal and cruel beyond measure. Their whole system of government was based on terrorism, and with massacre and destruction they built a great empire all over the Middle East. They were the imperialists of those days. And yet these people were highly cultured in some ways. An enormous library was collected at Nineveh, every department of current knowledge being represented. The library was not a paper one, I need hardly tell you, nor did it have anything like the modern book. The books of those days were on tablets. Thousands of these tablets from the old library at Nineveh are at present in the British Museum in London. Some of them are pretty ghastly; the monarch gives a vivid description of his cruelty to his enemies and how he enjoyed it.

In India the Aryans came after the Mohenjo Daro period. No ruins or statuary of their early days have yet been discovered, but their greatest monuments are their old books—the *Vedas* and others—which give us an insight into the minds of these happy warriors who came down to the Indian plains. These books are full of powerful Nature-poetry; the very gods are Nature-gods. It was natural that when art developed, this love of Nature should play a great part in it. The Sanchi gates, which are situated near Bhopal, are among the earliest artistic remains discovered. They date from the early Buddhist period, and the beautiful carvings on these gates, of flowers and leaves and animal forms, tell us of the love and understanding of Nature of the artists who made them.

And then from the north-west came Greek influence, for you will remember that after Alexander the Hellenic empires came up to the Indian frontier; and later on there was the borderland empire of the Kushans, which was also under Hellenic influence. Buddha was against image-worship. He did not call himself a god or ask to be worshipped. He wanted to rid society of the evils which priestcraft had brought into it; he was a reformer trying to raise the fallen and the unhappy. "I have come," he said, in his first sermon at Isipatana or Sarnath, near Benares, "I have come to satisfy the ignorant with wisdom. . . . The perfect man is nothing unless he spends himself in benefits to living beings, unless he consoles those who are abandoned. . . . My doctrine is a doctrine of pity; that is why the happy ones of the world find it hard. The way to salvation is open to all. The Brahman came forth from the womb of a woman even as the Chandala to whom he closes the way to salvation. Annihilate your passions as the elephant over- turns a hut made of reeds. . . . The only remedy against evil is sane reality." So Buddha taught the way of good conduct and the way of life. But, as is the way with foolish disciples who do not understand the inner meaning of the master, many of his followers observed the external rules of conduct that he had pre- scribed and did not appreciate their inner significance. Instead of following his advice they worshipped him. Still no statues of the Buddha rose, no images of him were made.

Then came ideas from Greece and other Hellenic countries, and in these countries beautiful statues of the gods were made, and these were worshipped. In Gandhara, on the north-west of India, this influence was greatest, and the Buddha infant appeared in sculpture. Like their own little and charming god Cupid he was, or as later the infant Christ was to be—the "sacro bambino", as the Italians call him. In this way image-worship began in Bud- dhism, and it developed till statues of Buddha were to be found in every Buddhist temple.

Iranian or Persian influence also affected Indian art. The Buddha legends and the rich mythology of the Hindus provided inexhaustible material for India's artists, and at Amaravati in the Andhradesh, in the Elephanta caves near Bombay, at Ajanta and Ellore, and many other places, you can trace these old legends and myths in stone and paint. Wonderfully worth visiting are these places, and I wish that every schoolgirl and schoolboy could visit at least some of them.

The Indian legends travelled across the seas to Farther India. In Java, at Borobudur, there is the whole Buddha story in a series of remarkable frescoes in stone. In the ruins of Angkor Vat there are still many beautiful statues which remind us of the days 800 years ago when the city was known in Eastern Asia as " Angkor the Magnificent ". The faces of these statues are gentle and full of life, and there hovers over most of them a strange and elusive smile which has come to be known as the " Smile of Angkor ". This smile persists though the racial type changes, and it never grows monotonous.

Art is a faithful mirror of the life and civilization of a period. When Indian civilization was full of life, it created things of beauty and the arts flourished, and its echoes reached distant countries. But, as you know, stagnation and decay set in, and as the country went to pieces the arts fell with it. They lost vigour and life and became overburdened with detail, and sometimes even grotesque. The coming of the Muslims gave a shock and brought new influences which rid the degraded forms of Indian art of over-ornamentations. The old Indian ideal remained at the back, but it was dressed up simply and gracefully in the new garments from Arabia and Persia. In the past, thousands of Indian master-builders had gone from India to Central Asia. Now the architects and painters came from western Asia to India. In Persia and Central Asia an artistic renaissance had taken place; in Constantinople great architects were putting up mighty buildings. This was also the period of the early Renaissance in Italy, when a galaxy of great masters produced beautiful paintings and statues.

Sinan was the famous Turkish architect of the day, and Babar sent for his favourite pupil, Yusuf. In Iran Bihzad was the great painter, and Akbar sent for several of his pupils and made them his Court painters. Persian influence became dominant both in architecture and painting. I have told you in a previous letter of some of the great buildings of this Indo-Moslem art of Moghal India, and you have seen many of them. The greatest triumph of this Indo-Persian art is the Taj Mahal. Many great artists helped to make it. It is said that the principal architect was a Turk or Persian named Ustad Isa, and that he was assisted by Indian architects. Some European artists, and especially an Italian, are supposed to have worked at the interior decoration. In spite of so many different masters working at it, there is no jarring or contradictory element in it. All the different influences are blended together to produce a wonderful harmony. Many people worked at the Taj, but the two influences which are predominant are the Persian and the Indian, and M. Grousset therefore calls it " the soul of Iran incarnate in the body of India ".

124

THE PERSISTENCE OF IRAN'S OLD TRADITIONS

January 20, 1933

LET us go now to Persia, the country whose soul is said to have come to India and found a worthy body here in the Taj. Persian Art has a remarkable tradition. This tradition has persisted for over 2000 years—ever since the days of the Assyrians. There have been changes of governments and dynasties and religion, the country has been under foreign rule and under its own kings, Islam has come and revolutionized much, but this tradition has persisted. Of course it has changed and developed in the course of ages. This persistence, it is said, is due to the connection of Persian Art with the soil and scenery of Persia.

I told you in the previous letter of the Assyrian Empire of Nineveh. This included Persia. About 500 or 600 years before Christ, the Iranians, who were Aryans, captured Nineveh and put an end to the Assyrian Empire. The Persian-Aryans then built for themselves a great empire from the banks of the Indus right up to Egypt. They dominated the ancient world, and their ruler is often referred to in Greek accounts as the " Great King ". Cyrus, Darius, Xerxes are the names of some of these " Great Kings ". You may remember that Darius and Xerxes tried to conquer Greece, and suffered defeat. This dynasty is called the Achæmenid dynasty. For 220 years it ruled a vast empire till Alexander the Great of Macedon put an end to it.

The Persians must have come as a great relief after the Assyrians and the Babylonians. They were civilized and tolerant masters, allowing different religions and cultures to flourish. The huge empire was well administered, and there was a network of good roads to facilitate communications from all parts. These Persians were closely related to the Indo-Aryans, those who had come to India. Their religion—that of Zoroaster or Zarathrustra—was related to the early Vedic religion. It seems clear that both had a common origin in the early home of the Aryans, wherever this may have been.

The Achæmenid kings were great builders. In their capital city of Persepolis they built huge palaces—they did not build temples—with vast halls supported by numerous columns. Some ruins can still give an idea of these enormous structures. Achæmenid art seems to have kept contact with Indian art of the Mauryan period (Ashoka, etc.), and influenced it.

Alexander defeated the " Great King " Darius and ended the Achæmenid dynasty. There followed a brief period of Greek rule under Seleucus (who had been Alexander's general) and his successors, and a much longer period of Hellenic influence under semi-foreign rulers. The Kushans sitting on the Indian borderland and stretching out south to Benares and north in Central Asia were contemporaries, and they also were under Hellenic influence. Thus the whole of Asia west of India was under Greek influence for more than 500 years after Alexander, right up to the third century after Christ. This influence was largely artistic. It did not interfere with the religion of Persia, which continued to be Zoroastrianism.

In the third century there was a national revival in Persia and a new dynasty came into power. This was the Sassanid dynasty, which was aggressively nationalistic and claimed to be the successor of the old Achæmenid kings. As usually happens with an aggressive nationalism, this was narrow and intolerant. It had to become so because it was wedged in between the Roman Empire and the Byzantine Empire of Constantinople on the west, and the advancing Turkish tribes on the east. Still, it managed to carry on for more than 400 years, right up to the coming of Islam. The Zoroastrian priesthood was all-powerful under the Sassanids, and their Church controlled the State and was intolerant of all opposition. It was during this period that the final version of their sacred book, the *Avestha*, is said to have been prepared.

In India at this time the Gupta Empire flourished, which was also a national revival after the Kushan and Buddhist periods. There was a renaissance of art and literature, and some of the greatest of Sanskrit writers, like Kalidas, lived then. There are many indications that Persia of the Sassanids had artistic contacts with India of the Guptas. Few paintings or sculptures of the Sassanid period have remained to our day; such as have been found are full of life and movement, the animals being very similar to those in the Ajanta frescoes. Sassanid artistic influence seems to have extended right up to China and the Gobi desert.

Towards the end of their long rule the Sassanids became weak and Persia was in a bad way. After long warfare with the Byzantine Empire both were thoroughly exhausted. It was not difficult for the Arab armies, full of ardour for their new faith, to conquer Persia. By the middle of the seventh century, within ten years of the death of the Prophet Mohammad, Persia was under the rule of the Caliph. As Arab armies spread to Central Asia and North Africa they carried with them not only their new religion, but a young and growing civilization. Syria, Mesopotamia, Egypt were all absorbed by Arabic culture. The Arabic language became their language, and even racially they were assimilated. Baghdad, Damascus, Cairo became the great centres of Arabic culture, and many fine buildings arose there under the impetus of the new civilization. Even to-day all these countries are the Arabic countries and, though separated from each other, they dream of unity.

Persia was similarly conquered by the Arabs, but they could not absorb or assimilate the people as they had done in Syria or Egypt. The Iranian race, being of the old Aryan stock, was further removed from the Semitic Arabs; their language was also an Aryan language. So the race remained apart and the language continued to flourish.

Islam spread rapidly and displaced Zoroastrianism, which ultimately had to seek shelter in India. But even in Islam the Persians took their own line. There was a split, and two parties arose, two branches of Islam—the Shias and the Sunnis. Persia became, and still is, predominantly a Shia country, while the rest of the Islamic world is mostly Sunni.

But though Persia was not assimilated, Arab civilization had a powerful influence on her; and Islam, as in India, gave new life to artistic activity. Arab art and culture were equally affected by Persian standards. Persian luxury invaded the households of the simple children of the desert, and the Court of the Arab Caliph became as gorgeous and magnificent as any other imperial Court had been. Imperial Baghdad became the greatest city of the day. North of it in Samarra on the Tigris the Caliphs built for themselves an enormous mosque and palace, the ruins of which still exist. The mosque had vast halls and courtyards with fountains. The palace was a rectangle, of which one side was over a kilometre in length.

In the ninth century the Empire of Baghdad decayed and split up into a number of States. Persia became independent, and Turkish tribes from the East formed many States, eventually seizing Persia itself and dominating the nominal Caliph of Baghdad. Mahmud of Ghazni arose at the beginning of the eleventh century and raided India and threatened the Caliph, and built for himself a brief-lived empire, to be ended by another Turkish tribe, the Seljuqs. The Seljuqs faced and fought long, and with success, the Christian Crusaders, and their empire lasted for 150 years. Towards the end of the twelfth century yet another Turkish tribe drove out the Seljuqs from Persia and established the kingdom of Khwarism or Khiva. But this had a brief life, for Chengiz Khan, indignant at the insult offered to his ambassador by the Shah of Khwarism, came with his Mongols and crushed the land and the people.

In a brief paragraph I have told of many changes and many empires, and you must be sufficiently confused. I have mentioned these ups and downs of dynasties and races, not to burden your mind with them, but to emphasize how the artistic tradition and life of Persia continued in spite of them. Tribe after tribe of Turks came from the East, and they succumbed to the mixed Perso-Arabian civilization which prevailed from Bokhara to Iraq. Those Turks who managed to reach Asia Minor, far from Persia, retained their own ways and refused to give in to Arabic culture. They made Asia Minor almost a bit of their native Turkestan. But in Persia and adjoining countries, such was the strength of the old Iranian culture that they accepted it and adapted themselves to it. Under all the various Turkish dynasties that ruled, Persian art and literature flourished. I have told you, I think, of the Persian poet Firdausi, who lived at the time of Sultan Mahmud of Ghazni. At Mahmud's request he wrote great national epic of Persia, the *Shāhnāma*, and the scenes described in this book lie in pre-Islamic days, and the great hero is Rustam. This shows us how closely tied up were Persian art and literature with the old national and traditional past. Most of the subjects for Persian paintings and beautiful miniatures are taken from the stories of the *Shāhnāma*.

Firdausi lived at the turn of the century and the millennium, from 932 to 1021. Soon after him came a name famous in English as it is in Persian—Omar Khayyám, the astronomer-poet of Nishapur in Persia. And Omar was followed by Sheikh Sadi of Shiraz, one of the greatest of Persian poets, whose *Gulistān* and *Būstān* schoolboys in Indian *maktabs* have had to learn by heart for generations past.

I mention just a few names of the great. There is no point in my giving you long lists of names. But I wish you to realize that the lamp of Persian art and culture was shining brightly right through these centuries from Persia to Transoxiana in Central Asia. Great cities like Bokhara and Balkh of Transoxiana rivalled the cities of Persia as centres of artistic and literary activity. It was at Bokhara that Ibn Sina or Avicenna, the most famous of Arab philosophers, was born at the end of the tenth century. It was in Balkh 200 years later that another great Persian poet was born, Jalaluddin Rumi. He is considered a great mystic, and he founded the order of the dancing dervishes.

So in spite of war and conflict and political changes the tradition of Perso-Arabian art and culture continued to be a living one and produced many masterpieces in literature, painting and architecture. Then came disaster. In the thirteenth century (about 1220) Chengiz Khan swept down and destroyed Khwarism and Iran, and a few years later Hulagu destroyed Baghdad, and the accumulations of long centuries of high culture were swept away. I have told you in some previous letter how the Mongols converted Central Asia almost into a wilderness, and how its great cities were deserted and became almost devoid of human life.

Central Asia never fully recovered from this calamity; and it is surprising enough that it recovered to the extent it did. You may remember that after Chengiz Khan's death his vast empire was divided up. The part of it in Persia and round about fell to Hulagu, who, after having had his fill of destruction, settled down as a peaceful and tolerant ruler, and founded the dynasty of the Il-khans. These Il-khans for some time continued to profess the old Sky religion of the Mongols; later they were converted to Islam. Both before and after this conversion they were completely tolerant of other religions. Their cousins in China, the Great Khan and his family, were Buddhists, and with them .they had the most intimate relations. They even sent for brides all the way from China.

These contacts between the two branches of the Mongols in Persia and China had considerable effect on art. Chinese influence crept. into Persia and a curious blend of Arabic, Persian, and Chinese influence appears in the paintings. But again the Persian element, in spite of all disasters, triumphed. In the middle of the fourteenth century Persia produced another great poet, Hafiz, who is still popular even in India.

The Mongol Il-khans did not last long. Their last remnants were destroyed by another great warrior, Timur, of Samarqand in Transoxiana. This terrible and most cruel savage, about whom I have written to you, was quite a patron of the arts, and was considered a learned man. His love of the arts seems to have consisted chiefly in sacking great cities like Delhi, Shiraz, Baghdad, and Damascus and carrying away the loot to adorn his own capital, Samarqand. But Samarqand's most wonderful and imposing structure is Timur's tomb, the Gur Amir. It is a fit mausoleum for him, for there is something of his commanding presence and strength and fierce spirit in its noble outlines.

The vast territories that Timur had conquered fell away after his death, but a relatively small domain, including Transoxiana and Persia, remained for his successors. For a full 100 years, right through the fifteenth century, these " Timurids ", as they were called, held sway over Iran and Bokhara and Herat, and, strangely enough, these descendants of a ruthless conqueror became famous for their generosity and humanity and encouragement of the arts. Timur's own son, Shah Rukh, was the greatest of them. He founded a magnificent library at Herat, which was his capital, and crowds of literary men were attracted to it.

This Timurid period of 100 years is so noteworthy for its artistic and literary movements that it is known as the " Timurid Renaissance ". There was a rich development of Persian literature, and large numbers of fine pictures were painted. Bihzad, the great painter, was head of a school of painting. It is interesting to note that side by side with Persian, Turkish literature also developed in the Timurid literary circles. This was also the period, to remind you again, of the Renaissance in Italy.

The Timurids were Turks, and they had succumbed largely to Persian culture. Iran, dominated by Turks and Mongols, imposed its own culture on the conquerors. At the same time Persia struggled to free herself politically, and gradually the Timurids were driven more and more to the east and their domain became smaller round Transoxiana. At the beginning of the sixteenth century Iranian nationalism triumphed, and the Timurids were finally driven out from Persia. A national dynasty, the Safavi or Safavids, came on the Persian throne. It was the second of this dynasty, Tahmasp I, who gave refuge to Humayun fleeing from India before Sher Khan.

The Safavi period lasted for 220 years from 1502 to 1722. It is called the golden age of Persian art. Isfahan, the capital, was filled with splendid buildings and became a famous artistic centre, especially noted for painting. Shah Abbas, who ruled from 1587 to 1629, was the outstanding sovereign of this dynasty, and he is considered one of Persia's greatest rulers. He was hemmed in by the Uzbegs on one side and the Ottoman Turks on the other. He drove away both and built up a strong State, cultivated relations with distant States in the West and elsewhere, and devoted himself to beautifying his capital. The town-planning of Shah Abbas in

Isfahan has been called " a masterpiece of classical purity and taste ". The buildings that were made were not only beautiful in themselves and finely decorated, but the charm of the setting enhanced the effect. European travellers who visited Persia at the time give glowing descriptions.

Architecture, literature, paintings, both frescoes and miniatures, beautiful carpets, fine faience work and mosaics, all flourished during this golden age of Persian art. Some of the fresco-paintings and miniatures are of an amazing loveliness. Art does not, or should not, know national boundaries, and many influences must have gone to enrich this Persian art of the sixteenth and seventeenth centuries. Italian influence, it is said, is evident. But behind all there is the old artistic tradition of Iran, which persisted through 2000 years. And the sphere of Iranian culture was not confined to Persia. It spread over a vast area from Turkey on the west to India on the east. The Persian language was the language of culture in the Moghal Courts in India, and in western Asia generally, as French used to be in Europe. The old spirit of Persian art has left an immortal emblem in the Taj Mahal at Agra. In much the same way this art has influenced Ottoman architecture as far west as Constantinople, and many a famous building grew up there with the impress of Persian influence.

The Safavis in Persia were more or less contemporaneous with the Great Moghals in India. Babar, the first of the Indian Moghals, was one of the Timurid princes of Samarqand. As the Persians had gained strength they had driven the Timurids away, and only parts of Transoxiana and Afghanistan remained under various Timurid princes. Babar had to fight from the age of twelve among these petty princes. He succeeded, and made himself ruler of Kabul, and then came to India. The high culture of the Timurids at the time can be judged from Babar, from whose memoirs I gave you some quotations in a previous letter. Shah Abbas, the greatest of the Safavi rulers, was a contemporary of Akbar and Jehangir. Between the two countries all along there must have been the most intimate contact. For long they had a common frontier, Afghanistan being part of the Moghal Indian Empire.

125

IMPERIALISM AND NATIONALISM IN PERSIA

January 21, 1933

You are entitled to have a grievance against me. I have given you sufficient provocation by rushing backwards and forwards in the various corridors of history. After having reached, by many different routes, the nineteenth century, I have suddenly taken you back a few thousand years and jumped about from Egypt to

India and China and Persia. This must be aggravating and confusing, and I have no good answer to the protest which I can almost hear you making. The reading of M. René Grousset's books suddenly started many lines of thought in my head, and I could not help sharing some of them with you. I felt also that I had neglected Persia in these letters, and I wanted to make some reparation for this omission. And now that we have been considering Persia, we might as well carry on her story to modern times.

I have told you of the old traditions and high accomplishments of Persian culture, of the golden age of Persian art, and so on and so forth. On looking at these phrases again, the language seems rather flowery and somewhat misleading. One might almost think that a real golden age had come to the people of Persia, and their miseries vanished away and they lived happily, like people in fairy-tales. Of course no such thing happened. Culture and art in those days, as even now to a large extent, were the monopoly of a few; the masses, the average person, had nothing to do with them. The life of the masses, indeed, from the earliest days has been a constant struggle for food and the necessaries of life; it has not differed greatly from the life of the animals. They had no time or leisure for anything else; sufficient and more than sufficient unto the day was the evil thereof; how could they think or appreciate art and culture? Art flourished in Persia and India and China and Italy and the other countries of Europe as a pastime for the Courts and the rich and leisured classes. Only religious art to some extent touched the life of the masses.

But an artistic Court did not signify good government; rulers who prided themselves on their patronage of art and literature were often enough incompetent and cruel as rulers. The whole system of society in Persia, as in most other countries at the time, was more or less feudal. Strong kings became popular because they stopped many of the petty exactions of the feudal lords. There were periods of relatively good rule and other periods of thoroughly bad rule.

Just when Moghal rule was in its last stages in India, the Safavi dynasty came to an end, about 1725. As usual, the dynasty had played itself out. Feudalism was gradually breaking up, and economic changes were going on in the country, upsetting the old order. Heavy taxation made matters worse, and discontent spread among the people. The Afghans, who were then under the Safavis, rose in revolt, and not only succeeded in their own country, but seized Isfahan and deposed the Shah. The Afghans were soon driven out by a Persian chief, Nadir Shah, who later took the crown himself. It was this Nadir Shah who raided India, during the last days of the decrepit Moghals, massacred the people of Delhi, and took away vast treasure, including the Peacock Throne of Shah Jehan. Persian history during the eighteenth century is a dismal record of civil war and changing rules and misrules.

The nineteenth century brought new troubles. Persia was coming into conflict with the expanding and aggressive imperialism of Europe. To the north, Russia was ceaselessly pressing, and the British were advancing from the Persian Gulf. Persia was not far

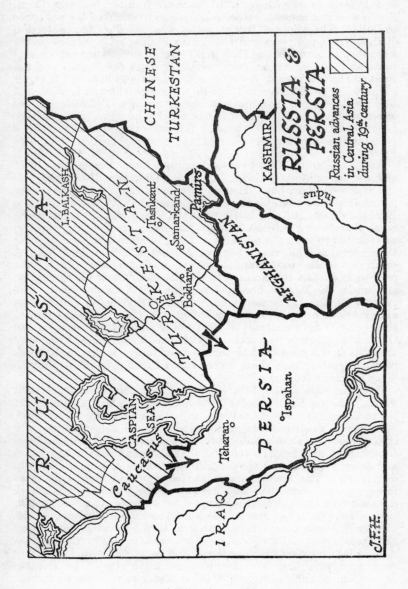

from India; their frontiers were gradually approaching each other, and indeed to-day there is a common frontier between them. Persia was on the direct route to India and overlooked the sea-route to India. The whole of British policy was based on the protection of their Indian Empire and the routes leading to it. In no event were they prepared to see their great rival Russia sitting astride this route and looking hungrily at India. So both the British and the Russians took a very lively interest in Persia and harassed the poor country. The Shahs were throughly incompetent and foolish, and usually played into their hands either by trying to fight them at the wrong moment or by fighting their own people. Persia might have been wholly occupied by Russia or England and annexed or made a protectorate like Egypt but for the rivalry between these two Powers.

At the beginning of the twentieth century Persia became the object of greed for another reason. Oil or petroleum was discovered, and this was very valuable. The old Shah was induced to give a very favourable concession for the exploitation of oil-fields in Persia to a British subject, D'Arcy, in 1901 for the long period of sixty years. Some years later a British company, the Anglo-Persian Oil Company, was formed to work the oil-fields. This Company has been working there since, and has made huge profits out of this oil business. A small part of the profits went to the Persian Government, but a great part went outside the country to the shareholders of the Company, and among the biggest shareholders is the British Government. The present Persian Government is strongly nationalistic, and objects very much to being exploited by foreigners. They cancelled the old sixty-year D'Arcy contract of 1901 under which the Anglo-Persian Oil Company had been working. The British Government was very annoyed at this, and tried to threaten and bully the Persian Government, forgetting that times have changed and it is not so easy to bully people in Asia now.[1]

But I am anticipating future history. As imperialism threatened Persia, and the Shah became more and more its tool, inevitably it led to the growth of nationalism. A nationalist party was formed. This party resented foreign interference, and objected equally strongly to the Shah's autocracy. They demanded a democratic constitution and modern reforms. The country was misgoverned and heavily taxed, and the British and Russians were continually interfering. The reactionary Shah felt more at ease with these foreign governments than with his own people who were demanding a measure of freedom. This demand for a democratic constitution came chiefly from the new middle classes and the intellectuals. The victory of Japan over Tsarist Russia in 1904 impressed and excited the Persian nationalists greatly, both because it was a victory of an Asiatic Power over a European one, and because Tsarist Russia was their own aggressive and troublesome neighbour. The Russian revolution of 1905, although it failed and was ruthlessly crushed,

---

[1] A new agreement, very much more favourable to the Iran Government, had ultimately to be accepted by the British Government and the Oil Company.

added to the enthusiasm and desire for action of the Persian nationalists. The pressure on the Shah was so great that he reluctantly agreed to a democratic constitution in 1906. The National Assembly called the " Mejlis ", was established, and the Persian Revolution seemed to have succeeded.

But there was trouble ahead. The Shah had no intention of effacing himself, and the Russians and British had no love for a democratic Persia which might become strong and troublesome. There was conflict between the Shah and the Mejlis, and the Shah actually bombarded his own parliament. But the people and the troops were with the Mejlis and the nationalists, and the Shah was only saved by Russian troops. Both Russia and England had, under some pretext or other—usually the excuse of protecting their subjects—brought their own troops and kept them. The Russians had their dreaded Cossacks, and the British utilized Indian troops to bully the Persians with whom we had no quarrel.

Persia was in great difficulties. She had no money, and the condition of the people was bad. The Mejlis tried hard to improve matters; but most of their efforts were scotched by the opposition of either the Russians or the British or both. Eventually they looked for help to America and appointed an able American financier to help them in reforming their finances. This American, Morgan Shuster, tried his best to do so, but always he came up against the solid walls of Russian or British opposition. Disgusted and disheartened, he left the country and returned home. In a book Shuster wrote afterwards he gave the story of how Russian and British imperialism was crushing the life out of Persia. The very name of the book is significant and tells a tale—*The Struggling of Persia*.

Persia seemed destined to disappear as an independent State. The first step towards this end had already been taken by Russia and England by dividing up the country into their " spheres of influence ". Their soldiers occupied important centres; a British company exploited the oil resources. Persia was in a thoroughly miserable condition. Outright annexation by a foreign Power might even have been better, for this would have brought some responsibility with it. Then came the outbreak of the World War in 1914.

Persia declared her neutrality in this war, but the declarations of the weak have little effect on the strong. Persia's neutrality was ignored by all the parties concerned, and foreign armies came and fought each other, regardless of what the unhappy Persian Government thought of the matter. All round Persia were countries who were in the war. England and Russia were allies on one side; Turkey, whose dominions included at the time Iraq and Arabia, was an ally of Germany. The war ended in the victory of England, France and their allies in 1918, and Persia was then wholly occupied by British forces. England was on the point of declaring a protectorate over Persia—a mild form of annexation—and there were also dreams of a vast British Middle Eastern Empire from the

Mediterranean to Baluchistan and India.   But the dreams did not come true.   Unfortunately for Britain, Tsarist Russia had vanished, and in her place there was now a Soviet Russia.   Also unfortunately for Britain, her plans went astray in Turkey, and Kemal Pasha rescued his country from the very jaws of the Allies.

All this helped the Persian nationalists, and Persia succeeded in remaining nominally free.   In 1921 a Persian soldier, Riza Khan, came into prominence by a *coup d'état*.   He gained control of the army and later became prime minister.   In 1925 the old Shah was deposed and Riza Khan was elected the new Shah by the vote of a Constituent Assembly.   He took the name and title of Riza Shah Pahlavi.

Riza Shah reached the throne peacefully and by methods which were outwardly democratic.   The Mejlis still functions, and the new Shah does not presume to be an autocratic monarch.   It is clear, however, that he is the strong man at the helm of the Persian Government.   Persia has changed greatly during the last few years, and Riza Shah is bent on many reforms so that the country might be modernized.   There is a strong national revival, which has put new life into the country, and which is taking the shape of an aggressive nationalism wherever foreign interests in Persia are concerned.

It is most interesting to note also that this national revival is in the true Iranian tradition of 2000 years.   It looks back to the early days, prior to Islam, of Iran's greatness, and tries to draw its inspiration from them.   The very name which Riza Shah has adopted is a dynastic name—" Pahlavi "—takes one back to the old days.   The people of Persia are, of course, Muslims—Shia Muslims—but in so far as their country is concerned, nationalism is a more powerful force.   All over Asia this is happening.   In Europe this took place 100 years earlier, in the nineteenth century; but already nationalism is considered by many people there to be an outworn creed, and they look for new faiths and beliefs which fit in more with existing conditions.

Iran is now the official designation of Persia.   Riza Shah has decreed that the name Persia must no longer be used.

126

ABOUT REVOLUTIONS GENERALLY, AND ESPECIALLY THOSE OF EIGHTEEN FORTY-EIGHT IN EUROPE

January 28, 1933
Idu'l-Fitr

WE must now go back to Europe and have another look at the intricate and ever-changing picture of this continent during the nineteenth century. Already in some letters written two months ago we surveyed this century and I pointed out some of its leading characteristics. You can hardly be expected to remember all the " isms " I mentioned then : industrialism and capitalism and imperialism and socialism and nationalism and internationalism— to repeat a few of them ! I told you also of democracy and science, and the tremendous revolutions in methods of transport, and popular education and its product, the modern newspaper. All these things, and many more, made up the civilization of Europe then— the *bourgeois* civilization in which the new middle classes controlled the industrial machine under the capitalist system. This civilization of *bourgeois* Europe went from success to success; it climbed height after height; and toward the end of the century it had impressed itself and all the world with its might, when disaster came.

In Asia we have also seen in some detail this civilization in action. Urged on by its growing industrialism, Europe stretched its arms to distant lands and tried to grab them and control them and generally to interfere with them to its own advantage. By Europe here I mean especially western Europe, which had taken the lead in industrialism, and, of all these western countries, England was for long the unquestioned leader, far ahead of the others, and profiting greatly by this lead.

All these vast changes that were going on in England and the West were not evident to the kings and emperors early in the century. They did not realize the importance of the new forces that were being generated. After Napoleon had been finally removed, the one thought of these rulers of Europe was to preserve themselves and their kind for ever more, to make the world safe for autocracy. They had not wholly recovered from the terrible fright of the French Revolution and Napoleon, and they wanted to take no more chances. As I have told you in a previous letter, they allied themselves in Holy Alliances and the like to preserve the " divine right of kings " to do what they chose, and to prevent the people from raising their heads. Autocracy and religion joined hands for this purpose, as they had often done before. The Tsar Alexander of Russia was the moving spirit in these alliances. No breath of industrialism or the new spirit had reached his country, and Russia was in a medieval and very backward condition. There were few big cities, commerce was little developed, and even handicrafts were not of a high order. Autocracy flourished unchecked. Conditions were different in other European countries. As one travelled west the middle classes were more and more in evidence. In England, as I have told you, there was no autocracy. The king was kept in check by Parliament; but Parliament itself was controlled by a handful of the rich. There was a great deal of difference between the autocrat of the Russias and this rich ruling oligarchy of England. But they had one thing in common—fear of the masses and of revolution.

So all over Europe reaction triumphed and everything that had a liberal look about it was ruthlessly suppressed. By the decisions of the Congress of Vienna in 1815 many nationalities—for instance those of Italy and Eastern Europe—had been placed under alien rule. They had to be kept down by force. But this kind of thing cannot be done successfully for long : there is bound to be trouble. It is like trying to hold the lid of a steaming kettle down. Europe simmered with steam, and repeatedly the steam forced itself out. I have told you in a previous letter of the risings on 1830, when several changes took place in Europe, notably in France, where the Bourbons were finally driven out. These risings frightened the kings and emperors and their ministers all the more, and they suppressed and repressed the people with greater energy.

In the course of these letters we have often come across great changes in countries brought about by wars and revolutions. Wars in the past were sometimes religious wars and sometimes dynastic ; often they were political invasions of one nationality by another. Behind all these causes there was usually some economic cause also. Thus most of the invasions by the Central Asian tribes of Europe and Asia were due to their being driven westward by hunger. Economic progress may strengthen a people or a nation and give them an advantage over others. I have pointed out to you that even in the so-called religious wars in Europe and elsewhere the economic factor was at work in the background. As we approach modern times we find that religious and dynastic wars cease. War, of course, does not end. Unhappily it becomes more virulent. But its causes now are obviously political and economic. The political causes are chiefly connected with nationalism : the suppression of one nation by another, or the conflict between two aggressive nationalisms. Even this conflict is largely due to economic causes, such as the demand by modern industrial countries for raw materials and markets. So we find that economic causes become more and more important in war, and indeed to-day they overshadow everything else.

Revolutions have undergone the same kind of change in the past. Early revolutions were usually palace revolutions : members of the ruling families intriguing against each other and fighting and murdering each other, or an exasperated populace rising and putting an end to a tyrant ; or an ambitious soldier seizing the throne with the help of the army. Many of these palace revolutions took place among a few, and the mass of the people were not much affected by them, and they seldom cared. The rulers changed, but the system remained the same, and the lives of the people continued unchanged. Of course a bad ruler might tyrannize a great deal and become unbearable ; a better ruler might be more tolerable. But whether the ruler was good or bad, the social and economic condition of the people would not usually be affected by a mere political change. There would be no social revolution.

National revolutions involve a greater change. When a nation is ruled by another, an alien ruling class is dominant. This is injurious in many ways, as the subject country is ruled for the benefit of another country, or of a foreign class benefiting by such rule. Of course it hurts greatly the self-respect of the subject-people. Besides this, the alien ruling class keeps out the upper classes of the subject country from positions of power and authority, which they might have otherwise occupied. A successful national revolution at least removes the foreign element, and the dominant elements in the country immediately take its place. Thus these classes profit greatly by the removal of the superior alien class; the country generally profits because it will not then be ruled in the interests of another country. Those lower in the scale may not profit much, unless the national revolution is accompanied by a social revolution also.

A social revolution is a very different affair from the other revolutions, which merely change things on the surface. It involves a political revolution also, but it is something much more than that, as it changes the fabric of society. The English Revolution, which made Parliament supreme, was not only a political revolution, but partly a social one also, as it meant the association of the richer *bourgeoisie* with those in power. This upper *bourgeois* class thus rose politically and socially; the lower *bourgeoisie* and the masses generally were not affected. The French Revolution was even more of a social revolution. As we have seen, it upset the whole order of society, and for a while even the masses functioned. Ultimately the *bourgeoisie* triumphed here also, and the masses were sent back to their place, having played their rôle in the revolution; but the privileged nobles were removed.

It is obvious that such social revolutions are much more far-reaching than merely political changes, and they are intimately connected with social conditions. An ambitious, over-eager person or group cannot bring about a social revolution, unless conditions are such that the masses are ready for it. By their being ready I do not mean that they are consciously prepared after being told to be so. I mean that social and economic conditions are such that life becomes too great a burden for them, and they can find no relief or adjustment except in such a change. As a matter of fact, for ages past, life has been such a burden for vast numbers of people, and it is amazing how they have tolerated it. Sometimes they have broken out in revolt, chiefly peasant revolts and *jacqueries*, and in their mad anger blindly destroyed what they could lay hands upon. But these people were not conscious of any desire to change the social order. In spite of this ignorance, however, there were repeated breakdowns of the existing social conditions in the past, in ancient Rome, in the Middle Ages in Europe, in India, in China, and many an empire has fallen because of them.

In the past, social and economic changes took place slowly, and, for long periods methods of production and distribution and transport remained much the same. People, therefore, did not notice the process of change, and thought that the old social order was permanent and unchangeable. Religion put a divine halo round this order and the customs and beliefs which accompanied it. People became so convinced of this that they never thought of changing the order even when conditions were so changed that it was manifestly inapplicable. With the coming of the Industrial

Revolution and the vast changes in methods of transport, social changes became much swifter. New classes came to the front and became wealthy. A new industrial working class arose, very different from the artisans and field-labourers. All this required a new economic arrangement and political changes. Western Europe was in a curious state of misfit. A wise society would make the necessary changes whenever the need for them arises, and so derive full benefit from changing conditions. But societies are not wise, and they do not think as a whole. Individuals think of themselves and of what will profit them; classes of people having similar interests do likewise. If a class dominates any society it wants to remain there and to profit by exploiting the other classes below it. Wisdom and foresight would demonstrate that in the long run the best way of profiting oneself is to profit society as a whole of which one is a member. But a person or class in power wants to hold on to what it possesses. The easiest method of doing so is to make the other classes and people believe that the existing social order is the very best possible. Religion is dragged in to impress this on the people; education is made to teach the same lesson; till at length, amazing as it is, almost every one believes in it absolutely and does not think of changing it. Even the people that suffer from this system actually believe that it is right for it to continue, and for them to be kicked and cuffed, and to starve while others live in plenty.

So people imagine that there is an unchanging social system and it it nobody's fault if the majority suffer under it. It is their own fault, it is kismet, it is fate, it is the punishment for past sins. Society is always conservative, and dislikes change. It loves to remain in the rut it has got into, and firmly believes that it was meant to remain there. So much so that it punishes most of those individuals who, wishing to improve its condition, tell it to come out of the rut.

But social and economic conditions do not wait for the pleasure of the complacent and unthinking in society. They march on, although people's ideas remain the same. The distance between these out-of-date notions and reality becomes greater, and if something is not done to reduce this distance and to bring the two together, the system cracks and there is a catastrophe. This is what brings about real social revolutions. If conditions are such, a revolution is bound to come, though it may be delayed by the drag of old-fashioned ideas. If these conditions do not exist, then a few individuals, however much they may try, cannot bring it about. When a revolution does break out, the veil that hides actual conditions from the people is removed and understanding comes to them very soon. Once they are out of the rut, they rush ahead. That is why during revolutionary periods people go forward with tremendous energy. Thus revolution is the inevitable result of conservatism and holding back. If society could avoid falling into the foolish error that there is an unchanging social order, but would always keep in line with changing conditions, there would be no social revolution. There would then be continuous evolution.

I have written, without any previous intention of doing so, at some length about revolutions.   The subject interests me, for to-day all over the world there appear to be misfits, and the social system seems to be breaking down in many places.   This has been the herald of social revolution in the past, and one is naturally led to believe that we are on the eve of great changes in the world.   In India, as in every country under foreign domination, nationalism and the desire to rid the country of alien rule are strong.   But to a great extent this nationalistic urge is confined to the well-to-do classes. The peasantry and the workers and others, who live in perpetual want, are naturally more interested in filling their empty stomachs than in vague nationalistic dreams.   For them nationalism or *Swaraj* has no meaning, unless it brings with it more food and better conditions.   Therefore, in India to-day the problem is not merely a political one ; even more so it is a social one.

I have been led to this long digression about revolutions because of the many revolts and other disturbances in Europe during the nineteenth century which I was considering.   Many of these revolts, and especially in the first half of the century, were nationalistic risings against foreign rule.   Side by side with these, in the industrialized countries, ideas of social revolt began to spread the conflict of the new working class with its capitalist masters.   People began to think about and work consciously for the social revolution.

The year 1848 is called the year of revolutions in Europe.   There were risings in many countries, some partly successful, but mostly ending in failure.   A suppressed nationalism was at the back of the risings in Poland, Italy, Bohemia and Hungary.   The Polish revolt was against Prussia, the Bohemian and the North Italian against Austria.   They were all suppressed.   The Hungarian revolt against Austria was the biggest of all.   Its leader was Lojos Kossuth, who is famous in Hungarian history as a patriot and a fighter for freedom. In spite of two years of resistance, this revolt also was suppressed. Some years later Hungary succeeded by a different method of fighting under another great leader, Déak.   It is interesting to note that Déak's methods were those of passive resistance.   In 1867 Hungary and Austria were joined together, more or less on an equal basis, to form what was called a " dual monarchy " under the Hapsburg Emperor, Francis Joseph.   Déak's methods of passive resistance became a model half a century later for the Irish against the English.   When the Non-co-operation movement was started in India in 1920, some people remembered Déak's struggle.   But there was a great deal of difference between the two methods.

There were revolts in Germany also in 1848, but they were not very serious ; they were suppressed and a promise of some reforms was made.   In France there was a big change.   Ever since the Bourbons had been driven out in 1830 Louis Philippe had been king, a kind of semi-constitutional monarch.   By 1848 the people grew weary of him and he was made to abdicate.   A republic was set up again. This was the Second Republic, as the first one was during the great Revolution.   Taking advantage of the confusion, a nephew of Napoleon, named Louis Bonaparte, came to Paris and, posing as a great friend of liberty, was elected as President of the Republic. This was just a pretence to obtain power. Having fully established himself, he gained control of the army, and in 1851 there was what is called a *coup d'état*. He overawed Paris by his soldiers, shot down many people and terrorized the Assembly. The next year he made himself emperor, calling himself Napoleon III, as the great Napoleon's son was supposed to be Napoleon II, although he had never reigned. So ended the Second Republic after a brief and inglorious career of a little over four years.

In England there was no revolt in 1848, but there was a great deal of trouble and disturbance. England has a way of bending when real trouble threatens, and so avoiding it. Her constitution, being flexible, helps in this, and long practice has made the English-man accept some compromise when there is no other way out. In this way he has managed to avoid big and sudden changes which have often come to other countries with more rigid constitutions and less compromising people. In 1832 there was great agitation in England over a Reform Bill, which gave the vote for electing members to Parliament to a larger number of people. Judged by modern standards, it was a very moderate and inoffensive Bill. Only some additional people of the middle classes were enfranchised; the workers and most others still did not have the vote. Parlia-ment was then in the hands of a small number of rich persons, and they were afraid of losing their privileges and their " rotten boroughs ", which returned them to the House of Commons without any trouble. So these people opposed the Reform Bill with all their might and said that England would go to the dogs, and the world would come to an end, if the Bill were passed. England was on the verge of civil war when the Opposition, frightened by popular agitation, consented to the Bill being passed. Needless to say England survived it and Parliament continued, as before, to be controlled by the rich. The well-to-do middle classes gained further power.

About 1848 another great agitation shook the country. This was called the Chartist Agitation, because it was proposed to present a monster petition to Parliament containing a " People's Charter " demanding various reforms. After frightening the ruling classes greatly, the movement was suppressed. There was a great deal of distress and discontent among the working classes in the factories. About this time some labour laws began to be passed, and these slightly improved the lot of the workers. England was making money fast by its rising trade; it was becoming the " workshop of the world ". Most of these profits went to the owners of the factories; but a small part of them trickled down to the workers. All this helped in preventing a rising in 1848. But at the time it seemed a near thing.

I have not finished with the year 1848 yet; the story of what hap-pened in Rome that year still remains to be told. I must carry that over to the next letter.

127

ITALY BECOMES A UNITED AND FREE NATION

January 30, 1933
Vasanta Panchami

IN my account of 1848 I have kept the story of Italy for the last. Of all the exciting happenings of the year 1848 the heroic struggle in Rome was the most fascinating.

Italy before Napoleon's time was a patchwork of little States and petty princes. Napoleon united it for a short while. After Napoleon it reverted to its previous state, or something even worse. The victorious allies at the Congress of Vienna of 1815 very considerately divided up the country among themselves. Austria took Venice and a great deal of territory round it; several Austrian princes were provided with choice morsels; the Pope came back to Rome and the States adjoining it, called the Papal States; Naples and the south formed the kingdom of the two Sicilies under a Bourbon king; to the north-west, near the French frontier, there was a King of Piedmont and Sardinia. All these petty kings and princes, with the exception of Piedmont, ruled in a most autocratic way, and oppressed their subjects even more than they or others had done before Napoleon came. But Napoleon's visit had stirred the country and inspired the youth with dreams of a free and united Italy. In spite of the oppression of the rulers, or perhaps because of it, there were many petty risings, and secret societies were formed.

Soon there emerged an ardent young man who came to be acknowledged as the leader of the movement for freedom. This was Giuseppe Mazzini, the prophet of Italian nationalism. In 1831 he organized a society, Giovane Italia—Young Italy—with the aim of an Italian Republic. For many years he worked for this cause in Italy and was an exile, often risking his life. Many of his writings became classics in the literature of nationalism. In 1848, when revolts were breaking out all over North Italy, Mazzini saw his chance and came to Rome. The Pope was driven away and a republic declared under a committee of three—Triumvirs they were called, a word from old Roman history. Mazzini was one of these three Triumvirs. This young Republic was attacked on all sides : by the Austrians, by the Neapolitans, even by the French, who came to restore the Pope. The chief fighter on the side of the Roman Republic was Garibaldi. He held the Austrians and defeated the Neapolitan armies, and even stopped the French. All this was done with the help of volunteers, and the bravest and best of the youth of Rome gave their lives in defence of the Republic. Eventually, after a heroic struggle, the Roman Republic fell to the French, who brought back the Pope.

So ended the first phase of the struggle. Mazzini and Garibaldi carried on their work in different ways, by propaganda and

preparation for the next big effort. They were very unlike each other; one was a thinker and an idealist, the other was a soldier with a genius for guerilla warfare. Both were fiercely devoted to Italian freedom and unity. A third player in this great game then became prominent. This was Cavour, the Prime Minister of Victor Emmanuel, King of Piedmont. Cavour was chiefly interested in making Victor Emmanuel King of Italy. As this involved the suppression and removal of many of the petty princes, he was perfectly prepared to take advantage of Mazzini's and Garibaldi's activities. He intrigued with the French—Napoleon III was the ruler in France then—and involved them in a war with his enemies the Austrians. This was in 1859. Garibaldi took advantage of the defeat of the Austrians by the French to lead an extraordinary expedition on his own account against the King of Naples and Sicily. This was the famous expedition of Garibaldi and his 1000 red-shirts, untrained men without proper arms or material, who met the trained armies pitched against them. The 1000 red-shirts were greatly outnumbered, but their enthusiasm and the good will of the populace led them from victory to victory. The fame of Garibaldi spread. Such was the magic of his name that armies melted away at his approach. Still his task was a difficult one, and many a time Garibaldi and his volunteers were on the verge of defeat and disaster. But even in the hour of defeat fortune smiled upon him, as it often does on desperate ventures, and turned defeat into victory.

Garibaldi and the 1000 landed in Sicily. From there slowly they worked their way up to Italy. As he marched through the villages of South Italy, Garibaldi appealed for volunteers, and the rewards he offered them were unusual. "Come!" he said, "come! He who stays at home is a coward. I promise you weariness, hardship, and battles. But we will conquer or die." Nothing succeeds like success. Garibaldi's early successes whipped up the spirit of nationalism of the Italians. Volunteers poured in, and they marched north singing Garibaldi's hymn :

> " The tombs are uncovered, the dead come from far,
> The ghosts of our martyrs are rising to war,
> With swords in their hands, and with laurels of fame,
> And dead hearts still glowing with Italy's name.
> Come join them ! Come follow, O youth of our land!
> Come fling out our banner, and marshal our band !
> Come all with cold steel, and come all with hot fire,
> Come all with the flame of Italia's desire !

> Begone from Italia, begone from our home !
> Begone from Italia, O stranger, begone."

How similar are national songs everywhere !

Cavour took advantage of Garibaldi's successes, and the result of all this was that Victor Emmanuel of Piedmont became King of Italy in 1861. Rome was still under French troops, Venice under the Austrians. Within ten years both Venice and Rome joined the rest of Italy, and Rome became the capital. Italy was at last one united nation. But Mazzini was not happy. All his life he had laboured for the republican ideal, and now Italy was but the kingdom of Victor Emmanuel of Piedmont. It is true that the new kingdom was a constitutional one and an Italian Parliament met at Turin immediately after Victor Emmanuel became king.

So Italy, the nation, was united again and free from foreign rule. Three men brought this about—Mazzini, Garibaldi and Cavour—and perhaps if any one of these had not been there, the freedom would have been longer in coming. George Meredith, the English poet and novelist, wrote many years afterwards :

> " We who have seen Italia in the throes,
> Half risen but to be hurled to the ground, and now,
> Like a ripe field of wheat where once drove plough
> All bounteous as she is fair, we think of those

> Who blew the breath of life into her frame :
> Cavour, Mazzini, Garibaldi : three :
> Her Brain, her Soul, her Sword ; and set her free
> From ruinous discords, with one lustrous aim."

I have told you briefly and in bold outline the story of the Italian struggle for freedom. This little account will read to you like any other bit of dead history. But I shall tell you how you can make this story live and fill yourself with the joy and anguish of the struggle. At least, so I felt when I was a boy at school, long, long ago, and I read the story in three books by Trevelyan—*Garibaldi and the Fight for the Roman Republic, Garibaldi and the Thousand*, and *Garibaldi and the Making of Italy*.

At the time of the Italian struggle the English people sympathized with Garibaldi and his red-shirts, and many an English poet wrote stirring poetry about the fight. It is strange how the sympathies of the English often enough go out to struggling peoples provided their own interests are not involved. To Greece, fighting for freedom, they send the poet Byron and others, to Italy they send all good wishes and encouragement; but next door to them in Ireland, and farther away in Egypt and India and elsewhere, their messengers bring maxim-guns and destruction. Many a beautiful poem was written about Italy at the time by Swinburne and Meredith and Elizabeth Barrett Browning. Meredith also wrote novels on this subject. I shall give you here a quotation from a poem of Swinburne *The Halt before Rome*—written while the Italian struggle was going on and meeting with many a check, and many a traitor was serving alien masters.

> " Gifts have your masters for giving,
> 　　Gifts hath not Freedom to give;
> She without shelter or station,
> 　　She beyond limit or bar,
> Urges to slumberless speed
> Armies that famish, that bleed,
> Sowing their lives for her seed,
> That their dust may rebuild her a nation,
> 　　That their souls may relight her a star."

128

THE RISE OF GERMANY

January 31, 1933

In our last letter we saw the building up of one of the great European nations with which we are so familiar to-day. We shall now see the making of another great modern nation—Germany.

In spite of a common language and many other common features, the German people continued to be split up into a large number of States, big and small. For many centuries Austria of the Hapsburgs was the leading German Power. Then Prussia came to the front, and there was rivalry for the leadership of the German people between these two Powers. Napoleon humbled both of them. As a consequence of this, German nationalism gained strength and helped in his final defeat. Thus both in Italy and in Germany Napoleon, un-consciously and without wishing it, gave an impetus to the spirit of nationalism and ideas of freedom. One of the leading German nationalists of the Napoleonic period was Fichte, a philosopher, but also an ardent patriot who did much to rouse up his people.

For half a century after Napoleon the little German States con-tinued. There were many attempts at federation, but they did not succeed because both the Austrian and Prussian rulers and govern-ments wanted to be leaders of it. Meanwhile there was a great deal of repression of all liberal elements, and there were revolts in 1830 and 1848, which were suppressed. Some petty reforms were also introduced to soothe the people.

In parts of Germany there were coal-fields and iron ore, as in England, and thus conditions were favourable for industrial develop-ment. Germany also was famous for her philosophers and scientists and soldiers. Factories were built and an industrial working class grew up.

At this stage, about the middle of the century, there rose a man in Prussia who was to dominate for many years not only Germany, but European politics. This man was Otto von Bismarck, a junker —that is, a landowner in Prussia. Born in the year of Waterloo, he served for many years as a diplomatic envoy in various Courts. In 1862 he became Prime Minister of Prussia and immediately he began to make his influence felt. Within a week of his becoming Prime Minister he said in the course of a speech : " The great ques-tions of the time will be decided, not by speeches and resolutions of majorities, but by iron and blood."

Blood and iron ! Those words, which became famous, truly represented the policy he pursued with foresight and relentlessness. He hated democracy, and treated parliaments and popular assemblies with scant courtesy. He seemed to be a relic from the past, but his ability and determination were such that he made the present bend to his will. He made modern Germany and moulded European history in the second half of the nineteenth century. The Germany of philosophers and scientists retired into the background and the new Germany of blood and iron, of military efficiency, began to dominate the continent of Europe. A prominent German of his day said " Bismarck makes Germany great and the Germans small." His policy of making Germany a great Power in Europe and in international affairs pleased the Germans, and the glamour of a growing national prestige made them put up with all manner of repression from him.

Bismarck came to power with clear ideas as to what he was to do and a carefully-worked-out plan. He adhered to this resolutely and met with amazing success. He wanted to make Germany and, through Germany, Prussia, dominant in Europe. At that time France, under Napoleon III, was considered the most powerful nation on the Continent. Austria was also a great rival. It is fascinating, as a lesson in the old style of international politics and diplomacy, to see how Bismarck played with the other Powers and then disposed of each of them by turn. The first thing he set out to do was to settle once for all the question of the leadership of the Germans. The old rivalry between Prussia and Austria could not be allowed to continue. The question must be finally decided in favour of Prussia, and Austria must realize that she would have to play second fiddle. After that would come the turn of France. (Please remember that when I talk of Prussia, Austria, and France I mean their governments. All these governments were more or less autocratic and the parliaments there had little power.)

So Bismarck quietly perfected his military machine. Meanwhile, Napoleon III attacked and defeated Austria. This defeat led to Garibaldi's campaign in South Italy, which finally resulted in the freedom of Italy. All this suited Bismarck, as it weakened Austria. A national revolt having occurred in Russian Poland, Bismarck actually offered his help to the Tsar to shoot down the Poles if necessary. This was a disgraceful offer to make, but it served its purpose, which was to gain the good will of the Tsar in any future complication in Europe. Then, in alliance with Austria, he defeated Denmark, and soon after turned on Austria, having taken care to obtain the support of France and Italy. Austria was overwhelmed by Prussia in a very short time in 1866. Having settled the question of German leadership and made it clear that Prussia was the leader, very wisely he treated Austria with generosity, so as to leave no bitterness. The way was now clear for the creation of a North German Federation under Prussia's leadership (Austria was not in it.) Bismarck became the Federal Chancellor. In these days, when some of our political and legal pandits talk and argue for months and years about federations and constitutions, it is interesting to note that Bismarck dictated the new constitution for the North German Federation in five hours. And this, with a few alterations, continued to be the German constitution for fifty years, till after the World War, when the Republic was established in 1918.

Bismarck had attained his first great objective. The next step was to establish a dominant European position by humbling France. Quietly and without fuss he prepared for this, trying to bring about German unity, and disarming the suspicions of the other European Powers. Even defeated Austria was treated so gently that there was not much ill-will left. England was the historical rival of France, and looked with great suspicion on Napoleon III's ambitious schemes. So it was not difficult for Bismarck to have the good will of England in any struggle against France. When he was fully prepared for war, he played his game so cleverly that it was Napoleon III who actually declared war on Prussia in 1870. The Prussian Government seemed to Europe the innocent victim of aggressive France. " A Berlin! A Berlin! " people shouted in Paris, and Napoleon III complacently imagined that he would actually be in Berlin soon at the head of a victorious army. But something very different happened. Bismarck's trained military machine hurled itself on the north-eastern frontier of France, and the French army

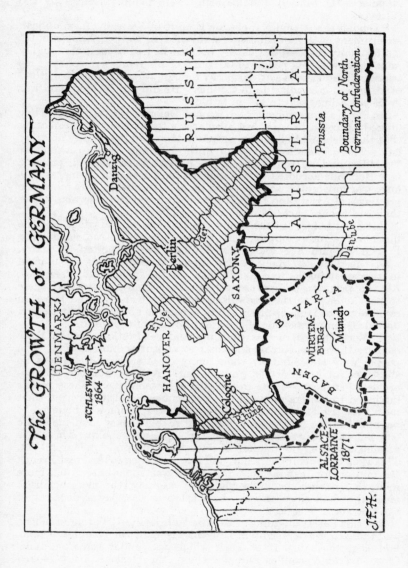

The GROWTH of GERMANY

Prussia

Boundary of North German Confederation.

RUSSIA

AUSTRIA

DENMARK

SCHLESWIG 1864

Danzig

Berlin

Oder

Elbe

HANOVER

Cologne

Rhine

SAXONY

BAVARIA

WÜRTEM-BURG

BADEN

Munich

Danube

ALSACE LORRAINE 1871

J.F.H.

crumpled up before it.   Within a few weeks, at Sedan, the Emperor
Napoleon III himself and his army were made prisoners by the
Germans.

So ended the second Napoleonic Empire of France.   A republican
government was immediately established in Paris.   Napoleon III
fell for many reasons, but chiefly because he had become thoroughly
unpopular with his people on account of his repressive policy.   He
tried to divert people's attention by foreign wars, a favourite method
of kings and governments in trouble.   He did not succeed, and war
itself put a final seal to his ambition.

In Paris a government of National Defence was formed.   They
offered peace to Prussia, but Bismarck's terms were so humiliating
that they decided to fight on, although they had practically no army
left.   There was a long siege of Paris with the German armies at
Versailles and all round the city.   At last Paris yielded, and the
new Republic accepted defeat and the hard terms of Bismarck.   A
huge war indemnity was agreed to be paid and, what hurt most, the
provinces of Alsace and Lorraine had to be given up to Germany after
they had been a part of France for over 200 years.

But even before the siege of Paris had ended, Versailles saw the
birth of a new empire.   In September 1870 Napoleon III's
French Empire had ended; in January 1871 a united Germany,
with the Prussian King as Kaiser or Emperor, was proclaimed
in the splendid hall of Louis XIV in the palace at Versailles.
All the princes and representatives of Germany assembled there
to pay homage to their new Emperor—the Kaiser.   The Prussian
royal house of Hohenzollern had now become an imperial house and
united Germany was one of the great Powers of the world.

In Versailles there was rejoicing and celebration, but in Paris
near by there was sorrow and distress and utter humiliation.   The
people were staggered by their many disasters and there was no
stable or well-established government.   A large number of monarchists had been elected to a National Assembly and these people
intrigued to restore monarchy.   To remove an obstacle from their
path they tried to disarm the National Guard, which was believed to
be republican.   All the democrats and revolutionary elements in the
city felt that this meant reaction and repression again.   There was
a rising, and the " Commune " of Paris was proclaimed in March 1871.
This was a kind of municipality, and it looked back to the great French
Revolution for inspiration.   But there was something much more
in it, and it embodied, though rather vaguely, the new socialistic
ideas that had since arisen.   In a sense it was the predecessor of
the Soviets in Russia.

But this Paris Commune of 1871 had a brief life.   The monarchists
and the *bourgeoisie*, frightened by this rising of the common people,
laid siege to that part of Paris which was under the Commune.
Close by, at Versailles and elsewhere, the German army looked
silently on.   As the French soldiers, who had been made prisoners
by the Germans and were now released returned to Paris, they took
the side of their old officers and fought against the Commune.   They

marched against the Communards, and on a summer day towards the end of May 1871 they defeated them, and shot down 30,000 men and women in the streets of Paris. Large numbers of captured Communards were shot down later in cold blood. So ended the Paris Commune, and at the time it stirred Europe greatly. This stir was caused not only by the bloody suppression of it, but also because it was the first socialistic revolt against the existing system. The poor had often risen against the rich, but they had not thought of changing the system under which they were poor. The Commune was both a democratic and an economic revolt, and is thus a landmark in the development of socialistic thought in Europe. In France the violent suppression of the Commune drove socialistic ideas underground and the recovery was slow.

Although the Commune was put down, France escaped more experiments in monarchy. After a while she settled down definitely to republicanism, and in January 1875 the Third Republic was proclaimed under a new constitution. This republic has continued since then and still exists. There are some people in France who talk even now of having kings; but they are very few, and France seems to be definitely committed to republicanism. The French Republic is a *bourgeois* republic, and is controlled by the well-to-do middle classes.

France recovered from the German war of 1870-71 and paid the huge indemnity, but in the heart of her people was anger at the humiliation they had been made to suffer. They are a proud people and have long memories and the idea of revenge—*la revanche*—obsessed them. Especially they felt the loss of Alsace and Lorraine. Bismarck had been wise in his generosity to Austria after her defeat, but there was no generosity or wisdom in his harsh treatment of France. At the cost of humbling a proud enemy he bought the terrible and ever-remembered enmity of those people. Just after the Battle of Sedan, even before the war had ended, Karl Marx, the famous socialist, issued a manifesto in which he prophesied that the annexation of Alsace would lead to "mortal enmity between the two countries, to a truce instead of a peace". In this, as in many other matters, he was a true prophet.

In Germany Bismarck was now the all-powerful Imperial Chancellor. The policy of "blood and iron" had succeeded for the time being, and Germany accepted it and liberal ideas were at a discount. Bismarck tried to keep power in the hands of the king, for he was no believer in democracy. The growth of German industry and the working class brought new problems as this class gained in strength and made radical demands. Bismarck dealt with it in two ways—by bettering the workers' conditions and suppressing socialism. He tried to win the workers over, or at any rate to prevent them from becoming extreme, by promoting social legislation. Germany thus took the lead in this kind of legislation, and laws for old-age pensions, insurance and medical aid for workers, and other improvements in workers' conditions, were passed before even England, with her older industry and workers' movement, had done much in this line. This policy had some success, but still the workers' organizations grew. They had able leaders : Ferdinand Lassalle, a very brilliant person, and said to be the greatest orator of the nineteenth century. He died quite young as the result of a duel. Wilhelm Liebknecht, a brave old fighter and rebel, who was almost shot, but escaped and lived to a good age ; his son, Karl, still carrying on the fight or liberty, was murdered a few years ago at the founding of the German Republic in 1918. And Karl Marx, about whom I shall have to tell you in another letter. But Marx was an exile from Germany for the greater part of his life.

The workers' organizations grew, and in 1875 they joined together to form the Socialist Democratic Party. Bismarck could not tolerate this growth of socialism. There was an attempt on the Emperor's life, and he made this the excuse for a fierce attack on socialists. In 1878 anti-socialist laws were passed suppressing every kind of socialist activity. There was a kind of martial law so far as socialists were concerned and thousands of persons were expelled from the country or sentenced to imprisonment. Many of those expelled went to America and were the pioneers of socialism there. The Socialist Democratic Party was hard hit, but it survived and later grew in strength again. Bismarck's terrorism could not kill it ; success proved much more harmful. As it grew in power it became a vast organization owning a great deal of property and with thousands of paid workers. When a person or organization gets wealthy he or it ceases to be revolutionary. And this was the fate which befell this Socialist Democratic Party in Germany.

Bismarck's skill in diplomacy did not leave him to the end, and he played a great game in the international politics of his day. These politics then were, and even now are, a curious and intricate web of intrigue and counter-intrigue and deception and bluff, all in secret and behind the veil. They would not last long if they saw the light of day. Bismarck made an alliance with Austria and Italy, called the Triple Alliance, for now he was beginning to fear the revenge of the French. And so each side went on arming and intriguing and glaring at each other.

In 1888 a young man became the German Kaiser as Emperor Wilhelm II. He fancied himself greatly as a strong man and soon he fell out with Bismarck. In his old age, and much to his wrath, the Iron Chancellor was dismissed from his office. As a sop he was given the title of prince, but he retired to his estate in disgust and disillusioned about kings. To a friend he said : " I took up office equipped with a great fund of royalist sentiments and veneration for the king; to my sorrow, I find that this fund is ever more and more depleted ! . . . I have seen three kings naked, and the sight was not always a pleasant one ! "

The grumpy old man lived for several years more, and died in 1898 at the age of eighty-three. Even after his dismissal by the Kaiser and his death, his shadow lay over Germany and his spirit moved his successors. But they were lesser men who came after him.

129

SOME FAMOUS WRITERS

February 1, 1933

As I was writing to you yesterday about the rise of Germany, it struck me that I had not told you anything about the greatest German of the early nineteenth century. This man was Goethe, a famous writer, the centenary of whose death was celebrated all over Germany a few months ago. And then I thought that I might tell you something about the famous writers of this period in Europe. But this was a dangerous subject for me, dangerous because I would only show my own ignorance. Just to give a list of well-known names would be rather silly, and to say something more would be difficult. I know little enough about English literature, and of the other European literatures my knowledge is confined to a few translations. What, then, was I to do?

The idea to say something on the subject had taken possession of my mind, and I could not rid myself of it. I felt that I should at least point out this direction to you, even though I cannot accompany you far along the way to this enchanted land. For art and literature often give greater insight into a nation's soul than the superficial activities of the multitude. They take us to a region of calm and serene thought which is not affected by the passions and prejudices of the moment. But to-day the poet and the artist are seldom looked upon as the prophets of to-morrow and they meet with little honour. If some honour comes to them at all, it usually comes after they are dead.

So I shall mention just a few names to you, some of which must be already familiar to you, and I shall only touch upon the early part of the century. This is just to whet your appetite. Remember that the nineteenth century has rich stores of fine writing in many of the European countries.

Goethe really belonged to the eighteenth century, for he was born in 1749, but he lived to the ripe old age of eighty-three, and thus saw a good third of the next century. He lived through one of the stormiest periods of European history, and saw his own country overrun by Napoleon's armies. In his own life he experienced much sorrow, but gradually he gained an inner command over life's difficulties and attained a detachment and calm which brought peace to him. Napoleon first saw him when he was over sixty. As he stood in the doorway, there was something in his face and figure, an untroubled look and a bearing so full of dignity, that Napoleon exclaimed: " *Voilà un homme !* " He dabbled in many things, and whatever he did, he did with distinction. He was a philosopher, a poet, a dramatist, and a scientist interested in many different sciences; and, besides all this, his practical job was that of a minister in the Court of a petty German prince ! He is best known to us as a writer, and his most famous book is *Faust*. His fame spread far during his long life, and in his own sphere of literature he came to be regarded by his country-men almost as a demi-god.

Goethe had a contemporary, somewhat younger than he was, named Schiller, who was also a great poet. Much younger was Heinrich Heine, yet another great and delightful poet in German, who has written very beautiful lyrics. All these three—Goethe, Schiller and Heine—were steeped in the classical culture of ancient Greece.

Germany has long been known as the land of philosophers, and I might as well mention one or two names to you, although perhaps they will not interest you greatly. Only those people who have a passion for the subject need try to read their books, for they are very abstruse and difficult. None the less these and other philosophers are interesting and instructive, for they kept alight the torch of thought, and through them one can follow the development of ideas. Immanuel Kant was the great German philosopher of the eighteenth century, and he lived on to the turn of the century, when he was eighty. Hegel is another great name in philosophy. He followed Kant, and is supposed to have greatly influenced Karl Marx, the father of communism. So much for the philosophers.

The early years of the nineteenth century produced quite a number of eminent poets, especially in England. Russia's best-known national poet, Pushkin, also lived then. He died young as the result of a duel. There were several poets in France also, but I shall mention only two French names. One is that of Victor Hugo, who was born in 1802 and lived, liked Goethe, to the age of eighty-three and, also like Goethe, became a kind of demi-god of literature in his own country. He had a varied career both as a writer and as a politician. He started life as an aggressive royalist and almost a believer in autocracy. Gradually he changed step by step till he became a republican in 1848. Louis Napoleon, when he became President of the short-lived Second Republic, exiled him for his republican views. In 1871 Victor Hugo favoured the Commune of Paris. From the extreme right of conservatism he had moved gradually but surely to the extreme left of socialism. Most people grow conservative and reactionary as they become older. Hugo did the exact opposite. But we are concerned here with him as a writer. He was a great poet, novelist and dramatist.

The second French name I shall mention to you is that of Honoré de Balzac. He was a contemporary of Victor Hugo's, but was very different from him. He was a novelist of tremendous energy, and wrote a huge number of novels during a fairly short life. His stories are connected with one another; the same characters often appear in them. His object was to mirror the whole of the French life of his day in his novels, and he called the whole series *La Comédie Humaine*. It was a very ambitious idea, and although he worked hard and long, he could not complete the enormous task he had set himself.

In England three brilliant young poets stand out in the early years of the nineteenth century. They were contemporaries, and they all died young within three years of each other.   These three were Keats, Shelley and Byron.   Keats had a hard tussle with poverty and discouragement, and when he died in Rome in 1821 at the age of twenty-six he was little known.   And yet he had written some very beautiful poetry.   Keats belonged to the middle classes, and it is interesting to note that if lack of money was an obstruction in his way, how much more difficult must it be for the poor to become poets and writers.   Indeed, the present Cambridge Professor of English Literature has some pertinent remarks to make about this :

> "It is ", he says, "certain that, by some fault in our common-wealth, the poor poet has not in these days, nor has had for two hundred years, a dog's chance.   Believe me—and I have spent a great part of ten years in watching some three hundred and twenty elementary schools,—we may prate of democracy, but actually, a poor child in England has little more hope than had the son of an Athenian slave to be emancipated into that intellectual freedom of which great writings are born."

I have given this quotation because we are apt to forget that poetry and fine writing, and culture generally, are monopolies of the well-to-do classes.   Poetry and culture have little place in a poor man's hut ; they are not meant for empty stomachs.   So our present-day culture becomes a reflection of the well-to-do *bourgeois* mind.   It may change greatly when the worker takes charge of it in a different social system where he has the opportunities and leisure to indulge in culture.   Some such change is being watched with interest in Soviet Russia to-day.

This also makes it clear to us that a great deal of our cultural poverty in India during the last few generations is due to our people's excessive poverty.   It is an insult to talk of culture to people who have nothing to eat.   This blight of poverty affects even those few who happen to be relatively well-to-do, and so unhappily even these classes in India are to-day singularly uncultured.   What a host of evils foreign rule and social backwardness have to answer for. But even in this general poverty and drabness, India can still produce splendid men and magnificent exemplars of culture like Gandhi and Rabindranath Tagore.

I have drifted away from my subject.

Shelley was a most lovable creature ; full of fire from his early youth and the champion of freedom in everything.   He was expelled from his college at Oxford for writing an essay on *The Necessity of Atheism*.   He (and Keats also) went through his brief life as a poet is supposed to do, living in his imagination and in the air and regardless of worldly difficulties.   He was drowned near the Italian coast a year after the death of Keats.   I need not tell you of his famous poems as you can easily find them out for yourself.   But I shall give you one of his shorter poems.   It is by no means among his best, but it brings out the awful fate of the poor worker in our present civilization.   He is in almost as bad a condition as the old slaves were. It is more than 100 years since the poem was written, and yet it applies to present-day conditions. It is called *The Mask of Anarchy.*

> What is Freedom ?—ye can tell
> That which slavery is, too well—
> For its very name has grown
> To an echo of your own.
>
> 'Tis to work and have such pay
> As just keeps life from day to day
> In your limbs, as in a cell
> For the tyrant's use to dwell.
>
> So that ye for them are made
> Loom, and plough, and sword, and spade,
> With or without your own will bent
> To their defence and nourishment.
>
> 'Tis to see your children weak
> With their mothers pine and peak,
> When the winter winds are bleak—
> They are dying, whilst I speak.
>
> 'Tis to hunger for such diet
> As the rich man in his riot
> Casts to the fat dogs that lie
> Surfeiting beneath his eye.
>
> 'Tis to be a slave in soul
> And to hold no strong contro
> Over your own wills, but be
> All that others make of ye.
>
> And at length, when ye complain
> With a murmur weak and vain,
> 'Tis to see the tyrant's crew
> Ride over your wives and you—
> Blood is on the grass like dew.

Byron has also written fine poetry in praise of freedom, but it is national freedom, and not economic freedom, as in Shelley's poem. He died, as I have told you, in the Greek national war of liberation against Turkey, two years after Shelley. I am rather prejudiced against Byron as a man, and yet I have a fellow-feeling for him, for did he not go to Harrow School and Trinity College, Cambridge—my school and college ? Unlike Keats and Shelley, fame came to him in his youth, and he was lionized by London society, only to be dropped later.

There were two other well-known poets about this time, both much longer-lived than this youthful trio. Wordsworth, who lived for eighty years from 1770 to 1850, is considered one of the great English poets. He was very fond of Nature, and much of his poetry is Nature-poetry. The other was Coleridge; a few of his poems are very good.

The early nineteenth century also saw three famous novelists. Walter Scott was the eldest of these, and his Waverley novels were very popular. I suppose you have read some of them. I remember liking them when I was a boy, but tastes change as one grows up, and I am sure they would bore me now if I read them. Thackeray and Dickens were the two other novelists. Both, I think, are far

superior to Scott. I hope they are both friends of yours. Thackeray
was born in Calcutta in 1811, and spent five or six years there.
Some of his books have got realistic descriptions of the Indian
nabobs—that is, the English people in India who, having collected
a huge fortune and become fat and peppery, returned to England
to enjoy themselves.

This is as much as I propose to write about the writers of the early
nineteenth century. It is ridiculously little about a big subject.
A person who knows the subject could write charmingly about it;
he would also, no doubt, tell you a lot about the music and art of
the period. All this requires telling and knowing, but they are
beyond me, and I shall wisely keep to solid ground.

I shall finish up this letter by giving you a poem from Goethe's
Faust. This is, of course, a translation from the German:

> Alas, alas!
> Thou hast smitten the world,
> Thou hast laid it low,
> Shattered, o'er thrown,
> Into nothingness hurled
> Crushed by a demi-god's blow
>
> We bear them away,
> The shards of the world,
> We sing well-a-day
> Over the loveliness gone,
> Over the beauty slain.
> Build it again,
> Great child of Earth,
> Build it again
> With a finer worth,
> In thine own bosom build it on high!
> Take up thy life once more:
> Run the race again!
> High and clear
> Let a lovelier strain
> Ring out than ever before!

130

DARWIN AND THE TRIUMPH OF SCIENCE

February 3, 1933

FROM the poets let us go to the scientists. The poets, I am afraid,
are still considered rather ineffectual beings; but the scientists are
the miracle-workers of to-day, and they have influence and honour.
This was not so before the nineteenth century. In the earlier centuries a scientist's life was a risky affair in Europe and sometimes
ended at the stake. I have told you of how Giordano Bruno was
burnt in Rome by the Church. A few years later, in the seventeenth
century, Galileo came very near the stake because he had stated that
the earth went round the sun. He escaped being burnt for heresy
because he apologized and withdrew his previous statements. In

this way the Church in Europe was always coming into conflict with science and trying to suppress new ideas. Organized religion, in Europe or elsewhere, has various dogmas attached to it which its followers are supposed to accept without doubt or questioning. Science has a very different way of looking at things. It takes nothing for granted and has, or ought to have, no dogmas. It seeks to encourage an open mind and tries to reach truth by repeated experiment. This outlook is obviously very different from the religious outlook, and it is not surprising that there was frequent conflict between the two.

Experiments of various kinds have, I suppose, been carried on by different peoples in all ages. In ancient India, it is said that chemistry and surgery were fairly advanced, and this could only have been so after a great deal of experimenting. The old Greeks also experimented to some extent. As for the Chinese, recently I read a most astonishing account, which gave extracts from Chinese writers of 1500 years ago, showing that they knew of the theory of evolution, and of the circulation of the blood through the body, and that Chinese surgeons gave anæsthetics. But we do not know enough about these times to justify any conclusions. If the ancient civilizations had discovered these methods, why did they forget them later ? And why did they not make greater progress ? Or was it that they did not attach enough importance to this kind of progress ? Many interesting questions arise, but we have no materials to answer them.

The Arabs were very fond of experimenting, and Europe in the Middle Ages followed them. But all their experimentation was not truly scientific. They were always looking for what was called the " Philosophers' Stone ", which was supposed to have the virtue of turning common metals into gold. People spent their lives in complicated chemical experiments to find the secret of such transmutation of metals; alchemy this was called. They also searched diligently for an " elixir of life " or *amrit*, which would give immortality. There is no record, outside fairy tales, of any one having ever succeeded in finding this *amrit* or the famous stone. This was really dabbling in some kind of magic in the hope of gaining wealth and power and long life. It had nothing to do with the spirit of science. Science has no concern with magic and sorcery and the like.

The real scientific method, however, developed gradually in Europe, and among the greatest names in the history of science is that of the Englishman, Isaac Newton, who lived from 1642 to 1727. Newton explained the law of gravitation—that is, of how things fall; and with the help of this, and other laws which had been discovered, he explained the movements of the sun and the planets. Everything, both big and small, seemed to be explained by his theories, and he received great honour.

The spirit of science was gaining on the dogmatic spirit of the Church. It could no longer be put down or its votaries sent to the stake. Many scientists patiently worked and experimented and collected facts and knowledge, especially in England and France, and later in Germany and America. The body of scientific knowledge thus grew. The eighteenth century in Europe, you will remember, was the century when rationalism spread among the educated classes. It was the century of Voltaire and Rousseau and many other able Frenchmen who wrote on all manner of subjects and created a ferment in the minds of the people. The great French Revolution was being hatched in the womb of the century. This rationalistic outlook fitted in with the scientific outlook, and both opposed the dogmatic outlook of the Church.

The nineteenth century, I have told you, was, among other things, the century of science. The Industrial Revolution, the Mechanical Revolution, and the amazing changes in the methods of transport, were all due to science. The numerous factories had changed the methods of production; railways and steamships had suddenly narrowed the world; the electric telegraph was an even greater wonder. Wealth poured into England from her far-flung empire. Old ideas were naturally much shaken by this, and the hold of religion grew less. Factory life, as compared to an agricultural life on the land, made people think more of economic relations than of religious dogmas.

In the middle of the century, in 1859, a book was published in England which brought the conflict between the dogmatic and the scientific outlook to a head. This book was the *Origin of Species*, by Charles Darwin. Darwin is not among the very great scientists; there was nothing very new in what he said. Other geologists and naturalists had been at work before Darwin, and had gathered much material. None the less Darwin's book was epoch-making; it produced a vast impression and helped in changing the social outlook more than any other scientific work. It resulted in a mental earthquake and made Darwin famous.

Darwin had wandered about in South America and the Pacific as a naturalist and had collected an enormous amount of material and data. He used this to show how each species of animals had changed and developed by natural selection. Many people had thought till then that every species or kind of animal, including man, had been separately created by God, and had remained apart and unchangeable since then—that is to say that one species could not become another. Darwin showed, by a mass of actual examples, that species did change from one to another, and that this was the normal method of development. These changes took place by natural selection. A slight variation in a species, if it happened to be profitable to it in any way or helped it to survive others, would gradually lead to a permanent change, as obviously more of this varied species would survive. After a while this varied species would be in the majority and would swamp the others. In this way changes and variations would creep in, one after the other, and after some time there would be an almost new species produced. So in course of time many new species would arise by this process of survival of the fittest by natural selection. This would apply to plants and animals, and even man. It is possible, according to this theory, that there might be a common ancestor of all the various plant and animal species we see to-day.

A few years later Darwin published another book—*The Descent of Man*—in which he applied his theory to man. This idea of evolution and of natural selection is accepted by most people now, though not exactly in the way Darwin and his followers put it forward. Indeed, it is quite a common thing for people to apply this principle of selection artificially to the breeding of animals and the cultivation of plants and fruits and flowers. Many of the prize animals and plants to-day are new species, artificially created. If man can produce such changes and new species in a relatively short time, what could not Nature do in this line in the course of hundreds of thousands or millions of years ? A visit to a natural history museum, say the South Kensington Museum in London, shows us how plants and animals are continually adapting themselves to nature.

All this seems obvious enough to us now. But it was not so obvious seventy years ago. Most people in Europe still believed at the time in the Biblical account of the creation of the world just 4004 years before Christ, and of each plant and animal being created separately, and finally man. They believed in the Flood and in Noah's Ark with its pairs of animals, so that no species might become extinct. All this did not fit in with the Darwinian theory. Darwin and the geologists talked of millions of years as the age of the earth, and not a paltry 6000 years. So there was a tremendous tussle in the minds of men and women, and many good people did not know what to do. Their old faith told them to believe in one thing, and their reason said another. When people believe blindly in dogmas and the dogmas receive a shock, they feel helpless and miserable and without any solid ground to stand upon. But a shock which wakes us to reality is good.

So there was a great argument and great conflict in England and elsewhere in Europe between science and religion. There could be no doubt of the result. The new world of industry and mechanical transport depended on science, and science thus could not be discarded. Science won all along the line, and " natural selection " and " survival of the fittest " became part of the ordinary jargon of the people, who used the phrases without fully understanding what they meant. Darwin had suggested in his *Descent of Man* that there might have been a common ancestor of man and certain apes. This could not be proved by examples showing various stages in the process of development. From this there grew the popular joke about the " missing link ". And, curiously enough, the ruling classes twisted Darwin's theory to suit their own convenience, and were firmly convinced that it supplied yet another proof of their superiority. They were the fittest to survive in the battle of life, and so by " natural selection " they had come out on top and were the ruling class. This became the justification for one class dominating over another, or one race ruling over another. It became the final argument of imperialism and the supremacy of the white race. And many people in the West thought that the more domineering they were, the more ruthless and strong, the higher up in the scale of human values they were likely to be.   It is not a pleasant philosophy, but it explains to some extent the conduct of western imperialist Powers in Asia and Africa.

Darwin's theories have been criticized subsequently by other scientists, but his general ideas still hold.   One of the results of a general acceptance of his theories was to make people believe in the idea of progress, which meant that man and society, and the world as a whole, were marching towards perfection and becoming better and better.   This idea of progress was not the result of Darwin's theory alone.   The whole trend of scientific discovery and the changes brought about by the Industrial Revolution and afterwards had prepared people's minds for it.   Darwin's theory confirmed it, and people began to imagine themselves as marching proudly from victory to victory to the goal of human perfection, whatever that might be.   It is interesting to note that this idea of progress was quite a new one.   There seems to have been no such idea in the past in Europe or Asia, or in any of the old civilizations.   In Europe, right up to the Industrial Revolution, people looked upon the past as the ideal period.   The old Greek and Roman classical period was supposed to be finer and more advanced and cultured than subsequent periods.   There was progressive deterioration or worsening of the race, so people thought, or at any rate there was no marked change.

In India there is much the same idea of deterioration, of a golden age that is past.   Indian mythology measures time in enormous periods, like the geological periods, but always it begins with the great age, *Satya Yuga*, and comes down to the present age of evil, the *Kali Yuga*.

So we see that the idea of human progress is quite a modern notion.   Our knowledge of past history, such as it is, makes us believe in this idea.   But, then, our knowledge is still very limited, and it may be that with fuller knowledge our outlook might change.   Even to-day there is not quite the same enthusiasm about " progress " as there was in the second half of the nineteenth century.   If progress leads us to destroy each other on a vast scale, as was done in the World War, there is something wrong with such progress.   Another thing worth remembering is that Darwin's " survival of the fittest " does not necessarily mean the survival of the best.   All these are speculations for the learned.   What we have to note is that the old and widespread idea of a static or unchanging, or even deteriorating, society was pushed aside by modern science in the nineteenth century, and in its place came the idea of a dynamic and changing society.   Also there came the idea of progress.   And indeed society did change out of all recognition during this period.

As I have been telling you of Darwin's theory of the origin of species, it might interest you to know what a Chinese philosopher wrote on the subject 2500 years ago.   Tson Tse was his name, and he wrote in the sixth century before Christ, about the time of the Buddha :

" All organizations are originated from a single species.   This

single species had undergone many gradual and continuous changes,
and then gave rise to all organisms of different forms. Such
organisms were not differentiated immediately, but, on the contrary, they acquired their differences through gradual change,
generation after generation.''

This is near enough to Darwin's theory, and it is amazing that the
old Chinese biologist should have arrived at a conclusion which it
took the world two and a half millennia to rediscover.

As the nineteenth century progressed the rate of change became
ever faster. Science produced wonder after wonder, and an endless
pageant of discovery and invention dazzled people's eyes. Many of
these discoveries changed the life of the people greatly, like the
telegraph, the telephone, the automobile and later the aeroplane.
Science dared to measure the farthest heavens and also the invisible
atom and its still smaller components. It lessened the drudgery of
man, and life became easier for millions. Because of science there
was a tremendous increase in the population of the world, and
especially of the industrial countries. At the same time science
evolved the most thoroughgoing methods of destruction. But this
was not the fault of science. It increased man's command over
Nature, but man with all this power did not know how to command
himself. And so he misbehaved often and wasted the gifts of
science. But the triumphant march of science went on, and within
150 years this changed the world more than all the previous many
thousand years had done. Indeed, in every direction and in every
department of life science has revolutionized the world.

This march of science is continuing even now, and it seems to
rush on faster than ever. There is no rest for it. A railway is built.
By the time it is ready to function it is already out of date. A
machine is bought and fixed up; within a year or two better and more
efficient machines of that very kind are being made. And so the
mad race goes on, and now in our time electricity is replacing steam,
and thus bringing about as great a revolution as the Industrial
Revolution of a century and a half ago.

Vast numbers of scientists and experts are continually at work in
the numerous highways and byways of science. The greatest name
in their ranks to-day is that of Albert Einstein, who has succeeded in
modifying to some extent the famous theory of Newton.

So vast has been the recent progress in science and so great the
additions and changes in scientific theory, that scientists themselves
have been taken aback. They have lost all their old complacency
and pride of certainty. They are hesitant now about their conclusions and their prophecies for the future.

But this is a development of the twentieth century and our own
day. In the nineteenth century there was full assurance, and
science, priding itself on its innumerable successes, imposed itself on
the people, and they bowed down to it as to a god.

131

THE ADVANCE OF DEMOCRACY

February 10, 1933

In my last letter I tried to give you a glimpse of the progress of science in the nineteenth century. Let us now look at another aspect of this century—the growth of the democratic idea.

You will remember my telling you of the war of ideas in eighteenth-century France; of Voltaire, the greatest thinker and writer of his day, and of others in France, who challenged many old notions of religion and society and boldly advanced new theories. Such political thinking was largely confined to France at the time. In Germany there were the philosophers who interested themselves in more abstruse questions of philosophy. In England, business and trade were increasing and most people were not fond of thinking unless circumstances made them do so. One notable book, however, came out in England in the second half of the eighteenth century. This was Adam Smith's *Wealth of Nations*. It was not a book on politics as such, but on political economy or economics. This subject, like all other subjects at the time, was mixed up with religion and ethics, and there was thus a great deal of confusion about it. Adam Smith dealt with it in a scientific way and, disregarding all ethical complications, tried to find natural laws which governed economics. Economics, as you perhaps know, deals with the management of the income and expenditure of the people or a country as a whole, of what they produce and what they consume, and their relations with each other and other countries and peoples. Adam Smith believed that all these rather complicated operations took place according to fixed natural laws, which he set down in his book. He also believed that full liberty should be given for the development of industry so that these laws might not be interfered with. This was the beginning of the doctrine of *laissez-faire* about which I have already told you something. Adam Smith's book had nothing to do with the new democratic ideas which were germinating in France at the time. But his attempt at scientific treatment of one of the most important problems which affected men and nations shows that men were going in a new direction, away from the old theological way of looking at everything. Adam Smith is considered the father of the science of economics, and he inspired many English economists of the nineteenth century.

The new science of economics was confined to professors and a few well-read men. But meanwhile the new ideas of democracy were spreading, and the American and French Revolutions gave them tremendous popularity and advertisement. The fine-sounding words and phrases of the American Declaration of Independence and the French Declaration of Rights stirred people to the depths. To the millions who were oppressed and exploited they brought a thrill and a message of deliverance. Both the declarations spoke of liberty and equality and of the right to happiness which every one has.   The proud declaration of these precious rights did not result in the people obtaining them.   Even now, a century and a half after these declarations, few can be said to enjoy them.   But even the declaration of these principles was extraordinary and life-giving.

The old idea in Europe as elsewhere, in Christianity as in other religions, was that sin and unhappiness were the common and inevitable lot of man.   Religion seemed to give a permanent and even an honoured place to poverty and misery in this world.   The promises and rewards of religion were all for some other world; here we were told to bear our lot with resignation and not to seek any fundamental change.   Charity was encouraged, the giving of crumbs to the poor, but there was no idea of doing away with poverty, or with a system which resulted in poverty.   The very ideas of liberty and equality were opposed to the authoritarian outlook of the Church and society.

Democracy did not, of course, say that all men were in fact equal. It could not say this, because it is obvious enough that there are inequalities between different men : physical inequalities which result in some being stronger than others, mental inequalities which are seen in some people being abler or wiser than others, and moral inequalities which make some unselfish and others not so.   It is quite possible that many of these inequalities are due to different kinds of upbringing and education or want of education.   Of two boys or girls who are similar in ability, give one a good education and the other no education, and after some years there will be a vast difference between the two.   Or give one of them healthy food and the other bad and insufficient food, and the former will grow properly, while the latter will be weak and ailing and under-developed.   So one's upbringing and surroundings and training and education make a vast deal of difference, and it may be that if we could give the same training and opportunities to everybody, there would be far less inequality than there is now.   This is indeed very likely.   But so far as democracy is concerned, it admitted that men were as a matter of fact unequal, and yet it stated that each one of them should be treated as having an equal political and social value.   If we accept this democratic theory in its entirety, we are led to all manner of revolutionary conclusions.   We need not go into these at this stage, but one obvious consequence of the theory was that each person should have a vote for the election of a representative to the governing assembly or parliament.   The vote was the symbol of political power, and it was assumed that if every one had a vote, each such person would have an equal share in political power.   Therefore one of the principal demands of democracy, right through the nineteenth century, was the extension of the franchise—that is, the right to vote.   Adult suffrage or franchise meant that every adult or grown-up person should have the vote.   For a long time women were not allowed to vote, and there was not very long ago a tremendous agitation by them, especially in Britain.   In most advanced countries now there is adult suffrage for both men and women.

But, curiously enough, when most people had got the vote they found that it did not make very much difference to them. In spite of having the vote, they had no power, or very little power, in the State. A vote is of little use to a hungry man. The people with real power were those who could take advantage of his hunger and make him work to do anything else that they wanted to their own advantage. Thus political power, which the vote was supposed to give, was seen to be a shadow with no substance, without economic power, and the brave dreams of the early democrats, that equality would follow from the vote, came to nothing.

This was, however, a much later development. In the early days —the end of the eighteenth and the beginning of the nineteenth centuries—there was great enthusiasm among the democrats. Democracy was going to make everybody a free and equal citizen and the government of the State would work for the happiness of everybody. There was a great reaction against the autocracy of kings and governments of the eighteenth century and the way they had abused their absolute power. This led people to proclaim the rights of individuals in their declarations. Probably these statements of the rights of individuals in the American and French declarations erred somewhat on the other side. In a complex society it is not an easy matter to separate individuals and give them perfect freedom. The interests of such an individual and of society may and do clash. However this may be, democracy stood for a great deal of individual freedom.

England, which was backward in political ideas in the eighteenth century, was greatly affected by the American and French Revolutions. The first reaction was one of fear against the new democratic ideas and the possibility of a social revolution at home. The ruling classes became even more conservative and reactionary. But still the new ideas spread among the intellectuals. Thomas Paine was an interesting Englishman of this period. He was in America at the time of the War of Independence and helped the Americans. He seems to have been partly responsible for converting the Americans to the idea of complete independence. On his return to England he wrote a book, *The Rights of Man,* in defence of the French Revolution which had just begun. In this book he attacked monarchy and pleaded for democracy. The British Government outlawed him because of this, and he had to fly to France. In Paris he soon became a member of the National Convention, but in 1793 he was put in prison by the Jacobins because he had opposed the execution of Louis XVI. In the Paris gaol he wrote another book called *The Age of Reason,* in which he criticized the religious outlook. Paine being out of reach of the English courts (he was discharged from the Paris prison after the death of Robespierre), his English publisher was sentenced to imprisonment for issuing this book. Such a book was considered dangerous to society, as religion was supposed to be necessary to keep the poor in their place. Several publishers of Paine's book, including women, were sent to prison. It is interesting to find that Shelley, the poet, wrote a letter of protest to the judge.

In Europe the French Revolution was the parent of the democratic ideas that spread throughout the first half of the nineteenth century. Indeed, the very ideas of the Revolution persisted, although conditions were rapidly changing. These democratic ideas were the intellectual reaction against kings and autocracy. They were based on conditions prior to industrialization. But the new industry—steam and big machinery—were completely upsetting the old order. Yet, strange to say, the radicals and democrats of the early nineteenth century ignored these changes and went on talking in the fine phrases of the Revolution and the Declaration of the Rights of Man. To them perhaps these changes were purely material and did not affect the high spiritual and moral and political demands of democracy. But material things have a way of refusing to be ignored. It is very interesting to find how extraordinarily difficult it is for people to give up old ideas and accept new ones. They will shut their eyes and their minds and refuse to see; they will fight to hold on to the old even when it harms them. They will do almost anything but accept the new ideas and adapt themselves to new conditions. The power of conservatism is prodigious. Even the radicals, who imagine themselves very advanced, often stick to old and exploded ideas, and shut their eyes to changing conditions. It is no wonder that progress is slow, and often there is a great lag between actual conditions and people's ideas—resulting in revolutionary situations.

Democracy was thus for many decades the carrying on of the traditions and ideas of the French Revolution. This failure to adapt itself to the new conditions led to the weakening of democracy towards the end of the century, and later, in the twentieth century, to its repudiation by many people. In India to-day many of our advanced politicians still talk in terms of the French Revolution and the Rights of Man, not appreciating that much has happened since then.

The early democrats naturally took to rationalism. Their demand for freedom of thought and speech could hardly be reconciled with dogmatic religion and theology. Thus democracy joined with science to weaken the hold of theological dogmas. People began to dare to examine the Bible, as if it was an ordinary book and not something that must be accepted blindly and without questioning. This criticism of the Bible was called the " higher criticism ". The critics came to the conclusion that the Bible was a collection of documents written by different persons in different ages. They also were of the opinion that Jesus had no intention of founding a religion. Many of the old beliefs were shaken by this criticism.

As the old religious foundations were being weakened by science and democratic ideas, attempts were made to formulate a philosophy to take the place of the old religion. One of these attempts was by a French philosopher, Auguste Comte, who lived from 1798 to 1857. Comte felt that the old theology and dogmatic religions were out of date, but he was convinced that some kind of religion was a social necessity. He therefore proposed a "religion of humanity" and called it "Positivism." This was to be based on love, order and progress. There was nothing supernatural about it; it was based on science. At its back, as indeed at the back of nearly all current ideas of the nineteenth century, was the idea of the progress of the human race. Comte's religion remained the belief of a few intellectuals only, but his general influence on European thought was great. He may be said to begin the study of the science of sociology, which deals with human society and culture.

A contemporary of Comte's, but surviving him by many years, was the English philosopher and economist, John Stuart Mill (1806–1873). Mill was influenced by Comte's teaching as well as by his socialistic ideas. He tried to give a new direction to the English school of political economy, which had grown up round the teachings of Adam Smith, and brought some socialistic principles into economic thought. But he is best known as the chief " utilitarian ". " Utilitarianism " was a new theory, started a little earlier in England, and brought into greater prominence by Mill. As its name suggests, its guiding philosophy was utility or usefulness. " The greatest happiness of the greatest number " was the fundamental principle of the Utilitarians. This was the only test of right and wrong. Actions were said to be right in proportion as they tended to promote happiness, and wrong in so far as they tended to promote the reverse of happiness. Society and government were to be organized with this point of view—the promotion of the greatest happiness of the greatest number. This view-point was not quite the same as the earlier democratic doctrine of equal rights for everybody. The greatest happiness of the greatest number might conceivably require the sacrifice or the unhappiness of a smaller number. I am merely pointing this difference out to you, but we need not discuss it here. Democracy thus came to mean the rights of the majority.

John Stuart Mill was a strong advocate of the democratic idea of liberty for the individual. He wrote a little book, *On Liberty*, which became famous. I shall give you an extract from this book in favour of freedom of speech and the free expression of opinion.

> " But the peculiar evil of silencing the expression of an opinion is, that it is robbing the human race; posterity as well as the existing generation; those who dissent from the opinion, still more than those who hold it. If the opinion is right, they are deprived of the opportunity of exchanging error for truth; if wrong, they lose, what is almost as great a benefit, the clearer perception and livelier impression of truth, produced by its collision with error. . . . We can never be sure that the opinion we are endeavouring to stifle is a false opinion; and if we were sure, stifling it would be an evil still."

Such an attitude could not be reconciled with that of dogmatic religion or despotism. It was the attitude of a philosopher, a seeker after truth.

I have given you just a few names of important thinkers in western Europe during the nineteenth century to show the way ideas were developing and to serve as landmarks in the world of thought. But the influence of these people, and the early democrats generally, was more or less confined to the intellectual classes. To some extent it

percolated through the intellectuals to the others. Although the
direct influence on the masses was slight, the indirect influence of
this democratic ideology was great. Even the direct influence in
some matters, such as the demand for the vote, was great.

As the nineteenth century grew older other movements and ideas
developed—the working-class movement and socialism. These had
their influence on current democratic notions and were themselves
affected by them. Some people looked upon socialism as an alternative to democracy; others considered it as a necessary part of it.
We have seen that the democrats were full of notions of liberty and
equality and every man's equal right to happiness. But they
realized soon that happiness did not come by merely making it a
fundamental right. Apart from other things, a certain measure of
physical well-being was necessary. A person who was starving was
not likely to be happy. This led them to think that happiness
depended on a better distribution of wealth among the people. This
leads to socialism, and that must wait till our next letter.

In the first half of the nineteenth century democracy and nationalism joined hands wherever subject nations or peoples were fighting
for freedom. Mazzini of Italy was typical of this kind of democratic
patriotism. Later in the century nationalism gradually lost this
democratic character and became more aggressive and authoritarian.
The State became the god which had to be worshipped by every one.

English business men were the leaders of the new industry. They
were not much interested in high democratic principles and the
people's right to liberty. But they discovered that greater liberty
for the people was good for business. It raised the standard of
the workers, and gave them an illusion of possessing some freedom,
and made them more efficient at their work. Popular education was
also required for industrial efficiency. Business men and industrialists, appreciating the expediency of this, piously agreed to confer these
favours on the people. In the second half of the century education
of a kind spread rapidly among the masses in England and western
Europe.

132

THE COMING OF SOCIALISM

February 13, 1933

I HAVE written to you about the advance of democracy; but
remember that it was a hard-fought advance. People who have
interests in an existing order do not want change, and resist it with
all their might. And yet progress or any betterment means such
change; an institution or a method of government has to give place
to a better one. Those who desire such progress must necessarily
attack the old institution or the old custom, and thus their path leads
to constant repudiation of existing conditions and conflict with those

who profit by them.   The ruling classes in western Europe resisted all advance step by step.   In England they gave in only when a refusal might have resulted in a violent revolution.   Another reason for them to advance was, as I have mentioned already, a feeling among the new business people that some democracy was expedient and good for business.

But again I shall remind you that these democratic ideas were, during the first half of the nineteenth century, largely confined to the intellectuals.   The common people had been powerfully affected by the growth of industrialism and driven from the land to the factories.   An industrial working class was growing, huddled up in ugly and insanitary factory towns, usually near the coalfields. These workers were changing rapidly and developing a new mentality. They were very different from the peasants and artisans who had flocked to the factories, urged by starvation.   As England had taken the lead in setting up these factories, she was also the first country to develop this industrial working class.   The conditions in the factories were appalling, the workers' houses or huts were even worse.   There was great misery among them.   Little children and women worked incredibly long hours.   And yet all attempts at improving these factories and houses by legislation were stoutly opposed by the owners.   Was not this a shameful interference, it was said, with the rights of property?   Even the compulsory sanitation of private houses was opposed on this ground.

The poor English workers were dying from slow starvation and overwork.   After the Napoleonic wars the country was exhausted, and there was an economic depression, the workers suffering most by this.   The workers naturally wanted to form associations to protect themselves and to fight for better conditions.   In the old days there had been guilds of artisans and skilled workers, but these were quite different.   Still the memory of these guilds must have been an inducement to the factory-workers to form associations of their own.   But they were prevented from doing so.   The British ruling classes were so frightened by the French Revolution that they made laws—Combination Acts they were called—to prevent the poor workers from even meeting together to discuss their own grievance.   " Law and order ", then in England as now in India, has always performed the very useful function of serving the ends and the pockets of the handful of those in authority.

But laws to prevent them from meeting did not better the conditions of the workers.   They simply exasperated them and made them desperate.   They formed secret associations, taking oaths binding each other to privacy and meeting at dead of night in out-of-way places.   When they were betrayed or found out there were conspiracy cases and terrible punishments.   Sometimes they destroyed the machines in their anger and set fire to the factories, and even killed some of their masters.   At last in 1825 the restrictions on workers' associations were partly removed and trade unions began to be formed.   These unions were formed by the better-paid skilled workers.   The large majority of the unskilled workers remained unorganized for a long time. The workers' movement thus took the shape of trade unions formed for the purpose of bettering the conditions of the workers by means of collective bargaining. The only effective weapon of the workers was the right to strike, that is to stop work and thus bring the factory to a standstill. This was no doubt a great weapon, but their employers had an even more powerful weapon, the ability to starve them into submission. So the struggle of the working class went on with great sacrifices on the part of the workers and slow gains. They had no direct influence on Parliament as they did not even have the vote. The great Reform Bill of 1832, which was so strongly opposed, only gave the vote to the well-to-do middle classes. Not only the workers, but the lower middle classes still had no vote.

Meanwhile there arose a man among the factory-owners of Manchester who was a humanitarian and who was pained at the shocking conditions of the workers. This man was Robert Owen. He introduced many reforms in his own factories and improved the condition of his workers. He carried on an agitation among his own class of employers and tried to convert them by argument to a better treatment of labour. Partly because of him, the British Parliament passed the first law to protect the workers against the greed and selfishness of the employers. This was the Factory Act of 1819. This Act laid down that little children of nine should not be made to work more than twelve hours a day. This provision itself will give you some idea of the terrible conditions to which the workers had to submit.

It was Robert Owen, it is said, who first used the word " socialism" somewhere about 1830. Of course the idea of a levelling-up between the rich and the poor, and a more or less equal distribution of property, was not a new one. Many people had advocated it in the past. In the early communities there had even been a kind of communism, the whole community or village holding land and other property in common. This is called primitive communism, and is to be found in many countries, including India. But the new socialism was something much more than a vague desire to equalize people. It was more definite and, to begin with, it was meant to apply to the new factory system of production. It was thus a child of the industrial system. Owen's idea was to have workers' co-operative societies, and that workers should have a share in the factories. He established model factories and settlements in England and America with more or less success. But he failed to convert his brother employers or the government. His influence during his time, however, was great, and he gave currency to a word, socialism, which has since captivated millions.

All this time capitalist industry was growing, and as it recorded success after success, the problem of the working class grew with it. Capitalism resulted in more and more production, and because of this the population grew with enormous speed, as more people could now be supported and fed. Huge businesses were built up with intricate co-operation between their different sections, and at the same time the competition of little businesses was crushed out. Wealth was poured into England, but much of this went to start new factories or railways or other such concerns. The workers tried to get better conditions by strikes, which usually failed miserably, and then joined the Chartist movement of the 'forties. This Chartist movement collapsed in the year of revolution, 1848.

The successes of capitalism dazzled people, but still there were some radicals or people with advanced views, or humanitarians, who were not happy at its cut-throat competition and the suffering it caused the workers in spite of the country's growing wealth. In England and Germany and France these people considered various alternatives to it. Several solutions were suggested, and they are all grouped together under the name of socialism or collectivism or social democracy, each of these words vaguely meaning the same thing. There was general agreement among these reformers that the trouble lay in the private ownership and control of industry. If instead of this the State could own and control this, or at any rate the principal means of production, like the land and the chief industries, then there would be no danger of the workers being exploited. So, rather vaguely, people sought an alternative to the capitalist system. But the capitalist system had no intention of collapsing. It was going from strength to strength.

These socialistic ideas were started by intellectuals and, in the case of Robert Owen, by a factory-owner. The workers' trade-union movement developed on different lines for a while, merely seeking higher wages and better conditions. But it was naturally influenced by these ideas, and in its turn it greatly influenced the development of socialism. In each of the three leading industrial countries in Europe—England, France and Germany—socialism developed somewhat differently, in accordance with the strength and character of the working class in each country. On the whole, English socialism was conservative and believed in evolutionary methods and slow progress; Continental socialism was more radical and revolutionary. In America conditions were very different because of the vastness of the country and the demand for labour, and so no strong working-class movement grew up for a long time.

From the middle of the century onwards, for a generation, British industry dominated the world, and wealth poured in both from profits of industry and the exploitation of India and other dependencies. A part of this great wealth managed to reach even the workers, and their standards of living rose to a height which they had never known before. Prosperity and revolution have little in common, and the old revolutionary spirit of the British workers disappeared. Even the British brand of socialism became the most moderate of all. Fabianism this was called, from an old Roman general who refused to give direct battle to the enemy, but gradually wore them out. In 1867 the British franchise was still further extended and some of the city workers got the vote. The trade unions were so well-behaved and prosperous that the labour vote was given to the British Liberal Party.

While England was smug and complacent with prosperity, on the Continent of Europe a new creed was finding enthusiastic and ardent support. This was anarchism, a word which seems to terrify many people who know nothing about it. Anarchism meant a society with, as far as possible, no central government and with a great deal of individual freedom. The anarchist ideal was extraordinarily high : " Faith in the ideal of a commonwealth based on altruism, solidarity, and voluntary respect for the other fellow's rights ". There was to be no force or compulsion on the part of the State. " That government is best which governs not at all; and when men are prepared for it that will be the kind of government which they will have ", said an American, Thoreau.

This seems a very fine ideal—perfect freedom for everybody, each person respecting the other, unselfishness all round, willing co-operation—but the present-day world, with all its selfishness and violence, is far removed from it. The anarchists' desire for no central government or a minimum of government must have arisen as a reaction from the autocracy and despotism under which people had suffered for so long. Governments had crushed them and tyrannized over them, therefore let there be no governments. The anarchists also felt that under some forms of socialism, the State, being master of all the means of production, might itself become despotic. The anarchists were therefore socialists of a kind, laying great stress on local and individual freedom. Many of the socialists, on the other hand, were prepared to agree to the anarchist creed as a distant ideal, but were of opinion that for some time it would be necessary to have a centralized and strong State government under socialism. Thus, although there was a great deal of difference between socialism and anarchism, there were many shades of each, gradually approaching and overlapping each other.

Modern industry gave rise to an organized working class. Anarchism, by its very nature, could not be a well-organized movement. Anarchistic ideas therefore had little chance of spreading in industrialized countries where trade unions and the like were growing up. England thus had no appreciable number of anarchists, nor had Germany. But southern and eastern Europe, which were backward in industrialism, were more fertile ground for these ideas. As modern industry spread to the south and east, anarchism became weaker and weaker. To-day it is practically a dead creed, but even now it is represented to some extent in a non-industrialized country like Spain.

Anarchism as an ideal may have been very fine, but it gave shelter not only to excitable and dissatisfied people, but also to selfish individuals who tried to seek profit for themselves under cloak of the ideal. And it led to a type of violence which has now become associated with the word in every one's mind and which has brought much discredit on it. Unable to do anything on a big scale to change society as they wanted, some anarchists decided to do propaganda in a novel way. This was the " propaganda by the deed ", the influence of courageous example, brave deeds to resist tyranny and sacrifice one's own life. There were risings in various place undertaken in this spirit. Those who took part in them expected no success at the time. Willingly they risked their lives to do this novel kind of propaganda for their cause. Of course these risings were put down, and then individual anarchists began to resort to terrorism, the throwing of the bomb, the shooting of kings and high officials. This foolish violence was obviously a sign of growing weakness and despair. Gradually, towards the end of the nineteenth century, anarchism as a movement faded away. The throwing of bombs and the " propaganda by the deed " were not approved of by many of the leading anarchists, who repudiated them.

I shall give you some well-known names of anarchists. It is interesting to note that most of these anarchist leaders were extraordinarily gentle, idealistic and likeable in their private lives. The earliest of the anarchist leaders was a Frenchman, Pierre Proudhon, who lived from 1809 to 1865. Slightly younger than him was a Russian noble, Michel Bakunin, who was a popular leader of European labour, especially in the south. He came into conflict with Marx, who drove him and his followers out of the international union he had formed. A third name, which brings us almost to our day, is that of Peter Kropatkin, another Russian, and a prince. He has written some very interesting books on anarchism and other subjects. The fourth and the last name I shall mention here is that of an Italian, Enrico Malatesta, over eighty years old, the last relic of the great anarchists of the nineteenth century.

There is a fine story about Malatesta which I must tell you. He was being prosecuted in a court of law in Italy. The government prosecutor argued that Malatesta's influence among the workers of the area was very great and that it had entirely changed their character. It was putting an end to criminality and crimes were getting rare. If all crime stopped, what would the courts do? So Malatesta ought to be sent to gaol ! And to gaol he was sent for six months.

Unfortunately anarchism has been identified too much with violence, and people have forgotten that it is a philosophy and an ideal which has appealed to many fine men. As an ideal it is still very far off from our present imperfect world, and our modern civilization is much too complicated for its simple remedies.

133

KARL MARX AND THE GROWTH OF WORKERS' ORGANIZATIONS

February 14, 1933

ABOUT the middle of the nineteenth century there appeared in the world of European labour and socialism a new and arresting personality. This man was Karl Marx, whose name has already appeared in these letters.   He was a German Jew, born in 1818, who became a student of law and history and philosophy.   He came into conflict with the German authorities because of a newspaper he brought out.   He went to Paris, where he came into touch with new people and read the new books on socialism and anarchism, and became a convert to the socialistic idea.   Here he met another German, Friedrich Engels, who had settled in England and had become a rich factory-owner in the growing cotton industry.   Engels was also unhappy and dissatisfied with existing social conditions, and his mind was seeking remedies for the poverty and exploitation he saw around him.   Robert Owen's ideas and attempts at reform appealed to him, and he became an Owenite, as Owen's followers were called.   The visit to Paris, which led to the first meeting with Karl Marx, changed him also.   Marx and Engels henceforward became close friends and colleagues, holding the same views, and working whole-heartedly together for the same cause.   They were about the same age.   So close was their co-operation that most of the books that they issued were joint books.

The French Government of the day—it was the time of Louis Philippe—expelled Marx from Paris.   He went to London, and there he lived for many years, burying himself in the books of the British Museum.   He worked hard and perfected his theories and wrote about them.   And yet he was by no means a mere professor or philosopher spinning theories and cut off from ordinary affairs. Whilst he developed and clarified the rather vague ideology of the socialist movement, and placed definite and clear-cut ideas and objectives before it, he also took an active and leading part in the organization of the movement and of the workers.   The events that took place in 1848, the year of revolution in Europe, naturally moved him greatly.   In that very year he and Engels jointly issued a manifesto which has become very famous.   This was the *Communist Manifesto*, in which they discussed the ideas which lay behind the great French Revolution as well as the subsequent revolts in 1830 and 1848, and pointed out how inadequate and inconsistent they were with actual conditions.   They criticized the then prevailing democratic cries of liberty, equality and fraternity, and pointed out that they meant little to the people, and merely gave a pious covering to the *bourgeois* State.   They then briefly developed their own theory of socialism, and ended the manifesto by an appeal to all workers :   "Workers of the World, unite.   You have nothing to lose but your chains, and have a world to win ! "

This appeal was a call to action.   Marx followed it up by ceaseless propaganda in newspapers and pamphlets and by efforts to bring the workers' organizations together.   He seems to have felt that a great crisis was coming in Europe, and he wanted the workers to be ready for it so that they might take full advantage of it.   According to his socialistic theory, the crisis was indeed bound to occur under the capitalistic system.   Writing in a New York newspaper in 1854 Marx said :

"Yet, we must not forget that a sixth power exists in Europe, maintaining at certain moments its domination over all five so-called ' great powers ', and causing them all to tremble.   This power is revolution.   After having long dwelt in quiet retirement, it is now again summoned to the field of battle by crises and starvation. . . . There is needed only a signal, and the sixth and greatest European power will step forth in shining armour, sword in hand, like Minerva from the brow of the Olympian.   The impending European war will give the signal."

Marx did not prove a correct prophet about the impending revolution in Europe.   It took more than sixty years, after he wrote this, and a World War, to bring about the revolution in one part of Europe. An attempt in 1871, the Paris Commune, was, as we have seen, mercilessly crushed.

In 1864 Marx succeeded in gathering a motley assembly in London.   There were many groups calling themselves, rather vaguely, socialists.   On the one side, there were democrats and patriots from several European countries under foreign rule whose belief in socialism was in something very distant and who were immediately more interested in national independence; on the other, there were the anarchists out for immediate battle.   Besides Marx, the outstanding personality was that of Bakunin, the anarchist leader, who had managed to escape from Siberia three years before after many years of imprisonment.   Bakunin's followers came chiefly from south Europe, the Latin countries like Italy and Spain, which were industrially backward and undeveloped.   They were unemployed intellectuals and other odd revolutionary elements who found no place in the existing social order.   Marx's followers came from the industrial countries, especially Germany, where the workers' conditions were better.   Marx thus represented the growing and organized and relatively well-to-do working class, Bakunin the poorer, unorganized workers and intellectuals and malcontents.   Marx was for patient organization and education of the workers in his socialistic theories till the hour came for action, which he expected soon enough. Bakunin and his followers were for immediate action.   On the whole Marx won.   An " International Working-Men's Association " was established.   This was the first of the Workers' " Internationals ", as they were called.

Three years later, in 1867, Marx's great book, *Das Kapital* or " Capital ", was published in German.   This was the product of his long years of labour in London, and in this he analysed and criticized existing theories of economics and explained at length his own socialistic theory.   It was a purely scientific work.   He dealt with the development of history and economics dispassionately and scientifically, avoiding all vagueness and idealism.   He discussed especially the growth of the industrial civilization of the big machine, and he drew certain far-reaching conclusions about evolution and history and the conflict of classes in human society.   This new clear-cut and cogently argued socialism of Marx was therefore called " scientific socialism ", as opposed to the vague " utopian " or " idealistic " socialism which had so far prevailed.   Marx's *Capital* is not an easy

book to read ; indeed, it is about as far removed from light reading
as one can imagine.   But none the less it is of the select company
of those few books which have affected the way of thinking of large
numbers of people, changed their whole ideology, and thus influenced
human development.

In 1871 came the tragedy of the Paris Commune, perhaps the first
conscious socialistic revolt.   This frightened European governments
and made them harsher to the workers' movement.   The next year
there was a meeting of the Workers' " International ", founded by
Marx, and he succeeded in transferring the headquarters of this to
New York.   Marx did this apparently to get rid of the anarchist
followers of Bakunin, and also perhaps because he thought that it
would have a safer lodging there than under the European governments, which were angry because of the Paris Commune.   But it was
not possible for the International to exist so far away from its nerve
centres.   All its strength lay in Europe, and even in Europe the
workers' movement was having a hard time.   So the First International gradually expired.

Marxism or Marxian socialism spread among European socialists,
especially in Germany and Austria, where it was generally known
as " social democracy ".   England, however, did not take to it
kindly.   It was too prosperous at the time for any advanced social
creed.   The British brand of socialism was represented by the Fabian
Society with a very mild programme of distant change.   The
Fabians had nothing to do with the workers.   They were advanced
liberal intellectuals.   George Bernard Shaw was one of the early
Fabians.   Their policy may be gathered from the famous phrase of
another noted Fabian, Sidney Webb : " the inevitability of
gradualness ".

In France it took a dozen years' slow recovery after the Commune
for socialism to become an active force again.   But it took a new
form there, a cross between anarchism and socialism.   This was
called " syndicalism " from the French *syndicat*, a working-men's
organization or trade union.   The socialistic theory was that the
State, representing society as a whole, should own and control the
means of production—that is, land and factories, etc.   There was
some difference of opinion as to how far this socialization should go.
There are obviously many personal things like tools and domestic
machines which it might be absurd to socialize.   But socialists were
agreed that anything which could be used for making private profit
out of other people's work should be socialized, that is, made the
property of the State.   Syndicalists, like anarchists, did not like
the State, and tried to limit its power.   They wanted each industry
to be controlled by the workers in that industry, by its *syndicat*.
The idea was that the various syndicates would elect representatives
to a general council.   This council would look after the affairs of the
whole country, and act as a kind of parliament for general affairs,
without the power to interfere with the inner arrangements of the
industry.   To bring about this state of affairs syndicalists advocated
the general strike, to bring the life of the country to a standstill, and

thus gain their objective. The Marxists did not approve of syndicalism at all, but, curiously enough, the syndicalists considered Marx (this was after his death) as one of themselves.

Karl Marx died in 1883, just fifty years ago. By that time powerful trade unions had grown up in England and Germany and other industrial countries. British industry had seen its best days and was declining in face of the growing competition of Germany and America. America of course had great natural advantages, which helped in rapid industrial growth. Germany was a curious mixture of political autocracy (tempered by a weak and powerless parliament) and industrial advance. The German Government under Bismarck, and even later, helped industry in many ways and tried to win over the working class by social reform which bettered their conditions. In the same way the English Liberals also passed some measures of social reform, lessening hours of work and improving the workers' lot to some extent. So long as prosperity lasted this method worked, and the English workers remained moderate and subdued and faithfully voted for the Liberals. But in the 'eighties the competition of other countries brought about an end to the long prosperous period, and a trade depression set in in England, and the wages of workers fell. So again there was an awakening of the working class, and a revolutionary spirit was in the air. Many people in England began to look to Marxism.

In 1889 another attempt was made to form a Workers' International. Many trade unions and labour parties were strong and wealthy now, with large numbers of paid officials. This International formed in 1889 (I think it was called the " Labour and Socialist International ") is called the " Second International ". It lasted for a quarter of a century, till the Great War came to test it and found it wanting. This International had many people in its ranks who later took high office in their countries. Some used the labour movement for their own advancement and then deserted it. They became prime ministers and presidents and the like; they had succeeded in life; but the millions who had helped them on and had faith in them were deserted and left where they were. These leaders, even those who swore by the name of Marx or were fiery syndicalists, went into parliaments, or became well-paid trade-union chiefs, and it became more and more difficult for them to risk their comfortable positions in rash undertakings. So they quietened down, and even when the masses of the workers, forced by desperation, became revolutionary and demanded action, they tried to keep them down. Social democrats of Germany became (after the War) president and chancellor of the Republic; in France Briand, fiery syndicalist preaching the General Strike, became prime minister eleven times and crushed a strike of his old comrades; in England, Ramsay MacDonald became prime minister, and deserted his own Labour Party which had made him; so also in Sweden, Denmark, Belgium, Austria. Western Europe to-day is full of dictators and people in authority who were socialists in their earlier days, but, as they aged, they mellowed down and forgot their old enthusiasm for

the cause, and sometimes even turned against their old-time colleagues.   Mussolini, the Duce of Italy, is an old socialist; so also is
Pilsudski, the Dictator of Poland.

The labour movement and almost every national movement for
independence has often suffered by such defections of its leaders and
prominent workers.   They grow tired after a while, weary of non-
success, and the empty crown of a martyr does not appeal for long.
They quieten down and the fire of their enthusiasm takes a duller
hue.   Some, who are more ambitious or more unscrupulous, walk across
to the other side and make individual truce with those they had so
far opposed and combated.   It is easy enough to reconcile one's
conscience to any step that one desires to take.   The movement
suffers and has a little setback by this defection, and because those
who fight labour and suppress nationalities know this well, they try
to win over individuals to their side by all manner of inducements
and fair words.   But individual preferment or fair words bring no
relief to the mass of the workers or to a suppressed nation striving to
be free.   So despite desertions and setbacks the struggle inevitably
goes on to its appointed end.

The Second International, started in 1889, grew in numbers and
respectability.   A few years later they turned out the anarchists
under Malatesta on the ground that they refused to take advantage
of the vote for parliaments.   The socialists of the International
showed that they preferred parliaments to association with their old
comrades in a common struggle.   Brave declarations were made by
them as to the duty of socialists in the event of war in Europe.
Socialists recognized no national boundaries so far as their work was
concerned.   They were not nationalists in the ordinary sense of
the word.   They said they would oppose war.   But when war did
come in 1914 the whole structure of the Second International broke
up, and socialists and labour parties in each country, and even
anarchists like Kropatkin, became rabid nationalists and haters of
the other country, as much as any one else.   Only a minority resisted,
and as a consequence were made to suffer greatly in many ways,
including long terms of imprisonment.

After the war was over, Lenin started a new Workers' International
in Moscow in 1919.   This was a purely communist organization, and
only declared communists could join it.   This exists now, and is
called the Third International.   The relics of the old Second
International also gradually collected themselves together after the
war.   A few allied themselves to the new Moscow Third International, but most of them disliked Moscow and its creed intensely
and refused to come anywhere near it.   They revived the Second
International.   This also exists now.   So that at present there are
two International Workers' organizations, briefly known as the
Second and Third Internationals.   Strangely enough, they both
swear by Marxism, but each has its own interpretation, and yet they
hate each other even more than they do their common enemy,
capitalism.

These Internationals do not include all the trade unions and working men's organizations in the world. Many of them do not belong to either. The American trade unions stand apart because most of them are very conservative. The Indian trade unions also do not belong to either International.

Perhaps you know the song *Internationale*. This is the accepted workers' and socialists' song all the world over.

134

MARXISM

February 16, 1933

I HAD intended telling you something in my last letter of the ideas of Marx which created so much commotion in the world of European socialism. But that letter had grown long enough, and I had to hold this over. It is not an easy subject for me to write about, as I am no expert in it, and, as it happens, even the experts and the pandits differ. I shall only give you some leading characteristics of Marxism, and avoid the difficult parts of it. This will give you rather a patchy picture, but, then, it is not my aim in these letters to provide full and detailed pictures of anything.

Socialism, I have told you, is of many kinds. There is general agreement, however, that it aims at the control by the State of the means of production—that is, land and mines and factories and the like—and the means of distribution, like railways, etc., and also banks and similar institutions. The idea is that individuals should not be allowed to exploit any of these methods or institutions, or the labour of others, to their own personal advantage. To-day most of these are privately owned and exploited, with the result that some people prosper and grow rich, while society as a whole suffers greatly and the masses remain poor. Also a great deal of the energy of even the owners and controllers of these means of production goes at present in fighting each other in cut-throat competition. If instead of this private war there was a sensible arranging of production and a well-thought-out distribution, waste and useless competition would be avoided, and the present great inequalities in wealth between different classes and peoples would disappear. Therefore production and distribution and other important activities should be largely socialized or controlled by the State—that is, by the people as a whole. That is the basic idea of socialism.

What the State or form of government should be like under socialism is a different question into which we need not go for the moment, although it is a very important matter.

Having agreed as to the ideal of socialism, the next thing to decide is how one is to achieve it. Here socialists part company with each other, and there are many groups pointing different ways. Roughly they may be divided into two classes : (1) the slow-change, evolutionary groups, which believe in going ahead step by step and working through parliaments, like the British Labour Party and the Fabians; and (2) the revolutionary groups, which do not believe in achieving results through parliaments. These latter groups are mostly Marxist.

The former evolutionary groups are now very small in number, and even those in England are weakening and the line dividing them from the Liberals and other non-socialist groups is thinning away. So Marxism might now be considered the general socialist creed. But among Marxists also there are two main divisions in Europe—there are the Russian communists on the one hand, and the old social democrats of Germany, Austria and elsewhere on the other —and between the two there is no love lost. These social democrats lost much of their old prestige by their failure to live up to their professions during the World War and afterwards. Many of their more ardent spirits have gone over to the communists, but they still control the great trade-union machines in western Europe. Communism, because of its success in Russia, is an advancing creed. In Europe and all over the world to-day it is the chief opponent of capitalism.

What, then, is this Marxism? It is a way of interpreting history and politics and economics and human life and human desires. It is a theory as well as a call to action. It is a philosophy which has something to say about most of the activities of man's life. It is an attempt at reducing human history, past, present and future, to a rigid logical system with something of the inevitability of fate or *kismet* about it. Whether life is so very logical, after all, and so dependent on hard-and-fast rules and systems does not seem very obvious, and many have doubted this. But Marx surveyed past history as a scientist and drew certain conclusions from it. He saw from the earliest days man struggling for a living; it was a struggle against Nature as well as against brother-man. Man worked to get food and the other necessities of life, and his methods of doing so gradually changed as time went on, and became more complex and advanced. These methods to produce the means of living were, according to Marx, the most important thing in man's life and society's life in every age. They dominated each period of history and influenced all activities and social relations of that period, and as they changed great historical and social changes followed them. To some extent we have traced the great effects of these changes in the course of these letters. For instance, when first agriculture was introduced, it made a vast difference. The wandering nomads settled down and villages and cities grew, and because of the greater yield of agriculture, there was a surplus left over, and population grew, and wealth and leisure, which gave rise to arts and handicrafts. Another obvious instance is the Industrial Revolution, when the introduction of big machinery for production made another tremendous difference. And there are many other instances.

The methods of production at a certain period of history correspond to a definite stage in the growth of the people. In the course of this work of production, and as a consequence of it, men enter into definite relations with each other (such as barter, buying, selling, exchange and so on), which are conditioned by, and which correspond to their methods of production. These relations taken as a whole constitute the economic structure of society. And on this economic basis are built up the laws, politics, social customs, ideas and everything else. Therefore, according to this view of Marx, as the methods of production change, the economic structure changes, and this is followed by a change in people's ideas, laws, politics, etc.

Marx also looked upon history as a record of struggles between different classes. "The history of all human society, past and present, has been the history of class struggles." The class which controls the means of production is dominant. It exploits the labour of other classes and profits by it. Those who labour do not get the full value of their labour. They get just a part of it for bare necessaries, the rest, the surplus, goes to the exploiting class. So the exploiting class gets wealthier from this surplus value. The State and government are controlled by this class which controls production, and the first object of the State thus becomes one of protecting this governing class. "The State is an executive committee for managing the affairs of the governing class as a whole", says Marx. Laws are made for this purpose, and people are led to believe by means of education, religion, and other methods, that the dominance of this class is just and natural. Every attempt is made to cover the class character of the government and the laws by these methods, so that the other classes that are being exploited may not find out the true state of affairs, and thus get dissatisfied. If any person does get dissatisfied and challenges this system, he is called an enemy of society and morality, and a subverter of old-established customs, and is crushed by the State.

But in spite of all efforts, one class cannot remain permanently dominant. The very factors that gave it dominance now work against it. It had become the ruling and exploiting class because it controlled the then existing means of production. Now, as new methods of production arise, the new classes which control these come into prominence, and they refuse to be exploited. New ideas stir men; there is what might be called an ideological revolution which breaks the fetters of the old ideas and dogmas. And then there is a struggle between this rising class and the old class which clings hard to power. The new class inevitably wins, because it controls the economic power now, and the old class, having played its part in history, fades away.

The victory of this new class is both political and economic; it symbolizes the triumph of the new methods of production. And from this follow changes in the whole fabric of society—new ideas, a new political structure, laws, customs, everything is affected. This new class becomes now the exploiting class to the classes under it, till in its turn it is displaced by one of them. So the struggle goes on, and must go on till there is no one class exploiting another.

Only when classes disappear and there is only one class left will the struggle end, for then there will be no further opportunity for exploitation. This one class cannot exploit itself. Only then will there be equilibrium in society and full co-operation, instead of ceaseless struggle and competition, as at present. And the State's chief business of coercion will no longer be required, for there will be no class to coerce, and so gradually the State itself will " wither away ", and thus the anarchist ideal will also be approached.

So Marx looked upon history as a grand process of evolution by inevitable class struggles. With a wealth of detail and example he showed how this had taken place in the past, how the feudal times had changed to the capitalist period with the coming of the big machine, and the feudal classes given place to the *bourgeoisie*. According to him, the last class struggle was taking place in our times between the *bourgeoisie* and the working class. Capitalism was itself producing and increasing the numbers and strength of this class, which would ultimately overwhelm it and establish the classless society and socialism.

This view of looking at history which Marx explained was called the " materialist conception of history ". It was called " materialist " because it was not " idealist ", a word which was used a great deal in a special sense by philosophers in Marx's day. The idea of evolution was becoming popular at the time. Darwin, as I have told you, established it in the popular mind so far as the origin and development of species were concerned. But this did not explain in any way human social relations. Some philosophers had tried to explain human progress by vague idealistic notions of the progress of the mind. Marx said that this was a wrong approach. Vague speculation in the air and idealism were, according to him, dangerous, as in this way people were likely to imagine all manner of things which had no real basis in fact. He proceeded therefore in a scientific way, examining facts. Hence the word " materialist ".

Marx constantly talks of exploitation and class struggles. Many of us become angry and excited at the injustice which we see around us. But, according to Marx, this is not a matter for anger or good virtuous advice. The exploitation is not the fault of the person exploiting. The dominance of one class over another has been the natural result of historical progress, and in due time gives place to another arrangement. If a person belonged to the dominant class, and as such exploited others, this was not a terrible sin for him. He was a part of a system, and it was absurd to call him unkind names. We are much too apt to forget this distinction between individuals and systems. India is under British imperialism, and we fight this imperialism with all our might. But the Englishmen who happen to support this system in India are not to blame. They are just little cogs in a huge machine, powerless to make any difference to its movement. In the same way, some of us may consider the *zamīndāri* system out of date and most harmful to the tenantry which is exploited terribly under it. But that again does not mean that the individual *zamindar* is to blame; so also the capitalists who are often blamed as exploiters. The fault always lies with the system, not with individuals.

Marx did not preach class conflict. He showed that in fact it existed, and had always existed in some form or other. His object in writing *Capital* was " to lay bare the economic law of motion of modern society ", and this uncovering disclosed these fierce conflicts between different classes in society. These conflicts are not always obvious as class struggles, because the dominant class always tries to hide its own class character. But when the existing order is threatened, then it throws away all pretence and its real character appears, and there is open warfare between the classes. Forms of democracy and ordinary laws and procedure all disappear when this happens. Instead of these class struggles being due to mis-understanding or the villainy of agitators, as some people say, they are inherent in society, and they actually increase with a better understanding of the conflict of interests.

Let us compare this theory of Marx's with existing conditions in India. The British Government has long claimed that its rule in India was based on justice and the good of the people of India, and there is no doubt that in the past many of our countrymen believed that there was some little truth in this claim. But now that this rule is seriously challenged by a great popular movement, its real character appears in all its crudity and nakedness, and any one can see the reality of this imperialist exploitation resting on the bayonet. All the covering of gilded forms and soft words has been removed. Special ordinances and the suppression of the most ordinary rights of speech, meeting, the Press, become the ordinary laws and procedure of the country. The greater the challenge to existing authority, the more will this happen. So also when one class seriously threatens another. We can see this happening in our country to-day in the savage sentences given to the peasants and workers and those who work for them.

Marx's theory of history was thus of an ever-changing and advancing society. There was no fixity in it. It was a dynamic conception. And it marched on inevitably whatever might happen, one social order being replaced by another. But a social order only disappeared after it had run its course and grown to its fullest extent. When society grew beyond this, then it simply tore the clothes of the old order, which it had outgrown and which fettered it, and put on new and bigger garments.

It was man's destiny, according to Marx, to help in this grand historical process of development. All the previous stages had been passed. The last class struggle between the capitalist *bourgeois* society and the working class was now taking place. (This was, of course, in the advanced industrial countries where capitalism was fully developed. Other countries where capitalism was not developed were backward, and their struggles were therefore of a somewhat mixed and different character. But essentially even there some aspect of this struggle was taking place, as the world was becoming more and more inter-related.) Marx said that capitalism would have to face difficulty after difficulty, crisis after crisis, till it toppled over, because of its inherent 'want of equilibrium. It is more than sixty years since Marx wrote, and capitalism has had many a crisis since then. But far from ending, it has survived them, and has grown more powerful, except in Russia, where it exists no longer. But now, as I write, it seems to be grievously sick all over the world, and doctors shake their heads about its chances of recovery.

It is said that capitalism managed to prolong its life to our day because of a factor which perhaps Marx did not fully consider. This was the exploitation of colonial empires by the industrial countries of the West. This gave fresh life and prosperity to it, at the expense, of course, of the poor countries so exploited.

We condemn often enough the exploitation of the poor by the rich, of the worker by the capitalist, under present-day capitalism. This is no doubt a fact, not because of the fault of the capitalist, but because the system itself is based on such exploitation. At the same time let us not imagine that this is a new thing under capitalism. Exploitation has been the hard and invariable lot of the workers and the poor in past ages under all systems. Indeed, it can be said that, in spite of capitalist exploitation, they are better off to-day than during any past period. But that is not saying very much.

The greatest modern exponent of Marxism has been Lenin. Not only did he expound it and explain it, but he lived up to it. And yet he has warned us not to consider Marxism as a dogma which cannot be varied. Convinced of the truth of its essence, he was not prepared to accept or apply its details everywhere unthinkingly. He tells us :

" In no sense do we regard the Marxist theory as something complete and unassailable. On the contrary, we are convinced that that theory is only the corner-stone of that science which socialists must advance in all directions if they do not wish to fall behind life. We think that it is especially necessary for Russian Socialists to undertake an independent study of the Marxist theory, for that theory gives only general guiding ideas, which can be applied differently in England, for instance, than in France, differently in France than in Germany, differently in Germany than in Russia."

I have tried to tell you in this letter something about Marx's theories, but I do not know if you can make much of this patchwork of mine, and whether it will convey any clear-idea to you. It is well to know these theories, because they are moving vast masses of men and women to-day and they may be of help to us in our own country. A great nation, Russia, as well as the other parts of the Soviet Union, have made Marx their major prophet, and in the world's great distress to-day many people in search of remedies look to him for possible inspiration.

I shall finish up this letter by quoting some lines from the English poet Tennyson :

> " The old order changeth yielding place to new,
> And God fulfils himself in many ways,
> Lest one good custom should corrupt the world."

135

THE VICTORIAN AGE IN ENGLAND

February 22, 1933

IN my letters dealing with the growth of the socialistic idea I have pointed out to you that the English type of socialism was the most moderate of all. It was the least revolutionary of the ideologies then prevalent in Europe, and it looked forward to a very gradual and step-by-step change to better conditions. Sometimes, when trade was bad, and there was a depression and unemployment increased and wages fell and people suffered, then a revolutionary wave would rise even in England. But with the return of better conditions this would subside. This moderation of English thought during the nineteenth century was intimately connected with the prosperity of England, for prosperity and revolution have little in common. Revolution means a great change, and those who are fairly satisfied with existing conditions have no desire to rush into risky and rash adventures on the off-chance of bettering them.

The nineteenth century was indeed the century of England's greatness. The lead she had taken in the eighteenth century, by having the Industrial Revolution and building the new factories in advance of other countries, she maintained for the greater part of the nineteenth. She was, as I have said, the workshop of the world, and wealth poured into her from far countries. The exploitation of India and other colonial possessions gave her a rich and unceasing tribute and added greatly to her prestige. While changes took place in almost all the countries of Europe, England seemed to continue without any revolution, strong and solid as a rock. There were crises from time to time, but they were overcome by giving a few more people the vote. Meanwhile, as we have seen, in France republics and empires gave way to each other in rapid succession; in Italy a new nation arose uniting the whole peninsula after long ages of disunion; in Germany a new empire came into being. The smaller countries, like Belgium, Denmark, Greece, also changed in many ways. Austria, the seat still of the oldest dynasty in Europe, the Hapsburg, had been humbled repeatedly by France, Italy and Prussia. Only Russia, in the east, appeared unchanging, with the autocratic Tsar ruling like a Great Moghal. But Russia was very backward industrially and was a peasant nation; the breath of the new ideas and the new industry had not yet touched her.

England's wealth and empire and sea-power gave her a

commanding position in Europe and the world. She was the leading nation, with her tentacles all over the world. The United States of America were still wrapped up in their own troubles and concerned more with their internal growth than with world affairs. Wonderful changes were taking place in methods of transport, making the world apparently smaller and more compact. These again helped England in tightening her hold on distant lands. In spite of all these changes England's form of government remained the same : a constitutional monarch—that is, a ruler with little power, and a parliament supposed to be supreme. The parliament was at first elected by a handful of landowners and rich merchants, but more and more people were given the vote in the course of the century to ward off trouble, whenever a crisis arose.

For a great part of the century Victoria was Queen of England. She belonged to the German House of Hanover, which had given a number of Georges to the English throne during the eighteenth century. She came to the throne in 1837, as a girl of eighteen, and she reigned for sixty-three years till the end of the century, 1900. This long period in England is often referred to as the Victorian Age. Queen Victoria thus saw many great changes in Europe and elsewhere, old landmarks disappearing and new ones taking their place. She saw the revolutions in Europe, the change in France, and the rise of the Italian kingdom and the German Empire. By the time she died she was a kind of grandmother to Europe and European monarchs. But there was one other ruler in Europe, a contemporary of Victoria's, who had a similar record. This was Francis Joseph of the house of Hapsburg of Austria. He was also eighteen when he came to the throne of his ramshackle empire in the year of revolution, 1848. For sixty-eight years he reigned, and managed to keep Austria and Hungary and other parts under him held together. But the World War put an end to him and his empire.

Victoria was more fortunate. During her reign she watched the power of England grow and her empire spread out. There was trouble in Canada when she came to the throne. The colony was in open rebellion, and many of the colonists wanted to break away from England and join their neighbours, the United States of America. But England had learnt a lesson from the American war, and she hastened to appease the Canadians by giving them a large measure of self-rule. Soon afterwards this developed into a full self-governing dominion. This was a new type of experiment in empire, for freedom and empire go ill together, but circumstances forced England's hand, as the alternative was the loss of Canada. As the majority of people in Canada were of English descent, there was a strong sentimental bond with the mother-country. The new country, being a vast undeveloped land with a sparse population, had to rely a great deal on English manufactures and English money for development. So there was no conflict then between the interests of the two countries, and the curious and novel relationship between them was not put to any strain.

Later in the century this method of giving self-government to

British settlements abroad was extended to Australia, which had been a convict settlement till almost the middle of the century. By the end of the century Australia was a free dominion in the Empire.

On the other hand, in India the British hold was tightened, and war after war of conquest extended the British Indian Empire. India was a dependency of the British. There was no shadow of self-government. The Revolt of 1857 was crushed, and India was made to feel the full weight of the Empire. I have told you else-where how she was exploited in a variety of ways by England. India, of course, was *the* Empire of Britain, and to proclaim this fact to the world Queen Victoria took the title of Empress of India. But, besides India, Britain also had many other smaller depen-dencies in various parts of the world.

The British Empire thus became a curious medley of two types of countries : the self-governing countries, which later became the free dominions, and the dependencies and protectorates. The former were more or less family members acknowledging the head-ship of the mother-country, the latter were definitely the servants and slaves of the establishment, looked down upon, ill treated and exploited. The self-governing dominions consisted of British people or other Europeans and their descendants, the dependencies were all non-British, non-European. This difference between the two parts of the British Empire has persisted till now.

England with her wealth and empire was more or less a satisfied Power; not wholly so, because the imperialist instinct is never satisfied with any frontier and always wants to expand. Still England's main worry was not to take more, but to protect what she had got. In particular, India was her star possession, to which she wanted to hold on to the last. All her foreign policy revolved round her possession of India and the safety of the sea-routes to the East. She meddled in Egypt, and ultimately dominated the country because of this; likewise she interfered in Persia and Afghanistan. By a clever move she bought up the shares of the Suez Canal Company, and thus gained control over the canal.

Most of the continental Powers of Europe did not worry her for the greater part of the nineteenth century, as they were full of their own troubles and were often fighting each other. England continued her traditional game of keeping the balance in Europe by playing off one country against another and taking advantage of conti-nental rivalries. Napoleon III of France seemed dangerous, but he collapsed, and France took some time to recover. Germany was still too young to be considered a serious rival. But one country seemed to challenge the British Empire, and this was Tsarist Russia, backward Russia, but on the map still a great country. As England had spread in India and south Asia, Russia had spread in north and Central Asia, and her frontier was not far from India. This nearness of Russia was a constant nightmare to the British. I have already told you, when dealing with India, of the British invasions of Afghanistan and the Afghan wars. These were almost entirely due to fear of Tsarist Russia.

In Europe also England and Russia came to blows. Russia longed to have a good seaport which was open all the year round and did not freeze in winter. In spite of her vast territories, all her ports were somewhere near the Arctic circle, and were frozen up for part of the year. In India and Afghanistan she was stopped by the British from reaching the sea; so also in Persia. The Black Sea was bottled up by the Turkish possession of the Bosphorus and the Dardanelles. In the past she had tried to take Constantinople, but the Turks were too strong for her. Now the Turks were weak and the coveted prize seemed almost within grasp. She tried to take it. But England stood in the way and, for entirely selfish reasons, she became the champion of the Turks. By war in 1854 in the Crimea, and later by the threat of another war, Russia was kept back.

It was during this Crimean War of 1854–1856 that Florence Nightingale led a gallant band of women volunteers to nurse the wounded. This was an unusual thing to do at the time, for Victorian middle-class women were stay-at-home folk. Florence Nightingale set a new example of active service to them and drew many out of their drawing-rooms. She has thus an important place in the development of the women's movement.

The form of government in Britain was what is called a constitutional monarchy or a " crowned republic ". This meant that the wearer of the crown had no real power, but was just the mouthpiece of the ministers whom Parliament trusted. Politically he (or she) was supposed to be just a puppet in the ministers' hands; he was " above politics ", it was said. As a matter of fact no man of intelligence or will can be a mere puppet, and the English king or queen has plenty of opportunity of interfering with public affairs. This is usually done behind the scenes, and the public seldom know of it till long afterwards. Any open interference would probably be greatly resented, and might imperil the monarchy. The one great virtue that a constitutional monarch must possess is tact; if he has this he can carry on and make himself felt in many ways.

Constitutionally and legally, the presidents of republics (like the President of the United States of America) have far more power than the crowned heads of parliamentary countries. But the former change frequently, and the latter remain for long periods and can influence affairs continuously, though quietly, in any particular direction. The king also has numerous opportunities of intriguing and exercising social pressure, for in the social world he is supreme. Indeed, the whole atmosphere of royal Courts is one of authoritarianism, of precedence and titles and classes, and this sets a standard for the whole country. It is not compatible with social equality and the abolition of classes. There can be no doubt that the presence of a royal court in England has had a great deal of influence in moulding the Englishman's mentality and in making him accept the class division of society. Or perhaps it is more correct to say that it is because of this acceptance of classes one above the other that the institution of royalty has managed to survive in England although it has disappeared from almost all the great countries of the world. "Every Englishman loves a lord" is an old saying, and there is much truth in it. Nowhere in Europe or America, and perhaps nowhere in Asia, except in Japan and India, are class distinctions so sharp as in England. It is strange that England should be so backward socially and so fundamentally conservative, when she was the leader in the past in political democracy and industrialism.

The British Parliament is called the "Mother of Parliaments". It has had a long and honourable career, and in many matters it was a pioneer in the fight against the king's autocracy. That autocracy gave place to the oligarchy of Parliament—that is, rule by a small landowning and governing class. Democracy then came with a flourish of trumpets and, after many a tussle, votes for electing members to the House of Commons were given to the majority of the population. In effect, this resulted not in real democratic control, but in the control of Parliament by the rich industrialists. Instead of democracy there was plutocracy.

The British Parliament developed a strange system for doing its business of governing and legislating. This was the two-party system. There was not much difference between the two parties, they did not stand out for any opposing principles. Both of them were rich men's parties accepting the existing social system. One of the parties had a greater number of the old landowning classes, the other had more of the rich factory-owners. But it was a question of Tweedledum and Tweedledee. They used to be called Tories and Whigs; later, in the nineteenth century, they came to be styled Conservatives and Liberals.

In other European countries it was very different, and real parties with different programmes and ideologies fought each other passionately in parliaments and outside. But in England it was all like a family affair, and opposition itself became a kind of co-operation, and each party took its turn of office and opposition. The real clash and class conflict between the rich and the poor did not show itself in Parliament, as both the big parties were rich men's parties. There were no religious questions of importance to rouse people's passions, nor were there any racial or national questions (as there were on the Continent). The only real element of excitement was brought in later in the century by the Irish Nationalist members, for with them Ireland's freedom was a national question.

When two such big parties run members for Parliament, it becomes very difficult for independent individuals or small groups to get elected. In spite of democracy and the vote, the poor voter has little say in the matter. He can either vote for the candidate of one of the parties or stay at home and not vote at all. And the members of the parties in Parliament have little independence left. They have to carry out the orders of their party chiefs and vote, and can do little else. For only in this way can they develop solidarity in the party and strength to defeat the rival party and thus gain office. This solidarity and uniformity is no doubt good in its own way, but it is very far from real democracy.

And we see that even in England, which is often held up as an example of democratic progress, democracy was not a brilliant success. The great problem of government, as to how the best men should be chosen by the people to govern them, was not satisfactorily solved. Democracy in action meant a great deal of shouting and public speaking and the poor voter being induced to choose a person about whom he knew nothing. General elections have been described as public auctions where all manner of promises are made. However, in spite of all these drawbacks, this pseudo or false democracy continued because England was prosperous and this prosperity prevented breakdowns of the system and brought a measure of content.

The two great leaders of the English political parties in the second half of the nineteenth century were Disraeli and Gladstone. Disraeli, who later became the Earl of Beaconsfield, was the leader of the Conservatives and many times Prime Minister. This was a remarkable feat for him, as he was a Jew with no important connections, and Jews are not liked by the English. But by sheer ability and perseverance he conquered the prejudice against him and forced his way to the front. He was a great imperialist, and it was he who made Victoria Empress of India. Gladstone belonged to one of the rich old English families. He became the leader of the Liberal party, and was also Prime Minister many times. So far as imperialism and foreign policy were concerned, there was no racial difference between Gladstone and Disraeli. But Disraeli was frank about his imperialism; Gladstone, typical Englishman as he was, covered it up with fine phrases and pious exhortations, and seemed to make out that God was his chief adviser in everything he did. He led a great campaign against Turkish atrocities in the Balkans, and of course Disraeli in sheer opposition took up the side of the Turks. As a matter of fact both the Turks and their subjects of different nationalities in the Balkans were to blame, and they indulged alternately in the most frightful massacres and atrocities.

Gladstone also championed Home Rule for Ireland. He did not succeed, and so great was the English opposition that the Liberal party itself split up, and one part of it joined the Conservatives, now called the Unionists, as they desired to continue the union with Ireland.

But I must tell you more of this and of other happenings in the Victorian Age in a subsequent letter.

136

ENGLAND BECOMES THE WORLD'S MONEY-LENDER

February 23, 1933

THE nineteenth-century prosperity of England was due to her industries and to her exploitation of her colonies and dependencies. In particular, her growing wealth was founded on four industries —" basic " industries they might be called; these were cotton, coal, iron, and ship-building. A host of other industries, heavy as well as light, grew up round these and apart from these. Great business houses and banking houses were built up. British merchant-ships were to be found in almost every part of the world, carrying not only British goods, but also the goods manufactured by other industrial countries. They became the chief carriers of merchandise in the world. The great insurance office of Lloyd's in London became the centre of the world's shipping. These industries and businesses dominated Parliament.

Wealth poured into the country, and the upper and middle classes grew richer and richer; some part of it reached the working classes also, and raised their standard of living. What was to be done with all the wealth that the rich were getting ? To keep it unused was folly, and everybody was keen on pushing industry, and thus producing more and more goods and getting more and more profits. A great part of this wealth went into new factories and railways and such-like undertakings in England and Scotland. After a while, when there was a very great number of factories and the country was thoroughly industrialized, the rate of profit naturally grew less, as there was more competition. Capitalists with money then looked abroad for more profitable fields of investment and found plenty of opportunities. All over the world railways were being built, and cables and telegraph lines and factories. The surplus money of Britain was poured into many of these undertakings in Europe, America, Africa, and the British dependencies. The United States of America, rich as they were in their resources, were rapidly growing, and they absorbed a good deal of British money for their railways, etc. In South America, and especially in the Argentine, the British owned huge plantations. Canada and Australia were built up with British capital. In China, I have told you something of the battle of concessions. In India, of course, the British were dominant, and lent money for railways and other works on their own rather extravagant terms.

Thus England became the money-lender to the world, and London was the world's money market. But do not think that this meant that huge bags full of gold or silver or cash were sent from England to other countries when money was lent. Modern business is not carried on in this way, or there would not be enough gold and silver to go round. Foolish people attach a great deal of importance to gold and silver, but they are just a means of exchange and of circulating goods. One cannot eat them or wear them or use them in any way, except of course as ornaments, which does little good to anybody. Real wealth consists in possessing goods which can be used. So when England, or rather British capitalists, advanced money, it meant that they had invested a sum in a foreign industry or railway, and instead of hard cash, British goods were sent out. British machinery or railway material would thus be sent to foreign countries. This helped British industry, and at the same time offered opportunities to the British investing class to invest their surplus cash at a handsome profit.

Money-lending is a profitable business; and the more England adopted this profession the richer she grew. A huge leisured class grew up, which lived entirely on the profits and dividends from this business. They did not have to work to produce anything. They held shares in some railway company or tea plantation or other concern, and dividends came to them regularly. English colonies of these leisured people grew up in many desirable places, like the French Riviera, Italy, and Switzerland; but of course most of them remained in England.

How did all the countries that had borrowed money from England in this way pay their interest on it or dividends ? Again, they could not send it in gold or silver. They did not have enough of these to pay year after year. They paid therefore in goods, not so much in manufactured goods, as England was herself the leading manufacturing country, but in food products and raw material. They poured into England in an unceasing stream wheat, tea, coffee, meat, fruit, wines, cotton, wool, etc.

Commerce between two nations consists of an exchange of articles. It is not possible for one country to go on buying and the other selling. If this were attempted, payment would have to be made in gold or silver, and soon there would be no more gold or silver left, or else the one-sided trade would stop of itself. In mutual trade an exchange takes place which adjusts itself, and is sometimes in favour of one country, sometimes in favour of the other. If we were to examine the trade of England during the nineteenth century, we would find that on the whole she received more goods than she sent out. That is, although she exported a vast quantity of goods, she actually imported more goods in value, with this difference, that she exported manufactured articles and imported principally food articles and raw materials. Thus apparently she bought more than she sold, which does not seem to be a good way of carrying on business. But as a matter of fact the excess of imports represented the profit on the money lent out. It was the tribute paid by debtor countries as well as dependencies like India.

All the profit from investments did not come over to England. Much of it remained in the debtor country and was re-invested by British capitalists. So that the total volume of British investments abroad went on increasing without any fresh money or goods being sent out from England. In India we are frequently reminded of the vast British investments in the railways, canals, and numerous other works, and an enormous sum is said to represent the " debt " of India to England on this account. Indians challenge this on many counts, but we need not go into that here. But it is worth noting that these huge investments do not represent much fresh capital from England. They represent the re-investment of profits made in India. In the days of Plassey and Clive, as I have told you, a huge amount of gold and treasure was actually taken away from India to England. After that the exploitation of India took different and less obvious forms, and part of the profits of it were invested in the country.

England found that the only possible way to carry on the profession of money-lending on a world scale was to accept payment of interest in goods. She could not insist on gold, as I have shown you above. This had two important results. England allowed foodstuffs to come from abroad to feed her population, and allowed her agriculture to suffer. She concentrated on manufacturing articles industrially for sale abroad, and ignored the plight of her farmers. If she could get cheap food from abroad, why should she trouble to raise it herself? And if she could make more profit by industry, why should she bother about agriculture? So England became a purely industrial country, dependent for her food on foreign countries.

The second result was that she adopted the policy of free trade —that is, she did not tax the foreign goods that came to her ports, or taxed them very little. As she was the leading industrial country, she had little to fear for a long time from any competition as regards manufactured goods. Taxing foreign goods thus meant taxing foreign food and raw material that came to her. This would have raised the price of the people's food and of her own manufactured articles. Besides, if she stopped foreign goods from coming in by heavy taxation, how were the foreign debtor countries to pay their tribute to England? They could only pay in goods. This was the reason why England adopted free trade when all other industrial countries were protectionist—that is, were protecting their growing industries by taxing foreign goods coming to them. The United States, France, Germany were all protectionist.

The nineteenth-century English policy of neglecting agriculture and concentrating on industry and getting food from outside and living in comfort on tribute from abroad seemed a profitable and agreeable one. But it had its dangers, as are obvious enough now. The policy was based on England's supremacy in industry and on her huge foreign trade. But if this supremacy should go, and with it her foreign trade dwindle, what then? How would she then pay for her food? And even if she could pay for the food, how would she get it from abroad if a powerful enemy stood in the way? During the last World War her people almost starved, because her food supply was nearly cut off. An even greater danger than this is the progressive dwindling of her foreign trade because of foreign competition. This competition became marked in the 'eighties of the nineteenth century, when the United States of America and

Germany began to seek foreign markets.   Gradually other nations
became industrialized and joined this quest, and now almost the
whole world is to some extent industrialized.   Each country is
trying to make most of the goods it needs and to keep out foreign
goods.   India wants to keep out foreign cloth.   What, then, is
Lancashire to do, and the other British industries dependent on
foreign trade ?

These are hard questions for England to answer, and there seem
to be hard times in store for her.   She cannot even retire into her
shell and live a self-sufficing existence, producing her own food and
necessities.   The modern world is far too complicated for this.
And even if she could cut herself off, it is doubtful if she could
produce enough food for her over-grown population.   But these
questions are of to-day ; they had little importance in the nineteenth century.   So England then gambled with her future and
banked on continued supremacy.   It was a great game, and the
stakes were high—to be the leading nation of the world or collapse.
There was no middle stage for her.   But the Victorian middle-class
Englishman was not lacking in self-confidence or conceit.   His long
prosperity and success, and leadership in industry and business, had
convinced him of his superiority over the rest of mankind.   He
looked down on all foreigners.   The peoples of Asia and Africa
were, of course, backward and barbarous, apparently created to
give the English an opportunity of exercising their inborn genius
for ruling and improving the backward races of mankind.   Even
the peoples of the European Continent were ignorant and superstitious foreigners.   The English were the chosen people at the
pinnacle of civilization, the vanguard marching at the head of
Europe, which itself was at the head of the rest of the world.   The
British Empire was a semi-divine institution which put the final
seal on the greatness of the race.   Lord Curzon, who was a Viceroy
of India thirty years ago, and who was one of the ablest Englishmen
of his time, dedicated a book of his to " those who believe that the
British Empire is, under Providence, the greatest influence for good
that the world has ever seen ".

All this that I am writing about the Victorian Englishman seems
rather far-fetched and extraordinary, and perhaps you may think
that I am trying to be humorous at his expense.   It is strange that
any sensible person should behave in this way and adopt this
amazing, conceited, and self-righteous attitude.   But national
groups will believe almost anything, if it tickles their vanity and is
to their advantage.   Individuals would never think of acting in
this crude and vulgar manner towards their neighbours, but nations
have no such compunction.   We are all, unfortunately, made that
way, and strut about praising our own national virtues.   The
Victorian Englishman was a type which is found, with minor
changes, almost everywhere.   All the European nations have had
their national prototypes of him, so also in America and Asia.

The prosperity of England and western Europe was due to the
growth of industrial capitalism.   This capitalism marched ahead

in its ceaseless search for profits. Success and profits were the only gods that drew the worship of the people, for capitalism had nothing to do with religion or morality. It was the doctrine of cut-throat competition between individuals and nations, and the devil take the hindmost ! The Victorians prided themselves on their tolerance in religion. They believed in progress and science, and their very success in business and empire proved to them that they were the elect who had survived in the struggle. Had not Darwin said so ? Their tolerance in matters of religion was really indifference. An English writer, R. H. Tawney, has described this state of affairs rather well. God, he says, had been put in His place, away from earthly matters. " There was a limited monarchy in Heaven, as well as upon earth ! " This was the view of the prosperous *bourgeoisie*, but church-going and religion were encouraged for the masses, in the hope that this might keep them from revolutionary ideas. Tolerance in religion did not mean tolerance in other matters. There was no tolerance in matters to which the majority attached importance, and under any strain all tolerance disappears. The British Government in India is supremely tolerant about religion, and makes a virtue of it. As a matter of fact it does not care in the least what happens to religion. But even a little criticism of its politics or anything that it does makes it prick up its ears, and no one can then accuse it of tolerance ! The greater the strain, the greater the fall; and if the strain is great enough, the government sets aside all pretence of tolerance and indulges in open and unabashed terrorism. We see this in India to-day. A short while ago I read in the papers that a boy hardly out of his 'teens had been sentenced to eight years' rigorous imprisonment for writing threatening letters to some British officials !

The growth of capitalist industry brought many changes. Capitalism functioned on a bigger and bigger scale; it was more profitable and more efficient for big concerns to function than small ones. So huge combines and trusts grew up, controlling whole industries, and they swallowed up the small independent producers and factories. The old ideas of *laissez-faire* collapsed before this, as there was far less chance or opportunity for individual initiative left. The powerful combines and corporations dominated governments.

Capitalism led also to another and fiercer phase of imperialism. As competition between the industrial Powers grew in the second half of the nineteenth century, they looked farther afield for markets and raw materials. All over the world there was a fierce scramble for empire. I have already told you in some detail of what happened in Asia—in India, China, Farther India and Persia. The European Powers now fell like vultures on Africa, and divided it amongst themselves. Here also England took the largest share —Egypt in the north and huge slices of territory east and west and south. France also did well. Italy wanted to share in the booty, but, much to every one's surprise, she was severely beaten by Abyssinia. Germany got a share, but was not satisfied. Everywhere imperialism, shouting, threatening, grasping, was rampant. Rudyard Kipling, the popular poet of British imperialism, sang of the " white man's burden ". The French talked of the *mission civilisatrice*, the civilizing mission of France. The Germans, of course, had to spread their *Kultur*. So these civilizers and improvers and bearers of other people's burdens went in a spirit of utter sacrifice and sat on the backs of the brown man and the yellow and the black. And nobody sang about the black man's burden.

The world was not big enough for all these grasping rival imperialisms. The fierce capitalistic urge for markets pushed each country on, and often they clashed with each other. Several times war seemed to hang in the balance between England and France. But the real clash of interests came between English and German industry. Germany had caught up with England in industry and shipping and challenged her in every market. But she found the best parts of the earth's surface already occupied by England. Proud and high-spirited and chafing at being kept back by other nations, she prepared strenuously for a great struggle with them. All Europe prepared, and armies and navies grew. Alliances were made between different countries, till there seemed to be two armed hosts facing each other—the Triple Alliance of Germany, Austria, and Italy, and the Dual Alliance of France and Russia, with England privately attached to them.

Meanwhile, at the end of the century England had a little war of her own in South Africa. The discovery of gold in the Boer republic of the Transvaal led to this war in 1899. The Boers fought with amazing courage and perseverance for three years against the leading Power of Europe. They were crushed and had to acknowledge defeat. But soon after the British (the Liberal Party was then in office) performed a wise and generous deed by offering full self-government to their recent enemies. A little later the whole of South Africa became a free Dominion of the British Empire.

137

CIVIL WAR IN AMERICA

February 27, 1933

THE Old World, with its conflicts and intrigues, its kings and its revolutions, its hates and its nationalisms, has taken up a great deal of our time. Let us now cross the Atlantic and visit the New World of America, and see how this fared after it had shaken off the grasping hand of Europe. The United States in particular demand our attention. From small beginnings they have grown and grown, till to-day they seem to dominate the world situation. England has no longer pride of place to-day; she is not the world's money-lender now, but is an unhappy debtor country, like all the others in Europe, asking the United States for kind and generous treatment. The mantle of the money-lender has fallen on America; wealth pours into her, and she breeds millionaires in surprising quantities. But, as in the case of Midas of old, her touch of gold has not brought her much joy, and her masses are suffering from want and poverty to-day in spite of her millionaires.

The thirteen seaboard States that broke off from England in 1775 had a population of well under four millions. To-day the city of New York alone has about double that population, and the whole of the United States have a population of a hundred and twenty-five millions. There are many more States now in the Union, and they extend right across the continent to the Pacific Ocean. The nineteenth century saw the growth of this great country, not only in extent and population, but also in modern industry and commerce, wealth and influence. The States had many difficulties and troubles and some wars and entanglements with Europe, but the greatest of their trials came from a bitter and devastating civil war between the States of the North and those of the South.

A few years after America became free there was the Revolution in France, followed by the wars of Napoleon. Both Napoleon and England tried to destroy each other's commerce, and in doing this came into conflict with the United States. American oversea commerce was quite paralysed, and this led to another war with England in 1812. Nothing much happened as a result of this two years' war. In the course of this war, when Napoleon had been disposed of at Elba and England had her hands free, the British managed to capture Washington, the capital city, and they burnt down and destroyed all the important public buildings including the Capitol, the building where Congress is held, and the White House, the residence of the presidents. Subsequently the British were defeated.

Even before this war the States had added a large slice of territory in the south. This was the old French colony of Louisiana, which Napoleon sold to them, as he was quite unable to defend it from British naval attacks. A few years later, in 1822, a purchase, from Spain this time, brought Florida to the States, and in 1848 a successful war with Mexico brought several States in the south-west, including California. Many of the names of cities in this south-western part are Spanish still, and remind one of the days when the Spaniards or the Spanish-speaking Mexicans ruled here. Everybody has heard of Los Angeles, the great city of Cinemadom, and of San Francisco.

While Europe was having its repeated attempts at revolution and repression, the United States kept on spreading westward. Repression in Europe helped immigration, and tales of vast territories and high wages attracted large numbers from the European countries. As the population spread to the west, new States were formed and added to the Union.

Between the northern States and the southern there was a great difference from the very beginning. The northern were industrial, where the new big machine-industry spread rapidly; in the south

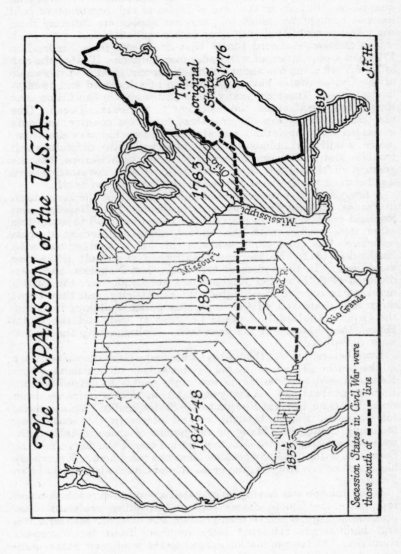

The EXPANSION of the U.S.A.

The original States
1776
1819
1783
Ohio
Mississippi
Missouri
1803
Red R.
Rio Grande
1845-48
1853

Secession States in Civil War were
those south of ▬▬▬ line

J.F.H.

there were large plantations worked by slave labour. Slavery was legal, but in the north it was not popular and had little importance. The South depended entirely on slave labour. The slaves were, of course, Negroes from Africa. No white people were slaves. " All men are born equal," says the Declaration of Independence, but this applied to the whites, not to the blacks.

The story of how these Negroes were brought from Africa is a very sad one. The slave trade began early in the seventeenth century, and a regular supply was kept up till 1863. At first, cargo-boats passing the West African coast—a part of it is still called the " Slave Coast "—picked up the Africans, whenever they could do so easily, and carried them to America. Among the Africans themselves there was very little slavery; only prisoners of war or debtors were so treated. It was found that this carrying of Africans to America and selling them as slaves was a very profitable business. The slave trade grew, and was subsidized as a business chiefly by the English, the Spanish, and the Portuguese. Special ships—slave-traders—were built with galleries between decks. In these galleries the unhappy Negroes were made to lie down, all chained up, and each couple fettered together. The voyage across the Atlantic lasted many weeks, sometimes months. During all these weeks and months these Negroes lay in these narrow galleries, shackled together, and all the space that was allowed to each of them was five and a half feet long by sixteen inches wide !

Liverpool became a great city on the foundation of the slave trade. As early as 1713, in the Peace of Utrecht, England extorted from Spain the privilege of carrying slaves between Africa and Spanish America. Even before this England had supplied slaves to the English territories in America. An attempt was thus made in the eighteenth century to make the Africa–America slave trade an English monopoly. In 1730 Liverpool had fifteen ships engaged in this trade. The number went on growing, till in 1792 there were 132 ships employed by Liverpool in the slave trade. The early days of the Industrial Revolution led to a great advance in cotton-spinning in Lancashire in England, and this led to a demand for more slaves in the United States. For the cotton used by the Lancashire mills came from the great cotton plantations of the southern States. These cotton plantations were rapidly extended, more slaves were brought over from Africa, and every effort was made to breed Negroes ! In 1790 there were 697,000 slaves in the United States; in 1861 the number rose to 4,000,000.

Early in the nineteenth century the British Parliament passed stringent laws against slavery. Other countries in Europe and America followed. But even when the slave trade was thus out-lawed, Negroes were still carried from Africa to America, with this difference, that the conditions of their journey were far worse. They could not be carried openly, so they were hidden away from sight on loose shelves, one on top of the other. Sometimes, an American writer tells us, " one crowded on to the lap of another, and with legs on legs, like riders on a crowded toboggan ! " It is difficult to imagine the full horror of all this. Conditions were so filthy that the slave ships had to be abandoned after four or five voyages. But the profits were huge, and during the height of the trade at the end of the eighteenth and the beginning of the nineteenth centuries as many as 100,000 slaves were carried every year from the African Slave Coast. And remember that the carrying away of this number meant the killing of far greater numbers in the raids to capture the Negroes.

All the principal countries made the trade illegal early in the nineteenth century or thereabouts. Even the United States did so. But although the slave trade was outlawed, slavery itself continued to be legal in America—that is to say, that the old slaves continued as slaves. And because slavery was legal, the slave trade also continued in spite of prohibition. When Britain put an end to slavery also, then New York became the principal port for the slave trade.

Although New York was the port for this trade for many years —till the middle of the century—the North was against slavery. The South, on the other hand, required these slaves for plantation work. Some of the States abolished slavery, others retained it. Negroes would often run away from a slavery State to a non-slavery one, and there would be disputes about them.

The economic interests of the North and the South were different, and as early as 1830 friction arose about tariffs and customs duties. Threats of breaking away from the Union were made. The States were jealous of their rights, and did not like too much interference from the Federal Government. Two parties arose in the country, one favouring State sovereignty, the other wanting a strong central government. All these points of difference divided the North and South farther from each other, and wherever new States were added to the Union, the question arose which side they would support. Where would the majority lie ? The population of the North was increasing rapidly because of the immigration from Europe, and this made southern people fear that soon they would be overwhelmed by the numbers of the North and out-voted on every question. So tension increased between the North and South.

Meanwhile an agitation grew up in the North for the total abolition of slavery. The people who were in favour of this were called the " Abolitionists ", and their principal leader was William Lloyd Garrison. In 1831 Garrison brought out a paper called the *Liberator* to support his anti-slavery agitation. In the very first issue of this paper he made it clear that he was not going to compromise on this issue, and would not be moderate about it. Some of his sentences from that issue have become famous, and I shall give them to you here :

> " I will be as harsh as truth, and as uncompromising as justice. On this subject I do not wish to think, or speak, or write with moderation. No ! No ! tell a man whose house is on fire to give a moderate alarm ; tell him to moderately rescue his wife from the hands of a ravisher ; tell the mother to gradually extricate her babe

from the fire into which it has fallen—but urge me not to use moderation in a cause like the present. I am in earnest—I will not equivocate—I will not excuse—I will not retreat a single inch—and I will be heard."

This brave attitude was, however, confined to a small minority. Most of those who opposed slavery did not want to interfere with it where it already existed. Still the tension grew between the North and the South, for this was due to their different economic interests, which conflicted especially on the tariff question.

In 1860 Abraham Lincoln was elected President of the United States, and his election was a signal for the South to break away. He was opposed to slavery, but even so he had made it clear that there would be no interference with it where it existed. He was not prepared to see it extended to new States or to give it legality. The South was not appeased by this assurance, and State after State seceded from the Union. The United States were going to pieces. Such was the terrible position that faced the new President. He made another effort to win over the South and prevent this break-up. He gave them all manner of assurances about allowing slavery to go on; he even said that he was prepared to make it (where it existed) a part of the constitution, which would give it permanence. In fact, he was prepared to go to almost any length for peace, but one thing he would not agree to, and that was the break-up of the Union. He denied absolutely the right of any State to withdraw from the Union.

Lincoln's attempts to avoid Civil War failed. The South had decided to break away, and eleven States did so, while some other border States also sympathized with them. The seceding States called themselves the " Confederate States " and elected their own President, Jefferson Davis. In April 1861 the Civil War began, and it lasted for four weary years, during which many a brother fought against his brother and many a friend against a friend. Huge armies grew up as the war continued. The North had many advantages; it had a much bigger population and greater wealth. Being a manufacturing and industrial area, its resources were far greater, and it had more railways. But the South had the better soldiers and generals, especially General Lee, and all the early victories went to the South. But ultimately the South was worn out. The Northern navy cut off the South completely from its market in Europe, and cotton and tobacco could not be exported. This crippled the South, but it also had a disastrous result on Lancashire, where many mills had to stop working because there was no cotton. There was great distress among the workers thrown out of employment in Lancashire.

English opinion about the war was generally in sympathy with the South, or at any rate the opinion of the wealthier classes was in favour of the South. The radical elements favoured the North.

Slavery was not the principal cause of the Civil War. As I have told you, to the last Lincoln gave assurances that he would respect slavery wherever it existed. The real trouble arose from the different and somewhat conflicting economic interests of the North and South, and finally Lincoln fought to preserve the Union. Even after war had begun, Lincoln made no clear pronouncement about slavery, as he was afraid of irritating many people in the North who were in favour of it. As the war went on, he became more definite. He proposed first that Congress should free the slaves after giving compensation to the owners. Later he gave up this idea of compensation, and finally, in September 1862, he issued the Proclamation of Emancipation, in which it was declared that the slaves in all the States in rebellion against the government should be free on and after January 1st, 1863. The principal reason for issuing this proclamation was probably the desire to weaken the South in the war. It resulted in 4,000,000 slaves being freed, and it was no doubt hoped that these would create trouble in the Confederate States.

The Civil War ended in 1865, after the South was thoroughly exhausted. War at any time is a terrible affair, but civil war is often more horrible still. The burden of four years of this awful struggle fell most of all on the President, Lincoln, and the result was largely due to his cool determination to persevere in spite of all disappointments and disasters. He was out not only to win, but to do so with as little ill-will as possible, so that the Union for which he was fighting might be a real union of hearts, and not a forced one. So, having won the war, he set out to be generous to the defeated South. But within a few days a crank shot him dead.

Abraham Lincoln is one of the greatest of American heroes. He has also taken his place among the world's great men. His beginnings were quite humble; he had little schooling, such education as he had was mostly his own work, and yet he grew up a great statesman and a great orator, and steered his country through a great crisis.

After Lincoln's death the American Congress was not as generous to the Southern Whites as he might have been. These Southern Whites were penalized in some ways and many were disfranchised —that is, their votes were taken away. On the other hand, the Negroes were given full rights as citizens, and this was made part of the American constitution. It was also laid down that no State could disfranchise a man on account of his race, colour, or previous slavery.

The Negroes were now legally free and had the vote. But this did them little good, for their economic status remained the same. All the freed Negroes were wholly without property, and it became a problem to know what to do with them. Some migrated to the northern towns, but most of them remained where they were, as much under the thumb of their old white masters in the South as ever. They worked as wage-labourers in the old plantations on such wages as the white employers chose to give them. The Southern Whites also organized themselves to keep down the Negroes in every way by terrorism. An extraordinary semi-secret organization, called the " Ku Klux Klan ", was formed, and its members went about in masks terrorizing the Negroes and preventing them from even voting at the elections.

During the last half-century the Negroes have made some progress. Many own property, and they have some fine educational institutions. But they are still very definitely the subject race. There are about 12,000,000 of them in the United States—just about 10 per cent. of the total population. Wherever they are in small numbers they are tolerated, as in parts of the North, but as soon as their numbers increase they are heavily sat upon and made to feel that they are little better than the slaves of old. Everywhere they are segregated and kept apart from the Whites—in hotels, restaurants, churches, colleges, parks, bathing-beaches, trams, and even in stores ! In railways they have to travel in special carriages called " Jim-Crow cars ". Marriage between the White and the Negro is forbidden by law. Indeed, there are all manner of strange laws. A law passed by the State of Virginia as recently as 1926 prohibited white and coloured persons from sitting on the same floor !

Sometimes there are terrible race riots between the Whites and the Negroes. Frequently in the south there are horrible cases of lynching—that is, when a mob gets hold of a person it suspects of some offence and kills him. Cases have occurred in recent years of Negroes being burned at the stake by white mobs.

All over America and especially in the southern States the lot of the Negro is still very hard. Often when labour is scarce innocent Negroes, in some States in the south, are sent to gaol on some trumped-up charge, and the convict labour is leased out to private contractors. This is bad enough, but the conditions accompanying it are shocking. So we see that legal freedom does not amount to very much, after all.

Have you read or heard of Harriet Beecher Stowe's *Uncle Tom's Cabin*? This book is about the old slave Negroes in the southern States, and gives their sad story. It came out ten years before the Civil War, and had great influence in rousing the American people against slavery.

138

THE INVISIBLE EMPIRE OF AMERICA

February 28, 1933

THE Civil War took a terrible toll of young men's lives in America, and it left a heavy burden of debt. But the country was young and full of energy, and its growth continued. It had tremendous natural resources, and was especially rich in minerals. The three articles which form the basis of modern industry and civilization were there in abundance—coal, iron, and petroleum. There was plenty of water-power from which electric power could be produced ;

the Niagara Falls is one instance of this which will come to your mind. It was a huge country with a relatively small population, and there was plenty of elbow-room for everybody. Thus it had every advantage to develop as a great manufacturing and industrial country, and it began to do so at a rapid pace. By the 'eighties of the nineteenth century American industry began to compete in foreign markets with British industry. America and Germany put an end to the easy supremacy which Britain had had for 100 years in foreign trade.

Immigrants poured into the country. They were all kinds of people from Europe : Germans, Scandinavians, Irish, Italians, Jews, Poles ; many were driven by political terrorism at home, and many in search of better living conditions. Overcrowded Europe poured out its surplus population to America. It was an extraordinary jumble of races, nationalities, languages, religions. In Europe they had all lived apart, each in its own little world, full of hatreds and animosities against the others ; here they were thrown together in a new atmosphere where the old hates did not seem to count for much. A uniform system of compulsory education soon rubbed off their national corners, and the American type began to grow out of this hotch-potch of races. The old Anglo-Saxon stock still considered itself the aristocrats ; they were the social leaders. Next to it, and not far from it, came the races from northern Europe. The people from southern Europe, especially from Italy, were looked down upon by these northern Europeans and called, rather contemptuously, " Dagos ". The Negroes, of course, were quite apart. They were at the bottom of the scale, and they did not mix with any of the white races. On the western coast there were some Chinese and Japanese and Indians, who had come when the demand for labour there was great. These Asiatic races also kept apart from the others.

The effect of the widespread net of railways and telegraphs was to knit together this huge country. This would have been impossible in the old days, when it took weeks and months to travel from one coast to another. In the past we have seen that there were often great empires in Asia and Europe. But these could not be closely knit together because of the difficulties of communications and transport. Different parts of the empire would be practically independent, leading their own separate lives, except that they acknowledged the supremacy of the emperor and paid tribute to him. They were loose associations of different countries under one head. There was no common outlook about them. The United States, however, because of railways and other methods of communication, as well as a uniform education, developed this common outlook amongst its different races. The races were gradually assimilated into a common stock. The process is by no means complete ; it is still going on. There is no other instance in history of assimilation on such a large scale.

The United States tried to keep away from European entanglements and the intrigues of European Powers, and they wanted

Europe to keep away from America, both North and South.   I have told you already of the " Monroe Doctrine ", the rule which President Monroe of the United States laid down when some European Powers —the " Holy Alliance "—wanted to interfere in South America to preserve Spain's empire.   Monroe declared that the United States could not tolerate any armed intervention in the whole of America by any European Power.   This declaration saved the young South American republics from Europe.   It almost led to war with England once, but America has successfully stuck to this policy for more than 100 years now.

South America was very different from the north, and 100 years have not lessened the differences.   Canada in the north is becoming more and more like the United States, but not so the southern republics.   As I told you once, these republics of South America, including Mexico, although it is in North America, are Latin republics.   The frontier of the United States and Mexico divides two different peoples and cultures.   South of it, across the thin band of Central America, and all over the great continent of South America, Spanish and Portuguese are the languages of the people. Spanish is really predominant, as Portuguese is, I believe, spoken only in Brazil.   Because of South America, Spanish is to-day one of the great world languages.   Latin America still looks to Spain for cultural inspiration.   Racial differences do not count there as much as they do in the United States and Canada.   Intermarriages between the Spanish stock and the original population, the Red Indians, and also to some extent the Negroes, have produced a mixed race.

In spite of 100 years of freedom, these Latin republics of the south refuse to settle down.   Periodically they have revolutions and military dictatorships and it is not easy to follow the course of their ever-changing politics and governments.   The three leading countries of South America are Argentina, Brazil, and Chile—the A, B, C countries they are called, from the first letters of their names. Mexico, in North America, is a leading Latin-American country.

The United States prevented interference in Latin America from Europe by means of the Monroe Doctrine.   But as they grew wealthy they began to look outside for fresh fields for expansion. Naturally their eyes first fell on Latin America.   They did not attempt to take possession of any of these countries by force in the old way of building up empires.   They sent their goods there and captured their markets.   They also invested their capital in railways, mines, and other undertakings in the south ; they lent money to governments and sometimes to warring factions at times of revolution.   By " they " I mean American capitalists and bankers, but behind them and supporting them was the American Government.   Gradually these bankers controlled, through the money they had lent or invested, many of the smaller South and Central American governments.   The bankers could even bring about revolutions by advancing money or arms to one party and not to another. Behind the bankers and capitalists was the great United States

Government, so what could the small and weak South American countries do? Sometimes the United States actually sent troops to help one party in a State, on the pretext of maintaining order.

In this way the American capitalists gained effective control of these smaller countries of the south and ran their banks, railways, and mines, and exploited them to their own advantage. Even in the larger countries of Latin America they had great influence because of their investments and money control. That is to say, the United States annexed the wealth, or a great part of it, of these countries. Now, this is worth noting, as it is a new kind of empire, the modern type of empire. It is invisible and economic, and exploits and dominates without any obvious outward signs. The South American republics are politically and internationally free and independent. On the map they are huge countries, and there is nothing to show that they are not free in any way. And yet most of them are dominated completely by the United States.

We have seen in our glimpses of history imperialism of various kinds in different ages. Right at the beginning the victory of one people over another in war meant that the victors could do what they liked with conquered land and people. They annexed both the land and its inhabitants—that is to say, the conquered people became slaves. This was the ordinary custom. In the Bible one reads of the Jews being taken away into captivity, because they were defeated in war by the Babylonians, and there are many other instances. Gradually this gave place to another type of imperialism, when only the land was annexed and the people were not made slaves. It was, no doubt, discovered that it was easier to make money out of them by taxation and other methods of exploitation. Most of us still think of empires of this kind, like the British in India, and we imagine that if the British were not in actual political control of India, India would be free. But this type of empire is already passing away, and giving place to a more advanced and perfected type. This latest kind of empire does not annex even the land; it only annexes the wealth or the wealth-producing elements in the country. By doing so it can exploit the country fully to its own advantage and can largely control it, and at the same time has to shoulder no responsibility for governing and repressing that country. In effect both the land and the people living there are dominated and largely controlled with the least amount of trouble.

In this way imperialism has perfected itself in the course of time, and the modern type of empire is the invisible economic empire. When slavery was abolished, and later when the feudal type of serfdom went, it was thought that men would be free. Soon, however, it was found that men were still exploited and dominated by those who controlled the money-power. From slaves and serfs, men became wage-slaves; freedom for them was still far off. So also in the case of countries. People imagine that the only trouble is the political domination of one country by another, and that if this was removed freedom would automatically come. But that is not so obvious, as we can see politically free countries entirely under the thumb of others because of economic domination. The British Empire in India is obvious enough. Britain has political control over India. Side by side with this visible empire, and as a necessary part of it, Britain has economic control over India. It is quite possible that Britain's visible hold over India might go before long, and yet the economic control might remain as an invisible empire. If that happens, it means that the exploitation of India by Britain continues.

Economic imperialism is the least troublesome form of domination for the dominating power. It does not give rise to so much resentment as political domination because many people do not notice it. But when the pinch is felt, people begin to appreciate its workings and resent it. In Latin America now there is not much love for the United States, and many efforts have been made to create a block of Latin-American nations to oppose the dominance of North America. They are not likely to do much till they get over their habit of frequent palace revolutions and mutual quarrels.

The visible empire of the United States extends to the Philippine Islands. I have told you in a previous letter how America got possession of them after a war with Spain. This war began in 1898 over the island of Cuba in the Atlantic. Cuba became independent, but in name only. Both Cuba and Haiti are dominated by America.

About a dozen years ago the Panama Canal was opened. This is in the narrow strip of Central America and connects the Atlantic with the Pacific Ocean. It was designed more than fifty years ago by Ferdinand de Lesseps, the man who màde the Suez Canal. But he got into trouble, and it was the Americans who made the canal. They had great difficulties with malaria and yellow fever, but they set out to put an end to these diseases there, and they succeeded. They removed all the sources which bred malarial mosquitoes and other carriers of disease, and made the canal zone quite healthy. The canal is situated in the tiny Republic of Panama, but the United States control it as well as the little republic. To America the canal is a great boon, as otherwise ships had to go all the way round South America. Still, the importance of the Panama Canal is not so great as that of the Suez Canal.

So the United States went on growing stronger and wealthier and producing, among other things, millionaires and sky-scrapers. They caught up to Europe in many ways and passed it. Industrially they became the leading nation of the world, and the standard of life of their workers became higher than anywhere else. Because of this prosperity, as in England in the nineteenth century, socialistic and other radical theories had little support. American labour, with some exceptions, was most moderate and conservative. It was relatively well paid; why should it risk present comfort for a doubtful betterment ? It consisted chiefly of Italians and other " Dagos ", as they were contemptuously called. They were weak and disorganized, and were looked down upon. Even the better-paid skilled workers considered themselves a class apart from these " Dagos ".

In American politics two parties grew up—the Republican and the Democratic. As in England, and even more so than in England, they represented the same rich classes, and there was little difference of principle between them.

So matters stood when the World War came and ultimately sucked America into the whirlpool of strife.

139

SEVEN HUNDRED YEARS OF CONFLICT BETWEEN IRELAND AND ENGLAND

March 4, 1933

LET us cross the Atlantic again and go back to the Old World. The first land that a traveller by sea or air sees is that of Ireland; let us therefore make this our first stop. This green and beautiful island dips into the Atlantic Ocean on the far west of Europe. It is a small island, lying away from the main currents of world history; but little as it is, it is full of romance, and for centuries past it has shown invincible courage and spirit of sacrifice in the struggle for national freedom. Ireland has put up an amazing record of perseverance in this struggle against a powerful neighbour. The quarrel began over 750 years ago, and it is not settled yet ! We have seen British imperialism in action in India, China, and elsewhere. But Ireland has had to bear the brunt of it from the earliest days. Yet she has never willingly submitted to it, and almost every generation has seen a rebellion against England. The bravest of her sons have died fighting for freedom or been executed by the English authorities. Vast numbers of Irishmen have left the home that they loved so passionately and emigrated to foreign countries. Many joined foreign armies that were fighting England, so that thus they might have a chance of pitting their strength against the country which was dominating and oppressing their homeland. The exiles of Ireland spread out in many distant countries, and wherever they went they carried a bit of Ireland in their hearts.

Unhappy individuals and oppressed and struggling countries, all those who are dissatisfied and have little joy in the present, have a way of looking back to the past and searching for consolation in it. They magnify this past and find comfort in thinking of bygone greatness. When the present is full of gloom, the past becomes a haven of refuge giving relief and inspiration. Old grievances also rankle and are not forgotten. This ever looking backward is not a sign of health in a nation. Healthy people and healthy countries act in the present and look to the future. But a person or nation which is not free cannot be healthy, and so it is natural that he or it should look back and live partly in the past.

So Ireland still lives in the past, and Irish people treasure the memory of the old days when she was free, and remember vividly her many struggles for freedom and her old grievances. They look back, 1400 years ago, to the sixth century after Christ, when Ireland was a centre of learning for western Europe and drew students from afar. The Roman Empire had fallen and Vandals and Huns had crushed Roman civilization. In those days, it is said, Ireland was one of the places which kept the lamp of culture burning till a fresh revival of culture took place in Europe. Christianity came early to Ireland. Ireland's patron saint, St. Patrick, is supposed to have brought it. It was from Ireland that it spread to the north of England. In Ireland many monasteries were founded and, like the old *ashrams* in India and the Buddhist monasteries, these became centres of learning, where teaching often took place in the open air. From these monasteries went out missionaries to northern and western Europe to preach the new religion of Christianity to the heathen. Beautiful manuscripts were written and illuminated by some of the monks in the Irish monasteries. There is kept in Dublin now one such beautiful manuscript book called the *Book of Kells*, probably written about 1200 years ago.

This period of 200 or 300 years, from the sixth century onwards, is looked upon by many Irishmen as a kind of Golden Age of Ireland when Gaelic culture was at its height. Probably the distance in time lends an enchantment to these old days and makes them seem greater than they actually were. Ireland was split up among many tribes then, and these tribes were continually fighting each other. The weakness of Ireland, as of India, was mutual strife. Then came the Danes and Norsemen and, as in England and France, harried the Irish and took possession of large territories. Early in the eleventh century an Irish king, Brian Boruma, who became famous, defeated the Danes and united Ireland for a while, but the country split up again after his death.

You will remember that the Normans under William the Conqueror conquered England in the eleventh century. A hundred years later these Anglo-Normans invaded Ireland, and the part they conquered was called the " Pale ", from which probably has come the common expression " beyond the pale ", meaning outside a privileged circle or a social group. This Anglo-Norman invasion in 1169 hit the old Gaelic civilization hard, and it was the beginning of almost continuous war with the Irish tribes. These wars, which lasted for hundreds of years, were barbarous and cruel in the extreme. The English (as the Anglo-Normans might be called now) always looked down upon the Irish as a kind of semi-savage race. There was the difference of race, the English being Anglo-Saxons, the Irish Celts ; later came the difference in religion, the English and Scotch becoming Protestants, and the Irish remaining faithful to Roman Catholicism. So these Anglo-Irish wars had all the bitterness of racial and religious wars. The English deliberately prevented the two races from mixing. A law was even passed (a statute of Kilkenny) prohibiting intermarriages between the English and Irish.

Rebellion followed rebellion in Ireland, and each was crushed with great cruelty. The Irish naturally hated their foreign rulers and oppressors, and rose in rebellion whenever they had the chance and even without it. " England's difficulty is Ireland's opportunity " is an old saying, and both for political and religious reasons Ireland often sided with England's enemies, like France and Spain. This enraged the English greatly and gave them a feeling of being stabbed in the back, and they retaliated with all manner of atrocities.

In Queen Elizabeth's time (the sixteenth century) it was decided to break the resistance of the rebellious Irish natives by planting English landlords among them to keep them down. So land was confiscated, and the old Irish landowning classes had to give place to foreigners. Thus Ireland became practically a peasant nation with foreign landlords. And these landlords remained foreign to the Irish people even after the lapse of hundreds of years.

Queen Elizabeth's successor, James I of England, went forward another step in this attempt to break the spirit of the Irish. He decided to have a regular plantation of foreign colonists in Ireland, and for this purpose nearly all the land in the six counties of Ulster in the north of Ireland was confiscated by the King. There was land to be had for nothing, and crowds of adventurers came over from England and Scotland. Many of these English and Scottish people got land and settled down as farmers. The city of London was also asked to help in this colonizing process, and it formed a special society for the new " Plantation of Ulster ". It was because of this that the city of Derry in the north became known as Londonderry.

So Ulster became a patch of Britain in Ireland, and it is not surprising to find that this was bitterly resented by the Irish. The new Ulsterites, on their part, hated the Irish, and looked down upon them. What an amazingly clever imperialist move this was of England to break up Ireland into two hostile camps ! The Ulster problem still remains unsolved after over 300 years.

Soon after this plantation of Ulster there was Civil War in England between Charles I and Parliament. On the side of Parliament were the Puritans and Protestants, and Catholic Ireland naturally sided with the King, Ulster backing Parliament. The Irish were afraid, not without reason, that the Puritans would crush Catholicism, and they rose in a great rebellion in 1641. This rebellion and its crushing were even more ferocious and barbarous than the earlier ones. The Irish Catholics had cruelly massacred Protestants. Cromwell's revenge was terrible. There were many massacres of the Irish, and especially of Catholic priests, and Cromwell is still remembered with bitterness in Ireland.

In spite of all this terrorism and cruelty, a generation later there was again rebellion and civil war, of which two incidents stand out, the sieges of Londonderry and Limerick. Protestant Londonderry in Ulster was besieged by the Catholic Irish in 1688, and it was most gallantly defended, though the defenders had no food left and were starving. English ships at last brought food and relief, after four months of siege and privation. In Limerick in 1690 it was the other way about; the Catholic Irish were besieged by the English. The hero of this siege was Patrick Sarsfield, who defended Limerick magnificently against great odds. Even Irish women fought in this defence, and Gaelic songs about Sarsfield and his gallant band are still sung in the countryside in Ireland. Sarsfield ultimately gave up Limerick, but only after an honourable treaty with the British. One of the clauses of this Treaty of Limerick was that the Irish Catholics would be given full civil and religious liberty.

This Treaty of Limerick was broken by the English, or rather by the English landowning families in Ireland. These Protestant families controlled a subordinate parliament in Dublin and, in spite of the solemn promise made at Limerick, they refused to give civil or religious liberty to the Catholics. Instead of this they passed special laws penalizing Catholics and deliberately ruining the Irish woollen trade. Their tenantry was pitilessly crushed and evicted from their lands. Remember that this was done by a handful of foreign Protestant landlords against the vast majority of the population, which was Catholic, and most of which formed the tenantry. But all power was in the hands of these English landlords, and these landlords lived away from their estates and left their tenantry to the cruel rapacity of their agents and rent-collectors.

The story of Limerick is an old one, but the bitterness and anger that the breaking of a solemn word gave rise to have not yet subsided, and even to-day Limerick stands foremost in an Irish nationalist's mind in the record of English perfidy in Ireland. At that time this breach of a covenant, and religious intolerance and repression, and the cruelty of the landlords, drove large numbers of the Irish to other countries. The pick of Irish youth went abroad and offered their services to any country that was fighting England. Wherever there was fighting against England, these Irishmen were sure to be found.

Jonathan Swift, the author of *Gulliver's Travels*, lived during this period (he lived from 1667 to 1745), and something of his anger against the English can be gathered from his advice to his Irish countrymen : " Burn everything English *except* their coal ! " More bitter still is the epitaph on his tomb in St. Patrick's Cathedral in Dublin. This epitaph was very probably written by himself :

> Here lies the body of
> Jonathan Swift
> for thirty years dean
> of this cathedral,
> where savage indignation can
> no longer gnaw his heart.
>
> Go, traveller, and
> imitate, if you can, one who
> played a man's part in defence
> of Liberty.

In 1774 the American War of Independence broke out, and British troops had to be sent across the Atlantic. For a change, Ireland had practically no British troops, and there was talk of a French invasion, for France had also declared war against England. So both Irish Catholics and Protestants raised volunteers for defence. For a while they forgot their old animosities and, co-operating together, discovered their power. England had to face the threat of another rebellion, and fearing that Ireland also might break away, as America was doing, an independent parliament was granted to Ireland. Thus in theory Ireland became independent of England, but continued under the same king. But the Irish Parliament was the same old landlord-ridden, narrow assembly, confined to Protestants, which had in the past sat so heavily on the Catholics. Catholics were still penalized in many ways. The only difference was that a better feeling seemed to prevail between the Protestants and Catholics. The leader of this parliament, Henry Grattan, himself a Protestant, wanted to do away with Catholic disabilities. He succeeded in doing very little.

Meanwhile the French Revolution took place, and this led to great hopes in Ireland. Curiously enough, this was welcomed by both Catholic and Protestant, who were gradually drawing closer to each other. An organization, called the " United Irishmen ", was started to bring them together and emancipate the Catholics. The " United Irishmen " were not approved of by the government and were crushed. So the inevitable and periodic rebellion came in 1798. This was not a religious fight between Ulster and the rest of the country, as some of the old rebellions had been; it was a national rising in which to some extent both joined. The rising was crushed by England, and the Irish hero of it, Wolfe Tone, was executed as a traitor.

Thus it was obvious that the granting of an independent parliament to Ireland had made little difference to the Irish people. The English Parliament at the time was itself a narrow, corrupt affair elected by pocket boroughs and the like, and controlled by a small landowning class and a few of the richer merchants. The Irish Parliament had all these evils, and, in addition, was confined to a handful of Protestants in a Catholic country. Even so, the British Government decided to put an end to this Irish Parliament and to join Ireland to Britain. This was strongly opposed in Ireland, but heavy bribery of the members of the Dublin Parliament induced them to vote their own parliament out of existence. The Act of Union was passed in 1800, and thus ended Grattan's short-lived parliament, and instead some Irish members were sent to the British Parliament in London.

The suppression of this corrupt Irish Parliament was probably no great loss, except in so far as it might have developed later into something better. But this Act of Union did one real harm, and perhaps it was intended to do this. It succeeded in putting an end to the movement for unity between the North and the South, Protestant and Catholic. Protestant Ulster looked away again from the rest of Ireland, and the two parts grew estranged from each other. Another difference had crept in between the two. Ulster, like England, took to modern industry; the rest of Ireland remained agricultural, and even agriculture did not flourish because of the land system and the continuous emigration. Thus while the north became industrialized, the south and east, and especially the west, remained industrially backward and medieval.

The Act of Union did not pass off without a rising in protest against it. The leader of this abortive rising was Robert Emmett, a brilliant young man, who, as so many of his countrymen before him, ended his days on the scaffold.

Irish members went to the British House of Commons. But not Catholics. Catholics were not permitted to do so either in England or Ireland. In 1829 these disabilities were removed and Catholics could sit in the British Parliament. The Irish leader, Daniel O'Connell, was successful in getting these disabilities removed, and was therefore called the "Liberator". Another change that took place gradually was the widening of the franchise, which gave the vote to more and more persons. Ireland now being joined on to Britain, the same laws applied to both. Thus the great Reform Bill of 1832 applied to Ireland as well as to Britain. So also the later Franchise Bill, and in this way the type of Irish member in the British House of Commons began to change. From being a representative of the landlords, he became a spokesman of the Catholic peasantry and of Irish nationalism.

In their poverty the landlord-ridden and rack-rented Irish tenantry had made the potato their chief article of diet. They practically lived on potatoes and, like the Indian peasantry to-day, they had no reserves; there was nothing to fall back upon. They lived on the verge of existence, and had no powers of resistance left. In 1846 the potato crop failed, and this resulted in a great famine. But despite the famine the landlords turned out their tenantry for non-payment of rent. Large numbers of Irishmen left their homes for America and other countries, and Ireland became almost a depopulated land. Many of her fields were tilled no longer and became pasture-lands.

This process of conversion of agricultural land that was ploughed into pasture-land for sheep was continuous in Ireland for over 100 years and right up to our times. The principal reason for this was the growth of factories in England for the manufacture of woollen textiles. The more machinery was used the greater the production and the more wool was required. It was more profitable for the landlords in Ireland to have pasture-lands for sheep rather than tilled fields with men working in them. Pasture-lands require very few workers, just a handful to look after the sheep. The agricultural workers thus became superfluous and were turned out by the landlords. Thus Ireland, which was in reality thinly populated, always had " superfluous " workers, and the process of depopulation went on. Ireland became just an area to supply raw material to " industrial " England. This old process of converting tilled land into pastures has now been reversed, and again the plough is getting back to its own. Curiously enough, this has resulted from a trade war between Ireland and England, which began in 1932.

The land question, the troubles of the unhappy tenants under absentee landlordism, was the chief question in Ireland for a great part of the nineteenth century. Ultimately the British Government decided to remove these landlords completely by buying up their land compulsorily and then giving it to their tenants. The landlords, of course, did not suffer at all. They got their full price from the government. The tenants got the land, but with the burden of the price attached to it. They were made to pay this price not in a lump sum, but by small annual payments.

After the national rising of 1798 there was no big rebellion in Ireland for over 100 years. The nineteenth century, unlike previous centuries, was free from this periodical occurrence in Ireland. But this was not due to a feeling of contentment. There was the exhaustion of the last rising and of the great famine, and the depopulation. To some extent, in the latter half of the century, people's minds were also turned to the British Parliament in the hope that the Irish members there might be able to do something. But still some Irishmen wanted to keep alive the tradition of a periodical rising. Only so, they thought, could the spirit and soul of Ireland remain fresh and unsullied. The Irish immigrants in America started a society there for Irish independence. These people, " Fenians " they were called, organized petty risings in Ireland. But the masses were not touched and the Fenians were soon crushed.

I must end this letter now because it is long enough. But Ireland's story is not yet over.

140

HOME RULE AND SINN FEIN IN IRELAND

March 9, 1933

AFTER so many armed insurrections, and because of famine and other calamities, Ireland was a little weary of this method of trying to gain freedom. In the second half of the nineteenth century, as the franchise for the British Parliament widened, many nationalist Irish members were returned to the House of Commons. People began to hope that perhaps these people might be able to do something for Irish freedom; they began to look to parliamentary action instead of the old-time method of armed rebellion.

The rift between Ulster in the north and the rest of Ireland had widened again. The racial and religious differences continued and, in addition to these, economic differences became more marked. Ulster, like England and Scotland, was industrialized, and big factory production was taking place. The rest of the country was agricultural and medieval and depopulated and poor. England's old policy of dividing Ireland into two parts had succeeded only too well; so well, indeed, that England herself could not get over the difficulty when she tried to in later years. Ulster became the greatest obstacle to Irish freedom. In a free Ireland rich Protestant Ulster was afraid of being submerged in a poor Catholic Ireland.

In the British Parliament and in Ireland two new words came to be used, the words "Home Rule". Ireland's demand was now called Home Rule. This was much less than, and very different from, the 700-year-old demand for independence. It meant a subordinate Irish Parliament dealing with local affairs, the British Parliament continuing to control certain important matters. Many Irishmen did not agree with this watering down of the old demand for independence. But the country was weary of rebellion and strife and refused to take part in several abortive attempts at insurrection.

One of the Irish members in the British House of Commons was Charles Stewart Parnell. Realizing that neither of the British parties, the Conservatives and the Liberals, paid the slightest attention to Ireland, he decided to make it difficult for them to carry on with their polite parliamentary game. Together with some other Irish members he started obstructing parliamentary business by long speeches and other tactics merely meant to cause delay. English people were very annoyed with these tactics; they said that they were not parliamentary, not gentlemanly. But Parnell was not affected by these criticisms. He had not come to Parliament to play the polite English parliamentary game in accordance with rules of the Englishman's making. He had come to serve Ireland, and if he could not do so in the normal way, he considered himself fully justified in adopting abnormal methods. In any event, he succeeded in drawing attention to Ireland.

Parnell became the leader of the Irish Home Rule Party in the British House of Commons, and this party became a nuisance to the two old British parties. When these two parties were more or less evenly matched, the Irish Home Rulers could make a difference either way. In this way the Irish question was always kept in the forefront. Gladstone at last agreed to Home Rule for Ireland, and he brought forward a Home Rule Bill in the House of Commons in 1886. This was a very mild measure of self-government, but even so it created a storm. The Conservatives were, of course, wholly opposed to it. Even Gladstone's party, the Liberals, did not like it and the party split into two, one part actually joining the Conservatives, who came to be called "Unionists" because they stood for union with Ireland. The Home Rule Bill fell, and with it fell Gladstone.

Seven years later in, 1893, Gladstone, then eighty-four years of age, again became Prime Minister. He brought forward his second Home Rule Bill, and this was just passed by a narrow majority in the House of Commons. But all Bills have also to pass the House of Lords before they can become law, and the House of Lords was full of Conservatives and reactionaries. It was not elected. It was a hereditary assembly of big landowners with some bishops added. This House of Lords rejected the Home Rule Bill which the Commons had passed.

So parliamentary efforts also had failed to bring what Ireland wanted. Still the Irish Nationalist Party (or the Home Rule Party) continued to work in Parliament in the hope that they might succeed and, on the whole, they had the confidence of the people of Ireland. But there were also many who lost faith in these methods and in the British Parliament. Many Irishmen became somewhat disgusted with politics, in the narrow sense of the word, and devoted themselves to cultural and economic activities. In the early years of the twentieth century there was a cultural renaissance in Ireland and, in particular, an effort to revive Gaelic, the old language of the country, which still flourished in the western country districts. This Celtic language had a rich literature, but centuries of English domination had driven it away from the towns, and it was gradually disappearing. Irish nationalists felt that Ireland could only retain her soul and her old culture through the medium of their own language, and so they worked hard to dig it out of the western villages and make it a living language. A Gaelic League was founded for the purpose. Everywhere, and especially in all subject countries, a national movement bases itself on the language of the country. No movement based on a foreign language can reach the masses or take root. In Ireland English was hardly a foreign language. It was almost universally known and spoken; certainly it was better known than Gaelic. And yet Irish nationalists considered it essential to revive Gaelic so that they might not lose touch with their old culture.

There was a feeling in Ireland then that strength came from within, and not from outside. There was disillusion at purely political activities in Parliament, and attempts were therefore made to build up the nation on a firmer basis. The new Ireland of the early years of the twentieth century was different from the old, and the renaissance made itself felt in many directions. In the literary and the cultural, as I have mentioned above, as also in the economic, where efforts were made, with success, to organize the farmers on a co-operative basis.

But behind all this was the craving for freedom, and although the Irish Nationalist Party in the British Parliament seemed to hold the confidence of the Irish people, faith in them was shaking. They began to be looked upon as just politicians fond of making speeches and powerless to do anything. The old Fenians and other believers in independence had, of course, never believed in these parliamentarians and their Home Rule. But now the new and young Ireland also began to look away from Parliament. Ideas of self-help were in the air; why not apply them to politics? Again ideas of armed rebellion began to play about in people's minds. But a new turn was given to this desire for action. A young Irishman, Arthur Griffith, began to preach a new policy, which came to be known as *Sinn Fein*, meaning " we ourselves ".

These words give an idea of the policy behind them. The Sinn Feiners wanted Ireland to rely on itself and not look for succour or charity from England; they wanted to build up the nation's strength from inside. They supported the Gaelic movement and the cultural revival. In politics they disapproved of the futile parliamentary action that was going on, and expected nothing from it. On the other hand, they did not consider armed rebellion feasible. They preached "direct action", as opposed to parliamentary action, by means of a kind of non-co-operation with the British Government. Arthur Griffith gave the instance of Hungary, where a policy of passive resistance had succeeded a generation earlier, and pleaded for the adoption of a similar policy to force England's hands.

During the last thirteen years we have had a great deal to do with various forms of non-co-operation in India, and it is interesting to compare this Irish precedent with ours. As all the world knows, the basis of our movement has been non-violence. In Ireland there was no such foundation or background; and yet the strength of the proposed non-co-operation lay in a peaceful passive resistance. The struggle was to be essentially a peaceful one.

Sinn Fein ideas spread slowly among the youth of Ireland. Ireland did not suddenly catch fire because of them. There were many people still who hoped from Parliament, especially as the Liberal Party had come back again in 1906 with a huge majority. In spite of this majority in the House of Commons, the Liberals had to face a permanent Conservative and Unionist majority in the House of Lords, and soon there was conflict between the two. The result of this conflict was to curb the power of the Lords. In money matters their interference could be got over by the Commons by passing the Bill objected to by the Lords in three successive sessions. In this way, by the Parliament Act of 1911, the Liberals took out the teeth of the House of Lords. But still the Lords remained with a great deal of power to hold up and interfere.

Having provided for the inevitable resistance of the Lords, the Liberals brought forward the third Home Rule Bill, and this was passed by the Commons in 1913. As expected, the Lords threw it out, and then the Commons went through the laborious process of passing it in three sessions. It became law in 1914, and it applied to the whole of Ireland, including Ulster.

Ireland seemed to have got Home Rule at last, but—there were many buts! While Parliament had debated Home Rule in 1912 and 1913 strange things were happening in the north of Ireland. The leaders of Ulster had proclaimed that they would not accept it and would resist it even if it became law. They talked of rebellion, and prepared for it. It was even stated that they would not hesitate to ask the help of a foreign Power, meaning Germany, to fight Home Rule! This was open and unabated treason. More interesting still, the leaders of the Conservative Party in England blessed this rebellious movement, and many helped it. Money from the rich Conservative classes poured into Ulster. It was obvious that the so-called " upper classes " or governing class were generally with Ulster, and so were many of the army officers who came from these classes. Arms were smuggled in and volunteers were openly drilled. A provisional government was even formed in Ulster to take charge when the time came. It is interesting to note that one of the leading " rebels " in Ulster was a prominent Conservative member of Parliament, F. E. Smith, who, later, as Lord Birkenhead, was Secretary of State for India and held other high offices.

Rebellions are common enough occurrences in history, and Ireland especially has had her full share of them. Still, these preparations for an Ulster rebellion have a special interest for us, as the party at the back of it was the very party which prided itself on its constitutional and conservative character. It was the party which always talked of " law and order " and was in favour of heavy punishment for those who offended against this law and order. Yet prominent members of this party talked open treason and prepared for armed rebellion, and the rank and file helped with money ! It is also interesting to note that this projected rebellion was against the authority of Parliament, which was considering, and which later passed, the Home Rule Bill. Thus the very foundations of democracy were attacked by it, and the old boast of the English people that they believed in the reign of law and in constitutional activity was set at nought.

The Ulster " rebellion " of 1912-14 tore the veil from these pretensions and high-sounding phrases and disclosed the real nature of government and modern democracy. So long as " law and order " meant that the privileges and interests of the governing class were preserved, law and order were desirable ; so long as democracy did not encroach on these privileges and interests, it could be tolerated. But if there were any attack on these privileges, then this class would fight. Thus " law and order " was just a fine phrase meaning to them their own interests. This made it clear that the British Government was in effect a class government, and not even a majority in Parliament against it would dislodge it easily. If such a majority tried to pass a socialistic law which lessened their privileges, they would rebel against it in spite of democratic principles. It is well to keep this in mind, as it applies to all countries, and we are apt to forget this reality in a fog of pious phrases and resounding words. There is no essential difference in this respect between a South American republic, where revolutions occur frequently, and England, where there is a stable government. The stability consists in the governing classes having dug themselves in and no other class being strong enough so far to remove them. In 1911 one of their defences, the House of Lords, was weakened, and they took fright and Ulster became the pretext for rebellion.

In India the charmed words " law and order " are, of course, with us every day and many times a day. It is well, therefore, to remember exactly what they mean. We might also remember that one of our mentors, a Secretary of State for India, was a leader of the Ulster rebellion.

So Ulster prepared for rebellion with arms and volunteers, and the government calmly looked on. There were no ordinances promulgated against these preparations ! After a while the rest of Ireland started copying Ulster and organizing " National Volunteers ", but in order to fight for Home Rule and, if necessary, against Ulster. So rival armies grew up in Ireland. It is curious to find that the British authorities, who had winked at the arming of the volunteers for the Ulster rebellion, were much more wide awake in suppressing the " National Volunteers ", although these were not against the Home Rule Bill.

A clash between these two sets of volunteers in Ireland seemed inevitable, and that meant civil war. Just then a greater war, the World War, broke out in August 1914, and everything else sank into insignificance before it. The Home Rule Act indeed became law, but at the same time it was provided that it must not come into operation before the end of the war ! So Home Rule was as far off as ever, and much was to happen in Ireland before the end of the war came.

I am bringing up my account of various countries to the outbreak of the World War. We have arrived at this stage in Ireland, and so we must stop for the present. But one thing I must tell you before I finish this letter. The leaders of the Ulster rebellion, instead of being punished for their activities, were rewarded soon after by being made Cabinet Ministers and holders of high offices under the British Government.

141

BRITAIN SEIZES AND HOLDS ON TO EGYPT

March 11, 1933

FROM America we took a long hop across the Atlantic to Ireland. Let us hop again now to a third continent, Africa, and to another victim of British imperialism, Egypt. In some of my letters to you, references were made to Egypt's early history. They were brief and scrappy because of my own ignorance. Even if I knew more about the subject than I do, I could not go back at this stage to the early days again. We have at last almost finished our account of the nineteenth century, and are on the threshold of the twentieth, and there we must remain. We cannot be going backwards and forwards all the time ! Besides, if I attempted to tell the story of each country's past, would these letters ever end ?

Still, I would not have you imagine that Egypt's story is more or less of a blank. For Egypt is the Ancient among nations, and carries us back farther than any other country, and counts its periods not in paltry centuries, but in thousands of years. Wonderful

and awe-inspiring remains still remind us of this remote past.
Egypt was the earliest and greatest field for archæological research,
and as stone monuments and other relics were dug out from under
the sand, they told a fascinating tale of the days long, long ago,
when they were young. This process of digging and discovery
continues still, and adds fresh pages to Egypt's ancient history.
We cannot yet say when it begins and how it begins. Already,
nearly 7000 years ago, civilized people lived in the valley of the Nile
with a long record of cultural progress behind them. They wrote
in their picture-language, the hieroglyphics; they made beautiful
pottery and vases, and vessels of gold and copper and ivory and
carved alabaster.

Even before Alexander of Macedon conquered Egypt in the fourth
century B.C., thirty-one Egyptian dynasties are said to have ruled
there. From out of this vast period of 4000 or 5000 years some
wonderful figures of men and women stand out, and seem almost alive
even to-day—men and women of action, great builders, great
dreamers and thinkers, warriors, despots and tyrants, proud and
vain rulers, beautiful women. The long succession of Pharaohs
passes before us, millennium after millennium. Women have full
freedom and are among the rulers. It was a priest-ridden country,
and the Egyptian people were always wrapped up in the future
and in the other world. The great Pyramids, which were built
with forced labour and with great cruelty to the workers, were a kind
of provision for this future for the Pharaohs. Mummies again were
a way of preserving one's body for the future. All this seems rather
dark and stern and joyless. And then we come across wigs for men,
for they used to shave their heads, and children's toys ! There
are dolls and balls and little animals with movable limbs, and these
toys suddenly make us remember the human side of the old Egyptians, and they seem to come nearer to us through the ages.

In the sixth century B.C., about the time of the Buddha, the
Persians conquered Egypt and made it a province of their vast
empire, which stretched from the Nile to the Indus. These were
the Achæmenid kings, whose capital was Persepolis, and who tried
and failed to subdue Greece, and who were finally defeated by
Alexander the Great. Alexander was welcomed in Egypt almost
as a deliverer from the harsh rule of the Persians. He left his
monument there in the city of Alexandria, which became a famous
centre of learning and Greek culture.

You will remember that after Alexander's death his empire was
split up amongst his generals and Egypt fell to the lot of Ptolemy.
The Ptolemies soon acclimatized themselves and, unlike the Persians,
accepted Egyptian customs. They behaved like the Egyptians,
and were accepted almost as if they continued the old line of the
Pharaohs. Cleopatra was the last of these Ptolemies, and with
her death Egypt became a province of the Roman Empire a few
years before the Christian Era is supposed to have begun.

Long before Rome adopted Christianity, Egypt took to it, and the
Egyptian Christians were persecuted by the Romans and had to

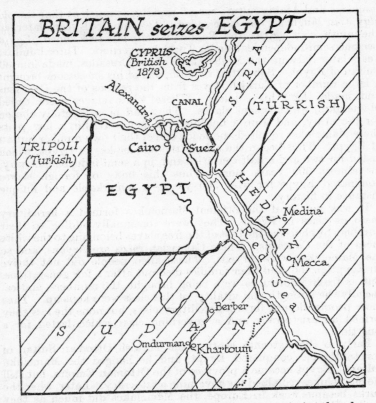

BRITAIN seizes EGYPT

CYPRUS
(British
1878)

Alexandria
CANAL
SYRIA
(TURKISH)

TRIPOLI
(Turkish)

Cairo
Suez

EGYPT

HEDJAZ
Red Sea

Medina

Mecca

S U D A N

Berber

Omdurman
Khartoum

hide in the desert. Secret monasteries grew up in the desert,
and the Christian world of those days was full of wonderful and
mysterious stories of the miracles performed by these hermits.
Later, when Christianity became the official religion of the Roman
Empire, after Constantine had adopted it, these Egyptian Christians
tried to revenge themselves by cruel persecutions of the non-
Christians, or pagans as they were called—those who confessed
the old Egyptian religion. Alexandria now became a famous
Christian centre of learning, but Christianity in Egypt, now that
it was the State religion, became a thing of sects and parties continually quarrelling with each other and fighting for mastery.
These bloody feuds became such a nuisance that the people generally
were thoroughly tired of all the Christian sects, and when, in the
seventh century, the Arabs came with a new religion, they were
welcomed. This was one of the reasons why the Arab conquest of
Egypt and North Africa was an easy one. Again the Christians
became a persecuted sect and were cruelly repressed.

So Egypt became a province of the Caliph's empire. The Arabic language and Arabic culture spread rapidly, so much so that the old Egyptian language was superseded. Two hundred years later, in the ninth century, as the Baghdad Caliphate weakened, Egypt became semi-independent under Turkish governors. Three hundred years later Saladin, the Moslem hero of the Crusades, made himself Sultan of Egypt. Soon after Saladin, one of his successors brought a large number of Turkish slaves from the regions of the Caucasus and made them his soldiers. These white slaves were called Mamelukes, which means slaves. They had been carefully chosen for the army, and were a fine body of men. Within a few years these Mamelukes revolted and made one of their own number Sultan of Egypt. Thus began the rule of the Mamelukes in Egypt, which lasted for two and a half centuries and, in a semi-independent way, for almost 300 years more. Thus this body of foreign slaves dominated Egypt for over 500 years—a remarkable and unique instance in history.

It was not as if the original Mamelukes formed a hereditary caste or class in Egypt. They were continually adding to their numbers by choosing the best of the free slaves belonging to the white races of the Caucasus. These Caucasian races are Aryans, and so the Mamelukes were Aryans. These alien people did not thrive on Egyptian soil, and their families died out after a few generations. But as fresh Mamelukes were being brought, the numbers, and especially the strength and vitality, of this class were kept up. Thus these people did not form a hereditary class, but none the less they formed an aristocracy and a governing class which lasted for a long time.

Early in the sixteenth century the Turkish Ottoman Sultan of Constantinople conquered Egypt, and he hanged the Mameluke Sultan. Egypt became a province of the Ottoman Empire, but still the Mamelukes remained the governing aristocracy. Later, when the Turks became weak in Europe, the Mamelukes did much as they liked in Egypt, although in theory Egypt continued to be part of the Ottoman Empire. When Napoleon came to Egypt at the end of the eighteenth century he met and defeated these Mamelukes. You may remember the story I told you of the Mameluke knight who rode up to the French army, and after the fashion of the Middle Ages and the days of chivalry, challenged its leader to single combat.

So we reach the nineteenth century. For the first half of this century Egypt was dominated by Mehemet Ali, an Albanian Turk, who had become governor of the country, or " Khedive " as these Turkish governors were called. Mehemet Ali is known as the founder of modern Egypt. The first thing he did was to break the power of the Mamelukes by having them treacherously massacred. He also defeated an English army in Egypt and made himself master of the country, just acknowledging the suzerainty of the Turkish Sultan for form's sake. He built up a new Egyptian army drawn from the peasantry (and not the Mamelukes); he built new canals; and he encouraged cotton-growing, which was to become Egypt's principal industry. He even threatened to take possession of Constantinople itself by driving out his nominal master, but refrained from doing so, and merely added Syria to Egypt.

Mehemet Ali died in 1849 at the age of eighty. His successors were feeble and extravagant and incompetent folk. But even if they had been better than they were, it would have been difficult for them to stand up against the rapacity of international financiers and the greed of European imperialisms. Money was lent by foreigners, especially English and French financiers, to the Khedives at exorbitant rates, mostly for their personal use, and then warships came to collect the interest when this was not paid in time ! It is an extraordinary story of international intrigue, of how financiers and governments work hand in glove with each other in order to despoil and dominate another country. In spite of the incompetence of several Khedives, Egypt made considerable progress. Indeed, the leading English newspaper, *The Times*, said in January 1876, " Egypt is a marvellous instance of progress. She has advanced as much in seventy years as other countries in five hundred." But in spite of all this, the foreign financiers insisted on their pound of flesh and, making it appear that the country was heading for bankruptcy, called for foreign intervention. The foreign governments, especially the English and French, were only too eager to intervene. They wanted an excuse, for Egypt was too tempting a morsel to be left to itself, and also Egypt was on the route to India.

Meanwhile the Suez Canal, built with forced labour and great inhumanity, had been opened for traffic in 1869. (It may interest you to know that there appears to have been such a canal between the Red Sea and the Mediterranean in the time of the old Egyptian dynasties about 1400 B.C. !) The opening of this canal immediately brought all the traffic between Europe and Asia and Australia to the Suez, and the importance of Egypt grew still more. For England, with her vital interests in India and the East, the control of the Canal and of Egypt became of paramount importance. The English Prime Minister in 1875, Disraeli, brought off a clever coup by buying up at a very low price all the Suez Canal shares of the insolvent Khedive. This was not only a good investment in itself, but it gave a great deal of the control of the Canal to the British Government. The rest of Egypt's shares in the Canal went to French financiers, so Egypt had practically no financial control left over the Canal. From these shares the British and the French have drawn enormous dividends, and have at the same time controlled the Canal and had this vital grip on Egypt. In 1932 the dividend of the British Government alone amounted to £3,500,000 on its original investment of £4,000,000.

It was inevitable that the British Government should try to gain further control of the country, and so in 1879 they started interfering continuously in Egyptian internal affairs, and put their own financiers in control. This was naturally resented by many Egyptians, and a nationalist party grew up bent on ridding Egypt of foreign interference. The leader of this was a young soldier,

Arabi Pasha, who came from poor working-class parents and had joined the Egyptian army as a private. His influence grew and he became Minister of War and, as such, he refused to carry out the directions of the English and French controllers. England's answer to this refusal to submit to foreign dictation was war, and in 1882 the British fleet bombarded and burnt the city of Alexandria. Having thus proclaimed the superiority of western civilization, and having also defeated the Egyptian forces on land, the British now took full control of Egypt.

In this way began the British occupation of Egypt. It was, in international law, an extraordinary position. Egypt was a province or a part of the Turkish dominions. England was supposed to be on friendly terms with Turkey, and yet she calmly occupied a part of these dominions. She put an agent of hers there. He was the boss over everybody, a kind of Great Moghal, like the Viceroy of India, and even the Khedive and his ministers were powerless before this British agent. The first British Agent was a Major Baring, who ruled in Egypt for twenty-five years and became Lord Cromer. Cromer ruled Egypt like a despot. His first concern was the payment of dividends to the foreign financiers and bond-holders. This was done regularly, and great praise was forthcoming for Egypt's sound finances. As in India, a measure of administrative efficiency was also brought about. But at the end of the twenty-five years the old Egyptian debt remained what it had been at the beginning. Practically nothing was done for education, and Cromer even stopped the starting of a national university. His outlook can be judged from a sentence in a letter of his written in 1892, to Lord Salisbury, who was then Prime Minister in England : " The Khedive is going to be very Egyptian " ! For an Egyptian to behave as an Egyptian should, was an offence in the eyes of Lord Cromer, just as for an Indian to behave as an Indian should is frowned upon and punished by the British.

The French did not like this British control of Egypt ; they had got no share of the loot. Nor did the other European Powers like it and, needless to say, the Egyptians did not like it at all. The British Government told everybody not to worry, as they were only in Egypt for a short while and would soon leave it. Again and again it was formally and officially declared by the British Government that they would evacuate Egypt. This solemn declaration was made about fifty times or more ; it is difficult to keep count of it. And yet the British stuck on, and are still there !

In 1904 the British came to an agreement with the French over many matters in dispute. They agreed to let the French have a free hand in Morocco, and in exchange for this the French agreed to recognize the British occupation of Egypt. It was a fair give and take, only Turkey, which was still supposed to be the suzerain Power, was not consulted, and of course there was no question of asking the Egyptian people !

Another feature of Egypt during this period was that the Egyptian courts had no power or jurisdiction over foreigners. These courts were not supposed to be good enough, and the foreigners were entitled to be tried by their own courts. So, what are called "extra-territorial" tribunals grew up, with foreign judges and with foreign interests at heart. One of these very foreign judges of the tribunal has written about them : *Leur justice a merveilleusement servie la coalition étrangère qui exploitait le pays.* I believe that the foreign residents of Egypt also escaped most of the taxation. A happy position—not to be taxed, not to be subject to the laws or courts of the country you are living in, and, at the same time to have every facility to exploit that country !

So Britain ruled and exploited Egypt, and her agents and representatives lived with all the pomp and pageantry of autocratic monarchs in their Residencies. Naturally nationalism grew and reform movements took shape. The greatest Egyptian reformer of the nineteenth century was Jamaluddin Afghani, a religious leader who sought to modernize Islam by reconciling it with modern conditions. He preached that all progress could be reconciled with Islam. His attempt to modernize Islam was similar in essence to attempts made in India to modernize Hinduism. These attempts are based on going back to certain basic teachings, and to finding new meanings and interpretations for old customs and dogmas. According to this, modern knowledge becomes a kind of addition to, or commentary upon, the old religious knowledge. This method is, of course, very different from the scientific method, which goes forward boldly without any such previous commitments. However, Jamaluddin's influence was very great not only in Egypt, but in the other Arabic countries.

With the growth of foreign trade a new middle class arose in Egypt, and this class became the backbone of the new nationalism. Out of this class came Saad Zaghlul Pasha, the greatest of modern Egyptian leaders. Egypt is predominantly a Muslim country, but there are still a considerable number of Copts who are Christians. These Copts are the purest of the old Egyptians. The new middle class contained both Muslims and Copts, and fortunately there was no antagonism between them. The British tried to create conflict between them, but they met with little success. The British also tried to divide the nationalist party. Occasionally they succeeded, as in India, in getting a few of the moderates to co-operate with them. But of this I shall tell you more in some subsequent letter.

This was the position of Egypt when the World War began in August 1914. Three months later Turkey joined Germany against England and France and their allies. Thereupon England actually decided on annexing Egypt, but some difficulties arose, and instead a British protectorate over Egypt was proclaimed.

So much for Egypt. The rest of Africa also fell a victim to European imperialism in the second half of the nineteenth century. There was a tremendous rush, and the huge continent was divided up among the European Powers. Like vultures they fell upon it, sometimes falling out with each other. Few met with any checks, but Italy was defeated in Abyssinia in 1896. Africa was predominantly under British or French control, and some parts were under Belgian, Italian, and Portuguese control. The Germans were there also till their defeat in the war. Only two independent States remained, Abyssinia in the East and little Liberia on the west coast. Morocco was under French and Spanish influence.

The story of how these vast territories were taken possession of is long and gruesome. It is by no means over yet. Worse still were the methods adopted to exploit the continent, and especially to extract rubber. Many years ago a shock of horror passed through the so-called civilized world at the tales of atrocities committed in the Belgian Congo. The Black Man's Burden has been a terrible one.

Africa, known as the Dark Continent, was an almost unknown land, so far as its interior was concerned, till the latter half of the nineteenth century. Many an adventurous and exciting journey across it had to be undertaken before this land of mystery could be put properly on the map. The greatest of its explorers was David Livingstone, a Scottish missionary. For years the continent swallowed him up and the outside world had no news of him. Connected with his name is that of Henry Stanley, a newspaper man and explorer, who went to look for him and found him at last in the heart of the continent.

142

TURKEY BECOMES THE "SICK MAN OF EUROPE"

March 14, 1933

FROM Egypt, across the Mediterranean, to Turkey is a small and natural step. The nineteenth century was to see the progressive crumbling away of the empire of the Ottoman Turks in Europe. The gradual decline had started in the previous century. Perhaps you remember my telling you of the Turkish sieges of Vienna, and of how, for a while, Europe trembled before the sword of the Turks. Pious Christians in the West considered the Turk as the "Scourge of God" sent to punish Christendom for its sins. But the final repulse of the Turks from the gates of Vienna turned the tide, and thenceforward they were on the defensive in Europe. The many nationalities they had subdued in south-eastern Europe were so many thorns in their side. No attempt was made to assimilate them, and probably this was not possible even if the attempt had been made, and the spirit of nationalism was coming into conflict with the heavy rule of the Turk. In the north-east Tsarist Russia was growing bigger and bigger, and always pressing hard on the Turkish dominions. She became the traditional and persistent enemy of the Turks, and for nearly 200 years waged intermittent war against them till both Tsar and Sultan went down almost together and took their empires with them.

The Ottoman Empire lasted long enough as empires go. After existing for a long period in Asia Minor, it was established in Europe in 1361. Although Constantinople itself did not fall to the Turks till 1453, all the territory round it went to them long before this date. The great city was saved for a while by the eruption of Timur in western Asia and his crushing defeat of the Turkish Sultan in 1402 at Angora. But the Turks soon recovered from this. From 1361 to the end of the Ottoman Empire in our own time is over five and a half centuries, and that is a long time.

And yet the Turk did not fit in at all with the new conditions that were developing in Europe after the end of the Middle Ages. Trade and commerce were growing, production was being organized on a bigger scale in the manufacturing cities of Europe. The Turk felt no attraction for this kind of thing. He was a fine soldier, a hard fighter and disciplinarian, easy-going in his intervals of leisure, but fierce and cruel when roused. Although he settled down in cities and beautified them with fine buildings, he carried something of his old nomadic way about him and fashioned his life accordingly. This way was perhaps the most suitable in the homelands of the Turks, but it did not fit in with the new surroundings in Europe or Asia Minor. The Turks refused to adapt themselves to the new surroundings, and so there was a continuous conflict between the two different systems.

The Ottoman Empire connected three continents—Europe, Asia, Africa; it covered all the ancient trade routes between East and West. If the Turks had been so inclined and had possessed the necessary capacity for it, they could have taken advantage of this favourable position and become a great commercial nation. But they had no such inclination or capacity, and they went out of their way to discourage this trade, probably because they did not like to see others profiting by it. It was partly owing to this stopping of the old trade routes that the seafaring and commercial peoples of Europe felt compelled to search for other routes to the East, and this led to the discoveries of new routes by Columbus in the west and Diaz and Vasco da Gama in the east. But the Turks remained indifferent to all this and controlled their empire by sheer discipline and military efficiency. The result was that commercial and wealth-producing activities gradually faded away in the European parts of the Ottoman Empire. Partly also this was brought about by the racial and religious conflict. The Turks and the Christian peoples of the Balkans had inherited the old religious feud from the time of the Crusades and before. The growth of the new nationalism added fuel to this fire, and there was continuous trouble. To give you an instance of how the European parts of the Ottoman dominions deteriorated : Athens, the famous city of old, was but a village of about 2000 inhabitants when Greece became free in 1829. (Now, 100 years later, Athens has a population of over 500,000.)

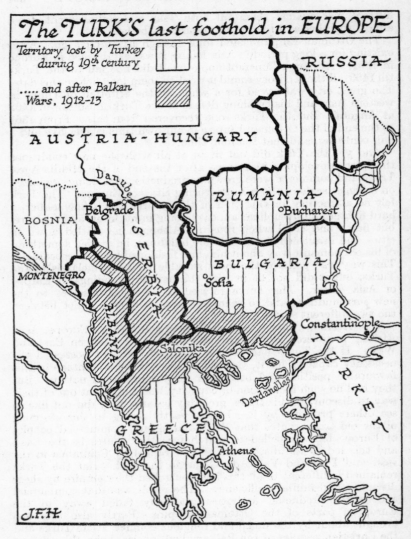

The TURK'S last foothold in EUROPE

Territory lost by Turkey
during 19th century

..... and after Balkan
Wars, 1912-13

RUSSIA

AUSTRIA-HUNGARY

Danube

RUMANIA

Belgrade   oBucharest

BOSNIA

SERBIA

MONTENEGRO   BULGARIA

                                      oSofia

ALBANIA   Constantinople

                    Salonika

                                      Dardanelles   TURKEY

GREECE

                    Athens

J.F.H.

This dropping away of commercial and other wealth-producing
activities was ultimately bad for the Turkish rulers themselves.
As the limbs of the empire grew weak and poor, the heart of the
empire also grew weak and suffered. It is surprising, indeed,
that in spite of all these conflicts and difficulties the empire lasted
so long.

The strength of the Ottoman Sultans for several hundred years

consisted in the " Janissaries ", a corps of Turkish soldiers consisting
of Christian slaves, who were carefully trained from boyhood upwards. These Janissaries remind one of the Egyptian Mamelukes,
but there was a difference between them. Although they remained
the flower of the Turkish army, they never became the ruling power
as in Egypt. But, like the Mamelukes, they did not form a hereditary
caste. As slaves they were favoured people with high posts and
offices reserved for them ; their sons, however, became free Muslims,
and for a long time they could not remain in this favoured corps,
which was confined to slaves. Recruitment to the corps was always
from new white Christian slaves. All this sounds very extraordinary,
does it not ? But remember that the word slave had not got quite
the same meaning in Islamic countries in those days, as it has now.
Slaves were often technically and legally slaves, but they rose
to the highest offices. In India you will remember the Slave Kings
of Delhi ; Saladin of Egypt also was originally a slave. The point
of view of the Turks seems to have been that a very thorough
training should be given to the ruling class to make them as efficient
as possible. They knew, as every teacher knows, that the best
period to train a person is from early childhood upwards. It
was perhaps not easy to take away the children of their Muslim
subjects and cut them off completely from their parents or make them
slaves. So they got hold of little Christian boys and made them
join the Sultan's slave household and gave them a rigorous training.
Of course the little boys became Muslims as they grew up.

This system was extended to the Sultans themselves. The
Sultan did not marry in the ordinary way. Carefully chosen
slave-girls were sent to his household, and they became the mothers
of his children. Thus all the Ottoman Sultans up to the early
eighteenth century were sons of slave mothers, and they had to
undergo the same rigorous training and severe discipline as any
other member of the slave household.

There was a certain amount of science in this careful selection
of slaves and their discipline and training for special functions,
from that of the Sultan downwards. It did result in a measure of
efficiency in particular spheres, and continually fresh blood came
from the new slaves, and a hereditary ruling caste could not grow
up. Perhaps the early strength of the empire depended on this
system. But it was obviously utterly out of keeping with European
or Asiatic conditions. It was quite different from the feudal system,
and it was even farther removed from the system which was replacing feudalism in Europe. Under this system, and in the absence of much trade and commerce, no real middle class could grow
up. The system could not continue in its original purity after the
second half of the sixteenth century, when a hereditary element
came into the slave household, and the sons of members of the
household could remain in it and follow their fathers' careers.
In many other ways also there was a gradual loosening of the
system. But the background remained, and this made Turkey
entirely different from, and a stranger in, Europe in spite of centuries

of close association. Within Turkey itself the foreign communities remained wholly apart, with their own laws and groupings.

I have told you so much about this extraordinary old Turkish system because it was unique and it helped to shape the Ottoman Empire. It does not, of course, exist now; it is a matter of history.

Turkey's history for the last 200 years is one of warfare against the continually advancing Russians and against revolts by subject nationalities. Greece, Rumania, Serbia, Bulgaria, Montenegro, Bosnia, were all Balkan countries and parts of the Ottoman Empire. Greece, as we saw, broke away in 1829 with the help of England, France and Russia. Russia is a Slav country, and so are Bulgaria and Serbia in the Balkans. Tsarist Russia tried to appear as the protector and champion of these Balkan Slavs. The real lure for Russia was Constantinople, and all its diplomacy was aimed at the eventual possession of this ancient seat of empire, the Tsar considering himself a successor of the Byzantine emperors. In 1730 began the series of Russo-Turkish wars, and they continued, with intervals of peace, in 1768, 1792, 1807, 1828, 1853, 1877 and, lastly, in 1914. In 1774 Russia got the Crimea from Turkey, and thus reached the Black Sea. But this was not much good, as the Black Sea is bottled up and Constantinople sits at the neck. In 1792 and 1807 the Russian frontier kept on advancing towards Constantinople and the Turkish frontier receding. During the Greek War of Independence, the Tsar tried to profit by it by attacking the Turks when they had their hands full elsewhere. He would have captured Constantinople if England and Austria had not intervened.

Why did England and Austria save Turkey from Russia? Not for love of Turkey, but because of rivalry and fear of Russia. I have told you before of the traditional rivalry of England and Russia in Asia and elsewhere. The possession of India especially brought the British right up to the Russian frontier, and they were continually having nightmares as to what Tsarist Russia might do to India. So it was their policy to thwart her and prevent her from adding to her strength. The possession of Constantinople would have given her a fine port in the Mediterranean and enabled her to keep a fleet of warships near the route to India. This was too much of a risk, and so England repeatedly stopped Russia from crushing Turkey. Austria also was interested in keeping Russia away. Austria is a tiny country now, but a few years ago it was a big empire adjoining the Balkans, and it wanted to have a big share in the Balkan countries itself when Turkey went to pieces. So it had to keep Russia away.

Poor Turkey seemed in a bad way with these powerful neighbours waiting for something to happen to her in order to pounce upon her and tear her to pieces. The Tsar of Russia, referring to Turkey, said to the British Ambassador in 1853: "We have on our hands a sick man—a very sick man. . . . He may die suddenly upon our hands. . . ." The phrase became a famous one, and Turkey was henceforth the "Sick Man of Europe". But the sick man took a mighty long time in dying!

In that very year, 1853, the Tsar made another attempt to put an end to him. That resulted in the Crimean War, in which England and France checked Russia. Twenty-one years later, in 1877, the Tsar again attacked Turkey and defeated her, but again foreign intervention saved Turkey to some extent, at any rate saved Constantinople from Russia. There was a famous international conference in Berlin in 1878 to consider the fate of Turkey, and Bismarck was there and Disraeli, and many other leading politicians of Europe, and they threatened and intrigued against each other. England seemed to be on the verge of war with Russia when the latter gave in. As a result of the Treaty of Berlin, the Balkan countries Bulgaria, Serbia, Rumania and Montenegro gained their independence; Austria occupied Bosnia and Herzegovina (which in theory remained under Turkish sovereignty); and Britain took the island of Cyprus, as a kind of commission from Turkey, for having sided with her to some extent.

The next Russo-Turkish war took place thirty-six years later, in 1914, as a part of the Great War.

Meanwhile considerable changes had been taking place in Turkey. The decisive defeat by Russia in 1774 had given the first shock to the Turks, and made them realize that they were getting left behind by the rest of Europe. Being a military nation, the first thing that struck them was that the army should be brought up to date. This was done to some extent and it was through the new officer class that western ideas crept into Turkey. As I have told you, there was not much of a middle class, and there was no other organized class. After the Crimean War of 1853–56 a real attempt at westernization was made. A movement favouring a constitutional form of government (which meant a democratic assembly instead of the autocracy of the Sultan) developed. Midhat Pasha was the leader of this. In 1876 there were riots in Constantinople in favour of having a constitution, and the Sultan granted it, only to set it aside almost immediately because of a revolt in Bulgaria and the Russian War. The heavy expense of this war and the cost of the reforms at the top without any fundamental economic change brought about the bankruptcy of the Turkish Government, with the result that money had to be borrowed from western financiers, and these people took control of part of the revenue. So the attempt at westernization and reform was not a success. It was difficult to fit this in with the old fabric of the empire.

Early in the twentieth century the demand for a constitution became strong. As before, the only organized people were the military officers, and it was among them that the new party, called the Young Turk Party, spread rapidly. Secret " Committees of Union and Progress " were formed and, having won over a great part of the army, they forced the Sultan in 1908 to restore the old constitution of 1876. There were great rejoicings, and Turks and Armenians and others, who had till then mutually killed each other, embraced and shed tears of joy at the dawn of a new era when all were going to be equal and the subject races would have full rights.

Enver Bey, handsome and vain, but also daring and adventurous, was the chief hero of this bloodless revolution. Mustapha Kemal, later to become the saviour of Turkey, was also an important Young Turk leader, but compared to Enver, he was in the background, and the two did not like each other.

The Young Turks did not have an easy time. The Sultan gave them trouble, and there was bloodshed, and the Sultan was deposed and another put in his place. There were economic difficulties and trouble with foreign Powers. Austria took advantage of the prevailing confusion to declare the annexation of Bosnia and Herzegovina (which she had occupied in 1878 after the Treaty of Berlin). Italy forcibly seized Tripoli in North Africa and declared war. The Turks could do little, as they had no proper navy, and had to submit to Italian demands. They had barely done so, when a new danger nearer home threatened them. Bulgaria, Servia, Greece and Montenegro, anxious to drive Turkey out of Europe and share the spoils, and seeing that the moment was favourable, allied themselves together in a Balkan League and attacked Turkey in October 1912. Turkey was exhausted and disorganized, and a contest for power was going on between the constitutionalists and the reactionaries. She collapsed completely before the Balkan League and had huge losses. Thus the first Balkan War ended in a few months, and Turkey was driven out of Europe almost completely, with only Constantinople remaining to her. Even Adrianople, the oldest of her European cities, was wrenched from her, much against her will.

Very soon, however, the victors fell out over the spoils and Bulgaria suddenly and treacherously attacked her previous allies. There was mutual slaughter then and, to profit by the confusion, Rumania, which had previously kept aloof, joined in. In the result, Bulgaria lost all she had gained, and Rumania, Greece and Serbia greatly increased their territories. Turkey also got back Adrianople. The hatred of the Balkan people for each other is something amazing. The Balkan countries are small, but they have been the storm-centre of Europe on many an occasion.

The Sultan who was deposed by the Young Turks in 1909 was an interesting person. His name was Abdul Hamid II, and he came to the throne in 1876. He had no love for reforms and modern innovations, but he was able in his way, and had a reputation for playing off the great Powers against one another. All the Ottoman Sultans, you will remember, were also Caliphs, or the religious heads of Islam. Abdul Hamid tried to exploit his position as such by attempting to build up a Pan-Islamic movement—that is, a movement in which Muslims of other countries could join, so that he could get their support. There was some talk of this Pan-Islamism for a few years in Europe and Asia, but it had no substantial foundation, and the Great War completely put an end to it. Pan-Islamism was opposed by nationalism in Turkey, and nationalism proved the greater force of the two.

Sultan Abdul Hamid became very unpopular in Europe, because

he was considered responsible for atrocities and massacres in Bulgaria and Armenia and elsewhere. Gladstone called him the "Great Assassin ", and led a great campaign in England against these atrocities. The Turks themselves consider his reign as the darkest period of their history. Massacres and atrocities seem to have been fairly regular occurrences in the Balkans and in Armenia, and both parties indulged in them. The Balkan peoples and the Armenians were as guilty of massacring Turks as the Turks were of massacring them. Centuries of racial and religious animosities had sunk deep into the very nature of these peoples, and they found terrible expression. Armenia was the worst sufferer. It is now one of the Soviet republics near the Caucasus.

So after the Balkan Wars Turkey found herself exhausted and with just a foothold left in Europe. The rest of her empire was also cracking up. Egypt, of course, belonged to her in name only; in reality Britain occupied and exploited the country. But even the other Arab countries were showing signs of a national movement. It is not surprising that Turkey felt dispirited and disillusioned. All the brave hopes of 1908 seem to have ended in ashes. Just then Germany seemed to sympathize with her. Germany was looking east, and had visions of German influence pervading the whole of the Middle East. Turkey also turned to Germany, and their contacts grew. This was the position when the World War of 1914 came, just a year after the second Balkan War had ended. Turkey was to have no rest.

143

THE RUSSIA OF THE TSARS

March 16, 1933

RUSSIA to-day is a Soviet country, and its government is run by representatives of the workers and peasants. In some ways it is the most advanced country in the world. Whatever actual conditions may be, the whole structure of government and society is based on the principle of social equality. That is so now. But some years ago, and right through the nineteenth century and before, Russia was the most backward and reactionary country in Europe. The purest forms of autocracy and authoritarianism flourished there; in spite of revolutions and changes in western Europe, the theory of the divine right of kings was still upheld by the Tsars. Even the Church, which was the old orthodox Greek Church and not the Roman or Protestant, was perhaps even more authoritarian than elsewhere, and it was a prop and a tool of the Tsarist government. " Holy Russia " the country was called, and the Tsar was the " Little White Father " of everybody, and these legends were used by the Church and the authorities to befog people's minds and turn their

attention from political and economic conditions. Holiness has
kept strange company in the course of history !

The typical symbol of this " Holy Russia " was the *knout*, and a
frequent occupation was *pogroms*—two words which Tsarist Russia
presented to the world. The *knout* was a whip used to punish serfs
and others. *Pogrom* means devastation and organized persecution;
in effect it meant massacres, especially of the Jews. And behind
Tsarist Russia were the vast lonely steppes of Siberia, a name which
had come be to associated with exile and prison and despair. Large
numbers of political convicts were sent to Siberia, and big exile
camps and colonies grew up, and near each of them were the graves
of suicides. Long and lonely terms of exile and prison are hard to
bear, and the mind of many a brave person has given way and the
body broken down under the strain. To live cut off from the world
and far away from one's friends and companions and those who
share one's hopes and lighten one's burden, one must have strength
of mind, and inner depths which are calm and steady, and the courage
to endure. So Tsarist Russia struck down every head that was raised
and crushed every attempt to gain freedom. Even travelling was
made difficult, so that liberal ideas might not come from abroad.
But freedom repressed has a way of adding compound interest
to itself, and when it moves forward, its progress is likely to be in
jumps, which upset the old apple-cart.

In our previous letters we have had some glimpses of the activities
and policies of Tsarist Russia in various parts of Asia and Europe—
in the Far East, in Central Asia, in Persia, and in Turkey. Let us
now fill in the picture a little and connect these separate activities
with the main theme. The geographical position of Russia is such
that it has always had two faces, one looking west and the other east.
It is, by virtue of its position, a Eurasian Power, and its later
history has been an alternation of its interest in East and West.
Repulsed in the west, it looked to the east; held up in the east,
it turned round again to the west.

I have told you of the breaking up of the old Mongol empires, the
legacy of Chengiz Khan, and of how the Mongols of the Golden
Horde were ultimately driven away from Russia by the Russian
princes under the leadership of the Prince of Moscow. This took
place at the end of the fourteenth century. The Princes of Moscow
gradually became the autocratic rulers of the whole country and
began to call themselves Tsars (or Cæsars). Their outlook and
customs remained largely Mongolian, and there was little in common between them and western Europe, which considered Russia
as barbarous. In 1689 came Tsar Peter to the throne, called Peter
the Great. He decided to make Russia face west, and he went on a
long tour of European countries to study conditions there. He
copied much that he saw and imposed his ideas of westernization
on his reluctant and ignorant nobility. The masses, of course,
were very backward and repressed, and there was no question for
Peter as to what they thought of his reforms. Peter saw that the
great nations of his day were strong on the sea, and he realized

the importance of sea-power. But Russia, huge as it was, had then no outlet on the sea except in the Arctic Ocean, which was not much good. So he pushed north-west to the Baltic and south to the Crimea. He did not reach the Crimea (his successors did that), but he got to the Baltic after defeating Sweden. He founded a new westernized city, called St. Petersburg, on the Neva, off the Gulf of Finland, which led to the Baltic Sea. He made this his capital, and so tried to break with the old traditions which clung to Moscow. Peter died in 1725.

More than half a century later, in 1782, another Russian ruler tried to " westernize " the country. This was a woman, Catherine II, also called the Great. She was an extraordinary woman, strong, cruel, able, and with a very unsavoury reputation about her personal life. Having disposed of her husband, the Tsar, by murder, she became the Autocrat of all the Russias and ruled for fourteen years. She posed as a great patron of culture and tried to make friends with Voltaire, with whom she corresponded. The French Court at Versailles was copied by her to some extent, and some educational reforms were introduced. But all this was at the top and for show purposes. Culture cannot be copied suddenly; it has to take root. A backward nation merely aping advanced nations changes the gold and silver of real culture into tinsel. The culture of western Europe was based on certain social conditions. Peter and Catherine, without trying to produce these conditions, tried to copy the super-structure, with the result that the burden of these changes fell on the masses and actually strengthened serfdom and the Tsar's autocracy.

So in Tsarist Russia an ounce of progress went hand in hand with a ton of reaction. The Russian peasants were practically slaves. They were tied to their lands and could not leave them without special permission. Education was limited to some officers and intellectuals, all drawn from the landed gentry. There was practically no middle class, and the masses were entirely illiterate and backward. In the past there had been frequent and bloody peasant revolts, blind revolts due to too much oppression, and they had been crushed. Now, with a bit of education at the top, some of the prevalent ideas of western Europe also trickled through. Those were the days of the French Revolution and then of Napoleon. Napoleon's fall, you will remember, resulted in reaction all over Europe, and Tsar Alexander I, with his " Holy Alliance " of emperors, was the champion of this reaction. His successor was even worse. Stung into action, a group of young officers and intellectuals rose in rebellion in 1825. They all belonged to the landowing class and had no backing in the masses or the army; they were crushed. They are called " Decembrists ", because their revolt took place in December, 1825. This revolt is the first outward sign of political awakening in Russia. It was preceded by secret political societies, as every kind of public political activity was prevented by the Tsar's government. These secret societies continued and revolutionary ideas began to spread, especially among the intellectuals and university students.

After Russia's defeat in the Crimean War, some reforms were introduced, and in 1861 serfdom was abolished. This was a great thing for the peasantry, and yet it did not bring them much relief, for the freed serfs were not given enough land to support them. Meanwhile, the spread of revolutionary ideas among the intelligentsia and their repression by the Tsar's government went on side by side. There was no link or common ground between these advanced intellectuals and the peasantry. So, in the early seventies, the socialistically inclined (they were all very vague and idealistic) students decided to carry their propaganda to the peasantry, and thousands of students descended upon the villages. The peasants did not know these students. They distrusted them and suspected some plot perhaps to restore serfdom. And so these peasants actually arrested many of these students, who had come at the peril of their lives, and handed them over to the Tsar's police ! This was an extraordinary example of trying to work in the air without being in touch with the masses.

This utter want of success with the peasantry was a great shock to these student intellectuals, and, in disgust and despair, they took to what is called " terrorism ", that is, throwing bombs and otherwise trying to kill those in authority. This was the beginning in Russia of terrorism and the cult of the bomb, and with it revolutionary activities took a new phase. These bomb-throwers called themselves " Liberals with a bomb ", and their terrorist organization was named " Will of the People ". This name was pretentious, as the people concerned were relatively small groups.

Thus began the new contest between these groups of determined young men and women and the Tsar's government. The revolutionary forces were swelled by the addition of people from the many subject races and national minorities in Russia. All these races and minorities were ill-treated by the government. They were not allowed to make public use of their own languages, and in many other ways they were harassed and humiliated. Poland, which was industrially more advanced than Russia, had been made just a province of Russia, and the very name of Poland had practically disappeared. The Polish language was prohibited. If this was the treatment accorded to Poland, worse treatment was given to other minorities and races. There was a rebellion in Poland in the sixties which was suppressed with great cruelty; and 50,000 Poles were sent to Siberia. Jews were continually being subjected to *pogroms*—that is, massacres, and large numbers of them migrated to other countries.

It was natural that these Jews and others, full of anger at the Tsarist oppression of their races, should join the Russian terrorists. Nihilism, as this terrorism was called, grew, and it met naturally with a bloody suppression, and long trains of political convicts trudged into the Siberian steppes, and many were executed. To meet this menace the Tsar's government adopted a method which was carried to extraordinary lengths. They sent *agents-provocateurs* to the ranks of the terrorists and revolutionaries, and these

people actually provoked bomb outrages, and sometimes committed them themselves, so that they might implicate others. One of these famous *agents-provocateurs* was Azeff, who was one of the leading bomb-throwing revolutionaries and was at the same time a chief of the Russian secret police ! There are other well-authenticated cases of this kind where Tsarist generals in the secret police took to bomb-throwing *as agents of the police* to get others into trouble !

While all this was happening, the Russian dominions were continually spreading eastwards and, as I have told you, they eventually reached the Pacific. In Central Asia they came to the frontiers of Afghanistan, and in the south they were pushing away at the Turkish frontier. Another important development, from the sixties onwards, was the rise of western industry. This was limited to a few areas only, like the Petersburg neighbourhood, and in Moscow, and the country as a whole remained completely agricultural. But the factories that were put up were quite up-to-date, and were usually under English management. Two results followed. Russian capitalism developed rapidly in these few industrial areas, and a working class also grew equally rapidly. As in the early days of the British factory system, the Russian workers were terribly exploited, and made to work almost night and day. But there was this difference. New ideas had now arisen, ideas of socialism and communism, and the Russian worker had a fresh mind and was receptive to these ideas. The British worker, with a long tradition behind him, had grown conservative and tied to old ideas.

These new ideas began to take shape, and a " Social Democratic Labour Party " was formed. This was based on the Marxist philosophy. These Marxists declared themselves against acts of terrorism. According to the theories of Karl Marx the working class had to be roused to action, and only by such mass action could they achieve their goal. The killing of individuals by terrorism would not move the working class to such action, for the goal was the overthrow of Tsarism, and not the assassination of the Tsar or his ministers.

As early as the 'eighties a young man, later to become known all over the world as Lenin, had participated in revolutionary activities even as a student at school. In 1887, when he was seventeen, he had to face a terrible blow. His elder brother Alexander, to whom Lenin was greatly attached, was executed on the scaffold for taking part in a terroristic attempt on the Tsar's life. In spite of the shock, Lenin said even then that freedom was not to be obtained by methods of terrorism; the way was through mass action only. And, grimly and with set teeth, this young man went on with his school work, appeared for his final school examination, and passed with distinction. Such was the stuff of which the leader and maker of the revolution of thirty years later was made !

Marx used to think that the working-class revolution which he predicted would begin in a highly industrialized country, like Germany, with a big and organized working class. He considered Russia

as the most unlikely place for this because of its backwardness
and medievalism. But in Russia he found faithful followers among
the young, who studied him with a passion for finding out what they
should do to put an end to their intolerable condition. The very
fact that in Tsarist Russia no open activity or constitutional methods
were open to them drove them to this study and to discussion among
themselves. These were sent in large numbers to prison, to Siberia,
or exile abroad. Wherever they went they continued this study
of Marxism and their preparation for the day of action.

<h1 style="text-align:center">144</h1>

THE RUSSIAN REVOLUTION OF 1905 THAT FAILED

March 17, 1933

THE Russian Marxists—the Social Democratic Party—had to
face a crisis in 1903, when they had to consider and answer a question
which every party based on certain principles and definite ideals
has, some time or other, to face and answer. Indeed, all men and
women who have such principles and beliefs have to face such crises
many times in their lives. The question was whether they should
stick to their principles completely and prepare for a revolution
of the working class, or whether they should compromise a little
with existing conditions, and thus prepare the ground for the
ultimate revolution. The question had arisen in all the western
European countries and everywhere, more or less, there had been
a weakening of the Social Democratic or similar parties and internal
conflicts. In Germany the Marxists had bravely declared for the
full loaf, the revolutionary view, but in effect they had toned down
and adopted the milder attitude. In France many leading socialists
deserted their parties and became Cabinet Ministers. So also in
Italy, Belgium, and elsewhere. In Britain Marxism was weak and
the question did not rise, but even there a Labour member became
a Cabinet Minister.

In Russia the position was different, as there was no room for
parliamentary action. There was no parliament. Even so, there
were possibilities of giving up what were called the " illegal "
methods of struggle against Tsarism and carrying on for a while
with quiet theoretical propaganda. But Lenin had clear and
definite views on the subject. He would countenance no weakening,
no compromise, because he was afraid that otherwise opportunists
would flood their party. He had seen the methods adopted by
western socialist parties, and he had not been impressed by them.
As he wrote later, in another connection, " the tactics of parliamentarism, as practised by western socialists, were incomparably
more demoralizing, having gradually converted each socialist
party into a little Tammany Hall with its climbers and job-hunters "

(Tammany Hall is in New York. It has become a symbol of political corruption.) Lenin did not care how many people he had with him—he even threatened at one period to stand alone—but he insisted that only those should be taken who were " whole-hoggers ", who were prepared to give everything for the cause, and even do without the applause of the multitude. He wanted to build up a body of experts in revolution who could develop the movement efficiently. He had no use for just sympathizers and fair-weather friends.

This was a hard line to take up, and many thought it was unwise. On the whole, however, the victory lay with Lenin, and the Social Democratic Party split up into two, and two names, which have since become famous, came into existence—*Bolsheviki* and *Mensheviki*. *Bolshevik* is now a terrible word for some people; but all it means is the majority. *Menshevik* means minority. Lenin's group in the party, after this split in 1903, being in the majority, was called Bolshevik—that is, the majority party. It is interesting to note that at that time Trotsky, then a young man of twenty-four, who was to be Lenin's great colleague in the 1917 revolution, was on the side of the Mensheviks.

All these discussions and debates took place far away from Russia, in London. A Russian party meeting had to be held in London because there was no room in Tsarist Russia for it, and most of its members were exiles, or escaped convicts from Siberia.

Meanwhile, in Russia itself trouble was brewing. Political strikes were signs of this. A political strike of workers means a strike not for economic betterment, such as higher wages, but to protest against some political action of government. It means some political consciousness on the part of the workers. Thus if Indian factory-workers strike because Gandhiji has been arrested, or some extraordinary bit of oppression has occurred, it is a political strike. Strangely enough, these political strikes were rare in western Europe, in spite of its powerful trade unions and workers' organizations. Or perhaps they were rare because the workers' leaders had toned down on account of their vested interests. In Russia the continuous tyranny of Tsarism kept the political side always in the forefront. As early as 1903 there were many spontaneous political strikes in South Russia. The movement was on a big mass scale, but, lacking leaders, it faded away.

The next year brought trouble in the Far East. I have told you in another letter of the long line of the Siberian Railway being built, across the northern Asiatic steppes, right up to the Pacific Ocean; of clashes with Japan from 1894 onwards; and of the Russo-Japanese War of 1904–5. I have also told you of " Red Sunday "—January, 22, 1905—when the Tsar's troops shot down a peaceful demonstration, led by a priest, which had gone to the " Little Father " to beg for bread. A thrill of horror ran through the country, and there were many political strikes. Ultimately there was a general strike throughout Russia. The new type of Marxist revolution had begun.

The workers who had struck, especially in big centres like Petersburg and Moscow, created a new organization—the " Soviet "—in each such centre. This was at first just a committee to run the general strike. Trotsky became the leader of the Petersburg Soviet. The Tsar's government was completely taken aback, and it surrendered to some extent, making promises about a constitutional assembly and a democratic franchise. The great citadel of autocracy seemed to have fallen. What the peasant revolts of the past had failed to do, what the terrorists with their bombs had not succeeded in doing, and what the moderate liberal constitutionalists with their cautious pleadings could not do, that the workers had done with their general strike. Tsardom, for the first time in its history, had to bow down to the common people. It turned out later to be an empty victory. But still the memory of it was a beacon of light for the workers.

The Tsar had promised a constitutional assembly, a *Duma*, as it was called, which means a thinking-place and not a talking-shop like a parliament (from the French *parler*). This promise cooled the ardour of the moderate liberals, who were satisfied. They are always easily satisfied. The landlords, frightened by the revolution, agreed to some reforms which benefited the richer peasants. The Tsar's government then faced the real revolutionaries and, realizing their weakness, played up to it. On the one side were the hungry workers, more interested in bread and higher wages than in political constitutions, and the poorer peasantry raising the dangerous slogan : " Give us land "; on the other were revolutionaries chiefly concerned with the political aspect and hoping to get a parliament after the western European model, and not thinking much of the real demands or feelings of the masses. Many of the better-class skilled workers who were organized in trade unions joined the revolution because they appreciated the political aspect. But the masses generally in the cities and the villages were apathetic. Thereupon the Tsarist government and police tried the time-honoured method of all despotisms : they created divisions and incited these hungry masses against some of the revolutionary groups. The unhappy Jews were massacred by the Russians, the Armenians by the Tartars, and there were even clashes between the revolutionary students and the poorer workers. Having broken the back of the revolution in this way in various parts of the country, the government attacked the two storm-centres—Petersburg and Moscow. The Petersburg Soviet was easily crushed. In Moscow the military helped the revolutionaries and there was a five-day battle before the Soviet was finally crushed. Then followed revenge. In Moscow it is said that the government put to death 1000 persons without trial and imprisoned 70,000. In the whole country about 14,000 died as a result of the various risings.

So ended, in defeat and disaster, the Russian revolution of 1905. It has been called the prologue to the 1917 revolution, which succeeded. " The masses need the schooling of big events " before their consciousness can be roused and they can act on a big scale.

The events of 1905 provided them, at a heavy cost, with this schooling.

The Duma was elected, and met in May 1906. It was far from being a revolutionary body, but it was too liberal for the Tsar's liking, and he sent it home after two and a half months. Having crushed the revolution, he cared little for the wrath of the Duma. The dismissed deputies of the Duma, who were middle-class liberal constitutionalists, took themselves to Finland (which was quite near Petersburg and which was then a semi-independent country under the Tsar's suzerainty), and called upon the Russian people to refuse to pay taxes and to resist recruitment to the army and navy as a mark of protest against the dismissal of the Duma. The deputies were out of touch with the masses, and there was no response to their appeal.

Next year, in 1907, a second Duma was elected. The police tried to prevent radical candidates from getting elected by putting all manner of difficulties in their way, and sometimes by the simple expedient of arresting them. Still the Duma was not to the Tsar's liking, and he dismissed it after three months. The Tsar's government now took steps to prevent all undesirables from getting elected by changing the electoral law. It succeeded, and the third Duma was a highly respectable and conservative body, and it had a long life.

You may wonder why the Tsar took the trouble to have these feeble Dumas when he was strong enough to carry on as he liked, after having crushed the 1905 revolution. The reason was partly to satisfy some small groups in Russia, chiefly the rich landlords and merchants. The situation in the country was bad. The people had, no doubt, been crushed, but they were sullen and angry. So it was thought worth while to keep at least the rich people at the top in hand. But a more important reason was to impress upon European countries that the Tsar was a liberal monarch. Tsarist misgovernment and tyranny were becoming bywords in western Europe. When the first Duma was dismissed, a leader of the British Liberal Party shouted out, in the House of Commons, I think, " The Duma is dead ! Long live the Duma ! " This showed how much sympathy there was for the Duma. And then the Tsar wanted money, and a great deal of it. The thrifty French had been lending it to him; it was, indeed, with the help of a French loan that the Tsar crushed the 1905 revolution. It was a strange contrast —republican France helping autocratic Russia to crush her radicals and revolutionaries. But republican France meant French bankers. Anyhow, appearances had to be kept up, and the Duma helped in this.

Meanwhile the European and the world situation was changing rapidly. After Russia's defeat by Japan England had ceased to fear Russia as she used to. A new fear had arisen for England, that of Germany, both in industry and on the sea, which for so long had been England's preserve. It was fear of Germany also that had made France so generous with her loans to Russia. This German menace, as it was called, drove two ancient enemies to embrace each other. In 1907 an Anglo-Russian treaty was signed which settled all their outstanding points of dispute, in Afghanistan, Persia, and elsewhere. Later, a triple *entente* developed between England, France, and Russia. In the Balkans, Austria was Russia's rival, and Austria was Germany's ally, and so was Italy on paper. So the triple *entente* of England, France, and Russia faced the triple alliance of Germany, Austria, and Italy. And the hosts prepared for action while peaceful people slumbered, not knowing the terrors that were in store for them.

These years in Russia, after 1905, were years of reaction. Bolshevism and the other revolutionary elements had been completely crushed. In foreign countries some of the Bolsheviks in exile, like Lenin, were carrying on patiently, writing books, and pamphlets, and trying to adapt the Marxist theory to changing conditions. The gulf between Menshevism (the more moderate minority party of the Marxists) and Bolshevism grew. Menshevism became more prominent during these years of reaction. Indeed, although it was called the minority party, it had far more people on its side then. From 1912 onwards again a change crept in the Russian world, and revolutionary activity grew, and with it grew Bolshevism. By the middle of 1914 the air of Petrograd was thick with talk of revolution and, as in 1905, large numbers of political strikes took place. And yet—such stuff are revolutions made of !—of the Petersburg Bolshevik Committee of seven, it was discovered later that three were in the Tsarist secret service ! The Bolsheviks had a small group in the Duma, and the leader of this was Malinowsky. He also was found to be a police agent ! And Lenin trusted him.

The World War began in August 1914, and this suddenly turned attention to the warring fronts, and conscription took away the chief workers, and the revolutionary movement died down. The Bolsheviks who raised their voices against the war were few, and they became extremely unpopular.

We have arrived at our appointed post—the World War—and we must stop here. But before I end this letter I should like to draw your attention to Russian art and literature. Tsarist Russia, with all its faults, managed to keep up, as most people know, wonderful dancing. It produced also a series of master-writers in the nineteenth century who built up a great literary tradition. In both the long novel and the short story they showed an amazing mastery. At the beginning of the century there lived Pushkin, the contemporary of Byron and Shelley and Keats, who is said to be the greatest of Russian poets. Of the novelists the famous writers of the nineteenth century are Gogol, Turgeniev, Dostoievsky, and Tchekhov. Then there is perhaps the greatest of them, Leo Tolstoy, who not only was a genius at writing novels, but became a religious and spiritual leader whose influence was far-reaching. Indeed, it reached Gandhiji, who was then in South Africa, and the two appreciated each other and corresponded with each other. The bond of union was the firm faith of both in non-resistance or non-violence. Accord-

ing to Tolstoy, this was the basic teaching of Christ, and Gandhiji
drew the same conclusion from the old Hindu writings. While
Tolstoy remained a prophet, living up to his convictions, but rather
cut off from the world, Gandhiji applied this seemingly negative
thing in an active way to mass problems in South Africa and India.

One of the great nineteenth-century Russian writers is still
living. He is Maxim Gorki.[1]

145

THE END OF AN EPOCH

March 22, 1933

THE nineteenth century ! What a long time we have been held
up by these 100 years ! For four months, off and on, I have written
to you about this period, and I am a little weary of it, and so perhaps
will you be when you read these letters. I began by telling you
that it was a fascinating period, but even fascination palls after a
while. We have really gone beyond the nineteenth century and
are fairly well advanced into the twentieth. The year 1914 was
our limit. It was in that year that the dogs of war, as the saying
goes, were let loose on Europe and the world. That year forms
a turning-point in history. It is the close of one epoch and the
beginning of another.

Nineteen hundred and fourteen ! Even that year is before your
time, and yet it was less than nineteen years ago, and that is not a
long period even in human life, much less in history. But the world
has changed so greatly during these years, and is changing still, that
it seems that an age has passed since then ; and 1914 and the years
that preceded it go back into the history of long ago and become parts
of a distant past of which we read in books, and which is so different
from our own day. Of these great changes I shall have something
to tell you later. One warning I shall give you now. You are
learning geography at school and the geography you learn is very
different from what I had to learn when I was at school in the years
before 1914. And it may be that much of this geography that you
are learning to-day, you may have to unlearn before long, even
as I had to do. Old landmarks, old countries disappeared in the
smoke of war, and new ones, with names difficult to remember,
took their place. Hundreds of cities changed their names almost
overnight; St. Petersburg became Petrograd and then Leningrad,
Constantinople must now be called Istambul, Peking is known as
Peiping and, Prague of Bohemia has become Praha of Czechoslovakia.

In my letters about the nineteenth century, I have necessarily
dealt separately with continents and countries; we have considered

[1] Gorki died in 1936.

different aspects and different movements also separately. But of course you will remember that all this was more or less simultaneous, and history marched all over the world with its thousands of feet together. Science and industry, politics and economics, abundance and poverty, capitalism and imperialism, democracy and socialism, Darwin and Marx, freedom and bondage, famine and pestilence, war and peace, civilization and barbarism—they all had their place in this strange fabric, and each acted and reacted on the other. So if we are to form a picture in our mind of this period or any other period, it must be a complex and ever-moving and changing picture, like a kaleidoscope, although many parts of the picture will not be pleasant to contemplate.

The dominant feature of this period was, as we have seen, the growth of capitalistic industry by large-scale power production— that is, production with the help of some mechanical power, like water, steam, or electricity (we have the name " power-house " for an electricity-generating plant). This had different effects in different parts of the world, and these effects were both direct and indirect. Thus the production of cloth by the power-loom in Lancashire upset conditions in remote Indian villages and put an end to many callings there. Capitalistic industry was dynamic; by its very nature it grew bigger and bigger and its hunger was never satisfied. Its distinguishing mark was acquisitiveness; it was always out to acquire and hold, and then acquire again. In- dividuals tried to do so, and so did nations. The society that grew up under this system is therefore called an acquisitive society. The aim was always to produce more and more, and to apply the surplus wealth thus produced to the building of more factories and railways and such-like undertakings, and also, of course, to enrich the owners. In the pursuit of this aim everything else was sacrificed. The workers who produced the wealth of industry benefited least from it, and they, including women and children, had to pass through a terrible time before their lot was improved a little. Colonies and dependencies were also sacrificed and exploited for the benefit of this capitalistic industry and the nations which possessed it.

So capitalism went blindly and ruthlessly forward, leaving many victims in its trail. None the less its march was a triumphant progress. Aided by science, it succeeded in many things, and this success dazzled the world, and seemed to atone for much of the misery it had caused. Incidentally, and without planning de- liberately for them, it also produced many of the good things of life. But underneath the bright surface and the good there was plenty of bad. Indeed, the most remarkable thing about it was the contrasts it produced, and the more it grew the greater were these contrasts : extreme poverty and extreme wealth; slum and sky- scraper; empire-state and dependent exploited colony. Europe was the dominant continent, and Asia and Africa the exploited ones. For the greater part of the century America was outside the currents of world events, but it was going ahead rapidly and building up vast resources. In Europe, England was the wealthy and proud

and smugly satisfied leader of capitalism, and especially of its imperial aspect.

The very pace and grasping nature of capitalistic industry brought matters to a head and produced opposition and agitation and ultimately some checks to protect workers. The early days of the factory system had meant terrible exploitation of the workers, and especially women and children. Women and children were employed in preference to men because they were cheaper, and they were made to work, sometimes eighteen hours a day, in the most unhealthy and abominable conditions. At last the State intervened and passed laws—factory legislation they are called—limiting hours of work per day and insisting on better conditions. Women and children were especially protected by these laws, but it was a long and a hard struggle to pass them in face of the strenuous opposition of the factory-owners.

Capitalistic industry further led to socialistic and communistic ideas which, while they accepted the new industry, challenged the basis of capitalism. Working-men's organizations and trade unions and internationals also developed.

Capitalism led to imperialism, and the impact of western capitalistic industry on long-established economic conditions in eastern countries caused havoc there. Gradually even in these eastern countries capitalistic industry took root and began to grow. Nationalism also grew there as a challenge to the imperialism of the West.

So capitalism shook up the world, and in spite of the terrible human misery it caused, it was, on the whole, a beneficent movement, at any rate in the West. It brought in its train great material progress and raised tremendously the standards of human well-being. The common man became far more important than he had ever been. In practice he did not have much of a say in anything, in spite of an illusory vote, but in theory his status grew in the State, and with this his self-respect increased. This applies, of course, to the western countries, where capitalistic industry had established itself. There was a vast accumulation of knowledge, and science did wonders, and its thousand applications to life made life easier for everybody. Medicine, especially in its preventive aspects, and sanitation, began to suppress and root out many diseases which had been a curse to man. To mention one instance : the origin and prevention of malaria were discovered, and there is no doubt now that it can be rooted out of an area if the necessary steps are taken. The fact that malaria still continues and has millions of victims in India and elsewhere is not the fault of science, but of a careless government and an ignorant populace.

Perhaps the most striking feature of the century was the progress in the methods of transportation and communication. The railway and the steamship and the electric telegraph and the motor-car changed the world completely, and made it for all human purposes a vastly different place from what it had always been. The world shrank, and its inhabitants grew nearer to each other, and could see much more of each other, and, with mutual knowledge, many barriers, born of ignorance, went down. Common ideas began to spread which produced some measure of uniformity all over the world. Right at the end of the period we are discussing came wireless telegraphy and flying. They are common enough now, and you have been up in an aeroplane several times, and journeyed by it, without thinking much of it. The development of wireless telegraphy and flying belongs to the twentieth century and our own times. People had often gone up in balloons, but no one, except in old myths and stories, the flying carpets of the Arabian Nights, and the *urankhatolā* of our Indian stories, had gone up on anything which was heavier than air. The first persons to succeed in going up in a heavier-than-air machine, the parent of the present aeroplane, were two American brothers, Wilbur and Orville Wright. They flew less than 300 yards in December 1903, but, even so, they had done something which had not been done before. After that there was continuous progress in flying, and I remember the excitement that was caused in 1909 when the Frenchman Blériot flew over the English Channel from France to England. Soon afterwards I saw the first aeroplane fly over the Eiffel Tower in Paris. And many years later, in May 1927, you and I were present in Paris when Charles Lindbergh came like a silver arrow flashing across the Atlantic and landed at Le Bourget, the aerodrome of Paris.

All this goes to the credit side of this period when capitalistic industry was dominant. Man certainly did wonderful things during this century. And one thing more to the credit side. As greedy and grasping capitalism grew, a check to it was devised in the co-operative movement. This was a combination of people to buy or sell goods in common and divide up the profits among themselves. The ordinary capitalist way was the competitive cut-throat way where each person tried to over-reach the other. The co-operative way was based on mutual co-operation. You must have seen many co-operative stores. The co-operative movement grew greatly in Europe in the nineteenth century. Perhaps it succeeded most in the little country of Denmark.

On the political side there was a growth of democratic ideas, and more and more people got the right to vote for their parliaments and assemblies. But this franchise, or right to vote, was limited to men, and women, however capable they might otherwise be, were not considered good or wise enough to have this right. Many women resented this, and in England a great agitation was organized by the women during the early years of the twentieth century. The woman suffrage movement this was called, and because men did not treat it seriously and paid little attention to it, the women suffragettes took to forcible and even violent methods to compel attention. They upset the business of Parliament by creating " scenes " and bodily attacked British Cabinet Ministers, so that these ministers had to be under continual police protection. Organized violence on a big scale also took place, and many women were sent to gaol, where they started hunger-striking. Thereupon they were let out, and as soon as they got well again they were put back in prison. Parliament passed a special law to permit this being done, and this was popularly called the "Cat and Mouse Act". These methods of the suffragettes, however, were certainly successful in attracting widespread attention. A few years later, after the World War began, women's right to the vote was recognized.

The women's movement, or the feminist movement as it is often called, was not confined to asking for votes. Equality with men in everything was demanded. The position of women in the West was very bad till quite recent times. They had few rights. English women could not even own property under the law, the husband took the lot, even his wife's earnings. They were thus even worse off legally than women are to-day under Hindu law, and that is bad enough. Women in the West were, indeed, a subject race, as in a host of ways Indian women are now. Long before the agitation for votes began, women had demanded equal treatment with men in other respects. At length, in the 'eighties, in England they were given some rights as to owning property. Women succeeded in this partly because factory-owners favoured it; they thought that if women could keep their earnings, this would be an inducement for them to work in the factories.

On every side we note great changes, but not so in the ways of governments. The great Powers continued to follow the methods of intrigue and deception recommended long ago by the Florentine Machiavelli, and 1800 years before him by the Indian minister, Chānakya. There was ceaseless rivalry between them, and secret treaties and alliances, and each Power was always trying to over-reach the other. Europe, as we have seen, played the active and aggressive rôle; Asia the passive. America's part in world politics was relatively small because of her own preoccupations.

With the growth of nationalism the idea of "my country right or wrong" developed, and nations gloried in doing things which, in the case of individuals, were considered bad and immoral. Thus a strange contrast grew between the morality of individuals and that of nations. There was a vast difference between the two, and the very vices of individuals became the virtues of nations. Selfishness, greed, arrogance, vulgarity were considered utterly bad and intolerable in the case of individual men and women. But in the case of large groups, of nations, they were praised and encouraged under the noble cloak of patriotism and love of country. Even murder and killing become praiseworthy if large groups of nations undertake it against one another. A recent author has told us, and he is perfectly right, that "civilization has become a device for delegating the vices of individuals to larger and larger communities".

146

THE WORLD WAR BEGINS

March 23, 1933

I FINISHED off my last letter by pointing out to you how vicious and immoral nations were when dealing with each other. They considered it a sign of their independence to adopt an offensive and intolerant attitude towards others, wherever they could afford to do this, and a dog-in-the-manger policy. There was no authority to tell them to behave, for were they not independent, and would not interference be resented ? The only check on their behaviour was fear of consequences. So the strong were respected to some extent and the weak were bullied.

This national rivalry was really an inevitable result of the growth of capitalistic industry. We have seen how an ever-growing demand for markets and raw materials made the capitalist Powers race round the world for empire. They rushed about in Asia and Africa seizing as much territory as possible in order to exploit it. Having covered the world, there was nowhere else to spread, so the imperialist Powers began glaring at each other and coveting each other's possessions. There were frequent clashes between these great Powers in Asia and Africa and Europe, and angry passions flared up, and war seemed to hang in the balance. Some of the Powers were better off than the others, and England, with her industrial lead and vast empire, seemed to be the most fortunate of all. But even England was not satisfied, for the more one has the more one wants. Vast schemes for the extension of her empire floated in the brains of her " empire-builders", schemes of an African empire extending without break from north to south, from Cairo to the Cape. England was also worried by the competition of Germany and the United States in industry. These countries were making manufactured goods cheaper than England, and were thus stealing England's markets from her.

If England the fortunate was not satisfied, the others were even more dissatisfied. And especially Germany, which had joined the great Powers rather late in the day and found all the ripe plums gone. She had made vast progress in science, education, and industry, and had at the same time built up a magnificent army. Even in social-reform legislation for her workers she was ahead of other countries, including England. Although the world was largely occupied by the other imperialist Powers when Germany came on the scene and the avenues of exploitation were limited, by sheer hard work and self-discipline she became the strongest and most efficient Power of the age of industrial capitalism. Her merchant-ships were to be seen in every port, and her own ports, Hamburg and Bremen, were among the greatest of world ports. The German mercantile marine not only carried German goods to distant countries, it captured also the carrying-trade of other countries.

It is not surprising that this new imperial Germany with this success achieved, and fully conscious of her strength, chafed at the limitations placed on her further growth. Prussia was the leader of the German Empire, and the Prussian landlord and military class which was in power has never been known for its humility. They were aggressive and took pride in being ruthlessly so, and they found an ideal leader of this assertive and bumptious spirit in their Emperor Kaiser Wilhelm II, of the house of Hohenzollern. The Kaiser went about proclaiming that Germany was going to be the leader of the world; that she wanted a place in the sun; that her future was on the sea; that it was her mission to spread her *Kultur*, or culture, throughout the world.

Now, all this had been said before by other people and other nations. England's "White Man's Burden" and France's "Civilizing Mission" were of the same family as Germany's *Kultur*. England claimed to be, and was in fact, supreme on the seas. The Kaiser said for Germany, rather crudely and bombastically, what many Englishmen had claimed for England, with this difference, that England was in possession and Germany was not. None the less the Kaiser's bombastic utterances greatly irritated the British; the idea that any other nation should even think of becoming the leading nation in the world was extremely distasteful to them. It was a kind of heresy, an obvious attack on England, which considered herself the leading nation. As for the sea, this had been considered a preserve of England ever since Napoleon's defeat at Trafalgar 100 years before, and to the English it seemed highly improper for Germany or any other nation to challenge this position. If Britain ceased to be strong at sea, what would become of her far-flung empire?

The Kaiser's challenges and threats were bad enough; what was worse was that he actually followed it up by increasing his navy. This completely upset the tempers and nerves of the British, and they also began to increase their navy. Thus a naval race began between the two, and newspapers of both countries kept up a shrieking agitation demanding more and more battleships and increasing national hatred.

This was one danger zone in Europe. There were many others. France and Germany were, of course, old rivals, and bitter memories of the defeat of 1870 rankled in the minds of the French, who dreamed of revenge. The Balkans were always a powder-box where various interests clashed. Germany also began to make friends with Turkey with a view to developing her influence in western Asia. It was proposed to build a railway to Baghdad connecting this city with Constantinople and Europe. The proposal was an eminently desirable one, but because Germany wanted to control this Baghdad Railway, national jealousies were aroused.

Gradually the fear of war spread in Europe and in self-defence the Powers sought alliances. The great Powers lined up in two groups: the Triple Alliance of Germany, Austria, and Italy, and the Triple Entente of England, France, and Russia. Italy was a very lukewarm member of the Triple Alliance and, as a matter of

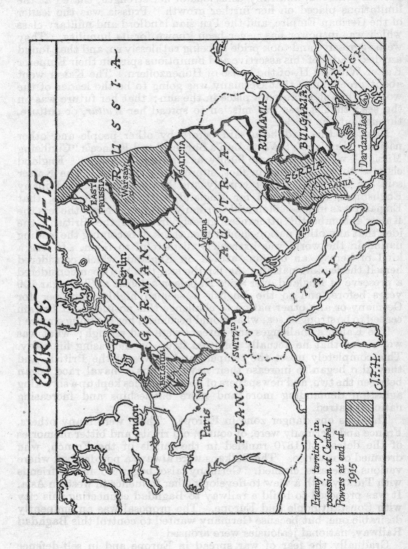

fact, in the event of war she broke her word and joined the other side. Austria was a ramshackle empire, big on the map, but full of discordant elements, with beautiful Vienna, a great centre of science and music and art, as the capital. So in effect the Triple Alliance meant Germany. But of course before the test came no one knew how Italy and Austria would shape.

So fear reigned in Europe, and fear is a terrible thing. Each country went on preparing for war and arming itself to the uttermost. There was an armament race, and the curious part of such competition is that if one country increases its armaments the other countries are forced to do likewise. The big private firms which made armaments—that is guns, battle-ships, ammunition, and all the other material for war—naturally reaped a rich harvest and waxed fat. They went further, and actually started war-scares to induce countries to purchase more arms from them. These armament firms were very rich and powerful, and many high officials and ministers in England, France, Germany, and elsewhere held shares in them, and were thus interested in their prosperity. Prosperity to an armament firm comes with war-scares and with wars. So this was the amazing position, that ministers and officials of many governments were financially interested in war ! These firms tried other ways also of promoting war expenditure by different countries. They bought up newspapers to influence public opinion, and often bribed government officials, and spread false reports to excite people. What a terrible thing is this armament industry which lives by the death of others, and which does not hesitate to encourage and bring about the horrors of war so that it may make profit out of it ! This industry helped to some extent to hasten the war of 1914. Even to-day it is playing the same game.

In the midst of this talk of war I must tell you of a curious attempt at peace. The Tsar Nicholas II of Russia, of all persons, suggested to the Powers that they should meet together to bring about an era of universal peace. This was the Tsar who was crushing every liberal movement in his empire and peopling Siberia with his convicts ! It seems almost a joke that he should talk of peace. But probably he was honest about it, for peace to him meant a perpetuation of existing conditions and his own autocracy. In response to his invitation, two Peace Conferences were held at the Hague in Holland in 1899 and 1907. Nothing of the least importance was done there. Peace cannot suddenly descend from the heavens. It can only come when the root-causes of trouble are removed.

I have told you a great deal about the rivalries and fears of the great Powers. The poor small nations are ignored, except those that misbehave. In the north of Europe there are some small countries which deserve attention because they are so very different from the greedy and grasping great Powers. There are Norway and Sweden in Scandinavia and Denmark just below them. These countries are not far from the Arctic regions; they are cold and hard to live in. They can support only a small population. But because they are outside the great Power circle of hatred and jealousy and rivalry, they live a peaceful life and spend their energies in civilized ways. Science flourishes there and fine literatures have grown. Norway and Sweden were joined together and formed one State till 1905. In that year Norway decided to break away and carry on a separate existence. So the two countries decided peacefully to break their bonds, and since then they have been separate independent States. There was no war or attempt to compel one country by another, and both continued to live as friendly neighbours.

Little Denmark has set an example to the big countries and small by abolishing her army and navy. It is a peasant nation, a country of small farmers, where the difference between rich and poor is not much. This equalization is largely due to the great development of the co-operative movement there.

But all the small countries of Europe are not paragons of virtue like Denmark. Holland, small itself, still holds sway over a large empire in the East Indies (Java, Sumatra, etc.). Next to it, Belgium exploits the Congo in Africa. Its real importance in European politics, however, comes from its position. It is almost on the highway between France and Germany, and in any war between these countries it is almost sure to be dragged in. Waterloo, you will remember, is near Brussels in Belgium. For this reason Belgium use l to be called the " cockpit of Europe ". The principal great Powers came to an agreement to respect the neutrality of Belgium in case of war, but, as we shall see, when war did come this agreement and promise went to pieces.

But the most troublesome of all small countries in Europe or elsewhere are in the Balkans. This hotch-potch of peoples and races, with generations of animosity and rivalry behind them, is full of mutual hatred and conflict. The Balkan Wars of 1912 and 1913 were extraordinarily bloody, and in a short time and within a short area there were enormous losses. The Bulgarians are said to have committed horrible atrocities on the refugee and retreating Turks. The Turks themselves had a very bad record in earlier years. Serbia (now a part of Yugoslavia) developed a most sinister reputation for assassination. A secret murder gang of so-called patriots, named the "Black Hand," and including among its members many high officials of the State, was responsible for a bunch of peculiarly horrible murders. The King and Queen of the country, King Alexander and Queen Draga, together with the Queen's brothers, the Prime Minister and some others, were all murdered in a disgusting manner. This was just a palace revolution and another person was made king.

So the twentieth century opened with thunder and lightning in the air of Europe, and as year succeeded year, the weather grew stormier. Complications and entanglements grew, and the life of Europe was tied up more and more in knots—knots which were to be cut ultimately by war. All the Powers expected war to come and prepared for it feverishly, and yet perhaps none of them was keen on it. They all feared it to some extent, for no one could prophesy with certainty what the result of war would be. And yet fear itself drove them on to war. As I have told you, the two sides in Europe lined up against each other. " The balance of power " it was called, a very delicate balance which a little push could throw over. Japan, although far away from Europe, and not much interested in its local problems, was also a party to its alliances and this balance of power. For Japan was England's ally. This alliance was meant to protect English interests in the East, and especially in India. It had been made in the days of Anglo-Russian rivalry, and still continued, although England and Russia were now on the same side. America was the only great Power which held aloof from this European system of alliances and balances.

So matters stood in 1914. You will remember that at this time England was having a lot of trouble in Ireland over the Home Rule Bill. Ulster was rebelling, volunteers were drilling in the north and in the south, and there was talk of civil war in Ireland. It is very likely that the German Government thought that the Irish trouble would keep England busy and that she would not interfere if a European war took place. The English Government was, as a matter of fact, privately committed to joining France in case of war, but this was not publicly known.

June 28, 1914—that was the date on which the spark was lighted which kindled the blaze. The Archduke Francis Ferdinand was the heir to the Austrian throne. He went to visit Serajevo, the capital of Bosnia in the Balkans. This Bosnia, as I have told you, had been annexed by Austria a few years earlier when the Young Turks were trying to get rid of their sultan. As the Archduke, with his wife sitting by him in an open carriage, was going along the streets of Serajevo, he was shot at and both he and his wife were killed. The government and people of Austria were in a rage and accused the Serbian Government (Serbia was the neighbour of Bosnia) of complicity in this crime. The Serbian Government of course denied this. Inquiries made long afterwards have gone to show that the Serbian Government, though not responsible for the murder, was not wholly ignorant of the preparations made for it. The responsibility for the murder must largely rest, however, with the Serbian " Black Hand " organization.

The Austrian Government, partly through anger and largely through policy, took up a very aggressive attitude towards Serbia. It had evidently decided to humble Serbia for good, and relied on the powerful help of Germany in case of a bigger war. So Serbian apologies were not accepted, and on July 23, 1914, Austria sent a final ultimatum to Serbia. Five days later, on July 28, Austria declared war on Serbia.

Austrian policy was largely in the hands of a vain and foolish minister who was bent on war. The aged Emperor Francis Joseph (who had been on the Austrian throne since 1848) was induced to agree, and a half-promise of help from Germany was construed to mean a full assurance. As a matter of fact, apart from Austria probably none of the other great Powers was eager for war just then. Germany, with all her readiness and pugnacity, was not keen, and

Kaiser Wilhelm II even tried in a half-hearted way to prevent it. England and France were not keen on war. The Russian Government meant the Tsar, a weak and foolish person, surrounded by knaves and fools of his own choice, and swayed by them hither and thither. Yet in the hands of this man lay the fate of millions. He himself was on the whole averse to the war, but his advisers frightened him with the consequences of delay and got him to agree to the mobilization of the army. This " mobilization " meant the calling up of the troops for active service, and in a vast country like Russia, this process took time. Fear of a German attack perhaps hurried Russian mobilization. News of this mobilization, which took place on July 30, frightened Germany, and she demanded that Russia should stop it. But there was no stopping the huge war machine now. Two days later, on August 1, Germany mobilized and declared war on Russia and France, and almost immediately vast German armies started invading Belgium to go to France that way, as it was easier. Poor Belgium had not harmed Germany, but when nations fight for life and death they care little for such trifles or for promises made. The German Government had asked Belgium's permission to send its army through Belgium; such permission was naturally and indignantly refused.

A great outcry arose in England and elsewhere on account of this violation of Belgian neutrality, and England made this the basis of declaring war herself against Germany. As a matter of fact England's choice had been made long ago, and the question of Belgium came as a convenient excuse. It now appears that even the French army had prepared plans in the pre-war years for taking their armies across Belgium to attack Germany, should this be considered necessary. Anyhow, England tried to pose as a great defender of right and truth and a champion of small nations, as against Germany, who was said to have treated her solemn promises and treaties as just " scraps of paper ". At midnight on August 4, England declared war against Germany, but she had taken the precaution of sending her army—the British Expeditionary Force—across the Channel secretly a day earlier to prevent any mishap. So that while the world thought that the question of England joining or not still hung in the balance, British troops were already on the Continent.

Austria, Russia, Germany, France, England, were all involved in the war now, and of course little Serbia also, who was partly the immediate cause of this outbreak. What of Italy, the ally of Germany and Austria? Italy, held aloof, Italy watched to see on which side the advantage lay, Italy bargained, and ultimately, six months later, Italy definitely joined the French-English-Russian side against her old allies.

So the first days of August 1914 saw the gathering and the marching of the armies of Europe. What were these armies? In the old days armies consisted of a number of professional soldiers. They were permanent armies. The French Revolution, however, made a great difference. When the Revolution was in danger from foreign attack, the ordinary citizens were enrolled and trained in large numbers. From that time onwards there was a tendency in Europe to replace the professional voluntary armies of limited numbers by conscript armies—that is, armies in which all the able-bodied men of the country were forced to serve. Thus this universal military service of the able-bodied men was a child of the French Revolution. It spread all over the Continent, where every young man for two years or more had to receive military training in camp and later was bound to serve when called upon to do so. Thus an army on active war service meant practically the whole of the male youth of the nation. This was so in France, Germany, Austria, and Russia, and mobilization in these countries meant the calling up of these young men from their homes in distant towns and villages. In England there was no universal service of this kind when the war began. Relying on her powerful navy, she kept a relatively small permanent and voluntary army. During the war, however, she fell into line with the other countries and introduced conscription, or compulsory military service.

This universal military service meant that the whole nation was in arms. The orders of mobilization affected every town, every village, every family. In the greater part of Europe, life suddenly stood still in those early days of August, and young men left millions of homes never to return. Everywhere there was a marching and a tramping, and cheers for the troops, and tremendous displays of patriotic fervour, and a tightening of the heart-strings, and also a certain light-heartedness, for the horrors of the years to come were little realized then.

This passionate patriotism swept everybody away. The socialists, who had talked so loudly of internationalism, the Marxists, who had called on the workers of the world to unite against the common enemy capitalism, were themselves swept off their feet and joined this capitalists' war as fervent patriots. Some few held their ground, but they were despised and cursed and often punished. Most people went mad with hatred of the enemy. While English and German workers killed each other, the learned men and scientists and professors of both countries, as well as of other warring countries, cursed each other, and believed the most horrible stories about each other.

So with the coming of the war ended the epoch of the nineteenth century. The majestic and calmly flowing river of western civilization was suddenly swallowed up in the whirlpool of war. The old world was gone for ever. Something new emerged from that whirlpool more than four years afterwards.

147

INDIA ON THE EVE OF THE WAR

March 29, 1933

It is a long time since I wrote to you about India.   I feel tempted to come back to this subject and to tell you how India fared on the eve of the war period.   I have decided to give in to the temptation.

In several long letters we have already examined some aspects of Indian life and of British rule in India during the nineteenth century. The dominant feature of this period appears to be the strengthening of the British hold on India and the accompanying exploitation of the country.   India was held down by a triple army of occupation— military, civil, and commercial.   The British military forces, and the Indian mercenary army under British officers, were obvious enough as an alien army of occupation.   But an even more powerful hold was that of the civil service, an irresponsible and highly centralized bureaucracy; and the third army, the commercial one, was supported by these two, and was the most dangerous of all, as most of the exploitation was done by this, or on its behalf, and its ways of exploiting the country were not so obvious as those of the other two.   Indeed, for a long time, and to some extent even now, eminent Indians objected far more to the first two, and did not seem to attach the same importance to the third.

One of the consistent aims of British policy in India was to create vested interests which, being of their own making, would rely upon them and become their supports in India.   In this way the feudal princes were strengthened and the big *zamindar* and *taluqadar* class created, and even social conservatism encouraged in the name of religious non-interference.   All these vested interests were themselves interested in the exploitation of the country, and indeed could exist only because of this exploitation.   The biggest vested interest created in India was that of British capital.

A statement made by an English statesman, Lord Salisbury, who was Secretary of State for India, has often been quoted, and, as it is illuminating, I shall give it to you here.   He said in 1875 :

> " As India must be bled, the lancet should be directed to the parts where the blood is congested, or at least is sufficient, not to those which are already feeble from want of it."

The British occupation of India and the policy they pursued here produced many results, some of which were not welcome to the British.   But even individuals can seldom control all the results of their actions, much less can nations.   Often enough among the results of certain activities are new forces which oppose those very activities, and fight them, and overcome them.   Imperialism produces nationalism; capitalism produces large aggregations of working men in factories, who unite and combat the capitalist owners. Government repression meant to stifle a movement and suppress a people actually results often in strengthening and steeling them, and thus preparing them for final victory.

We have seen that British industrial policy in India led to increasing ruralization—that is, more and more people, having no other occupations, drifted back from the towns to the villages. The burden on the land grew, and the holdings of the peasantry—that is, the area of their farms or fields—grew ever smaller. Most of these holdings became " uneconomic ", which means that they were not big enough to give the cultivator the minimum income for even the bare necessities of life. But he had no alternative; he could only carry on, usually getting more and more into debt. The land policy of the British Government made matters worse, especially in the *taluqadari* and big *zamīndārī* areas. Both in these areas and in the areas where, peasant proprietorship prevailed, peasants were evicted from their holdings for non-payment of revenue to government or rent to the *zamindar*. As a result of this, and because of the continual pressure of newcomers for land, a large class of landless labourers grew up in the rural areas, and there were, as I have told you, many dreadful famines.

This large dispossessed class was hungry for land to cultivate, but there was not enough land to go round. In the *zamīndārī* areas the landlords took advantage of this demand by raising rents. Some tenancy laws made to protect the tenant prohibited the sudden raising of rents beyond a certain percentage. But these were got over in a variety of ways and all manner of illegal dues were charged. In an Oudh *taluqadari* estate I was told once of over fifty different kinds of illegal dues ! The chief of these was *nazrāna*, a kind of premium which is paid by the tenant right at the beginning. How can the poor tenants make these various payments ? They can only do so by borrowing from the *bania*, the village banker. It is folly to borrow when there is no prospect of or ability to pay back. But what is the poor peasant to do ? He sees no hope anywhere; at any cost he wants land to till, hoping against hope that something will turn up. The result is that often enough in spite of his borrowings he cannot meet the demands of the landlord, and he is ejected from his holding, and again joins the class of landless labourers.

Both the peasant proprietor and the tenant, as well as many a landless labourer, become victims of the *bania*. They can never get rid of the debt. Whenever they earn a little they pay, but the interest swallows this up and the old debt remains. There are very few checks on the *bania* fleecing them. In effect they become bound down to him as serfs. The poor tenant is in a way doubly a serf—the *zamindar's* and the *bania's*.

Obviously this kind of thing cannot continue for very long. A time will come when the peasants are wholly unable to meet any of the demands made upon them, and the *bania* refuses to advance more money, and the *zamindar* also is hard hit. It is a system which on the face of it has elements of decay and instability. The recent agrarian troubles we have had all over the country would seem to point out that the system is now cracking up and cannot long survive.

I am afraid I have been repeating in this letter what I have said a trifle differently perhaps in a previous letter. But I wish you to appreciate that India means these millions of unhappy agriculturists, and not a handful of middle-class folk who fill the picture.

The existence of a large dispossessed class of landless labourers made the starting of big factories easy. Such factories can only be run if there are enough people (indeed more than enough) who are prepared to work for wages. The man who has got a bit of land does not want to leave it. Large numbers of landless unemployed are therefore necessary for the factory system, and the more there are, the easier it is for the factory-owners to beat down wages and control them.

Just about this time, as I think I have told you already, a new middle class gradually arose in India and accumulated some capital for investment. So that as the money was there and the labour was there, the result was factories. But most of the capital invested in India was foreign (British) capital. These factories were not encouraged by the British Government. They went contrary to its policy of keeping India a purely agricultural country, providing England with raw materials and consuming England's manufactured goods. But the conditions, which I have pointed out above, were such that big machine production had to begin in India, and the British Government could not easily stop it. So factories grew in spite of the government's disapproval. One of the ways of showing this disapproval was a tax on machinery entering India, another was the Cotton Excise duty, a tax actually on what Indian cotton mills produced.

The greatest of the early Indian industrialists was Jamshedji Nasarwanji Tata. He started many industries; the biggest of these was the Tata Iron and Steel Co. at Sakchi in Behar. This was started in 1907, and it began to function in 1912. The iron industry is one of the "basic" industries, as they are called. So much depends on iron nowadays that a country without an iron industry is largely dependent on others. The Tata iron-works are a huge affair. The village of Sakchi has now become the city of Jamshedpur, and the railway station a little way off is called Tatanagar. Iron-works are especially valuable in war-time, as they can produce munitions of war. It was fortunate for the British Government in India that the Tata works were in existence when the World War began.

Labour conditions in Indian factories were very bad. They resembled the conditions in English factories of the early nineteenth century. The wages were low because of the large numbers of unemployed landless people, and the hours of work were very long. In 1911 the first general Indian Factory Act was passed. Even this Act fixed a twelve-hour day for men, and six hours for children.

These factories did not swallow up all the landless labourers. Large numbers went to the tea and other plantations in Assam and other parts of India. The conditions under which they served in these plantations made them, for the time they were there, serfs of their employers.

Over 2,000,000 poverty-stricken Indian workers emigrated to foreign countries. Most of them went to the plantations of Ceylon and Malay. Many also went to the islands of Mauritius (in the Indian Ocean, off Madagascar), Trinidad (just north of South America), and Fiji (near Australia); and to South Africa, East Africa, and British Guiana (in South America). To many of these places they went as " indentured " workers, which meant practically that they were serfs. The " indenture " was the document which contained the contract made with these workers, and under which they were the slaves of their employers. Many horrible accounts of the indenture system reached India, especially from Fiji, so that there was an agitation here and the system was abolished.

So much for the peasantry, labour, and the emigrants. These were the poor, silent, and long-suffering masses of India. The really vocal class was the new middle class, which was practically a child of the British connection, but which none the less began criticizing it. It grew, and with it grew the national movement which, you will remember, came to a head in 1907–8, when a mass movement shook Bengal and the National Congress split up into two factions— the Extremists and the Moderates. The British followed their usual policy of crushing the advanced group and trying to win over the moderate group with some minor reforms. At this time also a new factor appeared on the scene—the political claims for separate and special treatment of the Muslims as a minority. It is well known now that then the government encouraged these demands, in order to create a division among Indians, and thus check the growth of nationalism.

For the moment the British Government succeeded in its policy. Lokamanya Tilak was in prison and his party suppressed; the Moderates had cordially welcomed some reforms in the administration (called the Minto–Morley reforms from the names of the Viceroy and the Secretary of State at the time), which gave no power to the Indians. A little later the annulment of the Partition of Bengal appeased Bengali sentiment. The political movement of 1907 and onwards became again the spare-time hobby of armchair people. So that in 1914, when the war came, there was little active political life in the country. The National Congress, representing the Moderates only, met once a year and passed some academic resolutions, and did nothing else. Nationalism was at a low ebb.

Apart from the political field, there had been other reactions from contact with the West. The religious ideas of the new middle classes (but not of the masses) were influenced, and new movements arose like the *Brahmo Samaj* and the *Arya Samaj*, and the caste system began to lose its rigidity. There was a cultural awakening also, especially in Bengal. Bengali writers made the Bengali language the richest of India's modern languages, and Bengal produced one of the greatest of our countrymen of this age, the poet Rabindra

Nath Tagore, who is happily still with us. Bengal also produced great men of science : Sir Jagadish Chandra Bose and Sir Prafulla Chandra Ray. Two other great Indian scientists whose names I might mention here are Ramanijam and Sir Chandrashekhara Venkata Raman. India was thus excelling in science, the very thing which had been the foundation of Europe's greatness.

One other name I might also mention here. It is of Sir Muhammad Iqbal, a poet of genius in Urdū, and especially Persian. He has written some beautiful poetry of nationalism. Unhappily he left poetry in his later years and devoted himself to other work.

While India was politically dormant in the pre-war years, a far country saw a gallant and a unique struggle for India's honour. This was South Africa, where large numbers of Indian labourers and some merchants had emigrated. They were humiliated and ill-treated in a host of ways, for racial arrogance reigned supreme there. It so happened that a young Indian barrister was taken to South Africa to appear in a law-case. He saw the condition of his fellow-countrymen, and he was humiliated and distressed by it. He resolved to do his best to help them. For many years he laboured quietly, giving up his profession and his belongings and devoting himself entirely to the cause he had espoused. This man was Mohandas Karamchand Gandhi. To-day every child in India knows him and loves him, but then he was little known outside South Africa. Suddenly his name flashed across to India, and people talked of him and of his brave fight with surprise and admiration and pride. The South African Government had tried to humiliate the Indian residents there still more, and under Gandhi's leadership they had refused to submit. This was strange enough, that a community of poor, down-trodden, ignorant workers and a group of petty merchants, far from their home country, should take up this brave attitude. What was stranger still was the method they had adopted, for as a political weapon this was a novel one in the world's history. We have heard of it often enough since. It was Gandhi's *satyagraha*, which means holding on to truth. It is sometimes called passive resistance, but that is not a correct translation, for it is active enough. It is not non-resistance merely, though *ahimsa* or non-violence is an essential part of it. Gandhi startled India and South Africa with this non-violent warfare, and people in India learnt with a thrill of pride and joy of the thousands of our countrymen and women who went willingly to gaol in South Africa. In our hearts we were ashamed of our subjection and our impotence in our own country, and this instance of a brave challenge on behalf of our own people increased our own self-respect. Suddenly India became politically awake on this issue, and money poured into South Africa. The fight was stopped when Gandhiji and the South African Government came to terms. Although at the time it was an undoubted victory for the Indian cause, many Indian disabilities have continued, and the old agreement, it is said, has not been kept by the South African Government. The question of Indians overseas is still with us, and it will remain with us till India is free.

How can Indians have honour elsewhere when they have not got it
in their own country ?   And how can we help them much so long as
we have not succeeded in helping ourselves to freedom in our own
country ?

So matters stood in India in the pre-war years.   When Turkey
was attacked by Italy in 1911 there was much sympathy in India
for Turkey, since Turkey was looked upon as an Asiatic and Oriental
power and, as such, had the good will of all Indians.   Indian
Muslims were especially affected, because they looked upon the
Sultan of Turkey as the Caliph, or Kalifa, or head of Islam.   In
those days there had also been some talk, fathered by Sultan Abdul
Hamid of Turkey, of Pan-Islamism.   The Balkan Wars of 1912 and
1913 agitated Indian Muslims even more, and as a gesture of friendship and good will a medical mission, called the Red Crescent
Mission, went from India to give assistance to the Turkish wounded.

Soon after, the World War began, and Turkey became involved
in it as an enemy of England.   But that takes us to the war period,
and I must stop here.

148

WAR 1914–1918

March 31, 1933

WHAT shall I write to you about this war, the World War, the
Great War, as it is called, which for over four years devastated
Europe and some parts of Asia and Africa, and wiped away millions
of young men in their prime ?   War is not a pleasant subject to
contemplate.   It is an ugly thing, but often it is praised and painted
in bright colours; and it is said that, like the fire which purifies
precious metals, war purifies and strengthens indolent nations,
grown soft and corrupt by too much ease and love of living. Instances
of high courage and moving sacrifice are pointed out to us, as if war
were the parent of these virtues.

I have tried to examine with you some of the causes of this war :
how the greed of capitalistic industrial countries, the rivalries of
imperialist Powers, clashed, and made conflict inevitable.   How the
leaders of industry in each of these countries wanted more and
more opportunities and areas to exploit; how financiers wanted to
make more money; how the makers of armaments wanted bigger
profits.   So these people plunged into the war, and, at their bidding,
and that of elderly politicians representing them and their class,
the youth of the nations rushed at each other's throats.   The vast
majority of these young men, and the common people of all the
countries concerned, knew nothing of these causes which had led
to the war.   They were really not concerned, and whether success
came or failure, they stood to lose by it.   It was a rich man's game
played with the lives of the people, and mostly of the young.   But

there could be no war unless the common people were prepared to fight. In all the Continental countries, as I have told you, there was conscription or compulsory service; in England it came later in the war. But even compulsion cannot force all the people in such a matter if they are really unwilling as a whole.

So elaborate efforts were made to whip up the enthusiasm and the love of country of the people in all the warring nations. Each party called the other the " aggressor ", and pretended to fight in self-defence only. Germany said that she was surrounded by a ring of enemies who were trying to strangle her. She accused Russia and France of taking the initiative in invading her. England based her action on a righteous defence of little Belgium, whose neutrality had been grossly violated by Germany. All the countries involved took up a self-righteous attitude and laid all the blame on the enemy. Each people was made to believe that their freedom was in danger and they must fight to defend it. The newspapers especially took a great part in creating this war atmosphere everywhere, which meant in effect bitter hatred of the people of the enemy countries.

So strong was this wave of hysteria that it swept everything before it. It was easy enough to rouse mass passions in the crowd; but even people of intellect and intelligence, men and women who were supposed to have a calm and equable temperament, thinkers, writers, professors, scientists—all of them, in all the countries involved, lost their balance and became filled with blood-lust and hatred of the enemy peoples. The clergymen, the men of religion, who are supposed to be men of peace, were as bloodthirsty, or even more so, than the others. Even pacifists and socialists lost their heads and forgot their principles. All—but not quite all. A tiny minority of people in each country refused to become hysterical, and would not allow themselves to be smitten by this war fever. They were jeered at and called cowards, and many were even sent to prison for refusal to do war service. Some of these were socialists, some were religious people, like the Quakers, who have conscientious objections to war. It has been truly said that when war breaks out nowadays the people involved go mad.

As soon as the war began, the governments of the various countries made it the excuse for suppressing truth and spreading all manner of lies. The personal liberties of the people were also suppressed. The other side was, of course, completely shut out. So that the people only got to know one side of the story, and that a greatly distorted and often completely false account. It was not difficult to fool the people in this way.

Even in peace-time narrow nationalist propaganda and the distortions of newspapers had fooled the people and prepared the ground for war. War itself had been glorified. In Germany, or rather in Prussia, this glorification of war became the definite philosophy of the rulers, from the Kaiser downwards. Learned books were written to justify it and to prove that war was a " biological necessity "—that is, it was necessary to human life and

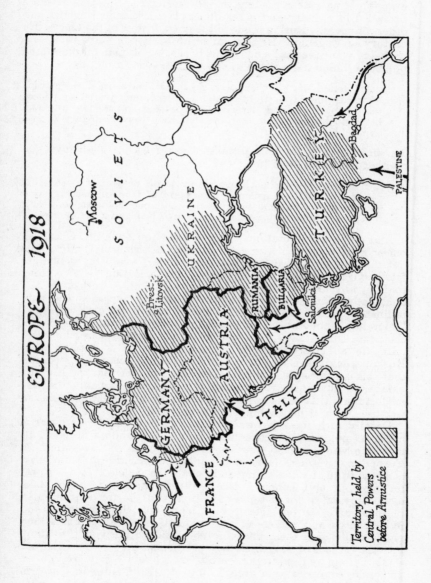

progress. The Kaiser received a lot of publicity because he was always posing rather crudely in the limelight. But similar ideas prevailed in military and other upper-class circles in England and other countries. Ruskin is one of the great writers of the nineteenth century in England. He is a favourite author of Gandhiji's, and probably you have read some of his books. This man of undoubted nobility of mind has written in one of his books :

> " I found, in brief, that all great nations learned their truth of words, and strength of thought, in war, and wasted by peace ; taught by war, and deceived by peace ; trained by war and betrayed by peace ; in a word, that they were born in war, and expired in peace."

To show what a frank imperialist Ruskin was, I shall give you another quotation from him :

> " That is what she (England) must do or perish : she must found colonies . . . seizing every piece of fruitful waste ground she can set foot on, and there teaching these her colonists that their first . . . aim is to advance the power of England by land or sea."

And one other quotation. This is from the book of an English officer who became a major-general in the British army. He points out that victory in war is almost impossible " except by deliberate falsehood, by acting a falsehood, or by prevarication ". According to him, any citizen who " refuses to adopt these measures . . . deliberately acts the part of a traitor to his comrades and subordinates " and " can only be termed a most despicable coward ". " Morality ; immorality—what are such things to great nations when their fate is at stake ? " A nation " must strike and strike again until its adversary receives its death-blow ". I wonder what Ruskin would have said to all this ! Do not imagine, of course, that this is a fair specimen of the English mind, or that the Kaiser's bombastic utterances represented the average German. But the misfortune is that people who think are so often in authority, and in war-time, almost invariably, they come to the front.

Usually such frank avowals are not made publicly, and war is made to put on a sanctimonious garb. So, while a tremendous massacre was going on over hundreds of miles of battle-front in Europe and elsewhere, fine high-sounding phrases were manufactured at home to justify the killing and delude the people. It was a war for freedom and honour ; the " war to end war " ; to make democracy safe ; for self-determination, and the freedom of small nations, and so on. Meanwhile many of the financiers and industrialists and makers of war material, who sat at home, and patriotically used these fine phrases to induce the young to jump into the furnace of war, made vast profits and become millionaires.

As the war went on from month to month and year to year, more and more countries were dragged into it. Both sides tried to win over neutrals by offering bribes secretly ; any such public offer would have put an end to the high ideals and the fine phrases which were shouted from the house-tops. The power of England and France to bribe was greater than that of Germany, and so most of the neutrals who joined the war came in on the Anglo-French-Russian side. Italy, the old ally of Germany, was won over by these Allies on their making a secret treaty promising her territory in Asia Minor and elsewhere. Another secret treaty promised Russia Constantinople. It was a pleasant task to divide up the world among themselves. These secret treaties were wholly opposed to the public statements of the statesmen of the Allies. Probably no one would have known of these treaties if the Russian Bolsheviks, when they seized power, had not published them.

Ultimately there were a dozen or more countries on the side of the Allies (I shall call the Anglo-French side the Allies for short). These were Britain and her empire, France, Russia, Italy, the United States of America, Belgium, Serbia, Japan, China, Rumania, Greece and Portugal. (There may be one or two more which I do not remember.) On the German side were Germany, Austria, Turkey, and Bulgaria. The United States came into the war in the third year. Even leaving them out of consideration for the time, it is obvious that the resources of the Allies were far greater than those of the German side. They had more men, far more money, more factories to make arms and munitions, and, above all, they had command of the seas, which made it easy for them to draw upon the resources of the neutral world. Thus the Allies could get war material or food or borrow money from America because of this sea power. Germany and her allies were surrounded and hemmed in by their enemies; and Germany's allies were weak countries which did not help much. They were often a drain on Germany and had to be propped up by her. So, practically, it was Germany alone against the greater part of the world in arms. It seems, from every point of view, a most unequal contest. And yet Germany held the world at bay for four years and repeatedly came near to victory. Year after year victory seemed to hang in the balance. It was an amazing effort for one nation, and it was only possible because of the magnificent military machine that Germany had built up. To the end, when Germany and her allies had been finally vanquished, the German army was still intact and much of it was on foreign territory.

On the side of the Allies the brunt of the fighting fell on the French army, and it was the French who, at tremendous cost of young lives, withstood the German military machine. England's great contribution was the navy and sea power, and also diplomacy and propaganda. Germany, proud of her army, was singularly crude in her diplomacy with neutral countries and in her methods of propaganda. There is no doubt that of all countries during the war, England took the palm in the efficiency and thoroughness of her propaganda of falsehood and distorted fact. Russia and Italy and the other allied countries played a comparatively minor, and not a distinguished, rôle in the fighting. And yet the Russian losses were perhaps the greatest of all countries. The United States, coming in towards the end, played the final decisive rôle in crushing Germany.

In the early months of the war there was great tension between England and America, and even war between them was mentioned. The friction was due to England's interference with American shipping on the seas, which she suspected of carrying goods to Germany. But then the British propaganda machine got busy and made a special effort to win over America. The first thing taken in hand was atrocity propaganda, and horrible stories of what the German army had done in Belgium were circulated. " Frightfulness " of the German *Hun* or *Boche* this was called. A few of these stories had some basis in fact, such as the destruction of the university and library of Louvain, but most of them were pure inventions. There was one amazing story of a corpse factory which the Germans were said to run ! And yet, such was the hatred of the enemy peoples for each other that they would believe anything.

You can form some idea of the vast scale on which British propaganda was carried on when I tell you that the British War Mission to America consisted of 500 officials and 10,000 assistants ! This was official; besides this a tremendous amount of unofficial work was done. All methods, fair and foul, were adopted for this propaganda work. In Stockholm in Sweden the British officially started a kind of English music-hall, giving a variety entertainment, to win the good will of the Swedes !

This propaganda, as well as the German submarine activities, about which I shall tell you something later, went a long way in bringing America to the side of the Allies. But ultimately the decisive factor was money.

War is an expensive business, a terribly expensive business. It swallows up mountains of valuable material, and only has devastation to show for it. It stops most wealth-producing activities and concentrates people's energy on destruction. Where was all this money to come from ? To begin with, on the side of the Allies, only England and France could be considered well off. They paid not only their own share of the war expense, but also paid for their allies by lending money and material to them. After some time Paris gave way; its financial resources were exhausted. London then financed the Allied side of the war alone. By the end of the second year of the war London also gave way. So towards the end of 1916 both French and English credit was at an end. Then an English mission consisting of prominent statesmen went to America to beg for financial help. America agreed to lend money, and thenceforward it was American money that carried on the war on the side of the Allies. The debt of the Allies to America grew by leaps and bounds to amazing figures, and, as it grew, the big banks and the financiers in America, who had lent the money, became more and more interested in an Allied victory. If the Allies were defeated by Germany, what would happen to the vast sums that America had lent to them ? The American banker's pocket was touched, and he reacted accordingly. Sentiment in favour of America joining the Allies in the war was developed, and ultimately America did so.

We hear a great deal now about the American debt question, and the newspapers are full of it. This debt, which hangs like a millstone round the necks of England and France, and which they cannot pay, was piled up in the days of the war. If that money had not been forthcoming at the time, their credit would have collapsed completely, and perhaps America would not have joined them.

149

THE COURSE OF THE WAR

April 1, 1933

WHEN the war began, early in August 1914, all the world looked at Belgium and the northern frontier of France. The vast German armies were marching on and on, sweeping away all the obstructions that came in their path. For a short while they were stopped by little Belgium and, angered at this, they tried to frighten the Belgians by acts of terrorism, which formed the basis of the atrocity stories of the Allies. They went on towards Paris, and the French army seemed to roll up in front of them and the small British army was swept aside. Within a month of the outbreak of the war Paris seemed to be doomed, and the French Government actually prepared to take its offices and valuables south to Bordeaux. Some Germans thought that they had practically won the war. Matters stood thus on the western front (that is the French front) of the war at the end of August.

Meanwhile Russian troops were invading East Prussia, and an attempt was made somehow to distract German attention from the western front. In France and England great hopes were placed in the Russian " steam-roller ", as it was called, rolling on to Berlin. But the Russian soldiers were badly armed and their officers were thoroughly incompetent, and behind them was the Tsar's corrupt government. Suddenly the Germans turned on them, and trapped a huge Russian army in the lakes and marshes of East Prussia, and destroyed it utterly. The Battle of Tannenburg is the name given to this tremendous German victory, and one of the chief generals associated with it was von Hindenburg, who became the President of the German Republic later.

It was a great victory, and yet indirectly it cost the German armies a great deal. In order to achieve it, and frightened a little by the Russian advance in the east, they had transferred some of their armies from the French side to the Russian. This had relieved the pressure on the western front somewhat, and the French army made a mighty effort to hurl back the invading Germans. At the Battle of the Marne, early in September 1914, they succeeded in pushing back the Germans about fifty miles. Paris was saved, and the French and the English had some breathing time.

The Germans made another attempt to break through, and nearly succeeded, but they were held. Both armies then dug themselves in, and a new kind of fighting, trench warfare, began. It was a kind of stalemate, and for over three years, and to some extent almost to the end of the war, this trench warfare continued on the western front, and huge armies dug themselves in like moles, and tried to exhaust each other. The German and French armies at this front ran into millions from the very beginning. The little British army, also at this front, grew rapidly till it could also be counted by the million.

On the eastern or Russian front there was more movement. Russian troops repeatedly defeated the Austrians, but were themselves invariably defeated by the Germans. The losses and casualties on this front were colossal. Do not imagine that at the western front, because of trench warfare, the losses were much less. The lives of men were treated with amazing unconcern, and hundreds of thousands were hurled to certain death in repeated attacks on the entrenched positions, with little result.

There were many other theatres of war. The Turks tried to attack the Suez Canal, but were repulsed. Egypt, as I have previously told you, was declared a British Protectorate in December 1914, and forthwith Britain suspended the new Legislative Assembly and filled the prisons with people they suspected. Nationalist newspapers were suppressed, and not more than five persons were allowed to meet. The censorship introduced there was described by the London *Times* as " savagely ruthless ". The country was, indeed, under martial law for the whole of the war period.

Britain attacked Turkey in many weak places of her ramshackle empire : in Iraq and, later on, in Palestine and Syria. In Arabia the national sentiment of the Arabs was taken advantage of by the British, and an Arab revolt against Turkey organized with the help of liberal bribes of money and material. Colonel T. E. Lawrence, a British agent in Arabia, was largely responsible for this revolt, and later he developed a reputation as a man of mystery, acting behind the scenes of many movements in Asia.

But the direct attack on the heart of Turkey began in February 1915, when the British fleet tried to force the Dardanelles, and thus to capture Constantinople. If they had succeeded in this, they would not only have put an end to Turkey in the war, but cut off all German influence from western Asia. But they failed. The Turks put up a brave fight and, it is interesting to note, Mustafa Kemal Pasha had a great share in this. For nearly a year the British carried on this attempt in Gallipoli ; after great losses they retired.

The German colonies in western and eastern Africa were also attacked by the Allies. These colonies were quite cut off from Germany and could not receive help. Gradually they succumbed. In China the German concession of Kiauchau was easily taken possession of by Japan. Japan, indeed, had a very easy time, as there was little doing in the Far East. So she tried to improve the occasion by bullying and threatening China into giving her all manner of valuable concessions and privileges.

Italy, for many months, watched the course of the war and tried to make out which side would win. Having decided at last that the chances of victory lay with the Allies, she agreed to the bribes they offered her and a secret pact was concluded. In May 1915 Italy formally joined the Allies in the war. For two years the Italians and the Austrians pegged away at each other without great results. Then the Germans came to help the Austrians, and the Italians collapsed before them. The Austro-German army almost reached to Venice.

Bulgaria joined Germany in October 1915. Soon after this the Austro-German army, co-operating with Bulgaria, crushed Serbia completely. The Serbian ruler with the remnants of his army had to leave the country and take refuge in Allied ships, and Serbia came under German rule.

Rumania had a special reputation for opportunism after her conduct in the Balkan wars. For two years she watched the course of the Great War, and ultimately, in August 1916, she threw in her lot with the Allies. Swift punishment came upon her, and the German army swept down upon her and crushed all resistance. Rumania also passed under Austro-German occupation.

So the Central Powers, Germany and Austria, came to occupy Belgium and a part of France in the north-east, and Poland, Serbia, and Rumania. In many of the minor theatres of the war they had triumphed. But the heart of the struggle lay on the western front and on the seas, and they were making no progress there. On that front the rival armies lay locked in the embrace of death. On the seas the Allies were supreme. Some German cruisers in the early days of the war had roamed about interfering with the shipping of the Allies. One of these was the famous *Emden*, which even bombarded Madras. But this was a petty diversion which made no difference to the fact that the Allies controlled the sea-routes. And with the help of this control they had tried to cut off the Central Powers from all food and other material from outside. This blockade of Germany and Austria was a terrible ordeal for them, for food grew scarce and hunger stared the whole population in the face.

Germany, on the other hand, started sinking the ships of the Allies by means of submarines. This submarine warfare was so successful that England's food supply was reduced and there was danger of famine. In May 1915 a German submarine sank the great English Atlantic liner *Lusitania*, and a large number of people were drowned in this. Many Americans also went down in her, and there was much indignation in America because of it.

Germany also attacked England by the air. Huge Zeppelin airships came on moonlit nights to throw bombs on London and places where there were munition factories. Later, aeroplanes did this bombing; and it became quite a usual thing for the whirring of the planes to be heard, and the firing of the anti-aircraft guns, and for people to rush down to cellars and underground places to protect themselves. The British people were very indignant at this bombing of civilian populations. They were rightly indignant, for it is a horrible thing. But there is little indignation in Britain when British aeroplanes drop bombs, and especially those devilish inventions " the time-delayed bombs ", in the North-West Frontier of India or in Iraq. This is called police work, and is done even in so-called peace-time.

So the war went on, month after month, consuming human lives as a forest fire consumes hordes of locusts, and as it went on, it became more destructive and barbarous. The Germans introduced poison gas, and soon both sides were using it. Aeroplanes came into greater use as bomb-throwers, and then came, first on the British side, the " tanks ", huge mechanical monsters, crawling over everything like caterpillars. Men died by the hundred thousand on the fronts, and behind them, in the home countries, women and children suffered from hunger and privation. In Germany and Austria especially, because of the blockade, starvation grew terrible. It became a test of endurance. Which side would outlast the other in this ordeal ? Would either army wear out the other ? Would the Allied blockade of Germany break her spirit ? Or would the German submarine campaign starve England and break her spirit and morale ? Behind each country lay a gigantic record of sacrifice and suffering. Was all this terrible sacrifice and suffering in vain, people wondered ? Are we to forget our dead and give in to the enemy ? The pre-war days seemed remote, even the causes of the war were forgotten ; only one thing remained to obsess the minds of men and women, the desire for revenge and victory.

The call of the dead, who have sacrificed themselves in a cause they held dear, is a terrible thing. Who that has any spirit in him or her can resist it ? Darkness reigned everywhere during these last years of war, and there was sorrow in every home in the warring countries, and a weariness, and disillusion, yet what could one do but hold the torch aloft ? Read this moving poem, written by a British officer, Major McCrae, and try to imagine how it must have affected the men and women of his race who read it in those black and dreary war days. And remember that similar poems were written in various countries and in many languages.

> We are the Dead. Short days ago
> We lived, felt dawn, saw sunset glow,
> Loved and were loved, and now we lie
>   In Flanders Fields.
>
> Take up our quarrel with the foe :
> To you from failing hands we throw
> The Torch ; be yours to hold it high.
> If ye break faith with us who die
> We shall not sleep, though Poppies grow
>   In Flanders Fields.

Towards the end of 1916 the advantage seemed to lie on the side of the Allies. Their new tanks had given them the initiative on the western front; the Zeppelin airships raiding England met with disasters; enough food managed to reach England on neutral ships in spite of German submarines. In May 1916 a naval battle had taken place in the North Sea (the Battle of Jutland), which was on the whole a success for the British. Meanwhile the blockade of Germany was bringing starvation nearer to the Austro-German people. Time seemed to be against the Central Powers, and quick results were considered necessary. Germany had even sent out some feelers for peace, but the Allies would have none of them; the Allied governments were committed too much by their secret treaties for the division of various countries to be satisfied with anything short of complete victory. Woodrow Wilson, the President of the United States, had also made some unsuccessful efforts to bring about peace.

The German leaders thereupon decided to intensify their submarine warfare, and thus starve England into submission. They proclaimed in January 1917 that they would sink even neutral ships in certain waters. This was to prevent these neutrals from taking food to England. This announcement greatly offended America; she could not tolerate her ships being sunk in this way. It made her entry into the war inevitable, and indeed the German Government must have known this when they made their decision about unrestricted submarining. Perhaps they had felt that there was no alternative left for them and the risk had to be taken. Or they might have thought that, as it was, American financiers were giving enough help to the Allies. In any event, the United States declared war in April 1917, and their entry, with their vast resources and fresh condition when all the other nations were jaded, made it certain that the German Powers would be defeated.

And yet, even before America had declared war, another event of vital importance had taken place. On March 15, 1917, the first Russian Revolution had resulted in the abdication of the Tsar. I shall write to you about this revolution separately. What I wish you to note now is that this revolution made a tremendous difference to the war. Russia obviously could not fight much now, if at all, against the German Powers; and this meant that Germany was relieved of all anxiety on the eastern front. She could transfer all or most of the eastern armies to the western front and hurl them against the French and British. Suddenly the position had become very favourable to Germany. If she had only known of the Russian revolution six or seven weeks before it occurred, what a difference it would have made. It might have meant no change in submarine warfare, and perhaps America remaining neutral. With Russia out of the lists and America neutral, it was highly likely that Germany would have crushed the British and French armies. Even as it was, German strength on the western front grew, and there was also a prodigious destruction of shipping, Allied and neutral, by German submarines.

The Russian Revolution seemed to help Germany. And yet it turned out to be one of the greatest causes of internal weakness. Within eight months of the first revolution came the second revolution, which gave power to the Soviets and the Bolsheviks, whose slogan was peace. They addressed the workers and soldiers of all warring nations and appealed for peace; they pointed out that it was a capitalists' war and that the workers must not allow themselves to be used as cannon-fodder for the advancement of imperialist aims. Some of these voices and appeals reached the soldiers of other nations at the front, and they produced a considerable impression. There were many mutinies in the French army, which the authorities just managed to suppress. The effect on German soldiers was even greater, for many regiments had actually fraternized with the Russian army after the revolution. When these regiments were transferred to the western front they carried this new message with them and spread it among other regiments. Germany was war-weary and utterly disheartened, and the seeds from Russia fell on ground that was prepared to receive them. In this way the Russian Revolution made Germany weak internally.

But the German military authorities were blind to these portents, and in March 1918 they forced a crushing and humiliating peace on Soviet Russia. The Soviets accepted because they had no alternative and they wanted peace at any price. In March 1918 also the German army made its last mighty effort on the western front. The Germans broke through the Anglo-French line, destroying armies in the process, and again reached the river Marne, from which they had been pushed back three and a half years before. It was a great effort, but it was the last one, and Germany was exhausted. Meanwhile, armies came from America across the Atlantic, and, learning from bitter experience, all the Allied armies on the western front—British, American, French—were put under one supreme command, so that there might be the fullest-co-operation and unity of effort. The French Marshal Foch was made the Generalissimo of the whole Allied army in the west. By the middle of 1918 the tide had definitely turned; the initiative and the offensive were with the Allies, and they marched on, pushing the Germans back. By October the end was near, and there was talk of an armistice.

On November 4 there was a German naval mutiny at Kiel, and five days later the German Republic was proclaimed in Berlin. The same day, November 9, the Kaiser Wilhelm II made an unseemly and ignominious exit from Germany to Holland, and with him passed away the house of Hohenzollern. Like the Manchus in China, " they had come in with the roar of a tiger, to disappear like the tail of a snake ".

On November 11, 1918, the armistice was signed and the war was at an end. This armistice was based on " Fourteen Points " which President Wilson of America had formulated. They were framed to a large extent on the principles of self-determination for the small nationalities involved, disarmament, no secret diplomacy, Russia to be helped by the Powers, and a League of Nations. We shall see later how many of these Fourteen Points were conveniently forgotten by the victors.

The war was over. But the blockade of Germany by England's fleet continued and food was not allowed to reach the starving German women and children. This amazing exhibition of hatred and desire to punish even the little children was supported by reputable British statesmen and public men, by great newspapers, even by so-called liberal journals. Indeed, the Prime Minister of England then was a Liberal, Lloyd George. The record of the four and quarter years of war is full of mad brutalities and atrocities. And yet perhaps nothing exceeds in sheer cold-blooded brutality this continuation of the blockade of Germany after the armistice. The war was over, and still a whole nation was starving and its little children were suffering terribly from hunger, and food was deliberately and forcibly kept away. How war distorts our minds and fills them with mad hatred! Bethmann Hollweg, the old Chancellor of Germany, said: "Our children, and our children's children, will bear traces of the blockade that England enforced against us, a refinement of cruelty nothing less than diabolic."

While the great statesmen and others in high places approved of this blockade, the poor British Tommy, who had done the fighting, could not stand the sight of it. After the armistice a British army had been stationed at Cologne in the Rhineland, and the English general commanding this army had to send a telegram to Prime Minister Lloyd George pointing out "how bad was the effect produced upon the British army by the spectacle of the sufferings of German women and children". For more than seven months after the armistice England continued this blockade of Germany.

The long years of war had brutalized the warring nations. They destroyed the moral sense of large numbers of people, and made many normal persons into half criminals. People got used to violence and to deliberate distortion of facts, and were filled with hatred and the spirit of revenge.

What was the balance-sheet of the war? No one knows yet; they are still making it up! I shall give you some figures to impress on you what modern war means.

The total casualties of the war have been calculated as follows :—

Known dead soldiers . . .	10,000,000
Presumed dead soldiers . .	3,000,000
Dead civilians	13,000,000
Wounded	20,000,000
Prisoners	3,000,000
War orphans	9,000,000
War widows	5,000,000
Refugees	10,000,000

Look at these tremendous figures and try to imagine the human suffering that underlies them. Add them up: the total of dead and wounded alone comes to 46,000,000.

And the cost in hard cash? They are still counting it! An

American estimate gives the total expenditure on the Allied side as £40,999,600,000—nearly forty-one thousand million pounds; and on the German side as £15,122,300,000—over fifteen thousand million pounds. Grand total, over fifty-six thousand million pounds ! These figures cannot be fully understood by us, as they are so utterly out of proportion to our daily life. They seem to remind us of astronomical figures like the distance to the sun or the stars. It is not surprising that the old warring nations, victors and vanquished alike, are still hopelessly involved in the after-effects of war finance.

The " war to end war ", and " make the world safe for democracy", and " ensure the freedom of small nationalities ", and for " self-determination ", and generally for freedom and high ideals, was over; and England, France, America, Italy, and their smaller satellites (Russia was of course out of it) had triumphed. How these high and noble ideals were translated into practice we shall see later. Meanwhile, we might repeat the lines which the English poet Southey wrote about another and an older victory.

> " And everybody praised the Duke
>   Who this great fight did win."
> " But what good came of it at last ? "
>   Quoth little Peterkin.
> " Why, that I cannot tell," said he,
>   " But 'twas a famous victory."

150

THE PASSING AWAY OF TSARDOM IN RUSSIA

April 7, 1933

In my account of the course of the war I referred to the Russian Revolution and to its effect on the war. Apart from its effect on the war, the Revolution was in itself a tremendous event, unique in world history. Although it was the first revolution of its kind, it may not long remain the only one of its type, for it has become a challenge to other countries and an example for many revolutionaries all over the world. It is therefore deserving of close study. It was undoubtedly the biggest outcome of the war; and yet, it was the most unthought of, and the least desired, by any of the governments and statesmen that plunged into the war. Or perhaps it would be more correct to say that it was the child of the historical and economic conditions prevailing in Russia, which were rapidly brought to a head by the vast losses and suffering caused by the war, and of which a master mind and a genius in revolution, Lenin, took advantage.

There were really two revolutions in the year 1917 in Russia, one in March, the other in November. Or the whole period may be looked upon as one continuous process of revolution with two high-water marks.

I have told you in my last letter on Russia about the 1905 revolution, which also arose at a time of war and defeat. This was suppressed with brutality, and the Tsar's government continued its career of unchecked autocracy, spying out and crushing all liberal opinion. The Marxists, and especially the Bolsheviks, were crushed, and all their principal men and women were either in the penal colonies of Siberia or in exile abroad. But even this handful of people abroad carried on their propaganda and study under the leadership of Lenin. They were all convinced Marxists, but the doctrine of Marx had been worked out for a highly industrialized country like England or Germany. Russia was still medieval and agricultural, with just a fringe of industry in the large towns. Lenin set about adapting the fundamentals of Marxism to Russia as it was. He wrote a great deal on this subject, and there were many arguments among the Russian exiles, and so they prepared themselves in the theory of revolution. Lenin believed in a job being done by experts and trained people, not merely by enthusiasts. If a revolution were to be attempted, it was his opinion that people should also be thoroughly trained for this job, so that when the time for action came, they should be clear in their minds as to what they should do. So Lenin and his colleagues utilized the dark years of repression after 1905 in training themselves for future action.

Already in 1914 the urban working class in Russia was waking up and becoming revolutionary again. There were numerous political strikes. Then came the war, and this absorbed all attention, and the most advanced workers were sent to the front as soldiers. Lenin and his group (most of the leaders were in exile outside Russia) opposed the war from the very beginning. They were not carried away by it like most of the socialists of other countries. They called it a capitalists' war, with which the working class had no concern except in so far as they could profit by it to win their own freedom.

The Russian army in the field met with terrible losses, probably the greatest of all the armies involved. The Russian generals were, even for military men, who are not usually supposed to be endowed with much intelligence, remarkably incompetent. Russian soldiers, ill equipped with arms and often with no ammunition and no supports, were hurled at the enemy and sent to certain death by the hundred thousand. Meanwhile in Petrograd—as St. Petersburg had come to be known—and other big cities, there was tremendous profiteering, and huge fortunes were made by speculators. These " patriotic " speculators and profiteers were of course loud in their demand for a war to the finish. It would no doubt have suited them to have a perpetual war ! But the soldiers and workers and the peasantry (which supplied the soldiers) became exhausted and hungry and full of discontent.

The Tsar Nicholas was a very foolish person, a great deal under the influence of his wife, the Tsarina, an equally foolish but stronger person. The two surrounded themselves with knaves and fools, and nobody dared to criticize them. Matters came to such a pass that a disgusting scoundrel, known as Gregory Rasputin, became the chief favourite of the Tsarina, and through her, of the Tsar. Rasputin (the word *Rasputin* means " dirty dog ") had been a poor peasant who had got into trouble over stealing horses. He decided to put on a garb of holiness and adopt the paying profession of an ascetic. As in India, this was an easy way of making money in Russia. He grew his hair long, and with his hair his fame also grew till it reached the imperial Court. The only son of the Tsar and Tsarina, called the Tsarevitch, was a bit of an invalid, and Rasputin somehow made the Tsarina believe that he would cure the boy. His fortune was made, and soon he dominated the Tsar and Tsarina, and the highest appointments were made at his instance. He lived a most depraved life, and took huge bribes, but for years he played this dominating part.

Everybody was disgusted by this. Even the moderates and the aristocracy began to murmur, and there was talk of a palace revolution—that is, a forcible change of Tsars. Meanwhile Tsar Nicholas had made himself the commander-in-chief of his army and was making a mess of everything. A few days before the end of the year 1916 Rasputin was murdered by a member of the Tsar's family. He was invited to dinner and asked to shoot himself; on his refusal to do so, he was shot down. Rasputin's murder was welcomed generally as a good riddance, but it resulted in greater oppression by the Tsar's secret police.

The crisis grew. There was a food famine and riots for food in Petrograd. And then, in the early days of March, out of the long agony of the workers, unexpectedly and spontaneously, grew the revolution. Five days in March, from the 8th to the 12th, saw the triumph of this revolution. It was no palace affair; it was not even an organized revolution carefully planned by its leaders at the top. It seemed to rise from below, from the most oppressed of the workers, and went groping blindly forward with no apparent plan or leadership. The various revolutionary parties, including the local Bolsheviks, were taken unawares and did not know what lead to give. The masses themselves took the initiative, and the moment they had won the soldiers stationed at Petrograd over to their side, success had come to them. These revolutionary masses must not, however, be mistaken for unorganized mobs bent on destruction, as the peasant outbreaks had often been in the past. The important fact about this March revolution was that the lead was taken in it, for the first time in history, by the class of factory-workers, the " proletariat ", as it has been called. And these workers, although they had no outstanding leaders with them at the time (Lenin and others being in prison or exile), had many an unknown worker who had been trained by Lenin's group. These unknown workers in dozens of factories gave backbone to the whole movement and directed it into definite channels.

We see here, as nowhere else, the rôle of the industrial masses in action. Russia of course was overwhelmingly an agricultural country, and even this agriculture was carried on in a medieval way. In the country as a whole there was little of modern industry; such of it as existed was concentrated in a few towns. Petrograd had many of these factories, and had thus a huge population of industrial workers. The March revolution was the work of these Petrograd workers and of the regiments stationed in that city.

March 8 hears the first rumblings of the revolution. The women take the lead, and the women workers of the textile factories march out and demonstrate in the streets. The next day the strikes spread; many men workers also come out; there are demands for bread and shouts of " Down with autocracy ". The authorities send the Cossacks, who had always in the past been the main support of Tsardom, to crush the demonstrating workers. The Cossacks push the people about but do not shoot, and the workers notice with joy that the Cossacks are really friendly behind their official masks. Immediately the enthusiasm of the people grows, and they try to fraternize with the Cossacks. But the police are hated and stoned. The third day, March 10, sees this spirit of fraternization with the Cossacks grow. A rumour even spreads that the Cossacks have fired at the police who have been shooting at the people. The police retire from the streets. Women workers go up to the soldiers and make fervent appeals to them; the soldiers' bayonets go up.

The next day, March 11, is a Sunday. The workers gather in the centre of the city, the police shooting at them from hidden places. Some soldiers also shoot at the people, who thereupon go to the barracks of this regiment and complain bitterly. The regiment is moved, and it comes out under its non-commissioned officers to protect the people; it fires on the police. The regiment is arrested, but too late. The revolt spreads to other regiments on March 12, and they come out with their rifles and machine guns. There is a great deal of shooting in the streets, but it was difficult to say who was shooting whom. The soldiers and workers then go and arrest some of the ministers (others have fled), and policemen, and secret service men. They liberate the old political prisoners in the gaols.

The revolution had triumphed in Petrograd. Moscow followed soon after. The villages watched developments. Slowly the peasantry accepted the new order, but without enthusiasm. For them, there were only two questions that mattered : to possess land and to have peace.

What of the Tsar ? What was happening to him during these eventful days ? He was not in Petrograd; he was far away in a small town from where, as Commander-in-Chief, he was supposed to be directing his armies. But his day was over, and, like an over-ripe fruit, he fell off almost unnoticed. The mighty Tsar, the great autocrat of all the Russias before whom millions trembled, the " Little Father " of " Holy Russia ", disappeared into the " dustbin of history ". It is strange how great systems collapse when they have fulfilled their destiny and lived their day. When the Tsar heard of the workers' strikes and disturbances in Petrograd, he ordered a declaration of martial law. This was formally declared by the general in command, but the declaration was not broadcast in the city or pasted up, as there was no one to do this job ! The government machinery had gone to pieces. The Tsar, still blind to what was happening, tried to return to Petrograd. The railway workers stopped his train on the way. The Tsarina, who was then in a suburb of Petrograd, sent a telegram to the Tsar. It was returned from the telegraph office with a note in pencil : " Whereabouts of addressee unknown " !

The generals at the front and the liberal leaders in Petrograd, frightened by these developments, and hoping to save something from the wreck, begged the Tsar to abdicate. He did so, nominating a relative to take his place. But there were to be no more Tsars; the house of Romanoff, after 300 years of autocratic rule, had left the Russian stage for good.

The aristocracy, the landowning classes, the upper middle classes, and even the liberals and reformers, looked upon the eruption of the working class with terror and dismay. They felt powerless before them when they saw that the army on which they relied had joined the workers. They were not yet sure on which side victory would lie, for it was possible that the Tsar might turn up with an army from the front and, with its help, crush the insurrection. So, fear of the workers on the one side and of the Tsar on the other, and an excessive anxiety to save their own skins, made their lot a miserable one. There was the Duma, which represented the landowning classes and the upper *bourgeoisie*. Even the workers looked up to it to some extent, but instead of taking the lead in the crisis or doing anything, its president and members sat in fear and trembling and could not make up their minds what to do.

Meanwhile the Soviet took shape. To the workers' representatives were added soldiers' representatives, and the new Soviet took possession of one wing of the huge Tauride Palace, part of which was occupied by the Duma. The workers and soldiers were full of enthusiasm at their victory. But then the question arose : what were they to do with it ? They had won power; who was to exercise it ? It did not strike them that the Soviet itself might do so; they took it for granted that the *bourgeoisie* should take power. So a deputation from the Soviet tramped up to the Duma to ask them to start governing. The president and members of the Duma thought that this deputation had come to arrest them ! They had no wish to be burdened with power; they were afraid of the risks involved. But what were they to do ? The Soviet deputation insisted, and they were afraid of refusing them. So most reluctantly, and in fear of the consequences, a committee of the Duma accepted power, and to the outside world it appeared that the Duma was leading the revolution. What an extraordinary mix-up it was; we would hardly believe that such things could happen if we read about them in a story. But fact is often stranger than fiction.

The Provisional Government which the committee of the Duma appointed was a very conservative body, and its prime minister was a prince. In another wing of the same building sat the Soviet, continually interfering with the work of the Provisional Government. But the Soviet itself was moderate to begin with, and the Bolsheviks in it were a mere handful. Thus there was a kind of double government—the Provisional Government and the Soviet —and behind both were the revolutionary masses which had carried through the revolution, and which were expecting great things from it. The only lead the hungry and war-weary masses got from the new government was that they must carry on the war till the Germans were beaten. Was it for this, they wondered, that they had gone through the revolution and driven away the Tsar ?

Just then, on April 17, Lenin arrived on the scene. He had been in Switzerland right through the war, and he was eager to come to Russia as soon as he heard of the revolution. How was he to do so ? The English and French would not allow him to pass their territories, nor would the Germans and Austrians. At length, for reasons of their own, the German Government agreed to let him pass in a sealed train from the Swiss to the Russian frontier. They hoped, of course, and with reason, that the arrival of Lenin in Russia would weaken the Provisional Government and the war party, for Lenin was against the war, and they hoped to profit by this. They did not imagine that this more or less obscure revolutionary would end by shaking Europe and the world.

There was no doubt or vagueness in Lenin's mind. His were the penetrating eyes which detected the moods of the masses ; the clear head which could apply and adapt well-thought-out principles to changing situations ; the inflexible will which held on to the course he had mapped out, regardless of immediate consequences. The very day he arrived he shook up violently the Bolshevik party, criticized their inaction, and pointed out in burning phrases what their duty was. His speech was an electric charge which pained but at the same time vivified. " We are not charlatans," he said ; " we must base ourselves only on the consciousness of the masses. Even if it is necessary to remain in a minority—so be it. It is a good thing to give up for a time the position of leadership ; we must not be afraid to remain in the minority." And so he stuck to his principles and refused to compromise. The revolution, which had drifted for so long leaderless and without guides, had at last got its leader. The hour had produced the man.

What were these differences in theory which separated the Bolsheviks from the Mensheviks and other revolutionary groups at this stage ? And what had paralysed the local Bolsheviks before Lenin's arrival ? And again, why had the Soviet, after having the power in its hands, made it over to the old-fashioned and conservative Duma ? I cannot go into these questions deeply, but we must give them some thought if we are to understand the continually changing drama of Petrograd and Russia in 1917.

Karl Marx's theory of human change and progress, called the

" materialist conception of history ", was based on new social forms taking the place of old forms as these latter became out of date. As the methods of technical production improved, the economic and political organization of society gradually caught up to them. The way this took place was by continual class struggles between the dominant class and the exploited classes. Thus the old feudal class had given place in western Europe to the *bourgeoisie*, which now controlled the economic and political structure in England, France, Germany, etc., and which, in its turn, would give place to the working class. In Russia the feudal class was still in command, and the change which had put the *bourgeoisie* in power in western Europe had not yet taken place. Most Marxists, therefore, thought that, inevitably, Russia would have to pass through this *bourgeois* and parliamentary stage before it could proceed to the last stage of the workers' republic. The middle stage could not be jumped over, according to them. Lenin himself, prior to the revolution of March 1917, had laid down an intermediate policy of co-operating with the peasants (and not opposing the *bourgeoisie*) against the Tsar and the landowners, for a *bourgeois* revolution.

The Bolsheviks and Mensheviks and all believers in Marx's theories were therefore full of this idea of having a *bourgeois* democratic republic after the English or French pattern. The leading workers' representatives also thought this inevitable, and it was because of this that the Soviet, instead of keeping power in its own hands, went and offered it to the Duma. These people, as is so often the case with all of us, had become the slaves of their own doctrines, and could not see that a new situation had arisen, which demanded a different policy or at any rate a different adaptation of the old policy. The masses were far more revolutionary than the leaders. The Mensheviks, who controlled the Soviet, even went so far as to say that the working class should not raise any social question then; their immediate task was to achieve political freedom. The Bolsheviks temporized. The March revolution succeeded in spite of its hesitating and cautious leaders.

With Lenin's arrival all this was changed. He sensed the position immediately and, with the genius of true leadership, adapted the Marxian programme accordingly. The fight was to be against capitalism itself now for the rule of the working class in co-operation with the poorer peasantry. The three immediate slogans of the Bolsheviks became (1) democratic republic, (2) confiscation of the landed estates, and (3) an eight-hour day for the workers. Immediately, these slogans brought reality into the struggle for the peasantry and workers. It was not a vague and empty ideal for them; it meant life and hope.

Lenin's policy was for the Bolsheviks to win over the majority of the workers to their side and thus to capture the Soviet; and for the Soviet then to seize power from the Provisional Government. He was not for another revolution immediately. He insisted on winning over a majority of the workers and the Soviet before the time came to overthrow the Provisional Government. He was hard on those who wished to co-operate with this government; that was betraying the revolution. He was equally hard on those who wanted to rush ahead to upset this government before the time for it had come; "a moment of action," he said, "is no time to aim 'a wee bit too far to the left.' We look upon that as the greatest crime, disorganization."

So, calmly but inexorably, like some agent of an inevitable fate, this lump of ice covering a blazing fire within went ahead to its appointed goal.

151

THE BOLSHEVIKS SEIZE POWER

April 9, 1933

DURING a revolutionary period history seems to march with seven-league boots. There are rapid changes outwardly, but an even greater change takes place in the consciousness of the masses. They learn little from books, as they have not much opportunity of a bookish education; and books, often enough, hide more than they reveal. Their school is the harder but truer one of experience. During the life-and-death struggle for power in a period of revolution, the masks that usually hide people's real motives come off, and the reality on which society is based can be seen behind them. So during this fateful year 1917 in Russia, the masses, and especially the industrial workers in the towns, who were at the heart of the revolution, learnt their lessons from events, and changed almost from day to day.

There was no stability or equilibrium anywhere. Life was dynamic and changing, and people and classes were pulling and pushing in different ways. There were still people hoping and conspiring for the return of Tsardom, but they did not represent an important class, and we can ignore them. The main conflict developed between the Provisional Government and the Soviet; and yet the majority in the Soviet were for co-operation and compromise with the government. Those anxious for compromise were afraid of being put in charge of the government and the State power. "Who will take the place of the goverment? We? But our hands tremble . . ." said a speaker in the Soviet. It is a familiar cry which we have heard in India also from many a possessor of palsied hands and a terrified heart. But strong hands and stout hearts are not lacking when the time comes for them.

The conflict between the Provisional Government and the Soviet was inevitable, however much the compromising elements on either side tried to avoid it. The government wanted to please the Allies by carrying on the war, and the possessing classes in Russia by protecting as far as possible their properties. The Soviet, being more in touch with the masses, sensed their demand for peace and land for the peasants, and many demands from the workers, such as the eight-hour day. Thus it happened that the government was paralysed by the Soviet, and the Soviet itself was paralysed by the masses, for the masses were far more revolutionary than the parties and their leaders.

An effort was made to bring the government more in line with the Soviet, and a radical lawyer and an eloquent orator, Kerensky, became the leading member of the government. He succeeded in forming a coalition government to which the Menshevik majority in the Soviet sent some representatives. He also tried hard to please England and France by launching an offensive against Germany. The offensive failed, as the army and the people were in no mood for more war.

Meanwhile, All-Russian Soviet Congresses were being held in Petrograd, and each subsequent Congress was more extreme than the last. More and more Bolshevik members were elected to them, and the two dominant parties, the Mensheviks and the Social Revolutionaries (an agrarian party), had their majority lessened. The Bolshevik influence increased, especially with the Petrograd workers. All over the country Soviets had sprung up, and they would not obey the orders of the government unless they were countersigned by the Soviet. One of the reasons why the Provisional Government was weak was the absence of a strong middle class in Russia.

While a tussle for power was going on in the capital, the peasantry took the law into their own hands. As I have told you, these peasants were not very enthusiastic about the March Revolution, nor were they against it. They waited and watched. But the landlords of the large estates, fearing that their property would be confiscated, divided it up into small holdings and gave it to dummy owners who would keep it on their behalf. They also transferred much of their property to foreigners. In this way they tried to save their lands. The peasantry did not like this at all, and they asked the government to stop all land sales by a decree. The government hesitated; what could it do? It did not want to irritate either party. Then the peasants began to take action themselves. As early as April some of them arrested their landlords and seized and divided the estates. The soldiers back from the front (who were, of course, peasants) played the leading part in this. The movement developed till the lands were seized on a mass scale. By June even the Siberian steppes had been affected. In Siberia there were no big landlords, so the peasantry took possession of Church and monastery lands.

It is interesting to note that this confiscation of the big estates took place entirely on the initiative of the peasants, and many months before the Bolshevik revolution. Lenin was in favour of the immediate transfer of the land to the peasants in an organized way. He was wholly against haphazard anarchist seizures. Thus, when the Bolsheviks came to power later on they found a Russia of peasant proprietors.

Exactly a month after Lenin's arrival another prominent exile came back to Petrograd. This was Trotsky, who had returned from New York after being detained on the way by the British. Trotsky was not one of the old Bolsheviks, nor was he now a Menshevik. But soon he lined up on the side of Lenin, and he took his place as the leading figure of the Petrograd Soviet. He was a great orator, a fine writer, and very much of an electric battery, full of energy, and he was of the greatest help to Lenin's party. I must give you rather a long extract from his autobiography—*My Life* the book is called—in which he describes the meetings he addressed in a building called the Modern Circus. This is not only a fine piece of writing, but it also brings a vivid and pulsating picture before our eyes of those strange revolutionary days of 1917 in Petrograd.

> "The air, intense with breathing and waiting, fairly exploded with shouts and with the passionate yells peculiar to the Modern Circus. Above and around me was press of elbows, chests, and heads. I spoke from out of a warm cavern of human bodies; whenever I stretched out my hands I would touch someone, and a grateful movement in response would give me to understand that I was not to worry about it, not to break off my speech but to keep on. No speaker, no matter how exhausted, could resist the electric tension of that impassioned human throng. They wanted to know, to understand, to find their way. At times it seemed as if I felt, with my lips, the stern inquisitiveness of this crowd that had become merged into a single whole. Then all arguments and words thought out in advance would break and recede under the imperative pressure of sympathy, and other words, other arguments utterly unexpected by the orator but needed by these people, would emerge in full array from my subconsciousness. On such occasions I felt as if I was listening to the speaker from the outside, trying to keep pace with his ideas, afraid that, like a somnambulist he might fall off the edge of the roof at the sound of my conscious reasoning.
>
> "Such was the Modern Circus. It had its own contours, fiery, tender and frenzied. The infants were peacefully sucking the breasts from which approving or threatening shouts were coming. The whole crowd was like that, like infants clinging with their dry lips to the nipples of the revolution. But this infant matured quickly."

So the ever-changing drama of revolution went on in Petrograd and in other cities and villages of Russia. The infant matured and grew big. Everywhere, as a result of the terrible strain of the war, economic collapse was becoming evident. And yet, profiteers went on making their war profits!

The Bolshevik strength and influence went on increasing in the factories and soviets. Alarmed by this, Kerensky decided to suppress them. At first there was a great campaign of slander against Lenin, who was described as a German agent sent to bring trouble to Russia. Had he not come across Germany from Switzerland with the connivance of the German authorities? Lenin became terribly unpopular with the middle classes, who considered him a traitor. Kerensky issued a warrant for Lenin's arrest, not as a revolutionary, but as a pro-German traitor. Lenin himself was keen on facing a trial to disprove this charge; his colleagues would not agree to this, and forced him to go into hiding. Trotsky was also arrested, but later released on the insistence of the Petrograd Soviet. Many other Bolsheviks were arrested; their newspapers were suppressed; workers, who were supposed to favour them, were disarmed. The attitude of these workers had been growing more and more aggressive and threatening towards the Provisional Government, and huge demonstrations had been held repeatedly against it.

There was an interlude when counter-revolution raised its head. An old general, Kornilov, advanced on the capital with an army to crush the whole revolution, including the Provisional Government. As he drew near to the city his army melted away. It had gone over to the side of the revolution.

Events were marching rapidly. The Soviet was becoming a definite rival to the government and often cancelled the government's orders or issued contrary directions. The Smolny Institute was now the seat of the Soviet and the headquarters of the Revolution in Petrograd. This place had been a private school for the girls of the nobility.

Lenin came to the outskirts of Petrograd, and the Bolsheviks decided that the time had come to seize power from the Provisional Government. Trotsky was put in charge of all the arrangements for the insurrection, and everything was carefully mapped, what vital points to seize and when. November 7th was fixed for the rising. On that day there was going to be a session of the All-Russian Congress of Soviets. Lenin fixed this date, and his reason for it is interesting. " November the 6th will be too early," he is reported to have said. " We must have an All-Russian basis for a rising, and on the 6th all the delegates to the Congress will not have arrived. On the other hand, November 8th will be too late. By that time the Congress will be organized, and it is difficult for a large body of people to take swift, decisive action. We must act on the 7th, the day the Congress meets, so that we may say to it, ' Here is the power ! What are you going to do with it ? ' " Thus spoke the clear-headed expert in revolution, knowing full well that the success of revolutions often depends on apparently trivial happenings.[1]

November 7 came, and Soviet soldiers went and occupied government buildings, especially the vital and strategic places like the telegraph office, telephone exchange, and the State Bank. There was no opposition. " The Provisional Government simply melted away," said the official report sent to England by a British agent.

[1] This story about November 7 being fixed by Lenin for the Bolshevik seizure of power has been given by Reed, the American journalist, who was present in Petrograd then. But other people who were present do not accept it. Lenin was in hiding and he was afraid that the other Bolshevik leaders might temporize and allow the right moment to pass. So he was continually urging them to action. Matters coming to a head on the 7th, this action took place then.

Lenin became the head of the new government, the President, and Trotsky, the Foreign Minister. The next day, November 8, Lenin came to the Soviet Congress at the Smolny Institute. It was evening. The Congress welcomed the leader with a mighty cheer. An American journalist, Reed, who was present on this occasion, has described what the " great Lenin " looked like when he marched to the platform.

" A short, stocky figure with a big head set down on his shoulders, bold and bulging. Little eyes, a snubbish nose, wide, generous mouth and heavy chin; clean-shaven now, but already beginning to bristle with the well-known beard of his past and future. Dressed in shabby clothes, his trousers much too long for him. Unimpressive to be the idol of the mob. A strange popular leader—a leader purely by virtue of intellect; colourless, humourless, uncompromising and detached, without picturesque idiosyncrasies —but with the power of explaining profound ideas in simple terms, of analysing a concrete situation. And combining with shrewdness the greatest intellectual audacity."

The second revolution within the year had succeeded, and it had been a remarkably peaceful one so far. The transfer of power took place with very little shedding of blood. There had been much more fighting and killing in March. The March Revolution had been a spontaneous, unorganized one, the November one had been carefully planned out. For the first time in history the representatives of the poorest classes, and especially of the industrial workers, were at the head of a country. But they were not going to have such an easy success. Tempests were gathering all round them, to burst on them with uncontrolled fury.

What was the situation that faced Lenin and his new Bolshevik Government ? The German war was still on, although the Russian army had gone to pieces and there was no chance of its fighting; there was disorder all over the country and roving bands of soldiers and brigands did much as they liked; the economic structure had broken down; food was scarce and people were hungry; all round him were representatives of the old order ready to crush the Revolution; the organization of the State was capitalist, and most of the old government servants refused to co-operate with the new government; bankers would not give money; even the telegraph office would not send telegrams. A difficult enough situation to frighten the bravest.

Lenin and his colleagues put their shoulders to the wheel. Peace with Germany was their first anxiety, and they immediately arranged for an armistice. The delegates of the two countries met at Brest Litovsk. The Germans knew well enough that there was no fight left in the Bolsheviks and, in their pride and folly, they made tremendous and humiliating demands. Much as the Bolsheviks desired peace, they were taken aback by this, and many of them were for a rejection of the terms. Lenin stood out for peace at any cost. There is a story that Trotsky, who was one of the Russian delegates at the peace conference, was asked by the Germans to go to a function in evening dress. He was perturbed; was it proper for a workers' delegate to put on this kind of *bourgeois* clothing? He telegraphed to Lenin for advice, and Lenin immediately replied : " If it will help to bring peace, go in a petticoat ! "

While the Soviet argued about the peace terms, the Germans started advancing on Petrograd, and they made their peace offer stiffer than before. Lenin's advice was accepted in the end by the Soviet, and they signed the peace of Brest-Litovsk in March 1918, much as they hated it. By this peace a huge slice of Russian territory on the west was annexed by Germany, but peace at any cost had to be accepted as, according to Lenin, " the army had voted for peace with its legs ".

The Soviet had tried at first to bring about a general peace among all the Powers involved in the World War. On the very next day after their seizure of power they had issued a decree offering peace to the world, and they made it quite clear that they renounced all claims under the Tsarist secret treaties. Constantinople, they said, must remain with the Turks, and there should be no other annexations. The Soviet's suggestion went unanswered, as both the warring parties still had hopes of success and were keen on taking the spoils of war. Partly the object of the Soviet in making the offer was no doubt propaganda. They wanted to influence the masses in each country and the war-weary soldiery, and to provoke social revolutions in other countries. For they were after world revolution; only thus, they thought, could they protect their own revolution. I have already told you that Soviet propaganda had great effect on the French and German armies.

Lenin looked upon the Brest-Litovsk peace with Germany as a temporary affair which would not last long. As it happened, it was annulled by the Soviet nine months later, as soon as Germany was defeated on the western front by the Allies. What Lenin wanted was to give a little rest, a breathing-space, to the weary workers and peasants in the army so that they might go back home and see with their own eyes what the Revolution had done. He wanted the peasants to realize that the landlords had gone and that the land belonged to them, and the industrial workers to feel that their exploiters had also gone. This would make them appreciate the gains of the Revolution and eager to defend them, and they would realize who their real enemies were. So Lenin thought, knowing full well that civil war was coming. His policy was triumphantly justified later. These peasants and workers went back from the front to their fields and factories; they were no Bolsheviks or socialists, but they became the staunchest supporters of the Revolution because they did not want to give up what they had got by it.

While they were trying to settle with the Germans somehow, the Bolshevik leaders also turned their attention to internal conditions. Large numbers of ex-army officers and adventurers with machine guns and war material were carrying on a brigand's trade, shooting and plundering in the heart of the big cities. There were also some members of the old Anarchist parties who disapproved of the Soviets and gave a lot of trouble. The Soviet authorities came down with a heavy hand on all these gangsters and others and crushed them.

A greater danger to the Soviet régime came from the members of the various civil services, many of whom refused to work under the Bolsheviks or co-operate with them in any way. Lenin laid down the principle that " he that will not work, neither shall he eat "; no work, no food. All civil servants who did not co-operate were immediately dismissed. The bankers refused to open their safes; they were opened by dynamite. But the supreme example of Lenin's contempt for the servants of the old order who refused to co-operate was seen when the Commander-in-Chief refused to obey orders. He was dismissed, and within five minutes a young Bolshevik lieutenant, Krylenko, was made the Commander-in-Chief!

In spite of these changes, much of the old structure of Russia remained. It is no easy matter to socialize a huge country suddenly, and it is possible that the process of change in Russia might have taken many long years if matters had not been forced by events. Just as the peasants had driven out the landlords, the workers in many instances, angry with their old bosses, drove them out and took possession of the factories. The Soviet could not possibly give back the factories to the old capitalistic owners, and so it took possession of them. In some cases these owners, during the civil war that followed, tried to damage the plants of the factories, and again the Soviet Government intervened and took possession of these factories to protect them. In this way the socialization of the means of production, that is, a kind of State socialism, or State ownership of the factories, etc.—went on much more rapidly than it might have done under normal conditions.

Life was not very different in Russia during the first nine months of Soviet rule. The Bolsheviks tolerated criticism and even abuse, and anti-Bolshevik papers continued to appear. The population generally was starving, but the rich still had plenty of money for ostentation and luxury. The night cabarets were crowded, and racing and other sports went on. The richer bourgeoisie was very much in evidence in the great towns, openly rejoicing at the expected downfall of the Soviet Government. These people, who were so patriotically keen on carrying on the war against Germany, now actually celebrated the advance of the Germans on Petrograd. They were quite cheerful at the prospect of German armies occupying their capital city. The dislike of social revolution was far greater for them than the fear of alien domination. This is almost always so, especially when classes are concerned.

Life was thus more or less normal, and there was certainly no Bolshevik terror at this stage. The famous Moscow ballet continued from day to day before crowded houses. The Soviet Government had moved to Moscow when Petrograd was threatened by the Germans, and Moscow has been their capital ever since. The

ambassadors of the Allies were still in Russia.   They had run away
from Petrograd when there was danger of the city falling into
German hands, and established themselves in safety in Vologda, a
small country town far from all activities.   There they sat together
in a continuous state of perturbation and excitement at the wild
rumours that reached them.   They would make anxious and
frequent inquiries from Trotsky whether the rumours were true.
Trotsky grew rather tired of this nervous agitation of these old
diplomats, and he offered to write " a bromide prescription to calm
the nerves of their Excellencies of Vologda " !   Doctors give
bromide to soothe the nerves of hysterical and excitable people.

Life seemed to go on normally on the surface, but below this
apparent calm were many currents and cross-currents.   No one,
not even they themselves, expected the Bolsheviks to survive for
long.   Every one was intriguing.   The Germans had set up a
puppet State in the Ukraine in South Russia, and in spite of the
peace, always seemed to threaten the Soviet.   The Allies, of course,
hated the Germans, but they hated the Bolsheviks even more.
President Wilson of America had indeed sent a cordial greeting to
the Soviet Congress early in 1918; he seems to have repented and
changed his mind later.   So the Allies privately subsidized and
helped counter-revolutionary activities, and even took a secret
share in them.   Moscow buzzed with foreign spies.   The chief
agent of the British secret service, known as the master spy of
Britain, was sent there to create trouble for the Soviet Government.
The dispossessed aristocrats and *bourgeoisie* were continually
fomenting counter-revolution with the help of money from the
Allies.

So matters stood about the middle of the year 1918.   The life
of the Soviet seemed to hang by a slender thread.

152

THE SOVIETS WIN THROUGH

April 11, 1933

THE month of July 1918 saw startling developments in the
situation in Russia.   The net round the Bolsheviks was gradually
closing in upon them.   The Germans threatened from the Ukraine
in the south, and a large number of old Czechoslovakian prisoners
of war in Russia were encouraged by the Allies to march on Moscow.
All over the western front in France the Great War was still going
on, but in Soviet Russia the strange spectacle was seen of both the
Allies and the German Powers working independently in a common
enterprise—the crushing of the Bolsheviks.   Again we see how
much greater is the force of class hatred than that of national
hatred, and national hatred is poisonous and bitter enough.   War
was not officially declared against Russia by these Powers; they

found many other ways of harassing the Soviet, notably by encouraging the counter-revolutionary leaders and helping them with arms and money. Several old Tsarist generals now took the field against the Soviet.

The Tsar and his family were being kept as prisoners in East Russia near the Ural mountains in the charge of the local soviet there. The advance of the Czech troops in this region frightened this local soviet, and they were alarmed at the possibility of the ex-Tsar being rescued and becoming a great centre of counter-revolution. So they took the law into their own hands and executed the whole family. It appears that the Central Committee of the Soviet was not responsible for this, and Lenin was opposed to the execution of the ex-Tsar on grounds of international policy and of his family on humanitarian grounds. The deed having been done, however, the Central Government justified it. Probably this upset the Allied Governments all the more and made them still more aggressive.

August saw a worsening of the situation, and two events brought anger, despair, and terror in their train. One of these was an attempt on Lenin's life, and the other was the landing of an Allied force at Archangel in North Russia. There was wild excitement in Moscow, and the end of the Soviet's existence seemed to be very near. Moscow itself was practically surrounded by enemies—Germans, Czechs, and the counter-revolutionary forces. Only a few districts round Moscow were under Soviet rule, and the landing of an Allied army seemed to make the end certain. The Bolsheviks did not have much of an army; it was barely five months since the Brest-Litovsk peace, and most of the old army had melted away to the fields. Moscow itself was full of conspiracies, and the *bourgeoisie* was openly rejoicing at the approaching fall of the Soviets.

Such was the terrible plight of the nine-month-old Soviet Republic. Despair seized the Bolsheviks and fear, and as they were going to die anyhow, they decided to die fighting. As the young French Republic had done a century and a quarter earlier, like a wild animal at bay, they turned on their enemies. There was to be no more tolerance, no mercy. The whole country was put under martial law, and early in September the Central Soviet Committee announced the Red Terror. " Death to all traitors, merciless war on the foreign invaders." They would fight with their backs to the wall both the enemy within and the enemy without. It was the Soviet against the world and against its own reactionaries. A period of what is called " militant communism " also began, and the whole country was turned into a kind of besieged camp. Every effort was made to build up the Red Army, and Trotsky was put in charge of this.

This was about the time, September and October 1918, when the German war-machine in the west was cracking up and there was talk of an armistice. President Wilson had laid down his Fourteen Points, which were supposed to embody the aims of the Allies. One of these points, it is interesting to remember, was that all

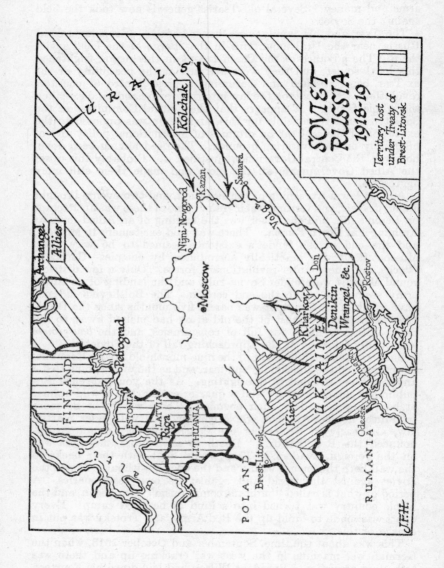

Russian territory was to be evacuated and Russia was to be given full opportunity for self-development with the aid of the Powers. A singular commentary on this was being provided by the Allied intervention in Russia and their landing of forces there. The Bolshevik Government sent a note to President Wilson pungently criticizing his Fourteen Points. In the course of this note they said : " You demand the independence of Poland, Serbia, Belgium, and freedom for the people of Austro-Hungary. . . . But, strangely, we do not notice in your demands any mention of freedom for Ireland, Egypt, India, or even the Philippine Islands."

Peace was made between the Allies and the German Powers on November 11, 1918, when the armistice was signed. But in Russia civil war raged throughout 1919 and 1920. Single-handed, the Soviets fought a host of enemies. At one time the Red Army was attacked on seventeen different fronts. England, America, France, Japan, Italy, Serbia, Czechoslovakia, Rumania, the Baltic States, Poland, and a host of counter-revolutionary Russian generals were all opposing the Soviet, and the fighting extended from eastern Siberia to the Baltic and the Crimea. Repeatedly, the end of the Soviet seemed near, Moscow itself was threatened, Petrograd was on the point of falling to the enemy, but it surmounted every crisis, and with each success grew its self-confidence and strength.

One of the counter-revolutionary leaders was Admiral Kolchak. He described himself as the ruler of Russia, and the Allies actually recognized him as such and helped him greatly. The way he behaved in Siberia is shown by an ally of his, General Graves, who commanded the United States army supporting Kolchak. This American general says :

> "There were horrible murders committed, but they were not committed by the Bolsheviks, as the world believes. I am well on the side of safety when I say that the anti-Bolsheviks killed one hundred people in Eastern Siberia to every one killed by the Bolsheviks."

It will interest you to know on what knowledge eminent statesmen conduct the affairs of great nations and make war and peace. Lloyd George, who was the British Prime Minister at the time, and perhaps the most powerful man in Europe, speaking about Russia in the British House of Commons, referred to Kolchak and other generals there. In the same breath he referred to " General Kharkov ". Kharkov, instead of being a general, happens to be an important city, the capital of Ukraine ! This ignorance of elementary geography, however, did not prevent these statesmen from cutting up Europe into bits and making a new map of it.

The Allies also blockaded Russia, and so effective was this that for the whole of 1919 Russia could neither buy nor sell anything abroad.

In spite of all these stupendous difficulties and numerous and powerful enemies, Soviet Russia survived and triumphed. This was one of the most astonishing feats in history. How did they manage it ? There is no doubt that if the Allied Powers had been united and bent on crushing the Bolsheviks, they could have done so in the early days. Having disposed of Germany, they had vast armies to play with. But it was not so easy to use these armies anywhere, and especially against the Soviets. They were all war-weary, and another demand on them for foreign warfare would have met with refusal. There was also a great deal of sympathy among the workers for the new Russia, and the Allied governments were afraid of having to face trouble at home if they declared open war against the Soviets. As it was, Europe seemed to be on the verge of revolt. And thirdly, there was the mutual rivalry of the Allied Powers. With the coming of peace they started bickering and quarrelling among themselves. All this prevented a determined attempt on their part to put an end to the Bolsheviks. They tried to bring this about indirectly as far as possible by getting others to fight for them and supplying them with money, arms, and expert advice. They felt sure that the Soviets could not last.

All this, no doubt, helped the Soviets and gave them time to strengthen themselves. But it would be unfair to them to imagine that their victory was due to outside circumstances. Essentially, it was a victory of the self-confidence, the faith, the self-sacrifice, and the unflinching determination of the Russian people. And the wonder of it is that these people were everywhere supposed, and rightly supposed, to be lazy and ignorant, demoralized and incapable of any great effort. Freedom is a habit, and if we are deprived of it for long, we are apt to forget it. These ignorant Russian peasants and workers had had little enough occasion to practise this habit. Yet the quality of the leadership of Russia was such in those days that it converted this poor human material into a strong, organized nation, full of faith in its mission and confidence in itself. The Kolchaks and others of that kind were defeated not only because of the ability and determination of the Bolshevik leaders, but also because the Russian peasant refused to put up with them. For him they were the representatives of the old order come to take away his newly won land and other privileges, and he decided to defend these to the death.

Towering above all others, and exercising an unchallenged supremacy, was Lenin. To the Russian people he became like a demi-god, the symbol of hope and faith, the wise one who knew a way out of every difficulty and whom nothing ruffled or perturbed. Next to him in those days (for he is discredited in Russia now) came Trotsky, a writer and an orator, without any previous military experience, who now set about building up a great army in the midst of civil war and blockade. Trotsky was recklessly brave, and frequently risked his life in fighting. There was no pity in him if others showed lack of courage or want of discipline. At a critical moment in the civil war he issued this order :

" I give warning that if any unit retreats without orders, the first to be shot down will be the commissary of the unit, and next the commander. Brave and gallant soldiers will be appointed in their places. Cowards, dastards and traitors will not escape the bullet. This I solemnly promise in the presence of the entire Red Army."

And he kept his word.

Another army order issued by Trotsky in October 1919 is interesting as it shows how the Bolsheviks always tried to distinguish between the people and the capitalist governments, and never took up a purely national attitude.

> " But even to-day," the order runs, " when we are engaged in a bitter fight with Yudenich, the hireling of England, I demand that you never forget that there are two Englands. Besides the England of profits, of violence, bribery and blood-thirstiness, there is the England of labour, of spiritual power, of high ideals of international solidarity. It is the base and dishonest England of the Stock Exchange manipulators that is fighting us. The England of labour and the people is with us."

Something of the doggedness with which the Red Army was made to fight can be seen in the decision to defend Petrograd when it was on the point of falling to Yudenich. The decree of the Council of Defence was : " To defend Petrograd to the last ounce of blood, to refuse to yield a foot, and to carry the struggle into the streets of the city ".

Maxim Gorki, the great Russian writer, tells us that Lenin once said of Trotsky :

> " Well, show me another man who would be able, within a year, to organize an almost exemplary army and moreover to win the respect of the military specialists. We have such a man. We have everything. And miracles are still going to happen."

This Red Army grew by leaps and bounds. In December 1917, soon after the Bolsheviks had seized power, the strength of the army was 435,000. After Brest-Litovsk much of this must have melted away and had to be built up afresh. By the middle of 1919 the strength was 1,500,000. A year later it had risen to the prodigious total of 5,300,000.

By the end of 1919 the Soviets had definitely got the better of their opponents in the civil war. For another year, however, the war continued, and there were many anxious moments. In 1920 the new State of Poland (freshly formed after the German defeat) fell out with Russia, and there was war between them. All these wars were practically over by the end of 1920, and Russia at last had some peace.

Meanwhile internal difficulties had grown. War and blockade and disease and famine had reduced the country to a miserable condition. Production had gone down greatly, for farmers cannot till the fields or workers run the factories when rival armies are constantly marching over them. War-communism had pulled the country through somehow, but everybody had to go on tightening his belt, till this process became very difficult to bear. The farmers were not interested in producing much, because they said that the

State would take away, under the militant communism then prevailing, all the extra stuff that they produced, so why should they
take the trouble? A very difficult and dangerous situation was
arising. There was even a revolt of the sailors at Kronstadt near
Petrograd, and strikes in Petrograd (or Leningrad) itself.

Lenin, with his genius for adapting fundamentals to existing
conditions, immediately took action. He put an end to war-
communism, and introduced a new policy called the New Economic
Policy, or NEP for short (from the first letters). This gave greater
freedom to the peasant to produce and sell his stuff, and it also
permitted some private trading. It was a break-away to some
extent from strict communistic principles, but Lenin justified it as
a temporary measure. It certainly brought great relief to the
people. But soon Russia had to face another terrible calamity.
This was a famine due to a great drought and consequent failure of
the crops over vast areas of south-east Russia. It was a dreadful
famine, one of the greatest that has been known, and millions of
people perished in it. Coming as it did after many years of war and
civil war and blockade and economic breakdown, and before the
Soviet Government had time to settle down to peace activities, it
might well have broken down the whole structure of government.
However, the Soviet survived it, as it had done its previous calamities.
There was a conference of representatives of European governments to consider what help they should give for famine relief.
They declared that they would give no help till the Soviet Government promised to pay the old Tsarist debts, which it had repudiated.
The money-lender was stronger than the humanitarian, and even a
heartrending appeal from Russian mothers for their dying children
went unheeded. But the United States of America made no
conditions and gave much help.

When England and other European countries refused to help in
the Russian famine, they were not otherwise boycotting the Soviet.
Early in 1921 an Anglo-Russian trade treaty had been signed, and
many other countries had followed this example and signed trade
treaties with the Soviet.

With eastern countries like China, Turkey, Persia, and Afghanistan, the Soviet adopted a very generous policy. They gave up old
Tsarist privileges and tried to be very friendly. This was in
accordance with their principles of freedom for all subject and
exploited peoples, but a more important motive for them was to
strengthen their own position. The imperialist Powers, like
England, were often put in a false position by this generosity of
Soviet Russia, and the eastern countries made comparisons which
were not to the advantage of England and the other Powers.

One other important event took place in 1919 about which I must
tell you. This was the founding of the Third International in
Moscow by the Communist Party. I have told you in previous
letters of the First International, which Karl Marx had founded,
and the Second International, which after many brave words came
to grief on the outbreak of the war of 1914. The Bolsheviks con-

sidered that the working class had been betrayed by the old workers' and socialist parties which formed this Second International. The Third International was therefore created by them, with a definitely revolutionary outlook, to wage war against capitalism and imperialism, and also against those opportunist socialists who followed a "middle-of-the-road" policy. This International is often called the Comintern (from Communist International), and it has played a great part in propaganda in many countries. As its name implies, it is an international organization elected by various communist parties in many different countries, but Russia, being the one country where communism has triumphed, naturally dominates the Comintern. The Comintern is of course different from the Soviet Government, though many persons occupy leading positions in both. As the Comintern is avowedly an organization for spreading revolutionary communism, it is bitterly disliked by the imperialist Powers, and they are always trying to suppress its activities in their territories.

The Second International (the "Labour and Socialist International") was also revived in western Europe after the war. To a great extent the Second and the Third Internationals have the same objective, in theory at any rate, but their ideology and methods are very different, and there is no love lost between them. They quarrel and fight and attack each other even more than they attack the common enemy, capitalism. The Second International is now a very respectable organization and has often provided cabinet ministers to European governments. The Third continues to be revolutionary, and is therefore far from respectable.

Right through the civil war in Russia the Red Terror and the White Terror competed with each other in their harsh cruelty, and probably the latter surpassed the former greatly. So one would conclude from the American general's account (which I have quoted above) about Kolchak's atrocities in Siberia, as well as other accounts. But there can be no doubt that the Red Terror was severe, and many innocent people must have suffered. The nerves of the Bolsheviks, attacked as they were on all sides, and surrounded by conspiracies and spies, gave way, and at the slightest suspicion they punished heavily. Their political police, called the *Cheka,* especially, got a bad name for this terror. It was the equivalent of the C.I.D. in India, but with greater powers.

This letter is getting long. But before I end it, I must tell you something more about Lenin. In spite of the injuries he had received when an attempt to take his life had been made in August 1918, he had not taken much rest. He went on working at tremendous pressure, and in May 1922 came the inevitable collapse. After a little rest he was again at work, but not for long. There was a worse collapse in 1923, from which he never recovered, and on January 21, 1924, he died near Moscow.

For many days his body lay in Moscow—it was winter, and the body was preserved by chemical treatment—and from all over Russia and the distant Siberian steppes came representatives of the common folk, peasants and workers, men and women and children, to pay their last homage to that beloved comrade of theirs who had pulled them out of the depths and pointed the way to a fuller life. They built him a simple and unadorned mausoleum in the beautiful Red Square of Moscow, and there his body still lies in a glass case, and every evening an unending procession passes silently by. It is not many years since he died, and already Lenin has become a mighty tradition, not only in his native Russia, but in the world at large. As time passes he grows greater; he has become one of the chosen company of the world's immortals. Petrograd has become Leningrad, and almost every house in Russia has a Lenin corner or a Lenin picture. But he lives, not in monuments or pictures, but in the mighty work he did, and in the hearts of hundreds of millions of workers to-day who find inspiration in his example, and the hope of a better day.

Do not imagine that Lenin was an inhuman kind of machine, wrapped up in his work and thinking of nothing else. Absolutely devoted to his work and life mission he certainly was, and at the same time wholly without self-consciousness; he was the very embodiment of an idea. And yet he was very human, with that most human of all traits, the capacity to laugh heartily. The British Agent in Moscow, Lockhart, who was there during the early, perilous days of the Soviet, says that, whatever happened, Lenin was always in good humour. " Of all the public figures I have ever met he possessed the most equable temperament," says this British diplomat. Simple and straight in his talk and his work, and a hater of big words and poses. He loved music, so much so that he was almost afraid that it might affect him too much and make him soft in his work.

A colleague of Lenin's, Lunacharsky, who was for many years the Bolshevik Commissar for Education, made a curious reference to him once. He compared Lenin's persecution of the capitalists with Christ's expulsion of the money-lenders from the temple, and added: " If Christ were alive to-day, he would be a Bolshevik." A curious comparison for irreligious people.

About women, Lenin once said : " No nation can be free when half the population is enslaved in the kitchen." Very revealing was the remark he made one day, as he was petting some children. His old friend Maxim Gorky tells us that he said, " These will have happier lives than we had. They will not experience much that we lived through. There will not be so much cruelty in their lives." Let us all hope so.

I shall finish up this letter with the words of a recent Russian composition for a full orchestra and people's chorus. It is said by people who have heard it that the music of this piece is full of vitality and power, and the song seems to represent the spirit of the revolting masses. Even the English translation of the words, which I give here, has something of this spirit in it. The song is called *October*, and this means the Bolshevik Revolution of November 1917. The Russian calendar in those days was what is called the unreformed calendar, and it was thirteen days behind the ordinary western calendar. According to this calendar the revolution of March 1917 took place in February, and it is therefore called the " February Revolution ", and similarly the Bolshevik Revolution, which took place early in November 1917 is called the " October Revolution ". Russia has changed its calendar now and adopted the reformed one, but these old names are still used.

> We went, asking for work and for bread,
> Our hearts were oppressed with anguish,
> The chimneys of the factories pointed toward the sky, like tired hands without strength to make a fist.
> Louder than the cannon, the silence was broken by the words of our grief and our pain.
> O Lenin ! the desire of calloused hands.
> We have understood, Lenin, we have understood that our lot is a struggle ! Struggle ! Struggle !
> You led us to the last fight. Struggle !
> You gave us the victory of labour.
> And no one shall take away from us this victory over ignorance and oppression.
> No one ! No one ! Never ! Never !
> Let every one be young and brave in the struggle, because the name of our victory is October !
> October ! October !
> October is a messenger from the sun.
> October is the will of the revolting centuries !
> October ! It is a labour, it is a joy and a song.
> October ! It is good fortune for the fields and machines !
> Here is the banner name of the young generation and Lenin.

153

JAPAN BULLIES CHINA

April 14, 1933

WHILE the World War was going on, certain events took place in the Far East which deserve our attention. I shall therefore take you to China now. In my last letter about China I told you about the establishment of a republic there, and of the troubles that followed. Attempts were made to re-establish the empire. These failed ; but the republic did not succeed in establishing its authority over the whole country, or rather, no single government succeeded in doing so. Ever since then there has been no authority which ruled without challenge over the whole of China. For some years there were two principal governments in the country, the Northern and the Southern. In the south Dr. Sun Yat-Sen and his national party, the Kuo-Min-Tang, were supreme. In the north there was Yuan Shih-Kai in command, and after him came a succession of generals and military men. *Tuchuns* these military adventurers were and are called ; they have been the curse of China during recent years.

China was thus in the unhappy condition of continuous disorder, and often of civil war between north and south or between rival *tuchuns*. It was an ideal opportunity for the imperialist Powers to intrigue and try to profit by these internal dissensions by encouraging one party or *tuchun* and then another. That was the way, you will remember, that the English established themselves in India. The European Powers took advantage of the opportunity, and started intriguing and playing off one *tuchun* against another. But soon their own troubles and the World War put an end to their activities in the Far East.

It was not so in the case of Japan. All the main fighting of the war was far away, and Japan felt perfectly safe in carrying on her old activities in China. Indeed, she was then in a far better position to do so because the other Powers were engaged elsewhere and were not likely to interfere. She declared war against Germany simply to get hold of the German concession of Kiauchau in China and then to push on farther inland.

Japanese policy in regard to China has shown a remarkable consistency for the last two score years. As soon as they had modernized their army and pushed on the industrialization of their country, they decided that they must become dominant in China. They wanted room to spread out and expand their industries, and Korea and China were both near and weak, and seemed to invite domination and exploitation. The first attempt they made was the war with China of 1894–95. They succeeded, but did not get as much as they wanted because of the opposition of certain European Powers. Then came the more difficult struggle with Russia in 1904. They won in this too, and established themselves firmly in Korea and Manchuria. Korea was soon afterwards annexed, and became a part of the Japanese Empire.

Manchuria, however, remained part of China. It forms, and is referred to, as the three eastern provinces of China. The Japanese simply took over the Russian concessions there, including the railway they had built, called till then the Chinese Eastern Railway. The name of this railway was changed to South Manchurian Railway. Japan now started getting a good grip of Manchuria. Meanwhile the railway attracted immigrants from the rest of over-populated China, and Chinese peasants poured in. A kind of bean, called the soya bean, flourished in Manchuria, and a world demand developed for this because of its valuable properties. Among other products, a kind of oil is made from this bean. This soya-bean cultivation also drew immigrants. So, while the Japanese tried to get full control of the economic machinery of Manchuria from the top, Chinese from the south poured in and peopled the land. The old Manchu people were drowned in this sea of Chinese peasants and others, and became fully Chinese in culture and outlook themselves.

Japan did not fancy the coming of the Republic in China. She disapproved of anything that might strengthen China, and her whole diplomacy was aimed at preventing the consolidation of China into one strong State. So she took a very active interest in helping one *tuchun* against another, so that the internal disorder might continue.

The young Republic of China had the most tremendous problems to face. It was not merely a question of seizing political power from the dying imperial government. There was little of political power to seize, for such central power hardly existed. It had to be created. The old China was an empire in name; in effect it was a collection of a large number of autonomous areas loosely strung together. The provinces were more or less autonomous, and so were even the towns and villages. The authority of the Central Government or Emperor was recognized, but this government did not interfere in local matters. There was no " unitary " State, as it is called, with power and the actual government concentrated in the centre, and uniformity in the various aspects of government. It was this loosely attached (in a political sense) State that had broken up because of the impacts of western industry and imperialist greed. If China were to survive, it was now felt that China must become a strong centralized State with a uniform system of government. The new Republic wanted to create such a State. It was something new, and hence it became one of the great difficulties facing the Republic. Her want of proper communications, roads and railways, has itself been a tremendous barrier in the way of political unity.

In the past the Chinese people had attached little importance to political power as such. Their whole mighty civilization was based on culture, and it taught, in a way which has not been equalled elsewhere, the art of living. They were so full of this old culture of theirs that even when their political and economic structure fell down they clung to the old cultural ways. Japan had deliberately adopted western industry and western ways, and yet at heart remained feudal. China was not feudal; she was full of rationalism and the spirit of science, and she looked with eagerness towards western developments in science and industry. And yet she did not rush in where Japan had rushed in. There were, no doubt, many difficulties in her way which Japan did not have. But still there was also a hesitation to do anything which might mean a complete break with the old culture. China has the philosopher's temperament, and philosophers do not act hastily. In her mind there was, and is, a great ferment; for the problems she had to face were not merely political, they were economic and social and intellectual and educational and so on.

And then again, the very size of huge countries like China and India creates difficulties. They are continental countries, and have something of the heaviness of a continent about them. When an elephant falls, he takes his time to get up; he cannot jump up like a cat or a dog.

When the World War began, Japan immediately joined the Allies and declared war on Germany. She took possession of Kiauchau and then began spreading out inland over the Shantung province, in which Kiauchau is situated. This meant that the Japanese were invading China proper. There was no question of operations against Germany, as Germany had nothing to do with this area. The Chinese Government politely asked them to go back. What arrogance ! said the Japanese, and forthwith they produced an official note containing twenty-one demands.

These " Twenty-one Demands " became famous. I shall not give them here. They meant the transfer of all manner of rights and privileges to Japan, especially in Manchuria, Mongolia, and in the province of Shantung. The result of agreeing to these demands would have been to convert China practically into a colony of Japan. The feeble Northern Chinese Government objected to these demands, but what could they do against the powerful Japanese army? And, then, this Chinese Government in the north was itself not a popular one with its own people. However, it did one thing which helped. The Japanese demands were published. There was a tremendous outcry immediately in China, and even the other Powers, busy as they were with the war, were much put out. America especially objected. The result was that Japan withdrew some of her demands and modified others, and, as to the rest, she succeeded in bullying the Chinese Government into accepting them in May 1915. This resulted in intense anti-Japanese feeling in China.

In August 1917, three years after the war had begun, China joined the Allies and declared war on Germany. This was rather ridiculous, as China could do nothing at all to Germany. The whole object was to put herself right with the Allies and to save herself from the further embraces of Japan.

The Bolshevik Revolution of November 1917 came soon after this and was followed by a great deal of disorder all over northern Asia. Siberia was one battleground for Soviet and anti-Soviet forces. Kolchak, the Russian white general, operated from Siberia against the Soviets. The Japanese, alarmed by the Soviet triumph, sent a large army to Siberia. British and American troops were also sent there. For a while Russian influence disappeared from Siberia and Central Asia. The British Government tried their best to put an end completely to Russian prestige in these areas. In the heart of Central Asia, in Kashgar, the British set up a wireless station for anti-Bolshevik propaganda.

In Mongolia also there was a fierce fight between Soviet and anti-Soviet people. As early as 1915, while the Great War was going on, Mongolia had succeeded, with help from Tsarist Russia, in gaining a great deal of autonomy from the Chinese Government. China remained suzerain, however, and Russia was also given a footing there in regard to Mongolia's foreign relations. It was a curious arrangement. After the Soviet Revolution there was civil war in Mongolia, in which the local soviets won after three years or more of struggle.

I have not told you yet about the peace conference that followed the World War. I shall have to deal with that in another letter.

I might mention here, however, that the big Powers at this conference —and this meant especially England, France, and the U.S.A.— decided to present the Shantung province of China to Japan. Thus, as a result of the war, China, their ally, was actually made to give up a part of her territory. The reason for this was some secret treaty made during the war between England, France, and Japan. Whatever the reason may have been, this shabby trick on China was deeply resented by the Chinese people, and they threatened the Peking Government with revolution if it compromised on the matter. A strict boycott of Japanese goods was also proclaimed and anti-Japanese riots took place. The Chinese Government (by which I mean the Northern, Peking Government, which was the principal Government) refused to sign the Peace Treaty.

Two years later a conference was held in Washington, United States, at which this question of Shantung cropped up. The conference was of all the Powers interested in Far Eastern questions, and they had met to discuss the strength of their navies. Several important results followed, so far as China and Japan were concerned, from this Washington Conference of 1922. Japan agreed to hand back Shantung, and so one question which had been agitating the Chinese people tremendously was disposed of. Two important agreements were also reached between the Powers.

One of these was known as the " Four-Power Pact ", between America, Great Britain, Japan, and France. These four Powers pledged themselves mutually to respect the territorial integrity of their various possessions in the Pacific—that is to say, they promised not to encroach on each other's territories. The other agreement, known as the " Nine-Power Treaty ", was between all the nine Powers attending—U.S.A., Belgium, Britain, France, Italy, Japan, Holland, Portugal, and China. The very first article of this treaty began thus :

" To respect the sovereignty, the independence and the territorial and administrative integrity of China. . . ."

Both these agreements were obviously meant to protect China from further aggression. They were meant to stop the old game of concession-hunting and annexations which the Powers had so far played. The western Powers had their hands full with the after-war problems and, for the moment, were not interested in China. Hence this self-denying ordinance to which they solemnly pledged themselves. Japan also pledged herself to this, although it conflicted with the deliberate policy which she had followed for many years. Before many years were over it was quite clear that Japan's old policy continued in spite of all agreements and pledges to the contrary, and a Japanese invasion of China took place. It has been an extraordinarily barefaced example of international lying and hypocrisy. To understand the background of what happened later, I had to take you to the Washington Conference.

About the time of the Washington Conference also, the final withdrawal of foreign troops from Siberia took place. The Japanese were the last to go. Immediately the local soviets came to the front and joined the Soviet Republic of Russia.

The Russian Soviet had early in its career addressed the Chinese Government and offered to give up all the special privileges which Tsarist Russia had enjoyed in China, in common with other imperialist Powers. Imperialism and communism could hardly go together, and, even apart from this, the Soviet deliberately adopted a generous policy towards eastern countries which had long been exploited or threatened by the western Powers. This was not only good morals but sound policy for Soviet Russia, as it created friends in the East. The Soviet's offer to give up special privileges was not a conditional one; it sought nothing in return. In spite of this, the Chinese Government was afraid of dealing with the Soviets, lest they might anger the western European Powers. At length, however, Russian and Chinese representatives met, and in 1924 agreed to certain terms. Learning of this agreement, the French, American, and Japanese Governments protested to the Peking Government, and Peking was so frightened at this that it actually disavowed the signature of its representative on the agreement. To such a pass was the unhappy Peking Government reduced ! Thereupon the Russian representative published the whole text of the agreement. It created quite a sensation. For the first time in her contacts with the Powers, China had been treated honourably and decently and had her rights recognized. It was her first equal treaty with a great Power. The Chinese people were delighted with it, and the government had to sign it. It was quite natural for the imperialist Powers to dislike it, for it put them in a very unfavourable light. While Soviet Russia gave generously, they stuck to all their special privileges.

The Soviet Government also got into touch with Dr. Sun-Yat-Sen's Southern Chinese Government, which had its headquarters at Canton, and they came to a mutual understanding. During most of this time a feeble kind of civil war was going on between the North and the South, and between various military commanders in the north. These northern *tuchuns*, or super-*tuchuns* as some of them were called, fought for no principles or programme; they fought for personal power. They allied themselves to each other and then crossed over to the other side, and formed a new combination. These ever-changing combinations were very confusing to the outsider. These *tuchuns*, or military adventurers, raised private armies, imposed private taxes, and carried on their private wars, and the burden of all this fell on the long-suffering Chinese people. Behind some of these super-*tuchuns*, it was said, were foreign Powers, and especially Japan. Help and money came to them also from the big foreign business houses in Shanghai.

The one bright spot was the south, where Dr. Sun-Yat-Sen's government functioned. This had ideals and a policy, and was not merely a brigand's affair, as some of the northern *tuchuns'* govern-ments were. In 1924 the first National Congress of the Kuo-Min-Tang, the People's Party, was held, and Dr. Sun placed a manifesto before it. In this manifesto he laid down the principles which should guide the nation. This manifesto and these principles have since been the basis of the Kuo-Min-Tang, and even now they are supposed to guide the general policy of the so-called National Government. In March 1925 Dr. Sun died, after a life worn out in China's service, and beloved by the Chinese people.

154

INDIA DURING WAR-TIME

April 16, 1933

INDIA, as a part of the British Empire, was of course directly involved in the World War. But there was no actual fighting in or near India. Nonetheless the war influenced developments in India in a variety of ways, both directly and indirectly, and thus brought about considerable changes. Her resources were used up to the fullest extent to help the Allies.

It was not India's war. India had no grievance against the German Powers, and, as for Turkey, there was great sympathy for her. But India had no choice in the matter. She was but a dependency of Britain, forced to toe the line of her imperialist mistress. And so, in spite of much resentment in the country, Indian soldiers fought against Turks and Egyptians and others, and made India's name bitterly disliked in western Asia.

As I have told you in a previous letter, politics were at a low ebb in India on the eve of the war. The coming of the war still further diverted attention from them, and numerous war measures, taken by the British Government, made real political activity difficult. A war period is always considered by governments a sufficient excuse for suppressing everybody else and doing just what they like themselves. The only licence permitted is licence for themselves. A censorship is established which suppresses truth, often spreads falsehoods, and prevents criticism. Special acts and regulations are passed to control almost every form of national activity. This was done in all the warring countries, and, naturally, it was done in India also, where a " Defence of India Act " was passed. Public criticism of the war or anything connected with it was thus effectively checked. Yet in the background there was universal sympathy with Turkey, and a desire that Britain should get a hard knock from Germany. This impotent wish was natural enough among those who had themselves been knocked about sufficiently. But there was no public expression of it.

In public, loud shouts of loyalty to Britain filled the air. Most of this shouting was done by the ruling princes, and some of it by the upper middle classes who came into contact with the government. To a slight extent the *bourgeoisie* was also taken in by the brave declarations of the Allies about democracy and liberty and the freedom of nationalities. Perhaps, it was thought, this might apply to India also, and it was hoped that help rendered then to Britain, in her hour of need, might meet with a suitable reward later. In any event, there was no choice in the matter, and there was no other safe way ; so they made the best of a bad job.

This outward display of loyalty in India was much appreciated in England in those days, and there was many an expression of gratitude. It was stated by those in authority that, after this, England would look at India with a " new angle of vision ".

But there were some Indians, both in India and in foreign countries, who did not adopt this " loyal " attitude. They did not even remain quiet and passive as the great majority did. They believed, according to the old Irish maxim, that England's difficulty was their country's opportunity. In particular, some Indians in Germany and in other countries of Europe gathered together in Berlin to devise means to help England's enemies, and formed a committee for this purpose. The German Government was naturally eager to accept help of every kind, and they welcomed these Indian revolutionaries. A regular written agreement was arrived at and signed by the two parties—the German Government and the Indian Committee—in which, among other things, the Indians promised to help the German Government during the war on the understanding that, in the event of victory, Germany would insist on Indian freedom. This Indian Committee thereupon worked on behalf of Germany throughout the war. They carried on propaganda among the Indian troops that were sent abroad, and their activities spread right up to Afghanistan and the north-west frontier of India. But, apart from causing a great deal of anxiety to the British, they did not succeed in doing much. An attempt to send arms to India by sea was frustrated by the British. The German defeat in the war put an end automatically to this committee and its hopes.

In India also there were some instances of revolutionary activity, and special tribunals were appointed to try conspiracy cases, and many were sentenced to death and many to long terms of imprisonment. Some of the persons sentenced then are still in prison—after eighteen years !

As the war proceeded, a handful of people made huge profits, as elsewhere, but the great majority felt the strain more and more and discontent grew. The demand for more men for the front went on growing, and recruiting for the army became very intense. All manner of inducements and rewards were offered to those who brought in recruits, and *zamindars* were made to supply fixed quotas of recruits from among their tenants. In the Punjab, especially, these " press-gang " methods—that is, forced recruiting—were employed to get men for the army and the labour corps. The total number of men that went from India to the various fronts, both as soldiers and in the labour corps, amounted to over a million. These methods were greatly resented by the people concerned and are supposed to have been one of the causes of the after-war troubles in the Punjab.

The Punjab was also affected in another way. Many Punjabis, and especially Sikhs, had emigrated to California in the United States and to British Columbia in western Canada. A stream of emigrants continued to go till it was stopped by the American and Canadian authorities. In order to put difficulties in the way of such immigrants, the Canadian Government made a rule that only such immigrants would be admitted as came direct from port to port without having changed ships on the way. This was meant to prevent Indian immigrants, as they had invariably to change ships in China or Japan. Thereupon a Sikh, Baba Gurdit Singh, engaged a whole ship, named the *Komagata Maru*, and carried a crowd of immigrants with him from Calcutta all the way to Vancouver in Canada. He had thus cleverly evaded the Canadian law, but none the less Canada was not going to have him, and none of the immigrants were allowed to land. They were sent back in the same ship, and they reached India destitute and very angry. There was quite a little battle with the police at Budge Budge, Calcutta, resulting in many deaths, chiefly amongst the Sikhs. Many of these Sikhs were subsequently shadowed and hunted all over the Punjab. These people also spread anger and discontent in the Punjab, and the whole *Komagata Maru* incident was resented all over India.

It is difficult to know all that happened in those war days, because the censorship would not allow many kinds of news to appear, and consequently wild rumours used to spread. It is known, however, that a big mutiny in an Indian regiment took place in Singapore, and there was trouble on a smaller scale in many other places.

Apart from supplying men for the war and helping in other ways, India was also made to provide hard cash. This was called a " gift " from India. A hundred million pounds was paid in this way on one occasion and, later, another big sum. To call this enforced contribution from a poor country a " gift " does credit to the sense of humour of the British Government.

All this that I have told you so far consisted of the less important consequences of the war, so far as India was concerned. But a far more fundamental change was being brought about by the war-time conditions. During the war, India's foreign trade, like the foreign trade of other countries, was wholly upset. The vast quantity of British goods that used to come to India was now very largely cut off. The German submarines were sinking ships in the Mediterranean and the Atlantic, and trade could not be carried on under these conditions. India had thus to provide for herself and supply her own needs. She had also to supply the government with all manner of things needed for the war. So that Indian industries grew rapidly, both the old industries, like the textile and jute, and new war-time industries. Tata's iron and steel works, which had so far been cold-shouldered by the government, now assumed tremendous importance, as they could produce war material. They were more or less run under government control.

For the war years, therefore, capitalists in India, both British and Indian, had an open field and little competition from abroad. They made full use of this opportunity and profited by it at the cost of the poor Indian masses. Prices of goods were put up and incredible dividends were declared. But the workers, whose labour produced these dividends and profit, saw little change in their miserable conditions. Their wages went up a little, but the prices of the necessaries of life went up far more, and so their position actually became worse.

But the capitalists prospered greatly and accumulated huge profits, which they wanted to invest again in industry. For the first time Indian capitalists were strong enough to exert pressure on the government. Even apart from this pressure, the force of events had forced the British Government to help Indian industry during war time. The demand for further industrialization of the country led to the importation of more machinery from abroad, as such machinery could not then be made in India. So that in place of manufactured goods coming from England to India, we find now more machinery coming.

All this involved a great change in British policy in India; a century-old policy was given up and a new one adopted in its place. British imperialism, adapting itself to changing conditions, changed its face completely. You will remember my telling you of the early stages of British rule in India. The first was the eighteenth-century stage of plunder and carrying away of hard cash. Then came the second stage when British rule was firmly established, and which lasted for over 100 years—right up to the war. This was to keep India as a field of raw material and a market for Britain's manufactured goods. Big industry was discouraged here in every way, and India's economic development prevented. Now, during war-time, comes the third stage, when big industry in India is encouraged by the British Government, and this is done in spite of the fact that it conflicts to some extent with Britain's manufacturers. Thus it is obvious that if the Indian textile industry is encouraged, Lancashire suffers to that extent, because India has been Lancashire's best customer. Why then should the British Government make this change in its policy to the detriment of Lancashire and other British industries ? I have already shown how its hands were forced by war conditions. Let us consider these reasons for the change in detail :

1. War-time demands automatically force the issue and push on industrialization in India.

2. This increases the Indian capitalist class and strengthens it, so that they demand more and more facilities for the growth of industry, to afford them an opportunity to invest their surplus funds. Britain is no longer in a position to ignore them completely, as this might alienate them and lead them to support the more extreme and revolutionary elements in the country, which are growing stronger. Therefore, it is desirable to keep them, if possible, on the British side by giving them some opportunities for growth.

3. The surplus money of the capitalist class in England also seeks opportunities for the investment in undeveloped countries, as profits are greater there. England itself being highly industrialized there are no such favourable opportunities of investment there. Profits are not so great and, owing to the strength of the organized labour movement, labour troubles are frequent. In undeveloped areas labour is weak, and hence wages are low and profits high. British capitalists naturally prefer investing in undeveloped areas under British control, such as India. Thus British capital comes to India, and this leads to still further industrialization.

4. The experience of the war showed that only highly industrialized countries can carry on a war effectively. Tsarist Russia broke down ultimately in the war because it was not sufficiently industrialized and had to rely on other countries. England fears that the next war may be a war with Soviet Russia at the Indian frontier. If India has not got her own big industries, the British Government will not be able to carry on the war properly on the frontier. This is too great a risk. Therefore, again, India should be industrialized.

For these reasons, inevitably, British policy changed and the industrialization of India was decided upon. The larger imperial policy of Britain demanded it, even at the cost of Lancashire and some other British industries. Of course Britain made out that this change was due to the British Government's exceeding love of India and her welfare. Having decided upon this policy, Britain took steps to ensure that the real control of the new industry in India would remain in the hands of British capitalists. The Indian capitalist is obligingly taken as a very junior partner in the concern.

In 1916, during war-time, an Indian Industrial Commission was appointed, and two years later it reported, recommending that industries should be encourged by government, and that new industrial methods should be introduced in agriculture. It also suggested that an attempt should be made to give universal primary education. As in the early days of factory development in England, mass elementary education was considered necessary in order to produce skilled labour.

This commission was followed after the war by a host of other commissions and committees. It was even suggested that Indian industries should be protected by duties or tariffs. All this was considered a great victory for Indian industry. And so, to some extent, it was. But a closer analysis revealed certain interesting features. It was proposed to encourage foreign capital, which meant in effect British capital, to come to India; and British capital poured in. It was not only predominant, but overwhelmingly so. The vast majority of the big concerns were financed by British capital. So that tariff duties and protection in India resulted in protecting British capital in India ! The great change in British policy in India had not proved so bad after all for the British capitalist. He had got a good sheltered market to spread out in and make his dividends with the help of low wages to his workers. This proved to be advantageous to him in another way also. Having invested his capital in India, China, Egypt, and such countries, where wages were low, he threatened the English workers in England with a reduction of wages. He told them that he could not otherwise compete with the products of low wages in India, China, etc. And if the English workman objected to having his wages cut down, the capitalist told him that he would be regretfully compelled to shut up his factory in England and invest the capital elsewhere.

The British Government in India also took many other steps to control industry in India. This is a complicated subject, and I do not propose to discuss it. But one thing I might mention. Banks play a very important part in modern industry, because big business often requires credit. The best of businesses may fail suddenly if these credit facilities are denied it. As the banks give this credit, you can appreciate what a lot of power they must have. They can make or mar a business. Soon after the war the British Government brought the entire banking system of the country under its control. In this way, and by the manipulation of the currency, the government can exercise vast power over Indian industries and firms. Further, in order to encourage British trade in India, they introduced " imperial preference ". This meant that if foreign goods are taxed for tariff purposes, British goods should be taxed less or not taxed at all, so that British goods may have an advantage over the others.

The growing strength of the Indian capitalist classes and upper *bourgeoisie* during the war began to show itself in the political movement also. Politics gradually came out of the pre-war and early war lull, and various demands for self-government and the like began to be made. Lokamanya Tilak came out of prison after completing his long term. The National Congress then, as I have told you, was in the hands of the moderate group, and was a small uninfluential body having little touch with the people. As the more advanced politicians were not in the Congress, they organized Home Rule Leagues. Two such leagues were started, one by Lokamanya Tilak and the other by Mrs. Annie Besant. For some years Mrs. Besant played an important part in Indian politics, and her great eloquence and powerful advocacy did much to revive interest in politics. The government considered her propaganda so dangerous that they even interned her, together with two of her colleagues, for some months. She presided over a session of the Congress in Calcutta, and was its first woman president. Some years later Mrs. Sarojini Naidu was the second woman president of the Congress.

In 1916 a compromise was arrived at between the two wings of the Congress, the Moderate and the Extremist, and both of them attended the Lucknow session held in December 1916. The compromise was of short duration, for within two years there was another split, and the Moderates, now calling themselves Liberals, walked away from the Congress, and they have kept away ever since.

The Lucknow Congress of 1916 marks the revival of the National Congress. From that time onwards it grew in strength and im-

portance and, for the first time in its history, began to be really a
national organization of the *bourgeoisie* or middle classes. It had
nothing to do with the masses as such, and they were not interested
in it till Gandhiji came. So that both the so-called Moderates and
Extremists represented more or less the same class, the *bourgeoisie*.
The Moderates represented, or rather were themselves, a handful
of prosperous people and those on the border-line of government
service; the Extremists had the sympathy of the greater part of
the middle classes and had many unemployed intellectuals within
their ranks. These intellectuals (and by this I mean simply more
or less educated people) stiffened their ranks and also provided
recruits to the ranks of the revolutionaries. There was no great
difference in the objective or ideals of the Moderates or the Extremists.
They both talked of self-government within the British Empire,
and both were prepared to accept a part of it for the time being, the
Extremist wanting more than the Moderate and using stronger
language. The handful of revolutionaries of course wanted a full
measure of freedom, but they had little influence with the leaders
of the Congress. The essential difference between the Moderates
and the Extremists was that the former were a prosperous party
of the Haves and some hangers-on of the Haves, and the Extremists
had a number of Have-nots also and, as the more extreme party,
naturally attracted the youth of the country, most of whom thought
that strong language was a sufficient substitute for action. Of
course these generalizations do not apply to all the individuals
on either side; for instance, there was Gopal Krishna Gokhale, a
very able and self-sacrificing leader of the Moderates, who was
certainly not a Have. It was he who founded the Servants of India
Society. But neither the Moderates nor the Extremists had anything to do with the real Have-nots, the workers and the peasants.
Tilak was, however, personally popular with the masses.

The Lucknow Congress of 1916 was notable for another reunion,
a Hindu-Muslim one. The Congress had always clung to a national
basis, but in effect it was predominantly a Hindu organization,
because of the overwhelming majority of Hindus in it. Some
years before the war the Muslim intelligentsia, egged on to some
extent by the government, had organized a separate body for themselves, called the All-India Muslim League. This was meant to keep
the Muslims away from the Congress, but soon it drifted towards
the Congress, and at Lucknow there was an agreement between the
two about the future constitution of India. This was called the
Congress-League Scheme, and it laid down, among other things,
the proportion of seats to be reserved for the Muslim minorities.
This Congress-League Scheme then became the joint programme
which was accepted as the country's demand. It represented the
views of the *bourgeoisie*, who were the only politically minded people
at the time. Agitation grew on the basis of this scheme.

The Muslims had grown more politically minded, and had joined
hands with the Congress largely because of their exasperation at
the British fighting Turkey. Because of sympathy for Turkey

and a vigorous expression of it, two Muslim leaders, the Maulanas Mohamad Ali and Shaukat Ali, had been interned early in the war. Maulana Abul Kalam Azad was also interned because of his connections with Arab countries, where he was very popular owing to his writings. All this served to irritate and annoy the Muslims, and they turned away from the government more and more.

As the demand for self-government grew in India, the British Government made various promises and started inquiries in India which occupied the people's attention. In the summer of 1918 the then Secretary of State for India and the Viceroy presented a joint report—called, from their respective names, the Montagu-Chelmsford Report—which embodied certain proposals for reforms and changes in India. Immediately a great argument arose in the country over these tentative proposals. The Congress strongly disapproved of them and considered them insufficient. The Liberals welcomed them, and, because of this, they parted company with the Congress.

So matters stood in India when the war ended. Everywhere there was a lively expectation of change. The political barometer was rising, and the mild and soothing, the somewhat apologetic and ineffective, whispers of the Moderates were giving place to the more confident, aggressive, direct, and truculent shouts of the Extremists. But both the Moderates and the Extremists thought and talked in terms of politics and the outward structure of government; behind them British imperialism went on quietly strengthening its hold on the economic life of the country.

155

THE NEW MAP OF EUROPE

April 21, 1933

AFTER we had considered briefly the course of the World War, we went on to the Russian Revolution, and then to the state of India during war-time. Let us now go back to the Armistice, which put an end to the war, and see how the victors behaved. Germany was prostrate. The Kaiser had run away, and a republic had been proclaimed. Still, to make sure that the German army would become quite powerless, many hard conditions were laid down in the terms of the Armistice. The German army had to leave not only all invaded territory, but also Alsace-Lorraine and part of Germany up to the Rhine. The Allies were to occupy the Rhineland—the territory round about Cologne. Germany had also to surrender many battleships and all her U-boats, as her submarines were called, and thousands of heavy guns and aeroplanes and railway engines and lorries and other material.

On the spot where the Armistice was signed, in the forest of

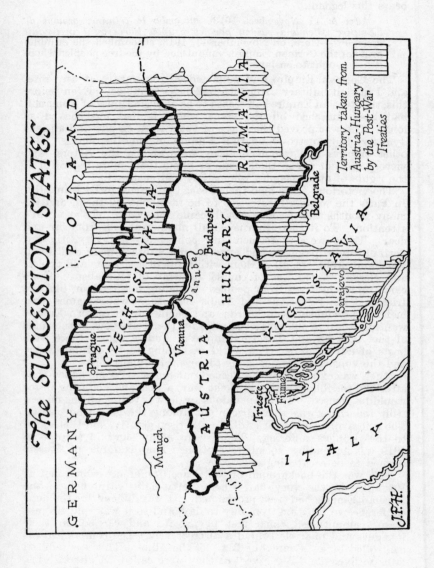

The SUCCESSION STATES

Territory taken from Austria-Hungary by the Post-War Treaties

GERMANY

POLAND

CZECHO-SLOVAKIA

oPrague

Munich
o

Vienna
o

AUSTRIA

Danube

Budapest
o

HUNGARY

RUMANIA

Belgrade
o

YUGO-SLAVIA

Sarajevo
o

Trieste

Fiume

ITALY

J.F.H.

Compiègne in northern France, there is a monument now which bears this legend :

" *Ici le* 11 *Novembre,* 1918, *succomba le criminel orgueil de l'Empire Allemand vaincu par les peuples libres qu'il prétendait asservir* "—Here, on November 11, 1918, succumbed the criminal pride of the German Empire, vanquished by the free peoples whom it had sought to enslave.

The German Empire had gone indeed, outwardly at any rate, and Prussian military arrogance had been humbled.   Even before this, the Russian Empire had ceased to be and the House of Romanoff had been marched off the stage where it had misbehaved so long.   The war proved the grave of yet a third empire and ancient dynasty, the Austro-Hungarian Empire of the Hapsburgs.   But other empires still remained—they were among the victors—and victory did not lessen their pride or make them more regardful of the rights of other peoples whom they had enslaved.

The victorious Allies held their Peace Conference in Paris in 1919. In Paris the world's future was to be fashioned by them, and for many months this famous city became the centre of the world's attention.   To it there journeyed all manner of folk from far and near.   There were statesmen and politicians, feeling vastly important, and diplomats, and experts, and military men and financiers, and profiteers, all of them with hosts of assistants and typists and clerks.   There was of course an army of journalists.   There came representatives from peoples struggling for freedom, like the Irish and the Egyptians and Arabs and others whose names even had not previously been heard; and peoples from eastern Europe wanting to carve out separate States for themselves out of the ruins of the Austrian and Turkish Empires.   And of course there were hosts of adventurers.   The world was going to be divided anew, and the vultures were not going to miss this opportunity.

Much was expected of the Peace Conference.   People hoped that after the terrible experience of the war, a just and enduring peace would be devised.   The tremendous strain was telling on the masses still, and there was great discontent among the labouring classes. The prices of the necessaries of life had risen greatly, and this added to the people's suffering.   There were many signs in Europe in 1919 of impending social revolution.   The example of Russia seemed to be a catching one.

This was the background of the Peace Conference which met at Versailles in the very hall where, forty-eight years before, the German Empire had been proclaimed.   It was difficult for the huge conference to function from day to day, and so it was split up into many committees, which met in private and carried on their intrigues and quarrels behind a discreet veil.   The conference was controlled by a " Council of Ten " of the Allies.   This was reduced later to five, the " Big Five " as they were called : United States, Britain, France, Italy, and Japan.   Japan dropped out of this, and so a " Council of Four " remained ; and lastly Italy dropped out, leaving the " Big Three " : America, Britain, and France.   These three countries were represented by President Wilson, Lloyd George, and Clemenceau, and to these three men fell the great task ot moulding the world afresh and healing its terrible wounds. It was a task worthy of supermen, demigods; and these three men were very far from being either. Men in authority—kings, statesmen, generals, and the like—are advertised and boomed up so much by the Press and otherwise that they often appear as giants of thought and action to the common people. A kind of halo seems to surround them, and in our ignorance we attribute to them many qualities which they are far from possessing. But on closer acquaintance they turn out to be very ordinary persons. A famous Austrian statesman once said that the world would be astounded if it knew with what little intelligence it is ruled. So these three, the " Big Three ", big as they seemed, were singularly limited in outlook and ignorant of international affairs, ignorant even of geography !

President Woodrow Wilson came with a vast reputation and popularity. He had used so many beautiful and idealistic phrases in his speeches and notes that people had begun to look upon him almost as a prophet of the new freedom that was to come. Lloyd George, the Prime Minister of Great Britain, was also a weaver of fine phrases, but he had a reputation for opportunism. Clemenceau, the " Tiger " as he was called, had no use for ideals and pious phrases. He was out to crush France's old enemy Germany, crush her and humble her in every way so that she might not be able to raise her head again.

So these three struggled with each other and pulled each his own way, and each in his turn was pulled and pushed by numerous other people in the Conference and outside. And behind them all lay the shadow of Soviet Russia. Russia was not represented at the Conference, neither was Germany; but Soviet Russia's very existence was a continuing challenge to all the capitalist Powers assembled in Paris.

Clemenceau won in the end, with the help of Lloyd George. Wilson got one of the things he was very keen on—a League of Nations—and having got the others to agree to this, he gave in on most other points. After many months of argument and debate, the Allies at the Peace Conference at last agreed to a draft treaty, and, having agreed amongst themselves, they summoned the German representatives to hear their commands. The enormous draft treaty of 440 articles was hurled at these Germans, and they were called upon to sign it. There was no argument with them, no opportunity was given them to make suggestions or changes. It was going to be a dictated peace; and they must either sign it as it was or take the consequences. The representatives of the new German Republic protested, and, on the very last day of grace, signed this Treaty of Versailles.

Separate treaties were drawn up and signed by the Allies with Austria, Hungary, Bulgaria, and Turkey. The Turkish treaty, though agreed to by the Sultan, fell through because of the

NEW COUNTRIES of EUROPE

splendid resistance of Kemal Pasha and his brave companions. But that is a story I must tell you separately.

What changes did these treaties bring about? Most of the territorial changes were in eastern Europe, western Asia, and Africa. In Africa the German colonies were seized by the Allies as spoils of war, England getting the choicest morsels. By adding Tanganyika and other territories in East Africa, the British succeeded in realizing a long-cherished dream of a continuous strip of empire right across Africa, from Egypt in the north to the Cape in the south.

In Europe the changes were considerable, and quite a large number of new States appeared on the map. Compare an old map with a new one, and you will see these great changes at a glance.

Some of the changes were the result of the Russian Revolution, as many of the peoples who lived on the borders of Russia, and were not themselves Russian, broke away from the Soviet and declared their independence. The Soviet Government recognized their rights of self-determination and did not interfere. Look at the new map of Europe. One big State, Austria-Hungary, has disappeared entirely, and in its place have risen several small States, which are often referred to as the Austrian Succession States. These are : Austria, reduced to a tiny fragment of its former self and with a great big city like Vienna as its capital; Hungary, also much reduced in size, Czechoslovakia, which includes the old Bohemia; part of Yugoslavia, which is our old and unpleasant acquaintance, Serbia, swollen out of all recognition; and parts have gone to Rumania, Poland, and Italy. It was a thorough dissection.

Farther to the north there is another new State, or rather an old State has reappeared—Poland. This was fashioned out of territories from Prussia, Russia, and Austria. In order to give Poland access to the sea, quite an extraordinary feat was accomplished. Germany, or rather Prussia, was cut into two and a corridor of land leading to the sea was given to Poland. So that in order to go from West to East Prussia one has to cross this Polish corridor. Near this corridor is the famous city of Danzig. This has been converted into a free city—that is, it belongs neither to Germany nor to the Polish State; it is a State by itself, directly under the League of Nations.

North of Poland are the Baltic States of Lithuania, Latvia, Estonia, and Finland, all successors of the old Tsarist Empire. They are small States, but each is a distinct cultural entity with a separate language. You will be interested to know that the Lithuanians are Aryans (like many others in Europe) and their language bears quite a close resemblance to Sanskrit. This is a remarkable fact, which probably many people in India do not realize, and which brings home to us the bonds which unite distant people.

The only other major territorial change in Europe was the transfer of the provinces of Alsace and Lorraine to France. There were some other changes also, but I shall not trouble you with them. Now you have seen that these changes resulted in the creation of many new States, most of these being quite small ones. Eastern Europe now resembles the Balkans, and therefore it is often said that the Peace treaties have " balkanized " Europe. There are many more frontiers now, and there is frequent trouble between these petty States. It is amazing how much they hate each other, especially in the Danube valley. A great deal of the responsibility for this lies on the Allies who divided up Europe all wrong, and thus created many new problems. Many national minorities are under foreign governments which oppress them. Poland has got a large territory which is really part of Ukraine, and the poor Ukrainians in this area have been subjected to all manner of atrocities in an attempt to " polonize " them forcibly. Yugoslavia and Rumania and Italy have all got foreign minorities in this way, and they ill-treat them. Austria and Hungary, on the other hand, are cut down to the bone, and most of their own people have been taken away from them. All these areas under foreign control naturally give rise to national movements and continuous friction.

Look at the map again. You will see that Russia is completely cut off from western Europe by a string of States—Finland, Estonia, Latvia, Lithuania, Poland, and Rumania. As I have told you, most of these States were not formed by the Versailles treaties, but were the result of the Soviet revolution. None the less they were welcomed by the Allies, as they formed a line separating Russia from non-Bolshevik Europe. They were a *cordon sanitaire* (by which infectious diseases are isolated) which would help in keeping off the Bolshevik infection! All these Baltic States are non-Bolshevik; otherwise they would of course join the Soviet Federation.

In western Asia parts of the old Turkish Empire tempted the western Powers. During the war the British had encouraged an Arab revolt against Turkey by promising to create a united Arab kingdom extending over Arabia, Palestine, and Syria. While this promise was being made to the Arabs, the British were making a secret treaty with France partitioning these very territories. It was not a very creditable thing to do and a British Prime Minister, Ramsay MacDonald, called it a tale of " crude duplicity ". But this was ten years ago, when he was not a minister, and so could afford, sometimes, to tell the truth.

There was almost a stranger sequel still when the British Government played with the idea of breaking not only its promise to the Arabs, but also its secret treaty with France. Before them rose the dream of a great Middle-Eastern empire, stretching from India to Egypt, an enormous block joining their Indian Empire to their vast African possessions. It was a tempting and tremendous dream. And yet it did not seem then very difficult to realize. At that time, in 1919, British troops held all this vast area—Persia, Iraq, Palestine, parts of Arabia, Egypt. They were trying to keep out the French from Syria. The city of Constantinople itself was in British possession. The dream vanished as the years 1920 and 1921 and 1922 unfolded what they had in store. The Soviet background and Kemal Pasha in the foreground put an end to these ambitious schemes of British ministers.

But still Britain held on to a great deal in western Asia—Iraq and Palestine—and tried to influence the course of events in Arabia by bribery and other means. Syria fell to the lot of the French. Of the new nationalism of the Arab countries and their struggle for freedom, I must tell you some other time.

We must go back to the Treaty of Versailles. This treaty laid down that Germany was the guilty party in causing the war, and the Germans were thus forced to admit their own war guilt by signing the treaty. Such forcible admissions have little value; they create bitterness, as they did in this case.

Germany was also called upon to disarm. She was allowed to keep only a small army, more or less for police purposes, and had to surrender her fleet to the Allies. As the German fleet was being taken for this surrender, its officers and men decided, on their own responsibility, to sink it rather than hand it over to the British. And so, in June 1919, at Scapa Flow, within sight of the British, who were making ready to take over, the whole German fleet was scuttled and sunk by its own crews.

Further, Germany was to pay a war indemnity and to make good the losses and damage caused to the Allies by the war. This was called " Reparations ", and for many years the word hung like a shadow over Europe. No definite sum was fixed by the treaty, but provision was made for the fixing of this sum. This undertaking to make good the war losses of the Allies was a stupendous affair. Germany was a conquered and ruined country at the time, faced with vast problems to make both ends meet for her domestic purposes. In addition to this, to have to shoulder the burden of the Allies was an impossible task, incapable of fulfilment. But the Allies were full of hatred and the spirit of revenge, and wanted not only their " pound of flesh ", but almost the last drop of blood from Germany's prostrate body. In England Lloyd George had won an election on the cry of " Hang the Kaiser ". In France feelings were even bitterer.

The whole purpose of all these clauses of the treaty was to tie up Germany in every possible way, to disable her, and to prevent her from becoming strong again. She was to remain for generations the economic serf of the Allies, paying vast sums as annual tribute. The obvious lesson of history that it is impossible to tie up a great people for long in this way did not strike the wise super-statesmen who laid the foundations of this peace of vengeance at Versailles. They are repenting it now.

Lastly, I must tell you of President Wilson's child, the League of Nations, which the Treaty of Versailles presented to the world. This was to be a league of free and self-governing States, and its purpose was " to prevent future wars by establishing relations on the basis of justice and honour and to promote co-operation, material and intellectual, between the nations of the world ". A very praiseworthy purpose ! Each member-State of the League undertook never to go to war with a fellow-State until all possibilities of a peaceful settlement had been exhausted, and then only after an interval of nine months. In case a member-State broke this pledge, the other States were pledged to discontinue financial and economic relations with that State. All this sounds very fine on paper ; in practice it has turned out to be very different. It is worth noting, however, that even in theory the League did not try to end war ; it sought to put difficulties in its way, so that the passage of time and efforts at conciliation might soothe away war passions. Nor did it try to remove the causes of war.

The League was to consist of an Assembly, where all its member-States would be represented, and a Council in which the great

Powers were to have permanent representatives and some additional ones were to be elected by the Assembly. There was to be a secretariat with its headquarters, as you know, at Geneva. There were also other departments of activity : an International Labour Office dealing with labour matters; a Permanent Court of International Justice at the Hague; and a Committee for Intellectual Cooperation. The League did not begin with all these activities. Some of them were added subsequently.

The original constitution of the League was contained in the Treaty of Versailles. This is called the " Covenant of the League of Nations ". In this covenant it was also laid down that armaments should be reduced by all States to the lowest point consistent with national safety. German disarmament (which of course was compulsory) was held to be the first step in this direction, the other countries were to follow. It was further stated that in case of aggression by any State, steps should be taken against it. But it was not stated what constituted aggression. When two people or two nations fight, each blames the other and calls it the aggressor.

The League could only decide important matters unanimously. Thus if even one member-State voted against a proposition, it fell through. This meant that there was to be no coercion by a majority vote. It further meant that national sovereignties remained as independent and almost as irresponsible as before; the League did not become a kind of super-State over them. This provision weakened the League greatly and made it practically an advisory body.

Any independent State could join the League, but four countries were definitely excluded : Germany, Austria, and Turkey—the defeated Powers—and Russia, the Bolshevik Power. It was laid down, however, that they might come in later under certain conditions. India, curiously enough, became an original member of the League, in flat contradiction of the provision that only self-governing States could be members. Of course by " India " was meant the British Government in India, and by this clever dodge the British Government managed to get an extra representative. On the other hand, America, which was in a sense a parent of the League, refused to join it. The Americans disapproved of President Wilson's activities and of European intrigues and complications, and decided to keep away.

Many people looked up to the League with enthusiasm and in the hope that it would end, or at any rate greatly lessen, the discords of our present-day world and bring an era of peace and plenty. League of Nations societies were founded in many countries to popularize the League and to spread, it was said, the habit of looking at things internationally. On the other hand, many other people described the League as a pious fraud, meant to further the designs of the great Powers. We have now had some actual experience of it, and perhaps it is easier to judge of its utility. The League started functioning on New Year's Day 1920. Its life has been a brief one so far, and yet it has been long enough to discredit it entirely. Undoubtedly it has done good work in various byways of modern life; and the mere fact that it has brought nations, or rather their governments, together to discuss international problems has been an advance on old methods. But it has failed completely in achieving its real object, the preservation of peace or even lessening the chances of war.

Whatever may have been the original intention of President Wilson about it, there can be no doubt that the League has been a tool in the hands of the great Powers, and especially of England and France. Its very basic function is the maintenance of the *status quo*—that is, the existing order. It talks of justice and honour between nations, but it does not inquire whether the existing relationships are based on justice and honour. It proclaims that it does not interfere in the " domestic matters " of nations. The dependencies of an imperialist Power are domestic matters for it. So that, as far as the League is concerned, it looks forward to a perpetual dominance by these Powers over their empires. In addition to this, fresh territories, taken from Germany and Turkey, were awarded to the Allied Powers under the name of " mandates ". This word is typical of the League of Nations, as it signifies the continuation of the old imperialist exploitation under a pleasant name. These mandates were supposed to be awarded in accordance with the wishes of the people of the mandated territory. Many of these unhappy peoples even rebelled against them, and carried on a bloody fight for long periods till they were bombed and shelled into submission. Such was the method of finding out the wishes of the people concerned !

Fine words and phrases were used. The imperialist Powers were " trustees " for the inhabitants of the mandated territories, and the League was to see that the conditions of the trust were fulfilled. As a matter of fact this made matters worse. The Powers did just what they liked, but they put on a more sanctimonious garb, and thus lulled the consciences of the unwary. When some little State offended in any way, the League put on a stern aspect and threatened it with its displeasure. When a great Power offended, the League looked away as far as possible or tried to minimize the offence.

Thus the great Powers dominated the League, and they used it whenever it served their purpose to do so, and ignored it when this was found more convenient. Perhaps the fault was not the League's; it lay with the system itself, which the League, by its very nature, had to put up with. The very essence of imperialism was bitter rivalry and competition between the different Powers, each of them bent on exploiting as much of the world as possible. If the members of a society are continually trying to pick each other's pockets and sharpening their knives in order to cut each other's throats, it is not likely that there will be much co-operation between them, or that the society will make remarkable progress. It is not surprising therefore that, in spite of an imposing array of sponsors and godparents, the League languished.

In the course of the treaty discussions at Versailles, it was posed on behalf of the Japanese Government that a clause recognizing racial equality be introduced into the treaty. This was not accepted. Japan was, however, consoled by the gift of Kiauchau in China. The " Big Three " were generous at the expense of a weak and humble ally like China. Because of this China did not sign the treaty.

Such was the Treaty of Versailles, which put an end to " the war which was to end war ". Philip Snowden, who later became Viscount Snowden, and a Cabinet Minister in England, made the following comment on the Treaty :

> " The Treaty should satisfy brigands, imperialists, and militarists. It is the death-blow to the hopes of those who expected the end of the war to bring peace. It is not a peace treaty, but a declaration of another war. It is the betrayal of democracy and of the fallen in the war. The Treaty exposes the true aims of the Allies."

Indeed, the Allies, in their hatred and pride and greed, overreached themselves. They began to repent in after years when the consequences of their own folly threatened to overwhelm them. But it was too late then.

156

THE POST-WAR WORLD

April 26, 1933

At last we have reached the last stage of our long wandering; we are on the threshold of to-day. We have to consider the post-war world, the world after the Great War. We are now in our own times, indeed your times ! It is the last stage, and a very short one as time goes, but still a difficult one. It is just fourteen and a half years since the war ended, and what is this tiny fraction of time to the long periods of history we have considered ? But we are in the very thick of it, and it is difficult to form correct opinions of events at such close range. We can neither get the right perspective nor the calm detachment which history demands. We are too excited about many happenings, and little things may seem big to us, and some of the really big things may not be fully appreciated. We may lose ourselves in a multitude of trees and miss seeing the wood.

And then again there is the difficulty of knowing how to measure the importance of events. What yardstick should we use for this purpose ? It is obvious enough that much will depend on the way we look at things. From one point of view an event may seem important to us, from another it may lose all importance and seem trivial. I am afraid I have to some extent evaded this question in the letters I have written to you; I have not answered it fairly and squarely. But still my general outlook has coloured all that I have written. Another person writing about the same periods and events might write something very different.

Now, I am not going into the question here of what our outlook on history should be. My own on the subject has changed greatly in recent years. And just as I have changed my views on this and other matters, so have many others. For the war gave a terrible shaking to everything and everybody. It upset the old world completely, and ever since then our poor old world is trying painfully to stand up again, without much success. It shook the whole system of ideas on which we had grown up and made us begin to doubt the very basis of modern society and civilization. We saw the terrible waste of young lives, the lying, violence, brutality, destruction, and wondered if this was the end of civilization. The Soviet rose in Russia—a new thing, a new social order, and a challenge to the old. Other ideas also floated in the air. It was a period of disintegration, of the breaking up of old beliefs and customs; an age of doubt and questioning which always come in a period of transition and rapid change.

All this makes it a little difficult for us to consider the post-war days as history. But while we may discuss and question various beliefs and ideas, and not accept any of them simply because it is said to be old, we cannot make this the excuse for just playing with ideas and not taking the trouble to think our hardest, so that we may know what to do. Such periods of transition in the world's history especially call for activity of mind and body. They are the times when the dull routine of life is livened up and adventure beckons, and we can all take our part in the building up of the new order. And in such times the youth have always played a dominating part, for they can adapt themselves to changing ideas and conditions far more easily than those who have grown old and hardened and fixed in the ancient beliefs.

Perhaps it will be as well to examine this post-war period in some detail. But in this letter I should like you to make a general survey of it. You will remember our survey of the nineteenth century after the fall of Napoleon. Inevitably one thinks of the Peace of Vienna of 1815 and its consequences, and compares it with the Peace of Versailles of 1919 and its consequences. The Peace of Vienna was not a happy one; it laid the seeds of future wars in Europe. Not learning by experience, our statesmen made the Versailles peace a far worse one, as we saw in the last letter. Over the post-war years has lain heavily the dark shadow of this so-called peace.

What are the outstanding events then of these past fourteen years? First in importance, I think, and most striking of all, has been the rise and consolidation of the Soviet Union, the U.S.S.R. or the Union of Socialist and Soviet Republics, as it is called. I have told you already something of the enormous difficulties which Soviet Russia had to face in its fight for existence. That it won in spite of them is one of the wonders of this century. The Soviet system spread all over the Asiatic parts of the former Tsarist pro-Empire, in Siberia right up to the Pacific, and in Central Asia to within hail of the Indian frontier. Separate Soviet republics were formed, but they federated together into one Union, and this is now the U.S.S.R. This Union covers an enormous area in Europe and Asia, which is about one-sixth of the total land area of the world. The area is very big, but bigness by itself does not mean much, and Russia, and much more so Siberia and Central Asia, were very backward. The second wonder that the Soviets performed was to transform great parts of this area out of all recognition by prodigious schemes of planning. There is no instance in recorded history of such rapid advance of a people. Even the most backward areas in Central Asia have gone ahead with a rush which we in India might well envy. The most notable advances have been in education and in industry. By vast Five Years' Plans the industrialization of Russia has been pushed on at a feverish pace and enormous factories have been put up. All this has meant a very great strain on the people, who have had to do without comforts, and even necessaries, so that the greater part of their earnings might go in this building up of the first socialist country. The burden has fallen especially on the peasantry.

The contrast between this progressive, go-ahead Soviet country and western Europe, with its ever-increasing troubles, is very marked. In spite of all its difficulties, western Europe is still far richer than Russia. In the long days of its prosperity, it accumulated a great deal of fat, on which it can live for some time. But the burden of debt which each country carries, the problem of Reparations, which under the Versailles Treaty Germany was to pay, and the continuous rivalry and conflicts of the Powers, great and small, have brought poor Europe to a terrible pass. Interminable conferences meet to find some way out of the difficulty, and no way is found, and daily the situation worsens. To compare Soviet Russia with western Europe to-day is to compare a youth, carrying a heavy burden but full of life and vigour, with an aged person with little hope or energy left, and going forward, not without pride, but inevitably, to the end of his present state.

The United States of America seemed, after the war, to have escaped this European contagion. For ten years they prospered exceedingly. They had in war-time pushed out England from being the boss of the money-lending business. America was now the money-lender to the world, and all the world was her debtor. In an economic sense she dominated the whole world, and she might have lived comfortably on the world's tribute, as, to some extent, England had done previously. But there were two difficulties. The debtor countries were in a bad way and could not pay their debts in cash; indeed, even if they had been in a good way they could not have paid these vast sums in cash. The only way they could try to pay them was to manufacture goods and send them to America. But America did not like the idea of foreign goods coming to her, and huge tariff walls were put up which stopped most of these goods from entering. How, then, were the poor

debtor countries to pay ? A brilliant way was found. America
would lend them more money to pay the interest due to her !
This was an extraordinary way of getting a debt paid, for it meant
the creditor paying more and more and the debt going up. It
became clear enough that most of the debtor countries would never
be able to shake off the debt, and then suddenly America stopped
lending, and immediately the whole paper structure came down
with a crash. And another very strange thing happened. America,
prosperous America, filled to the brim with gold, became suddenly
a land of vast numbers of unemployed workers, and the wheels of
industry stopped running, and destitution spread.

If rich America was so hard hit, it can be imagined what the
state of Europe was. Each country tried to keep out foreign goods
by heavy tariff rates and other devices and buy-home-made-goods
propaganda. Each country wanted to sell and not to buy, or to
buy as little as possible. This kind of thing cannot go on for long
without killing international trade, for trade and commerce depend
on exchange. This policy is called economic nationalism. It
spread to all countries, and so did other forms of aggressive nationalism. As trade and industry languished, the difficulties of each
country grew, and the great imperialist Powers tried to make both
ends meet by greater imperialist exploitation abroad and by cutting
down the wages of workers at home. Rival imperialisms, in their
desire and attempts to exploit various parts of the world, came
more and more into conflict. While the League of Nations talked
piously of disarmament and did nothing, the spectre of war seemed
ever to draw nearer. Again the Powers started grouping themselves
for the conflict that seemed inevitable.

So we seem to be nearing the end of the great period during
which capitalist civilization held sway in western Europe and
America and dominated the rest of the world. For the first ten
years after the war it appeared that perhaps capitalism might
recover and steady itself for another considerable period. But the
next three years or so have made this very doubtful. Not only
is the rivalry between capitalist States growing to dangerous dimensions, but, at the same time, within each State the conflict between
classes, between the workers and the capitalist owning class, which
controls the government, is becoming acute. As these conditions
worsen, a last desperate attempt is made by the owning classes to
crush the rising workers. This takes the form of fascism. Fascism
appears where the conflict between the classes has become acute
and the owning class is in danger of losing its privileged position.

Fascism began in Italy soon after the war. The workers were
getting out of hand there when the fascists, under the leadership of
Mussolini, gained control, and they have been in power ever since.
Fascism means naked dictatorship. It despises openly democratic
forms. Fascist methods have spread to a greater or lesser extent
in many countries of Europe, and dictatorship is quite a common
phenomenon there. Early in 1933 fascism triumphed in Germany
where the young Republic, proclaimed in 1918, was ended and

the most barbarous methods were adopted to kill the workers' movement.

So in Europe fascism faces democracy and the forces of socialism, and at the same time the capitalist Powers glare at each other and prepare to fight each other. And capitalism offers, further, the most remarkable sight of abundance and poverty side by side; food rotting away and even being thrown away and destroyed, and people starving.

One ancient country in Europe—Spain—has during the last few years turned herself into a republic and driven out her Hapsburg-Bourbon ruler. So there is one king the less in Europe and the world.

I have told you of three of the outstanding events of the fourteen years after the war : the rise of the Soviet Union; the economic world domination of America and her present crisis; and the European tangle. The fourth outstanding event of this period is the full awakening of eastern countries and their aggressive attempts to gain freedom. The East definitely enters world politics. These eastern nations might be considered in two classes : those that are considered independent, and those that are colonial countries controlled by some imperialist Power. In all these countries of Asia and North Africa nationalism has grown strong, and the desire for freedom insistent and aggressive. In all there have been powerful movements, and in some places even rebellions, against western imperialism. Many of these countries have received direct help and, what was of far greater importance, moral backing at a critical stage of their struggle, from the Soviet Union.

The most remarkable rebirth of a nation that seemed to be down and out is that of Turkey, and for that the credit must go in a large measure to Mustafa Kemal Pasha, the gallant leader who refused to submit even when all seemed against him. Not only did he win freedom for his country, but he modernized it and changed it out of all recognition. He put an end to the Sultanate and the Caliphate, and the seclusion of women and a host of other old customs. The moral and actual support of the Soviet was of great help to him. The Soviet also was of help to Persia in her efforts to get rid of British influence. A strong man, Riza Khan, rose there also, and he is the ruler now. Afghanistan also succeeded during this period in establishing its complete independence.

The Arab countries, with the exception of Arabia itself, are still under foreign control. The demand of the Arabs for unity has not been met. The greater part of Arabia has become independent under Sultan Ibn Saud. Iraq is independent on paper, but in effect is within the British sphere of influence and control. The little States of Palestine and Trans-Jordan are British mandates, and Syria a French mandate. There was an extraordinarily gallant rebellion in Syria against the French, and it partly succeeded. Egypt also had insurrections and a long-drawn-out struggle against the British. That struggle continues still, though Egypt is called independent and a king, supported by the British, reigns there.

To the far west of northern Africa there was also a gallant struggle for freedom in Morocco under the leadership of Abdel Krim. He succeeded in driving out the Spanish, but later the full force of the French crushed him.

All these struggles for freedom in Asia and Africa show how the new spirit was abroad and affecting the minds of men and women in distant countries of the East simultaneously. Two countries stand out because they have a world significance. They are China and India. Any radical change in either of these countries affects the whole great-Power system of the world; it is bound to produce enormous consequences in world politics. The struggles in China and India are thus far more than domestic struggles of the peoples concerned. The success of China means the emergence of a mighty State which makes a difference to the present balance of power, as it is called, and which automatically puts an end to the exploitation of China by the imperialist Powers. The success of India also means the appearance, at least potentially, of a great State, and inevitably it means the end of British imperialism.

China has had many ups and downs during the last ten years. An alliance of the Kuo-Min-Tang and the Chinese communists broke up, and ever since, China has been a prey to the *tuchuns* and similar brigand chiefs, who are often helped by foreign interests who want disorder in China to continue. For the last two years the Japanese have actually invaded China and taken possession of several provinces. This informal war is still going on. Meanwhile large areas in the interior of China have turned communist, and there is a Soviet government of a kind there.

In India the last fourteen years have been very full ones, and have seen an aggressive and yet a peaceful nationalism. Soon after the war, when expectations of great reforms ran high, we had martial law in the Punjab and the horrible massacre of Jallianwala Bagh. Anger at this and Muslim resentment at the treatment of Turkey and the Caliphate led to the non-co-operation movement of 1920–22 under Gandhi's leadership. Indeed, from 1920 onwards Gandhi has been the unquestioned leader of Indian nationalism. This has been the Gandhi Age in India, and his methods of peaceful revolt, by their novelty and efficacy, have attracted the world's attention. After a spell of quieter activities and preparation, the fight for freedom began again in 1930, with the definite adoption by the Congress of the goal of independence. Since then we have had, off and on, Civil Disobedience and overflowing prisons and the many other things that you know of. Meanwhile the British policy has consisted of petty reforms to win over some people if they can, and an attempt to crush the nationalist movement.

Burma had a great revolt of the starving peasantry in 1931. It was suppressed with great cruelty. In Java and the Dutch Indies there was also a revolt. In Siam there has been a ferment and some change has taken place limiting the King's powers. In French Indo-China nationalism is also on the move.

So all over the East nationalism struggles to find expression, and in some places it is mixed with a little communism. There is little in common between the two except the common hatred of imperialism. Soviet Russia's wise and generous policy towards all eastern countries, within her Union as well as outside, has found many friends for her even in non-communist countries.

One other outstanding feature of recent years has been the emancipation of women from the many bonds, legal, social, and customary, that held them. The war gave a great push to this in the West. And even in the East, from Turkey to India and China, woman is up and doing and taking a brave part in national and social activities.

Such are the times we live in. Every day brings news of change or important happening, of the friction between nations, of the conflict between capitalism and socialism, and fascism and democracy, of growing poverty and destitution, and over all lies the ever-lengthening shadow of war.

It is a stirring period of history, and it is good to be alive and to take one's share in it, even though the share may consist of solitude in the Dehra Dun Gaol!

157

IRELAND'S FIGHT FOR A REPUBLIC

April 28, 1933

WE shall now consider the important events of recent years in some greater detail. I shall begin with Ireland. From the point of view of world history and world forces, this little country of the far west of Europe has no great importance at present. But it is a brave and irrepressible country, and not all the might of the British Empire has been able to crush its spirit or cow it into submission.

In my last letter about Ireland I told you of the Home Rule Bill that was passed by the British Parliament just before the Great War. This was resented by the Protestant leaders of Ulster and by the Conservative Party in England, and a regular rebellion was organized against it. Thereupon the southern Irish also organized their " National Volunteers " to fight against Ulster if necessary. Civil war in Ireland seemed inevitable. Just then came the World War, and all attention was diverted to the battle-fields of Belgium and northern France. The Irish leaders in Parliament offered their help in the war, but the country was apathetic and by no means keen. Meanwhile the Ulster " rebels " were given high office in the British Government, and this made the Irish people still more dissatisfied.

Discontent grew in Ireland and a feeling that they must not be sacrificed in England's war. When a proposal was made that conscription be introduced in Ireland, as in England, and all the able-bodied young men be forced to join the army, there was an angry flare up of protest all over the country. Ireland prepared to resist with force, if necessary.

During Easter week in 1916 there was a rising in Dublin, and an Irish Republic was proclaimed. After a few days of fighting this was crushed by the British, and some of the bravest and finest young men of Ireland were shot down afterwards under martial law for their part in the brief rebellion. This rising—it is known as the " Easter Rising "—was hardly a serious attempt to challenge the British. It was more of a brave gesture to demonstrate to the world that Ireland still dreamt of a republic and refused to submit willingly to British domination. The gallant young men behind the rising deliberately sacrificed themselves in order to make this gesture to the world, well knowing that they would fail in the present, but hoping that their sacrifice would bear fruit later and bring freedom nearer.

About the time of this rising an Irishman was also caught by the British in an attempt to bring arms to Ireland from Germany. This man was Sir Roger Casement, who had been for long in the British consular service. Casement was tried in London and sentenced to death ; from his prisoner's dock in court he read out a statement which was extraordinarily moving and eloquent, and which laid bare the passionate patriotism of the Irish soul.

The Rising had failed, but in its very failure it triumphed. The repression by the British Government that followed it, and especially the shooting of the group of young leaders, created a powerful impression on the Irish people. Ireland seemed to be quiet on the surface, but anger blazed below, and soon this found its outlet in Sinn Fein. Sinn Fein ideas spread with great rapidity. In my last letter on Ireland I told you of this Sinn Fein. It had met with little success to begin with ; now it spread like a forest fire.

After the Great War was over there were elections all over the British Isles for the Parliament in London. In Ireland the Sinn Feiners captured the great majority of seats, displacing the old nationalists, who were for some co-operation with the British. But the Sinn Feiners did not get elected to the British Parliament in order to attend it. Their policy was entirely different; they believed in non-co-operation and boycott. So these elected Sinn Feiners stayed away from the London Parliament and instead set up their own republican assembly in Dublin in 1919. They proclaimed the Irish Republic, and called their assembly the " Dail Eireann ". It was supposed to be for the whole of Ireland, including Ulster, but the Ulsterites naturally kept away. They had no love for Catholic Ireland. The Dail Eireann elected De Valera as its president and Griffith as the vice-present. Both of these heads of the new republic happened to be in British gaols at the time.

Then began one of the most extraordinary of struggles, a fight that was unique and quite unlike any of the numerous former fights between Ireland and England. A mere handful of young men and women, with the sympathy of their people behind them, fought against fantastic odds; a great and organized empire was against them. The Sinn Fein struggle was a kind of non-co-operation with violence thrown in. They preached boycotts of English institutions and set up their own wherever possible, like arbitration courts to take the place of the ordinary law-courts. In the country-side a guerrilla warfare was carried on against the police outposts. The Sinn Fein prisoners gave a lot of trouble to the British Government by hunger-striking in gaols. The most famous hunger-strike, which thrilled Ireland, was that of Terence MacSwiney, the Lord Mayor of Cork. When put in gaol he declared that he would come out, alive or dead, and gave up taking food. After he had fasted for seventy-five days his dead body was carried out of the gaol.

Michael Collins was one of the more prominent organizers of the Sinn Fein rebellion. The British Government in Ireland was largely paralysed by the Sinn Fein tactics, and in the country districts it hardly existed. Gradually violence grew on both sides, and there were frequent reprisals. A special British force was enrolled to serve in Ireland; it was highly paid, and contained the more desperate and violent elements out of those recently discharged from the war armies. This force came to be known as the " Black and Tans ", from the colours of their uniforms. These Black and Tans started a campaign of cold-blooded murder, often shooting people in their beds, in the hope that they would thus terrorize the Sinn Feiners into submission. But the Sinn Feiners refused to submit, and carried on their guerrilla warfare. Thereupon the Black and Tans indulged in terrible reprisals, burning down whole villages and large parts of towns. Ireland became one huge field of conflict where both parties vied with each other in violence and destruction; behind one of the parties was the organized strength of an empire, behind the other was the iron resolve of a handful of men. For two years this Anglo-Irish War lasted, from 1919 to October 1921.

Meanwhile, in 1920, the British Parliament hurriedly passed a new Home Rule Bill. The old Act, passed just before the Great War, which nearly brought on rebellion in Ulster, was quietly dropped. The new Bill divided up Ireland into two parts : Ulster or North Ireland, and the rest of the country, and there were to be two separate parliaments. Ireland is a small country, and by dividing it up, the two parts became tiny areas in a small island. The new Parliament was set up in Ulster for the north, but in the south, in the rest of Ireland, nobody paid any attention to the Home Rule Act. They were all busy with the Sinn Fein rebellion.

In October 1921 Lloyd George, the British Prime Minister, appealed to the Sinn Fein leaders for a truce to talk over the possibility of a settlement, and this was agreed to. Britain could no doubt have ultimately crushed Sinn Fein in Ireland with her vast resources and by converting the whole country into a desert, but her policy in Ireland was making her very unpopular in America and elsewhere. Money had poured into Ireland from the Irish in America and even from the British Dominions, for carrying on the struggle. At the same time the Sinn Feiners were also tired out; the strain on them had been very great.

The English and Irish representatives met in London, and after two months of discussion and argument a provisional settlement was signed in December 1921. This did not recognize the Irish Republic, but it gave Ireland more freedom, except for one or two matters, than any Dominion had so far possessed. Even so, the Irish representatives were not willing to accept this, and only agreed when the threat of immediate and frightful war was held over them by England.

In Ireland there was a tremendous tussle over this treaty; some were for it, others violently against. The Sinn Fein party was split up into two over this question. The Dail Eireann at length accepted the treaty, and the Irish Free State, called officially in Ireland the "Saorstat Eireann", came into existence. But it brought in its train civil war between the old comrades of the Sinn Fein ranks. De Valera, the president of the Dail Eireann, was opposed to the treaty with England, and so were many others; Griffith and Michael Collins and others were in favour of it. For many months civil war raged in the country, and those in favour of the treaty and the Free State were helped by British forces to put down the others. Michael Collins was shot down by the republicans, and in the same way many a republican leader was shot down by the Free State people. The gaols were full of republicans. All this civil war and mutual hatred was a terribly tragic development of Ireland's brave struggle for freedom. English policy had won, where her arms had been checked, and Irishman was fighting Irishman, and England was to some extent quietly helping one party and generally looking on, well content with the new development.

The civil war gradually died away, but the republicans would not accept the Free State. Even those republicans who had been elected to the Dail (the parliament of the Free State) refused to attend, as they objected to taking an oath of allegiance which mentioned the King. So De Valera and his party kept away from the Dail, and the other Free State party, headed by Cosgrave, the president of the Free State, tried to crush the republicans in many ways.

The formation of the Irish Free State led to some far-reaching consequences in Britain's imperial politics. The Irish treaty had given to Ireland a greater measure of independence than was possessed at the time, in law, by the other Dominions. As soon as Ireland got this, the other Dominions automatically took it also, and the idea of Dominion status underwent a change. Further changes in the direction of greater independence of the Dominions followed some Imperial Conferences which were held between England and the Dominions. Ireland, with her strong republican movement, was always pulling towards complete independence. So also was South Africa with her Boer majority. In this way the position of the Dominions went on changing and improving till

they came to be considered as sister-nations with England in the
British Commonwealth of Nations. This sounds fine, and no
doubt it does represent a progressive growth towards an equal
political status. But the equality is more in theory than in fact.
Economically the Dominions are tied to Britain and British capital,
and there are many ways of bringing economic pressure to bear on
them. At the same time, as the Dominions grow, their economic
interests tend to conflict with those of England. Thus the Empire
gradually gets weaker. It was because of the imminent danger of
the cracking up of the Empire that England agreed to the loosening
of the bonds and admitting political equality with the Dominions.
By wisely going thus far in time, she saved much. But not for
long. The forces that separate the Dominions from England continue to work; they are in the main economic forces. And these
forces continually tend to weaken the Empire. It was because of
this, as well as the undoubted decline of England, that I wrote to
you of the fading away of the British Empire. If it is difficult for
the Dominions to remain tied to England for long, with all their
common traditions and culture and racial unity, how much more
difficult must it be for India to remain tied to her. For India's
economic interests come into direct conflict with British interests,
and one of them must bow to the other. Thus a free India is most
unlikely to accept this connection, with its corollary of subordinating
her economic policy to that of Britain.

The British Commonwealth, meaning thereby the free Dominions
and not poor, dependent India, means thus politically free units.
But all these units are still under the economic empire of Britain.
The Irish treaty meant the continuation of this exploitation of
Ireland to some extent by British capital, and this was the real
trouble behind the agitation for a republic. De Valera and the
republicans represented the poorer farmers, the lower middle-class
people, and the poor intellectuals; Cosgrave and the Free State
people represented the richer middle class and the richer farmers,
and both these classes were interested in the British trade, and
British capital was interested in them.

After some time De Valera decided to change his tactics. He
and his party went into the Dail Eireann and took the oath of
allegiance, announcing at the same time that they did so for form's
sake, and that they would do away with the oath as soon as they
had the majority. At the next election, early in 1932, De Valera
did get his majority in the Free State Parliament, and immediately
he began carrying out his programme. The fight for the republic
was still to go on, but the method of fighting was different. De
Valera proposed to abolish the oath of allegiance and also informed
the English Government that he would not pay the land annuities
any more to them. I think I wrote to you what these annuities
were. When the land in Ireland was taken from the big landlords,
they were compensated handsomely for it, and then the money for
this was realized year after year from the farmers who had taken
the land. This process had gone on for more than a generation,

but it still continued.   De Valera said that he would refuse to pay any more.

Immediately there was an outcry in England and a conflict with the British Government. They protested first of all that it was a breach of the Irish treaty of 1921 for De Valera to abolish the oath of allegiance. De Valera said that if Ireland and England were sister-nations, as the Dominions were proclaimed to be, and each was free to change its constitution, then obviously Ireland could change or remove the oath from the constitution. No question of the treaty of 1921 arose now. If Ireland did not have that right, then she was, to that extent, dependent on England.

Secondly, the British Government protested even more loudly about the stoppage of the annuities, and said that this was a gross breach of a contract and obligation. De Valera denied this, and there was a legal argument about it which need not trouble us. When the time for the payment of the annuities came and they were not paid, England started a new war against Ireland. This was an economic war. Heavy tariff duties were put on Irish goods coming to England so as to ruin the Irish farmer, whose products came to England, and thus force the Irish Government to come to terms. As usual with her, England began using her bludgeon in order to compel the other party, but such methods are not so useful now as they were. The Irish Government retaliated by putting duties on British goods going to Ireland. This economic war caused great loss to farmers and industries on both sides. But outraged nationalism and prestige stood in the way of either party giving in.

There was a fresh election in Ireland early in 1933 and, much to the disgust of the British Government, De Valera was even more successful than before and came back with a bigger majority. So it was obvious that the British policy of economic coercion had not succeeded. The curious part of it is that while the British Government proclaim the wickedness of the Irish in not paying their debts, they themselves do not want to pay their own debts to America.

So De Valera is head of the Irish Government now, and he is taking his country, step by step, towards a republic. The oath of allegiance has already gone; the payment of the annuities has been finally stopped; the old Governor-General has also gone, and De Valera has appointed a member of his party to this office, which has lost all its importance now. The fight for a republic goes on, but the methods are now different; the centuries-old Anglo-Irish struggle still continues, and it takes the shape of an economic war to-day.

Ireland may develop into a republic soon. But there is one great obstacle in the way. De Valera and his party want, above all, a unified Ireland, one republic, one central government for the whole island, including Ulster. Ireland is too small to be split up into two bits. How to get Ulster to join the rest of Ireland is the great problem before De Valera. It cannot be done by force. An attempt to do so by the British Government in 1914 nearly ended in a rebellion, and the Free State certainly cannot force Ulster, nor does it dream of doing so. De Valera hopes that he will be able to win the goodwill of Ulster, and thus bring about union. This hope seems to err on the side of optimism, for Protestant Ulster's bitter distrust of Catholic Ireland still continues.

Note (1938) :—The economic war between the two countries, after being carried on for some years, was ended by an agreement between the two governments. This agreement, which settled the problem of annuities and other financial obligations, was very advantageous to the Free State. Mr. De Valera has taken further steps towards the republic and has severed many links with the British Government and Crown. Ireland is now named Eire. The vital question before Eire is that of unity, which would include Ulster. But Ulster is still unwilling.

158

A NEW TURKEY RISES FROM THE ASHES

May 7, 1933

I TOLD you in my last letter of Ireland's brave fight for a republic. Between Ireland and Turkey there is no particular connection, but I have the new Turkey in mind to-day, and therefore I propose to write to you about her. In common with Ireland, she put up an amazing resistance against great odds. We have already seen three empires disappear as a result of the World War—Russia, Austria, and Germany. In Turkey we see the end of a fourth great empire, the Ottoman Empire. Ottoman and his successors had founded and built up this Empire 600 years ago; their dynasty was thus far older than the Romanoffs of Russia or the Hohenzollerns of Prussia and Germany. They were the contemporaries of the early Hapsburgs of the thirteenth century, and both these ancient houses went down together.

Turkey collapsed a few days before Germany in the World War and arranged a separate armistice with the Allies. The country had practically gone to pieces, the empire was no more, and the machinery of government had broken down. Iraq and the Arab countries were all cut off and were largely under the Allies. Constantinople itself was under the control of the Allies and, facing the great city, in the Bosphorus, British warships lay at anchor, proud emblems of victorious might. Everywhere there were English, French, and Italian troops, and British secret-service agents prowled all over the place. The Turkish forts were being dismantled, and the remains of the Turkish army were being made to deliver up their arms. The Young Turk leaders, Enver Pasha and Talaat Beg and others, had run away to other countries. On the Sultan's throne sat the puppet Caliph Wahid-ud-din, determined to save himself in the wreck, whatever happened to his country.

Another puppet, agreeable to the British Government, was made Grand Vizier. The Turkish Parliament was dissolved.

Such was the state of affairs in Turkey at the end of 1918 and the beginning of 1919. The Turks were thoroughly worn out and crushed in spirit. Remember what a terrible lot they had had to endure. Before the four years of the World War there was the Balkan War, and before that the war with Italy, and all this came hard on the heels of the Young Turk revolution, which removed Sultan Abdul Hamid and established a parliament. The Turks have always shown wonderful powers of endurance, but nearly eight years of continuous war was too much for them, as it would have been too much for any people. So they gave up all hope and, resigning themselves to an evil fate, waited for the decision of the Allies.

Nearly two years earlier, during war-time, the Allies had come to a secret agreement promising Smyrna and the western part of Asia Minor to Italy. Previous to this, Constantinople had been presented, on paper, to Russia, and the Arab countries divided up among the Allies. The last secret agreement, about Asia Minor being handed over to Italy, had to be agreed to by Russia. Unfortunately for Italy, the Bolsheviks seized power before this could be done, and so the agreement was never ratified, much to Italy's disgust and anger with her allies.

So matters stood. The Turks seemed to be down and out, from the craven Sultan downwards. The " sick man of Europe " had at last expired, or so it appeared. But there were a few Turks who refused to bow to fate or circumstance, however hopeless resistance might appear. They worked silently and secretly for a while, collecting arms and material from the depots actually under Allied control and shipping them to the interior of Anatolia (Asia Minor) via the Black Sea. Chief among these secret workers was Mustafa Kemal Pasha, whose name has already appeared in some of my previous letters.

The English did not like Mustafa Kemal at all. They suspected him and wanted to arrest him. The Sultan, who was wholly under the thumb of the English, did not like him either. But he thought it would be a safe policy to send him away far into the interior, and so Kemal Pasha was appointed Inspector-General of the army in Eastern Anatolia. There was practically no army to inspect, and his job was really supposed to be to help the Allies in getting arms from Turkish soldiers. This was an ideal opportunity for Kemal; he jumped at it and went off immediately. It was as well that he did so, for, within a few hours of his departure, the Sultan had changed his mind. His fears of Kemal suddenly got the better of him, and at midnight he sent word to the English to stop Kemal. But the bird had flown.

Kemal Pasha and a handful of other Turks began organizing national resistance in Anatolia. They proceeded quietly and cautiously at first, trying to win over the officers of the army who were stationed there. Outwardly they acted as the Sultan's agents,

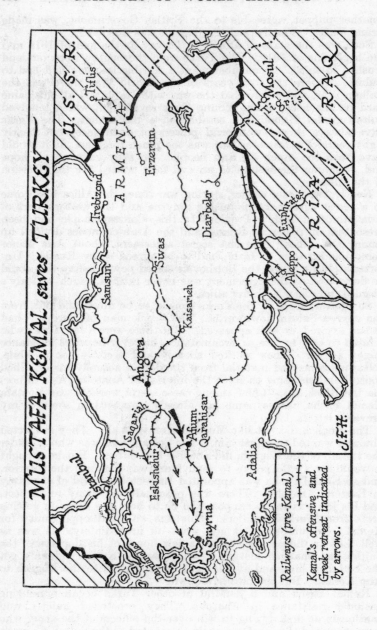

but they paid no attention to orders from Constantinople. The course of events helped them. In the Caucasus the English had created an Armenian Republic and promised to add the Turkish eastern provinces to it. (The Armenian Republic is now a part of the Soviet Union.) There was bitter enmity between the Armenians and the Turks, and many a massacre by the one of the other had taken place in the past. So long as the Turks were the bosses they had the best of this bloody game, during Abdul Hamid's time especially. For the Turks to be now put under the Armenians meant almost annihilation for them. They preferred fighting to this. So the Turks of the eastern provinces of Anatolia were willing enough to listen to Kemal Pasha's appeals and exhortations.

Meanwhile, another and a more important happening roused the Turks. Early in 1919 the Italians tried to make good their secret agreement with France and England, which had failed to materialize, by landing troops in Asia Minor. England and France did not like this at all; they did not want to encourage the Italians at the time. Not knowing what else to do, they agreed to Greek troops occupying Smyrna, so that the Italians might be forestalled.

Why were the Greeks chosen in this way? The French and English troops were war-weary and almost in a mutinous mood. They wanted to be demobilized and to go home as soon as possible. The Greeks were handy, and the Greek Government had dreams of annexing both Asia Minor and Constantinople and thus reviving the old Byzantine Empire. Two very able Greeks happened to be friends of Lloyd George, who was then Prime Minister in England and very powerful in the Allied councils. One of these was Venizelos, Prime Minister of Greece. The other is a very mysterious person, known as Sir Basil Zaharoff, although his original name was Basileios Zacharias. As a young man, as early as 1877, he became the agent in the Balkans for a British armament firm. When the World War ended, he was the richest man in Europe and perhaps in the world, and great statesmen and governments delighted to honour him. He was given high English titles as well as French titles; he owned many newspapers; and he seemed to influence governments considerably from behind the scenes. The public knew little about him and he kept away from the limelight. He was, indeed, the typical modern international financier who feels at home in many countries and influences and, to some extent, even controls governments of various democratic countries. People have a sensation of governing themselves in such countries, but behind them, unseen, stands the real power, international finance.

How did Zaharoff become so rich and important? His business was the selling of all kinds of armaments, and this was a profitable job, especially in the Balkans. But it is believed by many that from his early days he was a member of the British Secret Service. This helped him greatly in business and in politics, and repeated wars brought millions of profit to him, and so he grew into the mysterious giant of to-day.

This fabulously rich mystery man and Venizelos managed to get Lloyd George to agree to Greek troops being sent to Asia Minor. Zaharoff offered to finance the undertaking. It was one of his investments that did not pay, for it is said that he lost a hundred million dollars, which he had advanced to the Greeks, in their Turkish war.

Greek troops went across to Asia Minor in British ships and landed at Smyrna in May 1919, under cover of British, French and American warships. Immediately these troops, the gift of the Allies to Turkey, started massacre and outrage on a tremendous scale. There was a reign of terror which shocked even the jaded conscience of a war-weary world. In Turkey itself it had a most powerful effect, for the Turks saw the fate the Allies seemed to have in store for them. And to be massacred and treated like this by their old enemies and subjects, the Greeks! Anger blazed in the Turkish heart, and the nationalist movement grew. It is said, indeed, that although Kemal Pasha was the leader of this movement, the Greek occupation of Smyrna was its creator. Many of the Turkish officers, who had till then remained undecided, now joined it, even though this meant a defiance of the Sultan. For the Sultan had now ordered the arrest of Mustafa Kemal.

In September 1919 a Congress of elected representatives was held at Sivas in Anatolia. This put the seal on the new resistance, and an executive committee with Kemal as president was formed. A "National Pact" containing the minimum peace terms with the Allies, amounting to complete independence, was also adopted. The Sultan in Constantinople was impressed and a little frightened. He promised to convene a new session of Parliament and ordered elections. In these elections the people of the Sivas Congress got a big majority. Kemal Pasha did not trust the people at Constantinople, and he advised the newly elected deputies not to go there. But they did not agree and, headed by Rauf Beg, they went to Istanbul (as I shall call Constantinople in future). One of the reasons for their doing so was a declaration of the Allies that they would recognize the new Parliament if it met in Istanbul under the Sultan's presidentship. Kemal himself did not go, although he was a deputy.

The new Parliament met in Istanbul in January 1920, and immediately adopted the "National Pact" that had been drawn up at the Sivas Congress. The Allied representatives in Istanbul did not like this at all, nor did they like many other things that the Parliament did. So, six weeks later, they decided to apply their usual and rather coarse tactics which they have often applied in Egypt and elsewhere. The English General marched into Istanbul, took possession of the city, proclaimed martial law, arrested forty of the nationalist deputies, including Rauf Beg, and deported them to Malta! This gentle method of the British was merely meant to demonstrate that the "National Pact" was not approved of by the Allies.

Again Turkey was vastly excited. It was plain enough now that the Sultan was a puppet in British hands. Many Turkish deputies escaped to Angora, and the Parliament met there and called itself the Grand National Assembly of Turkey. It declared itself the government of the country and proclaimed that the Sultan and his government in Istanbul had ceased to function the day the British took possession of the city.

The Sultan retaliated by declaring Kemal Pasha and the others outlaws, and excommunicating them and condemning them to death. Further, he announced that any person murdering Kemal and the others would perform a sacred duty and would be rewarded here in this world as well as in the next. Remember that the Sultan was also the Caliph, the religious head, and this open invitation to murder, coming from him, was a terrible thing. Kemal Pasha was not only a hunted rebel but a backslider from the Faith whom any bigot or fanatic might assassinate. The Sultan did everything in his power to crush the nationalists. He proclaimed a *Jihād* or holy war against them, and organized a "Caliph's Army" of irregulars to fight them. Men of religion were sent out to organize risings. There were risings every where, and for a while civil war raged all over Turkey. It was bitter warfare, between town and town, brother and brother, and there was merciless cruelty on both sides.

Meanwhile, the Greeks in Smyrna were behaving as if they were the permanent masters of the country, and very barbarous masters. They laid waste fertile valleys and drove away thousands of homeless Turks. They advanced with little effective resistance from the Turks.

It was not a pleasant situation for the nationalists to face—civil war at home with the sanction of religion against them, and a foreign invader marching on them, and behind both the Sultan and the Greeks the great Allied Powers who were dominating the world after their victory over Germany. But Kemal Pasha's slogan to his people was "win or be wiped out". Asked by an American what he would do if the nationalists failed, he replied : "A nation which makes the ultimate sacrifices for life and independence does not fail. Failure means the nation is dead."

In August 1920 the treaty which the Allies had drawn up for unhappy Turkey was published; the Treaty of Sèvres it was called. It was the end of Turkish freedom; sentence of death was passed on Turkey as an independent nation. Not only was the country cut up into bits, but even in Istanbul itself an Allied commission was to sit and hold control. There was sorrow all over the country, and a day of national mourning was observed with prayers and a *hartāl*—a stoppage of all work. The newspapers came out with black borders. None the less the Sultan's representatives had signed this treaty. The nationalists, of course, rejected it with scorn, and the result of the publication of the treaty was that their power grew, and more and more Turks turned to them to save their country from utter degradation.

But who was to enforce this treaty on a rebellious Turkey ?

The Allies were not prepared to do it themselves. They had demobilized their armies, and at home they had to face an ugly temper among the demobilized soldiers and workers. There was still a spirit of revolution in the air in the western European countries. Besides, the Allies were falling out among themselves and quarrelling about the division of the spoils of war. In the East, England, and to some extent France, had to face a dangerous situation. Syria, under a French mandate, was seething with dissatisfaction, and promised trouble. Egypt had already had a bloody insurrection which the English had crushed. In India, the first great movement of rebellion, peaceful though this was, since the Revolt of 1857, was taking shape. This was the non-co-operation movement under Gandhi's leadership, and one of the main planks of this movement was the question of the Caliphate or *Khilafat* and the treatment given to Turkey.

So we see that the Allies were in no position to enforce their own treaty on Turkey; nor were they prepared to put up with an open flouting of it by the Turkish nationalists. They turned to their friends Venizelos and Zaharoff, and these two were perfectly prepared to undertake the job on behalf of Greece. No one expected the demoralized Turks to give much trouble, and the prize of Asia Minor was worth having. More Greek troops went over, and the Græco-Turkish War began on a big scale. Right through the summer and autumn of 1920 victory sided with the Greeks, and they drove the Turks before them. Kemal Pasha and his colleagues worked feverishly to build up an effective army out of the broken remnants at their disposal. Help, and most opportune help, came to them when it was most needed. Soviet Russia supplied them with arms and money. The common enemy of both was England.

As Kemal's strength grew the Allies began to feel a little doubtful of the issue of the struggle, and they offered better terms. But still they were not good enough for the Kemalists, who refused them. Thereupon the Allies washed their hands of the Græco-Turkish struggle and declared their neutrality. Having got the Greeks to entangle themselves, they left them in the lurch. Indeed, France, and to some extent even Italy, tried secretly to make friends with the Turks. The English still stood more or less, but unofficially, on the side of the Greeks.

In the summer of 1921 the Greeks made a great effort to capture the Turkish capital, Angora. They came near to it, taking possession of town after town, till at length they were stopped at the Saqariah river. Near this river for three weeks the two armies wrestled with each other, continuously fighting with all the racial bitterness of centuries, and giving no quarter to each other. It became a terrible test of endurance; the Turks just managed to hold on when the Greeks gave way and retired. As was their way, the Greek army went back burning and destroying everything and converting 200 miles of fertile country into a desert.

The battle of the Saqariah river had been just barely won. It was by no means a final victory, but still it is reckoned among the

decisive battles of recent history. It meant the turn of the tide.
It was yet another of the great conflicts between East and West
which have covered every inch of the soil of Asia Minor with human
blood during the past 2000 years and more.

Both armies were exhausted, and they sat down to recuperate
and reorganize. But the star of Kemal Pasha was undoubtedly
rising. The French Government made a treaty with. Angora.
There was also a treaty between Angora and the Soviet. Recognition by France was a great moral as well as physical gain to
Mustafa Kemal. The Turkish troops on the Syrian frontier were
thus released for service against Greece. The British Government
was still supporting the puppet Sultan and the effete Istanbul
Government, and so this French treaty was a blow to it.

In August 1922, suddenly, but after the most careful preparation,
the Turkish army attacked the Greeks and simply swept them into
the sea. In eight days the Greeks retired 160 miles, but, even so,
as they retired, they revenged themselves by killing every Turkish
man, woman, and child they came across. The Turks were equally
merciless, and few prisoners were taken. Among the prisoners,
however, was the Greek Commander-in-Chief and his staff. The
greater part of the Greek army escaped by sea from Smyrna, but
the city of Smyrna itself was largely burnt down.

Kemal Pasha followed up this victory by marching his troops
towards Istanbul. Not far from the city, at Chanak, British troops
stopped him, and for some days in September 1922 there was talk
of war between Turkey and Britain. But the British agreed to
nearly all the Turkish demands, and an armistice was signed, in
which the Allies actually promised to make all the Greek forces
still in Thrace evacuate the country. Always, behind the new
Turkey, was the spectre of Soviet Russia, and the Allies did not
like to provoke a war in which Russia might help Turkey.

Mustafa Kemal had triumphed, and the handful of rebels of 1919
now spoke on equal terms with representatives of the great Powers.
Many circumstances had gone to help this gallant band—the after-
war reaction, dissensions among the Allies, the preoccupation of
the English with trouble in India and Egypt, the help of Soviet
Russia, the insults offered by the English—but above all they owed
their triumph to their own iron determination and will to be free
and to the truly wonderful fighting qualities of the Turkish peasant
and soldier.

A peace conference was held in Lausanne, and it dragged on for
many months. There was a curious duel between imperious,
domineering Lord Curzon on behalf of England, and rather deaf
and stodgy Ismet Pasha, who quietly went on smiling and refusing
to hear what he did not want to hear, to the intense irritation of
Curzon. Curzon, used to Indian viceregal ways, and otherwise
also very pompous, tried blustering methods with no effect whatever on deaf and smiling Ismet. In disgust Curzon came away
and the conference broke up. Later it met again, but instead of
Curzon, another British representative came. All the Turkish

demands, as embodied in the " National Pact ", except one, were
agreed to, and the Treaty of Lausanne was signed in July 1923.
Again the support of Soviet Russia and the mutual jealousies of
the Allied Powers had helped Turkey.

Kemal Pasha, the Ghazi, the victorious, had got nearly all he had
set out for. But from the first he had shown great wisdom in
stating his minimum demands, and to these he stuck even in his
hour of victory. He had given up all idea of Turkish dominion
over non-Turkish lands like Arabia and Iraq and Palestine and
Syria. He wanted Turkey proper, the land inhabited by the Turkish
people, to be free. He did not want the Turks to interfere with
other people, nor was he prepared to tolerate any foreign interference in Turkey. Turkey thus became a compact and homogeneous country. Some years later, at Greek suggestion, an
extraordinary exchange of populations took place. The remaining
Greeks in Anatolia were sent over to Greece, and in exchange
Turks from Greece were brought over. About a million and a
half Greeks were thus exchanged, and most of these families had
lived for generations and centuries in Anatolia and Greece respectively. It was an amazing uprooting of peoples, and it completely
upset the economic life of Turkey, especially as the Greeks had a
great share in commerce. But this made Turkey even more homogeneous, and perhaps it is now one of the most homogeneous of
countries in Asia or Europe.

I have said above that the Turks got all their demands by the
Lausanne Treaty except one. This one exception was the *vilāyat*
or province of Mosul, near the Iraq frontier. As the parties could
not agree over this, the matter was referred to the League of
Nations. Mosul was important, partly because of its oil, but more
so because of its strategic importance. To hold the mountains of
Mosul meant to dominate, to some extent, Turkey and Iraq and
Persia, and even the Caucasus in Russia. For Turkey this was
obviously important. To Britain it was equally important, in
order to protect the land and air routes to India and as a line of
attack or defence against Soviet Russia. If you look at the map,
you will see how important the situation of Mosul is. The League
of Nations decided in favour of Britain on this question. The
Turks refused to agree, and again there was talk of war. A new
Russo-Turkish treaty was concluded just then in December 1925.
But the Angora Government gave way in the end, and Mosul went
to the new State of Iraq. Iraq is supposed to be independent, but
so far it is practically a protectorate of the British, and it swarms
with British officials and advisers.

I remember well how we rejoiced when we heard of Mustafa
Kemal's great victory over the Greeks, nearly eleven years ago.
This was the battle of Afium Qarahisar in August 1922, when he
broke the Greek front and drove the Greek army to Smyrna and
the sea. Many of us were in the Lucknow District Gaol then, and
we celebrated the Turkish triumph by decorating our prison barrack
with such odds and ends as we could gather, and there was even
an attempt, a feeble one, at illumination in the evening.

159

MUSTAFA KEMAL BREAKS WITH THE PAST

May 8, 1933

WE have followed the fortunes of the Turks from the dark period of their defeat to the day of their triumph, and we have seen that, strangely enough, the very steps that the Allies, and especially the British, took to suppress them and weaken them had the contrary effect on them, and actually strengthened the nationalists and steeled them to further resistance. The efforts of the Allies to dismember Turkey, the sending of the Greek troops to Smyrna, the British *coup d'état* of March 1920, when the nationalist leaders were arrested and deported, the British support of their puppet Sultan against the nationalists—all this went to fire the Turks with anger and enthusiasm. The attempt to humiliate and crush a brave people inevitably has that effect.

What did Mustafa Kemal and his colleagues do with the victory they had gained ? Kemal Pasha was no believer in sticking to the old ruts ; he wanted to change Turkey thoroughly. But immensely popular as he was after his victory, he had to proceed cautiously, for it is no easy matter to uproot a people from their ancient ways, founded on long tradition and religion. He wanted to put an end to the Sultanate as well as the Caliphate, but many of his colleagues did not agree with him, and the general Turkish sentiment was probably against such a change. No one wanted Wahid-ud-din, the puppet Sultan, to continue. He was hated as a traitor to the country who had tried to sell it to the foreigners. But many people wanted a kind of constitutional Sultanate and Caliphate with the real power resting in the National Assembly. Kemal Pasha would have no such compromise, and he waited for his chance.

As usual, the British provided this chance. When the Lausanne Peace Conference was being arranged, the British Government sent the invitation to it to the Sultan in Istanbul, asking him to send representatives to discuss peace terms, and further requested him to repeat this invitation to Angora. This casual treatment of the Nationalist Government at Angora which had won the war, and the deliberate attempt to push forward the puppet Sultan again, created a sensation in Turkey and angered the Turks. They suspected some further intrigue between the British and the treacherous Sultan. Mustafa Kemal took immediate advantage of this feeling and got the National Assembly to abolish the Sultanate in November 1922. But the Caliphate still remained by itself, and it was declared that it continued in the House of Othman. Soon after this a charge of high treason was brought against the ex-Sultan Wahid-ud-din. He preferred flight to a public trial, and escaped secretly in an English ambulance car which carried him to a British battle-ship. The National Assembly elected his cousin Abdul Majid Effendi as the new Caliph, who was merely the ceremonial religious head with no political power.

The next year, in 1923, there was a formal declaration of the Turkish Republic, with Angora for its capital. Mustâfa Kemal was elected president, and he concentrated all power in himself, so that he became a dictator. The Assembly carried out his mandates. He began now to attack many other old customs, and was not very courteous in his treatment of religion. Many people grew dissatisfied with his ways and his dictatorship, especially the religious folk, and these gathered round the new Caliph who was a quiet and inoffensive person. Kemal Pasha did not like this at all. He treated the Caliph rather shabbily and waited for a suitable opportunity to take the next big step.

Again he got his chance soon, and it came in a curious way. A joint letter was sent to him from London by the Aga Khan and an Indian ex-judge, Ameer Ali. They claimed to speak on behalf of the millions of Indian Muslims, and they protested against the treatment given to the Caliph, and requested that his dignity should be respected and better treatment given. They sent a copy of the letter to some Istanbul papers, and it was actually published there before the original reached Angora. There was nothing offensive in the letter, but Kemal Pasha seized hold of it and raised a tremendous outcry. He had got his chance at last, and he wanted to make the most of it. So it was announced that all this was another English intrigue to divide the Turks. The Aga Khan, it was said, was the special agent of the English; he lived in England, was chiefly interested in English horse-racing, and was always hobnobbing with English politicians. He was not even an orthodox Muslim, as he was the head of a special sect. It was further pointed out that during the World War the English had used him as a kind of counterpoise to the Sultan-Caliph in the East, and had increased his prestige by propaganda and otherwise and tried to make him the leader of the Indian Muslims, so that they might be kept in hand. If the Aga Khan was so solicitous about the Caliph, why had he not supported the Caliph in war time when a *jihād* or holy war had been declared against the English? He had sided with the English then and against the Caliph.

In this way Kemal Pasha created quite a little tempest over the joint letter which its authors, all unaware of its consequences, had sent from London, and he made the Aga Khan appear in a far from favourable light. The poor Istanbul editors who had printed the letter were dubbed traitors and agents of England, and were punished severely. Having raised strong feeling in this way, a Bill to abolish the Caliphate was presented to the National Assembly, and was passed the same day, in March 1924. Thus passed from the modern stage an ancient institution that had played a great rôle in history. There was to be no " Commander of the Faithful " now, at least so far as Turkey was concerned, for Turkey was now a secular State.

A short while before, India had been greatly agitated over the Caliphate when this was threatened by the British after the war. " Khilafat Committees " sprang up all over the country, and large numbers of Hindus joined the Muslims in this agitation, feeling that the British Government was doing an injury to Islam. Now the Turks themselves had deliberately ended the Caliphate; Islam stood without a Caliph. Kemal Pasha was firmly of opinion that Turkey must have no religious entanglements with the Arabic countries or with India. He wanted no leadership of Islam for his country or for himself. He had refused to become Caliph himself when asked to do so by some people from India and Egypt. He looked westward to Europe, and wanted Turkey to become westernized as soon as possible. He was entirely opposed to the Pan-Islamic idea. Pan-Turanianism was the new ideal, Turanian being the race of the Turks. That is, instead of the wider and looser international ideal of Islam, he preferred the stricter and more compact bond of pure nationalism.

I have told you that Turkey had now become a very homogeneous country with few foreign elements. But there was still one non-Turkish race in eastern Turkey, near the Iraq and Persian borders. These were the Kurds, an ancient race speaking an Iranian language. Kurdistan, where these people lived, was split up into Turkey, Persia, Iraq, and the Mosul area. Out of altogether 3,000,000 Kurds, nearly half still lived in Turkey proper. A modern nationalist movement had begun there soon after the Young Turk revolution of 1908. Even at the Versailles Peace Conference, Kurdish representatives had demanded national independence.

In 1925 a great rebellion broke out in the Kurdish area of Turkey. This was just the time when the Mosul dispute was creating friction between England and Turkey, and Mosul was itself a Kurdish area adjoining the part of Turkey that had rebelled. The Turks naturally concluded that England was behind the rebellion and that British agents had incited the more religious Kurds against the reforms of Kemal Pasha. It is not possible to say if British agents had anything to do with the rebellion, though it was obvious enough that Kurdish trouble in Turkey just then was welcome to the British Government. It is clear, however, that religious orthodoxy had much to do with the rising, and it is equally clear that Kurdish nationalism had also much to do with it. Probably the nationalistic motive was the strongest.

Kemal Pasha immediately raised the cry that the Turkish nation was in danger, as England was behind the Kurds. He got the National Assembly to pass a law providing that the use of religion as a means of exciting popular sentiment, whether in speech or in print, should be deemed high treason, and as such should be subject to the most extreme penalties. The teaching of religious doctrines which might subvert loyalty to the Republic was also prohibited in mosques. He then crushed the Kurds without pity, and set up special Tribunals of Independence to try them by the thousand. The Kurdish leaders, Sheikh Said and Doctor Fuad and many others, were executed. They died with the plea for the independence of Kurdistan on their lips.

So the Turks, who had only recently been fighting for their own freedom, crushed the Kurds, who sought theirs. It is strange how a defensive nationalism develops into an aggressive one, and a fight for freedom becomes one for dominion over others. In 1929 there was another revolt of the Kurds, and again it was crushed, for the time being at least. But how can one crush for ever a people who insist on freedom and are prepared to pay the price for it?

Kemal Pasha then turned on all those who had opposed his policy in the National Assembly or outside. The appetite for power of a dictator always grows with its use; it is never satisfied; it cannot brook any opposition. So Mustafa Kemal resented all opposition, and an attempt to kill him by some fanatic brought matters to a head. The Tribunals of Independence now went all over Turkey trying and punishing heavily all who opposed the Ghazi Pasha. Even the biggest people in the Assembly, old nationalist colleagues of Kemal's, were not spared if they were in the opposition. Rauf Beg, whom the British had deported to Malta, and who was later the prime minister of Turkey, was condemned in his absence. Many other important leaders and generals who had fought in the war for independence were disgraced and punished, and some were even executed. The charge against them was that they had conspired with the Kurds, and perhaps even with the old enemy, England, against the safety of the State.

Having swept away all opposition, Mustafa Kemal was now the unchallenged dictator, and Ismet Pasha was his right-hand man. He now began to put into practice many of the ideas that had filled his head. He started with a small enough thing, and yet a typical one. He attacked the *fez*, the head-dress which had become the symbol of a Turk and to some extent of a Muslim. He began cautiously with the army. Then he himself appeared in a hat in public, to the vast astonishment of the crowd; and he finished up by making the wearing of a *fez* a criminal offence! It sounds rather silly to attach so much importance to a head-dress. What is much more important is what is inside the head, not what is on top of it. But little things sometimes become symbols of big things, and Kemal Pasha apparently attacked old custom and orthodoxy by means of the inoffensive *fez*. There were riots over this question. They were suppressed and heavy punishments awarded.

Having won this first round, Mustafa Kemal went a step further. He closed and dissolved all the monasteries and religious houses and confiscated all their wealth for the State. The dervishes who lived in these houses were told to work for their living. Even their distinctive dress was prohibited.

Even earlier than this the Muslim religious schools had been abolished and State secular (non-religious) schools started instead. There were many foreign schools and colleges in Turkey. These were also made to give up their religious teaching, and if they refused to do so, they were made to close up.

A wholesale change was made in the law. So far, in many matters the law was based on the teachings of the Koran, the *Shariat* as it is called. Now the Swiss Civil Code and the Italian Penal Code and the German Commercial Code were bodily adopted. This meant a complete change in the personal law which governed marriage, inheritance, etc. The old Islamic law was changed in regard to these matters. Polygamy was abolished.

Another change which went against old religious custom was the encouragement of drawing, painting, and sculpture of the human form. This practice is not approved of in Islam. Mustafa Kemal opened schools of art for this purpose for boys and girls.

Turkish women had played quite an important part in the struggle for freedom ever since the days of the Young Turks. Kemal Pasha was particularly keen on their emancipation from all kinds of bonds. A " Society for the Defence of the Rights of Women " was formed and professions were thrown open to them. The veil was the first to be attacked vigorously, and it disappeared with remarkable rapidity. Women have only to be given a chance to tear this veil aside. Kemal Pasha gave them this chance, and off they came. He encouraged European dancing very much. Not only was he fond of it himself, but it came to represent in his mind the emancipation of women and western civilization. The hat and dancing became the slogans of progress and civilization ! Rather poor symbols of the West, but at least they worked on the surface, and Turkey changed its headgear and its clothes and its way of life. A generation of women, brought up in seclusion, was suddenly turned in the course of a few years into lawyers, teachers, doctors, and judges. There are even women police in the streets of Istanbul ! It is interesting to find how one thing reacts on another. The adoption of the Latin alphabet led to a great increase in the use of typewriters in Turkey, and this meant more short-hand typists, which led to the greater employment of women.

Children were also encouraged in various ways to develop themselves fully as self-reliant and capable citizens, instead of the old learn-by-heart type of the religious schools. One remarkable institution was the " Children's Week ". For one week in each year, it is said, each government official was nominally replaced by a child and the whole State was administered by children. I do not know how this works, but it is a fascinating idea, and I am sure that, however silly and inexperienced some of the children may be, they cannot behave in a more foolish way than many of our grown-up and staid and solemn-looking rulers and officials do.

A small change, but still an important indication of the new view-point of Turkey's rulers was the discouragement of " salaaming ". It was made clear by them that hand-shaking was a more civilized form of greeting and should be indulged in in future.

Kemal Pasha then launched a great attack on the Turkish language, or rather what he considered the foreign elements in it. Turkish was written in the Arabic script, and Kemal Pasha considered this both difficult and foreign. The Soviets had been faced by a similar problem in Central Asia, as many of the Tartar peoples had scripts derived from the Arabic or Persian. In 1924 the Soviets held a Conference at Baku to consider this question, and it was decided there to adopt the Latin script for the various Tartar languages of central Asia. That is to say, the languages remained unchanged, but they were written in the Latin or Roman letters. A special system of notation was devised to give expression to the special sounds of these languages. Mustafa Kemal was attracted to this system, and he learnt it. He applied it to the Turkish language, and personally started a vigorous campaign in its favour. After a couple of years of propaganda and teaching, a date was fixed by law after which the use of the Arabic script was forbidden and the Latin script made compulsory. Newspapers, books, everything, had to appear in the Latin script. Every one between the ages of sixteen and forty was made to attend school to learn the Latin alphabet. Officials who did not know it were liable to be dismissed. Prisoners would not be released even at the end of their sentences unless they could read and write in the new script ! A dictator can be very thorough, especially if he happens to be popular. Few other governments would dare to interfere so much with people's lives.

The Latin script was thus established in Turkey, but soon another change followed. It was found that Arabic and Persian words could not be easily written in this script; their special sounds and *nuances* could not be expressed in it. Pure Turkish words were not so fine; they were rougher, more direct and vigorous, and could be written easily in the new script. The decision was therefore taken to drop Arabic and Persian words from the Turkish language and replace them with pure Turkish words. At the back of this decision was, of course, a nationalist reason. Kemal Pasha, as I have told you, wanted to cut Turkey off as far as possible from Arabian and other eastern influences. The old Turkish language, full of Arabic and Persian words and phrases, might have been suitable enough for the ornate and pompous life of the imperial Ottoman Court. It was considered unsuitable for the new, vigorous, republican Turkey. So the fine words were given up, and learned professors and others went to the villages to learn the language of the peasants and hunt for words of good old Turkish stock. This change is going on now. Such a change for us in northern India would mean our giving up to a large extent our ornate and rather artificial Hindustani of Lucknow and Delhi—a relic of old court life—and adopting instead many of the rustic *ganvārū* words of the village.

These changes in the language have meant changes in the names of towns and persons also. Constantinople, as you know, is now Istanbul, Angora is Ankara, Smyrna is Ismir. People's names in Turkey have been usually taken from the Arabic—Mustafa Kemal itself is an Arabic name. The new tendency is to give pure Turkish names.

A change which has caused trouble has been the law that Islamic prayers and the *azān*, the call to prayer, must also be in

Turkish. These prayers have always been recited by Muslims in the original Arabic; this is done even now in India. It was felt therefore by many *moulvis* and people in charge of mosques that this was an improper innovation, and they continued prayers in Arabic. There were, and there still are sometimes, riots over this question. But the Turkish Government under Kemal Pasha has crushed this as all other opposition.

All these vast social upsets of the past ten years have completely changed the life of the people, and a new generation, cut off from the old customs and religious associations, is growing up. But important as these changes are, they have not affected the economic life of the country greatly. With some minor changes at the top, the basis of this remains the same as it was. Kemal Pasha is no economist, nor is he in favour of such radical changes as have taken place in Soviet Russia. So that although politically he is on terms of alliance with the Soviets, economically he keeps far from communism. His political and social ideas seem to be derived from a study of the great French Revolution.

There is no strong middle class in Turkey, yet, apart from the professional class. The sending away of the Greek and other foreign elements has weakened commercial life. But the Turkish Government definitely prefers national poverty and slow industrial growth to the sacrifice of its economic independence. And because it fears that if foreign capital came into Turkey on a large scale it would mean such a sacrifice, and a consequent exploitation of the country by the foreigner, it has discouraged foreign enterprises. Heavy duties have been put on foreign goods. Many of the industries have been nationalized—that is the government owns and controls them on behalf of the people. Railway construction is going on at a fair pace.

Kemal Pasha is more interested in agriculture, for the Turkish peasant has been the backbone of the Turkish nation and army. Model farms have been made and tractors introduced, and farmers' co-operative societies encouraged.

Turkey, like the rest of the world, was involved in the great depression and found it difficult to make both ends meet. But she goes ahead slowly and steadily under Mustafa Kemal, who continues to be the supreme leader and dictator of the country. He has been given the tital of Ataturk, the Father of the Country, and by this he is now known.

160

INDIA FOLLOWS GANDHI

May 11, 1933

I MUST tell you now something about recent events in India. We are naturally interested in them far more than in outside happenings, and I have to keep guard on myself so that I do not enter into too many details. Apart from our personal interest, however, India is to-day, as I have told you, one of the major problems of the world. It is the typical and classical country of imperialist domination. The whole structure of British imperialism has rested on it, and other countries have been lured on to the paths of imperialist adventure by this successful British example.

I have told you in my last letter on India of the war-time changes that occurred here; of the growth of Indian industry and the Indian capitalist class, and of the change in British policy towards Indian industry. The industrial and commercial pressure from India on England was increasing, so also was the political pressure. All over the East there was a political awakening, all over the world there was ferment and a *malaise* after the war. In India there was occasional evidence of violent revolutionary activity. The expectations of the people ran high. The British Government itself had felt that something must be done, and it had taken steps in the political field by an inquiry, followed by certain proposals for changes contained in the Montagu-Chelmsford Report, and in the economic field by throwing out many sops to the rising *bourgeoisie*, while taking care to keep the citadels of power and exploitation in its own hands.

For a short while after the war trade prospered and there was quite a boom period, during which enormous profits were made, especially in jute in Bengal. The dividends often amounted to over 100 per cent. Prices went up, and to some extent, but comparatively little, wages increased also. With the prices rose the rent to be paid by tenants to their *zamindars*. Then came a slump, and trade began to languish. The condition of the industrial workers and the agriculturists became worse and discontent grew rapidly. There were many strikes in the factories owing to increasingly hard conditions. In Oudh, where the condition of the tenantry was particularly bad under the *taluqadari* system, a mighty agrarian movement grew almost spontaneously. Among the educated lower middle classes unemployment increased, and resulted in much suffering.

This was the economic background in the early days of the post-war period, and if you keep this in view, it will help you to understand the political developments. There was a militant spirit in the country which was manifesting itself in a variety of ways. Industrial labour was organizing itself into trade unions and later building up an All-India Trade Union Congress; small *zamindars* and peasant proprietors were dissatisfied with the Government and were looking favourably towards political action; even tenants, like the proverbial worm, were trying to turn; and the middle classes, especially the unemployed, were definitely turning to politics, and a handful of them to revolutionary activities. Hindus, Muslims, Sikhs, and others were all equally affected by these conditions, for economic conditions pay little heed to religious cleavages. But Muslims had been, in addition, greatly shaken up by the war against Turkey and the expectation that the British Government would take possession of the *jazīrat-ul-Arab*, the islands of Arabia, as they are called, the holy cities of Mecca, Medina, and Jerusalem (for Jerusalem is a holy city for the Jews, Christians and Muslims).

So India waited after the war; resentful, rather aggressive, not very hopeful, but still expectant. Within a few months, the first fruits of the new British policy, so eagerly waited for, appeared in the shape of a proposal to pass special laws to control the revolutionary movement. Instead of more freedom, there was to be more repression. These Bills were based on the report of a committee and were known as the Rowlatt Bills. But very soon they were called the " Black Bills " all over the country, and were denounced everywhere and by every Indian, including even the most moderate. They gave great powers to the government and the police to arrest, keep in prison without trial, or to have a secret trial of, any person they disapproved of or suspected. A famous description of these Bills at the time was : *na vakīl, na appeal, na dalīl*. As the outcry against the Bills gained volume, a new factor appeared, a little cloud on the political horizon which grew and spread rapidly till it covered the Indian sky.

This new factor was Mohandas Karamchand Gandhi. He had returned to India from South Africa during war-time and settled down with his colony in an *ashram* in Sabarmati. He had kept away from politics. He had even helped the government in recruiting men for the war. He was, of course, very well known in India since his *satyagraha* struggle in South Africa. In 1917 he had championed with success the miserable down-trodden tenants of the European planters in the Champaran District of Bihar. Later he had stood up for the peasantry of Kaira in Gujrat. Early in 1919 he was very ill. He had barely recovered from it when the Rowlatt Bill agitation filled the country. He also joined his voice to the universal outcry.

But this voice was somehow different from the others. It was quiet and low, and yet it could be heard above the shouting of the multitude; it was soft and gentle, and yet there seemed to be steel hidden away somewhere in it; it was courteous and full of appeal, and yet there was something grim and frightening in it; every word used was full of meaning and seemed to carry a deadly earnestness. Behind the language of peace and friendship there was power and the quivering shadow of action and a determination not to submit to a wrong. We are familiar with that voice now; we have heard it often enough during the last fourteen years. But it was new to us in February and March 1919; we did not quite know what to make of it, but we were thrilled. This was something very different from our noisy politics of condemnation and nothing else, long speeches always ending in the same futile and ineffective resolutions of protest which nobody took very seriously. This was the politics of action, not of talk.

Mahatma Gandhi organized a *Satyagraha Sabhā* of those who were prepared to break chosen laws and thus court imprisonment. This was quite a novel idea then, and many of us were excited but

many shrank back. To-day it is the most commonplace of occurrences, and for most of us it has become a fixed and regular part
of our lives !

As usual with him, Gandhi sent a courteous appeal and warning
to the Viceroy. When he saw that the British Government were
determined to pass the law in spite of the opposition of a united
India, he called for an all-India day of mourning, a *hartāl*, a stoppage
of business, and meetings on the first Sunday after the Bills became
law. This was to inaugurate the *Satyagraha* movement, and so
Sunday, April 6, 1919, was observed as the Satyagraha Day all over
the country, in town and village. It was the first all-India demonstration of the kind, and it was a wonderfully impressive one, in
which all kinds of people and communities joined. Those of us
who had worked for this *hartāl* were amazed at its success. It
had been possible for us to approach only a limited number of
people in the cities. But a new spirit was in the air, and somehow the message managed to reach the remotest villages of our
huge country. For the first time the villager as well as the town
worker took part in a political demonstration on a mass scale.

A week before April 6, Delhi, mistaking the date, had observed
the *hartāl* on the previous Sunday, March 31. Those were days of
an amazing comradeship and good-will among the Hindus and
Muslims of Delhi, and the remarkable sight was witnessed of Swami
Shraddhanand, a great leader of the Arya-Samaj, addressing huge
audiences in the famous Jāme Masjid of Delhi. On March 31,
the police and the military tried to disperse the great crowds in
the streets and shot at them, killing some people. Swami Shraddhanand, tall and stately in his *sanyāsin's* garb, faced with bared
chest and unflinching look the bayonets of the Gurkhas in the
Chandni Chowk. He survived them, and India was thrilled by the
incident; but the tragedy of it is that less than eight years later
he was treacherously stabbed to death by a Muslim fanatic, as he
lay on his sick-bed.

Events marched rapidly after that Satyagraha Day on April 6.
There was trouble in Amritsar on April 10, when an unarmed and
bareheaded crowd, mourning for the arrest of its leaders, Drs.
Kitchlew and Satyapal, was shot at by the military and many
were killed; it thereupon took its mad revenge by killing five
or six innocent Englishmen, sitting in their offices, and burning
their bank buildings. And then a curtain seemed to drop on the
Punjab. It was cut off from the rest of India by a rigid censorship; hardly any news came, and it was very difficult for people
to enter or leave the province. There was martial law there, and
the agony of this continued for many months. Slowly, after weeks
and months of agonized suspense, the curtain lifted and the horrible
truth was known.

I shall not tell you here of the horrors of the martial-law period
in the Punjab. All the world knows of the massacre that took place
on April 13 in the Jallianwala Bagh in Amritsar, when thousands
fell dead and wounded, in that trap of death from which there was

no escape. The very word " Amritsar " has become a synonym
for massacre. Bad as this was, there were other and even more
shameful deeds all over the Punjab.

It is difficult to forgive all this barbarity and frightfulness even
after so many years, and yet it is not difficult to understand it.
The British in India, by the very nature of their domination, feel
always that they live on the edge of a volcano. They have seldom
understood or tried to understand the mind or heart of India.
They have lived their life apart, relying on their vast and intricate
organization and the force behind it. But behind all their confidence there is always a fear of the unknown, and India, in spite of
a century and a half of rule, is an unknown land to them. Memories
of the Revolt of 1857 are still fresh in their minds, and they feel as
if they lived in a strange and hostile country which might turn at
any moment on them and rend them. Such is their general background. When they saw a great movement rising in the country,
hostile to them, their fears grew. When news of the bloody deeds
that took place in Amritsar on April 10 reached the high officials
of the Punjab in Lahore, their nerve failed them completely. They
thought that this was another bloody revolt on a big scale, like the
one of 1857, and that the lives of all English people were in danger.
They saw red, and they determined to strike terror. Jallianwala
Bagh and martial law and all that followed were the consequences
of this attitude of mind.

One can understand, although one cannot excuse, a frightened
person misbehaving, even though there was no real reason for his
fright. But what amazed and angered India even more was the
contemptuous justification of the deed many months afterwards
by General Dyer, who had been responsible for the firing at Amritsar,
and his subsequent barbarous neglect of the thousands of the
wounded. " That was none of my business," he had said. Some
people in England and the government mildly criticized Dyer, but
the general attitude of the British ruling class was displayed in a
debate in the House of Lords in which praise was showered on
him. All this fed the flames of wrath in India, and a great bitterness arose all over the country over the Punjab wrongs. Inquiry
committees had been appointed both by the government and the
Congress to find out what had actually occurred in the Punjab.
The country awaited their report.

From that year April 13 has been a National Day for India, and
the eight days from April 6 to April 13 the National Week. Jallianwala Bagh is now a place for political pilgrimage. It is an attrac-
tively laid out garden now, and much of the old horror of it has
gone. But the memory lingers.

That year, in December 1919, by a curious coincidence, the
Congress was held in Amritsar. No great decision was arrived at
by this Congress because the result of the inquiries was awaited,
but it was evident that the Congress had changed. There was
now a mass character about it and a new, and for some of the old
Congressmen a disturbing, vitality. There was Lokamanya Tilak,

uncompromising as ever, attending his last Congress, for he was to die before the next one was held. There was Gandhi, popular with the crowd, and just beginning his long period of domination over the Congress and Indian politics. There came also to the Congress, straight from prison, many leaders who had been involved in monstrous conspiracy cases during the martial-law days and sentenced to long terms of imprisonment, but were now amnestied, and the famous Ali Brothers just released after many years' detention.

The next year the Congress took the plunge, and adopted Gandhi's programme of non-co-operation. A special session in Calcutta adopted this, and later the annual session in Nagpur confirmed it. The method of struggle was a perfectly peaceful one, non-violent as it was called, and its basis was a refusal to help the government in its administration and exploitation of India. To begin with there were to be a number of boycotts—of titles given by the foreign government, of official functions and the like, of law-courts both by lawyers and litigants, of official schools and colleges, and of the new councils under the Montagu-Chelmsford reforms. Later the boycotts were to extend to the civil and military services and the payment of taxes. On the constructive side stress was laid on hand-spinning and *khaddar*, and on arbitration courts to take the place of the law-courts. Two other most important planks were Hindu-Muslim unity and the removal of untouchability among the Hindus.

The Congress also changed its constitution and became a body capable of action, and at the same time it laid itself out for a mass membership.

Now, this programme was a totally different thing from what the Congress had so far been doing; indeed, it was quite a novel thing in the world, for the *Satyagraha* in South Africa had been very limited in its scope. It meant immediate and heavy sacrifices for some people, like the lawyers, who were called upon to give up their practices, and the students who were asked to boycott the government colleges. It was difficult to judge it, as there were no standards of comparison. It is not surprising that the old and experienced Congress leaders hesitated and were filled with doubt. The greatest of them, Lokamanya Tilak, had died a little before this. Of the other prominent Congress leaders only one, Motilal Nehru, supported Gandhi in the early stages. But there was no doubting the temper of the average Congressman, or the man in the street, or the masses. Gandhi carried them off their feet, almost hypnotized them, and with loud shouts of *Mahatma Gandhi kī jai*, they showed their approval of the new gospel of non-violent non-co-operation. The Muslims were as enthusiastic about it as the others. Indeed, the Khilafat Committee, under the leadership of the Ali Brothers, had adopted the programme even before the Congress did so. Soon the mass enthusiasm and the early successes of the movement brought most of the old Congress leaders into it.

I cannot examine, in these letters, the virtues and defects of this novel movement or the philosophy underlying it. That would be too intricate a question, and perhaps no one can do it satisfactorily enough except the author of the movement, Gandhi. Still, let us look at it from an outsider's point of view and try to understand why it spread so rapidly and successfully.

I have told you of the economic pressure on the masses and their steadily worsening condition under foreign exploitation and the growth of unemployment among the middle classes. What was the remedy for this? The growth of nationalism turned people's minds to the necessity for political freedom. Freedom was not only necessary because it was degrading to be dependent and enslaved, not only because, as Tilak had put it, it was our birthright and we must have it, but also to lessen the burden of poverty from our people. How was freedom to be obtained? Obviously, we were not going to get it by remaining quiet and waiting for it. It was equally clear that methods of mere protest and begging, which the Congress had so far followed with more or less vehemence, were not only undignified for a people, but were also futile and ineffective. Never in history had such methods succeeded or induced a ruling or privileged class to part with power. History, indeed, showed us that peoples and classes who were enslaved had won their freedom through violent rebellion and insurrection.

Armed rebellion seemed out of the question for the Indian people. We were disarmed, and most of us did not even know the use of arms. Besides, in a contest of violence, the organized power of the British Government, or any State, was far greater than anything that could be raised against it. Armies might mutiny, but unarmed people could not rebel and face armed forces. Individual terrorism, on the other hand, the killing by bomb or pistol of individual officers, was a bankrupt's creed. It was demoralizing for the people, and it was ridiculous to think that it could shake a powerfully organized government, however much it might frighten individuals. As I have told you, this kind of individual violence was even given up by the Russian revolutionaries.

What, then, remained? Russia had succeeded in her revolution and established a workers' republic, and her methods had been mass action backed by army support. But even in Russia the Soviets had succeeded at a time when the country and the old government had simply gone to pieces, as a result of the war, and there was little left to oppose them. Besides, few people in India knew at that time about Russia or Marxism, or even thought in terms of the workers or peasants.

So all these avenues led nowhere, and there seemed to be no way out of the intolerable conditions of a degrading servitude. People who were at all sensitive felt terribly depressed and helpless. This was the moment when Gandhi put forward his programme of non-co-operation. Like Sinn Fein in Ireland, it taught us to rely on ourselves and build up our own strength, and it was obviously a very effective method of bringing pressure on the government. The government rested very largely on the co-operation, willing or unwilling, of Indians themselves, and if this co-operation were with-drawn and the boycotts practised, it was quite possible, in theory, to bring down the whole structure of government. Even if the non-co-operation did not go so far, there was no doubt that it could exert tremendous pressure on the government, and at the same time increase the strength of the people. It was to be per-fectly peaceful, and yet it was not mere non-resistance. *Satyagraha* was a definite, though non-violent, form of resistance to what was considered wrong. It was, in effect, a peaceful rebellion, a most civilized form of warfare, and yet dangerous to the stability of the State. It was an effective way of getting the masses to function, and it seemed to fit in with the peculiar genius of the Indian people. It put us on our best behaviour and seemed to put the adversary in the wrong. It made us shed the fear that crushed us, and we began to look people in the face as we had never done before, and to speak out our minds fully and frankly. A great weight seemed to be lifted from our minds, and this new freedom of speech and action filled us with confidence and strength. And, finally, the method of peace prevented to a large extent the growth of those terribly bitter racial and national hatreds which had always so far accompanied such struggles, and thus made the ultimate settlement easier.

It is not surprising, therefore, that this programme of non-co-operation, coupled with the remarkable personality of Gandhi, caught the imagination of the country and filled it with hope. It spread, and at its approach the old demoralization vanished. The new Congress attracted most of the vital elements in the country and grew in power and prestige.

Meanwhile new councils and assemblies had been put up under the Montagu-Chelmsford scheme of reform. The Moderates, now called Liberals, had welcomed them, and had become ministers and other officials under them. They had practically merged into the government and had no popular backing. The Congress had boy-cotted these legislatures, and little attention was paid to them in the country. All eyes were turned to the real struggle outside, in the towns and villages. For the first time, large numbers of Con-gress workers had gone to the villages and established Congress committees there and helped in the political awakening of the villagers.

Matters were coming to a head and, inevitably, the clash occurred, in December 1921. The occasion for this was the visit of the Prince of Wales to India, which had been boycotted by the Con-gress. Mass arrests took place all over India, and the gaols were filled with thousands of " politicals ". Most of us had our first experience of the inside of a prison then. Even the president-elect of the Congress, Deshbandhu Chittaranjan Das, was arrested, and Hakim Ajmal Khan presided in his place at the Ahmedabad session. But Gandhi himself was not arrested then, and the movement prospered, and the number of those offering themselves for arrest always exceeded those who were arrested. As the well-known leaders and workers were removed to prison, new and inexperienced and sometimes even undesirable men (and sometimes even secret police agents!) took their place, and there was disorganization and some violence. Early in 1922 a collision occurred at Chauri Chaura near Gorakhpur in the U.P. between a crowd of peasants and the police, and this ended in the peasants burning the police station with some policemen inside it. Gandhi was greatly shocked at this and some other incidents, which showed that the movement was becoming disorganized and violent, and, at his suggestion, the Congress Executive suspended the law-breaking part of non-co-operation. Soon after this Gandhi was himself arrested, tried, and sentenced to six years' imprisonment. This was in March 1922, and thus ended the first phase of the non-co-operation movement.

161

INDIA IN THE NINETEEN-TWENTIES

May 14, 1933

THE first phase of the non-co-operation movement ended when civil disobedience was suspended in 1922, but this suspension gave great dissatisfaction to many Congressmen. There had been a great awakening, and about 30,000 civil resisters had gone to gaol. Was all this to count for nothing and the movement to be suddenly suspended in mid-career before it had achieved its object, simply because some poor excitable peasants had misbehaved? Freedom was still far off and the British Government was functioning as before. In Delhi and in the Provinces there were Legislative Councils, but with no real power; the Congress had boycotted them. Gandhi was in gaol.

There was much argument in the Congress ranks about the next step and a party, called the Swaraj Party, was formed to advocate a change in the policy of the Congress. They suggested that while the fundamental non-co-operation programme should be adhered to, it should be varied in one particular. The boycott of the Legislative Councils should be ended. This led to a split in the Congress, but ultimately the Swaraj Party had its way.

Congressmen entered the Councils and made brave speeches and refused supplies. But their resolutions and votes were ignored by the Government and the Viceroy certified the Budget, which the Assembly had thrown out. These activities of Congressmen in the Legislatures were good propaganda for a while, but they meant a lowering of the tone of the movement. They led to a divorce from the masses and to unsavoury compromises with reactionary groups.

Let us try to understand some of the different forces and movements which were stirring India in these nineteen-twenties.

Dominating almost everything else was the Hindu-Muslim question. Friction was increasing, and riots had occurred in many places in northern India over petty questions like the right of playing music before mosques. This was a strange and sudden change after the remarkable unity of the non-co-operation days. How did this occur, and what was the basis of that unity ?

The basis of the national movement was largely economic distress and unemployment. This gave rise to a common anti-British Government feeling in all groups and a vague desire for Swaraj or freedom. This feeling of hostility formed the common link, and thus there was common action, but the motives of different groups were different. Swaraj had a different meaning for each such group—the unemployed middle class looked forward to employment, the peasant to a relief from the many burdens imposed on him by the landlord, and so on. Looking at this question from the point of view of religious groups, the Muslims had joined the movement, as a body, chiefly because of the *Khilafat*. This was a purely religious question affecting Muslims only, and non-Muslims had nothing to do with it. Gandhi, however, adopted it, and encouraged others to do so, because he felt it his duty to help a brother in distress. He also hoped in this way to bring the Hindus and Muslims nearer each other. The general Muslim outlook was thus one of Muslim nationalism or Muslim internationalism, and not of true nationalism. For the moment the conflict between the two was not apparent.

On the other hand, the Hindu idea of nationalism was definitely one of Hindu nationalism. It was not easy in this case (as it was in the case of the Muslims) to draw a sharp line between this Hindu nationalism and true nationalism. The two overlapped, as India is the only home of the Hindus and they form a majority there. It was thus easier for the Hindus to appear as full-blooded nationalists than for the Muslims, although each stood for his own particular brand of nationalism.

Thirdly, there was what might be called real or Indian nationalism, which was something quite apart from these two religious and communal varieties and, strictly speaking, was the only form which could be called nationalism in the modern sense of the word. In this third group there were, of course, both Hindus and Muslims and others. All these three kinds of nationalism happened to come together from 1920 to 1922, during the non-co-operation movement. The three roads were separate, but for the moment they ran parallel.

The British Government was greatly taken aback by the mass movement of 1921. In spite of the long notice they had had, they did not know how to deal with it. The usual direct way of arrest and punishment was ineffective, as this was the very thing wanted by the Congress. So their secret service evolved a technique to weaken the Congress from within. Police agents and Secret-Service men entered Congress Committees and created trouble by encouraging violence. Another method adopted was to send secret agents as *sādhus* and *faqīrs* to create communal trouble.

Similar methods are, of course, always adopted by governments ruling against the will of the people. They are the stock-in-trade of imperialist Powers. The fact that these methods succeed indicates the weakness and backwardness of the people, and not so much the sinfulness of the government concerned. To be able to divide other people and make them clash with each other, and thus weaken them and exploit them, is in itself a sign of better organization. This policy can only succeed when there are rifts and cleavages on the other side. To say that the British Government created the Hindu-Muslim problem in India would be patently wrong, but it would be equally wrong to ignore their continuous efforts to keep it alive and to discourage the coming together of the two communities.

In 1922, after the suspension of the non-co-operation campaign, the ground was favourable for such intrigue. There was the reaction after a strenuous campaign which had suddenly ended without apparent results. The three different roads which had run parallel to each other began to diverge and go apart. The *Khilafat* question was out of the way. Communal leaders, both Hindu and Muslim, who had been suppressed by the mass enthusiasm of the non-co-operation days, rose again and began taking part in public life. The unemployed middle-class Muslims felt that the Hindus monopolized all the jobs and stood in their way. They demanded, therefore, separate treatment and separate shares in everything. Politically, the Hindu-Muslim question was essentially a middle-class affair, and a quarrel over jobs. Its effect, however, spread to the masses.

The Hindus were on the whole the better-off community. Having taken to English education earlier, they had got most of the government jobs. They were richer also. The village financier or banker was the *bania* who exploited the small landholders and tenants and gradually reduced them to beggary and himself took possession of the land. The *bania* exploited Hindu and Muslim tenants and land-holders alike, but his exploitation of the Muslims took a communal turn, especially in provinces where the agriculturists were mainly Muslim. The spread of machine-made goods probably hit the Muslims harder than the Hindus, as there were relatively more artisans among the Muslims. All these factors went to increase the bitterness between the two major communities of India and to strengthen Muslim nationalism, which looked to the community rather than to the country.

The demands of the Muslim communal leaders were such as to knock the bottom out of all hope of true national unity in India. To combat them on their own communal lines, Hindu communal organizations grew into prominence. Posing as true nationalists, they were as sectarian and narrow as the others.

The Congress, as a body, kept away from the communal organizations, but many individual Congressmen were infected. The real nationalists tried to stop this communal frenzy, but with little success; and big riots occurred.

To add to the confusion, a third type of sectional nationalism arose—Sikh nationalism. In the past the dividing line between the Sikhs and the Hindus had been rather vague. The national awakening also shook up the virile Sikhs, and they began to work for a more distinct and separate existence. Large numbers among them were ex-soldiers, and these gave a stiffening to a small but highly organized community, which, unlike most groups in India, was more used to action than to words. The bulk of them were peasant proprietors in the Punjab, and they felt themselves menaced by the town bankers and other city interests. This was the real motive behind their desire for a separate group recognition. To begin with, the *Akāli* movement, so called because the Akālis formed the active and aggressive group among the Sikhs, interested itself in religious questions, or rather in the possession of property belonging to shrines. They came into conflict with the Government over this, and an amazing exhibition of courage and endurance was seen at the Guru-ka-bagh near Amritsar. The *Akāli jathās* were beaten most brutally by the police, but they never retreated a step, nor did they raise their hands against the police. The Akālis won in the end and gained possession of their shrines. They then turned to the political field and rivalled the other communal groups in making extreme demands for themselves.

These narrow communal feelings of different communities, or group nationalisms, as I have called them, were very unfortunate. And yet they were natural enough. Non-co-operation had stirred up India thoroughly, and the first results of this shaking-up were these group-awakenings and Hindu and Muslim and Sikh nationalisms. There were also many other smaller groups which gained self-consciousness, and especially there were the so-called " Depressed Classes ". These people, long suppressed by the upper-class Hindus, were chiefly the landless labourers in the fields. It was natural that when they gained self-consciousness a desire to get rid of their many disabilities should possess them and a bitter anger against those Hindus who had for centuries oppressed them.

Each awakened group looked at nationalism and patriotism in the light of its own interests. A group or a community is always selfish, just as a nation is selfish, although individuals in the community or nation may take an unselfish view. So each group wanted far more than its share and, inevitably, there was conflict. As intercommunal bitterness increased, the more extreme communal leaders of each group came to the front, for, in moments of anger, each group chooses as its representative the person who pitches his group demands highest and curses the others most. The conflict was aggravated in a variety of ways by the Government, especially by their encouraging the more-extreme communal leaders. So the poison went on spreading, and we seemed to be in a vicious circle from which there was no obvious way out.

While these forces and disruptive tendencies were taking shape in India, Gandhi fell very ill in Yarvada prison and had to undergo an operation. He was discharged from prison early in 1924. He was greatly distressed by the communal troubles and, many months later, a big riot shocked him so much that he fasted for twenty-one days. Many " unity " conferences were held to bring about peace, but with little result.

The effect of these communal wranglings and group nationalisms was to weaken the Congress as well as the *Swaraj* Party in the Councils. The ideal of *Swaraj* went into the background, as most people thought and talked in terms of their groups. The Congress, trying to avoid siding with any group, was attacked by communalists on every side. The principal work of the Congress during these days was one of quiet organization and cottage industries (*khaddar*), etc., and this helped it to keep in touch with the peasant masses.

I have written at some length about our communal troubles. because they played an important part in our political life during the nineteen-twenties. And yet we must not exaggerate them. There is a tendency to give them far more importance than they deserve, and every quarrel between a Hindu boy and a Muslim boy is considered a communal quarrel, and every petty riot is given great publicity. We must remember that India is a very big country, and in tens of thousands of towns and villages Hindus and Muslims live at peace with each other, and there is no communal trouble between them. Usually this kind of trouble is confined to a limited number of cities, though sometimes it has spread to the villages. It must also be remembered that the communal question is essentially a middle-class question in India, and because our politics are dominated by the middle classes—in the Congress, in the Councils, in newspapers, and in almost every other form of activity—it assumes an undue prominence. The peasantry are hardly articulate; they have only begun to function politically in recent years in the village Congress Committees and in some *Kisān Sabhās* and the like. The town workers, especially in the big factories, are a little more wide awake, and have organized themselves into trade unions. But even these industrial workers, and far more so the peasantry, look for leadership to individuals drawn from the middle classes. Let us now consider the condition of the masses, the peasantry and industrial labour, during this period.

The rapid growth of Indian industry, which the war had brought about, continued for some years after the peace. British capital poured into India and a great number of new companies were registered to work new factories and industries. The larger industrial concerns and factories especially were financed by foreign capital, and thus big-scale industry was practically controlled by British capitalists. A few years ago it was estimated that 87 per cent. of the capital of companies working in India was British, and probably even this is an under-estimate. Thus the real economic hold of Britain over India increased. Big towns grew up, at the expense of smaller towns, and not of the villages. The textile industry grew especially, and so also mining.

There were many committees and commissions appointed by the Government to consider the new problems of growing industrialization. These recommended that foreign capital should be encouraged, and generally favoured British industrial interests in India. A Tariff Board was appointed protecting Indian industries. But this protection meant, as I have told you, protecting in many cases British capital in India. The price of these protected goods naturally rose in the markets, and this helped in raising to that extent the cost of living. So that the burden of protection fell on the masses or the purchasers of these goods, and the factory-owners got a sheltered market from which competition had been removed or lessened.

With the growth of factories, there was naturally a growth in the numbers of the industrial wage-earning class. The Government estimate, as long ago as 1922, was that there were as many as 20,000,000 in this class in India. The landless unemployed of the rural areas drifted to the industrial towns to join this class, and they had to put up as a rule with shameful conditions of exploitation. Conditions which had existed in England 100 years earlier, in the beginnings of the factory system, were now found in India— terrible long hours of work, miserable wages, degrading and insanitary living conditions. The class of factory-owners had one end in view : to make the most of the boom period by piling up profits; and they did so with great success for some years, paying huge dividends, while the condition of the workers remained miserable. The workers had no share in these mighty profits which they had created, but later, when the boom period was followed by a slump and trade declined, the workers were asked to share in the common misfortune by accepting lower wages.

As the workers' organizations, the trade unions, grew, the agitation for better labour conditions, shorter hours of work, and higher wages grew with them. Influenced by this partly, and partly by the general world demand that labour should be treated better, the government passed a number of laws, improving the lot of the factory-worker. I have told you already, in a previous letter, of the Factory Act that was passed. In this it was laid down that children from twelve to fifteen should not work more than six hours a day. There was to be no night work for women and children. For grown-up men and women a maximum of eleven hours a day, and sixty hours a week (a working week consisting of six days) was fixed. This factory law, with some subsequent amendments, still holds.

An Indian Mines Act was passed in 1923 to give some protection to the unhappy workers who have to labour in the mines, chiefly coal-mines, underground. Children under thirteen were prohibited from working underground, but women continued doing so, and indeed formed nearly half the total number of workers. For grown-ups the maximum of work fixed for a week of six days was : for above-ground work, sixty, and for underground work, fifty-four. The maximum hours for a day are, I think, twelve hours. I am giving you these figures of hours of work to give you some idea of labour conditions. Even with their help you can have only a very partial idea, for in addition you must also know many other things, like the amount of wages, living conditions, etc., before a real idea is formed. We cannot go into such matters here. But it is something to realize how boys and girls and men and women have to work as long as eleven hours a day in the factories for a paltry wage which just keeps them alive. The kind of monotonous work they do in the factories is terribly depressing; there is no joy in it; and when they go home, dead tired, a whole family has usually to crowd into a small mud hovel with no sanitary conveniences.

Some other laws were also passed which were of help to the workers. There was a Workmen's Compensation Act in 1923, which laid down that in case of accidents, etc., some compensation had to be paid to the injured worker. And there was a Trade Union Act in 1926, dealing with the formation and recognition of trade unions. The trade-union movement grew in India with some rapidity during these days, especially in Bombay. An All-India Trade-Union Congress was formed, but after a few years of existence this split up into two groups. All over the world, ever since the war and the Russian Revolution, labour has been pulled in two different directions. There are the old orthodox and moderate trade unions attached to the Second International (about which I have told you previously), and there is the new and powerful attraction of Soviet Russia and the Third International. So, everywhere, the moderate and usually better-off factory-workers incline towards safety and the Second International, and the more revolutionary towards the Third. This pull took place in India also, and at the end of 1929 there was a split. Ever since then the labour movement in India has been weak.

Of the peasantry I cannot add much here to what I have already written in previous letters. Their condition worsens, and they are getting more and more hopelessly involved in debt to the money-lender. The smaller landlords, the peasant proprietors and the tenants, all get caught in the clutches of the money-lender, the *bania*, the *sāhūkār*. Gradually, as the debt cannot be paid up, the land passes to this money-lender, and the tenant becomes doubly his serf, both as the landlord and as the *sāhūkār*. Usually this *bania* landlord resides in the city, and there are no intimate contacts between him and his tenantry. His continuous attempts are directed to getting as much money as is possible from the starving peasantry. The old *zamindar*, living in the midst of his tenantry, might have shown some pity occasionally; the banker-*zamindar*, living in the city and sending agents for collections, hardly ever shows this weakness.

Various official estimates of the debts of the agricultural classes have been made by Government committees. In 1930 it was estimated that the total indebtedness of these classes in the whole of India (excluding Burma) amounted to the prodigious figure of 8,030,000,000 rupees. This includes the debts of both landlords and cultivators. This figure went up greatly during the years of economic slump and later.

Thus the agricultural classes, the smaller *zamindars* and tenants alike, are sinking deeper and deeper into the morass, and there is no way out except a radical way which would cut at the root of the present land system. Taxation is so arranged that the greatest burden of it falls on the class which is the poorest and the least able to bear it. Expenditure goes largely to the army, to the civil services and to other British charges, from which the masses do not benefit. The expenditure on education is about ninepence per head, as compared with £2 15s. per head in Britain; thus the British rate of educational expenditure is 73⅓ times the Indian.

Attempts have often been made in the past to estimate the national income per head of population in India. This is a difficult matter, and estimates vary greatly. Dadabhai Naoroji calculated it in 1870 as Rs. 20 per head. Recent estimates have gone up to Rs. 67, and even the most favourable, made by some Englishmen, do not go beyond Rs. 116. It is interesting to compare this with other countries. In the United States of America the corresponding figure is Rs. 1,925, and even this has been greatly exceeded since; in Britain it is Rs. 1,000 per head.[1]

162

PEACEFUL REBELLION IN INDIA

May 17, 1933

I HAVE written many letters to you about India and her past—far more than about any other country. But the past is now merging into the present, and this letter that I am beginning will, I hope, bring up the story to the India of to-day. I shall refer to some recent happenings which are fresh in our minds. The time for writing about them is not yet, for the tale is but half told. But all history ends rather abruptly in the present, and the remaining chapters of the story remain hidden in the future. And indeed the story has no ending; it goes on and on.

Towards the end of 1927 the British Government announced that they would send a commission to India to make inquiries about future reforms and changes in the structure of government. This announcement was received by all political India with anger and condemnation. The Congress objected to it because it resented the idea that India should be periodically examined for her fitness of self-government. This was the phrase used by the British to cover their desire to hold on to the country as long as possible. The Congress had long claimed for the country the right of self-determination, which had been so much advertised by the Allies during the World War, and it refused to admit the right of the British Parliament to dictate to India or to be the final arbiter of her future

[1] A rupee, at the present rate of exchange, is equal to one shilling and sixpence.

destiny.   On these grounds the Congress objected to the new parliamentary commission.   The moderate groups in India objected to the
commission on other grounds, chiefly because there was no Indian
member of it.   It was a purely British commission.   Although the
grounds of objection were different, the fact remains that almost
every group in India, including the most moderate, joined together
in condemning it and in advocating its boycott.

About that time, in December 1927, the Congress met in annual
session in Madras, and resolved that its goal was national independence for India.   This was the first time that the Congress had
declared for independence.   Two years later, in Lahore, independence became definitely the creed of the National Congress.
The Madras Congress also created the All-Parties Conference which
had a brief but active career.

The next year, 1928, saw the British commission in India.   As I
have said, it was generally boycotted, and there were big demonstrations against it wherever it went.   The Simon Commission it was
called, from the name of its chairman, and " *Simon go back* " became
a familiar cry all over India.   On many occasions the police indulged
in *lathi* charges on the demonstrators; in Lahore even Lala Lajpat
Rai was beaten by the police.   Some months later Lalaji died, and
it was considered probable by doctors that the police beating had
hastened his death.   All this naturally created great excitement
and anger in the country.

Meanwhile, the All-Parties Conference was trying to draw up a
constitution and to find a solution for the communal tangle.   It
produced a report containing proposals for a constitution and the
communal question.   This report is known as the *Nehru Report*, as
Pandit Motilal Nehru was the chairman of the committee which
drafted it.

Another notable event of the year was a great peasant campaign
at Bardoli in Gujrat against the increase in the revenue assessment
by the Government.   Gujrat has no big *zamindārī* system, as in the
United Provinces; there are peasant proprietors there.   Under the
leadership of Sardar Vallabhbhai Patel, these peasants put up a
remarkably gallant fight and won a great victory.

The Calcutta Congress of December 1928 adopted the Nehru
Report, which recommended a constitution similar to that of the
British Dominions.   But even in adopting it, the Congress did so
provisionally, and fixed a time-limit of one year.   If there were no
agreement with the British Government on this basis within a year,
than the Congress was to revert to independence.   Thus the Congress and the country were inevitably heading towards a crisis.

Labour also was very restive, and in some of the big industrial
centres was becoming aggressive as attempts were made to reduce
wages.   In Bombay it was particularly well organized, and great
strikes took place in which 100,000 or more workers took part.
Socialistic, and to some extent communistic, ideas began to spread
among the workers, and the Government, frightened by the revolutionary development, and by labour's growing strength, suddenly

arrested thirty-two labour leaders early in 1929 and started a big conspiracy case against them. This case became famous all over the world as the Meerut case. After a trial lasting nearly four years almost all the accused were sentenced to prodigious terms of imprisonment. And the curious part of it was that none of them was charged with any actual act of rebellion or even breach of the peace. Their offence seems to have been the holding of and the attempt to spread certain opinions. These sentences were greatly reduced on appeal.

Another form of activity, smouldering underneath and sometimes appearing on the surface, was that of the people believing in violent methods to bring about a revolution. This was chiefly in Bengal, to some extent in the Punjab, and a little in the United Provinces. The British Government tried to suppress it in many ways and there were numerous conspiracy cases. A special law, called the " Bengal Ordinance ", was issued by the Government to enable them to arrest and keep in prison without trial any one they chose to suspect. Under this ordinance many hundreds of Bengali youths were arrested and imprisoned; "detenus" they were called, and there was no time-limit to the period of their imprisonment. It is interesting to note that when this extraordinary ordinance was issued a Labour Government was in office in England, and was thus responsible for the ordinance.

There were a number of acts of terrorism by these revolutionaries, most of them in Bengal. Three events, however, attracted special attention. One was the shooting of a British police officer in Lahore, who was supposed to have hit Lala Lajpat Rai at the demonstration against the Simon Commission. The second was the throwing of a bomb in the Assembly building in Delhi by Bhagat Singh and Batukeshwara Dutt. This bomb, however, did little damage and seems to have been meant merely to create a big noise and attract the country's attention. The third occurrence was in Chittagong in 1930 just about the time when the Civil Disobedience movement was beginning. It was a daring and big-scale raid on the armoury, and it met with some success. The government adopted every conceivable device to crush this movement. There were spies and informers and large numbers of arrests and conspiracy cases, and detenus (sometimes people, acquitted in a court of law, were immediately re-arrested and kept as detenus under the Ordinance), and parts of East Bengal were under military occupation, and people could not move without permits, nor could they go on bicycles, or even wear any dress they chose. There were heavy fines on whole towns and villages for the offence of not giving information to the police.

In one of the conspiracy cases in Lahore in 1929 one of the prisoners, Jatindranath Das, went on hunger strike as a protest against gaol treatment. This boy stuck to it to the very end, and died of it on the sixty-first day. Jatin Das's self-immolation deeply affected India. Another event that shocked and pained the country was the execution of Bhagat Singh early in 1931.

I must go back to Congress politics now. The year of grace fixed by the Calcutta Congress was expiring. Towards the end of 1929 the British Government made an effort to prevent the serious developments which were in the air. It made a vague declaration about future progress. Even then the Congress offered its co-operation, subject to certain conditions. These conditions not being fulfilled, the Lahore Congress of December 1929 inevitably decided in favour of independence and a struggle to attain it.

So 1930 opened with the air dark with the shadow of coming events. There were preparations for Civil Disobedience. The Assembly and Councils were boycotted again and Congress members resigned from them. On January 26, a special pledge of independence was taken all over the country at innumerable gatherings in the cities and villages, and the anniversary of that day is celebrated annually as Independence Day. In March began Gandhi's famous march to Dandi on the sea coast to break the salt law there. He had chosen the salt tax to initiate his campaign, because this tax fell heavily on the poor, and was thus an especially bad tax.

By the middle of April 1930 the Civil Disobedience campaign was in full swing; and not only was the salt law violated everywhere, but other laws also. There was peaceful rebellion all over the country, and new laws and ordinances came in rapid succession in order to crush it. But these very ordinances became the objects of Civil Disobedience. There were mass arrests, and brutal *lathi* charges became frequent occurrences, and firing at peaceful crowds, and a proscription of Congress committees, and gagging of the Press, and censorship, and beatings, and harsh gaol treatment. There was ordinance rule on the one side, and a determined and systematic breach of these ordinances on the other, as well as a boycott of foreign cloth and British goods. Nearly 100,000 persons went to prison, and for a while this peaceful and yet determined struggle in India held the world's attention.

Three facts I should like to bring to your notice. The first was the remarkble political awakening of the North-West Frontier Province. Right at the beginning of the struggle, in April 1930 there was a tremendous shooting down of peaceful crowds in Peshawar, and right through the year our frontier countrymen endured an amazing amount of brutal treatment with gallant fortitude. This was doubly remarkable, as the frontier people are very far from being peaceful and they flare up at the slightest provocation. And yet they held their peace. It was surprising, and most creditable, for newcomers to the political field, like the Pathans, to come immediately to the forefront and play such a brave part.

The second noteworthy fact, and certainly the most outstanding event of a great year, was the remarkable awakening of Indian women. The way hundreds of thousands of them shed their veils and, leaving their sheltered homes, came into the street and the marketplace to fight side by side in the struggle with their brothers, and often put to shame their menfolk, was something that could hardly be believed by those who did not see it.

The third fact worth noting was that, as the movement developed, economic factors came into play so far as the peasantry were concerned. The year 1930 was the first year of a great world crisis, and prices of agricultural produce fell greatly. The peasantry were hard hit by this, as their income depends on their selling their produce. The non-payment of taxes, therefore, fitted in with their distress, and *Swaraj* became for them not just a distant political goal but, what was more important, an immediate economic question. Thus the movement began to have a new and a more intimate meaning for them, and an element of class conflict, as between landlords and tenants, came in. This was so especially in the United Provinces and in western India.

While Civil Disobedience was flourishing in India, across the seas in London a Round Table Conference was held by the British Government with much pomp and circumstance. The Congress had nothing to do with it. The Indians who went to it were all Government nominees. Like marionettes, or shadow figures without substance, they flitted about that London stage, well realizing that the real struggle was taking place in India. The Government kept the communal problem in the forefront of the discussions to show up the weaknesses of the Indians ; they had taken care to nominate the most extreme communalists and reactionaries to the conference, so that there was no chance whatever of a settlement.

In March 1931 there came a truce or a provisional settlement between the Congress and the Government to enable further discussions to take place. The Gandhi-Irwin Pact this was called. Civil Disobedience was discontinued and thousands of Civil-Disobedience prisoners were released and the ordinances were withdrawn.

The year 1931 saw Gandhi attend the second Round Table Conference in London on behalf of the Congress. In India itself three problems assumed importance and held the attention both of the Congress and the Government. The first was Bengal, where the Government carried on a severe campaign against political workers under the guise of putting down terrorism. A new and far stiffer ordinance was issued, and Bengal knew no peace in spite of the Delhi settlement.

The second problem was in the Frontier Province, where the political awakening was still driving the people to action. Under the leadership of Khan Abdul Ghaffar Khan, a huge, disciplined but peaceful organization was spreading. The *Khudāi Khidmatgār* they were called, and sometimes "Red-shirts ", because they wore a red uniform (and not because of any affiliation with socialists or communists). Government did not like this movement at all. It was afraid of it, as it knew the worth of a good Pathan fighter.

The third problem arose in the United Provinces. The poor tenant had been very hard hit by the world depression and the fall in prices. He could not pay his rent. Some remissions were given to him, but they were not considered enough. The Congress tried to mediate for him, without much result. Matters came to a head when the time for rent collections came in November 1931. The Congress, beginning with Allahabad district, advised the tenants as well as the *zamindars* to withhold the payment of rent and revenue pending a settlement of the question of remissions. Forthwith the Government countered this by an ordinance for the United Provinces. It was a very stiff and comprehensive ordinance, giving full powers to the district officials to crush every kind of activity, and even to prevent the movements of individuals.

Close on the heels of this came two amazing ordinances for the Frontier Province, and both there and in the U.P. arrests of leading Congress-men took place.

Such was the position that faced Gandhi when he returned, without success, from London in the last week of the year. Three provinces under ordinance rule and several of his colleagues already in prison. Within a week the Congress had declared Civil Disobedience again and the Government, on its part, had outlawed thousands of Congress committees and a host of allied organizations.

This struggle was far stiffer than the one of 1930. The Government prepared themselves carefully for it, profiting by previous experience. The veil of legality and the forms of law were set aside and, under all-embracing ordinances, a kind of martial law under civil officers prevailed over the country. The real brute force of the State was very much in evidence. This was a natural development, for the more powerful grows the nationalist movement, and the more it threatens the very basis of the foreign Government, the fiercer becomes the latter's resistance. The pious phrases of trusteeship and goodwill are put aside, and the bludgeon and the bayonet appear as the real props of foreign rule. Law becomes the will not only of the Viceroy at the top, but of each petty official, who can do what he wills, well knowing that he will be supported by his superiors. The Secret Service and the C.I.D. especially spread out everywhere, as in the Russia of Tsarist days, and grow in power. There are no checks, and the appetite for unrestrained power grows with use. A government which governs chiefly through its Secret Service, and a country which suffers under this, are soon demoralized. For every Secret Service luxuriates in an atmosphere of intrigue, spies, lies, terrorism, provocation, frame-ups, blackmail and the like. During the last three years in India the excessive powers given to petty officials and the police and the C.I.D. and the use made of them have resulted in a progressive brutalization and deterioration of these services. The object aimed at was terrorization.

I must not go into details. One interesting feature of the Government's policy on this occasion was a widespread confiscation of property, houses, motor-cars, moneys in banks, etc., both of organizations and individuals. This was meant to strike at the middle-class supporters of the Congress. A minor but striking feature of one of the ordinances was that parents and guardians were to be punished for the offences of their children or wards !

While all this was taking place, the British propaganda machine was busy in painting a rosy picture of India. In India itself no newspaper dared to print the truth for fear of consequences—even the publication of the names of persons arrested was an offence.

But the most revealing feature of British policy in India has been its attempt to form an alliance with all the most reactionary elements in India. The British Empire stands to-day relying on feudal and other extreme forces of reaction in its attempt to fight the forces of progress. They have tried to rally " vested interests " to their support, frightening them with fear of social revolution if the British authority were removed from India. The feudal princes are the first line of defence; then come the big *zamindar* classes. By clever manœuvring and pushing the extreme communalists to the front, the problem of minorities has been made a barrier to Indian freedom. Recently, the remarkable sight was witnessed of the British Government expressing every sympathy and cordiality with the extreme religious reactionaries among the Hindus over the temple entry question. Everywhere the British seek their support in reaction and narrow bigotry and a misguided self-interest.

A mass struggle has one great advantage. It is the best and swiftest method, though perhaps a painful one, of giving political education to the masses. For the masses need the " schooling of big events ". Ordinary peace-time political activity, such as elections in democratic countries, often confuses the average person. There is a deluge of oratory, and every candidate promises all manner of fine things, and the poor voter, or the man in the field or factory or shop, is confused. There are no very clear lines of cleavage for him between one group and another. But when a mass struggle comes, or in time of revolution, the real position stands out clearly, as if lit up by lightning. In such moments of crisis, groups or classes or individuals cannot hide their real feelings or character. Truth will out. Not only is a time of revolution a test of character, of courage, endurance, and selflessness, it also brings out the real conflicts between different classes and groups, which had so far been covered up by fine and vague phrases.

Civil Disobedience in India has been a national struggle; it has certainly not been a class struggle. It has definitely been a middle-class movement with peasant backing. It could not therefore separate the classes as a class movement would have done. And yet even in this national movement there was to some extent a lining up of classes. Some of these, like the feudal princes, the *taluqadars* and big *zamindars*, aligned themselves completely with the government, preferring their class interest to national freedom.

The growth of the national movement, under the leadership of the Congress, resulted in the peasant masses joining the Congress and looking to it for relief from their many burdens. This increased the power of the Congress greatly and at the same time it gave it a mass outlook. While the leadership remained middle class, this was tempered by pressure from below, and agrarian and social problems occupied the Congress more and more. A gradual leaning towards socialism also developed. This was evidenced by an important resolution on fundamental rights and economic programme, which was passed by the Karachi Congress in 1931. This resolution laid down that the constitution should guarantee certain well-recognized democratic rights and liberties as well as the rights of minorities. It further stated that key and basic industries and services should be State-controlled. The struggle for independence began to mean something much more than political freedom, and a social content was given to it. The real question became one of ending the poverty and exploitation of the masses, and independence was a means to this end.

While the Civil Disobedience struggle was going on in India and vast numbers of political workers were in prison, the British Government put forward their proposals for Indian constitutional reform. A restricted form of provincial autonomy was suggested and a Federation in which the feudal princes would have a dominating voice. Every conceivable safeguard that the wit of man could devise was proposed by the Government, not only to hold on to their interests, but to strengthen their threefold occupations of India—military, civil, and commercial. Every vested interest was fully protected, and the most important, that of Britain, was most effectively safeguarded. Only the interests of the three hundred and fifty odd millions of India seemed to have been overlooked. These proposals met with a storm of opposition in India.

I have neglected Burma, and must tell you something about her. The Burmese people did not take part in the Civil Disobedience movements of 1930 or 1932. But in 1930 and 1931 there was a great peasant revolt in North Burma due to great economic distress. This revolt was put down with considerable barbarity by the British Government. Attempts are now being made to separate Burma from India politically, so that, in the event of India gaining freedom, Burma might continue to be exploited by British imperialism. Burma has considerable importance because of her oil and timber and mineral resources.

Note (*October* 1938):

Since this letter was written, five and a half years ago in prison, many changes have taken place in India. At that time the Civil Disobedience movement was still being carried on, though in an attenuated form, and large numbers of Congress-men were in gaol. The Congress itself, with its thousands of committees and allied organizations, had been declared illegal. In 1934 Civil Disobedience was stopped by the Congress and the Government withdrew the ban against the Congress. The old policy of boycotting the legislatures was varied by the Congress and elections to the Central Assembly were contested with considerable success.

In 1935, after long debate, the British Parliament passed the Government of India Act, which laid down a new constitution for India. According to this, there was a measure of provincial autonomy, with numerous safeguards, and a federation between the Provinces and the Indian States. The Act met with widespread opposition in India, and the Congress rejected it. The safeguards and " special powers " in the hands of the Governors and the

Viceroy were especially objected to as taking the substance out of provincial autonomy; the Federation was even more strongly opposed, as this perpetuated the autocratic régime in the States and brought about an unnatural and unworkable union between feudal and autocratic units and the semi-democratic provinces. It was looked upon as a deliberate attempt to smother the political and social progress of India and to strengthen the hold of British Imperialism, both directly and through the feudal princes. A communal arrangement was also made a part of the new constitution which created numerous separate electorates. This was welcomed by some minorities, which profited to some extent by it, but was condemned on the ground of being anti-democratic and a barrier to progress.

The part of the Government of India Act dealing with Provincial Autonomy was applied early in 1937, and general elections were held all over India in accordance with it. The Congress, although rejecting the Act, decided to participate in these elections, and a very vigorous and widespread election campaign was conducted throughout the country. In the great majority of provinces the Congress had overwhelming success, and Congress-men formed the majority party in most of the new provincial legislatures. The question whether they should accept office as ministers in the Provincial Governments or not was hotly debated. Ultimately the Congress decided to accept office, but it made it clear that the old objective of independence and the old policy remained, and office was to be accepted to further that policy and to strengthen the country in its struggle for independence. Further, it laid down that the safeguards should not be used by the Governors.

As a result of this decision, Congress ministries were formed in seven provinces : Bombay, Madras, United Provinces, Bihar, Central Provinces, Orissa, and the North-West Frontier Province. A coalition ministry was formed some time later by the Congress in Assam. The two principal provinces where there were non-Congress ministries were Bengal and the Punjab.

The formation of Congress Ministries led to the release of political prisoners and the removal of restrictions on civil liberties in those areas. The masses welcomed the change and looked forward expectantly to a rapid improvement in their condition. Political consciousness among the people increased rapidly and agrarian and workers' movements gathered momentum. There were many strikes. The ministries immediately undertook agrarian and debt legislation to lighten the burden on the peasantry, and tried to better the condition of the industrial workers. Something was done but, circumstanced as they were and working within the limitations of the Act, no far-reaching social changes could be attempted.

There were frequent conflicts between the Congress Ministers and the Governors, and on two occasions the ministers offered their resignations. An acceptance of these resignations would have led to a major clash between the Congress and the British Government.

This was not desired by the latter, and the view-point of the ministers prevailed. The situation is, however, essentially unstable and conflicts are inevitable. For the Congress this is a passing phase and the objective remains independence.

A major conflict may be precipitated by an attempt on the part of the British Government to impose Federation. This has so far not been done because of the strong opposition to it. The Congress to-day is more powerful than at any previous period of its existence and it cannot be ignored. It is determined not to submit to the proposed Federation. The Congress demand is for a Constituent Assembly, elected by adult franchise, which would frame a constitution for a free India.

The communal problem has again assumed importance in India and has caused friction. There is a tendency, however, for economic and social questions to come to the forefront and to divert attention from communal and religious cleavages.

The mass awakening in India has spread to the Indian States, and powerful movements are growing in many States demanding responsible government. This has been notably so in Mysore, Kashmir, and Travancore among the major states. These demands have been met, especially in Travancore recently, by brutal suppression and violence on the part of the State authorities. In many of these semi-feudal states (such as Kashmir), the administration is controlled by British officials.

During the last few years India has taken a growing interest in international affairs and has sought to see its own problem in relation to the world problem. The events in Abyssinia, Spain, China, Czechoslovakia, and Palestine have moved the people of India deeply, and the Congress is beginning to develop a foreign policy. This policy is one of peace and of support of democracy. It is equally opposed to imperialism and fascism.

Burma was separated from India in 1937. It has been given a legislative assembly which is similar to the provincial assemblies in India.

163

EGYPT'S FIGHT FOR FREEDOM

May 20, 1933

LET us now go to Egypt and follow another struggle between a growing nationalism and an imperialist Power. The Power there, as in India, is Britain. Egypt is, in many ways, very different from India, and Britain has been there for a comparatively short period, and yet there are numerous parallels and common features in the two countries. The nationalist movements of India and Egypt have adopted different methods, but, fundamentally, the urge to national freedom is the same and the objective is the same. And the way imperialism functions in its efforts to suppress these nationalist movements is also much the same. So each of us can learn much from the other's experiences. For us in India there is an especial lesson, for we can see, in the example of Egypt, what British grants of " freedom " amount to, and what they lead to.

Of all the Arab countries (Arabia, Iraq, Syria, Palestine), Egypt is the most advanced. It has been the highway between East and West, the great trade route for steamships ever since the building of the Suez Canal. With the new Europe of the nineteenth century it has had far more contacts than any of the countries of western Asia. It forms a very distinct national unit, quite separate from the other Arab countries, but with the closest cultural ties with them, for they all have the same language, traditions, and religion. The daily newspapers of Cairo go to all the Arab countries and have great influence there. Among all these countries the nationalist movement first took shape in Egypt, and it was thus natural for Egyptian nationalism to become a model for the other Arab countries.

I have told you, in my last letter on Egypt, about the nationalist movement of 1881–2 headed by Arabi Pasha and how this was crushed by Britain. I have also told you of the early reformers, of Jemal-ud-din Afghani, and of the impact of the new ideas from the West on orthodox Islam. These reformers tried to harmonize Islam with modern progress by going back to old principles and discarding many of the accretions of religion, the many things that get added on to it in the course of centuries. The next step among progressive people was to separate religion from social institutions. The old religions have a way of covering and regulating every aspect of our day-to-day lives. Thus Hinduism and Islam, quite apart from their purely religious teachings, lay down social codes and rules about marriage, inheritance, civil and criminal law, political organization, and indeed almost everything else. In other words, they lay down a complete structure for society and try to perpetuate this by giving it religious sanction and authority. Hinduism has gone farthest in this respect by its rigid system of caste. This religious perpetuation of a social structure makes change difficult. So in Egypt, as elsewhere, progressive people tried to separate religion from the social structure and institutions. The reason they gave was that these old institutions, which religion or custom had imposed on the people in the past, were no doubt proper and suitable for the conditions that prevailed at the time of the Scriptures. But these conditions had greatly changed now, and the old institutions did not fit in with them. Ordinary common sense tells us that a rule made for a bullock-cart would not suit a motor car or a railway train.

Such was the argument used by these progressives and reformers. This led to increasing secularization of the State and of many institutions—that is to say, they were separated from religion. This process went farthest, as we have seen, in Turkey. The President of the Turkish Republic does not even take his oath of office in the name of God ; he takes it on his honour. Matters have not developed to this extent in Egypt, but the same tendency is at work there and in other Islamic countries. The Turks, Egyptians, Syrians, Persians, etc., speak to-day far more in the new language of nationalism than in the old one of religion. Probably the Muslims of India have resisted this nationalizing process more than any other large group of Muslims in the world, and they are thus far more conservative and religious-minded than their co-religionists of the Islamic countries. This is a curious and striking fact. The new nationalism has usually gone hand in hand with the development of the *bourgeoisie*, the middle classes under the capitalist economic system. The Muslims in India have been backward in developing this *bourgeoisie*, and this failure may have obstructed their march towards nationalism. It is also possible that the fact of being a minority community in India has so worked on their fears as to make them more conservative and tied to old tradition, and suspicious of new-fangled notions and ideas. It must have been some such psychology which made the Hindus draw into their shells and become a very rigid caste-bound community when the early Islamic invasions took place, nearly 1000 years ago.

The new middle class grew in Egypt, with the growth of foreign trade, during the last quarter of the nineteenth century and afterwards. A member of this class, having risen to it from a *fellah* or peasant family, was Saad Zaghlul. He was a young man when Arabi Pasha challenged the British in 1881–2, and he served under Arabi. From that time onwards until his death in 1927, for forty-five years he worked for Egyptian freedom, and became the leader of the Egyptian independence movement. He was Egypt's unquestioned leader, beloved of the peasantry from which he had sprung, and idolized by the middle classes to which he belonged. But the so-called aristocracy, the old feudal landlord class, did not take to him kindly. They did not like the rising middle class, which was gradually pushing them away from their dominant position in the country. Zaghlul was an upstart in their eyes, and he had to struggle against them as a leader and representative of his own class. As in India, the British tried to find support for themselves in this feudal landowning class. This class was really more Turkish than Egyptian, and represented the old governing nobility.

Thus the British in Egypt, in the approved and well-tried fashion of imperialism, tried to attach to themselves some social group or political section, and obstructed the development of a single nationality by setting one class or section against another. As in India, they tried to raise a minority question, the Christian Copts forming a minority in Egypt, but in this they failed. And all this they did, also in the approved fashion, with pious phrases on their lips and pleas that everything that they did was for the benefit of the other party; they were the " trustees " of the " dumb millions ", and all would be well if " agitators " and such-like people with " no stake in the country " would not create trouble. Incidentally, this process of conferring benefits often resolved itself into shooting down large numbers of the people benefited. Perhaps in this way they were made to escape the miseries of this world, and their departure for paradise was hastened.

Egypt had been under martial law right through the war and for long afterwards. During war-time a Disarmament Act had been passed and a Conscription Act. The country was full of British troops. It had been declared a British protectorate at the beginning of the war.

With the coming of peace in 1918 the nationalists in Egypt became active again, and drew up Egypt's case for independence to place before the British Government as well as before the Peace Conference in Paris. There were no real parties in Egypt then. One national Party, called the *Watanists*, existed with a small membership. It was proposed to send a big deputation under Saad Zaghlul Pasha to London and Paris to plead for Egypt's independence, and in order to make this deputation a national one with strong backing, a widespread organization was set up. This was the origin of the great *Wafd* party of Egypt, for *wafd* means deputation. The British Government refused to permit this deputation to go to London, and, in March 1919, arrested Zaghlul and other leaders.

This resulted in the outbreak of a bloody revolution. Some British people were killed, and the city of Cairo and other centres passed into the hands of the revolutionary committee. Nationalist Committees of Public Safety were formed in many places. The university students took a great part in this rebellion. After these initial successes, however, the rebellion was to a large extent suppressed, though occasionally English officials were killed. But though the active insurrection was suppressed, the movement was far from being crushed, It changed its tactics and entered upon a second phase—that of passive resistance. So successful was this that the British Government were forced to take some steps to meet the Egyptian demand. A commission was sent from England under Lord Milner. The Egyptian nationalists decided to boycott this commission, and they did so with remarkable success. Again the students played an important part in the boycott of the Milner Commission. The Commission were so impressed by the national resistance that they made some far-reaching recommendations. The British Government ignored these, and the struggle in Egypt continued for three years, from early in 1919 to early in 1922. The Egyptians would agree to nothing short of complete independence—*istiqlāl el-tām*.

Zaghlul Pasha had been released some time after his arrest in 1919. In December 1921 he was again arrested, and was deported. But this did not improve the situation in Egypt from the point of view of the British, and they were compelled to take some action to conciliate the Egyptians. All attempts at compromise had failed, although Zaghlul was far from being an uncompromising extremist. Indeed, an actual attempt at assassinating Zaghlul was made once by some people who accused him of betraying his country by trying to make weak compromises with the British. But the real reasons for the failure of the British Government and the Egyptian nationalists to agree were then, and still continue to be, fundamental. They are similar to the reasons which prevent a compromise in India. The Egyptian nationalists did not wish to ignore all British interests in Egypt. They were perfectly prepared to discuss these and to make allowances for Britain's special interest in her imperial trade and strategic routes and other matters, but they would discuss these questions only after their full independence was acknowledged and without prejudice to that independence. England, on the other hand, thought that it was her business to say exactly how much freedom was to be given, and this freedom was to be subject to her own interests, which must first be protected.

So there was no common ground for agreement. But the British Government felt that something had to be done soon, and so, even without an agreement, they made a declaration on February 28, 1922. They stated that in future they would recognize Egypt as an "independent sovereign State", but—and this was a big but—four matters were reserved for further consideration. These were :

1. Security of the communications of the British Empire in Egypt.
2. Defence of Egypt against all foreign aggression or interference, direct or indirect.
3. Protection of foreign interests in Egypt and the protection of minorities.
4. The question of the future of the Sudan.

These reservations bear a family likeness to their cousins in India; we call them "safeguards", and their brood is far more numerous here. These reservations were not accepted, for, simple and innocent as they looked, they meant that there would be no real independence either in domestic or foreign matters. So that the declaration of independence of February 28, 1922, was a one-sided act of the British Government which was not recognized by Egypt. What even independence can mean with reservations or safeguards in favour of Britain has been amply demonstrated in Egypt during the years that followed.

In spite of this " independence ", martial law under British officers continued for a year and a half more. It was only ended after the Egyptian Government had passed an Act of Indemnity—that is to say, a law freeing all officials from all liabilities for illegal acts committed by them during the martial law period.

The new "independent" Egypt was presented with a most reactionary constitution with great powers in the hands of the King —King Fuad, who was imposed on the poor Egyptians. King Fuad and the British officials got on excellently together; they both disliked the nationalists, and they both objected to the idea of freedom for the people, or even of real parliamentary government. Fuad considered himself the Government, and did much as he pleased, dismissed Parliament and ruled as a dictator, relying on British bayonets, which never failed him.

The first altruistic action of the British Government after their declaration of Egyptian independence was to demand enormous sums as compensation for the officials who were retiring under the new régime. King Fuad, as the Egyptian Government, readily agreed, and the huge sum of £6,500,000 was thus paid out—one high official getting as much as £8,500. And the interesting part is that some of these officials, who were so heavily compensated for retirement, were immediately re-engaged under special contracts. Remember that Egypt is not a big country, and that it has a population of less than one-third that of the United Provinces.

The Egyptian constitution bravely lays down that " all power emanates from the nation ". As a matter of fact ever since the new constitution came into force, the Egyptian Parliament has had a very thin time. So far as I know, not a single parliament has lived to the end of its normal term. Again and again it has met with sudden death at the hands of King Fuad, who has suspended the constitution and ruled as an autocratic monarch.

The first elections to the new parliament were held in 1923, and Zaghlul Pasha and his party, now known as the *Wafd* Party, swept the country. They gained 90 per cent. of the votes and 177 out of 214 seats. An effort was made to come to terms with England, Zaghlul going to London for the purpose. The two view-points could not be reconciled, and the negotiations broke down over several questions, one of these being that of the Sudan. The Sudan is a country south of Egypt; it is very different from Egypt; the people are different, and so is the language. Through the Sudan flows the Nile in its upper regions. The river Nile has been from the beginning of recorded history—and that means 7000 or 8000 years—the life-blood of Egypt. The whole of Egyptian agriculture and life have revolved round the annual Nile floods which brought the rich soil from the highlands of Abyssinia and thus converted a desert into a rich and fertile land. Lord Milner (of the commission that was boycotted) wrote about the Nile as follows :—

> " It is an uncomfortable thought that the regular supply of water by the great river, which is to Egypt not a question of convenience and prosperity, but of life, must always be exposed to some risks as long as the upper reaches of the river are not under Egyptian control."

The upper reaches of the Nile are in the Sudan; hence the vital importance of the Sudan to Egypt.

In the past the Sudan was supposed to be under the joint control of England and Egypt. It was called the Anglo-Egyptian Sudan. As Britain was actually ruling Egypt, there was no conflict of interests, and a great deal of Egyptian money was spent in the Sudan. Indeed, it was stated in the British Parliament by Lord Curzon in 1924 that the Sudan would be bankrupt if it were not for the financial expenditure undertaken by Egypt. When the question of leaving Egypt had at last to be faced by the British, they wanted to hold on to the Sudan. The Egyptians, on the other hand, felt that their existence was bound up with the control of the upper waters of the Nile in the Sudan. Hence the conflict of interests.

In 1924, when the question of the Sudan was being discussed between Saad Zaghlul and the British Government, the Sudanese people showed their attachment to Egypt in many ways. For this they were severely punished by the British, who did just what they liked without consulting the Egyptian Government, in spite of the joint administration, for which Egypt had to pay a good deal.

Another reservation made by Britain in the so-called declaration of Egyptian independence was the protection of foreign interests. What were these foreign interests? I have told you something about them in a previous letter. When the Turkish Empire was weakening, the great Powers had imposed various rules on it under which special treatment was to be given to their citizens in Turkey. These European foreigners were not to be subject to Turkish laws or courts, whatever offence they might commit. They were to be tried by their own consuls or diplomatic representatives, or by special courts consisting of foreigners. They had other privileges also, such as freedom from most kinds of taxation. These special and very valuable privileges of the foreigners were called " capitulations ", from capitulate, to surrender, as they were, to some extent, surrenders of sovereignty by the State concerned. Because Turkey had to put up with them, the various parts of the Turkish dominions had also to submit to them. Egypt, which was wholly under British rule, and where Turkey did not even possess nominal authority, was, however, in this respect made to suffer as a part of the Turkish Empire, and the capitulations were enforced there. Under these most fortunate conditions for them, important foreign settlements of business men and capitalists grew up in the cities. It was natural enough that they should oppose the abolition of a system which protected them in every way and allowed them to grow rich and prosperous without having to pay taxes even. These were the foreign vested interests which the British Government had undertaken to protect. Egypt could not possibly agree to a system which not only was wholly inconsistent with independence, but meant a tremendous loss of revenue to her. It was hardly possible to do anything on a big scale in the way of reform in social conditions if the richest people escaped taxation. During the long period of direct British rule, they had practically done nothing for primary education or the sanitation and improvement of village conditions.

It so happened that Turkey, which had been the original cause of the capitulations, got rid of them after Kemal Pasha's victory. I might mention here that China is also still struggling with something similar to these capitulations. Japan had them also for a short while in the nineteenth century, but as soon as she became powerful, she rejected them.

Thus the question of foreign vested interests was another obstruction in the way of a settlement between Britain and Egypt. Vested interests are always in the way of freedom.

With their usual magnanimity, the British Government had also decided to protect the interests of minorities, and this was also a reservation in the declaration of independence of February 1922. The chief minority was that of the Copts. These people are supposed to be the descendants of the ancient Egyptians, and are thus the oldest race in Egypt. They are Christians, and have been so from the early days of Christianity, before Europe became Christian. Instead of thanking the British Government for their great solicitude for the minorities, the Copts were ungrateful enough to tell them not to trouble about them. Soon after the British declaration of February 1922, the Copts gathered together at a great meeting and resolved " that they renounce all minority representation and minority protection in the interest of national unity and the attainment of the national aim ". This decision of the Copts was criticized by the British as a very foolish one ! But, wise or foolish, it put an end to the British claim to protect them, and the question of minorities ceased to be a subject for discussion. As a matter of fact the Copts took a great part in the national struggle for freedom, and some of Zaghlul Pasha's most trusted colleagues in the *Wafd* were Copts.

Because of these opposing view-points and the actual conflicts of interests, the negotiations between Egypt, as represented by Saad Zaghlul and his colleagues, and the British, in 1924, broke down. The British Government was very angry at this. They were used to having their way in Egypt, and found the obstinacy of the new parliament in Cairo, and especially of the *Wafd* leaders, most irritating. They decided to teach a lesson, after their own imperialist manner, to the *Wafd* and the Egyptian Parliament. An opportunity came to them soon, and of the extraordinary way in which they seized it and profited by it, I shall tell you in my next letter. That remarkable incident, holding up as it were a mirror to the working of modern imperialism, deserves a letter to itself.

164

WHAT INDEPENDENCE UNDER THE BRITISH MEANS

May 22, 1933

I TOLD you in my last letter of the failure of the negotiations in 1924 between the Egyptian Government, as represented by the nationalists, and the British, and the anger of the British Government at this. Before I proceed to the remarkable developments that followed, I must remind you that, in spite of so-called independence, Egypt continued to be under British military occupation. Not only was the British army stationed there, but the Egyptian army was also under British control, and had an Englishman, with the title of the Sirdar of the Army, at its head. The chief police officials were also Englishmen, and, under the plea of protecting foreigners in Egypt, the British Government controlled the departments of Finance, Justice and the Interior; that is to say, they controlled every vital thing in the Government. The Egyptians were naturally insisting on the British giving up this control.

On November 19, 1924, an Englishman, Sir Lee Stack, who held the office of Sirdar of the Egyptian Army and was also the Governor-General of the Sudan, was murdered by some Egyptians. Naturally this gave a shock to the British people in Egypt and in England; perhaps it gave an even greater shock to the leaders of the Egyptian nationalist party, the *Wafd*, for they knew that it would mean an attack on them. This attack came swiftly enough. Within three days, on November 22, the British High Commissioner in Egypt, Lord Allenby, presented an ultimatum to the Egyptian Government, making the following immediate demands :

1. An apology.
2. The punishment of the criminals.
3. Prohibition of all political demonstrations.
4. Payment of an indemnity of £500,000.
5. Withdrawal within twenty-four hours of all Egyptian troops from the Sudan.
6. The removal of the limitations that had, in the interest of Egypt, been placed on the area to be irrigated in the Sudan.
7. Withdrawal of all further opposition to the assumption by the British Government of the right to protect all foreigners in Egypt. This specially referred to the retention of British authority in the departments of Finance, Justice and Interior.

These seven demands are worthy of some attention. Because some people had murdered Sir Lee Stack, the British Government immediately, and without even the possibility of an inquiry, treated the Egyptian Government as a whole, that is the Egyptian people, as if they had been guilty of the murder. Further, they made a handsome financial profit out of the whole affair, and, most significant of all, made it the occasion to settle forcibly all the matters in dispute between themselves and the Egyptian Government, over which the negotiations had broken down in London only a few months before. As if this were not enough, they added that all political demonstrations should be prohibited, thus preventing even the normal public life of the country from continuing.

Now, all this was rather an extraordinary development out of the murder, and it required a vigorous and fertile imagination to make a murder yield so much profit to the British. What makes it still more curious was that the two chief officials (nominally under the Egyptian Government) who might have been considered especially responsible for the prevention of crime and outrage, the Chief of Police of Cairo and the Director-General of the European Department of Public Safety, were both Englishmen. No one considered them responsible for the murder. But the poor Egyptian

Government, which had immediately after the murder expressed its deep sorrow and regret, was made to feel the heavy, but coldly calculated and profitable, anger of the British Government.

The Egyptian Government humbled itself to the dust. Zaghlul Pasha agreed to nearly all the conditions of the ultimatum, and even paid up the indemnity of £500,000 within twenty-four hours. Only about the Sudan the Egyptian Government said it could not waive its rights. Even this humility and apology were not enough for Lord Allenby and, because the Sudan conditions had not been accepted, he took forcible possession, on behalf of the British, of the customs house at Alexandria, thereby controlling the customs revenue. Further, in spite of Egyptian protests, he enforced these conditions in the Sudan and made the Sudan a British colony. There were revolts of the Egyptian troops in the Sudan, but they were suppressed with extreme severity.

Zaghlul Pasha and his Government had immediately resigned as a protest against the British action and, also in that very month of November 1924, King Fuad dissolved Parliament. So the British had succeeded in driving out Zaghlul and his *Wafd* party from office and in putting an end to Parliament for the time being at least. They had also annexed the Sudan, and were thus in an easy position to strangle Egypt's throat by controlling the waters of the Nile in the Sudan.

The unhappy Egyptian Parliament had appealed to the League of Nations against " the exploitation of a tragic incident for im-perialist purposes ", but the League is blind and deaf to complaints against the great Powers.

From this time onwards there was a continuous struggle in Egypt, a tussle between the *Wafd* party, practically representing the whole nation, on the one side, and a combination of King Fuad and the British High Commissioner, backed by the other foreign interests and the hangers-on of the Court, on the other. Most of the time the country was ruled, in defiance of the constitution, by dictatorships, King Fuad acting as an autocratic monarch. Whenever Parliament was allowed to meet it demonstrated that nearly the whole country stood behind the *Wafd* party, and so it was dissolved. Fuad could not possibly act in this way if he did not have the backing of the British and the army and police under their control. Egypt, the " independent ", is treated more or less like an Indian State, with the British Resident, the real authority, pulling the strings.

Parliament had been dissolved in November 1924. In March 1925 the new Parliament met. This had a big *Wafd* majority, and it immediately elected Zaghlul Pasha the president of the Chamber of Deputies. Neither the English nor King Fuad approved of this, and so on that very day, this brand-new, one-day-old Parliament was dissolved ! For a whole year after this there was no Parliament, in spite of the constitution, and Fuad governed as a dictator, the real power behind him being the British Commissioner. The whole country resented this, and Saad Zaghlul succeeded in uniting all groups to oppose the combination of King Fuad and the English. In November 1925 there was even a meeting of the members of Parliament in defiance of the Government prohibition. The Parliament House itself was occupied by troops. So the members met elsewhere.

Fuad then tried to change the whole constitution by just issuing a decree from his palace. His object was to make it still more conservative, so that future parliaments might be easier to control and most of the Zaghlulists might be kept out. But there was a tremendous outcry against this and it was clear that elections under the new system would be wholly boycotted. Thereupon King Fuad had to give way and elections were held under the old system. Result : vast majority for Zaghlul's party—200 to 14 ! There could not have been a greater proof of Zaghlul's hold on the nation and of what Egypt wanted. In spite of this the British Commissioner (who was Lord Lloyd, an ex-Indian governor) said he objected to Zaghlul becoming Prime Minister and another person was, therefore, appointed. What business the English had to interfere in the matter it is a little difficult to understand. The new Government was, however, largely controlled by Zaghlul's party and, in spite of all attempts at moderation, they often came into conflict with Lloyd, who was a most imperious and domineering individual, and who often threatened them with British warships.

Another attempt was made in 1927 to come to an agreement with Britain, but even the very moderate Prime Minister of King Fuad was surprised at Britain's conditions. Under cover of a paper independence they really meant a British protectorate. So the negotiations again failed.

While these negotiations were going on, Egypt's great leader, Saad Zaghlul Pasha, died, on August 23, 1927, at the age of seventy. He died, but his memory lives in Egypt as a bright and precious heritage, and inspires the people. His wife, Madame Safia Zaghlul, is still living, loved and revered by the entire nation, which has given her the title of the " mother of the people ". And his house in Cairo—the " People's House " it is called—has long been the headquarters of the Egyptian nationalists.

Mustafa Nahas Pasha succeeded Zaghlul as the leader of the *Wafd*. Later, in March 1928, he became Prime Minister. He tried to bring in some simple domestic reforms concerning civil liberties and the right of the people to possess arms. These rights had been curtailed by the British during the martial-law period. As soon as the Egyptian Parliament began considering this question, there came threats from England that this must not be done. It seems extraordinary that England should thus intervene in a purely domestic matter; but Lord Lloyd, in the approved old fashion, presented an ultimatum, and British warships steamed into Alexandria harbour from Malta. Nahas Pasha gave way to some extent, and agreed to postpone consideration of the measures to the next session, a few months later.

But there was to be no next session. The King and the British

Commissioner, reaction and imperialism, saw to it that the Parliament should be given no further chance to misbehave. The intrigue worked out in a novel way. Nahas Pasha was especially noted for his high character and his incorruptibility. Suddenly, on the basis of a letter (which later turned out to be forged), a charge of corruption was brought against Nahas Pasha and a Coptic leader of the *Wafd*. There was tremendous propaganda by palace circles and by the British. Not only in Egypt, but in foreign countries, British agencies and newspaper correspondents spread these false accusations. Under cover of this charge King Fuad asked Nahas Pasha to resign from the premiership. He refused to do so, and thereupon he was dismissed by Fuad. The next step in the Lloyd-Fuad intrigue was now taken. There was a *coup d'état*, and by a decree the King suspended Parliament and altered the constitution. The articles in the constitution dealing with the freedom of the Press and other liberties were abolished and a dictatorship was proclaimed. There were rejoicings in the English Press and among the Europeans in Egypt.

The members of Parliament met together, in spite of the dictatorship, and declared the new Government illegal, but neither Lloyd nor Fuad was worried about such matters. The function of " law and order " is to support reaction and imperialism, not to be used as a weapon against them.

The case brought by the Government against Nahas Pasha collapsed in spite of Government pressure. The charges against him were held to be false. And the Government (how amazingly fair and chivalrous it was !) issued orders forbidding the publication of the judgment in the Press. But of course the news spread immediately, and everywhere there was great joy.

The dictatorship, backed by Lloyd and the British forces, tried hard to crush and break up the *Wafd* party, which meant Egyptian nationalism. There was a regular terror and a complete censorship of news. In spite of this, great national demonstrations took place in which the women took a special part. There was a week's strike, the lawyers and others taking part in it, but owing to the censorship, the Press could not even report this.

So the year 1928 passed in storm and stress. Towards the end of the year a change in the political situation in England had its immediate reaction in Egypt. A Labour Government had come into office there, and one of the first steps it took was to recall Lloyd, who had become insufferable, even to the British Government. Lloyd's removal broke up for a while the Fuad-English alliance. Without English support Fuad could not carry on, and so he allowed fresh elections to Parliament in December 1928. Again the *Wafd* party captured nearly all the seats.

The English Labour Government started negotiations again with Egypt, and Nahas Pasha went to London in 1929 for this purpose. The Labour Government went a little farther this time than its predecessors, and Nahas Pasha's view-point on the three of the reservations was accepted. But on the fourth—the Sudan—again there was no agreement, and so the negotiations broke down.   On this occasion, however, there had been far greater agreement than before; and the parties remained friendly to each other, and promised to have discussions again.   This was on the whole a success for Nahas Pasha and the *Wafd*, and the British and other foreign business men and financiers in Egypt did not fancy it at all. Neither did King Fuad.   A few months later, in June 1930, there was a conflict between the King and Parliament, and Nahas Pasha resigned from the premiership.

Fuad again stepped into the breach with a dictato ship—the third dictatorship of his reign.   Parliament was dissolved, the *Wafd* newspapers were suspended and generally the dictatorship began to function with a heavy hand.   All the members of Parliament, of both Houses, the Chamber and the Senate, defied the Palace Government, and forcing their way into the Parliament House, held a session there.   Solemnly they took the oath, on June 23, 1930, of loyalty to the constitution, and they swore that they would defend it with all their strength.   Great demonstrations were held all over the country.   These were forcibly broken up by the troops, and a good deal of blood was shed.   Nahas Pasha himself was injured.   In this way the troops and police under British officers upheld a dictatorship which was bitterly resented by the whole nation excepting a handful of aristocrats and rich men who clung to the King.   Even others besides the *Wafdists*, even the moderates and liberals, who, as in India, proclaimed their opposition to all strong action on behalf of the people, even they protested against the dictatorship.

Later in the same year, 1930, the King published a decree proclaiming a new constitution, in which he cut down the powers of Parliament and increased his own !   It was so easy to do this kind of thing.   Issue a proclamation and it was done, for behind the King was the grim shadow of an imperialist Power.

I have told you the story of these nine years in Egypt, from 1922 to 1930, in some detail, because it has seemed to me to be an extraordinary story.   These were the years of Egypt's " independence ", according to the British declaration of February 1922.   There could be no question of what the Egyptian people wanted.   Whenever they were given the chance, the vast majority of them, Muslims and Copts, elected the *Wafdists*.   But because what they wanted was to lessen the power of foreigners, and especially of the British, to exploit the country, all these foreign vested interests opposed them in every way—by force and violence, by fraud and intrigue —and put up a puppet king to do their bidding.

The *Wafd* movement has been a purely nationalist *bourgeois* movement.   It has fought for national independence, and has not interfered with social problems.   Whenever Parliament has functioned, it has done some good work in educational and other departments.   Indeed, in spite of the national struggle, Parliament did more in this brief period than the English administration had done in the previous forty years.   The *Wafd's* popularity with the peasantry has been shown by the elections and by the great demonstrations. And yet, as the movement is essentially a middle-class one, it has not aroused the masses to the extent that a movement aiming at social change would do.

Before I end this letter I must tell you of the women's movement. All over the Arab countries, except probably in Arabia itself, there has been a great awakening of women. Egypt is in this, as in many other matters, more advanced than Iraq or Syria or Palestine. But in all these countries there is an organized women's movement, and in July 1930 the first Arab Women's Congress met at Damascus. They laid stress more on cultural and social progress than on political matters. In Egypt women are more politically inclined. They take part in political demonstrations, and have a strong Women Suffrage Union. They claim a reform of the marriage law in their own favour, and equal opportunities for women in professions, etc. Muslim and Christian women co-operate with each other fully. The habit of veiling the face is lessening everywhere, more especially in Egypt. The veil has not disappeared, as in Turkey, but it is going to pieces.

Note (*October* 1938) :

From 1930 onwards Egypt was under a dictatorial government controlled from the Palace. In theory it was a " sovereign independent State ", but in reality it was almost a colony of Great Britain, with foreign garrisons in Cairo and Alexandria and Britain controlling the Suez Canal and the Sudan. These were the years of the great economic slump all over the world, and Egypt suffered greatly owing to the fall in cotton prices.

In 1935 Fascist Italy invaded Abyssinia, and this new danger to Egypt, as well as to British interests in the upper Nile valley, brought about a change in the relations between Egypt and England. England could not now afford to have a rebellious and unfriendly Egypt, and Egyptian leaders began to look at England as a possible friend. The *Wafd* Party triumphed during the elections for the Parliament, and Nahas Pasha became Prime Minister. In the new atmosphere that was created as a result of Italian aggression in Abyssinia, Egypt and England came to terms, and a treaty was signed in August 1936. Egypt, for the sake of peace, agreed to give up much that she had insisted on previously, and accepted the *status quo* in the Sudan and England's right to defend the Suez Canal. Further, Egypt's foreign policy was to be linked up to that of England. England, on the other hand, withdrew her troops from Cairo and Alexandria, promised to help in abolishing the Mixed Courts and extra-territoriality, and to support Egypt's admission to the League of Nations.

There were great rejoicings at this settlement, but they were somewhat premature. The Palace, in spite of a change of kings, continued to hate the *Wafd* and to intrigue against it. British imperialism still continued to function behind the scenes. A very large part of the land of Egypt is owned by a handful of persons,

and the royal family itself owns a tremendous share.   These landed
magnates are strongly opposed to progressive legislation and to the
growth of the people's power.   Thus there was continuous friction,
and the King dismissed Nahas Pasha and dissolved Parliament.

New elections were held after an interval of Palace government,
and, to every one's surprise, the *Wafd* sustained a heavy defeat.
Subsequently it appeared that this election was largely a bogus
affair and false returns had been engineered.   The *Wafd* Party,
under Nahas Pasha's leadership, continues to be very popular, but
the Government of to-day is run by the Palace clique with the
support of British imperialism.

165

WESTERN ASIA RE-ENTERS WORLD POLITICS

May 25, 1933

ONLY a tiny strip of blue separates Egypt and Africa from
western Asia.   Let us cross this Suez Canal and visit Arabia and
Palestine and Syria and Iraq—all Arab countries—and, a little
beyond them, Persia.   Western Asia, as we have seen, has played a
mighty part in history, and has often been the pivot of world
affairs.   And then there came a period, lasting several hundred
years, when politically it retired into the background.   It became
a backwater, and the current of life rushed by, hardly creating a
ripple on its still surface.   And now we are witnesses of yet another
change which is bringing the countries of the Middle East again into
world affairs; again the highway between East and West passes
through them.   This is a fact which deserves our attention.

Whenever I think of western Asia I am apt to lose myself in the
past; so many images of the old days crowd into my mind, and I
find it difficult to resist their fascination.   I shall try not to give in
to this attraction, but I must remind you again—lest you forget !
—of the importance, for many thousands of years from the very
beginning of history, of this part of the earth's surface.   Old
Chaldea dimly appears in history 7000 years ago.   (This corresponds
to modern Iraq.)   And then comes Babylon, and after the Babylonians appear the cruel Assyrians, with their great capital at Nineveh.
The Assyrians are in their turn pushed away, and a new dynasty
and a new people, coming from Persia, impose their will on the
whole of the Middle East from the Indian frontier to Egypt.   These
were the Achæmenids of Persia, with their capital at Persepolis.
They produced the " Great Kings " Cyrus and Darius and Xerxes,
who threatened little Greece, but failed to overcome her.   They
met their fate later at the hands of a son of Greece, or rather of
Macedonia, Alexander.   A curious incident took place in Alexander's career when, in this meeting-place of Asia and Europe, he
planned what has been called a " marriage " of the two continents.

He himself (although he had a few wives already) married the daughter of the Persian King, and thousands of Alexander's officers and soldiers also married Persian girls.

After Alexander, Greek culture prevailed in the Middle East from the Indian frontier to Egypt for many centuries. The power of Rome arose during this period, and it spread towards Asia. It found a check in a new Persian Empire—that of the Sassanids. The Roman Empire itself split up into two, the Western and the Eastern, and Constantinople came to be the seat of the latter. The old struggle between East and West continued on these plains of western Asia, and the chief combatants were the Byzantine Empire of Constantinople and the Persian Sassanid Empire. And all this time great caravans of people, carrying merchandise on the backs of camels, crossed these plains from east to west and west to east, for the Middle East was then one of the world's great highways.

Three great religions had seen the light of day in these lands of western Asia—Judaism (that is the religion of the Jews), Zoro-astrianism (the religion of the modern Parsees), and Christianity. A fourth now appeared in the deserts of Arabia, and soon it dominated the other three in this part of the world. Then there came the Arab Empire of Baghdad and a new form of the old struggle—Arabs against Byzantines. After a long and brilliant career, Arab civilization wanes before the coming of the Seljuk Turks, and is finally crushed by the successors of Chengiz Khan, the Mongol.

But before the Mongols came west a fierce struggle had already commenced on the western coasts of Asia between the Christian West and the Muslim East. These were the Crusades, which lasted, off and on, for 250 years, almost to the middle of the thirteenth century. These Crusades are looked upon as wars of religion, and so they were. But religion was more of an excuse for the wars than a cause. The people of Europe in those days were backward as compared to the East. These were the Dark Ages of Europe. But Europe was waking up, and the more advanced and cultured East drew it like a magnet. This pull towards the East took many shapes, and among these the Crusades were the most important. As a result of these wars Europe learnt much from the western Asiatic countries. She learnt many fine arts and crafts and habits of luxury, and, what was more important, methods of scientific work and thought.

The Crusades were hardly over when the Mongols swept down on western Asia, bringing destruction in their train. And yet we must not think of the Mongols just as destroyers. Their vast movements from China to Russia brought together distant peoples and en-couraged trade and intercourse. Under their huge empire the old caravan routes became safe to travel by, and not only merchants but diplomatists, religious missionaries and others went up and down them on their tremendous journeys. The Middle East was in the direct line of these ancient world highways : it was the link between Asia and Europe.

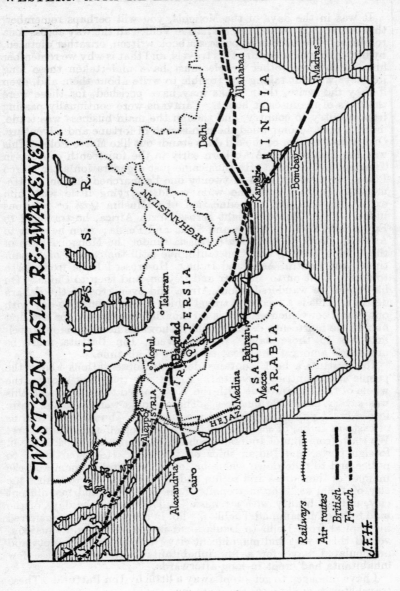

It was in the days of the Mongols, you will perhaps remember, that Marco Polo went from his native Venice all the way across Asia to China.   We happen to possess a book written, or rather dictated, by him giving an account of his travels, and that is why we remember him.   But many other people must have undertaken these long journeys without taking the trouble to write about them and, even if they did write, their books may have perished, for those were the days of manuscript books.   Caravans were continually passing from country to country, and though the main business was trade, many a man accompanied them in search of fortune and adventure. One great traveller of the old days stands out like Marco Polo.   This was Ibn Battuta, an Arab born early in the fourteenth century in Tangiers in Morocco.   He thus came just a generation after Marco Polo.   As a young man of twenty-one he marched out on his tremendous journey into the wide world, carrying little with him except his wits and the education of a Muslim *Qazi* or religious judge.   From Morocco, right across North Africa, he travelled to Egypt, and then to Arabia and Syria and Persia; then he went to Anatolia (Turkey), and South Russia (under the Mongol Khans of the Golden Horde), and Constantinople (still the capital of Byzantium), and Central Asia, and India.   He crossed India from north to south, went on to Malabar and Ceylon, and then to China.   On his return he wandered about Africa and even crossed the Sahara desert !   This is a record of travel which is rare enough to-day with our many conveniences.   It is an amazing eye-opener for the first half of the fourteenth century, and it shows us how common travelling was in those days.   In any event, Ibn Battuta must be numbered amongst the great travellers of all time.

Ibn Battuta's book contains delightful observations about the people and countries he visited.   Egypt was rich then because the whole of the Indian trade with the West passed through it, and this was a very profitable business.   These profits went to make Cairo into a great city with beautiful monuments.   Ibn Battuta tells us of caste in India, of *sati*, and of the custom of offering *pān-supārī* ! We learn from him of Indian merchants carrying on a brisk trade in foreign ports, and Indian ships on the seas.   He is particular to notice and to note down where he found beautiful women, and the manner of their dress and scents and ornaments.   He describes the city of Delhi as " the metropolis of India, a vast and magnificent city, uniting beauty with strength ".   Those were the days of the mad Sultan Mohammad Tughlaq, who, in a fit of anger, transferred his capital from Delhi to Daulatabad in the south, and thus converted this " vast and magnificent city " into a desert " empty and unpopulated, save for a few inhabitants ", and even these few inhabitants had crept in long afterwards.

I have managed to get swept away a little by Ibn Battuta.   These travel-stories of old days fascinate me.

So we see that up till the fourteenth century the Middle East, or western Asia, played a great part in world affairs and was the main link between East and West.   The next 100 years saw a change.

The Ottoman Turks took possession of Constantinople and spread all over these countries of the Middle East, including Egypt. They did not encourage continental trade, partly because this trade was in the hands of their rivals in the Mediterranean, the Viennese and the Genoese. Trade itself took to new ways, for new sea routes were opened out, and these sea routes took the place of the old land caravan routes. So these land routes across western Asia, which had done good service for many thousands of years, fell into disuse, and the lands through which they had passed faded into unimportance.

For nearly 400 years, from early in the sixteenth century to the end of the nineteenth, the sea routes were all-important, and they dominated the land routes, especially where there were no railways, and there were no railways in western Asia. A little before the World War, proposals were made, backed by the German Government, for a railway connecting Constantinople with Baghdad. The other Powers were very jealous of Germany doing this, as it would have led to the increase of German influence in the Middle East. The war intervened.

When the war ended in 1918, Britain was supreme in western Asia and, as I have told you, for a brief while, visions of a great Middle Eastern Empire, from India to Turkey, floated before the dazzled eyes of British statesmen. That was not to be. Bolshevik Russia and Kemal Pasha and other factors prevented its realization, but still Britain managed to hold on to a good deal. Iraq and Palestine continued under British influence or control. So that although the British were unable to realize their vast ambitions, they succeeded in holding on to their old policy of controlling the routes and approaches to India. It was with this object that British armies fought during war-time in Mesopotamia and Palestine, and encouraged and helped the Arab revolt against Turkey. It was because of this that great friction arose between England and Turkey over the Mosul question after the war. And this is one of the chief reasons for the bad blood between England and Soviet Russia, for England hates the idea of a great Power like Russia sitting on the garden wall, overlooking the road to India.

The two railways about which there was so much dispute before the war—the Baghdad Railway and the Hejaz Railway—have now been built. The Baghdad Railway connects Baghdad with the Mediterranean Sea and Europe. The Hejaz Railway connects Medina in Arabia to the Baghdad Railway at Aleppo. (The Hejaz is the most important part of Arabia, containing the holy cities of Islam, Mecca and Medina.) So that many important cities of western Asia are now connected by the railway system to Europe and Egypt, and are thus easily accessible. The city of Aleppo is developing into an important railway junction, for the railway systems of three continents will meet there ; the line from Europe, from Asia *via* Baghdad, and from Africa *via* Cairo. British policy has long aimed at controlling these routes in Asia and Africa. The Asiatic route, when extended from Baghdad, may reach India. The

African route is meant to go right across the African continent from
Cairo to Cape Town in the far south.   The all-red Cape-to-Cairo
line has long been the dream of British imperialists, and it is well
on the way to realization now—" all-red " means that it should pass
British territory along the whole route, as red is the colour on the
map monopolized by the British Empire.

But these developments may or may not take place in the future,
for the railway has got serious rivals now in the motor-car and the
aeroplane.   Meanwhile it is worth remembering that both these
two new railways in western Asia, the Baghdad and the Hejaz, are
largely controlled by the British, and serve British policy in opening
out a new and shorter route, under their control, to India.   Part of
the Baghdad Railway passes through Syria, which is under French
control.   Not liking this dependence on the French, the British
intend building a new line through Palestine to take its place.
Another little railway is being built in Arabia between Jeddah, the
port in the Red Sea, and Mecca.   This will be a great convenience
to the tens of thousands of pilgrims who go to Mecca every year.

So much for the railway system which is opening out these
countries of western Asia to the world.   And yet even before it has
done its job it is losing some of its importance, and is being pushed
aside by the motor-car and the aeroplane.   The motor-car has
taken very readily to the desert, and rushes along the same old
caravan routes along which trudged for thousands of years the patient
camel.   A railway is very costly, and it takes time to build.   The
motor is cheap and can function immediately whenever required.
But motor-cars and lorries do not usually serve long distances;
they go backwards and forwards in comparatively small areas of
100 miles at most.

For the great distances there is, of course, the aeroplane, which is
both cheaper than the railway and far swifter.   There can be no
doubt that the use of aircraft will go on increasing rapidly for purposes of transport.   Already great progress has been made, and
huge air-liners go regularly from continent to continent.   Western
Asia again becomes a meeting-place of these great air routes, and
Baghdad is especially the centre of them.   The British Imperial
Airways line from London to India and Australia passes Baghdad;
also the K.L.M. Dutch line from Amsterdam to Batavia, and the
French line—Air France—from Paris to Indo-China.   Moscow and
Iran are also connected with Baghdad by air.   A passenger to
China and the Far East by air has to pass Baghdad.   From Baghdad
also aeroplanes go to Cairo, connecting with the African service to
Cape Town.

Most of these air lines do not pay and are heavily subsidized by
their governments, for air-power is all-important to empires to-day.
With the development of air-power, the importance of sea-power
has diminished greatly.   England, which was so proud of its navy,
and considered itself secure from attack, has ceased to be an island
from the point of view of defence.   It is as vulnerable from the air
as France or any other country.   And so all the great Powers are

keen on becoming strong in the air, and the old rivalry on the sea has given place to air rivalry. Passenger traffic by air is encouraged and subsidized by each country in peace-time, as this builds up a service of trained pilots who can be used in time of war. Civil aviation helps the development of military aviation. A rapid development in civil aviation is therefore taking place, and there are hundreds of air services in Europe and America. The progress made is probably greatest in the United States of America; in the Soviet Union also great progress has been made and many air-services run across its vast territories.

In this age of air-power, western Asia attains a new importance because of the many long-distance lines that cross there. It re-enters again world politics and becomes a pivot of inter-continental affairs. This means also that it becomes the scene of friction and conflict between the great Powers, for their ambitions clash, and each tries to overreach the other. If we keep this in mind, we can understand the policy which has shaped British and other activities in the Middle East and elsewhere.

Mosul, besides being situated on this new high road to India, possesses oil, and oil is even more important in the age of air-power than it was before. Iraq possesses important oilfields and, as we have seen, is the very heart of the inter-continental air-system. Hence the great importance for the British of controlling Iraq. Persia has vast oilfields which have long been exploited by the Anglo-Persian Oil Company, which is partly owned by the British Government. The importance of oil and petrol grows and affects imperialist policies. Indeed modern imperialism has sometimes been called " oil imperialism ".

We have considered in this letter some of the factors which have given a new prominence to the Middle East and brought it back into the whirlpool of world politics. But behind all this is the awakening of the whole of the Asiatic East.

166

THE ARAB COUNTRIES—SYRIA

May 28, 1933

WE have seen what a powerful force nationalism has been in binding together and strengthening groups of people living in countries usually with a common language and traditions. While this nationalism binds together one such group, it marks it off and separates it still further from other groups. Thus nationalism makes of France a strong, solid national unit, closely bound together and looking on the rest of the world as something different; so also it makes the different German peoples into one powerful German nation. But this very drawing together separately of France and Germany cuts them off from each other still more.

In a country which has several distinct national groups, nationalism is often a disruptive force which, instead of strengthening and binding together the country, actually weakens it and tends to break it up. The Austro-Hungarian Empire before the World War was such a country with many nationalities, of which two, the German-Austrians and the Hungarians, were the dominant ones, and the others were dependent. The growth of nationalism therefore weakened Austria-Hungary, as it infused fresh life into each of these nationalities separately, and with this came the desire for freedom. The war made matters worse, and the country broke up into little bits when defeat followed the war, each national area forming a separate State. (The division was not a very happy or logical one, but we need not go into that here.) Germany, on the other hand, in spite of a severe defeat, did not break up into bits. It held together even in disaster under the powerful stress of nationalism.

The Turkish Empire before the World War was, like Austria-Hungary, a collection of many nationalities. Apart from the Balkan races, there were the Arabs and the Armenians and others. Nationalism, therefore, proved a disruptive force in this Empire also. The Balkans were first affected by it and, right through the nineteenth century, Turkey had to struggle with the Balkan races, one after the other, beginning with Greece. The great Powers, and especially Tsarist Russia, tried to profit by this awakening nationalism and intrigued with it. They also used the Armenians as a tool to hammer and weaken the Ottoman Empire, and hence the repeated conflicts between the Turkish Government and the Armenians, resulting in bloody massacres. These Armenians were exploited and used for propaganda purposes by the great Powers, but after the World War, when there was no further use for them, they were left to their own fate. Later, Armenia, which lies to the east of Turkey, touching the Black Sea, became a Soviet republic and joined the Russian Soviet Union.

The Arab parts of the Turkish dominions took more time to wake up, although there was little love lost between the Arabs and the Turks. At first there was a cultural awakening and a renaissance of the Arabic language and literature. This began in Syria, as early as the 'sixties of the nineteenth century, and spread to Egypt and other Arabic-speaking countries. Political movements grew up after the Young Turk revolution in Turkey in 1908 and the fall of Sultan Abdul Hamid. Nationalist ideas spread among the Arabs, both Muslim and Christian, and the idea of freeing the Arab countries from Turkish rule and uniting them in one State took shape. Egypt, though an Arabic-speaking country, was more or less apart politically, and was not expected to join this proposed Arab State, which was meant to include Arabia, Syria, Palestine, and Iraq. The Arabs also wanted to get back the religious leadership of Islam by getting the Caliphate transferred from the Ottoman Sultan to an Arab dynasty. Even this was looked upon more as a national move, as redounding to the greater importance and glory

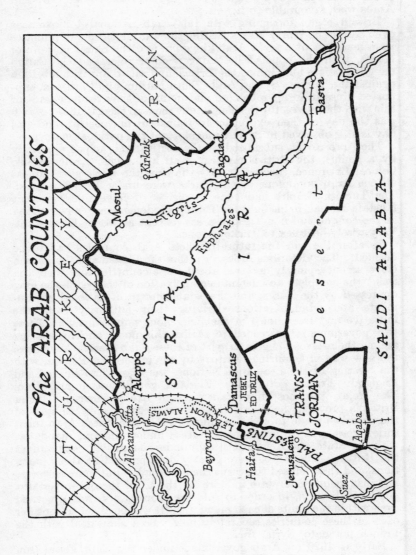

of the Arabs, than as a religious one, and even the Syrian Christian Arabs were favourable to it.

Britain began intriguing with this Arab nationalist movement even before the World War. During the war all manner of promises were made about a great Arab kingdom, and the Sherif Hussein of Mecca, with the hope of becoming a great ruler and the Caliph dangling before him, joined the British and raised an Arab rebellion against the Turks. Syrian Arabs, both Muslim and Christian, supported Hussein in his rebellion, and many of their leaders paid for this with their lives, for the Turks sent them to the gallows. May 6 was the day of their execution in Damascus and Beirut, and this day is still observed in Syria in memory of the national martyrs.

The Arab revolt, subsidized by the British, and helped especially by a genius, the British mystery man and secret service agent, Colonel Lawrence, succeeded. By the time the war ended, almost all the Arab dominions of the Turks were under British control. The Turkish Empire had gone to pieces. I have told you that Mustafa Kemal, in his fight for Turkey's independence, never aimed at the conquest of non-Turkish areas (except a part of Kurdistan). Very wisely he stuck to Turkey proper.

So after the war the future of these Arab countries had to be decided. The victorious Allies, or rather the British and the French Governments, piously declared about these countries that their aim was " the complete and definite emancipation of the peoples so long oppressed by the Turks, and the establishment of national governments and administrations deriving their authority from the initiative and free choice of the indigenous populations ". These two governments proceeded to realize this noble aim by sharing among themselves the greater part of these Arab areas. Mandates, the new way of acquiring territory by the imperialist Powers, with the blessing of the League of Nations, were issued to France and England. France got Syria; England got Palestine and Iraq. The Hejaz, the most important part of Arabia, was put under Britain's protégé, the Sherif Hussein of Mecca. Thus, in spite of the promises made to create a single Arab State, these Arab territories were split up into separate areas under different mandates, with one State, the Hejaz, outwardly independent, but really under the British. The Arabs were greatly disappointed at these partitions, and they refused to accept them as final. But more surprises and disappointments were in store for them, for the old imperialist policy of division, in order to rule the more easily, was practised even within the limits of each mandate. It will be easier to consider each of these countries separately now. So I shall deal with the French mandate, Syria, first.

Early in 1920 an Arab government under the Emir Feisal (son of King Hussein of the Hejaz) was set up in Syria with the help of the British. A Syrian National Congress met and adopted a democratic constitution for a united Syria. But all this was a few months' show only, and in the summer of 1920, the French, with the League of Nations mandate for Syria in their pocket, came and

drove out Feisal and took forcible possession of the country.   Syria,
even taken as a whole, is a small country with a population of less
than 3,000,000.   But it proved to be a hornets' nest for the French,
for the Syrian Arabs, both Muslim and Christian, now that they
had resolved on independence, refused to submit easily to the
domination of another Power.   There was continuous trouble, and
local insurrections took place, and a huge French army was required
in Syria to carry on French rule.   The French Government then
tried the usual tactics of imperialism and sought to weaken Syrian
nationalism by dividing up the country into even smaller States
and giving importance to religious and minority differences.   It was
a deliberate policy, almost proclaimed officially, " to divide in order
to rule ".

Syria, small as it was, was now split up into five separate States.
On the western sea coast and near the Lebanon mountains, the
State of Lebanon was created.   The majority of the population
here consisted of a sect of Christians called the Maronites, and the
French gave them a special status to win them over against the
Syrian Arabs.

North of Lebanon, also along the coast, another little State was
created in the mountains where some Muslim people, called the
Alawis, lived.   Farther north still, a third State, Alexandretta,
was established; this adjoined Turkey and was largely inhabited
by Turkish-speaking people.

Thus Syria proper, as it now remained, was deprived of some of
its most fertile districts and, what was much worse, completely cut
off from the sea.   For thousands of years Syria had been one of the
great Mediterranean countries, and now this ancient alliance was
broken up and it had to face the inhospitable desert.   Even from
this Syria another mountainous bit was cut off and made into a
separate State, the Jebel ed Druz, where a tribal people, the Druzes,
lived.

From the very beginning the Syrians had not taken kindly to
the French mandate.   There had been conflicts and big demonstrations, in which Arab women had taken part, and the French
had repressed these with a heavy hand.   The division of the
country, and the deliberate attempt to raise religious and minority
problems, made matters worse, and dissatisfaction grew.   To put
this down, the French, like the British in India, suppressed personal
and political liberties and covered the country with their spies and
secret service men.   They appointed as their officials " loyal "
Syrians who had no influence whatever with the people and who
were generally regarded as renegades by their own countrymen.
All this was done, of course, with the most pious of motives, and
the French proclaimed that they considered it " their duty to
educate the Syrians to political maturity and independence "—the
phrase has a familiar ring in India !

Matters were coming to a head, especially among the fighting
and somewhat primitive people of the Jebel ed Druz (who are not
unlike the tribes of our north-west frontier).   The French Governor

played a dirty trick on the leaders of these Druzes. He invited them and then made them prisoners and kept them as hostages. This was in the summer of 1925, and immediately an insurrection broke out in the Jebel ed Druz. This local revolt spread all over the country, and became a general rising for Syrian freedom and unity.

This war of Syrian independence was a remarkable affair. A small country, about the size of two or three districts in India, stood up to fight France, which was then the greatest military Power in the world. Of course the Syrians could not fight pitched battles with the huge and well-equipped French armies, but they made it difficult for them to hold the rural areas. Only the large towns were in French possession, and even these were often raided by the Syrians. The French tried their utmost to terrorize the people by shooting down large numbers and burning down numerous villages. The famous old city of Damascus itself was bombarded and largely destroyed in October 1925. The whole of Syria was a military camp. In spite of all this the rising was not put down for two years. It was crushed at last by the mighty French military machine, but the great sacrifices of the Syrians had not been in vain. They had established their right to freedom, and the world knew what stuff they were made of.

It is interesting to notice that while the French tried to give a religious colouring to the rising and tried to use the Christians against the Druzes, the Syrians made it quite clear that they fought for national freedom, and not for a religious objective. Right at the beginning of the insurrection a provisional government was established in the Druze country, and this government issued a proclamation appealing to the people to join the war of independence and win " the complete independence of Syria, one and indivisible . . . the free election of a Constituent Assembly to draft the constitution, the withdrawal of the foreign army of occupation, and the creation of a national army to guarantee security and apply the principles of the French Revolution and the Rights of Man ". So the French Government and the French army tried to put down a people who were standing up for the principles of the French Revolution and the rights which it had proclaimed !

Early in 1928 martial law was ended in Syria; also the censorship of the Press. Many political prisoners were released. In accordance with the demand of the nationalists, a Constituent Assembly was convened in order to draw up the constitution. But the French sowed the seeds of trouble by arranging for separate religious electorates (as in India now). Separate compartments were created for Muslims, Greek Catholics, Greek Orthodox Church, and Jews, and each voter was compelled to vote for one of his own religious group. A curious and revealing situation arose in Damascus. The leader of the nationalists was a Protestant Christian. Being a Protestant, he did not fall into any of the special electorates, and could not therefore be elected, although he was one of the most popular men in Damascus. The Muslims, who had ten seats, offered to give up one seat, so that it might be given to the Protestants, but the French Government would not agree.

In spite of all these attempts of the French, the nationalists controlled the Constituent Assembly, and they drafted a constitution for an independent and sovereign State. Syria was to be a republic in which all authority was derived from the people. There was no reference in this draft constitution to the French or their mandate. The French protested at this, but the Assembly would not budge an inch, and a tussle went on for many months. At last the French High Commissioner suggested that the draft constitution should be adopted with just one transitional clause to the effect that during the continuance of the mandate no article in the constitution should be applied so as to conflict with France's obligations under the mandate. This was rather vague, but still it was a great climb down for the French. The Constituent Assembly, however, would not agree even to this. The French Government thereupon, in May 1930, dissolved this Assembly and at the same time proclaimed the constitution drafted by it, with the addition of their transitional clause.

So Syria proper had succeeded in obtaining much that it wanted, and yet it had not compromised or given up a single one of its demands. Two things remained : the ending of the mandate, with which would go the transitional clause, and the larger question of Syrian unity. Otherwise the constitution itself is a progressive one, and designed for a perfectly free country. The Syrians showed themselves brave and determined fighters during the great insurrection, and afterwards as equally determined and persistent negotiators, refusing to modify or qualify in any way their demand for full freedom.

In November 1933 France offered a treaty to the Syrian Chamber of Deputies. This Chamber had been packed and consisted of a majority of moderates favourable to the French Government. In spite of this, the treaty was rejected by the Chamber. This was due to France insisting on continuing the existing partition of Syria into five States, and on maintaining camps, barracks, aerodromes, and military forces in Syria.

Note (October) 1938 :

The Nazi triumph in Czechoslovakia, and the increasing domination of Europe by Germany and her demand for colonies, have brought about a new situation all over the world. France has sunk back into the second rank of Powers and can hardly maintain for long a vast overseas empire. The difficult situation in Palestine has led to suggestions that Syria and Palestine and Trans-Jordan might be united together in an Arab federation.

167

PALESTINE AND TRANS-JORDAN

May 29, 1933

ADJOINING Syria is Palestine, for which the British Government holds a mandate from the League of Nations. This is an even smaller country, with a total population of less than a million, but it attracts a great deal of attention because of its old history and associations. For it is a holy land for the Jews as well as Christians and, to some extent, even the Muslims. The people inhabiting it are predominantly Muslim Arabs, and they demand freedom and unity with their fellow-Arabs of Syria. But British policy has created a special minority problem here—that of the Jews—and the Jews side with the British and oppose the freedom of Palestine, as they fear that this would mean Arab rule. The two pull different ways, and conflicts necessarily occur. On the Arab side are numbers, on the other side great financial resources and the world-wide organization of Jewry. So England pits Jewish religious nationalism against Arab nationalism, and makes it appear that her presence is necessary to act as an arbitrator and to keep the peace between the two. It is the same old game which we have seen in other countries under imperialist domination; it is curious how often it is repeated.

The Jews are a very remarkable people. Originally they were a small tribe, or several tribes, in Palestine, and their early story is told in the Old Testament of the Bible. Rather conceited they were, thinking themselves the Chosen People. But this is a conceit in which nearly all people have indulged. They were repeatedly conquered and suppressed and enslaved, and some of the most beautiful and moving poems in English are the songs and laments of these Jews as given in the authorized translation of the Bible. I suppose in the original Hebrew they are equally, or even more, beautiful. I shall give you just a few lines from one of the Psalms:—

> " By the waters of Babylon we sat down and wept : when we remembered thee, O Sion.
> As for our harps we hanged them up : upon the trees that are therein.
> For they that led us away captive required of us then a song, and melody, in our heaviness : Sing us one of the songs of Sion.
> How shall we sing the Lord's song : in a strange land ?
> If I forget thee, O Jerusalem : let my right hand forget her cunning.
> If I do not remember thee, let my tongue cleave to the roof of my mouth : yea, if I prefer not Jerusalem in my mirth."

These Jews were finally dispersed all over the world. They had no home or nation, and everywhere they went they were treated as unwelcome and undesirable strangers. They were made to live in special areas of cities, apart from the others—" ghettos " these areas were called—so that they might not pollute others. Sometimes they were made to put on a special dress. They were humiliated, reviled, tortured, and massacred; the very word " Jew " became a word of abuse, a synonym for a miser and a grasping money-lender. And yet these amazing people not only survived all this, but managed to keep their racial and cultural characteristics, and prospered and produced a host of great men. To-day they hold leading positions as scientists, statesmen, literary men, financiers, business men, and even the greatest socialists and communists have been Jews. Most of them, of course, are far from prosperous; they crowd in the cities of eastern Europe and, from time to time, suffer " pogroms " or massacres. These people without home or country, and especially the poor among them, have never ceased to dream of old Jerusalem, which appears to their imaginations greater and more magnificent than it ever was in fact. Zion they call Jerusalem, a kind of promised land, and Zionism is this call of the past which pulls them to Jerusalem and Palestine.

Towards the end of the nineteenth century this Zionist movement took gradual shape as a colonizing movement, and many Jews went to settle in Palestine. There was also a renaissance of the Hebrew language. During the World War the British armies invaded Palestine and, as they were marching on Jerusalem, the British Government made a declaration in November 1917, called the Balfour Declaration. They declared that it was their intention to establish a " Jewish National Home " in Palestine. This declaration was made to win the good will of international Jewry, and this was important from the money point of view. It was welcomed by Jews. But there was one little drawback, one not unimportant fact seems to have been overlooked. Palestine was not a wilderness, or an empty, uninhabited place. It was already somebody else's home. So that this generous gesture of the British Government was really at the expense of the people who already lived in Palestine, and these people, including Arabs, non-Arabs, Muslims, Christians, and, in fact, everybody who was not a Jew, protested vigorously at the declaration. It was really an economic question. These people felt that the Jews would compete with them in all activities and, with the great wealth behind them, would become the economic masters of the country; they were afraid that the Jews would take the bread out of their mouths and the land from the peasantry.

The story of Palestine ever since has been one of conflict between Arabs and Jews, with the British Government siding with one or the other as occasion demanded, but generally supporting the Jews. The country has been treated as a British colony with no self-government. The Arabs, supported by the Christians and other non-Jewish peoples, have demanded self-determination and complete freedom. They have taken strong objection to the mandate and to fresh immigrants on the ground that there is no room for more. As Jewish immigrants have poured in, their fear and anger have increased. They (the Arabs) have declared that " Zionism had been an accomplice of British imperialism; responsible Zionist leaders had constantly urged what an advantage a strong Jewish National Home would be to the English in guarding the road to India, just

because it was a counteracting force to Arab national aspirations ".
How India crops up in odd places !

The Arab Congress decided to non-co-operate with the British
Government and to boycott the elections to a Legislative Council
which the British were forming.   This boycott was very successful,
and the Council could not be formed.   The policy of non-co-operation of a kind lasted for several years ; than it weakened to some
extent and some groups gave partial co-operation to the British.
Even so, the British could not get an elective council, and the High
Commissioner governed as an all-powerful sultan.

In 1928 the different Arab groups again united in the Arab
Congress and demanded a democratic parliamentary system of
government " as of right ".   They further very bravely stated that
" the people of Palestine cannot and will not tolerate the present
absolute colonial system of government ".   An interesting feature
of this new wave of Arab nationalism was the stress laid on economic
questions.   This is always a sign of a growing appreciation of the
realities of the situation.

In August 1929 there were big Arab-Jew riots.   The real cause
was Arab bitterness and fear due to the growing wealth and numbers
of the Jews, as well as the Jewish opposition to Arab demands for
freedom.   The immediate cause, however, was a dispute about the
" Wailing Wall ", as it is called.   This is part of the wall which
surrounded Herod's temple in old times, and is thus sacred to the
Jews, who look upon it as a monument of the days when they were a
great people.   Subsequently a mosque was built there, and this wall
was made part of the structure.   The Jews say their prayers near
this wall and, especially, recite their lamentations in a loud voice—
hence the name the " Wailing Wall ".   The Muslims object to this
practice near a part of one of their most famous mosques.

After the riots were put down, the struggle continued in other
ways, and the curious part of it is that the Arabs had the full support
of all Christian churches in Palestine.   Both Muslims and Christians
thus joined together in great strikes and demonstrations.   Even
women took a prominent part.   This shows that the real trouble
was not religious, but economic conflict between the newcomers and
the old residents.   The League of Nations strongly criticized the
British administration for its failure to fulfil its mandatory duties,
and especially for having failed to prevent the riots of 1929.

So Palestine continues to be practically a British colony, and in
some ways worse even than a full-fledged colony, and the British
are continuing this state of affairs by playing the Jew against the
Arab.   It is full of British officials, and all the high posts are occupied
by them.   As usual with British dependencies, very little has been
done for education, in spite of the strong desire of the Arabs for
it.   The Jews, with their great financial resources, have fine
schools and colleges.   The Jewish population is already nearly a
quarter of the Muslim population, and their economic power is far
greater.   They seem to look forward to the day when they will be
the dominant community in Palestine.   The Arabs tried to gain their

co-operation in the struggle for national freedom and democratic government, but they rejected these advances. They have preferred to take sides with the foreign ruling Power, and have thus helped it to keep back freedom from the majority of the people. It is not surprising that this majority, comprising the Arabs chiefly and also the Christians, bitterly resent this attitude of the Jews.

TRANS-JORDAN

Adjoining Palestine, across the river Jordan, is yet another little State, a post-war creation of the British. This is called Trans-Jordan. It is a tiny area, bordering on the desert and lying between Syria and Arabia. The total population of the State is about 300,000, barely equal to a moderate-sized city ! The British Government could have easily joined it on to Palestine, but imperial policy always prefers division to consolidation. This State plays an important part as a step in the overland and air route to India. It is also a useful border State between the desert and the fertile lands leading to the sea on the west.

Small as the State is, the same succession of events takes place there as in the larger adjoining countries. There is the popular demand for a democratic parliament which is not agreed to, demonstrations suppressed, censorship, deportations of leaders, boycotts of government measures, and so on. The British cleverly made the Emir Abdullah (another son of King Hussein of the Hejaz and brother of Feisal) the ruler of Trans-Jordan, a puppet ruler entirely under their control. But he is useful in screening the British from the people. He gets the blame for much that happens, and he is very unpopular. Trans-Jordan under Abdullah is in fact something like the many small Indian States we have.

In theory the State is independent, but by a treaty which Abdullah signed with the British in 1928, all manner of military and other privileges are given to Britain. Trans-Jordan, in fact, becomes part of the British Empire. This is another instance, on a small scale, of the new type of independence which flourishes under the British. This treaty and generally this state of affairs is bitterly resented by the people, both Muslim and Christian. The agitation against the treaty was suppressed, even the newspapers supporting it being forbidden, and, as I have mentioned above, the leaders being deported. Thereupon opposition increased, and a National Congress met and adopted a National Pact and denounced the treaty. When the electoral roll for the new elections was being prepared, it was boycotted by the overwhelming majority of the people. Abdullah and the British, however, managed to gather together a few supporters to make a show ratification of the treaty.

During the troubles in Palestine in 1929 there were great demonstrations in Trans-Jordan against the British and the Balfour Declaration.

I go on writing to you, at great length, of happenings in different countries, and they seem to be the same tale repeated again and again. I do so to make you realize that we have not to deal so much with national peculiarities, as all of us are apt to imagine in our respective countries, as with world forces, with an awakening nationalism all over the East, and with the same technique of imperialism to combat it. As nationalism grows and advances, the tactics of imperialism change slightly; there is an outward attempt to appease and give in so far as forms are concerned. Meanwhile, as this national struggle progresses in the different countries, the social struggle, the class conflict between different classes in each country, also grows more obvious, and the feudal, and to some extent the possessing, classes side more and more with the imperialist Power.

Note (October 1938):

The triangular conflict in Palestine between Arab Nationalism, Jewish Zionism, and British Imperialism has continued and grown more and more desperate. The triumph of the Nazis in Germany drove out vast numbers of Jews from Central Europe, and the Jewish pressure on Palestine increased. This intensified the apprehensions of the Arabs that they would be submerged in floods of Jewish immigration and that Palestine would be dominated by the Jews. The Arabs fought against this, and some of them took to terrorist activities. Later some of the extremer Zionists retaliated in kind.

In April 1936 the Palestine Arabs declared a general strike which lasted for nearly six months, in spite of every attempt by the British authorities, through military force and reprisals, to crush it. Huge concentration camps grew up after the well-known Nazi pattern. Failing in this endeavour, the government appointed a Royal Commission to inquire into Palestine affairs. This Commission reported that the mandate had been a failure and should be surrendered, and suggested a partition of the country into three areas—a large area under Arab control, a small one near the sea under Jewish control, and a third area, including Jerusalem, under direct British control. This scheme of partition was objected to by almost everybody, Arab and Jew, but many of the Jews were prepared to work it. The Arabs, however, would have nothing to do with it, and their national resistance grew. During the last few months this has taken the form of a vast national movement, aggressively hostile to British rule, and gradually displacing it in large areas of Palestine, which passed under the control of the Arab Nationalists. The British Government has sent fresh armies for the re-conquest of the country, and a state of terror and frightfulness exists there.

The Arabs unfortunately indulged in a great deal of terrorism. To some extent the Jews did likewise against the Arabs. The British Government has pursued and is pursuing a ruthless policy of destruction and killing, thereby seeking to crush the national struggle for freedom. Methods which are even worse than those employed in the Black and Tan era in Ireland are being practised in Palestine, and a heavy censorship hides them from the rest of the world. Yet what comes through is bad enough. I have just read of Arab

" suspects " being herded together by the British military forces in huge barbed-wire enclosures called iron cages, each of these " cages " holding 50 to 400 prisoners, who are fed by their relations, literally like animals in a cage.

Meanwhile the whole Arab world is aflame with indignation, and the East, Muslim and non-Muslim alike, has been deeply affected by this brutal attempt to crush a people struggling for their freedom. These people have committed many wrong and terroristic deeds, but it must be remembered that they are essentially fighting for national freedom and have been cruelly suppressed by the forces of British imperialism.

It is a tragedy that two oppressed peoples—the Arabs and the Jews—should come into conflict with each other. Every one must have sympathy for the Jews in the terrible trials they are passing through in Europe, where vast numbers of them have become homeless wanderers, unwanted in any country. One can understand them being attracted to Palestine. And it is a fact that the Jewish immigrants there have improved the country, introduced industries, and raised standards of living. But we must remember that Palestine is essentially an Arab country, and must remain so, and the Arabs must not be crushed and suppressed in their own homelands. The two peoples could well co-operate together in a free Palestine, without encroaching on each other's legitimate interests, and help in building up a progressive country.

Unfortunately Palestine, being on the sea and air route to India and the East, is a vital factor in the British imperial scheme, and Jews and Arabs have both been exploited to further this scheme. The future is uncertain. The old scheme of partition is likely to fall through and a larger Arab federation with a Jewish autonomous enclave is in the air. It is certain, however, that Arab nationalism in Palestine will not be crushed, and the future of the country can only be built up on the stable foundation of Arab-Jew co-operation and the elimination of imperialism.

168

ARABIA—A JUMP FROM THE MIDDLE AGES

June 3, 1933.

I HAVE been writing to you about the Arab countries, but I have not so far dealt with the fountain-head of the Arabic language and culture and the birthplace of Islam, Arabia itself. The source of Arab civilization though it was, it has remained backward and medieval, and has been far outstripped, according to the tests of our modern civilization, by the neighbouring Arab countries— Egypt, Syria, Palestine, and Iraq. Arabia is an enormous country ; in size and area it is about two-thirds as big as India. And yet the population of the whole country is estimated to be 4,000,000 or 5,000,000 only—that is, about one-seventieth or one-eightieth of the

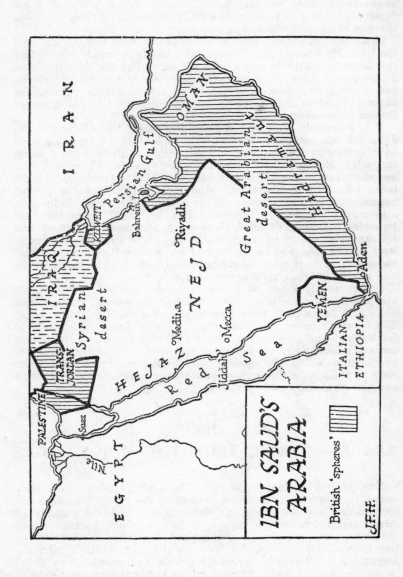

IRAN

Persian Gulf

KUWEIT

Bahrein

IRAQ

Riyadh

Oman

Great Arabian desert

Hadramaut

NEJD

TRANS-JORDAN

Syrian desert

PALESTINE

Suez

HEJAZ

Medina

Mecca

Jiddah

Aden

YEMEN

ITALIAN ETHIOPIA

Red Sea

EGYPT

Nile

IBN SAUD'S ARABIA

British 'spheres'

J.F.H.

population of India. It is obvious from this that it is very thinly populated; most of it is indeed a desert, and it was because of this that it escaped the attentions of greedy adventurers in the past, and remained a relic of medievalism, without railways or telegraphs or telephones or the like, in the midst of a changing world. It was largely inhabited by wandering nomad tribes—the Bedouins they are called—and they travelled across the desert sands on their swift camels, the " ships of the desert ", and on the backs of their beautiful Arab horses, known the world over. They lived a patriarchal life which had changed little in 1000 years. The World War changed all this, as it changed many other things.

If you will look at the map you will find that the great Arabian peninsula lies between the Red Sea and the Persian Gulf. To the south of it lies the Arabian Sea, to the north lie Palestine and Trans-Jordan and the Syrian desert, and to the north-east the green and fertile valleys of Iraq. Along the west coast, bordering the Red Sea, lies the land of Hejaz, which is the cradle of Islam, containing the holy cities Mecca and Medina and the port, Jeddah, where thousands of pilgrims land every year on their way to Mecca. In the centre of Arabia and towards the east up to the Persian Gulf lies Nejd. The Hejaz and Nejd are the two main divisions of Arabia. In the south-west lies Yemen, known from the old Roman times as Arabia Felix, Arabia the Fortunate, the Happy, because it was fertile and fruitful, in contrast with the rest, which was largely barren and desert. This part is, as one would expect, thickly populated. Almost at the south-western tip of Arabia lies Aden, a British possession and a port of call for ships passing between East and West.

Before the World War nearly the whole country was under Turkish control or acknowledged Turkish overlordship. But in Nejd the Emir Ibn Saud was gradually emerging as an independent ruler and was spreading out by conquest to the Persian Gulf. This was in the years preceding the war. Ibn Saud was the head of a particular community or sect of Muslims known as Wahabis, which was founded in the eighteenth century by Abdul Wahab. This was really a reform movement in Islam, something like the Puritans in Christianity. The Wahabis were against many ceremonies and the saint-worship that had become so popular with the Muslim masses, in the form of worship of tombs and what were supposed to be the relics of holy men. The Wahabis called this idolatry, just as the Puritans of Europe had called the Roman Catholics, who worshipped the images and relics of saints, idolaters. Thus, even apart from political rivalry, there was a religious feud between the Wahabis and the other Muslim sects in Arabia.

During the World War Arabia became a hotbed of British intrigue, and British and Indian money was lavishly spent in subsidizing and bribing the various Arab chiefs. All manner of promises were made to them, and they were encouraged to revolt against Turkey. Sometimes two rival chiefs, who were fighting each other, were both receiving British subsidies ! The British succeeded in getting the

Sherif Hussein of Mecca to raise the Arab standard of revolt. Hussein's importance consisted in the fact that he was a descendant of the Prophet Mohammad, and was therefore greatly respected. Hussein was promised by the British the kingdom of a united Arabia.

Ibn Saud was cleverer. He got himself recognized as an independent sovereign by the British, accepted a tidy little sum of £5000 or about Rs. 70,000 per month from them, and promised to remain neutral. So, while others were fighting, he consolidated his position and strengthened it, to some extent with the help of British gold. The Sherif Hussein was becoming unpopular in Islamic countries, including India, because of his rebellion against the Sultan of Turkey, who was also then the Caliph. Ibn Saud, by quietly remaining neutral, took full advantage of changing conditions and slowly built up a reputation for himself of being the strong man of Islam.

In the south was Yemen. The Imam, or ruler, of Yemen remained loyal to the Turks right through the war. But he was cut off from the scene of operations and could not do much. After Turkey's defeat he became independent. Yemen is still an independent State.

The end of the war found England dominating Arabia and trying to use both Hussein and Ibn Saud as her tools. Ibn Saud was too clever to allow himself to be exploited. The Sherif Hussein's family, however, suddenly blossomed out in full glory, backed as it was by British force. Hussein himself became King of the Hejaz; one of his sons, Feisal, became ruler of Syria; and another son, Abdullah, was made by the British the ruler of the small new state Trans-Jordan. The glory was short-lived, for, as we have seen, Feisal was driven out of Syria by the French, and Hussein's kingship vanished away before the advancing Wahabis of Ibn Saud. Feisal, having joined the unemployed again, was provided by the British with the rulership of Iraq, reigning there by the grace of his patrons.

During the brief period of Hussein's kingship of the Hejaz, the Turkish Parliament at Angora abolished the Caliphate in 1924. There was no Caliph, and Hussein, greatly daring, jumped on to the empty throne and proclaimed himself the Caliph of Islam. Ibn Saud saw that his time had come, and he appealed both to Arab nationalism and to Muslim internationalism against Hussein. He stood out as the champion of Islam against an ambitious usurper, and with the help of careful propaganda managed to gain the good will of Muslims in other countries. The Khilafat Committee in India sent him their good wishes. Seeing which way the wind was blowing, and realizing that the horse they had so far backed was not likely to win, the British quietly withdrew their support of Hussein. Their subsidies were stopped, and poor Hussein, who had been promised so much, was left almost friendless and helpless before a powerful and advancing enemy.

Within a few months, in October 1924, the Wahabis entered Mecca and, in accordance with their puritan faith, destroyed some tombs. There was a good deal of consternation in Muslim countries at this destruction; even in India much feeling was aroused. Next year Medina and Jeddah fell to Ibn Saud, and Hussein and his family were driven away from the Hejaz. Early in 1926 Ibn Saud proclaimed himself King of the Hejaz. In order to consolidate his new position and to keep the good will of Muslims abroad, he held an Islamic World Congress at Mecca in June 1926, to which he invited representative Muslims from other countries. Apparently he had no desire to become Caliph, and in any event he was not likely to be accepted as such by large numbers of Muslims because of his Wahabism. King Fuad of Egypt, whose anti-national and despotic record we have already examined, was keen on becoming the Caliph, but nobody would have him, not even his own people of Egypt. Hussein, after his defeat, had abdicated from the Caliphate he had assumed.

The Islamic Congress held at Mecca did not come to any important decision, and it was perhaps not meant to do so. It was a device adopted by Ibn Saud to strengthen his position, especially before foreign Powers. Indian representatives of the Khilafat Committee, and I think Maulana Mohammad Ali was one of them, returned disappointed and angry with Ibn Saud. But this did not make much difference to him. He had exploited the Indian Khilafat Committee when he wanted its help, and now he could well do without its good will.

Ibn Saud was soon master of nearly the whole country with the exception of Yemen, which continued as an independent State under its old Imam. But for this corner in the south-west, he was lord of Arabia and he took the title of King of Nejd, thus becoming a double king, King of Hejaz and King of Nejd. Foreign Powers recognized his independence, and foreigners were not allowed any special privileges, as they are in Egypt still. Indeed, they could not even take wines and other alcoholic drinks.

Ibn Saud had succeeded as a soldier and a fighter. He now set himself the much harder task of adapting his State to modern conditions. From the patriarchal stage it was to jump into the modern world. It appears that Ibn Saud has met with considerable success in this task also, and has thus shown to the world that he is a far-seeing statesman.

His first success was in the putting down of internal disorder. Within a very short time the great caravan and pilgrim routes were perfectly safe. This was a great triumph, and was naturally welcomed by the large numbers of pilgrims who had so far often had to face robbery on the highways.

An even more striking success was the settling of the nomad Bedouins. He started these settlements even before his conquest of the Hejaz, and in this way he laid the foundations of a modern State. It was not easy to settle the restless and wandering and freedom-loving Bedouins, but Ibn Saud has largely succeeded. The administration of the State has been improved in many ways, and aeroplanes and motors and telephones and many other symbols of modern civilization have appeared. Slowly but surely the Hejaz is becoming modernized. But it is not an easy matter to jump from the Middle Ages to the present day, and the greatest difficulty lies in changing people's ideas. This new progress and change were not to the liking of many of the Arabs; the new-fangled machinery of the West, their engines and motors and aeroplanes, struck them as the inventions of the evil one. They protested against these innovations, and they even rose against Ibn Saud in 1929. Ibn Saud tried to win them over by tact and argument, and succeeded with many. Some continued in their revolt, and were defeated by Ibn Saud.

Another difficulty then faced Ibn Saud, but this was a difficulty which all the world had to face. From 1930 onwards there has been a tremendous slump in trade everywhere. The great industrial countries of the West have felt this most, and are still struggling in its ever-tightening grip. Arabia has little to do with world trade, but the slump made itself felt in another way. The chief source of revenue of Ibn Saud has been the income derived from the great annual pilgrimage to Mecca. About 100,000 pilgrims from foreign countries used to visit Mecca every year. In 1930 there was a sudden drop to 40,000 and the fall continued in subsequent years. This resulted in a complete upsetting of the economic structure of the State, and there was great misery in many parts of Arabia. The lack of money has handicapped Ibn Saud in many ways and put a stop to many of his schemes of reform. He would not give concessions to foreigners, for he rightly feared that foreign exploitation óf the country's resources would lead to an increase of foreign influence. And this would mean foreign interference and a lessening of independence. His fears were perfectly justified, for most of the ills from which colonial dependent countries have suffered have arisen from this foreign exploitation. Ibn Saud preferred poverty and freedom to a measure of progress and riches minus freedom.

The pressure due to the trade slump, however, led Ibn Saud to revise his policy a little, and he began to give some concessions to foreigners. But even so he was careful to safeguard his independence, and conditions were laid down for this. For the present concessions are only to be given to foreign Muslim groups. Thus one of the first concessions to be given was to an Indian Muslim group of capitalists for the building of a railway between the port, Jeddah, and Mecca. This railway is a tremendous thing in Arabia, for it revolutionizes the annual pilgrimage. It not only benefits the pilgrims, but also helps greatly in modernizing the Arabs' outlook.

I have already told you in a previous letter of the one railway which exists at present in Arabia—the Hejaz Railway, which connects Medina to the Baghdad Railway in Aleppo in Syria.

I have mentioned in the early part of this letter that Yemen in the south-west was known as Arabia Felix. As a matter of fact this name was also applied to a great part of Southern Arabia, stretching almost to the Persian Gulf. But the name is most inappropriate for this area, as it is an inhospitable desert. Perhaps it was not known sufficiently in the past, and thus a mistake was made. Till recently it was unknown territory, one of the few places on the earth's surface which had not been charted and mapped out.

169

IRAQ AND THE VIRTUES OF AERIAL BOMBING

June 7, 1933

ONE Arab country remains for us to consider. This is Iraq or Mesopotamia, the rich and fertile land between the two rivers, the Tigris and the Euphrates, the land of old story, of Baghdad and Harounal-Rashid and the Arabian Nights. It lies between Persia and the Arabian desert; to the south is its principal port Basra, a little way up the river from the Persian Gulf; in the north it touches Turkey. Iraq and Turkey meet in Kurdistan, the area inhabited by the Kurds. Most of these Kurds are in Turkey now, and I have told you of their struggle for freedom against the Turks. But many Kurds are in Iraq also, and they form an important minority there. Mosul, which was long a bone of contention between Turkey and England, now lies in this northern Kurdish area of Iraq, which means that it is under British control. Near Mosul lie the ruins of ancient Nineveh of the Assyrians.

Iraq was one of the countries for which England received a " mandate " from the League of Nations, a " mandate " being, in the pious language of the League, a " sacred trust " of civilization on behalf of the League of Nations. The idea was that the inhabitants of the mandated territory were not advanced enough or capable of looking after their own interests, and were therefore to be helped in doing so by the great Powers. A comparable procedure perhaps would be to appoint a tiger to look after the interests of a number of cows or deer. These mandates were supposed to be given at the desire of the people concerned. The mandates of the countries freed from Turkish rule in western Asia fell to the lot of England and France. The governments of these two countries declared, as I have already told you, that their sole aim was " the complete and definite emancipation of the peoples . . . and the establishment of national governments and administrations deriving their authority from the initiative and free choice of the indigenous populations ". What steps have been taken to realize this noble aim during the last dozen years, we have briefly seen so far in Syria, Palestine and Trans-Jordan, where there were repeated disturbances and non-co-operation and boycott. The " initiative and free choice " of the people were then encouraged by shooting them down, deporting and exiling their leaders, suppressing their newspapers, destroying their cities and villages, and often proclaiming martial law. There is nothing novel in such happenings. Imperialist Powers have indulged in violence and destruction and terrorism from the earliest days of historic record. The novel feature of the modern type of imperialism is its attempt to hide its terrorism and exploitation behind pious phrases about " trusteeship " and the " good of the masses " and " the training of backward peoples in self-government " and the like. They shoot and kill and destroy only for the good of the people shot down. This hypocrisy may be perhaps a sign of advance, for hypocrisy is a tribute to virtue, and it shows that the truth is not liked, and is therefore wrapped up in these comforting and deluding phrases, and thus hidden away. But somehow this sanctimonious hypocrisy seems far worse than the brutal truth.

Let us now see how the wishes of the inhabitants were given effect to in Iraq, and how this country has marched to freedom under the British mandate. During the World War the English had made Iraq, or Mesopotamia as it used to be called then, their base for operations against Turkey. They flooded the country with British and Indian troops. They suffered one big defeat in April 1916, when a British army under General Townshend had to surrender to the Turks at Kutal-Amara. There was terrible waste and mismanagement in the whole of the Mesopotamian campaign, and as the Indian Government was largely responsible for this, it came in for a great deal of strong criticism for its inefficiency and stupidity. However, the great resources of the British told in the long run, and they drove the Turks north and captured Baghdad and later almost reached Mosul. At the end of the war the whole of Iraq was under British military occupation.

The first reaction of the grant of the Iraq mandate to England was seen early in 1920. There were strong protests against this, and the protests soon developed into disturbances, and the disturbances into a rebellion, which spread to the whole country. It is a curious and interesting fact that this first half of 1920 saw more or less simultaneous disturbances in Turkey, Egypt, Syria, Palestine, Iraq, and Persia. Even in India in those days non-co-operation was in the air. The rebellion in Iraq was ultimately crushed, largely with the help of troops from India. It has long been the function of the Indian Army to do the dirty work of British imperialism, and because of this, our country has been made sufficiently unpopular in the Middle East and elsewhere.

The Iraq rebellion was put down by the British, partly by force and partly by assurances of future independence. They established a provisional government with Arab ministers, but behind each minister was a British adviser, who was the real power. Even these tame and nominated ministers proved to be too aggressive for British liking. British plans demanded a complete subservience of Iraq, and some of the ministers refused to be parties to this. Therefore, in April 1921 the British arrested and exiled the leading minister, Sayyid Talib Shah, who was the ablest of the lot, and another step was thus taken in preparing the country for independence. In the summer of 1921, Feisal, the son of Hussein of the Hejaz, was brought over by the British and presented to the Iraqis as their future king. Feisal, you will remember, was just then unemployed, as his Syrian venture had collapsed before the French attack. He was a good friend of the British, and had taken a leading part in the Arab revolt against Turkey during the World War. He was thus likely to be more amenable to British plans than the local ministers had so far been. The " notables ", the rich middle class and other leading personalities, agreed to have Feisal as king on condition that the government was a constitutional one with a democratic parliament. They had little choice in the matter. What they wanted was a real parliament, and as Feisal was likely to be king anyhow, they made this parliament a condition. The people generally were not consulted. So Feisal became king in August 1921.

But this was no solution of the problem, for the Iraqi people were very much opposed to the British mandate and wanted complete independence and then unity with the other Arab countries. Agitation and demonstrations continued, and matters came to a head a year later, in August 1922. The British authorities then gave a further lesson in independence to the Iraqis. The British High Commissioner, Sir Percy Cox, put an end to the power of the King (who was ill then) as well as that of the ministry and of the council which Iraq had been given, and took full charge of the government himself. In fact he became the absolute dictator, and he enforced his will and suppressed disturbances with the help of British forces, and especially the British Air Force. The old story, which we find everywhere with variations—India, Egypt, Syria, etc.—was repeated. Nationalist newspapers were suspended, the parties were dissolved, leaders were exiled, and British aeroplanes with their bombs established the might of the British Empire.

Again this was no solution of the problem. After a few months Sir Percy Cox permitted the King and the ministry to function outwardly, and got them to agree to a treaty with Britain. Assurances were again given that England would help Iraq to independence, and even make her a member of the League of Nations. Behind these beautiful and comforting promises lay the solid fact that the Iraq Government was made to agree to run the administration with the help of British officers, or those approved by Britain. This treaty of October 1922 was made over the heads of the people, and was condemned by them. It was pointed out that the Arab Government was a sham and that the real power continued to be the British authority. The leaders decided to boycott the elections to the National Constituent Assembly, which was called to draw up the future constitution. This non-co-operation was successful and the Assembly could not meet. There were also disturbances and difficulties in collecting taxes.

For over a year, right through 1923, these troubles continued. At length some changes, favourable to Iraq, were made in the treaty, and some of the leading agitators were exiled. The agitation lessened, and early in 1924 elections for the Constituent Assembly could be held. This Assembly also opposed the British treaty. Strong pressure was brought to bear upon it by the British, and at last the treaty was ratified by a little over a third of the members, a large number of the deputies not even attending this session.

The Constituent Assembly drafted a new constitution for Iraq, and on paper it seemed a fair one, laying down that Iraq was a sovereign and independent free State with a constitutional hereditary monarchy and a parliamentary form of government. But of the two houses of parliament one, the Senate, was to be nominated by

the King. Thus the King had great power, and behind the King
were the British officials who occupied the key positions. This
constitution came into force in March 1925, and for some years the
new Parliament functioned, but the protest against the mandate
continued. A great deal of attention was concentrated on the
dispute between England and Turkey about Mosul, for Iraq was
also a claimant of this area. This dispute was finally settled in
June 1926, by a joint treaty between England, Iraq, and Turkey.
Mosul went to Iraq, and as Iraq itself lies in the shadow of British
imperialism, British interests were thus safeguarded.

In June 1930 there was a fresh treaty of alliance between Britain
and Iraq. Again Iraq's·full independence, both in home and foreign
affairs, was recognized. But the safeguards and the exceptions
were such as to convert this independence into a veiled protectorate.
In order to safeguard the route to India, Britain's " essential communications ", as the treaty says, Iraq provides England with sites
for air bases. Britain also maintains troops in Mosul and elsewhere. Iraq is only to have British military instructors, and British
officers are to serve in an advisory capacity with the Iraq forces.
Arms, ammunitions, aircraft, etc., are to be obtained from Britain.
In case of war Britain is to have all facilities in the country in order
to carry on warlike operations against the enemy. Thus from the
strategic area round Mosul England can strike easily at Turkey,
Persia, or at the Soviets in Azerbaijan.

This treaty was followed by 1931 by a Judicial Agreement
between Britain and Iraq, in which Iraq undertakes to employ a
British Judicial Adviser, a British President of the Court of Appeal,
and British presidents at Baghdad, Basra, Mosul, and other places.

Besides these provisions it appears that British officials occupy
many high offices. In effect, therefore, this " independent " country
is practically a protectorate of England, and the treaty of alliance of
1930, which ensures this, is for twenty-five years.

Although the new Parliament functioned after the adoption of the
new constitution in 1925, the people were far from satisfied, and in
the outlying areas disturbances sometimes took place. This was
especially the case in Kurdish areas, where there were repeated
outbreaks, which were suppressed by the British Air Force by the
gentle practice of bombing and destroying whole villages. After
the treaty of 1930 the question arose of Iraq being made a member
of the League of Nations under British auspices. But the country
was not at peace, and disturbances continued. This was neither
to the credit of the mandatory Power, England, nor to that of the
existing government of King Feisal, for these revolts were proof
enough that the people were not satisfied with the government that
had been thrust upon them by the British. It was considered very
undesirable that these matters should come up before the League,
and so a special effort was made to put an end to these disturbances
by force and terrorism. The British Air Force was used for this
purpose, and the result of its attempts to bring peace and order may
be appreciated to some extent from the description of an eminent

English officer. Lt.-Col. Sir Arnold Wilson, in the course of the anniversary lecture to the Royal Asian Society in London on June 8, 1932, referred to

" the pertinacity with which (notwithstanding declarations at Geneva) the R.A.F. has been bombing the Kurdish population for the last ten years, and in particular the last six months. Devastated villages, slaughtered cattle, maimed women and children bear witness to the spread, in the words of the special correspondent to *The Times*, of a uniform pattern of civilization."

Finding that the people of the villages often ran away and hid themselves on the approach of an aeroplane, and were not sporting enough to wait for the bombs to kill them, a new type of bomb—the time-delayed bomb—was used. This did not burst on falling, but was so wound up as to burst some time afterwards. This devilish ruse was meant to mislead the villagers into returning to their huts after the aeroplanes had gone and then being hit by the bursting of the bomb. Those who died were the comparatively fortunate ones. Those who were maimed, whose limbs were torn away sometimes, or who had other serious injuries, were far more unfortunate, for there was no medical aid available in those distant villages.

So peace and order were restored, and the Government of Iraq presented itself under British auspices before the League of Nations and was admitted as a member. It has been said, truly enough, that Iraq was " bombed " into the League.

Iraq having become a member State of the League, the British mandate is over. It has been replaced by the treaty of 1930, which ensures effective British control of the State. Dissatisfaction at this state of affairs continues, for the people of Iraq want complete freedom and the unity of Arab nations. Membership of the League of Nations does not interest them much, for they consider, as do most other oppressed people in the East, that the League is just an instrument in the hands of the great European Powers to further their own colonial and other ends.[1]

We have now finished our survey of the Arab nations. You will have noticed how all of them, in common with India and other Eastern countries, were powerfully moved by waves of nationalism after the World War. It was like an electric current passing through them all at the same time. Another remarkable feature was the similarity of methods adopted. There were insurrections and violent rebellions in many of these countries, but gradually they came to rely more and more on a policy of non-co-operation and boycott. There is no doubt that the fashion in this new method of resistance was set by India in 1920, when the Congress followed Mahatma Gandhi's lead. The idea of non-co-operation and the boycott of legislatures has spread from India to other countries of the East, and become one of the well-recognized and frequently practised methods of the struggle for national freedom.

[1] King Feisal died in September 1933 and was succeeded by his son Gazi I, who was killed in an accident in 1939, and who was succeeded by his baby son.

I should like to draw your attention to an interesting contrast between English and French methods of imperialist control. England, in all her colonial countries, tried to form an alliance with the feudal, the landowning, and the most conservative and backward classes. We have seen this in India, in Egypt, and elsewhere. She created shaky thrones in her colonial countries and put reactionary rulers on them, well knowing that they would support her. Thus she put Fuad in Egypt, Feisal in Iraq, Abdullah in Trans-Jordan, and she tried to put Hussein in the Hejaz. France, on the other hand, being herself a typical *bourgeois* country, tries to find support in some parts of the *bourgeoisie* of the colonial countries, the rising middle classes. In Syria, for instance, she looked to the Christian middle classes for support. Both England and France in all the colonial countries under them rely principally on the policy of weakening the nationalism opposed to them by dividing it and creating minority, racial, and religious problems. Nationalism is, however, gradually surmounting these divisions all over the East, and nowhere more so perhaps than in the Arab countries of the Middle East, where religious groups are becoming weaker before the ideal of a common nationality.

I have told you above about the activities of the British R.A.F. (Royal Air Force) in Iraq. For the last dozen years or so it has become the definite policy of the British Government to use aeroplanes to do " police work ", as it is called, in their semi-colonial countries. This is done especially where a measure of self-government is given and the administration is largely indigenous. Armies of occupation are not kept now in these countries, or are reduced greatly. This has many advantages. A great deal of money is saved, and the military occupation of a country is less in evidence. At the same time aeroplanes and bombs give them complete control over the situation. In this way the use of bombing from aeroplanes has increased greatly in independent areas, and the British probably use this method far more than any other Power. I have told you about Iraq. The same story can be repeated for the North-West Frontier of India, where this kind of bombing is a regular and frequent occurrence.

This method may be cheaper and more expeditious than the old one of sending an army. But it is a terribly cruel and ghastly method. Indeed, it is difficult to imagine anything more disgustingly barbarous than to throw bombs, and especially time-delayed bombs, on whole villages, and destroy innocent and guilty alike. This method also makes an invasion of another country very easy. So an outcry has arisen against it, and eloquent speeches are delivered at Geneva at the League of Nations against the barbarity of attacking civilian populations by air. All the nations, including the United States, were in favour of the total abolition of aerial bombardment. But the British insisted on reserving the right to use aircraft for " police purposes " in the colonies, and this prevented agreement in the League as well as at the Disarmament Conference held in 1933.

170

AFGHANISTAN AND SOME OTHER COUNTRIES OF ASIA

June 8, 1933

To the east of Iraq lies Iran or Persia, and to the east of Persia lies Afghanistan. Both Persia and Afghanistan are India's neighbours, for the Persian frontier touches India (in Baluchistan) for several hundred miles, and Afghanistan and India lie side by side for about 1000 miles from the extreme western tip of Baluchistan to the northern mountains of the Hindu Kush, where India rests her snowy head on the heart of Central Asia, and looks down upon the territories of the Soviets. Not only are these three countries neighbours, but racially they are akin, for the old Aryan stock dominates in all of them. Culturally, as we have seen, they have had much in common in the past. Till recently, Persian was the language of the learned in northern India, and even now it is popular, especially among the Muslims. In Afghanistan Persian is still the Court language, the popular language of the Afghans being Pashtu.

About Persia I do not wish to add to what I have already told you in previous letters. But recent events in Afghanistan deserve a brief mention. Afghan history is almost a part of Indian history; indeed, for long Afghanistan was part of India. Since its separation, and especially during the last 100 years or more, it has been a buffer State between the two great empires of Russia and England. The Russian Empire has gone and given place to the Soviet Union, but Afghanistan still plays its old part of buffer, where Englishmen and Russians intrigue and try to gain the mastery. The nineteenth century saw these intrigues develop into wars between England and Afghanistan, which resulted in many British disasters but the ultimate supremacy of England. Many Afghan *detenus*, members of the Afghan royal family, are still scattered about northern India, and remind us of England's interventions in Afghanistan. Amirs friendly to the British came to rule, and Afghanistan's foreign policy was definitely put under British control. But, however friendly these Amirs were, they could not be wholly relied upon, and subsidies of large sums of money were given to them annually by the British. Such was the Amir Abdur Rahman, who had a long reign, ending in 1901. He was followed by the Amir Habibullah, who was also well inclined towards the British.

One of the reasons for Afghanistan's dependence on the British in India was the position of the country. You will see in the map that it is cut off from the sea by Baluchistan. It was thus like a house with no means of reaching the highway except through someone else's grounds, and this is a troublesome affair. Its easiest way of

communicating with the outside world was through India.   There
were no proper communications in those days in the Russian
territory to the north of Afghanistan.   I believe that the Soviet
Government has recently developed these communications, both by
building railways and encouraging air and motor services.   India
thus being Afghanistan's window to the world, the British Government could take advantage of this fact by exerting pressure in many
ways.   This difficulty of Afghanistan's access to the sea is still one
of the major problems confronting the country.

Early in 1919 the intrigues and rivalries of the Afghan Court
broke out on the surface, and there were two palace revolutions in
quick succession.   I do not know exactly what happened behind
the scenes or who was responsible for these changes.   The Amir
Habibullah was assassinated, and thereupon his brother Nasrullah
became Amir.   But very soon Nasrullah was removed and Amanullah, one of the younger sons of Habibullah, became Amir.   He
followed this up in May 1919 by a petty invasion of India.   Exactly
what the immediate provocation for this was or who took the initiative I do not know.   Probably Amanullah resented any kind of
dependence on the British and wanted to establish the full independence of his country.   Probably also he thought that the
conditions were favourable.   Those were the days, you will remember, of martial law in the Punjab and general discontent in India,
and a growing agitation among the Muslims over the Khilafat
question.   Whatever the causes and inducements, an Afghan war
with the British resulted.   But this war was of a remarkably short
duration, and there was very little fighting.   In a military sense the
British in India were, of course, far stronger than Amanullah, but
they were in no mood for war, and some petty incidents were
enough to make them come to terms with the Afghans.   The result
was the recognition of Afghanistan as an independent country, with
full control of its foreign relations with other countries.   Thus
Amanullah had gained his object, and his prestige went up everywhere in Europe and Asia.   Naturally he was not in the good books
of the British.

Amanullah began to attract still more attention by the new policy
he pursued in his country.   This was one of rapid reforms on
Western lines—the " westernization " of Afghanistan as it is called.
In this work his wife, Queen Souriyah, helped him greatly.   She had
been educated partly in Europe, and the seclusion of women behind
the veil irked her.   Thus began the strange process of changing a
very backward country in quick time, of pushing and driving the
Afghan out of his old ruts into the new ways.   Mustafa Kemal
Pasha was evidently Amanullah's ideal, and he tried to copy him in
many ways, even making Afghans put on coats and trousers and
European hats, and making them shave off their beards.   But
Amanullah did not have the grit or the ability of Mustafa Kemal.
Kemal Pasha had made his position perfectly secure, internationally
and nationally, before he started his sweeping reforms.   He had an
efficient and hardened army at his back and a tremendous prestige

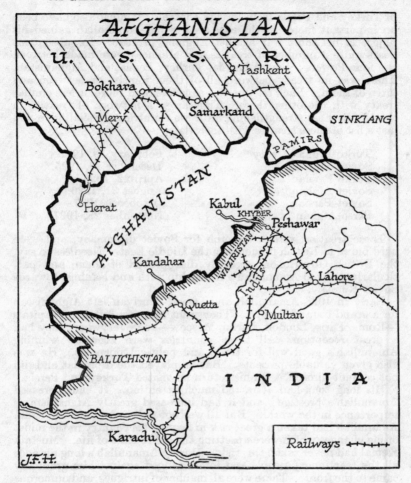

with all his people. Amanullah went ahead without these precautions, and his task was far harder, for the Afghans were much more backward than any of the Turks.

But it is easy to be wise after the event. In the early years of his reign, Amanullah seemed to be carrying everything before him. He sent many Afghan boys and girls to Europe for education. He started many reforms in his administration. He strengthened his international position by treaties with his neighbours and with Turkey. The Soviets had deliberately adopted a generous and friendly policy with all Eastern countries from China to Turkey, and this Soviet friendliness and help had been a great factor in the freeing

of Turkey and Persia from foreign control. It must also have been
an important factor in the ease with which Amanullah gained his
object in his short war against England in 1919. In subsequent
years quite a number of treaties and alliances were made between
the four Powers : Soviet Russia, Turkey, Persia, and Afghanistan.
There was no treaty between all of them jointly, or between any
three of them. Each one made a separate, and more or less similar
treaty with the other three. Thus arose a network of treaties in
the Middle East strengthening all these countries. I shall give you
just a list of these treaties with their dates :—

Turko-Afghan treaty	..	..	February 19, 1921.
Soviet-Turkish ,,	..	..	December 17, 1925.
Turko-Persian ,,	..	..	April 22, 1926.
Soviet-Afghan ,,	..	..	August 31, 1926.
Soviet-Persian ,,	..	..	October 1, 1927.
Perso-Afghan ,,	..	..	November 28, 1927.

These treaties were a triumph for Soviet diplomacy, and were
hard blows to British influence in the Middle East. Needless to say,
the British Government strongly disapproved of them, and particularly disliked Amanullah's friendship with and leanings towards
Soviet Russia.

Early in 1928 Amanullah and Queen Souriyah left Afghanistan
for a grand tour of Europe. They went to many European capitals
—Rome, Paris, London, Berlin, Moscow—and everywhere they had
a great reception. All these countries were keen on winning
Amanullah's good will for trade and political purposes. He was
also given valuable presents. But he played the diplomat and did
not commit himself. On his return he visited Turkey and Persia.

His long tour had attracted much attention. It had increased
Amanullah's prestige; and it had increased greatly Afghanistan's
importance in the world. But all was not well in Afghanistan itself.
Amanullah had taken a great risk in leaving his country in the midst
of big changes which were upsetting the old routine of life. Mustafa
Kemal had never taken this risk. During Amanullah's long absence
all the reactionary people and forces ranged against him gradually
came to the front. There were all manner of intrigues, and numerous
rumours to discredit him. Money seemed to flow in for this anti-
Amanullah propaganda, nobody knew from where. Many *mullahs*,
the priestly ones, seemed to be paid for this work, and they spread
all over the country denouncing Amanullah as a *kafir*, an enemy of
the faith. Curious pictures of Queen Souriyah in European evening
dress or some negligé were circulated by the thousand in the villages
—to show how improperly she used to dress herself. Who was
responsible for this widespread and expensive propaganda ? The
Afghans had neither the money for it nor the training; they were
just suitable material for it. It was widely believed and stated in
the Middle East and in Europe that the British Secret Service was at
the back of this propaganda. Such things can seldom be proved,

and no definite evidence was forthcoming to connect the British with this work, though it is said that the Afghan rebels were armed with British rifles. But it was obvious enough that England was interested in weakening Amanullah in Afghanistan.

While his foundations were being sapped in Afghanistan, Amanullah was enjoying splendid receptions in European capitals. He returned to his country full of fresh zeal for his reforms, full of new ideas, and more impressed than ever by Kemal Pasha, whom he had met at Angora. He set to work immediately to push on these reforms. He abolished the titles of the nobility and tried to curtail the powers of the religious heads. He even tried to make a Cabinet council responsible for the government, thus reducing his own autocratic powers. The emancipation of women was also slowly pushed on.

Suddenly the smouldering fire broke out, and rebellion flared up towards the end of 1928. Under the leadership of an ordinary water-carrier, Bacha-i-Saqao, this rebellion spread, and in 1929 it triumphed. Amanullah and his Queen ran away, and the water-carrier became the Amir. For five months Bacha-i-Saqao reigned in Kabul, when he was removed by Nadir Khan, a general and minister of Amanullah. Nadir Khan played his own hand, and when he had triumphed he took the ruler's place himself as Nadir Shah. There were recurring troubles and disturbances in the country, but Nadir Shah continued as the ruler, as he was friendly to England and received help from her. The British Government lent him a large sum of money without interest and provided him with rifles and ammunition. The unsettled conditions in Afghanistan are largely due to its being a buffer State between two powerful rivals.[1]

And now I have done with Afghanistan and with western and southern Asia. I shall tell you briefly about some recent happenings in the south-east corner of Asia, and then end this letter.

East of Burma lies Siam, the only country which has managed to keep its independence in this part of the world. It is jammed in between British Burma and French Indo-China. The country is full of old Indian remains, and its traditions and culture and ceremonies still bear the old Indian impress. Till recently it was an autocratic monarchy, and social conditions were largely feudal, with a small and growing middle class. The title of the kings was frequently, I believe, Rama, another word which brings us back to India. Thus they were Rama I, Rama II, and so on. During the World War Siam joined the Allies, when the victory of the Allies seemed assured, and later it became a member of the League of Nations.

In June 1932 there was a *coup d'état* in Bangkok, the capital of Siam, and the autocratic form of government was ended, giving place to the beginnings of democracy under the control of the Siam People's Party. A group of young Siamese military officers and others, under the leadership of a lawyer, Luang Pradit, arrested

[1] In November 1933 Nadir Shah was assassinated, and was succeeded by his young son, who became King Zahir Shah.

members of the royal family and the principal ministers, and made
King Prajadhipok accept a constitution.   The King's powers were
limited and a People's Assembly came into existence.   This change
had popular support, but it was not due 'to a mass upheaval.   It
resembled the military *coup* by which the Young Turks had ended the
depotism of Sultan Abdul Hamid.   The King's quick submission
ended the crisis, but the King's readiness to submit to change was
not genuine, and in April 1933 he suddenly dissolved the Assembly
and expelled Luang Pradit.   Two months later there was another
coup d'état and the Assembly was revived.   The new government
in Siam has not developed any close contacts with England, but
inclines much more towards Japan.[1]

Nationalism has spread also, and is growing in strength, in French
Indo-China to the east of Siam.   In trying to suppress the nationalist
movement, the French Government have had many conspiracy cases
and given long terms of imprisonment to large numbers of people.
A revealing statement was made in Geneva at a meeting of the
Disarmament Conference in March 1933, by the French representative.   This representative, M. Sarraut, had himself been the
Governor of French Indo-China.   He referred to " the development
of nationalism in colonial possessions which were becoming extremely
difficult to administer ".   He gave the instance of French Indo-
China, where 10,000 men were now required to maintain order, as
compared to 1500 when he was Governor there.

Lastly, Java in the Dutch East Indies, famous for its sugar and
rubber, and famous also for the terrible exploitation of the people
that used to take place on its plantations.   With the growth of
nationalism have come jointly, as in India, a small measure of reform
and a great deal of repression.   The great majority of the Javanese
are Muslims, and they were affected by the events in western Asia
during the World War and after.   The growth of the Chinese
revolutionary movement in Canton influenced them greatly and they
were interested in the non-co-operation movement in India.   In
1916 the Javanese were promised constitutional reforms by the Dutch
Government, and a People's Council was set up in Batavia.   But this
was largely nominated and had little power, and agitation against it
continued.   A new constitution was granted in 1925, but this made
little change and failed to satisfy the people.   There were strikes
and riots in Java and Sumatra, and in 1927 there was a rising against
the Dutch Government.   This was crushed with great cruelty.
The nationalist movement, however, went on and, on its constructive
side, built many national schools and encouraged, as in India,
cottage industries and craftsmanship.   The struggle for freedom
continues.   The sugar industry of Java has suffered greatly owing
to the world economic slump and the restriction of markets abroad
by the imposition of heavy protective duties.

Early in 1933 a curious incident took place in the eastern seas off
Java.   The crew of one of the Dutch warships, protesting against a
wage-cut, took charge of the ship and sailed away.   They did no

[1] In October 1933 there was a right-wing insurrection. but this was suppressed, and Luang Pradit continued to lead the government.

damage, and they made it clear that they were merely holding out for their wages. It was a kind of aggressive strike. Dutch aeroplanes thereupon bombed this warship, killing many of the crew, and thus took possession of it.

And now we must leave Asia with its ever-recurring conflicts between nationalism and imperialism, and go to Europe, for Europe demands attention. We have not considered post-war Europe yet, and you must remember that European conditions are still the key to world conditions. So our next few letters will be about Europe.

Two parts of Asia remain to be considered, two huge areas, the Chinese area and the Soviet area in the north. We must come back to them some time later.

171

THE REVOLUTION THAT DID NOT COME OFF

June 13, 1933

A WELL-KNOWN English writer, G. K. Chesterton, has said somewhere that the greatest event of the nineteenth century in England was the revolution which did not happen. You will remember that on several occasions during that century England was on the verge of revolution—that is, a social revolution brought about by the petty *bourgeoisie* and the workers. But always the ruling classes yielded just a little at the last moment, gave an outward share in the parliamentary structure by extending the vote, and also gave a small share in the profits of imperialist exploitation abroad, and thus kept down the impending revolution. They could afford to do so because of their expanding empire and the money they made out of it. The revolution therefore did not take place in England, but its shadow frequently lay over the country, and the fear of it shaped events. Thus a thing that did not actually happen is said to have been the greatest event of the last century.

In the same way, perhaps, it might be said that the greatest event of the post-war period in Western Europe was the revolution that did not come off. The conditions that produced the Bolshevik Revolution in Russia were present in the central and western European countries also, though in a lesser degree. The principal difference between Russia and the industrialized countries of the West—England, Germany, France, etc.—was the absence of a strong *bourgeoisie* in Russia. As a matter of fact, according to the Marxist theory, a workers' revolution was expected to break out first in these advanced industrial countries, and certainly not in backward Russia. But the World War smashed up the rotten old structure of Tsarism, and just because there was no strong middle class to step in and control the government through a parliament of the Western type, the workers' Soviets seized the power. Thus, curiously enough, the very backwardness of Russia, the very cause of her weakness, became a reason for her to take a bigger step forward than the more advanced countries. The Bolsheviks under Lenin took this step, but they were under no illusions. They knew that Russia was backward and would take a time to catch up to the more advanced countries. They hoped that their example in establishing a workers' republic would spur on the workers of other European countries to revolt against the existing régimes. In this general European social revolution they felt, lay their only hope of survival, for otherwise the young Soviet Government of Russia would be suppressed by the rest of the capitalist world.

It was in this hope and belief that they broadcast their appeals to the workers of the world in the early days of their revolution. They denounced all imperialist designs to annex territory; they said that they would not make any claim on the basis of the secret treaties between Tsarist Russia and England and France; they made it clear that Constantinople must remain with the Turks. They offered the most generous terms to the Eastern countries and to the many oppressed nationalities of the Tsarist Empire. And, above all, they stood out as the champions of the international working class, calling upon the workers everywhere to follow their example and establish socialist republics. Nationalism, and Russia as a nation, meant nothing to them, except as that part of the world where, for the first time in history, a workers' government had been established.

The Bolshevik appeals were suppressed by the German and Allied governments, but they managed to trickle down to the various fronts and the factory areas. Their effect was considerable everywhere, and a noticeable cracking up of the French army was visible. The German army and workers were even more affected. There were even risings and revolts in Germany and Austria and Hungary —the defeated countries—and for many months, or even a year or two, Europe seemed to be on the verge of a mighty social revolution. The victorious Allied countries were a little better off than the defeated ones, for success had toned them up and given them hopes (which were empty enough as subsequent events proved) of making good some of their losses at the expense of the defeated Powers. But even in the Allied countries there was the temper of revolution. Indeed, all over Europe and Asia the air was thick with discontent, and the fire of revolution smouldered beneath the surface, and often threatened to break out. There was a difference, however, in the types of discontent in Asia and Europe and in the classes which threatened revolution. In Asia the middle classes were the leaders in the national revolts against Western imperialism; in Europe the working classes threatened to upset the existing *bourgeois* capitalist social order and to seize power from the middle classes.

In spite of all these rumblings and portents, nothing like the Russian Revolution broke out in central or western Europe   The old structure was strong enough to resist the attacks made upon it, but these attacks weakened it and frightened it sufficiently to protect Soviet Russia. The Soviets would, in all likelihood, have collapsed before the imperialist Powers in 1919 or 1920 but for this powerful help behind the lines.

Gradually, as year followed year after the end of the World War, things appeared to settle down to some extent. The revolutionary elements were suppressed by a curious alliance of the reactionary conservatives, monarchists and feudal landlords on the one side, and the moderate socialists or social democrats on the other. This was indeed a strange alliance, for the social democrats proclaimed their faith in Marxism and a workers' government. Their ideal thus appeared to be, on the surface, the same as that of the Soviets and communists. And yet these social democrats feared the communists more than the capitalists, and combined with the latter to crush the former. Or it may be that they feared the capitalists so much that they did not dare to go against them; they hoped to consolidate their position by peaceful and parliamentary means, and thus bring in socialism almost imperceptibly. Whatever their motives may have been, they helped the reactionary elements to crush the revolutionary spirit, and thus actually brought about a counter-revolution in many of the European countries. This counter-revolution in its turn crushed these very social democratic parties, and new and aggressively anti-socialist forces came into Power. Roughly, events shaped themselves in this way in Europe during the years which followed the World War.

But the conflict has not ended, and the fight between the two rival forces—capitalism and socialism—goes on. There can be no permanent compromise between the two, although there have been, and there may be in the future, temporary arrangements and treaties between the two. Russia and communism stand at one pole, and the great capitalist countries of Western Europe and America stand at the other. Between the two, the liberals, the moderates, and the centre parties are disappearing everywhere. The conflict and the discontent are really caused by complete economic upsets and increasing misery all over the world, and till some equilibrium establishes itself this tussle must continue.

Of the many abortive revolutions that have taken place since the war, the German one is the most interesting and revealing, and I shall therefore tell you something about it. I have already told you of the failure of the socialists in all European countries to live up to their ideals and promises, when the war came. They were swept away by the fierce nationalism of each country, and forgot the international ideal of socialism in the mad blood-lust of war. On the very verge of the World War, on July 30, 1914, the German Social Democratic Party leaders declared against the sacrifice of " a single drop of blood of a German soldier " for the imperialist designs of the Hapsburgs. (The quarrel at the time was between Austria and Serbia over the murder of the Archduke Franz-Ferdinand of Austria.) Five days later the party supported the war, and so did other similar parties in other countries. Indeed, the Austrian socialist leader actually talked of adding Poland and Serbia to the Austrian Empire, and said that this would be no annexation !

Early in 1918 the Bolshevik appeals to the workers of Europe produced a marked effect on German workers, and there were big strikes in the munition factories. This produced a very serious situation for the German imperial government, and might even have resulted in disaster. The socialist leaders thereupon saved the situation by joining the strike committee and breaking the strike from within.

On November 4, 1918, a naval mutiny broke out in Kiel in northern Germany. The great battleships of the German navy had been ordered to put out to sea, but the sailors and stokers refused to do so. The troops that were sent out to suppress them went over to them and made common cause. The officers were deposed or arrested, and councils (Soviets) of workers and soldiers were formed. It was just like the early beginnings of the Soviet Revolution in Russia, and it seemed to be spreading all over Germany. Immediately the Social Democratic leaders appeared at Kiel and succeeded in diverting the sailors' and workers' attention into other channels. These sailors, however, left Kiel with their arms and spread out all over the country carrying the seeds of revolt.

The revolutionary movement was spreading. In Bavaria (South Germany) a republic was proclaimed. Still the Kaiser stuck on. On November 9 a general strike began in Berlin. All work was stopped, and there was hardly any violence, as the whole garrison of the city went over to the side of the revolution. The old order had visibly collapsed, and the question was, what would take its place. Some communist leaders were on the point of proclaiming a Soviet or republic, when a Social Democrat leader forestalled them by proclaiming a parliamentary republic.

So the German Republic came into existence. But it was a shadow republic, for nothing was really changed. The Social Democrats who were in command of the situation left almost everything as it was; they took a few high posts, ministerships, etc., and the army, the civil service, the judicial service, and the whole administration continued as it was in the Kaiser's days. Thus, as the title of a recent book says, " The Kaiser Goes : The Generals Remain ". Revolutions are not made or strengthened in this way. A real revolution must change the political, the social, and the economic structure. It is absurd to expect that a revolution will survive if power is left in the hands of its enemies. The German Social Democrats, however, did this very thing and gave full opportunities to opponents of the Revolution to prepare for and organize its downfall. The old militarists were still the bosses in Germany.

The new Social Democratic government did not like the Kiel sailors wandering about the country spreading revolutionary ideas. They tried to suppress these sailors in Berlin, and there were violent conflicts early in January 1919. The German communists thereupon tried to establish a Soviet government, and called upon the city masses for help. They got some help from the people and took possession of government buildings, and for about a week in January

—known as the " Red Week " in Berlin—they seemed to be in power in the city.   But the response from the masses was not sufficient, as most of the people were puzzled and did not know what to do.   The regular soldiers in Berlin were also puzzled, and they remained neutral.   As these soldiers could not be relied upon, the Social Democrats enrolled some special volunteer troops for the purpose, and with their help they crushed the communist rising.   The fighting was cruel, and no quarter was given.   Some days after the fighting was over, two of the communist leaders, Karl Liebknecht and Rosa Luxemburg, were tracked down to a place where they were in hiding and murdered in cold blood.   This murder, and the subsequent acquittal of the people who had been responsible for it, created great bitterness between the communists and the Social Democrats.   Karl Liebknecht was the son of Wilhelm Liebknecht, the famous old socialist fighter of the nineteenth century, whose name has already appeared in a previous letter of mine.   Rosa Luxemburg was also an old worker, and a great friend of Lenin. As it happened, both Liebknecht and Luxemburg had been opposed to the communist rising which resulted in their death.

The communists had been crushed by the Social Democratic Republic, and, soon after, a constitution for the Republic was drawn up at Weimar; hence it is known as the Weimar Constitution. Within three months a fresh change threatened the Republic, this time from the other side.   The reactionaries staged a counter-revolution against the Republic, and the old generals figured prominently in it.   This revolt is known as the " Kapp Putsch "—Kapp was the leader and " putsch " is the German word for such a rising. The Social Democratic government ran away from Berlin, but the workers of Berlin put an end to the " putsch " by a sudden general strike, a complete stoppage of all activities, which brought the life of the great city to a standstill.   Kapp and his friends had now to run away from Berlin before the organized workers, and the Social Democratic leaders returned again to take charge of the government.   In marked contrast with their treatment of the communists, the government was quite gentle with the Kappist rebels.   Many of them were officers drawing pensions, and, in spite of their rebellion, even the pensions continued.

A similar counter-revolutionary " putsch " or rising was organized in Bavaria.   It failed, but the chief interest of it is that the organizer was a petty Austrian officer, Hitler, who to-day is the Dictator of Germany.

The result of all this was that although the German Republic carried on in name, it grew weaker and weaker.   The split between the socialists, the Social Democrats and communists, weakened both, and the reactionaries, who openly denounced the Republic, grew more and more organized and aggressive.   The big landowners— " Junkers " they are called in Germany—and the big industrialists gradually pushed out the few socialist elements that had remained in the government.   The Peace Treaty of Versailles came as a great shock to the German people, and this was exploited by the reactionaries to their own advantage.   Under this treaty Germany had to disarm and to give up her huge army.   She was only allowed to keep a small army of 100,000.   The result was that outwardly there was disarmament and in reality a great quantity of arms were hidden away.   Huge " private armies " grew up—that is, volunteers belonging to different parties.   The conservative nationalists volunteer army was called the *Steel helmets*; the communists workers' volunteers were the *Red Front*; and later Hitler's followers formed the " Nazi " troops.

I have told you a lot about these early post-war years in Germany, and I could tell you much more to show how revolution hovered in the air and fought with the counter-revolution.   In different parts of Germany, in Bavaria and Saxony, there were also risings.   Much the same conditions prevailed in Austria, which the peace treaty reduced to a tiny fraction of its former self.   This small country, with a huge capital city, Vienna, was entirely German, in language and culture.   It became a republic on November 12, 1918, the day after the Armistice.   It wanted to become a part of Germany, but the Allied Powers strictly prohibited this, although this was a natural thing to do.   This proposed union of Austria and Germany is referred to by the German word " anschluss ".[1]

In Austria, as in Germany, the Social Democrats were in power to begin with, but fearful and lacking confidence in themselves, they followed a policy of compromise with the *bourgeois* parties. The result was a great weakening of the Social Democrats and the passing of the government into other hands.   As in Germany, private armies grew up, and finally a reactionary dictatorship was established.   For a long time there was a conflict between the socialist city of Vienna and the conservative farmers of the countryside.   The socialist Vienna municipality became famous for its fine housing and other schemes for the working classes.

In Hungary a revolution broke out as early as October 3, 1918, five weeks before the war ended.   In November a republic was proclaimed.   Four months later, in March 1919, a second revolution took place.   This was a Soviet revolution under the leadership of a communist, Bela Kun, who had been associated with Lenin previously.   A Soviet government was established, and it was in power for some months.   Thereupon the conservative and reactionary elements in the country invited a Rumanian army to come to their help.   The Rumanians came most willingly, helped to crush Bela Kun's government, and then settled down to loot the country. They only left when the Allied Powers threatened to take action against them.   As the Rumanians withdrew, the Hungarian conservatives organized a private army or bands of volunteers to terrorize over all the liberal or advanced elements in the country, so as to prevent any further attempt at revolution.   Thus began in 1919 the " White Terror " of Hungary, as it is called, which is considered " one of the bloodiest pages of post-war history ".   Hungary is still partly feudal, and these feudal landlords combined with the big

[1] This " anschluss " took place in March 1938.

industrialists, who had made huge fortunes during the war, to murder and terrorize not only communists but workers generally and social democrats and liberals and pacifists and even Jews. Ever since then Hungary has been under a reactionary dictatorship. There is a parliament for show purposes, but the ballot is open—that is, voting for members of parliament is public—and the police and the army see to it that only persons welcome to the dictatorship are elected. No public meetings on political questions are tolerated.

I have considered in this letter some of the post-war happenings in Central Europe, the reactions of the war and defeat and the Russian Revolution on what used to be the Central Powers. The amazing economic effects of the war, and how they have brought capitalism to its present unhappy pass, we shall have to deal with separately. The net result of what I have written about in this letter is that social revolution seemed to be imminent in Europe during those post-war days. This fact helped Soviet Russia, because none of the great imperialist Powers dared to attack her whole-heartedly for fear of the bad effect on its own working class. The revolution, however, did not come off, except in little bits which were crushed. In the crushing and the avoiding of this social revolution the social democrats played a prominent part, although their whole party was based on the theory of such a social revolution. It would appear that these social democrats hoped or believed that capitalism would die a natural death. Therefore, instead of attacking it vigorously, they helped to preserve it for the time being. Or it may be that their huge and wealthy party machine was comfortable enough and too much involved in the existing order to take the risk of social upheaval. They tried to steer a middle course, with the result that they bungled the job completely and lost even what they had. Recent events in Germany have made this clearer than ever.

Another factor dominating these post-war years is the growth of the spirit of violence. It is curious that while in India the gospel of non-violence was being preached, nearly all over the world violence was in action, naked and unabashed, and was being glorified. The war was largely responsible for this, and afterwards the clashes between different class interests. As these clashes became more obvious and intense, violence grew. Liberalism almost disappeared and nineteenth-century democracy fell into disfavour. Dictators appeared on the scene.

I have dealt with the defeated Powers in this letter. The victorious Powers had similar troubles, though England and France escaped having any rising or upheaval as in Central Europe. Italy had a great upheaval, producing strange results which deserve separate treatment.

172

A NEW WAY OF PAYING OLD DEBTS

June 15, 1933

WE find thus that after the World War, Europe, as indeed the whole world to some extent, was like a seething cauldron. The peace of Versailles and the other treaties did not improve matters. The new map of Europe settled some old national problems by freeing the Poles and the Czechs and the Baltic peoples. But at the same time it created fresh national problems by putting part of the Austrian Tyrol under Italy, and part of Ukraine under Poland, and by other unhappy territorial distributions in eastern Europe. The most curious and irritating arrangement was that of the Polish Corridor and Danzig. Central and eastern Europe was " balkanized " by the creation of many small new states, which meant more frontiers, more customs barriers, more brutal hatreds.

Apart from these treaties of 1919, Rumania managed to take Bessarabia, which used to be a part of south-western Russia. This has since been a matter of dispute and argument between the Soviets and Rumania. Bessarabia has been called " the Alsace-Lorraine on the Dnieper ".

A far bigger question than that of territorial changes was that of Reparations—that is, the amount defeated Germany was to be made to pay to the victorious Allies as costs and damages caused by the war. No exact sum was laid down in the Treaty of Versailles, but subsequent conferences fixed these reparations at the enormous sum of £6,600,000,000, to be paid in annual instalments. It was impossible for any country to pay this vast sum, much less could defeated and exhausted Germany do so. Germany protested without result, and then, having no choice, paid two or three instalments by borrowing from the United States. She did so to gain time, and hoped to get the whole question reconsidered. It was obvious to her and to most others that she could not go on paying huge sums for generations.

Very soon Germany's financial system went to pieces, and the government did not have enough money either to pay external debts, like reparations, or even to meet internal obligations. Payments to other countries had to be made in gold. When these payments were not made on the fixed dates, there was default. Within Germany, however, the government could pay in currency notes, and so they adopted the device of printing more and more paper notes. By printing paper notes money is not created; what is created is credit. People use these notes because they know that they can get them changed for gold or silver if they want to. Behind these notes there is always some amount of gold kept in the banks to keep up the value of the notes. Paper money thus performs a very useful function, as it saves a lot of gold and silver from day-to-day use and increases credit. But if a government goes on printing paper money and issuing these notes without any limit and without any regard to the amount of gold in the banks, then the value of this money is bound to fall. The more the printing the less the value, the less does it perform its function of credit. This process is called inflation. This is exactly what happened in Germany in 1922 and 1923. The German Government, wanting more money for its expenses, printed more notes. This resulted in sending up prices of everything else, but in lowering the price of the German mark itself as compared to the pound, the dollar, or the franc. So the government had to print more marks, and again the mark fell. This process went on to fantastic lengths, till a dollar or pound came to be worth billions of paper marks. In fact the paper mark almost ceased to have any value. A postage stamp for a letter cost a million paper marks! And all other prices were similarly graded and constantly changing.

This German inflation and astounding fall of the mark did not take place of its own accord. It was deliberately brought about by the German Government to help them to get out of their financial difficulties and to a large extent it did so. For the government and municipalities and other debtors easily paid off all their internal German debts with the worthless paper marks. Of course they could not pay off debts in and to foreign countries in this way, as no one there would accept their paper money. In Germany they could enforce acceptance by law. In this way the government and every debtor got rid of a troublesome burden of debt. But they did so at a tremendous cost of suffering. All the people suffered during this inflation, but most of all the middle classes suffered, for most of these people were getting fixed salaries or had other fixed incomes. Of course as the mark fell these salaries went up, but they never went up enough to keep pace with the falling mark. The lower middle classes were almost wiped off by this inflation, and we have to remember this when we consider the remarkable happenings in Germany in subsequent years. For these discontented *déclassé* middle classes now formed a powerful army of the disaffected, full of revolutionary possibilities. They drifted into the private armies that were growing up round the principal parties, and most of them went to Hitler's new party, the National Socialists or Nazis.

The old mark, having become perfectly useless for any purpose, was then abolished, and a new currency, the "rentenmark", was introduced. There was no inflation with this, and it was worth its value in gold. So Germany, after making a clean sweep of her lower middle classes, returned again to a stable currency.

Germany's financial troubles led to important international consequences. There was a default in paying reparations to the Allies. These reparations were being divided up between these Allied Powers, the biggest share going to France. Russia was not taking any part of them; in fact she renounced any claim that she might have had. When the German default occurred, France and Belgium took military possession of the Ruhr area in Germany.

The Allies were already in possession of the Rhineland under the Versailles Treaty. In January 1923 an additional area was occupied by the French and Belgians (England refused to join in this undertaking). This Ruhr area adjoins the Rhineland and contains rich coalfields and factories. The French wanted to pay themselves by taking possession of the coal and other articles produced. But here a difficulty presented itself. The German Government decided to oppose the French occupation by passive resistance, and they called upon the mine-owners and workers of the Ruhr to stop work and not help the French in any way. They further helped these mine-owners and industrialists by paying them millions of marks for the losses caused to them. After nine or ten months, which were very expensive both for the French and the Germans, the German Government withdrew passive resistance and began co-operating with the French in working the mines and factories in the area. In 1925 the French and Belgians left the Ruhr.

German passive resistance had broken down in the Ruhr, but it had demonstrated that the reparations question must again be considered and more reasonable figures of payments fixed. So conferences and commissions followed each other in quick succession, and fresh plans were evolved one after another. There was the Dawes Plan in 1924, and five years later, in 1929, the Young Plan, and three years later, in 1932, it was practically acknowledged by all concerned that no further payments could be made for reparations, and the whole idea was scrapped.

For these few years from 1924 Germany made regular payments of reparations. But how was this done when Germany had no money and was not solvent? Simply by borrowing from the United States of America. The Allies (England, France, Italy, etc.) owed money to America, the money they had borrowed in war-time; Germany owed money to the Allies as reparations. So America lent money to Germany, and Germany could pay the Allies, so that the Allies might in their turn pay America. It was a very pretty arrangement, and everybody seemed to be satisfied ! Indeed, there was no other way of getting payments. Of course the whole round of borrowings and lendings depended on one little thing—America continuing to lend money to Germany. If this stopped, the whole arrangement collapsed.

These lendings and borrowings did not mean actual payments in hard cash ; they were all paper transactions. America credited a certain sum to Germany, Germany transferred this to the Allies, and the Allies re-transferred it to America. The actual money did not move at all, only a number of book entries were made. Why did America go on lending to impoverished countries which could not even pay the interest on previous debts ? America did so to help them to carry on somehow and prevent them from going bankrupt, for America feared the collapse of Europe, which, apart from other bad consequences, would have meant the end of the whole debt due to America. So, like a prudent creditor, America kept her debtors alive and functioning. But after some years

America got rather tired of this policy of continuous lending and put an end to it. Immediately the whole structure of reparations and debts came down with a crash and there were defaults, and all the nations of Europe and America fell into a morass.

Reparations were thus a problem which shadowed Europe for over a dozen years after the war. And at the same time there was the question of war debts—that is, the debts of countries other than Germany. As I told you in a letter dealing with the World War, England and France financed the war in the early days and lent money to their smaller allies; then France's resources were exhausted and she could lend no more. England, however, continued lending. Later England collapsed financially and could lend no more. Only the United States could do so, and they lent generously and with advantage to themselves, to England, France, and other Allies. Thus at the end of the war some countries owed money to France. Many were the debtors of England; and all, Allied countries owed large sums to America. America was the only country that owed money to no other country. It was then a great creditor nation. It had taken up England's old position and become the money-lender to the world. Some figures will perhaps make this clearer. Before the war America was a debtor nation owing three thousand million dollars to other countries. By the time the war had ended, this debt had been wiped off, and instead, America had advanced huge sums of money. In 1926 America was a creditor nation to the tune of twenty-five thousand million dollars.

These war debts were a tremendous burden on the debtor countries, England, France, Italy, etc., as the debts were all official debts for which the governments were responsible. They tried to get special favourable terms from America, and some concessions were obtained, but still the burden continued. So long as Germany paid reparations, these payments (which were really American credits) were transferred to America by the debtor countries. But when reparations became irregular or stopped coming, it became very difficult to pay the debts. The European debtor countries tried to connect reparations and war debts; they said that both must be considered together, and if one stopped the other must automatically stop also. America, however, refused to connect the two. She said that she had lent money and she wanted it back, quite apart from the question of reparations from Germany, which stood upon a separate footing. This attitude of America was very much resented in Europe, and hard things were said of her. She was Shylock and wanted her pound of flesh, it was said. It was stated, in France especially, that the money borrowed from America had been spent in a common undertaking, the war, and therefore should not be looked upon as an ordinary debt. The Americans, on the other hand, were greatly disgusted with the after-war rivalries and intrigues in Europe. They saw France and England and Italy continue to spend vast sums on their armies and navies, and even lend money to some of the smaller countries for arming. If these countries of Europe had so much money for armaments, why should they, the Americans, let them off their debts? If they did so, probably this money would also be thrown into armaments. So argued America, and she stuck to her claims on the debts.

As with the reparations, it was difficult enough to pay the war debts anyhow. International debts can either be paid in gold or in goods or services (like transport, shipping and many other services). It was impossible to pay these huge sums in gold; there was not enough gold to be had. And payment in goods and services became almost impossible also, both for reparations and debts, as America and the European countries set up huge tariff barriers which kept out foreign goods. This created an impossible situation, and was the real difficulty. And yet no country was prepared to lower the tariff barriers or take goods in payment for the sum due to it, as this meant injury to the home industries. It was a curious and vicious circle.

Europe was not the only continent which owed money to the United States of America. American bankers and business men invested enormous sums of money in Canada and in Latin America (that is, South and Central America and Mexico). These Latin American countries were greatly impressed during the World War with the power of modern industry and machinery. So they concentrated on industrial development, and money, of which there was an abundance in the United States, poured in from the north. They borrowed so much that they could hardly pay the interest on it. Dictators appeared everywhere, and so long as the borrowing went on, it was well, just as it was well so long as America went on lending to Germany. When the lending to Latin America stopped, there was a crash there, as in Europe.

To give you some idea of American investments and how they grew rapidly in Latin America, I shall give you two figures. In 1926 these investments amounted to four and a quarter thousand million dollars. Three years later in 1929 they amounted to over five and a half thousand millions.

So America in these post-war years was undoubtedly the banker of the world; rich, prosperous, and bursting with wealth. She dominated the world, and her people looked upon Europe, and much more so on Asia, rather contemptuously as old and quarrelsome continents in their dotage. Try to form some idea of American wealth in those peak days of prosperity in the nineteen-twenties. In the fifteen years from 1912 to 1927 the total national wealth of America went up from $187,239,000,000 to $400,000,000,000. The population in 1927 was about 117 millions, and the wealth per head of population was $3428. Progress has been so rapid that these figures are changing from year to year. In a previous letter when comparing the national incomes of India and other countries I gave a much lower figure for America. That was for annual income, not wealth, and it was probably for an earlier year. The figure for 1927 given above is based on a statement made in November 1926 by President Coolidge of America.

Some other figures may interest you. They are all for 1927. The number of families in the United States was 27,000,000. They owned 15,923,000 electrically-lighted homes, and 17,780,000 telephones were in use. There were 19,237,171 motor cars in use, and this figure was 81 per cent. of the world total. America produced 87 per cent. of the world's automobiles, 71 per cent. of the world's petroleum, and 43 per cent. of the world's coal. And yet the population of the United States was only 6 per cent. of the world's population. The general standard was thus very high, and yet it was not as high as it might have been, for wealth was concentrated in the hands of a few thousand millionaires and multi-millionaires. This " Big Business " ruled the country. They chose the President, they made the laws, and often enough they broke the laws. There was tremendous corruption in this Big Business, but the American people did not mind so long as there was general prosperity.

I have given you these figures of American prosperity in the nineteen-twenties partly to show you to what heights modern industrial civilization has taken a country as compared with backward, non-industrial countries like India and China, and partly to contrast this prosperity with the subsequent crisis and collapse in America, about which I shall tell you later.

This crisis was to come later. Right up to 1929 America seemed to have escaped the ills of suffering Europe and Asia. The defeated Powers were in a very bad way. I have told you something about Germany's misery. Most of the small countries of central Europe, and especially Austria, were in an even worse state. Austria also suffered from inflation, and so did Poland, and both had to change their currencies.

But this trouble was not confined to the defeated countries. Even the victorious countries were gradually involved in it. It had always been known that to be a debtor was not a good thing. A new and strange realization now came : that it was not a good thing either to be a creditor ! For the victorious Powers, to whom Germany owed reparations, got into great difficulties because of these reparations, and the very act of receiving them got them into further trouble. Of this I must tell you in my next letter.

173

THE STRANGE BEHAVIOUR OF MONEY

June 16, 1933

One of the most remarkable characteristics of the post-war period is the strange behaviour of money. Before the war, money in each country had a more or less fixed value. Each country had its own currency, such as the rupee in India, the pound in England, the dollar in America, the franc in France, the mark in

Germany, the rouble in Russia, the lira in Italy, and so on; and these currencies bore a steady relation to each other. They were connected to each other by what is called the international gold standard—that is, each currency had a definite gold value. Within the boundaries of each country its own currency was good enough, but not so outside. The connecting link between two currencies was gold, and international payments or settlements were thus made in gold. So long as the currencies had fixed gold values, they could not vary much, as gold is a fairly stable metal so far as value is concerned.

War-time necessities, however, made the warring governments leave this gold standard, and thus made their currencies cheaper. There was a measure of inflation. This was helpful in carrying on business, but it upset the international relations of currencies. During the war the world was divided up into two huge camps, the Allied camp and the German camp, and within each camp there was co-operation and co-ordination, and everything was subordinated to the war. Difficulties arose after the war, and the changing economic conditions and the mutual distrusts of nations resulted in the extraordinary behaviour of different currencies. The whole money system of to-day is largely based on credit; a banknote and a cheque are both promises to pay which are accepted as good money. Credit depends on confidence, and when confidence goes, credit goes with it. This is one of the reasons why the money system misbehaved so much during the post-war years, as the troubled conditions of Europe had shaken all confidence. The modern world is inter-dependent, each part is intimately connected with the other and there are ever so many international activities. This means that the troubles of one country have their immediate reactions in other countries. If the German mark falls or a German bank fails, the people of London and Paris and New York may be put out by it in many ways.

Because of these and other reasons, which I shall not trouble you with, currency or money difficulties arose in nearly all countries, and the more advanced the country industrially, the greater often was the difficulty. For industrial advance meant a highly complicated and delicate international structure. Obviously a backward and isolated place like Tibet would not be affected by the behaviour of the mark or pound. But the fall in the value of the dollar might immediately upset Japan.

Then, again, in each industrial country the interests of various groups were different. Thus some wanted cheap money and inflation (not, of course, a limitless inflation such as had taken place in Germany), while some wanted the exact opposite, deflation—that is, a high gold value of money. For instance, the creditors, the bankers and the like were in favour of a high money value, as they were owed money; the debtors naturally wanted cheaper money to pay their debts. The industrialists and manufacturers were in favour of cheap money, as they were usually the debtors of the bankers and, more important still, this encouraged the sale of their goods abroad. Cheaper British money would mean that the price of British goods would be less as compared to German or American or other foreign goods in the foreign market, and this would result in an advantage to British industrialists and a greater sale of their goods. So you will notice that different groups pulled different ways, the principal tug-of-war being between the industrialists and the bankers. I am trying to put this as simply as I can. As a matter of fact there were many complicating factors.

Both in France and Italy there was inflation, and the franc and lira fell in value. The old value of the franc used to be about 25 to the pound sterling (as the British pound is called). This fell to 275 to the pound. Later it was fixed at about 120 to the pound.

After the war when America stopped helping England, the pound fell in value a little. England was then faced by a difficulty. Was she to accept this natural fall in the value of the pound and fix the pound at this new value? This would have helped industry by cheapening goods, but it would have caused loss to the bankers and creditors. More important still, it would have put an end to London's position as the financial centre of the world. New York would then step into this position, and borrowers would go there instead of coming to London. The alternative was to force up the pound to its original value. This would raise the prestige of the pound and London would continue its financial leadership. But industry would suffer and, as the event proved, many other undesirable things would happen.

The British Government chose the latter course in 1925 and raised the pound to its former gold value. Thus they sacrificed to some extent their industry to their bankers. The real issue before them was a more important one still, for it vitally affected the continuance of their empire. If London lost the financial headship of the world, the various parts of the Empire would not look to it for leadership or help, and the Empire would gradually melt away. So that this question became one of imperial policy, and this wider imperialism won at the cost of British industry and immediate domestic interests. It was in this same way, you may remember, that imperial considerations induced Britain to encourage the industrialization of India after the war, even at some cost to Lancashire and British industry.

Thus a brave attempt was made by Britain to keep leadership and empire, but it was an attempt which proved most costly and it was foredoomed to failure. The British Government, or any other government, could not control the inevitable developments of economic destiny. The pound had regained its ancient prestige for a while, but at the cost of a growing paralysis of industry. Unemployment grew, and the coal industry was especially hard hit. The deflation of the pound (as this process of raising its gold value is called) was largely responsible for this. There were other reasons also. Some German coal had been received in payment for reparations, and this meant that less British coal was required, which resulted in greater unemployment in the coal-mines. Thus the creditor and victor countries came to realize that it was not an unmixed blessing to receive a tribute of this kind from the defeated country. The British coal industry was also very badly organized. It was split up into hundreds of small companies, and could not easily compete with the larger and better organized groups on the Continent and in America.

As the coal industry went from bad to worse, the mine-owners decided to reduce the wages of their workers. This was fiercely resented by the miners, and they had the support of the workers in other industries. The whole labour movement in Britain got ready to fight on behalf of the miners, and a " Council of Action " was formed. Previous to this a powerful " triple alliance " had been formed between the three great trade unions, the miners, the railway workers, and the transport workers, which comprised millions of well-organized and trained workers. This aggressive attitude of the working class rather frightened the government, and they postponed the crisis by giving a subsidy to the mine-owners to enable them to continue the old scale of wages for another year. An inquiry commission was also appointed. But nothing came of all this, and next year in 1926 the crisis came again when the mine-owners wanted to reduce wages. This time the government were ready for the fight with labour ; they had made every preparation for it during the past months.

The coal-owners decided to lock out the miners because they would not agree to a wage-cut. This precipitated a general strike in England called by the Trade Union Congress. There was a remarkable response to this call, and almost all organized workers throughout the country stopped working. The life of the country was brought almost to a standstill, railways did not run, newspapers could not be printed and most other activities stopped. Government managed to carry on some essential services with the help of volunteers. The General Strike began at midnight May 3–4, 1926. After ten days the moderate leaders of the Trade Union Congress, who had no love for this kind of revolutionary strike, suddenly called it off on the pretext of some vague promise made to them. The miners were left in the lurch, but they carried on for many long and weary months. They were starved out and beaten down in the end. This was a signal defeat not only for the miners, but for British workers generally. Wages were lowered in many cases, hours of work were increased in some industries, and the living standards of the working class went down. The government took advantage of its victory to pass new laws to weaken labour, and especially to prevent any general strike in the future. This General Strike of 1926 failed because of the irresolution and weakness of the labour leaders and their want of preparation for it. Indeed, their whole object was to avoid it, and when they could not do so they ended it at the first opportunity. On the other hand, the government was fully prepared and it received the support of the middle classes.

The General Strike in England and the long coal lock-out created great interest in Soviet Russia, and the Russian trade unions sent very large sums of money, especially subscribed by the Russian workers to help the English miners.

Labour had been crushed in England for the moment. But this was no solution of the problem of a declining industry and growth of unemployment. Unemployment meant widespread suffering among the workers; it also meant a great burden on the State, for a system of unemployment insurance had grown up in many countries. It was recognized that it was the duty of the State to support a worker who was unemployed for no fault of his own. So some relief or doles were given to the registered unemployed, and this meant the expenditure of huge sums of money by the government and by local bodies.

Why was all this happening? Why was industry deteriorating, trade languishing, unemployment increasing, and conditions worsening not only in England, but in almost all countries? Conference after conference was held, the statesmen and the rulers were obviously keen on improving conditions, but no success came to them. It was not as if some natural calamity had occurred, like an earthquake, or floods, or want of rains, causing famine and suffering. The world was getting on in much the same way as before. There was actually more food and more factories and more of everything required, and yet there was more human misery. Something was obviously very radically wrong, to bring about this contrary result. There was gross mismanagement somewhere. Socialists and communists said that it was all the fault of capitalism, which was on its last legs. They pointed to Russia, where, though many troubles and difficulties existed, there was no unemployment, at least.

These questions are rather intricate, and doctors and pandits differ greatly as to the remedies for human ailments. But let us nevertheless look at them and examine some of their outstanding features.

The world to-day is becoming, and has largely become, a single unit—that is to say, that life, activities, production, distribution, consumption, etc., all tend to be international and world-wide, and this tendency is increasing. Trade, industry, the money system, are also largely international. There is the closest connection and interdependence between different countries, and an event in any one of them has reactions in others. In spite of all this internationalism, governments and their policies continue to be narrowly nationalistic. Indeed, this narrow nationalism has become worse and more aggressive during the post-war years, and is to-day a dominating factor in the world. The result is a continuous conflict between the actual international events of the world and the nationalistic policy of governments. You may look upon the international activities of the world as a river flowing down to the sea, and the national policies as attempts to stop it and dam it and divert it, and even to make it flow backwards. It is obvious that the river is not going to flow backwards, nor is it going to be stopped. But it may occasionally be diverted a little, or a dam may result in floods. So these nationalisms of to-day are interfering with the even flow of the river and creating floods and backwaters and stagnant pools, but they cannot stop the ultimate progress of the river.

In trade and the economic sphere we thus have what is called " economic nationalism ". This means that a country is to sell more than it buys, and to produce more than it consumes. Every nation wants to sell its goods, but, then, who is to buy ? For every sale there must be a seller as well as a buyer. It is obviously absurd to have a world of sellers only. And yet this is the basis of economic nationalism. Every country puts up tariff walls, economic barriers to keep out foreign goods, and at the same time it wants to develop its own foreign trade. These tariff walls interfere with and kill international trade, on which the modern world is built up. As trade languishes, industry suffers and unemployment increases. This again results in a fiercer attempt to keep out foreign goods, which are supposed to interfere with home industries, and tariff walls are raised higher. International trade suffers still more and the vicious circle goes on.

The modern industrial world has really advanced beyond the stage of nationalism. The whole machinery of production of goods and distribution does not fit into the nationalist structure of governments and countries. The shell is too small for the growing body inside, and it cracks.

These tariffs and obstacles in the way of trade really profit some classes only in each country, but as these classes are dominant in their respective countries, they shape the country's policy. So each country tries to overreach the other, and in the result all of them suffer together, and national rivalries and hatreds increase. Repeated attempts are made to settle mutual differences by conferences, and the best of intentions are expressed by the statesmen of different countries, but success eludes them. Does this not remind you of the repeated attempts to settle the communal problem, the Hindu-Muslim-Sikh problems, in India ? Perhaps in both the cases failure is due to wrong assumptions and to wrong premises, as well as to wrong objectives.

These classes that profit by tariffs and other methods of encouraging economic nationalism, such as bounties and subsidies and special railway freights, etc., are the owning and manufacturing classes, who profit by these protected home markets. Vested interests are thus built up under protection and tariffs, and, like all vested interests, they object very strongly to any change which might injure them. This is one of the reasons why tariffs, once introduced, stay on, and why economic nationalism goes on in the world although most people are convinced that it is bad for everybody. It is not easy to put an end to vested interests once created, and it is still less easy for any nation to take a solitary lead in such a matter. If all the countries would agree to act together and put an end to, or greatly reduce, the tariffs, perhaps it might be done. Even then there would be difficulties, as industrially backward countries would suffer, as they would not be able to compete on equal terms with advanced countries. New industries are often built up under the shelter of a protective duty.

Economic nationalism discourages and prevents trade between nations. Thus the world market suffers. Each nation becomes a monopoly area with a protected market; the free market goes. Within each nation also, monopolies increase and the free and open market tends to disappear. Big trusts, big factories, big shops swallow up the smaller producers and the petty shopkeepers, and thus put an end to competition. In America, Britain, Germany, Japan, and other industrial countries these national monopolies developed at a tremendous pace, and power was thus concentrated in a few hands. Petrol, soap, chemical goods, armaments, steel, banking, and ever so many other things were monopolized. All this has a curious result. It is the inevitable consequence of the growth of science and the development of capitalism, and yet it cuts at the root of this very capitalism. For capitalism began with the world market and the free market. Competition was the breath of life of capitalism. If the world market goes, and so also the free market and competition within national boundaries, the bottom is knocked out of this old capitalist structure of society. What will take its place is another matter, but it seems that the old order cannot continue for long with these mutually contradictory tendencies.

Science and industrial progress have gone far ahead of the existing system of society. They produce enormous quantities of food and the good things of life, and capitalism does not know what to do with them. Indeed, it sits down often to destroy them or to limit production. And so we have the extraordinary spectacle of abundance and poverty existing side by side. If capitalism is not advanced enough for modern science and technology, some other system must be evolved more in keeping with science. The only other alternative is to strangle science and keep it from going ahead. But that would be rather silly, and in any event it is hardly conceivable.

It is not surprising that with economic nationalism, and the growth of monopolies and national rivalries, and the other products of a decaying capitalism, there should be trouble all over the world. Modern imperialism itself is a form of this capitalism, for each imperialist Power tries to solve its national problems by exploiting other people. This again leads to rivalries and conflicts between the imperialist Powers. Everything seems to lead to conflict in the topsy-turvy world of to-day !

I began this letter by telling you that money had behaved strangely during the post-war period. Can we blame money when everything else is behaving in a most extraordinary way ?

174

MOVE AND COUNTER-MOVE

June 18, 1933

My last two letters have dealt with economic and currency questions. These subjects are supposed to be very mysterious and difficult to understand. It is true that they are not easy and they require hard thinking, but they are not so terrible, after all; and economists and experts are partly responsible for the air of mystery that surrounds these subjects. In the old days priests used to have a monopoly of mystery, and they imposed their will on the ignorant populace by all manner of rites and ceremonials, often in archaic language which few understood, and by pretending to be in communication with unseen powers. The power of priest-craft is very much less to-day, and in industrial countries it has almost gone. In place of the priests have arisen the expert economists and bankers and the like, who talk in a mysterious language, consisting chiefly of technical terms, which a layman finds it difficult to understand. And so the average man has to leave the decision of these questions to the experts. But the experts often attach themselves, consciously or unconsciously, to the ruling classes and serve their interests. And experts differ.

It is as well, therefore, that we should all try to understand something about these economic questions which seem to dominate politics and everything else to-day. There are many ways of dividing human beings into groups and classes. One possible way would be to have two classes : the drifters, who have little will of their own and allow themselves to be carried hither and thither like straw on the surface of the waters, and those who try to play an effective rôle in life and to influence their surroundings. For the latter class, knowledge and understanding are essential, for effective action can only be based on these. Mere good will or pious hopes are not enough. When there is a natural calamity, or an epidemic, or a failure of the rains, or almost any other misfortune, we often see, not only in India, but in Europe also, people praying for relief. If the prayer soothes them and gives them confidence and courage, it is a good thing, and no one need object to it. But the idea that prayer will stop an epidemic of disease is giving place to the scientific notion that the root causes of disease should be wiped out by sanitation and other means. When there is a breakdown in the machinery of a factory or there is a puncture in the tyre of a car, whoever heard of people sitting down and just hoping or piously wishing, or even praying, that the break might right itself or the puncture mend itself ? They set to work and mend the machinery or the tyre, and soon the machinery is functioning again or the car running smoothly along the road.

So also in the human and the social machine, we require besides good will, good knowledge of its working and its possibilities. This knowledge is seldom exact, as it deals with indefinite things, such as human wishes and desires and prejudices and wants, and these become still more indefinite when we deal with people in the mass, with society as a whole, or with different classes of people. But study and experience and observation gradually bring order even into this rather indefinite mass, and knowledge grows, and with it grows our capacity to deal with our surroundings.

Now I should like to say something about the political aspect of Europe during these post-war years. The first thing that strikes one is the division of the Continent into three parts : the victors of the war, the vanquished, and Soviet Russia. There were some small countries, like Norway and Sweden and Holland and Switzerland, which did not fall into any of these three divisions, but they were not important from the larger political point of view. Soviet Russia, of course, stood by herself, with her workers' government, a source of continuous irritation and annoyance to the victorious Powers. This irritation was caused not only by her system of government, which was an invitation to revolution to workers in other countries, but also by her coming in the way of many of the designs of the victorious Powers in the East. I have already told you of the wars of intervention during which, in 1919 and 1920, most of these victorious Powers tried to crush the Soviets. Soviet Russia, however, survived, and the imperialist Powers of Europe had to put up with her existence, but they did so with as little good will or grace as possible. In particular, the old rivalry between England and Russia, dating from the Tsarist period, continued, and occasionally burst forth into alarms and incidents which threatened war. The Soviets were convinced that England was continually intriguing against them and trying to build up an anti-Soviet *bloc* of Powers in Europe, and there were several war scares.

In western and Central Europe the distinction between the victor Powers and the defeated ones was very marked, and France especially represented the spirit of victory. The defeated countries were naturally dissatisfied with many of the provisions of the peace treaties, and, though they were powerless to do anything, they dreamed of future changes. Austria and Hungary were very sick countries, and their condition seemed to worsen. Yugoslavia, on the other hand, was a Serbia bloated up, and had become a collection of incongruous elements and nationalities. It did not take many years for the different parts to get tired of each other, and to develop a tendency to split up. In Croatia (which is now a province of Yugoslavia), there is a strong movement for independence, and this has been vigorously repressed by the Serbian Government. Poland is big enough on the map now, but its imperialists cherish extraordinary dreams of stretching out to the Black Sea in the south, and thus restoring the ancient Polish frontier of 1772. Meanwhile Poland includes a part of the Russian Ukraine and this has been and is still being, " pacified " or " polonized " by a reign of terror, with torture, death penalties, and many other barbarous punishments. These are some of the little fires that go

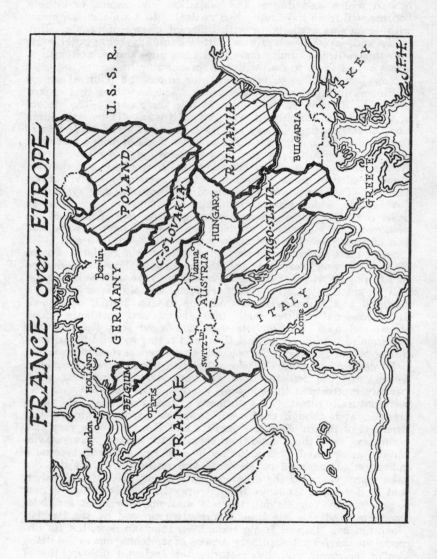

on smouldering in eastern Europe. Their importance lies in the danger of the fire spreading.

Politically, and in a military sense also, France was the dominant Power in Europe in the after-war years. She had gained much of what she had wanted in the shape of territory and the promise at least of reparations, but she was far from happy. A great fear haunted her, the fear of Germany becoming strong enough to fight her again and perhaps defeat her. The principal reason for this fear was the much bigger population of Germany. France is actually bigger in size than Germany and is perhaps even more fertile. Yet the population of France is under 41,000,000, and it is almost steady. The population of Germany is over 62,000,000, and it is growing. The Germans have also the reputation of being an aggressive and warlike nation, and they have twice invaded France within living memory.

So the fear of a German revenge obsessed France and the foundation and governing idea of her whole policy was " security ", the security for France to hold and keep what she had got. It was French military supremacy that kept in check all the countries disappointed by the Versailles peace, for a maintenance of this peace was considered necessary for French security. Further to strengthen her position, France built up a *bloc* of nations, who were also interested in maintaining the Treaty of Versailles. These countries were Belgium, Poland, Czechoslovakia, Rumania, and Yugoslavia.

In this way France established her hegemony or leadership of Europe. This was not to the liking of England, for England does not like any Power, except herself, to be predominant in Europe. There was a great cooling off in the love and friendship which England had for her ally France ; France was criticized in the English Press as being selfish and hard-hearted, and friendly references were made to the old enemy Germany. We must forget and forgive, said the English people, and not allow ourselves to be governed in peace-time by memories of war days. Admirable sentiments these were, and doubly admirable from the English point of view because they happened to fit in with English policy. It has been said by an Italian statesman, Count Sforza, that this is " a precious gift bestowed by divine grace upon the British people ", for all classes to justify with the highest moral reasons any political advantage that may come to England or any diplomatic action that the British Government might take.

From early in 1922 Anglo-French friction became a chronic feature of European politics. On the surface there were smiles and courteous words, and their statesmen and prime ministers met frequently and were photographed together, but the two Governments often pulled in different directions. England was not in favour of the Allied occupation of the Ruhr valley, when Germany defaulted in the payment of reparations in 1922, but France had her way in spite of England. The British, however, did not take part in the occupation.

Another old ally, Italy, fell out with the French, and there was constant friction between the two countries. The reason for this was the seizure of power by Mussolini in 1922, and his imperialist ambitions, which were obstructed by France. Of Mussolini and fascism I shall tell you in my next letter.

The post-war years also brought into evidence certain disruptive tendencies in the British Empire. I have discussed some aspects of this question in other letters. Here I shall only refer to one aspect. Both Australia and Canada were being drawn more and more into the American sphere of cultural and economic influence, and one of the joint dislikes of all three countries were the Japanese, and especially Japanese immigration. Australia is in special danger from this, as it has vast uninhabited areas, and Japan is not far, and has an overflowing population. Neither these two Dominions nor the United States liked England's alliance with Japan. England wanted to please America, for America was dominating the world both as creditor and otherwise, and also wanted to keep the Empire going as long as possible. So she sacrificed the Anglo-Japanese alliance at the Washington Conference in 1922. I have written to you about this conference in my last letter on China. It was there that the Four-Power Agreement and the Nine-Power Treaty were made. These treaties related to China and the Pacific coast, but Soviet Russia, which was vitally interested, was not invited, in spite of her protest.

This Washington Conference marked a change in England's eastern policy. So far England had relied on Japan to help her in the Far East, and even in India if need arose. But now the Far East was becoming a very important factor in world affairs, and there were conflicts of interest between the different Powers. China was rising, or so it seemed, and Japan and America were becoming more and more hostile to each other. Many people thought that the Pacific would be the chief centre of the next great war. As between Japan and America, England changed over to the side of America, or rather it would be more correct to say that she left the side of Japan. Her policy was definitely one of keeping friends with powerful and wealthy America, without making any commitments. Having ended the Japanese Alliance, England started preparing for a possible Far Eastern war. She built enormous and very expensive docks at Singapore, and made of this place a great naval base. From this place she can control the traffic between the Indian Ocean and the Pacific. She can dominate India and Burma on the one side, and the French and Dutch colonies on the other; and most important of all, she can take effective part in a Pacific conflict, whether it be against Japan or any other Power.

This breaking up of the Anglo-Japanese Alliance at Washington in 1922 isolated Japan. The Japanese were driven to look towards Russia, and they began cultivating better relations with the Soviets. Three years later, in January 1925, there was a treaty between Japan and the Soviet Union.

In the early years after the war, Germany was treated by the victorious Powers very much as an outcast nation. Not finding much sympathy with these Powers, and with a view to frightening them a little, she turned to Soviet Russia and made a treaty—the Treaty of Rapallo—with her in April 1922. The negotiations for this had been secret, and so when publicity was given to the treaty, the Allied Governments had a shock. The British Government was especially put out, as the English ruling class disliked the Soviet Government intensely. It was really the realization that if Germany was not treated well and conciliated, she might go over to Russia, that brought about a change in British policy towards Germany. They became quite appreciative of Germany's difficulties, and made friendly unofficial advances to her in many ways. They stood apart from the Ruhr adventure. All this was not because of a sudden love for Germany, but because of a desire to keep Germany away from Russia and in the anti-Soviet group of nations. This became the keystone of British policy for some years, and success came to them in 1925 at Locarno. A conference of the Powers was held at Locarno, and for the first time since the war there was a real agreement between the victorious Powers and Germany on some points, which were embodied in a treaty. There was no complete agreement; the tremendous question of reparations as well as other questions remained. But a good beginning was made, and many mutual assurances and guarantees were given. Germany accepted her western French frontier as defined by the Treaty of Versailles; as to her eastern frontier, with the Polish Corridor to the sea, she refused to accept it as final, but she promised to use peaceful means only in her attempts to get it changed. If any party broke the agreement, then the others bound themselves to stand together to fight it.

Locarno was a triumph for British policy. It made Britain to some extent the arbiter in a dispute between France and Germany, and it brought Germany away from Russia. The chief importance of Locarno was, indeed, that it brought together the western European nations in an anti-Soviet *bloc*. Russia got nervous, and within a few months she countered with an alliance with Turkey. This Russo-Turkish Treaty was signed in December 1925, just two days after the decision of the League of Nations against Mosul, which decision, you may remember, was against Turkey. In September 1926 Germany entered the League of Nations, and there was much embracing and hand-shaking, and everybody in the League smiled and complimented everybody else.

And so these moves and counter-moves went on between the European nations, often influenced by their domestic policies. In England a general election, in December 1923, resulted in a Conservative defeat, and the Labour Party in Parliament, although it had no clear majority, formed the government for the first time. Ramsay MacDonald was the Prime Minister. This government had a brief life of nine and a half months. During this period, however, it came to an agreement with Soviet Russia, and diplomatic and trade relations were established between the two countries.

The conservatives were opposed to any recognition of the Soviets, and in the next British general election, which came within a year of the last one, Russia figured greatly. This was due to the fact that a certain letter, known as the *Zinoviev letter*, was made a trump card by the conservatives in the election. In this letter communists in England were urged to work secretly for revolution. Zinoviev was a leading Bolshevik in the Soviet Government; he denied absolutely having written the letter and said that it must be a forgery. But still the conservatives exploited the letter fully and, partly with its help, managed to win the election. A Conservative Government was now formed with Stanley Baldwin as the Prime Minister. This government was repeatedly asked to investigate the truth or falsity of the " Zinoviev letter ", but it refused to do so. Subsequent disclosures in Berlin showed that it was a forgery made by a " white " Russian—that is, an anti-Bolshevik *émigré* Russian. The forgery, however, had done its work in England and put an end to one government and brought in another. By such trivial incidents are international affairs influenced !

Later in the same year a new development, this time in the Far East, was a source of great irritation to the British Government. A strong united national government suddenly appeared in China, and this seemed to be on intimate terms with the Soviets. For many months the British were in great difficulties in China, and they had to swallow their prestige and do many things that they disliked. And then the Chinese movement, after a brief day of success, split up and went to pieces. The generals massacred and drove out the radical elements in the movement, and preferred to place their reliance on the foreign bankers in Shanghai. This was a great defeat for Russia in the international game, and her prestige went down in China and elsewhere. For England it was a triumph, and she sought to improve the occasion by pressing home the defeat on the Soviet. Attempts were again made to organize the anti-Soviet *bloc* and to encircle Russia.

About the middle of 1927 action was taken against the Soviets in different parts of the world. In April 1927, on the same day, raids took place on the Soviet embassy in Pekin and the Soviet consulate in Shanghai. Two different Chinese governments controlled these areas, yet they acted together in this matter. It is a very unusual thing for an embassy to be raided and an ambassador insulted; almost inevitably it leads to war. It was the Russian belief that the Chinese governments had been made to act in this way by England and other anti-Soviet Powers to force a war on Russia. But Russia did not fight. A month later, in May 1927, another extraordinary raid took place, this time on Russian trade offices in London. This is called the " Arcos " raid, as Arcos was the name of the Russian official trading company in England. This was also a great and, as the event proved, a wholly unjustified insult to another Power. It was immediately followed by a break in diplomatic and trade relations between the two countries. Next month, in June, the Soviet Minister in Poland was assassinated in

Warsaw. (Four years earlier the Soviet minister in Rome had been assassinated in Lausanne.) All these events, each coming quickly after the other, upset the nerves of the Russian people, and they fully expected a combined attack on them by the imperialist Powers. Russia had a big war scare, and in many of the western European countries the workers demonstrated in favour of Russia and against the war that seemed to be coming. The scare passed, and there was no war.

In that very year, 1927, Soviet Russia celebrated on a big scale the tenth anniversary of the Bolshevik Revolution. England and France were very hostile to Russia then, but Soviet Russia's friendship with eastern nations was shown by the fact that official delegations from Persia, Turkey, Afghanistan, and Mongolia took part in the celebrations.

While these alarms and war preparations were going on in Europe and elsewhere, there was also a great deal of talk of disarmament. The Covenant of the League of Nations had laid down that " members of the League recognize that the maintenance of peace requires the reduction of national armaments to the lowest point consistent with national safety and the enforcement by common action of international obligations ". Apart from laying down this pious principle, the League did nothing else at the time, but it called upon its Council to take necessary steps in this matter. Germany and the other defeated Powers were, of course, disarmed by the peace treaties. The victorious Powers had undertaken to follow, but repeated conferences failed to bring about any solid result. This was not surprising, when each Power aimed at a kind of disarmament which would result in making it relatively stronger than the others. To this, naturally, the others would not agree. The French stuck all along to their demand for security before disarmament.

Of the great Powers neither America nor the Soviet Union were members of the League. Indeed, the Soviet looked upon the League as a rival and hostile show, a group of capitalist powers ranged against the Soviet Union. The Soviet Union was itself considered (just as the British Empire is sometimes spoken of) as a League of Nations, as there were many republics federated together in the Union. The eastern nations also looked upon the League of Nations with suspicion, and considered it a tool of the imperialist Powers. Nevertheless America, Russia, and nearly all countries took part in the League conferences to consider disarmament. In 1925, the League appointed a Preparatory Commission which was to prepare the ground for a great World Conference on Disarmament. This commission went on interminably for seven years, examining plan after plan, without any result. In 1932 the World Conference itself met and, after many months of futile talk, faded away.

America not only took part in these disarmament discussions, but her interest in Europe and European affairs increased because of her dominating economic position in the world. All Europe was her debtor, and she was interested in preventing the European countries from cutting each other's throats again, for, apart from higher considerations, what would happen to her debts and trade if this happened ? The disarmament discussions not yielding any quick results, a new proposal to help in the preservation of peace appeared in 1928, as a result of talks between the French and American Governments. This proposal bravely attempted to " outlaw " war. The original idea was for a pact between France and America only; but this developed, and ultimately included nearly all the nations of the world. In August 1928 the pact was signed in Paris, and it is therefore known as the Paris Pact of 1928, or the Kellogg-Briand Pact, or simply as the Kellogg Pact. Kellogg was the American Secretary of State who took a lead in the matter, and Aristide Briand was the French Foreign Minister. The Pact was quite a short document condemning recourse to war for the solution of international controversies and renouncing war as an instrument of national policy in the mutual relations of the signatories of the Pact. This language, which is almost the wording of the Pact itself, sounds very fine, and if honestly meant would put an end to war. But it was soon evident how insincere were the Powers. Both the French and the English, and especially the English, made many reservations before signing it, which practically nullified the Pact for them. The British Government excluded from the Pact any warlike activity it might have to undertake in connection with its empire, which meant that it could really make war just when it wanted to. It declared a kind of British " Monroe Doctrine " over its areas of dominance and influence.

While war was being thus " outlawed " in public, a secret Anglo-French Naval Compromise took place in 1928. News of this managed to leak out, and shocked Europe and America. This was evidence enough of the real state of affairs behind the scenes.

The Soviet Union accepted the Kellogg Pact and signed it. Its real reason for doing so was to prevent in this way, to some extent at least, the formation of an anti-Soviet *bloc* which might attack the Soviet under cover of the Pact. The British reservations to the Pact seemed to be especially aimed at the Soviet. In signing the Pact, Russia took strong objection to these British and French reservations.

Russia was so keen on avoiding war that she took the additional precaution of having a special peace pact with her neighbours—Poland, Rumania, Estonia, Latvia, Turkey, and Persia. This is known as the Litvinov Pact. It was signed in February 1929, six months before the Kellogg Pact became international law.

So these pacts and alliances and treaties continued to be made in a desperate attempt to steady a quarrelsome and collapsing world, as if such pacts or patchwork on the surface could remedy a deep-seated disease. This was a period in the nineteen-twenties, when socialists and social democrats were often in office in European countries. The more they tasted of office and power, the more they merged themselves into the capitalist structure. Indeed, they became the best defenders of capitalism, and often enough as keen imperialists as any conservative or other reactionary had been. To some extent the European world had quietened down after the revolutionary ferment of the early post-war years. Capitalism seemed to have adjusted itself to the new conditions for another period of time, and there appeared to be no immediate prospect of a revolutionary change anywhere.

So matters stood in the year 1929 in Europe.

175

MUSSOLINI AND FASCISM IN ITALY

June 21, 1933.

I HAVE brought up the outline of our story of Europe to 1929. But one important chapter has been omitted so far, and I must go back a little to deal with it. This relates to events in Italy after the war. These events are important not so much because they tell us what happened in Italy, but because they are of a new kind and give warning of a novel phase of activity and conflict all over the world. They have thus much more than a national significance, and I have therefore reserved them for a separate letter. So this letter will deal with Mussolini, one of the outstanding personalities of to-day, and with the rise of fascism in Italy.

Even before the World War began, Italy was in the grip of severe economic trouble. Her war with Turkey in 1911–12 had ended in her victory, and the annexation of Tripoli in northern Africa was very pleasing to her imperialists. But this little war had not done much good internally and had not improved the economic situation. Matters worsened, and in 1914, on the eve of the World War, Italy seemed to be on the brink of revolution. There were many big strikes in the factories, and the workers were only kept in check by the moderate socialist leaders of labour, who succeeded in putting down the strikes. Then came the war. Italy refused to join her German allies, and tried to take advantage of her neutral position to squeeze out concessions from both sides. This attitude of offering her services to the highest bidder was not a very edifying one, but nations are quite callous, and have a way of behaving in a manner which would shame any private individual. The Allies, England and France, could offer the bigger bribe, both immediate cash and promise of territory, and so in May 1915 Italy joined the war on the side of the Allies. I think I have told you of the secret treaty that was made subsequently, allotting Smyrna and a bit of Asia Minor to Italy. The Russian Bolshevik Revolution came before this treaty could be ratified and upset the little game. This was one of the grievances of Italy, and there was some dissatisfaction also at the peace treaties of Paris, a feeling that Italian " rights " had been ignored. The imperialists and *bourgeoisie* had looked forward to the annexation and exploitation of fresh colonial territories, and thereby easing the economic strain in their own country.

For conditions in Italy after the war were very bad, and the country was more exhausted than any other Allied country. The economic system seemed to be breaking down, and the advocates of socialism as well as communism were increasing. There was, of course, the Russian Bolshevik example before them. On the one side there were the factory-workers, who were suffering from the economic conditions, on the other there were the large numbers of soldiers who had been demobilized and who were often without any job. Disorders grew, and the middle-class leaders tried to organize these soldiers to oppose the growing power of the workers. In the summer of 1920 a crisis developed. The great Metal Workers' Union, with a membership of half a million workers, demanded higher wages. This demand was rejected, and thereupon the workers decided to strike in a novel way—" striking on the job " this was called. This meant that the workers went to their factories, but instead of working did nothing, and indeed obstructed work. This was the syndicalist programme which had been advocated by French labour long ago. The factory-owners replied to this obstructionist strike by having a lock-out—that is, closing their factories. The workers thereupon took possession of the factories and tried to work them on socialist lines.

This action of the workers was definitely revolutionary, and if persisted in was bound to lead to a social revolution or to failure. No middle position was possible for long. The Socialist Party was very strong in Italy then. Apart from its control of the trade unions, it controlled 3000 municipalities, and sent 150 members, that is about one-third of the total number, to Parliament. A powerful and well-established party owning property and holding many positions in the State is seldom revolutionary. Even so, this party, including its moderates, approved of the workers' action in taking possession of the factories. Having done so, it did nothing else. It did not want to go back, but it did not dare to go ahead; it chose the middle path of least resistance and, like all doubters and people who hesitate and cannot make up their minds at the right time, they suffered time to go ahead without them, and were crushed in the process. Because of the hesitation of the labour leaders and radical parties, the workers' occupation of the factories fizzled out.

This encouraged the owning classes greatly. They had measured the strength of the workers and their leaders and found it less than they had expected, and now they planned a revenge to crush the labour movement and the Socialist Party. They turned especially to certain volunteer groups that had been formed in 1919, out of the demobilized soldiers, by Benito Mussolini. *Fasci di combatti-menti*, " fighting groups," they were called, and their chief function was to attack, whenever an opportunity arose, socialists and radicals and their institutions. Thus they would destroy the printing press of a socialist newspaper, or attack a municipality or co-operative association under socialist or radical control. The big industrialists

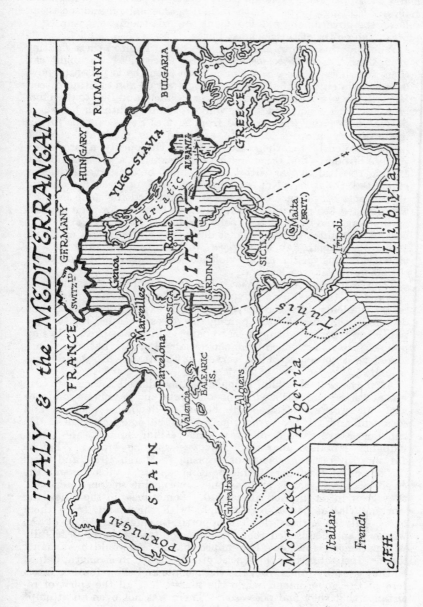

ITALY & the MEDITERRANEAN

Italian

French

J.F.H.

and the upper *bourgeoisie* generally, began to patronize and finance these " fighting groups ", in their fight against labour and socialism. Even the government was indulgent towards them, as it wanted to break the power of the Socialist Party.

Who was this Benito Mussolini who had organized these fighting groups or *Fasci di combattimenti,* or fascists, as we might call them for short ? He was a young man then (he is just fifty now, having been born in 1883) who had had a varied and exciting career. His father was a blacksmith who was a socialist, and Benito therefore grew up with a socialist background. In his youth he became a fiery agitator, and was expelled from several Swiss cantons for his revolutionary propaganda. He attacked the moderate socialist leaders violently for their moderation. He openly approved of the use of bombs and other methods of terrorism against the State. During the Italian war with Turkey, most of the socialist leaders supported the war. Not so Mussolini, who opposed it ; and for certain acts of violence he was even imprisoned for some months. He attacked the moderate socialist leaders bitterly, for their support of the war, and got them expelled from the Socialist Party. He became the editor of the socialist daily paper, the *Avanti* of Milan, and from day to day he advised workers to meet violence with violence. This incitement to violence was strongly objected to by the moderate Marxist leaders.

Then came the World War. For some months Mussolini was opposed to the war and advocated Italy's neutrality. He then, rather suddenly, changed his views, or his expression of them, and declared in favour of Italy joining the Allies. He left the socialist paper, and began editing a new paper which preached this new policy. He was expelled from the Socialist Party. Later he volunteered as a common soldier, served at the Italian front, and was wounded.

After the war Mussolini stopped calling himself a socialist. He was at a loose end, disliked by his old party and having no influence with the working classes. He began to denounce pacifism and socialism and, at the same time, even the *bourgeois* State. He denounced every kind of State and, calling himself an " individualist ", praised anarchy. This was what he wrote. What he did was to found *Fascismo* or fascism, in March 1919, and enrol the out-of-work soldiers in his fighting squads. Violence was the creed of these groups and, as the government seldom interfered, they grew in daring and aggression. Sometimes, in the cities, the working classes had a regular fight with them and drove them out. But the socialist leaders opposed this fighting spirit of the workers, and counselled them to meet the fascist terror peacefully with patient resignation. They hoped that fascism would thus exhaust itself. Instead of this the fascist groups gained in strength, helped as they were by funds from the rich people and the refusal to interfere of the government, while the masses lost all the spirit of resistance that they had possessed. There was not even an attempt to meet fascist violence by the labour weapon, the strike.

The fascists under Mussolini's leadership managed to combine two contradictory appeals. First and foremost they were the enemies of socialism and communism, and thus they gained the support of the propertied classes. But Mussolini was an old socialist agitator and revolutionary, and he was full of popular anti-capitalist slogans which were appreciated by many of the poorest classes. He had also learnt much of the technique of agitation from those experts in this business, the communists. Fascism thus became a strange mixture and could be interpreted in different ways. Essentially a capitalist movement, it shouted many slogans which were dangerous for capitalism. And thus it drew into its fold a motley crowd. The middle classes were its backbone, especially the unemployed of the lower-middle class. Unemployed and unskilled workers who were not organized in labour unions began to drift into it as it grew in power. For nothing succeeds like success. The fascists violently forced the shopkeepers to keep down prices, and thus gained the good will of the poor also. Many adventurers of course flocked to the fascist standards. In spite of all this, fascism remained a minority movement.

And so, while the socialist leaders doubted and hesitated and quarrelled among themselves and there were divisions and splits in their party, fascist power grew. The regular army was very friendly to fascism, and Mussolini had won over the army generals to his side. It was a remarkable feat for Mussolini to win to his side and hold together such diverse and conflicting elements, and to make each group within his ranks imagine that fascism was especially meant for it. The rich fascist looked upon him as the defender of his property, and considered his anti-capitalist speeches and slogans as empty phrases meant to delude the masses. The poor fascist believed that the real thing in fascism was this very anti-capitalism, and that the rest was just intended to humour the rich people. So Mussolini tried to play one off against the other, and spoke in favour of the rich one day, and in favour of the poor the next day, but essentially he was the champion of the propertied classes, who were financing him, and who were out to destroy the power of labour and socialism, which had threatened them for so long.

At last, in October 1922, the fascist bands, directed by regular army generals, marched on Rome. The Prime Minister, who had so far tolerated fascist activities, now declared martial law. But it was too late, and the King himself was now on Mussolini's side. He (the King) vetoed the martial law decree, accepted his Prime Minister's resignation, and invited Mussolini to become the next Prime Minister and form his ministry. The fascist army reached Rome on October 30, 1922, and on the same day Mussolini arrived by train from Milan to become the Prime Minister.

Fascism had triumphed and Mussolini was in control. But what did he stand for? What was his programme and policy? Great movements are almost invariably built up round a clear-cut ideology which grows up round certain fixed principles and has definite objectives and programmes. Fascism had the unique distinction of having no fixed principles, no ideology, no philosophy behind it, unless the mere opposition to socialism, communism, and liberalism might be considered to be a philosophy. In 1920, a year after the fascist groups were formed, Mussolini declared about the fascists :

> "not being tied down to any fixed principles, they proceed unceasingly towards one goal, the future well-being of the Italian people."

That, of course, is no distinctive policy, for every person can say that he is prepared to stand by the well-being of his people. In 1922, just a month before the march on Rome, Mussolini said : " Our programme is very simple, we want to rule Italy."

Mussolini has made this clearer still in an article he has written on the origin of fascism in an Italian encyclopædia. He says in it that he had no definite plans for the future when he embarked on his march on Rome. He was impelled to set out on his adventure by the dominant urge to act in a political crisis, the result of his past socialist training.

Fascism and communism though violently opposed to each other, have some activities in common. But so far as principles and ideology are concerned there can be no greater contrast than between these two. For fascism, we have seen, has no basic principles; it starts off from a blank. Communism or Marxism, on the other hand, is an intricate economic theory and interpretation of history, which requires the hardest mental discipline.

Although fascism had no principles or ideals, it had a definite technique of violence and terrorism, and it had a certain outlook on the past which helps us a little to understand it. Its symbol was an old imperial Roman symbol which used to be carried in front of the Roman Emperors and magistrates. This was a bundle of rods (*fasces* they were called, hence *Fascismo*) with an axe at the centre. The fascist organization is also based on the old Roman model, even the names used being the old ones. The fascist salute, called the *fascista*, is the old Roman salutation with the raised and outstretched arm. Thus the fascists looked back to imperial Rome for inspiration; they had the imperialist outlook. Their motto was : " No discussion—only obedience ", a motto suited to an army perhaps, but certainly not to a democracy. Their leader, Mussolini, was *il Duce*, the dictator. As their uniform they adopted a black shirt, and they were thus known as the " Black-shirts ".

As the only positive programme of the fascists was to gain power, they had achieved this when Mussolini became Prime Minister. He then devoted himself to consolidating his position by crushing his opponents. An extraordinary orgy of violence and terrorism took place. Violence is a common enough phenomenon in history, but usually it is considered a painful necessity and it is excused and explained. Fascism, however, did not believe in any such apologetic attitude towards violence. They accepted it and praised it openly, and they practised it even though there was no resistance

to them.   The opposition members in Parliament were terrorized
by beatings, and a new electoral law, quite changing the constitution,
was forced through.   In this way a great majority was obtained in
favour of Mussolini.

It was strange that when they were actually in power and in
command of the police and the State machine, the fascists should
still continue their illegal violence.   Yet they did so, and of course
they had a free field, as the State police would not interfere.   There
were murders and torture and beatings and destruction of property,
and especially there was a new method widely practised by these
fascists.   This was to give enormous doses of castor oil to anyone
who dared to oppose them.

In 1924 Europe was shocked by the murder of Giacomo Matteoti,
a leading socialist who was a member of Parliament.   He spoke
in Parliament and criticized fascist methods during the election
that had just been held.   Within a few days he was murdered.
The murderers were tried for form's sake, but they got off practically
without punishment.   A moderate leader of the liberals, Amendola,
died as a result of a beating.   A liberal ex-Prime Minister, Nitti,
just managed to escape from Italy, but his house was destroyed.
These are just a few instances which attracted world attention,
but the violence was continuous and widespread.   This violence
was apart from and in addition to legal methods of suppression,
and yet it was not just emotional mob violence.   It was disciplined
violence undertaken deliberately against all opponents, not only
socialists and communists but peaceful and very moderate liberals
also.   Mussolini's order was that life should be rendered difficult
" or impossible " for his opponents.   It was faithfully carried
out.   No other party was to exist, no other organization or institution.   Everything must be fascist.   And all the jobs must go to
the fascists.

Mussolini became the all-powerful dictator of Italy.   He was not
only the Prime Minister, but at the same time he was the Minister
for Foreign Affairs, the Interior, the Colonies, War, Marine, Air,
and Labour !   He was practically the whole Cabinet.   The poor
King retired into the background and was seldom heard of.   Parliament was gradually pushed aside and became a pale shadow of
itself.   The Fascist Grand Council dominated the stage, and
Mussolini dominated the Fascist Grand Council.

Mussolini's early speeches on foreign affairs created a great deal
of surprise and consternation in Europe.   They were extraordinary
speeches—bombastic, full of threats, and wholly unlike the diplomatic
utterances of statesmen.   He always seemed to be spoiling for a
fight.   He talked of Italy's imperial destiny, of Italian aeroplanes
darkening the sky with their numbers, and he openly threatened his
neighbour France on several occasions.   France was, of course, far
more powerful than Italy, but no one wanted to fight, and so
much that Mussolini said was tolerated.   The League of Nations
became a special target for Mussolini's satire and contempt, although
Italy was a member of it, and on one occasion he defied it in the most

aggressive way.   Yet the League and the other Powers put up with this.

Many outward changes have taken place in Italy, and a tourist is favourably impressed by the appearance of order and punctuality everywhere.   Rome, the imperial city, is being beautified, and many ambitious schemes for betterment have been undertaken. Visions of a new Roman Empire float before Mussolini.

In 1929 the old quarrel between the Pope and the Italian Government was ended by an agreement between Mussolini and the Pope's representative.   Ever since the Italian kingdom made Rome its capital in 1871, the Pope had refused to recognize it or to give up his claim to the sovereignty of Rome.   The Popes, therefore, as soon as they were elected, retired into their enormous palace of the Vatican in Rome, which includes St. Peter's, and never came out of it on Italian territory.   They made themselves voluntary prisoners.   By the agreement of 1929 this little Vatican area in Rome was recognized as an independent and sovereign State. The Pope is the absolute monarch of this State, and the total number of citizens is about 500 !   The State has its own courts, coinage, postage stamps, and public services, and it has the most expensive little railway in the world.   The Pope is no longer a self-made prisoner ; he sometimes comes out of the Vatican.   This treaty with the Pope made Mussolini popular with the Catholics.   The illegal phase of fascist violence lasted intensively for a year or so, and then to some extent until 1926.   In 1926 " exceptional laws " were passed to deal with political opponents which gave great powers to the State and made illegal action unnecessary.   They were something like the ordinances and the laws based on these ordinances which we have had in such abundance in India.   Under these " exceptional laws " people continue to be punished, sent to prison, and deported in large numbers.   According to official figures, between November 1926 and October 1932 as many as 10,044 persons were brought before the special tribunals.   Three penal islands were set apart for the deportees—Ponza, Ventolene, and Tremiti—and conditions were very bad there.

Repression and arrests on a large scale have continued, and it is clear from these that a secret and revolutionary opposition exists in the country in spite of all the attempts to crush it.   Financial burdens increase, and the economic condition of the country continues to deteriorate.

176

DEMOCRACY AND DICTATORSHIPS

June 22, 1933

BENITO MUSSOLINI'S example of setting himself up as a dictator in Italy seemed to be a catching one in Europe.   " There is a vacant throne," he had said, " in every country in Europe waiting for a capable man to fill it." Dictatorships arose in many countries, and parliaments were either dissolved or forcibly made to fall in with the dictator's wishes. A notable instance was that of Spain.

Spain was not involved in the World War. She made money out of it by selling goods to the fighting nations. But she had her own troubles, and she was industrially a very backward country. The days of her greatness in Europe, when the wealth of the Americas and the East poured into her ports, were long past, and she hardly counted as an important Power in Europe. There was a feeble parliament, called the Cortes, and the Roman Church was strong. As had happened in other industrially backward countries in Europe, syndicalism and anarchism spread, rather than the solid Marxism and moderate socialism of Germany and England. In 1917, when the Bolsheviks in Russia were struggling for power, the workers and radicals of Spain tried to establish a democratic republic by having a general strike. This strike and the whole movement were crushed by the King's government and the army, and as a result the army became all-powerful in the country. The King, relying on the army, also became a little more independent and autocratic.

Morocco had been more or less divided up into two spheres of influence by France and Spain. In 1921 an able leader, Abdel Krim, rose among the Riffs of Morocco against Spanish rule. He showed great ability and gallantry and defeated Spanish troops repeatedly. This led to an internal crisis in Spain. Both the King and the army leaders wanted to put an end to the constitution and the Parliament and have a dictatorship. They agreed about this, but they disagreed as to who was to be the dictator, the King wanting to be a dictator or absolute monarch himself, and the army leaders wanting a military dictatorship. In September 1923 there was a military revolt, and this decided the issue in favour of the army, and General Primo de Rivera became the Dictator. He suspended the Cortes (Parliament) and ruled frankly on the basis of force—that is, the army. The Morocco campaign against the Riffs, however, did not prosper, and Abdel Krim continued to defy the Spanish aggressively. The Spanish Government even offered him favourable terms, but he refused them, holding out for complete independence. It is probable that the Spanish Government would not have been able to subdue him single-handed. In 1925 the French, who had great interests in Morocco, decided to intervene, and they brought their vast resources to bear against Abdel Krim. By the middle of 1926 he had been defeated, and his long and gallant struggle ended by his surrender to the French.

In Spain, during all these years, Primo de Rivera's dictatorship continued with all the usual accompaniments of military force, censorship, repression, and sometimes martial law. This dictatorship, it must be remembered, was different from that of Mussolini, as it was based solely on the army, and not, as in Italy, on some classes of population. As soon as the army got tired of Primo de Rivera he had no other support left. Early in 1930 the King dismissed

Primo. The same year there was a revolution that was suppressed, but the republican and revolutionary sentiment was too widespread to be kept down. In 1931 the republicans showed their great strength in the municipal elections, and, soon after, King Alfonso, holding that discretion was the better part of valour, abdicated and fled from the country. A provisional government was established, and Spain, the old symbol of autocratic monarchy and Church rule in Europe, became the youngest of Europe's republics, outlawing the ex-King Alfonso and fighting the influence of the Church.

But I was telling you about dictators. Among the other countries besides .Italy and Spain that gave up the democratic forms of government and established dictatorships were : Poland, Yugoslavia, Greece, Bulgaria, Portugal, Hungary, and Austria. In Poland, Pilsudski, the old socialist of Tsarist days, was the Dictator, owing to his control of the army, and he was in the habit of using the most amazingly offensive language to the legislators of the Polish Parliament, and sometimes indeed they were arrested and bundled away. In Yugoslavia, the King, Alexander, is himself the Dictator. It is stated that in some parts of the country conditions became worse, and there was more oppression than there ever was even when the Turks governed them.

All the countries I have mentioned above have not been continuously under open dictatorships. Sometimes their parliaments wake up for a while and are allowed to function; sometimes, as recently happened in Bulgaria, the government in power arrests any group of deputies it does not like, such as the communists, and removes them forcibly from the Parliament, leaving the others to carry on as best they can. Always they live either under dictatorship or on the verge of it, and such governments of individuals or small groups, resting on force, must find support in continuing repression, murders and imprisonments of opponents, a strict censorship, and a widespread system of spies.

Dictatorships sprang up outside Europe also. I have already told you of Turkey and Kemal Pasha. In South America there were many dictators, but they are an old institution there, for the South American republics have never taken kindly to the processes of democracy.

I have not included the Soviet Union in the above list of dictatorships, because the dictatorship there, although as ruthless as any other, is of a different type. It is not the dictatorship of an individual or a small group, but of a well-organized political party basing itself especially on the workers. They call it the " dictatorship of the proletariat ". Thus we have three kinds of dictatorships—the communist type, the fascist, and the military. There is nothing peculiar about the military one; it has existed from the earliest days. The communist and fascist types are new in history, and are the special products of our own times.

The first thing that strikes one is that all these dictatorships and their variations are the direct opposite of democracy and the parliamentary form of government. You will remember my telling you that the nineteenth century was the century of democracy, the century when the Rights of Man of the French Revolution governed advanced thought, and individual freedom was the aim. Out of this developed the parliamentary form of government, in varying degrees, in most countries of Europe. In the economic field this led to the theory of *laissez-faire*. The twentieth century, or rather the post-War years, put an end to this great tradition of the nineteenth century, and fewer and fewer people do reverence now to the idea of formal democracy. And with this fall of democracy the so-called liberal groups everywhere have suffered a like fate, and they have ceased to count as effective forces.

Both communism and fascism have opposed and criticized democracy, though each has done so on entirely different grounds. Even in countries which are neither communist nor fascist, democracy is far less in favour than it used to be. Parliament has ceased to be what it was, and commands no great respect. Great powers are given to executive heads to do what they consider necessary without further reference to Parliament. Partly this is due to the critical times we live in, when swift action is necessary and representative assemblies cannot always act swiftly. Germany has recently thrown her Parliament overboard completely and is now exhibiting the worst type of fascist rule. The United States of America have always given a great deal of power to their President, and this has recently been increased. England and France are about the only two countries at present where Parliament still functions outwardly as in the old days; their fascist activities take place in their dependencies and colonies—in India we have British fascism at work, in Indo-China there is French fascism " pacifying " the country. But even in London and Paris, parliaments are becoming hollow shells. Only last month a leading English liberal said :

> " Our representative Parliament is rapidly becoming merely the machinery of registration for the dictates of a governing caucus elected by an imperfect and badly working electoral machine."

Nineteenth-century democracy and parliaments are thus losing ground everywhere. In some countries they have been openly and rudely discarded, in others they have lost real significance and tend to become a bit of " solemn and empty pageantry ". A historian has compared this degeneration of parliament to the degeneration of kingship in the nineteenth century. Just as the king in England and elsewhere lost real power and became a constitutional monarch, more or less for show purposes, so also, according to this historian, parliaments are likely to become, and are becoming, powerless and dignified symbols, looking big and important but meaning little.

Why has this happened ? Why has democracy, which was for a century or more the ideal and inspiration of countless people, and which can count its martyrs by the thousand, why has it fallen into disfavour now? Such changes do not happen without sufficient reason; they are not just due to the whims and fancies of a fickle public. There must be something in modern conditions of life which does not fit in with the formal democracy of the nineteenth century. The subject is interesting and intricate. I cannot go into it here, but I shall put one or two considerations before you.

I have referred to democracy as "formal" in the preceding paragraph. The communists say that it was not real democracy; it was only a democratic shell to hide the fact that one class ruled over the others. According to them, democracy covered the dictatorship of the capitalist class. It was plutocracy, government by the wealthy. The much-paraded vote given to the masses gave them only the choice of saying once, in four or five years, whether a certain person, X, might rule over them and exploit them or another person, Y, should do so. In either event the masses were to be exploited by the ruling class. Real democracy can only come when this class rule and exploitation end and only one class exists. To bring about this socialist State, however, a period of the dictatorship of the proletariat is necessary so as to keep down all capitalist and *bourgeois* elements in the population and prevent them from intriguing against the workers' State. In Russia this dictatorship is exercised by the Soviets in which all the workers and peasants and other " active " elements are represented. Thus it becomes a dictatorship of the 90 per cent. or even 95 per cent. over the remaining 10 or 5 per cent. That is the theory. In practice the Communist Party controls the Soviets and the ruling clique of communists control the Party. And the dictatorship is as strict, so far as censorship and freedom of thought or action are concerned, as any other. But as it is based on the good will of the workers it must carry the workers with it. And, finally, there is no exploitation of the workers or any other class for the benefit of another. There is no exploiting class left. If there is any exploitation, it is done by the State for the benefit of all. Russia, it is worth remembering, never had the democratic form of government. It jumped in 1917 from autocracy to communism.

The fascist attitude is entirely different. As I have told you in my last letter, it is not easy to find out what fascist principles are, as they do not seem to possess any fixed principles. But that they are opposed to democracy there is no doubt, and their opposition is not on the communist ground that democracy is not the real article but a sham. Fascists object to the whole principle underlying the democratic idea, and they curse democracy with all the vigour at their command. Mussolini has called it a " putrefying corpse " ! The idea of individual liberty is equally disliked by the fascists, the State is everything, the individual does not count. (Communists also do not attach much value to individual liberties.) What would poor Mazzini, the prophet of nineteenth century-democratic liberalism, have said to his fellow-countryman Mussolini !

Not only communists and fascists, but many others, who have thought over the troubles of the present age, have become dissatisfied with the old idea of giving a vote and calling it a democracy. Democracy means equality, and democracy can only flourish in an equal society. It is obvious enough that the giving of votes to everybody does not result in producing an equal society. In spite of adult suffrage and the like, there is to-day tremendous inequality. Therefore, in order to give democracy a chance, an equal society must be created, and this reasoning leads them to various other ideals and methods. But all these people agree that present day parliaments are highly unsatisfactory.

Let us look a little more deeply into fascism and try to find out what it is. It glories in violence and hates pacifism. Mussolini, writing in the *Enciclopedia Italiana*, says :

> " Fascism does not believe in the necessity or utility of perpetual peace. Therefore it repudiates pacifism, which conceals a refusal to struggle and an essential cowardice—in face of sacrifice. War, and war only, raises human energies to the maximum of tension and seals with its nobility the peoples who have the courage to accept it. All other trials are substitutes; they do not place the individual before the choice of life and death."

Fascism is intensely nationalistic, while communism is international. Fascism actually opposes internationalism. It makes of the State a god on whose altar individual freedom and rights must be sacrificed; all other countries are alien and almost like enemies. Jews, being considered as foreign elements, are ill-treated. In spite of certain anti-capitalist slogans and a revolutionary technique, fascism is allied with property-owning and reactionary elements.

These are some odd aspects of fascism. The philosophy underlying it, if it has any, is difficult to grasp. It began, as we have seen, with the simple desire for power. When success came, an attempt was made to build up a philosophy round it. Just to give you an idea of how very involved this is and to puzzle you, I shall give you an extract from the writings of an eminent fascist philosopher. His name is Giovanni Gentile, and he is considered the official philosopher of fascism; he has also been a fascist minister in the government. Gentile says that people should not seek self-realization through their personality or individual selves, as in democracy, but, according to fascism, through the acts of the transcendental ego as the world's self-consciousness (whatever this may mean—it is wholly beyond me). Thus in this view there is no room for individual liberty and personality, for the true reality and freedom of the individual is that which he gains by losing himself in something else—the State.

> " My personality is not suppressed, but uplifted, strengthened, enlarged by being merged and restored in that of the family, the state, the spirit."

Again Gentile says :

> " Every force is moral force in so far as capable of influencing the will, whatever be the argument applied, the sermon or the cudgel."

So now we know what a lot of moral force the British Government in India uses up whenever it indulges in a *lathi* charge !

All these are subsequent attempts to justify or explain a thing that has happened. It is also said that fascism aims at a " Corporative State ", in which I suppose everybody pulls together for the common good. But no such State has so far appeared in Italy or elsewhere. Capitalism functions in Italy more or less in the same way as in other capitalist countries, though some restrictions have been introduced.

As fascism has spread in other countries, it has become clear that it is not a peculiar Italian phenomenon, but that it is something which appears when certain social and economic conditions prevail in a country. Whenever the workers become powerful and actually threaten the capitalistic State, the capitalist class naturally tries to save itself. Usually such a threat from the workers comes in times of violent economic crisis. If the owning and ruling class cannot put down the workers in the ordinary democratic way by using the police and army, then it adopts the fascist method. This consists in creating a popular mass movement, with some slogans which appeal to the crowd, meant for the protection of the owning capitalist class. The backbone for this movement comes from the lower-middle class, most of them suffering from unemployment, and many of the politically backward and unorganized workers and peasants are also attracted to it by the slogans and hopes of bettering their position. Such a movement is financially helped by the big *bourgeoisie* who hope to profit by it, and although it makes violence a creed and a daily practice, the capitalist government of the country tolerates it to a large extent because it fights the common enemy—socialist labour. As a party, and much more so if it becomes the government in a country, it destroys the workers' organizations and terrorizes all opponents.

Fascism thus appears when the class conflicts between an advancing socialism and an entrenched capitalism become bitter and critical. This social war is due not to misunderstanding, but to a better appreciation of the inherent conflicts and diversities of interests in our present-day society. These conflicts cannot be resolved by ignoring them. And the more people who suffer by the present system understand this diversity of interests, the more do they resent being deprived of what they consider their share. The owning class has no intention of giving up what it has got, and so the conflict becomes intense. So long as capitalism can use the machinery of democratic institutions to hold power and keep down labour, democracy is allowed to flourish. When this is not possible, then capitalism discards democracy and adopts the open fascist method of violence and terror.

Fascism exists in varying degrees in all countries of Europe except, I suppose, Russia. Its latest triumph has been won in Germany. Even in England fascist ideas are spreading among the ruling classes, and we see their application often enough in India. On the world-stage to-day fascism, the last resort of capitalism, faces communism.

But fascism, apart from its other aspects, does not even offer to solve the economic troubles that afflict the world. By its intense and aggressive nationalism it goes against the world tendency towards inter-dependence, aggravates the problems that the decline of capitalism has created, and adds to national friction which often leads to war.

177

REVOLUTION AND COUNTER-REVOLUTION IN CHINA

June 26, 1933

Let us now take leave of Europe with its discontents and visit another area of even greater trouble—the Far East, China and Japan. In my last letter on China I told you of the many difficulties of the young republic which had been grafted on to one of the world's most ancient and vital cultures. The country seemed to be splitting up, and unscrupulous war-lords, *tuchuns* and super-*tuchuns*, were coming into prominence, often encouraged and helped by the imperialist Powers, who were interested in keeping China weak and disunited. These *tuchuns* had no principles; each one of them stood for his own personal aggrandizement, and they were frequently changing sides in the petty civil wars that were continually going on. Meanwhile they lived with their armies on the unhappy peasantry. I have also told you of the nationalist government organized in the south at Canton by Dr. Sun Yat-Sen the great leader who had worked for China's freedom all his life.

The whole country was dominated by the economic interests of the foreign imperialist Powers, who sat at the great port towns, like Shanghai and Hongkong, and controlled all the foreign trade of China. Dr. Sun had said quite truly that China was economically the colony of these Powers. It was bad enough to have one master, to have many masters was sometimes even worse. Dr. Sun tried to get foreign help to develop the country industrially and to put his house in order. In particular he looked to America and Britain, but neither of them, nor any other imperialist Power, came to his help. They were all interested in the exploitation of China, and not in her well-being or strengthening. Dr. Sun then turned to Soviet Russia in 1924.

Communism had been growing secretly and rapidly among the students and intellectual classes in China. A Communist Party had been formed in 1920, and it worked as a secret society because it was not allowed to function openly by the various governments. Dr. Sun was far from being a communist; he was a mild socialist, as his famous " Three Principles of the People " show. He was, however, impressed by the generous and straightforward behaviour of the Soviets towards China and other Eastern countries, and he developed friendly relations with them. He engaged some Russian advisers, the best known of whom was a very able Bolshevik, Borodin. Borodin became a tower of strength to the Kuomintang at Canton, and he worked to build up a powerful national party organization with mass support. He did not seek to work on communist lines entirely. He kept the national basis of the party, but communists were now admitted to the Kuomintang as members. There was thus a kind of informal alliance between the nationalist Kuomintang and the Communist Party. Many of the conservative and richer members of the Kuomintang, especially the landlords, did not like this association with the communists. On the other hand, many of the communists did not like it either, because it meant their toning down their programme and not doing many things they might otherwise have done. The alliance was not a very stable one, and, as we shall see, it broke down at a critical moment, and this brought disaster to China. It is always difficult to hold together in one group two or more classes whose interests clash. But while this alliance lasted it prospered exceedingly, and the Kuomintang and the Canton Government grew in power. Tenants' organizations were encouraged, and they spread rapidly, so also workers' trade unions. It was this mass support which gave the Canton Kuomintang real power, and it was this which frightened the landlord leaders and induced them to break up the party at a later stage.

Conditions in China bear many resemblances to those in India, although there are many radical differences also. China is essentially an agricultural country with vast numbers of farmers. Capitalist industry is confined chiefly to half a dozen cities and is under foreign control. The millions of farmers and tenants are crushed under a terrible burden of debt. Rents are very high and, as in India, the agriculturists have long periods of enforced idleness when they have little work in the fields. Cottage industries are thus needed by them to fill in this time and add to their income. Indeed, there are many such industries now. There are very few great estates. When such an estate is formed it is soon divided up among the heirs. About half the peasantry own their farms, the other half work under landlords. China is thus a country of vast numbers of small farms. For hundreds of years Chinese farmers have had the reputation of being able to extract the utmost possible sustenance from the land. They were forced to do so because of the small parcels of land they possessed, and so they exercised an amazing ingenuity and worked tremendously hard. They had none of the labour-saving devices which modern agriculture possesses, and this made them work harder than they need have done for the results obtained.

Even with all this ingenuity and hard work nearly half of them could not make both ends meet, and were half starved through their short and stunted lives, as happens to the great numbers of peasants in India. They lived on the verge of destitution, and calamities came, famines and floods, and swept them away by the million. Dr. Sun's Government, at Borodin's suggestion, passed decrees giving

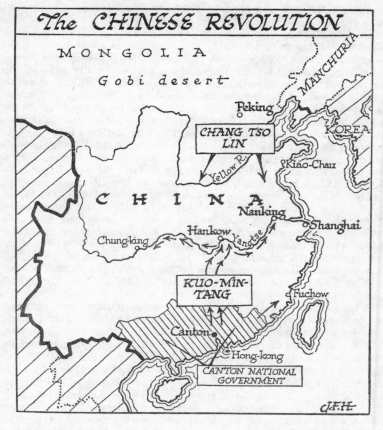

The CHINESE REVOLUTION

MONGOLIA

Gobi desert

MANCHURIA

Peking

CHANG TSO LIN

KOREA

Yellow R.

Kiao-Chau

C H I N A

Nanking

Shanghai

Chung-king   Hankow   Yangtse

KUO-MIN-TANG

Fuchow

Canton

Hong-kong

CANTON NATIONAL GOVERNMENT

relief to the peasants and the workers.   The land rent was reduced by 25 per cent., an eight-hour working day and a minimum wage were fixed for the workers, and peasant unions were established.   It was natural that these reforms should be welcomed by the masses and fill them with enthusiasm.   They flocked to the new unions and to the support of the Canton Government.

So Canton consolidated itself and prepared for a tussle with the *tuchuns* of the north.   A military academy was opened and an army built up.   An interesting development not only in Canton but all over China, and to some extent all over the East, was the displacement of religious authority by secular authority.   China, of course, had never been a religious country in the narrow sense of the word.   It now became even more secular.   Education, which used to be religious, was secularized.   The most obvious examples of this process are afforded by the use to which many old temples are now put.   In Canton a famous old temple is now used as a police training institute ! In another place temples have been converted into vegetable markets.

Dr. Sun Yat-Sen died in March 1925, but the Canton Government went on adding to its strength, with Borodin as its adviser. Soon afterwards, some incidents took place which filled the Chinese people with anger against foreign imperialists, and especially against the British. There were strikes in the cotton mills of Shanghai and a worker was killed in a demonstration in May 1925. A great memorial service was organized for him, and this was made the occasion for anti-imperialist demonstrations by students and workers. A British police officer, with Sikh policemen under him, ordered firing on this crowd—the order was " Shoot to kill "—and several students were killed. Anger at the British blazed out all over China, and a subsequent incident made matters far worse. This took place in June 1925, in the foreign area (known as the Shameen area) of Canton, where a Chinese crowd, chiefly of students, was fired on by machine-guns and fifty-two persons were killed and many more wounded. The British were held to be mainly responsible for this " Shameen massacre " as it was called. A political boycott of British goods was proclaimed at Canton, and Hongkong trade was held up for many months, causing great losses to British firms and the British Government. Hongkong, as you perhaps know, is a British possession in South China. It is quite near to Canton, and through it passes an enormous trade.

After the death of Dr. Sun there was a continuous tussle between the conservative right wing and the advanced left wing of the Canton Government. Sometimes one and then the other was in power. About the middle of 1926 Chiang Kai-Shek, a right-winger, became commander-in-chief, and he started pushing out the communists. But still to some extent the two groups worked together, although they distrusted each other. Then began the advance of the Canton army to the north to fight and expel the various *tuchuns* and establish one national government in the whole country. This northern advance was an extraordinary thing, and soon it attracted the world's attention. There was little actual fighting, and the army of the south marched on swiftly from victory to victory. The north was disunited, but the real strength of the south came from its popularity with the peasants and workers. A little army of propagandists and agitators went ahead of the army, organizing peasant's and workers' unions and telling them of the benefits they would have under the Canton Government. And so cities and villages welcomed the advancing armies and helped them in every way. The troops sent against the Canton army hardly fought, and often went over, bag and baggage, to them. Before the year 1926 was over the nationalists had crossed half China and taken possession of the great city of Hankow on the Yangtse river. They shifted their capital from Canton to Hankow, renaming it Wuhan. The northern warlords had been defeated and driven away, and the imperialist Powers suddenly realized, much to their annoyance, that a new and agressive nationalist China stood before them claiming equality and refusing to be bullied.

Early in 1927 there was a conflict between the Chinese and the British when the nationalists tried to take possession of the British concession at Hankow. Ordinarily such an aggressive attitude on the part of the Chinese would have led to war and the British Government would have crushed them and terrorized them into giving indemnities, and more concessions. Such had been the invariable practice, as we have already seen, for nearly a century, since the Opium War of 1840. But times had changed, and a different China faced them now, and so immediately, and for the first time in China, British policy underwent a change also and became conciliatory towards the new China. The Hankow concession affair was a minor matter and could be easily settled. But not very far, and on the line of the nationalist advance, was the great port of Shanghai, the biggest and the richest foreign concession area in China. Enormous foreign vested interests were interested in the fate of Shanghai. The city itself, or rather the concession area, was under foreign control and practically independent of the Chinese Government. These foreigners in Shanghai and their governments became very anxious when the nationalist armies approached them, and warships and troops were hurried to the port. The British Government especially sent a large expeditionary force, consisting partly of Indian troops, to Shanghai early in January 1927.

The nationalist Government, now established at Hankow or Wuhan, were faced with a difficult problem—to advance or not to advance, to take Shanghai or not to do so. Their easy successes so far had emboldened them and filled them with enthusiasm, and Shanghai was a very tempting prize. On the other hand, they had simply marched on and on over more than 500 miles of territory, and had not consolidated their position there. To attack Shanghai might involve them in difficulties with foreign Powers, and this might endanger the gains they had already achieved. Borodin advised caution and consolidation. He was of opinion that the nationalists should keep away from Shanghai and strengthen their position in the southern half of China which was already under their control, and prepare the ground in the north with propaganda. Very soon, within a year or so, he expected the whole of China to be ready to welcome a nationalist advance. That would be the time to take Shanghai, march to Peking, and face the foreign imperialist Powers. Borodin, the revolutionary, gave this cautious advice, because he was experienced in judging the various factors in a situation. The right-wing leaders of the Kuomintang, however, and especially the commander-in-chief, Chiang Kai-Shek, insisted on marching to Shanghai. The real reason for this desire to take Shanghai appeared later when the Kuomintang split up into two. The growing power of the tenants' and workers' unions was not liked by these right-wing leaders. Many of the generals were themselves landlords. They had therefore decided to crush these unions, even at the cost of breaking up the party into two and weakening the nationalist cause. Shanghai was an important centre of the big Chinese *bourgeoisie*, and the right-wing generals counted upon it to help them, with money and otherwise, in their fight against the more advanced elements in their party, and especially against the communists. In such a fight they knew they could also rely on the support of the foreign bankers and industrialists in Shanghai.

So they marched on Shanghai, and on March 22, 1927, the Chinese part of the city fell to them, the foreign concession areas not being attacked. This fall of Shanghai also took place without much fighting, Opposing troops went over to the nationalists, and a general strike of the workers in the city in favour of the nationalists, completed the downfall of the existing Government in Shanghai. Two days later the great city of Nanking was also occupied by the nationalist armies. And then came the split in the Kuomintang, between the left wing and the right wing, which put an end to the nationalist triumph and brought disaster. The revolution had ended; counter-revolution now began.

Chiang Kai-Shek had marched on Shanghai against the wishes of many members of the Hankow Government. Both parties intrigued against each other. The Hankow people tried to undermine Chiang's influence in the army and so to get rid of him; Chiang set up a rival government in Nanking. All this happened within a few days of the capture of Shanghai. Having rebelled against his own Government at Hankow, Chiang now made war on communists, left-wingers, and trade-unionist workers. The very workers who had made it easy for him to take Shanghai and had welcomed him joyously there were now hunted out and crushed. Large numbers of people were shot down or beheaded, thousands were arrested and imprisoned. The freedom that the nationalists were supposed to have brought to Shanghai was soon converted into a bloody terror.

It was during these very April days of 1927 that simultaneously raids took place on the Soviet embassy in Peking and the Soviet consulate in Shanghai. It seemed obvious enough that Chiang Kai-Shek was acting in concert with the northern war-lord Chang Tso Lin, with whom he was supposed to be at war. In Peking, as in Shanghai, a " clean-up " of communists and advanced workers was carried out. The imperialist Powers of course welcomed this development, because it broke up and weakened the ranks of the Chinese nationalists. Chiang Kai-Shek sought to co-operate with the representatives of the Powers in Shanghai. You will remember that it was about this time, in May 1927, that the British Government carried out the Arcos raid on Soviet premises in London and then broke off relations with Russia.

And so, within a month or two, the picture had changed completely in China. From being a united and a triumphant party representing the Chinese nation and, flushed with success, facing the foreign Powers, the Kuomintang had broken up into warring groups, and the workers and peasants, who had been its life and strength, were now being persecuted and hunted down. The foreign interests in Shanghai breathed happily again and graciously helped one group against another, especially in the pleasant and profitable pastime of baiting and harassing the workers. These workers in the Shanghai factories (and indeed throughout China) were terribly exploited by the owners, and their standards and living conditions were miserable. Trade unionism gave them strength and had already forced the hands of the owners in giving higher wages. Trade unions therefore were not approved of by the factory-owners—European, Japanese, or Chinese.

Borodin was strongly criticized in Moscow for the turn events had taken in China, and in July 1927 he left for Russia. With his departure the left wing of the Kuomintang at Hankow went to pieces. The Nanking Government now controlled the Kuomintang completely, and the war against communists specially and against all left-wingers and workers' leaders continued. Among those who left China, or were driven out, at this stage, was Madame Sun, the revered widow of the great leader, Sun Yat-Sen. She declared in sorrow that her husband's great work for China's freedom had been betrayed by the militarists and others. And yet these militarists continued to swear by Dr. Sun's three famous principles—Nationalism, Democracy, and Social Justice.

Again China became a maze of war-lords and generals fighting each other. Canton broke off from the Nanking Government and established a government of its own in the south. In 1928 Peking fell into the hands of the Nanking Government. Its name was changed to Peiping, which means " Northern Peace". Peking had meant " Northern Capital ", but it was no longer the capital.

In spite of the fall of Peking or Peiping, as we must call it now, civil war continued in various parts of the country. Canton formed a separate government, but even in the north various war-lords did much as they pleased, and carried on personal quarrels, and sometimes came to terms with each other for a while. In theory the so-called " National " Government at Nanking ruled China, except for Canton. There were, however, many areas which were beyond its control, notably a big area in the interior where a communist government was set up. The Nanking Government relied chiefly on the Shanghai bankers for financial support. The large armies of various generals became a terrible burden on the peasantry. Vast numbers of ex-soldiers also roamed about the countryside in search of employment and, finding none, often took to banditry.

Relations between the Nanking Government and Soviet Russia were broken off in December 1927, and, under the patronage of the imperialist Powers, Nanking adopted an aggressive anti-Soviet policy. This would have led to war in 1927 but for the persistent refusal of Russia to go to war. In 1929 the Chinese Government again became aggressive, this time in Manchuria. The Soviet consulate was raided and the Russian officials of the Chinese Eastern Railway were dismissed. This railway was largely Russian property, and the Soviet Government immediately took action against the Chinese. For a few months a kind of war existed, and then the Chinese Government agreed to the Soviet demand to restore the old arrangement.

Manchuria and the railway running through it have led to many international complications, as many interests clash there, especially

Chinese, Japanese, and Russian. Recently Japan has gained control over these north-eastern provinces of China, in spite of world disapproval. I shall tell you of this in my next letter.

I have referred above to a communist government being set up in some parts of China. It appears that the first communist government to be established was in November 1927, in the district of Haifeng in the province of Kwantung in the south. This was the " Haifeng Soviet Republic ", which developed out of various peasants' unions. The Soviet area grew in the interior of China till by the middle of 1932 about a sixth of the total area of China proper— that is, an area of 250,000 square miles with a population of 50,000,000 —was included in it. This government built up a Red Army of 400,000 men, and this army had auxiliary units of boys and girls. Both the Nanking and Canton governments tried their utmost to crush these Chinese Soviets, and Chiang Kai-Shek led repeated expeditions against them without much success. The soviets sometimes retreated and consolidated themselves elsewhere in the interior.[1]

178

JAPAN DEFIES THE WORLD

June 29, 1933

WE have followed the dismal story of the disintegration of China, of the revolution that seemed to have triumphed and then, suddenly, collapsed and was swallowed up by a fierce counter-revolution. The tale is not ended yet, there is much more to come. The revolution failed because the conflicts of conscious class interests were greater than the binding force of nationalism. The rich landed and other interests preferred to break the nationalist movement rather than risk the dominance of the peasant and worker masses.

Apart from her internal troubles, China had now to face a determined attack from a foreign enemy. This was Japan, bent on profiting by the weakness of China and the preoccupation of other Powers.

Japan is an extraordinary example of a mixture of modern industrialism and medieval feudalism, of parliamentarism and autocracy and military control. The ruling landowning and military classes have deliberately tried to build up a State on the lines of a clan, with themselves as the chiefs and the Emperor as the supreme head. Religion, education, everything has been made to help in this process. Religion is an officially controlled affair, the temples and shrines being directly under official control, and the priests holding official posts. Thus a huge propaganda machine, working through the temples and schools, is constantly teaching the people, not only

[1] The conflict between Chiang Kai-Shek and the Chinese Soviets, their joining together against Japanese aggression, and Japan's invasion of China and the war that followed, are dealt with in the Postscript at the end of this book.

patriotism to the country, but obedience to the will of the Emperor who is to be considered semi-divine. The old Japanese term for something corresponding to the old chivalry was "*Bushido*", a kind of clan loyalty. This idea has been extended to cover the whole State, and with it is connected the Emperor at the top. The Emperor is really a symbol in whose name the ruling big landlord and military classes exercise power. Industrialization has developed a *bourgeoisie* in Japan, but the big industrial magnates happen to come from the old landowning families, and thus there has so far been no transfer of power to the *bourgeoisie* as such. In effect, there is so much monopoly in Japan that a few powerful families control the industry as well as the politics of the country.

Buddhism has long been a popular faith in Japan, but Shinto is more of a national religion, with its stress on ancestor-worship. This worship includes the past emperors and heroes of the nation, and especially those who have died in war. In this way it becomes a powerful and effective method for spreading a love of country and the idea of obedience to the reigning emperor. The Japanese people are famous for their amazing patriotism and their capacity for sacrifice for their country. It is not so well known that this patriotism is of a very aggressive kind, and dreams of world empire. About 1915 a new sect was started in Japan. It was called the "Omoto-Kyo" sect, and it spread very rapidly all over the country. The principal doctrine of this sect was that Japan should become the ruler of the whole world, the Emperor being the supreme head. On behalf of the sect it was stated :

"We are only aiming at making the Emperor of Japan ruler and governor of the whole world, as he is the only ruler in the world who retains the spiritual mission inherited from the remotest ancestor in the divine world."

During the World War, as we have seen, Japan tried to bully China by her twenty-one demands. She did not get all she wanted, because of the outcry in America and Europe, but she got a great deal. After the war Japan saw in the collapse of the Tsarist Empire an ideal opportunity for spreading out in Asia. Her armies entered Siberia and her agents came right up to Samarqand and Bokhara in Central Asia. That adventure failed because of the recovery of Soviet Russia and to some extent the opposition and distrust of America. For it must always be remembered that there is little love lost between Japan and the United States of America. They dislike each other greatly, and glare at each other across the Pacific Ocean. The Washington Conference of 1922 was a blow to Japanese ambitions and a victory for American diplomacy. At this conference nine Powers, including Japan, pledged themselves to respect the integrity of China, which meant that Japan must give up all hopes of spreading out in China. At this Conference also the Anglo-Japanese alliance came to an end and Japan stood isolated in the Far East. The British Government started building a mighty naval base at Singapore, and this was obviously a threat to Japan. In

1924 the United States of America passed an anti-Japanese immigration Bill, as they wanted to keep out Japanese workers from the States. This racial discrimination was greatly resented in Japan, and to some extent all over the East. But Japan could do nothing against America. Feeling isolated and surrounded by a hostile ring, Japan turned to Russia, and in January 1925 signed a treaty with her.

I must tell you of a great disaster that befell Japan during this period and which weakened her very much. This was a terrible earthquake which took place on September 1, 1925, and was followed by a tidal wave and a fire in the great capital city of Tokyo. This huge city was destroyed and so also the port of Yokohama. Over 100,000 people died and enormous damage was done. The Japanese people met the disaster with courage and resolution and built a new city of Tokyo on the ruins of the old.

Japan had come to terms with Russia because of her difficulties, but this did not mean approval of communism. Communism meant the end of emperor-worship, and feudalism, and the exploitation of the masses by the ruling class, and indeed almost everything that the existing order stood for. This communism was growing in Japan because of the increasing misery of the people, who were being exploited more and more by powerful industrial interests. The population was growing rapidly. It could not emigrate to America or Canada or even the barren wastes of Australia; the doors were closed. China was near, but China was over full of people. There was some emigration to Korea and Manchuria. Besides her own especial troubles, Japan had to face the common troubles of industrialism and trade depression which all the world was experiencing. As the internal situation grew more serious, severe repression of communist and all radical ideas began. In 1925 a " Peace Preservation Law " was passed and, as the wording is interesting, I shall give you the first article of this law. It runs thus :

> "That those who have organized an association or fraternity with the object of altering the national constitution, or of repudiating the private property system, or those who have joined such an organization with full knowledge of its object, are to be punished with penalties, ranging from death to servitude of over five years."

The extreme severity of this law, which bars not only communism but all forms of socialistic or radical or constitutional reform, is a measure of the fright of the Japanese Government at the rise of communism.

But communism is the outcome of widespread misery due to social conditions, and unless these conditions are improved, mere repression can be no remedy. There is a terrible misery in Japan at present. The peasantry, as in China and India, are crushed under a tremendous burden of debt. Taxation, especially because of heavy military expenditure and war needs, is very heavy. Reports come of starving peasants trying to live on grass and roots, and of selling even their children. The middle classes are also in a bad way owing to unemployment, and suicides have increased.

The campaign against communism began on a big scale early in 1928, when over 1000 arrests were made in the course of one night, and yet newspapers were not allowed to publish this fact for over a month. Police raids and mass arrests have taken place frequently year after year. One of the biggest raids took place in October 1932, when 2250 persons were arrested. Most of these people were not labourers, but students and teachers. There were among them hundreds of graduates and women. It is curious to notice that many rich young people have been attracted to communism in Japan. Advanced thinkers there, as in India and elsewhere, are considered more dangerous than criminals. Like the Meerut trial in India, some of the Japanese communist trials have gone on for years.

I have told you all this about conditions in Japan so that you may have some idea of the background of the Manchurian adventure of Japan, about which I propose to tell you something now.

You have read in previous letters of Japan's persistent attempts to get a footing on the Asiatic mainland, first in Korea and then in Manchuria. The war with China of 1894 and the Russian war of ten years later were both waged with this object in view. Success came to Japan and step by step she went ahead. Korea was absorbed and became just a part of the Japanese Empire. In Manchuria, which is a general name for China's three eastern provinces, the Russian lease and concessions round about Port Arthur were transferred to Japan. Part of the railway built by Russia across Manchuria, the Chinese Eastern Railway, also came under Japanese control, and was named the South Manchuria Railway. In spite of all these changes Manchuria as a whole still continued to be under the Chinese Government, and because of the railway Chinese immigrants poured in. Indeed, this immigration to the three north-eastern provinces is supposed to be one of the greatest migrations in world history. Within seven years, from 1923 to 1929, over 2,500,000 Chinese went across. The population of Manchuria is about 30,000,000 now and of these 95 per cent. are Chinese. The three provinces are thus thoroughly Chinese. The remaining 5 per cent. are Russians, Mongol nomads, Koreans, and Japanese. The old Manchus have become absorbed in the Chinese, and have even forgotten their language.

You will remember my telling you of the Nine-Power Treaty signed at the Washington Conference of 1922. This was specially made, at the suggestion of the Western Powers, to check Japanese designs in China. Explicitly and unambiguously, all the nine Powers (of which Japan was one) agreed " to respect the sovereignty, the independence and the territorial and administrative integrity of China ".

For some years Japan held her hand. Behind the scenes, however, she helped, with money and otherwise, some of the Chinese warlords, or *tuchuns*, to carry on the civil war and thus weaken China. In particular, she helped Chang Tso Lin, who dominated Manchuria and even Peking till the victory of the southern nationalists. In 1931 the Japanese Government adopted an openly aggressive

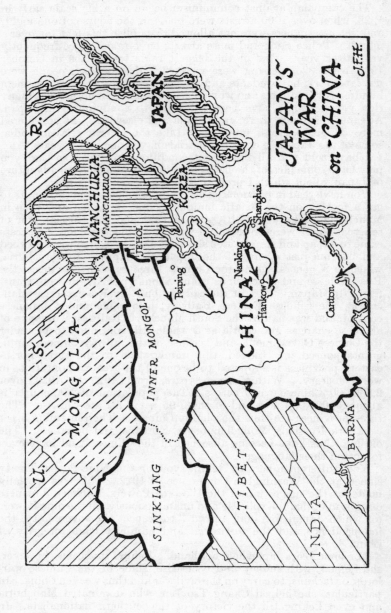

attitude in Manchuria. This may have been due to their intense economic crisis, which forced them to do something abroad in order to divert attention as well as relieve the tension at home, or to the dominance of the military party in the Government, or to the feeling that all the other Powers were busy with their own troubles and the trade depression and were not likely to interfere. Probably all these reasons worked together to induce the Japanese Government to take a step which was a very serious one. For this step was a distinct breach of the Nine-Power Treaty of 1922. It was also a breach of the League of Nations Covenant, for both China and Japan were members of the League, and, as such, could not attack each other without reference to the League. And, lastly, it was a clear breach of the Paris (or Kellogg) Pact of 1928 for the outlawry of war. By carrying on warlike operations against China, the Japanese Government deliberately broke these treaties and pledges and defied the world.

Of course they did not say so. They put up some feeble, and obviously untrue, excuse of bandits in Manchuria and some petty incidents which compelled them to send their troops to maintain order and protect their interests. There was no open declaration of war, but nevertheless there was a Japanese invasion of Manchuria. The Chinese people were very angry at this. The Chinese Government protested and appealed to the League of Nations and the other Powers, but no one paid any attention to them. Each country was full of its own troubles and unwilling to add to them by opposing Japan. It is also probable that some Powers, and notably England, had a secret arrangement with Japan. Chinese irregular troops gave a lot of trouble to the Japanese in Manchuria. And yet there was supposed to be no war between the two countries ! More troublesome to Japan was a great movement in China for the boycott of Japanese goods.

In January 1932 a Japanese army suddenly descended on Chinese soil near Shanghai, and perpetrated one of the most ghastly massacres of modern times. They avoided the foreign concession areas, so as not to irritate the western Powers, and attacked the densely populated Chinese quarters. A huge area near Shanghai (I think its name was Chapei) was bombed and shelled and utterly destroyed, thousands being killed and vast numbers rendered homeless. Remember that this was not a fight against an army. It was the bombing of innocent civilians. The Japanese admiral who was in charge of this gallant operation, when asked about it, stated that Japan had mercifully decided that there should be " only two more days of indiscriminate bombing of civilians " ! Even the pro-Japanese correspondent of the London *Times* in Shanghai was shocked by this " wholesale massacre ", as he called it, of the Chinese by the Japanese. What the Chinese people felt about it may well be imagined. A wave of horror and anger passed through China, and the various war-lords and governments in the country forgot, or seemed to forget, their mutual rivalries before this barbarous foreign invasion. There was talk of a united front against Japan, and even the communist

Government of the Chinese interior offered its services to the Nanking
Government.   And yet, strange to say, Nanking, or its leader Chiang
Kai-Shek, made no move to defend Shanghai from the advancing
Japanese troops.   All that Nanking did was to protest to the League.
It did not even try to build up a united resistance against the Japanese.
It almost appears that it had no desire to resist, in spite of its tall
talk and the burning indignation of the country.

And then there appeared at Shanghai an odd army from the south
—the Nineteenth Route Army it was called.   It consisted of Canton-
ese people, but it was not under the orders of either the Nanking or
the Canton Government.   It was a ragged army with little equipment, no big guns, poor uniforms, and not enough clothing to protect
it from the bitter cold of a Chinese winter.   There were many boys
of fourteen and sixteen serving in it; some were only twelve years
old.   This ragged army decided to fight and hold the Japanese in
defiance of Chiang Kai-Shek's orders.   For two weeks in January
and February 1932 they fought without any help from the Nanking
Government, and they fought with such remarkable heroism that
the far stronger and better-equipped Japanese were, much to their
surprise, held up.   Not only the Japanese but everybody was surprised, the foreign Powers and the Chinese people themselves.   After
two weeks' unaided fighting, when everybody was full of praises of
this army, Chiang Kai-Shek sent some of his troops to help in the
defence.

The 19th Route Army made history and became famous the world
over.   Their defence upset Japanese plans, and as the Western
Powers were also anxious about their interests in Shanghai, the
Japanese troops were gradually withdrawn from the Shanghai area
and shipped away.   It is worth noting that these Western Powers
were far more concerned with their financial or other interests than
with odd massacres like the Chapei one, in which thousands of Chinese
had been killed, or with the breach of solemn treaties and international covenants.   The League of Nations was repeatedly moved
in the matter, but always it found some excuse for postponing action.
The fact that an actual war was going on and thousands had been
and were being killed was not a matter of urgency for the League.
It was said that there was no real war because it had not been
officially declared to be a war !   The reputation and prestige of the
League suffered greatly by this weakness and almost deliberate
connivance at wrong-doing.   The responsibility for this of course
lay with some of the great Powers, and England especially adopted a
pro-Japanese attitude in the League.   Ultimately the League
appointed an international commission of inquiry into the Manchurian affair, under the chairmanship of Lord Lytton.   This was
readily agreed to by the Powers, as it meant postponing any decision
for many months.   Manchuria was far off, and it would take a long
time for the commission to go there and report, and perhaps the
matter might blow over by then.

The Japanese withdrew from Shanghai, but they paid more attention now to Manchuria.   They set up a puppet government there

and proclaimed that Manchuria had exercised its right of self-determination. This new puppet State was named Manchukuo, and a seedy-looking youth, a descendant of the old Manchu rulers of China, was made the monarch of the new domain. Of course the whole thing was for show purposes only, and Japan was the real ruler. Everybody knew that if the Japanese army were removed the State of Manchukuo would topple over in a day.

The Japanese had great trouble in Manchuria, for volunteer Chinese bands were continually fighting them. These bands are called by the Japanese " bandits ". Manchukuo armies, consisting of the local Chinese, were trained and equipped by the Japanese. When they were sent against the " bandits ", they walked over and joined the " bandits " with all their up-to-date equipment! Manchuria suffered greatly because of this incessant warfare, and the soya bean trade began to die out.

After many months of inquiry the Lytton Commission presented its report to the League of Nations. It was a careful, moderate, and judicially worded document, but it was dead against Japan. This upset the British Government very much, as they were bent on protecting Japan. The consideration of the matter was put off for several months again. At last the question had to be faced by the League. The American attitude had been very different from that of England; it was much more against Japan. America had declared that she would not recognize any change brought about forcibly by Japan in Manchuria or elsewhere. In spite of this strong American attitude, England, and to some extent France, Italy, and Germany, supported Japan.

While the League was doing its best to avoid a decision, Japan took a new step. On New Year's Day 1933, a Japanese army suddenly appeared in China proper and attacked the town of Shanhaikwan, which stands on the Chinese side of the Great Wall. There was shelling from big guns and destroyers, and bombing from aeroplanes; it was a thoroughly up-to-date attack, and Shanhaikwan was reduced to a " smoking ruin ", and a large number of its civilian inhabitants lay dead and dying. And then the Japanese army marched on into the Chinese province of Jehol and approaching Peiping. The excuse was that the " bandits " used to make Jehol their headquarters for attacking Manchukuo, and that anyway Jehol was part of Manchukuo!

This fresh aggression and the New-Year-Day massacre woke up the League and, largely because of the insistence of the smaller Powers, the League passed a resolution adopting the Lytton report and condemning Japan. The Japanese Government did not care in the least (for did it not know that some great Powers, including England, were backing it secretly?) and marched out of the League. Having resigned from the League, Japan quietly went on advancing on Peiping. It met with little or no resistance, and when the Japanese army almost reached the gates of Peiping, in May 1933, an armistice between China and Japan was announced. Japan had triumphed. It is not surprising that the Nanking Government and the present Kuomintang became very unpopular in China, after the pitiful exhibition which they gave against Japanese aggression.

I have said a lot about this Manchurian affair. It is important because it affects the future of China. But it is more important still because it shows up the League of Nations and its utter ineffectiveness and futility in the face of proved international wrong-doing. It also shows up the duplicity of the big European Powers and their intrigues. In this particular matter America (not a member of the League) tried to take up a strong attitude against Japan and almost drifted into war with her. But then the secret support that England and other Powers gave to Japan nullified America's attitude, and, fearing isolation against Japan, America became more cautious. The League piously condemned Japan but did nothing to follow this up. The puppet State of Manchukuo was not to be recognized by the League members, but this non-recognition became little more than a farce.

In spite of the League's condemnation of Japan, British ministers and ambassadors go out of their way to justify Japanese action. This is a strange contrast to England's behaviour towards Russia. In April 1933 some English engineers were tried in Russia for espionage. Some were acquitted, and two were sentenced to light terms of imprisonment. There was a great outcry at this, and the British Government immediately put an embargo on the entry of Russian goods into Britain. Russia responded by keeping out British goods.[1]

So China lost Manchuria and much else, and Japan continued to threaten the rest of the country. Tibet was independent. Mongolia was a Soviet country allied to the Russian Soviet Union. China also had trouble in another huge province, Sinkiang or Chinese Turkestan, which lies between Tibet and Siberia. To Yarkand and Kashgar in this province go caravans regularly from Srinagar in Kashmir, via Leh in Ladakh. The population of this province consists largely of Muslim Turks. They are Chinese in their outlook and culture and even names. But they are very far from the heart of China and are cut off by the Gobi desert. Communications are very primitive. The bonds that tie them to China are not strong and there is a feeling of Turkish nationalism which breaks out from time to time. This vast area has been the scene of international intrigue ever since the Great War. England and Russia and Japan spy and intrigue against each other and the Chinese government, and support rival chiefs locally.

Early in 1933 there was a Turkish revolt in Sinkiang; Yarkand and Kashgar fell and a republic was proclaimed. The British accused the Soviet of encouraging this revolt, but the Soviet openly charged the British with having instigated it with the object of creating a buffer State between China and Russia, like Manchukuo. Even the name of the British army officer who organized the revolt in Sinkiang is mentioned.

Note.—This revolt in Sinkiang was suppressed by the supporters

[1] This trade war between England and Russia was brought to an end later by an agreement between the two countries.

of the Chinese Government, apparently with some unofficial help given by the Soviet authorities. Soviet prestige went up in Central Asia in consequence and British prestige fell.

179

THE UNION OF SOCIALIST SOVIET REPUBLICS

July 7, 1933

LET us now go back to Russia, the land of the Soviets, and take up the thread of her story from where we had left off. We had reached January 1924, when Lenin, the leader and inspirer of the revolution, died. In the many subsequent letters that I have written to you since about other countries, Russia has frequently found mention. In considering European problems, or the Indian frontier, or the Middle-Eastern countries, Turkey and Persia, or the Far East, China and Japan, Russia has cropped up again and again. The fact must be becoming evident to you that it is very difficult, and indeed impossible, to separate the politics and economics of one nation from those of others. The inter-relations and interdependence of nations have grown tremendously in recent years, and the world is becoming, in many ways, a single unit. History has become international, a world history, and can only be understood even as regards one country if we keep looking at the world as a whole.

The enormous area covered by the Soviet Union in Europe and Asia stands apart from the capitalist world, and yet everywhere it comes into contact, and often into conflict, with this other world. I have told you in previous letters of the Soviet's generous Eastern policy, of the help given to Turkey, Persia, and Afghanistan, and of its intimate relations with China, followed by a sudden break. I have also told you of the Arcos raid in England, and of the " Zinoviev letter " which turned out to be a forgery, but which none the less influenced a British general election. Now I want to take you to the centre of Soviet land to watch the development of the strange and fascinating social experiment that was taking place there.

The first four years after the Revolution, from 1917 to 1921, had been a period of fighting to preserve the Revolution from a host of enemies. It was a thrilling and dramatic period of war and revolt and civil war and starvation and death, brightered up by the crusading zeal of the masses and the heroism shown in defence of an ideal. The immediate reward was nothing, but great hopes and promises filled the people and made them bear their terrible sufferings and forget even, for a while, their empty stomachs. This was the period of " militant communism ".

Then came a slight relaxation when Lenin introduced the New Economic Policy, or NEP, in 1921. It was a going back from communism, a compromise with *bourgeois* elements in the country. This did not mean that the Bolshevik leaders had changed their objective. All it meant was that they had taken a step back to rest and recuperate in order to be able to take several steps forward again later. So the Soviets settled down and faced the mighty problem of building up a nation that had been largely destroyed and ruined. In order to build and do constructive work, they wanted machinery and material, such as railway-engines and carriages and motor-trucks and tractors and factory equipments. They had to buy these in foreign countries, and they had little money for them. They tried therefore to get credits in these foreign countries so that they might be able to pay for the goods they bought in convenient instalments. Credits could only be obtained when the countries were on speaking terms with each other, not if they did not recognize each other officially. Soviet Russia was therefore very keen on getting recognition from the big Powers and having diplomatic and trade relations with them. But these big imperialist Powers hated the Bolsheviks and all their works; to them communism was an abomination that must be put down. They had, indeed, tried their best to put it down during the wars of intervention, and they had failed. They would have preferred to have no dealings with the Soviets. But it is difficult to ignore a government which happens to control one-sixth of the whole surface of the earth. It is still more difficult to ignore a good customer who is prepared to buy a great deal of expensive machinery. Trade between an agricultural country like Russia and industrial countries like Germany, England, and America was beneficial to both sides, for Russia wanted machinery and could supply cheap food and raw material.

The pull of the pocket was at last greater than the hatred of communism, and nearly all countries recognized the Soviet Government, and many of them made trade treaties with it. The only Power that consistently refused to recognize the Soviets was America. There has, however, been trade between Russia and the United States of America.[1]

In this way the Soviets established relations with most of the capitalist and imperialist Powers, and to some extent they profited by the rivalries of these Powers, as they did when defeated Germany turned to them in 1922 and the Rapallo Treaty was signed. But the compromise was a very unstable one, and there was a fundamental incompatibility between the two systems—capitalist and communist. The Bolsheviks were always encouraging the oppressed and exploited people, both the subject peoples in colonial countries and the workers in factories, to rise against their exploiters. They did not do so officially, but through the Comintern or Communist International. The imperialist Powers, on the other hand, and especially England, were continually intriguing against the very existence of the Soviets. So there was bound to be trouble, and there was frequent conflict,

---

[1] The Soviet Union was recognized by the United States in 1933, and diplomatic relations were established between the two countries.

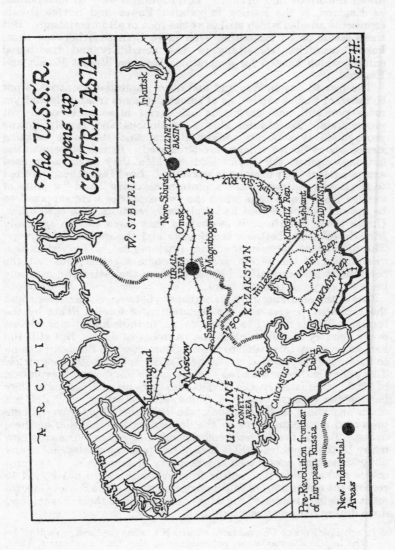

The U.S.S.R. opens up CENTRAL ASIA

ARCTIC

W. SIBERIA

Irkutsk

KUZNETZ BASIN

Novo-Sibirsk

Omsk

Magnitogorsk

URAL AREA

Turk-Sib. Riy.

Tashkent

KIRGHIZ Rep.

TADJIKISTAN

UZBEK Rep.

TURKMEN Rep.

KAZAKSTAN

1750 miles

Samara

Moscow

Volga

Baku

CAUCASUS

UKRAINE

DONETZ AREA

Leningrad

Pre-Revolution frontier of European Russia.

New Industrial Areas

J.F.H.

resulting in a break of diplomatic relations and in war scares. You will remember my telling you of the breach with England that followed the Arcos raid in 1927. This friction is easy to understand, as England is the leading imperialist Power and Soviet Russia represents an idea which strikes at the root of all imperialism. But there seems to be something even more than that between these hostile countries, something of the hereditary and traditional enmity which existed for generations between Tsarist Russia and England.

The fear to-day in England and other capitalist countries is not so much of Soviet armies, as of something more intangible and yet more powerful and dangerous, of Soviet ideas and communist propaganda. To counter this a continuous and largely untrue propaganda is kept up against Russia, and the most amazing stories about Soviet villainy are circulated. British statesmen use language against the Soviet leaders which they have never used except against their enemies in war-time. Lord Birkenhead referred to the Soviet statesmen as "a junta of assassins" and "a junta of swollen frogs" at a time when the two countries were supposed to be not only at peace, but had diplomatic relations with each other. Under these conditions it is obvious that there can be no really friendly relations between the Soviets and the imperialist Powers. The differences between them are fundamental. The victors and vanquished of the World War may come together, but not the communist and capitalist. Peace between the latter two can only be temporary; it is but a truce.

One of the recurring grounds of dispute between Soviet Russia and the capitalist powers was the repudiation of foreign debts by the former. This is not a live issue now, as, in these hard times, almost every country is defaulting in the payment of debt. But still the subject crops up from time to time. Soon after the Bolsheviks came to power they repudiated the former Tsarist debts to other countries. This policy had been declared as early as the unsuccessful revolution of 1905. Consistently, the Soviets also gave up such claims as they had on the eastern countries, China, etc. Further, they did not claim any share in Reparations. In 1922 the Allied governments presented a memorandum to the Soviets on the question of these debts. To this the Soviets replied reminding the governments how many of the capitalist States had in the past repudiated debts and obligations, and confiscated the property of foreigners. "Governments and systems that spring from revolutions are not bound to respect the obligations of fallen governments." The Soviet Government especially reminded the Allies of what one of them, France, had done during her great revolution.

"The French Convention, of which France declares herself to be the legitimate successor, proclaimed on the 22nd December, 1792, that the 'sovereignty of people is not bound by the treaties of tyrants'. In accordance with this declaration, revolutionary France not only tore up the political treaties of former régimes with foreign countries, but also repudiated her national debt."

In spite of this justification of repudiation, the Soviet Government was so keen to come to terms with the other Powers that it was perfectly prepared to discuss the question of debt with them. But it took up the position that such discussion could take place only after the foreign government had given unconditional recognition to the Soviets. As a matter of fact the Soviet gave many assurances about payment of obligations to England, France, and America, but there was no great eagerness on the part of the capitalist Powers to come to terms with Russia.

As against the British claim the Soviet had made an interesting counter-claim. The total British claim against Russia for government and war debts and railway bonds and commercial investments amounted to about £840,000,000. The Bolsheviks counter-claimed from Britain for her share of the damage done during the Russian Civil War, as Britain and British forces had supported the enemies of the Soviets. The total damage was estimated at £4,067,226,040, and of this Britain's share was said to be approximately £2,000,000,000. So that the counter-claim was nearly two and a half times as great as the claim.

In making this counter-claim the Bolsheviks were not on very weak ground. They gave the famous instance of the *Alabama* cruiser. This cruiser was built in England for the Southern States during the American Civil War of the 'sixties. The cruiser left Liverpool after the Civil War had begun, and it did a great deal of damage to the shipping and trade of the Northern States. England and America were on the verge of war. The United States Government claimed that England had no business to hand over the cruiser to the Southern States during war-time, and they claimed compensation for all the damage it had caused. The matter was referred to arbitration, and ultimately England had to pay £3,229,166 to the United States as damages.

England's part in the Russian Civil War was far more important and effective than this supply of a cruiser for which she had had to pay such heavy damages. During the wars of foreign intervention in Russia, it has been officially stated by the Soviet that 1,350,000 lives were lost.

This question of Russia's old debts has only been partly decided so far, but it is losing all importance through sheer lapse of time. Meanwhile, we see great capitalist and imperialist countries like England, France, Germany, and Italy doing almost the very thing which had shocked them so much in Russia's case. It is true they do not repudiate their debts or challenge the basis of the capitalist system. They merely default and do not pay.

Soviet policy with other nations was one of peace at almost any cost, for they wanted time to recuperate, and the great task of building up a huge country on socialistic lines absorbed their attention. There seemed to be no near prospect of social revolution in other countries, and so the idea of a " world revolution " faded out for the time being. With Eastern countries Russia developed a policy of friendship and co-operation, although they were governed under the capitalist system. I h..ve told you of the network of treaties between Russia and Turkey and Persia and Afghanistan. A common fear and dislike of the great imperialist Powers were the link that joined them.

The New Economic Policy which Lenin introduced in 1921 was meant to win over the middle peasantry to socialization. The rich peasants, or *kulaks*, as they are called—the word *kulak* means a fist— were not encouraged, as they were capitalists on a small scale and resisted the process of socialization. Lenin also started a huge scheme for the electrification of rural areas, and mighty electric plants were put up. This was meant to help the peasants in many ways and to prepare the way for the industrialization of the country. Above all, it was meant to produce an industrial mentality among the peasantry, and thus to bring them nearer to the town workers or proletariat. The peasants, whose villages were lighted up by electricity and much of whose farm work was done by electric power, began to get out of the old ruts and superstitions and to think on new lines. There is always a conflict between the interests of the city and the village, the town-dweller and the peasant. The worker in the city wants cheap food and raw material from the countryside and high prices for the factory goods he makes; the peasant, on the other hand, wants cheap tools and other factory goods from the city and high prices for the food and raw materials he produces. This conflict was becoming acute in Russia as a result of the four years of militant communism. It was largely because of this and in order to relieve the tension that the NEP was introduced and the peasants were given facilities for private trading.

Lenin was so keen on his scheme for electrification that he used a formula that became famous. He said that " electricity plus soviets equals socialism ". Even after Lenin's death this electrification continued at a tremendous pace. Another way of influencing the peasantry and improving agricultural methods was to introduce large numbers of tractors for ploughing and other purposes. The Ford Company of America supplied them. The Soviets also entered into a very big contract with Ford for the construction of a huge motor plant in Russia which could produce as many as 100,000 automobiles every year. This plant was meant chiefly for tractors.

Another activity of the Soviets, which brought them into conflict with foreign interests, was the production and sale abroad of oil and petrol. In Azerbaijan and Georgia in the Caucasus there is a rich oil-producing area. Probably this is part of the larger oil area which spreads to Persia, Mosul, and Iraq. Baku, on the Caspian Sea, is the great oil city of South Russia. The Soviets started selling their oil and petrol abroad at cheaper rates than those charged by the great oil companies. These oil companies, like the Standard Oil Co. of America, and the Anglo-Persian, the Royal Dutch Shell Co., and others, are very powerful, and practically control the petrol supply of the world. The under-selling by the Soviets caused great loss to them and angered them greatly. They started a campaign against Soviet oil, calling it " stolen oil ", because the oil wells in the Caucasus had been confiscated by the Soviet from their previous capitalist owners. After a while, however, they came to terms with this "stolen oil".

I have been constantly referring to the "Soviet" or "Soviets", in this and other letters. Sometimes I have talked of "Russia" doing this or that. I have used all these words rather loosely to mean the same thing, and I must now tell you what this thing is. Of course you know that the Soviet Republic was proclaimed in November 1917, in Petrograd, after the Bolshevik Revolution. The Tsarist Empire was not a compact national State. Russia proper dominated over a large number of subject nationalites both in Europe and in Asia. There were nearly 200 of such nationalities, and they varied tremendously. In the Tsar's time they were treated as subject peoples; and their languages and cultures were to a greater or less extent suppressed. Practically nothing was done for the improvement of the backward peoples in central Asia. The Jews, although they had no special area to call their own, were one of the worst treated of the minority communities, and Jewish *pogroms*, or massacres, were notorious. This led to many people from these oppressed nationalities joining the Russian revolutionary movement, although their chief interest was in a national revolution and not a social one. The Provisional Government after the February Revolution of 1917 made many promises to these nationalities, but in effect did nothing. Lenin had, on the other hand, from the early days of the Bolshevik Party, long before the Revolution, insisted on giving each nationality the full right of self-determination even to the extent of complete separation and independence. This was a part of the old Bolshevik programme. Immediately after the Revolution the Bolsheviks, now the Government of the country, reaffirmed their faith in this principle of self-determination.

During the Civil War the Tsarist Empire went to pieces and, for a while, the Soviet Republic controlled only a small area round Moscow and Leningrad. Encouraged by the western Powers, several nationalities bordering the Baltic Sea—Finland, Estonia, Latvia, and Lithuania—became independent States. So also of course did Poland. As the Russian Soviet triumphed in the Civil War and foreign armies withdrew, separate and independent Soviet governments grew up in Siberia and Central Asia. These governments, having common aims, were naturally closely allied to each other. In 1923 they joined together to form the Soviet Union, or, to give it its full official title, the Union of Socialist Soviet Republics. This is often known by its capital letters—the U.S.S.R.

Since 1923 there have been some changes in the number of Union republics, as in one or two cases republics have split up into two.

At present there are seven Union republics :

(1) Russian Socialist Federative Soviet Republic, or the R.S.F.S.R.
(2) White Russia S.S.R.
(3) Ukrainian S.S.R.
(4) Trans-Caucasian Socialist Federative S.R.

2 E

(5) Turkmenistan, or Turkemen, S.S.R.
(6) Uzbek S.S.R.
(7) Tadjikistan, or Tadjik, S.S.R.

Mongolia is also in some kind of alliance with the Soviet Union.
The Soviet Union is thus a federation of several republics. Some
of these federating republics are themselves federations. Thus the
Russian S.F.S.R. is a federation of twelve autonomous republics, and
the Trans-Caucasian S.F.S.R. is a federation of three republics :
the Azerbaijan S.S.R., Georgia S.S.R., and Armenia S.S.R.   Besides
these numerous interrelated and interdependent republics, there are
many " national " and " autonomous " regions within the republics.
The object of introducing so much autonomy everywhere is to encourage each nationality to keep its own culture and language and
to have as much freedom as possible. As far as possible, an attempt
has been made to avoid the domination of one national or racial
group over another. This Soviet solution of the minorities problem
has interest for us, as we have to face a difficult minority problem
ourselves. The Soviets' difficulties appear to have been far greater
than ours, for they had 182 different nationalities to deal with. Their
solution of the problem has been very successful. They went to the
extreme length of recognizing each separate nationality and encouraging it to carry on its work and education in its own language.   This
was not merely to please the separatist tendencies of different
minorities, but because it was felt that real education and cultural
progress could take effect for the masses only if the native tongue
were used. And the results achieved already have been remarkable.

In spite of this tendency to introduce lack of uniformity in the
Union, the different parts are coming far nearer to each other than
they ever did under the centralized government of the Tsars.   The
reason is that they have common ideals and they are all working
together in a common enterprise. Each Union Republic has in
theory the right to separate from the Union whenever it wants to,
but there is little chance of its doing so, because of the great advantages of federation of socialist republics in the face of the hostility of
the capitalist world.

The principal republic of the Union is of course the Russian—the
R.S.F.S.R. This spreads out from Leningrad right across Siberia.
White Russia S.S.R. lies next to Poland. Ukraine is in the south
along the shores of the Black Sea; it is the granary of Russia.
Trans-Caucasia is, as its name tells us, across the Caucasus mountains, between the Caspian Sea and the Black Sea.   One of the Trans-
Caucasian republics is Armenia, which was for so long the scene of
frightful massacres by Turk and Armenian. Now as a Soviet
republic it seems to have settled down to peaceful activities.   On the
other side of the Caspian Sea we have the three Central Asian
republics—Turkmenistan, Uzbekistan, which has the famous cities
of Bokhara and Samarqand, and Tadjikistan. Tadjikistan lies
just north of Afghanistan, and is the nearest Soviet territory to
India.

These Central Asian republics have a special interest for us because of our age-old contact with Middle Asia. They are even more fascinating because of the remarkable progress they have made during the past few years. Under the Tsars they were very backward and superstitious countries with hardly any education and their women mostly behind the veil. To-day they are ahead of India in many respects.

180

THE PIATILETKA, OR RUSSIA'S FIVE YEAR PLAN

July 9, 1933

LENIN, so long as he lived, was the unchallenged leader of Soviet Russia. To his final decision every one bowed; when there were conflicts, his word was law and brought together the warring sections in the Communist Party. Trouble came inevitably after his death when rival groups and rival forces fought for mastery. To the outside world, and to a lesser extent in Russia also, Trotsky was the outstanding personality among the Bolsheviks after Lenin. It was Trotsky who had taken a leading part in the October Revolution, and it was he who, faced by stupendous difficulties, created the Red Army which triumphed in the Civil War and against foreign intervention. And yet, Trotsky was a new-comer to the Bolshevik Party, and the old Bolsheviks, Lenin apart, neither liked him nor trusted him greatly. One of these old Bolsheviks, Stalin, had become general secretary of the Communist Party, and as such he was in control of the dominant and most powerful organization in Russia. Between Trotsky and Stalin there was no love lost. They hated each other, and they were wholly unlike each other. Trotsky was a brilliant writer and orator, and had also proved himself a great organizer and man of action. He had a keen and flashing intellect, evolving theories of revolution, and hitting out at his opponents with words that stung like whips and scorpions. Stalin seemed to be a commonplace man beside him, silent, unimposing, far from brilliant. And yet he was also a great organizer, a great and heroic fighter, and a man of iron will. Indeed, he has come to be known as " the man of steel ". While Trotsky was admired, it was Stalin who inspired confidence. He came from the masses himself, being a Georgian of peasant origin. There was no room in the Communist Party for both these towering personalities.

The conflict between Stalin and Trotsky was a personal one, but it was really something more than that. Each of them represented a different policy, a different method of developing the revolution. Trotsky had, many years before the Revolution, worked out a theory of " Permanent Revolution ". According to this, it was not possible for a single country, however advantageously situated it might be, to establish full socialism. Real socialism would only come after a world revolution, as only then could the peasantry be effectively socialized. Socialism was the next higher stage in economic development after capitalism. As capitalism became international, it broke down, as we see happening in the greater part of the world to-day. Only socialism could work this international structure to advantage, hence the inevitability of socialism. That was the Marxist theory. But if an attempt were made to work socialism in a single country—that is, nationally and not internationally—this would mean a going back to a lower economic stage. Internationalism was the necessary foundation for all progress, including socialist progress, and to go back from it was neither possible nor desirable. According to Trotsky, therefore, it was not economically possible to build up socialism in a separate country, even in the Soviet Union, big as it was. There was so much for which the Soviets had to rely on the industrial countries of Western Europe. It was like the co-operation of the city and the village or rural areas; the industrial West was the city, and Russia was largely rural. Politically, also, Trotsky was of opinion that a separate socialist country could not survive for long in a capitalist environment. The two were—and we have seen how true this is—wholly incompatible with each other. Either the capitalist countries would crush the socialist country, or there would be social revolutions in the capitalist countries and socialism would be established everywhere. For some time, of course, or some years, the two might exist side by side in an unstable equilibrium.

To a large extent this seems to have been the view of all the Bolshevik leaders before and after the Revolution. They waited impatiently for world revolution, or at any rate revolutions in some European countries. For many months there was thunder in the air of Europe, but the storm passed off without bursting. Russia settled down to NEP and a more or less humdrum life. Trotsky thereupon raised the cry of alarm, and pointed out that the Revolution was in danger unless a more aggressive policy aiming at world revolution were followed. This challenge resulted in a mighty duel between Trotsky and Stalin, a conflict which shook the Communist Party for some years. The conflict resulted in the complete victory of Stalin, chiefly because he was the master of the Party machine. Trotsky and his supporters were treated as enemies of the Revolution and driven out from the Party. Trotsky was at first sent to Siberia, and then exiled outside the Union.

The immediate conflict between Stalin and Trotsky had taken place on Stalin's proposal to adopt an aggressive agrarian policy to win over the peasant to socialism. This was an attempt to build up socialism in Russia, apart from what happened in other countries, and Trotsky rejected it and stuck to his theory of "permanent revolution", without which, he said, the peasantry could not be fully socialized. As a matter of fact Stalin adopted many of Trotsky's suggestions, but he did so in his own way, not in Trotsky's. Referring to this, Trotsky has written in his autobiography: "In politics, however, it is not merely *what*, but *how* and *who* that decides."

So the great struggle between the two giants ended and Trotsky was pushed off the stage on which he had played such a brave and brilliant part. He had to leave the Soviet Union, of which he had been one of the principal architects. Nearly all the capitalist countries were afraid of this dynamic personality, and would not admit him. England refused him admittance, as did most other European countries. At last he found temporary refuge in Turkey in the little island of Prinkipo, off Istanbul. He devoted himself to writing, and produced a remarkable *History of the Russian Revolution*. His hatred of Stalin possessed him still, and he continued to criticize and attack him in biting language. A regular Trotskyist party grew up in some parts of the world, and this ranged itself against the Soviet Government and the official communism of the Comintern.

Having disposed of Trotsky, Stalin devoted himself to his new agrarian policy with extraordinary courage. He had to face a difficult situation. There was distress and unemployment among the intellectuals and there had even been strikes of workers. He taxed the *kulaks*, or the rich peasants, heavily, and then devoted this money to building up rural collective farms—that is, big co-operative farms in which large numbers of farmers worked together and shared the profits. The *kulaks* and richer peasants resented this policy and became very angry with the Soviet Government. They were afraid that their cattle and farm materials would be pooled with those of their poorer neighbours, and because of this fear they actually destroyed their livestock. There was such a great destruction of livestock that in the following year there was an acute shortage of foodstuffs, meat, and dairy produce.

This was an unexpected blow to Stalin, but he clung on grimly to his programme. Indeed, he developed it and made it into a mighty plan, covering the whole Union, for both agriculture and industry. The peasant was to be brought near to industry by means of enormous model State farms and collective farms, and the whole country was to be industrialized by the erection of huge factories, hydro-electric power works, the working of mines, and the like; and side by side with this, a host of other activities relating to education, science, co-operative buying and selling, building houses for millions of workers and generally raising their standards of living, etc., were to be undertaken. This was the famous " Five Year Plan ", or the *Piatiletka*, as the Russians called it. It was a colossal programme, ambitious and difficult of achievement even in a generation by a wealthy and advanced country. For backward and poor Russia to attempt it seemed to be the height of folly.

This Five Year Plan had been drawn up after the most careful thought and investigation. The whole country had been surveyed by scientists and engineers, and numerous experts had discussed the problem of fitting in one part of the programme into another. For the real difficulty came in this fitting in. There was not much point in having a huge factory if the raw material for it was lacking; and even when raw material was available, it had to be brought to the factory. So the problem of transport had to be tackled and railways built, and railways required coal, so coal-mines had to be worked. The factory itself wanted power for its working. To supply it with this power, electricity was produced by the water-power obtained from damming up great rivers, and this electric power was then sent over the wires to the factories and farms, and for the lighting of cities and villages. Then again, all this required engineers, mechanics, and trained workers, and it is no easy matter to produce scores of thousands of trained men and women within a short time. Motor tractors could be sent to the farms by the thousand, but who was to work them?

These are but a few instances to give you an idea of the amazing complexity of the problems raised by the Five Year Plan. A single mistake would have far-reaching results; a weak or backward link in the chain of activity would delay or stop a whole series. But Russia had one great advantage over the capitalist countries. Under capitalism all these activities are left to individual initiative and chance, and owing to competition there is waste of effort. There is no co-ordination between different producers or different sets of workers, except the chance co-ordination which arises in the buyers and sellers coming to the same market. There is, in brief, no planning on a wide scale. Individual concerns may and do plan their future activities, but most of this individual planning consists in attempts to overreach or get the better of other individual concerns. Nationally, this results in the very opposite of planning; it means excess and want, side by side. The Soviet Government had the advantage of controlling all the different industries and activities in the whole Union, and so it could draw up and try to work a single co-ordinated plan in which every activity found its proper place. There would be no waste in this, except such waste as might come from errors of calculation or working, and even such errors could be rectified far sooner with a unified control than otherwise.

The object of the Plan was to lay down the solid foundations of industralism in the Soviet Union. The idea was not to put up some factories to produce the goods which every one needs, such as cloth, etc. This would have been easy enough by getting machinery from abroad, as is done in India, and fixing it up. Such industries, producing consumable goods, are called " light industries ". These light industries necessarily depend on the " heavy industries ", the iron and steel and machine-making industries, which supply the machinery and equipment for the light industries, as well as engines, etc. The Soviet Government looked far ahead and decided to con-centrate on these basic or heavy industries in the Five Year Plan. In this way the foundations of industrialism would be firmly laid, and it would be easy to have the light industries afterwards. The heavy industries would also make Russia less dependent on foreign countries for machinery or war material.

This choice in favour of heavy industry seems to have been the obvious one under the circumstances, but it meant a far greater effort and tremendous suffering for the people. Heavy industries

are far more expensive than light ones, and—a more vital difference—
they do not begin to pay for a much longer time. A textile factory
starts making cloth, and this can be sold to the people immediately;
so also in regard to other light industries producing consumable
goods. But an iron and steel factory might produce steel rails and
locomotives. These cannot be consumed, or even used, till a
railway line is built. This takes time, and till then a great deal
of money is locked up in the concern, and the country is the poorer
for it.

For Russia, therefore, this building of heavy industries at a tremendous
pace meant a very great sacrifice. All this construction, all this
machinery that came from outside, had to be paid for, and paid for
in gold and cash. How was this to be done? The people of the
Soviet Union tightened their belts and starved and deprived themselves
of even necessary articles so that payment could be made
abroad. They sent their food-stuffs abroad, and with the price
obtained for them paid for the machinery. They sent everything
they could find a market for: wheat, rye, barley, corn, vegetables,
fruits, eggs, butter, meat, fowls, honey, fish, caviare, sugar, oils,
confectionery, etc. Sending these good articles outside meant that
they themselves did without them. The Russian people had no
butter, or very little of it, because it went abroad to pay for machinery.
And so with many other goods.

This mighty effort embodied in the Five Year Plan began in
1929. Again the spirit of revolution was abroad, the call of an ideal
stirred the masses and made them devote all their energy to the new
struggle. This struggle was not against a foreign enemy or an
internal foe. It was a struggle against the backward conditions of
Russia, against the remains of capitalism, against the low standards
of living. Almost with enthusiasm they put up with further sacrifices
and lived a hard, ascetic life; they sacrificed the present for the
great future that seemed to beckon to them and of which they were
the proud and privileged builders.

Nations have, in the past, concentrated all their efforts on the
accomplishment of one great task, but this has been so in times of
war only. During the World War, Germany and England and France
lived for one purpose only—to win the war. To that purpose everything
else was subordinated. Soviet Russia, for the first time in
history, concentrated the whole strength of the nation in a peaceful
effort to build, and not to destroy, to raise a backward country
industrially and within a framework of socialism. But the privation,
especially of the upper and middle-class peasantry, was very great,
and often it seemed that the whole ambitious scheme would collapse,
and perhaps carry the Soviet Government with it. It required
immense courage to hold on. Many prominent Bolsheviks thought
that the strain and suffering caused by the agricultural programme
were too great and there should be a relaxation. But not so Stalin.
Grimly and silently he held on. He was no talker: he hardly spoke
in public. He seemed to be the iron image of an inevitable fate going
ahead to the predestined goal. And something of his courage and

determination spread among the members of the Communist Party and other workers in Russia.

A continuous propaganda in favour of the Five Year Plan kept up the enthusiasm of the people and whipped them up to fresh endeavour. Great public interest was taken in the building of the huge hydro-electric works and dams and bridges and factories and communal farms. Engineering was the most popular profession, and newspapers were full of technical details about great feats of engineering. The desert and the steppes were peopled and large new towns grew up round each big industrial concern. New roads, new canals, and new railways, mostly electric railways, were built and air services developed. A chemical industry was built up, a war industry, and a tool industry, and the Soviet Union began producing tractors, automobiles, high-power locomotives, motor engines, turbines, aeroplanes. Electricity spread over large areas, and the radio came into common use. Unemployment disappeared completely, as there was so much building and other work to be done that all available workers were absorbed. Indeed, many qualified engineers came from foreign countries and were welcomed. It is worth remembering that this was the time when depression spread all over western Europe and America and unemployment increased to enormous figures.

The work of the Five Year Plan did not go on smoothly. There was often great trouble and lack of co-ordination and upsets and waste. But in spite of all this the tempo of work went on increasing, and the demand always was for more and more work. And then came the slogan " The Five Year Plan in Four Years ", as if five years had not been a short enough time for this amazing programme ! The Plan formally came to an end on December 31, 1932—that is, at the end of four years. And immediately from January 1, 1933, a new Five Year Plan was started.

People often argue about the Five Year Plan, and some say it was a tremendous success, and others call it a failure. It is easy enough to point out where it has failed, for in many respects it has not come up to expectations. There is a vast disproportion in many things in Russia to-day, and the chief lack is that of trained and expert workers. There are more factories than qualified engineers to run them, more restaurants and kitchens than qualified cooks ! These disproportions will no doubt soon disappear, or at any rate lessen. One thing is clear : that the Five Year Plan has completely changed the face of Russia. From a feudal country it has suddenly become an advanced industrial country. There has been an amazing cultural advance ; and the social services, the system of social health and accident insurance, are the most inclusive and advanced in the world. In spite of privation and want, the terrible fear of unemployment and starvation which hangs over workers in other countries has gone. There is a new sense of economic security among the people.

The argument about the success or otherwise of the Five Year Plan is rather a pointless one. The answer to it is really the present state of the Soviet Union. And a further answer is the fact that this Plan has impressed itself on the imagination of the world. Everybody talks of " planning " now, and of Five-Year and Ten-Year and Three-Year plans. The Soviets have put magic into the word.

181

THE SOVIET UNION'S DIFFICULTIES, FAILURES AND SUCCESSES

July 11, 1933

THE Five Year Plan of Soviet Russia was a colossal undertaking. It was really a number of big revolutions tacked on together, especially an agricultural revolution which substituted large-scale collective and mechanized farming for the old-fashioned small-scale methods, and an industrial revolution which industrialized Russia at a tremendous pace. But the most interesting feature of the Plan was the spirit that lay behind it, for this was a new spirit in politics and industry. This spirit was the spirit of science, an attempt to apply a thought-out scientific method to the building up of society. No such thing had been done before in any country, even the most advanced ones, and it is this application of the methods of science to human and social affairs that is the outstanding feature of Soviet planning. It is because of this that all the world is talking of planning now, but it is difficult to plan effectively when the very basis of the social system, like the capitalistic system, rests on competition and the protection of vested rights in property.

But, as I have told you, this Five Year Plan brought much suffering, and difficulties, and dislocation. And people paid a terrible price for it. Most of them paid this price willingly and accepted the sacrifices and sufferings for a few years in the hope of a better time afterwards; some paid the price unwillingly and only because of the compulsion of the Soviet Government. Among those who suffered most were the *kulaks* or richer peasants. With their greater wealth and special influence, they did not fit into the new scheme of things. They were capitalistic elements which prevented the collective farms from developing on socialist lines. Often they opposed this collectivization, sometimes they entered the collectives to weaken them from inside or to make undue personal profits out of them. The Soviet Government came down heavily on them. The Government was also very hard on many middle-class people whom it suspected of espionage and sabotage on behalf of its enemies. Because of this, large numbers of engineers were punished and sent to gaol. As engineers were specially wanted for the numerous big schemes that were in hand, this meant injury to the Plan itself.

Disproportions there were almost everywhere. The transport

system lagged behind, and so the goods that were produced in factories and fields often had to wait for transport facilities, and this upset work elsewhere. The greatest difficulty was the lack of competent experts and engineers.

During these years of the Five Year Plan the world, or rather the capitalistic world, was experiencing the greatest depression that it had ever known. Trade was sinking, factories closing up, unemployment growing. Agriculturists all over the world had been very hard hit by a great fall in prices of food-stuffs and raw materials. The tremendous activity and employment in the Soviet Union contrasted remarkably with the inactivity and unemployment elsewhere. The Union seemed to be unaffected by the world depression, the basis of its economy was quite different. But the Soviet did not escape the results of the depression; they crept in indirectly, and added greatly to the Soviet's difficulties. I have told you that the Soviet was buying machinery abroad, and it paid for this by selling its agricultural produce in foreign countries. As the price of food-stuffs, etc., fell in the world market, the Soviet got less money for its exports. But it had to raise enough gold to pay for the machinery bought by it, and so it exported more and more food-stuffs. In this way the world trade depression and fall in prices caused loss to the Soviet and upset many of its calculations. And this led to a further shortage of many necessaries in the country, and greater hardship.

While on the one hand there was a growing shortage of food-stuffs, on the other hand there was a tremendous growth of population all over the Union. This rapid growth, out of all proportion to the relatively slow progress of agricultural production, was the Soviet's chief problem. The population of the present territory of the U.S.S.R. before the Revolution was 130,000,000. Observe the growth in the subsequent years, in spite of the enormous losses of the Civil War:

In 1917 the population was   130,000,000
In 1926   „   „   „   149,000,000
In 1929   „   „   „   154,000,000
In 1930   „   „   „   158,000,000
In 1933 (spring-estimate) was 165,000,000

Thus there has been an increase of 35,000,000 in a little over fifteen years—that is an increase of 26 per cent., which is extraordinary.

Not only did the population grow as a whole all over the Soviet Union, but it grew especially in the cities. The old cities grew bigger and bigger, and new industrial towns rose up even in the deserts and the steppes. Vast numbers of peasants flocked to the cities from their villages, attracted by the work to be done in the building up of the many huge enterprises of the Five Year Plan. In 1917 there were twenty-four cities in the U.S.S.R. each with a population of over 100,000. In 1926 there were thirty-one such cities, and in 1933 there were over fifty. Within fifteen years the

Soviet had built over 100 industrial towns. From 1913 to 1932 Moscow doubled its population, going up from 1,600,000 to 3,200,000; Leningrad added another 1,000,000, and nearly reached the 3,000,000 mark; Baku in Trans-Caucasia also doubled its population from 334,000 to 660,000. Altogether the urban population went up from 20,000,000 in 1913 to 35,000,000 in 1932.

A peasant who goes to a city and becomes a labourer there ceases to be a food producer as he was in his village. As a labourer or worker in a factory he may produce machine goods or tools, but, so far as food is concerned, he is only a consumer now. The great exodus of peasants from villages thus meant the transformation of food producers into food consumers only. This became another factor in making the food situation difficult.

There was yet another factor. The growing industry of the country wanted more and more raw materials for the factories. Thus, cotton was required by the cloth factories. Cotton and other raw materials therefore were sown in many areas instead of food crops. This again reduced the food supply.

The tremendous growth of the population of the Soviet Union was in itself a remarkable sign of prosperity. It was not due, as in America, to immigration from outside. It showed that in spite of the privations and hardships of the people there was, as a general rule, no actual starvation. A severe system of rationing managed to supply the absolutely necessary articles of food to the population. Competent observers tell us that this rapid growth of population is largely due to a feeling of economic security among the people. Children are no longer a burden to the family, as the State is prepared to look after them, to feed them and educate them. Another reason is the growth of sanitation and medical facilities, which have resulted in reducing the infant mortality rate from 27 to 12 per cent. In Moscow the general mortality rate in 1913 was over twenty-three per thousand; in 1931 it was under thirteen per thousand.

To add to the many difficulties about the shortage of food, there was a drought in some parts of the Union in 1931. In 1931 and 1932 there were also war scares in the Far East, and the Soviet, fearing a war brought on by a Japanese attack in conjunction with other capitalist Powers, began to hoard grain and other food-stuffs for the army in case of need. There is an old Russian saying : "Fear has big eyes"—how very true it is, whether you apply it to little children or to communities and nations ! Because there can be no real peace between communism and capitalism, and the imperialist nations are very keen on suppressing communism, and manœuvre and intrigue to that end, the nerves of the Bolsheviks are always on edge and their eyes grow big at the least provocation. Often enough they have reason for anxiety and they have had to meet, even internally, widespread attempts at sabotage or destruction of their factories or other big concerns.

Nineteen-thirty-two was a very critical year for the Soviet Union. The Government took the most drastic steps against sabotage and against the stealing of communal property, which had occurred in many of the communal farms. Ordinarily there is no death penalty in Russia, but it was introduced in cases of counter-revolution. The Soviet Government decreed that the stealing of communal property is equivalent to counter-revolution, and is therefore punishable by death. For, says Stalin : " If the capitalists have pronounced *private* property sacred and inviolable, thus achieving in their time a strengthening of the capitalist order, then we communists must so much the more pronounce *public* property sacred and inviolable, in order thus to strengthen the new socialist forms of economy."

The Soviet Government also took steps to ease the strain in other ways. The most important of these was the permission given to the collective and individual farms to sell their surplus produce directly in the city markets. This reminds one, to some extent, of NEP coming after the period of militant communism in 1921, but the Soviet Union is very different from what it was then. It has gone a good way on the road to socialism; it is industrialized and its agriculture has been largely communalized.

Between 1929 and 1933 200,000 collective farms were organized and there were also about 5000 State farms. These State farms are supposed to be models for the others, and some of them are enormous. During this period 120,000 more tractors were introduced, and nearly two-thirds of the peasants became members of these collectives.

Another activity that has grown astonishingly is that of the co-operative organization. The Consumers' Co-operative Society had a membership of 26,500,000 in 1928; in 1932 the membership was 75,000,000. This society has a chain of wholesale and retail stores stretching from one end of the Union to the other, even to the remotest corner.

The 1st of January, 1933, saw the commencement of the second Five Year Plan. It was directed towards the building up of light industries, which will result in raising the standard of living rapidly. It was hoped to provide some rewards in the shape of more comfort and better living-conditions after the strain and privation of the first Five Year Plan. It was no longer necessary to go abroad for most of the machinery required, as the Soviet heavy industries could supply this machinery. This also relieved the Soviet from having to send large quantities of food abroad to help in payment for goods purchased.

Stalin, addressing a congress of peasants from collective farms in 1933, said :

> "Our immediate task is to make all collectivized peasants well-to-do. Yes, comrades, well-to-do. . . . Sometimes people say : if there is socialism why should we still work ? We worked before; we work now. Isn't it time we quit working ? . . . No, socialism is built on labour. . . . Socialism demands that all men work honestly, not for others, not for the rich, not for the exploiters, but for themselves, for society."

Work remains, and must remain, though in the future it is likely to be pleasanter and lighter than in the trying early years of planning. Indeed, the maxim of the Soviet Union is : " He that will not work, neither shall he eat." But the Bolsheviks have added a new motive for work : the motive to work for social betterment. In the past, idealists and stray individuals have been moved to activity by this incentive, but there is no previous instance of society as a whole accepting and reacting to this motive. The very basis of capitalism was competition and individual profit, always at the expense of others. This profit motive is giving place to the social motive in the Soviet Union, and, as an American writer says, workers in Russia are learning that " from the acceptance of mutual dependence comes independence of want and fear ". This elimination of the terrible fear of poverty and insecurity, which bears down upon the masses everywhere, is a great achievement. It is said that this relief has almost put an end to mental diseases in the Soviet Union.

And so these strenuous years in the U.S.S.R. have seen growth everywhere and in almost everything, painful and disproportionate growth, but still a spreading of cities and industry, and huge collective farms and mighty co-operatives, and trade and population, and also culture and science and learning. Above all, they have seen the growth of a unity and solidarity among the numerous different peoples that inhabit the U.S.S.R. from the Baltic Sea to the Pacific Ocean and the Pamir and Hindu Kush mountains of Central Asia.

I feel tempted to write to you about the progress in education and science and culture generally in the U.S.S.R., but I must restrain myself. I shall tell you just a few odd facts which might interest you. The educational system in Russia is supposed by many competent judges to be the best and most up-to-date in existence. Illiteracy has almost been ended, and the most surprising advances have been made in backward areas like Uzbekistan and Turkmenistan in Central Asia. In this Central Asian area there were 126 schools with 6200 pupils in 1913; in 1932 there were 6975 schools with 700,000 pupils, of whom over one-third were girls. Universal compulsory education has been introduced. To appreciate this remarkable progress, you must remember that till recently girls were kept in seclusion, and not allowed to appear in public in this part of the world. It is said that this rapid progress has been due to the use of the Latin alphabet, which made primary education far easier than with the various local alphabets. You will remember my telling you about Kemal Pasha's adoption of the Latin script or alphabet in place of the old Arabic one. He got the idea and the alphabet, varied to suit other languages, from the Soviet experiment. In 1924 the Caucasian republics discarded the Arabic script and adopted the Latin one. This was very successful in removing illiteracy, and most of the other nationalities in the Soviet Union adopted the Latin script—the Chinese, Mongols, Turks, Tartars, Buriats, Bashkirs, Tadjiks, and many others. The language used was always the local one; only the script was changed.

You will be interested to learn that over two-thirds of all the school-children in the Soviet Union are served with hot luncheons in schools. This is, of course, free of charge, and education itself is quite free, as it must be in a workers' State.

The growth of literacy and the progress of education have created a huge reading class, and probably more books and newspapers are printed than in any other country. Mostly these books are serious and " heavy " books and not the light novels of other countries. The Russian worker is so excited about engineering and electricity that he prefers reading books about them to reading story-books. But for children there are the most delightful books, including even fairy-tales, though, I believe, orthodox Bolsheviks do not approve of fairy stories.

In science Soviet Russia is already in the first rank, both in pure science and in its numerous applications. Numerous huge institutes in various branches of science and experimental stations have grown up. In Leningrad there is an enormous Institute of Plant Industry, which possesses as many as 28,000 different varieties of wheat. This institute has been experimenting with methods of sowing rice by aeroplane.

The old palaces of the Tsars and the nobility have now become museums and rest-houses and sanatoria for the people. Near Leningrad there is a small town which used to be called Tsarkoe Selo (meaning " The Tsar's Village "), as it contained two imperial palaces and the Tsar used to live there in summer. The name has now been changed to Detskoe Selo (" The Children's Village "), and I suppose the old palaces now serve the purposes of children and young people. Children and the young are the favoured persons in Soviet land to-day, and they get the best of everything, even though others might suffer lack. It is for them that the present generation labours, for it is they who will inherit the socialized and scientific State, if that finally comes into existence in their time. In Moscow there is a great " Central Institute for the Protection of Mother and Child "

Women in Russia have perhaps more freedom than in any other country, and at the same time they have special protection from the State. They enter all professions, and quite large numbers of them are engineers. The first woman ambassador appointed by any government was the old Bolshevik Madame Kollontai. Lenin's widow, Krupskaya, is the head of a branch of the Soviet education department.

The Soviet Union is an exciting land with all these changes taking place from day to day and hour to hour. But no part of it is so exciting and fascinating as the desert steppes of Siberia and the old-world valleys of Central Asia, both cut off for genera-tions from the drift of human change and advance, and now bounding ahead at a tremendous pace. To give you some idea of these rapid changes, I shall tell you something about Tadjikistan, which was perhaps one of the most backward areas of the Soviet Union.

Tadjikistan lies in the valleys of the Pamir mountains, north of the River Oxus, bordering Afghanistan and Chinese Turkestan, and not far from the Indian frontier.   It used to be under the Emirs of Bokhara, who were vassals of the Russian Tsars.   In 1920 there was a local revolution in Bokhara and the Emir was overthrown and a Bokhara People's Soviet Republic established.   Civil war followed, and it was during these disorders that Enver Pasha, the once-popular leader of Turkey, met his death.   The Bokhara Republic came to be called the Uzbek Socialist Soviet Republic, and it became one of the constituent sovereign republics of the U.S.S.R.   In 1925 an autonomous Tadjik Republic was formed within the Uzbek area. In 1929 Tadjikistan became a sovereign republic and one of the seven member States of the Soviet federation—the U.S.S.R.

Tadjikistan had attained this dignity, but it was a small and backward area with a population of under 1,000,000, and hardly any proper communications, the only roads being camel-tracks.   Under the new régime immediate steps were taken to improve roads, irrigation and agriculture, industries, education, and health services. Motor roads were built, cotton-growing begun and made highly successful owing to irrigation.   By the middle of 1931 over 60 per cent. of the cotton plantations were collectivized, and a great part of the grain area was also organized under communal farms.   An electric power-station was established and eight cotton-mills and three oil-mills grew up.   A railway line was built connecting the country through Uzbekistan to the Soviet Union railway system, and an aeroplane service established making connections with the principal air lines.

In 1929 there was only one dispensary in the country.   In 1932 there were sixty-one hospitals and thirty-seven dental clinics, with 2125 beds and twenty doctors.   The progress of education can be judged from the following figures :

In 1925 : only six modern schools.
End of 1926 : 113 schools with 2300 students.
In 1929 : 500 schools.
      1931 : over 2000 educational institutions with over 120,000 students.

Of course the money spent on education has gone up with a júmp. The school budget for 1929–30 was for 8,000,000 roubles (a rouble at par is about two shillings, but the actual value varies) ; for 1930–31 the budget was 28,000,000 rubles.   Besides the ordinary schools, kindergartens, training-schools, libraries and reading-rooms were being opened.   There was a tremendous hunger for knowledge among the people.

Under these conditions the seclusion of women behind the veil could hardly continue, and this was rapidly giving way.

All this sounds almost incredible.   I have taken this information and figures from the report of a competent American observer who visited Tadjikistan early in 1932.   Probably many additional changes have taken place since.

It appears that the Soviet Union helped the young Tadjik Republic with money for educational and other purposes, because it is the policy of the Union to pull up backward areas. The country, however, seems to be rich in mineral deposits. Gold, oil, and coal have been found, and it is even believed that the gold reserves are very big. In the old days, up to the time of Chengiz Khan, these gold mines were worked, but apparently they have not been exploited since.

In 1931 there was a counter-revolutionary rising in Tadjikistan, and many of the richer landowning classes who had run away from the country to Afghanistan invaded the country. The rising fizzled out because the peasants did not support it.

This letter is getting long and very mixed. But I must tell you something more about the Soviet Union's activities in the international sphere. You know already that the Soviet signed the Kellogg Peace Pact which was supposed to " outlaw " war. There was also the Litvinov Pact of 1929 between the Soviet and its neighbours. In her desire to ensure peace, Russia went on making " non-aggression " pacts with various countries. Japan was the only one of the Soviet's neighbours which refused to agree to such a pact. In November 1932 Russia and France concluded a non-aggression pact, and this was an important event in world politics, as it brought Russia into the orbit of Western European politics.

China, after a long period of silent hostility, and no diplomatic relations, recognized afresh the Soviet Government, when she was hard pressed by Japan in Manchuria. With Japan, Russia has had normal diplomatic contacts, but their relations with each other have been consistently bad. The Soviet stands as a check to Japanese ambitions on the mainland of Asia, and frequent border conflicts occur. The Japanese Government constantly provokes the Soviet, and there has often been talk of war between them, but Russia preferred to pocket even insults rather than go to war.

Anglo-Russian friction has been a permanent feature of international politics. The trial of the British engineers in April 1933 in Moscow led to reprisals and counter-reprisals, but the storm blew over and normal relations were re-established. But the Conservative Government of Britain dislikes the Soviet, and there is always tension between them. In the United States of America friendlier feelings are growing towards Russia, and President Roosevelt is establishing normal relations. The interests of America and Russia hardly come into conflict anywhere in the world.

The rise of the Nazi Government in Germany has, however, brought a new and aggressively violent enemy for Russia. Though unable to do much direct harm to Russia, it is a great future danger. In Europe fascist tendencies are on the increase.

Soviet Russia has been behaving internationally very much as a satisfied Power, avoiding all trouble, and trying to keep peace at all costs. This is the opposite of a revolutionary policy which would aim at fomenting revolution in other countries. It is a national policy of building up socialism in a single country and avoiding all complications outside. Necessarily this results in compromises with imperialist and capitalist Powers. But the essential socialist basis of Soviet economy continues, and the success of this is itself the most powerful argument in favour of socialism.

This was the position of Soviet Russia in July 1933. A World Economic Conference being held in London then, Russia took advantage of the presence of others to get another non-aggression pact between herself and her neighbours—Afghanistan, Estonia, Latvia, Persia, Poland, Rumania, Turkey, and Lithuania. Japan, as before, kept out of it.

182

SCIENCE GOES AHEAD

July 13, 1933

I HAVE written to you at great length about political happenings, and a little about the economic changes that took place all over the world during the post-war years. In this letter I want to write about other matters, and especially about science and its effects.

But before I go on to science, I would remind you again of the very great change in woman's position since the World War. This so-called " emancipation " of women from legal, social and customary bonds began in the nineteenth century with the coming of big industries which employed women workers. It made slow progress, and then war conditions hurried up the process, and the after-war years almost completed it. To-day even Tadjikistan, about which I wrote to you in my last letter, has its women doctors and teachers and engineers, who only a few years back lived in seclusion. You and your generation will probably take all this for granted. And yet it is quite a novel thing not only in Asia, but in Europe also. Less than 100 years ago, in 1840, the first " World's Anti-Slavery Convention " was held in London. Women came as delegates to it from America, where the existence of negro slavery was agitating many people. The Convention, however, refused to admit these " female delegates ", on the ground that for any woman to take part in a public meeting was improper and degrading to the sex !

And now let us go to science. In dealing with the Five Year Plan in Soviet Russia, I told you that it was the application of the spirit of science to social affairs. To some extent, though only partly, this spirit has been at the back of Western civilization for the past 150 years or so. As its influence has grown, the ideas based on unreason and magic and superstition have been pushed aside, and methods and processes alien to those of science have been opposed. This does not mean that the spirit of science has triumphed completely over unreason and magic and superstition. Far from it. But it has undoubtedly advanced a long way, and the nineteenth century saw many of its resounding victories.

I have written to you already of the stupendous changes brought about in the nineteenth century by the application of science to industry and life. The world, and especially western Europe and North America, were changed out of all recognition; far more than they had changed for thousands of years previously. A surprising enough fact is the enormous increase in the population of Europe during the nineteenth century. In 1800 the population was 180 millions for the whole of Europe. Slowly in the course of ages it had risen to that figure. And then it shoots ahead, and in 1914 it was 460 millions. During this period also millions of Europeans emigrated to other continents, particularly to America, and we may put their number at about 40 millions. Thus Europe's population went up to about 500 millions from 180 millions, in the course of a little over 100 years. This increase was especially marked in the industrial countries of Europe. England, at the beginning of the eighteenth century, had a population of 5 millions only, and was the poorest country in western Europe. It became the richest country in the world, with a population of 40 millions.

This growth and wealth resulted from greater control over, or rather understanding of, the processes of Nature which scientific knowledge made possible. There was great increase in knowledge, but do not imagine that this necessarily means an increase in wisdom. Men began to control and exploit the forces of Nature without having any clear ideas of what their aim in life was or should be. A powerful automobile is a useful and desirable thing, but one must know where to go in it. Unless properly guided, it may jump over a precipice. The President of the British Association of Science said recently : " The command of Nature has been put into man's hands before he knows how to command himself."

Most of us use the products of science—railways, aeroplanes, electricity, wireless, and thousands of others—without thinking of how they came into existence. We take them for granted, as if we were entitled to them as of right. And we are very proud of the fact that we live in an advanced age and are ourselves so very " advanced ". Now, there is no doubt that our age is a very different one from previous ages, and I think it is perfectly correct to say that it is far more advanced. But that is a different thing from saying that we as individuals or groups are more advanced. It would be the height of absurdity to say that because an engine-driver can run an engine and Plato or Socrates could not, therefore the engine-driver is more advanced than, or is superior to, Plato or Socrates. But it would be perfectly correct to say that the engine itself is a more advanced method of locomotion than Plato's chariot was.

We read so many books nowadays, most of them, I am afraid, rather silly books. In the old days people read few books, but they were good books, and they knew them well. One of the greatest of European philosophers, a man full of learning and wisdom, was Spinoza. He lived in the seventeenth century in Amsterdam. It is said that his library consisted of less than sixty volumes.

It is well, therefore, for us to realize that the great increase in knowledge in the world does not necessarily make us better or wiser. We must know how to use that knowledge properly before we can fully profit by it. We must know whither to go before we rush ahead in our powerful car. We must, that is, have some idea of what the aim and object of life should be. Vast numbers of people to-day have no such notion, and never worry themselves about it. They live in an age of science, but the ideas that govern them and their actions belong to ages long past. It is natural that difficulties and conflicts should arise. A clever monkey may learn to drive a car, but he is hardly a safe chauffeur.

Modern knowledge is amazingly intricate and widespread. Tens of thousands of investigators work away continuously, each experimenting in his particular department, each burrowing away in his own patch, and adding tiny bit by bit to the mountain of knowledge. The field of knowledge is so vast that each worker has to be a specialist in his own line. Often he is unaware of other departments of knowledge, and thus, though he is very learned in some branches of knowledge, he is unlearned about many others. It becomes difficult for him to take a wise view of the whole field of human activity. He is not cultured in the old sense of the word.

There are, of course, individuals who have risen above this narrow specialization and, while being specialists themselves, can take a wider view. Undeterred by war and human troubles, these people have been carrying on scientific researches, and during the last fifteen years or so have made remarkable contributions to knowledge. The greatest scientist of the day is supposed to be Albert Einstein, a German Jew, who has been turned out of Germany by the Hitler Government because they do not approve of Jews.

Einstein discovered some new fundamental laws of physics, affecting the whole universe, through intricate calculations in mathematics, and thereby he varied some of Newton's laws which had been accepted without question for 200 years. Einstein's theory was confirmed in a most interesting way. According to this theory, light behaves in a particular way, and this could be tested during an eclipse of the sun. When such an eclipse occurred, it was found that light-rays did behave in that way, and so a conclusion reached by mathematical reasoning was confirmed by actual experiment.

I am not going to try to explain this theory to you, because it is very abstruse. It is called the Theory of Relativity. In dealing with the universe, Einstein found that the idea of time and the idea of space were, separately, not applicable. So he discarded both and put forward a new idea in which both were wedded together. This was the idea of space-time.

Einstein dealt with the universe. At the other end of the scale, scientists investigated the infinitely small. Take a pin's point—about as small a thing as you can see with the unaided eye. This pin's point, it was proved by scientific methods, is, in a way, like a universe in itself! It has molecules buzzing round each other; and each molecule consists of atoms which also go round and round without touching each other; and each atom consists of large numbers of electric particles or charges, or whatever they are, protons and electrons, which are also in constant and tremendously fast motion. Smaller still are positrons and neutrons and dentons; and the average life of a positron has been estimated to be about a thousand-millionth part of a second! All this is, on an infinitely small scale, like the planets and the stars going round and round in space. Remember that the molecule is far too small to be seen even by the most powerful microscope. As for the atoms and the protons and electrons, it is difficult even to imagine them. And yet so advanced is scientific technique that quite a lot of information has been collected about these protons and electrons, and recently the atom was split.

In considering the latest theories of science one's head reels, and it is very difficult to appreciate them. I shall now tell you something even more amazing. We know that our earth, which seems so big to us, is but a minor planet of the Sun, which is itself a very insignificant little star. The whole solar system is but a drop in the ocean of space. Distances are so great in the universe that it takes thousands and millions of years for light to reach us from some parts of it. Thus when we see a star at night, what we see is not what it is now, but what it was when the ray of light, which now reaches us, left it on its long journey, which may have taken hundreds or thousands of years. This is all very confusing to one's ideas of time and space, and that is why Einstein's space-time is far more helpful in considering such matters. If we leave out space and consider only time, the past and present get mixed up. For the star we see is present for us, and yet it is the past that we see. For ought we know it may have ceased to exist long ago, after the light-ray started on its journey.

I have said that our Sun is an unimportant little star. There are about 100,000 other stars, and all these together form what is called a galaxy. Most of the stars that we see at night form this galaxy. But we only see very few of the stars with our unaided eyes. Powerful telescopes help us to see far more. It is calculated by the experts in this science that there are as many as 100,000 different galaxies of stars in the universe!

Another astonishing fact. We are told that this universe is an expanding one. A mathematician, Sir James Jeans, compares it to a soap-bubble which is getting bigger and bigger, the universe being the surface of the bubble. And this bubble-like universe is so big that it takes millions and millions of years for light to travel across it.

If your capacity for astonishment is not exhausted, I have something more to tell you about this truly amazing universe. A famous Cambridge astronomer, Sir Arthur Eddington, tells us that our universe is gradually going to pieces, like a clock that is run down, and unless wound up again somehow, will disintegrate. Of course all this happens in millions of years, so we need not worry.

Physics and chemistry were the leading sciences of the nineteenth century. They helped man to gain command over Nature or the outside world. Then scientific man began to look inside and to study himself. Biology became important; this was the study of life in man and animals and plants. Already it has made extraordinary progress, and biologists say that it will be possible soon to produce changes in the character or temperament of a person by injections, or other means. Thus it may perhaps be possible for a coward to be converted into a man of courage, or, what is more likely, for a government to deal with its critics and opponents by reducing their powers of resistance in this way.

From biology the next step has been psychology, the science which deals with the mind, with the thoughts and motives and fears and desires of human beings. Science is thus invading new fields and telling us more about ourselves, and so perhaps helping us to command ourselves.

Eugenics is also a step from biology. It is the science of race improvement.

It is interesting to notice how the study of certain animals has helped in the development of science. The poor frog was cut up to find out how nerves and muscles functioned. The tiny and insignificant little fly which often sits on over-ripe bananas, hence called the banana fly, has led to more knowledge about heredity than anything else. From careful observations of this fly it has been found how the characteristics of one generation pass on by inheritance to the next generation. To some extent this helps in understanding the working of heredity in human beings.

An even more absurd animal to teach us much is the common grasshopper. Long and careful study of grasshoppers by American observers has shown how sex is determined in animals as well as in human beings. We know a great deal now as to how the little embryo, right at the beginning of its career, becomes male or female, developing gradually into a tiny male or female animal, a little boy or girl.

The fourth instance is that of the ordinary household dog. A famous Russian scientist of our time, Pavlov, began observing dogs carefully, especially noting when their mouths watered at the sight of food. He actually measured this saliva in the dog's mouth. This watering of the dog's mouth at the sight of food is an automatic occurrence, an " unconditioned reflex " as it is called. Just as when an infant sneezes or yawns or stretches itself without previous experience.

Then Pavlov tried to produce " conditioned reflexes "—that is, he taught the dog to expect food at a certain signal. The result was that this signal became associated in the dog's mind with food, and produced the same result as food, although no food was present.

These experiments on dogs and their saliva have been made the basis of human psychology, and it has been shown how a human being in infancy has a number of " unconditioned reflexes ", and as he grows he develops more and more " conditioned reflexes ". In fact, all we learn is based on this. We form habits in this way, and we learn languages, etc. Our actions are governed by our reflexes, which of course are both pleasant and unpleasant. There is the common reflex of fear. No knowledge of Pavlov's experiments is necessary for a man to jump away with great rapidity, and without thinking, when he sees a snake near him, or even a bit of a string looking like a snake.

Pavlov's experiments have revolutionized the whole science of psychology. Some of them are very interesting, but I cannot go into this question any further here. I must add, though, that there are several other important methods of psychological inquiry.

I have mentioned these few instances to give you some idea of the methods of scientific work. The old metaphysical way was to talk vaguely about big things which it was not easy, or even possible, to analyse or understand fully. People argued and argued about them and got very heated, but as there was no final test of the truth or otherwise of their arguments, the matter always remained in the air. They were so busy in arguing about the other world that they did not deign to observe the common things of this world. The method of science is the exact opposite. Careful observations are made of what appear to be trivial and insignificant facts, and these lead to important results. Theories are then framed on these results, and these theories are again checked by further observations and experiments.

This does not mean that science does not go wrong. It often goes wrong, and has to retrace its steps. But the scientific method seems to be the only correct way of approaching a question. Science to-day has lost all the arrogance and self-sufficiency which it had during the nineteenth century. It is proud of its achievements, and yet it is humble before the vast and ever-widening ocean of knowledge that still lies unexplored. The wise man realizes how little he knows; it is the foolish person who imagines that he knows everything. And so with science. The more it advances, the less dogmatic does it get, and the more hesitating is its answer to the questions that may be put to it. "The progress of science," says Eddington, "is to be measured not by the number of questions we can answer, but by the number of questions we can ask." That is perhaps so, but still science does answer more and more questions, and helps us to understand life, and thus enables us, if we will but take advantage of it, to live a better life, directed to a purpose worth having. It illumines the dark corners of life and makes us face reality, instead of the vague confusion of unreason.

183

THE GOOD AND BAD APPLICATIONS OF SCIENCE

July 14, 1933

In my last letter I gave you a peep into the wonderland of the latest developments of science. I do not know if this glimpse will interest you and attract you to these realms of thought and achievement. If you have the desire to know more of these subjects, you can easily find your way to many books. But remember that human thought is ever advancing, ever grappling with and trying to understand the problems of Nature and the universe, and what I tell you to-day may be wholly insufficient and out-of-date to-morrow. To me there is a great fascination in this challenge of the human mind, and how it soars up to the uttermost corners of the universe and tries to fathom its mysteries, and dares to grasp and measure what appear to be the infinitely big as well as the infinitely small.

All this is what is called " pure " science—that is, science which has no direct or immediate effect on life. It is obvious that the Theory of Relativity, or the idea of Space-time, or the size of the universe, have nothing to do with our day-to-day lives. Most of these theories depend on higher mathematics, and these intricate and upper regions of mathematics are, in this sense, pure science. Most people are not much interested in this kind of science; they are naturally far more attracted by the applications of science to every-day life. It is this applied science that has revolutionized life during the last 150 years. Indeed, life to-day is governed and conditioned entirely by these offshoots of science, and it is very difficult for us to imagine existence without them. People often talk about the good old days of the past, of a golden age that is gone. Some periods of past history are singularly attractive, and in some ways they may even have been superior to our time. But even this attraction is probably due more to distance and to a certain vagueness than to anything else, and we are apt to think of an age as being great because of some great men who adorned it and dominated it. The fate of the common people right through history has been a miserable one. Science brought them some relief from their age-long burdens.

Look around you, and you will find that most of the things that you can see are somehow connected with science. We travel by the methods of applied science, we communicate with each other in the same way, our food is often produced that way and carried from one place to another. The newspaper we read could not be produced, nor our books, nor the paper I write on or the pen I write with, by methods other than those of science. Sanitation and health and the conquest over some diseases depend on science. For the modern world it is quite impossible to do without applied science. Apart from all other reasons, one reason is a final and conclusive one : without science there would not be enough food for the world's population, and half of it, or more, would die off from starvation. I have told you how population has gone up with a bound during the last 100 years. This swollen population can only live if the help of science is taken to produce food and transport it from one place to another.

Ever since science introduced the big machine into human life there has been a continuous process of improving it. Innumerable little changes are being made from year to year, and even month to month, which go to make the machine more efficient and less dependent on human labour. These improvements in technique, these advances in technology, as it is called, have become especially rapid during the last thirty years of the twentieth century. The rate of change in recent years—and it is still going on—has been so tremendous, that it is revolutionizing industry and methods of production as much as the Industrial Revolution of the second half of the eighteenth century. This new revolution is largely due to the increasing use of electricity in production. Thus we have had a great Electrical Revolution in the twentieth century, especially in the United States of America, and this is leading to entirely new conditions of life. Just as the Industrial Revolution of the eighteenth century led to the Machine Age, the Electrical Revolution is now leading to the Power Age. Electric power, which is used for industries, railways, and numerous other purposes, dominates everything. It was because of this that Lenin, looking far ahead, decided to build all over Soviet Russia huge hydro-electric power works.

This application of electric power to industry, together with other improvements, often results in a great change without costing much. Thus a slight re-arrangement of electrically-driven machinery might double the production. This is largely due to the progressive elimination of the human factor which is slow and liable to err. Thus, as machines go on improving, fewer workers are employed in them. Huge machines are now controlled by one man handling some levers and switches. This results in increasing the production of manufactured goods enormously, and at the same time throwing out many workers from the factory, as they are no longer required. At the same time advances in technology are so rapid, that, often by the time a new machine is installed in a factory, it is itself partly obsolete because of new improvements.

The process of machines replacing workers had, of course, occurred from the early days of machinery, and, as I think I have told you, there were many riots in those days, and angry workmen broke the new machines. It was found, however, that ultimately machinery resulted in more employment. As a worker could produce far more goods with the help of machinery, his wages went up and the prices of goods went down. The workers and common people could thus buy more of these goods. Their standards of living went up and the demands for manufactured goods grew. This resulted in more factories being built and more men being employed. Thus, although machinery displaced workers in each factory as a whole, far more workers were employed because there were many more factories.

This process went on for a long time, helped as it was by the exploitation by industrial countries of distant markets in backward countries. During the past few years this process seems to have stopped. Perhaps no further expansion is possible under the present capitalistic system, and some change in the system is necessary. Modern industry goes in for " mass production ", but this can only be carried on if the goods so produced are bought by the masses. If the masses are too poor or are unemployed, then they cannot buy these goods.

In spite of all this, technical improvements go on ceaselessly, and result in machinery displacing men and adding to the unemployed. From 1929 onwards there was a great depression in trade all over the world, but even this did not prevent technology from advancing. It is said that there have been so many improvements *since* 1929 in the United States that millions of people who have been thrown out of work can never be employed, even if the production of 1929 were to be kept up.

This is one of the reasons—there are many others also—that has produced the great problem of the unemployed all over the world, and especially in the advanced industrial countries. It is a curious and inverted problem, for greater production by up-to-date machinery means, or ought to mean, greater wealth for the nation and higher standards of living for every one. Instead, it has resulted in poverty and terrible suffering. One would have thought that a scientific solution of the problem would not be difficult. Perhaps it is not. But the real difficulty comes in trying to solve it scientifically and reasonably. For in doing so many vested interests are affected, and they are powerful enough to control their governments. Then, again, the problem is essentially an international one, and to-day national rivalries prevent an international solution. Soviet Russia is applying the methods of science to similar problems, but because she has to proceed nationally, the rest of the world being capitalist and hostile to her, she has far greater difficulties than she would otherwise have had. The world is essentially international to-day, although its political structure lags behind and is narrowly national. For socialism to succeed finally, it will have to be international world socialism. The hands of the clock cannot be put back, nor can the international structure of to-day, incomplete as it is, be suppressed in favour of national isolation. An attempt at the intensification of nationalism, as the fascists are trying to do in various countries, is bound to fail in the end, because it runs counter to the fundamental international character of world economy to-day. It may be, of course, that in so failing it may carry the world with it, and involve what is called modern civilization in a common disaster.

The danger of such a disaster is by no means remote and unthinkable. Science, as we have seen, has brought many good things in its train, but science has also added enormously to the horrors of war. States and governments have often neglected many branches of science, pure and applied. But they have not neglected the warlike aspects of science, and they have taken full advantage of the latest scientific technique to arm and strengthen themselves. Most States rest, in the final analysis, on force, and scientific technique is making these governments so strong that they can tyrannize over people without, as a rule, any fear of consequences. The old days of popular risings against tyrannical governments and the building of barricades and fights in the open streets, such as occurred in the great French Revolution, are long past. It is impossible now for an unarmed or even armed crowd to fight with an organized and well-equipped State force. The State army itself may turn against the Government, as happened in the Russian Revolution, but, unless this happens, it cannot be forcibly defeated. Hence the necessity has arisen for people, struggling for freedom, to seek other and more peaceful methods of mass action.

Science thus leads to groups or oligarchies controlling States, and to the destruction of individual liberty and the old nineteenth century ideas of democracy. Such oligarchies arise in different States, sometimes outwardly paying homage to the principles of democracy, at other times openly condemning them. These different State oligarchies come into conflict with each other and nations go to war. Such a big war to-day or in the future may well destroy not only these oligarchies, but civilization itself. Or it may be that out of its ashes an international socialist order might arise, as expected by the Marxist philosophy.

War is not a pleasant subject to contemplate in all its horrid reality, and because of this the reality is hidden behind fine phrases and brave music and bright uniforms. But it is necessary to know something of what war means to-day. The last war—the World War—brought home to many the horror of war. And yet it is said that the last war was nothing compared to what the next one is likely to be. For if industrial technique has advanced tenfold during the last few years, the science of war has advanced a hundred-fold. War is no longer an affair of infantry charges and cavalry dashes; the old foot-soldier and cavalry man are almost as useless now in war as the bow and arrow. War to-day is an affair of mechanized tanks (a kind of moving battleship on caterpillar wheels), aeroplanes and bombs, and especially the latter two. Aeroplanes are increasing in speed and efficiency from day to day.

If war breaks out, it is expected that the warring nations will immediately be attacked by hostile aircraft. These aeroplanes will come immediately after the declaration of war, or they may even come before, to steal an advantage over the enemy, and hurl high-explosive bombs at the great cities and factories. Some of the enemy aeroplanes might be destroyed, but the remaining ones will be quite enough to bomb the city. Poison gases will come out of the bombs thrown from aeroplanes, and these will spread and envelop whole areas, suffocating and killing every living thing within their reach. It will be a large-scale destruction of the civilian population in the cruellest and most painful way, causing intolerable suffering and mental distress. And this kind of thing might be done simultaneously in the great cities of the rival Powers at war with each other. In a European war, London, Paris, Berlin might be a heap of smouldering ruins within a few days or weeks.

There is worse to come. The bombs thrown from the aeroplanes might contain germs and bacteria of various horrible diseases, so that a whole city might be infected with these diseases. This kind of " bacteriological warfare " can be carried on in other ways also : by infecting food and drinking-water and by animal-carriers—for instance, a rat which carries plague.

All this sounds monstrous and incredible, and so it is. Not even a monster would like to do it. But incredible things happen when people are thoroughly afraid and are fighting a life-and-death struggle. The very fear that the enemy country might adopt such unfair and monstrous methods induces each country to be first in the field. For the weapons are so terrible that the country that uses them first has a great advantage. Fear has big eyes !

Indeed, poison gas was used extensively during the last war, and it is well known that all the great Powers have now got large factories to manufacture this gas for war purposes. A curious result of all this is that the real fighting in the next big war will take place not at the front, where some armies might dig themselves in and face each other, but behind the fronts, in the cities and homes of the civilian population. It may even be that the safest place during the war will be the front, for the troops will be fully protected there from air attacks and poison gases and infection ! There will be no such protection for the men left behind, or the women, or the children.

What will be the result of all this ? Universal destruction ? The end of the fine structure of culture and civilization that centuries of effort have built up ?

What will happen no one knows. We cannot tear the veil from the future. We see two processes going on to-day in the world, two rival and contradictory processes. One is the progress of co-operation and reason, and the building up of the structure of civilization ; the other a destructive process, a tearing up of everything, an attempt by mankind to commit suicide. And both go faster and faster, and both arm themselves with the weapons and technique of science. Which will win ?

184

THE GREAT DEPRESSION AND WORLD CRISIS

July 19, 1933

THE more one thinks of the powers that science has placed at the disposal of man, and the use that man is putting them to, the more one wonders. For the plight of the capitalist world to-day is indeed an astonishing one. By means of the radio, science carries our voices to distant lands, by wireless telephone we speak to people at the other ends of the earth, and soon we shall be able to see them by means of the " television ". By its wonderful technique science can produce all that mankind needs in abundance, and rid the world for ever of the ancient curse of poverty. From the earliest days in the dawn of history, men had tried to find some relief from their daily toil which crushed them, giving little return, in dreams of an El Dorado, a land flowing with milk and honey and with every kind of plenty. They had imagined a golden age that was past, and they had looked forward to a paradise to come where they would at last have peace and joy. And then came science and placed the means of creating plenty at their disposal, and yet in the midst of this actual and possible plenty, the majority of mankind still lived in misery and destitution. Is this not an amazing paradox ?

Our present-day society is actually embarrassed by science and its abundant gifts. They do not fit in with each other; there is conflict between the capitalist form of society and the latest scientific technique and methods of production. Society has learnt how to produce but not how to distribute what it has produced.

After this little preamble, let us have a look at Europe and America again. I have told you something already of their troubles and difficulties during the first ten years after the World War. The defeated countries—Germany and the small countries of central Europe—were very badly hit by the post-war conditions, and their currencies collapsed, ruining their middle classes. The victor and creditor Powers of Europe were little better off. Each of them owed money to America and had a tremendous internal national war debt, and the burden of these two debts made them stumble and stagger. They lived in the hope of getting money from Germany as Reparations, and using this for payment of their foreign debts at least. This hope was not a very reasonable one, for Germany was not even a solvent country. But the difficulty was got over by America lending money to Germany, who then paid England, France, etc., their share of the Reparations, and they in their turn paid America part of their debts.

The United States was the only country during this decade, that was prosperous. It seemed to be overflowing with money, and this very prosperity led to extravagant hopes and gambling in securities and shares.

The general impression in the capitalist world was that the economic crisis would pass as previous slumps had done, and that the world would gradually settle down to another period of prosperity. Indeed, the life of capitalism seems to have been an alternation between prosperity and crisis. It had been pointed out long ago that this was in the very nature of the unplanned and unscientific methods of capitalism. Prosperity in industry led to a boom period, and then everybody wanted to produce as much as possible to take advantage of this. The result was that there was over-production—that is, more was produced than could be sold. Stocks mounted up, there was a crisis, and industry slowed down again. After a period of stagnation, during which the accumulated stocks were gradually disposed of, industry woke up again, and soon there was another period of prosperity. This was the usual cycle, and most people hoped that some time or other prosperity would come back.

In 1929, however, came a sudden change for the worse. America stopped lending money to Germany and the South American States, and thus put an end to the paper structure of loans and debt payments. It was obvious that the American capitalists would not go on lending money for ever, for this only increased their debtors' liabilities, and made it impossible for the debts ever to be paid. They had only lent money so far because of the abundance of cash with them for which they had no use. This superfluity of spare money also led them to tremendous speculation in the Stock Exchange. There was a regular gambling fever and every one wanted to get rich quickly.

The stoppage of loans to Germany immediately brought on a crisis, and some German banks failed. Gradually the circle of payments of reparations and debts stopped. Many of the South American governments and other small States began to default. President Hoover of the United States, observing with alarm that the whole structure of credit was collapsing, declared a year's moratorium in July 1931. This meant that all inter-governmental debt and reparation payments were to cease for a year in order to give relief to all the debtors.

Meanwhile, in October 1929, a striking event had taken place in America. The gambling on the Stock Exchange led to ridiculously high prices of shares, etc., and then to sudden collapse. There was a great crisis in financial circles in New York, and from that day America's period of prosperity ended. The United States lined up with the other nations who were suffering from the slump. The depression of trade and industry now became the Great Depression, which spread all over the world. Do not think that the Stock Exchange gambling or financial crisis in New York brought on the fall of America or the depression. That was just the last straw on the camel's back. The real reasons went far deeper.

Trade began to shrink all over the world, and prices, especially of agricultural produce, to fall rapidly. There was said to be over-production of almost everything, which really meant that people had no money to buy the goods produced; there was under-consumption. As manufactured articles could not be sold, they accumulated, and, naturally, the factories making them had to be closed. They could not go on making things which did not sell. This led to a great and unprecedented growth in unemployment in Europe and America and elsewhere. All industrial countries were hard hit. So also were agricultural countries which supplied food-stuffs or raw materials for industries to the world market.

Thus India's industries suffered to some extent, but far greater suffering was caused to the agricultural classes by the fall in prices. Ordinarily such a fall in the price of food-stuffs would have been a great boon to the people, for they could get their food cheap. But this is a topsy-turvy world under the capitalist system, and this boon turned out to be a scourge. The peasantry had to pay their rent to their landlord or revenue to the government in cash, and to get this cash they had to sell their produce. Prices were so extraordinarily low that they could not raise enough money sometimes even by selling all the stuff they had produced. And often they were turned out of their lands and their mud huts, and even their few household goods were auctioned to provide the rent. And in this way, even when food was very cheap, they, who had produced it, starved and were made homeless.

The very interdependence of the world made this depression world-wide. Only a place like Tibet, cut off from the outside world, was, I suppose, free from it. Month by month the depression spread and trade declined. It was like paralysis creeping along and incapacitating the whole social structure. Perhaps the best way to form an idea of this decline is to examine the actual figures for world trade which the League of Nations has published. The figures represent millions of gold dollars and they are for the first three months of each year :

First quarter of	Imports Value	Exports Value	Imports & Exports Value
1929	7972	7317	15289
1930	7364	6520	13884
1931	5154	4531	9685
1932	3434	3027	6461
1933	2829	2552	5381

These figures show us how world trade progressively declined and was, in the first quarter of 1933, 35 per cent., or about one-third, of what it had been four years earlier.

What do these abstract figures about trade tell us in human terms ? They tell us that the mass of the people are so poor that they cannot buy what they produce. They tell us that vast numbers of workers are unemployed and, with the best will in the world, cannot find work. In Europe and the United States alone there were 30,000,000 unemployed workers, Britain having as many as 3,000,000 and the United States 13,000,000. Nobody knows how many unemployed there are in India or in other countries of Asia. Probably in India alone they far exceed the total for Europe and America. Think of the vast numbers of these unemployed all over the world, and their family members who depend on them, and then you will have some idea of the human suffering caused by the trade depression. In many European countries a system of State insurance gave a subsistence allowance to all the registered unemployed; in the United States charity was doled out to them. But these allowances and doles did not go far, and many did not even get them and starved. In some parts of central and eastern Europe conditions became terrible.

Of all the great industrial countries America was hit last by the depression, but the reaction there was greater than elsewhere. The people of America were not used to long-continuing trade depression and hardship. Proud, purse-proud America was stunned by the blow, and as the number of unemployed increased, million after million, and hunger and slow starvation became a common sight, the morale of the nation began to crack up. Confidence in banks and investments was shaken, and money was drawn out from banks and hoarded. Banks exist on the basis of confidence and credit: if this confidence goes, so does the bank. There were thousands of bank failures in the United States, and each failure added to the crisis and generally made matters worse.

Large numbers of unemployed men and women took to vagrancy and wandered about from town to town in search of employment. They walked along the high roads, asking passing motorists to give them a lift, or often hung on to the foot-boards of slow goods-trains. Even more striking were the numbers of young boys and girls, and even children, wandering alone or in small groups up and down the huge country. Meanwhile, grown-up and able-bodied men sat idle, waiting and hoping for work, and model factories were closed down. Yet such is the nature of capitalism that, at this very time, dark and filthy sweat-shops grew up, and children of twelve and sixteen were made to work there as much as ten or twelve hours a day for a small wage. Some employers took advantage of the tremendous pressure of unemployment on these young boys and girls and made them work hard and long in their mills and factories. The depression thus brought back child labour to America, and labour laws prohibiting this as well as other abuses were openly flouted.

Remember that there was no lack of food or manufactured goods in America or in the rest of the world. The complaint was that there was too much, there was over-production. A well-known English economist, Sir Henry Strakosch, stated that in July 1931—that is, in the second year of the depression—there were, in the markets of the world, goods sufficient to maintain the people of the world, on the standards to which they had been accustomed, for two years and three months following, supposing that not a stroke of work was done during this interval. And yet during this very period there was privation and starvation on a scale that the modern industrial world had never seen. Side by side with this privation took place an actual destruction of food-stuffs. Crops were not gathered and were allowed to rot in the fields, fruit was left on the trees, and many articles were actually destroyed. To give you just one instance : From June 1931 to February 1933 over 14,000,000 bags of coffee were destroyed in Brazil. As each bag contains 132 lb., over 1,848,000,000 lb. of coffee were thus destroyed ! This was more than enough for the total population of the world, giving every person a pound to himself. And yet we know that millions of people who would welcome coffee cannot afford it.

Besides coffee, wheat was destroyed, and cotton, and many other things. Steps were also taken to lessen production in future by restricting the sowing of cotton, rubber, tea, etc. All this destruction and restriction was done to raise prices of agricultural produce, so that a shortage might create a demand and push prices up. For the farmer who sells his goods in the market this would no doubt be profitable, but for the consumers? Truly, this world of ours is curious. If there is under-production, prices are so high that most people cannot afford to buy, and there is privation. If there is over-production, prices fall so low that industry and agriculture cannot function, and there is unemployment, and how can the unemployed buy anything, for they have no money to buy with! In either event, whether there is scarcity or abundance, the lot of the masses is privation.

As I have said, there was no lack of goods in America or elsewhere during the depression. The farmers had agricultural produce which they could not dispose of, and the city people had manufactured goods which they could not sell. And yet each wanted the other's goods. The process of exchange got held up because of the lack of money on either side. And then, in highly industrialized, advanced, capitalistic America, many people took to the ancient method of barter, which had existed in the old days before money came into use. Hundreds of barter organizations developed in America. As the capitalistic system of exchange broke down for lack of money, people began to do without money and to exchange goods and services. Exchange associations arose to help this barter by issuing certificates. An interesting instance of barter was that of a dairyman who gave milk, butter, and eggs to a university in exchange for the education of his children.

Barter also developed to some extent in other countries. There were also many instances of barter between nations as the complicated system of international exchanges broke down. Thus England bartered coal for Scandinavian timber; Canada gave aluminium for Soviet oil; the United States bartered wheat for Brazilian coffee.

The farmers in America were hard hit by the slump, and they could not pay back the money they had borrowed from banks on mortgages on their farms. The banks thereupon tried to realize the money by getting the farms sold up. But the farmers would not allow this, and they organized themselves in committees of action to prevent such sales. The result was that no one dared to bid for a farmer's property at such an auction and the banks were forced to agree to the farmers' terms. This farmers' revolt spread in the Middle-West agricultural regions of America and was significant as showing how the development of the crisis was making these conservative farmers of old American stock, who had long been the backbone of the country, more aggressive and revolutionary in outlook. Their movement was native to the country and had no connection with socialism or communism. Economic distress was changing these middle-class farmers with property rights into peasants who are just tillers of the soil and own little property. Among their slogans were : " Human rights are above legal and property rights ", and " Wives and children have the first mortgage ".

I have dealt at some length with conditions in the United States because America is in many ways a fascinating country. It is the most advanced of capitalist countries, and it has no feudal roots in the past such as Europe and Asia have. Changes there are thus apt to be rapid. Other countries are more used to privation for the masses ; in America this was a new and staggering phenomenon on such a big scale. You can judge of the state of other countries during the depression from what I have told you about America. Some were far worse, others were a little better. On the whole, agricultural and backward countries were not so badly hit as advanced industrial ones. Their very backwardness saved them to some extent. Their chief trouble was the collapse of agricultural prices, which brought great hardship to the peasantry. Australia, which is mainly agricultural, could not pay her debts to the English banks, and was on the verge of bankruptcy because of this fall in prices. To save herself she had to agree to hard conditions from the English bankers. In a depression the class which flourishes and dominates over others is the banker class.

In South America the stoppage of loans from the United States and the depression brought a crisis which upset most of the republican governments, or rather the dictators that ruled there. There were revolutions all over the south, including the three leading countries—the ABC countries—Argentine, Brazil, and Chile. These revolutions were, like all South American revolutions, palace affairs, just changing dictators and governments at the top. The person or group that controls the army and police governs the country. All the South American governments were heavily in debt and most of them defaulted.

185

WHAT CAUSED THE CRISIS

July 21, 1933

THE great depression held the world by the throat and strangled or slowed up almost all activities. The wheels of industry stopped running in many places ; fields that used to produce food and other crops lay fallow and untilled ; rubber-trees oozed out rubber, but there was none to collect it ; hillsides that were covered with well-looked-after tea-bushes ran wild and there was no one to tend them. And those who used to do all this work joined the great armies of the unemployed, and waited for work and employment that did not come and, helpless and almost hopeless, faced hunger and privation. In many countries the number of suicides greatly increased.

All industries, I have said, came under the shadow of the depression. But there was one that did not; this was the armaments industry, which supplied arms and war material to the different national armies and navies and air services. This trade prospered, and paid fat dividends to its shareholders. It was not affected by the depression, for it trafficked in national rivalries and conflicts, and these grew worse under the crisis.

One great area also escaped the direct effects of the depression—the Soviet Union. There was no unemployment there, and work went on harder than ever under the Five Year Plan. It was outside the area controlled by capitalism, and its economy was different. But, as I have told you, it suffered indirectly from the depression because of the fall in prices of agricultural produce which it sold abroad.

What was the cause of this great depression, this world crisis, which in its own way was almost as terrible as the World War itself? It is called the crisis of capitalism because the vast and intricate capitalist machine cracked badly under it. Why did capitalism behave in this way? And was it a temporary crisis which capitalism will survive, or was it rather the beginnings of the final death agony of this great system which has dominated the world for so long? Many such questions arise, and they fascinate us, for on their answer depends the future of humanity, and incidentally ourselves. In December 1932 the British Government sent a note to the American Government pleading to be let off the payment of their war debt. In this note they pointed out how the remedies that had been tried had aggravated the disease. "Everywhere," they said, "taxation has been ruthlessly increased and expenditure drastically curtailed, and yet the control restrictions intended to remedy the trouble have merely aggravated it." Further, they pointed out, that "this loss and suffering is not due to the niggardliness of Nature. The triumphs of physical science are growing and the vast potentialities of the production of real wealth remain unimpaired." The fault did not lie in Nature, but in man and in the system he had created.

It is not easy to give a correct diagnosis of this disease of capitalism or to prescribe a remedy for it. Economists, who ought to know all about it, differ among themselves and suggest a variety of causes and remedies. The only people who are quite clear in their minds about it seem to be the communists and socialists, who find a justification for their views and theories in the breakdown of capitalism. Capitalist experts were frankly puzzled and perplexed. One of the greatest and ablest of British financiers, Montagu Norman, who is the Governor of the Bank of England, said at a public function : " The economic problem is too great for me. The difficulties are so vast, so novel, precedents so lacking, that I approach the whole subject in ignorance and humility. It is too great for me. When it comes to the future, I hope that we may see the light at the end of the tunnel which some are able already to point out to us." But this light is, like the will-o'-the-wisp, a deceptive phantom, raising hopes in us only to disappoint. A well-known British politician, Sir Auckland Geddes, has said that " thinking people believe that the disintegration of society has begun. In Europe we know that an age is dying."

The Germans used to hold that the real cause of the crisis was Reparations ; many others held that the depression came because of the war debts, between nations as well as within nations, which have become too great a burden to be borne and are crushing all industry. Thus the war is made primarily responsible for the world's troubles. Some economists were of opinion that the real trouble lay in the strange behaviour of money and the great fall in prices which, in turn, was caused by the scarcity of gold, gold having become scarce partly because enough is not produced from the mines for the world's needs, and more so because of the hoarding of gold by different governments. Yet others said that all troubles were due to economic nationalism, to tariffs and heavy duties which prevent international trade. Another suggested cause was the advance in technology or scientific technique which has reduced the number of workers required, and thus increased unemployment.

Much may be said for all these and other suggestions, and it may be that all of them have contributed to the world's distemper. But it seems hardly right or reasonable to lay the blame for the crisis on any one of them or all of them. Indeed, many of these so-called causes were the results of the crisis, though each one of them helped to aggravate it. The basic trouble must lie deeper. It was not due to defeat in war, as the victors were themselves involved in it ; it was not due to national poverty, because the richest country in the world, America, was one of the worst sufferers. There can be no doubt that the World War has been a powerful factor in hastening the crisis, both because of the great burden of debt and the manner of its distribution among the creditors. Also because the high prices of commodities during the war and some years after the war were artificial and there was bound to be a collapse. But let us look deeper.

Over-production, it is said, is the trouble. This is a misleading word, for there can be no over-production when millions suffer from lack of even absolutely necessary articles. Hundreds of millions of people in India have not got enough clothes to wear, and yet one hears of large stocks in Indian cloth mills and *khadi* stores, and of " over-production " of cloth. The real explanation is that the people are much too poor to buy the cloth, not that they do not require it. It is lack of money among the masses. This lack of money does not mean that money has disappeared from the world. It means that the distribution of money among the world's people has changed and is continually changing—that is, there is inequality in the distribution of wealth. On the one side there is an excess of wealth and the owners of it do not know how to utilize all of it; they merely save it up and swell up their bank accounts. This money is not used for buying commodities in the market. On the other side there is a greater lack of wealth, and even the commodities that are required cannot be bought, for want of money.

This seems to be a roundabout way of saying that there are rich and poor; a very obvious fact that requires no argument. These rich and poor have existed all along from the beginning of history. Why, then, should they be made responsible for the present crisis? I think I have told you in some previous letter that the whole tendency of the capitalist system is to aggravate inequalities in the distribution of wealth. Under feudal conditions the position was almost static or slowly changing; capitalism, with the big machine and the world market, was dynamic, and swift changes took place as wealth was accumulated by individuals and groups. The growth of inequality in the distribution of wealth, added to some other factors, led to the new struggle between labour and capital in the industrial countries. The capitalists in these countries eased the tension by various concessions to labour—higher wages, better living conditions, etc.—at the expense of the exploitation of colonial and backward areas. In this way the exploitation of Asia and Africa and South America and eastern Europe helped the industrial countries of western Europe and North America to accumulate wealth and pass on a bit of it to their workers. As new markets were discovered, new industries were developed or old industries grew. Imperialism took the form of an aggressive search for these markets and for raw materials, and the rivalries of different industrial Powers brought them into conflict. When the whole world was practically under capitalist exploitation, this process of spreading out came to an end, and the conflicts of the Powers led to war.

I have already told you all this, but I am repeating it to help you to understand the world crisis. During this period of a developing capitalism and a growing imperialism there were many crises in the West, due to too much saving on the one side and too little money to spend on the other. But these crises passed off because the spare money with the capitalists went to develop and exploit backward areas, and thus created new markets there, which increased consumption of goods. Imperialism was called the final phase of capitalism. Ordinarily this process of exploitation might have gone on till the whole world had been industrialized. But difficulties and checks arose. The chief difficulty was the fierce competition of the imperialist Powers, each wanting the biggest share for itself. Another was the new nationalism in the colonial countries and the growth of colonial industries, which began to supply their own markets. All these processes, as we have seen, led to the war. But the war did not and could not solve the difficulties of capitalism. One huge area, the Soviet Union, went out of the capitalist world completely and ceased to be a market which could be exploited.

In the East nationalism grew more aggressive and industrialization spread. The tremendous advance in scientific technique during and after the war also helped in the unequal distribution of wealth and in creating unemployment. The war debts were also a powerful factor.

These war debts were enormous, and it is worth remembering that they represented no solid wealth of any other kind. If a country borrows money to build a railway or irrigation works, or anything else beneficial for the country, it has got something solid in exchange for the money borrowed and spent. Indeed, these works may actually produce more wealth than was spent on them; they are therefore called "productive works". The money borrowed in war-time was not spent for any such purpose. It was not only unproductive, but it was destructive. Vast amounts were spent, and they left a trail of destruction behind. The war debts were thus a pure and unmitigated burden. There were three kinds of war debts : Reparations, which the defeated countries were forced to agree to pay; inter-governmental debts, which the Allied countries owed to each other, and especially to America, and national debts, which each country had borrowed from its own citizens.

Each of these three different kinds of debts was huge, but the biggest of all for each country was its national debt. Thus the British national debt after the war amounted to the prodigious figure of £6,500,000,000. Even to pay interest on such debts was a great burden and meant very heavy taxation. Germany wiped off her big internal debt by the inflation which put an end to the old mark, and so, in this respect, she escaped a burden at the expense of the people who had lent her money. France, adopting the same method of inflation, but not to the same extent, reduced the value of her franc to almost a fifth of what it was, and thus at one stroke reduced her internal national debt to one-fifth. It was not possible to play this game with the debts owing to other countries (the Reparations or inter-governmental debts), which had to be paid in solid gold.

The payment of these inter-governmental debts by one country to another meant that the paying country lost so much money and became poorer. But the repayment of the internal national debt did not make any such difference to the country, as the money remained in the country anyhow. And yet it made a big difference. Such debts were paid by raising money by taxation from all the taxpayers in the country, rich and poor. The bond-holders who had lent money to the State were the rich. So that the result was that the rich and poor were both taxed to pay the rich; the rich got back what they paid in taxation to the State and much more; the poor paid, but did not get back anything. The rich became richer, and the poor poorer.

If the European debtor countries paid up some of their debts to America, all this money went to the big bankers and financiers there. Thus the war debts resulted in aggravating an already bad situation and in over-burdening the rich people with money at the expense of the poor. The rich wanted to invest this, for no business man likes to see his money idle. They over-invested this money in fresh factories and machinery and other capital expenditure, which was not justified by the impoverished state of the people generally. They also went in for speculation on the Stock Exchange. They prepared to produce goods on a bigger and bigger mass scale, but what was the good of it when the masses had no money to buy ? So there was over-production, and goods could not be sold, and industries began losing money, and many of them shut up shop. Business men, frightened by their losses, stopped investing in industry and held on to their money, which lay idle in banks. And thus unemployment became general and the depression world-wide.

I have discussed the different suggested causes of the crisis separately, but, of course, they all worked together, and thus made the trade depression a greater one than any before. Essentially it was due to the unequal distribution of the surplus income produced by capitalism. To put it differently, the masses did not get enough money as wages and salaries to buy the goods they had produced by their work. The value of the products was greater than their total income. The money which, if it had been with the masses, would have gone to buy these goods, was concentrated in the hands of relatively few very rich persons, who did not know what to do with it. It was this superfluous money that flowed out in loans from America to Germany and central Europe and South America. It was this foreign lending that kept war-worn Europe and the capitalist machine functioning for some years, and was yet a cause of the crisis. And it was a stoppage of these foreign loans that finally brought the crash.

If this diagnosis of the crisis of capitalism is correct, then the remedy can only be one which equalizes incomes, or at least tends in that direction. To do so fully would be to adopt socialism, but capitalists are not likely to do that till circumstances compel them. People talk of a planned capitalism, of international combines to exploit backward areas, but behind this talk, national rivalries and the struggle of imperialist Powers for world markets grows fierce. Planning for what ? For profiting one at the expense of another ? The motive of capitalism is individual profit, and competition has been its watchword, and competition and planning go ill together.

Even apart from socialists and communists many thinking people have begun to question the efficacy of capitalism under present conditions. Startling remedies have been suggested by some to do away not only with the present profit system, but also the price system itself, under which one pays for goods with money. These are too intricate to mention here, and some of them are rather fantastic. I am referring to them to make you realize how people's minds have been shaken up, and revolutionary proposals are being made by men who are far from being revolutionary.

The I.L.O. (International Labour Office) of Geneva recently made a simple proposal to reduce unemployment immediately by limiting the workers' hours of work to forty per week. This would have resulted in millions of additional workers being engaged, and thus reducing unemployment to that extent. All the representatives of workers welcomed this, but the British Government opposed it, and with the help of Germany and Japan managed to get the proposal shelved. Britain's record in the I.L.O. has been a consistently reactionary one during all this post-war period.

The crisis and depression are world-wide, and one would imagine that the remedy must also be an international world remedy. Attempts have been made by different countries to find some way of co-operation, but they have all failed so far. And so each country, despairing of a world solution, has sought a national remedy in economic nationalism. If world trade is shrinking away, it has been argued, let us at least keep our own country's trade to ourselves and prevent foreign goods from coming. Export trade being doubtful and variable, each country has tried to concentrate on the home market. Tariffs have been put on or raised to keep out foreign goods, and they have succeeded in doing so. They have also succeeded in injuring international trade, for every country's tariff was a barrier to world trade. Europe and America and, to some extent, Asia are full of these high tariff walls. Another result of the tariffs was the increased cost of living, for the prices of food-stuffs and everything that was protected by the tariff went up. A tariff creates a national monopoly and prevents, or makes more difficult, competition from outside. Under a monopoly, prices are bound to rise. The particular industry protected by the tariff may benefit, or rather its owners may benefit, by the protection given to it, but this is largely at the cost of the people who buy the goods, as they have to pay higher prices. Tariffs thus bring some relief to certain classes and they create vested interests, for the industries profiting by the tariffs want to keep them. Thus in India the cloth industry is protected very heavily against Japan. This is very profitable to the Indian mill-owners, who could not otherwise compete with Japan, and who can thus charge higher prices. The sugar industry is also protected here, with the result that large numbers of sugar factories have grown up all over India and especially in the United Provinces and Bihar. A vested interest is thus created, and if the sugar duties were removed, this interest would suffer and many of the new sugar mills might collapse.

Two kinds of monopolies increased: external monopolies as between nations helped by tariffs, and internal monopolies, large concerns swallowing up smaller ones. Of course the growth of monopolies was no new process. It had been taking place for many years past, even before the World War. This became swifter now. Tariffs also had been functioning in many countries. England was the one big country that had so far relied on free trade and done without tariffs. But now she had to break her old tradition and fall into line with other countries by imposing tariff duties. These brought some immediate relief to some of her industries.

All this, though it brought local and temporary relief, really made matters worse in the world as a whole. Not only did it further lessen international trade, but it maintained and increased the unequal distribution of wealth. It led to continuous friction between rival nations, each raising its tariffs against the other—tariff wars, as they are called. As the world markets became fewer and more and more protected, the struggle for them grew harder, and employers began to press for wage-cuts for their workers, so that they might be able to compete with other countries. And so the depression grew and the ranks of the unemployed swelled. Every wage-cut reduced the purchasing power of the workers.

186

THE STRUGGLE OF AMERICA AND ENGLAND FOR LEADERSHIP

July 25, 1933

I HAVE told you of the shrinkage of international trade during the depression till only a third of it has remained. Domestic trade also lessened because of the decreasing buying power of the people. Unemployment went on increasing, and the support of these millions of unemployed workers became a great burden on the various governments. In spite of high taxes, many governments found it almost impossible to make both ends meet; their revenue went down; their expenditure, in spite of economy and salary-cuts, remained high. For the greater part of this expenditure was tied up with armies and navies and the air force, and with the payment of debts, internal as well as external. There were deficits in the national budgets—that is, expenditure exceeded income. These deficits, which could only be made good by borrowing more money or diverting money from other reserve funds, weakened the financial position of the countries concerned.

At the same time large stocks of goods remained unsold because people did not have enough money to buy them, and in many instances these " superfluous " food-stuffs and other articles were actually destroyed, though people elsewhere were in sore need of them. The crisis and collapse were world-wide (excluding the Soviet Union), and yet the different nations failed to co-operate internationally to end them. Each country has shifted for itself, has tried to overreach the others, and even attempted to profit by another's misfortune. This individual and selfish action as well as the other partial remedies tried have only aggravated the situation. Quite apart from this trade depression, but influencing it considerably, are two dominant facts or tendencies in world affairs. One is the rivalry of the capitalist world with the Soviet Union; the other is Anglo-American rivalry.

The capitalist crisis has weakened and impoverished all the

capitalist countries and, in a sense, has lessened the chances of war. Each country is busy putting its own house in order, and has no money for adventures. And yet, paradoxically, this very crisis has increased the war danger, for it is making nations and their governments desperate, and desperate people often seek a solution for their internal difficulties in war abroad. This is especially so when a dictator or a small oligarchy is in power. Sooner than give up power he will plunge his country into war, and thus divert his people's attention away from troubles at home. Thus a crusade against the Soviet Union and communism is always likely, as it might be hoped that this will bring many of the capitalist countries together. The Soviet Union, as I have told you, was not directly affected by the crisis of capitalism. Busy with its five-year plans, it was intent on avoiding war at any cost.

Rivalry between England and America was inevitable after the war. They are the two greatest world Powers, and each of them wants to dominate world affairs. England had unchallenged supremacy before the world war. The war made the United States the richest and most powerful nation, and naturally they wanted to take henceforth what they considered was their rightful position in the world—that is, the leading place. They were not going to permit England to boss everything in future. England herself fully realized that times had changed, and she tried to adapt herself to them by seeking the friendship of America. She even went to the length of giving up her Japanese alliance to please America, and made other soothing advances. But England was not prepared to give up her special interests and position, and especially her financial leadership, as her greatness and empire were bound up with these. And it was precisely this financial leadership that America wanted. Friction between the two countries was inevitable. Behind soft words and pleasant phrases, the bankers of the two countries, backed by their governments, fought for this great prize, the world leadership in finance and industry. In this game America seemed to have most of the winning cards and trumps, but long experience and good play were on the side of England.

The war debts added to the bitterness between the two Powers, and Americans were cursed in England for being Shylocks after their pound of flesh. As a matter of fact the American debt was due from the British Government to private bankers who had lent the money, or advanced credit, during war-time. The United States Government had merely guaranteed it. It was thus not a question of the U.S. Government wiping off the debt. If England were excused from paying it, the U.S. Government, who were the guarantors, would have to pay it. The American Congress saw no reason why they should undertake this additional liability, especially in time of crisis.

Thus the economic interests of England and America pulled in different ways, and the pull of economic interest is stronger than any other pull. There is so much in common between the two peoples, and yet there is this inevitable conflict, in which the strength and resources of the United States are far greater. The conflict may result in acuter forms of struggle or, in the alternative, in a gradual but continuous transfer of England's special privileges and dominating position to the United States. To give up a great deal that they value, to lose their ancient prestige as well as the profits of imperialist exploitation, to take a back place in the world, dependent on the good will of America, is no pleasant thought to Englishmen, and they are not likely to submit without a struggle. This is the tragedy of England's present position. All the sources of her old strength are drying up, and the future seems to point inevitably to decline. But, used to dominion for generations, the English people are not prepared to accept this fate, and they are fighting, and will fight, bravely against it.

I have pointed out to you two dominant rivalries in the world to-day, as they go to explain much that is happening. There are, of course, ever so many rivalries; the whole capitalist and imperialist system is based on competition and rivalry.

To go back to our account of the progress of events under the depression. The Rhineland was evacuated by the French in June 1930, much to the relief of the Germans. But it had come too late to be accepted as a sign of good will, and the shadow of the depression darkened everything. As trade conditions worsened money became scarcer with the debtors, and the payment of reparations and debts more difficult, or even impossible. To get over the difficulty of paying, President Hoover had declared a moratorium for a year. Attempts were made to get the whole question of war debts reviewed, but the United States Congress refused to reconsider it. The French Government were equally hard on the question of reparations from Germany. The British Government, being both creditor and debtor, were in favour of wiping off both reparations and debts, and having a clean slate. Each country thought in its own terms, with the result that there was no common action. About the middle of 1931 there was a financial collapse in Germany and bank failures. This led to a crisis in England, who could not meet her liabilities. The country was on the verge of financial collapse also. Under threat of this, the Labour Government was turned out by its own chief MacDonald, who now appeared as the head of a "National Government", which was dominated by conservatives. But even this National Government could not save the pound. About that time there was also a mutiny of the British sailors of the Atlantic Fleet on the question of wage-cuts. This peaceful mutiny had a tremendous effect on Britain and Europe. Memories of the Russian Revolution and the mutinies of the sailors there came to people's minds and put the fear of a coming Bolshevism into them. The British capitalists decided to save their capital before any disaster came, and sent it in large quantities to foreign countries. Patriotism among wealthy people does not apparently stand the strain of a risk to money or vested interest.

As British capital went abroad, the pound fell lower, and at last on September 23, 1931, England had to abandon the gold standard—

that is, in order to save her gold, to separate the pound from gold. Henceforth no one who had pounds sterling could claim to be paid in gold, as he could before.

This devaluation of the pound was a tremendous event from the point of view of the British Empire and England's world position. It meant the abandonment, at least for the time being, of the financial leadership which had made London the centre and capital of the world in money matters. To preserve this England had reverted to the gold standard in 1925, even at the cost of loss to her industry, and had faced unemployment, coal strike, etc. But all this had been of no avail, and the pound was forced away from gold by the actions of other countries. This seemed to mark the beginning of the end of the British Empire, and so it was interpreted the world over. The date, September 23, 1931, became quite important as fixing this historic event.

But England was a tough fighter, and had still a dependent and helpless empire to draw upon. She recovered from the crisis largely by drawing out gold from India and Egypt, two countries under her full control. Her industries benefited by the fall of the pound, as she could sell her goods cheaper abroad. It was a remarkable recovery.

The question of reparations and war debts still remained. It was obvious that Germany could not pay reparations, and indeed she formally refused to do so. At last, at a conference held in Lausanne in 1932, reparations were reduced to a nominal figure in the hope and expectation that the United States would reduce debts similarly also. But the U.S. Government refused to mix up debts with reparations or to write off the former. This upset the apple-cart again, and people in Europe were very angry with America.

The time for payment of the instalments due to the United States came in December 1932, and America insisted on them despite eloquent pleading on behalf of England, France, etc. After a great deal of argument, England paid up, but said it was for the last time. France and some other countries refused to pay and defaulted. No fresh settlement followed this, and last month, in June 1933, the payment of the next instalment of the debt became due. France again refused to pay; America was, however, generous to England and accepted a token payment of a small sum, leaving the larger question to be decided later.[1]

In this connection, when great and rich capitalist Powers like England and France are trying to get out of the debts they owe, according to their own standards and system, it is interesting to think of the Soviet repudiation of debts which has been so strongly condemned by them. In India also a cry of pious horror goes up from government circles when it is suggested, as has been done on behalf of the Congress, that an impartial tribunal should consider

---

[1] During the next five years, from 1933 to 1938, no further payment of debt to the United States was made by England or France. Not even token payments were made. It seems to be taken for granted that the debt can be ignored and will not be paid.

the whole question of India's debt to England. A similar question of the payment of a nation's liabilities has led to serious friction between Ireland and England, and to a trade war between them which is still going on.

I have repeatedly referred above to England's financial leadership and America's fight for it, and to banking crises, and to the collapse financially of various countries. What does all this jargon mean? You may well ask, for I doubt if you understand it. Perhaps the subject does not interest you. But now that I have said so much about it, I feel I ought to try to explain it more fully. Whether we are interested or not, we are vastly influenced, both nationally and individually, by these financial happenings, and it is as well to understand something that moulds our present and future. Many people look upon the financial system of the capitalist world with awe and reverence, so impressed are they by its mysterious workings. It seems to them too intricate and delicate and complicated for them even to try to understand it, and so they leave it to experts and bankers and the like. It is undoubtedly intricate and complicated, and to be complicated is not necessarily a virtue in anything, but still we must have some idea of it if we are to understand our present world. I am not going to try to explain the whole system to you. That is more than I can do, for I am no expert at it, and am just a learner. I shall just tell you a few facts, which I hope will help you to follow intelligently some of the world happenings and the news that we see in the papers. I shall probably have to repeat much that I have already said, but you will not mind that if it helps to make you understand. Remember that this is the capitalist system, with its private companies with shares, its private banks, and stock exchanges where shares are bought and sold. In the Soviet Union the financial and industrial system is quite different. There are no such companies or private banks or stock exchanges there; almost everything is owned and controlled by the State, and foreign trade is essentially barter.

You know that within each country business is carried on almost entirely by means of cheques and, to a lesser extent, bank-notes; gold and silver are seldom used except for petty purchases (gold indeed is hardly obtainable). This paper money represents credit, and it serves the purpose of hard cash so long as people have confidence in the banks or the government of the country issuing the currency notes. But this paper money is no good in making payments from one country to another, as each country has its own national currency. The basis of international payments is therefore gold, which has an intrinsic value as a rare metal, either gold coins or uncoined gold (bullion it is called in the mass) being used. But if the actual gold had to be used for every payment from one country to another, it would be a tremendous nuisance, and international trade could hardly develop. Besides, the amount of actual gold available in the world would limit the amount or value of international trade, for when this limit was reached, there being no more gold available for payments, no further foreign trade transactions could take place till some of the gold was released and brought back.

But this is not so.   In 1929 the total gold money in the world was eleven thousand million dollars.   In the same year the total value of goods sent from one country to another was thirty-two thousand million dollars;   there were also foreign loans amounting to four thousand million;   and other foreign payments, like tourist expenditure, freight charges, money sent home by emigrants, etc., also amounting to about four thousand million.   Thus the total international payments amounted to about forty thousand million dollars, which is nearly four times the total amount of gold money.

How were foreign payments made then?   Obviously all of them could not be made in gold.   Usually they were made in a kind of auxiliary money, or credit papers like cheques or bills of exchange, which merchants sent abroad in acknowledgment of their debts. This business was done through the medium of banks doing exchange business.   The exchange bank would be in touch with buyers and sellers in different countries and would adjust its payments and receipts through the bills of exchange received by it.   If the bank ran short of bills of exchange at any moment, it could make payments by means of well-known securities, such as government bonds or loans or shares in international companies.   These shares could be sold or transferred by a telegraphic message, and so payment could be made at the other end immediately.

Thus actual payments in international trade are made through the medium of the central exchange banks by means of commercial paper (bills of exchange, etc.) and financial paper (securities, etc.). These banks must keep a big supply of both these kinds of paper, bills of exchange and securities, to meet the day-to-day needs of business.   They publish weekly lists showing how much gold and such foreign paper they have got.   Ordinarily gold will never be sent abroad for payment abroad.   But whenever it so happens that it is actually cheaper to send gold abroad than to make payment in any other way, then the banker will send gold metal.

In the gold-standard countries the value of the national currency was fixed in terms of gold, and any one could demand payment in gold.   These currencies therefore were practically fixed and interchangeable, as they could be converted into gold.   The only possible variation was the cost of sending the gold metal from one country to another, for if the price in his own country was higher, a business man could easily get the gold from another country.   This was the gold-standard system.   Under this system different national currencies were stable, and international trade grew up in the nineteenth century, right up to the World War.   This system has broken down to-day, and, in consequence, money has behaved strangely, and most national currencies are unstable.

The exports of a country roughly balance its imports.   In other words, a country pays for the goods it receives by the goods it sends abroad.   But this is not quite true, and often there is a small balance either way, when the imports are greater in value than the exports;

this is called an " adverse balance ", and the country has to make an
extra payment to settle accounts.

The stream of goods moving between the different countries is
by no means a regular one. It changes frequently and there are
ups and downs, and as this varies, the demand for and supply of
bills of exchange also vary. It often happens that a country has
plenty of bills of exchange of a kind that it does not need at the
time, and not enough of another kind that it needs. Thus France
may have more than enough bills of exchange in German marks
in Germany, but not enough to settle accounts in dollars with
America. France would then want to sell the former and buy
instead bills in dollars on the United States. To be able to do this
there must be a central market for bills of exchange where these
international exchanges can take place. Such a market can only
exist in a country which has three qualifications :

1. Its foreign trade must be widespread and of a varied kind, so
that it has an abundant supply of bills of exchange of all kinds.

2. Securities of every kind must be available there—that is, it
must be the greatest market for capital.

3. It must also be the greatest market for gold, so that in case
both bills of exchange and securities are lacking, gold may be easily
procurable.

Right through the nineteenth century, England was the only
country which satisfied those three conditions. Being first in the
field in industry and having a large empire as a monopoly area, she
developed the biggest volume of foreign trade in the world. To
her growing industry she sacrificed her agriculture. Her ships
carried merchandise and bills of exchange from every port. Because
of this great industrial development, she naturally became the
greatest market for capital and accumulated all kinds of foreign
securities. Another factor that helped her was the presence of
two-thirds of the gold supply of the world within the British Empire
—in South Africa, Australia, Canada, and India. These gold mines
found a ready market in London, where the Bank of England bought
all the gold they produced at a fixed price.

Thus the City of London became the central market for bills of
exchange, securities, and gold. It became the financial capital of
the world, and every government or banker who wanted to settle an
account abroad and could not find the means to do so in his own
country came to London, where he found every kind of commercial
and financial paper as well as gold. The pound sterling became the
solid symbol of commerce. If Denmark or Sweden wanted to
buy something from South America, the contract was made out
pounds sterling although the goods never came to London.

This was a tremendously profitable business for England, for the
whole world paid some tribute to her for this service. There were
the direct profits ; and then foreign business houses kept balances
or receipts on deposit in English banks with a view to future payments. These deposits were profitably lent out by these banks to
other clients for short periods. The English banks also got to

know all about the business of foreign industrialists. From the bills of exchange that passed through their hands they found out the prices charged by German or other foreign business men, and even the names of their clients in foreign countries. This information was very useful to British industry, for it enabled it to cut out its foreign competitors.

To increase and strengthen this international business, English banks opened branches and agencies all over the world. Apart from helping to bring foreign countries under the influence of British industry, these banks performed another very useful service from the British point of view. They made inquiries and kept records about all the well-known local firms and businesses. So that when such a local firm issued a bill of exchange, the British bank or agent on the spot knew the worth of this bill, and could guarantee it if he thought it safe. This was called "accepting" it, as the bank wrote "accepted" on it. As soon as the bank assumed responsibility for it, the bill could easily be sold or transferred, as it had the bank's reputation behind it. Without such a guarantee or acceptance the bill of exchange of an unknown foreign firm would not find any buyers in a distant market like London or elsewhere, as no one would know the firm. The bank accepting the bill took a risk in doing so, but it did so after full inquiry through its branch offices on the spot. In this way this system of "acceptances" helped to facilitate the transfer of bills of exchange and business generally, and at the same time tightened the grip of the City of London on world trade. No other country was in a position to do this acceptance work on a large enough scale, as none had many branches abroad.

Thus, for over 100 years London was the financial and economic capital of the world, and all the strings of international finance and trade passed through her hands. Money was abundant there, and, because of this, could be had on cheaper terms. This attracted all bankers there. To the Governor of the Bank of England came all the information about trade and finance from the four corners of the world, and, by a glance at his books and papers, he could tell what the economic condition of any country was. Indeed, he sometimes knew more about it than the government of that country. And by little dodges of buying or selling securities in which a foreign government was interested, or by the way short-term loans were given, pressure could be brought to bear on the political policy of this foreign government. High Finance, as this was called, was, and still is, one of the most effective of the methods of coercion of the imperialist Powers.

Such was the state of affairs before the World War. The City of London was the seat and symbol of the power and prosperity of the British Empire. The war brought many changes and upset the old order. It brought a great victory, but a victory which cost London and England dear.

What happened after the war I shall tell you in my next letter.

187

THE DOLLAR, THE POUND, AND THE RUPEE

July 27, 1933

THE World War cut up the world into three parts : the two warring parts and the neutral countries. No trade or other contracts were left between the rival warring areas, except the secret traffic of spying on each other. International trade was, of course, wholly upset. Owing to their command of the seas, the Allies could carry on some trade with neutral countries and colonies, but even this was greatly restricted by the German submarine campaign.

All the resources of the warring countries went into the war, and huge sums were spent. For nearly a year and a half England and France financed their poorer allies, both of them borrowing money from their own people as well as running up bills in America. Then France was exhausted and could not help others. England carried on the burden for another year and a quarter, and in its turn became exhausted in March 1917, when it was unable to meet a payment of £50,000,000 due to the United States. Fortunately for England and France and their Allies, America entered the war on their side at this critical moment, when no one else had any financial resources left. From then onwards till the end of the war, the United States supplied the funds for the war to all their Allies. They raised prodigious sums from their own people in " Liberty " and " Victory " loans, and spent these lavishly themselves and lent them to the Allies. The result was, as I have told you, that when the war ended, the United States were the world's money-lenders, to whom all the nations owed money. When the war began, the American Government owed Europe five thousand million dollars; when the war ended Europe owed America ten thousand million dollars.

This was not the only financial gain of America during the war. American foreign trade had grown at the expense of English and German trade, and now equalled British trade. . The United States had also accumulated two-thirds of the world's gold, and an enormous amount of foreign government stocks and bonds.

The United States were thus in an overpowering financial position. They could reduce any of their debtor countries to bankruptcy by simply demanding payment of their debts. It was natural therefore that they should envy London's old position of financial world capital and desire it for themselves. They wanted New York, the richest city in the world, to take the place of London. Thus began a fierce struggle between the bankers and financiers of New York and London, backed by their governments.

Pressure from America shook the English pound. The Bank of England was unable to deliver gold on its currency, and the pound sterling (which was thus off the gold standard) began to vary and fall. The French franc also fell. In an unstable world only the American dollar seemed to be firm as a rock.

One would have thought that under these circumstances the money business and gold would have turned away from London and gone to New York. But, strange to say, this did not happen, and foreign bills of exchange and the gold from the mines still went to London. This was not because people preferred the pound to the dollar, but because dollars were not easily available.

You will remember my telling you of the system of " acceptances " which the British banks worked all over the world through branches and agencies. The American banks had no such branches or foreign agencies, and so they had no means at their disposal of getting the foreign bills of exchange by " accepting " them, and naturally the bills drifted to London through the British banks. Coming up against this difficulty, American bankers immediately set about opening branches and agencies in foreign countries, and fine buildings grew up in many places. But there was yet another difficulty. The work of " acceptances " could only be done by a trained personnel who had full information about local conditions and local business. British banks had built up their service in 100 years of growth, and it was not easy to catch them up in this respect quickly.

The Americans then combined with some French, Swiss, and Dutch banks against London, but with no great success. France, although a very rich country exporting a great deal of capital abroad, had never paid attention to organizing a traffic in foreign bills of exchange. So the tussle between New York and the city of London went on, and on the whole the latter was not affected. In 1924 a new factor in favour of New York appeared. The German mark was stabilized after the great inflation was over, and German capital which had run away to Switzerland and Holland during the inflation (capital always runs away in times of risk or danger !) returned to German banks. The addition of Germany now to the American financial *bloc* made a great deal of difference to London. For now vast numbers of American bills of exchange could be exchanged for European bills of exchange without reference to London. And London had still an unstable currency—that is, the pound had no fixed gold value; it was off the gold standard.

The financiers of the City of London were now alarmed. They saw all the good business in international exchange going over to New York and its European allies, and London having only the leavings. The first thing to be done to prevent this happening was to fix up the pound again in relation to gold—that is, to stabilize it. This would again attract good exchange business. So in 1925 the pound was stabilized at the old level. This was a great triumph for the English bankers and creditors, for a more valuable pound meant a bigger income for them. It was bad for English industry, as it raised the prices of English goods abroad, and industrialists found great difficulty in competing with America, Germany, and other industrial countries on the foreign market. But England deliberately sacrificed to some extent her industry to her banking system, or rather to her financial supremacy in the world exchange market. The prestige of the pound went up, but you will remember that this was followed in England by domestic troubles due partly to the blow to industry. There was unemployment and the long-drawn-out Coal-Strike and the General Strike.

The pound was stabilized, but this was not enough. The British Government owed an enormous sum of money to America, which was a floating debt and could be demanded back at almost any time. By making such a demand the United States could put England in a very difficult position and force the pound down again. So the leading British statesmen (among them Stanley Baldwin) rushed to New York to come to terms with America about the repayment of the war debt in instalments ("funding", this process is called). All the European countries were America's debtors, and the proper course for them would have been to consult together and then approach the United States for the best terms that they could get. But the British Government were so anxious to save the pound and keep London's financial leadership that they had no time to consult France or Italy and wanted some arrangement with America quickly and at any cost. They got the arrangement, but at a heavy cost, and they agreed to the severe conditions laid down by the United States Government. Subsequently France and Italy got far better terms from the United States for their debts.

These strenuous efforts and sacrifices saved the pound and the City of London, but the struggle with New York continued in all the world markets. Having an abundance of money, New York offered long-term loans at low interest, and many countries which used to borrow in the London money market (including Canada, South Africa and Australia) were thus enticed away to New York. London could not compete in these long-term loans with New York, and it thereupon tried giving short-term loans to the banks of Central Europe. In short-term loans the banker's experience and prestige count for more, and this was in favour of London. So London banks established close relations with Viennese banks and through them with the banks in central and south-eastern Europe (the Danube and Balkan areas). New York also continued to do some business there.

This was a period of frenzied finance when, partly because of the competition of London and New York, money poured into Europe, and millionaires and multi-millionaires cropped up with amazing rapidity. The way things were done was simple. Some enterprising person would get a concession in one of these countries to build railways or other public works, or a monopoly like that of the manufacture and sale of matches. A company would be formed to hold this concession or monopoly, and this would issue stock or shares. On the basis of this stock or shares the big banks in New York or London would give advances. Financiers would thus borrow money in dollars in New York at 2 per cent. and then lend this in Berlin at 6 per cent. and in Vienna at 8 per cent. By this clever shifting about of other people's money these financiers became very wealthy. One of the most famous of them was Ivan Kreugar, a Swede who was known as the Match King because of his monopoly in matches. Kreugar had tremendous prestige at one time, but it was later proved that he was a thorough fraud and that he embezzled huge sums of money. He committed suicide when he was on the point of being found out. Several other famous financiers of the time also got into trouble because of their shady methods.

This Anglo-American competition in central and eastern Europe did one good. The money that was poured in contributed greatly to the revival of Europe during the years before the depression began in 1929.

Meanwhile France had had an inflation in 1926 and 1927, and the franc had fallen greatly in value. Frenchmen with money—and every French petty *bourgeois* has his savings—sent their money abroad for fear of losing it as the franc fell. They bought a vast quantity of foreign securities and foreign bills of exchange. In 1927 the franc was stabilized again and fixed in relation to gold, but at about one-fifth of its previous value. The French holders of foreign securities were now all keen on changing them for something in francs. They had done a good stroke of business, for now they were getting five times as many francs as they possessed originally, and thus they had not suffered at all from the inflation, as they would have done if they had stuck to francs right through. The French Government decided to profit by the occasion, and it bought up all such foreign bills of exchange or securities, giving instead freshly printed bills in francs. Thus the French Government suddenly became very wealthy in the possession of these foreign bills and securities—in fact, it possessed at that time the greatest number of them. It had no desire or sufficient qualification to become a competitor with England and America for financial leadership. But it was in a position to influence both.

The French are a cautious people, and so is their government. They prefer small profits and safety to the chance of big profits with the risk of losing even what they have. So, cautiously, the French Government lent out its superfluous money to good firms in London at a low rate of interest. Thus they would only charge the British bank 2 per cent. interest; the British would pass on the money at 5 or 6 per cent. to German banks, who in their turn would advance it to Vienna at 8 or 9 per cent., and finally the money might reach Hungary or the Balkans at 12 per cent ! The rate of interest increased with the risk, but the Bank of France preferred to face no risk and to deal with safe British banks. In this way France kept a very large sum of money (consisting of the foreign sterling bills of exchange it had bought up) in London, and this helped London in its fight against New York.

Meanwhile the trade crisis and depression had been growing and agricultural prices falling. Wheat prices fell so long in the autumn of 1930 that banks in eastern Europe could not realize moneys from their debtors, and so could not pay back the money they had borrowed in pounds and dollars in Vienna. This led to a banking crisis in Vienna, and the greatest Viennese bank, the Credit-Anstalt, failed and collapsed. This again shook up the German banks, and a collapse of the mark seemed to be imminent. This would have meant danger to American and British capital in Germany, and it was to avoid this that President Hoover proclaimed a moratorium on debts and reparations. To have insisted on payment of reparations then would have meant the complete financial collapse of Germany. As it happened, even this was not enough, and Germany could not even pay her private debts to other countries and a moratorium for these had also to be given her.

This meant that plenty of English money, which had been given in short-term loans to Germany, was locked up there—" frozen " as it is called. The position of the London bankers became difficult, as they had to meet their liabilities, and they had been counting on getting their money from Germany. France and America came to their help by lending £130,000,000, but this came too late. Panic spread in London financial circles, and when such a panic occurs everybody wants to take out his money. The £130,000,000 vanished quickly. You must remember that the pound was on the gold standard, and anyone who had sterling could demand gold.

The British Government, which was a Labour Government at the time, wanted to borrow more money, and anxiously asked New York and Paris bankers for it. It appears that they agreed to help subject to certain conditions, one of these being that the British Government must economize in labour matters, in social services, etc., and perhaps wage-cuts were also suggested. This was interference by foreign bankers in Britain's domestic affairs. The situation was exploited against the Labour Government, and Ramsay MacDonald, the Prime Minister and head of that government, betrayed it and his own party, and formed another government with the support chiefly of the Conservatives. This was called the " National Government " formed to meet the crisis. This action of Ramsay MacDonald is one of the most remarkable instances of desertion in the history of the European labour movement.

The National Government had come in to save the pound. It got the promised loan from France and America, but even with its help it could not save the pound. On September 23, 1931, the government was forced to abandon the gold standard and the pound again became unstable currency. The pound fell rapidly and was worth only about 14s. in gold—that is, roughly two-thirds of its former value.

This was the event and the date which produced a great impression in the world. It was looked upon by Europe as a sign of the approaching disruption of the British Empire, for it meant the end of London's domination of the world money market. These expectations or wishes (for there is little love for the British Empire in Europe or America, not to mention Asia) proved somewhat premature.

The fall of the pound shook up the currencies of many countries which had kept sterling paper money as if it were gold, because it could be changed for gold at any time. Now that sterling could not be changed for gold and had fallen 30 per cent. in value, the currencies of some of these other countries fell also, and they were dragged down by England to abandon the gold standard.

France was now in a strong position; its cautious policy had paid. While America, and even more so England, had their credits frozen in Germany and were in need of money, France had plenty of money in foreign bills as well as in gold francs. Both the American and British governments made love to France and tried hard to induce her to side with each against the other. But France, over-cautious, refused to fall in with either scheme, and so let the chance of bargaining go by.

In England there was a General Election for Parliament at the end of 1931, and this resulted in an overwhelming victory for the "National Government", in reality for the Conservative Party. The Labour Party was almost wiped out. Frightened by stories that Labour might confiscate their capital, and perhaps also terrified by the short-lived mutiny of the British sailors of the Atlantic Fleet over wage reductions, the British *bourgeoisie* flocked to the Conservative National Government.

In spite of crisis and danger, after the fall of the pound, the three leading nations, America, Britain, and France, or their bankers, could not co-operate together. Each played a lone hand, hoping to better its own position at the cost of the others. Instead of fighting for financial leadership, they could have joined together to form a joint international exchange market. But each preferred to go its own way. The Bank of England set out to recover for London its lost position and, to the world's astonishment, it succeeded to a large extent in doing so, although the pound was still off gold.

When England went off the gold standard, the official banks of other countries (these banks are called central banks) sold off the sterling bills of exchange that they possessed to get gold instead. They had kept the sterling bills so far because they were at any time changeable into gold, and could thus be counted as gold. When large numbers of these bills were sold suddenly, the value of the pound fell rapidly by 30 per cent. This fall in value induced debtors (including some governments and big businesses) who owed their debts in sterling to pay up in gold, as they had to pay 30 per cent. less now. A good deal of gold thus came into England.

But the real flow of gold to England was from India and Egypt. These poor and dependent countries were made to come to rich England's assistance, and their hidden resources were utilized to strengthen England's financial position. They had not much say in the matter; their desire or interests counted for little in face of England's need.

The story of the poor rupee in India is a long and sad one from India's point of view. It has been made to change about in value repeatedly to serve the interests of the British Government and British financiers. I am not going into these currency matters here, except to tell you that the post-war activities of the British Govern-

ment in India in regard to currency matters cost India vast sums of
money.   Then in 1927 a great controversy arose in India about the
fixing of the value of the rupee in relation to the pound sterling and
gold (the pound was then on the gold standard).   This was called
the " ratio controversy ", because the government wanted to fix
the value at one shilling and sixpence and Indian opinion almost
unanimously wanted it fixed at one shilling and fourpence.   The
question was the old one of giving a higher value to money, and thus
profiting bankers and creditors and holders of money and encouraging foreign imports, or a lower value and lessening the burden on
debtors and encouraging home industries and exports.   The
government, of course, had its way in spite of Indian opinion, and
one and six was fixed as the gold rupee value.   There was thus, in
the opinion of many, a slight deflation, an over-valuation of the
rupee.   Only England had gone in for deflation, when bringing the
pound on the gold standard in 1925, and this was, as we have seen,
to retain her financial leadership of the world, for which she was
prepared to sacrifice much.   France, Germany, and other countries
preferred inflation to ease their economic situation.

This higher value of the rupee meant an increased value of the
British capital invested in India.   It also meant a burden on Indian
industry, as the prices of Indian goods went up slightly.   Above all,
it meant an added burden on all the peasants and landowners who
were indebted to the moneylender, for, as the value of money went
up, the value of these debts also went up.   The difference between
eighteen pence and sixteen pence—that is twopence—represented a
rise of $12\frac{1}{2}$ per cent.   Suppose the agricultural indebtedness of
India is 10,000 million rupees ; a $12\frac{1}{2}$ per cent, addition to it means
an addition of the enormous sum of 1250 million rupees.

In terms of money, of course, the debts remained the same as
before.   But in terms of prices of agricultural produce the debts
went up.   The real value of money is what it will buy, so much
wheat, or clothes, or other articles or commodities.   This value
adjusts itself if allowed to do so.   A fall in the buying power of
money results in a fall in currency.   To fix an artificially higher
value is to give it an artificial buying power which it does not really
possess.   Thus the peasant found that more of his income now went
to the payment of his debts and interest on them, and he had less
left over.   In this way the one and six ratio added to the depression
in India.

When the pound sterling was forced off gold in September 1931,
the rupee also went off, but it was kept tied to the pound.   Thus the
one and six ratio remained, but this now represented a smaller
amount of gold.   The rupee was kept linked to sterling so that
British capital might not suffer in India, for if the rupee had been
left to itself, it might have fallen lower, and thus caused loss to sterling capital.   As it was, loss was only caused to non-British foreign
capital in India—American, Japanese, etc., because of the lesser
gold value.   Another great advantage to England in having the
rupee linked with the pound was that this enabled her to pay for

raw material purchased for her industries in British currency. The
bigger the sterling area, the better for the pound.

As the rupee fell in value with the pound, the internal price of
gold naturally went up—that is, gold could fetch more rupees.
The great hardships and privation in the country induced people
to sell whatever gold they possessed in the shape of ornaments, etc.,
to get more rupees for it in order to pay their debts.   So gold flowed
in innumerable tiny streamlets from all over the country to the
banks, and the banks made a profit by selling it on the London
market.   In this way Indian gold flowed continuously to England
and a vast quantity was sent.   The process still continues.   It is
this gold, as well as the gold that came from Egypt, that saved the
situation for the Bank of England and British finance, and enabled
them to pay back the money borrowed in September 1931 from
America and France.

Now, it is a strange fact that while every country in the world,
including the richest countries, is trying hard to keep its own gold
and to add to it, India is doing the very opposite.   The American
and French governments have hoarded up a huge amount of gold
in their bank vaults.   It has been a strange process of digging out
the gold from the mine only to bury it again deep down in the
underground bank vaults.   Many countries, including British
Dominions, have declared embargoes on gold—that is, no one is
permitted to take it out of the country.   England went off
the gold standard to preserve her gold.   But not so India, because
India's financial policy is governed in the interests of England.

There is often talk of gold and silver hoarding in India, and to
some extent, among the handful of the rich, this is correct.   But
the masses are far too poor to hoard anything.   The better-class
peasantry have a few odd ornaments which represent their " hoard ".
They have no banking facilities.   These petty ornaments and reserves of gold in India have been drawn away by the depression
and the rise in the price of gold.   A national government would
have kept this gold in the country as a reserve, as gold is the only
recognized international medium of payment.

To go back to our story of the pound's struggle with the dollar.
By these methods and other clever devices, which I need not mention here, the Bank of England strengthened its position greatly.
Early in 1932 it had a bit of luck, as there was a banking crisis in
the United States owing to American money also being frozen in
Germany.   During this crisis many Americans sold their dollars and
bought sterling bonds.   Thus the British Government got plenty of
foreign bills of exchange in dollars, which it then presented in New
York to the government bank there and took gold instead.   The
dollar being on the gold standard, anyone could demand gold for it.
In this way the British gold reserve mounted up without any
mishap or further decline of the pound, which remained unstable
and off gold.   With plenty of foreign bills of exchange and securities
also, the City of London became again the great central market of
international exchange.   New York was defeated for the time being,

chiefly because of its great banking crisis, in which, as I have told
you in an earlier letter, thousands of small banks perished.

188

THE CAPITALIST WORLD FAILS TO PULL
TOGETHER

July 28, 1933

WHAT a long story of financial rivalry and manœuvring I have
told you, and I am afraid you will not thank me for it ! It is such a
tangled web of international intrigue that it is no easy matter to
unravel it or, having entered it, to get out of it. I have only tried
to give you the barest glimpse of what appears more or less on the
surface, and much of what happens never sees the surface or the light
of day.

In the modern world the banker's and financier's part is a tremendous one. Even the days of the lords of industry are past ; it is the
big banker who controls industry, agriculture, railways, and the
transport system, indeed, to some extent everything, including the
government. For as industry and trade have advanced they have
required ever-increasing sums, and the banks have supplied them.
Much of the world's work is now done on credit, and it is the big bank
that enlarges or restricts and controls credit. The industrialist and
the agriculturist both have to go to the bank for loans of money to
carry on work. Not only is this lending business a profitable one
for the bankers, but it increases their control gradually over industry
and agriculture. By refusing to lend or by demanding their money
back at a critical moment, they can upset the borrower's business or
force him to agree to any terms. This applies both within a country
and in the international sphere, for the big central banks lend money
to the governments of different countries, and thus exercise pressure
on them. New York bankers in this way control many of the governments of Central and South America.

A remarkable feature of these big banks is that they prosper both
in good times and bad. In good times they share in the general
prosperity of business, and money rolls in, and is lent out by them at
profitable rates. In bad times of depression and crises they hold
tight to money and do not risk it (and thus add to the depression for
without credit it is difficult to run many businesses), but they profit
in another way. Prices of everything fall—of land, factories, etc.—
and many industries go bankrupt. The bank thereupon comes and
buys everything up cheap ! It is thus to the bankers' interest to
have cycles of prosperity and depression.

In the present great depression the big banks have continued to do
well and have paid good dividends. It is true that thousands of
banks have failed in the United States, and some big ones in Austria

and Germany. The banks that have failed in America were all small ones; the American banking system seems to have been wrong. But even so the big banks of New York have done fairly well. There was no bank failure in England.

Bankers therefore are the real bosses in the capitalist world to-day, and people have called our times the " Financial Age ", coming after the purely Industrial Age. Millionaires and multi-millionaires crop up in Western countries, and especially in America, the land of millionaires, and are much admired. But daily it is becoming more evident that the methods of " high finance " are most shady, and differ from what is usually considered robbery and deception only in the big scale of their operations. Huge monopolies crush all small concerns, and big financial operations, which few people can understand, fleece the poor confiding investor. Some of the biggest financiers in Europe and America have been exposed recently, and the sight was not a pleasant one.

We have seen that the struggle for financial leadership between England and America ended for the time being in the City of London's victory. But what was the prize of this victory ? While the struggle had gone on for a dozen years this prize itself had been gradually vanishing. As international trade declined, the profits attaching to financial leadership also declined. Bills of exchange became scarcer, and, at the same time, securities fell in value, and fresh shares and securities were seldom issued. And yet the interest payments on huge public and private debts remained constant, and the debtor countries found it exceedingly difficult to pay them. There being little else available for international payments, the demand for gold increased. But gold flowed away from the poor countries to the richer ones with stabler currencies.

But all the accumulation of gold and wealth, and the latest technique of industry, did not help America much when the depression grew. The great land of opportunity, which had attracted men and women from afar, became a land of despair. Big Business, which had ruled the country, was found to be thoroughly corrupt, and confidence in the leaders of finance and industry was shaken. President Hoover, who had been the friend of Big Business, became very unpopular, and at the presidential election held in November 1932, he was defeated by Franklin Roosevelt.

Early in March 1933 another banking crisis attacked America. This led the United States to abandon the gold standard and to allow the dollar to fall in value, although America had more gold than any other country. The object of this was to lessen the burden on industry and agriculture and to relieve the debtors at the cost of the banks and the creditors. This was the exact opposite of what the British Government had done in India, in spite of the unanimous opposition of the Indian people.

In June 1933 another attempt was made to get the capitalist world to co operate together for the solution of the many problems that were crushing it. A World Economic Conference was held in London, and delegates to it talked of the " panic-ridden world "

and issued warnings that " if the conference fails, the whole capitalist
structure will go smash ".   But in spite of all these warnings and
dangers, the great Powers could not co-operate, and each tried to
pull its own way.   The Conference failed, and left each country to
pursue its policy of economic nationalism.

It was impossible for England to be self-sufficient, as she did not
grow enough food for herself, and the raw materials for her industries
came from abroad.   So the British Government tried to develop
economic nationalism on an empire basis, trying to make the British
Empire one economic unit based on sterling prices.   With this idea
in view, a British Empire Conference was held in Ottawa in 1932.
But even there difficulties arose, as Canada, Australia, and South
Africa were not prepared to give up anything for the benefit of England.   It was England that had to concede their demands.   India,
however, was officially made to agree to give preferential treatment
to British goods, although there was strong popular opposition to
this.   Subsequent events have shown that the Ottawa Agreement
has not been a success, and there has been much friction over it,
both between the Dominions and England, and India and England.

Meanwhile a new terror arose for Empire industries and markets.
Cheap Japanese goods flooded in everywhere, and they were so
exceedingly cheap that even tariffs could not keep them out.   This
cheapness was due to the fall of the yen, as well as to the low wages
paid to the girl factory-workers in Japan.   Japanese industry was
also helped by government subsidies, and by Japanese shipping
companies charging very low freights.   It was also a fact that Japanese industry was very efficient, which many of the older British
industries were not.

Tariffs failing to keep out Japanese goods, markets were definitely
closed to them or a quota system was introduced, under which only
a limited quantity of goods was allowed in.   If Japanese goods
were thus to be shut out from other countries, what was to happen to
Japan's enormous industries ?   Her whole economic system would
be upset, and attempts to find outlets would lead to economic
reprisals, and even to war.   This is the inevitable course of events
under the wasteful competition of capitalism.

In the same way if the British markets were closed to the other
countries of Europe, it would mean the ruin of some of these countries.
So that we find that all the steps that each country takes for its own
immediate good hurt other countries and international trade, and
lead to friction and trouble.

189

REVOLUTION IN SPAIN

July 29, 1933

I SHALL take you away now from the long and depressing account of the trade slump and crisis, and tell you of two outstanding events of recent times. These two events are : the revolution in Spain and the triumph of the Nazis in Germany.

Spain and Portugal form the south-western corner of Europe, and, as we have seen, they have played an important part in European and world history. They exhausted themselves in their adventures in empire and, while western Europe progressed industrially and otherwise in the nineteenth century, they remained backward and priestridden. Nationalist Spain had triumphed over Napoleon, but it did not profit by the ideas released by the French Revolution. While France rid herself of feudalism and changed her land system completely, Spain remained semi-feudal, with nobles owning vast estates and having all manner of special privileges. The Roman Catholic Church was dominant, not only in religion, but on the land, in trade, and in education. The Church was the largest landowner, and carried on trade on an extensive scale. Education was completely controlled by it.

The army officers were a caste by themselves with special privileges. The proportion of officers to other ranks was very great ; it was one in seven. Among the intellectuals there were progressive, liberal-minded elements ; and a labour movement, split up into syndicalists, socialists, and anarchists, was growing. But all real power rested with the Church, the Army, and the Nobles. In Catalonia and the Basque country in the north there were strong movements aiming at autonomy.

The governments of both Spain and Portugal were more or less autocratic monarchies with feeble parliamentary assemblies. In Spain this assembly was called the " Cortes ". For a brief period in the early seventies of the nineteenth century, Spain had a republic, but this was not a success, and the king came back again with all his previous autocracy. The Spanish war with the United States of America in 1898 resulted in Spain losing almost the last of her colonies. All the colonial domain that she had left was in part of Morocco, adjoining her.

Portugal has still large colonies in Africa, besides tiny bits of India, like Goa. In 1910 the king was dethroned and a republic was established in Portugal. There have been many revolts since then, both royalist, trying to get back the king, and left-wing, attempting to get rid of dictators and reactionary governments. The Republic has, however, continued, in some form or other, and has usually been dominated by a military group. It took the part of the Allies during the Great War, and came out of it with a heavy debt which brought it near bankruptcy. The present Government is very reactionary

and pro-fascist.   In Goa every public activity is repressed, and there
is a complete denial of civil liberty.

Spain remained neutral during the Great War and profited by
this.   It supplied goods to the warring countries and industrialization spread.   In the after-war years there was a slump and unemployment and social unrest.   About the same time, in 1921, there was the
Riff War in Morocco, in which Abdel Krim completely defeated the
Spanish Army.   But the French came in later and overwhelmed
Abdel Krim and saved Spanish Morocco for Spain.   During the
Moroccan War Primo de Rivera emerged and became dictator in
1923, suspending the constitution.   He continued for six years, but
gradually he lost the confidence of the army and had to resign in
1929 after a financial crisis.   Meanwhile King Alfonso had all the
time been there, supporting reactionary groups and trying to consolidate his own position.

The Spanish people are strongly individualist, and their advanced
groups had often quarrelled with one another.   From the days of
Bakunin, the anarchist philosophy had appealed to the new working
class, and trade unions, after the English or German fashion, had
not been popular.   The Anarcho-Syndicalists formed a strong group,
especially in Catalonia.   Other advanced groups were the liberal-
democrats, the socialists, and a small but growing Communist
Party.   All these groups stood for a republic.   The experience of
Primo de Rivera's dictatorship brought all these republican groups
together, and they began to co-operate with one another.

Success came to them in the municipal elections in 1931, which
resulted in a sweeping republican victory.   This was enough to
frighten the King (who was both a Bourbon and a Hapsburg), and
he left the country hastily.   A republic was proclaimed and a
Provisional Government established on April 14, 1931.   The
revolution had been a peaceful one.

The Spanish Revolution bears a striking resemblance to the first
Russian Revolution, that of March 1917.   The old monarchical
structure, like Tsardom in Russia, was thoroughly rotten, and it
fell to pieces without even an attempt to face its opponents.   In
both cases the revolution represented a belated attempt to wipe out
feudalism and change the land system, the chief pressure coming
from the poverty-stricken peasantry.   In Spain, even more than in
Russia, the power of the Church was felt as a terrible burden.   Both
the revolutions produced unstable conditions, with various classes
pulling in different directions.   There were frequent risings both
from the right and the extreme left.   In Russia this instability led
to the November Revolution; in Spain it still continues.

The new Spanish constitution had some interesting features.
There is only one chamber, the Cortes, and universal suffrage is
provided for.   A unique feature is that the President is forbidden to
declare war without the sanction of the League of Nations.   All
international covenants recorded in the League of Nations and ratified
by Spain become Spanish law immediately, and even overrule
positive legislation that conflicts with them.

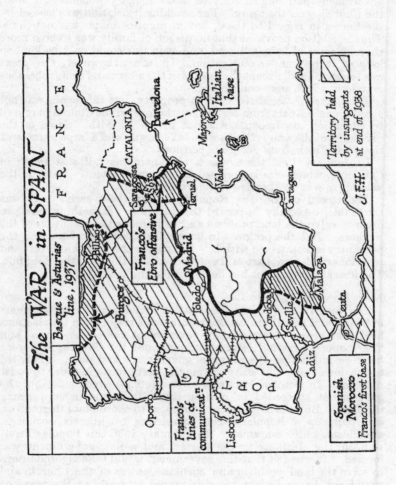

The WAR in SPAIN

FRANCE

Barcelona

Italian base

CATALONIA

Majorca

Saragossa

Valencia

Franco's Ebro offensive

Teruel

Cartagena

Basque & Asturias line, 1937

Bilbao

Madrid

Burgos

Toledo

Cordoba

Malaga

Seville

Ceuta

Franco's lines of communicat*n*

Oporto

P O R T

Cadiz

Lisbon

Spanish Morocco
Franco's first base

Territory held by insurgents at end of 1938

J.F.H.

The government of the new Republic was described as a left-liberal democracy with a tinge of socialism. The Prime Minister and the strong man of the government was Manuel Azana. This government had immediately to face difficult problems—the land, the Church, and the army. Far-reaching legislation was passed by the Cortes in regard to these, but in practice much was not done. Thus legislation provided that no person or family was to hold more than 25 acres of irrigated land, and even this could only be kept so long as it was under cultivation. In effect, however, the great estates continued, except the estates of the crown and some rebellious grandees, which were confiscated.

The Cortes nationalized Church property, but this again was not acted upon. Apart from certain restrictions on the Church in regard to education, its freedom was not interfered with. Some of the privileges of the army officers were taken away and a large number of them were retired on generous pensions.

In January 1932 there was a big anarcho-syndicalist rising in Catalonia, which was suppressed by the government. Later in the year there was an abortive rising from the right.

The record of the new Republic during these early years was creditable, especially in regard to education. Something was also done to solve the land problem and to improve the condition of the workers. But the progress in land reform has been slow and the peasantry is dissatisfied with it. Meanwhile the vested interests and reactionary elements are still entrenched and threaten the Republic. The liberal government has dealt with them leniently.

Note (November 1938) :
The year 1933 saw the consolidation of the reactionary elements in Spain, and this Right coalition obtained a majority in the elections held that year. A reactionary government came into power, and this stopped agrarian reform, strengthened the Church, and went back on much that the previous government had done. This led to the development of unity among the Left groups in order to resist reaction. In October 1934 there were riots all over Spain, but the government succeeded in putting them down and in suppressing the Left. But the Left forces continued to consolidate themselves, and built up a Popular Front consisting of liberals, socialists, anarchists, and communists. In February 1936 this Popular Front won in the elections to the Cortes, and a new government was formed. It was felt that this government would take vigorous steps to solve the land problem and curb the power of the Church, and would not be so lenient towards vested interests as the previous liberal administration had been. Conflict therefore grew, and the forces of reaction decided to strike. They obtained support from Mussolini and Nazi Germany.

In July 1936 General Franco started the rebellion in Spanish Morocco with the help of the Moorish army which was promised the independence of Spanish Morocco. The army officers and the greater part of the army were with Franco, and the government appeared defenceless.   Thereupon the government called upon the masses to fight, with bare fists if nothing else was available.   There was a splendid response to this, especially in Madrid and Barcelona. The government and the Republic were saved, but Franco took possession of large parts of Spain.

Since then the war has gone on, Franco being aided to a very great extent by Italy and Germany, who sent large armies, aeroplanes and aviators and ammunition.   The Republic also had foreign volunteers to help it, but at the same time it built up a magnificent new Spanish army.   The British and French Governments have stated that they follow a policy of non-intervention, but this in effect has helped Franco.

The Spanish War has been full of horror, and vast numbers have been killed by aerial bombardments on open towns and civilian populations by Italian and German aeroplanes in Franco's service. The defence of Madrid has become famous.   At present Franco occupies three-fourths of Spain, but he has been effectively held by the Republic, which, in a military sense, is strong.   Its chief difficulty is lack of food.

The war in Spain has been considered as something much more than a national conflict.   It has become symbolical of the struggle between democracy and fascism and has thus attracted widespread attention and sympathy.

190

THE NAZI TRIUMPH IN GERMANY

July 31, 1933

THE Spanish Revolution surprised some people, but in reality there was nothing surprising in it.   It took place in the natural order of events, and close observers knew that it was inevitable.   The old structure of king-feudalism-Church was moth-eaten, and had no strength left.   It was quite out of keeping with modern conditions and so, like a ripe fruit, it fell down almost at a push.   In India also there are still many such feudal relics of a bygone age; they would probably disappear quickly enough if they were not bolstered up by a foreign Power.

The recent changes in Germany are, however, of a totally different kind, and there is no doubt that they have shaken up Europe and stupefied numbers of people.   That a cultured and highly advanced people like the Germans should have indulged in brutal and barbarous behaviour has been an amazing experience.

Hitler and his Nazis have triumphed in Germany.   They have been called fascist, and their victory a victory of counter-revolution, a going-back on the German revolution of 1918 and what followed it. All this is perfectly true, and you will find all the elements of fascism in Hitlerism, and a fierce reaction, and a savage attack on all liberal elements and especially workers.   And yet it is something much more than just reaction, and something broader and more based on mass sentiment than Italian fascism. That mass sentiment is not that of the workers, but of a starving, dispossessed middle class turned revolutionary.

In a previous letter dealing with Italy I discussed fascism, and I pointed out that it occurred when a capitalist State was threatened during an economic crisis by social revolution. The owning capitalist classes tried to protect themselves by creating a mass movement, round a nucleus of the lower-middle class, using misleading anti-capitalist slogans to attract the unwary peasants and workers. Having seized power and gained control of the State, they scrap all democratic institutions and crush their enemies and especially break up all workers' organizations. Their rule is thus primarily based on violence. The middle-class supporters are given jobs in the new State, and usually some measure of State control of industry is introduced.

We find all this taking place in Germany, and it was even expected. But what is surprising is the tremendous urge behind it, and the numbers of people who joined Hitler.

The Nazi counter-revolution took place in March 1933. But I shall take you a little farther back to watch the beginnings of the movement.

The German Revolution of 1918 was an unreal affair; it was no revolution at all. The Kaiser went and a republic was proclaimed, but the old political, social, and economic system continued. For a few years the Social Democrats controlled the government. They were greatly afraid of the old reactionary and vested interests, and were always trying to compromise with them. They had a tremendously powerful machine behind them in their party, with millions of members, and the trade unions, and they had the sympathy of many others. But their policy was always a defensive one before the reactionary elements; they were only aggressive towards their own extreme wing and the Communist Party. They bungled their job so badly that many of their supporters left them. The workers who left them went over to the Communist Party, which became quite powerful with several million members, and the middle-class supporters went off to join reactionary parties. Between the Social Democrats and the Communists there was continuous war which weakened both.

When the great German inflation came in the post-war years, the German industrialists and big landowners were in favour of it. The landlords, who were heavily in debt, with their estates mortgaged, paid off their debts in the inflated currency, which was almost worthless, and recovered possession of their estates. The big factory-owners improved their plants, and huge trusts were built up. German goods became so cheap that they found a ready market everywhere and unemployment vanished. The working class was strongly organized in trade unions, and it succeeded in keeping up wages even though the mark fell. The inflation hit the middle class and reduced it to abject poverty. It was this dispossessed middle class of

1923–24 that joined Hitler first.   As the depression spread owing to failures of banks and increase of unemployment, many others joined Hitler.   He became a refuge for the discontented.   Another big class he drew from were the officers of the old army.   This army had been disbanded after the war, under the terms of the Treaty of Versailles, and thousands of officers were unemployed and had nothing to do.   They drifted to the various private armies that were growing up—the Nazi " Storm Troops ", as they were called, and the " Steel helmets " of the Nationalists, who were conservatives in favour of the Kaiser's return.

Who was Adolf Hitler ?   Surprising as it is, he was not even a German citizen till a year or two before he came to power.   He was a German-Austrian who had served in the war in a humble capacity. He took part in an abortive rising against the German Republic— a " putsch "—and though sentenced to imprisonment, was leniently treated by the authorities.   He then organized his party called the " National Sozialist " (National Socialist) to oppose the Social Democrats.   The word Nazi comes from this name: Na from *N*ational and zi from So*zi*alist.   Although the party was called socialist, it had absolutely nothing to do with socialism.   Hitler was and is a sworn enemy of socialism as it is ordinarily understood.   The party adopted as a symbol the *swastika*, a Sanskrit word, but the sign has been well known all over the world from ancient times.   This sign, as you know, is very popular in India, and is considered a symbol of auspiciousness.   The Nazis also organized a fighting force, the " Storm Troops ", with a brown shirt for uniform.   The Nazis are thus often called the " Brown-shirts ", just as the Italian Fascists are known as the " Black-shirts ".

The programme of the Nazis was not a clear or a positive one. It was intensely nationalistic, and laid stress on the greatness of Germany and the Germans, and for the rest it was a hotch-potch of various hatreds.   It was against the Treaty of Versailles, which was considered a humiliation for Germany, and this attracted many people to the Nazis.   It was anti-Marxist-Communist-Socialist and opposed to workers' trade unions and the like.   It was anti-Jew because Jews were considered an alien race which defiled and lowered the high standards of the " Aryan " German race.   It was vaguely anti-capitalist, but this only amounted to cursing profiteers and the rich.   The only socialism it talked of rather loosely was a measure of State control.

Behind all this lay an extraordinary philosophy of violence.   Not only was violence praised and encouraged, but it was considered the highest duty of man.   A famous German philosopher, Oswald Spengler, is an exponent of this philosophy.   Man, he says, is a " beast of prey, brave and crafty and cruel ". . . . " Ideals are cowardice." . . . " The animal of prey is the highest form of mobile life."   He refers to " the toothless feeling of sympathy and reconciliation and quiet ", and to " hate, the most genuine of all race-feelings in the beast of prey ".   Man should be like the lion, never tolerating an equal in his den, and not like the meek cow, living

2 G

in herds and driven hither and thither.   For such a man, war is, of course, the supreme occupation and joy.

Oswald Spengler is one of the most learned men of the day; the books he has written surprise one by the enormous amount of learning they contain.   And all this vast learning has led him to these astounding and hateful conclusions.   I have quoted him because he enables us to understand the mentality behind Hitlerism and explains the cruelty and brutality of the Nazi régime.   Of course one should not imagine that every Nazi thinks in this way. But the leaders and the aggressive elements certainly think so, and they set the fashion.   It will perhaps be more correct to say that the average Nazi did not think at all.   He felt roused up by his own misery and the national humiliation (the French occupation of the Ruhr was bitterly resented in Germany) and angry at things as they were.   Hitler is a powerful orator, and he played on the emotions of his vast audiences and cast all the blame for everything that was happening on the Marxists and the Jews.   If Germany was treated badly by France or other foreign countries, this became a reason for more people to join the Nazis, for the Nazis would protect the honour of Germany.   If the economic crisis became worse, recruits poured in.

The Social Democratic Party soon lost control over the government, and another group, the Catholic Centre Party, came into power because of the rivalries of others.   No single party was strong enough to ignore others in the Reichstag (the Parliament), and so there were frequent elections and intrigues and party manœuvres.   The growth of the Nazis frightened the Social Democrats so much that they supported the capitalist Centre Party and the election of the old General von Hindenburg for the presidentship. In spite of the growth of the Nazis, the two workers' parties, the Social Democratic and the Communist, were strong, and each had millions of supporters to the last, but they could not co-operate even in face of the common danger.   The Communists remembered with bitterness the persecution they had been subjected to by the Social Democrats in the days of their power, from 1918 onwards, and how, at every moment of crisis, they, the Social Democrats, had sided with the reactionary groups.   The Social Democratic Party, on the other hand, like the British Labour Party, with whom it was associated in the Second International, was a wealthy, widespread organization with plenty of patronage at its command, and it disliked taking any risk to endanger its security and position. It was very much afraid of doing anything against the law, or of indulging in what is known as direct action.   It spent most of its energy in combating the Communists.   And yet both of these parties were Marxists of a kind.

Germany thus became an armed camp of evenly balanced forces, and there were frequent riots and murders, especially by the Nazis of Communist workers.   Sometimes the workers retaliated.   Hitler was remarkably successful in holding together a motley crew, the various elements of which had little in common with each other.

It was a curious alliance of the lower middle classes with the big industrialists on the one hand and the richer peasantry on the other. The industrialists supported Hitler and gave him money because he cursed socialism and seemed to be the only bulwark against an advancing Marxism or Communism. The poorer middle classes and peasantry and even some workers were attracted by the anti-capitalistic slogans.

On January 30, 1933, old President Hindenburg (he was eighty-six years old then) made Hitler Chancellor, which is the highest executive office in Germany, corresponding to the Prime Minister. There was an alliance between the Nazis and the Nationalists, but very soon it was obvious that the Nazis were in full command and no one else counted. A general election gave the Nazis, with their allies the Nationalists, just a bare majority in the Reichstag. Even if they had not got this majority, it would not have mattered much, for the Nazis arrested their opponents in the Parliament and put them in jail. All the Communist members were thus removed, and many of the Social Democrats. Just then the Reichstag building caught fire and was burnt down. The Nazis stated that this was the work of the Communists and that it was a plot to undermine the State. The Communists denied this vigorously and, in fact, they accused the Nazis' leaders of having caused the fire to find an excuse for attacking them.

Then began the Nazi or the Brown Terror all over Germany. To begin with, Parliament was wound up (although the Nazis had a majority in it), and all power was vested in Hitler and his Cabinet. They could make laws or do anything they liked. The Weimar Constitution of the Republic was thus scrapped and all forms of democracy were openly scorned. Germany was a kind of federation; this, too, was ended, and all power was concentrated in Berlin. Everywhere dictators were appointed, who were responsible only to the dictator next above them. Hitler was, of course, the dictator-in-chief.

While these changes were taking place, the Nazi Storm Troops were let loose all over Germany, and they began a reign of violence and terror, amazingly savage and brutal. It was unique of its kind. There have been Terrors before, Red Terrors and White Terrors, but they always took place when a country, or a dominant group was fighting for its life in a civil war. The Terror was a reaction of terrible danger and constant fear. The Nazis had no such danger to face, nor had they any reason to be afraid. They controlled the government, and there was no armed opposition or resistance to them. The Brown Terror was thus not an outcome of passion and fear, but a deliberate, cold-blooded, and incredibly brutal suppression of all who did not fall in line with the Nazis.

It would serve no purpose to give a list of the atrocities that have taken place in Germany since the Nazis came to power, and that still take place behind the scenes. There have been savage beatings and tortures and shooting and murder on a vast scale, both men and women being victims. Enormous numbers of people have been put in gaols and concentration camps, and are said to be treated very badly there. The attack has been fiercest on the Communists, but the more moderate Social Democrats have fared little better. A dead set has been made at the Jews, and others attacked have been pacifists, liberals, trade unionists, and internationalists. The Nazis proclaim that it is a war of extermination against Marxism and the Marxists and indeed the entire " Left ". Jews must also be eliminated from all posts and professions. Thousands of Jewish professors, teachers, musicians, lawyers, judges, doctors, and nurses, have been turned out. Jewish shopkeepers have been boycotted and Jewish workers dismissed from factories. There has been a wholesale destruction of books that the Nazis do not approve of, public burnings taking place. Newspapers have been ruthlessly suppressed for the slightest difference of opinion or criticism. No news of the Terror is allowed to be published, and even a whisper of it is punished heavily.

All organizations and parties, other than the Nazi Party, of course, have been suppressed. The Communist Party went first, then the Social Democratic, later the Catholic Centre Party, and lastly even the Nazis' allies, the Nationalists. The mighty German trade unions, representing the labour and savings and sacrifices of generations of workers, were broken up and all their funds and properties confiscated. Only one party, one organization, was to remain—the Nazi Party.

The strange Nazi philosophy is forced down every one's throat, and such is the fear of the Terror that no one dare raise his head. Education, the theatre, art, science—everything is being given the Nazi stamp. " The true German thinks with his blood ! " says Hermann Goering, one of Hitler's chief men. " The age of pure reason and of unprejudiced science is over," says another Nazi leader. Children are taught that Hitler is a second Jesus, but greater than the first. The Nazi Government does not favour too much extension of education among the people, and especially among women. Indeed, woman's place, according to the Hitlerite, is the home and kitchen, and her chief job is to provide children to fight and die for the State. Dr. Joseph Goebbels, another Nazi leader, who is Minister for " Public Enlightenment and Propaganda ", has said that " woman's place is in the family; her proper task is to provide her country and her people with children. . . . The liberation of women is a danger to the State. She must leave to man the things that belong to man." This same Dr. Goebbels has also told us what his method is of enlightening the public : " It is my intention to play on the Press as on a piano."

Behind all this barbarism and brutality and fire and thunder lay the privation and hunger of the dispossessed middle classes. It was really a fight for jobs and bread. Jewish doctors, lawyers, teachers, nurses, etc., were turned out because the " Aryan " Germans had not been able to compete with them and looked hungrily at their success and wanted their jobs. Jewish shops were closed because they were successful rivals. Many of the non-Jewish shops were also closed and their owners were arrested by the Nazis because they were suspected of profiteering and charging unreasonably high prices. The peasant supporters of the Nazis have been casting longing eyes on the big estates in East Prussia, which they want parcelled out among themselves.

An interesting feature of the original Nazi programme was a proposal to limit all salaries to 12,000 marks per year, which is equivalent to Rs. 8000, or Rs. 666 per month. I do not know how far this has been given effect to. The present salary of the Chancellor is 26,000 marks per year (= Rs. 1440 per month). It is proposed that not even the directors or employers of private companies, which are subsidized by government, are to be paid a higher salary than 18,000 marks per year, and these people have often been paid huge sums in the past. Compare these figures with the bloated salaries which poor India pays her officials. The Congress proposed at Karachi to fix the salary limit at Rs. 500 per month.

It must not be imagined that behind the Nazi movement there is only brutality and terror, prominent as these are. There is undoubtedly a very real enthusiasm for Hitler among large numbers of Germans, apart from the vast majority of the workers. If the figures of the last election are taken as a guide, he has 52 per cent. of the population behind him, and this 52 per cent. is terrorizing the remaining 48 per cent., or part of it. With this 52 per cent., or perhaps more now, Hitler is very popular. People who go to Germany talk of a strange psychological atmosphere there, as of a religious revival. Germans feel that the long years of humiliation and suppression, caused by the Treaty of Versailles, are past, and they can breathe freely again.

But the other half, or thereabouts, of Germany feels very differently. The German working class is dominated by an intense hatred and fury, hidden and controlled by fear of the terrible reprisals of the Nazis. They have submitted as a whole to force and terrorism, and watched with sorrow and despair the destruction of what they had built up with vast labour and sacrifice. Of all that has taken place during the last few months in Germany, not the least amazing has been the complete collapse of the great Social Democratic Party without the slightest effort to resist. This was the oldest, the biggest, and the most highly organized party of the working class in Europe. It was the backbone of the Second International. And yet it submitted tamely and with hardly a protest —though protests alone would have been singularly futile—to every insult and indignity, and finally to extinction. Step by step the Social Democratic leaders submitted to the Nazis, hoping each time that their submission and humiliation might save them something at least. But their very submission was made a weapon against them, and the Nazis pointed out to the workers how their leaders had basely deserted them when danger threatened. In the long history of the struggle of the European working class there are some triumphs and many defeats, but never had there been such a disgraceful surrender and betrayal of the workers' cause without the least effort to resist. The Communist Party tried to resist and called for a general strike. They were not supported by the Social Democratic leaders, and the strike fizzled out. The workers' movement, though broken up, is still carrying on with a secret organization which appears to be widespread. In spite of the Nazi spy system, secretly published newspapers are supposed to have a circulation of several hundred thousand. Some of the Social Democratic leaders who managed to escape from Germany are also trying to carry on some propaganda from abroad by secret methods.

The working class was by far the greatest sufferer from the Brown Terror. World opinion was, however, more agitated by the treatment of the Jews. Europe is partly used to class warfare, and sympathy always goes along class lines. But the attack on the Jews was a racial attack, something of the kind that used to occur in the Middle Ages or, in recent times, unofficially, in backward countries like Tsarist Russia. The official persecution of a whole race shocked Europe and America. To add to the shock, the German Jews had among their number many world-famed men, brilliant scientists, doctors, lawyers, musicians, and writers, headed by the great name of Albert Einstein. These people considered Germany their home, and they were looked upon everywhere as Germans. Any country would have felt honoured to own them, but the Nazis, in their mad racial obsession, hunted them out, and a mighty outcry rose against this all over the world. Then the Nazis instituted a boycott of Jewish shops and professional men, and yet, strangely enough, they would not allow these Jews as a rule to leave Germany. The only result of such a policy must be to starve them out. The world outcry made the Nazis tone down their public methods against the Jews, but the policy continues.

But Jewry, although it is scattered all over the world and can call no nation its own, is not so helpless as not to be able to retaliate. It controls a great deal of business and finance and, quietly and without much fuss, it proclaimed a boycott of German goods. And not only that, but something more, as a resolution, passed in May 1933, at a New York conference, declared. It was resolved " to boycott all goods, materials, or products manufactured, raised or improved in Germany, or any part thereof; all German shipping, freight, and traffic services, as well as all German health, pleasure, and other resorts, and generally to abstain from any act which would in any manner lend material support to the present régime in Germany ".

This was one of the reactions of Hitlerism abroad; there were other reactions which were even more far-reaching. The Nazis had all along denounced the Treaty of Versailles and demanded its revision, especially on the eastern frontier, where there is the absurd arrangement of a Polish corridor to Danzig cutting off a bit of Germany from the rest of the country. They also loudly asked for complete equality in arming. (You may remember that they were largely disarmed by the Peace Treaty.) Hitler's blood-and-thunder speeches and threats of rearming upset Europe completely, especially France, which had most to fear from a powerful Germany, and for some days Europe seemed to be on the brink of war. Suddenly this Nazi fear led to a new grouping of Powers in Europe. France began to feel quite friendly towards Soviet Russia. Fearing a revision of the Treaty of Versailles, all the countries that had been created by it or had profited by it, like Poland, Czechoslovakia, Yugoslavia, and Rumania, drew together, and at the same time drew nearer to Russia. In Austria a surprising situation arose. A fascist Chancellor, Dolfuss, was already in control there, but his brand of fascism was different from that of Hitler's. The Nazis are strong in Austria, but Dolfuss has opposed them. Italy welcomed Hitler's triumph, but did not encourage all Hitler's ambitions. In England, which for many years had been pro-German, the people became anti-German and even began to talk again of " Huns ". Hitler's Germany was quite isolated in Europe. It was obvious that a war would have meant a crushing of unarmed Germany by the powerful army of France. Hitler changed his tactics and began to talk in terms of peace, and Mussolini came to his rescue by proposing a Four-Power Pact between France, England, Germany, and Italy.

This Pact was ultimately signed by the four Powers in June 1933, though France hesitated before doing so. As far as the language of the Pact goes, it is inoffensive enough, and all it says is that the four Powers will consult each other in certain international matters, especially in regard to any proposal to revise the Treaty of Versailles. This Pact is looked upon, however, as an attempt to form an anti-Soviet block. France apparently signed it most unwillingly. Perhaps a result of and an answer to this Pact has been the non-Aggression Pact which was signed in London on July 1, 1933, between the Soviet and her neighbours. It is interesting to notice that France has expressed her great sympathy and agreement with this Soviet Pact.

Hitler's fundamental programme—and it is the programme of German capitalism—is to pose as the champion of Europe against Soviet Russia. If Germany is to have more territory, it can only get it in eastern Europe or at the expense of the Soviet Union. Before this can be done Germany must be armed, and it is therefore necessary to get the Treaty of Versailles revised to this effect or, at any rate, to have the assurance that nobody will interfere. Hitler counts on Italian support. If he can win over England's support also, it will be easy, so he probably hopes, to neutralize France's opposition in any discussions under the Four-Power Pact.

Hitler is thus trying to win British support. In order to do so he has even publicly stated that it would be a calamity if the British hold on India was weakened. His anti-Sovietism is itself an attraction to the British Government, for, as I have told you, there is nothing that British imperialism dislikes quite so much as Soviet Russia. But the British people have been so disgusted with Nazi activities that it will take some time to win them over to any proposal involving an approval of Hitlerism.

Nazi Germany has thus become a storm centre in Europe, adding to the multitude of fears of this " panic-stricken world ". What will happen in Germany itself ? Will this Nazi régime last ? There is plenty of hatred and opposition to the Nazis in Germany, but it is clear enough that all organized opposition has been crushed. There is no party or organization left in Germany, and the Nazis are supreme. Among the Nazis themselves there appear to be two parties : the capitalist element and the business community forming the right wing, and the majority of the rank and file of the party, who have added to their number many workers who have recently joined them, forming the left wing. The people who gave the revolutionary urge to Hitler's movement had a great deal of anti-capitalist radicalism, and they have subsequently accepted many socialists and Marxists. The right wing and the left wing of the Nazi movement had little in common. Hitler's great success consisted in keeping them together and playing one off against the other. This could be done as long as a common enemy was in sight. Now that the enemy has been crushed or absorbed, the conflict between the right and left wing is bound to develop.

Already there are rumblings. The left-wing Nazis demanded that the first revolution having been successfully completed, the " Second Revolution " should now be begun, this being against capitalism, landlordism, etc. Hitler has, however, come down with a threat to suppress ruthlessly this " Second Revolution ". So he has ranged himself definitely with the capitalist right wing. Most of his principal lieutenants now occupy high offices, and being comfortably installed, they are not eager for change.

This account of Hitlerism has been a long one. But you will agree that this Nazi triumph and its consequences have been most important for Europe and the world and will have far-reaching results. Undoubtedly it is fascism, and Hitler himself is a typical fascist. But the Nazi movement has been something more wide-spread and radical than Italian fascism was. Whether these radical elements will make any difference or will simply be crushed, remains to be seen.

To some extent orthodox Marxist theory has been confounded by the growth of the Nazi movement. Orthodox Marxists have believed that the only genuinely revolutionary class was the working class and, as economic conditions worsened, this class would draw to itself the discontented and dispossessed elements of the lower-middle class and ultimately bring about a workers' revolution. As a matter of fact, something very different has happened in Germany. The workers were far from revolutionary when the crisis came, and a new revolutionary class was formed chiefly from the dispossessed lower-middle classes and other discontented elements. This does not fit in with orthodox Marxism. But, say other Marxists, Marxism must not be looked upon as a dogma or religion or creed which authoritatively lays down the final truth, as religions do. It is a philosophy of history, a way of looking at history which explains much and makes it hang together, and a method of action to achieve socialism or social equality. Its fundamental principles have to be applied in a variety of ways to meet the changing conditions of different times and different countries.

Note (November 1938) :

Since the above letter was written, five and a quarter years ago, there has been nothing so remarkable in world politics as the growth in power and prestige of Nazi Germany under Hitler. Hitler dominates Europe to-day, and the great Powers, or those who were great, bow down to him and tremble at his threats. Twenty years ago Germany was defeated, humbled, crushed. And now, without a military victory or war, Hitler has made her the victorious nation, and the Treaty of Versailles is dead and buried.

Hitler's first concern, after coming into power, was to crush opponents in Germany and consolidate the Nazi Party. Having "Nazified" Germany, he decided to end the leftist tendencies within the Nazi ranks, which had been looking forward to a second and anti-capitalist revolution. The Brown-shirts were disbanded and their leaders shot down on June 30, 1934. Many others were also killed off, including General von Schleicher, who had once been Chancellor.

In August 1934 President von Hindenburg died, and Hitler took his place, becoming the Chancellor-President. He was all-powerful in Germany then, the Fuehrer or Leader of the German people. There was great distress among the people and private charity was organized, almost compulsorily, on a vast scale to relieve distress. Compulsory labour camps were also started where the unemployed were sent to work. Large numbers of Jews, who had been forcibly removed, gave place to Germans. The economic condition of Germany did not improve, indeed it grew worse, but unemployment, as such, disappeared. Meanwhile secret rearmament went on, and the fear of Germany grew.

Early in 1935 the plebiscite in the Saar basin went overwhelmingly in favour of union with Germany, and this area was joined on to Germany. In May that year, Hitler publicly repudiated the disarmament clauses of the Treaty of Versailles and decreed compulsory military service. A huge rearmament programme was launched. None of the League Powers did anything; fear gripped them, especially France. France negotiated an alliance with Soviet Russia. The British Government preferred to line up with Nazi Germany and signed a naval pact with her in June 1935.

This had curious consequences. France, feeling that England was deserting her, made overtures to Italy, and Mussolini, thinking that the moment was opportune, launched the invasion of Abyssinia.

In March 1938 Hitler marched into Austria and proclaimed the *anschluss* or union with Germany. Again the League Powers submitted. In Austria an aggressive and brutal anti-Jew campaign was launched by the Nazis.

Czechoslovakia now became the target for Nazi aggression, and for several months the problem of the Sudeten Germans agitated

Europe. British policy helped the Nazis greatly, and France dared not go against this policy. Ultimately, under threat of immediate war from Germany, France deserted her ally Czechoslovakia and England was a party to the betrayal. By the Pact of Munich between Germany, England, France, and Italy, the fate of Czechoslovakia was sealed on September 29, 1938. The Sudeten areas and much else were occupied by Germany, and, profiting by the occasion, Poland and Hungary took parts of the country.

A new division of Europe was thus begun, a Europe in which France and England were becoming second-class Powers, and Nazi Germany, under Hitler, was triumphantly dominant.

191

DISARMAMENT

August 2, 1933

I HAVE told you of the failure of the World Economic Conference which met in London. The Conference was wound up and its members went home, expressing the pious hope that they might meet again under more favourable circumstances.

Another great failure at world efforts at co-operation has been the Disarmament Conference. This conference was the outcome of the Covenant of the League of Nations. The Treaty of Versailles had decided that Germany (as well as the other defeated Powers like Austria, Hungary) was to disarm. She was not to keep a navy or air force or have a big army. It was further proposed that other countries should also gradually disarm, so that armaments might be reduced everywhere to the lowest point consistent with national safety. The first part of the programme—German disarmament—was immediately enforced; the second part—general disarmament—remained, and still remains, a pious hope. It was to fulfil this second part of the programme that the Disarmament Conference was ultimately called nearly thirteen years after the Treaty of Versailles. But before the full conference met, Preparatory Commissions explored the whole subject for years.

The World Disarmament Conference met at last early in 1932. Month after month, year after year, it went on, considering many proposals and rejecting them, reading innumerable reports, listening to interminable arguments. From being a disarmament conference it almost became an armaments conference. No agreement could be reached, for no country was prepared to consider the question from the wider international point of view; for each country disarmament meant that other countries should disarm or lessen their armaments while it kept up its own strength. Nearly all countries adopted a selfish attitude, but Japan and Great Britain were pre-eminent in this respect, and put great difficulties in the way of any agreement. While this Conference was proceeding, Japan was defying the League and carrying on a bloody and aggressive war in Manchuria, two South American Republics were fighting each other, and Britain continued to bomb the tribesmen on the north-west frontier of India. American opposition to Japanese aggression in China was largely neutralized by the British attitude, which was consistently friendly to Japan.

Of the many proposals made, three of the most important came from Soviet Russia, the United States of America, and France, respectively. Russia proposed that there should be a 50 per cent. reduction of armaments all round. America suggested a general reduction of one-third. But Britain opposed both these proposals, maintaining that she could not reduce her forces, and especially her navy, as these were meant for police purposes only.

France, with past memories of German aggression, has always laid stress on " security "—that is, some arrangement which would make aggression difficult, if not impossible. She suggested the creation of an international force under the League of Nations, which could be used against the aggressor, each nation keeping small and lightly-armed forces only; all air forces to be under the League. But this proposal was objected to on the ground that it would give all power to the great Powers that controlled the League, and in effect France would dominate Europe.

Who was the aggressor? This was a difficult question, for it is the habit of every aggressor nation to claim that it is acting on the defensive. Japan in Manchuria, Italy in Abyssinia, did not admit that they were aggressors. In the Great War every nation referred to the enemy as aggressors. So some clear and precise definition was necessary if action was to be taken against the aggressor. Soviet Russia put forward a definition according to which if a nation sent an armed force across the frontier to another country, or blockaded the coast of another country, it would become an aggressor nation. President Roosevelt and a committee of the League of Nations also defined " aggressor " in similar terms. The Soviet definition was accepted in the non-aggression pact between Russia and her neighbours. Most of the Powers, big and small, including France, agreed to this definition. Japan of course was highly embarrassed by it, and England refused to agree to it, and wanted to leave the matter vague. Italy supported her.

The British proposal for disarmament proceeded on the basis that it was not necessary for Britain to reduce her armaments; it was for other nations to disarm. In regard to bombing from the air, everybody approved of its complete abolition, but Britain added a proviso : " except for police purposes in outlying areas ", which meant a free hand to bomb in her Empire. This proviso was not acceptable to others, and so the whole proposal for abolition fell through.

Germany, very naturally, demanded equality with the other Powers; either she must be allowed to rearm to the limit allowed to others, or the others must disarm down to her limit. This was an unanswerable argument. Had not the League Covenant said that German disarmament was a prelude to others? While these discussions were proceeding, the Nazis came into power in Germany and their aggressive and threatening attitude frightened France and hardened her as well as the other Powers. Neither of the alternatives proposed on behalf of Germany were agreed to.

To add to the difficulties of disarmament, there are numerous intrigues behind the scenes, especially by the highly paid agents of armament firms. In the modern capitalist world the business of making arms and instruments of destruction is one of the most prosperous of industries. These arms are made for the governments of various countries, for only governments wage war as a rule, and yet, curiously enough, private firms make these arms. The principal owners of these firms grow enormously rich, and they are usually in close touch with governments. I told you something about one of these, Sir Basil Zaharoff, in one of my earlier letters. Shares in armament concerns, bringing high dividends, are often sought after, many persons prominent in public life are shareholders in these firms.

War and the preparation for war mean profit to these armament firms. They traffic in wholesale death, and, impartially, they sell their engines of destruction to all who pay for them. When the League of Nations was condemning Japan for aggression in China, English and French and other armament firms were supplying arms freely to both Japan and China. It is obvious that real disarmament will mean ruin for these firms. Their trade will be gone. They try their best, therefore, to prevent what is, from their point of view, a catastrophe. Indeed, they go further. A League of Nations Commission, specially appointed to inquire into the private manufacture of arms, came to the conclusion that these firms had been active in fomenting war scares and in persuading their own countries to adopt warlike policies. It was also found that the firms spread false reports about the military and naval expenditure of various countries so as to induce other countries into increasing their expenditure on armaments. They tried to play off one country against another, and helped in promoting an armaments' race between them. They bribed government officials and bought up newspapers in order to influence public opinion. And then they formed international trusts and monopolies to increase the price of arms, etc. The League Commission suggested that the private manufacture of armaments should be stopped. This was also proposed in the Disarmament Conference, but here again persistent opposition has come from the British Government.

These armament firms of different countries are closely associated with each other. They exploit patriotism and play with death, and yet they are themselves international in their operations—the " Secret International " they have been called. It is natural that these people should object strongly to disarmament, and they have done their best to prevent any agreement. Their agents move in the highest diplomatic and political circles, and these sinister figures have been in evidence at Geneva,. trying to pull the wires from behind the scenes.

Often closely allied with this " Secret International " are the Intelligence Departments or Secret Services of various governments. Every government employs spies to get secret information from other countries. Sometimes the spies get caught, and then they are promptly disowned by their own government. Referring to these secret services, Arthur Ponsonby (who was some years ago Under-Secretary for Foreign Affairs in the British Government, and who is now Lord Ponsonby) said in May 1927 in the House of Commons : " We must really face the facts, when we are getting on our high moral horse, that forgery, theft, lying, bribery, and corruption exist in every Foreign Office and every Chancellory of the world. . . . I say that according to the recognized moral code our representatives abroad would be neglectful in their duty if they were not finding out secrets from the archives of those countries."

Because these Sécret Services work in secret, they are difficult to control. They influence the foreign policy of their respective countries greatly. They are widespread and powerful organizations. The British Intelligence Service to-day is probably the most powerful, and with the widest ramifications. There is an instance on record of a famous British spy becoming a high Soviet official in Russia ! Sir Samuel Hoare, the British Cabinet Minister, was during war-time the head of the British Intelligence and Secret Service department in Russia, and he has recently stated publicly, with some pride, that his system of getting information was so good that he learnt of Rasputin's murder long before any one else did.

The real difficulty before the Disarmament Conference has been that there are two classes of countries—the satisfied Powers and the unsatisfied Powers, the dominant Powers and those that are suppressed, the Powers that want the present state of affairs to continue and those that want a change. Between the two there can be no stable equilibrium, just as there can be no real stability between a dominant class and a suppressed class. The League of Nations represents on the whole the dominant Powers, and so it tries to maintain the *status quo*. Security pacts and attempts to define an " aggressor " nation are all meant to preserve existing conditions. Probably, whatever might happen, the League will never denounce one of the Powers that control it as an " aggressor ". It will always so manœuvre as to declare the other party as an " aggressor ".

Pacifists and others who want to prevent war welcome these security pacts, and thereby in a sense they help in the maintenance of an unjust *status quo*. If this is so in Europe, much more is it so in Asia and Africa, where imperialist Powers have annexed large portions of territory. The *status quo* thus in Asia and Africa means the continuance of imperialist exploitation.

The United States of America have been, so far, free of any alliances or commitments in Europe regarding the maintenance of this *status quo*.

Nothing proves the unreality and mockery of international

politics to-day so much as the failure of all attempts at disarmament. Everybody talks of peace, and yet prepares for war. The Kellogg-Briand Pact outlaws war, but who remembers it now or cares for it ?

Note.—The German proposals before the Disarmament Conference were rejected, and in October 1933 Germany walked out of the Conference, and also resigned from the League of Nations. Since then she has been out of the League. Japan also left the League on the Manchurian issue, and Italy left because of the League's attitude towards her invasion of Abyssinia. So that three great Powers were out of the League and, under these circumstances, any international decision on disarmament, under the League's auspices, became almost impossible. Indeed, soon after the Disarmament Conference rearmament began on an intensive scale in all countries. Germany began building up a colossal army and air force, and England, France, the United States of America, and other countries voted huge credits for additional armaments.

192

PRESIDENT ROOSEVELT TO THE RESCUE

August 4, 1933

I WANT you to have another look at the United States of America before I wind up this story (and the winding up cannot be long delayed). A great and rather fascinating experiment is taking place there now, and the world is on the watch, for on its results depends the future turn that capitalism will take. America, let me repeat, is by far the most advanced capitalist country; she is the wealthiest, and her industrial technique is ahead of the others. She owes money to no other country, and her only debt is to her own citizens. Her export trade has been considerable and growing, and yet it was only a small part (about 15 per cent.) of her enormous internal trade. The country is nearly as big as the continent of Europe, but there is this big difference, that Europe is cut up into a large number of little nations, each having high customs duties at its frontiers, while the United States have no such trade barriers within their own territories. It was thus far easier for a huge internal trade to develop in America than it was in Europe. America had all these advantages over the impoverished, debt-ridden countries of Europe. She had plenty of gold, plenty of money, plenty of goods.

And yet, in spite of all this, the crisis of capitalism caught her and took all the pride out of her. Fatalism descended on a people whose vitality and energy knew no bounds. The country as a whole remained rich, money did not disappear, but it piled up in a few places. Hundreds of millions were still in evidence in New York; the great banker J. Pierpont Morgan still sported his private luxury yacht, which is reported to have cost £6,000,000. And yet New York has been described recently as "Hunger Town". Great city municipalities like Chicago have been practically bankrupt, unable to pay the salaries of thousands of their employees. And this very Chicago is now running a magnificent exhibition or "world fair" called "The Century of Progress".

These contrasts are not confined to America. Go to London and the overflowing wealth and luxury of the British upper classes are everywhere in evidence, except of course in the slums. Visit Lancashire or northern or central England, or parts of Wales and Scotland, and you see long lines of unemployed, and pinched and haggard faces, and miserable living conditions.

A marked feature of recent years in America was the growth of crime, especially of the "gangster" variety—that is, gangs working together and frequently shooting people who came in their way. Crime is said to have increased greatly ever since a law was passed prohibiting the sale of intoxicating drinks. This "prohibition", as it is called, became law soon after the World War, partly because the big employers wanted their workers to keep away from such drinks so that they might work better. But the rich themselves ignored the law and continued to get drinks illegally from abroad. Gradually an enormous illegal trade in alcoholic drinks was built up. "Bootlegging" this was called, and it consisted both of smuggling wines and spirits from abroad and of secretly manufacturing them. Usually this secretly manufactured stuff was far worse and more harmful than the real article. "Speak-easy" was the name for the place where such drinks could be bought at very high prices, and thousands of such private bars grew up in all the big cities. All this was, of course, illegal, and to enable it to exist policemen and politicians were bribed and sometimes terrorized. This widespread contempt of the law led to the growth of the gangster groups. Thus "prohibition" resulted on the one side in doing good to the workers and rural population, on the other it did great harm, and a very powerful boot-legging interest grew up. The whole country was split up into two parties : those in favour of prohibition called the "Drys", and those against it called the "Wets".

Among gangster crimes the most notorious and shocking were those of kidnapping little children of rich people and holding them for ransom. Some time ago Lindbergh's baby son was so kidnapped and, to the world's horror, was brutally done to death.

All this, in addition to the trade depression and the realization that many of the high officials and big business people were corrupt and incompetent, upset the nerves of the American people. During the presidential election of November 1932 they turned in their millions to Roosevelt, hoping that he would bring them relief. Roosevelt was a "wet", and belonged to the Democratic Party, which has very seldom provided presidents to the United States.

It is always interesting and helpful to compare different countries, always keeping in mind their distinctive features. One is tempted, therefore, to compare recent events in the United States with those in Germany and England. The comparison with Germany is a closer one, because both countries, in spite of being highly industrialized, have a large farming population. Germany's farmers are 25 per cent. of her total population; in the United States they form 40 per cent. These farmers count in the making of national policy. Not so in England, where the small proportion of farmers are neglected, although some effort is now being made to revive them.

One of the outstanding causes of the Nazi movement in Germany was the growth in numbers of the dispossessed lower-middle classes, and this growth became rapid after the German inflation. It was this class that became revolutionary in Germany. This is precisely the class which is growing in America now; it is called the " white-collar proletariat ", to distinguish it from the working-class proletariat, which seldom indulges in white collars

Other comparisons are the currency crises, the fall of the mark, the pound, and the dollar from gold and inflation, and bank failures. In England there have been no bank failures because there are not many small banks and a few big banks control the banking business. In other respects the courses of events in the three countries resemble each other; Germany having her crisis first, then England, then the United States. More or less the same class of people, in their respective countries, were behind the Nazis, the British National Government in the election in 1931, and President Roosevelt in his election in November 1932. This was the lower-middle class, many of whom had previously belonged to other parties. This comparison must not be taken too far, not only because of national differences, but because the situation in England and America has not yet developed as it has in Germany. But the point is that very similar economic influences have been at work in these three highly advanced industrial countries, and the results they produce are therefore likely to be similar. This is not so in France (or other countries) to the same extent, for France is still more agricultural and less advanced industrially.

Roosevelt took office as President early in March 1933, and he was immediately faced by a tremendous banking crisis in addition to the great depression that was going on. Some weeks later he described the state of the country when he took office and he said that the country was " dying by inches " then.

Roosevelt took swift and decisive action. He asked the American Congress for powers to deal with banks, industry, and agriculture, and the Congress, quite unnerved by the crisis, and influenced by popular feeling in favour of Roosevelt, gave him these powers. He became practically a dictator (though a democratic one), and everybody looked to him for immediate and effective action to save them from disaster. He did act with lightning rapidity, and within a few weeks he had shaken up the whole of the United States by his various activities, and produced an even greater feeling of confidence in himself.

Among President Roosevelt's many decisions were :

1. He went off gold and allowed the dollar to fall, thus reducing the burden on debtors. This was a measure of inflation.

2. Relieved farmers by subsidies, and got a huge loan of $2,000,000,000 issued to relieve agriculture.

3. Enlisted 250,000 workers immediately for forestry services and for flood-control work. This was to relieve unemployment a little.

4. He asked Congress for $800,000,000 for unemployment relief. This was granted him.

5. He set aside the enormous sum of about $3,000,000,000, which was to be borrowed, for public works to promote employment.

6. He hurried up the repeal of Prohibition.

All these enormous sums were to be obtained by borrowing from the rich people. Roosevelt's whole policy was, and is, to increase the buying power of the people; when they have the money they will buy, and the trade depression will automatically lessen. It is with this object in view that he is having huge schemes of public works where the workers can be employed and earn money. It is also with this object that he is trying to raise the wages of workers and lessen their hours of work. A shorter working day would mean the employment of more people.

This attitude is in direct opposition to the usual attitude of employers during times of crisis and depression. Almost invariably they try to cut down wages and lengthen hours of work, so as to cheapen their costs of production. But, says Roosevelt, if we are to resume mass production of goods, we must give the masses the capacity to buy them by a mass distribution of high wages.

The Roosevelt Government has also given a loan to Soviet Russia for the purpose of buying American cotton. The two governments are also discussing the possibilities of large-scale barter between the two countries.

America has so far been a purely capitalistic State with full and unrestricted competition; an " individualistic " State, as it is called. Roosevelt's new policy does not fit in with this, as he is interfering with business in a variety of ways. He is therefore practically introducing a great deal of State control over industry, though he calls it by another name. It is really a measure of State socialism, regulating hours and conditions of labour, controlling industry and preventing " cut-throat competition ". He has called it " a partnership in planning, and seeing that plans are carried out ".

This work is being carried on now with the usual American push and energy. Child labour has been abolished. (The child's age for this purpose is up to sixteen.) Higher wages is the slogan, more pay, less hours of work. " Prosperity Push " this campaign is called, and the whole country, it is reported, has become a giant recruiting poster for this campaign. Aeroplanes dash about broadcasting appeals to employers and others. Each separate big industry is being induced to draw up " codes " fixing higher wages, etc., and pledging itself to carry them out; if it fails to draw up a suitable code there is the gentle threat that the government will

do it.   Individual employers are asked to sign pledge forms promising
to raise wages and shorten the hours of work of their employees.
To those employers who take a lead in this matter the government
proposes to give badges of honour, and, to shame slackers, a roll of
honour will be kept in the post office of every town.

All this has resulted in some improvement in prices and trade.
But the real improvement, which is marked, is in business sentiment
and morale.   The feeling of defeat has largely gone, and there is,
among the large masses of the people, and especially the middle
classes, an abounding faith in President Roosevelt.   He is compared already to America's great hero, President Lincoln, who also
took office at a time of a great crisis, the Civil War.

Even in Europe many people began to look up to him and expected
a world leadership against the depression.   But at the World
Economic Conference he became rather unpopular with the delegates
of other countries because he directed his representatives to refuse
to fix the dollar in terms of gold, or to agree to anything else
which might interfere with his great schemes in the United States.

Roosevelt's policy is definitely one of economic nationalism, and
he is bent on improving conditions in America.   Some European
governments do not like it, and bankers are particularly annoyed.
The British Government does not approve of Roosevelt's progressive
tendencies.   They prefer Big Business.

And yet Roosevelt is taking a more active part in world affairs
than his predecessor did.   On the question of disarmament and
other international questions, he has taken up a definite and more
advanced attitude than that of England.   His polite warning to
Hitler made Hitler tone down.   He is also getting into touch with
Soviet Russia.

The great question in America to-day, and even elsewhere, is :
will Roosevelt succeed ?   He is making a brave attempt to keep
capitalism going.   But his success means the dethronement of
Big Business, and it is far from likely that Big Business will take
this lying down.   American Big Business is held to be the most
powerful vested interest in the modern world, and it is not going
to give up its power and privileges merely at the bidding of President
Roosevelt.   For the present it is quiet, for public opinion and the
President's popularity have rather overwhelmed it.   But it is
waiting for its opportunity.   If there is no great improvement
within a few months, public opinion, it is expected, will turn against
Roosevelt, and then Big Business will come out into the open.

Many competent observers think that President Roosevelt is
facing an impossible task and that he cannot succeed.   His failure
will make Big Business supreme again, and with perhaps even greater
power than before.   For Roosevelt's state socialism apparatus will
then be utilized for the private profit of Big Business.   The labour
movement is not strong in America, and can easily be crushed.

Note.—President Roosevelt's great attempt to overcome the
crisis, and to adapt capitalism to the new conditions, met with
partial success, though there was no fundamental change.   There

was an improvement in the situation. This attempt was in effect based on huge schemes of relief and on transferring to some extent the profits of industry to the workers by persuading the employers to give higher wages and shorter hours. The employers, especially Ford, resisted this as an attack on their freedom. The Codes for industry and agriculture failed, and there were many strikes. But American Labour grew stronger and more class-conscious and a new spirit pervaded it. Trade Unions increased their membership greatly.

As economic recovery took place, Big Business became more aggressive and resisted Roosevelt. The Supreme Court declared most of the effective clauses of Roosevelt's two principal Acts, the National Recovery Act, and the Agricultural Adjustment Act, as opposed to the Constitution and therefore inoperative. Roosevelt's New Deal was thus undermined.

In 1936 Roosevelt was elected President for a second time by a big majority. His struggle with Big Business continues. The Congress is no longer dominated by him, and it has opposed him in many matters.

193

THE FAILURE OF PARLIAMENTS

August 6, 1933

WE have examined recent events in some detail and considered many forces and tendencies that are shaping our changing world to-day. Among the facts that stand out there are two which I have already mentioned but which will bear further consideration. These two are : the failure of labour and the old type of socialism during the post-war years, and the failure or decline of parliaments.

I have told you how organized labour failed and the Second International went to pieces when the World War broke out in 1914. This was explained by the sudden shock of war, when fierce national passions are aroused and a temporary madness takes possession of peoples. Something very different, and even more revealing, has happened during the last four years. These four years have seen the greatest slump that the capitalist world has ever known, and they have in consequence brought ever-increasing misery to the workers. And yet this has not resulted in creating a real revolutionary sentiment among the masses of the workers generally everywhere, and especially in England and the United States.

The old type of capitalism is obviously breaking down. Objectively—that is, so far as external facts are concerned—conditions seem to be fully ripe for a change to a socialist economy. But the great majority of the very people who might have desired this most —the workers—have no will for revolution. Revolutionary sentiments have been far more in evidence among the conservative farmers of America and, as I have repeatedly told you, among the lower-middle classes in most countries, who are far more aggressive than the workers. This is most in evidence in Germany, but to a lesser degree it is to be seen also in England, the United States, and elsewhere. The differences in degree are due to national characteristics, as well as to various stages in the development of the crisis.

Why has labour, which was so aggressive and revolutionary in the early post-war years, become so quiescent and resigned to any fate that may be in store for it? Why did the German Social Democratic Party break down without a struggle and allow itself to be shattered by the Nazis? Why is English labour so moderate and reactionary? and even more so American labour? Labour leaders are often blamed for their incompetence and for their betrayal of the interests of the working class. Many of them no doubt deserve this blame, and it is sad to find them turning renegades and making the Labour Movement a stepping-stone to gratify personal ambition. Opportunism there is unhappily in every department of human activity; but the opportunism which exploits the hopes and ideals and sacrifices of the down-trodden and suffering millions for personal advantage is one of the greatest of human tragedies.

Leaders may be to blame. But leaders are, after all, the products of existing conditions. A country usually gets the rulers it deserves, and a movement the leaders which in the final analysis represent its real wishes. In reality neither the leaders of labour nor their followers in these imperialistic countries looked upon socialism as a living creed, something to be desired immediately. Their socialism got too much entangled and bound up with the capitalistic system. The exploitation of colonial countries brought them a small share in the profits, and they looked to the continuance of capitalism for a higher standard of life. Socialism became a distant ideal, a kind of heaven to dream of, a hereafter, not the present. And, like the old idea of heaven, it became a handmaid of capital.

And so Labour Parties, Trade Unions, Social Democrats, the Second International, and all similar organizations, pottered away at petty attempts to reform leaving the whole structure of capitalism intact. Their idealism left them, and they became huge bureaucratic organizations without a soul and with little real strength.

The new Communist Party was differently situated. It had a message for the worker which was more vital, more appealing, and behind it the attractive background of the Soviet Union. But even so it had singularly little success. It failed to move the labour masses in Europe or America. In England and the United States it was amazingly weak. In Germany and in France it had some strength, and yet we have seen how little it could profit by it, in Germany at least. Internationally its two great defeats have been in China in 1927 and in Germany in 1933. Why did the Communist Party fail during these days of trade depression and repeated crisis and low wages and unemployment? It is difficult to say.

Some say that it was just bad tactics, wrong methods of work. Others suggest that the Party was too much bound down to the Soviet Government, and its policy was thus more a national policy for the Soviet than an international policy as it should have been. This may have been so, but it is hardly a satisfactory explanation.

The Communist Party as such did not grow among the workers, but communist ideas spread widely, especially among the intellectual classes. Everywhere, even among the supporters of capitalism, there was an expectation, a fear, that the crisis might lead inevitably to some form of communism. It was generally recognized that the old type of capitalism had had its day. This acquisitive economy, this policy of individual grab, with no planning, with its waste and conflicts and periodical crises, must go. In its place some form of planned socialistic economy or co-operative economy must be established. This does not mean necessarily the victory of the working class, for a State may be organized on semi-socialistic lines for the benefit of the owning classes. A State socialism and a State capitalism are much the same thing; the real question is who is in command in the State and who profits by it, the whole community or a particular possessing class.

While the intellectuals argued, the lower-middle classes, or the petty *bourgeoisie*, in the Western industrial countries took action. These classes felt vaguely that capitalism and capitalists exploited them, and therefore felt some resentment against them. But they were far more afraid of the working class and of communism taking command. Capitalists usually made terms with this fascist wave, as they felt that there was no other way of stopping communism. Gradually almost everybody who was afraid of communism allied himself to this fascism. In this way, to a greater or less extent, fascism spreads wherever capitalism is in danger and faces communism or the possibility of it. Between the two, parliamentary government goes to pieces.

And this leads us to the second outstanding fact which I mentioned at the beginning of this letter—the failure or decline of parliaments. I have already told you a good deal in previous letters about dictatorships and the failure of old-style democracy. This is obvious enough in Russia, Italy, Central Europe, and now in Germany, where parliamentary government had collapsed even before the Nazis seized power. In the United States we have seen how Congress has given the fullest powers to President Roosevelt. This process is evident even in France and England, the two countries of Europe with the longest and most stable tradition of democracy. Let us consider England's case.

The English way of doing things is very different from the Continental method. Always they try to keep up old appearances, and the changes are thus not very obvious. To an ordinary observer the British Parliament continues as before, but as a matter of fact it has changed greatly. In the old days the House of Commons exercised power directly, and the average member had a good say in the matter. Now it is the Cabinet or the Government that decides every big question, and the House of Commons can only say yes or no to it. Of course the House can turn out the Government by saying no, but this is a drastic step which is seldom taken, as it would result in a lot of trouble and a general election. So that if a government has got a majority in the House of Commons, it can do almost anything it likes and get the House to agree to it and thus make it law. Power has thus been transferred, and is still being transferred, from the legislature to the executive.

Again, there is so much work to be done by Parliament nowadays, so many complicated questions to be faced, that a practice has grown for Parliament to decide only the general principles of any measure or law, and to leave it to the executive government, or to some department of it, to fill in the details. In this way the executive has got enormous powers and can do what it likes in an emergency. Parliament thus is getting more and more out of touch with important activities of the State. Its chief functions are now being reduced to criticism of government measures, questions, and inquiries, and finally approval of the general policy of government. As Harold J. Laski says : " Our government has become an executive dictatorship tempered by fear of Parliamentary revolt."

The sudden fall of the Labour Government in August 1931 was brought about in a curious way, which shows how little Parliament had to do with the matter. Ordinarily a government in England falls because it is defeated in the House of Commons. In 1931 nothing came before the House; no one knew what was happening, not even most of the members of the Cabinet itself. The Prime Minister, Ramsay MacDonald, had some secret conversations with the leaders of other parties; they saw the King, and the old Cabinet suddenly disappeared and a new one was announced in the newspapers ! Some of the members of the old Cabinet learnt of all this for the first time from these newspapers. All this was an extraordinary and most undemocratic method of procedure, and the fact that the House of Commons ultimately ratified it does not alter this fact. This was the method of dictatorship.

The Labour Government thus overnight gave place to a " National Government " in which the Conservatives predominated and a few Liberals and Labourites tried to give a national colouring. Ramsay MacDonald continued as Prime Minister, although he was repudiated and expelled by the Labour Party. Such " national " governments come into existence when there is fear that far-reaching socialistic changes might shake the position of the owning classes, or cast too great a burden on them. Such a position arose in England in August 1931, when the crisis came which later drove the pound from gold, and the reaction to this was the consolidation of the forces of capitalism against socialism. By playing upon the fears of the middle-class masses that all their savings would go if Labour were to win, the National Government thoroughly frightened this petty *bourgeoisie* and got returned by a tremendous majority. MacDonald and his supporters said that the only alternative to the National Government was communism.

Thus in England also old-time democracy has broken down and Parliament is on the decline. Democracy fails when vital issues which move people's passions have to be faced, such as religious clashes, or national and racial (Aryan German *versus* Jew), and above all economic conflicts (between the Haves and the Have-Nots). You will remember that when such a religio-national issue arose in Ireland between Ulster and the rest in 1914, the British Conservative Party actually refused to accept Parliament's decision, and even encouraged civil war. Thus so long as an apparently democratic procedure serves the purposes of the possessing classes, they use it to their advantage to protect their own interests. When this comes in their way and challenges these special privileges and interests, then they discard democracy and take to methods of dictatorship. It is quite possible that the British Parliament might in the future get a majority in favour of sweeping social changes. If such a majority attacks vested interests, the owners of these interests may repudiate Parliament itself, and even encourage a revolt against its decision, as they did in 1914 over the Ulster issue.

So we see that parliament and democracy are only considered desirable by the possessing classes so long as they maintain existing conditions. That is, of course, not real democracy; it the exploitation of the democratic idea for undemocratic purposes. Real democracy has had no chance to exist so far, for there is an essential contradiction between the capitalist system and democracy. Democracy, if it means anything, means equality; not merely the equality of possessing a vote, but economic and social equality. Capitalism means the very opposite : a few people holding economic power and using this to their own advantage. They make laws to keep their own privileged position secure, and anybody who breaks these laws becomes a disturber of law and order whom society must punish. Thus there is no equality under this system, and the liberty allowed is only within the limits of capitalist laws meant to preserve capitalism.

The conflict between capitalism and democracy is inherent and continuous; it is often hidden by misleading propaganda and by the outward forms of democracy, such as parliaments, and the sops that the owning classes throw to the other classes to keep them more or less contented. A time comes when there are no more sops left to be thrown, and then the conflict between the two groups comes to a head, for now the struggle is for the real thing, economic power in the State. When that stage comes, all the supporters of capitalism, who had so far played with different parties, band themselves together to face the danger to their vested interests. Liberals and such-like groups disappear, and the forms of democracy are put aside. This stage has now arrived in Europe and America, and fascism, which is dominant in some form or other in most countries, represents that stage. Labour is everywhere on the defensive, not strong enough to face this new and powerful consolidation of the forces of capitalism. And yet, strangely enough, the capitalist system itself totters and cannot adjust itself to the new world. It

seems certain that even if it succeeds in surviving, it will do so in a
greatly changed and a harsher form.   And this, of course, will be
but another stage in the long conflict.   For modern industry and
modern life itself, under any form of capitalism, are battlefields
where armies are continually clashing against each other.

Some people imagine that all this trouble and conflict and misery
could be avoided if a few sensible persons were in charge of various
governments, and that it is the folly or knavery of politicians and
statesmen that is at the bottom of everything.   They think that if
good people would but get together they could convert the wicked
by moral exhortations and pointing out to them the error of their
ways.   This is a very misleading idea, for the fault does not lie
with individuals, but with a wrong system.   So long as that system
endures, these individuals must act in the way they do.   Groups
that occupy dominant or privileged positions, either foreign national
groups governing another nation, or economic groups within a
nation, convince themselves by an amazing self-deception and
hypocrisy that their special privileges are a just reward of merit.
Any one who challenges this position seems to them a knave and a
scoundrel and an upsetter of settled conditions.   It is impossible
to convince a dominant group that its privileges are unjust, and that
it should give them up.   Individuals may sometimes be so convinced, though rarely, but groups never.   And so, inevitably, come
clashes and conflicts and revolution, and infinite suffering and
misery.

194

A FINAL LOOK ROUND THE WORLD

August 7, 1933

OF the writing of letters there is no end so long as pen and paper
and ink hold out.   And of writing on world happenings also there
is no end, for this world of ours rolls on, and the men and women
and children in it laugh and weep, and love and hate, and fight each
other unceasingly.   It is a story that goes on and on and has no
ending.   And in the to-day in which we live, life seems to be flowing
faster than ever, its tempo is swifter, and changes come rapidly one
after the other.   Even as I write it changes, and what I write to-day
may be out of date, distant, and perhaps out of place, to-morrow.
The river of life is never still; it flows on, and sometimes, as now,
it rushes forward, pitilessly, with a demon energy, ignoring our little
wills and desires, making cruel mock of our petty selves, and tossing
us about like straws on its turbulent waters, rushing on and on no
one knows whither—to a great precipice which will shatter it into a
thousand bits, or to the vast and inscrutable, stately and calm,
ever-changing and yet changeless sea.

I have written already far more than I ever intended or than I ought to have done. My pen has run on. We have finished our long wandering and have completed the last long stage. We have reached to-day and stand on the threshold of to-morrow, wondering what it will be like when it also, in its turn, becomes to-day. Let us pause a little and look round the world. How does it stand on this seventh day of August nineteen hundred and thirty-three?

In India Gandhiji has again been arrested and sentenced and is back in Yervada Prison. Civil Disobedience has been resumed, though in a restricted form, and our comrades go to gaol again. A brave and dear comrade, a friend whom I first met a quarter of a century ago when I was new at Cambridge, Jatindra Mohan Sen-Gupta, has just left us, dying as a prisoner of the British Government. Life merges into death, but the great work to make life worth living for the people of India goes on. Many thousands of India's sons and daughters, the most spirited and often the most gifted, lie in prison or internment camps, spending their youth and energy in conflict against the existing system which enslaves India. All this life and energy might have gone in a building up, in construction; there is so much to be done in this world. But before the construction must come destruction, so that the ground may be cleared for the new structure. We cannot put up a fine building on top of the mud walls of a hovel. The state of India to-day can best be appreciated by the fact that in certain parts of India in Bengal even the manner of dress is regulated by government order, and to dress otherwise means prison. And in Chittagong even little boys (and presumably little girls also) of twelve and upwards have to carry about identity cards with them wherever they go. I do not know if such an extraordinary order has ever been enforced elsewhere, even in Nazi-ridden Germany, or in a war area occupied by enemy troops. We are indeed a ticket-of-leave nation to-day under British rule. And across our north-west frontier our neighbours are being bombed by British aeroplanes.

Our fellow-countrymen in other countries have little honour shown to them; they are seldom made welcome anywhere. And this is not surprising, for how can they have honour elsewhere when they have no honour at home? They are being turned out of South Africa where they were born and bred, and some parts of which, especially in Natal, they had built up with their labour. Colour prejudice, racial hatred, economic conflict, all combine to make these Indians in South Africa castaways with no home or refuge. They must be shipped away to some other place, to British Guiana, or back to India, where they can but starve, or anywhere else, says the Government of the Union of South Africa, so long as they leave South Africa for good.

In East Africa, Indians have played a great part in building up Kenya and the surrounding territories. But they are no longer welcome there; not because the Africans object, but because the handful of European planters object to them. The best areas, the highlands, are reserved for these planters, and neither African nor Indian may possess land there. The poor Africans are far worse off. Originally all the land was in their possession and was their only source of income. Huge areas of this were confiscated by the government, and free grants of land were made to the European settlers. These settlers or planters are thus big landholders there now. They pay no income-tax and hardly any other tax. Almost the whole burden of taxation falls on the poor down-trodden African. It was not easy to tax the African, for he possesses next to nothing. A tax was put on certain necessaries of life for him, like flour and clothing, and indirectly he had to pay it when he bought them. But the most extraordinary tax of all was a direct hut and poll tax on every male over sixteen years old and his dependants, which included women. The principle of taxation is that people should be taxed out of what they earn or possess. As the African possessed practically nothing else, his body was taxed! But how was he to pay this poll tax of twelve shillings per person per year if he had no money? Therein lay the craftiness of this tax, for it forced him to earn some money by working on the plantations of the European settlers, and thus paying the tax. It was a device not only to get money, but also cheap labour for the plantations. So these unhappy Africans sometimes have to travel enormous distances, coming from the interior 700 or 800 miles away to the plantations near the coast (there are no railways in the interior and just a few near the coast), in order to earn enough wages to pay their poll tax.

There is so much more that I could tell you of these poor exploited Africans who do not even know how to make their voices heard by the outside world. Their tale of misery is a long one, and they suffer in silence. Driven off from their best lands, they had to return to them as tenants of the Europeans, who got the land free at the expense of these Africans. These European landlords are semi-feudal masters, and every kind of activity which they dislike has been suppressed. The Africans cannot form any association even to advocate reforms as the collection of any money is forbidden. There is even an ordinance proscribing dancing, because the Africans sometimes mimicked and made fun of European ways in their songs and dances! The peasantry are very poor, and they are not allowed to grow tea or coffee because this would compete with the European planters.

Three years ago the British Government solemnly announced that they were trustees for the African, and that in future he would not be deprived of his lands. Unfortunately for the Africans, gold was discovered in Kenya last year. The solemn promise was forgotten; the European planters made a rush for this land, turned out the African farmers, and started digging for gold. So much for British promises. We are told that all this will eventually work out for the advantage of the Africans, and that they are quite happy at losing their lands!

This capitalist method of exploiting a gold-bearing area is most extraordinary. People are actually made to run for it from a prescribed place, and each one takes possession of part of the area and then works it.   Whether he finds much gold or not in that particular bit depends on his luck.   This method is typical of capitalism. The obvious way to deal with a gold-field seems to be for the government of the country to take possession of it and work it for the advantage of the whole State.   This is what the Soviet Union is doing with its gold-fields in Tadjikistan and elsewhere.

I have said something about Kenya in this final survey of ours because we have ignored Africa in these letters.   Remember it is a vast continent full of the African races who have been cruelly exploited by foreigners for hundreds of years, and are still exploited. They are terribly backward, but they have been kept down, and not given the chance to go ahead.   Where this chance has been given them, as recently at a university founded on the west coast, they have made remarkable progress.

Of the countries of western Asia I have told you enough.   There, and in Egypt, the struggle for freedom goes on in various forms and in various stages.   So also in south-east Asia, in Farther India and Indonesia—Siam, Indo-China, Java, Sumatra and the Dutch Indies, the Philippine Islands.   And everywhere, except in Siam, which is independent, the struggle has two aspects :   the nationalist urge against foreign domination and the urge of the down-trodden classes for social equality or at least economic betterment.

In the Far East of Asia, giant China lies helpless before her aggressors, and is torn by internal dissension into many bits.   One of her faces is turned towards communism, and the other is turned violently away from it, and meanwhile Japan marches forward, almost inexorably, and establishes her hold on large areas of Chinese territory.   But China has survived many a mighty invasion and danger in the long course of her history, and there is little doubt that she will survive the Japanese invasion.

Imperialist Japan, semi-feudal, military-ridden, and yet industrially highly advanced, a strange mixture of the past and the present, nurses ambitious dreams of world empire.   But behind these dreams lies the reality of threatening economic collapse and terrible misery for her teeming population, which is shut out from America and the vast uninhabited spaces of Australia.   And a tremendous check to these dreams also lies in the hostility of the United States, the most powerful of modern nations.   Soviet Russia is another powerful check to Japanese expansion in Asia. In Manchuria and over the deep waters of the Pacific Ocean many keen-eyed observers can already see the approaching shadow of a great war.

The whole of northern Asia is part of the Soviet Union, and is absorbed in planning and building a new world and a new social order.   It is strange that these backward countries that civilization had left behind in its march, and where a kind of feudalism still prevailed, should have jumped forward to a stage which is ahead of the advanced nations of the West.   The Soviet Union in Europe and Asia stands to-day a continuing challenge to the tottering capitalism of the western world.   While trade depression and slump and unemployment and repeated crises paralyse capitalism, and the old order gasps for breath, the Soviet Union is a land full of hope and energy and enthusiasm, feverishly building away and establishing the socialist order. And this abounding youth and life, and the success the Soviet has already achieved, are impressing and attracting thinking people all over the world.

The United States of America, another vast area, is typical of the failure of capitalism. In the midst of great difficulties, crises, labour strikes, and unexampled unemployment, she is making a brave effort to pull together and preserve the capitalist system. The result of this great experiment remains to be seen. But whatever that may be, nothing can take away from America the great advantages that she possesses in her wide territories, rich in almost everything that man requires, and in her technical resources, which are greater than those of any other country, and in her skilled and highly-trained people. The United States, as also the Soviet Union, is bound to play a vastly important part in the world affairs of the future.

And the great continent of South America, with its Latin nations so entirely different from the north ? Unlike the north, there is little racial prejudice here and a great melting of different races— southern Europeans, Spanish, Portuguese, Italians, and Negroes and the so-called Red Indians, the original inhabitants of the American continents. These Red Indians have almost died out in Canada and the United States, but here in the South they still exist in large numbers, especially in Venezuela. They live mostly away from the great cities. You may be surprised to learn that some of these South American cities, like Buenos Aires and Rio de Janeiro, are not only very big, but very beautiful, with magnificent boulevards. Buenos Aires, the capital of Argentina, has a population of two and a half millions, and Rio de Janeiro, the capital of Brazil, has nearly two millions.

Although there is a melting of races, the governing classes belong to the white ruling aristocracy. The clique or group that controls the army and police usually governs, and, as I have told you, there have been frequent revolutions at the top. All the South American countries have abundant mineral resources, and are thus potentially very rich. But meanwhile they are sunk in debt, and as soon as the United States stopped lending money to them four years ago, they got into a hopeless muddle, and there were revolutions all over the place. The three chief countries, the ABC countries as they are called, Argentina, Brazil, and Chile, also succumbed to revolutions, owing to financial difficulties.

Since the summer of 1932 South America has had two little wars of its own, but, like the Japanese war in Manchuria, they are not officially called wars. Ever since the League of Nations covenant and the Kellogg Peace Pact and other pacts, wars hardly occur. When one nation invades another and kills its citizens, this is called a " conflict ", and as a conflict is not prohibited by the pacts, everybody is happy ! These little wars have no world importance, such as the Manchurian one had, but they serve to prove how weak and futile the whole much-vaunted peace machinery of the world is, from the League of Nations to the numerous pacts and agreements. One member of the League invades another member, and the League sits helplessly by, or makes feeble and utterly useless efforts to settle the quarrel.

One of these wars or " conflicts " in South America is between Bolivia and Paraguay over a piece of jungle territory called the Chaco. A witty Frenchman has said : " The struggle between Bolivia and Paraguay over the Chaco jungle reminds me of two bald-headed men fighting for a comb." The struggle is foolish, but it is not quite so silly as this. There are oil interests involved in this vast jungle territory, and the river Paraguay, which runs through it, connects Bolivia with the Atlantic Ocean. The two countries have refused to compromise, and have sacrificed thousands of lives already.

The other conflict is between Colombia and Peru over a little village named Laticia, which Peru seized very improperly. I think that Peru was strongly criticized by the League of Nations.

Latin America (and this includes Mexico) is Catholic in religion. In Mexico violent conflicts have taken place between the State and the Catholic priests. As in Spain, the Mexican Government wanted to curb the great power of the Roman Church in education and in almost everything.

The language of South America is Spanish, except in Brazil, where Portuguese is the official language. Because of this enormous area where it flourishes, Spanish is to-day one of the greatest of world languages. It is a beautiful and sonorous language, with a fine modern literature, and now, because of South America, it is a commercial language of great importance.

195

THE SHADOW OF WAR

August 8, 1933

In our last letter we surveyed rapidly the continents of Asia, Africa, and the Americas. Europe remains, troublesome and quarrelsome Europe, and yet possessing many virtues.

England, so long the leading world Power, has lost her old supremacy and is trying hard to hold on to what remains. Her sea-power, which gave her security and dominance over others and enabled her to build up her empire, is no longer what it was. There was a time, not so long ago, when her navy was bigger and more powerful than that of any other two great Powers. To-day it claims equality only with that of the United States and, in case of need, the United States have the resources to outbuild England rapidly. Even more important than sea-power is air-power to-day, and in this respect England is weaker still; there are several Powers which have more fighting aeroplanes than she has. Her trade supremacy is also gone without hope of recovery, and her great export trade progressively declines. By means of high tariffs and preferences she is trying to preserve the Empire market for her goods. This in itself means a giving up of ambitious ideas of world trade outside the Empire. Even if success comes to her in this more limited sphere, it does not bring back to her the old supremacy. That is gone for ever. Even the limited success within the Empire is of doubtful extent and duration.

England is still, after her fierce duel with America, the financial centre of world trade, and the City of London is the central exchange for it. But this prize is losing all its lustre and value as world trade shrinks and disappears. England and other countries, by their policies of economic nationalism, tariffs, etc., are themselves helping in this shrinkage of world trade. Even if a large measure of world trade continues and the present capitalist system endures, there can be no doubt that the financial leadership of it will eventually shift to New York from London. But very probably before that happens vast changes will have taken place in the capitalist system.

England has a reputation of adapting herself to changing circumstances. The reputation is justified so long as her social basis receives no shock and her possessing classes retain their privileged position. Whether this capacity for adaptation will carry her through fundamental social changes has still to be seen. It is highly unlikely that such a change will be quietly and peacefully effected. Those who have power and privilege do not give them up willingly.

Meanwhile England is shrinking from the bigger world to her Empire, and to preserve this Empire she has agreed to great changes in its structure. The Dominions have a measure of independence, though they are tied in many ways to the British financial system. England has sacrificed much to please her growing Dominions, and yet conflicts arise between them. Australia is bound hand and foot to the Bank of England, and fear of Japanese invasion keeps her closely tied to England; Canada's growing industries compete with some of England's and refuse to give in to them, and Canada has also numerous associations with her great neighbour, the United States; in South Africa there is no great sentiment in favour of the Empire, though the old bitterness has now gone. Ireland stands by herself, and the Anglo-Irish trade war is still going on. The English duties on Irish goods, which were meant to frighten and coerce Ireland into submission, have had a contrary effect. They have given a tremendous push to Irish industries and agriculture, and Ireland is succeeding in becoming to a large extent a self-reliant and self-sufficient nation. Fresh factories have sprung up and grass-land is again becoming corn-land. The food that used to be exported to England is now consumed by the people, and their standards are rising. De Valera has thus triumphantly vindicated his policy, and Ireland to-day is a thorn in British Imperial policy, aggressive, defiant, and not fitting in at all with the Ottawa deals. England thus does not stand to gain much by her trade associations with her Dominions. She could gain much from India, for India still offers a vast market. But political conditions in India, as well as economic distress, are not favourable to British trade. By sending people to gaol one cannot force them to buy British goods. Mr. Stanley Baldwin said recently in Manchester :

> "The day when we could dictate to India and tell her when and where to buy her goods was gone. The safeguard for trade was good will. We should never sell goods to India by cotton streamers on the end of a bayonet."

Apart from internal conditions in India, England has to face fierce Japanese competition here and elsewhere in the East and in some of the Dominions.

So England is trying hard to hold on to what she has got by making of her Empire an economic unit, and adding to this such other small countries as come to terms with her, such as Denmark or the Scandinavian countries. This policy is being forced on her by the very logic of events; there is no other way. Even to protect herself in times of war she must be more self-contained. She is therefore developing her agriculture now also. How far this imperial policy of economic nationalism will succeed no one can say now. I have suggested many difficulties which will come in the way of success. If failure comes, then the whole structure of Empire must collapse, and the English people will have to face a much lower standard of living, unless they change over to a socialist economy. But even the success of the policy is full of dangers, for it may result in the ruin of many European countries, whose trade will thus not have a sufficient outlet, and the bankruptcy of England's debtors will in its turn do harm to England's position.

Economic conflicts are also bound to arise against Japan and America. With the United States there is rivalry in many fields, and, as the world stands to-day, the United States, with her vast resources, must go ahead while England declines. This process can only lead to a quiet acceptance of defeat in the struggle by England, or to the risk of war to make a final effort to save what she has before that too goes and she is too weak to challenge her rivals.

Yet another great rival of England is the Soviet Union. They stand for diametrically opposite policies, and they glare at each other and intrigue against each other all over Europe and Asia. The two Powers may live at peace with each other for a while, but it is quite impossible to reconcile the two, for they stand for wholly different ideals.

England is a satisfied Power to-day because she has got all she wants. Her fear is that she will lose this, and the fear is justified. She tries hard to maintain the *status quo*, and thereby her present position, by using the League of Nations for this purpose. But events are too strong for her or for any Power. Undoubtedly she is strong to-day but equally undoubtedly she weakens and declines as an imperialist Power, and we are witnessing the evening of her great Empire.

Crossing over to the continent of Europe, there is France, also an imperialist Power with a great empire in Africa and Asia. In a military sense she is the most powerful nation in Europe.[1] She has a mighty army, and she is the leader of a group of other nations : Poland, Czechoslovakia, Belgium, Rumania, Yugoslavia. And yet she fears the militant spirit of Germany, especially since the Hitler régime. Hitler has indeed succeeded in bringing about a remarkable change of feelings between capitalist France and Soviet Russia. A common enemy has made them quite friendly to each other.

In Germany the Nazi Terror still continues, and reports of new cruelties and atrocities come daily. How long this brutality will continue it is impossible to say ; it has already lasted many months, and there is no abatement of it. Such repression can never be the sign of a stable government. Probably if Germany had been strong enough in a military sense there would have been a war already in Europe. This war may yet come. Hitler is fond of saying that he is the last refuge from communism, and this may be true, for the only alternative to Hitlerism in Germany now is communism.

Italy, under Mussolini, takes a very cold, matter-of-fact, and selfish view of international politics, and does not indulge in pious phrases about peace and good will, as other nations do. She prepares for war strenuously, for she is convinced that war is bound to come before long, and meanwhile she manœuvres for position. Being fascist, she welcomes fascism in Germany, and keeps on friendly terms with the Hitlerites ; and yet she opposes the great aim of German policy—the union with Austria. Such a union would bring the German frontier right up to the Italian, and Mussolini does not fancy this nearness of his brother fascist of Germany.[2]

Central Europe is a heaving mass of petty nations suffering in the grip of the slump and from the after-effects of the World War, and now thoroughly upset and frightened by Hitler and his Nazis. In all these Central European countries, and especially where there are Germans, as in Austria, Nazi parties are growing. But anti-Nazi feeling is also growing, and the result is conflict. Austria is at present the chief field for this conflict.

Some time back, in 1932, I think, the three pro-French States of Central Europe and the Danube area—Czechoslovakia, Rumania, and Yugoslavia—formed a union or alliance. All these three States had profited by the World War settlement, and they wanted to keep what they had got. For this purpose they joined together and formed what was in reality an alliance for war. This is called the " Little *Entente* ". This Little *Entente* comprising the three

---

[1] This is no longer so since German rearmament. After the Munich Pact of September 1938, France has almost become a second-class Power. Her group of alliances in Central Europe has also broken up.

[2] Austria was invaded and absorbed by Germany in March 1938. Mussolini was compelled by circumstances to agree to it, but Italy strongly disapproved of the change.

States practically forms a new Power in Europe, which is pro-French and anti-German and opposed to Italian policy also.

The triumph of the Nazis in Germany was a danger signal to the Little Entente as well as to Poland, for the Nazis not only wanted a revision of the Versailles Peace Treaty (all Germans wanted this), but talked in terms which seemed to bring war near. So aggressive and violent were the Nazi language and other tactics that even such States as wanted a treaty revision, like Austria and Hungary, got frightened. As a result of Hitlerism and in fear of it, all the States of Central Europe and the East which had so far bitterly hated each other drew nearer to one another—the Little Entente, Poland, Austria, Hungary, and the Balkan States. There has even been talk of an economic union between them. These countries, and notably Poland and Czechoslovakia, have also become more friendly towards Soviet Russia since the Nazi eruption in Germany. A consequence of this was the general non-aggression pact signed between them and Russia some weeks ago.

Spain, as I have told you, has recently had a revolution. It cannot settle down, and seems to hover on the brink of another change.

So you see what a curious chequer-board Europe is at present, with its conflicts and hatreds, and rival groups of nations glaring at each other. There is interminable talk of disarmament, and yet everywhere there is arming going on and new and terrible weapons of war and destruction are being invented. There is also plenty of talk of international co-operation, and conferences without number have been held. All to little purpose. The League of Nations itself is a pitiful failure, and the last effort to pull together at the World Economic Conference has also come and gone with no success. There is a proposal that the various countries of Europe, or rather Europe without Russia, should join together to form a kind of United States of Europe. The " Pan-Europe " movement this is called, and it is really an effort to form an anti-Soviet *bloc*, as well as to get over the innumerable difficulties and tangles due to there being such a large number of little nations. But national hatreds are far too powerful for any one to pay attention to such a proposal.

In reality each country is drifting farther apart from the others. The slump and world crisis have quickened this process by pushing all countries along the lines of economic nationalism. Each sits behind high tariff barriers and tries to keep out as far as possible foreign goods. It cannot, of course, keep out all foreign goods, because no country is self-sufficient—that is, capable of producing everything it requires. But the tendency is for it to grow or manufacture everything it needs. Some essential articles it may not be able to grow because of its climate. For instance, England cannot grow cotton or jute or tea or coffee and many other articles which require a warmer climate. This means that in future trade will be largely confined between countries having different climates, and therefore growing and making different articles. Countries manufacturing the same type of articles will have little use for each other's

2 H

goods. Thus trade will go north and south, and not east and west, for climates vary north and south. A tropical country may deal with a temperate or cold country, but not two tropical countries with each other, or two temperate countries. Of course there may be other considerations also, such as the mineral resources of a country. But in the main the north and south considerations will apply to international trade. All other trade will be stopped by tariff barriers.

This seems to be an inevitable tendency to-day. It is called the final phase in the industrial revolution when each country is sufficiently industrialized. It is true that Asia and Africa are far from industrialized yet. Africa is too backward and too poor to absorb manufactured goods in any quantity. The three large areas which might continue to absorb such foreign goods are India, China, and Siberia. Foreign industrial countries are looking eagerly towards these three huge potential markets. Having been cut off from many of their usual markets, they are thinking of this " push towards Asia " in order to dispose of their surplus goods, and thus prop up their tottering capitalism. But it is not so easy to exploit Asia now, partly because of the development of Asiatic industries, and partly because of international rivalry. England wants to keep India as a market for her own goods, but Japan and the United States and Germany want a look in also. So also in China; and to add to this is her present disturbed state and want of proper communications, which make trade difficult. Soviet Russia is prepared to take quite a lot of manufactured goods from abroad if she is given credit and not asked to pay for them immediately. But very soon the Soviet Union will make almost everything it requires.

The whole past tendency has been towards greater interdependence between nations, a greater internationalism. Even though separate independent national States remained, an enormous and intricate structure of international relations and trade grew up. This process went so far as to conflict with the national States and with nationalism itself. The next natural step was a socialized international structure. Capitalism, having had its day, had reached the stage when it was time for it to retire in favour of socialism. But unhappily such a voluntary retirement never takes place. Because crisis and collapse threatened it, it has withdrawn into its shell and tried to reverse the past tendency towards interdependence. Hence economic nationalism. The question is if this can succeed, and even if it does so, for how long ?

The whole world is a strange mix-up, a terrible tangle of conflicts and jealousies, and the new tendencies but increase the field of these conflicts. In every continent, in every country, the weak and the oppressed want to share in the good things of life which they themselves help to produce. They claim payment of their debt, long overdue to them. In some places they are doing so loudly and harshly and aggressively; in other places more quietly. Can we blame them if, angry and bitter at the treatment and exploitation they have been subjected to for so long, they act in a manner we do not like? They were ignored and looked down upon; no one took the trouble to teach them drawing-room manners.

This upheaval of the weak and the oppressed frightens the possessing classes everywhere, and they band themselves together to suppress it. And thus fascism grows and imperialism crushes all opposition. The fine phrases about democracy and the people's good and trusteeship retire into the background, and the naked rule of the possessing classes and vested interests becomes more obvious, and in many places it seems to meet with triumph. A harsher age appears, an age of iron and aggressive violence, for everywhere the fight is one of life and death between the old order and the new. Everywhere, whether it is in Europe or America or India, the stakes are high and the fate of the old régime hangs in the balance, even though for the moment it may be strongly entrenched. Partial reform does not meet or solve the problems of the day when the whole imperialist-capitalist system is shaken to its foundation and cannot even meet its liabilities or the demands made upon it.

All these innumerable conflicts, political, economic, racial, darken the world to-day, and carry the shadow of war with them. It is said that the greatest of these conflicts, the most fundamental of them, is the one between imperialism and fascism on the one side and communism on the other. These face each other all over the world, and between them there is no room for compromise.

Feudalism, capitalism, socialism, syndicalism, anarchism, communism—so many isms! And behind them all stalks opportunism! But there is also idealism for those who care to have it; not the idealism of empty fancies and an imagination run riot, but the idealism of working for a great human purpose, a great ideal which we seek to make real. Somewhere George Bernard Shaw has said :—

> "This is the true joy in life, the being used for a purpose recognized by yourself as a mighty one; the being thoroughly worn out before you are thrown on the scrap heap; the being a force of nature, instead of a feverish, selfish little clod of ailments and grievances, complaining that the world will not devote itself to making you happy."

Our incursions into history have shown us how the world has grown more and more compact, how different parts have come together and become interdependent. The world has indeed become one single inseparable whole, each part influencing, and being influenced by, the other. It is quite impossible now to have a separate history of nations. We have outgrown that stage, and only a single world history, connecting the different threads from all the nations, and seeking to find the real forces that move them, can now be written with any useful purpose.

Even in past times, when nations were cut off from each other by many physical and other barriers, we have seen how common international and inter-continental forces shaped them. Great individuals have always counted in history, for the human factor is important in every crisis of destiny; but greater than any individual are the mighty forces at work which, almost blindly and sometimes cruelly, forge ahead, pushing us hither and thither.

So it is to-day with us. Mighty forces are at work moving the hundreds of millions of human beings, and they go ahead like an earthquake or some other upheaval of Nature. We cannot stop them, however much we may try, and yet we may, in our own little corner of the world, make some slight difference to them in speed or direction. According to our different temperaments we meet them—some frightened by them, others welcoming them, some trying to combat them, others submitting helplessly to the heavy hand of fate, while still others try to ride the tempest and control it a little and direct it, willingly facing the perils that this involves for the joy of helping actively in a mighty process.

There is no peace for us in this turbulent twentieth century, a third of which has already passed with its full complement of war and revolution. " The whole world is in revolution," says the great fascist, Mussolini. " Events themselves are a tremendous force pushing us on like some implacable will." And the great Communist, Trotsky, also warns us of this century not to expect too much of peace and comfort. " It is clear," he says, " that the twentieth century is the most disturbed century within the memory of humanity. Any contemporary of ours who wants peace and comfort before everything else has chosen a bad time to be born."

The whole world is in labour, and the shadow of war and revolution lies heavy everywhere. If we cannot escape from this inevitable destiny of ours, how shall we face it ? Ostrich-like, shall we hide our heads from it ? Or shall we play a brave part in the shaping of events and, facing risks and perils if need be, have the joy of great and noble adventure, and the feeling that our " steps are merging with those of history " ?

All of us, or at any rate those who think, are looking forward expectantly to the future as it unrolls itself and becomes the present. Some await the outcome with hope, others with fear. Will it be a fairer and a happier world, where the good things of life will not be reserved for a few, but are freely enjoyed by the masses. Or a harsher world than even to-day, from which many of the amenities of present-day civilization have gone after fierce and destructive wars ? These are two extremes. Either may occur, it seems improbable that a middle course will prevail.

While we wait and watch, we work for the kind of world we would like to have. Man has not progressed from his brute stage by helpless submission to the ways of Nature, but often by a defiance of them and a desire to dominate them for human advantage.

Such is To-day. The making of To-morrow lies with you and your generation, the millions of girls and boys all over the world who are growing up and training themselves to take part in this To-morrow.

196

THE LAST LETTER

August 9, 1933

WE have finished, my dear; the long story has ended. I need write no more, but the desire to end off with a kind of flourish induces me to write another letter—the Last Letter !

It was time I finished, for the end of my two-year term draws near. In three and thirty days from to-day I should be discharged, if indeed I am not released sooner, as the gaoler sometimes threatens to do. The full two years are not over yet, but I have received three and a half months' remission of my sentence, as all well-behaved prisoners do. For I am supposed to be a well-behaved prisoner, a reputation which I have certainly done nothing to deserve. So ends my sixth sentence, and I shall go out again into the wide world, but to what purpose ? *A quoi bon ?* When most of my friends and comrades lie in gaol and the whole country seems a vast prison.

What a mountain of letters I have written ! And what a lot of good *swadeshi* [1] ink I have spread out on *swadeshi* paper. Was it worth while, I wonder ? Will all this paper and ink convey any message to you that will interest you ? You will say, yes, of course, for you will feel that any other answer might hurt me, and you are too partial to me to take such a risk. But whether you care for them or not, you cannot grudge me the joy of having written them, day after day, during these two long years. It was winter when I came. Winter gave place to our brief spring, slain all too soon by the summer heat; and then, when the ground was parched and dry and men and beasts panted for breath, came the monsoon, with its bountiful supply of fresh and cool rain-water. Autumn followed, and the sky was wonderfully clear and blue and the afternoons were pleasant. The year's cycle was over, and again it began : winter and spring and summer and the rainy season. I have sat here, writing to you and thinking of you, and watched the seasons go by, and listened to the pitapat of the rain on my barrack roof—

> " *O doux bruit de la pluie,*
> *Parterre et sur les toits !*
> *Pour un cœur qui s'ennuie,*
> *Oh ! le chant de la pluie !* "

Benjamin Disraeli, the great English statesman of the nineteenth century, has written : " Other men condemned to exile and captivity, if they survive, despair; the man of letters may reckon those days as the sweetest of his life." He was writing about Hugo Grotius, a famous Dutch jurist and philosopher of the seventeenth century, who was condemned to imprisonment for life, but managed to escape after two years. He spent these two years in

---

[1] *Swadeshi* means made in one's own country.

prison in philosophic and literary work. There have been many famous literary gaolbirds, the two best known perhaps being the Spaniard, Cervantes, who wrote *Don Quixote*, and the Englishman, John Bunyan, the author of *The Pilgrim's Progress*.

I am not a man of letters, and I am not prepared to say that the many years I have spent in gaol have been the sweetest in my life, but I must say that reading and writing have helped me wonderfully to get through them. I am not a literary man, and I am not a historian; what, indeed, am I? I find it difficult to answer that question. I have been a dabbler in many things; I began with science at college, and then took to the law, and, after developing various other interests in life, finally adopted the popular and widely practised profession of gaol-going in India!

You must not take what I have written in these letters as the final authority on any subject. A politician wants to have a say on every subject, and he always pretends to know much more than he actually does. He has to be watched carefully! These letters of mine are but superficial sketches joined together by a thin thread. I have rambled on, skipping centuries and many important happenings, and then pitching my tent for quite a long time on some event which interested me. As you will notice, my likes and dislikes are pretty obvious, and so also sometimes are my moods in gaol. I do not want you to take all this for granted; there may, indeed, be many errors in my accounts. A prison, with no libraries or reference books at hand, is not the most suitable place in which to write on historical subjects. I have had to rely very largely on the many note-books which I have accumulated since I began my visits to gaol twelve years ago. Many books have also come to me here; they have come and gone, for I could not collect a library here. I have shamelessly taken from these books facts and ideas; there is nothing original in what I have written. Perhaps occasionally you may find my letters difficult to follow; skip those parts, do not mind them. The grown-up in me got the better of me sometimes, and I wrote as I should not have done.

I have given you the barest outline; this is not history; they are just fleeting glimpses of our long past. If history interests you, if you feel some of the fascination of history, you will find your way to many books which will help you to unravel the threads of past ages. But reading books alone will not help. If you would know the past you must look upon it with sympathy and with understanding. To understand a person who lived long ago, you will have to understand his environment, the conditions under which he lived, the ideas that filled his mind. It is absurd for us to judge of past people as if they lived now and thought as we do. There is no one to defend slavery to-day, and yet the great Plato held that slavery was essential. Within recent times scores of thousands of lives were given in an effort to retain slavery in the United States. We cannot judge the past from the standards of the present. Every one will willingly admit this. But every one will not admit the equally absurd habit of judging the present by the standards of the past. The various religions have especially helped in petrifying old beliefs and faiths and customs, which may have had some use in the age and country of their birth, but which are singularly unsuitable in our present age.

If, then, you look upon past history with the eye of sympathy, the dry bones will fill up with flesh and blood, and you will see a mighty procession of living men and women and children in every age and every clime, different from us and yet very like us, with much the same human virtues and human failings. History is not a magic show, but there is plenty of magic in it for those who have eyes to see.

Innumerable pictures from the gallery of history crowd our minds. Egypt—Babylon—Nineveh—the old Indian civilizations — the coming of the Aryans to India and their spreading out over Europe and Asia—the wonderful record of Chinese culture—Knossos and Greece—Imperial Rome and Byzantium—the triumphant march of the Arabs across two continents—the renaissance of Indian culture and its decay—the little-known Maya and Aztec civilizations of America—the vast conquests of the Mongols—the Middle Ages in Europe with their wonderful Gothic cathedrals—the coming of Islam to India and the Moghal Empire—the Renaissance of learning and art in western Europe—the discovery of America and the sea-routes to the East—the beginnings of Western aggression in the East—the coming of the big machine and the development of capitalism—the spread of industrialism and European domination and imperialism—and the wonders of science in the modern world.

Great empires have risen and fallen and been forgotten by man for thousands of years, till their remains were dug up again by patient explorers from under the sands that covered them. And yet many an idea, many a fancy, has survived and proved stronger and more persistent than the empire.

> " Egypt's might is tumbled down,
> Down a-down the deeps of thought;
> Greece is fallen and Troy town,
> Glorious Rome hath lost her crown,
> Venice' pride is nought.
> But the dreams their children dreamed,
> Fleeting, unsubstantial, vain,
> Shadowy as the shadows seemed,
> Airy nothing, as they deemed,
> These remain."

So sings Mary Coleridge.

The past brings us many gifts; indeed, all that we have to-day of culture, civilization, science, or knowledge of some aspects of the truth, is a gift of the distant or recent past to us. It is right that we acknowledge our obligation to the past. But the past does not exhaust our duty or obligation. We owe a duty to the future also, and perhaps that obligation is even greater than the one we owe to the past. For the past is past and done with, we cannot change it; the future is yet to come, and perhaps we may be able to shape it a little. If the past has given us some part of the truth, the future also hides many aspects of the truth, and invites us to search for them. But often the past is jealous of the future and holds us in a terrible grip, and we have to struggle with it to get free to face and advance towards the future.

History, it is said, has many lessons to teach us; and there is another saying that history never repeats itself. Both are true, for we cannot learn anything from it by slavishly trying to copy it, or by expecting it to repeat itself or remain stagnant; but we can learn something from it by prying behind it and trying to discover the forces that move it. Even so, what we get is seldom a straight answer. "History," says Karl Marx, "has no other way of answering old questions than by putting new ones."

The old days were days of faith, blind, unquestioning faith. The wonderful temples and mosques and cathedrals of past centuries could never have been built but for the overpowering faith of the architects and builders and people generally. The very stones that they reverently put one on top of the other, or carved into beautiful designs, tell us of this faith. The old temple spire, the mosque with its slender minarets, the Gothic cathedral—all of them pointing upward with an amazing intensity of devotion, as if offering a prayer in stone or marble to the sky above—thrill us even now, though we may be lacking in that faith of old of which they are the embodiments. But the days of that faith are gone, and gone with them is that magic touch in stone. Thousands of temples and mosques and cathedrals continue to be built, but they lack the spirit that made them live during the Middle Ages. There is little difference between them and the commercial offices which are so representative of our age.

Our age is a different one; it is an age of disillusion, of doubt and uncertainty and questioning. We can no longer accept many of the ancient beliefs and customs; we have no more faith in them, in Asia or in Europe or America. So we search for new ways, new aspects of the truth more in harmony with our environment. And we question each other and debate and quarrel and evolve any number of " isms " and philosophies. As in the days of Socrates, we live in an age of questioning, but that questioning is not confined to a city like Athens; it is world-wide.

Sometimes the injustice, the unhappiness, the brutality of the world oppress us and darken our minds, and we see no way out. With Matthew Arnold, we feel that there is no hope in the world and that all we can do is to be true to one another.

> " For the world which seems
> To lie before us, like a land of dreams,
> So various, so beautiful, so new,
> Hath really neither joy, nor love, nor light,
> Nor certitude, nor peace, nor help for pain;
> And we are here, as on a darkling plain
> Swept with confused alarms of struggle and flight,
> Where ignorant armies clash by night."

And yet if we take such a dismal view we have not learnt aright
the lesson of life or of history. For history teaches us of growth
and progress and of the possibility of an infinite advance for man.
And life is rich and varied, and though it has many swamps and
marshes and muddy places, it has also the great sea, and the
mountains, and snow, and glaciers, and wonderful starlit nights
(especially in gaol !), and the love of family and friends, and the
comradeship of workers in a common cause, and music, and books
and the empire of ideas. So that each one of us may well say :—

> " Lord, though I lived on earth, the child of earth,
> Yet was I fathered by the starry sky."

It is easy to admire the beauties of the universe and to live in a
world of thought and imagination. But to try to escape in this
way from the unhappiness of others, caring little what happens to
them, is no sign of courage or fellow-feeling. Thought, in order to
justify itself, must lead to action. " Action is the end of thought ",
says our friend Romain Rolland. " All thought which does not
look towards action is an abortion and a treachery. If then we are
the servants of thought we must be the servants of action."

People avoid action often because they are afraid of the consequences, for action means risk and danger. Danger seems terrible
from a distance ; it is not so bad if you have a close look at it.
And often it is a pleasant companion, adding to the zest and delight
of life. The ordinary course of life becomes dull at times, and we
take too many things for granted and have no joy in them. And
yet how we appreciate these common things of life when we have
lived without them for a while ! Many people go up high mountains
and risk life and limb for the joy of the climb and the exhilaration
that comes from a difficulty surmounted, a danger overcome ; and
because of the danger that hovers all around them, their perceptions
get keener, their joy of the life which hangs by a thread, the more
intense.

All of us have our choice of living in the valleys below, with their
unhealthy mists and fogs, but giving a measure of bodily security ;
or of climbing the high mountains, with risk and danger for companions, to breathe the pure air above, and take joy in the distant
views, and welcome the rising sun.

I have given you many quotations and extracts from poets and
others in this letter. I shall finish up with one more. It is from
the Gitanjali ; it is a poem, or prayer, by Rabindra Nath Tagore :—

> " Where the mind is without fear and the head is held high;
> Where knowledge is free;
> Where the world has not been broken up into fragments by narrow
> domestic walls;
> Where words come out from the depth of truth;
> Where tireless striving stretches its arms towards perfection;
> Where the clear stream of reason has not lost its way into the dreary
> desert sand of dead habit;
> Where the mind is led forward by thee into ever-widening thought and
> action—
> Into that heaven of freedom, my Father, let my country awake."

We have finished, *carissima*, and this last letter ends.   The last letter !   Certainly not.   I shall write you many more.   But this series ends, and so

Tamām Shud !

POSTSCRIPT

Arabian Sea
November 14, 1938

FIVE and a quarter years ago I wrote to you the last letter of this series from my cell in the District Gaol of Dehra Dun.   My two-year sentence of imprisonment was nearing its end, and I put away the huge pile of the letters that I had written to you during that long period of solitary living (but with you always as my companion in thought), and prepared my mind for my release to the outer world of movement and action.   That discharge came soon afterwards, but five months later I was back again in the familiar surroundings of prison with another sentence of two years.   Again I took the pen and wrote a story, a more personal one this time.

I came out again, and we shared sorrow together, a sorrow that has shadowed my life ever since.   But personal misfortune is of little account in this world of sorrow and strife, which demands from us all our strength in the struggles that convulse it.   And so we parted, and you went to the sheltered paths of study, and I to the din and tumult of the struggle.

Five years and more have passed with their burden of war and suffering, and ever the contrast grows between the world we live in and the world of our dreams.   Hope itself sometimes gasps for breath, throttled by the evil that pursues us.   And yet as I write, the Arabian Sea stretches out before me in all its strength and beauty, silent as a dream, shimmering in the silver of the moonlight.

I am supposed to tell you in this Postscript the story of these five years, for these Letters are going to appear in a new garb, and my publisher demands that they should be brought up to date.   It is a difficult task, for so much has happened during this period that if I took to writing about it, and had the time for it, I would exceed all bounds and produce another book.   Even a mere record of the principal events would be long and burdensome.   I must therefore give you the barest outline of what has happened.   I have added some notes to the Letters already written, giving additional facts, and now we shall have a brief survey of these years.

In my concluding Letters I drew your attention to the tremendous contradictions and rivalries of the modern world, to the growth of fascism and naziism, and to the shadow of war.   These five years have intensified these rivalries and conflicts, and though World War has so far been avoided, great and horrible wars have taken place in Africa, in Europe, and in the Far East of Asia.   Every year, and sometimes every month, brings its tale of fresh aggression and horror. The world grows more and more disorganized, international relations become anarchical, and the League of Nations and the other attempts made at international co-operation have ended as dismal failures. Disarmament is a thing of the past, and each nation arms feverishly, night and day, to the utmost of its capacity. Fear grips the world, and Europe, lashed by aggressive and triumphant naziism and fascism, deteriorates rapidly and takes the road to barbarism.

We examined at length in our previous letters the issues that lay behind the Great War of 1914–18. War came, and out of it emerged the Treaty of Versailles and the Covenant of the League. But the old problems were unsolved, and many new ones arose: reparations, war debts, disarmament, collective security, economic crisis, and unemployment on a vast scale. Behind the problems of the peace there still remained vital social problems which had upset the equilibrium of the world. In the Soviet Union the new social forces had proved victorious, and were trying to build up, in face of enormous difficulties and world opposition, a new kind of world. Elsewhere deep social changes went on, but found no outlet, and were held back by the existing political and economic structure. Abundance came to the world, a vast expansion of production; the dream of ages was realized. But the slave long used to his bondage is afraid of freedom, and foolish humanity has grown so used to scarcity that it cannot easily think in other terms. And so the new wealth is deliberately thrown away, restricted and confined, and actually there is more unemployment and misery.

Conference after conference met and the nations of the world gathered together to solve this amazing paradox and to ensure peace. There were pacts and agreements and alliances—Washington, Locarno, the Kellogg Pact, non-aggression pacts—but the basic problems were not touched, and at the first touch of brutal reality these agreements and pacts vanished away, leaving the naked sword as the arbiter of Europe's destiny. The Treaty of Versailles is dead, the map of Europe has changed again, and a new division of the world is taking place. The question of war debts has faded away and the richest nations have decided not to pay them.

So we come back to the pre-war age of 1914 and before, with all its problems and conflicts, but intensified a hundredfold by what has happened since. The capitalist system in decay leads to economic nationalism as well as the growth of greater monopolies; it becomes aggressive and violent, and cannot even tolerate parliamentary democracy. Fascism and naziism arise in all their naked brutality, and make war the end and aim of all their policy. At the same time a great new Power arises in the Soviet areas, which is a continuing challenge to the old order and a powerful check to imperialism and fascism alike.

We live in an age of revolution, a revolution which started when the War broke out in 1914, and continues from year to year with the world in the throes of conflict everywhere. The French Revolution of 150 years ago gradually ushered in an age of political equality, but the times have changed, and that by itself is not enough to-day. The boundaries of democracy have to be widened now so as to include economic equality also. This is the great revolution through which we are all passing, the revolution to ensure economic equality, and thus to give democracy its full meaning, and to bring ourselves in line with the advance of science and technology.

This equality does not fit in with imperialism or with capitalism, which are based on inequality and the exploitation of nation or class. Therefore it is resisted by those who profit by this exploitation, and when the conflict grows, even the conception of political equality and parliamentary democracy is repudiated. That is fascism, which in many ways takes us back to the Middle Ages. It exalts the domination of Race, and in place of the divine right of an autocratic king has the divine right of an all-powerful Leader. The growth of fascism during the last five years, and its attack on every democratic principle and conception of freedom and civilization have made the defence of democracy the vital question to-day. The present world conflict is not between communism and socialism on the one hand and fascism on the other. It is between democracy and fascism, and all the real forces of democracy line up and become anti-fascists. Spain to-day is the supreme example of this.

But behind that democracy lies inevitably the idea of an extension of democracy, and for fear of this, reactionaries everywhere, even though paying lip-service to democracy, give their sympathy or allegiance to fascism. The rôle of the fascist Powers is clear enough; there is no doubt about their aims or policy. But the governing factor of the situation has been the rôle of the so-called democratic Powers, more especially England. The British Government has throughout played a reactionary rôle in Asia, Africa, and Europe, and given every encouragement to fascism and naziism. It has done so, curiously enough, even at the cost of endangering the security of the British Empire, so great was its fear of the growth of real democracy and its class sympathy with the leaders of fascism. If fascism has grown and begun to dominate the world, the credit for this must largely go to the British Government. The United States of America, with a keener sense of democracy, more than once offered to co-operate with other Powers to check fascist aggression, but England refused that offer. France has become so utterly dependent on the City of London and on British foreign policy that it dare not adopt an independent policy.

In Labour matters also Britain has been consistently reactionary at the International Labour Conferences. In June 1937 the I.L.O. adopted a convention of forty hours a week for the textile industry. It did so in spite of the opposition of Great Britain. Even the British Dominions deserted Britain and supported the United States. But of course the delegate for India, nominated by the British Government, sided with Britain. The members of the United States delegation, including employers and Government representatives, remarked that " until they came to Geneva they had no idea how reactionary the British Government was." "Great Britain," one of them further added, " has become the spear-head of reaction."

The League of Nations, with all its weaknesses, still embodied the international idea, and its covenant laid down penalties for aggression. It had failed to take any action (except for appointing a commission of inquiry and subsequent condemnation of aggression) when Japan invaded Manchuria. The British Government had indeed encouraged Japan in this adventure, and ever since then, with a few minor lapses in the right direction, it followed a policy of ignoring and weakening the League. The rise of naziism, with its avowed policy of aggression, was a direct challenge to the League, but England and, to a certain extent, France, submitted to this challenge and allowed the League to fade away. The fascist Powers left the League, Germany doing so in October 1933, and Japan and Italy later. In September 1934 the Soviet Union joined the League and put fresh blood into it. Fear of Nazi Germany led France to an alliance with the Soviets, but England preferred an alignment with Nazi Germany to co-operation with the Soviet Union even on the basis of the League Covenant. Each successful aggression emboldened the fascist Powers and convinced them that they could defy the League with impunity, for they realized that the British Government would not go against them.

It is this progressive alignment of the British Government with the fascist Powers that explains much that has happened in China, Abyssinia, Spain, and Central Europe. It makes us understand why the proud structure of the League of Nations, which represented so much the hope of peace and progress of mankind, lies in ruins to-day.

We have seen how Japan successfully defied the League and the world in Manchuria and set up a puppet State, Manchukuo, there. Although there was actual military invasion, there was no declaration of war. Internal revolts were fomented, and these were made the excuse for intervention. This new technique was subsequently perfected by Italy and Nazi Germany, and to it was added false propaganda abroad on an unprecedented scale. There are no declarations of war now; they belong to a past age. As Hitler, speaking at Nuremburg in 1937, said : " If ever I wanted to attack an opponent, I would not negotiate and prepare for months, but would do as I always did : emerge out of the dark and with the swiftness of lightning throw myself upon my opponent."

In January 1935 Germany occupied the Saar basin after a plebiscite. In May that year Hitler finally repudiated the disarmament clauses of the Treaty of Versailles and decreed compulsory military service for Germans. This open and one-sided breach of Versailles frightened France. But England tacitly accepted it, and indeed went a long step further a month later by concluding secretly a naval pact with Germany. This pact itself was a breach of Versailles, and thus England herself ignored the Peace Treaty. The amazing part of this was that she did so without reference to her old ally, France, and just when German rearmament on a colossal scale was threatening Europe. France was terrified at what it considered the perfidy of England, and rushed to Mussolini to come to terms with him, so as to minimize the danger on her Italian frontier.

Abyssinia.—This gave Mussolini the chance for which he had long waited. For years past he had planned the invasion of Abyssinia, but he had hesitated because he was not sure of the British and French attitude. There had been great tension between France and Italy, and in October 1934 King Alexander of Yugoslavia and the French Foreign Minister, Louis Barthou, were murdered in Marseilles, apparently by an Italian agent. Now Mussolini felt confident that neither France nor England would offer any effective opposition to his invasion of Abyssinia. In October 1935 this invasion began, when the League of Nations was actually in session. Abyssinia was a member State of the League, and the world was shocked. The League declared Italy to be the aggressor, and after much delay applied some economic sanctions against her—that is member States were forbidden to deal with her in regard to many commodities. But the really important articles, which were essential for the war, such as oil, iron, steel, and coal, were not included in this list. The Anglo-Iranian Oil Co. worked hard and over-time to supply oil to Italy. Italy was inconvenienced by the sanctions, but no great difficulty was placed in her way. The United States of America suggested an embargo on oil, but Britain would not agree.

The British Foreign Minister, Sir Samuel Hoare, and Monsieur Laval, the French Minister, came to an agreement to hand over a great part of Abyssinia to Italy, but there was such a public outcry that Sir Samuel Hoare had to resign. Meanwhile the Abyssinians fought bravely, but they were powerless against wholesale bombing from low-flying aeroplanes. Incendiary bombs and gas bombs were used on civilians, women and children, ambulances and hospitals, and the most brutal massacres took place. In May 1936 the Italian Army entered Addis Ababa, the capital, and later occupied large areas of the country. Two and a half years have passed since then, but Abyssinian resistance still continues in outlying areas. Abyssinia is far from conquered yet, although England and France have now recognized the conquest.

The tragedy and betrayal of Abyssinia by the League Powers showed the world that the League was powerless. Hitler could now defy it without fear, and in March 1936 he marched his troops into the demilitarized zone of the Rhineland. This was another violation of Versailles.

Spain.—The year 1936 witnessed another step in the fascist attempt to dominate Europe, and this was destined to become a vital struggle for democracy and freedom. We have seen how rival forces fought for mastery in Spain, and how the young Republic struggled against clerical and semi-feudal reaction. At last the progressive parties joined together, and in February 1936 formed a Popular Front. Previous to this a Popular Front had been established in France in order to combat the growing forces of fascism which openly threatened the French Republic and even organized an abortive rising. The French Popular Front came on a crest of great popular enthusiasm and, succeeding in the elections, formed a government which passed many laws giving relief to the workers.

The Spanish Popular Front also succeeded in the elections to the Cortes and formed a government. It was pledged to various and reforms, which had been too long delayed, and to curb the power of the Church. Fearing these reforms, the reactionary elements banded together and decided to strike. They sought and obtained aid from Italy and Germany, and on July 18, 1936, General Franco began his revolt with the help of the Spanish Moorish army, to which lavish promises were made. Franco expected to win easily and rapidly. He had the army on his side and help from two powerful countries. The Republic seemed helpless, but in the hour of its peril it called upon the masses of Spain to defend their freedom, and distributed arms to them. The common people answered that call and fought almost barehanded against the guns and aeroplanes of Franco. They checked him. Volunteers from abroad also poured into Spain to fight for democracy, and formed an International Brigade, which rendered invaluable service to the Republic at a time when it most needed it. But while volunteers came to the Republic, the regular Italian Army came in large numbers to help Franco, and aeroplanes and pilots and technicians and arms came from Italy and Germany. Behind Franco were the experienced general staffs of these two great Powers; on the side of the Republic there was enthusiasm and courage and sacrifice. The Rebels, advanced till they reached the gates of Madrid in November 1936, but then a supreme effort of the people of the Republic stopped them there. " No Pasaran "—they shall not pass—was the cry of the people, and Madrid, bombarded daily from the air and by heavy artillery, with her fine buildings in ruins, with numerous fires, caused by incendiary bombs, continually breaking out, with the bravest of her children dying in thousands for her sake, Madrid remained unconquered and victorious. Two years have passed since the rebel troups reached the outskirts of Madrid. Still they remain there and hear that cry—No Pasaran—and Madrid, in her sorrow and desolation, holds her head high in freedom, and has become the embodiment of the proud and unconquerable spirit of the Spanish people.

We must understand this Spanish struggle, for it is infinitely more than a local or national struggle. It began by a revolt against a democratically elected parliament. A cry of communism and religion in danger was raised, but there were very few communists among the Popular Front deputies, and the great majority were socialists and Republicans. As for religion, the bravest fighters for the Republic have been the Catholics of the Basque country. The Republic guarantees the freedom of religion—unlike Hitler in Germany—but the vested interests in land and education of the Church were certainly objected to. The revolt was against democracy as such when it was feared that it would attack and put an end to feudalism in land and large estates. When this happens, as I have said before, then reactionaries do not take the trouble to observe democratic forms or to try to convert the electorate. They take to arms and endeavour to force their will on the mass of the people by violence and terrorism.

The Spanish military and clerical clique which rebelled found willing allies in the two fascist Powers, Italy and Germany, who wanted to gain supremacy over Spain in order to have control over the Mediterranean and establish naval bases there. The mineral resources of Spain also attracted them. Thus the Spanish War was not a civil war, but was in reality an European War in the game of power politics to disable France and weaken Britain, and thus establish the domination of fascism over Europe. The interests of Germany and Italy conflicted to some extent, but they pulled together for the time being.

A fascist Spain would be fatal for France, and would threaten both the British Mediterranean route to the East and the Cape route. Gibraltar would then be useless and the Suez Canal of no great value. Thus, even from the point of view of self-interest, if not from love of democracy, one would have expected England and France to give every legitimate aid to the Spanish Government to put down the rebellion. But here again we see how class interests move governments even at the cost of their national interests. The British Government evolved a scheme of non-intervention which has been the supreme farce of our times. Germany and Italy belong to the Non-Intervention Committee, and yet openly aid the Rebels and recognize them as the lawful government. Their armies are sent to Franco and their airmen bomb Spanish towns. Non-intervention has thus meant that help should only reach the Rebels. The French Government, at the instigation of the British, has closed the Pyrenees frontier, thus stopping any help from trickling in to the Spanish Republic.

British ships carrying food to the Republic have been sunk by Franco's aeroplanes or navy and the British Prime Minister, Mr. Chamberlain, has actually defended Franco's action. To such a pass has the British Government come in its fear of the spread of democracy. A few days ago it concluded an agreement with Italy by which it went a step further in recognizing Franco and in giving a free hand to Italy to intervene in Spain. The Spanish Republic, indeed, would have long been dead if it had relied on England and France or acted on their advice. But in spite of British and French policy, the Spanish people refused to submit to fascism. For them it is a national struggle for independence against the foreign invaders, a struggle which has become epic in character, and which has astonished the world by miracles of courage and endurance. Most horrible of all have been the aerial bombardment by Italian and German aeroplanes on Franco's side of cities and villages and civilian populations.

During the past two years the Republic has built up a fine army, and recently they have sent away all their foreign volunteers.

While Franco occupies nearly three-quarters of Spain, and has cut off Madrid and Valencia from Catalonia, the new Republican Army holds him now in check, and has proved its worth during the great battle of the Ebro, which has lasted almost continuously for several months. It is clear that Franco cannot defeat this army unless he has overwhelming foreign aid.

The Republic's greatest ordeal now is lack of food, especially during the winter months. For the Republic has not only to provide food for its army and the normal population in the area under its control, but also for the millions of refugees who have come to it from the areas occupied by Franco's troops.

China.—From the tragedy of Spain let us now go to the tragedy of China.

Japan's aggression in Manchuria was continuous and, as I have told you, she had the official good will of Britain. Britain rejected the offer of American co-operation against Japanese aggression. Why did Britain encourage Japan in this way, and thus strengthen a powerful rival? From the early days of the twentieth century Japan has forged ahead as an imperialist Power almost under British protection. At first this was aimed against Tsarist Russia. After the Great War, England's two great rivals were the United States of America and the Soviet Union, and so the old policy of supporting Japan was continued, till now, when Japan herself threatens important British interests. One of the reasons for America recognizing the Soviet Union in 1933 was American rivalry to Japan.

In China from 1933 onwards there were several governments : there was Chiang Kai-Shek's Nationalist Government, which was recognized by the Powers, and the Canton Government in the south, which also claimed to follow the Kuomintang, and a large Soviet area in the interior, besides a number of semi-independent war-lords in the interior. North of Peiping there was Japan continually nibbling away at China. Instead of facing Japanese aggression, Chiang Kai-Shek spent all his energy in sending, year after year, powerful military expeditions to crush the Soviet areas. Most of these expeditions failed, and even when they occupied these regions, the Chinese Soviet armies escaped them and went and established themselves farther inland. The story of the amazing 8000-mile trek of the Eighth Route Army under Chu Teh across China has become a classic in military annals.

So this conflict continued, year after year, although Soviet China offered to co-operate with Chiang Kai-Shek in resisting Japanese aggression. In 1937 Japan launched a major offensive, and this at last induced the warring factions to unite and present a united front to Japan. China also drew closer to the Soviet Union, and in November 1937 a non-aggression pact was signed by the two countries.

Japan met with fierce resistance, and tried to break it by vast and horrible massacres from the air and other methods of un-believable barbarity. But in this fiery ordeal a new nation was

forged in China, and the old lethargy of the Chinese people dropped
away from them. Great cities were reduced to ashes by Japanese
bombers and vast numbers of people slain. The strain on Japan
was great, and her financial and economic system showed signs of
cracking up. The sympathy of the people of India was naturally
with the Chinese people, as it was also with the Spanish Republic,
and in India and America and elsewhere great movements for the
boycott of Japanese goods grew.

Still the great military machine of Japan advanced in China, and
the Chinese people adopted guerrilla tactics to harass the Japanese
armies, with great effect. Japan occupied Shanghai and Nanking,
and when she approached Canton and Hankow, the Chinese themselves set fire to and destroyed their great cities. The Japanese
army occupied their charred ruins, as Napoleon had occupied
Moscow, but they are far from having crushed Chinese resistance,
which grows harder with every fresh disaster.

Austria.—Let us now go back to Europe, and follow the story of
Austria to its tragic end. This little republic was bankrupt and
divided, with Nazi Germany pressing on one side and Fascist Italy
on the other. Although Vienna had a progressive socialist municipality, the country was under an internal brand of clerical fascism
with Dollfuss as Chancellor, who placed his reliance on Mussolini to
protect him against Nazi aggression. Italy sent arms to Dollfuss
in contravention of the Treaty of Versailles, and Mussolini advised
him to suppress the socialists. Dollfuss decided to disarm these
socialist workers of Vienna, and this led to the counter-revolution
of February 1934. For four days there was fighting in Vienna, and
the famous workers' houses were shelled and partly destroyed.
Dollfuss won, but at the cost of breaking up the only strong group
that could have resisted external aggression.

Meanwhile Nazi intrigues continued, and in June 1934 Dollfuss
was assassinated by the Nazis in Vienna. This coup was meant to
be followed by a Nazi invasion from Germany. Hitler was on the
point of sending his army across the frontier when he was checked
by Mussolini's threat to send his troops to defend Austria against
the Germans. Mussolini had no desire to see Austria absorbed by
Germany, and the German frontier coming right up to Italy. Hitler
formally declared in 1935 that he would not annex Austria or have
the *anschluss*.

But Italy's Abyssinian adventure weakened her, and as friction
with Great Britain and France increased, Mussolini had to come to
terms with Hitler. Hitler now had a free hand in Austria, and
Nazi activities grew. Early in 1938 Chamberlain, the British
Prime Minister, made it clear that England would not intervene
to save Austria. Events moved fast then, and when the Austrian
Chancellor Schuschnigg decided to have a plebiscite, Hitler objected
to this, and invaded Austria in March 1938. There was no resistance,
and the *anschluss*, or union with Germany, was proclaimed. Thus
ended this ancient country, which had long been the seat of empire,
and Austria disappeared from the map of Europe. Her last Chan-

cellor, Schuschnigg, was made a prisoner by the Germans, and a trial was threatened as he had not completely fallen in with Nazi wishes. He is still a prisoner of the Nazis.

The coming of the German Nazis to Austria let loose a terror on the people which was worse even than the early days of the Nazi terror in Germany. The Jews suffered, and still suffer terribly, and in the once beautiful and cultured city of Vienna barbarism reigns and horror piles on horror.

Czechoslovakia.—Europe was numbed by the Nazi triumph in Austria, but the effect was greatest in Czechoslovakia, which was now enclosed on three sides by Nazi Germany. Many people thought that an invasion of this country would follow, and the preliminaries to this, Nazi intrigues and attempts to foment trouble in the frontier districts, began in the approved fascist way.

The Sudetenland of Czechoslovakia, the Bohemia of old, had a German-speaking population, which had been dominant in the Austro-Hungarian Empire. They had not taken kindly to a Czech State, and they had a number of legitimate grievances. They wanted a measure of autonomy; they had no desire to join Germany, and there were many Germans amongst them who were wholly opposed to the Nazi regime. Bohemia had never previously formed part of Germany. After the disappearance of Austria it was expected that Hitler would invade Czechoslovakia, and large numbers of people were frightened at this prospect, and joined the local Nazi party in order to put themselves on the safe side.

Internationally, Czechoslovakia's position was a strong one. She was an advanced industrial State, highly organized, with a powerful and efficient army. She had alliances with France and the Soviet Union, and England was supposed to be on her side in case of conflict. Being the only democratic State left in Central Europe, she had the sympathy of democrats all over the world, including America. There could be no doubt that, in case of war, the fascist Powers would suffer defeat if the democratic forces pulled together.

The question of the Sudeten minority had been raised, and it was right that their grievances should be remedied. It was a fact, however, that the minorities in Czechoslovakia were far better treated than any other minority in Central Europe. The real question was not a minority one, but Hitler's desire to dominate the whole of South-east Europe and to enforce his will by violence and threat of violence.

The Czech Government tried their hardest to solve the minority question, and agreed to almost all the demands made, but as one demand was accepted, a new and more far-reaching one appeared, till the very existence of the State was threatened. It was obvious that Hitler's object was to put an end to this democratic State which was a thorn in his side. British policy, under the guise of helping in a peaceful solution of the problem, encouraged Hitler in his aggression. Lord Runciman was sent to Prague by the British Government to act as a " mediator ", but in effect this so-called mediation led to continuous pressure on the Czech Government to give in to the Nazi demands. Ultimately the Czechs accepted Lord Runciman's own proposals, which were very far-reaching, but the Nazis now wanted more, and in order to enforce their demands, mobilized the German Army. Mr. Chamberlain thereupon intervened personally, and paid a visit to Hitler at Berchtesgaden, where he agreed to Hitler's ultimatum, which demanded a cession of large areas of Czechoslovakia to Germany. England and France then presented their own ultimatum to their friend and ally Czechoslovakia, asking her to agree immediately to Hitler's terms, and threatening to desert her completely if she refused to do so. The Czech people were amazed and shocked at this betrayal by their friends, but eventually, in sorrow and despair, their Government bowed to this ultimatum. Mr. Chamberlain went again to Hitler, this time to Godesberg on the Rhine, and found that he wanted still much more. Even Mr. Chamberlain could not agree to this, and in the last week of September 1938, war, world war, threw its heavy shadow all over Europe, and people rushed to get their gas-masks and dug trenches in parks and gardens as a protection against air-raids. Again Mr. Chamberlain went to Hitler, this time to Munich, and Monsieur Daladier and Signor Mussolini also went there. Russia, the ally of France and Czechoslovakia, was not invited, and Czechoslovakia, whose fate was to be decided and who was also an ally, was not even consulted. Hitler's new and far-reaching demands, backed by the threat of immediate war and invasion, were practically accepted in full, and on September 29 the Munich Agreement, embodying these, was signed by the four Powers.

War was averted for the time being, and a great feeling of relief spread among the peoples of all countries. But the price paid for this was the shame and dishonour of France and England, a terrible blow to democracy in Europe, the dismemberment of Czechoslovakia, the end of the League of Nations as an instrument for peace, and a resounding triumph for naziism in central and south-eastern Europe. And the peace that had been purchased was an armistice during which every country armed feverishly for the war to come.

The Munich Agreement was a turning-point in Europe and world history. A new division of Europe had begun, and the British and French Governments had ranged themselves openly on the side of naziism and fascism. Britain hastened to ratify the Anglo-Italian Agreement, recognizing the Italian conquest of Abyssinia and giving Italy a free hand in Spain. A four-Power pact between England, France, Germany, and Italy began to take shape, a common front against Russia and the democratic forces in Spain and elsewhere.

Russia.—It is remarkable that during all these years and months of intrigues and the breaking of solemn pledges by great Powers, Soviet Russia consistently honoured her international obligations, stood for peace and against aggression, and to the last did not desert her ally Czechoslovakia. But England and France ignored her and made friends with the aggressors, and even Czechoslovakia, betrayed by France and England, fell into the Nazi orbit and put an end to her alliance with Russia. Czechoslovakia has been split up, and Hungary and Poland, like hungry vultures, have profited by the occasion. Internally also there have been great changes and Slovakia claims autonomy. The remains of Czechoslovakia function now almost as a German colony.

Thus the foreign policy of the Soviet Union has received a severe setback. And yet it stands to-day as a powerful, and as the only effective, barrier in Europe and Asia to fascism and the anti-democratic forces. For Russia, though ignored in recent months by England and France, is to-day a mighty Power. The first Five Year Plan met with general success, though it failed in particulars, especially in regard to the quality of the goods produced. There were untrained mechanics, and transport also largely failed. The concentration on heavy industry led to shortage of goods for consumption and to a lowering of standards. But this plan laid the foundations of future progress by rapidly industrializing Russia and collectivizing her agriculture. The second Five Year Plan (1933–1937) changed the emphasis from heavy to light industry, and aimed at getting rid of the deficiencies of the first plan and at producing consumers' goods. Great progress was made, and the standards of life went up, and are continually going up. Culturally and educationally, and in many other ways, the advance all over the Soviet Union has been remarkable. Anxious to continue this advance and to consolidate its socialist economy, Russia consistently followed a peace policy in international affairs. In the League of Nations it stood for substantial disarmament, collective security, and corporate action against aggression. It tried to accommodate itself to the capitalist Great Powers and, in consequence, Communist Parties sought to build up " popular fronts " or " joint fronts " with other progressive parties.

In spite of this general progress and development, the Soviet Union passed through a severe internal crisis during this period. I have already told you of the conflict between Stalin and Trotsky. Various people, dissatisfied with the existing régime, gradually drew together and it is said that some of them even conspired with the fascist Powers. Even Yagoda, the chief of the Soviet Intelligence (the G.P.U.), is stated to have been associated with these people. In December 1934 Kirov, a leading member of the Soviet Government, was murdered. The Government took stern action against its opponents, and from 1937 there were a series of trials which provoked great controversy all over the world, as many famous and prominent individuals were involved in them. Among those tried and sentenced were those who were called Trotskyites, and rightist leaders (Rykov, Tomsky, Bukharin), and some high army officers, the chief of whom was Marshal Tuchachevsky.

It is difficult for me to express a definite opinion about these trials or the events that led up to them, as the facts are complicated and not clear. But it is undoubted that the trials disturbed large numbers of people, including many friends of Russia, and added to the prejudice against the Soviet Union. Close observers are of opinion that there was a big conspiracy against the Stalinist régime and that the trials were *bona fide*. It also seems to be established that there was no mass support behind the conspiracy, and that the reaction of the people was definitely against the opponents of Stalin. Nevertheless the extent of the repression, which may have hit many innocent persons also, was a sign of ill-health, and injured the Soviet's position internationally

Economic Recovery.—The great trade slump which began in 1930, and paralysed the capitalist world for several years, at last showed signs of improvement. There was partial recovery in most countries; in Britain recovery was more marked than elsewhere. The devaluation of the pound, tariffs, and the exploitation of Empire markets and resources helped Britain. The home market was developed by tariffs and subsidies and by agricultural reforms and organization of producers to reduce competition. An effort was made to plan production and wholesale distribution. Pressure was also brought to bear on Denmark and the Scandinavian countries to buy British goods.

This recovery, though it was considerable, was at the expense of international trade. Thus it was only a relative and partial recovery. Real recovery depends on the revival of international trade. It should be remembered also that Britain has not paid, and does not intend to pay, her debt to America. The economic recovery is partly due to the intensive rearmament programmes of various countries. Such a recovery is obviously insecure and unstable. Mass unemployment still continues.

The British Empire.—But though England has tided over the economic crisis for the present, the British Empire is very sick, and the political and economic forces working for its disintegration grow stronger. Its rulers have even lost their faith in it and their hope in its continuance. They cannot solve their internal problems; India, intent on independence, grows ever stronger, little Palestine shakes them up. America, the great rival of England in the capitalist world, challenges British supremacy, and drifts farther away from England as the British Government inclines towards the fascist Powers. Soviet Russia successfully builds socialism, which is opposed to all imperialisms. Germany and Italy look with greedy eyes on the rich prize of the British Empire. The submission of England to their threats at Munich has led them to treat her almost as a second-class Power and to address her in arrogant language. England might have consolidated her position by an extension of democracy and by adhering to collective security. Instead she chose to abandon this and to support Hitler, and now British Imperialism is in a hopeless quandary, involved in the numerous contradictions that flow from the Munich policy.

Colonies.—Germany demands colonies now, and we are told that is a " have-not " and " dissatisfied " Power. What of the many smaller Powers that have no colonies? And what of the real " have-nots ", the people of the colonies? The whole argument is based on the continuation of the imperialist system. The satisfaction or otherwise of a country depends on the economic policy pursued there, and under imperialism there will always be dissatisfaction, because there will always be inequality. Tsarist Russia before the Revolution was said to be a dissatisfied, expanding Power. Soviet Russia to-day is smaller in territory, but is " satisfied " because it has no imperialist ambitions and pursues a different economic policy.

Germany wants colonies not because she cannot get her raw materials otherwise, for the open market is there for her to buy, but because she wants to exploit the people of these colonies to her own advantage. She wants to pay them in her own depreciated currency, in so-called " frozen " marks, and then compel them to buy German goods for them.

I have written to you about some of the principal events of the past five years and of the consequences that flowed from them. I do not know where to stop, for everywhere there is ferment and change and conflict, and it is becoming impossible to consider, much less to solve, the world's problems on local or national lines. World solutions are necessary. Meanwhile the world grows from bad to worse, and war and violence dominate it. Europe, proud leader of the modern world, rattles back to barbarism. Her old governing classes are impotent and wholly incapable of finding a way out of the difficulties that encompass them.

The Munich Agreement upset the unstable equilibrium of the world. South-eastern Europe began to succumb to Nazi Power, and Nazi intrigues grew in every country. The smaller countries of Europe, called the Oslo group (Denmark, Norway, Sweden, Finland, the Netherlands, Belgium and Luxemburg), realizing that Britain's friendship was of no value to them, declared their neutrality, and refused to undertake any collective responsibility. Japan grew more aggressive in the Far East, captured Canton and came into conflict with British interests in Hongkong; in Palestine the situation deteriorated rapidly. Relations between America and England became cooler than ever. While Mr. Chamberlain was lining up with the fascist Powers, President Roosevelt was denouncing the aims and methods of Naziism. Disgusted with European conflicts and Britain's and France's attitude to fascist aggression, America held aloof, and at the same time started rearmament on a vast scale. So also the Soviet Union. Her policy of alliances and non-aggression pacts in the West had not succeeded, and she may be forced into isolation. Yet both America and Russia know that there can be no isolation or neutrality in this distracted world of to-day, and if conflict comes, they are bound to be dragged into it. For that they prepare.

America.—President Roosevelt's internal policy in the United States has met with many checks, and the Supreme Court and the reactionary elements have come in his way. Recent elections give an increasing strength to his Republican opponents in the Congress. And yet Roosevelt's personal popularity and his hold of the American public continue.

Roosevelt has also followed a policy of developing friendly relations with the South American governments. In Mexico there has been conflict between the Government and American and British oil interests. A far-reaching revolution has taken place in Mexico, which has established the right of the people to the land. The Church and the vested interests in oil and land lost many of their special rights and privileges, and therefore opposed these changes.

Turkey.—In a world of conflict, Turkey seems to be a singularly peaceful country to-day, with no external enemies. The age-long feud with Greece and the Balkan countries has been settled. Relations with the Soviet Union and with England are good. There was a conflict with France over Alexandretta, which, you will remember, was one of the five States into which the French Government divided its mandated area of Syria. Alexandretta has a predominantly Turkish population, and the French accepted the Turkish contention and created an autonomous State there.

So Turkey, under the wise guidance of Kemal Ataturk, freed from its racial and other problems, devoted herself to internal development. The Ataturk had served his people well, and when he died on November 10, 1938, he had the good fortune to know that his work had been crowned with remarkable success. He was succeeded in the presidentship of Turkey by his old colleague General Ismet Ineunu.

Islam.—Kemal Ataturk gave a new turn to the vital impulse of Islam in the Middle East. It put on a modern dress and shed medievalism, and thus brought itself into line with the world of to-day. The Ataturk's example has had a powerful effect on all the Islamic countries of the Middle East, and modern nation States have grown up, basing themselves on nationalism rather than on religion. This effect has not so far been equally marked in countries like India, where Muslim populations, in common with others, are under imperialist domination.

The World in Conflict.—Europe and the Pacific are the two great scenes of conflict to-day, and in both these great areas an aggressive fascism seeks to crush democracy and freedom and dominate the world. A kind of fascist international has grown up which not only carries on open, though undeclared, wars, but is always intriguing in various countries and fomenting trouble so as to give it an opportunity to intervene. There is open glorification of war and violence, and a false propaganda on an unprecedented scale. Under cover of the slogan of anti-communism, it advances its imperialist designs, although international communism is nowhere on the aggressive, and has been on the side of world peace and democracy for many years. In the United States of America there have been Nazi conspiracies and trials. In France in December 1937 a conspiracy against the Republic was discovered. This was organized by the Cagoulards, or the Hooded Men as they were called, aided by supplies of arms from Germany and Italy. Bomb outrages and murders were committed by these men. In England influential groups influence British foreign policy in a fascist direction.

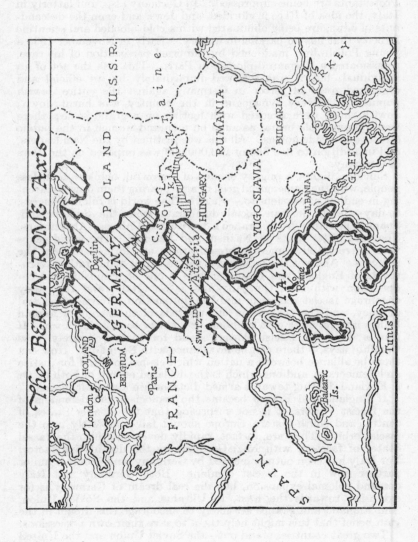

This international fascism is not only imperialism in its most extreme form, but, as in the Middle Ages, it has produced religious and racial conflicts. In Germany both the Catholic Church and the Protestants are being suppressed. In Germany also, and latterly in Italy, the idea of Race is glorified, and Jews, and even the descendants of Jews, are being eliminated with a cold-blooded and scientific ferocity that has no parallel in history. Early in November 1938 a young Polish Jew, maddened by the cruel persecution of his race, assassinated a German diplomat in Paris. This was the act of an individual, but it was followed immediately by an official and organized reign of terror in Germany against the entire Jewish population. Every synagogue in the country was burnt down; Jewish shops were wrecked with looting on a grand scale; there were innumerable brutal assaults on men and women in the public streets and inside homes. All this was justified by the Nazi leaders, and in addition to it a fine of £80,000,000 was imposed on the Jews of Germany.

Suicides, flights, a mighty exodus of sorrowful, helpless, homeless people, with the immemorial grief of ages bearing them down, marching in endless processions to—where ? The world is full of refugees, to-day—Jews, German social democrats from the Sudetenland, Spanish peasants from Franco's territories, Chinese, Abyssinians. They are bitter fruits of Naziism and Fascism. The world gasps with horror, and numerous organizations are formed to help the refugees. And yet the policy that the so-called democratic governments of England and France pursue is one of friendship and co-operation with Nazi Germany and fascist Italy, and thus they encourage fascist terrorism and the destruction of civilization and decency, and the conversion of hundreds of thousands of human beings into refugees with no home or country to call their own. If this is what the fascist Powers stand for to-day, " surely ", as Gandhiji says, " there can be no alliance with Germany. How can there be alliance between a nation which claims to stand for justice and democracy, and one which is the declared enemy of both ? Or is England drifting towards armed dictatorship and all it means ? "

If England and France became the apologists and defenders of the fascist Powers, it is not surprising that the smaller States of central and south-eastern Europe should fall completely into the fascist orbit. They are, in fact, rapidly developing into the vassal States of fascism, with Nazi Germany as the dominating factor. For Italy has been outmanœuvred by Germany, and is only a junior partner now in the fascist combine. Both Germany and Italy demand colonial expansion, but the real dream of Germany is for extension towards the East, to Ukraine and the Soviet Union. And England and France are likely to encourage this dream in the vain belief that this might help them to save their own possessions.

Two great countries stand out—the Soviet Union and the United States of America, the two most powerful nations of the modern world, almost self-sufficient within their far-flung territories, almost unbeatable. For varying reasons both are opposed to Fascism and

Naziism. In Europe Soviet Russia remains the sole barrier to fascism; if she were destroyed there would be a complete end of democracy in Europe, including France and England. The United States are far from Europe and cannot easily, and have no desire to, intervene in its affairs. But when such intervention comes in Europe or the Pacific, the tremendous strength of America will make itself felt effectively.

On the side of freedom are also the rising democracies of India and the East, and some of the British Dominions are far more advanced than the British Government. Democracy and freedom are in grave peril to-day, and the peril is all the greater because their so-called friends stab them in the back. But Spain and China have given us wonderful and inspiring examples of the true spirit of democracy, and in both these countries, through the horror of war, a new nation is being created, and there is a revival and a renaissance in many fields of national life and activity.

In 1935 there was the invasion of Abyssinia; in 1936 Spain was attacked; in 1937 China was invaded afresh; in 1938 Austria was invaded and removed from the map by Nazi Germany, and Czechoslovakia was broken up and reduced to vassalage. Each year has brought its full crop of disaster; what of 1939 on whose threshold we stand? What will it bring to us and to the world?

INDEX

972

INDEX